The Legal Environment of Business

Text and Cases

Ethical, Regulatory, and Corporate Issues

Frank B. Cross | Roger LeRoy Miller

CENGAGE
Learning·

Australia • Brazil • Japan • Korea • Mexico • Singapore • Spain • United Kingdom • United States

Cengage Learning
20 Channel Center Street
Boston, MA 02210
USA

Cengage Learning is a leading provider of customized learning solutions with office locations around the globe, including Singapore, the United Kingdom, Australia, Mexico, Brazil, and Japan. Locate your local office at:
www.international.cengage.com/region.

Cengage Learning products are represented in Canada by Nelson Education, Ltd.

For your lifelong learning solutions, visit **www.cengage.com/custom.**

Visit our corporate website at **www.cengage.com.**

Brief Contents

For

The Legal Environment of Business: Text and Cases,
Text and Cases, Ethical, Regulatory, and Corporate Issues

Contents

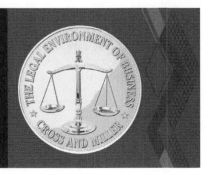

UNIT THREE
THE COMMERCIAL ENVIRONMENT 183

UNIT FOUR
THE BUSINESS
ENVIRONMENT 379

UNIT FIVE
THE EMPLOYMENT
ENVIRONMENT 449

UNIT SIX
THE REGULATORY ENVIRONMENT 537

CONCEPT SUMMARIES

EXHIBITS

SHIFTING LEGAL PRIORITIES FOR BUSINESS

INSIGHT INTO ETHICS

TUDENTS: Accessing Your Aplia

ourse Through CengageBrain

CENGAGE**brain**.com

What is login.cengagebrain.com? Imagine that you are using Aplia along with another online study tool from Cengage Learning. Rather than having separate logins and passwords for both applications, Cengage offers a single access point through login.cengagebrain.com.

When you visit login.cengagebrain.com, you will see the following:

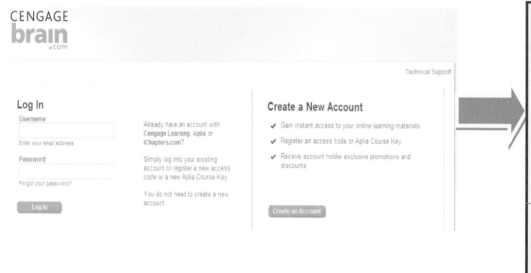

A Single Sign-On (SSO) account provides for one login to access Cengage Learning digital resources.

For the purpose of this document, we will focus on the right side of this screen or **"Create a New Account"**.

Note: If you *do* have an existing account, CengageBrain accepts all prior login credentials, including Aplia and iChapters.

Step 1 | Begin by Creating an Account

1. Click the "Create an Account" button
2. The following page will load. Enter in the Aplia Course Key

YOUR COURSE KEY IS PROVIDED BY YOUR INSTRUCTOR TO ACCESS APLIA.

Instructors often provide the Aplia Course Key on their **syllabus**, or the course web site. If you need help locating the **Aplia Course Key**, ask your instructor.

Your Aplia Course Key will look like this.

ep 2 | Confirm Your Course Information

e graphic below serves as an illustration for what you will see. Please confirm the displayed
een represents your enrolled course.

ck to Log In / Register / Confirm Course

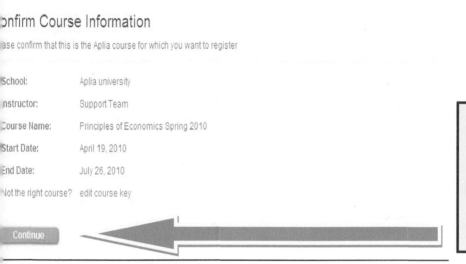

er Your Code or Key   Account Information   Access Materials

onfirm Course Information

ase confirm that this is the Aplia course for which you want to register

School:	Aplia university
nstructor:	Support Team
Course Name:	Principles of Economics Spring 2010
Start Date:	April 19, 2010
End Date:	July 26, 2010
Not the right course?	edit course key

Continue

Confirm that the course
information shown matches
the course you are enrolled in.
If yes, click the "**Continue**"
button.   If not, click on the
"edit course key" link to re-
enter the correct Course Key.

ep 3 | Complete Registration Form

a new user, you must complete all fields in the registration form and click "Continue"

k to Log In / Register / Enter Your Code or Key / Account Information

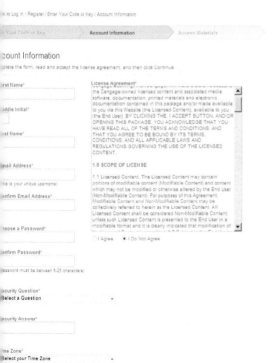

Your Code or Key   Account Information   Access Materials

count Information

plete the form, read and accept the license agreement, and then click Continue

irst Name*

iddle Initial*

st Name*

mail Address*

his is your unique username)

anfirm Email Address*

noose a Password*

anfirm Password*

assword must be between 8-25 characters)

curity Question*
Select a Question

ecurity Answer*

ne Zone*
Select your Time Zone

I am at least 13 years of age

Sign up and be the first to receive exclusive CengageBrain discounts and promotions

Continue   Cancel

Please complete all fields to
establish your account and select a
security question.   Select
"Continue" to proceed with your
Aplia registration.

Step 4 | My Home Dashboard Review

You have arrived at your **"My Home"** page. Here you can verify your e-Mail address with CengageBrain and pay for your course **(See Step 5).** Note that any prior (and future) Cengage Learning purchases will appear on this page. Additionally, the page provides support resources and a transaction history of your Cengage purchases – digital products, textbooks or rentals.

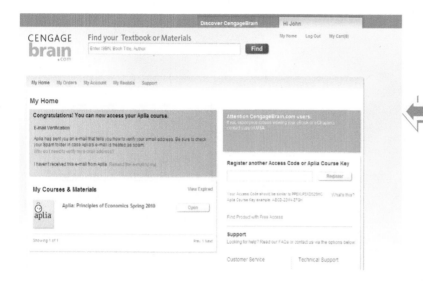

IMPORTANT: CengageBrain requires you to verify your e-mail address. Please go to your e-mail and check for a message from CengageBrain.com with the Subject **"Aplia Verification E-Mail"**. If you don't see the message, check your SPAM folder.

Click the link to verify your e-mail. **Once verified, you will be prompted to log back in again with your e-mail and password from Step 3 above. Once you do, you will be brought back to your "My Home" Dashboard as shown below.**

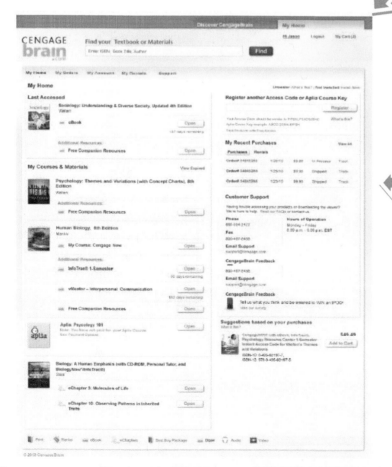

Here is a complete view of the Dashboard showing all Cengage Learning resources instantly available in one spot. Also note transaction history and support options in the right hand field.

TE: YOUR APLIA PAYMENT CODES ARE BOUND WITHIN THIS BOOK. THERE ARE <u>NO</u> <u>DITIONAL CHARGES TO ACCESS APLIA</u>. SIMPLY COMPLETE THE PAYMENT PROCESS BY KING ON THE "SEE PAYMENT OPTIONS LINK" CIRCLED IN **GREEN**.

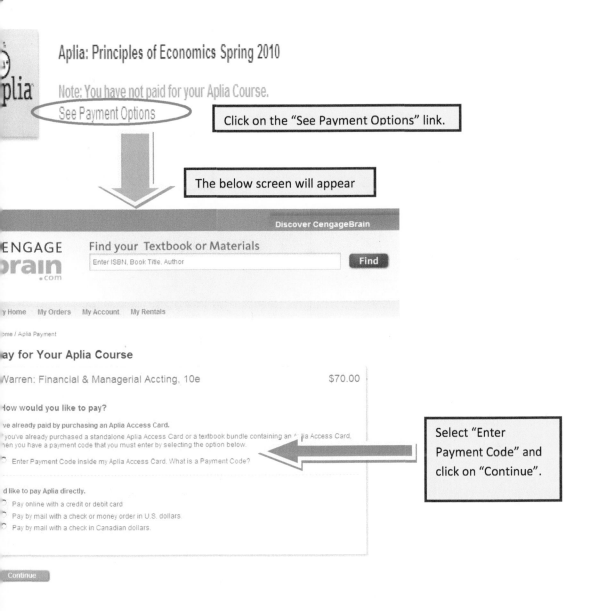

y Courses & Materials

Aplia: Principles of Economics Spring 2010

Note: You have not paid for your Aplia Course.

See Payment Options

Click on the "See Payment Options" link.

The below screen will appear

Discover CengageBrain

ENGAGE
rain
.com

Find your Textbook or Materials

Enter ISBN, Book Title, Author

Find

y Home   My Orders   My Account   My Rentals

ome / Aplia Payment

ay for Your Aplia Course

Warren: Financial & Managerial Accting, 10e $70.00

How would you like to pay?

ve already paid by purchasing an Aplia Access Card.

you've already purchased a standalone Aplia Access Card or a textbook bundle containing an A lia Access Card,
nen you have a payment code that you must enter by selecting the option below.

Enter Payment Code inside my Aplia Access Card. What is a Payment Code?

Select "Enter Payment Code" and click on "Continue".

d like to pay Aplia directly.

Pay online with a credit or debit card
Pay by mail with a check or money order in U.S. dollars.
Pay by mail with a check in Canadian dollars.

Continue

Step 5 | Completing Payment For Your Aplia Course (cont.)

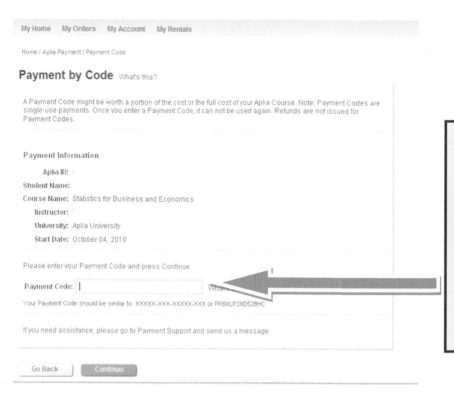

My Home   My Orders   My Account   My Rentals

Home / Aplia Payment / Payment Code

Payment by Code   What's this?

A Payment Code might be worth a portion of the cost or the full cost of your Aplia Course. Note: Payment Codes are single-use payments. Once you enter a Payment Code, it can not be used again. Refunds are not issued for Payment Codes.

Payment Information

Aplia ID:

Student Name:

Course Name: Statistics for Business and Economics

Instructor:

University: Aplia University

Start Date: October 04, 2010

Please enter your Payment Code and press Continue.

Payment Code: [   ]   What's

Your Payment Code should be similar to XXXXX-XXX-XXXXX-XXX or PP8XLP3XD528HC

If you need assistance, please go to Payment Support and send us a message.

Go Back   Continue

Enter the payment code that is **bound within your book**. Your payment code will look like the one shown below.

Payment Code
BQQFF-FNB-JPCPQ-PXH

NOTE: Your payment code *is not* the same as your Course Key provided by your Instructor.

My Home   My Orders   My Account   My Rentals

Payment Confirmation

Please print this page for your records.

Your Payment Code has been accepted as payment for your Aplia course.

Order Summary

Student name:

Aplia ID:

Course: Statistics for Business and Economics

Instructor:

School: Aplia University

Course start date: 10/04/10

Course end date: 12/26/10

Grace period ends: 10/25/10

Payment code used: ZTRKF-FNB-JPGNP-PCB

Date and time of payment: 10/19/10, 08:21 AM

Please note that your Payment Code has now been used and will no longer work for any subsequent Aplia course.

Refund Policy

There are no refunds for Payment Codes. For more information, please read Aplia's Terms

If you have questions about your payment, please contact Aplia Supp

Continue

This is a **Payment Confirmation** screen. Feel free to print the screen by clicking on the link that says "print" in blue at the top of the page.

Click "Continue" to return to your **My Home Dashboard** and click on the **"OPEN"** button next to your Aplia course.

ep 6 | Accessing Your Course

e click on the "Open" button, you will be directed to your Aplia course as shown below.

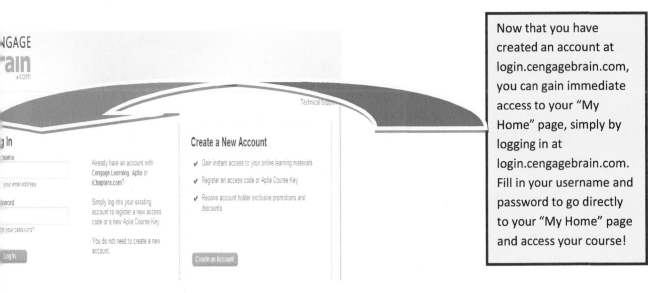

Congratulations!

You have successfully accessed your Aplia course! This page is your Aplia Home Page. Make note of Assignments, Instructor Announcements, access your eBook, etc.

ep 7 | Re-Entering Your Course After Logging Out

Now that you have created an account at login.cengagebrain.com, you can gain immediate access to your "My Home" page, simply by logging in at login.cengagebrain.com. Fill in your username and password to go directly to your "My Home" page and access your course!

Still Need Help?

Problems with your CengageBrain account?

- Check the FAQs in the Support area of your CengageBrain home.

  OR

- Write to cengagebrain.support@cengage.com

  OR

- Call 866-994-2427 Monday through Friday from 8 AM to 6 PM EST

Problems with your Aplia course?

- Click on the Support link in your Aplia course

  OR

- Write to support@aplia.com

  OR

- Start a chat with a Support representative Monday through Friday from 8 AM to 5 PM PST.

Preface to the Instructor

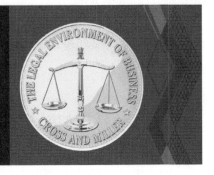

The study of the legal environment of business has universal applicability. A student entering any field of business must have at least a passing understanding of business law in order to function in the real world. Additionally, students preparing for a career in accounting, government and political science, economics, and even medicine can use much of the information that they learn in a legal environment of business course. In fact, every individual throughout his or her lifetime can benefit from a knowledge of contracts, employment relationships, real property law, land-use control, and other legal topics. Consequently, we have fashioned this text as a useful "tool for living" for all of your students (including those taking the CPA exam).

For the Eighth Edition, we have spent a great deal of effort making this book more contemporary, exciting, and visually appealing than ever before. We have also added many new features and special pedagogical devices that focus on legal, ethical, global, and corporate issues, while addressing core curriculum requirements.

WHAT IS NEW IN THE EIGHTH EDITION

Instructors have come to rely on the coverage, accuracy, and applicability of *The Legal Environment of Business*. To make sure that our text engages your students, solidifies their understanding of legal concepts, and provides the best teaching tools available, we now offer the following items either in the text or in conjunction with the text:

➤ New *Shifting Legal Priorities for Business* Feature

For the Eighth Edition, we have created a new feature that shows students how legal priorities are shifting in the business world. Special emphasis is given to sustainability, ethical trends, and changing managerial responsibilities. Each discussion ends with a short section entitled *Managerial*

Implications that points out why the changing priorities examined are significant to businesspersons. Topics examined include:

- Prosecuting White-Collar Crime with the Honest-Services Fraud Law (Chapter 7)
- The National Export Initiative (Chapter 8)
- Fair Trade and Environmental Sustainability (Chapter 11)
- The Law of Building "Green"—Sustainable Real Estate Development (Chapter 26)
- SEC Disclosures and Climate Change (Chapter 29)

➤ New *Case in Point* Feature

Many instructors use cases to illustrate how the law applies to business. For this edition, we have expanded our in-text discussion of case law by adding at least one new *Case in Point* feature in every chapter. This feature presents, in paragraph format, the facts and issues of an actual case and then describes the court's decision and rationale. Citations to the cases are included for further reference. The *Case in Point* features are integrated throughout the text to help students better understand how courts apply the principles under discussion in the real world.

➤ New *Debate This* Feature

To encourage student participation and motivate your students to think critically about the rationale underlying the law on a particular topic, we have created a special new feature for the Eighth Edition. Entitled *Debate This*, it consists of a brief statement or question concerning the chapter material that can be used to spur lively classroom or small group discussions, or can be a written assignment. This feature follows the *Reviewing* feature (discussed shortly) at the end of each chapter. **Suggested pro and con responses to the *Debate This* features can be found in both the *Instructor's Manual* and the *Answers Manual* that accompany this text.** (The full title of this manual is *Answers to Questions* *and Case Problems and Alternate Problem Sets with Answers.*)

➤ New Chapter on *Mortgages and Foreclosures after the Recession*

For the Eighth Edition, we have included an entirely new chapter (Chapter 16) titled *Mortgages and Foreclosures after the Recession.* This chapter examines some of the mortgage-lending practices that contributed to the latest recession and discusses the legal reforms enacted in response to it.

➤ New *Insight into Ethics* Feature

For the Eighth Edition, we have created many new *Insight into Ethics* features, which appear in selected chapters and examine the ethical implications of various topics. This feature provides valuable insights into how the courts and the law are dealing with specific ethical issues. Each discussion ends with a critical-thinking question that explores some cultural, environmental, political, social, or technological aspect of the issue. The following are some of the topics explored in this feature:

* Should Pharmaceutical Companies Be Allowed to Tweet? (Chapter 6)
* Some Consequences of Caps on Medical Malpractice Awards (Chapter 12)
* Warning Labels for Video Games (Chapter 13)
* Fiduciary Duties of LLC Managers (Chapter 18)

➤ *Managerial Implications in Selected Cases*

We have devised a special new item of case pedagogy for this edition. At the end of selected cases that have particular importance for business managers, we have included a new section entitled *Managerial Implications.* This section points out the significance of the court's ruling in the case for business owners and managers.

➤ Emphasis on Critical Thinking and Legal Reasoning

Today's business leaders must often think "outside the box" when making business decisions. For this reason, we have included **numerous critical-thinking elements** in the Eighth Edition that are designed to challenge students' understand-ing of the materials beyond simple retention. Your students' critical-thinking and legal reasoning skills will be increased as they work through the numerous pedagogical aids in the book. The new *Debate This* feature (discussed previously) requires critical thinking. In addition, nearly every feature and every case presented in the text conclude with some type of critical-thinking question.

For the Eighth Edition, we continue to offer one longer excerpt—labeled an *Extended Case*—with two critical-thinking questions in every chapter. These *Extended Cases* may be used for case-briefing assignments and are also tied to the *Special Case Analysis* questions found in every unit of this text.

Because of the popularity of the case-ending questions, we've also included two questions for all cases. These questions may include:

* *What If the Facts Were Different?*
* *Impact of This Case on Today's Law*
* *The Ethical Dimension*
* *The E-Commerce Dimension*
* *The Global Dimension*
* *The Legal Environment Dimension*

Suggested answers to all questions following cases can be found in both the *Instructor's Manual* and the *Answers Manual* that accompany this text.

➤ *Special Case Analysis* Questions

Through the years, instructors have frequently requested that we help them teach their legal environment of business students how to analyze case law. We discuss the fundamental topic of how to read and understand case law in Chapter 1 and cover *How to Brief Cases and Analyze Case Problems* in Appendix A. For every unit in the text, in the *Questions and Case Problems* at the end of selected chapters, we also provide a *Special Case Analysis* question that is based on the *Extended Case* excerpt in that chapter. These questions are designed to build students' analytical skills.

The *Special Case Analysis* questions test students' ability to perform IRAC (Issue, Rule, Application, and Conclusion) case analysis. Students must identify the legal issue presented in the chapter's *Extended Case,* understand the rule of law, determine how the rule applies to the facts of the case, and describe the court's conclusion. Instructors can assign these questions as homework or use them in class to elicit student participation and teach case analysis.

➤ *Reviewing* Feature in Every Chapter

In the Eighth Edition of *The Legal Environment of Business*, we continue to offer the *Reviewing* feature at the end of every chapter to help solidify students' understanding of the chapter materials. Each *Reviewing* feature presents a hypothetical scenario and then asks a series of questions that require students to identify the issues and apply the legal concepts discussed in the chapter.

This feature is designed to help students review the chapter topics in a simple and interesting way and see how the legal principles discussed in the chapter affect the world in which they live. You can use this feature as the basis for in-class discussion or can encourage students to use it for self-study prior to completing homework assignments. **Suggested answers to the questions posed in the *Reviewing* feature can be found in both the *Instructor's Manual* and the *Answers Manual* that accompany this text.**

The *Reviewing* feature is also tied to a set of questions for each chapter in the Web-based CengageNOW system, to be discussed next. Students can read through the scenario in the text and then answer the four questions online (called Applications and Analysis questions). By using the CengageNOW system, students can receive instant feedback on their answers to these questions, and instructors will obtain automatically graded assignments that enable them to assess students' understanding of the materials.

➤ Improved CengageNOW for *The Legal Environment of Business:* Interactive Assignment System

To help students learn how to identify and apply the legal principles they study, we have created an easy-to-use Web-based product for this text. The system provides interactive, automatically graded assignments for every chapter and unit. For each of the twenty-nine chapters, we have devised several categories of multiple-choice questions that stress different aspects of the chapter materials. By using the optional **CengageNOW** system, students can complete the assignments from any location via the Internet and can receive instant feedback on why their answers to questions were incorrect or correct (if the instructor wishes to allow feedback). Instructors can customize the system to meet their own specifications and can track students' progress. CengageNOW offers all of the following:

- **Chapter Review Questions**—The first set of ten to fifteen questions reviews the basic concepts and principles discussed in the chapter. This set often includes questions based on the cases presented in the text.
- **Brief Hypotheticals**—The next group of seven to ten questions gives students practice in spotting the issue and rule of law in the context of a short factual scenario.
- **Legal Reasoning**—The third set contains five questions that require students to analyze the factual situation provided and apply the rules of law discussed in the chapter to arrive at an answer.
- **IRAC Case Analysis**—The next set of four questions for each chapter requires students to perform all the basic elements of legal reasoning (identify the *issue*, determine the *rule* of law, *apply* the rule to the facts presented, and arrive at a *conclusion*). These questions are based on the *Extended Case* excerpts that appear in each chapter.
- **Application and Analysis**—The final set of four questions is linked to the *Reviewing* feature (discussed previously) that appears in every chapter of the text. The student is required to read through the hypothetical scenario, analyze the facts presented, identify the issues in dispute, and apply the rules discussed in the chapter to answer the questions.
- **Essay Questions**—In addition to the multiple-choice questions, we now provide essay questions that allow students to compose and submit essays online. Students' essays are automatically recorded to the gradebook so that instructors can quickly and easily evaluate the essays and record grades.
- **Video Questions**—CengageNOW also provides links to the Business Law Digital Video Library (discussed shortly) for *The Legal Environment of Business* so that students can access and view the video clips and answer questions related to the topics in the chapter.
- **Cumulative Questions for Each Unit**—In addition to the questions relating to each chapter, the CengageNOW system provides a set of cumulative questions, entitled "Synthesizing Legal Concepts," for each of the six units in the text.
- **Additional Advantages of CengageNOW**—Instructors can utilize the system to upload their course syllabi, create and customize homework assignments, keep track of their students' progress, communicate with their students about assignments and due dates, and create reports

summarizing the data for an individual student or for the whole class.

➤ Aplia for *The Legal Environment of Business:* Online Homework and Gradebook System

Aplia is an online homework system dedicated to improving learning by increasing student effort and engagement. Aplia encourages legal environment of business students to read their text, stay engaged with course material, and master critical-thinking and legal reasoning skills that will serve them well in their future business careers.

Originally created by a professor to enhance his own courses, Aplia has been specially tailored to cover the topics in each chapter of this text. Immediate, detailed feedback for every question helps students learn and improves their performance. Aplia's numerous interactive features keep students interested in the legal environment, prepare them for classes, and connect the concepts they have learned across chapters. Aplia also allows instructors to spend more time teaching and less time reviewing and grading assignments. As your students complete assignments, their scores are imported automatically into your gradebook, where you can easily track class and individual student performance.

Aplia Text, an interactive textbook, contains all the contents of the printed textbook but takes advantage of the digital environment. Features such as flipbook-style navigation allow students to scan through the text easily. They can also highlight the text; listen to audio clips; and view movies, simulations, graphs, and slideshows.

➤ CourseMate

CourseMate brings the legal environment of business concepts to life with interactive learning, study, and exam preparation tools that support the printed textbook. Built-in engagement tracking tools allow you to assess the study activities of your students. Additionally, CourseMate includes an interactive online textbook, which contains the complete content of the printed textbook enhanced by the many advantages of a digital environment.

➤ Improved Ethics Coverage

For the Eighth Edition of *The Legal Environment of Business,* we have significantly revised and updated the chapter on ethics and business decision mak-

ing (Chapter 4). The chapter now presents a more practical, realistic case-study approach to business ethics and the dilemmas facing businesspersons today.

It also provides step-by-step guidance for making ethical business decisions. The emphasis on ethics is reiterated in materials throughout the text, particularly the *Insight into Ethics* feature, the *Focus on Ethics* feature that concludes every unit, and the pedagogy that accompanies selected cases and features. We also discuss **corporate governance issues** in the ethics chapter, the chapter on investor protection, and the *Focus on Ethics* feature at the end of Unit Six. Finally, each chapter includes a **Question of Ethics** case problem that provides a modern-day example of the kinds of ethical issues faced by businesspersons and explores the ways that courts can resolve them.

➤ More on the Sarbanes-Oxley Act of 2002

In a number of places in this text, we discuss the Sarbanes-Oxley Act of 2002 and the corporate scandals that led to the passage of that legislation. For example, Chapter 4 contains a section examining the requirements of the Sarbanes-Oxley Act relating to confidential reporting systems. In Chapter 29, we discuss this act in the context of securities law and present an exhibit (Exhibit 29–4) containing some of the key provisions of the act relating to corporate accountability with respect to securities transactions.

Because the Sarbanes-Oxley Act is a topic of significant concern in today's business climate, we include excerpts and explanatory comments on the act as Appendix E. Students and instructors alike will find it useful to have the provisions of the act immediately available for reference.

THE LEGAL ENVIRONMENT OF BUSINESS ON THE WEB

For the Eighth Edition of *The Legal Environment of Business,* we offer a Companion Web site so that users can easily locate the resources they seek.

Resources at *The Legal Environment of Business* Web Site

When you visit **www.cengage.com/blaw/cross**, you will find a broad array of teaching/learning resources, including the following:

- **Sample answers** to the *Case Problem with Sample Answer,* which appears in the *Questions and Case Problems* section at the end of every chapter. This problem/answer set is designed to help your students learn how to answer case problems by acquainting them with model answers to selected problems. In addition, we offer the answers to the hypothetical *Questions with Sample Answers* on the Web site, as well as in the text (Appendix F).
- **Videos** referenced in the *Video Questions* that appear in selected chapters.
- **Internet exercises** for every chapter in the text (at least two per chapter). These exercises have been refocused to provide more practical information to legal environment of business students on topics covered in the chapters and to acquaint students with the resources that are available online.
- **Interactive quizzes** for every chapter in this text.
- **Legal reference materials** including a "Statutes" page that offers links to the full text of selected statutes referenced in the text, a Spanish glossary, and links to other important legal resources available for free on the Web.
- **Law on the Web** features that provide links to URLs that discuss topics related to each chapter in the text.
- **Link to our Business Law Digital Video Library** that provides a compendium of more than seventy-five video scenarios (see below).
- **Online Legal Research Guide** that offers complete yet brief guidance to using the Internet and evaluating information obtained from the Internet, as well as hyperlinks to the Web sites discussed.
- **Court case updates** that present summaries of new cases from various legal publications are continually updated and are specifically keyed to chapters in this text.

Business Law Digital Video Library

Video Questions appear at the end of selected chapters of this text. In response to popular demand, we have created some new *Video Questions* for this edition. Each of these questions directs students to the text's Web site at **www.cengage.com/blaw/cross** to view a video relevant to a topic covered in the chapter. This instruction is followed by a series of questions based on the video.

The videos can be used for homework assignments, discussion starters, or classroom demonstrations, and are useful for generating student interest. Some of the new videos are clips from actual movies or television series, such as *Field of Dreams, Midnight Run,* and *Mary Tyler Moore.* Others are from a new Real World Legal series of videos. By watching a video and answering the questions, students will gain an understanding of how the legal concepts they have studied in the chapter apply to the real-life situation portrayed in the video.

The videos are part of our Business Law Digital Video Library. An access code for the videos can be packaged with each new copy of this textbook for no additional charge. If Business Law Digital Video Library access did not come packaged with the textbook, students can purchase it online at **www.cengage.com/blaw/dvl**.

Suggested answers for all of the *Video Questions* are given in both the *Instructor's Manual* and the *Answers Manual* that accompany this text.

THE MOST COMPLETE SUPPLEMENTS PACKAGE AVAILABLE TODAY

This edition of *The Legal Environment of Business* is accompanied by a vast number of teaching and learning supplements. We have already mentioned CengageNOW, Aplia, CourseMate, and the supplemental resources available on the text's Web site at **www.cengage.com/blaw/cross**. In addition, the complete teaching/learning package for the Eighth Edition contains numerous other supplements, including those listed below. For further information on *The Legal Environment of Business* teaching/learning package, contact your local sales representative or visit the text's Web site.

Printed Supplements

- **Instructor's Manual**—Includes sections titled "Additional Cases Addressing This Issue" at the end of selected case synopses. (Also available on the *Instructor's Resource CD-ROM,* or IRCD.)
- **Study Guide**—Includes essay questions and sample CPA exam questions.
- **Two comprehensive Test Banks**—Offers a complete set of questions for every chapter to provide instructors with even greater flexibility in teaching. *Test Bank 1* and *Test Bank 2* each contain multiple-choice questions with answers, true/false questions with answers,

and two short essay questions per chapter. Additionally, there is one question for every *Shifting Legal Priorities for Business* and *Insight into Ethics* feature, and there are two multiple-choice questions for each *Focus on Ethics*. (Also available on the IRCD.)

- **Answers to Questions and Case Problems and Alternate Problem Sets with Answers**— Provides answers to all questions presented in the text, including the questions in each *Focus on Ethics,* the *Critical Thinking* questions concluding the *Insight into Ethics* feature, and alternate problem sets. (Also available on the IRCD.)

Software, Video, and Multimedia Supplements

- **Instructor's Resource CD-ROM (IRCD)**— The IRCD includes the following supplements: *Instructor's Manual, Answers Manual, Test Bank 1* and *Test Bank 2,* Case-Problem Cases, Case Printouts, Lecture Outline System, PowerPoint slides, ExamView, *Instructor's Manual* for the *Drama of the Law* video series, *Handbook of Landmark Cases and Statutes in Business Law and the Legal Environment, Handbook on Critical Thinking in Business Law and the Legal Environment,* and *A Guide to Personal Law.*
- **ExamView Testing Software** (also available on the IRCD).
- **Lecture Outline System** (also available on the IRCD).
- **PowerPoint slides** (also available on the IRCD).
- **WebTutor Advantage and WebTutor Toolbox**—Feature chat, discussion groups, testing, student progress tracking, and legal environment of business course materials.
- **Case-Problem Cases** (available only on the IRCD).
- **Transparency acetates** (available only on the IRCD).
- **Westlaw®**—Ten free hours for qualified adopters.
- **Business Law Digital Video Library**— Provides access to more than seventy-five videos, including the *Drama of the Law* videos and video clips from Hollywood movies. Access to our Business Law Digital Video Library is available in an optional package with each new text at no additional cost. If this access did not come with the textbook, your students can purchase it at **www.cengage.com/blaw/dvl**.

FOR USERS OF THE SEVENTH EDITION

First of all, we want to thank you for helping make *The Legal Environment of Business* the best-selling legal environment text in America today. Second, we want to make you aware of the numerous additions and changes that we have made in this new edition—many in response to comments from reviewers. For example, we have added more examples and new *Case in Point* features, and have incorporated the latest United States Supreme Court decisions throughout the text as appropriate.

Significantly Revised Chapters

Every chapter of the Eighth Edition has been revised as necessary to incorporate new developments in the law or to streamline the presentations. New trends in the law are also addressed in the cases and special features of the Eighth Edition. Other major changes and additions for this edition include the following:

- Chapter 4 (Ethics and Business Decision Making)—This chapter has been significantly revised, and a new section on the ethical transgressions of financial institutions discusses well-known companies, such as American International Group (AIG). The chapter also provides step-by-step guidance on making ethical business decisions, materials on global business ethics, and a new video question concerning marketing strategies in the pharmaceutical industry. The 2010 United States Supreme Court case involving Jeffrey Skilling, former CEO of Enron Corporation, is presented in the chapter. Other topics include recent bribery scandals, bribery by foreign companies, and Internet attacks on corporate reputations. A new *Shifting Legal Priorities for Business* feature titled *Corporate Social Responsibility May Mean Outbehaving the Competition* has been added.
- Chapter 5 (Constitutional Law)—This chapter has been thoroughly revised and updated to be more business oriented. New *Case in Point* examples have been added throughout, and the privacy materials have been updated to include a new subsection on pretexting.
- Chapter 6 (Administrative Law)—This chapter has been reworked to underscore the practical significance of administrative law for business-persons. We present the United States Supreme

Court case on fleeting expletives in this chapter and an *Insight into Ethics* titled *Should Pharmaceutical Companies Be Allowed to Tweet?*

- Chapter 7 (Criminal Law and Cyber Crime)—This chapter has been streamlined and updated. We have added discussions of criminal negligence and strict liability. A *Shifting Legal Priorities for Business* feature titled *Prosecuting White-Collar Crime with Honest-Services Fraud Law* includes a discussion of how the Supreme Court limited the application of this federal law in 2010.
- Chapter 11 (Sales, Leases, and E-Contracts)—We have streamlined and simplified our coverage of the Uniform Commercial Code. We have added numerous new *Case in Point* features and examples throughout the chapter to increase student comprehension. We have also expanded our discussion of international sales and lease contracts.
- Chapter 12 (Torts and Cyber Torts)—Our torts coverage has been revised to be more up to date and business oriented. We have added new materials on tort reform, cyber torts, spam, and the U.S. Safe Web Act. We also have reorganized the presentation of causation and damages and included additional coverage on comparative negligence, as well as a new *Insight into Ethics* feature titled *Some Consequences of Caps on Medical Malpractice Awards.*
- Chapter 14 (Intellectual Property and Internet Law)—The materials on intellectual property rights have been thoroughly revised and updated to reflect the most current laws and trends. We have reworked our discussion of descriptive, generic, and suggestive trademarks for clarity and included an updated discussion of software and business process patents. We have also updated the materials on copyrights in digital information and added a description of cloud computing. The chapter also includes updates on international treaties protecting intellectual property and a *Shifting Legal Priorities for Business* feature on the Anti-Counterfeiting Trade Agreement.
- Chapter 15 (Creditor-Debtor Relations and Bankruptcy)—This chapter has been revised to be more up to date and streamlined to focus on materials that students need to know. The bankruptcy law materials have been substantially revised and include updated dollar amounts of various provisions of the Bankruptcy Code.
- Chapter 16 (Mortgages and Foreclosures after the Recession)—This chapter is entirely new to this edition and provides a timely look at the mortgage crisis, predatory lending practices, and the laws enacted to address some of the problems that became evident during the recession.
- Chapter 19 (Corporations)—This chapter has been substantially revised and updated to provide more practical information and recent examples. We have reworked our coverage to reflect modern trends in corporate law. The chapter includes a new *Shifting Legal Priorities for Business* feature titled *The Latest Recession Re-Ignites the Internet Taxation Debate*. We have updated the materials on the Sarbanes-Oxley Act and added discussions of new e-proxy rules and shareholder access.
- Chapter 21 (Employment Relationships), Chapter 22 (Employment Discrimination), and Chapter 23 (Immigration and Labor Law)—These three chapters covering employment law have been thoroughly updated to include discussions of legal issues facing employers today.

  - Chapter 21 includes a new section on layoffs and the WARN Act and covers recent amendments to the FMLA. We have updated minimum wage figures, Social Security rates, and Medicare percentages, and include current information on privacy rights and genetic testing. The chapter also includes a new *Shifting Legal Priorities for Business* feature titled *The Online Creation and Modification of Employment Contracts*.
  - Chapter 22 includes the latest developments in age and disability discrimination and equal pay legislation. We discuss relevant United States Supreme Court decisions and have reworked the text to simplify and add clarity.
  - Chapter 23 includes coverage of labor law and new material on immigration law, which is of increasing importance to employers.

- Chapter 24 (Consumer Protection)—The materials on food labeling and credit cards have been significantly updated. This chapter discusses the Consumer Financial Protection Bureau, a new agency established by the 2010 financial reform package. A *Shifting Legal Priorities for Business* feature titled *New Health-Care Law Requires Caloric Information* is also included.
- Chapter 25 (Environmental Law)—The materials on air pollution and water pollution have been updated. New subsections discuss how environmental self-audits can help businesses minimize their liability and explain the innocent landowner, or third party, defense to Superfund liability.

- Chapter 26 (Real Property and Land-Use Control)—This chapter has been revised to include more discussion of zoning and includes a new *Shifting Legal Priorities for Business* feature titled *The Law of Building "Green"—Sustainable Real Estate Development.*
- Chapter 28 (Antitrust and Restraint of Trade)—We have added new examples and coverage of leading cases throughout the chapter, particularly in the discussions of price fix-

ing, relevant product market, and relevant geographic market.
- Chapter 29 (Investor Protection and Corporate Governance)—The materials on securities law and investor protection were revamped to make this difficult topic more understandable to students. The chapter now includes revised materials on the registration process to account for well-known seasoned issuers and updated coverage of securities fraud.

Acknowledgments for Previous Editions

Since we began this project many years ago, a sizable number of legal environment of business professors and others have helped us in various phases of the undertaking. The following reviewers offered numerous constructive criticisms, comments, and suggestions during the preparation of the previous editions.

Peter W. Allan
Victor Valley College

William Dennis Ames
Indiana University of Pennsylvania

Thomas M. Apke
California State University, Fullerton

Linda Axelrod
Metropolitan State University

Jane Bennett
Orange Coast College

Sam Cassidy
University of Denver

Angela Cerino
Villanova University

David Cooper
Fullerton College

Steven R. Donley
Cypress College

Paul F. Dwyer
Siena College

Joan Gabel
Florida State University

Gamewell Gant
Idaho State University

Arlene M. Hibschweiler
SUNY Fredonia

Barbara W. Kincaid
Southern Methodist University

Marty P. Ludlum
Oklahoma City Community College

Marty Salley McGee
South Carolina State University

Robert Mitchum
Arkansas State University, Beebe

Kathleen A. Phillips
University of Houston

David Redle
University of Akron

Larry A. Strate
University of Nevada–Las Vegas

Dawn Swink
Minnesota State University, Mankato

Brian Terry
Johnson and Wales University

John Theis
Mesa State College

Michael G. Walsh
Villanova University

Glynda White
Community College of Southern Nevada

LeVon E. Wilson
Western Carolina University

John A. Wrieden
Florida International University

Mary-Kathryn Zachary
State University of West Georgia

We would also like to give credit to the following reviewers for their useful input during development of CengageNOW for *The Legal Environment of Business:* Interactive Assignment System:

Nena Ellison
Florida Atlantic University

Jacqueline Hagerott
Franklin University

Melanie Morris
Raritan Valley Community College

William H. Volz
Wayne State University

We also wish to extend special thanks to the following individuals for their contributions to the Eighth Edition, specifically for their valuable input for new Chapter 16 and for helping revise Chapter 26:

Robert C. Bird
University of Connecticut

Corey Ciocchetti
University of Denver

Joan Gabel
Florida State University

Dean Bredeson
University of Texas at Austin

Thomas D. Cavenagh
North Central College–Naperville, Illinois

Eric D. Yordy
Northern Arizona University

As in all past editions, we owe a debt of extreme gratitude to the numerous individuals who worked directly with us or at Cengage Learning. In particular, we wish to thank Vicky True and Rob Dewey for their helpful advice and guidance during all of the stages of this new edition. We extend our thanks to Jan Lamar, our longtime developmental editor, for her many useful suggestions and for her efforts in coordinating reviews and ensuring the timely and accurate publication of all supplemental materials. We are also indebted to Laura-Aurora Stopa for her support and excellent marketing advice.

Our production manager and designer, Bill Stryker, made sure that we came out with an error-free, visually attractive Eighth Edition. We appreciate his efforts more than he can ever imagine. We are also indebted to the staff at Parkwood Composition, our compositor. Their ability to generate the pages for this text quickly and accurately made it possible for us to meet our ambitious printing schedule. We also wish to thank Joy Westberg for her creation of the visual preface.

We especially wish to thank Katherine Marie Silsbee for her management of the entire project, as well as for the application of her superb research and editorial skills. We also thank Lavina Leed Miller for her case research and Roger Meiners for his assistance in finding new case problems. We also wish to thank William Eric Hollowell, who co-authored the *Instructor's Manual,* the *Study Guide,* and the two *Test Banks,* for his excellent research efforts. We were fortunate enough to have the copy-editing of Jeanne Yost and the proofreading services of Susan Bradley and Pat Lewis. We are grateful for the efforts of Vickie Reierson and Roxanna Lee for their proofreading and other assistance, which helped to ensure an accurate text. Finally, we thank Suzanne Jasin of K & M Consulting for her many special efforts on this project.

In addition, we would like to give special thanks to all of the individuals who were instrumental in developing and implementing the new CengageNOW for *The Legal Environment of Business:* Interactive Assignment System. These include Rob Dewey, Vicky True, Jan Lamar, and Kristen Meere at Cengage Learning, and Katherine Marie Silsbee, Roger Meiners, Lavina Leed Miller, William Eric Hollowell, Kimberly Wallan, Kristi Wiswell, and Joseph Zavaleta.

Through the years, we have enjoyed an ongoing correspondence with many of you who have found points on which you wish to comment. We continue to welcome all comments and promise to respond promptly. By incorporating your ideas, we can continue to write a legal environment of business text that is best for you and best for your students.

F. B. C.
R. L. M.

Preface to the Student

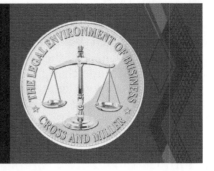

Welcome to the legal environment of business. You are about to embark on the study of one of the more important topics you can master in today's changing world. A solid understanding of the legal environment of business will, of course, help you if you are going into the world of business. If you decide on a career in accounting, economics, finance, political science, or history, understanding how the legal environment works is crucial.

Moreover, in your role as a consumer, you will be faced with some legal issues throughout your lifetime—renting an apartment, buying a house, obtaining a mortgage, and leasing a car, to mention only a few. In your role as an employee (if you don't go into business for yourself), you will need to know what rights you have and what rights you don't have. Even when you contemplate marriage, you will be faced with legal issues.

WHAT YOU WILL FIND IN THIS TEXT

As you thumb through the pages in this text, you will see that we have tried to make your study of the legal environment of business as efficient and enjoyable as possible. To this end, you will find the following aids on how to:

- **Master Terminology**—through *Key Terms* that are boldfaced, listed at the end of each chapter, and explained fully in the *Glossary* at the end of the book.
- **Understand Concepts**—through numerous *Concept Summaries* and *exhibits*.
- **Observe the Law in the Context of the Real World**—through new *Case in Point* examples within each chapter's text and the *Reviewing* feature at the end of every chapter.
- **See How Legal Issues Can Arise**—through *Video Questions* based on Web-available short videos, including some from Hollywood movies.
- **Figure out How the Law Is Evolving**—through a new feature called *Shifting Legal Priorities for Business*.

- **Determine How the Law Applies to Business Managers**—through the new *Managerial Implications* sections that appear in selected features and cases.
- **Gain Insight into How the Law Affects or Is Affected by Ethical Issues**—through the *Insight into Ethics* feature.

The above list, of course, is representative only. You will understand much more of what the legal environment of business is about as you read through the *court cases* presented in this book, including *Extended Case excerpts*, which will give you a feel for how the courts really decide cases. We present them in the courts' language (and provide bracketed definitions to clarify certain terms in the opinion).

IMPROVE YOUR ABILITY TO PERFORM LEGAL REASONING AND ANALYSIS

Although the legal environment of business may seem to be a mass of facts, your goal in taking this course should also be an increased ability to use legal reasoning and analysis to figure out how legal situations will be resolved. To this end, you will find the following key learning features to assist you in mastering legal reasoning and analysis:

- ***Find and Analyze Case Law***—In Chapter 1, you will find a section with this title that explains:

  - Legal citations.
  - The standard elements of a case.
  - The different types of opinions a court can issue.
  - How to read and understand cases.

- ***Brief a Case***—In Appendix A, you will see how to brief and analyze case problems. This explanation will teach you how to break down the elements of a case and will improve your ability to answer the *Case Problems* in each chapter.

XXVI PREFACE *TO THE STUDENT*

- *Questions with Sample Answers*—At the end of each chapter, there is one hypothetical factual scenario that presents a legal question for which you can access a *sample answer* in Appendix F (and also on the text's Web site). This allows you to practice and to see if you are answering the hypothetical questions correctly.
- *Case Problems with Sample Answers*—Each chapter has a series of chapter-ending *Case Problems*. You can find an answer to one problem in each chapter on this book's Companion Student Web site (discussed below). You can easily compare your answer to the court's opinion in each real case.
- *Impact of This Case on Today's Law*—Each case that is considered a landmark concludes with a short section that explains the relevance of older case law to the way courts reason today.
- *What If the Facts Were Different?*—This section, found at the end of selected cases, encourages you to think about how the outcome of a case might be different if the facts were altered.
- *The Ethical [E-Commerce, Global, or Legal Environment] Dimension*—Every case in this text concludes with two critical-thinking questions. These *Dimension* questions ask you to explore the law in a variety of contexts to help you meet the specific curriculum requirements for legal environment students.
- *Managerial Implications*—When a case has particular importance for business managers, we point out its significance in these special sections.

THE COMPANION STUDENT WEB SITE

The Companion Student Web site at **www.cengage.com/blaw/cross** provides you with short videos on various legal topics and with sample answers to selected case problems. In addition, you will find the following:

- *Interactive quizzes* for every chapter.
- *Appendix A: How to Brief and Analyze Case Problems* that will help you analyze

cases. This useful appendix in the book can also be downloaded from the Web site.
- *Legal reference materials* including a "Statutes" page that offers links to the full text of selected statutes referenced in the text, a Spanish glossary, and links to other important legal resources available free on the Web.
- *Internet exercises* for every chapter in the text (at least two per chapter) that help you learn how to research the law online.
- *Law on the Web* features that provide links to Web sites that discuss topics related to each chapter in the text.
- *Online Legal Research Guide* that offers complete yet brief guidance to using the Internet and evaluating information obtained from the Internet, as well as hyperlinks to the Web sites discussed.
- *Court case updates* that follow up on decisions presented in the text.

INTERACTIVE ASSIGNMENTS ON THE WEB

Some of you may have instructors who provide assignments using either of our interactive Web-based systems: **Aplia or CengageNOW for *The Legal Environment of Business:* Interactive Assignment System.**

Both Aplia and CengageNOW allow you to improve your mastery of legal concepts and terminology, legal reasoning and analysis, and much more. Your instructor will give you further information if she or he decides to use a Web-based system.

Of course, whether or not you are using Aplia or CengageNOW, you will wish to consider purchasing the *Study Guide*, which can help you get a better grade in your course (see the inside cover for details).

The law is all around you—and will be for the rest of your life. We hope that you begin your first course in the legal environment of business with the same high degree of excitement that we, the authors, always have when we work on improving this text, now in its Eighth Edition. *The Legal Environment of Business* has withstood the test of time—hundreds of thousands of students before you have already used and benefited from it.

Dedication

To my parents and sisters.

F. B. C.

To Dave VanHoose,

You represent the highest
level of professionalism
and dedication to academic
standards that I have ever
encountered.

Thanks,

R. L. M.

UNIT ONE

THE
FOUNDATIONS

CONTENTS

CHAPTER 1

Business and Its Legal Environment

One of the important functions of law in any society is to provide stability, predictability, and continuity so that people can know how to order their affairs. If any society is to survive, its citizens must be able to determine what is legally right and legally wrong. They must know what sanctions will be imposed on them if they commit wrongful acts. If they suffer harm as a result of others' wrongful acts, they must know how they can seek redress. By setting forth the rights, obligations, and privileges of citizens, the law enables individuals to go about their business with confidence and a certain degree of predictability. The stability and predictability created by the law provide an essential framework for all civilized activities, including business activities.

What do we mean when we speak of "the law"? Although the law has various definitions, they are all based on the general observation that **law** consists of *enforceable rules governing relationships among individuals and between individuals and their society.* These "enforceable rules" may consist of unwritten principles of behavior established by a nomadic tribe. They may be set forth in a law code, such as the Code of Hammurabi in ancient Babylon (c. 1780 B.C.E.) or the law code of one of today's European nations. They may consist of written laws and court decisions created by modern legislative and judicial bodies, as in the United States. Regardless of how such rules are created, they all have one thing in common: they establish rights, duties,

and privileges that are consistent with the values and beliefs of their society or its ruling group.

In this introductory chapter, we first look at an important question for any student reading this text: How does the legal environment affect business decision making? We next describe the major sources of American law, the common law tradition, and some basic schools of legal thought. We conclude the chapter with sections offering practical guidance on several topics, including how to find the sources of law discussed in this chapter (and referred to throughout the text) and how to read and understand court opinions.

SECTION 1
BUSINESS ACTIVITIES AND THE LEGAL ENVIRONMENT

As those entering the world of business will learn, laws and government regulations affect virtually all business activities—from hiring and firing decisions to workplace safety, the manufacturing and marketing of products, business financing, and more. To make good business decisions, a basic knowledge of the laws and regulations governing these activities is beneficial—if not essential. Realize also that in today's world, a knowledge of "black-letter" law is not enough. Businesspersons are also pressured to

make ethical decisions. Thus, the study of business law necessarily involves an ethical dimension.

Many Different Laws May Affect a Single Business Transaction

As you will note, each chapter in this text covers a specific area of the law and shows how the legal rules in that area affect business activities. Though compartmentalizing the law in this fashion promotes conceptual clarity, it does not indicate the extent to which a number of different laws may apply to just one transaction.

Consider an example. Suppose that you are the president of NetSys, Inc., a company that creates and maintains computer network systems for business firms, and also markets related software. One day, Hernandez, an operations officer for Southwest Distribution Corporation (SDC), contacts you by e-mail about a possible contract concerning SDC's computer network. In deciding whether to enter into a contract with SDC, you should consider, among other things, the legal requirements for an enforceable contract. Are there different requirements for a contract for services and a contract for products? What are your options if SDC **breaches** (breaks, or fails to perform) the contract? The answers to these questions are part of contract law and sales law.

Other questions might concern payment under the contract. How can you ensure that NetSys will be paid? For example, if payment is made with a check that is returned for insufficient funds, what are your options? Answers to these questions can be found in the laws that relate to negotiable instruments (such as checks) and creditors' rights. Also, a dispute may occur over the rights to NetSys's software, or there may be a question of liability if the software is defective. Questions may even be raised as to whether you and Hernandez had the authority to make the deal in the first place. A disagreement may arise from

other circumstances, such as an accountant's evaluation of the contract. Resolutions of these questions may be found in areas of the law that relate to intellectual property, e-commerce, torts, product liability, agency, business organizations, or professional liability.

Finally, if any dispute cannot be resolved amicably, then the laws and the rules concerning courts and court procedures spell out the steps of a lawsuit. Exhibit 1–1 below illustrates the various areas of law that may influence business decision making.

Ethics and Business Decision Making

Merely knowing the areas of law that may affect a business decision is not sufficient in today's business world. Businesspersons must also take ethics into account. As you will learn in Chapter 4, *ethics* generally is defined as the study of what constitutes right or wrong behavior. Today, business decision makers need to consider not just whether a decision is legal, but also whether it is ethical.

Throughout this text, you will learn about the relationship between the law and ethics, as well as about some of the types of ethical questions that

EXHIBIT 1–1 • Areas of the Law That May Affect Business Decision Making

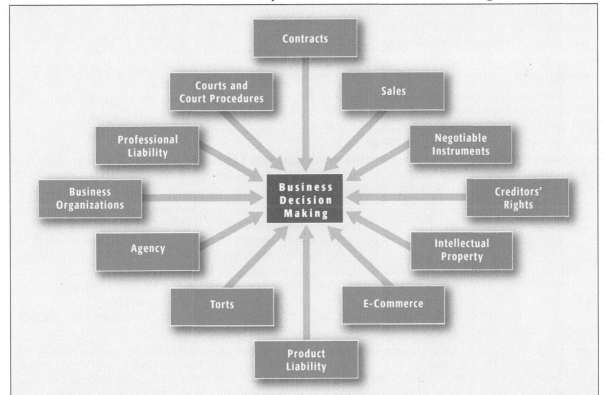

often arise in the business context. For example, the unit-ending *Focus on Ethics* features are devoted solely to the exploration of ethical questions pertaining to topics treated within the unit. We have also included *Ethical Dimension* questions for selected cases that stress the importance of ethical considerations in today's business climate and *Insight into Ethics* features that appear in selected chapters. A *Question of Ethics* case problem is included at the conclusion of every chapter to introduce the ethical aspects of specific cases involving real-life situations. Additionally, Chapter 4 offers a detailed look at the importance of ethical considerations in business decision making.

SECTION 2
SOURCES OF AMERICAN LAW

There are numerous sources of American law. *Primary sources of law,* or sources that establish the law, include the following:

1. The U.S. Constitution and the constitutions of the various states.
2. Statutory law—including laws passed by Congress, state legislatures, or local governing bodies.
3. Regulations created by administrative agencies, such as the Food and Drug Administration.
4. Case law and common law doctrines.

We describe each of these important sources of law in the following pages.

Secondary sources of law are books and articles that summarize and clarify the primary sources of law. Examples include legal encyclopedias, treatises, articles in law reviews, and compilations of law, such as the *Restatements of the Law* (which will be discussed shortly). Courts often refer to secondary sources of law for guidance in interpreting and applying the primary sources of law discussed here.

Constitutional Law

The federal government and the states have separate written constitutions that set forth the general organization, powers, and limits of their respective governments. **Constitutional law** is the law as expressed in these constitutions.

According to Article VI of the U.S. Constitution, the Constitution is the supreme law of the land. As such, it is the basis of all law in the United States. A law in violation of the Constitution, if challenged,

will be declared unconstitutional and will not be enforced, no matter what its source. Because of its importance in the American legal system, we present the complete text of the U.S. Constitution in Appendix B.

The Tenth Amendment to the U.S. Constitution reserves to the states all powers not granted to the federal government. Each state in the union has its own constitution. Unless it conflicts with the U.S. Constitution or a federal law, a state constitution is supreme within the state's borders.

Statutory Law

Laws enacted by legislative bodies at any level of government, such as the statutes passed by Congress or by state legislatures, make up the body of law generally referred to as **statutory law.** When a legislature passes a statute, that statute ultimately is included in the federal code of laws or the relevant state code of laws (these codes are discussed later in this chapter).

Statutory law also includes local **ordinances**—statutes (laws, rules, or orders) passed by municipal or county governing units to govern matters not covered by federal or state law. Ordinances commonly have to do with city or county land use (zoning ordinances), building and safety codes, and other matters affecting the local community.

A federal statute, of course, applies to all states. A state statute, in contrast, applies only within the state's borders. State laws thus may vary from state to state. No federal statute may violate the U.S. Constitution, and no state statute or local ordinance may violate the U.S. Constitution or the relevant state constitution.

UNIFORM LAWS The differences among state laws were particularly notable in the 1800s, when conflicting state statutes frequently made trade and commerce among the states difficult. To counter these problems, in 1892 a group of legal scholars and lawyers formed the National Conference of Commissioners on Uniform State Laws (NCCUSL) to draft **uniform laws,** or model laws, for the states to consider adopting. The NCCUSL still exists today and continues to issue uniform laws.

Each state has the option of adopting or rejecting a uniform law. *Only if a state legislature adopts a uniform law does that law become part of the statutory law of that state.* Note that a state legislature may adopt all or part of a uniform law as it is written, or the legislature may rewrite the law however the legislature wishes. Hence, even though many states may have adopted a uniform law, those states' laws may not be entirely "uniform."

The earliest uniform law, the Uniform Negotiable Instruments Law, was completed by 1896 and adopted in every state by the early 1920s (although not all states used exactly the same wording). Over the following decades, other acts were drawn up in a similar manner. In all, more than two hundred uniform acts have been issued by the NCCUSL since its inception. The most ambitious uniform act of all, however, was the Uniform Commercial Code.

THE UNIFORM COMMERCIAL CODE The Uniform Commercial Code (UCC), which was created through the joint efforts of the NCCUSL and the American Law Institute,[1] was first issued in 1952. All fifty states,[2] the District of Columbia, and the Virgin Islands have adopted the UCC. It facilitates commerce among the states by providing a uniform, yet flexible, set of rules governing commercial transactions. The UCC assures businesspersons that their contracts, if validly entered into, normally will be enforced.

As you will read in later chapters, from time to time the NCCUSL revises the articles contained in the UCC and submits the revised versions to the states for adoption. During the 1990s, for example, four articles (Articles 3, 4, 5, and 9) were revised, and two new articles (Articles 2A and 4A) were added. Amendments to Article 1 were approved in 2001 and have now been adopted by a majority of the states. Because of its importance in the area of commercial law, we cite the UCC frequently in this text. We also present excerpts of the UCC in Appendix C.

Administrative Law

Another important source of American law is **administrative law,** which consists of the rules, orders, and decisions of administrative agencies. An **administrative agency** is a federal, state, or local government agency established to perform a specific function. Administrative law and procedures, which will be examined in detail in Chapter 6, constitute a dominant element in the regulatory environment of business.

Rules issued by various administrative agencies now affect almost every aspect of a business's

operations, including its capital structure and financing, its hiring and firing procedures, its relations with employees and unions, and the way it manufactures and markets its products. Regulations enacted to protect the environment often play a significant role in business operations. See this chapter's *Shifting Legal Priorities for Business* feature on the following page for a discussion of the concept of sustainability and how some environmental regulations encourage it.

FEDERAL AGENCIES At the national level, the cabinet departments of the executive branch include numerous **executive agencies.** The U.S. Food and Drug Administration, for example, is an agency within the U.S. Department of Health and Human Services. Executive agencies are subject to the authority of the president, who has the power to appoint and remove their officers. There are also major **independent regulatory agencies** at the federal level, such as the Federal Trade Commission, the Securities and Exchange Commission, and the Federal Communications Commission. The president's power is less pronounced in regard to independent agencies, whose officers serve for fixed terms and cannot be removed without just cause.

STATE AND LOCAL AGENCIES There are administrative agencies at the state and local levels as well. Commonly, a state agency (such as a state pollution-control agency) is created as a parallel to a federal agency (such as the Environmental Protection Agency). Just as federal statutes take precedence over conflicting state statutes, so federal agency regulations take precedence over conflicting state regulations.

Case Law and Common Law Doctrines

The rules of law announced in court decisions constitute another basic source of American law. These rules include interpretations of constitutional provisions, of statutes enacted by legislatures, and of regulations created by administrative agencies. Today, this body of judge-made law is referred to as **case law.** Case law—the doctrines and principles announced in cases—governs all areas not covered by statutory law or administrative law and is part of our common law tradition. We look at the origins and characteristics of the common law tradition in some detail in the pages that follow.

See *Concept Summary 1.1* on page 7 for a review of the sources of American law.

---

1. This institute was formed in the 1920s and consists of practicing attorneys, legal scholars, and judges.
2. Louisiana has not adopted Articles 2 and 2A (covering contracts for the sale and lease of goods), however.

By now, almost everyone is aware that at the federal, state, and local levels there are numerous statutes that deal with the environment (environmental law will be discussed in Chapter 25). In the last few years, federal, state, and local statutes and administrative regulations have started to embrace the concept of sustainability.

What Does Sustainability Mean?

Although there is no one official definition, *sustainability* generally has been defined as economic development that meets the needs of the present while not compromising the ability of future generations to meet their own needs. By any definition, sustainability is a process rather than a tangible outcome. For business managers, it means that they should engage in long-range planning rather than focusing only on short-run profitability.

Federal Law and Sustainability

Certain provisions of federal environmental laws directly address the topic of sustainability. For example, the Resource Conservation and Recovery Act[a] requires waste minimization as the preferred means of hazardous waste management. Facilities that generate or manage hazardous waste must certify that they have a waste minimization program that reduces the toxicity and quantity of the hazardous waste.

The Pollution Prevention Act (PPA)[b] requires that facilities minimize or eliminate the release of pollutants into the environment whenever feasible. The PPA established a national policy to recycle any pollutants that cannot be prevented.

Finally, the federal Environmental Protection Agency (EPA) has undertaken a major effort to encourage sustainability. The agency's Web site (www.epa.gov) devotes numerous pages to sustainability, sustainable development, and sustainable agriculture. The EPA also has a "sector strategies program" that seeks industry-wide environmental gains through innovative actions.

Other nations have enacted legislation that requires sustainability to be taken into account when protecting the environment. An example is the Environmental Protection and Bio-Diversity Conservation Act in Australia.[c]

State Law and Sustainability

At least one state has legislatively committed itself to the concept of sustainable policies. More than a decade ago, the Oregon Sustainability Act was passed. This act officially defines *sustainability* as:

Using, developing, and protecting resources in a manner that enables people to meet current needs and provides that future generations can also meet future needs, from the joint perspective of environmental, economic, and community objectives.

Oregon's seven-member sustainability board recommends and proposes sustainability legislation and also develops policies and programs related to sustainability.

Where Does the United States Rank in the World Sustainability Index?

Environmental experts from Yale and Columbia universities have created an Environmental Sustainability Index (ESI) that ranks countries according to how well they manage their environments, protect the global commons, and have the capacity to improve their environmental performance. Finland and Norway are at the top of the ESI. The United States ranks forty-fifth. This low ranking is due mainly to excessive waste generation and greenhouse gas emissions in this country.

Some Corporations Take the Lead by Creating the Position of a Chief Sustainability Officer

The giant chemical company DuPont has an official chief sustainability officer (CSO)—a position that did not exist a few years ago. This corporate officer is responsible not only for ensuring that the company complies with all federal, state, local, and international environmental regulations, but also for discovering so-called megatrends that can affect different markets.

DuPont, though best known as a chemical company, also sells agricultural seeds and crop-protection products. One megatrend that its CSO has identified is a growing world population that is going to require more production of corn, soybeans, and other crops from limited acreage. That is where sustainability comes in—producing more with less.

MANAGERIAL IMPLICATIONS

Managers cannot wait until the government tells them what sustainable business practices they must follow. A company that adopts sustainable business practices today not only will promote desirable economic, social, and environmental results, but at the same time will enhance productivity, reduce costs, and thereby increase profitability. A company that has a clear understanding of sustainability will be more competitive as increasing consumer demand for "green" products and global concerns about the environment put pressure on all producers.

a. 42 U.S.C. Sections 6901 *et seq.* (1976).
b. 42 U.S.C. Sections 13101 *et seq.* (1990).
c. This act became effective in 1999 and has been amended many times since.

CONCEPT SUMMARY 1.1
Sources of American Law

Source	Description
Constitutional Law	The law as expressed in the U.S. Constitution and the state constitutions. The U.S. Constitution is the supreme law of the land. State constitutions are supreme within state borders to the extent that they do not violate a clause of the U.S. Constitution or a federal law.
Statutory Law	Laws (statutes and ordinances) enacted by federal, state, and local legislatures and governing bodies. None of these laws may violate the U.S. Constitution or the relevant state constitution. Uniform laws, when adopted by a state, become statutory law in that state.
Administrative Law	The rules, orders, and decisions of federal, state, or local government administrative agencies.
Case Law and Common Law Doctrines	Judge-made law, including interpretations of constitutional provisions, of statutes enacted by legislatures, and of regulations created by administrative agencies.

SECTION 3
THE COMMON LAW TRADITION

Because of our colonial heritage, much of American law is based on the English legal system, which originated in medieval England and continued to evolve in the following centuries. Knowledge of this system is necessary to understanding the American legal system today.

Early English Courts

The origins of the English legal system—and thus the U.S. legal system as well—date back to 1066, when the Normans conquered England. William the Conqueror and his successors began the process of unifying the country under their rule. One of the means they used to do this was the establishment of the king's courts, or *curiae regis*. Before the Norman Conquest, disputes had been settled according to the local legal customs and traditions in various regions of the country. The king's courts sought to establish a uniform set of customs for the country as a whole. What evolved in these courts was the beginning of the **common law**—a body of general rules that applied throughout the entire English realm. Eventually, the common law tradition became part of the heritage of all nations that were once British colonies, including the United States.

COURTS OF LAW AND REMEDIES AT LAW The early English king's courts could grant only very limited kinds of **remedies** (the legal means to enforce a right or redress a wrong). If one person wronged another in some way, the king's courts could award as compensation one or more of the following: (1) land, (2) items of value, or (3) money. The courts that awarded this compensation became known as **courts of law,** and the three remedies were called **remedies at law.** (Today, the remedy at law normally takes the form of monetary **damages**—an amount given to a party whose legal interests have been injured.) Even though the system introduced uniformity in the settling of disputes, when a complaining party wanted a remedy other than economic compensation, the courts of law could do nothing, so "no remedy, no right."

COURTS OF EQUITY AND REMEDIES IN EQUITY Equity is a branch of law—founded on what might be described as notions of justice and fair dealing—that seeks to supply a remedy when no adequate remedy at law is available. When individuals could not obtain an adequate remedy in a court of law, they petitioned the king for relief. Most of these petitions were decided by an adviser to the king, called a **chancellor,** who had the power to grant new and unique remedies. Eventually, formal chancery courts, or **courts of equity,** were established.

The remedies granted by the equity courts became known as **remedies in equity,** or equitable remedies. These remedies include *specific performance* (ordering a party to perform an agreement as promised), an *injunction* (ordering a party to cease engaging in a specific activity or to undo some wrong or injury), and *rescission* (the cancellation of a contractual obligation). We will discuss these and other equitable remedies in more detail at appropriate points in the chapters that follow, particularly in Chapter 10.

As a general rule, today's courts, like the early English courts, will not grant equitable remedies unless the remedy at law—monetary damages—is inadequate. Suppose that Ted forms a contract (a legally binding agreement—see Chapter 9) to purchase a parcel of land that he thinks will be just perfect for his future home. Further suppose that the seller breaches this agreement. Ted could sue the seller for the return of any deposits or down payment he might have made on the land, but this is not the remedy he really seeks. What Ted wants is to have the court order the seller to perform the contract. In other words, Ted wants the court to grant the equitable remedy of specific performance because monetary damages are inadequate in this situation.

EQUITABLE MAXIMS In fashioning appropriate remedies, judges often were (and continue to be) guided by so-called **equitable maxims**—propositions or general statements of equitable rules. Exhibit 1–2 below lists some important equitable maxims. The last maxim listed in that exhibit—"Equity aids the vigilant, not those who rest on their rights"—merits special attention. It has become known as the equitable doctrine of **laches** (a term derived from the Latin *laxus*, meaning "lax" or "negligent"), and it can be used as a defense. A **defense** is an argument raised by the **defendant** (the party being sued) indicating why the **plaintiff** (the suing party) should not obtain the remedy sought. (Note that in equity proceedings, the party bringing a lawsuit is called the **petitioner**, and the party being sued is referred to as the **respondent**.)

The doctrine of laches arose to encourage people to bring lawsuits while the evidence was fresh.

What constitutes a reasonable time, of course, varies according to the circumstances of the case. Time periods for different types of cases are now usually fixed by **statutes of limitations.** After the time allowed under a statute of limitations has expired, no action (lawsuit) can be brought, no matter how strong the case was originally.

Legal and Equitable Remedies Today

The establishment of courts of equity in medieval England resulted in two distinct court systems: courts of law and courts of equity. The courts had different sets of judges and granted different types of remedies. During the nineteenth century, however, most states in the United States adopted rules of procedure that resulted in the combining of courts of law and equity. A party now may request both legal and equitable remedies in the same action, and the trial court judge may grant either or both forms of relief.

The distinction between legal and equitable remedies remains relevant to students of business law, however, because these remedies differ. To seek the proper remedy for a wrong, one must know what remedies are available. Additionally, certain vestiges of the procedures used when there were separate courts of law and equity still exist. For example, a party has the right to demand a jury trial in an action at law, but not in an action in equity. Exhibit 1–3 on the facing page summarizes the procedural differences (applicable in most states) between an action at law and an action in equity.

The Doctrine of *Stare Decisis*

One of the unique features of the common law is that it is *judge-made* law. The body of principles and doctrines that form the common law emerged over time as judges decided legal controversies.

EXHIBIT 1–2 • Equitable Maxims

1. *Whoever seeks equity must do equity.* (Anyone who wishes to be treated fairly must treat others fairly.)
2. *Where there is equal equity, the law must prevail.* (The law will determine the outcome of a controversy in which the merits of both sides are equal.)
3. *One seeking the aid of an equity court must come to the court with clean hands.* (The plaintiff must have acted fairly and honestly.)
4. *Equity will not suffer a wrong to be without a remedy.* (Equitable relief will be awarded when there is a right to relief and there is no adequate remedy at law.)
5. *Equity regards substance rather than form.* (Equity is more concerned with fairness and justice than with legal technicalities.)
6. *Equity aids the vigilant, not those who rest on their rights.* (Equity will not help those who neglect their rights for an unreasonable period of time.)

EXHIBIT 1-3 • Procedural Differences between an Action at Law and an Action in Equity

PROCEDURE	ACTION AT LAW	ACTION IN EQUITY
Initiation of Lawsuit	By filing a complaint	By filing a petition
Parties	Plaintiff and defendant	Petitioner and respondent
Decision	By jury or judge	By judge (no jury)
Result	Judgment	Decree
Remedy	Monetary damages	Injunction, specific performance, or rescission

CASE PRECEDENTS AND CASE REPORTERS When possible, judges attempted to be consistent and to base their decisions on the principles suggested by earlier cases. They sought to decide similar cases in a similar way and considered new cases with care because they knew that their decisions would make new law. Each interpretation became part of the law on the subject and served as a legal **precedent**—that is, a decision that furnished an example or authority for deciding subsequent cases involving identical or similar legal principles or facts.

In the early years of the common law, there was no single place or publication where court opinions, or written decisions, could be found. By the early fourteenth century, portions of the most important decisions from each year were being gathered together and recorded in *Year Books,* which became useful references for lawyers and judges. In the sixteenth century, the *Year Books* were discontinued, and other forms of case publication became available. Today, cases are published, or "reported," in volumes called **reporters,** or *reports*. We describe today's case reporting system in detail later in this chapter.

STARE DECISIS AND THE COMMON LAW TRADITION The practice of deciding new cases with reference to former decisions, or precedents, became a cornerstone of the English and American judicial systems. The practice formed a doctrine known as **stare decisis**[3] (a Latin phrase meaning "to stand on decided cases").

Under this doctrine, judges are obligated to follow the precedents established within their jurisdictions. The term *jurisdiction* refers to a geographic area in which a court or courts have the power to apply the law—see Chapter 2. Once a court has set forth a principle of law as being applicable to a certain set of facts, that court and courts of lower rank (within the same jurisdiction) must adhere to that principle and apply it in future cases involving similar fact patterns. Thus, *stare decisis* has two aspects: first, that decisions made by a higher court are binding on lower courts; and second, that a court should not overturn its own precedents unless there is a compelling reason to do so.

Controlling precedents in a jurisdiction are referred to as binding authorities. A **binding authority** is any source of law that a court must follow when deciding a case. Binding authorities include constitutions, statutes, and regulations that govern the issue being decided, as well as court decisions that are controlling precedents within the jurisdiction. United States Supreme Court case decisions, no matter how old, remain controlling until they are overruled by a subsequent decision of the Supreme Court, by a constitutional amendment, or by congressional legislation (that has not been held unconstitutional).

STARE DECISIS AND LEGAL STABILITY The doctrine of *stare decisis* helps the courts to be more efficient because if other courts have carefully analyzed a similar case, their legal reasoning and opinions can serve as guides. *Stare decisis* also makes the law more stable and predictable. If the law on a given subject is well settled, someone bringing a case to court can usually rely on the court to make a decision based on what the law has been in the past.

DEPARTURES FROM PRECEDENT Although courts are obligated to follow precedents, sometimes a court will depart from the rule of precedent if it decides that the precedent should no longer be followed. If a court decides that a ruling precedent is simply incorrect or that technological or social changes have rendered the precedent inapplicable, the court might rule contrary to the precedent. Cases that overturn precedent often receive a great deal of publicity.

---

3. Pronounced *ster*-ay dih-*si*-ses.

CASE IN POINT The United States Supreme Court expressly overturned precedent when it concluded that separate educational facilities for whites and blacks, which it had previously upheld as constitutional,[4] were inherently unequal.[5] The Court's departure from precedent in this case received a tremendous amount of publicity as people began to realize the ramifications of this change in the law.

Note that judges do have some flexibility in applying precedents. For example, a lower court may avoid applying a precedent set by a higher court in its jurisdiction by distinguishing the two cases based on their facts. When this happens, the lower court's ruling stands unless it is appealed to a higher court and that court overturns the decision.

WHEN THERE IS NO PRECEDENT Occasionally, the courts must decide cases for which no precedents exist, called *cases of first impression.* For example, as you will read throughout this text, the extensive use of the Internet has presented many new and challenging issues for the courts to decide. In deciding cases of first impression, courts often look at *persuasive authorities* (precedents from other jurisdictions) for guidance. A court may also consider a number of factors, including legal principles and policies underlying previous court decisions or existing statutes, fairness, social values and customs, **public policy** (governmental policy based on widely held societal values), and data and concepts drawn from the social sciences. Which of these sources is chosen or receives the greatest emphasis depends on the nature of the case being considered and the particular judge or judges hearing the case.

Stare Decisis and Legal Reasoning

Legal reasoning is the reasoning process used by judges in deciding what law applies to a given dispute and then applying that law to the specific facts or circumstances of the case. Through the use of legal reasoning, judges harmonize their decisions with those that have been made before, as the doctrine of *stare decisis* requires.

Students of business law and the legal environment also engage in legal reasoning. For example, you may be asked to provide answers for some of the case problems that appear at the end of every chapter in this text. Each problem describes the facts of a particular dispute and the legal question at issue. If you are assigned a case problem, you will be asked to determine how a court would answer that question, and why. In other words, you will need to give legal reasons for whatever conclusion you reach.[6] We look here at the basic steps involved in legal reasoning and then describe some forms of reasoning commonly used by the courts in making their decisions.

BASIC STEPS IN LEGAL REASONING At times, the legal arguments set forth in court opinions are relatively simple and brief. At other times, the arguments are complex and lengthy. Regardless of the length of a legal argument, however, the basic steps of the legal reasoning process remain the same. These steps, which you can also follow when analyzing cases and case problems, form what is commonly referred to as the *IRAC method* of legal reasoning. IRAC is an acronym formed from the first letters of the following words: *Issue, Rule, Application,* and *Conclusion.* To apply the IRAC method, you would ask the following questions:

1. *What are the key facts and issues?* Suppose that a plaintiff comes before the court claiming *assault* (the act of wrongfully and intentionally making another person fearful of immediate physical harm—part of a class of actions called *torts*). The plaintiff claims that the defendant threatened her while she was sleeping. Although the plaintiff was unaware that she was being threatened, her roommate heard the defendant make the threat. The legal issue, or question, raised by these facts is whether the defendant's action constitutes the tort of assault, given that the plaintiff was not aware of that action at the time it occurred.

2. *What rules of law apply to the case?* A rule of law may be a rule stated by the courts in previous decisions, a state or federal statute, or a state or federal administrative agency regulation. In our hypothetical case, the plaintiff **alleges** (claims) that the defendant committed a tort. Therefore, the applicable law is the common law of torts—specifically, tort law governing assault (see Chapter 12 for more detail on intentional torts). Case precedents involving similar facts and issues thus would be relevant. Often, more than one rule of law will be applicable to a case.

---

4. See *Plessy v. Ferguson,* 163 U.S. 537, 16 S.Ct. 1138, 41 L.Ed. 256 (1896). A later section in this chapter explains how to read legal citations.

5. *Brown v. Board of Education of Topeka,* 347 U.S. 483, 74 S.Ct. 686, 98 L.Ed. 873 (1954).

6. See Appendix A for further instructions on how to analyze case problems.

3. *How do the rules of law apply to the particular facts and circumstances of this case?* This step is often the most difficult because each case presents a unique set of facts, circumstances, and parties. Although cases may be similar, no two cases are ever identical in all respects. Normally, judges (and lawyers and law students) try to find **cases on point**— previously decided cases that are as similar as possible to the one under consideration. (Because of the difficulty—and importance—of this step in the legal reasoning process, we discuss it in more detail in the next subsection.)

4. *What conclusion should be drawn?* This step normally presents few problems. Usually, the conclusion is evident if the previous three steps have been followed carefully.

FORMS OF LEGAL REASONING Judges use many types of reasoning when following the third step of the legal reasoning process—applying the law to the facts of a particular case. Three common forms of reasoning are deductive reasoning, linear reasoning, and reasoning by analogy.

Deductive Reasoning. Deductive reasoning is sometimes called *syllogistic reasoning* because it employs a **syllogism**—a logical relationship involving a major premise, a minor premise, and a conclusion. For example, consider the hypothetical case presented earlier. In deciding whether the defendant committed assault by threatening the plaintiff while she was sleeping, the judge might point out that "under the common law of torts, an individual must be *aware* of a threat of danger for the threat to constitute assault" (major premise); "the plaintiff in this case was unaware of the threat at the time it occurred" (minor premise); and "therefore, the circumstances do not amount to an assault" (conclusion).

Linear Reasoning. A second form of legal reasoning that is commonly employed might be thought of as "linear" reasoning because it proceeds from one point to another, with the final point being the conclusion. To understand this form of reasoning, imagine a knotted rope, with each knot tying together separate pieces of rope to form a tightly knotted length. As a whole, the rope represents a linear progression of thought logically connecting various points, with the last point, or knot, representing the conclusion. For example, a tenant in an apartment building sues the landlord for damages for an injury resulting from an allegedly inadequately lit stairway.

The court may engage in a reasoning process involving the following "pieces of rope":

1. The landlord, who was on the premises the evening the injury occurred, testifies that none of the other nine tenants who used the stairway that night complained about the lights.
2. The fact that none of the tenants complained is the same as if they had said the lighting was sufficient.
3. That there were no complaints does not prove that the lighting was sufficient but does prove that the landlord had no reason to believe that it was not.
4. The landlord's belief was reasonable because no one complained.
5. Therefore, the landlord acted reasonably and was not negligent with respect to the lighting in the stairway.

From this reasoning, the court concludes that the tenant is not entitled to compensation on the basis of the stairway's allegedly insufficient lighting.

Reasoning by Analogy. Another important type of reasoning that judges use in deciding cases is reasoning by *analogy*. To reason by **analogy** is to compare the facts in the case at hand to the facts in previous cases and, to the extent that the patterns are similar, to apply the same rule of law to the present case. To the extent that the facts are unique, or "distinguishable," different rules may apply. For example, in Case A, the court held that a driver who crossed a highway's center line was negligent. Case B involves a driver who crossed the line to avoid hitting a child. In determining whether Case A's rule applies in Case B, a judge would consider what the reasons were for the decision in A and whether B is sufficiently similar for those reasons to apply. If the judge holds that B's driver is not liable, that judge must indicate why Case A's rule is not relevant to the facts presented in Case B.

There Is No One "Right" Answer

Many people believe that there is one "right" answer to every legal question. In most legal controversies, however, there is no single correct result. Good arguments can often be made to support either side of a legal controversy. Quite often, a case does not involve a "good" person suing a "bad" person. In many cases, both parties have acted in good faith in some measure or in bad faith to some degree.

Additionally, each judge has her or his own personal beliefs and philosophy (see the discussion of schools of jurisprudential thought later in this chapter), which shape the process of legal reasoning, at least to some extent. This means that the outcome of a particular lawsuit before a court cannot be predicted with absolute certainty. In fact, in some cases, even though the weight of the law would seem to favor one party's position, judges, through creative legal reasoning, have found ways to rule in favor of the other party in the interests of preventing injustice.

Legal reasoning and other aspects of the common law tradition are reviewed in *Concept Summary 1.2* below.

The Common Law Today

Today, the common law derived from judicial decisions continues to be applied throughout the United States. Common law doctrines and principles, however, govern only areas *not* covered by statutory or administrative law. In a dispute concerning a particular employment practice, for example, if a statute regulates that practice, the statute will apply rather than the common law doctrine that applied prior to the enactment of the statute.

COURTS INTERPRET STATUTES Even in areas governed by statutory law, though, judge-made law continues to be important because there is a significant interplay between statutory law and the common law. For example, many statutes essentially codify existing common law rules, and regulations issued by various administrative agencies usually are based, at least in part, on common law principles. Additionally, the courts, in interpreting statutory law, often rely on the common law as a guide to what the legislators intended.

Furthermore, how the courts interpret a particular statute determines how that statute will be applied. If you wanted to learn about the coverage and applicability of a particular statute, for example, you would necessarily have to locate the statute and study it. You would also need to see how the courts in your jurisdiction have interpreted and applied the statute. In other words, you would have to learn what precedents have been established in your jurisdiction with respect to that statute. Often, the applicability of a newly enacted statute does not become clear until a body of case law develops to clarify how, when, and to whom the statute applies.

RESTATEMENTS OF THE LAW CLARIFY AND ILLUSTRATE THE COMMON LAW The American Law Institute has drafted and published compilations of the common law called *Restatements of the Law*, which generally summarize the common law rules followed by most states. There are *Restatements of the Law* in the

CONCEPT SUMMARY 1.2
The Common Law Tradition

Aspect	Description
Origins of the Common Law	The American legal system is based on the common law tradition, which originated in medieval England. Following the conquest of England in 1066 by William the Conqueror, king's courts were established throughout England, and the common law was developed in these courts.
Legal and Equitable Remedies	The distinction between remedies at law (money or items of value, such as land) and remedies in equity (including specific performance, injunction, and rescission of a contractual obligation) originated in the early English courts of law and courts of equity, respectively.
Case Precedents and the Doctrine of *Stare Decisis*	In the king's courts, judges attempted to make their decisions consistent with previous decisions, called precedents. This practice gave rise to the doctrine of *stare decisis*. This doctrine, which became a cornerstone of the common law tradition, obligates judges to abide by precedents established in their jurisdictions.
Stare Decisis and Legal Reasoning	Legal reasoning is the reasoning process used by judges in applying the law to the facts and issues of specific cases. Legal reasoning involves becoming familiar with the key facts of a case, identifying the relevant legal rules, applying those rules to the facts, and drawing a conclusion. In applying the legal rules to the facts of a case, judges may use deductive reasoning, linear reasoning, or reasoning by analogy.

areas of contracts, torts, agency, trusts, property, restitution, security, judgments, and conflict of laws. The *Restatements,* like other secondary sources of law, do not in themselves have the force of law, but they are an important source of legal analysis and opinion on which judges often rely in making their decisions.

Many of the *Restatements* are now in their second, third, or fourth editions. We refer to the *Restatements* frequently in subsequent chapters of this text, indicating in parentheses the edition to which we are referring. For example, we refer to the third edition of the *Restatement of the Law of Contracts* as simply the *Restatement (Third) of Contracts.*

SECTION 4
SCHOOLS OF JURISPRUDENTIAL THOUGHT

How judges apply the law to specific cases, including disputes relating to the business world, depends in part on their philosophical approaches to law. Part of the study of law, often referred to as **jurisprudence,** involves learning about different schools of jurisprudential thought and discovering how the approaches to law characteristic of each school can affect judicial decision making.

Clearly, a judge's function is not to *make* the laws—that is the function of the legislative branch of government—but to interpret and apply them. From a practical point of view, however, the courts play a significant role in defining the laws enacted by legislative bodies, which tend to be expressed in general terms. Judges thus have some flexibility in interpreting and applying the law. It is because of this flexibility that different courts can, and often do, arrive at different conclusions in cases that involve nearly identical issues, facts, and applicable laws.

The Natural Law School

An age-old question about the nature of law has to do with the finality of a nation's laws, such as the laws of the United States at the present time. For example, what if a particular law is deemed to be a "bad" law by a substantial number of that nation's citizens? Those who adhere to the **natural law** theory believe that a higher or universal law exists that applies to all human beings and that written laws should imitate these inherent principles. If a written law is unjust, then it is not a true (natural) law and need not be obeyed.

The natural law tradition is one of the oldest and most significant schools of jurisprudence. It dates back to the days of the Greek philosopher Aristotle (384–322 B.C.E.), who distinguished between natural law and the laws governing a particular nation. According to Aristotle, natural law applies universally to all humankind.

The notion that people have "natural rights" stems from the natural law tradition. Those who claim that a specific foreign government is depriving certain citizens of their human rights are implicitly appealing to a higher law that has universal applicability. The question of the universality of basic human rights also comes into play in the context of international business operations. For example, U.S. companies that have operations abroad often hire foreign workers as employees. Should the same laws that protect U.S. employees apply to these foreign employees? This question is rooted implicitly in a concept of universal rights that has its origins in the natural law tradition.

The Positivist School

In contrast, *positive,* or national, law (the written law of a given society at a particular point in time) applies only to the citizens of that nation or society. Those who adhere to **legal positivism** believe that there can be no higher law than a nation's positive law. According to the positivist school, there is no such thing as "natural rights." Rather, human rights exist solely because of laws. If the laws are not enforced, anarchy will result. Thus, whether a law is "bad" or "good" is irrelevant. The law is the law and must be obeyed until it is changed—in an orderly manner through a legitimate lawmaking process. A judge with positivist leanings probably would be more inclined to defer to an existing law than would a judge who adheres to the natural law tradition.

The Historical School

The **historical school** of legal thought emphasizes the evolutionary process of law by concentrating on the origin and history of the legal system. This school looks to the past to discover what the principles of contemporary law should be. The legal doctrines that have withstood the passage of time—those that have worked in the past—are deemed best suited for shaping present laws. Hence, law derives its legitimacy and authority from adhering to the standards that historical development has shown to be workable. Adherents of the historical school are more likely than those of other schools to strictly follow decisions made in past cases.

Legal Realism

In the 1920s and 1930s, a number of jurists and scholars, known as *legal realists,* rebelled against the historical approach to law. **Legal realism** is based on the idea that law is just one of many institutions in society and that it is shaped by social forces and needs. The law is a human enterprise, and judges should take social and economic realities into account when deciding cases. Legal realists also believe that the law can never be applied with total uniformity. Given that judges are human beings with unique personalities, value systems, and intellects, different judges will obviously bring different reasoning processes to the same case.

Legal realism strongly influenced the growth of what is sometimes called the **sociological school** of jurisprudence. This school views law as a tool for promoting justice in society. In the 1960s, for example, the justices of the United States Supreme Court played a leading role in the civil rights movement by upholding long-neglected laws calling for equal treatment for all Americans, including African Americans and other minorities. Generally, jurists who adhere to this philosophy of law are more likely to depart from past decisions than are those jurists who adhere to the other schools of legal thought.

Concept Summary 1.3 below reviews the schools of jurisprudential thought.

SECTION 5

CLASSIFICATIONS OF LAW

The law may be broken down according to several classification systems. For example, one classification system divides law into substantive law and procedural law. **Substantive law** consists of all laws that define, describe, regulate, and create legal rights and obligations. **Procedural law** consists of all laws that delineate the methods of enforcing the rights established by substantive law. Other classification systems divide law into federal law and state law, private law (dealing with relationships between private entities) and public law (addressing the relationship between persons and their governments), and national law and international law. Here we look at still another classification system, which divides law into civil law and criminal law, as well as at what is meant by the term *cyberlaw.*

Civil Law and Criminal Law

Civil law spells out the rights and duties that exist between persons and between persons and their governments, as well as the relief available when a person's rights are violated. Typically, in a civil case, a private party sues another private party

CONCEPT SUMMARY 1.3
Schools of Jurisprudential Thought

School of Thought	Description
Natural Law School	One of the older and more significant schools of legal thought. Those who believe in natural law hold that there is a universal law applicable to all human beings. This law is discoverable through reason and is of a higher order than positive (national) law.
Positivist School	A school of legal thought centered on the assumption that there is no law higher than the laws created by the government. Laws must be obeyed, even if they are unjust, to prevent anarchy.
Historical School	A school of legal thought that stresses the evolutionary nature of law and looks to doctrines that have withstood the passage of time for guidance in shaping present laws.
Legal Realism	A school of legal thought that advocates a less abstract and more realistic and pragmatic approach to the law and takes into account customary practices and the circumstances surrounding the particular transaction. Legal realism strongly influenced the growth of the *sociological school* of jurisprudence, which views law as a tool for promoting social justice.

(although the government can also sue a party for a civil law violation) to make that other party comply with a duty or pay for the damage caused by failure to comply with a duty. Much of the law that we discuss in this text is civil law. Contract law, for example, covered in Chapters 9 and 10, is civil law. The whole body of tort law (see Chapter 12) is also civil law.

Criminal law, in contrast, is concerned with wrongs committed *against the public as a whole.* Criminal acts are defined and prohibited by local, state, or federal government statutes. Criminal defendants are thus prosecuted by public officials, such as a district attorney (D.A.), on behalf of the state, not by their victims or other private parties. (See Chapter 7 for a further discussion of the distinction between civil law and criminal law.)

Cyberlaw

As mentioned, the use of the Internet to conduct business transactions has led to new types of legal issues. In response, courts have had to adapt traditional laws to situations that are unique to our age. Additionally, legislatures at both the federal and the state levels have created laws to deal specifically with such issues. Frequently, people use the term **cyberlaw** to refer to the emerging body of law that governs transactions conducted via the Internet. Cyberlaw is not really a classification of law, nor is it a new *type* of law. Rather, it is an informal term used to describe both new laws and modifications of traditional laws that relate to the online environment. Throughout this book, you will read how the law in a given area is evolving to govern specific legal issues that arise in the online context.

SECTION 6
HOW TO FIND PRIMARY SOURCES OF LAW

This text includes numerous references, or *citations,* to primary sources of law—federal and state statutes, the U.S. Constitution and state constitutions, regulations issued by administrative agencies, and court cases. A **citation** identifies the publication in which a legal authority—such as a statute or a court decision or other source—can be found. In this section, we explain how you can use citations to find primary sources of law. Note that in addition to being published in sets of books, as described next, most federal and state laws and case decisions are available online.

Finding Statutory and Administrative Law

When Congress passes laws, they are collected in a publication titled *United States Statutes at Large.* When state legislatures pass laws, they are collected in similar state publications. Most frequently, however, laws are referred to in their codified form—that is, the form in which they appear in the federal and state codes. In these codes, laws are compiled by subject.

UNITED STATES CODE The *United States Code* (U.S.C.) arranges all existing federal laws by broad subject. Each of the fifty subjects is given a title and a title number. For example, laws relating to commerce and trade are collected in Title 15, "Commerce and Trade." Titles are subdivided by sections. A citation to the U.S.C. includes both title and section numbers. Thus, a reference to "15 U.S.C. Section 1" means that the statute can be found in Section 1 of Title 15. ("Section" may be designated by the symbol §, and "Sections," by §§.) In addition to the print publication of the U.S.C., the federal government provides a searchable online database of the *United States Code* at www.gpoaccess.gov/uscode.

Commercial publications of federal laws and regulations are also available. For example, West Group publishes the *United States Code Annotated* (U.S.C.A.). The U.S.C.A. contains the official text of the U.S.C., plus notes (annotations) on court decisions that interpret and apply specific sections of the statutes. The U.S.C.A. also includes additional research aids, such as cross-references to related statutes, historical notes, and library references. A citation to the U.S.C.A. is similar to a citation to the U.S.C.: "15 U.S.C.A. Section 1."

STATE CODES State codes follow the U.S.C. pattern of arranging law by subject. They may be called codes, revisions, compilations, consolidations, general statutes, or statutes, depending on the preferences of the states. In some codes, subjects are designated by number. In others, they are designated by name. For example, "13 Pennsylvania Consolidated Statutes Section 1101" means that the statute can be found in Title 13, Section 1101, of the Pennsylvania code. "California Commercial Code Section 1101" means that the statute can be found under the subject heading "Commercial Code" of the California code in Section 1101. Abbreviations are often used. For example, "13 Pennsylvania Consolidated Statutes Section 1101" is abbreviated "13 Pa. C.S. § 1101," and "California Commercial Code Section 1101" is abbreviated "Cal. Com. Code § 1101."

ADMINISTRATIVE RULES Rules and regulations adopted by federal administrative agencies are initially published in the *Federal Register,* a daily publication of the U.S. government. Later, they are incorporated into the *Code of Federal Regulations* (C.F.R.). Like the U.S.C., the C.F.R. is divided into fifty titles. Rules within each title are assigned section numbers. A full citation to the C.F.R. includes title and section numbers. For example, a reference to "17 C.F.R. Section 230.504" means that the rule can be found in Section 230.504 of Title 17.

Finding Case Law

Before discussing the case reporting system, we need to look briefly at the court system (which will be discussed in detail in Chapter 2). There are two types of courts in the United States, federal courts and state courts. Both the federal and the state court systems consist of several levels, or tiers, of courts. *Trial courts,* in which evidence is presented and testimony given, are on the bottom tier (which also includes lower courts that handle specialized issues). Decisions from a trial court can be appealed to a higher court, which commonly is an intermediate *court of appeals,* or an *appellate court.* Decisions from these intermediate courts of appeals may be appealed to an even higher court, such as a state supreme court or the United States Supreme Court.

STATE COURT DECISIONS Most state trial court decisions are not published in books (except in New York and a few other states, which publish selected trial court opinions). Decisions from state trial courts are typically filed in the office of the clerk of the court, where the decisions are available for public inspection. Written decisions of the appellate, or reviewing, courts, however, are published and distributed (both in print and via the Internet). As you will note, most of the state court cases presented in this book are from state appellate courts. The reported appellate decisions are published in volumes called *reports* or *reporters,* which are numbered consecutively. State appellate court decisions are found in the state reporters of that particular state. Official reports are published by the state, whereas unofficial reports are privately published.

Regional Reporters. State court opinions appear in regional units of the National Reporter System, published by West Group. Most lawyers and libraries have the West reporters because they report cases more quickly and are distributed more widely than the state-published reporters. In fact, many states

have eliminated their own reporters in favor of West's National Reporter System. The National Reporter System divides the states into the following geographic areas: *Atlantic* (A. or A.2d), *North Eastern* (N.E. or N.E.2d), *North Western* (N.W. or N.W.2d), *Pacific* (P., P.2d, or P.3d), *South Eastern* (S.E. or S.E.2d), *South Western* (S.W., S.W.2d, or S.W.3d), and *Southern* (So., So.2d, or So.3d). (The *2d* and *3d* in the preceding abbreviations refer to *Second Series* and *Third Series,* respectively.) The states included in each of these regional divisions are indicated on the facing page in Exhibit 1–4, which illustrates West's National Reporter System.

Case Citations. After appellate decisions have been published, they are normally referred to (cited) by the name of the case; the volume, name, and page number of the state's official reporter (if different from West's National Reporter System); the volume, name, and page number of the National Reporter; and the volume, name, and page number of any other selected reporter. (Citing a reporter by volume number, name, and page number, in that order, is common to all citations; often, as in this book, the year the decision was issued will be included in parentheses, just after the citations to reporters.) When more than one reporter is cited for the same case, each reference is called a *parallel citation.*

Note that some states have adopted a "public domain citation system" that uses a somewhat different format for the citation. For example, in Wisconsin, a Wisconsin Supreme Court decision might be designated "2010 WI 40," meaning that the case was decided in the year 2010 by the Wisconsin Supreme Court and was the fortieth decision issued by that court during that year. Parallel citations to the *Wisconsin Reports* and West's *North Western Reporter* are still included after the public domain citation.

Consider the following case citation: *State v. Favoccia,* 119 Conn.App. 1, 986 A.2d 1081 (2010). We see that the opinion in this case can be found in Volume 119 of the official *Connecticut Appellate Reports,* on page 1. The parallel citation is to Volume 986 of the *Atlantic Reporter, Second Series,* page 1,081. In presenting appellate opinions in this text (starting in Chapter 2), in addition to the reporter, we give the name of the court hearing the case and the year of the court's decision. Sample citations to state court decisions are explained in Exhibit 1–5 on pages 18–20.

FEDERAL COURT DECISIONS Federal district (trial) court decisions are published unofficially in West's

EXHIBIT 1-4 • West's National Reporter System—Regional/Federal

Regional Reporters	Coverage Beginning	Coverage
Atlantic Reporter (A. or A.2d)	1885	Connecticut, Delaware, District of Columbia, Maine, Maryland, New Hampshire, New Jersey, Pennsylvania, Rhode Island, and Vermont.
North Eastern Reporter (N.E. or N.E.2d)	1885	Illinois, Indiana, Massachusetts, New York, and Ohio.
North Western Reporter (N.W. or N.W.2d)	1879	Iowa, Michigan, Minnesota, Nebraska, North Dakota, South Dakota, and Wisconsin.
Pacific Reporter (P., P.2d, or P.3d)	1883	Alaska, Arizona, California, Colorado, Hawaii, Idaho, Kansas, Montana, Nevada, New Mexico, Oklahoma, Oregon, Utah, Washington, and Wyoming.
South Eastern Reporter (S.E. or S.E.2d)	1887	Georgia, North Carolina, South Carolina, Virginia, and West Virginia.
South Western Reporter (S.W., S.W.2d, or S.W.3d)	1886	Arkansas, Kentucky, Missouri, Tennessee, and Texas.
Southern Reporter (So., So.2d, or So.3d)	1887	Alabama, Florida, Louisiana, and Mississippi.
Federal Reporters		
Federal Reporter (F., F.2d, or F.3d)	1880	U.S. Circuit Courts from 1880 to 1912; U.S. Commerce Court from 1911 to 1913; U.S. District Courts from 1880 to 1932; U.S. Court of Claims (now called U.S. Court of Federal Claims) from 1929 to 1932 and since 1960; U.S. Courts of Appeals since 1891; U.S. Court of Customs and Patent Appeals since 1929; U.S. Emergency Court of Appeals since 1943.
Federal Supplement (F.Supp. or F.Supp.2d)	1932	U.S. Court of Claims from 1932 to 1960; U.S. District Courts since 1932; U.S. Customs Court since 1956.
Federal Rules Decisions (F.R.D.)	1939	U.S. District Courts involving the Federal Rules of Civil Procedure since 1939 and Federal Rules of Criminal Procedure since 1946.
Supreme Court Reporter (S.Ct.)	1882	United States Supreme Court since the October term of 1882.
Bankruptcy Reporter (Bankr.)	1980	Bankruptcy decisions of U.S. Bankruptcy Courts, U.S. District Courts, U.S. Courts of Appeals, and the United States Supreme Court.
Military Justice Reporter (M.J.)	1978	U.S. Court of Military Appeals and Courts of Military Review for the Army, Navy, Air Force, and Coast Guard.

NATIONAL REPORTER SYSTEM MAP

Federal Supplement (F.Supp. or F.Supp.2d), and opinions from the circuit courts of appeals (reviewing courts) are reported unofficially in West's *Federal Reporter* (F., F.2d, or F.3d). Cases concerning federal bankruptcy law are published unofficially in West's *Bankruptcy Reporter* (Bankr. or B.R.).

EXHIBIT 1-5 • How to Read Citations

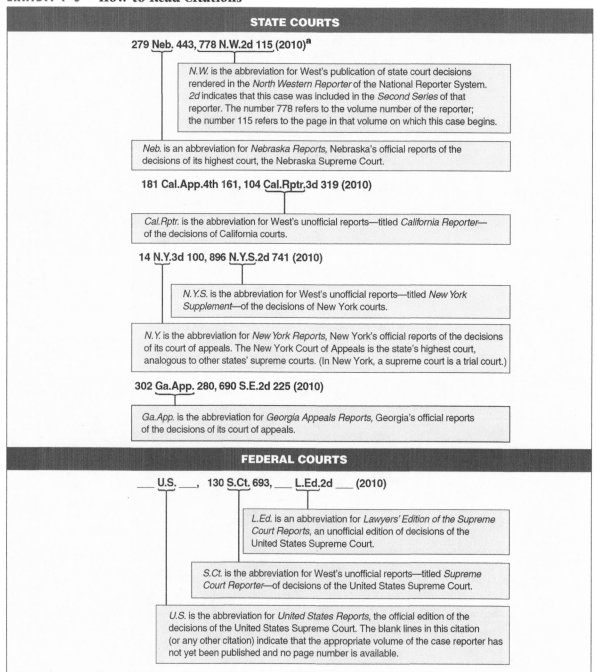

STATE COURTS

279 Neb. 443, 778 N.W.2d 115 (2010)[a]

N.W. is the abbreviation for West's publication of state court decisions rendered in the *North Western Reporter* of the National Reporter System. *2d* indicates that this case was included in the *Second Series* of that reporter. The number 778 refers to the volume number of the reporter; the number 115 refers to the page in that volume on which this case begins.

Neb. is an abbreviation for *Nebraska Reports,* Nebraska's official reports of the decisions of its highest court, the Nebraska Supreme Court.

181 Cal.App.4th 161, 104 Cal.Rptr.3d 319 (2010)

Cal.Rptr. is the abbreviation for West's unofficial reports—titled *California Reporter*— of the decisions of California courts.

14 N.Y.3d 100, 896 N.Y.S.2d 741 (2010)

N.Y.S. is the abbreviation for West's unofficial reports—titled *New York Supplement*—of the decisions of New York courts.

N.Y. is the abbreviation for *New York Reports,* New York's official reports of the decisions of its court of appeals. The New York Court of Appeals is the state's highest court, analogous to other states' supreme courts. (In New York, a supreme court is a trial court.)

302 Ga.App. 280, 690 S.E.2d 225 (2010)

Ga.App. is the abbreviation for *Georgia Appeals Reports,* Georgia's official reports of the decisions of its court of appeals.

FEDERAL COURTS

___ U.S. ___, 130 S.Ct. 693, ___ L.Ed.2d ___ (2010)

L.Ed. is an abbreviation for *Lawyers' Edition of the Supreme Court Reports,* an unofficial edition of decisions of the United States Supreme Court.

S.Ct. is the abbreviation for West's unofficial reports—titled *Supreme Court Reporter*—of decisions of the United States Supreme Court.

U.S. is the abbreviation for *United States Reports,* the official edition of the decisions of the United States Supreme Court. The blank lines in this citation (or any other citation) indicate that the appropriate volume of the case reporter has not yet been published and no page number is available.

a. The case names have been deleted from these citations to emphasize the publications. It should be kept in mind, however, that the name of a case is as important as the specific page numbers in the volumes in which it is found. If a citation is incorrect, the correct citation may be found in a publication's index of case names. In addition to providing a check on errors in citations, the date of a case is important because the value of a recent case as an authority is likely to be greater than that of older cases from the same court.

The official edition of the United States Supreme Court decisions is the *United States Reports* (U.S.), which is published by the federal government. Unofficial editions of Supreme Court cases include West's *Supreme Court Reporter* (S.Ct.) and the *Lawyers' Edition of the Supreme Court Reports* (L.Ed. or L.Ed.2d). Sample citations for federal court decisions are also listed and explained in Exhibit 1–5.

EXHIBIT 1–5 • How to Read Citations, Continued

FEDERAL COURTS (Continued)

590 F.3d 259 (4th Cir. 2010)

> *4th Cir.* is an abbreviation denoting that this case was decided in the U.S. Court of Appeals for the Fourth Circuit.

683 F.Supp.2d 918 (W.D.Wis. 2010)

> *W.D.Wis.* is an abbreviation indicating that the U.S. District Court for the Western District of Wisconsin decided this case.

ENGLISH COURTS

9 Exch. 341, 156 Eng.Rep. 145 (1854)

> *Eng.Rep.* is an abbreviation for *English Reports, Full Reprint,* a series of reports containing selected decisions made in English courts between 1378 and 1865.

> *Exch.* is an abbreviation for *English Exchequer Reports*, which includes the original reports of cases decided in England's Court of Exchequer.

STATUTORY AND OTHER CITATIONS

18 U.S.C. Section 1961(1)(A)

> *U.S.C.* denotes *United States Code*, the codification of *United States Statutes at Large*. The number 18 refers to the statute's U.S.C. title number and 1961 to its section number within that title. The number 1 in parentheses refers to a subsection within the section, and the letter A in parentheses to a subsection within the subsection.

UCC 2–206(1)(b)

> *UCC* is an abbreviation for *Uniform Commercial Code*. The first number 2 is a reference to an article of the UCC, and 206 to a section within that article. The number 1 in parentheses refers to a subsection within the section, and the letter b in parentheses to a subsection within the subsection.

Restatement (Third) of Torts, Section 6

> *Restatement (Third) of Torts* refers to the third edition of the American Law Institute's *Restatement of the Law of Torts*. The number 6 refers to a specific section.

17 C.F.R. Section 230.505

> *C.F.R.* is an abbreviation for *Code of Federal Regulations*, a compilation of federal administrative regulations. The number 17 designates the regulation's title number, and 230.505 designates a specific section within that title.

Continued

UNPUBLISHED OPINIONS Many court opinions that are not yet published or that are not intended for publication can be accessed through Westlaw® (abbreviated in citations as "WL"), an online legal database maintained by West Group. When no citation to a published reporter is available for cases cited in this text, we give the WL citation (see Exhibit 1–5 on the next page for an example).

EXHIBIT 1–5 • How to Read Citations, Continued

WESTLAW® CITATIONS[b]

<u>2010 WL 348005</u>

WL is an abbreviation for Westlaw. The number 2010 is the year of the document that can be found with this citation in the Westlaw database. The number 348005 is a number assigned to a specific document. A higher number indicates that a document was added to the Westlaw database later in the year.

UNIFORM RESOURCE LOCATORS (URLs)

http://www.<u>westlaw</u>.<u>com</u>[c]

The suffix *com* is the top level domain (TLD) for this Web site. The TLD *com* is an abbreviation for "commercial," which usually means that a for-profit entity hosts (maintains or supports) this Web site.

westlaw is the host name—the part of the domain name selected by the organization that registered the name. In this case, West registered the name. This Internet site is the Westlaw database on the Web.

www is an abbreviation for "World Wide Web." The Web is a system of Internet servers that support documents formatted in *HTML* (hypertext markup language) and other formats as well.

http://www.<u>uscourts.gov</u>

This is "The Federal Judiciary Home Page." The host is the Administrative Office of the U.S. Courts. The TLD *gov* is an abbreviation for "government." This Web site includes information and links from, and about, the federal courts.

http://www.<u>law.cornell.edu</u>/<u>index.html</u>

This part of a URL points to a Web page or file at a specific location within the host's domain. This page is a menu with links to documents within the domain and to other Internet resources.

This is the host name for a Web site that contains the Internet publications of the Legal Information Institute (LII), which is a part of Cornell Law School. The LII site includes a variety of legal materials and links to other legal resources on the Internet. The TLD *edu* is an abbreviation for "educational institution" (a school or a university).

http://www.<u>ipl2.org</u>/<u>div</u>/<u>news</u>

This part of the URL points to a static *news* page at this Web site, which provides links to online newspapers from around the world.

div is an abbreviation for "division," which is the way that ipl2 tags the content on its Web site as relating to a specific topic.

The site *ipl2* was formed from the merger of the Internet Public Library and the Librarians' Internet Index. It is an online service that provides reference resources and links to other information services on the Web. The site is supported chiefly by the *iSchool* at Drexel College of Information Science and Technology. The TLD *org* is an abbreviation for "organization" (normally nonprofit).

b. Many court decisions that are not yet published or that are not intended for publication can be accessed through Westlaw, an online legal database.

c. The basic form for a URL is "service://hostname/path." The Internet service for all of the URLs in this text is *http* (hypertext transfer protocol). Because most Web browsers add this prefix automatically when a user enters a host name or a hostname/path, we have generally omitted the *http://* from the URLs listed in this text.

OLD CASE LAW On a few occasions, this text cites opinions from old, classic cases dating to the nineteenth century or earlier; some of these are from the English courts. The citations to these cases may not conform to the descriptions given above because the reporters in which they were originally published were often known by the names of the persons who compiled the reporters.

SECTION 7
HOW TO READ AND UNDERSTAND CASE LAW

The decisions made by the courts establish the boundaries of the law as it applies to almost all business relationships. It thus is essential that businesspersons know how to read and understand case law. The cases that we present in this text have been condensed from the full text of the courts' opinions and are presented in a special format. In approximately two-thirds of the cases, we have summarized the background and facts, as well as the court's decision and remedy, in our own words and have included only selected portions of the court's opinion ("in the language of the court"). In the remaining one-third of the cases, we have provided a longer excerpt from the court's opinion without summarizing the background and facts or decision and remedy. The following sections will provide useful insights into how to read and understand case law.

Case Titles and Terminology

The title of a case, such as *Adams v. Jones,* indicates the names of the parties to the lawsuit. The *v.* in the case title stands for *versus,* which means "against." In the trial court, Adams was the plaintiff—the person who filed the suit. Jones was the defendant. If the case is appealed, however, the appellate court will sometimes place the name of the party appealing the decision first, so the case may be called *Jones v. Adams* if Jones is appealing. Because some appellate courts retain the trial court order of names, it is often impossible to distinguish the plaintiff from the defendant in the title of a reported appellate court decision. You must carefully read the facts of each case to identify the parties. Otherwise, the discussion by the appellate court may be difficult to understand.

The following terms, phrases, and abbreviations are frequently encountered in court opinions and legal publications. Because it is important to understand what is meant by these terms, phrases, and abbreviations, we define and discuss them here.

PARTIES TO LAWSUITS As mentioned previously, the party initiating a lawsuit is referred to as the *plaintiff* or *petitioner,* depending on the nature of the action, and the party against whom a lawsuit is brought is the *defendant* or *respondent.* Lawsuits frequently involve more than one plaintiff and/or defendant.

When a case is appealed from the original court or jurisdiction to another court or jurisdiction, the party appealing the case is called the **appellant.** The **appellee** is the party against whom the appeal is taken. (In some appellate courts, the party appealing a case is referred to as the *petitioner,* and the party against whom the suit is brought or appealed is called the *respondent.*)

JUDGES AND JUSTICES The terms *judge* and *justice* are usually synonymous and represent two designations given to judges in various courts. All members of the United States Supreme Court, for example, are referred to as justices, and justice is the formal title often given to judges of appellate courts, although this is not always the case. In New York, a *justice* is a judge of the trial court (which is called the Supreme Court), and a member of the Court of Appeals (the state's highest court) is called a *judge.* The term *justice* is commonly abbreviated to J., and *justices,* to JJ. A United States Supreme Court case might refer to Justice Sotomayor as Sotomayor, J., or to Chief Justice Roberts as Roberts, C.J.

DECISIONS AND OPINIONS Most decisions reached by reviewing, or appellate, courts are explained in written **opinions.** The opinion contains the court's reasons for its decision, the rules of law that apply, and the judgment. When all judges or justices unanimously agree on an opinion, the opinion is written for the entire court and can be deemed a *unanimous opinion.* When there is not a unanimous agreement, a *majority opinion* is written; the majority opinion outlines the view supported by the majority of the judges or justices deciding the case.

Often, a judge or justice who wishes to make or emphasize a point that was not made or emphasized in the unanimous or majority opinion will write a *concurring opinion.* This means that the judge or justice agrees, or concurs, with the majority's decision, but for different reasons. When there is not a unanimous opinion, a *dissenting opinion* presents the views of one or more judges who disagree with the majority's decision. The dissenting opinion is important because it may form the basis of the arguments used years later in overruling the precedential majority opinion. Occasionally, a court issues a *per curiam* (Latin for "by the whole court") opinion, which does not indicate the judge or justice who authored the opinion.

A Sample Court Case

To illustrate the various elements contained in a court opinion, we present an annotated court opinion in Exhibit 1–6 on pages 23–25. The opinion is from an actual case decided by the U.S. Court of Appeals for the Seventh Circuit in 2010.

BACKGROUND OF THE CASE Kevin T. Singer, an inmate at a Wisconsin correctional facility, was a devoted player of Dungeons and Dragons (D&D), a popular fantasy role-playing game. While incarcerated, Singer was able to order and possess D&D materials for two years. In November 2004, however, the prison's gang expert received an anonymous letter stating that Singer and three other inmates were trying to recruit others to join a "gang" dedicated to playing D&D. Prison officials immediately searched Singer's cell, confiscated all of his D&D materials, and prohibited him and other inmates from playing D&D. Singer filed a lawsuit in federal district court against the Wisconsin prison, alleging that these actions violated his free speech and due process rights. The district court found in favor of the prison when it concluded that the D&D ban was rationally related to a legitimate government interest. Singer appealed to the U.S. Court of Appeals for the Seventh Circuit.

EDITORIAL PRACTICE You will note that triple asterisks (* * *) and quadruple asterisks (* * * *) frequently appear in the opinion. The triple asterisks indicate that we have deleted a few words or sentences from the opinion for the sake of readability or brevity. Quadruple asterisks mean that an entire paragraph (or more) has been omitted. Additionally, when the opinion cites another case or legal source, the citation to the case or other source has been omitted to save space and to improve the flow of the text. These editorial practices are continued in the other court opinions presented in this book. In addition, whenever we present a court opinion that includes a term or phrase that may not be readily understandable, a bracketed definition or paraphrase has been added.

BRIEFING CASES Knowing how to read and understand court opinions and the legal reasoning used by the courts is an essential step in undertaking accurate legal research. A further step is "briefing," or summarizing, the case. Legal researchers routinely brief cases by reducing the texts of the opinions to their essential elements. Generally, when you brief a case, you first summarize the background and facts of the case, as we have done for the cases presented within this text. You then indicate the issue (or issues) before the court. An important element in the case brief is, of course, the court's decision on the issue and the legal reasoning used by the court in reaching that decision. Detailed instructions on how to brief a case are given in Appendix A, which also includes a briefed version of the sample court case presented in Exhibit 1–6.

THE SAMPLE COURT CASE STARTS ON THE FACING PAGE.

EXHIBIT 1–6 • A Sample Court Case

> This section contains the citation—the name of the case, the name of the court that heard the case, the year of the decision, and reporters in which the court's opinion can be found.

SINGER v. RAEMISCH

United States Court of Appeals,

Seventh Circuit,

593 F.3d 529 (2010).

> This line provides the name of the justice (or judge) who authored the court's opinion.

TINDER, Circuit Judge.

* * * *

> The court divides the opinion into three sections, each headed by a Roman numeral and an explanatory heading. The first section summarizes the factual background of the case.

I. Background

Kevin T. Singer is an inmate at Wisconsin's Waupun Correctional Institution. He is also a devoted player of D&D [Dungeons and Dragons], a fantasy role-playing game in which players collectively develop a story around characters whose personae they adopt.

* * * Singer was able to order and possess his D&D materials without incident from June 2002 until November 2004. This all changed on or about November 14, 2004, when Waupun's long-serving Disruptive Group Coordinator, Captain Bruce Muraski, received an anonymous letter from an inmate. The letter expressed concern that Singer and three other inmates were forming a D&D gang and were trying to recruit others to join by passing around their D&D publications and touting the "rush" they got from playing the game. Muraski, Waupun's expert on gang activity, decided to heed the letter's advice and "check into this gang before it gets out of hand."

On November 15, 2004, Muraski ordered Waupun staff to search the cells of the inmates named in the letter. The search of Singer's cell turned up twenty-one books, fourteen magazines, and Singer's handwritten D&D manuscript, all of which were confiscated. * * * In a December 6, 2004, letter to Singer, Muraski informed Singer that "inmates are not allowed to engage in or possess written material that details rules, codes, dogma of games/activities such as 'Dungeons and Dragons' because it promotes fantasy role playing, competitive hostility, violence, addictive escape behaviors, and possible gambling."

Continued

EXHIBIT 1-6 • A Sample Court Case, Continued

To *lodge a complaint* is to file the appropriate legal documents with the clerk of a court to initiate a lawsuit.

The First Amendment to the U.S. Constitution guarantees the right of *free speech*—to express one's views without governmental restrictions. The Fifth and Fourteenth Amendments guarantee the right to *due process*—to enjoy life, liberty, and property without unfair government interference.

An *affidavit* is a written or printed voluntary statement of fact, confirmed by the oath or affirmation of the party making it and made before a person having the authority to administer the oath or affirmation.

A *summary judgment* is a judgment that a court enters without continuing a trial. This judgment can be entered only if no facts are in dispute and the only question is how the law applies to the facts.

The second major section of the opinion responds to the plaintiff's appeal.

The court applies the principle established by the *Turner* case—which the United States Supreme Court decided—to the facts of the Singer case. The rulings in cases decided by higher courts are binding on the decisions of lower courts, according to the doctrine of *stare decisis* (see page 9).

Penological interests relate to the branch of criminology dealing with prison management and the treatment of offenders.

* * * *

* * * Singer **lodged a** * * * **complaint** in federal court * * * . He alleged that his **free speech** and **due process** rights were violated when Waupun officials confiscated his D&D materials and enacted a categorical ban against D&D. * * *

Singer collected fifteen **affidavits**—from other inmates, his brother, and three role-playing game experts. He contends that the affidavits demonstrate that there is no connection between D&D and gang activity. * * * The prison officials countered Singer's affidavit evidence by submitting an affidavit from Captain Bruce Muraski * * * . Muraski testified * * * that fantasy role-playing games like D&D have "been found to promote competitive hostility, violence, and addictive escape behavior, which can compromise not only the inmate's rehabilitation and effects of positive programming, but endanger the public and jeopardize the safety and security of the institution."

The prison officials moved for **summary judgment** on all of Singer's claims. The district court granted the motion in full, but Singer limits his appeal to the foreclosure of his First Amendment claims.

II. Discussion

* * * *

In [*Turner v. Safley*], the [United States] Supreme Court determined that prison regulations that restrict inmates' constitutional rights are nevertheless valid if they are reasonably related to legitimate **penological interests.**

* * * *

[Singer] attacks the district court's conclusion that the D&D ban bears a rational relationship to a legitimate governmental interest * * * .

The sole evidence the prison officials have submitted on this point is the affidavit of Captain Muraski, the gang specialist. Muraski testified that Waupun's prohibition on role-playing and fantasy games * * * was intended to promote prison security because co-operative games can mimic

EXHIBIT 1-6 • A Sample Court Case, Continued

Thereof here means "of gangs."

Something that is organized by a rigid, ranked order—here, by a ranked order of inmates depending on who is winning the most.

A *trove* is a collection or treasure.

An *affiant* is a person who swears to an affidavit.

In the third major section of the opinion, the court states its decision and gives its order.

A *large quantum* is a sizeable quantity.

To *affirm* a judgment is to declare that it is valid.

the organization of gangs and lead to the actual development **thereof.** * * * At bottom, his testimony about this policy aim highlighted Waupun's worries about cooperative activity among inmates, particularly that carried out in an organized, **hierarchical** fashion * * * . He [also] testified that D&D can "foster an inmate's obsession with escaping from the real life, correctional environment, fostering hostility, violence and escape behavior," which in turn "can compromise not only the inmate's rehabilitation and effects of positive programming but also endanger the public and jeopardize the safety and security of the institution."

* * * *

It is true that Singer procured an impressive **trove** of affidavit testimony, including some from role-playing game experts, but none of his **affiants'** testimony addressed the inquiry at issue here. The question is not whether D&D has led to gang behavior in the past; the prison officials concede that it has not. The question is whether the prison officials are rational in their belief that, if left unchecked, D&D could lead to gang behavior among inmates and undermine prison secu- rity in the future. Singer's affiants * * * lack the qualifications necessary to determine whether the relationship between the D&D ban and the maintenance of prison security is so remote as to render the policy arbitrary or irrational. In other words, none of them is sufficiently versed in prison security concerns to raise a genuine issue of material fact about their relationship to D&D.

* * * *

III. Conclusion

Despite Singer's **large quantum** of affidavit testimony * * *, he has failed to demonstrate a genuine issue of material fact concerning the reasonableness of the relationship between Waupun's D&D ban and the prison's clearly legitimate peno- logical interests. The district court's grant of summary judg- ment is therefore **AFFIRMED.**

REVIEWING
Business and Its Legal Environment

Suppose that the California legislature passes a law that severely restricts carbon dioxide emissions from automobiles in that state. A group of automobile manufacturers files suit against the state of California to prevent the enforcement of the law. The automakers claim that a federal law already sets fuel economy standards nationwide and that fuel economy standards are essentially the same as carbon dioxide emission standards. According to the automobile manufacturers, it is unfair to allow California to impose more stringent regulations than those set by the federal law. Using the information presented in the chapter, answer the following questions.

1. Who are the parties (the plaintiffs and the defendant) in this lawsuit?
2. Are the plaintiffs seeking a legal remedy or an equitable remedy?
3. What is the primary source of the law that is at issue here?
4. Where would you look to find the relevant California and federal laws?

DEBATE THIS: *Under the doctrine of* stare decisis, *courts are obligated to follow the precedents established in their jurisdiction unless there is a compelling reason not to. Should U.S. courts continue to adhere to this common law principle, given that our government now regulates so many areas by statute?*

TERMS AND CONCEPTS

administrative agency 5
administrative law 5
allege 10
analogy 11
appellant 21
appellee 21
binding authority 9
breach 3
case law 5
case on point 11
chancellor 7
citation 15
civil law 14

common law 7
constitutional law 4
court of equity 7
court of law 7
criminal law 15
cyberlaw 15
damages 7
defendant 8
defense 8
equitable maxims 8
executive agency 5
historical school 13
independent regulatory
  agency 5

jurisprudence 13
laches 8
law 2
legal positivism 13
legal realism 14
legal reasoning 10
natural law 13
opinion 21
ordinance 4
petitioner 8
plaintiff 8
precedent 9
procedural law 14

public policy 10
remedy 7
remedy at law 7
remedy in equity 7
reporter 9
respondent 8
sociological school 14
stare decisis 9
statute of limitations 8
statutory law 4
substantive law 14
syllogism 11
uniform law 4

QUESTIONS AND CASE PROBLEMS

1–1. Sources of Law How does statutory law come into existence? How does it differ from the common law?

1–2. QUESTION WITH SAMPLE ANSWER: Schools of Jurisprudential Thought.

After World War II, an international tribunal of judges convened at Nuremberg, Germany and convicted several Nazis of "crimes against

humanity." Assuming that these convicted war criminals had not disobeyed any law of their country and had merely been following their government's orders, what law had they violated? Explain.

• **For a sample answer to Question 1–2, go to Appendix F at the end of this text.**

1–3. Reading Citations Assume that you want to read the entire court opinion in the case of *Pinard v. Dandy Lions,*

LLC, 119 Conn.App. 368, 987 A.2d 406 (2010). Refer to the subsection entitled "Finding Case Law" in this chapter, and then explain specifically where you would find the court's opinion.

1–4. Sources of Law This chapter discussed a number of sources of American law. Which source of law takes priority in the following situations, and why?

(a) A federal statute conflicts with the U.S. Constitution.

(b) A federal statute conflicts with a state constitutional provision.

(c) A state statute conflicts with the common law of that state.

(d) A state constitutional amendment conflicts with the U.S. Constitution.

1–5. *Stare Decisis* In this chapter, we stated that the doctrine of *stare decisis* "became a cornerstone of the English and American judicial systems." What does *stare decisis* mean, and why has this doctrine been so fundamental to the development of our legal tradition?

1–6. Court Opinions What is the difference between a concurring opinion and a majority opinion? Between a concurring opinion and a dissenting opinion? Why do judges and justices write concurring and dissenting opinions, given that these opinions will not affect the outcome of the case at hand, which has already been decided by majority vote?

1–7. The Common Law Tradition Courts can overturn precedents and thus change the common law. Should judges have the same authority to overrule statutory law? Explain.

1–8. Schools of Judicial Thought "The judge's role is not to make the law but to uphold and apply the law." Do you agree or disagree with this statement? Discuss fully the reasons for your answer.

1–9. Remedies Assume that Arthur Rabe is suing Xavier Sanchez for breaching a contract in which Sanchez promised to sell Rabe a painting by Vincent van Gogh for $3 million.

(a) In this lawsuit, who is the plaintiff and who is the defendant?

(b) Suppose that Rabe wants Sanchez to perform the contract as promised. What remedy would Rabe seek from the court?

(c) Now suppose that Rabe wants to cancel the contract because Sanchez fraudulently misrepresented the painting as an original Van Gogh when in fact it is a copy. What remedy would Rabe seek?

(d) Will the remedy Rabe seeks in either situation be a remedy at law or a remedy in equity? What is the difference between legal and equitable remedies?

(e) Suppose that the trial court finds in Rabe's favor and grants one of these remedies. Sanchez then appeals the decision to a higher court. On appeal, which party will be the appellant (or petitioner), and which party will be the appellee (or respondent)?

1–10. A QUESTION OF ETHICS: The Common Law Tradition.

 On July 5, 1884, Dudley, Stephens, and Brooks— "all able-bodied English seamen"—and a teenage English boy were cast adrift in a lifeboat following a storm at sea. They had no water with them in the boat, and all they had for sustenance were two one-pound tins of turnips. On July 24, Dudley proposed that one of the four in the lifeboat be sacrificed to save the others. Stephens agreed with Dudley, but Brooks refused to consent—and the boy was never asked for his opinion. On July 25, Dudley killed the boy, and the three men then fed on the boy's body and blood. Four days later, a passing vessel rescued the men. They were taken to England and tried for the murder of the boy. If the men had not fed on the boy's body, they would probably have died of starvation within the four-day period. The boy, who was in a much weaker condition, would likely have died before the rest. [Regina v. Dudley and Stephens, 14 Q.B.D. (Queen's Bench Division, England) 273 (1884)]

(a) The basic question in this case is whether the survivors should be subject to penalties under English criminal law, given the men's unusual circumstances. Were the defendants' actions necessary but unethical? Explain your reasoning. What ethical issues might be involved here?

(b) Should judges ever have the power to look beyond the written "letter of the law" in making their decisions? Why or why not?

LEGAL RESEARCH EXERCISES ON THE WEB

Go to this text's Web site at **www.cengage.com/blaw/cross**, select "Chapter 1," and click on "Practical Internet Exercises." There you will find the following Internet research exercises that you can perform to learn more about the topics covered in this chapter.

Practical Internet Exercise 1–1: **Legal Perspective**
Internet Sources of Law

Practical Internet Exercise 1–2: **Management Perspective**
Online Assistance from Government Agencies

Practical Internet Exercise 1–3: **Social Perspective**
The Case of the Speluncean Explorers

The Court System

oday, in the United States there are fifty-two court systems— one for each of the fifty states, one for the District of Columbia, and a federal system. Keep in mind that the federal courts are not superior to the state courts; they are simply an independent system of courts, which derives its authority from Article III, Section 2, of the U.S. Constitution. By the power given to it under Article I of the U.S. Constitution, Congress has extended the federal court system beyond the boundaries of the United States to U.S. territories such as Guam, Puerto Rico, and the Virgin Islands.[1] As we shall see, the United States Supreme Court is the final controlling voice over all of these fifty-two systems, at least when questions of federal law are involved.

Every businessperson will likely face a lawsuit at some time in his or her career. Thus, anyone involved in business needs to have an understanding of the American court systems, as well as the various methods of dispute resolution that can be pursued outside the courts.

In this chapter, after examining the judiciary's role in the American governmental system, we discuss some basic requirements that must be met before a party may bring a lawsuit before a particular court. We then look at the court systems of the United States in some detail. We will examine some alternative methods of settling disputes, including online dispute resolution, in Chapter 3.

---

1. In Guam and the Virgin Islands, territorial courts serve as both federal courts and state courts; in Puerto Rico, they serve only as federal courts.

THE JUDICIARY'S ROLE IN AMERICAN GOVERNMENT

As you learned in Chapter 1, the body of American law includes the federal and state constitutions, statutes passed by legislative bodies, administrative law, and the case decisions and legal principles that form the common law. These laws would be meaningless, however, without the courts to interpret and apply them. This is the essential role of the judiciary—the courts— in the American governmental system: to interpret the laws and apply them to specific situations. (See this chapter's *Insight into Ethics* feature on the facing page for a discussion of how the availability of "unpublished opinions" over the Internet is changing what some judges consider to be persuasive precedent.)

As the branch of government entrusted with interpreting the laws, the judiciary can decide, among other things, whether the laws or actions of the other two branches are constitutional. The process for making such a determination is known as **judicial review.** The power of judicial review enables the judicial branch to act as a check on the other two branches of government, in line with the system of checks and balances established by the U.S. Constitution.[2]

The power of judicial review is not mentioned in the U.S. Constitution (although many constitutional scholars conclude that the founders intended the judiciary to have this power). Rather, this power was explicitly established by the United States Supreme Court in 1803 by its decision in *Marbury v. Madison.*[3] In that decision, the Court stated, "It is emphatically

---

2. In a broad sense, judicial review occurs whenever a court "reviews" a case or legal proceeding—as when an appellate court reviews a lower court's decision. When discussing the judiciary's role in American government, however, the term *judicial review* refers to the power of the judiciary to decide whether the actions of the other two branches of government violate the U.S. Constitution.
3. 5 U.S. (1 Cranch) 137, 2 L.Ed. 60 (1803).

INSIGHT INTO ETHICS
How the Internet Is Expanding Precedent

The notion that courts should rely on precedents to decide the outcome of similar cases has long been a cornerstone of U.S. law. Nevertheless, the availability of "unpublished opinions" over the Internet is changing what the law considers to be precedent. An *unpublished opinion* is a decision made by an appellate court that is not intended for publication in a reporter (the bound books that contain court opinions).[a] Courts traditionally have not considered unpublished opinions to be "precedent," binding or persuasive, and attorneys often have not been allowed to refer to these decisions in their arguments.

Increased Online Availability

The number of court decisions not published in printed books has risen dramatically in recent years. Nearly 80 percent of the decisions of the federal appellate courts are unpublished, and the number is equally high in some state court systems. Even though certain decisions are not intended for publication, they are posted ("published") almost immediately on online legal databases, such as Westlaw and Lexis. With the proliferation of free legal databases and court Web sites, the general public also has almost instant access to the unpublished decisions of most courts. This situation has caused many to question why these opinions have no precedential effect.

Should Unpublished Decisions Establish Precedent?

Before the advent of the Internet, not considering unpublished decisions as precedent might have been justified on the ground of fairness. How could lawyers know about unpublished decisions if they were not printed in the case reporters? Now that opinions are

so readily available on the Web, however, this justification is no longer valid. Moreover, it now seems unfair *not* to consider these decisions as precedent, given that they are so publicly accessible. Some claim that unpublished decisions could make bad precedents because these decisions frequently are written by staff attorneys and law clerks rather than by judges, so the reasoning may be inferior. If an unpublished decision is considered merely as persuasive precedent, however, then judges who disagree with the reasoning are free to reject the conclusion.

The United States Supreme Court Changed the Federal Rules on Unpublished Opinions

The United States Supreme Court made history in 2006 when it announced that it would allow lawyers to cite unpublished decisions in all federal courts. Rule 32.1 of the Federal Rules of Appellate Procedure states that federal courts may not prohibit or restrict the citation of federal judicial opinions that have been designated as "not for publication," "non-precedential," or "not precedent." The rule applies only to federal courts and only to unpublished opinions issued after January 1, 2007. It does not specify the effect that a court must give to one of its unpublished opinions or to an unpublished opinion from another court.

Basically, Rule 32.1 simply establishes a uniform rule for all of the federal courts that allows attorneys to cite—and judges to consider as persuasive precedent—unpublished decisions. The rule is a clear example of how technology—the availability of unpublished opinions over the Internet—has affected the law.

CRITICAL THINKING
INSIGHT INTO THE LEGAL ENVIRONMENT
Now that the United States Supreme Court is allowing unpublished decisions to form persuasive precedent in federal courts, should state courts follow? Why or why not?

---

a. Recently decided cases that are not yet published are also sometimes called *unpublished opinions*, but because these decisions will eventually be printed in reporters, we do not include them here.

---

the province and duty of the Judicial Department to say what the law is. . . . If two laws conflict with each other, the Courts must decide on the operation of each. . . . [I]f both [a] law and the Constitution apply to a particular case, . . . the Court must determine which of these conflicting rules governs the case. This is of the very essence of judicial duty." Since the *Marbury v. Madison* decision, the power of judicial review has remained unchallenged. Today, this power is exercised by both federal and state courts.

SECTION 2
BASIC JUDICIAL REQUIREMENTS

Before a lawsuit can be brought before a court, certain requirements must be met. These requirements relate to *jurisdiction, venue,* and *standing to sue.*

Jurisdiction

In Latin, *juris* means "law," and *diction* means "to speak." Thus, "the power to speak the law" is the literal meaning of the term **jurisdiction.** Before any court can hear a case, it must have jurisdiction over the person (or company) against whom the suit is brought (the defendant) or over the property involved in the suit. The court must also have jurisdiction over the subject matter of the dispute. The Internet has raised certain issues regarding jurisdiction.

JURISDICTION OVER PERSONS OR PROPERTY A particular court generally can exercise **in personam jurisdiction** (personal jurisdiction) over any person or business that resides in a certain geographic area. A state trial court, for example, normally has jurisdictional authority over residents (including businesses) of a particular area of the state, such as a county or district. A state's highest court (often called the state supreme court[4]) has jurisdictional authority over all residents within the state.

A court can also exercise jurisdiction over property that is located within its boundaries. This kind of jurisdiction is known as **in rem jurisdiction,** or "jurisdiction over the thing." Suppose that a dispute arises over the ownership of a boat in dry dock in Fort Lauderdale, Florida. The boat is owned by an Ohio resident, over whom a Florida court normally cannot exercise personal jurisdiction. The other party to the dispute is a resident of Nebraska. In this situation, a lawsuit concerning the boat could be brought in a Florida state court on the basis of the court's *in rem* jurisdiction.

Long Arm Statutes. Under the authority of a state **long arm statute,** a court can exercise personal jurisdiction over certain out-of-state defendants based on activities that took place within the state. Before a court can exercise jurisdiction over an out-of-state defendant under a long arm statute, though, it must be demonstrated that the defendant had sufficient contacts, or *minimum contacts,* with the state to justify the jurisdiction.[5] Generally, this means that the defendant must have enough of a connection to the state for the judge to conclude that it is fair for the state to exercise power over the defendant. For example, if an out-of-state defendant caused an automobile accident or sold defective goods within the state, a court usually will find that minimum contacts

exist to exercise jurisdiction over that defendant. Similarly, a state may exercise personal jurisdiction over a nonresident defendant who is sued for breaching a contract that was formed within the state.

CASE IN POINT An Xbox game system caught fire in Bonnie Broquet's home in Texas and caused substantial personal injuries. Broquet filed a lawsuit in a Texas court against Ji-Haw Industrial Company, a nonresident company that made the Xbox components. Broquet alleged that Ji-Haw's components were defective and had caused the fire. Ji-Haw argued that the Texas court lacked jurisdiction over it, but a state appellate court held that the Texas long arm statute authorized the exercise of jurisdiction over the out-of-state defendant.[6]

Corporate Contacts. Because corporations are considered legal persons, courts use the same principles to determine whether it is fair to exercise jurisdiction over a corporation.[7] A corporation normally is subject to personal jurisdiction in the state in which it is incorporated, has its principal office, and/or is doing business. Courts apply the minimum-contacts test to determine if they can exercise jurisdiction over out-of-state corporations.

The minimum-contacts requirement usually is met if the corporation advertises or sells its products within the state, or places its goods into the "stream of commerce" with the intent that the goods be sold in the state. Suppose that a business is incorporated under the laws of Maine but has a branch office and manufacturing plant in Georgia. The corporation also advertises and sells its products in Georgia. These activities would likely constitute sufficient contacts with the state of Georgia to allow a Georgia court to exercise jurisdiction over the corporation.

Some corporations, however, do not sell or advertise products or place any goods in the stream of commerce. Determining what constitutes minimum contacts in these situations can be more difficult.

In the following case, the defendant was a New Jersey corporation that performed machining services on component parts that it received from a North Carolina firm. The North Carolina firm claimed that the services were defective and wanted to sue for breach of contract in a North Carolina court. Did the New Jersey firm have minimum contacts with North Carolina? That was the issue before the court.

---

4. There are exceptions. For example, in New York the supreme court is a trial court.
5. The minimum-contacts standard was first established in *International Shoe Co. v. State of Washington*, 326 U.S. 310, 66 S.Ct. 154, 90 L.Ed. 95 (1945).

---

6. *Ji-Haw Industrial Co. v. Broquet*, 2008 WL 441822 (Tex.App.—San Antonio 2008).
7. In the eyes of the law, corporations are "legal persons"—entities that can sue and be sued. See Chapter 19.

✳ EXTENDED CASE 2.1 ✳
Southern Prestige Industries, Inc. v. Independence Plating Corp.

Court of Appeals of North Carolina, 690 S.E.2d 768 (2010).

IN THE LANGUAGE OF THE COURT
CALABRIA, Judge.
* * * *

The facts in the instant case [the case before the court] are undisputed. Defendant (Independence Plating Corporation) is a New Jersey corporation that provides anodizing[a] services. Defendant's only office and all of its personnel are located in the state of New Jersey. Defendant does not advertise or otherwise solicit business in North Carolina. Prior to July 2007, defendant had engaged in a long-standing business relationship with Kidde Aerospace ("Kidde"), a North Carolina company.
* * * *

Plaintiff and defendant engaged in frequent transactions between 27 July 2007 and 25 April 2008.

On 18 November 2008, plaintiff initiated an action for breach of contract in [a North Carolina state court]. Plaintiff alleged that defects caused by defendant's anodizing process caused plaintiff's machined parts to be rejected by Kidde. On 6 February 2009, defendant filed, with a supporting affidavit [a written statement, made under oath], a motion to dismiss pursuant to [North Carolina statutory law] for lack of personal jurisdiction. On 18 March 2009, plaintiff filed an affidavit, with supporting exhibits, challenging the assertions in defendant's motion to dismiss. On 4 May 2009, after reviewing the evidence submitted by the parties, the trial court entered an order denying defendant's motion to dismiss. Defendant appeals.

Defendant's only argument on appeal is that the trial court erred in denying its motion to dismiss for lack of personal jurisdiction. Specifically, defendant argues there are insufficient contacts to satisfy the due process [see page 111] of law requirements that are necessary to subject defendant to the personal jurisdiction of North Carolina's courts. We disagree.
* * * *

Neither party contests the findings of fact contained in the trial court's order. * * * Therefore, the only issue to be determined is "whether the trial court's findings of fact support its conclusion of law that the court has personal jurisdiction over defendant. We conduct our review of this issue *de novo* [anew]."

North Carolina courts utilize a two-prong analysis in determining whether personal jurisdiction against a nonresident is properly asserted. Under the first prong of the analysis, we determine if statutory authority for jurisdiction exists under our long arm statute. If statutory authority exists, we consider under the second prong whether exercise of our jurisdiction comports [is in accordance] with standards of due process.

Defendant has conceded that the facts are sufficient to confer jurisdiction under the North Carolina long arm statute. Therefore, "the inquiry becomes whether plaintiffs' assertion of jurisdiction over defendants complies with due process."

In order to satisfy due process requirements, there must be "certain minimum contacts [between the nonresident defendant and the forum state—that is, the state in which the court is located] such that the maintenance of the suit does not offend 'traditional notions of fair play and substantial justice.'"

In order to establish minimum contacts with North Carolina,

the defendant must have purposefully availed itself of the privilege of conducting activities within the forum state and invoked the benefits and protections of the laws of North Carolina. The relationship between the defendant and the forum state must be such that the defendant should reasonably anticipate being haled into a North Carolina court.

* * * *

* * * *Our courts look at the following factors in determining whether minimum contacts exist: (1) the quantity of the contacts, (2) the nature and quality of the contacts, (3) the source and connection of the cause of action to the contacts, (4) the interest of the forum state, and (5) the convenience to the parties.* [Emphasis added.]

In the instant case, the trial court found that the parties "had an ongoing business relationship characterized by frequent transactions between July 27, 2007, and April 25, 2008, as reflected by thirty-two purchase orders." Plaintiff would ship machined parts to defendant, who would then anodize the parts and return them to plaintiff in North Carolina. Defendant sent invoices totaling $21,018.70 to plaintiff in North Carolina, and these invoices were paid from plaintiff's corporate account at a North Carolina bank. Plaintiff filed a breach of contract action against defendant because the machined parts that were shipped to defendant from North Carolina and then anodized by defendant and shipped back to North Carolina were defective.

"It is generally conceded that a state has a manifest interest in providing its residents with a convenient forum for

---

a. *Anodizing* is a process in which metal is subjected to electrolytic action in order to coat the metal with a protective or decorative film.

EXTENDED CASE CONTINUES ➡

redressing injuries inflicted by out-of-state actors. Thus, North Carolina has a 'manifest interest' in providing the plaintiff 'a convenient forum for redressing injuries inflicted by' defendant, an out-of-state merchant." As for the remaining factor, there is no evidence in the record that would indicate that it is more convenient for the parties to litigate this matter in a different forum. "Litigation on interstate business transactions inevitably involves inconvenience to one of the parties. When [t]he inconvenience to defendant of litigating in North Carolina is no greater than would be the inconvenience [to] plaintiff of litigating in [the defendant's state] . . . no convenience factors . . . are determinative[.]" [Emphasis added.]

Therefore, after examining the ongoing relationship between the parties, the nature of their contacts, the interest of the forum state, the convenience of the parties, and the cause of action, we conclude defendant has "purposely availed" itself of the benefits of doing business in North Carolina and "should reasonably anticipate being haled" into a North Carolina court. We hold that defendant has sufficient minimum contacts with North Carolina to justify the exercise of personal jurisdiction over defendant without violating the due process clause.

Affirmed.

QUESTIONS

1. What are the factors that the court looked at in determining whether minimum contacts existed between the defendant and the state of North Carolina?
2. Why did the court state that the convenience of the parties was not "determinative" in this case?

JURISDICTION OVER SUBJECT MATTER Subject-matter jurisdiction refers to the limitations on the types of cases a court can hear. Certain courts are empowered to hear certain kinds of disputes.

General and Limited Jurisdiction. In both the federal and the state court systems, there are courts of *general* (unlimited) *jurisdiction* and courts of *limited jurisdiction.* A court of general jurisdiction can decide cases involving a broad array of issues. An example of a court of general jurisdiction is a state trial court or a federal district court. An example of a state court of limited jurisdiction is a probate court. **Probate courts** are state courts that handle only matters relating to the transfer of a person's assets and obligations after that person's death, including issues relating to the custody and guardianship of children. An example of a federal court of limited subject-matter jurisdiction is a **bankruptcy court,** which handles only bankruptcy proceedings (see Chapter 15).

A court's jurisdiction over subject matter is usually defined in the statute or constitution creating the court. In both the federal and the state court systems, a court's subject-matter jurisdiction can be limited not only by the subject of the lawsuit but also by the sum in controversy, whether the case is a felony (a more serious type of crime) or a misdemeanor (a less serious type of crime), or whether the proceeding is a trial or an appeal.

Original and Appellate Jurisdiction. A court's subject-matter jurisdiction is also frequently limited to hearing cases at a particular stage of the dispute. Courts in which lawsuits begin, trials take place, and evidence is presented are referred to as *courts of original jurisdiction.* Courts having original jurisdiction are courts of the first instance, or trial courts. In the federal court system, the *district courts* are trial courts. In the various state court systems, the trial courts are known by different names. Courts having appellate jurisdiction act as reviewing, or appellate, courts. The distinction between courts of original jurisdiction and courts of appellate jurisdiction normally lies in whether the case is being heard for the first time.

JURISDICTION OF THE FEDERAL COURTS Because the federal government is a government of limited powers, the jurisdiction of the federal courts is limited. Federal courts have subject-matter jurisdiction in two situations: *federal questions* and *diversity of citizenship.*

Federal Questions. Article III of the U.S. Constitution establishes the boundaries of federal judicial power. Section 2 of Article III states that "the judicial Power shall extend to all Cases, in Law and Equity, arising under this Constitution, the Laws of the United States, and Treaties made, or which shall be made, under their Authority." In effect, this clause means that whenever a plaintiff's cause of action is based, at least in part, on the U.S. Constitution, a treaty, or a federal law, a **federal question** arises. Any lawsuit involving a federal question comes under the judicial authority of the federal courts and can originate in a federal court. People who claim that their constitutional rights have been violated, for example, can begin their suits in a federal court. Note that in a case based on a federal question, a federal court will apply federal law.

Diversity of Citizenship. Federal district courts can also exercise original jurisdiction over cases involving **diversity of citizenship.** This term applies whenever a federal court has jurisdiction over a case that does not involve a question of federal law. The most common type of diversity jurisdiction has two requirements: (1) the plaintiff and defendant must be residents of different states, and (2) the dollar amount in controversy must exceed $75,000.[8] For purposes of diversity jurisdiction, a corporation is a citizen of both the state in which it is incorporated and the state in which its principal place of business is located. A case involving diversity of citizenship can be filed in the appropriate federal district court. If the case starts in a state court, it can sometimes be transferred to a federal court. A large percentage of the cases filed in federal courts each year are based on diversity of citizenship. In a case based on diversity of citizenship, a federal court will apply the relevant state law (which is often the law of the state in which the court sits).

EXCLUSIVE VERSUS CONCURRENT JURISDICTION
When both federal and state courts have the power to hear a case, as in suits involving diversity of citizenship, **concurrent jurisdiction** exists. When cases can be tried only in federal courts or only in state courts, **exclusive jurisdiction** exists. Federal courts have exclusive jurisdiction in cases involving federal crimes, bankruptcy, and most patent and copyright claims; in suits against the United States; and in some areas of admiralty law (law governing transportation on ocean waters). State courts also have exclusive jurisdiction over certain subjects— for example, divorce and adoption.

When concurrent jurisdiction exists, a party may choose to bring a suit in either a federal court or a state court. Factors affecting a party's decision to litigate in a federal versus a state court include the availability of different remedies, the distance to the respective courthouses, and the experience or reputation of a particular judge. For example, if the dispute involves a trade secret, a party might conclude that a federal court—which has exclusive jurisdiction over copyrights, patents, and trademarks—would have more expertise in the matter. The concepts of exclusive and concurrent jurisdiction are illustrated in Exhibit 2–1 below.

JURISDICTION IN CYBERSPACE The Internet's capacity to bypass political and geographic boundaries undercuts the traditional basis on which courts assert personal jurisdiction. This basis includes a party's contacts with a court's geographic jurisdiction. For a court to compel a defendant to come before it, there must be at least minimum contacts. Are there sufficient minimum contacts if the only connection to a jurisdiction is an ad on a Web site originating from a remote location?

The "Sliding-Scale" Standard. Gradually, the courts are developing a "sliding-scale" standard for determining when the exercise of personal

---

8. Diversity jurisdiction also exists in cases between (1) a foreign country and citizens of a state or of different states and (2) citizens of a state and citizens or subjects of a foreign country. These bases for diversity jurisdiction are less commonly used.

EXHIBIT 2-1 • Exclusive and Concurrent Jurisdiction

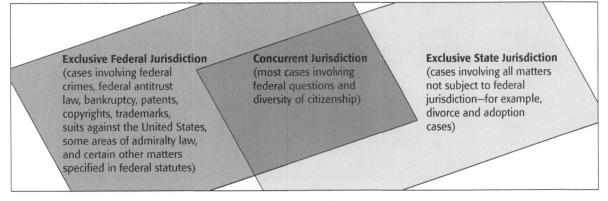

Exclusive Federal Jurisdiction
(cases involving federal crimes, federal antitrust law, bankruptcy, patents, copyrights, trademarks, suits against the United States, some areas of admiralty law, and certain other matters specified in federal statutes)

Concurrent Jurisdiction
(most cases involving federal questions and diversity of citizenship)

Exclusive State Jurisdiction
(cases involving all matters not subject to federal jurisdiction—for example, divorce and adoption cases)

jurisdiction over an out-of-state Internet-based defendant is proper. In developing this standard, the courts have identified three types of Internet business contacts: (1) substantial business conducted over the Internet (with contracts and sales, for example), (2) some interactivity through a Web site, and (3) passive advertising. Jurisdiction is proper for the first category, is improper for the third, and may or may not be appropriate for the second.[9] In certain situations, even a single contact can satisfy the minimum-contacts requirement.

CASE IN POINT A Louisiana resident, Daniel Crummey, purchased a used recreational vehicle (RV) from sellers in Texas after viewing photos of it on eBay. The sellers' statements on eBay claimed that "Everything works great on this RV and will provide comfort and dependability for years to come. This RV will go to Alaska and back without problems!" Crummey picked up the RV in Texas, but on the drive back to Louisiana, the RV quit working. He filed a suit in Louisiana against the sellers alleging that the vehicle was defective, but the sellers claimed that the Louisiana court lacked jurisdiction. Because the sellers had used eBay to market and sell the RV to a Louisiana buyer—and had regularly used eBay to sell vehicles to remote parties in the past—the court found that jurisdiction was proper.[10]

International Jurisdictional Issues. Because the Internet is international in scope, international jurisdictional issues understandably have come to the fore. The world's courts seem to be developing a standard that echoes the requirement of minimum contacts applied by the U.S. courts. Most courts are indicating that minimum contacts—doing business within the jurisdiction, for example—are enough to compel a defendant to appear and that a physical presence is not necessary. The effect of this standard is that a business firm has to comply with the laws in any jurisdiction in which it targets customers for its products. This situation is complicated by the fact that many countries' laws on particular issues—free speech, for example—are very different from U.S. laws.

Concept Summary 2.1 on the facing page reviews the various types of jurisdiction, including jurisdiction in cyberspace.

---

9. For a leading case on this issue, see *Zippo Manufacturing Co. v. Zippo Dot Com, Inc.,* 952 F.Supp. 1119 (W.D.Pa. 1997).

10. *Crummey v. Morgan,* 965 So.2d 497 (La.App. 1 Cir. 2007). But note that a single sale on eBay does not necessarily confer jurisdiction. Jurisdiction depends on whether the seller regularly uses eBay as a means for doing business with remote buyers. See also *Boschetto v. Hansing,* 539 F.3d 1011 (9th Cir. 2008).

Venue

Jurisdiction has to do with whether a court has authority to hear a case involving specific persons, property, or subject matter. **Venue**[11] is concerned with the most appropriate location for a trial. For example, two state courts (or two federal courts) may have the authority to exercise jurisdiction over a case, but it may be more appropriate or convenient to hear the case in one court than in the other.

Basically, the concept of venue reflects the policy that a court trying a case should be in the geographic neighborhood (usually the county) where the incident leading to the lawsuit occurred or where the parties involved in the lawsuit reside. Venue in a civil case typically is where the defendant resides, whereas venue in a criminal case normally is where the crime occurred. Pretrial publicity or other factors, though, may require a change of venue to another community, especially in criminal cases in which the defendant's right to a fair and impartial jury has been impaired.

Standing to Sue

To bring a lawsuit before a court, a party must have **standing to sue,** or a sufficient stake in a matter to justify seeking relief through the court system. In other words, a party must have a legally protected and tangible interest at stake in the litigation. The party bringing the lawsuit must have suffered a harm or been threatened with a harm by the action about which she or he has complained. At times, a person can have standing to sue on behalf of another person. For example, a parent or a legal guardian can bring a lawsuit on a child's behalf.

Standing to sue also requires that the controversy at issue be a **justiciable**[12] **controversy**—a controversy that is real and substantial, as opposed to hypothetical or academic.

CASE IN POINT James Bush went to the Federal Bureau of Investigation's (FBI's) office in San Jose, California, and filled out complaint forms indicating that he was seeking records under the Freedom of Information Act (FOIA—see Chapter 24). When the FBI failed to provide the requested records, Bush filed a lawsuit against the U.S. Department of Justice. The court dismissed the suit, however, finding that no actual controversy existed for the court to decide. Bush had failed to comply with certain requirements of the FOIA when he filled out the forms, so the FBI was not obligated to provide any records.[13]

---

11. Pronounced *ven*-yoo.

12. Pronounced jus-*tish*-a-bul.

13. *Bush v. U.S. Department of Justice,* 2008 WL 5245046 (N.D.Cal. 2008).

CONCEPT SUMMARY 2.1
Jurisdiction

Type of Jurisdiction	Description
Personal	Exists when a defendant is located within the territorial boundaries within which a court has the right and power to decide cases. Jurisdiction may be exercised over out-of-state defendants under state long arm statutes. Courts have jurisdiction over corporate defendants that do business within the state, as well as corporations that advertise, sell, or place goods into the stream of commerce in the state.
Property	Exists when the property that is subject to a lawsuit is located within the territorial boundaries within which a court has the right and power to decide cases.
Subject Matter	Limits the court's jurisdictional authority to particular types of cases. 1. *Limited jurisdiction*—Exists when a court is limited to a specific subject matter, such as probate or divorce. 2. *General jurisdiction*—Exists when a court can hear cases involving a broad array of issues.
Original	Exists with courts that have the authority to hear a case for the first time (trial courts).
Appellate	Exists with courts of appeal and review. Generally, appellate courts do not have original jurisdiction.
Federal	1. *Federal questions*—A federal court can exercise jurisdiction when the plaintiff's cause of action is based at least in part on the U.S. Constitution, a treaty, or a federal law. 2. *Diversity of citizenship*—A federal court can exercise jurisdiction in cases between citizens of different states when the amount in controversy exceeds $75,000, between a foreign country and citizens of a state or of different states, or between citizens of a state and citizens or subjects of a foreign country.
Concurrent	Exists when both federal and state courts have authority to hear the same case.
Exclusive	Exists when only state courts or only federal courts have authority to hear a case.
In Cyberspace	Gradually, the courts are developing standards to use in determining when jurisdiction over a Web site owner or operator in another state is proper. Jurisdictional disputes involving international cyberspace transactions present a significant legal challenge.

In the following case—involving a suit between a state and an agency of the federal government—the court was asked to determine whether the state's allegations rose to the level of a "concrete, particularized, actual or imminent" injury against the state independent of any harm to private parties.

CASE 2.2
Oregon v. Legal Services Corp.

United States Court of Appeals, Ninth Circuit, 552 F.3d 965 (2009).
www.ca9.uscourts.gov[a]

BACKGROUND AND FACTS • The U.S. government established the Legal Services Corporation (LSC) to provide federal funds to local legal assistance programs for individuals who cannot afford legal services. LSC restricts the use of the funds for some purposes, including participating

---

a. In the left-hand column, in the "Decisions" pull-down menu, click on "Opinions." On that page, click on "Advanced Search"; in the "by Case No.:" box, type "06-36012" and click on "Search." In the result, click on the appropriate link to access the opinion. The U.S. Court of Appeals for the Ninth Circuit maintains this Web site.

CASE CONTINUES ➡

CASE 2.2 CONTINUED ▶ in class-action lawsuits. The recipients must maintain legal, physical, and financial separation from organizations that engage in these activities. In 2005, to cut costs, the state of Oregon directed legal assistance programs to consolidate in situations in which separate organizations provided services in the same geographic area. LSC did not approve of the integration of programs that received its funds with programs that engaged in restricted activities. Oregon filed a suit in a federal district court against LSC, alleging that the state's ability to provide legal services to its citizens was frustrated. The court dismissed the suit "on the merits." Oregon appealed to the U.S. Court of Appeals for the Ninth Circuit.

IN THE LANGUAGE OF THE COURT
Milan D. *SMITH,* Jr., Circuit Judge:
* * * *

 * * * In this case there is no burden or injury placed on Oregon. * * * Oregon has not accepted federal funds, nor is it bound by the accompanying restrictions. Oregon is not injured by the federal government's decision to subsidize certain private activities, even if the government attaches impermissible conditions, as is alleged, to the recipients of those funds. *Oregon is only affected by virtue of its interest in the effect of the grant and the conditions on its citizens; it has no independent claim of injury.* [Emphasis added.]

Oregon cannot claim injury simply on the basis that federal subsidies to private parties do not [complement] Oregon's policies. *The state has no standing to sue the federal government to provide voluntary federal subsidies to private parties, and certainly has no standing to sue the federal government to change its conditions for those federal subsidies.* [Emphasis added.]
* * * *

Oregon argues * * * that it has been injured by LSC's regulations, which thwart Oregon's efforts at policy making with regards to Oregon's Legal Service Program. Oregon attempts to analogize [draw comparisons to] its situation to cases recognizing a state's standing to defend its statutes when they are alleged to be unconstitutional or pre-empted by federal regulation. However, those cases are distinguishable, because in this case there is no dispute over Oregon's ability to regulate its legal services program, and no claim that Oregon's laws have been invalidated as a result of the LSC restrictions.

The core of the dispute is whether Oregon should have the ability to control the conditions surrounding a voluntary grant of federal funds to specifically delineated private institutions. Because Oregon has no right, express or reserved, to do so, there is no judicially cognizable [able to be known] injury. Oregon may continue to regulate its legal service programs as it desires, but it cannot depend on voluntary financial support from LSC to * * * any * * * legal services provider within the state if it makes choices that conflict with the LSC * * * regulations.
* * * *

Oregon has failed to allege generalized facts sufficient to show an actual injury for the purposes of establishing its standing in this case. Oregon is not directly affected by the * * * LSC regulations, and is free to avoid any or all indirect effects of those regulations by simply increasing its own taxes to fund its desired policies. * * * Oregon * * * is, therefore, without standing to pursue its claims in this action.

DECISION AND REMEDY • *The U.S. Court of Appeals for the Ninth Circuit agreed that Oregon's complaint should be dismissed, but vacated the judgment and remanded the case for an entry of dismissal based on the plaintiff's lack of standing.*

THE LEGAL ENVIRONMENT DIMENSION • *Under what circumstances might a state suffer an injury that would give it standing to sue to block the enforcement of restrictions on the use of federal funds?*

THE ETHICAL DIMENSION • *Would it be ethical for a state to alter its policies to align with LSC's restrictions in order to continue the funding of local legal services programs? Explain.*

═══════ SECTION 3 ═══════
THE STATE AND FEDERAL COURT SYSTEMS

Each state has its own court system. Additionally, there is a system of federal courts. Although no two state court systems are exactly the same, the right-hand side of Exhibit 2–2 below illustrates the basic organizational framework characteristic of the court systems in many states. The exhibit also shows how the federal court system is structured.

The State Court Systems

Typically, a state court system includes several levels, or tiers, of courts. As indicated in Exhibit 2–2, state courts may include (1) local trial courts of limited jurisdiction, (2) state trial courts of general jurisdiction, (3) state courts of appeals (intermediate appellate courts), and (4) the state's highest court (often called the state supreme court). Generally, any person who is a party to a lawsuit has the opportunity to plead the case before a trial court and then, if he or she loses, before at least one level of appellate court. Finally, if the case involves a federal statute or federal constitutional issue, the decision of a state supreme court on that issue may be further appealed to the United States Supreme Court.

The states use various methods to select judges for their courts. Usually, voters elect judges, but in some states judges are appointed. For example, in Iowa, the governor appoints judges, and then the general population decides whether to confirm their appointment in the next general election. The states normally specify the number of years that judges will serve.

TRIAL COURTS Trial courts are exactly what their name implies—courts in which trials are held and testimony is taken. State trial courts have either general or limited jurisdiction. Trial courts that have general jurisdiction as to subject matter may be called county, district, superior, or circuit courts.[14] State trial courts of general jurisdiction have jurisdiction over a wide variety of subjects, including both civil disputes and criminal prosecutions. In some states, trial courts of general jurisdiction may hear appeals from courts of limited jurisdiction.

Courts of limited jurisdiction as to subject matter are often called special inferior trial courts or minor judiciary courts. **Small claims courts** are inferior trial courts that hear only civil cases involving claims of less than a certain amount, such as $5,000. Suits brought in small claims courts generally are conducted informally, and lawyers are not required. Decisions of small

---

14. The name in Ohio and Pennsylvania is Court of Common Pleas; the name in New York is Supreme Court, Trial Division.

EXHIBIT 2–2 • The State and Federal Court Systems

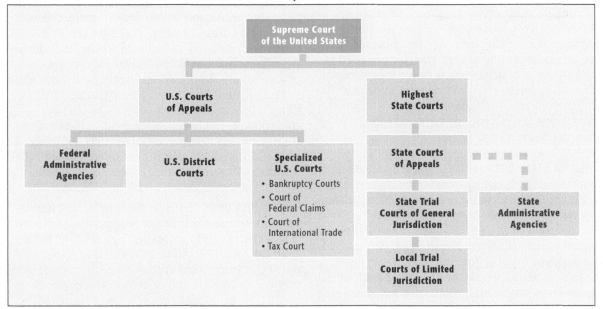

claims courts and municipal courts may sometimes be appealed to a state trial court of general jurisdiction. Other courts of limited jurisdiction include domestic relations courts, local municipal courts, and probate courts. A few states have also established Islamic law courts, which are courts of limited jurisdiction that serve the American Muslim community.[15]

APPELLATE, OR REVIEWING, COURTS Every state has at least one court of appeals (appellate court, or reviewing court), which may be an intermediate appellate court or the state's highest court. About three-fourths of the states have intermediate appellate courts. Generally, courts of appeals do not conduct new trials, in which evidence is submitted to the court and witnesses are examined. Rather, an appellate court panel of three or more judges reviews the record of the case on appeal, which includes a transcript of the trial proceedings, and then determines whether the trial court committed an error.

Usually, appellate courts focus on questions of law, not questions of fact. A **question of fact** deals with what really happened in regard to the dispute being tried—such as whether a party actually burned a flag. A **question of law** concerns the application or interpretation of the law—such as whether flag-burning is a form of speech protected by the First Amendment to the U.S. Constitution. Only a judge, not a jury, can rule on questions of law. Appellate courts normally defer (or give weight) to the trial court's findings on questions of fact because the trial court judge and jury were in a better position to evaluate testimony—by directly observing witnesses' gestures, demeanor, and other nonverbal behavior during the trial. At the appellate level, the judges review the written transcript of the trial, which does not include these nonverbal elements. Thus, an appellate court will not tamper with a trial court's finding of fact unless it is clearly erroneous (contrary to the evidence presented at trial) or when there is no evidence to support the finding.

HIGHEST STATE COURTS The highest appellate court in a state often is called the supreme court but may be designated by some other name. In New York and Maryland, the highest state court is called the Court of Appeals; in Maine and Massachusetts, it is the Supreme Judicial Court; and in West Virginia, it is the Supreme Court of Appeals.

The decisions of each state's highest court on all questions of state law are final. Only when issues of federal law are involved can the United States Supreme Court overrule a decision made by a state's highest court. Suppose that a city ordinance prohibits citizens from engaging in door-to-door advocacy without first obtaining a permit. Further suppose that a religious group sues the city, arguing that the law violates the freedoms of speech and religion guaranteed by the First Amendment. If the state supreme court upholds the law, the group could appeal the decision to the United States Supreme Court—because a constitutional (federal) issue is involved.

The Federal Court System

The federal court system is basically a three-tiered model consisting of (1) U.S. district courts (trial courts of general jurisdiction) and various courts of limited jurisdiction, (2) U.S. courts of appeals (intermediate courts of appeals), and (3) the United States Supreme Court. Unlike state court judges, who are elected, federal court judges—including the justices of the Supreme Court—are appointed by the president and confirmed by the U.S. Senate. All federal judges receive lifetime appointments under Article III of the U.S. Constitution, which states that federal judges "hold their offices during good Behaviour."

U.S. DISTRICT COURTS At the federal level, the equivalent of a state trial court of general jurisdiction is the district court. U.S. district courts have original jurisdiction in matters involving a federal question and concurrent jurisdiction with state courts when diversity jurisdiction exists. Federal cases typically originate in district courts. There are other federal courts with original, but special (or limited), jurisdiction, such as the federal bankruptcy courts.

There is at least one federal district court in every state. The number of judicial districts can vary over time, primarily owing to population changes and corresponding changes in caseloads. Today, there are ninety-four federal judicial districts. Exhibit 2–3 on the facing page shows the boundaries of both the U.S. district courts and the U.S. courts of appeals.

U.S. COURTS OF APPEALS In the federal court system, there are thirteen U.S. courts of appeals—referred to as U.S. circuit courts of appeals. Twelve of the federal courts of appeals (including the Court of Appeals for the D.C. Circuit) hear appeals from the federal district courts located within their respective judicial circuits, or geographic boundaries.[16] The Court of

---

15. See, for example, *Jabri v. Qaddura,* 108 S.W.3d 404 (Tex.App.—Fort Worth 2003); and *Abd Alla v. Mourssi,* 680 N.W.2d 569 (Minn.App. 2004).

16. Historically, judges were required to "ride the circuit" and hear appeals in different courts around the country, which is how the name "circuit court" came about.

Appeals for the Thirteenth Circuit, called the Federal Circuit, has national appellate jurisdiction over certain types of cases, such as those involving patent law and those in which the U.S. government is a defendant. The decisions of a circuit court of appeals are binding on all courts within the circuit court's jurisdiction and are final in most cases, but appeal to the United States Supreme Court is possible.

UNITED STATES SUPREME COURT At the highest level in the three-tiered federal court system is the United States Supreme Court. According to the language of Article III of the U.S. Constitution, there is only one national Supreme Court. All other courts in the federal system are considered "inferior." Congress is empowered to create other inferior courts as it deems necessary. The inferior courts that Congress has created include the second tier in our model—the U.S. circuit courts of appeals—as well as the district courts and the various federal courts of limited, or specialized, jurisdiction.

The United States Supreme Court consists of nine justices. Although the Supreme Court has original, or trial, jurisdiction in rare instances (set forth in Article III, Sections 1 and 2), most of its work is as an appeals court. The Court can review any case

decided by the federal courts of appeals, and it also has appellate authority over cases involving federal questions that have been decided in the state courts. The Court is the final arbiter of the Constitution and federal law.

Appeals. To bring a case before the Court, a party requests that it issue a writ of *certiorari*.[17] A **writ of certiorari** is an order issued by the Court to a lower court requiring the latter to send it the record of the case for review. The Court will not issue a writ unless at least four of the nine justices approve of it. This is called the **rule of four.** Whether the Court will issue a writ of *certiorari* is entirely within its discretion, and most petitions for writs are denied. (Thousands of cases are filed with the Court each year, yet it hears, on average, fewer than one hundred of these cases.)[18] A denial of the request to issue a writ of *certiorari* is not a decision on the merits of a case, nor does it

---

17. Pronounced sur-shee-uh-*rah*-ree.
18. From the mid-1950s through the early 1990s, the Supreme Court reviewed more cases per year than it has since then. In the Court's 1982–1983 term, for example, the Court issued written opinions in 151 cases. In contrast, during the Court's 2009–2010 term, the Court issued written opinions in only 92 cases.

EXHIBIT 2-3 • Geographic Boundaries of the U.S. Courts of Appeals and U.S. District Courts

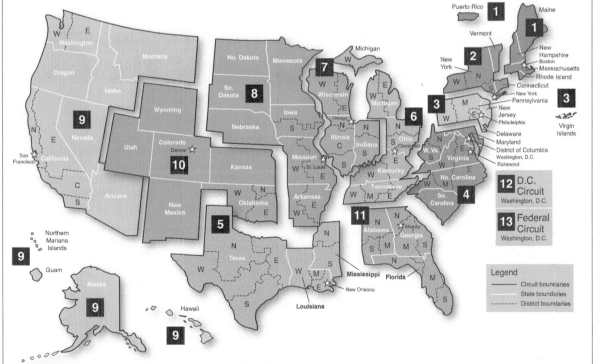

Source: Administrative Office of the United States Courts.

indicate agreement with the lower court's opinion. Also, denial of the writ has no value as a precedent. Denial simply means that the lower court's decision remains the law in that jurisdiction.

Petitions. Typically, the Court grants petitions in cases that raise important constitutional questions or when the lower courts have issued conflicting decisions on a significant issue. The justices, however, never explain their reasons for hearing certain cases and not others, so it is difficult to predict which type of case the Court might select.

See *Concept Summary 2.2* below to review the various types of courts in the federal and state court systems.

SECTION 4
JUDICIAL PROCEDURES: FOLLOWING A CASE THROUGH THE COURT

American and English courts follow the *adversarial system of justice.* Although clients are allowed to represent themselves in court (called *pro se* representation),[19] most parties to lawsuits hire attorneys to represent them. Each lawyer acts as his or her client's advocate, presenting the client's version of the facts in such a way as to convince the judge (or the judge and jury, in a jury trial) that this version is correct.

Most of the judicial procedures in the following pages are rooted in the adversarial framework of the American legal system. In this section, which provides an overview of judicial procedures, we illustrate the steps involved in a lawsuit with a hypothetical civil case. Criminal procedures will be discussed in Chapter 7.

Procedural Rules

The parties to a lawsuit must comply with the procedural rules of the court in which the lawsuit is filed. Although most people, when considering the outcome of a case, think of matters of substantive law, procedural law can have a significant impact on the ability to assert a legal claim. Procedural rules provide a framework for every dispute and specify what must be done at each stage of the litigation process. Procedural rules are complex, and they vary from court to court and from state to state. There is a set of federal rules of procedure as well as various sets of rules for state courts. Additionally, the applicable procedures will depend on whether the case is a civil or criminal proceeding. All civil trials held in federal

---

19. This right was definitively established in *Faretta v. California,* 422 U.S. 806, 95 S.Ct. 2525, 45 L.Ed.2d 562 (1975).

CONCEPT SUMMARY 2.2	
Types of Courts	
Type of Court	**Description**
Trial Courts	Trial courts are courts of original jurisdiction in which actions are initiated. 1. *State courts*—Courts of general jurisdiction can hear any case that has not been specifically designated for another court; courts of limited jurisdiction include domestic relations courts, probate courts, and small claims courts. 2. *Federal courts*—The federal district court is the equivalent of the state trial court. Federal courts of limited jurisdiction include the bankruptcy courts and others shown in Exhibit 2–2 on page 37.
Intermediate Appellate Courts	Courts of appeals are reviewing courts; generally, appellate courts do not have original jurisdiction. About three-fourths of the states have intermediate appellate courts; in the federal court system, the U.S. circuit courts of appeals are the intermediate appellate courts.
Supreme Courts	The highest state court is that state's supreme court (it may be called by another name). Appeal from state supreme courts to the United States Supreme Court is possible only if a federal question is involved. The United States Supreme Court is the highest court in the federal court system and the final arbiter of the Constitution and federal law.

district courts are governed by the **Federal Rules of Civil Procedure (FRCP).**[20]

Broadly speaking, the litigation process has three phases: pretrial, trial, and posttrial. Each phase involves specific procedures, as discussed throughout this chapter. To illustrate the procedures involved in a civil lawsuit, we will use a simple hypothetical case. The case arose from an automobile accident, which occurred when a car driven by Antonio Carvello, a resident of New Jersey, collided with a car driven by Jill Kirby, a resident of New York. The accident took place at an intersection in New York City. Kirby suffered personal injuries, which caused her to incur medical and hospital expenses as well as lost wages for four months. In all, she calculated that the cost to her of the accident was $100,000.[21] Carvello and Kirby have been unable to agree on a settlement, and Kirby now must decide whether to sue Carvello for the $100,000 compensation she feels she deserves.

Consultation with an Attorney

The rules of procedure often affect the outcome of a dispute—a fact that highlights the importance of obtaining the advice of counsel. Thus, almost anyone contemplating a lawsuit seeks the guidance of a qualified attorney. In the hypothetical Kirby-Carvello case, assume that Kirby consults with a lawyer, who advises her regarding what she can expect in a lawsuit, her probability of success at trial, and the procedures that will be involved. If more than one court has jurisdiction over the matter, the attorney will also discuss the advantages and disadvantages of filing in a particular court. Depending on the court hearing the case, the attorney will give Kirby an idea of how much time it will take to resolve the dispute through litigation and provide an estimate of the costs involved.

The attorney will also inform Kirby of the legal fees that she will have to pay in an attempt to collect damages from the defendant, Carvello. Attorneys base their fees on such factors as the difficulty of a matter, the amount of time involved, the experience and skill of the attorney in the particular area of the law, and the cost of doing business. In the United States, legal fees range from $175 to $700 per hour or even higher. The client is also responsible for paying various expenses related to the case (called out-of-pocket costs), such as court filing fees, travel expenses, and the cost of expert witnesses and investigators.

TYPES OF ATTORNEYS' FEES For a particular legal matter, an attorney may charge one type of fee or a combination of several types. *Fixed fees* may be charged for the performance of such services as drafting a simple will. *Hourly fees* may be computed for matters that will involve an indeterminate period of time. *Contingency fees* are fixed as a percentage (usually between 25 and 40 percent) of a client's recovery in certain types of lawsuits, such as a personal-injury lawsuit.[22] If the lawsuit is unsuccessful, the attorney receives no fee, but the client will have to reimburse the attorney for any out-of-pocket costs incurred. Because Kirby's claim involves a personal injury, her lawyer will likely take the case on a contingency-fee basis, but she may have to pay an amount up front to cover the court costs.

SETTLEMENT CONSIDERATIONS Once an attorney has been retained, the attorney is required to pursue a resolution of the matter on the client's behalf. Nevertheless, the amount of energy an attorney will spend on a given case is also determined by the time and funds the client wishes to devote to the process. If the client is willing to pay for a lengthy trial and one or more appeals, the attorney may pursue those actions. Often, however, after learning of the substantial costs that litigation entails, a client decides to pursue a settlement of the claim. Attempts to settle the case may be ongoing throughout the litigation process.

Another important factor in deciding whether to pursue litigation is the defendant's ability to pay the damages sought. Even if Kirby is awarded damages, it may be difficult to enforce the court's judgment if, for example, the amount exceeds the limits of Carvello's automobile insurance policy.

Pretrial Procedures

The pretrial litigation process involves the filing of the *pleadings*, the gathering of evidence (called *discovery*), and possibly other procedures, such as a pretrial conference and jury selection.

---

20. The United States Supreme Court has authority to establish these rules, as spelled out in 28 U.S.C. Sections 2071–2077. Generally, though, the federal judiciary appoints committees that make recommendations to the Supreme Court. The Court then publishes any proposed changes in the rules and allows for public comment before finalizing the rules.
21. In this example, we are ignoring damages for pain and suffering and for permanent disabilities. Often, plaintiffs in personal-injury cases seek such damages.

---

22. Note that attorneys may charge a contingency fee in only certain types of cases and are typically prohibited from entering into this type of fee arrangement in criminal cases, divorce cases, and cases involving the distribution of assets after death.

THE PLEADINGS The *complaint* and *answer* (and other legal documents discussed below), taken together, are known as the **pleadings.** The pleadings inform each party of the other's claims and specify the issues (disputed questions) involved in the case. Because the rules of procedure vary depending on the jurisdiction of the court, the style and form of the pleadings may be different from those shown in this chapter.

The Plaintiff's Complaint. Kirby's action against Carvello commences when her lawyer files a **complaint**[23] with the clerk of the appropriate court. The complaint contains a statement alleging (1) the facts showing that the court has subject-matter and personal jurisdiction, (2) the facts establishing the plaintiff's basis for relief, and (3) the remedy the plaintiff is seeking. Complaints can be lengthy or brief, depending on the complexity of the case and the rules of the jurisdiction.

Exhibit 2–4 on the facing page illustrates how a complaint in the Kirby-Carvello case might appear. The complaint asserts facts indicating that the federal district court has subject-matter jurisdiction because of diversity of citizenship. It then gives a brief statement of the facts of the accident and alleges that Carvello negligently drove his vehicle through a red light, striking Kirby's car and causing serious personal injury and property damage. The complaint goes on to state that Kirby is seeking $100,000 in damages, although in some state civil actions the plaintiff need not specify the amount of damages sought.

Service of Process. Before the court can exercise personal jurisdiction over the defendant (Carvello)—in effect, before the lawsuit can begin—the court must have proof that the defendant was notified of the lawsuit. Formally notifying the defendant of a lawsuit is called **service of process.** The plaintiff must deliver, or serve, a copy of the complaint and a **summons** (a notice requiring the defendant to appear in court and answer the complaint) to the defendant. The summons notifies Carvello that he must file an answer to the complaint within a specified time period (twenty days in the federal courts) or suffer a default judgment against him. A **default judgment** in Kirby's favor would mean that she would be awarded the damages alleged in her complaint because Carvello failed to respond to the allegations.

Method of Service. How service of process occurs depends on the rules of the court or jurisdiction in which the lawsuit is brought. Under the FRCP, anyone who is at least eighteen years of age and is not a party to the lawsuit can serve process in federal court cases. In state courts, the process server is often a county sheriff or an employee of an independent company that provides process service in the local area. Usually, the server hands the summons and complaint to the defendant personally or leaves it at the defendant's residence or place of business. In some states, process can be served by mail if the defendant consents (accepts service). When the defendant cannot be reached, special rules provide for alternative means of service, such as publishing a notice in the local newspaper. In cases involving corporate defendants, the summons and complaint may be served on an officer or on a *registered agent* (representative) of the corporation.

Waiver of Formal Service of Process. In many instances, the defendant is already aware that a lawsuit is being filed and is willing to waive (give up) her or his right to be served personally. The FRCP and many states' rules allow defendants to waive formal service of process, provided that certain procedures are followed. Kirby's attorney, for example, could mail to defendant Carvello a copy of the complaint, along with "Waiver of Service of Summons" forms for Carvello to sign. If Carvello signs and returns the forms within thirty days, formal service of process is waived. Moreover, under the FRCP, defendants who agree to waive formal service of process receive additional time to respond to the complaint (sixty days, instead of twenty days). Some states provide similar incentives to encourage defendants to waive formal service of process and thereby reduce associated costs and foster cooperation between the parties.

The Defendant's Response. In an **answer,** the defendant either admits or denies each of the allegations in the plaintiff's complaint and may also set forth defenses to those allegations. Under the federal rules, any allegations that are not denied by the defendant will be deemed by the court to have been admitted.

If Carvello admits to all of Kirby's allegations in his answer, a judgment will be entered for Kirby. If Carvello denies Kirby's allegations, the matter will proceed further. Carvello can also admit the truth of Kirby's complaint but raise new facts to show that he

---

23. Sometimes, the complaint is called a *petition* or a *declaration.*

EXHIBIT 2-4 • A Typical Complaint

```
              IN THE UNITED STATES DISTRICT COURT
           FOR THE SOUTHERN DISTRICT OF NEW YORK


                                           CIVIL NO. 12-1047

  JILL KIRBY

                        Plaintiff,

  v.                                       COMPLAINT

  ANTONIO CARVELLO

                        Defendant.


     The plaintiff brings this cause of action against the defendant, alleging as
  follows:

  1. This action is between the plaintiff, who is a resident of the State of
     New York, and the defendant, who is a resident of the State of New Jersey.
     There is diversity of citizenship between the parties.
  2. The amount in controversy, exclusive of interest and costs, exceeds the
     sum of $75,000.
  3. On September 10th, 2011, the plaintiff, Jill Kirby, was exercising good
     driving habits and reasonable care in driving her car through the
     intersection of Boardwalk and Pennsylvania Avenue, New York City, New York,
     when the defendant, Antonio Carvello, negligently drove his vehicle through
     a red light at the intersection and collided with the plaintiff's vehicle.
  4. As a result of the collision, the plaintiff suffered severe physical injury,
     which prevented her from working, and property damage to her car.

     WHEREFORE, the plaintiff demands judgment against the defendant for the sum
  of $100,000 plus interest at the maximum legal rate and the costs of this action.


                         By  _____
                                 Joseph Roe
                                 Attorney for Plaintiff
                                 100 Main Street
       1/3/12                    New York, New York
```

should not be held liable for Kirby's damages. This is called raising an **affirmative defense.** For example, Carvello could assert Kirby's own negligence as a defense by alleging that Kirby was driving recklessly at the time of the accident. If Carvello makes such a claim against Kirby, he can then say that she owes him for damage to his car. This is appropriately called a **counterclaim.** If Carvello files a counterclaim, Kirby will have to submit an answer to the counterclaim.

DISMISSALS AND JUDGMENTS BEFORE TRIAL Many actions for which pleadings have been filed never come to trial. The parties may negotiate a settlement of the dispute at any stage of the litigation process. There are also numerous procedural avenues for disposing of a case without a trial. Many of them involve one or the other party's attempts to get the case dismissed through the use of various motions.

A **motion** is a procedural request submitted to the court by an attorney on behalf of her or his client.

When one party files a motion with the court, that party must also send to, or serve on, the opposing party a *notice of motion,* which informs the opposing party that the motion has been filed. **Pretrial motions** include the *motion to dismiss,* the *motion for judgment on the pleadings,* and the *motion for summary judgment.*

Motion to Dismiss. Either party can file a **motion to dismiss,** asking the court to dismiss the case for the reasons stated in the motion, although normally it is the defendant who requests dismissal. A defendant can file a motion to dismiss if the plaintiff's complaint fails to state a claim for which relief (a remedy) can be granted. Such a motion asserts that even if the facts alleged in the complaint are true, they do not give rise to any legal claim against the defendant. For example, if the allegations in Kirby's complaint do not constitute negligence on Carvello's part, Carvello can move to dismiss the case for failure to state a claim. Defendant Carvello could also file a motion to dismiss on the grounds that he was not properly served, that the court lacked jurisdiction, or that the venue was improper.

If the judge grants the motion to dismiss, the plaintiff generally is given time to file an amended complaint. If the judge denies the motion, the suit will go forward, and the defendant must then file an answer. Note that if Carvello wishes to discontinue the suit because, for example, an out-of-court settlement has been reached, he can likewise move for dismissal. The court can also dismiss a case on its own motion.

Motion for Judgment on the Pleadings. At the close of the pleadings, either party may make a **motion for judgment on the pleadings,** which asks the court to decide the issue solely on the pleadings without proceeding to trial. The judge will grant the motion only when there is no dispute over the facts of the case and the sole issue to be resolved is a question of law. In the Kirby-Carvello case, if Carvello admits to all of Kirby's allegations in his answer and raises no affirmative defenses, Kirby can file a motion for judgment on the pleadings. In deciding a motion for judgment on the pleadings, the judge may consider only the evidence contained in the pleadings.

Motion for Summary Judgment. Either party can file a **motion for summary judgment,** which asks the court to grant a judgment in that party's favor without a trial. A court will grant a motion for summary judgment only if it determines that no facts are in dispute and the only question is how the law applies to the facts. A motion for summary judgment can be made before or during a trial, but it will be granted only if, when the evidence is viewed in the light most favorable to the other party, there clearly are no facts in contention.

To support a motion for summary judgment, a party can submit evidence obtained at any point before the trial that refutes the other party's factual claim. The evidence may consist of **affidavits** (sworn statements by parties or witnesses) or copies of documents, such as contracts, e-mails, and letters obtained through the course of discovery. Of course, the evidence must be *admissible* evidence—that is, evidence that the court would allow to be presented during the trial. The use of additional evidence is one feature that distinguishes the motion for summary judgment from the motion to dismiss and the motion for judgment on the pleadings.

DISCOVERY Before a trial begins, the parties can use a number of procedural devices to obtain information and gather evidence about the case. Kirby, for example, will want to know how fast Carvello was driving, whether he had been drinking or was under the influence of any medication, and whether he was wearing corrective lenses if he was required by law to do so while driving. The process of obtaining information from the opposing party or from witnesses prior to trial is known as **discovery.** Discovery includes gaining access to witnesses, documents, records, and other types of evidence. In federal courts, the parties are required to make initial disclosures of relevant evidence to the opposing party.

Discovery prevents surprises at trial by giving both parties access to evidence that might otherwise be hidden. This allows the litigants to learn as much as they can about what to expect at a trial before they reach the courtroom. Discovery also serves to narrow the issues so that trial time is spent on the main questions in the case.

The main question in the following case was what a court could do when a plaintiff failed to identify and disclose the names of expert witnesses, even though the court deemed that such witnesses were necessary to establish the plaintiff's claim against the defendants.

CASE 2.3

Blankenship v. Collier

Supreme Court of Kentucky, 302 S.W.3d 665 (2010).
www.courts.ky.gov/supremecourt/minutes.htm[a]

BACKGROUND AND FACTS • Horace Collier was admitted to Caritas Medical Center with abdominal pain. The following day, after undergoing tests and being diagnosed by Dr. Robert Blankenship as having appendicitis, Collier had an appendectomy. One year later, Collier sued Blankenship and Caritas in a Kentucky state court, contending that they had been negligent. Specifically, Collier claimed that he had been ignored for several hours, causing severe abdominal pain, and that his X-ray had not been stored properly, further delaying his diagnosis and treatment. More than nine months later, Collier had not yet disclosed the identities of any expert witnesses who would testify on his behalf, and the court ordered him to do so by January 30, 2006. At Collier's request, this deadline was extended to February 28. Finally, on March 14, 2006, after Collier still had not disclosed any names, the defendants filed motions for summary judgment, arguing that there could be no issue of material fact in this medical malpractice[b] case without expert testimony. The trial court granted the motions. Collier appealed, arguing that summary judgment was inappropriate because it was being used only as a sanctioning tool to punish him for failing to timely disclose his experts and that there was a "serious question" as to whether he would even need experts to prove his medical malpractice claim. The intermediate appellate court agreed and reversed the trial court's decision. The defendants appealed the decision to the Supreme Court of Kentucky.

IN THE LANGUAGE OF THE COURT
Opinion of the court by Justice *ABRAMSON*.
* * * *

* * * Although a defendant is permitted to move for a summary judgment at any time, this Court has cautioned trial courts not to take up these motions prematurely and to consider summary judgment motions "only after the opposing party has been given ample opportunity to complete discovery." Thus, even though an appellate court always reviews the substance of a trial court's summary judgment ruling *de novo* [anew] * * * to determine whether the record reflects a genuine issue of material fact, *a reviewing court must also consider whether the trial court gave the party opposing the motion an ample opportunity to respond and complete discovery before the court entered its ruling.* In a medical malpractice action, where a sufficient amount of time has expired and the plaintiff has still "failed to introduce evidence sufficient to establish the respective applicable standard of care," then the defendants are entitled to summary judgment as a matter of law. The trial court's determination that a sufficient amount of time has passed and that it can properly take up the summary judgment motion for a ruling is reviewed for an abuse of discretion. [Emphasis added.]

In this case, the issue before this Court is not simply whether Collier had failed to establish a genuine issue of material fact at the time Dr. Blankenship and Caritas filed their summary judgment motions—without a doubt, there is no genuine issue of material fact in the record because Collier has no expert to support his claim of medical negligence. Rather, the more specific issue is whether the trial court was correct to take up the defendants' summary judgment motions and enter a ruling when it did and, secondarily, whether the court was required first either to enter a separate order requiring Collier to obtain expert testimony or to enter an order sanctioning Collier for failing to meet the court's expert disclosure deadline.

Having carefully reviewed the record, we conclude that the defendants' summary judgment motions were properly before the trial court and it did not abuse its discretion in taking them

---

a. On the page that opens, select "January 21" under the "2010" heading. Scroll down the list to the case title to access the court's opinion. The Supreme Court of Kentucky maintains this Web site.

b. *Medical malpractice* is the term used for the tort of negligence when committed by medical professionals—see Chapter 12.

CASE CONTINUES ➡

CASE 2.3 CONTINUED ▶ up and deciding to rule on the motions approximately four months after they were filed and seventeen months after the lawsuit was initiated. Collier had completely failed to identify any expert witnesses and could not sustain his burden of proof without expert testimony and, thus, no material issue of fact existed in the record and the defendants were entitled to summary judgment as a matter of law. Because Collier never disputed that a medical expert was necessary to prove his claim of medical negligence and continually represented to the trial court that he would obtain an expert witness, no separate ruling stating the obvious—the need for an expert witness—was required before the court ruled on the defendants' summary judgment motions. Further, * * * the trial court was not required to enter a sanctions order prior to granting the defendants' summary judgment motions.

DECISION AND REMEDY • *The Supreme Court of Kentucky reversed the decision of the lower appellate court and reinstated the trial court's decision. The trial court had not abused its discretion by granting summary judgment for the defendants.*

THE ETHICAL DIMENSION • *Collier contended that there was a "serious question" as to whether he would even need experts to prove his medical malpractice claim. Is it fair to Collier to prevent the trial from proceeding, even though the lack of expert testimony might have made it difficult—if not impossible—for him to win the case? Explain.*

MANAGERIAL IMPLICATIONS • *Business owners and managers should be aware that initiating discovery procedures and responding to discovery requests in a timely fashion are important in any litigation. Although the court in this case claimed that summary judgment was not a sanction imposed on the plaintiff for delays during discovery, one could argue (as a dissenting judge did) that it was indeed a sanction—and a very harsh one. Courts have also dismissed cases when the plaintiffs have caused undue delay by not meeting procedural deadlines.*

Discovery Rules. The FRCP and similar state rules set forth the guidelines for discovery activity. Generally, discovery is allowed regarding any matter that is relevant to the claim or defense of any party. Discovery rules also attempt to protect witnesses and parties from undue harassment, and to safeguard privileged or confidential material from being disclosed. Only information that is relevant to the case at hand—or likely to lead to the discovery of relevant information—is discoverable. If a discovery request involves privileged or confidential business information, a court can deny the request and can limit the scope of discovery in a number of ways. For example, a court can require the party to submit the materials to the judge in a sealed envelope so that the judge can decide if they should be disclosed to the opposing party.

Depositions. Discovery can involve the use of depositions. A **deposition** is sworn testimony by a party to the lawsuit or by any witness, recorded by an authorized court official. The person deposed gives testimony and answers questions asked by the attorneys for both sides. The questions and answers are recorded, sworn to, and signed. These answers not only help the attorneys prepare their cases but also give them the opportunity to ask immediate follow-up questions and to evaluate how their witnesses will conduct themselves at trial. In addition, depositions

can be employed in court to *impeach* (challenge the credibility of) a party or a witness who changes testimony at the trial. A deposition can also be used as testimony if the witness is not available at trial.

Interrogatories. Another aspect of discovery can also involve **interrogatories,** which are written questions for which written answers are prepared and then signed under oath. The main difference between interrogatories and written depositions is that interrogatories are directed to a party to the lawsuit (the plaintiff or the defendant), not to a witness, and the party usually has thirty days to prepare answers. The party's attorney often drafts the answers to interrogatories in a manner calculated to give away as little information as possible. Whereas depositions are useful for eliciting candid responses and answers not prepared in advance, interrogatories are designed to obtain accurate information about specific topics, such as how many contracts were signed and when. The scope of interrogatories is also broader because parties are obligated to answer questions, even if that means disclosing information from their records and files. Note that a court can impose sanctions on a party who fails to answer interrogatories (or who refuses to respond to other discovery requests).

CASE IN POINT Computer Task Group, Inc. (CTG), hired William Brotby as an information technology consultant. As a condition of his employment, Brotby signed an agreement that restricted his ability to work for CTG's customers if he left CTG. Less than two years later, Brotby left CTG and began working for Alyeska Pipeline Service Company, a CTG client, in breach of the agreement. CTG sued Brotby. During discovery, Brotby refused to respond fully to CTG's interrogatories. He gave contradictory answers, made frivolous objections, filed baseless motions, and never disclosed all the information that CTG sought. The court ordered Brotby to comply with discovery requests five times, but Brotby continued to make excuses and changed his story repeatedly, making it impossible for CTG to establish basic facts with any certainty. Eventually, CTG requested and the court granted a default judgment against Brotby based on his failure to cooperate.[24]

Requests. One party can serve the other party with a written request for an admission of the truth of matters relating to the trial. Any fact admitted under such a request is conclusively established as true for the trial. For example, Kirby can ask Carvello to admit that his driver's license was suspended at the time of the accident. A request for admission shortens the trial because the parties will not have to spend time proving facts on which they already agree.

A party can gain access to documents and other items not in her or his possession in order to inspect and examine them. Carvello, for instance, can gain permission to inspect and copy Kirby's car repair bills. Likewise, a party can gain "entry upon land" to inspect the premises.

When the physical or mental condition of one party is in question, the opposing party can ask the court to order a physical or mental examination by an independent examiner. If the court agrees to make the order, the opposing party can obtain the results of the examination. Note that the court will make such an order only when the need for the information outweighs the right to privacy of the person to be examined.

Electronic Discovery. Any relevant material, including information stored electronically, can be the object of a discovery request. The federal rules and most state rules (as well as court decisions) specifically allow individuals to obtain discovery of electronic "data compilations." Electronic evidence, or **e-evidence,** consists of all computer-generated or electronically recorded information, such as e-mail, voice mail, spreadsheets, word-

processing documents, and other data. E-evidence can reveal significant facts that are not discoverable by other means. For example, computers automatically record certain information about files—such as who created the file and when, and who accessed, modified, or transmitted it—on their hard drives. This information can only be obtained from the file in its electronic format—not from printed-out versions.

The FRCP deals specifically with the preservation, retrieval, and production of electronic data. Although traditional means, such as interrogatories and depositions, are still used to find out whether e-evidence exists, a party usually must hire an expert to retrieve the evidence in its electronic format. An expert uses software to reconstruct e-mail exchanges and recover computer files that the user thought had been deleted. Reviewing back-up copies of documents and e-mail can provide useful information about how a particular matter progressed over time.

Electronic discovery, or e-discovery, has significant advantages over paper discovery, but it is also time consuming and expensive. These costs are amplified when the parties involved in the lawsuit are large corporations with many offices and employees. Who should pay the costs associated with e-discovery? For a discussion of how the courts are handling this issue, see this chapter's *Shifting Legal Priorities for Business* feature on the next page.

PRETRIAL CONFERENCE After discovery has taken place and before the trial begins, the attorneys may meet with the trial judge in a **pretrial conference,** or hearing. Usually, the conference consists of an informal discussion between the judge and the opposing attorneys after discovery has taken place. The purpose of the conference is to explore the possibility of a settlement without trial and, if this is not possible, to identify the matters that are in dispute and to plan the course of the trial. In particular, the parties may attempt to establish ground rules to restrict the number of expert witnesses or discuss the admissibility or costs of certain types of evidence.

JURY SELECTION Before a jury trial commences, a panel of jurors must be selected. Although some types of trials require twelve-person juries, most civil matters can be heard by six-person juries. The jury selection process is known as ***voir dire***.[25] During *voir dire* in most jurisdictions, attorneys for the plaintiff and the defendant ask prospective jurors

---

24. *Computer Task Group, Inc. v. Brotby*, 364 F.3d 1112 (9th Cir. 2004).

25. Pronounced *vwahr deehr*. These verbs based on Old French mean "to speak the truth." In legal language, the phrase refers to the process of questioning jurors to learn about their backgrounds, attitudes, and similar attributes.

Today, less than 0.5 percent of new information is created on paper. Instead of sending letters and memos, people send e-mails and text messages, creating a massive amount of electronically stored information (ESI). The law requires parties to preserve ESI whenever there is a "reasonable anticipation of litigation."

Why Companies Fail to Preserve Electronic Evidence

Preserving electronic evidence, or e-evidence, can be a challenge, particularly for large corporations that have electronic data scattered across multiple networks, servers, desktops, laptops, handheld devices, and even home computers. Although many companies have policies regarding back-up of office e-mail and computer systems, these may cover only a fraction of the e-discovery requested in a lawsuit.

Technological advances further complicate the situation. Users of BlackBerry devices, for example, can configure them so that messages are transmitted with limited or no archiving rather than going through a company's servers and being recorded. How can a company preserve e-evidence that is never on its servers? In one case, the court held that a company had a duty to preserve transitory "server log data," which exist only temporarily on a computer's memory.[a]

Potential Sanctions and Malpractice Claims

A court may impose sanctions (such as fines) on a party that fails to preserve e-evidence or to comply with e-discovery requests. A firm may be sanctioned if it provides e-mails without the attachments, does not produce all of the e-evidence requested, or fails to suspend its automatic e-mail deletion procedures.[b] Nearly 25 percent of the reported opinions on e-discovery from 2008 involved sanctions for failure to preserve e-evidence.[c] Attorneys who fail to properly advise their clients concerning the duty to preserve e-evidence also often face sanctions and malpractice claims.[d]

Lessons from Intel Corporation

A party that fails to preserve e-evidence may even find itself at such a disadvantage that it will settle a dispute rather than continue litigation. For example, Advanced Micro Devices, Inc. (AMD), sued Intel Corporation, one of the world's largest microprocessor suppliers, for violating antitrust laws. Immediately after the lawsuit was filed, Intel began collecting and preserving the ESI on its servers. Although the company instructed its employees to retain documents and e-mails related to competition with AMD, many employees saved only copies of the e-mails that they had received and not e-mails that they had sent. In addition, Intel did not stop its automatic e-mail deletion system, causing other information to be lost. In the end, although Intel produced data that, on paper, would have been equivalent to "somewhere in the neighborhood of a pile 137 miles high," its failure to preserve e-evidence led it to settle the dispute in 2008.[e]

MANAGERIAL IMPLICATIONS

Clearly, companies can be accused of intentionally failing to preserve electronic data. As a manager, you have to weigh the cost of retaining data, such as e-mails, against the benefits of having those data available if your company is ever sued.

a. See *Columbia Pictures Industries v. Brunnell*, 2007 WL 2080419 (C.D.Cal. 2007).

b. See, for example, *John B. v. Goetz*, 531 F.3d 448 (6th Cir. 2008); and *Wingnut Films, Ltd. v. Katija Motion Pictures*, 2007 WL 2758571 (C.D.Cal. 2007).

c. Sheri Qualters. "25% of Reported E-Discovery Opinions in 2008 Involved Sanction Issues," *National Law Journal*. 12 December 2008: n.p.

d. See, for example, *Qualcomm, Inc. v. Broadcom Corp.*, 539 F.Supp.2d 1214 (S.D.Cal. 2007).

e. See *In re Intel Corp. Microprocessor Antitrust Litigation*, 2008 WL 2310288 (D.Del. 2008). See also *Adams v. Gateway, Inc.*, 2006 WL 2563418 (D. Utah 2006).

oral questions to determine whether a potential jury member is biased or has any connection with a party to the action or with a prospective witness.

During *voir dire*, a party may challenge a certain number of prospective jurors *peremptorily*—that is, ask that an individual not be sworn in as a juror without providing any reason. Alternatively, a party may challenge a prospective juror *for cause*—that is, provide a reason why an individual should not be sworn in as a juror. If the judge grants the challenge, the individual is asked to step down. A prospective juror, however, may not be excluded by the use of discriminatory challenges, such as those based on racial criteria or gender.

See *Concept Summary 2.3* on the facing page for a review of pretrial procedures.

The Trial

Various rules and procedures govern the trial phase of the litigation process. There are rules governing what kind of evidence will or will not be admitted during the trial, as well as specific procedures that the participants in the lawsuit must follow.

OPENING STATEMENTS At the beginning of the trial, both attorneys are allowed to make **opening statements** setting forth the facts that they expect to prove during the trial. The opening statement provides an opportunity for each lawyer to give a brief version of the facts and the supporting evidence that will be used during the trial. Then the plaintiff's case is presented. In our hypothetical case, Kirby's lawyer would introduce evidence (relevant documents, exhibits, and the testimony of witnesses) to support Kirby's position.

RULES OF EVIDENCE Whether evidence will be admitted in court is determined by the **rules of evidence**—a series of rules that have been created by the courts to ensure that any evidence presented during a trial is fair and reliable. The Federal Rules of Evidence govern the admissibility of evidence in federal courts.

Evidence will not be admitted in court unless it is relevant to the matter in question. **Relevant evidence** is evidence that tends to prove or disprove a fact in question or to establish the degree of probability of a fact or action. For example, evidence

CONCEPT SUMMARY 2.3
Pretrial Procedures

Procedure	Description
The Pleadings	1. *The plaintiff's complaint*—The plaintiff's statement of the cause of action and the parties involved, filed with the court by the plaintiff's attorney. After the filing, the defendant is notified of the suit through service of process. 2. *The defendant's response*—The defendant's response to the plaintiff's complaint may take the form of an answer, in which the defendant admits or denies the plaintiff's allegations. The defendant may raise an affirmative defense and/or assert a counterclaim.
Pretrial Motions	1. *Motion to dismiss*—May be made by either party; requests that the judge dismiss the case for reasons that are provided in the motion (such as failure to state a claim for which relief can be granted). 2. *Motion for judgment on the pleadings*—May be made by either party; will be granted only if no facts are in dispute and only questions of law are at issue. 3. *Motion for summary judgment*—May be made by either party; will be granted only if no facts are in dispute and only questions of law are at issue. Unlike the motion for judgment on the pleadings, the motion for summary judgment may be supported by evidence outside the pleadings, such as testimony and other evidence obtained during the discovery phase of litigation.
Discovery	The process of gathering evidence concerning the case; involves (1) *depositions* (sworn testimony by either party or any witness); (2) *interrogatories* (in which parties to the action write answers to questions with the aid of their attorneys); and (3) requests for admissions, documents, examinations, or other information relating to the case. Discovery may also involve electronically recorded information.
Pretrial Conference	A pretrial hearing, at the request of either party or the court, to identify the matters in dispute after discovery has taken place and to explore the possibility of settling the dispute without a trial. If no settlement is possible, the parties plan the course of the trial.
Jury Selection	In a jury trial, the selection of members of the jury from a pool of prospective jurors. During *voir dire*, the attorneys for both sides may challenge prospective jurors either for cause or peremptorily (for no cause).

that the defendant's gun was in the home of another person when the victim was shot would be relevant because it would tend to prove that the defendant did not shoot the victim.

Generally, hearsay is not admissible as evidence. **Hearsay** is testimony someone gives in court about a statement made by someone else who was not under oath at the time of the statement. Literally, it is what someone heard someone else say. For example, if a witness in the Kirby-Carvello case testified in court concerning what he or she heard another observer say about the accident, that testimony would be hearsay, or secondhand knowledge. Admitting hearsay into evidence carries many risks because, even though it may be relevant, there is no way to test its reliability.

EXAMINATION OF WITNESSES Because Kirby is the plaintiff, she has the burden of proving that her allegations are true. Her attorney begins the presentation of Kirby's case by calling the first witness for the plaintiff and examining, or questioning, the witness. (For both attorneys, the types of questions and the manner of asking them are governed by the rules of evidence.) This questioning is called **direct examination.** After Kirby's attorney is finished, the witness is subject to **cross-examination** by Carvello's attorney. Then Kirby's attorney has another opportunity to question the witness in *redirect examination,* and Carvello's attorney may follow the redirect examination with a *recross-examination.* When both attorneys have finished with the first witness, Kirby's attorney calls the succeeding witnesses in the plaintiff's case, each of whom is subject to examination by the attorneys in the manner just described.

Expert Witnesses. Both the plaintiff and the defendant may present testimony from one or more expert witnesses—such as forensic scientists, physicians, and psychologists—as part of their cases. An *expert witness* is a person who, by virtue of education, training, skill, or experience, has scientific, technical, or other specialized knowledge in a particular area beyond that of an average person. In Kirby's case, her attorney might hire an accident reconstruction specialist to establish Carvello's negligence or a physician to confirm the extent of Kirby's injuries.

Normally, witnesses can testify only about the facts of a case—that is, what they personally observed. When witnesses are qualified as experts in a particular field, however, they can offer their opinions and conclusions about the evidence in that field. Expert testimony is an important component of litigation today.

Because numerous experts are available for hire and expert testimony is powerful and effective with juries, there is tremendous potential for abuse. Therefore, in federal courts and most state courts, judges act as gatekeepers to ensure that the experts are qualified and that their opinions are based on scientific knowledge. If a party believes that the opponent's witness is not qualified as an expert in the relevant field, that party can make a motion asking the judge to exclude this evidence and prevent the expert witness from testifying in front of the jury.

Potential Motion and Judgment. At the conclusion of the plaintiff's case, and before presenting any witnesses, the defendant's attorney has the opportunity to ask the judge to direct a verdict for the defendant on the ground that the plaintiff has presented no evidence to support her or his claim. This is called a **motion for a judgment as a matter of law** (or a **motion for a directed verdict** in state courts). In considering the motion, the judge looks at the evidence in the light most favorable to the plaintiff and grants the motion only if there is insufficient evidence to raise an issue of fact. (Motions for directed verdicts at this stage of a trial are seldom granted.)

Defendant's Evidence. The defendant's attorney then presents the evidence and witnesses for the defendant's case. Witnesses are called and examined by the defendant's attorney. The plaintiff's attorney has the right to cross-examine them, and there may be a redirect examination and possibly a recross-examination. At the end of the defendant's case, either attorney can move for a directed verdict, and the test again is whether the jury can, through any reasonable interpretation of the evidence, find for the party against whom the motion has been made. After the defendant's attorney has finished introducing evidence, the plaintiff's attorney can present a **rebuttal** by offering additional evidence that refutes the defendant's case. The defendant's attorney can, in turn, refute that evidence in a **rejoinder.**

CLOSING ARGUMENTS, JURY INSTRUCTIONS, AND VERDICT After both sides have rested their cases, each attorney presents a closing argument. In the **closing argument,** each attorney summarizes the facts and evidence presented during the trial and indicates why the facts and evidence support his or her client's claim. In addition to generally urging a verdict in favor of the client, the closing argument typically reveals the shortcomings of the points made by the opposing party during the trial.

Attorneys generally present closing arguments whether or not the trial was heard by a jury. If it was a jury trial, the attorneys will have met with the judge prior to closing arguments to determine how the jury will be instructed on the law. The attorneys can refer to these instructions in their closing arguments. After closing arguments are completed, the judge instructs the jury in the law that applies to the case (these instructions are often called *charges*), and the jury retires to the jury room to deliberate a verdict. In most civil cases, the standard of proof is a *preponderance of the evidence*.[26] In other words, the plaintiff (Kirby in our hypothetical case) need only show that her factual claim is more likely to be true than the defendant's. (As you will read in Chapter 7, in a criminal trial the prosecution has a higher standard of proof to meet—it must prove its case *beyond a reasonable doubt*.)

Once the jury has reached a decision, it issues a **verdict** in favor of one party; the verdict specifies the jury's factual findings. In some cases, the jury also decides on the amount of the *award* (the compensation to be paid to the prevailing party). After the announcement of the verdict, which marks the end of the trial itself, the jurors are dismissed.

See *Concept Summary 2.4* below for a review of trial procedures.

Posttrial Motions

After the jury has rendered its verdict, either party may make a posttrial motion. The prevailing party usually requests that the court enter a judgment in accordance with the verdict. The nonprevailing party frequently files either a *motion for a new trial* or a *motion for judgment n.o.v.*

MOTION FOR A NEW TRIAL At the end of the trial, the losing party may make a motion to set aside the adverse verdict and any judgment and to hold a new trial. After looking at all the evidence, the judge will grant the **motion for a new trial** only if she or he believes that the jury was in error and that it is not appropriate to grant judgment for the other side. Usually, this occurs when the jury verdict is obviously the result of a misapplication of the law or a

---

26. Note that some civil claims must be proved by "clear and convincing evidence," meaning that the evidence must show that the truth of the party's claim is *highly* probable. This standard is often applied in situations that present a particular danger of deception, such as allegations of fraud.

CONCEPT SUMMARY 2.4
Trial Procedures

Procedure	Description
Opening Statements	Each party's attorney is allowed to present an opening statement indicating what the attorney will attempt to prove during the course of the trial.
Examination of Witnesses	1. Plaintiff's introduction and direct examination of witnesses, cross-examination by defendant's attorney, possible redirect examination by plaintiff's attorney, and possible recross-examination by defendant's attorney. 2. Both the plaintiff and the defendant may present testimony from one or more expert witnesses. 3. At the close of the plaintiff's case, the defendant may make a motion for a directed verdict (or judgment as a matter of law), which, if granted by the court, will end the trial before the defendant presents witnesses. 4. Defendant's introduction and direct examination of witnesses, cross-examination by plaintiff's attorney, possible redirect examination by defendant's attorney, and possible recross-examination by plaintiff's attorney. 5. Possible rebuttal of defendant's argument by plaintiff's attorney, who presents more evidence. 6. Possible rejoinder by defendant's attorney to meet that evidence.
Closing Arguments, Jury Instructions, and Verdict	Each party's attorney argues in favor of a verdict for his or her client. The judge instructs (or charges) the jury as to how the law applies to the issue, and the jury retires to deliberate. When the jury renders its verdict, this brings the trial to an end.

misunderstanding of the evidence presented at trial. A new trial can also be granted on the grounds of newly discovered evidence, misconduct by the participants during the trial (such as when a juror has made prejudicial and inflammatory remarks), or an error by the judge.

MOTION FOR JUDGMENT *N.O.V.*   If Kirby wins, and if Carvello's attorney has previously moved for a directed verdict, then Carvello's attorney can now make a **motion for judgment** *n.o.v.*—from the Latin *non obstante veredicto,* meaning "notwithstanding the verdict." (Federal courts use the term *judgment as a matter of law* instead of *judgment n.o.v.)* Such a motion will be granted only if the jury's verdict was unreasonable and erroneous. If the judge grants the motion, then the jury's verdict will be set aside, and a judgment will be entered in favor of the opposing party (Carvello). If the motion is denied, Carvello may then appeal the case. (Kirby may also appeal the case, even though she won at trial. She might appeal, for example, if she received a smaller monetary award than she had sought.)

The Appeal

Either party may appeal not only the jury's verdict but also the judge's ruling on any pretrial or post-trial motion. Many of the appellate court cases that appear in this text involve appeals of motions for summary judgment or other motions that were denied by trial court judges. Note that a party must have legitimate grounds to file an appeal (some legal error) and that few trial court decisions are reversed on appeal. Moreover, the expenses associated with an appeal can be considerable.

FILING THE APPEAL   If Carvello decides to appeal the verdict in Kirby's favor, then his attorney must file a *notice of appeal* with the clerk of the trial court within a prescribed period of time. Carvello then becomes the *appellant* or *petitioner.* The clerk of the trial court sends to the reviewing court (usually an intermediate court of appeals) the *record on appeal.* The record contains all the pleadings, motions, and other documents filed with the court and a complete written transcript of the proceedings, including testimony, arguments, jury instructions, and judicial rulings.

Carvello's attorney will file an appellate *brief* with the reviewing court. The **brief** is a formal legal document outlining the facts and issues of the case, the judge's rulings or jury's findings that should be reversed or modified, the applicable law, and arguments on Carvello's behalf (citing applicable statutes and relevant cases as precedents). The attorney for

the *appellee* (Kirby, in our hypothetical case) usually files an answering brief. Carvello's attorney can file a reply, although it is not required. The reviewing court then considers the case.

APPELLATE REVIEW   A court of appeals does not hear any evidence. Rather, it reviews the record for errors of law. Its decision concerning a case is based on the record on appeal and the briefs and arguments. The attorneys present oral arguments, after which the case is taken under advisement. The court then issues a written opinion. In general, appellate courts do not reverse findings of fact unless the findings are unsupported or contradicted by the evidence.

An appellate court has the following options after reviewing a case:

1. The court can *affirm* the trial court's decision. (Most decisions are affirmed.)
2. The court can reverse the trial court's judgment if it concludes that the trial court erred or that the jury did not receive proper instructions.
3. The appellate court can *remand* (send back) the case to the trial court for further proceedings consistent with its opinion on the matter.
4. The court might also affirm or reverse a decision *in part.* For example, the court might affirm the jury's finding that Carvello was negligent but remand the case for further proceedings on another issue (such as the extent of Kirby's damages).
5. An appellate court can also *modify* a lower court's decision. If the appellate court decides that the jury awarded an excessive amount in damages, for example, the court might reduce the award to a more appropriate, or fairer, amount.

HIGHER APPELLATE COURTS   If the reviewing court is an intermediate appellate court, the losing party may decide to appeal the decision to the state's highest court, usually called its supreme court. Although the losing party has a right to ask (petition) a higher court to review the case, the party does not have a right to have the case heard by the higher appellate court. Appellate courts normally have discretionary power and can accept or reject an appeal. Like the United States Supreme Court, state supreme courts generally deny most petitions for appeal.

If the petition is granted, new briefs must be filed before the state supreme court, and the attorneys may be allowed or requested to present oral arguments. Like the intermediate appellate courts, the supreme court can reverse or affirm the lower appellate court's decision or remand the case. At this point, the case typically has reached its end (unless a federal question is at issue and one of the parties has legitimate grounds to seek review by a federal appellate court).

Enforcing the Judgment

The uncertainties of the litigation process are compounded by the lack of guarantees that any judgment will be enforceable. Even if the jury awards Kirby the full amount of damages requested ($100,000), Carvello's auto insurance coverage might have lapsed, in which event the company would not pay any of the damages. Alternatively, Carvello's insurance policy might be limited to $50,000, meaning that Carvello personally would have to pay the remaining $50,000.

If the defendant does not have the funds available to pay the judgment, the plaintiff can go back to the court and request that the court issue a *writ of execution*. A **writ of execution** is an order directing the sheriff to seize and sell the defendant's nonexempt assets, or property (certain assets are exempted by law from creditors' actions). The proceeds of the sale are then used to pay the damages owed, and any excess proceeds are returned to the defendant. Alternatively, the nonexempt property itself could be transferred to the plaintiff in lieu of an outright payment.

The problem of collecting a judgment is less difficult when a party is seeking to satisfy a judgment against a defendant with substantial assets that can be easily located, such as a major corporation. Usually, one of the factors considered by the plaintiff and his or her attorney before a lawsuit is initiated is whether the defendant has sufficient assets to cover the amount of damages sought. In addition, during the discovery process, attorneys routinely seek information about the location of the defendant's assets that might be used to satisfy a judgment.

Exhibit 2–5 below illustrates the specific stages of a typical lawsuit.

EXHIBIT 2–5 • Stages in a Typical Lawsuit

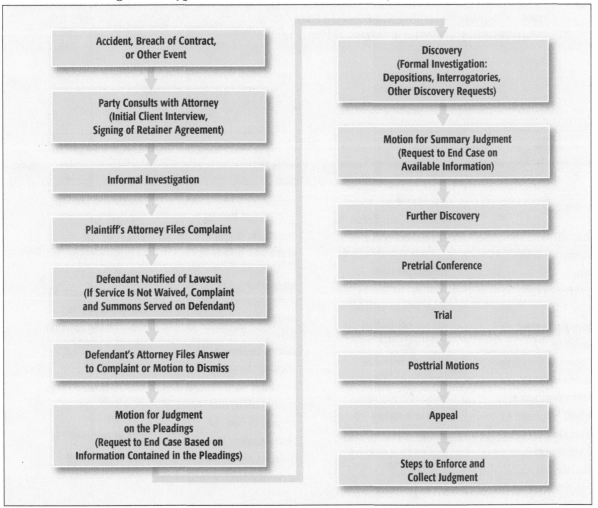

- Accident, Breach of Contract, or Other Event
- Party Consults with Attorney (Initial Client Interview, Signing of Retainer Agreement)
- Informal Investigation
- Plaintiff's Attorney Files Complaint
- Defendant Notified of Lawsuit (If Service Is Not Waived, Complaint and Summons Served on Defendant)
- Defendant's Attorney Files Answer to Complaint or Motion to Dismiss
- Motion for Judgment on the Pleadings (Request to End Case Based on Information Contained in the Pleadings)
- Discovery (Formal Investigation: Depositions, Interrogatories, Other Discovery Requests)
- Motion for Summary Judgment (Request to End Case on Available Information)
- Further Discovery
- Pretrial Conference
- Trial
- Posttrial Motions
- Appeal
- Steps to Enforce and Collect Judgment

REVIEWING
The Court System

Ronald Metzgar placed his fifteen-month-old son, Matthew, awake and healthy, in his playpen. Ronald left the room for five minutes and on his return found Matthew lifeless. A toy block had lodged in the boy's throat, causing him to choke to death. Ronald called 911, but efforts to revive Matthew were to no avail. There was no warning of a choking hazard on the box containing the block. Matthew's parents hired an attorney and sued Playskool, Inc., the manufacturer of the block, alleging that the manufacturer had been negligent in failing to warn of the block's hazard. Playskool filed a motion for summary judgment, arguing that the danger of a young child choking on a small block was obvious. Using the information presented in the chapter, answer the following questions.

1. Suppose that the attorney the Metzgars hired agreed to represent them on a contingency-fee basis. What does that mean?
2. How would the Metzgars' attorney likely have served process (the summons and complaint) on Playskool, Inc.?
3. Should Playskool's request for summary judgment be granted? Why or why not?
4. Suppose that the judge denied Playskool's motion and the case proceeded to trial. After hearing all the evidence, the jury found in favor of the defendant. What options do the plaintiffs have at this point if they are not satisfied with the verdict?

DEBATE THIS: *Some consumer advocates argue that attorneys' high contingency fees—sometimes reaching 40 percent—unfairly deprive winning plaintiffs of too much of their awards. Should the government put a cap on contingency fees at, say, 20 percent of the award? Why or why not?*

TERMS AND CONCEPTS

affidavit 44
affirmative defense 43
answer 42
bankruptcy court 31
brief 52
closing argument 50
complaint 42
concurrent jurisdiction 33
counterclaim 43
cross-examination 50
default judgment 42
deposition 46
direct examination 50
discovery 44
diversity of citizenship 33

e-evidence 47
exclusive jurisdiction 33
Federal Rules of Civil Procedure (FRCP) 41
federal question 33
hearsay 50
in personam jurisdiction 30
in rem jurisdiction 30
interrogatories 46
judicial review 28
jurisdiction 30
justiciable controversy 34
long arm statute 30
motion 43
motion for a directed verdict 50

motion for a judgment as a matter of law 50
motion for a new trial 51
motion for judgment *n.o.v.* 52
motion for judgment on the pleadings 44
motion for summary judgment 44
motion to dismiss 44
opening statement 49
pleadings 42
pretrial conference 47
pretrial motion 44
probate court 31
question of fact 38

question of law 38
rebuttal 50
rejoinder 50
relevant evidence 49
rule of four 39
rules of evidence 49
service of process 42
small claims court 37
standing to sue 34
summons 42
venue 34
verdict 51
voir dire 47
writ of *certiorari* 39
writ of execution 53

QUESTIONS AND CASE PROBLEMS

2–1. Discovery Rules In the past, the rules of discovery were very restrictive, and trials often turned on elements of surprise. For example, a plaintiff would not necessarily know until the trial what the defendant's defense was going to be. In the last several decades, however, new rules of discovery have substantially changed this situation. Now each attorney can access practically all of the evidence that the other side intends to present at trial, with the exception of certain information—namely, the opposing attorney's work product. Work product is not a precise concept. Basically, it includes all of the attorney's thoughts on the case. Can you see any reason why such information should not be made available to the opposing attorney? Discuss fully.

2–2. QUESTION WITH SAMPLE ANSWER: Motions.

The defendant in a lawsuit is appealing the trial court's decision in favor of the plaintiff. On appeal, the defendant claims that the evidence presented at trial to support the plaintiff's claim was so scanty that no reasonable jury could have found for the plaintiff. Therefore, argues the defendant, the appellate court should reverse the trial court's decision. Will an appellate court ever reverse a trial court's findings with respect to questions of fact? Discuss fully.

• **For a sample answer to Question 2–2, go to Appendix F at the end of this text.**

2–3. Jurisdiction Marya Callais, a citizen of Florida, was walking along a busy street in Tallahassee, Florida, when a large crate flew off a passing truck and hit her, causing numerous injuries. She experienced a great deal of pain and suffering, incurred significant medical expenses, and could not work for six months. She wants to sue the trucking firm for $300,000 in damages. The firm's headquarters are in Georgia, although the company does business in Florida. In what court might Callais bring suit—a Florida state court, a Georgia state court, or a federal court? What factors might influence her decision?

2–4. CASE PROBLEM WITH SAMPLE ANSWER: Appellate Review.

BSH Home Appliances Corp. makes appliances under the Bosch, Siemens, Thermador, and Gaggenau brands. To make and market the "Pro 27 Stainless Steel Range," a restaurant-quality range for home use, BSH gave specifications for its burner to Detroit Radiant Products Co. and requested a price for 30,000 units. Detroit quoted $28.25 per unit, offering to absorb all tooling and research and development costs. In 2001 and 2003, BSH sent Detroit two purchase orders, for 15,000 and 16,000 units, respectively. In 2004, after Detroit had shipped 12,886 units, BSH stopped scheduling deliveries. Detroit filed a suit against BSH, alleging breach of contract. BSH argued, in part, that the second purchase order had not added to the first but had replaced it. After a trial, a federal district court issued its "Findings of Fact and Conclusions of Law." The court found that the two purchase orders "required BSH to purchase 31,000 units of the burner at $28.25 per unit." The court ruled that Detroit was entitled to $418,261 for 18,114 unsold burners. BSH appealed to the U.S. Court of Appeals for the Sixth Circuit. Can an appellate court set aside a trial court's findings of fact? Can an appellate court come to its own conclusions of law? What should the court rule in this case? Explain. *[Detroit Radiant Products Co. v. BSH Home Appliances Corp., 473 F.3d 623 (6th Cir. 2007)]*

• **To view a sample answer for Problem 2–4, go to this book's Web site at www.cengage.com/blaw/cross, select "Chapter 2," and click on "Case Problem with Sample Answer."**

2–5. Discovery In October 2004, Rita Peatie filed a suit in a Connecticut state court against Wal-Mart Stores, Inc., to recover for injuries to her head, neck, and shoulder. Peatie claimed that she had been struck two years earlier by a metal cylinder falling from a store ceiling. The parties agreed to nonbinding arbitration. Ten days before the hearing in January 2006, the plaintiff asked for, and was granted, four more months to conduct discovery. On the morning of the rescheduled hearing, she asked for more time, but the court denied this request. The hearing was held, and the arbitrator ruled in Wal-Mart's favor. Peatie filed a motion for a new trial, which was granted. Five months later, she sought through discovery to acquire any photos, records, and reports held by Wal-Mart regarding her alleged injury. The court issued a "protective order" against the request, stating that the time for discovery had long been over. On the day of the trial—four years after the alleged injury—the plaintiff asked the court to lift the order. Should the court do so? Why or why not? *[Peatie v. Wal-Mart Stores, Inc., 112 Conn.App. 8, 961 A.2d 1016 (2009)]*

2–6. Jury Misconduct Michelle Fleshner worked for Pepose Vision Institute (PVI), a surgical practice. She was fired after she provided information to the Department of Labor about PVI's overtime pay policy. She sued for wrongful termination, and the jury awarded her $125,000. After the trial, a juror told PVI's attorneys that another juror had made anti-Semitic statements during jury deliberations. The comments concerned a witness who testified on PVI's behalf. According to the juror, the other juror said, about the witness: "She is a Jewish witch." "She is a penny-pinching Jew." "She was such a cheap Jew that she did not want to pay Plaintiff unemployment compensation." Another juror confirmed the remarks. PVI filed a motion for a new trial on the basis of juror misconduct. The trial judge held that the comments did not prevent a fair trial from occurring. PVI appealed. Do you think such comments are sufficient to require a new trial, or must a juror's bias be discovered during *voir dire* for it to matter? Explain. *[Fleshner v. Pepose Vision Institute, 304 S.W.3d 81 (Mo. 2010)]*

2–7. A QUESTION OF ETHICS: Service of Process.

Narnia Investments, Ltd., filed a suit in a Texas state court against several defendants, including Harvestons Securities, Inc., a securities dealer. (Securities *are documents evidencing the ownership of a corporation, in the form of stock, or debts owed by it, in the form of bonds.) Harvestons is registered with the state of Texas, and thus a party may serve a summons and a copy of a complaint on Harvestons by serving the Texas Securities Commissioner. In this case, the return of service indicated that process was served on the commissioner "by delivering to JoAnn Kocerek defendant, in person, a true copy of this [summons] together with the accompanying copy(ies) of the [complaint]." Harvestons did not file an answer, and Narnia obtained a default judgment against the defendant for $365,000, plus attorneys' fees and interest. Five months after this judgment, Harvestons filed a motion for a new trial, which the court denied. Harvestons appealed to a state intermediate appellate court, claiming that it had not been served in strict compliance with the rules governing service of process.* [Harvestons Securities, Inc. v. Narnia Investments, Ltd., *218 S.W.3d 126 (Tex.App.—Houston 2007)]*

(a) Harvestons asserted that Narnia's service was invalid, in part, because "the return of service states that process was delivered to 'JoAnn Kocerek'" and did not show that she "had the authority to accept process on behalf of Harvestons or the Texas Securities Commissioner." Should such a detail, if it is required, be strictly construed and applied? Should it apply in this case? Explain.

(b) Whose responsibility is it to see that service of process is accomplished properly? Was it accomplished properly in this case? Why or why not?

2–8. VIDEO QUESTION: Jurisdiction in Cyberspace.

Go to this text's Web site at **www.cengage.com/ blaw/cross** and select "Chapter 2." Click on "Video Questions" and view the video titled *Jurisdiction in Cyberspace.* Then answer the following questions.

(a) What standard would a court apply to determine whether it has jurisdiction over the out-of-state computer firm in the video?

(b) What factors is a court likely to consider in assessing whether sufficient contacts existed when the only connection to the jurisdiction is through a Web site?

(c) How do you think the court would resolve the issue in this case?

2–9. SPECIAL CASE ANALYSIS: Jurisdiction.

Go to Extended Case 2.1, *Southern Prestige Industries, Inc. v. Independence Plating Corp.,* 690 S.E.2d 768 (2010) on pages 31 and 32. Read the excerpt and answer the following questions.

(a) **Issue:** The issue in this case concerned jurisdictional requirements. Why did this issue arise, and how will its outcome affect the parties?

(b) **Rule of Law:** What rule of law determined whether personal jurisdiction over the defendant existed in this case?

(c) **Applying the Rule of Law:** What factors did the court evaluate in determining how the rule of law applied to this case?

(d) **Conclusion:** In which party's favor did the court rule? Why?

LEGAL RESEARCH EXERCISES ON THE WEB

Go to this text's Web site at **www.cengage.com/blaw/cross**, select "Chapter 2," and click on "Practical Internet Exercises." There you will find the following Internet research exercises that you can perform to learn more about the topics covered in this chapter.

Practical Internet Exercise 2–1: **Legal Perspective**
Civil Procedure

Practical Internet Exercise 2–2: **Historical Perspective**
The Judiciary's Role in American Government

CHAPTER 3

Alternative and Online Dispute Resolution

Trials are costly and time consuming. It has been said that this is the result of "too many lawyers, too many lawsuits, and too many laws." In fact, since 1960, the number of lawyers has tripled, the number of lawsuits has tripled, and the number of laws has multiplied, while the numbers of judges and courts have not kept pace.

Although it is true that the number of lawsuits filed has grown rapidly, only 5 to 10 percent of lawsuits filed actually go to trial. Most cases are settled or dismissed long before the parties enter a courtroom. Moreover, the number of cases that are litigated does not appear to be growing any faster than the population. When compared with the large number of transactions that occur in our highly complex economy, the rate of litigation appears low to some.

Nevertheless, in any individual case, it may be months before a hearing can be scheduled. Depending on the complexity of the case, the extent of discovery proceedings required, the delaying tactics of the opposing party, and the backlog of cases pending in the particular court, several years may pass before a case is actually tried. Even in the best of situations, the civil procedures discussed in Chapter 2 all require much time and expense, particularly when electronic discovery is involved.

As the cost and complexity of litigation have grown, businesspersons and other individuals have asked, "Is there a more appropriate way to resolve disputes?"

SECTION 1
THE SEARCH FOR ALTERNATIVES TO LITIGATION

A number of solutions have been proposed, and some have been implemented, to reduce the congestion in our court system and to reduce the litigation costs facing all members of society. The enforcement of arbitration clauses, the use of court-referred arbitration and mediation, and the emergence of an increasing number of private forums for dispute resolution have all helped to reduce the caseload of the courts.

Another solution to the problem involves putting caps on damage awards, particularly for pain and suffering. Without the probability of obtaining multimillion-dollar judgments for pain and suffering, some potential litigants will be deterred from undertaking lawsuits to obtain damages. Another avenue of attack is to penalize those who bring frivolous lawsuits. Rule 11 of the Federal Rules of Civil Procedure allows for disciplinary sanctions against lawyers and litigants who bring frivolous lawsuits in federal courts.

Many courts require *mediation* or *arbitration* before a case goes to trial. There are proposals to further reduce delay and expenses in federal civil cases, and proposals are being considered by the states as well. Some of the proposals can be viewed as case-management plans. One proposal, for example, would require each federal district court to implement procedures for placing cases on different tracks, with simple cases being handled more quickly than complex ones.

Politics and Law

Because reforms of any system affect individuals and groups differently, they seldom are accomplished easily and quickly. Reform of the court system is a prime example. At the federal level, members of Congress long have been concerned with bringing court costs and delay under control. These concerns led to legislation that required the federal courts to develop a plan to cut costs and reduce delay within the federal judicial system.

New Methods and Arrangements

The search for alternative means to resolve disputes has produced several distinct methods and arrangements. These range from neighbors sitting down over a cup of coffee to work out their differences to huge multinational corporations agreeing to resolve a dispute through a formal hearing before a panel of experts. All of these alternatives to traditional litigation make up what is broadly termed **alternative dispute resolution (ADR).**

ADR describes any procedure or device for resolving disputes outside the traditional judicial process. ADR normally is a less expensive and less time-consuming process than formal litigation. In some instances, it also has the advantage of being more private. Except in disputes involving court-annexed arbitration (as will be discussed later in this chapter), no public record of ADR proceedings is created; only the parties directly involved are privy to the information presented during the process. This is a particularly important consideration in many business disputes, because such cases may involve sensitive commercial information. Today, ADR also includes online methods of resolving disputes.

The great advantage of ADR is its flexibility. Normally, the parties themselves can control how the dispute will be settled, what procedures will be used, whether a neutral third party will be present or make a decision, and whether that decision will be legally binding or nonbinding. ADR also offers more privacy than court proceedings and allows disputes to be resolved relatively quickly.

Today, more than 90 percent of civil lawsuits are settled before trial using some form of ADR. Indeed, most states either require or encourage parties to undertake ADR prior to trial. Many federal courts have instituted ADR programs as well. In the following pages, we examine the basic forms of ADR. Keep in mind, though, that new methods of ADR—and new combinations of existing methods—are constantly being devised and employed.

SECTION 2
NEGOTIATION AND MEDIATION

Alternative dispute resolution methods differ in the degree of formality involved and the extent to which third parties participate in the process. Generally,

negotiation is the least formal method and involves no third parties. Mediation may be similarly informal but does involve the participation of a third party.

Negotiation

The simplest form of ADR is **negotiation.** In the process of negotiation, the parties come together informally, with or without attorneys to represent them. Within this informal setting, the parties air their differences and try to reach a settlement or resolution without the involvement of independent third parties. Because no third parties are involved and because of the informal setting, negotiation is the simplest form of ADR. Even if a lawsuit has been initiated, the parties may continue to negotiate their differences at any time during the litigation process and attempt to settle their dispute.

PREPARATION FOR NEGOTIATION In spite of the informality of negotiation, each party must carefully prepare his or her side of the case. The elements of the dispute should be considered, documents and other evidence should be collected, and witnesses should be prepared to testify. Negotiating from a well-prepared position improves the odds of obtaining a favorable result. Even if a dispute is not resolved through negotiation, preparation for negotiation will reduce the effort required to prepare for the next step in the dispute-resolution process.

ASSISTED NEGOTIATION To facilitate negotiation, various forms of what might be called "assisted negotiation" have emerged in recent years. Assisted negotation, as the term implies, involves the assistance of a third party. Forms of ADR associated with the negotation process include *mini-trials, early neutral case evaluation,* and *facilitation.* Another form of assisted negotiation—the summary jury trial—will be discussed later in this chapter.

A **mini-trial** is a private proceeding in which each party's attorney briefly argues the party's case before the other party. Typically, a neutral third party, who acts as an adviser and an expert in the area being disputed, is also present. If the parties fail to reach an agreement, the adviser renders an opinion as to how a court would likely decide the issue. The proceeding assists the parties in determining whether they should negotiate a settlement of the dispute or take it to court.

In **early neutral case evaluation,** the parties select a neutral third party (generally an expert in the subject matter of the dispute) to evaluate their respective positions. The parties explain their positions to the case evaluator however they wish. The evaluator then assesses the strengths and weaknesses of the parties' positions, and this evaluation forms the basis for negotiating a settlement.

Disputes may also be resolved in a friendly, non-adversarial manner through **facilitation,** in which a third party assists disputing parties in reconciling their differences. The facilitator helps to schedule negotiating sessions and carries offers back and forth between the parties when they refuse to face each other in direct negotiations. Technically, facilitators are not to recommend solutions. (In practice, however, they often do.) In contrast, a mediator is expected to propose solutions.

Mediation

One of the oldest forms of ADR is mediation. In **mediation,** a neutral third party acts as a **mediator** and works with both sides in the dispute to facilitate a resolution. The mediator normally talks with the parties separately as well as jointly, emphasizes points of agreement, and helps the parties to evaluate their options. Although the mediator may propose a solution (called a mediator's proposal), he or she does not make a decision resolving the matter. The mediator, who need not be a lawyer, usually charges a fee for his or her services (which can be split between the parties). States that require parties to undergo ADR before trial often offer mediation as one of the ADR options or (as in Florida) the only option.

Mediation is essentially a form of assisted negotiation. We treat it separately here because traditionally it has been viewed as an alternative to negotiation. Additionally, a mediator usually plays a more active role than the neutral third parties in negotiation-associated forms of ADR.

Today, characteristics of mediation are being combined with those of arbitration (to be discussed next). In *binding mediation,* for example, the parties agree that if they cannot resolve the dispute, the mediator can make a legally binding decision on the issue. In *mediation-arbitration,* or "med-arb," the parties first attempt to settle their dispute through mediation. If no settlement is reached, the dispute will be arbitrated.

ADVANTAGES OF MEDIATION Few procedural rules are involved in the mediation process—far fewer than in a courtroom setting. The proceedings can be tailored to fit the needs of the parties—the mediator can be told to maintain a diplomatic role or be asked to express an opinion about the dispute, lawyers can be excluded from the proceedings, and the exchange of a few documents can replace the more expensive and time-consuming process of pretrial discovery. Disputes are often settled far more quickly in mediation than in formal litigation.

One of the bigger advantages of mediation is that it is not as adversarial in nature as litigation. In mediation, the mediator takes an active role and attempts to bring the parties together so that they can come to a mutually satisfactory resolution. The mediation process tends to reduce the antagonism between the disputants, allowing them to resume their former relationship while minimizing hostility. For this reason, mediation is often the preferred form of ADR for disputes involving business partners, employers and employees, or other parties involved in long-term relationships.

Another important benefit of mediation is that the mediator is selected by the parties. In litigation, the parties have no control over the selection of a judge. In mediation, the parties may select a mediator on the basis of expertise in a particular field as well as for fairness and impartiality. To the degree that the mediator has these attributes, he or she will more effectively aid the parties in reaching an agreement over their dispute.

DISADVANTAGES OF MEDIATION Mediation is not without disadvantages. A mediator is likely to charge a fee. (This can be split between the parties, though, and thus may represent less expense than would both sides' hiring lawyers.)

Informality and the absence of a third party referee can also be disadvantageous. (Remember that a mediator can only help the parties reach a decision, not make a decision for them.) Without a deadline hanging over the parties' heads, and without the threat of sanctions if they fail to negotiate in good faith, they may be less willing to make concessions or otherwise strive honestly and diligently to reach a settlement. This can slow the process or even cause it to fail.

SECTION 3
ARBITRATION

A more formal method of ADR is **arbitration,** in which an **arbitrator** (a neutral third party or a panel of experts) hears a dispute and imposes a resolution on the parties. Arbitration differs from other forms of ADR in that the third party hearing the dispute makes a decision for the parties. Exhibit 3–1 on the following page outlines the basic differences among

EXHIBIT 3–1 • **Basic Differences in the Traditional Forms of ADR**

TYPE OF ADR	DESCRIPTION	NEUTRAL THIRD PARTY PRESENT	WHO DECIDES THE RESOLUTION
Negotiation	Parties meet informally with or without their attorneys and attempt to agree on a resolution. This is the simplest and least expensive method of ADR.	No	The parties themselves reach a resolution.
Mediation	A neutral third party meets with the parties and emphasizes points of agreement to bring them toward resolution of their dispute. 1. This method of ADR reduces hostility between parties. 2. Mediation is preferred for resolving disputes between business partners, employers and employees, or others involved in long-term relationships.	Yes	The parties, but the mediator may suggest or propose a resolution.
Arbitration	The parties present their arguments and evidence before an arbitrator at a hearing, and the arbitrator renders a decision resolving the parties' dispute. 1. This ADR method is the most formal and resembles a court proceeding because some rules of evidence apply. 2. The parties are free to frame the issues and set the powers of the arbitrator. 3. If the parties agree that the arbitration is binding, then the parties' right to appeal the decision is limited.	Yes	The arbitrator imposes a resolution on the parties that may be either binding or nonbinding.

the three traditional forms of ADR. The key difference between arbitration and the forms of ADR just discussed is that in arbitration, the third party's decision may be legally binding on the parties. Usually the parties in arbitration agree that the third party's decision will be *legally binding,* although the parties can also agree to *nonbinding* arbitration.

When a dispute arises, the parties can agree to settle their differences informally through arbitration rather than formally through the court system. Alternatively, the parties may agree ahead of time that, if a dispute should arise, they will submit to arbitration rather than bring a lawsuit. If the parties agree that the arbitrator's decision will be legally binding, they are obligated to abide by the arbitrator's decision regardless of whether or not they agree with it. (See this chapter's *Insight into Ethics* feature on the facing page for a discussion of some potential ethical implications of the use of arbitration.)

The federal government and many state governments favor arbitration over litigation. The federal policy favoring arbitration is embodied in the Federal Arbitration Act (FAA) of 1925.[1] The FAA requires that courts give deference to all voluntary

arbitration agreements in cases governed by federal law. Virtually any dispute can be the subject of arbitration. A voluntary agreement to arbitrate a dispute normally will be enforced by the courts if the agreement does not compel an illegal act or contravene public policy.

The Federal Arbitration Act

The Federal Arbitration Act does not establish a set arbitration procedure. The parties themselves must agree on the manner of resolving their dispute. The FAA provides the means for enforcing the arbitration procedure that the parties have established for themselves.

Section 4 allows a party to petition a federal district court for an order compelling arbitration under an agreement to arbitrate a dispute. If the judge is "satisfied that the making of the agreement for arbitration or the failure to comply therewith is not in issue, the court shall make an order directing the parties to proceed with arbitration in accordance with the terms of the agreement."

Under Section 9 of the FAA, the parties to the arbitration may agree to have the arbitrator's decision confirmed in a federal district court. Through

---

1. 9 U.S.C. Sections 1–15.

INSIGHT INTO ETHICS
Implications of an Increasingly Private Justice System

Downtown Houston boasts a relatively new courthouse with thirty-nine courtrooms, but often, many of those courtrooms stand empty. Has litigation in Texas slowed down? Indeed, it has not—the courtrooms are empty because fewer civil lawsuits are going to trial. A similar situation is occurring in the federal courts. In 1984, more than 12,000 civil trials were heard in our federal courts. Today, only about 3,500 federal civil trials take place annually. Two developments in particular are contributing to the disappearance of civil trials—arbitration and private judges.

Corporations Use Arbitration Instead of Courts

Since the 1980s, corporations have been avoiding the public court system and taking cases to arbitration instead. Every day, millions of Americans sign arbitration agreements, often unknowingly committing themselves to allow private arbitrators to solve their disputes with employers and the corporations with which they do business.

This trend raises some troublesome ethical issues, however. For instance, arbitration agreements may force consumers to travel long distances to participate in these private forums. Perhaps more disturbing is that the supposedly neutral arbitrators may actually be captive to the industries they serve. Arbitrators are paid handsomely and typically would like to serve again. Thus, they may be reluctant to rule against a company that is involved in a dispute. After all, the company may well need arbitrators to resolve a subsequent dispute, whereas the other party—a consumer or employee—is unlikely to need the arbitrators again.

Private Judges Reduce Court Cases, Too

Another reason for the decline in the number of civil trials in our public courts is the growing use of private judges. A private judge, usually a retired judge, has the power to conduct trials and grant legal resolutions of disputes. Private judges increasingly are being used to resolve commercial disputes, as well as divorces and custody battles, for two reasons: (1) a case can be heard by a private judge much sooner than it would be heard in a public court, and (2) proceedings before a private judge can be kept secret.

The Consequences of Private Judges

In Ohio, a state statute allows the parties to any civil action to have their dispute tried by a retired judge of their choosing who will make a decision in the matter.[a] Recently, though, private judging came under criticism in that state because private judges were conducting jury trials in county courtrooms at taxpayers' expense. One public judge refused to give up jurisdiction over a case on the ground that private judges are not authorized to conduct jury trials. Private judging raises significant public-policy issues that legislatures might wish to resolve.

Another issue is that private judges charge relatively large fees. This means that litigants who are able to pay the extra cost can have their case heard long before they would be able to obtain a trial date in a regular court. Is it fair for those who cannot afford private judges to wait longer for justice? Similarly, is it ethical to allow parties to pay extra for secret proceedings before a private judge and thereby avoid the public scrutiny of a regular trial? Some suggest that the use of private judges is leading to two different systems of justice.

A Threat to the Common Law System?

As discussed in Chapter 1, courts are obligated to consider precedents—the decisions rendered in previous cases with similar facts and issues—when deciding the outcome of a dispute. If fewer disputes go to trial because they are arbitrated or heard by a private judge, then they will never become part of the body of cases and appeals that form the case law on that subject. With fewer precedents on which to draw, individuals and businesses will have less information about what constitutes appropriate business behavior in today's world.

Furthermore, private dispute resolution does not allow our case law to keep up with new issues related to areas such as biotechnology and the online world. Thus, the long-term effects of the decline of public justice could be a weakening of the common law itself.

CRITICAL THINKING

INSIGHT INTO THE SOCIAL ENVIRONMENT
If wealthier individuals increasingly use private judges, how will our justice system be affected in the long run?

---

a. See Ohio Revised Code Section 2701.10.

confirmation, one party obtains a court order directing another party to comply with the terms of the arbitrator's decision. Section 10 establishes the grounds by which the arbitrator's decision may be set aside (canceled). The grounds for setting aside a decision are limited to misconduct, fraud, corruption, or abuse of power in the arbitration process itself; a court will not review the merits of the dispute or the arbitrator's judgment.

The FAA covers any arbitration clause in a contract that involves interstate commerce. Business activities that have even remote connections or minimal effects on commerce between two or more states are considered to be included. Thus, arbitration agreements involving transactions only slightly connected to the flow of interstate commerce may fall under the FAA, even if the parties, at the time of contracting, did not expect their arbitration agreement to involve interstate commerce.

CASE IN POINT Buckeye Check Cashing, Inc., cashes personal checks for consumers in Florida. Buckeye would agree to delay submitting a consumer's check for payment if the consumer paid a "finance charge." For each transaction, the consumer signed an agreement that included an arbitration clause. A group of consumers filed a lawsuit claiming that Buckeye was charging an illegally high rate of interest in violation of state law. Buckeye filed a motion to compel arbitration, which the trial court denied, and the case was appealed. The plaintiffs argued that the entire contract—including the arbitration clause—was illegal and therefore arbitration was not required. The United States Supreme Court found that the arbitration provision was *severable,* or capable of being separated, from the rest of the contract. The Court held that when the challenge is to the validity of a contract as a whole, and not specifically to an arbitration clause within the contract, an arbitrator must resolve the dispute. This is true even if the contract later proves to be unenforceable, because the FAA established a national policy favoring arbitration and that policy extends to both federal and state courts.[2]

State Arbitration Statutes

Nearly all states follow the federal approach to voluntary arbitration. Most of the states and the District of Columbia have adopted the Uniform Arbitration Act, which was drafted by the National Conference of Commissioners on Uniform State Laws in 1955. Those states that have not adopted the uniform act nonetheless follow many of the practices specified in it.

Under the uniform act, the basic approach is to give full effect to voluntary agreements to arbitrate disputes between private parties. The act supplements private arbitration agreements by providing explicit procedures and remedies for enforcing arbitration agreements. The uniform act does not, however, dictate the terms of the agreement. Moreover, under both federal and state statutes, the parties are afforded considerable latitude in deciding the subject matter of the arbitration and the methods for conducting the arbitration process. In the absence of a controlling statute, the rights and duties of the parties are established and limited by their agreement.

The Arbitration Process

The arbitration process begins with a *submission.* **Submission** is the act of referring a dispute to an arbitrator. The next step is the *hearing,* in which evidence and arguments are presented to the arbitrator. The process culminates in an *award,* which is the decision of the arbitrator.

The right to appeal the award to a court of law is limited. If the award was made under a voluntary arbitration agreement, a court normally will not set it aside even if it was the result of an erroneous determination of fact or an incorrect interpretation of law by the arbitrator.

This limitation is based on at least two grounds. First, if an award is not treated as final, then rather than speeding up the dispute-resolution process, arbitration would merely add one more layer to the process of litigation. Second, the basis of arbitration—the freedom of parties to agree among themselves how to settle a controversy—supports treating an award as final. Having had the opportunity to frame the issues and to set out the manner for resolving the dispute, one party should not complain if the result was not what that party had hoped it would be.

SUBMISSION The parties may agree to submit questions of fact, questions of law, or both to the arbitrator. The parties may even agree to leave the interpretation of the arbitration agreement to the arbitrator. In the case of an existing agreement to arbitrate, the clause itself is the submission to arbitration.

The submission typically states the identities of the parties, the nature of the dispute to be resolved,

---

2. *Buckeye Check Cashing, Inc. v. Cardegna,* 546 U.S. 440, 126 S.Ct. 1204, 163 L.Ed.2d 1038 (2006).

the monetary amounts involved in the controversy, the location at which the arbitration is to take place, and the intention of the parties to be bound by the arbitrator's award. Exhibit 3–2 on the next page contains a sample submission form.

Most states require that an agreement to submit a dispute to arbitration be in writing. Moreover, because the goal of arbitration is speed and efficiency in resolving controversies, most states require that matters be submitted within a definite period of time, generally six months from the date on which the dispute arises.

THE HEARING Because the parties are free to construct the method by which they want their dispute resolved, they must state the issues that will be submitted and the powers that the arbitrator will exercise. The arbitrator may be given power at the outset of the process to establish rules that will govern the proceedings. Typically, these rules are much less restrictive than those governing formal litigation. Regardless of who establishes the rules, the arbitrator will apply them during the course of the hearing.

Restrictions on the kind of evidence and the manner in which it is presented may be less rigid in arbitration, partly because the arbitrator is likely to be an expert in the subject matter involved in the controversy. Restrictions may also be less stringent because there is less fear that the arbitrator will be swayed by improper evidence. In contrast, evidence in a jury trial must sometimes be presented twice: once to the judge, outside the presence of the jury, to determine if the evidence may be heard by the jury, and—depending on the judge's ruling—again, to the jury.

In the typical hearing format, the parties begin as they would at trial by presenting opening arguments to the arbitrator and stating what remedies should or should not be granted. After the opening statements have been made, evidence is presented. Witnesses may be called and examined by both sides. After all the evidence has been presented, the parties give their closing arguments. On completion of the closing arguments, the arbitrator closes the hearing.

THE AWARD After each side has had an opportunity to present evidence and to argue its case, the arbitrator reaches a decision. The final decision of the arbitrator is referred to as an **award,** even if no monetary payment is conferred on a party as a result of the proceedings. Under most statutes, the arbitrator must render an award within thirty days of the close of the hearing.

In most states, the award need not state the arbitrator's findings regarding factual questions in the case. Nor must the award state the conclusions that the arbitrator reached on any questions of law that may have been presented. All that is required for the award to be valid is that it completely resolve the controversy.

Most states do, however, require that the award be in writing, regardless of whether any conclusions of law or findings of fact are included. If the arbitrator does state his or her legal conclusions and factual findings, then a letter or an opinion will be drafted containing the basis for the award. Even when there is no statutory requirement that the arbitrator state the factual and legal basis for the award, the parties may impose the requirement in their submission or in their predispute agreement to arbitrate.

Enforcement of Agreements to Submit to Arbitration

The role of the courts in the arbitration process is limited. One important role is played at the prearbitration stage. A court may be called on to order one party to an arbitration agreement to submit to arbitration under the terms of the agreement. The court in this role is essentially interpreting a contract. The court must determine what the parties have committed themselves to before ordering that they submit to arbitration.

THE ISSUE OF ARBITRABILITY When a dispute arises as to whether or not the parties have agreed in an arbitration clause to submit a particular matter to arbitration, one party may file suit to compel arbitration. The court before which the suit is brought will not decide the basic controversy but must decide the issue of arbitrability—that is, whether the issue is one that must be resolved through arbitration. If the court finds that the subject matter in controversy is covered by the agreement to arbitrate, then a party may be compelled to arbitrate the dispute involuntarily.

Although the parties may agree to submit the issue of arbitrability to an arbitrator, the agreement must be explicit; a court will never *infer* an agreement to arbitrate. Unless a court finds an *explicit* agreement to have the arbitrator decide whether a dispute is arbitrable, the court will decide the issue. This is an important initial determination, because no party will be ordered to submit to arbitration unless the court is convinced that the party has consented to do so.

EXHIBIT 3-2 • **Sample Submission Form**

American Arbitration Association
SUBMISSION TO RESOLUTION SERVICES

The named parties hereby submit the following dispute for resolution, under the rules of the American Arbitration Association:

Procedure Selected: ☐ Binding Arbitration ☐ Early Neutral Evaluation

☐ Mediation ☐ Mini-Trial

☐ Fact-Finding

☐ Other_____

(describe)

Rules to Apply: ☐ Commercial ☐ Construction

☐ International ☐ Employment

☐ Other_____

(describe)

Nature and Type of Dispute (attach additional sheets if necessary): _____

Amount of Monetary Claim or Nature of Non-Monetary Claim:_____

Type of Business: Claimant: _____Respondent: _____

Place of Hearing or Conference: _____

We agree that, if arbitration is selected, we will abide by and perform any award rendered hereunder and that a judgment may be entered on the award.

To be completed and signed by all parties
(attach additional sheets if necessary, please remember to obtain signatures)

Name of Party	Name of Party
Address	Address
City, State and Zip Code	City, State and Zip Code
(___) _____	(___) _____
Telephone Fax	Telephone Fax
Email address	Email address
Name of the Party's Attorney or Representative	Name of the Party's Attorney or Representative
Name of Firm (if applicable)	Name of Firm (if applicable)
Address	Address
City, State and Zip Code	City, State and Zip Code
(___) _____	(___) _____
Telephone Fax	Telephone Fax
Email address	Email address
Signed† (may be signed by a representative) Title	Signed† (may be signed by a representative) Title
Date: _____	Date: _____

Please file two signed copies and the non-refundable filing fee with the AAA.
For additional information, please visit our website at www.adr.org

† *SIGNATURES OF ALL PARTIES ARE REQUIRED*   Form SRS 6/05

The terms of an arbitration agreement can limit the types of disputes that the parties agree to arbitrate. When the parties do not specify limits, however, disputes can arise as to whether the particular matter is covered by the arbitration agreement, and it is up to the court to resolve the issue of arbitrability.

In the following case, the parties had previously agreed to arbitrate disputes involving their contract to develop software, but the dispute involved claims of copyright infringement (see Chapter 14). The question was whether the copyright infringement claims were beyond the scope of the arbitration clause.

CASE 3.1
NCR Corp. v. Korala Associates, Ltd.

United States Court of Appeals, Sixth Circuit, 512 F.3d 807 (2008).
www.ca6.uscourts.gov[a]

COMPANY PROFILE • In 1884, John H. Patterson founded the National Cash Register Company (NCR), maker of the first mechanical cash registers. In 1906, NCR created a cash register run by an electric motor. By 1914, the company had developed one of the first automated credit systems. By the 1950s, NCR had branched out into transistorized business computers, and later it expanded into liquid crystal displays and data warehousing. Today, NCR is a worldwide provider of automated teller machines (ATMs), integrated hardware and software systems, and related maintenance and support services. More than 300,000 NCR ATMs are installed throughout the world.

BACKGROUND AND FACTS • To upgrade the security of its ATMs, NCR developed a software solution to install in all of its machines. At the same time, Korala Associates, Ltd. (KAL), claimed to have developed a similar security upgrade for NCR's ATMs. Indeed, KAL had entered into a contract with NCR in 1998 (the "1998 Agreement") to develop such software. To facilitate that process, NCR had loaned to KAL a proprietary ATM that contained copyrighted software called APTRA XFS. NCR alleged that KAL had "obtained access to, made unauthorized use of, and engaged in unauthorized copying of the APTRA XFS software." NCR further claimed that KAL had developed its version of the security upgrade only by engaging in this unauthorized activity. When NCR brought a suit claiming copyright infringement, KAL moved to compel arbitration under the terms of the 1998 Agreement. At trial, KAL prevailed. NCR appealed the order compelling arbitration.

IN THE LANGUAGE OF THE COURT
Chief Justice *BATCHELDER* delivered the opinion of the court.
* * * *

The arbitration clause contained within the 1998 Agreement provides that:

Any controversy or claim arising out of or relating to this contract, or breach thereof, shall be settled by arbitration and judgment upon the award rendered by the arbitrator may be entered in any court having jurisdiction thereof. The arbitrator shall be appointed upon the mutual agreement of both parties failing which both parties will agree to be subject to any arbitrator that shall be chosen by the President of the Law Society.

The parties do not dispute that a valid agreement to arbitrate exists; rather the issue of contention is whether NCR's claims fall within the substantive scope of the agreement.

As a matter of federal law, any doubts concerning the scope of arbitrable issues should be resolved in favor of arbitration. Despite this strong presumption in favor of arbitration, "arbitration is a matter of contract between the parties, and one cannot be required to submit to arbitration a dispute which it has not agreed to submit to arbitration." *When faced with a broad arbitration clause, such as one covering any dispute arising out of an agreement, a court should follow the presumption of arbitration and resolve doubts in favor of arbitration. Indeed, in such a case, only an express provision excluding a specific dispute, or the most forceful evidence of a purpose to exclude*

---

a. Click on "Opinions Search" and then on "Short Title," and type "NCR." Click on "Submit Query." Next, click on the opinion link in the first column of the row corresponding to the name of this case.

CASE CONTINUES ⇒

CASE 3.1 CONTINUED ➡ *the claim from arbitration, will remove the dispute from consideration by the arbitrators.* [Emphasis added.]

* * * It is sufficient that a court would have to reference the 1998 Agreement for part of NCR's direct [copyright] infringement claim. Under these circumstances, we find that the copyright infringement claim as to APTRA XFS falls within the scope of the arbitration agreement.

DECISION AND REMEDY • *The U.S. Court of Appeals for the Sixth Circuit affirmed the part of the district court's decision compelling arbitration of NCR's claims of direct copyright infringement relating to the APTRA XFS software.*

THE LEGAL ENVIRONMENT DIMENSION • *Why did NCR not want its claims decided by arbitration?*

THE ETHICAL DIMENSION • *Could NCR have a claim that KAL engaged in unfair competition because KAL engaged in unethical business practices? (Hint: Unfair competition may occur when one party deceives the public into believing that its goods are the goods of another.) Why or why not?*

COMPULSORY ARBITRATION AGREEMENTS A significant question in the last several years has concerned compulsory arbitration agreements. For example, many claim that employees' rights are not sufficiently protected when they are forced, as a condition of being hired, to agree to arbitrate all disputes and thus waive their rights under statutes specifically designed to protect employees. The United States Supreme Court, however, has held that mandatory arbitration clauses in employment contracts generally are enforceable.[3]

Arbitration clauses in contracts for consumer goods and services have also been a source of controversy. Generally, the criticism of compulsory arbitration in these contexts has to do with the parties' unequal bargaining power. For example, an employment contract that provides for mandatory arbitration of any disputes might be presented to a job applicant on a take-it-or-leave-it basis. In

other words, if the applicant wants the job, he or she will have to sign the contract. As you will read in Chapter 9, a contract or clause drafted by one party (the dominant party) and presented to the other party on a take-it-or-leave-it basis is referred to as an *adhesion contract*. Although the courts normally enforce contractual agreements, when enforcement would be manifestly unfair or oppressive, a court may deem the contract *unconscionable*—that is, contrary to public policy—and refuse to enforce it.

Compulsory arbitration agreements often spell out the rules for a mandatory proceeding. For example, an agreement may address in detail the amount and payment of filing fees and other expenses. When an individual worker lacks the ability to pay, some courts have overturned provisions in employment-related agreements that require the parties to split the costs.

In the following case, a travel agency included an arbitration clause in its contract with two clients who participated in an agency expedition to Mt. Kilimanjaro, the highest mountain in Africa. The court had to determine whether the agreement to arbitrate should be enforced.

---

3. For a landmark decision on this issue, see *Gilmer v. Interstate/ Johnson Lane Corp.,* 500 U.S. 20, 111 S.Ct. 1647, 114 L.Ed.2d 26 (1991).

✻ EXTENDED CASE 3.2 ✻
Lhotka v. Geographic Expeditions, Inc.

California Court of Appeal, First District, 181 Cal.App.4th 816, 104 Cal.Rptr.3d 844 (2010).

IN THE LANGUAGE OF THE COURT
SIGGINS, J. [Judge]
* * * *
Jason Lhotka was thirty-seven years old when he

died of an altitude-related illness while on a GeoEx [Geographic Expeditions, Inc.] expedition up Mount Kilimanjaro with his mother, plaintiff Sandra Menefee. GeoEx's limitation of liability and release form, which both Lhotka and

Menefee signed as a requirement of participating in the expedition, provided that each of them released GeoEx from all liability in connection with the trek and waived any claims for liability "to the maximum extent permitted by law." The release * * * reads: "I understand that all Trip Applications are subject to acceptance by GeoEx in San Francisco, California, USA. I agree that in the unlikely event a dispute of any kind arises between me and GeoEx, the following conditions will apply: (a) the dispute will be submitted to a neutral third-party mediator in San Francisco, California, with both parties splitting equally the cost of such mediator. If the dispute cannot be resolved through mediation, then (b) the dispute will be submitted for binding arbitration to the American Arbitration Association in San Francisco, California; (c) the dispute will be governed by California law; and (d) the maximum amount of recovery to which I will be entitled under any and all circumstances will be the sum of the land and air cost of my trip with GeoEx. I agree that this is a fair and reasonable limitation on the damages, of any sort whatsoever, that I may suffer. I agree to fully indemnify [compensate] GeoEx for all of its costs (including attorneys' fees) if I commence an action or claim against GeoEx based upon claims I have previously released or waived by signing this release." Menefee paid $16,831 for herself and Lhotka to go on the trip.

A letter from GeoEx president James Sano that accompanied the limitation of liability and release explained that the form was mandatory and that, on this point, "our lawyers, insurance carriers and medical consultants give us no discretion. A signed, unmodified release form is required before any traveler may join one of our trips. * * * My review of other travel companies' release forms suggests that our forms are not a whole lot different from theirs."

After her son's death, Menefee sued GeoEx for wrongful death and alleged various theories of liability including fraud, gross negligence and recklessness, and intentional infliction of emotional distress. GeoEx moved to compel arbitration.

The trial court found the arbitration provision was unconscionable

* * * and on that basis denied the motion. It ruled: "The agreement at issue is both procedurally and substantively unconscionable * * * .

This appeal timely followed.
* * * *

We turn * * * to GeoEx's contention that the court erred when it found the arbitration agreement unconscionable. Although the issue arises here in a relatively novel setting, the basic legal framework is well established.

"Unconscionability has generally been recognized to include an absence of meaningful choice on the part of one of the parties together with contract terms which are unreasonably favorable to the other party. Phrased another way, *unconscionability has both a procedural and a substantive element. The procedural element requires oppression or surprise. * * * The substantive element concerns whether a contractual provision reallocates risks in an objectively unreasonable or unexpected manner."* * * * [Emphasis added.]

GeoEx argues the arbitration agreement involved neither the oppression nor surprise aspects of procedural unconscionability. GeoEx argues the agreement was not oppressive because plaintiffs made no showing of an "industry-wide requirement that travel clients must accept an agreement's terms without modification" and "they fail[ed] even to attempt to negotiate" with GeoEx. We disagree. GeoEx's argument cannot reasonably be squared with its own statements advising participants that they must sign an *unmodified* release form to participate in the expedition; that GeoEx's "lawyers, insurance carriers and medical consultants give [it] no discretion" on that point; and *that other travel companies were no different.* In other words, GeoEx led the plaintiffs to understand not only that its terms and conditions were nonnegotiable, but that plaintiffs would encounter the same requirements with any other travel company. This is a sufficient basis for us to conclude the plaintiffs lacked bargaining power.

GeoEx also contends its terms were not oppressive, apparently as a

matter of law, because Menefee and Lhotka could have simply decided not to trek up Mount Kilimanjaro. It argues that contracts for recreational activities can *never* be unconscionably oppressive because, unlike agreements for necessities such as medical care or employment, a consumer of recreational activities *always* has the option of [forgoing] the activity. The argument has some initial resonance [significance], but on closer inspection we reject it as unsound.
* * * *

Here, certainly, plaintiffs could have chosen not to sign on with the expedition. That option, like any availability of market alternatives, is relevant to the existence, and degree, of oppression. But we must also consider the other circumstances surrounding the execution of the agreement. GeoEx presented its limitation of liability and release form as mandatory and unmodifiable, and essentially told plaintiffs that any other travel provider would impose the same terms. "Oppression arises from an inequality of bargaining power which results in no real negotiation and an absence of meaningful choice * * * ." GeoEx presented its terms as both nonnegotiable and *no different than what plaintiffs would find with any other provider.* Under these circumstances, plaintiffs made a sufficient showing to establish at least a minimal level of oppression to justify a finding of procedural unconscionability. [Emphasis in original.]

* * * [We now] address whether the substantive unconscionability of the GeoEx contract warrants the trial court's ruling.
* * * *

The arbitration provision in GeoEx's release * * * guaranteed that plaintiffs could not possibly obtain anything approaching full recompense for their harm by limiting any recovery they could obtain to the amount they paid GeoEx for their trip. In addition to a limit on their recovery, plaintiffs, residents of Colorado, were required to mediate

EXTENDED CASE CONTINUES ➡

EXTENDED CASE 3.2 CONTINUED ▼

and arbitrate in San Francisco—all but guaranteeing both that GeoEx would never be out more than the amount plaintiffs had paid for their trip, and that any recovery plaintiffs might obtain would be devoured by the expense they incur in pursuing their remedy. The release also required plaintiffs to indemnify GeoEx for its costs and attorney fees for defending any claims covered by the release of liability form. Notably, there is no reciprocal limitation on damages or indemnification obligations imposed on GeoEx. Rather than providing a neutral forum for dispute resolution, GeoEx's arbitration scheme provides a potent disincentive for an aggrieved client to pursue any claim, in any forum—and may well guarantee that GeoEx wins even if it loses. Absent reasonable justification for this arrangement—and none is apparent—we agree with the trial court that the arbitration clause is so one-sided as to be substantively unconscionable.

* * * *

The order denying GeoEx's motion to compel arbitration is affirmed.

QUESTIONS

1. What did the judge mean when he said that GeoEx's one-sided arbitration scheme "may well guarantee that GeoEx wins even if it loses"?
2. Did the fact that the terms of the release were nonnegotiable contribute to its procedural unconscionability or its substantive unconscionability? Explain.

Setting Aside an Arbitration Award

After the arbitration has been concluded, the losing party may appeal the arbitrator's award to a court, or the winning party may seek a court order compelling the other party to comply with the award. The scope of review in either situation is much more restricted than in an appellate court's review of a trial court decision. The court does not look at the merits of the underlying dispute, and the court will not add to or subtract from the remedies provided by the award. The court's role is limited to determining whether there exists a valid award. If so, the court will order the parties to comply with the terms. The general view is that because the parties were free to frame the issues and set the powers of the arbitrator at the outset, they cannot complain about the result.

FACT FINDINGS AND LEGAL CONCLUSIONS The arbitrator's fact findings and legal conclusions are normally final. That the arbitrator may have erred in a ruling during the hearing or made an erroneous fact finding is normally no basis for setting aside an award: the parties agreed that the arbitrator would be the judge of the facts. Similarly, no matter how obviously the arbitrator was mistaken in a conclusion of law, the award is normally nonetheless binding: the parties agreed to accept the arbitrator's interpretation of the law. A court will not look at the merits of the dispute, the sufficiency of the evidence presented, or the arbitrator's reasoning in reaching a particular decision.

This approach is consistent with the underlying view of all voluntary arbitration—that its basis is really contract law. If the parties freely contract with one another, courts will not interfere simply because one side feels that it received a bad bargain. Any party challenging an award must face the presumption that a final award is valid. But is an award final or binding if the parties did not agree that it would be?

PUBLIC POLICY AND ILLEGALITY In keeping with contract law principles, no award will be enforced if compliance with the award would result in the commission of a crime or would conflict with some greater social policy mandated by statute. A court will not overturn an award, however, simply because the arbitrator was called on to resolve a dispute involving a matter of significant public concern. For an award to be set aside, it must call for some action on the part of the parties that would conflict with or in some way undermine public policy.

DEFECTS IN THE ARBITRATION PROCESS There are some bases for setting aside an award when there is a defect in the arbitration process. These bases are typified by those set forth in the Federal Arbitration Act. Section 10 of the act provides four grounds on which an arbitration award may be set aside.

1. The award was the result of corruption, fraud, or other "undue means."
2. The arbitrator exhibited bias or corruption.

3. The arbitrator refused to postpone the hearing despite sufficient cause, refused to hear evidence pertinent and material to the dispute, or otherwise acted to substantially prejudice the rights of one of the parties.

4. The arbitrator exceeded his or her powers or failed to use them to make a mutual, final, and definite award.

The first three bases for setting aside the award include actions or decisions that are more than simply mistakes in judgment. Each requires some "bad faith" on the part of the arbitrator. Bad faith actions or decisions are ones that affect the integrity of the arbitration process. The honesty and impartiality, rather than the judgment, of the arbitrator are called into question.

Sometimes, it is difficult to make the distinction between honest mistakes in judgment and actions or decisions made in bad faith. A bribe is clearly the kind of "undue means" included in the first basis for setting aside an award. Letting only one side argue its case is likewise a clear violation of the second basis.

Meetings between the arbitrator and one party outside the presence of the other party also taint the arbitration process. Although meetings might not involve the kind of corruption that results from taking a bribe, they do affect the integrity of the process; the third basis for setting aside an award is meant to protect against this.

Not every refusal by an arbitrator to admit certain evidence is grounds for setting aside an award under the third basis. As noted, to provide a basis for overturning an award, the arbitrator's decision must be more than an error in judgment, no matter how obviously incorrect that judgment might appear to another observer. The decision must be so obviously wrong or unfair as to imply bias or corruption. Otherwise, the decision normally cannot be a basis for setting aside an award.

The fourth basis for setting aside an award is that the arbitrator exceeded his or her powers in arbitrating the dispute. This issue involves the question of arbitrability. An arbitrator exceeds his or her powers and authority by attempting to resolve an issue that is not covered by the agreement to submit to arbitration.[4]

WAIVER Although a defect in the arbitration process is sufficient grounds for setting aside an award,

a party sometimes forfeits the right to challenge an award by failing to object to the defect in a timely manner. The party must object when he or she learns of the problem. After making the objection, the party can proceed with the arbitration process and still challenge the award in court after the arbitration proceedings have concluded. If, however, a party makes no objection and proceeds with the arbitration process, then a later court challenge to the award may be denied on the ground that the party *waived* the right to challenge the award on the basis of the defect.

Frequently, this occurs when a party fails to object that an arbitrator is exceeding his or her powers in resolving a dispute because the subject matter is not arbitrable or because the party did not agree to arbitrate the dispute. The question of arbitrability is one for the courts to decide. If a party does not object on this issue at the first demand for arbitration, however, a court may consider the objection waived.

CONFLICTS OF LAW Parties are afforded wide latitude in establishing the manner in which their disputes will be resolved. Nevertheless, an agreement to arbitrate may be governed by the Federal Arbitration Act (FAA) or one of the many state arbitration acts, even though the parties do not refer to a statute in their agreement. Recall that the FAA covers any arbitration clause in a contract that involves interstate commerce. Frequently, however, transactions involving interstate commerce also have substantial connections to particular states, which may in turn have their own arbitration acts. In such situations, unless the FAA and state arbitration law are nearly identical, the acts may conflict. How are these conflicts to be resolved?

As a general principle, the supremacy clause and the commerce clause of the U.S. Constitution are the bases for giving federal law preeminence; when there is a conflict, state law is preempted by federal law. Thus, in cases of arbitration, the strong federal policy favoring arbitration can override a state's laws that might be more favorable to normal litigation.

CHOICE OF LAW Notwithstanding federal preemption of conflicting state laws, the FAA has been interpreted as allowing the parties to choose a particular state law to govern their arbitration agreement. The parties may choose to have the laws of a specific state govern their agreement by including in the agreement a **choice-of-law clause.** The FAA does not mandate any particular set of rules that parties must follow in arbitration; the parties are free to agree on the manner best suited to their needs.

---

4. See, for example, *Major League Baseball Players Association v. Garvey*, 532 U.S. 1015, 121 S.Ct. 1724, 149 L.Ed.2d 740 (2001).

Consistent with this view that arbitration is at heart a contractual matter between private parties, the United States Supreme Court has upheld arbitration agreements containing choice-of-law provisions.

Disadvantages of Arbitration

Arbitration has some disadvantages. The result in any particular dispute can be unpredictable, in part because arbitrators do not need to follow any previous cases in rendering their decisions. Unlike judges, arbitrators do not have to issue written opinions or facilitate a participant's appeal to a court. Arbitrators must decide disputes according to whatever rules have been provided by the parties, regardless of how unfair those rules may be. In some cases, arbitration can be nearly as expensive as litigation. In part, this is because both sides must prepare their cases for presentation before a third party decision maker, just as they would have to do to appear in court. Discovery usually is not available in arbitration, however, which means that during the hearing the parties must take the time to question witnesses whom, in a lawsuit, they would not need to call.

SECTION 4
THE INTEGRATION OF ADR AND FORMAL COURT PROCEDURES

Increasingly, courts are requiring that parties attempt to settle their differences through some form of ADR before proceeding to trial. For example, several federal district courts encourage nonbinding arbitration for cases involving amounts less than $100,000. Less than 10 percent of the cases referred for arbitration ever go to trial. About half of all federal courts have adopted formal rules regarding the use of ADR, and many other courts without such rules use ADR procedures.

Most states have adopted programs that allow them to refer certain types of cases for negotiation, mediation, or arbitration. Typically—as in California and Hawaii—court systems have adopted mandatory mediation or nonbinding arbitration programs for certain types of disputes, usually involving less than a specified threshold dollar amount. Only if the parties fail to reach an agreement, or if one of the parties disagrees with the decision of a third party mediating or arbitrating the dispute, will the case be heard by a court. South Carolina was the first state to institute a voluntary arbitration program at the appellate court level. In the South Carolina system, litigants must waive a court hearing when requesting arbitration. All decisions by the arbitrators are final and binding.

Court-Annexed Arbitration

Court-annexed arbitration differs significantly from the voluntary arbitration process discussed above. There are some disputes that courts will not allow to go to arbitration. Most states, for example, do not allow court-annexed arbitration in disputes involving title to real estate or in cases in which a court's equity powers are involved.

A FUNDAMENTAL DIFFERENCE The fundamental difference between voluntary arbitration and court-annexed arbitration is the finality and reviewability of the award. With respect to court-annexed arbitration, either party may reject the award for any reason. In the event that one of the parties does reject the award, the case will proceed to trial, and the court will hear the case *de novo*—that is, the court will reconsider all the evidence and legal questions as though no arbitration had occurred.

Everyone who has a recognizable cause of action or against whom such an action is brought is entitled to have the issue decided in a court of law. Because court-annexed arbitration is not voluntary, there must be some safeguard against using it in a way that denies an individual his or her "day in court." This safeguard is provided by permitting either side to reject the award regardless of the reason for so doing.

The party rejecting the award may be penalized, however. Many statutes providing for court-annexed arbitration impose court costs and fees on a party who rejects an arbitration award but does not improve his or her position by going to trial. Thus, for example, if a party rejects an arbitration award, and the award turns out to be more favorable to that party than the subsequent jury verdict, the party may be compelled to pay the costs of the arbitration or some fee for the costs of the trial.

In court-annexed arbitration, discovery of evidence occurs before the hearing. After the hearing has commenced, a party seeking to discover new evidence must usually secure approval from the court that mandated the arbitration. This is intended to prevent the parties from using arbitration as a means of previewing each other's cases and then rejecting the arbitrator's award.

THE ROLE OF THE ARBITRATOR Notwithstanding the differences between voluntary and court-annexed arbitration, the role of the arbitrator is essentially the same in both types of proceedings. The arbitrator determines issues of both fact and law. The arbitrator also makes all decisions concerning applications of the rules of procedure and evidence during the hearing.

WHICH RULES APPLY Regarding the rules of evidence, there are differences among the states. Most states impose the same rules of evidence on an arbitration hearing as on a trial. Other states allow all evidence relevant to the dispute regardless of whether the evidence would be admissible at trial. Still other jurisdictions leave it to the arbitrator to decide what evidence is admissible.

WAIVER Once a court directs that a dispute is to be submitted to court-annexed arbitration, the parties must proceed to arbitration. As noted above, either side may reject the award that results from the arbitration for any reason. If a party fails to appear at, or participate in, the arbitration proceeding as directed by the court, however, that failure constitutes a waiver of the right to reject the award.

Court-Related Mediation

Mediation is proving to be more popular than arbitration as a court-related method of ADR, and mediation programs continue to increase in number in both federal and state courts. Today, more court systems offer or require mediation, rather than arbitration, as an alternative to litigation.

Mediation is often used in disputes relating to employment law, environmental law, product liability, and franchises. One of the most important business advantages of mediation is its lower cost, which can be 25 percent (or less) of the expense of litigation. Another advantage is the speed with which a dispute can go through mediation (possibly one or two days) compared with arbitration (possibly months) or litigation (possibly years).

Part of the popularity of mediation is that its goal, unlike that of litigation and some other forms of ADR, is for opponents to work out a resolution that benefits both sides. The rate of participants' satisfaction with the outcomes in mediated disputes is high.

Summary Jury Trials

Another means by which the courts have integrated alternative dispute-resolution methods into the traditional court process is through the use of summary jury trials. A **summary jury trial** is a mock trial that occurs in a courtroom before a judge and jury. Evidence is presented in an abbreviated form, along with each side's major contentions. The jury then presents a verdict.

The fundamental difference between a traditional trial and a summary jury trial is that in the latter, the jury's verdict is only advisory. A summary jury trial's goal is to give each side an idea of how it would fare in a full-blown jury trial with a more elaborate and detailed presentation of evidence and arguments. At the end of the summary jury trial, the presiding judge meets with the parties and may encourage them to settle their dispute without going through a standard jury trial.

SECTION 5
ADR FORUMS AND SERVICES

Services facilitating dispute resolution outside the courtroom are provided by both government agencies and private organizations, as well as by companies conducting business online.

Nonprofit Organizations

The major source of private arbitration services is the **American Arbitration Association (AAA).** Most of the largest law firms in the nation are members of this association. Founded in 1926, the AAA now settles more than 200,000 disputes a year and has offices in every state. Cases brought before the AAA are heard by an expert or a panel of experts—of whom usually about half are lawyers—in the area relating to the dispute. To cover its costs, this nonprofit organization charges a fee, paid by the party filing the claim. In addition, each party to the dispute pays a price for each hearing day, as well as a special additional fee in cases involving personal injuries or property loss.

In addition to the AAA, hundreds of other state and local nonprofit organizations provide arbitration services. For example, the Arbitration Association of Florida provides ADR services in that state. The Better Business Bureau offers ADR programs to aid in the resolution of certain types of disagreements. Many industries—including the insurance, automobile, and securities industries—also now have mediation or arbitration programs to facilitate timely and inexpensive settlement of claims.

For-Profit Organizations

Those who seek to settle their disputes quickly can turn to private, for-profit organizations to act as mediators or arbitrators. The leading firm in this private system of justice is JAMS/Endispute, which is based in California. The private system of justice includes hundreds of firms throughout the country offering dispute-resolution services by hired judges.

Procedures in these private courts are fashioned to meet the desires of the clients seeking their services. For example, the parties might decide on the date of the hearing, the presiding judge, whether the judge's decision will be legally binding, and the site of the hearing—which could be a conference room, a law school office, or a leased courtroom complete with the American flag and Bible. The judges may follow procedures similar to those of the federal courts and use similar rules. Each party to the dispute may pay a filing fee and a designated fee for a half-day hearing session or a special, one-hour settlement conference.

Online Organizations

An increasing number of companies and organizations are offering dispute-resolution services using the Internet. The settlement of disputes in these online forums is known as **online dispute resolution (ODR).** To date, the disputes resolved in these forums have most commonly involved disagreements over the rights to domain names (Web site addresses—see Chapter 14) and disagreements over the quality of goods sold via the Internet, including goods sold through Internet auction sites.

ODR may be best for resolving small- to medium-sized business liability claims, which may not be worth the expense of litigation or even traditional methods of alternative dispute resolution. Rules being developed in online forums, however, may ultimately become a code of conduct for everyone who does business in cyberspace. Most online forums do not automatically apply the law of any specific jurisdiction. Instead, results are often based on general, more universal legal principles. As with traditional offline methods of dispute resolution, any party may appeal to a court at any time.

NEGOTIATION AND MEDIATION SERVICES The online negotiation of a dispute generally is simpler and more practical than litigation. Typically, one party files a complaint, and the other party is notified by e-mail. Password-protected access is possible twenty-four hours a day, seven days a week. Fees are usually low (often 2 to 4 percent, or less, of the disputed amount).

CyberSettle.com, National Arbitration and Mediation (NAM), and other Web-based firms offer online forums for negotiating monetary settlements. The Better Business Bureau also provides online dispute settlement. The parties to a dispute may agree to submit offers. If the offers fall within a previously agreed-on range, they will end the dispute. Special software keeps secret any offers that are not within the range. If there is no agreed-on range, typically an offer includes a deadline when the offer will expire, and the other party must respond before then. The parties can drop the negotiations at any time.

ARBITRATION PROGRAMS A number of organizations, including the American Arbitration Association, offer online arbitration programs. For example, the Internet Corporation for Assigned Names and Numbers (ICANN), a nonprofit corporation that the federal government set up to oversee the distribution of domain names, has issued special rules for the resolution of domain name disputes. ICANN has also authorized several organizations to arbitrate domain name disputes in accordance with ICANN's rules.

SECTION 6
INTERNATIONAL DISPUTE RESOLUTION

Businesspersons who engage in international business transactions normally take special precautions to protect themselves in the event that a party with whom they are dealing in another country breaches an agreement. Often, parties to international contracts include special clauses in their contracts providing for how any disputes arising under the contracts will be resolved.

Forum-Selection and Choice-of-Law Clauses

Parties to international contracts often include *forum-selection clauses*. These clauses designate the jurisdiction (court or country) in which any dispute arising under the contract will be litigated and the nation's law that will be applied. Choice-of-law clauses are also frequently included in international contracts. If no forum and choice-of-law clauses have been included in an international contract, however, legal proceedings will be more complex and attended by much more uncertainty. For example, litigation may take place in two or more countries, with each country applying its own national law to the particular transactions.

Furthermore, even if a plaintiff wins a favorable judgment in a lawsuit litigated in the plaintiff's country, there is no guarantee that the court's judgment will be enforced by judicial bodies in the defendant's country. As will be discussed in Chapter 8, for reasons of courtesy, the judgment may be enforced in the defendant's country, particularly if the defendant's country is the United States and the foreign court's decision is consistent with U.S. national law and policy. Other nations, however, may not be as accommodating as the United States, and the plaintiff may be left empty-handed.

Arbitration Clauses

In an attempt to prevent such problems, parties to international contracts often include arbitration clauses in their contracts, requiring that any contract disputes be decided by a neutral third party. In international arbitration proceedings, the third party may be a neutral entity (such as the International Chamber of Commerce), a panel of individuals representing both parties' interests, or some other group or organization. The United Nations Convention on the Recognition and Enforcement of Foreign Arbitral Awards[5]—which has been implemented in more than fifty countries, including the United States—assists in the enforcement of arbitration clauses, as do provisions in specific treaties among nations. The American Arbitration Association provides arbitration services for international as well as domestic disputes.

---

5. June 10, 1958, 21 U.S.T. 2517, T.I.A.S. No. 6997 (the "New York Convention").

REVIEWING
Alternative and Online Dispute Resolution

Adrian Reese, a resident of New York, owned a strip mall located in Ohio, which he leased out to different businesses. The tenants in the building had complained that the two public restrooms were substandard and in need of repair. Reese therefore contracted with Lyle Copeland, a licensed contractor in Ohio, to remodel the bathrooms and fix the outdated plumbing. Copeland began the work on the date promised but progressed very slowly. Then, while ripping out the existing pipes, Copeland accidentally broke the main pipe, which caused flooding and water damage to the building. Several of the tenants immediately vacated the property after the incident. Reese claimed that Copeland was legally responsible for $300,000 in property damage because his actions were reckless and incompetent. Copeland maintained that it was an accident and refused to pay for the damage. Using the information presented in the chapter, answer the following questions.

1. What types of assisted negotiation might the parties use to settle this dispute?
2. Does the fact that the parties reside in different jurisdictions have any effect on whether they might try mediation or negotiation? Why or why not?
3. Why would the parties wish to use some method of alternative dispute resolution (ADR) rather than filing a traditional lawsuit?
4. Suppose that one of the parties rejects any attempt at using ADR and instead files a lawsuit in a federal district court. That court happens to require that this dispute be arbitrated prior to any trial on the matter. Explain whether this arbitration is likely to be legally binding on the parties.

DEBATE THIS: *Prior to all litigation, the opposing parties must submit to mediation or arbitration.*

TERMS AND CONCEPTS

alternative dispute
  resolution (ADR) 58
American Arbitration
  Association 71

arbitration 59
arbitrator 59
award 63
choice-of-law clause 69
early neutral case
  evaluation 58

facilitation 59
mediation 59
mediator 59
mini-trial 58
negotiation 58

online dispute
  resolution (ODR) 72
submission 62
summary jury trial 71

QUESTIONS AND CASE PROBLEMS

3–1. Arbitration In an arbitration proceeding, the arbitrator need not be a judge or even a lawyer. How, then, can the arbitrator's decision have the force of law and be binding on the parties involved?

3–2. QUESTION WITH SAMPLE ANSWER: Choice-of-Law.

Two private U.S. corporations enter into an agreement to conduct mining operations in the newly formed Middle Eastern nation of Euphratia. As part of the agreement, the companies include an arbitration clause and a choice-of-law provision. The first states that any controversy arising out of the performance of the agreement will be settled by arbitration. The second states that the agreement is to be governed by the laws of the location of the venture, Euphratia. A dispute arises, and the parties discontinue operations. One of the parties claims sole ownership to the Euphratian mines and orders the other party to remove its equipment from the mines. The other party disputes the claim of sole ownership and seeks an order from a U.S. federal court compelling the parties to submit to arbitration over the ownership issue and alleged breaches of the agreement. How should the court rule if the laws of Euphratia state that, whereas arbitration agreements are to be enforced generally, matters of ownership of natural resources can only be resolved in a Euphratian court of law? Does it matter that two U.S. companies engaged in international commerce would be governed by the Federal Arbitration Act? Explain.

• **For a sample answer to Question 3–2, go to Appendix F at the end of this text.**

3–3. Award Two brothers, both of whom are certified public accountants (CPAs), form a professional association to provide tax-accounting services to the public. They also agree, in writing, that any disputes that arise between them over matters concerning the association will be submitted to an independent arbitrator, whom they designate to be their father, who is also a CPA. A dispute arises, and the matter is submitted to the father for arbitration. During the course of arbitration, which occurs over several weeks, the father asks the older brother, who is visiting one evening, to explain a certain entry in the brothers' association accounts. The younger brother learns of the discussion at the next meeting for arbitration; he says nothing about it, however. The arbitration is concluded in favor of the older brother, who seeks a court order compelling the younger brother to comply with the award. The younger brother seeks to set aside the award, claiming that the arbitration process was tainted by bias because "Dad always liked my older brother best." The younger brother also seeks to have the award set aside on the basis of improper conduct in that matters subject to arbitration were discussed between the father and older brother without the younger brother's being present. Should a court confirm the award or set it aside? Why or why not?

3–4. Award After resolving their dispute, the two brothers encountered in Question 3–3 decide to resume their tax-accounting practice according to the terms of their original agreement. Again a dispute arises, and again it is decided by the father (now retired except for numerous occasions on which he acts as an arbitrator) in favor of the older brother. The older brother files a petition to enforce the award. The younger brother seeks to set aside the award and offers evidence that the father, as arbitrator, made a gross error in calculating the accounts that were material to the dispute being arbitrated. If the court is convinced that the father erred in the calculations, should the award be set aside? Why or why not?

3–5. Arbitration Agreement Licensed real estate brokers in Colorado who belong to the Denver Metropolitan Commercial Association of Realtors (DMCAR) agree, as a condition of membership, to submit all disputes about real estate transactions to binding arbitration in accordance with procedures of the National Association of Realtors. Some realtors challenged the arbitration agreement, contending it was invalid because the parties did not execute arbitration agreements with each other and because membership in DMCAR is voluntary, so it does not create a binding obligation to arbitration if a member resigns from the association. Would such a condition of membership be valid and binding on members in the event a dispute arose? [*Lane v. Urgitus,* 145 P.3d 672 (Colo.Sup.Ct. 2006)]

3–6. Arbitration Clause Kathleen Lowden sued cellular phone company T-Mobile USA, Inc., contending that its service agreements were not enforceable under Washington state law. Lowden requested that the court allow a class-action suit, in which her claims would extend to similarly affected customers. She contended that T-Mobile had improperly charged her fees beyond the advertised price of service and charged her for roaming calls that should not have been classified as roaming. T-Mobile moved to force arbitration in accordance with the provisions that were clearly set forth in the service agreement. The agreement also specified that no class-action suit could be brought, so T-Mobile also asked the court to dismiss the request for a class-action suit. Was T-Mobile correct that Lowden's only course of action was to file arbitration personally? Why or why not? [*Lowden v. T-Mobile USA, Inc.*, 512 F.3d 1213 (9th Cir. 2008)]

3–7. CASE PROBLEM WITH SAMPLE ANSWER: Arbitration.

Thomas Baker and others who bought new homes from Osborne Development Corp. sued for multiple defects in the houses they purchased. When Osborne sold the homes, it paid for them to be in a new home warranty program administered by Home Buyers Warranty (HBW). When the company enrolled a home with HBW, it paid a fee and filled out a form that stated the following: "By signing below, you acknowledge that you . . . consent to the terms of these documents including the binding arbitration provision contained therein." *HBW then issued warranty booklets to the new homeowners that stated:* "Any and all claims, disputes and controversies by or between the Homeowner, the Builder, the Warranty Insurer and/or HBW . . . shall be submitted to arbitration." *Were the new homeowners bound by the arbitration agreement, or could they sue the builder, Osborne, in court? Explain.* [Baker v. Osborne Development Corp., *159 Cal.App.4th 884, 71 Cal.Rptr.3d 854 (2008)*]

- To view a sample answer for Problem 3–7, go to this book's Web site at www.cengage.com/blaw/cross, select "Chapter 3," and click on "Case Problem with Sample Answer."

3–8. Arbitration PRM Energy Systems, Inc. (PRM), owned technology patents that it licensed to Primenergy to use and to sublicense in the United States. The agreement stated that all disputes would be settled by arbitration. Kobe Steel of Japan was interested in using the technology at its U.S. subsidiary. PRM directed Kobe to talk to Primenergy about that. Kobe talked to PRM directly about using the technology in Japan, but no agreement was reached. Primenergy then agreed to let Kobe use the technology in Japan without telling PRM. The dispute between PRM and Primenergy about Kobe went to arbitration, as required by the license agreement. In addition, PRM sued Primenergy for fraud and theft of trade secrets. PRM also sued Kobe for using the technology in Japan without its permission. The district court ruled that PRM had to take all complaints about Primenergy to arbitration. PRM also had to take its complaint about Kobe to arbitration because the complaint involved a sublicense Kobe was granted by Primenergy. PRM appealed, contending that the fraud and theft of trade secrets went beyond the license agreement with Primenergy and that Kobe had no right to demand arbitration because it never had a right to use the technology under a license from PRM. Is PRM correct, or must all matters go to arbitration? Why or why not? [*PRM Energy Systems, Inc. v. Primenergy,* 592 F.3d 830 (8th Cir. 2010)]

3–9. A QUESTION OF ETHICS: Agreement to Arbitrate.

Nellie Lumpkin, who suffered from various illnesses, including dementia, was admitted to the Picayune Convalescent Center, a nursing home. Because of her mental condition, her daughter, Beverly McDaniel, filled out the admissions paperwork and signed the admissions agreement. It included a clause requiring parties to submit to arbitration any disputes that arose. After Lumpkin left the center two years later, she sued, through her husband, for negligent treatment and malpractice during her stay. The center moved to force the matter to arbitration. The trial court held that the arbitration agreement was not enforceable. The center appealed. [Covenant Health & Rehabilitation of Picayune, LP v. Lumpkin, *23 So.3d 1092 (Miss.App. 2009)*]

(a) Should a dispute involving medical malpractice be forced into arbitration? This is a claim of negligent care, not a breach of a commercial contract. Is it ethical for medical facilities to impose such a requirement? Is there really any bargaining over such terms?

(b) Should a person with limited mental capacity be held to the arbitration clause agreed to by the next-of-kin who signed on behalf of that person?

LEGAL RESEARCH EXERCISES ON THE WEB

Go to this text's Web site at **www.cengage.com/blaw/cross**, select "Chapter 3," and click on "Practical Internet Exercises." There you will find the following Internet research exercises that you can perform to learn more about the topics covered in this chapter.

Practical Internet Exercise 3–1: **Legal Perspective**
Alternative Dispute Resolution

Practical Internet Exercise 3–2: **Management Perspective**
Resolve a Dispute Online

CHAPTER 4

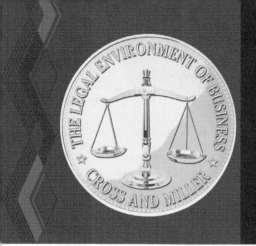

Ethics and Business Decision Making

In the early part of the first decade of the 2000s, ethics scandals erupted throughout corporate America. Heads of major corporations (some of which no longer exist) were tried for fraud, conspiracy, conspiracy to commit securities fraud, grand larceny, and obstruction of justice. Former multimillionaires (and even billionaires) who once ran multinational corporations are now serving sentences in federal penitentiaries. The giant energy company Enron in particular dominated headlines. Its investors lost around $60 billion when the company ceased to exist.

Fast-forward to 2009. One man, Bernard Madoff, was convicted of bilking investors out of more than $50 billion through a Ponzi scheme[1] that he had perpetrated for decades. Madoff's victims included not only naïve retirees but also some of the world's biggest and best-known financial institutions, including the Royal Bank of Scotland, France's BNP Paribas, Spain's Banco Santander, and Japan's Nomura. But ethical lapses were not limited to Madoff. Ethical problems in many financial institutions contributed to the onset of the deepest recession since the Great Depression of the 1930s. Not only did some $9 trillion in investment capital evaporate, but millions of workers lost their jobs. The point is clear: the scope and scale of corporate unethical behavior, especially in the financial sector, skyrocketed in the first decade of the twenty-first century—with enormous repercussions for everyone.

The ethics scandals of the last fifteen years have taught businesspersons all over the world that business ethics cannot be taken lightly. Acting ethically in a business context can mean billions of dollars—made or lost—for corporations, shareholders, and employees and can have far-reaching effects on society and the global economy.

---

1. A Ponzi scheme is a type of illegal pyramid scheme named after Charles Ponzi, who duped thousands of New England residents into investing in a postage-stamp speculation scheme in the 1920s.

SECTION 1
BUSINESS ETHICS

As you might imagine, business ethics is derived from the concept of ethics. **Ethics** can be defined as the study of what constitutes right or wrong behavior. It is a branch of philosophy focusing on morality and the way moral principles are derived. Ethics has to do with the fairness, justness, rightness, or wrongness of an action.

Business ethics focuses on what is right and wrong behavior in the business world. It has to do with how businesses apply moral and ethical principles to situations that arise in the workplace. Because business decision makers often address more complex ethical issues than they face in their personal lives, business ethics may be more complicated than personal ethics.

Why Is Business Ethics Important?

All of the corporate executives who are sitting behind bars could have avoided these outcomes had they engaged in ethical decision making during their careers. As a result of their crimes, all of their companies suffered losses, and some, such as Enron, were forced to enter bankruptcy, causing thousands of workers to lose their jobs. The corporations, shareholders, and employees who suffered because of those individuals' unethical and criminal behavior certainly paid a high price. Thus, an in-depth understanding of business ethics is important to the long-run viability of any corporation today.

It is also important to the well-being of individual officers and directors and to the firm's employees. Finally, unethical corporate decision making can negatively affect suppliers, consumers, the community, and society as a whole.

At the end of every unit in this book, a series of ethical issues will be presented in features called *Focus on Ethics*. In each of these unit-ending features, we expand on the concepts of business ethics that we present in this chapter.

The Moral Minimum

The minimum acceptable standard for ethical business behavior—known as the **moral minimum**—is normally considered to be compliance with the law. In many corporate scandals, had most of the businesspersons involved simply followed the law, they would not have gotten into trouble. Note, though, that in the interest of preserving personal freedom, as well as for practical reasons, the law does not—and cannot—codify all ethical requirements.

As they make business decisions, businesspersons must remember that just because an action is legal does not necessarily make it ethical. For instance, no law specifies the salaries that publicly held corporations can pay their officers. Nevertheless, if a corporation pays its officers an excessive amount relative to other employees, or relative to what officers at other corporations are paid, the executives' compensation might be challenged as unethical. (Executive bonuses can also present ethical problems—see the discussion later in this chapter.)

"Gray Areas" in the Law

In many situations, business firms can predict with a fair amount of certainty whether a given action would be legal. For instance, firing an employee solely because of that person's race or gender would clearly violate federal laws prohibiting employment discrimination. In some situations, though, the legality of a particular action may be less clear. In part, this is because there are so many laws regulating business that it is increasingly possible to violate one of them without realizing it. The law also contains numerous "gray areas," making it difficult to predict with certainty how a court will apply a given law to a particular action.

In addition, many rules of law require a court to determine what is "foreseeable" or "reasonable" in a particular situation. Because a business has no way of predicting how a specific court will decide these issues, decision makers need to proceed with caution and evaluate an action and its consequences from an ethical perspective. The same problem often occurs in cases involving the Internet because it is often unclear how a court will apply existing laws in the context of cyberspace. Generally, if a company can demonstrate that it acted in good faith and responsibly under the circumstances, it has a better chance of successfully defending its action in court or before an administrative law judge in an agency hearing.

Short-Run Profit Maximization

Some people argue that a corporation's only goal should be profit maximization, which will be reflected in a higher market value. When all firms strictly adhere to the goal of profit maximization, resources tend to flow to where they are most highly valued by society. Ultimately, profit maximization, in theory, leads to the most efficient allocation of scarce resources.

Corporate executives and employees have to distinguish, though, between *short-run* and *long-run* profit maximization. In the short run, a company may increase its profits by continuing to sell a product, even though it knows that the product is defective. In the long run, however, because of lawsuits, large settlements, and bad publicity, such unethical conduct will cause profits to suffer. Thus, business ethics is consistent only with long-run profit maximization. An overemphasis on short-term profit maximization is the most common reason that ethical problems occur in business.

CASE IN POINT When the powerful narcotic painkiller OxyContin was first marketed, its manufacturer, Purdue Pharma, claimed that it was unlikely to lead to drug addiction or abuse. Internal company documents later showed that the company's executives knew that OxyContin could be addictive, but kept this risk a secret to boost sales and maximize short-term profits. In 2007, Purdue Pharma and three former executives pleaded guilty to criminal charges that they misled regulators, patients, and physicians about OxyContin's risks of addiction. Purdue Pharma agreed to pay $600 million in fines and other payments. The three former executives agreed to pay $34.5 million in fines and were barred from federal health programs for a period of fifteen years—a ruling that was upheld by an administrative law judge in 2009. Thus, the company's focus on maximizing profits in the short run led to unethical conduct that hurt profits in the long run.

The following case provides an example of unethical conduct that was designed to enhance a company's short-term outlook but in the end destroyed the firm.

CASE 4.1
Skilling v. United States

Supreme Court of the United States, ___ U.S. ___, 130 S.Ct. 2896, 177 L.Ed.2d 619 (2010).

COMPANY PROFILE • In the 1990s, Enron Corporation was an international, multibillion-dollar enterprise consisting of four businesses that bought and sold energy, owned energy networks, and bought and sold bandwidth capacity. "Wholesale," the division that bought and sold energy, was the most profitable and accounted for 90 percent of Enron's revenues. Jeffrey Skilling—Enron's president, its chief operating officer, and a member of its board of directors—boasted at a conference with financial analysts in January 2001 that Enron's retail energy and bandwidth sales divisions had "sustainable high earnings power." Skilling became Enron's chief executive officer (CEO) in February 2001.

BACKGROUND AND FACTS • In August 2001, Jeffrey Skilling resigned his position as Enron's CEO. Four months later, Enron filed for bankruptcy. An investigation uncovered a conspiracy to deceive investors about Enron's finances to ensure that its stock price remained high. Among other things, Skilling had shifted more than $2 billion in losses from Enron's struggling divisions to Wholesale. He had overstated Enron's profits in telephone calls to investors and in press releases. To hide more losses, he had arranged deals between Enron's executives and third parties, which he falsely portrayed to Enron's accountants and to the Securities and Exchange Commission as producing income. Skilling was convicted in a federal district court of various crimes, including conspiracy to commit fraud to deprive Enron and its shareholders of the "honest services" of its employees. He was sentenced to 292 months in prison and three years of supervised release, and was ordered to pay $45 million in restitution. Skilling appealed, and the U.S. Court of Appeals for the Fifth Circuit affirmed the trial court's ruling. Skilling appealed to the United States Supreme Court, arguing, among other things, that the honest-services statute is unconstitutionally vague or, in the alternative, that his conduct did not fall within the statute's compass.

IN THE LANGUAGE OF THE COURT
Justice *GINSBURG* delivered the opinion of the Court.
* * * *

[In 1988,] Congress enacted a new statute "specifically to cover * * * the intangible right of honest services" [as a "scheme or artifice to defraud" in laws prohibiting mail and wire fraud].
* * * *

[Before 1988,] the "vast majority" of the honest-services cases involved offenders who, in violation of a fiduciary duty participated in bribery or kickback schemes.

* * * The honest-services doctrine had its genesis [origin] in prosecutions involving bribery allegations.

In view of this history, there is no doubt that Congress intended [the law] to reach *at least* bribes and kickbacks. Reading the statute to proscribe [rule out] a wider range of offensive conduct, we acknowledge, would raise the due process concerns underlying the vagueness doctrine. To preserve the statute without transgressing [breaching] constitutional limitations, we now hold that [the statute] criminalizes *only* the bribe-and-kickback core of the [case law prior to 1988]. [Emphases added by the Court.]
* * * *

The government did not, at any time, allege that Skilling solicited or accepted side payments from a third party in exchange for making * * * misrepresentations [concerning Enron's fiscal health]. It is therefore clear that, as we read [the statute], Skilling did not commit honest-services fraud.

Because the indictment alleged three objects of the conspiracy—honest-services wire fraud, money-or-property wire fraud, and securities fraud—Skilling's conviction is flawed. This determination, however, does not necessarily require reversal of the conspiracy conviction * * *. We leave this dispute for resolution on remand.

CASE 4.1 CONTINUED ➡ **DECISION AND REMEDY** • *The United States Supreme Court vacated the federal appellate court's ruling that Skilling's actions had violated the honest-services statute. The Court remanded the case for further proceedings to determine how its decision would affect the other charges against Skilling.*

THE ETHICAL DIMENSION • *During Skilling's tenure at Enron, the mood among the employees must have been upbeat because the company's situation would have appeared "rosy." Is there anything unethical about this situation? Discuss.*

MANAGERIAL IMPLICATIONS • *Just because the Court has reduced the scope of the honest-services fraud doctrine does not mean that federal prosecutors will be unable to indict businesspersons who egregiously violate ethical business practices. There are more than four thousand federal crimes on the books today. Consequently, the federal government will continue to pursue actions that it deems are illegal business practices. The government will simply charge those who are its targets with other federal crimes.*

The Importance of Ethical Leadership

Talking about ethical business decision making is meaningless if management does not set standards. Furthermore, managers must apply the same standards to themselves as they do to the company's employees.

ATTITUDE OF TOP MANAGEMENT One of the more important ways to create and maintain an ethical workplace is for top management to demonstrate its commitment to ethical decision making. A manager who is not totally committed to an ethical workplace rarely succeeds in creating one. Management's behavior, more than anything else, sets the ethical tone of a firm. Employees take their cues from management. For example, an employee who observes a manager cheating on her expense account quickly learns that such behavior is acceptable.

Managers who set unrealistic production or sales goals increase the probability that employees will act unethically. If a sales quota can be met only through high-pressure, unethical sales tactics, employees will try to act "in the best interest of the company" and will continue to behave unethically.

A manager who looks the other way when he knows about an employee's unethical behavior also sets an example—one indicating that ethical transgressions will be accepted. Managers have found that discharging even one employee for ethical reasons has a tremendous impact as a deterrent to unethical behavior in the workplace.

BEHAVIOR OF OWNERS AND MANAGERS Business owners and managers sometimes take more active roles in fostering unethical and illegal conduct. This may indicate to their co-owners, co-managers, employees, and others that unethical business behavior will be tolerated.

Business owners' misbehavior can have negative consequences for themselves and their business. Not only can a court sanction the business owners and managers, but it can also issue an injunction that prevents them from engaging in similar patterns of conduct in the future.

CASE IN POINT Douglas and Brian Baum, along with their father, ran an asset recovery business. The Baums researched various unclaimed funds, tried to locate the rightful owners, and received either a finder's fee or the right to some or all of the funds recovered. The Baums convinced investors—through misrepresentation—to file a meritless lawsuit in a federal district court in Texas. The court later determined that the Baums had maliciously attempted to extort funds and sanctioned them for pretending to be lawyers, lying to the parties and the court, and generally abusing the judicial system. The judge also issued a permanent injunction against all three Baums to prohibit them from filing claims related to the same case without express permission from the judge. When the Baums continued their business in the same manner, the judge expanded the injunction to apply to all claims filed in Texas. The Baums appealed, claiming that the court lacked the power to expand the injunction. The appellate court ruled that federal courts have the power to enjoin (prevent) plaintiffs from future filings when those plaintiffs consistently abuse the court system and harass their opponents.[2]

The following case shows how a manager's sexist attitudes and actions affected the workplace environment. The case also underscores the limitations of the law with respect to this type of unethical business behavior.

---

2. *Baum v. Blue Moon Ventures, LLC,* 513 F.3d 181 (5th Cir. 2008).

✹ EXTENDED CASE 4.2 ✹
Krasner v. HSH Nordbank AG[a]

United States District Court, Southern District of New York, 680 F.Supp.2d 502 (2010).

IN THE LANGUAGE OF THE COURT

Gerard E. *LYNCH,* Circuit Judge.

Plaintiff David Krasner brings this action against his former employer, HSH Nordbank AG ("HSH"), and his supervisor while employed there, Roland Kiser, alleging [among other things] sexual discrimination * * * in violation of Title VII of the Civil Rights Act of 1964.[b]

* * * *

Defendant HSH is an international commercial bank, headquartered in Germany, and has offices worldwide, including a branch in New York City.

There, Krasner alleges, he encountered an atmosphere infected with overt sexism, where career "advancement based on sexual favoritism" was accepted, and where male supervisors promoted a sexist and demeaning image of women in the workplace in which women's advancement was governed by a "casting couch." * * * Kiser also pressured male subordinates, such as Krasner, to go to strip clubs with him when on business trips abroad.

* * * *

* * * The primary offender in Krasner's estimation is Kiser, and what takes center stage in the complaint are allegations of a relationship between Kiser and a woman named Melissa Campfield * * *. Kiser, it is alleged, "advance[ed] and promot[ed]" Campfield's career "at the expense of the career advancement and reputations of other far more senior and qualified employees," Krasner included.

* * * *

* * * On September 6, 2007, Krasner lodged a verbal, in-person complaint with * * * the Head of Human Resources, articulating his belief that "Kiser was violating [HSH's] ethics policy by creating a personal conflict of interest" and generally "creating an unprofessional environment."

* * * *

* * * On September 19, Krasner again turned to the Human Resources department, this time with a written complaint, reiterating his belief that Kiser was violating the company's ethics policy and creating an unprofessional environment through his relationship with Campfield.

* * * *

On October 3, HSH concluded its internal investigation of Krasner's complaints and found no violation of law or internal ethics policy. A month later, on November 5, 2007, Krasner was summarily terminated * * *.

Krasner subsequently sought and received a right to sue letter from the Equal Employment Opportunity Commission ("EEOC") and thereafter commenced this lawsuit * * *. Defendants—HSH and Kiser—move to dismiss.

* * * *

The substantive anti-discrimination provision of Title VII prohibits employers from "discriminat[ing] against any individual with respect to his compensation, terms, conditions, or privileges of employment, because of such individual's * * * sex. *One form of gender discrimination prohibited by Title VII is sexual harassment that results in a 'hostile or abusive work environment.'* " Under this doctrine,

even if an *"employee does not experience a specific negative action,"* he may have a viable claim under Title VII for sexual discrimination where *"the harassment is so pervasive that it changes the conditions of employment."* [Emphasis added.]

* * * *

Krasner's discrimination claim is founded on allegations that he was subject to a sexually hostile work environment through a combination of "(1) widespread sexual favoritism resulting from Kiser's affair with Campfield; (2) widespread sexual favoritism resulting from other affairs at [HSH]; and (3) sexually harassing and offensive conduct perpetrated by Kiser * * * unrelated to sexual affairs." In addressing these contentions, the parties argue as though a hostile environment is something that exists in some absolute way, like poisonous chemicals in the air, affecting everyone who comes in contact with it. In doing so, the parties all but ignore the prohibited causal factor requirement, which is critical to liability.

Title VII does not prohibit employers from maintaining nasty, unpleasant workplaces, or even ones that are unpleasant for reasons that are sexual in nature. Rather, it prohibits employers from discriminating against an employee (including by subjecting him or her to hostile working conditions) "because of such individual's * * * sex."

* * * *

An examination of Krasner's allegations reveals that he does not contend that he was disparaged or badly treated or subjected to an unpleasant work atmosphere in any way because he is a man. Rather, his complaint is primarily

---

a. *AG* stands for *Actiengesellschaft,* a German term denoting a corporation.

b. Title VII of the federal Civil Rights Act of 1964 prohibits employment discrimination on the basis of race, color, national origin, religion, or gender—see Chapter 22.

EXTENDED CASE 4.2 CONTINUED ⬇

that Kiser and other supervisors advanced a demeaning view of women in the workplace, which Krasner was exposed to and found "objectionable," and which denied "him the opportunity to work in an employment setting free of unlawful harassment."

* * * *

* * * Krasner's claim fails because "none of the alleged acts of harassment committed directly against [Krasner]"—either when viewed in isolation or in conjunction with any potential discrimination against women— "support a claim that [he] is being harassed because he is a *male* employee."

The primary animator of the complaint is what Krasner terms the "egregious effects of Kiser's favoritism" towards Campfield upon plaintiff himself.

Assuming that these actions * * * systematically and pervasively altered the conditions of Krasner's working environment sufficiently to satisfy the objective component of a hostile environment claim, the claim must nevertheless fail because the complaint does not allege that these incidents are in any way related to his gender. Krasner does not allege, and proffers [presents or offers] no facts that remotely suggest, that a female supervisor in his position would not have experienced exactly the same consequences from Kiser's preferential treatment of Campfield.

* * * *

For the foregoing reasons, defendants' motions to dismiss the complaint * * * are granted.

SO ORDERED.

QUESTIONS

1. Why did the court conclude that Krasner did not have a valid claim for "hostile environment" discrimination?
2. Suppose that a female employee had experienced the same type of treatment that Krasner had. Would the female employee succeed in a Title VII claim of gender-based discrimination? Why or why not?

Creating Ethical Codes of Conduct

One of the most effective ways of setting a tone of ethical behavior within an organization is to create an ethical code of conduct. A well-written code of ethics explicitly states a company's ethical priorities and demonstrates the company's commitment to ethical behavior.

The code of conduct indicates the company's commitment to legal compliance, as well as to the welfare of its customers or clients, its employees, and its suppliers. The code also details some specific ways in which the interests and welfare of these different groups will be protected.

ETHICS TRAINING FOR EMPLOYEES For an ethical code to be effective, its provisions must be clearly communicated to employees. Most large companies have implemented ethics training programs, in which managers discuss with employees on a face-to-face basis the firm's policies and the importance of ethical conduct. Some firms hold periodic ethics seminars during which employees can openly discuss any ethical problems that they may be experiencing and learn how the firm's ethical policies apply to those specific problems. Smaller firms should also offer some form of ethics training to employees because if a firm is accused of an ethics violation, the court will consider the presence or absence of such training in evaluating the firm's conduct.

THE SARBANES-OXLEY ACT The Sarbanes-Oxley Act of 2002[3] requires companies to set up confidential systems so that employees and others can "raise red flags" about suspected illegal or unethical auditing and accounting practices. (Excerpts and explanatory comments of the Sarbanes-Oxley Act appear in Appendix E of this text.)

Some companies have implemented online reporting systems to accomplish this goal. In one such system, employees can click on an icon on their computers that anonymously links them with EthicsPoint, an organization based in Portland, Oregon. Through EthicsPoint, employees can report suspicious accounting practices, sexual harassment, and other possibly unethical behavior. EthicsPoint, in turn, alerts management personnel or the audit committee at the designated company to the possible problem. Those who have used the system say that it is less inhibiting than calling a company's toll-free number.

---

3. 15 U.S.C. Sections 7201 *et seq.*

ETHICAL TRANSGRESSIONS BY FINANCIAL INSTITUTIONS

One of the best ways to learn the ethical responsibilities inherent in operating a business is to look at the mistakes made by other companies. In the following subsections, we describe some of the worst ethical failures of financial institutions during the latter part of the first decade of the 2000s. Many of these ethical wrongdoings received wide publicity and raised public awareness of the need for ethical leadership in all businesses.

Corporate Stock Buybacks

By now, you are probably aware that many of the greatest financial companies in the United States have either gone bankrupt, been taken over by the federal government, or been bailed out by U.S. taxpayers. What most people do not know is that those same corporations were using their own cash funds to prop up the value of their stock in the years just before the economic crisis that started in 2008.

THE RATIONALE UNDERLYING BUYBACKS The theory behind a **stock buyback** is simple—the management of a corporation believes that the market price of its shares is "below their fair value." Therefore, instead of issuing dividends to shareholders or reinvesting profits, management uses the company's funds to buy its shares in the open market, thereby boosting the price of the stock.

Who benefits from stock buybacks? Although all shareholders benefit somewhat, the main individual beneficiaries are often corporate executives who have been given **stock options,** which enable them to buy shares of the corporation's stock at a set price. When the market price rises above that level, the executives can profit by selling their shares. Although stock buybacks are legal and can serve legitimate purposes, they can easily be abused if managers use them just to increase the stock price in the short term so that they can profit from their options without considering the long-term needs of the company.

THE PREVALENCE OF BUYBACKS From 2005 to 2007, stock buybacks for the top five hundred U.S. corporations added up to $1.4 *trillion.* From 2003 to 2007, the five largest U.S banks bought back close to $100 *billion* in stock. Bank of America Corporation alone bought back $40 billion of its stock (nearly

40 percent of its common stock equity at the end of 2009) during that time period.[4]

In the investment banking business, which almost disappeared entirely in the latter half of 2008, stock buybacks were particularly egregious. In the first half of 2008, Lehman Brothers Holdings was buying back its own stock—in September of that year, it filed for bankruptcy. According to financial writer Liam Denning, Lehman's buybacks were "akin to giving away the fire extinguisher even as your house begins to fill with smoke." Goldman Sachs, another investment bank, bought back $15 billion of its stock in 2007. By the end of 2008, U.S. taxpayers had provided $10 billion in bailout funds to that same company.

Startling Executive Decisions at American International Group

For years, American International Group (AIG) was a respected, conservative, worldwide insurance company based in New York. Then, during the first decade of the 2000s, its managers decided to enter an area in which they had little expertise—the issuance of insurance contracts guaranteeing certain types of complicated financial contracts. When many of those insured contracts failed, AIG experienced multibillion-dollar losses. Ultimately, the company sought a federal bailout that eventually amounted to almost $200 billion of U.S. taxpayers' funds.

While some company executives were testifying before Congress after receiving the funds, other AIG executives spent almost $400,000 on a weeklong retreat at a resort in Monarch Beach, California. In essence, U.S. taxpayers were footing the bill. To most observers, such arrogance was as incomprehensible as it was unethical.

Executive Bonuses

Until the economic crisis began in the latter half of the first decade of the 2000s, the bonuses paid in the financial industry did not make headlines. After all, times were good, and why shouldn't those responsible for record company earnings be rewarded? When investment banks and commercial banks began to fail, however, or had to be bailed out or taken over by the federal government, executive bonuses became an issue of paramount importance.

---

4. This amount was almost as much as the $45 million that Bank of America received from the government bailout under the Troubled Asset Relief Program.

Certainly, the system of rewards in banking became perverse. Executives and others in the industry were paid a percentage of their firm's profits, no matter how risky their investment actions had been. In other words, commissions and bonuses were based on profits from transactions involving risky assets, such as collateralized debt obligations and securities based on subprime and other low-quality mortgages. In some instances, the assets were sold off to investors, but sometimes the firms themselves invested in the risky assets, which in the short run provided high returns. When the subprime mortgage crisis started in 2007, the worldwide house of cards came tumbling down, but those who had created and sold those risky assets suffered no liability—and even received bonuses. Of course, some of those firms that had enjoyed high short-run returns from their risky investments—and paid bonuses based on those profits—found themselves facing bankruptcy.

Consider Lehman Brothers before its bankruptcy. Its chief executive officer, Richard Fuld, Jr., earned almost $500 million between 2000 and the firm's demise in 2008. Even after Lehman Brothers entered into bankruptcy, its new owners, Barclays and Nomura, legally owed $3.5 billion in bonuses to employees still on the payroll. In 2006, Goldman Sachs awarded its employees a total of $16.5 billion in bonuses, or an average of almost $750,000 for each employee.

By 2007, profits on Wall Street had already begun to drop—sometimes dramatically. Citigroup's profits, for example, were down 83 percent from the previous year. Bonuses, in contrast, declined by less than 5 percent. The bonus payout in 2007 for all Wall Street firms combined was $33.2 billion.

SECTION 3
APPROACHES TO ETHICAL REASONING

Each individual, when faced with a particular ethical dilemma, engages in **ethical reasoning**—that is, a reasoning process in which the individual examines the situation at hand in light of his or her moral convictions or ethical standards. Businesspersons do likewise when making decisions with ethical implications.

How do business decision makers decide whether a given action is the "right" one for their firms? What ethical standards should be applied? Broadly speaking, ethical reasoning relating to business traditionally has been characterized by two fundamental

approaches. One approach defines ethical behavior in terms of duty, which also implies certain rights. The other approach determines what is ethical in terms of the consequences, or outcome, of any given action. We examine each of these approaches here.

In addition to the two basic ethical approaches, a few theories have been developed that specifically address the social responsibility of corporations. Because these theories also influence today's business decision makers, we conclude this section with a short discussion of the different views of corporate social responsibility.

Duty-Based Ethics

Duty-based ethical standards often are derived from revealed truths, such as religious precepts. They can also be derived through philosophical reasoning.

RELIGIOUS ETHICAL STANDARDS In the Judeo-Christian tradition, which is the dominant religious tradition in the United States, the Ten Commandments of the Old Testament establish fundamental rules for moral action. Other religions have their own sources of revealed truth. Religious rules generally are absolute with respect to the behavior of their adherents. For example, the commandment "Thou shalt not steal" is an absolute mandate for a person who believes that the Ten Commandments reflect revealed truth. Even a benevolent motive for stealing (such as Robin Hood's) cannot justify the act because the act itself is inherently immoral and thus wrong.

KANTIAN ETHICS Duty-based ethical standards may also be derived solely from philosophical reasoning. The German philosopher Immanuel Kant (1724–1804), for example, identified some general guiding principles for moral behavior based on what he believed to be the fundamental nature of human beings. Kant believed that human beings are qualitatively different from other physical objects and are endowed with moral integrity and the capacity to reason and conduct their affairs rationally. Therefore, a person's thoughts and actions should be respected. When human beings are treated merely as a means to an end, they are being treated as the equivalent of objects and are being denied their basic humanity.

A central theme in Kantian ethics is that individuals should evaluate their actions in light of the consequences that would follow if *everyone* in society acted in the same way. This **categorical imperative** can be applied to any action. Suppose that you are deciding whether to cheat on an examination. If you have adopted Kant's categorical imperative, you will decide *not* to cheat because if everyone cheated, the examination (and the entire education system) would be meaningless.

THE PRINCIPLE OF RIGHTS Because a duty cannot exist without a corresponding right, duty-based ethical standards imply that human beings have basic rights. The principle that human beings have certain fundamental rights (to life, freedom, and the pursuit of happiness, for example) is deeply embedded in Western culture. As discussed in Chapter 1, the natural law tradition embraces the concept that certain actions (such as killing another person) are morally wrong because they are contrary to nature (the natural desire to continue living). Those who adhere to this **principle of rights,** or "rights theory," believe that a key factor in determining whether a business decision is ethical is how that decision affects the rights of others. These others include the firm's owners, its employees, the consumers of its products or services, its suppliers, the community in which it does business, and society as a whole.

A potential dilemma for those who support rights theory, however, is that they may disagree on which rights are most important. When considering all those affected by a business decision, for example, how much weight should be given to employees relative to shareholders, customers relative to the community, or employees relative to society as a whole?

In general, rights theorists believe that whichever right is stronger in a particular circumstance takes precedence. Suppose that a firm can either keep a plant open, saving the jobs of twelve workers, or shut the plant down and avoid contaminating a river with pollutants that would endanger the health of thousands of people. In this situation, a rights theorist can easily choose which group to favor. (Not all choices are so clear-cut, however.)

Outcome-Based Ethics: Utilitarianism

"The greatest good for the greatest number" is a paraphrase of the major premise of the utilitarian approach to ethics. **Utilitarianism** is a philosophical theory developed by Jeremy Bentham (1748–1832) and modified by John Stuart Mill (1806–1873)—both British philosophers. In contrast to duty-based ethics, utilitarianism is outcome oriented. It focuses on the consequences of an action, not on the nature of the action itself or on any set of preestablished moral values or religious beliefs.

Under a utilitarian model of ethics, an action is morally correct, or "right," when, among the people it affects, it produces the greatest amount of good for the greatest number. When an action affects the majority adversely, it is morally wrong. Applying the utilitarian theory thus requires (1) a determination of which individuals will be affected by the action in question; (2) a **cost-benefit analysis,** which involves an assessment of the negative and positive effects of alternative actions on these individuals; and (3) a choice among alternative actions that will produce maximum societal utility (the greatest positive net benefits for the greatest number of individuals).

Corporate Social Responsibility

For many years, groups concerned with civil rights, employee safety and welfare, consumer protection, environmental preservation, and other causes have pressured corporate America to behave in a responsible manner with respect to these causes. Thus was born the concept of **corporate social responsibility**—the idea that those who run corporations can and should act ethically and be accountable to society for their actions. Just what constitutes corporate social responsibility has been debated for some time, and there are a number of different theories today.

STAKEHOLDER APPROACH One view of corporate social responsibility stresses that corporations have a duty not just to shareholders, but also to other groups affected by corporate decisions ("stakeholders"). Under this approach, a corporation would consider the impact of its decision on the firm's employees, customers, creditors, suppliers, and the community in which the corporation operates. The reasoning behind this "stakeholder view" is that in some circumstances, one or more of these other groups may have a greater stake in company decisions than the shareholders do. Although this may be true, it is often difficult to decide which group's interests should receive greater weight if the interests conflict.

CORPORATE CITIZENSHIP Another theory of social responsibility argues that corporations should behave as good citizens by promoting goals that society deems worthwhile and taking positive steps toward solving social problems. The idea is that because business controls so much of the wealth and power of this country, business in turn has a responsibility to society to use that wealth and power in socially beneficial ways. Under a corporate citizenship view, companies are judged on how much they donate to social causes, as well as how they conduct their operations with respect to employment discrimination, human rights, environmental concerns, and similar issues.

Some corporations publish annual social responsibility reports, which may also be called corporate sustainability (*sustainability* refers to the capacity to endure) or citizenship reports. For example, the Hitachi Group releases an Annual Corporate Social Responsibility Report that outlines its environmental strategy, including its attempts to reduce carbon dioxide emissions (so-called greenhouse gases). It typically discusses human rights policy and its

commitment to human rights awareness. The software company Symantec Corporation issued its first corporate responsibility report in September 2008 to demonstrate its focus on critical environmental, social, and governance issues. Among other things, Symantec pointed out that it had adopted the Calvert Women's Principles, the first global code of corporate conduct designed to empower, advance, and invest in women worldwide.

In the following case, a corporation's board of directors focused solely on the shareholders' profits and failed to check the actions of the firm's chief executive officer. If the board had applied a different set of priorities, the shareholders might have been in a better financial position.

CASE 4.3
Fog Cutter Capital Group, Inc. v. Securities and Exchange Commission

United States Court of Appeals, District of Columbia Circuit, 474 F.3d 822 (2007).

BACKGROUND AND FACTS • The National Association of Securities Dealers (NASD) operates the Nasdaq, an electronic securities exchange, on which Fog Cutter Capital Group was listed.[a] Andrew Wiederhorn had founded Fog Cutter in 1997 to manage a restaurant chain and make other investments. With family members, Wiederhorn controlled more than 50 percent of Fog Cutter's stock. The firm agreed that if Wiederhorn was terminated "for cause," he was entitled only to his salary through the date of termination. If terminated "without cause," he would be owed three times his $350,000 annual salary, three times his largest annual bonus from the previous three years, and any unpaid salary and bonus. "Cause" included the conviction of a felony. In 2001, Wiederhorn became the target of an investigation into the collapse of Capital Consultants, LLC. Fog Cutter then redefined "cause" in his termination agreement to cover only a felony involving Fog Cutter. In June 2004, Wiederhorn agreed to plead guilty to two felonies, serve eighteen months in prison, pay a $25,000 fine, and pay $2 million to Capital Consultants. The day before he entered his plea, Fog Cutter agreed that while he was in prison, he would keep his title, responsibilities, salary, bonuses, and other benefits. It also agreed to a $2 million "leave-of-absence payment." In July, the NASD delisted Fog Cutter from the Nasdaq. Fog Cutter appealed this decision to the Securities and Exchange Commission (SEC), which dismissed the appeal. Fog Cutter petitioned the U.S. Court of Appeals for the District of Columbia Circuit for review.

IN THE LANGUAGE OF THE COURT
RANDOLPH, Circuit Judge.
* * * *

Fog Cutter's main complaint is that the Commission failed to take into account the company's sound business reasons for acting as it did. The decision to enter into the leave-of-absence agreement was, Fog Cutter argues, in the best interest of its shareholders. The company tells us that Wiederhorn's continuing commitment to the company and his return to an active role in the company after his incarceration were essential to preserving Fog Cutter's core business units.
* * * *

* * * Fog Cutter made a deal with Wiederhorn that cost the company $4.75 million in a year in which it reported a $3.93 million net loss. We know as well that Fog Cutter handed

---

a. Securities (stocks and bonds) can be bought and sold through national exchanges. Whether a security is listed on an exchange is subject to the discretion of the organization that operates it. The Securities and Exchange Commission oversees the securities exchanges.

CASE 4.3 CONTINUED ➡ Wiederhorn a $2 million bonus right before he went off to prison, a bonus stemming directly from the consequences of Wiederhorn's criminal activity.

* * * *

Here there was ample evidence supporting the NASD's grounds for taking action against Fog Cutter: Wiederhorn's guilty plea, the leave-of-absence deal and its cost to the company, the Board's determination that Wiederhorn should retain his positions with Fog Cutter, and the concern that Wiederhorn would continue to exert influence on company affairs even while he was in prison. *The decision was in accordance with NASD rules giving the organization broad discretion to determine whether the public interest requires delisting securities in light of events at a company. That rule is obviously consistent with the [law], and NASD's decision did not burden competition.* [Emphasis added.]

Fog Cutter claims that it had to pay Wiederhorn and retain him because if it fired him in light of his guilty plea, it would have owed him $6 million. This scarcely speaks well for the company's case. The potential obligation is a result of an amendment the Board granted Wiederhorn in 2003 while he was under investigation. * * * Before the amendment to Wiederhorn's employment agreement in 2003, termination "for cause" included the conviction of any felony other than a traffic offense. In the 2003 amendment, the relevant provision allowed the Board to terminate Wiederhorn "for cause" upon conviction of a felony involving Fog Cutter. The Board had known about the investigation of Wiederhorn in connection with Capital Consultants for more than two years when it agreed to this amendment.

Fog Cutter thinks NASD's action was "unfair." But it was the company that bowed to Wiederhorn's demand for an amendment to his employment agreement, knowing full well that it was dramatically increasing the cost of firing him. Now it argues that terminating Wiederhorn would have been too expensive. One is reminded of the old saw about the child who murders his parents and then asks for mercy because he is an orphan. The makeup of Fog Cutter's Board was virtually unchanged between the time it amended the employment agreement and entered into the leave-of-absence agreement. It was, to say the least, not arbitrary or capricious for the Commission to find that Wiederhorn exercised thorough control over the Board, and to find this troubling. We agree that the Board provided little or no check on Wiederhorn's conduct, and that the Board's actions only aggravated the concerns Wiederhorn's conviction and imprisonment raised.

That Fog Cutter did not itself violate the [law] and that it disclosed the relevant events does not demonstrate any error in the delisting decision. The NASD's rules state that it may apply criteria more stringent than the minimum [legal] standards for listing. Fog Cutter's disclosure of its arrangements with Wiederhorn did not change the nature of those arrangements, which is what led the NASD to find that the company's actions were contrary to the public interest and a threat to public confidence in the Nasdaq exchange.

DECISION AND REMEDY • *The U.S. Court of Appeals for the District of Columbia Circuit denied Fog Cutter's petition for review of the SEC's decision. The NASD was concerned with "the integrity and the public's perception of the Nasdaq exchange" in light of Wiederhorn's legal troubles and the Fog Cutter board's acquiescence to his demands. The SEC "amply supported these concerns and was well within its authority to dismiss Fog Cutter's" appeal.*

THE ETHICAL DIMENSION • *Should more consideration have been given to the fact that Fog Cutter was not convicted of a violation of the law? Why or why not?*

THE GLOBAL DIMENSION • *What does the decision in this case suggest to foreign investors who may be considering investments in securities listed on U.S. exchanges?*

A WAY OF DOING BUSINESS A survey of U.S. executives undertaken by the Boston College Center for Corporate Citizenship found that more than 70 percent of those polled agreed that corporate citizenship must be treated as a priority. More than 60 percent said that good corporate citizenship added to their companies' profits. Strategist Michelle Bernhart has argued that corporate social responsibility cannot attain its maximum effectiveness unless it is treated as a way of doing business rather than as a special program.

Not all socially responsible activities can benefit a corporation, however. Corporate responsibility is most successful when a company undertakes activities that are relevant and significant to its stakeholders and related to its business operations. For example, the Brazilian firm Companhia Vale do Rio Doce is one of the world's largest diversified metals and mining companies. In 2008, it invested more than $150 million in social projects involving health care, infrastructure, and education. At the same time, it invested more than $300 million in environmental protection. One of its projects involves the rehabilitation of native species in the Amazon Valley. To that end, the company is planting almost 200 million trees in an attempt to restore 1,150 square miles of land where cattle breeding and farming have caused deforestation.

EMPLOYEE RECRUITING AND RETENTION A key corporate stakeholder is a company's workforce, which may include potential employees—job seekers. Surveys of college students about to enter the job market confirm that young people are looking for socially responsible employers. Younger workers are generally altruistic. They want to work for a company that allows them to participate in community projects.

Corporations that engage in meaningful social activities retain workers longer, particularly younger ones. At the accounting firm PKF Texas, for instance, employees support a variety of business, educational, and philanthropic organizations. As a result, this company is able to recruit and retain a younger workforce. Its turnover rate is half the industry average.

_____ SECTION 4 _____
MAKING ETHICAL BUSINESS DECISIONS

As Dean Krehmeyer, executive director of the Business Roundtable's Institute for Corporate Ethics, once said, "Evidence strongly suggests being ethical—doing the right thing—pays." Instilling ethical business decision making into the fabric of a business organization is no small task, even if ethics "pays." The job is to get people to understand that they have to think more broadly about how their decisions will affect employees, shareholders, customers, and even the community. Great companies,

such as Enron and the worldwide accounting firm Arthur Andersen, were brought down by the unethical behavior of a few. A two-hundred-year-old British investment banking firm, Barings Bank, was destroyed by the actions of one employee and a few of his friends. Clearly, ensuring that all employees get on the ethical business decision-making "bandwagon" is crucial in today's fast-paced world.

The George S. May International Company has provided six basic guidelines to help corporate employees judge their actions. Each employee—no matter what her or his level in the organization—should evaluate every action using the following six guidelines:

1. *The law.* Is the action you are considering legal? If you do not know the laws governing the action, then find out. Ignorance of the law is no excuse.
2. *Rules and procedures.* Are you following the internal rules and procedures that have already been laid out by your company? They have been developed to avoid problems. Is what you are planning to do consistent with your company's policies and procedures? If not, stop.
3. *Values.* Laws and internal company policies reinforce society's values. You might wish to ask yourself whether you are attempting to find a loophole in the law or in your company's policies. Next, you have to ask yourself whether you are following the "spirit" of the law as well as the letter of the law or the internal policy.
4. *Conscience.* If you feel any guilt, let your conscience be your guide. Alternatively, ask yourself whether you would be happy to be interviewed by national news media about the action you are going to take.
5. *Promises.* Every business organization is based on trust. Your customers believe that your company will do what it is supposed to do. The same is true for your suppliers and employees. Will your action live up to the commitments you have made to others, both inside the business and outside?
6. *Heroes.* We all have heroes who are role models for us. Is what you are planning on doing an action that your "hero" would take? If not, how would your hero act? That is how you should be acting.

Globalization makes it increasingly difficult for major corporations to differentiate themselves from the competition based solely on their products. See this chapter's *Shifting Legal Priorities for Business* feature on the following page for another way that corporations may gain an edge over their competitors.

The worldwide explosion of information technology has made socially responsible behavior more important simply because it has become increasingly difficult to hide bad corporate behavior. In our transparent global economy, corporations that "outbehave" their competition ethically may also outperform them financially.

The Difficulty of Managing a Company's Reputation

Before the advent of the Internet, a corporation that faced an ugly public relations situation—a product that had injured several consumers, for example—simply hired crisis-management consultants and then hid behind lawyers. Today, corporations can no longer manage their reputations the old-fashioned way. Now, when customers are unhappy or employees are disgruntled, they let the entire world know by dashing off a blog posting or putting a video clip on YouTube. In this online environment, corporations cannot control their stories. They can, however, control the way management operates.

Differentiation through "Doing Good"

In today's global economy, companies need to find ways other than through their products or services to differentiate themselves from their competitors. Even if they produce a quality product, chances are that another company somewhere in the world will copy it and sell it for less. Companies must now compete in other areas, including how responsible their behavior is. For instance, how does the company treat its customers and employees?

A key component of responsible behavior is the creation of trust between companies and their customers, employees, and suppliers. Companies that build trust also enjoy higher profits. Numerous studies have shown a strong correlation between the cost of obtaining supplies and the level of trust between the buyer of those raw materials and the seller. The less trust there is between the purchaser and the seller, the higher the procurement costs—and sometimes by a significant margin.

Online Access to the Best Leadership Practices

Fortunately, managers no longer have to create from scratch the best socially responsible leadership practices. The Boston College Center for Corporate Citizenship sponsors an online community where member companies share their best practices for corporate social responsibility. This online community offers user-generated advice and access to numerous business case studies from Boston College's Carroll School of Management. Some of this advice is particularly useful for companies attempting to expand into other countries. Their managers need to understand what social issues matter most in those countries. They can obtain this information from the Center for Corporate Citizenship.

Sustainability Counts, Too

MIT's Sloan School of Management offers custom courses on sustainability. These courses can help managers understand that sustainability is a business opportunity and how to integrate sustainability into their evaluation of risk. One of the first companies to send its executives and directors to this course was Itaú Unibanco S.A., a large Brazilian financial services corporation.

MANAGERIAL IMPLICATIONS

We live in a small world, and it is getting smaller. Managers must recognize that everything they and their co-workers do can be instantaneously communicated around the world. Whenever a manager considers acting in a socially irresponsible way, he or she should envision a YouTube video exposing those actions to millions of viewers.

SECTION 5
PRACTICAL SOLUTIONS TO CORPORATE ETHICS QUESTIONS

Corporate ethics officers and ethics committees require a practical method to investigate and solve specific ethics problems. Ethics consultant Leonard H. Bucklin of Corporate-Ethics.US™ has devised a procedure that he calls Business Process Pragmatism™. It involves five steps:

1. *Inquiry.* Of course, the process must begin with an understanding of the facts. The parties involved might include the mass media, the public, employees, or customers. At this stage, the ethical problem or problems are specified. A list of relevant ethics principles is created.

2. *Discussion.* Here, a list of action options is developed. Each option carries with it certain ethical

principles. In addition, resolution goals should be listed.

3. *Decision.* In this step, those participating in the process craft a consensus decision, or a consensus plan of action, for the corporation.

4. *Justification.* Will the consensus solution withstand moral scrutiny? At this point in the process, reasons should be attached to each proposed action or series of actions. Will the stakeholders involved accept these reasons?

5. *Evaluation.* Do the solutions to the corporate ethics issue satisfy corporate values, community values, and individual values? Ultimately, can the consensus resolution withstand moral scrutiny of the decisions made and the process used to reach those decisions?

SECTION 6
BUSINESS ETHICS ON A GLOBAL LEVEL

Given the various cultures and religions throughout the world, conflicts in ethics frequently arise between foreign and U.S. businesspersons. For example, in certain countries the consumption of alcohol and specific foods is forbidden for religious reasons. Under such circumstances, it would be thoughtless and imprudent for a U.S. businessperson to invite a local business contact out for a drink.

The role played by women in other countries may also present some difficult ethical problems for firms doing business internationally. Equal employment opportunity is a fundamental public policy in the United States, and Title VII of the Civil Rights Act of 1964 prohibits discrimination against women in the employment context (see Chapter 22). Some other countries, however, offer little protection for women against gender discrimination in the workplace, including sexual harassment.

We look here at how the employment practices that affect workers in other countries, particularly developing countries, have created some difficult ethical problems for U.S. sellers of goods manufactured in foreign nations. We also examine some of the ethical ramifications of the U.S. law prohibiting bribery of foreign officials.

The Monitoring of Employment Practices of Foreign Suppliers

Many U.S. businesses contract with companies in developing nations to produce goods, such as shoes and clothing, because the wage rates in those nations are significantly lower than those in the United States. Yet what if a foreign company hires women and children at below-minimum-wage rates, for example, or requires its employees to work long hours in a workplace full of health hazards? What if the company's supervisors routinely engage in workplace conduct that is offensive to women?

Given today's global communications network, few companies can assume that their actions in other nations will go unnoticed by "corporate watch" groups that discover and publicize unethical corporate behavior. As a result, U.S. businesses today usually take steps to avoid such adverse publicity—either by refusing to deal with certain suppliers or by arranging to monitor their suppliers' workplaces to make sure that the employees are not being mistreated.

By providing a forum for complaints, the Internet has increased the potential for damage to the reputation of any major (or minor) corporation at the hands of disgruntled employees or consumers, as well as special interest groups. Wal-Mart and Nike in particular have been frequent targets for advocacy groups that believe that those corporations exploit their workers. Although some of these complaints may be unfounded or exaggerated, the courts generally have refused to consider them defamatory (the tort of defamation will be discussed in Chapter 12). Most courts have regarded online attacks as simply the expression of opinion and therefore a form of speech protected by the First Amendment.

The Foreign Corrupt Practices Act

Another ethical problem in international business dealings has to do with the legitimacy of certain side payments to government officials. In the United States, the majority of contracts are formed within the private sector. In many foreign countries, however, government officials make the decisions on most major construction and manufacturing contracts because of extensive government regulation and control over trade and industry. Side payments to government officials in exchange for favorable business contracts are not unusual in such countries, nor are they considered to be unethical. In the past, U.S. corporations doing business in these nations largely followed the dictum "When in Rome, do as the Romans do."

In the 1970s, however, the U.S. media uncovered a number of business scandals involving large side payments by U.S. corporations to foreign representatives for the purpose of securing advantageous international trade contracts. In response to this unethical behavior, in 1977 Congress passed the Foreign Corrupt Practices Act[5] (FCPA), which prohibits U.S. businesspersons from bribing foreign officials to secure beneficial contracts.

PROHIBITION AGAINST THE BRIBERY OF FOREIGN OFFICIALS The first part of the FCPA applies to all U.S. companies and their directors, officers, shareholders, employees, and agents. This part prohibits the bribery of most officials of foreign governments if the purpose of the payment is to get the official to act in his or her official capacity to provide business opportunities.

The FCPA does not prohibit payment of substantial sums to minor officials whose duties are ministerial. These payments are often referred to as "grease," or facilitating payments. They are meant to accelerate the performance of administrative services that might otherwise be carried out at a slow pace. Thus, for example, if a firm makes a payment to a minor official to speed up an import licensing process, the firm has not violated the FCPA. Generally, the act, as amended, permits payments to foreign officials if such payments are lawful within the foreign country. The act also does not prohibit payments to private foreign companies or other third parties unless the U.S. firm knows that the payments will be passed on to a foreign government in violation of the FCPA.

BRIBERY BY FOREIGN COMPANIES Until a few years ago, the application of the FCPA was confined to

---

5. 15 U.S.C. Sections 78dd-1 *et seq.*

U.S. companies that allegedly bribed foreign officials. More recently, the act has become an instrument for prosecuting foreign companies suspected of bribing officials outside the United States. The U.S. Department of Justice estimates that more than fifty such cases are under investigation or prosecution within this country. Today, the Federal Bureau of Investigation has a five-member team to examine possible violations of U.S. laws by foreign corporations in their attempts to secure business.

ACCOUNTING REQUIREMENTS In the past, bribes were often concealed in corporate financial records. Thus, the second part of the FCPA is directed toward accountants. All companies must keep detailed records that "accurately and fairly" reflect their financial activities. In addition, all companies must have accounting systems that provide "reasonable assurance" that all transactions entered into by the companies are accounted for and legal. These requirements assist in detecting illegal bribes. The FCPA further prohibits any person from making false statements to accountants or false entries in any record or account.

PENALTIES FOR VIOLATIONS The FCPA provides that business firms that violate the act may be fined up to $2 million. Individual officers or directors who violate the FCPA may be fined up to $100,000 (the fine cannot be paid by the company) and may be imprisoned for up to five years.

REVIEWING
Ethics and Business Decision Making

Isabel Arnett was promoted to chief executive officer (CEO) of Tamik, Inc., a pharmaceutical company that manufactures a vaccine called Kafluk, which supposedly provides some defense against bird flu. The company began marketing Kafluk throughout Asia. After numerous media reports that bird flu could soon become a worldwide epidemic, the demand for Kafluk increased, sales soared, and Tamik earned record profits. Tamik's CEO, Arnett, then began receiving disturbing reports from Southeast Asia that in some patients, Kafluk had caused psychiatric disturbances, including severe hallucinations, and heart and lung problems. Arnett was informed that six children in Japan had committed suicide by jumping out of windows after receiving the vaccine. To cover up the story and prevent negative publicity, Arnett instructed Tamik's partners in Asia to offer cash to the Japanese families whose children had died in exchange for their silence. Arnett also refused to authorize additional research within the company to study the potential side effects of Kafluk. Using the information presented in the chapter, answer the following questions.

1. This scenario illustrates one of the main reasons why ethical problems occur in business. What is that reason?

REVIEWING
Ethics and Business Decision Making, Continued

2. Would a person who adheres to the principle of rights consider it ethical for Arnett not to disclose potential safety concerns and to refuse to perform additional research on Kafluk? Why or why not?

3. If Kafluk prevented fifty Asian people who were infected with bird flu from dying, would Arnett's conduct in this situation be ethical under a utilitarian model of ethics? Why or why not?

4. Did Tamik or Arnett violate the Foreign Corrupt Practices Act in this scenario? Why or why not?

⚙ DEBATE THIS: *Executives in large corporations are ultimately rewarded if their companies do well, particularly as evidenced by rising stock prices. Consequently, shouldn't we just let those who run corporations decide what level of negative side effects of their goods or services is "acceptable"?*

TERMS AND CONCEPTS

business ethics 76
categorical imperative 83

corporate social
    responsibility 84
cost-benefit analysis 84
ethical reasoning 83

ethics 76
moral minimum 77
principle of rights 84

stock buyback 82
stock options 82
utilitarianism 84

QUESTIONS AND CASE PROBLEMS

4–1. Business Ethics Jason Trevor owns a commercial bakery in Blakely, Georgia, that produces a variety of goods sold in grocery stores. Trevor is required by law to perform internal tests on food produced at his plant to check for contamination. On three occasions, the tests of food products containing peanut butter were positive for salmonella contamination. Trevor was not required to report the results to U.S. Food and Drug Administration officials, however, so he did not. Instead, Trevor instructed his employees to simply repeat the tests until the results were negative. Meanwhile, the products that had originally tested positive for salmonella were shipped out to retailers. Five people who ate Trevor's baked goods that year became seriously ill, and one person died from a salmonella infection. Even though Trevor's conduct was legal, was it unethical for him to sell goods that had once tested positive for salmonella? If Trevor had followed the six basic guidelines for making ethical business decisions, would he still have sold the contaminated goods? Why or why not?

4–2. QUESTION WITH SAMPLE ANSWER: Approaches to Ethical Reasoning.

Shokun Steel Co. owns many steel plants. One of its plants is much older than the others. Equipment at the old plant is outdated and inefficient, and the costs of production at that plant are now twice as high as at any of Shokun's other plants. Shokun cannot increase the price of its steel because of competition, both domestic and international. The plant employs more than a thousand workers; it is located in Twin Firs, Pennsylvania, which has a population of about forty-five thousand. Shokun is contemplating whether to close the plant. What factors should the firm consider in making its decision? Will the firm violate any ethical duties if it closes the plant? Analyze these questions from the two basic perspectives on ethical reasoning discussed in this chapter.

• **For a sample answer to Question 4–2, go to Appendix F at the end of this text.**

4–3. Ethical Conduct Unable to pay more than $1.2 billion in debt, Big Mountain Metals, Inc., filed a petition to declare bankruptcy in a federal bankruptcy court in July 2009. Among Big Mountain's creditors were several banks, including Bank of New London and Suzuki Bank. The court appointed Morgan Crawford to work as a "disinterested" (neutral) party with Big Mountain and the creditors to resolve their disputes; the court set an hourly fee as Crawford's compensation. Crawford told the banks that he wanted them to pay him an additional percentage fee based on his "success" in finding "new value" to pay Big Mountain's debts. He said that without such a deal, he would not perform his mediation duties. Suzuki Bank agreed; the other banks disputed the deal, but no one told the court. In October 2010, Crawford asked the court for nearly $2.5 million in compensation, including the hourly fees, which totaled about $531,000, and the percentage fees. Big Mountain and others asked the court to deny Crawford any fees on the basis that he had improperly negotiated "secret side agreements." How did Crawford violate his duties as a "disinterested" party? Should he be denied compensation? Why or why not?

4–4. Ethical Conduct Ernest Price suffered from sickle-cell anemia. In 1997, Price asked Dr. Ann Houston, his physician, to prescribe OxyContin, a strong narcotic, for the pain. Over the next several years, Price saw at least ten different physicians at ten different clinics in two cities, and used seven pharmacies in three cities, to obtain and fill simultaneous prescriptions for OxyContin. In March 2001, when Houston learned of these activities, she refused to write more prescriptions for Price. As other physicians became aware of Price's actions, they also stopped writing his prescriptions. Price filed a suit in a Mississippi state court against Purdue Pharma Co. and other producers and distributors of OxyContin, as well as his physicians and the pharmacies that had filled the prescriptions. Price alleged negligence, among other things, claiming that OxyContin's addictive nature caused him injury and that this was the defendants' fault. The defendants argued that Price's claim should be dismissed because it arose from his own wrongdoing. Who should be held *legally* liable? Should any of the parties be considered ethically responsible? Why or why not? [*Price v. Purdue Pharma Co.*, 920 So.2d 479 (Miss. 2006)]

4–5. CASE PROBLEM WITH SAMPLE ANSWER: Ethical Leadership.

In 1999, Andrew Fastow, chief financial officer of Enron Corp., asked Merrill Lynch, an investment firm, to participate in a bogus sale of three barges so that Enron could record earnings of $12.5 million from the sale. Through a third entity, Fastow bought the barges back within six months and paid Merrill for its participation. Five Merrill employees were convicted of conspiracy to commit wire fraud, in part, on an "honest-services" theory. Under this theory, an employee deprives his or her employer of "honest services" when the employee promotes his or her own interests, rather than the interests of the employer. Four of the employees appealed to the U.S. Court of Appeals for the Fifth Circuit, arguing that this charge did not apply to the conduct in which they engaged. The court agreed, reasoning that the barge deal was conducted to benefit Enron, not to enrich the Merrill employees at Enron's expense. Meanwhile, Kevin Howard, chief financial officer of Enron Broadband Services (EBS), engaged in "Project Braveheart," which enabled EBS to show earnings of $111 million in 2000 and 2001. Braveheart involved the sale of an interest in the future revenue of a video-on-demand venture to nCube, a small technology firm, which was paid for its help when EBS bought the interest back. Howard was convicted of wire fraud, in part, on the "honest-services" theory. He filed a motion to vacate his

conviction on the same basis that the Merrill employees had argued. Did Howard act unethically? Explain. Should the court grant his motion? Discuss. [United States v. Howard, 471 F.Supp.2d 772 (S.D.Tex. 2007)]

- **To view a sample answer for Problem 4–5, go to this book's Web site at www.cengage.com/blaw/cross, select "Chapter 4," and click on "Case Problem with Sample Answer."**

4–6. Corporate Social Responsibility Methamphetamine (meth) is an addictive, synthetic drug made chiefly in small toxic labs (STLs) in homes, tents, barns, or hotel rooms. The manufacturing process is dangerous and often results in explosions, burns, and toxic fumes. The government has spent considerable resources to find and eradicate STLs, imprison meth dealers and users, treat addicts, and provide services for families affected by these activities. Meth cannot be made without ephedrine or pseudoephedrine, which are ingredients in cold and allergy medications. Arkansas has one of the highest numbers of STLs in the United States. In an effort to recoup the costs of dealing with the meth epidemic, twenty counties in Arkansas filed a suit in a federal district court against Pfizer, Inc., and other companies that make or distribute cold and allergy medications. What is the defendants' ethical responsibility in this case, and to whom do they owe it? Why? [*Ashley County, Arkansas v. Pfizer, Inc.*, 552 F.3d 659 (8th Cir. 2009)]

4–7. Business Ethics on a Global Scale In the 1990s, Pfizer, Inc., developed a new antibiotic called Trovan (trovafloxacin mesylate). Tests showed that in animals Trovan had life-threatening side effects, including joint disease, abnormal cartilage growth, liver damage, and a degenerative bone condition. In 1996, an epidemic of bacterial meningitis swept across Nigeria. Pfizer sent three U.S. physicians to test Trovan on children who were patients in Nigeria's Infectious Disease Hospital. Pfizer did not obtain the patients' consent, alert them to the risks, or tell them that Médecins Sans Frontières (Doctors Without Borders) was providing an effective conventional treatment at the same site. Eleven children died in the experiment, and others were left blind, deaf, paralyzed, or brain damaged. Rabi Abdullahi and other Nigerian children filed a suit in a U.S. federal district court against Pfizer, alleging a violation of a customary international law norm prohibiting involuntary medical experimentation on humans. Did Pfizer violate any ethical standards? What might Pfizer have done to avert the consequences? Explain. [*Abdullahi v. Pfizer, Inc.*, 562 F.3d 163 (2d Cir. 2009)]

4–8. Violation of Internal Ethical Codes Havensure, LLC, an insurance broker, approached York International to determine whether it could provide insurance for York at a better rate. At the time, York was obtaining its group insurance from Prudential Insurance Co. through Universal Life Resources (ULR), another insurance broker. York allowed Havensure to study its policies. Havensure discovered that the premium Prudential charged included a hidden broker's fee that it used to pay ULR. When Havensure claimed that it could get the insurance at a lower price, York agreed that Havensure could send requests for proposals to various insurance companies. To keep York's business, Prudential offered to match the lowest rate quoted. Prudential also informed York that it must continue to buy the policy through ULR, not through Havensure. York agreed. Havensure then sued Prudential for wrongful interference with a business relationship (a tort that will be discussed in Chapter 12). The trial court held for Prudential. Havensure appealed. The appeals court held that although Prudential had violated its own code of ethics by having a hidden fee for a broker, and might have violated New York insurance law, Havensure still had no case. Why would a court find that a firm that violated its own rules, and might have violated the law, had no obligation for the loss it might have imposed on another firm trying to compete for business? Does this ruling make sense? Why or why not? [*Havensure, LLC v. Prudential Insurance Co. of America*, 595 F.3d 312 (6th Cir. 2010)]

4–9. A QUESTION OF ETHICS: Copyrights.

Steven Soderbergh is the Academy Award–winning director of Erin Brockovich, Traffic, *and many other films. CleanFlicks, LLC, filed a suit in a federal district court against Soderbergh, fifteen other directors, and the Directors Guild of America. The plaintiff asked the court to rule that it had the right to sell DVDs of the defendants' films altered without the defendants' consent to delete scenes of "sex, nudity, profanity and gory violence." CleanFlicks sold or rented the edited DVDs under the slogan "It's About Choice" to consumers, sometimes indirectly through retailers. It would not sell to retailers that made unauthorized copies of the edited films. The defendants, with DreamWorks, LLC, and seven other movie studios that own the copyrights to the films, filed a counterclaim against CleanFlicks and others engaged in the same business, alleging copyright infringement. Those filing the counterclaim asked the court to prevent CleanFlicks and the others from making and marketing altered versions of the films. [CleanFlicks of Colorado, LLC v. Soderbergh, 433 F.Supp.2d 1236 (D.Colo. 2006)]*

(a) Movie studios often edit their films to conform to content and other standards and sell the edited versions to network television and other commercial buyers. In this case, however, the studios objected when CleanFlicks edited the films and sold the altered versions directly to consumers. Similarly, CleanFlicks made unauthorized copies of the studios' DVDs to edit the films, but objected to others' making unauthorized copies of the altered versions. Is there anything unethical about these apparently contradictory positions? Why or why not?

(b) CleanFlicks and its competitors asserted, among other things, that they were making "fair use" of the studios' copyrighted works. They argued that by their actions "they are criticizing the objectionable content commonly found in current movies and that they are providing more socially acceptable alternatives to enable families to view the films together, without exposing children to the presumed harmful effects emanating from the objectionable content." If you were the judge, how would you view this argument? Is a court the appropriate forum for making determinations of public or social policy? Explain.

4–10. VIDEO QUESTION: Business Ethics.

Go to this text's Web site at **www.cengage.com/ blaw/cross** and select "Chapter 4." Click on "Video Questions" and view the video titled *Real World Legal: Pharzime, Scene 1 and Scene 2.* Then answer the following questions.

(a) In *Scene 1,* two employees discuss whether to market their company's drug as a treatment for other conditions—even though the U.S. Food and Drug Administration (FDA) approved the drug for treating only epilepsy. One employee argues that marketing the drug for more than the one treatment will increase the company's short-term profits and that obtaining the FDA approval for the other treatments will take too long. What theory describes this employee's perspective?

(b) In *Scene 2,* a new sales rep discusses the company's off-label marketing strategy with a veteran sales rep. Is it unethical or illegal for a sales rep to represent that he is a doctor when he has a doctorate degree in chemistry but is not actually a physician? Explain.

(c) In *Scene 2,* when the new sales rep suggests that they talk with the corporation's legal or human resources department about the drug's safety for off-label uses, how does the woman respond? Does her response encourage ethical conduct? Discuss fully.

LEGAL RESEARCH EXERCISES ON THE WEB

Go to this text's Web site at **www.cengage.com/blaw/cross**, select "Chapter 4," and click on "Practical Internet Exercises." There you will find the following Internet research exercises that you can perform to learn more about the topics covered in this chapter.

Practical Internet Exercise 4–1:   **Legal Perspective**
                                    Ethics in Business

Practical Internet Exercise 4–2:   **Management Perspective**
                                    Environmental Self-Audits

In Chapter 4, we examined the importance of ethical standards in the business context. We also offered suggestions on how business decision makers can create an ethical workplace. Certainly, it is not wrong for a businessperson to try to increase his or her firm's profits. But there are limits, both ethical and legal, to how far businesspersons can go. In preparing for a career in business, you will find that a background in business ethics and a commitment to ethical behavior are just as important as a knowledge of the specific laws that are covered in this text. Of course, no textbook can give an answer to each and every ethical question that arises in the business environment. Nor can it anticipate the types of ethical questions that will arise in the future, as technology and globalization continue to transform the workplace and business relationships.

The most we can do is examine the types of ethical issues that businesspersons have faced in the past and that they are facing today. In the *Focus on Ethics* sections in this book, we provide examples of specific ethical issues that have arisen in various areas of business activity.

In this initial *Focus on Ethics* feature, we look first at the relationship between business ethics and business law. We then examine various obstacles to ethical behavior in the business context. We conclude the feature by exploring the parameters of corporate social responsibility through a discussion of whether corporations have an ethical duty to the community or society at large.

Business Ethics and Business Law

Business ethics and business law are closely intertwined because ultimately the law rests on social beliefs about right and wrong behavior in the business world. Thus, businesspersons, by complying with the law, are acting ethically. Mere legal compliance (the "moral minimum" in terms of business ethics), however, is often not enough. This is because the law does not—and cannot—provide the answers for all ethical questions.

In the business world, numerous actions may be unethical but not necessarily illegal. Consider an example. Suppose that a pharmaceutical company is banned from marketing a particular drug in the United States because of the drug's possible adverse side effects. Yet no law prohibits the company from selling the drug in foreign markets—even though some consumers in those markets may suffer serious health problems as a result of using the drug. At issue here is not whether it would be legal to market the drug in other countries but whether it would be *ethical* to do so. In other words, the law has its limits—it cannot make all ethical decisions for us. Rather, the law

assumes that those in business will behave ethically in their day-to-day dealings. If they do not, the courts will not come to their assistance.

Obstacles to Ethical Business Behavior

People sometimes behave unethically in the business context, just as they do in their private lives. Some businesspersons knowingly engage in unethical behavior because they think that they can "get away with it"—that is, no one will ever learn of their unethical actions.

Examples of this kind of unethical behavior include padding expense accounts, casting doubts on the integrity of a rival co-worker to gain a job promotion, stealing company supplies or equipment, and so on. Obviously, these acts are unethical, and many of them are illegal as well. In some situations, however, businesspersons who would choose to act ethically may be deterred from doing so because of situational circumstances or external pressures.

Ethics and the Corporate Environment   Individuals in their personal lives normally are free to decide ethical issues as they wish and to follow through on those decisions. In the business world, and particularly in the corporate environment, rarely is such a decision made by *one* person. If you are an officer or a manager of a large company, for example, you will find that the decision as to what is right or wrong for the company is not totally yours to make. Your input may weigh in the decision, but ultimately a corporate decision is a collective undertaking.

Additionally, collective decision making, because it places emphasis on consensus and unity of opinion, tends to hinder individual ethical assertiveness. For example, suppose that a director has ethical misgivings about a planned corporate venture that promises to be highly profitable. If the other directors have no such misgivings, the director who does may be swayed by the others' enthusiasm for the project and downplay her or his own criticisms.

Furthermore, just as no one person makes a collective decision, so no one person (normally) is held accountable for the decision. The corporate enterprise thus tends to shield corporate personnel from both individual exposure to the consequences of their decisions (such as direct contact with someone who suffers harm from a corporate product) and personal accountability for those decisions.

Ethics and Management   Much unethical business behavior occurs simply because management does not always make clear what ethical standards and behaviors are expected of the firm's employees. Although most firms now issue ethical policies or codes of conduct, these policies and codes are not always effective in creating an ethical workplace. At times, this is because the firm's ethical policies are not communicated clearly to employees or do not bear on the real ethical issues confronting decision makers. Additionally, particularly in a large corporation, unethical behavior in one corporate department may simply escape the attention of those in control of the corporation or the corporate officials responsible for implementing and monitoring the company's ethics program.

Unethical behavior may also occur when corporate management, by its own conduct, indicates that ethical considerations take a second seat. If management makes no attempt to deter unethical behavior—through reprimands or employment terminations, for example—it will be obvious to employees that management is not very serious about ethics. Likewise, if a company gives promotions or salary increases to those who clearly use unethical tactics to increase the firm's profits, then employees who do not resort to such tactics will be at a disadvantage. An employee in this situation may decide that because "everyone else does it," he or she might as well do it too.

Of course, an even stronger encouragement of unethical behavior occurs when employers engage in blatantly unethical or illegal conduct and expect their employees to do so as well. An employee in this situation faces two options, neither of which is satisfactory: participate in the conduct or "blow the whistle" on (inform authorities of) the employer's actions—and, of course, risk being fired. (See Chapter 21 for a more detailed discussion of whistleblowing and its consequences for employees.)

Corporate Social Responsibility

As discussed in Chapter 4, just what constitutes corporate social responsibility has been debated for some time. In particular, questions arise concerning a corporation's ethical obligations to its community and to society as a whole.

A Corporation's Duty to the Community In some circumstances, the community in which a business enterprise is located is greatly affected by corporate decisions and therefore may be considered a stakeholder. Assume, for example, that a company employs two thousand workers at one of its plants. If the company decides that it would be profitable to close the plant, the employees—and the community—would suffer as a result. To be considered ethical in that situation (and, in some circumstances, to comply with laws governing plant shutdowns), a corporation must take both the employees' needs and the community's needs into consideration when making its decision.

Another ethical question sometimes arises when a firm moves into a community. Does the company have an obligation to evaluate first how its presence will affect that community (even though the community is not a stakeholder yet)? This question has surfaced in regard to the expansion of Wal-Mart Stores, Inc., into smaller communities. Generally, most people in such communities welcome the lower prices and wider array of goods that Wal-Mart offers relative to other, smaller stores in the area. A vocal minority of people in some communities, however, claim that smaller stores often find it impossible to compete with Wal-Mart's prices and thus are forced to go out of business. Many of these smaller stores have existed for years and, according to Wal-Mart's critics, enhance the quality of community life. These critics claim that it is unethical of Wal-Mart to disregard a town's interest in the quality and character of its community life.

In addition to expanding, Wal-Mart has been consolidating some of its smaller stores into large "superstores." As it consolidates, Wal-Mart is closing stores in some of the very towns in which it drove its smaller competitors out of business. This development raises yet another ethical question: Does a store such as Wal-Mart have an obligation to continue operations in a community once it has driven its competitors out of business?

A Corporation's Duty to Society Perhaps the most disputed area of corporate social responsibility is the nature of a corporation's duty to society at large. Those who contend that corporations should first and foremost attend to the goal of profit maximization would argue that it is by generating profits that a firm can best contribute to society. Society benefits from profit-making activities because profits can only be realized when a firm markets products or services that are desired by society. These products and services enhance the standard of living, and the profits accumulated by successful business firms generate national wealth. Our laws and court decisions promoting trade and commerce reflect the public policy that the fruits of commerce (wealth) are desirable and good. Because our society values wealth as an ethical goal, corporations, by contributing to that wealth, automatically are acting ethically.

Those arguing for profit maximization as a corporate goal also point out that it would be inappropriate to use the power of the corporate business world to further society's goals by promoting social causes. Determinations as to what exactly is in society's best interest involve questions that are essentially political, and therefore the public, through the political process, should have a say in making those determinations. Thus, the legislature—not the corporate boardroom—is

FOCUS ON ETHICS CONTINUES ➡

the appropriate forum for making such decisions.

Critics of the profit-maximization view believe that corporations should become actively engaged in seeking and furthering solutions to social problems. Because so much of the wealth and power of this country is controlled by business, business in turn has a responsibility to society to use that wealth and power in socially beneficial ways. Corporations should therefore promote human rights, strive for equal treatment of minorities and women in the workplace, take steps to preserve the environment, and generally not profit from activities that society has deemed unethical. The critics also point out that it is ethically irresponsible to leave decisions concerning social welfare up to the government, because many social needs are not being met sufficiently through the political process.

It Pays to Be Ethical

Most corporations today have learned that it pays to be ethically responsible—even if this means less profit in the short run (and it often does). Today's corporations are subject to more intensive scrutiny—by both government agencies and the public—than corporations of the past. "Corporate watch" groups monitor the activities of U.S. corporations, including activities conducted in foreign countries. Through the Internet, complaints about a corporation's practices can easily be disseminated to a worldwide audience. Similarly, dissatisfied customers and employees can voice their complaints about corporate policies, products, or services in Internet chat rooms and other online forums. Thus, if a corporation fails to conduct its operations ethically or to respond quickly to an ethical crisis, its goodwill and reputation (and future profits) will likely suffer as a result.

There are other reasons as well for a corporation to behave ethically. For example, companies that demonstrate a commitment to ethical behavior—by implementing ethical programs, complying with environmental regulations, and promptly investigating product complaints, for example—often receive more lenient treatment from government agencies and the courts. Additionally, investors may shy away from a corporation's stock if the corporation is perceived to be socially irresponsible. Finally, unethical (and/or illegal) corporate behavior may result in government action, such as new laws imposing further requirements on corporate entities.

DISCUSSION QUESTIONS

1. What might be some other deterrents to ethical behavior in the business context, besides those discussed in this *Focus on Ethics* feature?
2. Can you think of a situation in which a business firm may be acting ethically but not in a socially responsible manner? Explain.
3. Why are consumers and the public generally more concerned with ethical and socially responsible business behavior today than they were, say, fifty years ago?
4. Suppose that an automobile manufacturing company has to choose between two alternatives: contributing $1 million annually to the United Way or reinvesting the $1 million in the company. In terms of ethics and social responsibility, which is the better choice?
5. Have Internet chat rooms and online forums affected corporate decision makers' willingness to consider the community and public interest when making choices? Are corporate decision makers more apt to make ethical choices in the cyber age? Explain.

UNIT TWO

THE PUBLIC AND INTERNATIONAL ENVIRONMENT

CONTENTS

Constitutional Law

The U.S. Constitution is the supreme law in this country.[1] As mentioned in Chapter 1, neither Congress nor any state may pass a law that conflicts with the Constitution. Laws that govern business have their origin in the lawmaking authority granted by this document.

In this chapter, we examine some basic constitutional concepts and clauses and their significance for businesspersons. We then look at certain freedoms guaranteed by the first ten amendments to the Constitution—the Bill of Rights—and discuss how these freedoms affect business activities.

1. See Appendix B for the full text of the U.S. Constitution.

SECTION 1

THE CONSTITUTIONAL POWERS OF GOVERNMENT

Following the Revolutionary War, the states—through the Articles of Confederation—created a *confederal form of government* in which the states had the authority to govern themselves and the national government could exercise only limited powers. When problems arose because the nation was facing an economic crisis and state laws interfered with the free flow of commerce, a national convention was called, and the delegates drafted the U.S. Constitution. This document, after its ratification by the states in 1789, became the basis for an entirely new form of government.

A Federal Form of Government

The new government created by the U.S. Constitution reflected a series of compromises made by the convention delegates on various issues. Some delegates wanted sovereign power to remain with the states; others wanted the national government alone to exercise sovereign power. The end result was a compromise—a **federal form of government** in which the national government and the states *share* sovereign power.

The Constitution sets forth specific powers that can be exercised by the national government and provides that the national government has the implied power to undertake actions necessary to carry out its expressly designated powers (or *enumerated powers*). All other powers are expressly "reserved" to the states under the Tenth Amendment to the U.S. Constitution.

As part of their inherent sovereignty, state governments have the authority to regulate affairs within their borders. As mentioned, this authority stems, in part, from the Tenth Amendment, which reserves all powers not delegated to the national government to the states or to the people. State regulatory powers are often referred to as **police powers.** The term does not relate solely to criminal law enforcement but rather refers to the broad right of state governments to regulate private activities to protect or promote the public order, health, safety, morals, and general welfare. Fire and building codes, antidiscrimination laws, parking regulations, zoning restrictions, licensing requirements, and thousands of other state statutes covering almost every aspect of life have been enacted pursuant to states' police powers. Local governments, including cities, also exercise police powers.[2] Generally, state laws enacted pursuant to a state's police powers carry a strong presumption of validity.

---

2. Local governments derive their authority to regulate their communities from the state, because they are creatures of the state. In other words, they cannot come into existence unless authorized by the state to do so.

Relations among the States

The U.S. Constitution also includes provisions concerning relations among the states in our federal system. Particularly important are the *privileges and immunities clause* and the *full faith and credit clause*.

THE PRIVILEGES AND IMMUNITIES CLAUSE Article IV, Section 2, of the U.S. Constitution provides that the "Citizens of each State shall be entitled to all Privileges and Immunities of Citizens in the several States." This clause is often referred to as the interstate **privileges and immunities clause.**[3] It prevents a state from imposing unreasonable burdens on citizens of another state—particularly with regard to means of livelihood or doing business. When a citizen of one state engages in basic and essential activities in another state (the "foreign state"), the foreign state must have a *substantial reason* for treating the nonresident differently from its own residents. Basic activities include transferring property, seeking employment, or accessing the court system. The foreign state must also establish that its reason for the discrimination is *substantially related* to the state's ultimate purpose in adopting the legislation or regulating the activity.[4]

THE FULL FAITH AND CREDIT CLAUSE Article IV, Section 1, of the U.S. Constitution provides that "Full Faith and Credit shall be given in each State to the public Acts, Records, and judicial Proceedings of every other State." This clause, which is referred to as the **full faith and credit clause,** applies only to civil matters. It ensures that rights established under deeds, wills, contracts, and similar instruments in one state will be honored by other states. It also ensures that any judicial decision with respect to such property rights will be honored and enforced in all states.

The full faith and credit clause was originally included in the Articles of Confederation to promote mutual friendship among the people of the various states. In fact, it has contributed to the unity of American citizens because it protects their legal rights as they move about from state to state. It also protects the rights of those to whom they owe obligations, such as a person who is awarded monetary damages by a court. The ability to enforce such rights is extremely important for the conduct of business in a country with a very mobile citizenry.

The Separation of the National Government's Powers

To guard against the possibility that the national government might use its power arbitrarily, the Constitution provided for three branches of government. The legislative branch makes the laws, the executive branch enforces the laws, and the judicial branch interprets the laws. Each branch performs a separate function, and no branch may exercise the authority of another branch.

Additionally, a system of **checks and balances** allows each branch to limit the actions of the other two branches, thus preventing any one branch from exercising too much power. Some examples of these checks and balances include the following:

1. The legislative branch (Congress) can enact a law, but the executive branch (the president) has the constitutional authority to veto that law.
2. The executive branch is responsible for foreign affairs, but treaties with foreign governments require the advice and consent of the Senate.
3. Congress determines the jurisdiction of the federal courts and the president appoints federal judges, with the advice and consent of the Senate, but the judicial branch has the power to hold actions of the other two branches unconstitutional.[5]

The Commerce Clause

To prevent states from establishing laws and regulations that would interfere with trade and commerce among the states, the Constitution expressly delegated to the national government the power to regulate interstate commerce. Article I, Section 8, of the U.S. Constitution explicitly permits Congress "[t]o regulate Commerce with foreign Nations, and among the several States, and with the Indian Tribes." This clause, referred to as the **commerce clause,** has had a greater impact on business than any other provision in the Constitution. The commerce clause provides the basis for the national government's extensive regulation of state and even local affairs.

One of the early questions raised by the commerce clause was whether the word *among* in the

---

3. Interpretations of this clause commonly use the terms *privilege* and *immunity* synonymously. Generally, the terms refer to certain rights, benefits, or advantages enjoyed by individuals.

4. This test was first announced in *Supreme Court of New Hampshire v. Piper,* 470 U.S. 274, 105 S.Ct. 1272, 84 L.Ed.2d 205 (1985). For another example, see *Lee v. Miner,* 369 F.Supp.2d 527 (D.Del. 2005).

5. As discussed in Chapter 2, the power of judicial review was established by the United States Supreme Court in *Marbury v. Madison,* 5 U.S. (1 Cranch) 137, 2 L.Ed. 60 (1803).

phrase "among the several States" meant *between* the states or *between and within* the states. For some time, the courts interpreted the commerce clause to apply only to commerce between the states (*interstate* commerce) and not commerce within the states (*intrastate* commerce). In 1824, however, the United States Supreme Court decided the landmark case of *Gibbons v. Ogden*.[6] The Court ruled that commerce within the states could also be regulated by the national government as long as the commerce *substantially affected* commerce involving more than one state.

THE EXPANSION OF NATIONAL POWERS UNDER THE COMMERCE CLAUSE As the nation grew and faced new kinds of problems, the commerce clause became a vehicle for the additional expansion of the national government's regulatory powers. Even activities that seemed purely local in nature came under the regulatory reach of the national government if those activities were deemed to substantially affect interstate commerce.

In 1942, for example, the Supreme Court held that wheat production by an individual farmer intended wholly for consumption on his own farm was subject to federal regulation.[7] In *Heart of Atlanta Motel v. United States*,[8] a landmark case decided in 1964, the Supreme Court upheld the federal government's authority to prohibit racial discrimination nationwide in public facilities, including local motels, based on its powers under the commerce clause. The Court noted that "if it is interstate commerce that feels the pinch, it does not matter how local the operation that applies the squeeze."

THE COMMERCE CLAUSE TODAY Today, the national government continues to rely on the commerce clause for its constitutional authority to regulate business activities in the United States. The breadth of the commerce clause permits the national government to legislate in areas in which Congress has not explicitly been granted power. In the last twenty years, however, the Supreme Court has begun to curb somewhat the national government's regulatory authority under the commerce clause. In 1995, the Court held—for the first time in sixty years—that Congress had exceeded its regulatory authority under the commerce clause. The Court struck down an act that banned the possession of guns within one thousand feet of any school because the

act attempted to regulate an area that had "nothing to do with commerce."[9] Subsequently, the Court invalidated key portions of two other federal acts on the ground that they exceeded Congress's commerce clause authority.[10]

MEDICAL MARIJUANA LAWS AND THE COMMERCE CLAUSE In one notable case, however, the Supreme Court did allow the federal government to regulate noncommercial activities taking place wholly within a state's borders.

CASE IN POINT About a dozen states, including California, have adopted "medical marijuana" laws that legalize marijuana for medical purposes. Marijuana possession, however, is illegal under the federal Controlled Substances Act (CSA).[11] After the federal government seized the marijuana that two seriously ill California women were using on the advice of their physicians, the women filed a lawsuit. They argued that it was unconstitutional for the federal statute to prohibit them from using marijuana for medical purposes that were legal within the state. In 2005, however, the United States Supreme Court held that Congress has the authority to prohibit the *intra*state possession and noncommercial cultivation of marijuana as part of a larger regulatory scheme (the CSA).[12] In other words, state laws that allow the use of medical marijuana do not insulate the users from federal prosecution.

THE "DORMANT" COMMERCE CLAUSE The United States Supreme Court has interpreted the commerce clause to mean that the national government has the *exclusive* authority to regulate commerce that substantially affects trade and commerce among the states. This express grant of authority to the national government, which is often referred to as the "positive" aspect of the commerce clause, implies a negative aspect—that the states do *not* have the authority to regulate interstate commerce. This negative aspect of the commerce clause is often referred to as the "dormant" (implied) commerce clause.

The dormant commerce clause comes into play when state regulations affect interstate commerce.

---

6. 2 U.S. (9 Wheat.) 1, 6 L.Ed. 23 (1824).

7. *Wickard v. Filburn*, 317 U.S. 111, 63 S.Ct. 82, 87 L.Ed. 122 (1942).

8. 379 U.S. 241, 85 S.Ct. 348, 13 L.Ed.2d 258 (1964).

9. The Court held the Gun-Free School Zones Act of 1990 to be unconstitutional in *United States v. Lopez*, 514 U.S. 549, 115 S.Ct. 1624, 131 L.Ed.2d 626 (1995).

10. *Printz v. United States*, 521 U.S. 898, 117 S.Ct. 2365, 138 L.Ed.2d 914 (1997), involving the Brady Handgun Violence Prevention Act of 1993; and *United States v. Morrison*, 529 U.S. 598, 120 S.Ct. 1740, 146 L.Ed.2d 658 (2000), concerning the federal Violence Against Women Act of 1994.

11. 21 U.S.C. Sections 801 *et seq.*

12. *Gonzales v. Raich*, 545 U.S. 1, 125 S.Ct. 2195, 162 L.Ed.2d 1 (2005).

In this situation, the courts weigh the state's interest in regulating a certain matter against the burden that the state's regulation places on interstate commerce. Because courts balance the interests involved, it is difficult to predict the outcome in a particular case.

In the following case, the plaintiffs—a group of California wineries and others—contended that a 2006 Massachusetts statute discriminated against out-of-state wineries in violation of the dormant commerce clause. A federal district court agreed and enjoined (prevented) the enforcement of the statute. The commonwealth of Massachusetts appealed the trial court's decision.

✳ EXTENDED CASE 5.1 ✳
Family Winemakers of California v. Jenkins[a]

United States Court of Appeals, First Circuit, 592 F.3d 1 (2010).
www.ca1.uscourts.gov/opinions/main.php[b]

IN THE LANGUAGE OF THE COURT
LYNCH, Chief Judge.
* * * *

The ratification of the Twenty-first Amendment ended Prohibition[c] and gave states substantial control over the regulation of alcoholic beverages. Most states, including Massachusetts, then imposed a three-tier system to control the sale of alcoholic beverages within their territories. The hallmark of the three-tier system is a rigid, tightly regulated separation between producers, wholesalers, and retailers of alcoholic beverages. Producers can ordinarily sell alcoholic beverages only to licensed in-state wholesalers. Wholesalers then must obtain licenses to sell to retailers. Retailers, which include stores, taverns, restaurants, and bars, must in turn obtain licenses to sell to consumers or to serve alcohol on their premises. Recently, as to wine, Massachusetts has adjusted the separation between these three tiers * * *.
* * * *

Wineries have heralded direct shipping as a supplemental avenue of distribution because of its economic advantages, especially for wineries that do not rank among the fifty to one hundred largest producers. Direct shipping lets consumers directly order wines from the winery, with access to their full range of wines, not just those a wholesaler is willing to distribute. Direct shipping also avoids added steps in the distribution chain, eliminating wholesaler and retailer price markups.

Before 2005, Massachusetts's * * * winery licensing law * * * allowed only in-state wineries to obtain licenses to combine distribution methods through wholesalers, retailers, and direct shipping to consumers. [After the United States Supreme Court] invalidated similar facially discriminatory state laws, [the 2005 Massachusetts law] was held to be invalid under the Commerce Clause.

In 2006, the Massachusetts legislature enacted [a new law regulating wineries, which] does not distinguish on its face between in-state and out-of-state wineries' eligibility for direct shipping licenses, but instead distinguishes between "small" or "large" wineries through [a] 30,000 gallon cap.

* * * *

* * * All wineries producing over 30,000 gallons of wine—all of which are located outside Massachusetts— can apply for a "large winery shipment license[.]" * * * "Large" wineries can either choose to remain completely within the three-tier system and distribute their wines solely through wholesalers, or they can completely opt out of the three-tier system and sell their wines in Massachusetts exclusively through direct shipping [to consumers]. They cannot do both. * * * By contrast, "small" wineries can simultaneously use the traditional wholesaler distribution method, direct distribution to retailers, and direct shipping to reach consumers.

* * * *

* * * *Discrimination under the Commerce Clause "means differential treatment of in-state and out-of-state economic interests that benefits the former and burdens the latter," as opposed to state laws that "regulate * * * evenhandedly with only incidental effects on interstate commerce[.]"* [Emphasis added.]

* * * Plaintiffs argue that Massachusetts's choice of 30,000 gallons as the demarcation [separation]

---

a. The case was brought against Eddie J. Jenkins, the chair of the Massachusetts Alcoholic Beverages Control Commission, in his official capacity.

b. When the page opens, type "Family Winemakers" in the "Short Title *contains*" box and then click on "Submit Search." Select Opinion Number 09-01169P.01A to access the case. The U.S. Court of Appeals for the First Circuit maintains this Web site.

c. The Eighteenth Amendment to the U.S. Constitution, adopted in 1919, prohibited the sale of alcoholic beverages, giving rise to the so-called Prohibition Era. The Twenty-first Amendment, ratified in 1933, repealed the Eighteenth Amendment.

EXTENDED CASE CONTINUES ➡

EXTENDED CASE 5.1 CONTINUED ⬇

point between "small" and "large" wineries, along with [a] production exception for fruit wine, has both a discriminatory effect and [a] purpose. The discriminatory effect is because [the law's] definition of "large" wineries encompasses the wineries which produce 98 percent of all wine in the United States, all of which are located out-of-state and all of which are deprived of the benefits of combining distribution methods. All wines produced in Massachusetts, on the other hand, are from "small" wineries that can use multiple distribution methods. Plaintiffs also say that [the law] is discriminatory in purpose because the gallonage cap's particular features, along with legislators' statements and [the law's] process of enactment, show that [the law's] true purpose was to ensure that Massachusetts's wineries obtained advantages over their out-of-state counterparts.

* * * *

* * * State laws that alter conditions of competition to favor in-state interests over out-of-state competitors in a market have long been subject to invalidation.

* * * Here, the totality of the evidence introduced by plaintiffs demonstrates that [the law's] preferential treatment of "small" wineries that produce 30,000 gallons or less of grape wine is discriminatory. Its effect is to significantly alter the terms of competition between in-state and out-of-state wineries to the detriment of the out-of-state wineries that produce 98 percent of the country's wine.

[The 2006 law] confers a clear competitive advantage to "small" wineries, which include all Massachusetts's wineries, and creates a comparative disadvantage for "large" wineries, none of which are in Massachusetts. "Small" wineries that obtain a * * * license can use direct shipping to consumers, retailer distribution, and

wholesaler distribution simultaneously. Combining these distribution methods allows "small" wineries to sell their full range of wines at maximum efficiency because they serve complementary markets. "Small" wineries that produce higher-volume wines can continue distributing those wines through wholesaler relationships. They can obtain new markets for all their wines by distributing their wines directly to retailers, including individual bars, restaurants, and stores. They can also use direct shipping to offer their full range of wines directly to Massachusetts consumers, resulting in greater overall sales.

* * * *

We conclude that [the 2006 law] altered the competitive balance to favor Massachusetts's wineries and disfavor out-of-state competition by design.

* * * *

We *affirm* the judgment of the district court.

QUESTIONS

1. The court held that the Massachusetts statute discriminated against out-of-state wineries "by design" (intentionally). How can a court determine legislative intent?
2. Suppose that most "small" wineries, as defined by the 2006 Massachusetts law, were located out of state. How could the law be discriminatory in that situation?

The Supremacy Clause and Federal Preemption

Article VI of the U.S. Constitution, commonly referred to as the **supremacy clause,** provides that the Constitution, laws, and treaties of the United States are "the supreme Law of the Land." When there is a direct conflict between a federal law and a state law, the state law is rendered invalid. Because some powers are *concurrent* (shared by the federal government and the states), however, it is necessary to determine which law governs in a particular circumstance.

When Congress chooses to act exclusively in an area in which the federal government and the states have concurrent powers, **preemption** occurs. A valid federal statute or regulation will take precedence over a conflicting state or local law or regulation on

the same general subject. Often, it is not clear whether Congress, in passing a law, intended to preempt an entire subject area against state regulation, and it is left to the courts to determine whether Congress intended to exercise exclusive power over a given area. No single factor is decisive as to whether a court will find preemption. Generally, congressional intent to preempt will be found if a federal law regulating an activity is so pervasive, comprehensive, or detailed that the states have no room to regulate in that area. Also, when a federal statute creates an agency to enforce the law, the agency's rulings on matters that come within its jurisdiction will likely preempt state laws.

CASE IN POINT The United States Supreme Court heard a case involving a man who alleged that he had been injured by a faulty medical device (a balloon catheter that had been inserted into his artery following a heart attack). The Court found that the Medical Device Amendments of 1976 had included a preemption provision and that the device had passed the U.S. Food and Drug Administration's rigorous premarket approval process. Therefore, the Court ruled that the federal regulation of medical devices preempted the injured party's state common law claims for negligence, strict liability, and implied warranty.[13]

The Taxing and Spending Powers

Article I, Section 8, of the U.S. Constitution provides that Congress has the "Power to lay and collect Taxes, Duties, Imposts, and Excises." Section 8 further requires uniformity in taxation among the states, and thus Congress may not tax some states while exempting others. Traditionally, if Congress attempted to regulate indirectly, by taxation, an area over which it had no authority, the courts would invalidate the tax. Today, however, if a tax measure is reasonable, it generally is held to be within the national taxing power. Moreover, the expansive interpretation of the commerce clause almost always provides a basis for sustaining a federal tax.

Article I, Section 8, also gives Congress its spending power—the power "to pay the Debts and provide for the common Defence and general Welfare of the United States." Congress can spend revenues not only to carry out its expressed powers but also to promote any objective it deems worthwhile, so long as it does not violate the Bill of Rights. The spending power necessarily involves policy choices, with which taxpayers may disagree.

SECTION 2
BUSINESS AND THE BILL OF RIGHTS

The importance of a written declaration of the rights of individuals eventually caused the first Congress of the United States to submit twelve amendments to the U.S. Constitution to the states for approval. Ten of these amendments, commonly known as the **Bill of Rights,** were adopted in 1791 and embody a series of protections for the individual against various types of interference by the federal government.[14] The protections guaranteed by these ten amendments are summarized in Exhibit 5–1 on the following page.[15] Some of these constitutional protections apply to business entities as well. For example, corporations exist as separate legal entities, or *legal persons,* and enjoy many of the same rights and privileges as *natural persons* do.

Limits on Federal and State Governmental Actions

As originally intended, the Bill of Rights limited only the powers of the national government. Over time, however, the United States Supreme Court "incorporated" most of these rights into the protections against state actions afforded by the Fourteenth Amendment to the Constitution. That amendment, passed in 1868 after the Civil War, provides, in part, that "[n]o State shall . . . deprive any person of life, liberty, or property, without due process of law." Starting in 1925, the Supreme Court began to define various rights and liberties guaranteed in the U.S. Constitution as constituting "due process of law," which was required of state governments under the Fourteenth Amendment. Today, most of the rights and liberties set forth in the Bill of Rights apply to state governments as well as the national government. In other words, neither the federal government nor state governments can deprive persons of those rights and liberties.

The rights secured by the Bill of Rights are not absolute. As you can see in Exhibit 5–1 on the next page, many of the rights guaranteed by the first ten amendments are set forth in very general terms. For example, the Second Amendment states that people have a right to keep and bear arms, but it does not explain the extent of this right. As the Supreme Court noted in 2008, this does not mean that people can "keep and carry any weapon whatsoever in any manner whatsoever and for whatever purpose."[16] Legislatures can prohibit the carrying of concealed weapons or certain types of weapons, such as machine guns. Ultimately, it is the United States Supreme Court, as the final interpreter of the Constitution, that gives meaning to these rights and determines their boundaries.

Freedom of Speech

A democratic form of government cannot survive unless people can freely voice their political opinions and criticize government actions or policies.

---

13. *Riegel v. Medtronic, Inc.,* 552 U.S. 312, 128 S.Ct. 999, 169 L.Ed.2d 892 (2008).

14. Another of these proposed amendments was ratified more than two hundred years later (in 1992) and became the Twenty-seventh Amendment to the Constitution. See Appendix B.

15. See the Constitution in Appendix B for the complete text of each amendment.

16. *District of Columbia v. Heller,* ___ U.S. ___, 128 S.Ct. 2783, 171 L.Ed.2d 637 (2008).

EXHIBIT 5–1 • Protections Guaranteed by the Bill of Rights

First Amendment: Guarantees the freedoms of religion, speech, and the press and the rights to assemble peaceably and to petition the government.

Second Amendment: States that the right of the people to keep and bear arms shall not be infringed.

Third Amendment: Prohibits, in peacetime, the lodging of soldiers in any house without the owner's consent.

Fourth Amendment: Prohibits unreasonable searches and seizures of persons or property.

Fifth Amendment: Guarantees the rights to indictment by grand jury, to due process of law, and to fair payment when private property is taken for public use; prohibits compulsory self-incrimination and double jeopardy (being tried again for an alleged crime for which one has already stood trial).

Sixth Amendment: Guarantees the accused in a criminal case the right to a speedy and public trial by an impartial jury and with counsel. The accused has the right to cross-examine witnesses against him or her and to solicit testimony from witnesses in his or her favor.

Seventh Amendment: Guarantees the right to a trial by jury in a civil case involving at least twenty dollars.[a]

Eighth Amendment: Prohibits excessive bail and fines, as well as cruel and unusual punishment.

Ninth Amendment: Establishes that the people have rights in addition to those specified in the Constitution.

Tenth Amendment: Establishes that those powers neither delegated to the federal government nor denied to the states are reserved to the states and to the people.

a. Twenty dollars was forty days' pay for the average person when the Bill of Rights was written.

Freedom of speech, particularly political speech, is thus a prized right, and traditionally the courts have protected this right to the fullest extent possible.

Symbolic speech—gestures, movements, articles of clothing, and other forms of expressive conduct— is also given substantial protection by the courts. For example, the Supreme Court has held that the burning of the American flag as part of a peaceful protest is a constitutionally protected form of expression.[17] Similarly, wearing a T-shirt with a photo of a presidential candidate is a constitutionally protected form of expression.

REASONABLE RESTRICTIONS Expression—oral, written, or symbolized by conduct—is subject to reasonable restrictions. A balance must be struck between a government's obligation to protect its citizens and those citizens' exercise of their rights. Reasonableness is analyzed on a case-by-case basis. If a restriction imposed by the government is content neutral, then a court may allow it. To be content neutral, the restriction must be aimed at combatting some societal problem, such as crime, and not be aimed at suppressing the expressive conduct or its message. Courts have often protected nude dancing as a form of symbolic expression but typically allow content-neutral laws that ban all public nudity.

CASE IN POINT Ria Ora was charged with dancing nude at an annual "anti-Christmas" protest in Harvard Square in Cambridge, Massachusetts, under a statute banning public displays of open and gross lewdness. Ora argued that the statute was overbroad and unconstitutional, and a trial court agreed. On appeal, a state appellate court upheld the statute as constitutional in situations in which there was an unsuspecting or unwilling audience.[18]

CORPORATE POLITICAL SPEECH Political speech by corporations also falls within the protection of the First Amendment. For example, many years ago the United States Supreme Court struck down as unconstitutional a Massachusetts statute that prohibited corporations from making political contributions or expenditures that individuals were permitted to make.[19] Similarly, the Court has held that a law forbidding a corporation from including inserts with its bills to express its views on controversial issues violates the First Amendment.[20] Corporate political speech continues to be given significant protection under the First Amendment. For example, in 2010 the Court overturned a twenty-year-old precedent when it ruled that corporations can spend freely to support or oppose candidates for president and Congress.[21]

---

17. *Texas v. Johnson*, 491 U.S. 397, 109 S.Ct. 2533, 105 L.Ed.2d 342 (1989).

18. *Commonwealth v. Ora*, 451 Mass. 125, 883 N.E.2d 1217 (2008).

19. *First National Bank of Boston v. Bellotti*, 435 U.S. 765, 98 S.Ct. 1407, 55 L.Ed.2d 707 (1978).

20. *Consolidated Edison Co. v. Public Service Commission*, 447 U.S. 530, 100 S.Ct. 2326, 65 L.Ed.2d 319 (1980).

21. *Citizens United v. Federal Election Commission*, ___ U.S. ___, 130 S.Ct. 876, ___ L.Ed.2d ___ (2010).

COMMERCIAL SPEECH The courts also give substantial protection to *commercial speech,* which consists of communications—primarily advertising and marketing—made by business firms that involve only their commercial interests. The protection given to commercial speech under the First Amendment is less extensive than that afforded to noncommercial speech, however. A state may restrict certain kinds of advertising, for example, in the interest of preventing consumers from being misled. States also have a legitimate interest in roadside beautification and therefore may impose restraints on billboard advertising. For example, in one Florida case, the court found that a law preventing a nude dancing establishment from billboard advertising was constitutionally permissible because it directly advanced a substantial government interest in highway beautification and safety.[22]

Generally, a restriction on commercial speech will be considered valid as long as it meets three criteria: (1) it must seek to implement a substantial government interest, (2) it must directly advance that interest, and (3) it must go no further than necessary to accomplish its objective.

At issue in the following case was whether a government agency had unconstitutionally restricted commercial speech when it prohibited the inclusion of a certain illustration on beer labels.

---

22. *Café Erotica v. Florida Department of Transportation,* 830 So.2d 181 (Fla.App. 1 Dist. 2002); review denied by *Café Erotica/We Dare to Bare v. Florida Department of Transportation,* 845 So.2d 888 (Fla. 2003).

CASE 5.2
Bad Frog Brewery, Inc. v. New York State Liquor Authority

United States Court of Appeals, Second Circuit, 134 F.3d 87 (1998).
www.findlaw.com/casecode/index.html[a]

BACKGROUND AND FACTS • Bad Frog Brewery, Inc., makes and sells alcoholic beverages. Some of the beverages feature labels that display a drawing of a frog making the gesture generally known as "giving the finger." Bad Frog's authorized New York distributor, Renaissance Beer Company, applied to the New York State Liquor Authority (NYSLA) for brand label approval, as required by state law before the beer could be sold in New York. The NYSLA denied the application, in part, because "the label could appear in grocery and convenience stores, with obvious exposure on the shelf to children of tender age." Bad Frog filed a suit in a federal district court against the NYSLA, asking for, among other things, an injunction against the denial of the application. The court granted summary judgment in favor of the NYSLA. Bad Frog appealed to the U.S. Court of Appeals for the Second Circuit.

IN THE LANGUAGE OF THE COURT
Jon O. *NEWMAN,* Circuit Judge:
* * * *
* * * To support its asserted power to ban Bad Frog's labels [NYSLA advances] * * * the State's interest in "protecting children from vulgar and profane advertising" * * * .

[This interest is] substantial * * * . *States have a compelling interest in protecting the physical and psychological well-being of minors* * * * . [Emphasis added.]
* * * *

* * * NYSLA endeavors to advance the state interest in preventing exposure of children to vulgar displays by taking only the limited step of barring such displays from the labels of alcoholic beverages. *In view of the wide currency of vulgar displays throughout contemporary society, including comic books targeted directly at children, barring such displays from labels for alcoholic beverages cannot realistically be expected to reduce children's exposure to such displays to any significant degree.* [Emphasis added.]

* * * If New York decides to make a substantial effort to insulate children from vulgar displays in some significant sphere of activity, at least with respect to materials likely to be seen by

---

a. Under the heading "US Court of Appeals," click on "2nd Circuit Court of Appeals." Enter "Bad Frog Brewery" in the "Party Name Search" box and click on "search." On the resulting page, click on the case name to access the opinion.

CASE CONTINUES ➡

CASE 5.2 CONTINUED ➡ children, NYSLA's label prohibition might well be found to make a justifiable contribution to the material advancement of such an effort, but its currently isolated response to the perceived problem, applicable only to labels on a product that children cannot purchase, does not suffice. * * * A state must demonstrate that its commercial speech limitation is part of a substantial effort to advance a valid state interest, not merely the removal of a few grains of offensive sand from a beach of vulgarity.

    * * * *

    * * * Even if we were to assume that the state materially advances its asserted interest by shielding children from viewing the Bad Frog labels, it is plainly excessive to prohibit the labels from all use, including placement on bottles displayed in bars and taverns where parental supervision of children is to be expected. Moreover, to whatever extent NYSLA is concerned that children will be harmfully exposed to the Bad Frog labels when wandering without parental supervision around grocery and convenience stores where beer is sold, that concern could be less intrusively dealt with by placing restrictions on the permissible locations where the appellant's products may be displayed within such stores.

DECISION AND REMEDY • *The U.S. Court of Appeals for the Second Circuit reversed the judgment of the district court and remanded the case for the entry of a judgment in favor of Bad Frog. The NYSLA's ban on the use of the labels lacked a "reasonable fit" with the state's interest in shielding minors from vulgarity, and the NYSLA did not adequately consider alternatives to the ban.*

WHAT IF THE FACTS WERE DIFFERENT? • *If Bad Frog had sought to use the offensive label to market toys instead of beer, would the court's ruling likely have been the same? Why or why not?*

THE LEGAL ENVIRONMENT DIMENSION • *Whose interests are advanced by the banning of certain types of advertising?*

UNPROTECTED SPEECH The United States Supreme Court has made it clear that certain types of speech will not be protected under the First Amendment. Speech that violates criminal laws (threatening speech and pornography, for example) is not constitutionally protected. Other unprotected speech includes *fighting words* (speech that is likely to incite others to respond violently).

Speech that harms the good reputation of another, or defamatory speech (see Chapter 12), also is not protected under the First Amendment. To constitute defamation, the speech in question must be an assertion of fact and not merely an opinion. Unlike an opinion, a statement of purported fact can be proved true or false.

Obscene Speech. The First Amendment, as interpreted by the Supreme Court, also does not protect obscene speech. Establishing an objective definition of obscene speech has proved difficult, however, and the Court has grappled from time to time with this problem. In *Miller v. California,*[23] the Supreme Court created a test for legal obscenity, including a set of requirements that must be met for material to be legally obscene. Under this test, material is obscene if (1) the average person finds that it

violates contemporary community standards; (2) the work taken as a whole appeals to a prurient (arousing or obsessive) interest in sex; (3) the work shows patently offensive sexual conduct; and (4) the work lacks serious redeeming literary, artistic, political, or scientific merit.

Because community standards vary widely, the *Miller* test has had inconsistent applications, and obscenity remains a constitutionally unsettled issue. Numerous state and federal statutes make it a crime to disseminate obscene materials, including child pornography.

Online Obscenity. In 2000, Congress enacted the Children's Internet Protection Act (CIPA),[24] which requires public schools and libraries to install **filtering software** on computers to keep children from accessing adult content. Such software is designed to prevent persons from viewing certain Web sites based on a site's Internet address or its **meta tags,** or key words. The CIPA was challenged on constitutional grounds, but in 2003 the Supreme Court held that the act does not violate the First Amendment. The Court concluded that because libraries can disable the filters for any patrons who ask, the system is reasonably flexible

---

23. 413 U.S. 15, 93 S.Ct. 2607, 37 L.Ed.2d 419 (1973).   **24.** 17 U.S.C. Sections 1701–1741.

and does not burden free speech to an unconstitutional extent.[25]

Due to the difficulties of policing the Internet as well as the constitutional complexities of prohibiting online obscenity through legislation, online obscenity remains a continuing problem in the United States (and worldwide). In 2005, the Federal Bureau of Investigation established an Anti-Porn Squad to target and prosecute companies that distribute child pornography in cyberspace. The Federal Communications Commission has also established new obscenity regulations for television networks. See this chapter's *Insight into Ethics* feature below for a discussion of some problems surrounding virtual child pornography.

---

25. *United States v. American Library Association,* 539 U.S. 194, 123 S.Ct. 2297, 156 L.Ed.2d 221 (2003).

INSIGHT INTO ETHICS
Is It Illegal to Distribute Virtual Pornography?

Millions of pornographic images of children are available on the Internet. Some are images of actual children engaged in sexual activity. Others are virtual (computer-generated) pornography—that is, images made to look like children engaged in sexual acts. Whereas child pornography is illegal, the Supreme Court has ruled that virtual pornography is legally protected under the First Amendment because it does not involve the exploitation of real children.[a]

This ruling and the difficulty in distinguishing between real and virtual pornography have created problems for prosecutors. Before they can convict someone of disseminating child pornography on the Internet, they must prove that the images depict real children. To help remedy this problem, Congress enacted the Protect Act of 2003 (here, *Protect* stands for "Prosecutorial Remedies and Other Tools to end the Exploitation of Children Today").[b]

The Protect Act's Pandering Provisions

One of the Protect Act's many provisions prohibits misrepresenting virtual child pornography as actual child pornography. The act's "pandering" provision makes it a crime to knowingly advertise, present, distribute, or solicit "any material or purported material in a manner that reflects the belief, or that is intended to cause another to believe, that the material or purported material" is illegal child pornography.[c] Thus, it may be a crime to intentionally distribute virtual child pornography.

This "pandering" provision was challenged in a 2008 case, *United States v. Williams.*[d] The defendant, Michael Williams, sent a message to an Internet chat room that read "Dad of Toddler has 'good' pics of her an [sic] me for swap of your toddler pics." A law enforcement agent responded by sending Williams a private message that contained photos of a college-aged female, which were computer altered to look like photos of a ten-year-old girl. Williams requested explicit photos of the girl, but the agent did not respond. After that, Williams sent another public message that accused the agent of being a cop and included a hyperlink containing seven pictures of minors engaging in sexually explicit conduct.

Williams was arrested and charged with possession of child pornography and pandering material that appeared to be child pornography. He claimed that the Protect Act's pandering provision was unconstitutionally overbroad and vague. (He later pleaded guilty to the charges but preserved the issue of constitutionality for appeal.)

Is the Protect Act Constitutional?

On appeal, the federal appellate court held that the pandering provision of the Protect Act was unconstitutional because it criminalized speech regarding child pornography. The United States Supreme Court reversed that decision, ruling that the Protect Act was neither unconstitutionally overbroad nor impermissibly vague. The Court held that the statute was valid because it does not prohibit a substantial amount of protected speech. Rather, the act generally prohibits offers to provide, and requests to obtain, child pornography—both of which are unprotected speech. Thus, the act's pandering provision remedied the constitutional defects of its predecessor, which had made it illegal to possess virtual child pornography.

---

a. *Ashcroft v. Free Speech Coalition,* 553 U.S. 234, 122 S.Ct. 1389, 152 L.Ed.2d 403 (2002).
b. 18 U.S.C. Section 2252A(a)(5)(B).
c. 18 U.S.C. Section 2252A(a)(3)(B).
d. 535 U.S. 285, 128 S.Ct. 1830, 170 L.Ed.2d 650 (2008).

CRITICAL THINKING

INSIGHT INTO THE LEGAL ENVIRONMENT
Why should it be illegal to "pander" virtual child pornography when it is not illegal to possess it?

Freedom of Religion

The First Amendment states that the government may neither establish any religion nor prohibit the free exercise of religious practices. The first part of this constitutional provision is referred to as the **establishment clause,** and the second part is known as the **free exercise clause.** Government action, both federal and state, must be consistent with this constitutional mandate.

THE ESTABLISHMENT CLAUSE The establishment clause prohibits the government from establishing a state-sponsored religion, as well as from passing laws that promote (aid or endorse) religion or that show a preference for one religion over another. Although the establishment clause involves the separation of church and state, it does not require a complete separation. Rather, it requires the government to accommodate religions. Federal or state laws that do not promote or place a significant burden on religion are constitutional even if they have some impact on religion. For a government law or policy to be constitutional, it must not have the primary effect of promoting or inhibiting religion.

Can a secular court resolve an internal church dispute over property ownership without becoming impermissibly entangled with questions of religion? The court in the following case faced that question.

CASE 5.3
In re Episcopal Church Cases

California Supreme Court, 45 Cal.4th 467, 87 Cal.Rptr.3d 275 (2009).

BACKGROUND AND FACTS • The Episcopal Church of the United States is divided into regions called dioceses. In 2003, an openly gay man was ordained as bishop of an Episcopal diocese in New Hampshire. Some members of St. James Parish—an Episcopal parish in Los Angeles, California—did not agree with this ordination. The parish's vestry (a board of elected laypersons that, with a rector, governs an Episcopal parish) voted to end its affiliation with the Episcopal Church and to affiliate with the Anglican Church of Uganda. After the disaffiliation, a dispute arose as to who owned the church building that the parish used for worship and the property on which the building stands. To resolve this dispute, the Episcopal Church and others filed a suit in a California state court against St. James and others, with both sides claiming ownership. The court ruled that the parish owned the building and the property, but a state intermediate appellate court reversed this judgment. St. James appealed to the California Supreme Court, arguing, in part, that the parish's name was on the deed to the property.

IN THE LANGUAGE OF THE COURT
CHIN, J. [Justice]
* * * *

* * * State courts must not decide questions of religious doctrine; those are for the church to resolve. Accordingly, if resolution of a property dispute involves a point of doctrine, the court must defer to the position of the highest ecclesiastical authority that has decided the point. *But to the extent the court can resolve a property dispute without reference to church doctrine, it should apply neutral principles of law. The court should consider sources such as the deeds to the property in dispute, * * * the general church's constitution, canons, and rules, and relevant statutes* * * *. [Emphasis added.]
* * * *

St. James Parish holds * * * title to the property in question. That is the fact that defendants rely on most heavily in claiming ownership. On the other hand, from the beginning of its existence, St. James Parish promised to be bound by the constitution and canons of the Episcopal Church. Such commitment is found in the original application to the higher church authorities to organize as a parish * * *.
* * * *

* * * The Episcopal Church's adoption of Canon I.7.4 * * * strongly supports the conclusion that, once defendants left the general church, the property reverted to the general church.
* * * *

[A California state statute] permits the governing instruments of the general church to create an express trust in church property, which Canon I.7.4 does. * * * This statute also compels

CASE 5.3 CONTINUED ➡ the conclusion that the general church owns the property now that defendants have left the general church.

       * * * *

    Defendants state that, over the years, St. James Parish "purchased additional parcels of property in its own name, with funds donated exclusively by its members." They contend that it would be unjust and contrary to the intent of the members * * * to cause the local parish to "lose its property simply because it has changed its spiritual affiliation." But the matter is not so clear. * * * Did they act over the years intending to contribute to a church that was part of the Episcopal Church or to contribute to St. James Parish even if it later joined a different church? It is impossible to say for sure. Probably different contributors over the years would have had different answers if they had thought about it and were asked. The only intent a secular court can effectively discern is that expressed in legally cognizable documents.

    * * * The individual defendants are free to disassociate themselves from the parish and the Episcopal Church and to affiliate themselves with another religious denomination. No court can interfere with or control such an exercise of conscience. The problem lies in defendants' efforts to take the church property with them. This they may not do.

DECISION AND REMEDY • *The California Supreme Court affirmed the appellate court's judgment. The state supreme court applied "neutral principles of law" and concluded that the Episcopal Church, not St. James Parish, owned the property in question.*

THE LEGAL ENVIRONMENT DIMENSION • *Should the court have considered whether the Episcopal Church had abandoned or departed from the tenets of faith and practice that it had held at the time of St. James's affiliation? Why or why not?*

WHAT IF THE FACTS WERE DIFFERENT? • *Suppose that before this property dispute was finally resolved, the church's rules were changed to declare that "all property is held in trust for the local churches." Would the result in this case have been different? Explain.*

THE FREE EXERCISE CLAUSE The free exercise clause guarantees that a person can hold any religious belief that she or he wants, or a person can have no religious belief. This constitutional guarantee generally prevents the government from compelling a person to do something that is contrary to her or his religious beliefs. (Note that the clause applies only to the government—not to individuals and private businesses. See Chapter 22 for a discussion of laws that promote religious freedom in the employment context.)

When religious practices work against public policy and the public welfare, though, the government can act. For example, the government can require that a child receive certain types of vaccinations or medical treatment if his or her life is in danger—regardless of the child's or parent's religious beliefs. When public safety is an issue, an individual's religious beliefs often have to give way to the government's interest in protecting the public. The government's interest must be sufficiently compelling, however.

CASE IN POINT A religious sect in New Mexico follows the practices of a Brazil-based church. Its members ingest hoasca tea as part of a ritual to connect with and better understand God. Hoasca tea, which is brewed from plants native to the Amazon rain forest, contains an illegal hallucinogenic drug. When federal drug agents confiscated the church's shipment of hoasca tea as it entered the country, the church filed a lawsuit claiming that the government had violated its members' right to freely exercise their religion. Ultimately, the Supreme Court ruled that the government had failed to demonstrate a sufficiently compelling interest in barring the sect's sacramental use of hoasca.[26]

Searches and Seizures

The Fourth Amendment protects the "right of the people to be secure in their persons, houses, papers, and effects." Before searching or seizing private property, law enforcement officers must usually obtain a **search warrant**—an order from a judge or other public official authorizing the search or seizure.

SEARCH WARRANTS AND PROBABLE CAUSE To obtain a search warrant, law enforcement officers must

---

26. *Gonzales v. O Centro Espirita Beneficiente Uniao Do Vegetal*, 546 U.S. 418, 126 S.Ct. 1211, 163 L.Ed.2d 1017 (2006).

convince a judge that they have reasonable grounds, or probable cause, to believe a search will reveal evidence of a specific illegality. To establish **probable cause,** the officers must have trustworthy evidence that would convince a reasonable person that the proposed search or seizure is more likely justified than not. Furthermore, the Fourth Amendment prohibits *general* warrants. It requires a particular description of whatever is to be searched or seized. General searches through a person's belongings are impermissible. The search cannot extend beyond what is described in the warrant. Although search warrants require specificity, if a search warrant is issued for a person's residence, items that are in that residence may be searched even if they do not belong to that individual.

CASE IN POINT Paycom Billing Services, Inc., an online payment service, stores vast amounts of customer credit-card information. Christopher Adjani, a former Paycom employee, threatened to sell Paycom's confidential client information if the company did not pay him $3 million. Pursuant to an investigation, the Federal Bureau of Investigation (FBI) obtained a search warrant to search Adjani's person, automobile, and residence, including computer equipment. When the FBI agents served the warrant, they discovered evidence of the criminal scheme in the e-mail communications on a computer in Adjani's residence that belonged to Adjani's live-in girlfriend. The court held that the search of the computer was proper given the involvement of computers in the alleged crime.[27]

SEARCHES AND SEIZURES IN THE BUSINESS CONTEXT Because of the strong governmental interest in protecting the public, a warrant normally is not required for seizures of spoiled or contaminated food. Nor are warrants required for searches of businesses in such highly regulated industries as liquor, guns, and strip mining. The standard used for highly regulated industries is sometimes applied in other contexts as well, such as screening for airline travel.

CASE IN POINT Christian Hartwell was attempting to board a flight from Philadelphia to Phoenix, Arizona. When he walked through the security checkpoint, he set off the alarm. Airport security took him aside and eventually discovered that he had two packages of crack cocaine in his pocket. When Hartwell was convicted of possession of drugs, he appealed, claiming that the airport search was suspicionless and violated his Fourth Amendment rights. A federal appellate court held that airports can be treated as highly regulated industries and that suspicionless checkpoint screening of airline passengers is constitutional.[28]

Generally, government inspectors do not have the right to enter business premises without a warrant, although the standard of probable cause is not the same as that required in nonbusiness contexts. The existence of a general and neutral enforcement plan will normally justify issuance of the warrant. Lawyers and accountants frequently possess the business records of their clients, and inspecting these documents while they are out of the hands of their true owners also requires a warrant.

Self-Incrimination

The Fifth Amendment guarantees that no person "shall be compelled in any criminal case to be a witness against himself." Thus, in any federal or state (because the due process clause extends the protection to state courts) proceeding, an accused person cannot be forced to give testimony that might subject him or her to any criminal prosecution.

The Fifth Amendment's guarantee against self-incrimination extends only to natural persons. Therefore, neither corporations nor partnerships receive Fifth Amendment protection. When a partnership is required to produce business records, it must do so even if the information provided incriminates the individual partners of the firm. In contrast, sole proprietors and sole practitioners (those who fully own their businesses) cannot be compelled to produce their business records. These individuals have full protection against self-incrimination because they function in only one capacity; there is no separate business entity.

SECTION 3
DUE PROCESS AND EQUAL PROTECTION

Other constitutional guarantees of great significance to Americans are mandated by the *due process clauses* of the Fifth and Fourteenth Amendments and the *equal protection clause* of the Fourteenth Amendment.

27. *United States v. Adjani,* 452 F.3d 1140 (9th Cir. 2006); *cert.* denied, 549 U.S. 1025, 127 S.Ct. 568, 166 L.Ed.2d 420 (2006).

28. *United States v. Hartwell,* 436 F.3d 174 (3d Cir. 2006).

Due Process

Both the Fifth and Fourteenth Amendments provide that no person shall be deprived "of life, liberty, or property, without due process of law." The **due process clause** of these constitutional amendments has two aspects—procedural and substantive. Note that the due process clause applies to "legal persons" (that is, corporations), as well as to individuals.

PROCEDURAL DUE PROCESS *Procedural* due process requires that any government decision to take life, liberty, or property must be made equitably; that is, the government must give a person proper notice and an opportunity to be heard. Fair procedures must be used in determining whether a person will be subjected to punishment or have some burden imposed on her or him. Fair procedure has been interpreted as requiring that the person have at least an opportunity to object to a proposed action before an impartial, neutral decision maker (which need not be a judge). Thus, for example, if a driver's license is construed as a property interest, the state must provide some sort of opportunity for the driver to object before suspending or terminating the person's license.

SUBSTANTIVE DUE PROCESS *Substantive* due process protects an individual's life, liberty, or property against certain government actions regardless of the fairness of the procedures used to implement them. Substantive due process limits what the government may do in its legislative and executive capacities. Legislation must be fair and reasonable in content and must further a legitimate governmental objective. Only when state conduct is arbitrary, or shocks the conscience, however, will it rise to the level of violating substantive due process.[29]

If a law or other governmental action limits a fundamental right, the state must have a legitimate and compelling interest to justify its action. Fundamental rights include interstate travel, privacy, voting, marriage and family, and all First Amendment rights. Thus, a state must have a substantial reason for taking any action that infringes on a person's free speech rights.

In situations not involving fundamental rights, a law or action does not violate substantive due process if it rationally relates to any legitimate government purpose. Under this test, almost any business regulation will be upheld as reasonable.

Equal Protection

Under the Fourteenth Amendment, a state may not "deny to any person within its jurisdiction the equal protection of the laws." The United States Supreme Court has interpreted the due process clause of the Fifth Amendment to make the **equal protection clause** applicable to the federal government as well. Equal protection means that the government cannot enact laws that treat similarly situated individuals differently.

Both substantive due process and equal protection require review of the substance of the law or other governmental action rather than review of the procedures used. When a law or action limits the liberty of all persons to do something, it may violate substantive due process; when a law or action limits the liberty of some persons but not others, it may violate the equal protection clause. Thus, for example, if a law prohibits all advertising on the sides of trucks, it raises a substantive due process question; if it makes an exception to allow truck owners to advertise their own businesses, it raises an equal protection issue.

In an equal protection inquiry, when a law or action distinguishes between or among individuals, the basis for the distinction, or classification, is examined. Depending on the classification, the courts apply different levels of scrutiny, or "tests," to determine whether the law or action violates the equal protection clause. The courts use one of three standards: strict scrutiny, intermediate scrutiny, or the "rational basis" test.

STRICT SCRUTINY If a law or action prohibits or inhibits some persons from exercising a fundamental right, the law or action will be subject to "strict scrutiny" by the courts. Under this standard, the classification must be necessary to promote a *compelling state interest*. Also, if the classification is based on a *suspect trait*—such as race, national origin, or citizenship status—it must be necessary to promote a compelling government interest.[30]

Compelling state interests include remedying past unconstitutional or illegal discrimination but do not include correcting the general effects of "society's discrimination." For instance, for a city to give preference to minority applicants in awarding

---

29. See, for example, *Breen v. Texas A&M University,* 485 F.3d 325 (5th Cir. 2007); *Hart v. City of Little Rock,* 432 F.3d 801 (8th Cir. 2005); and *County of Sacramento v. Lewis,* 523 U.S. 833, 118 S.Ct. 1708, 140 L.Ed.2d 1043 (1998).

30. See, for example, *Johnson v. California,* 543 U.S. 499, 125 S.Ct. 1141, 160 L.Ed.2d 949 (2005).

construction contracts, it normally must identify past unconstitutional or illegal discrimination against minority construction firms. Because the policy is based on suspect traits (race and national origin), it will violate the equal protection clause *unless* it is necessary to promote a compelling state interest. Generally, few laws or actions survive strict-scrutiny analysis by the courts.

INTERMEDIATE SCRUTINY Another standard, that of *intermediate scrutiny,* is applied in cases involving discrimination based on gender or legitimacy. Laws using these classifications must be *substantially related to important government objectives.* For example, an important government objective is preventing illegitimate teenage pregnancies. Therefore, because males and females are not similarly situated in this regard—only females can become pregnant—a law that punishes men but not women for statutory rape will be upheld, even though it treats men and women unequally.

The state also has an important objective in establishing time limits (called *statutes of limitation*) for how long after an event a particular type of action can be brought. Such limits prevent persons from bringing fraudulent and stale (outdated) claims.

THE "RATIONAL BASIS" TEST In matters of economic or social welfare, a classification will be considered valid if there is any conceivable *rational basis* on which the classification might relate to a legitimate government interest. It is almost impossible for a law or action to fail the rational basis test. Thus, for example, a city ordinance that in effect prohibits all pushcart vendors, except a specific few, from operating in a particular area of the city will be upheld if the city provides a rational basis—such as reducing the traffic in the particular area—for the ordinance. In contrast, a law that provides unemployment benefits only to people over six feet tall would clearly fail the rational basis test because it could not further any legitimate government objective.

SECTION 4
PRIVACY RIGHTS

The U.S. Constitution does not explicitly mention a general right to privacy. In a 1928 Supreme Court case, *Olmstead v. United States,*[31] Justice Louis

Brandeis stated in his dissent that the right to privacy is "the most comprehensive of rights and the right most valued by civilized men." The majority of the justices at that time, however, did not agree with Brandeis. It was not until the 1960s that the Supreme Court endorsed the view that the Constitution protects individual privacy rights. In a landmark 1965 case, *Griswold v. Connecticut,*[32] the Supreme Court held that a constitutional right to privacy was implied by the First, Third, Fourth, Fifth, and Ninth Amendments.

Federal Statutes Affecting Privacy Rights

In the 1960s, Americans were sufficiently alarmed by the accumulation of personal information in government files that they pressured Congress to pass laws permitting individuals to access their files. Congress responded in 1966 with the Freedom of Information Act, which allows any person to request copies of any information on her or him contained in federal government files. In 1974, Congress passed the Privacy Act, which also gives persons the right to access such information. Since then, Congress has passed numerous other laws protecting individuals' privacy rights with respect to financial transactions, electronic communications, and other activities in which personal information may be gathered and stored by organizations.

Since the 1990s, one of the major concerns of individuals has been how to protect privacy rights in cyberspace and to safeguard private information that may be revealed online (including credit-card numbers and financial information). The increasing value of personal information for online marketers—who are willing to pay a high price for such information to those who collect it—has exacerbated the situation.

PRETEXTING A *pretext* is a false motive put forth to hide the real motive, and *pretexting* is the process of obtaining information by false means. Pretexters may try to obtain personal data by claiming that they are taking a survey for a research firm, a political party, or even a charity. Congress passed the Gramm-Leach-Bliley Act,[33] which made pretexting

---

31. 277 U.S. 438, 48 S.Ct. 564, 72 L.Ed. 944 (1928).

32. 381 U.S. 479, 85 S.Ct. 1678, 14 L.Ed.2d 510 (1965).
33. Also known as the Financial Services Modernization Act, Pub. L. No. 106-102 (1999), 113 Stat. 1338, codified in numerous sections of 12 U.S.C.A. and 15 U.S.C.A.

to obtain financial information illegal. Initially, it was not clear whether that law prohibited lying to obtain *nonfinancial* information for purposes other than identity theft.

This gray area in the law led to a highly publicized scandal involving Patricia C. Dunn, who was then chair of Hewlett-Packard. To find out who had leaked confidential company information to the press, Dunn hired private investigators who used false pretenses to access individuals' personal cell phone records. Dunn claimed that she had not been aware of the investigators' methods and had assumed that they had obtained the information from a public record. Although she was indicted in 2006 for her role in the pretexting, the criminal charges were later dropped. Several civil lawsuits followed. In 2007, the company paid $14.5 million in fines to settle a lawsuit filed by the California attorney general. In 2008, Hewlett-Packard reached a settlement with the New York Times Company and three *BusinessWeek* magazine journalists in connection with the scandal.

To clarify the law on pretexting to gain access to phone records, Congress enacted the Telephone Records and Privacy Protection Act.[34] This act makes it a federal crime to pretend to be someone else or to make false representations for the purpose of obtaining another person's confidential phone records. The Federal Trade Commission investigates and prosecutes violators, who can be fined and sentenced to up to ten years in prison.

MEDICAL INFORMATION Responding to the growing need to protect the privacy of individuals' health records—particularly computerized records—Congress passed the Health Insurance Portability and Accountability Act (HIPAA) of 1996.[35] This act defines and limits the circumstances in which an individual's "protected health information" may be used or disclosed.

HIPAA also requires health-care providers and health-care plans, including certain employers who sponsor health plans, to inform patients of their privacy rights and of how their personal medical information may be used. The act also states that a person's medical records generally may not be used for purposes unrelated to health care—such

as marketing, for example—or disclosed to others without the individual's permission. Covered entities must formulate written privacy policies, designate privacy officials, limit access to computerized health data, physically secure medical records with lock and key, train employees and volunteers on their privacy policies, and sanction those who violate the policies.

THE USA PATRIOT ACT Today, individuals face additional concerns about government intrusions into their privacy. The USA Patriot Act was passed by Congress in the wake of the terrorist attacks of September 11, 2001, and then reauthorized in 2006.[36] The Patriot Act has given government officials increased authority to monitor Internet activities (such as e-mail and Web site visits) and to gain access to personal financial information and student information. Law enforcement officials may now track the telephone and e-mail communications of one party to find out the identity of the other party or parties. To gain access to these communications, the government must certify that the information likely to be obtained by such monitoring is relevant to an ongoing criminal investigation but does not need to provide proof of any wrongdoing.[37] Privacy advocates argue that this law adversely affects the constitutional rights of all Americans, and it has been widely criticized in the media.

Other Laws Affecting Privacy

State constitutions and statutes also protect individuals' privacy rights, often to a significant degree. Privacy rights are also protected under tort law (see Chapter 12). Additionally, the Federal Trade Commission has played an active role in protecting the privacy rights of online consumers (see Chapter 24). The protection of employees' privacy rights, particularly with respect to electronic monitoring practices, is an area of growing concern (see Chapter 21).

34. Pub. L. No. 109-476, (2007), 120 Stat. 3568, codified at 18 U.S.C.A. Section 1039.

35. HIPAA was enacted as Pub. L. No. 104-191 (1996) and is codified in 29 U.S.C.A. Sections 1181 *et seq.*

36. The Uniting and Strengthening America by Providing Appropriate Tools Required to Intercept and Obstruct Terrorism Act of 2001, also known as the USA Patriot Act, was enacted as Pub. L. No. 107-56 (2001) and reauthorized by Pub. L. No. 109-173 (2006).

37. See, for example, *American Civil Liberties Union v. National Security Agency*, 493 F.3d 644 (6th Cir. 2007), in which a federal appeals court upheld the government's warrantless monitoring of electronic communications.

REVIEWING
Constitutional Law

A state legislature enacted a statute that required any motorcycle operator or passenger on the state's highways to wear a protective helmet. Jim Alderman, a licensed motorcycle operator, sued the state to block enforcement of the law. Alderman asserted that the statute violated the equal protection clause because it placed requirements on motorcyclists that were not imposed on other motorists. Using the information presented in the chapter, answer the following questions.

1. Why does this statute raise equal protection issues instead of substantive due process concerns?
2. What are the three levels of scrutiny that the courts use in determining whether a law violates the equal protection clause?
3. Which standard of scrutiny, or test, would apply to this situation? Why?
4. Applying this standard, or test, is the helmet statute constitutional? Why or why not?

✹ **DEBATE THIS:** *Legislation aimed at "protecting people from themselves" concerns the individual as well as the public in general. Protective helmet laws are just one example of such legislation. Should individuals be allowed to engage in unsafe activities if they choose to do so?*

TERMS AND CONCEPTS

Bill of Rights 103
checks and balances 99
commerce clause 99
due process clause 111
equal protection clause 111

establishment clause 108
federal form of
  government 98
filtering software 106
free exercise clause 108
full faith and credit
  clause 99

meta tags 106
police powers 98
preemption 102
privileges and immunities
  clause 99

probable cause 110
search warrant 109
supremacy clause 102
symbolic speech 104

QUESTIONS AND CASE PROBLEMS

5–1. Commerce Clause A Georgia state law requires the use of contoured rear-fender mudguards on trucks and trailers operating within Georgia state lines. The statute further makes it illegal for trucks and trailers to use straight mudguards. In approximately thirty-five other states, straight mudguards are legal. Moreover, in Florida, straight mudguards are explicitly required by law. There is some evidence suggesting that contoured mudguards might be a little safer than straight mudguards. Discuss whether this Georgia statute violates any constitutional provisions.

5–2. QUESTION WITH SAMPLE ANSWER: Freedom of Religion.

Thomas worked in the nonmilitary operations of a large firm that produced both military and nonmilitary goods. When the company discontinued the production of nonmilitary

goods, Thomas was transferred to a plant producing military equipment. Thomas left his job, claiming that it violated his religious principles to participate in the manufacture of goods to be used in destroying life. In effect, he argued, the transfer to the military equipment plant forced him to quit his job. He was denied unemployment compensation by the state because he had not been effectively "discharged" by the employer but had voluntarily terminated his employment. Did the state's denial of unemployment benefits to Thomas violate the free exercise clause of the First Amendment? Explain.

• **For a sample answer to Question 5–2, go to Appendix F at the end of this text.**

5–3. Equal Protection With the objectives of preventing crime, maintaining property values, and preserving the quality of urban life, New York City enacted an ordinance to regulate the locations of commercial establishments that featured adult entertainment. The ordinance expressly applied to female, but not male, topless entertainment. Adele Buzzetti owned the Cozy Cabin, a New York City cabaret that featured female topless dancers. Buzzetti and an anonymous dancer filed a suit in a federal district court against the city, asking the court to block the enforcement of the ordinance. The plaintiffs argued, in part, that the ordinance violated the equal protection clause. Under the equal protection clause, what standard applies to the court's consideration of this ordinance? Under this test, how should the court rule? Why?

5-4. Freedom of Speech Henry Mishkoff is a Web designer whose firm does business as "Webfeats." When Taubman Co. began building a mall called "The Shops at Willow Bend" near Mishkoff's home, Mishkoff registered the domain name "shopsatwillowbend.com" and created a Web site with that address. The site featured information about the mall, a disclaimer indicating that Mishkoff's site was unofficial, and a link to the mall's official site. Taubman discovered Mishkoff's site and filed a suit in a federal district court against him. Mishkoff then registered various other names, including "taubmansucks.com," with links to a site documenting his battle with Taubman. (A Web name with a "sucks.com" moniker attached to it is known as a *complaint name*, and the process of registering and using such names is known as *cybergriping*.) Taubman asked the court to order Mishkoff to stop using all of these names. Should the court grant Taubman's request? On what basis might the court protect Mishkoff's use of the names? [*Taubman Co. v. Webfeats*, 319 F.3d 770 (6th Cir. 2003)]

5-5. CASE PROBLEM WITH SAMPLE ANSWER: Privacy.

To protect the privacy of individuals identified in information systems maintained by federal agencies, the Privacy Act of 1974 regulates the use of the information. The statute provides for a minimum award of $1,000 for "actual damages sustained" caused by "intentional or willful actions" to the "person entitled to recovery." Buck Doe filed for certain disability benefits with an office of the U.S. Department of Labor (DOL). The application form asked for Doe's Social Security number, which the DOL used to identify his claim on documents sent to groups of claimants, their employers, and the lawyers involved in their cases. This disclosed Doe's Social Security number beyond the limits set by the Privacy Act. Doe filed a suit in a federal district court against the DOL, alleging that he was "torn . . . all to pieces" and "greatly concerned and worried" because of the disclosure of his Social Security number and its potentially "devastating" consequences. He did not offer any proof of actual injury, however. Should damages be awarded in such circumstances solely on the basis of the agency's conduct, or should proof of some actual injury be required? Why? [Doe v. Chao, 540 U.S. 614, 124 S.Ct. 1204, 157 L.Ed.2d 1122 (2004)]

• **To view a sample answer for Problem 5–5, go to this book's Web site at www.cengage.com/blaw/cross, select "Chapter 5," and click on "Case Problem with Sample Answer."**

5-6. Supremacy Clause The Federal Communications Act of 1934 grants the right to govern all *interstate* telecommunications to the Federal Communications Commission (FCC) and the right to regulate all *intrastate* telecommunications to the states. The federal Telephone Consumer Protection Act of 1991, the Junk Fax Protection Act of 2005, and FCC rules permit a party to send unsolicited fax ads to recipients with whom the party has an "established business relationship" if those ads include an "opt-out" alternative. Section 17538.43 of California's Business and Professions Code (known as "SB 833") was enacted in 2005 to provide the citizens of California with greater protection than that afforded under federal law. SB 833 omits the "established business relationship" exception and requires a sender to obtain a recipient's express consent (an "opt-in" provision) before faxing an ad to that party into or out of California. The Chamber of Commerce of the United States filed a suit against Bill Lockyer, California's state attorney general, seeking to block the enforcement of SB 833. What principles support the plaintiff's position? How should the court resolve the issue? Explain. [*Chamber of Commerce of the United States v. Lockyer*, 463 F.3d 1076 (E.D.Cal. 2006)]

5-7. Freedom of Speech For decades, New York City has had to deal with the vandalism and defacement of public property caused by unauthorized graffiti. Among other attempts to stop the damage, in December 2005 the city banned the sale of aerosol spray-paint cans and broad-tipped indelible markers to persons under twenty-one years of age and prohibited them from possessing such items on property other than their own. By May 1, 2006, five people—all under age twenty-one—had been cited for violations of these regulations, and 871 individuals had been arrested for actually making graffiti. Some artists, including college student Lindsey Vincenty, who was studying visual arts, wished to create graffiti on legal surfaces, such as canvas, wood, and clothing. Unable to buy her supplies in the city or to carry them in the city if she bought them elsewhere, Vincenty and others filed a suit in a federal district court on behalf of themselves and other young artists against Michael Bloomberg, the city's mayor, and others. The plaintiffs claimed that, among other things, the new rules violated their right to freedom of speech. They asked the court to enjoin the enforcement of the rules. Should the court grant this request? Why or why not? [*Vincenty v. Bloomberg*, 476 F.3d 74 (2d Cir. 2007)]

5-8. Due Process In 2006, at the Russ College of Engineering and Technology of Ohio University, a university investigative report found "rampant and flagrant plagiarism" in the theses of mechanical engineering graduate students. Faculty singled out for "ignoring their ethical responsibilities and contributing to an atmosphere of negligence toward issues of academic misconduct" included Jay Gunasekera, professor of mechanical engineering and chair of the department. These findings were publicized in a press conference on May 31. The university prohibited Gunasekera from advising graduate students. He filed a suit in a federal district court against Dennis Irwin, the dean of Russ College, and others, for violating his "due-process rights when they publicized accusations about his role in plagiarism by his graduate student advisees without providing him with a meaningful opportunity to clear his name" in public. Irwin asked the court to dismiss the suit. What does due process require in these circumstances? Why? [*Gunasekera v. Irwin*, 551 F.3d 461 (6th Cir. 2009)]

5–9. Commerce Clause Under the federal Sex Offender Registration and Notification Act (SORNA), sex offenders must register as sex offenders and update their registration when they travel from one state to another. David Hall, a convicted sex offender in New York, moved from New York to Virginia, lived there for part of a year, and then returned to New York. When he returned, he was charged with the federal offense of failing to register as a sex offender while in Virginia, as required by SORNA. In his defense, he claimed that SORNA was unconstitutional because Congress had no authority to criminalize interstate travel where no commerce was involved. The federal district court dismissed the indictment. The government appealed, contending that the statute is valid under the commerce clause. Does that contention seem reasonable? Why or why not? [*United States v. Hall*, 591 F.3d 83 (2d Cir. 2010)]

5–10. A QUESTION OF ETHICS: Defamation.

Aric Toll owns and manages the Balboa Island Village Inn, a restaurant and bar in Newport Beach, California. Anne Lemen owns the "Island Cottage," a residence across an alley from the Inn. Lemen often complained to the authorities about excessive noise and the behavior of the Inn's customers, whom she called "drunks" and "whores." Lemen referred to Theresa Toll, Aric's wife, as "Madam Whore." Lemen told the Inn's bartender Ewa Cook that Cook "worked for Satan," was "Satan's wife," and was "going to have Satan's children." She told the Inn's neighbors that it was "a whorehouse" with "prostitution going on inside" and that it sold illegal drugs, sold alcohol to minors, made "sex videos," was involved in child pornography, had "Mafia connections," encouraged "lesbian activity," and stayed open until 6:00 A.M. Lemen also voiced her complaints to potential customers, and the Inn's sales dropped more than 20 percent. The Inn filed a suit in a California state court against Lemen, asserting defamation and other claims. [Balboa Island Village Inn, Inc. v. Lemen, 40 Cal.4th 1141, 156 P.3d 339 (2007)]

(a) Are Lemen's statements about the Inn's owners, customers, and activities protected by the U.S. Constitution? Should such statements be protected? In whose favor should the court rule? Why?

(b) Did Lemen behave unethically in the circumstances of this case? Explain.

LEGAL RESEARCH EXERCISES ON THE WEB

Go to this text's Web site at **www.cengage.com/blaw/cross**, select "Chapter 5," and click on "Practical Internet Exercises." There you will find the following Internet research exercises that you can perform to learn more about the topics covered in this chapter.

Practical Internet Exercise 5–1: **Legal Perspective**
Commercial Speech

Practical Internet Exercise 5–2: **Management Perspective**
Privacy Rights in Cyberspace

CHAPTER 6
✳
Administrative Law

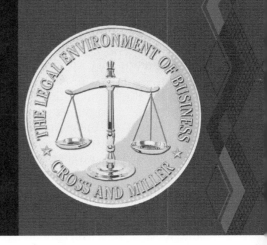

Government agencies established to administer the law have a great impact on the day-to-day operations of the government and the economy. In its early years, the United States had a relatively simple, nonindustrial economy with few political demands for detailed regulations and therefore relatively few administrative agencies. Today, in contrast, rules cover almost every aspect of a business's operation. Consequently, agencies have multiplied.

Administrative agencies issue rules, orders, interpretations, and decisions. The regulations make up the body of *administrative law.* You were introduced briefly to some of the main principles of administrative law in Chapter 1. In the following pages, we look at these principles in much greater detail.

THE PRACTICAL SIGNIFICANCE OF ADMINISTRATIVE LAW

Unlike statutory law, administrative law is created by administrative agencies, not by legislatures, but it is nevertheless of paramount significance for businesses. When Congress—or a state legislature—enacts legislation, it typically adopts a rather general statute and leaves its implementation to an administrative agency, which then creates the detailed rules and regulations necessary to carry out the statute. The administrative agency, with its specialized personnel, has the time, resources, and expertise to make the detailed decisions required for regulation.

Administrative Agencies Exist at All Levels of Government

Administrative agencies are spread throughout the government. At the federal level, the Securities and Exchange Commission regulates a firm's capital structure and financing, as well as its financial reporting. The National Labor Relations Board oversees relations between a firm and any unions with which it may deal. The Equal Employment Opportunity Commission also regulates employer-employee relationships. The Environmental Protection Agency and the Occupational Safety and Health Administration affect the way a firm manufactures its products, and the Federal Trade Commission influences the way it markets those products.

Added to this layer of federal regulation is a second layer of state regulation that, when not preempted, may cover many of the same activities as federal regulation or regulate independently the activities that federal regulation does not cover. If the actions of parallel state and federal agencies conflict, the actions of the federal agency will prevail under the supremacy clause of the U.S. Constitution. Agency regulations at the county or municipal level can also affect certain types of business activities.

Agencies Provide a Comprehensive Regulatory Scheme

Often, administrative agencies at various levels of government work together and share the responsibility of creating and enforcing particular regulations. For example, when Congress enacted the Clean Air Act (to be discussed in Chapter 25), it provided only general directions for the prevention of air pollution. The specific pollution-control requirements imposed on business are almost entirely the product of decisions made by the Environmental Protection Agency (EPA). Moreover, the EPA works with parallel environmental agencies at the state level to analyze existing data and determine the appropriate pollution-control standards.

Legislation and regulations have significant benefits—in the example of the Clean Air Act, a cleaner environment than existed in decades past. At the same time, these benefits entail considerable costs for business. The EPA has estimated the costs of compliance with the Clean Air Act at many tens of billions of dollars yearly. Although the agency has calculated that the overall benefits of its regulations often exceed their costs, the burden on business is substantial. Additionally, the costs are proportionately higher for small businesses because they cannot take advantage of the economies of scale (cost advantages that a firm obtains due to expansion) available to larger operations.

Given the costs that regulation entails, business has a strong incentive to try to influence the regulatory environment. Whenever new regulations are proposed, as happens constantly, companies may lobby the agency to try to persuade it not to adopt a particular regulation or to adopt one that is more cost-effective. At the same time, public-interest groups may be lobbying in favor of more stringent regulation.

SECTION 2
AGENCY CREATION AND POWERS

Congress creates federal administrative agencies. By delegating some of its authority to make and implement laws, Congress can monitor indirectly a particular area in which it has passed legislation without becoming bogged down in the details relating to enforcement—details that are often best left to specialists.

To create an administrative agency, Congress passes **enabling legislation,** which specifies the name, purposes, functions, and powers of the agency being created. Federal administrative agencies can exercise only those powers that Congress has delegated to them in enabling legislation. Through similar enabling acts, state legislatures create state administrative agencies, which commonly parallel federal agencies.

An agency's enabling statute defines its legal authority. An agency cannot regulate beyond the powers granted by the statute, and it may be required to take some regulatory action by the terms of that statute. When regulated groups oppose a rule adopted by an agency, they often bring a lawsuit arguing that the rule was not authorized by the enabling statute and is therefore void. Conversely, a group may file suit claiming that an agency has illegally *failed* to pursue regulation required by the enabling statute.

Enabling Legislation—An Example

Congress created the Federal Trade Commission (FTC) by enacting the Federal Trade Commission Act of 1914.[1] The act prohibits unfair methods of competition and deceptive trade practices. It also describes the procedures that the FTC must follow to charge persons or organizations with violations of the act, and it provides for judicial review of agency orders. The act grants the FTC the power to do the following:

1. To create "rules and regulations for the purpose of carrying out the Act."
2. To conduct investigations of business practices.
3. To obtain reports from interstate corporations concerning their business practices.
4. To investigate possible violations of federal antitrust statutes.[2]
5. To publish findings of its investigations.
6. To recommend new legislation.
7. To hold trial-like hearings to resolve certain kinds of trade disputes that involve FTC regulations or federal antitrust laws.

The authorizing statute for the FTC allows it to prevent the use of "unfair methods of competition," but does not define *unfairness*. Congress delegated that authority to the commission, thereby providing it with considerable discretion in regulating competition. The commission that heads the FTC is composed of five members, each of whom the president appoints, with the advice and consent of the Senate, for a term of seven years.

Types of Agencies

As discussed in Chapter 1, there are two basic types of administrative agencies: executive agencies and independent regulatory agencies. Federal *executive agencies* include the cabinet departments of the

---

1. 15 U.S.C. Sections 41–58.
2. The FTC shares enforcement of the Clayton Act with the Antitrust Division of the U.S. Department of Justice (see Chapter 27).

executive branch, which were formed to assist the president in carrying out executive functions, and the subagencies within the cabinet departments. The Occupational Safety and Health Administration, for example, is a subagency within the U.S. Department of Labor. Executive agencies usually have a single administrator, director, or secretary who is appointed by the president to oversee the agency and can be removed by the president at any time. Exhibit 6–1 below lists the cabinet departments and some of their most important subagencies.

Independent regulatory agencies are outside the federal executive departments (those headed by a cabinet secretary). Examples of independent agencies include the Federal Trade Commission and the Securities and Exchange Commission (SEC). Rather than having a single person as its head, an independent agency usually is run by a commission or board made up of several members, one of whom serves as the agency's chair. Commissioners or board members typically serve for fixed terms and cannot be removed without just cause. The SEC has five

EXHIBIT 6-1 • Executive Departments and Important Subagencies

DEPARTMENT AND DATE FORMED	SELECTED SUBAGENCIES
State (1789)	Passport Office; Bureau of Diplomatic Security; Foreign Service; Bureau of Human Rights and Humanitarian Affairs; Bureau of Consular Affairs; Bureau of Intelligence and Research
Treasury (1789)	Internal Revenue Service; U.S. Mint
Interior (1849)	U.S. Fish and Wildlife Service; National Park Service; Bureau of Indian Affairs; Bureau of Land Management
Justice (1870)[a]	Federal Bureau of Investigation; Drug Enforcement Administration; Bureau of Prisons; U.S. Marshals Service
Agriculture (1889)	Soil Conservation Service; Agricultural Research Service; Food Safety and Inspection Service; Forest Service
Commerce (1913)[b]	Bureau of the Census; Bureau of Economic Analysis; Minority Business Development Agency; U.S. Patent and Trademark Office; National Oceanic and Atmospheric Administration
Labor (1913)[b]	Occupational Safety and Health Administration; Bureau of Labor Statistics; Employment Standards Administration; Office of Labor-Management Standards; Employment and Training Administration
Defense (1949)[c]	National Security Agency; Joint Chiefs of Staff; Departments of the Air Force, Navy, Army; service academies
Housing and Urban Development (1965)	Office of Community Planning and Development; Government National Mortgage Association; Office of Fair Housing and Equal Opportunity
Transportation (1967)	Federal Aviation Administration; Federal Highway Administration; National Highway Traffic Safety Administration; Federal Transit Administration
Energy (1977)	Office of Civilian Radioactive Waste Management; Office of Nuclear Energy; Energy Information Administration
Health and Human Services (1980)[d]	Food and Drug Administration; Centers for Medicare and Medicaid Services; Centers for Disease Control and Prevention; National Institutes of Health
Education (1980)[d]	Office of Special Education and Rehabilitation Services; Office of Elementary and Secondary Education; Office of Postsecondary Education; Office of Vocational and Adult Education
Veterans Affairs (1989)	Veterans Health Administration; Veterans Benefits Administration; National Cemetery System
Homeland Security (2002)	U.S. Citizenship and Immigration Services; Directorate of Border and Transportation Services; U.S. Coast Guard; Federal Emergency Management Agency

a. Formed from the Office of the Attorney General (created in 1789).
b. Formed from the Department of Commerce and Labor (created in 1903).
c. Formed from the Department of War (created in 1789) and the Department of the Navy (created in 1798).
d. Formed from the Department of Health, Education, and Welfare (created in 1953).

commissioners who serve for five-year terms that are staggered so that one term ends on June 5 of every year. The SEC's commissioners oversee its four divisions and nineteen offices. Selected independent regulatory agencies, as well as their principal functions, are listed in Exhibit 6–2 below.

Agency Powers and the Constitution

Administrative agencies occupy an unusual niche in the U.S. legal scheme because they exercise powers that are normally divided among the three branches of government. As mentioned earlier, agencies' powers include functions associated with the legislature (*rulemaking*), the executive branch (*enforcement*), and the courts (*adjudication*).

The constitutional principle of *checks and balances* allows each branch of government to act as a check on the actions of the other two branches. Furthermore, the U.S. Constitution authorizes only the legislative branch to create laws. Yet administrative agencies, to which the Constitution does not specifically refer, can make **legislative rules,** or *substantive rules,* that are as legally binding as laws that Congress passes. (Administrative agencies also issue **interpretive rules,** which simply declare policy and do not affect legal rights or obligations.)

THE DELEGATION DOCTRINE Article I of the U.S. Constitution authorizes Congress to delegate powers to administrative agencies. In fact, courts generally hold that Article I is the basis for all administrative law. Section 1 of that article grants all legislative powers to Congress and requires Congress to oversee the implementation of all laws. Article I, Section 8, gives Congress the power to make all laws necessary for executing its specified powers. The courts interpret these passages, under what is known as the **delegation doctrine,** as granting Congress the power to establish administrative agencies that can create rules for implementing those laws.

The three branches of government exercise certain controls over agency powers and functions, as discussed next, but in many ways administrative agencies function independently. For this reason, administrative agencies, which constitute the **bureaucracy,** are sometimes referred to as the "fourth branch" of the U.S. government.

EXHIBIT 6–2 • Selected Independent Regulatory Agencies

NAME AND DATE FORMED	PRINCIPAL DUTIES
Federal Reserve System Board of Governors (the Fed)–1913	Determines policy with respect to interest rates, credit availability, and the money supply; starting in 2008, the Federal Reserve became involved in various "bailouts" of firms in the financial sector, including a "conservatorship" of two large mortgage institutions (Fannie Mae and Freddie Mac) and control of the world's largest insurance company, AIG.
Federal Trade Commission (FTC)–1914	Prevents businesses from engaging in unfair trade practices; stops the formation of monopolies in the business sector; protects consumer rights.
Securities and Exchange Commission (SEC)–1934	Regulates the nation's stock exchanges, in which shares of stock are bought and sold; enforces the securities laws, which require full disclosure of the financial profiles of companies that wish to sell stock and bonds to the public.
Federal Communications Commission (FCC)–1934	Regulates all communications by telegraph, cable, telephone, radio, satellite, and television.
National Labor Relations Board (NLRB)–1935	Protects employees' rights to join unions and bargain collectively with employers; attempts to prevent unfair labor practices by both employers and unions.
Equal Employment Opportunity Commission (EEOC)–1964	Works to eliminate discrimination in employment based on religion, gender, race, color, disability, national origin, or age; investigates claims of discrimination.
Environmental Protection Agency (EPA)–1970	Undertakes programs aimed at reducing air and water pollution; works with state and local agencies to help fight environmental hazards. (It has been suggested recently that its status be elevated to that of a department.)
Nuclear Regulatory Commission (NRC)–1975	Ensures that electricity-generating nuclear reactors in the United States are built and operated safely; regularly inspects operations of such reactors.

EXECUTIVE CONTROLS The executive branch of government exercises control over agencies both through the president's power to appoint federal officers and through the president's veto power. The president may veto enabling legislation presented by Congress or congressional attempts to modify an existing agency's authority. In addition, the president has created a process whereby the Office of Information and Regulatory Affairs (OIRA) of the Office of Management and Budget reviews the cost-effectiveness of agency rules. The OIRA also reviews agencies' compliance with the Paperwork Reduction Act,[3] which requires agencies to minimize the paperwork burden on regulated entities.

LEGISLATIVE CONTROLS Congress also exercises authority over agency powers. Congress gives power to an agency through enabling legislation and can take power away—or even abolish an agency altogether—through subsequent legislation. Legislative authority is required to fund an agency, and enabling legislation usually sets certain time and monetary limits on the funding of particular programs. Congress can always revise these limits. In addition to its power to create and fund agencies, Congress has the authority to investigate the implementation of its laws and the agencies that it has created. Congress also has the power to "freeze" the enforcement of most federal regulations before the regulations take effect. Another legislative check on agency actions is the Administrative Procedure Act, which will be discussed shortly.

JUDICIAL CONTROLS The judicial branch exercises control over agency powers through the courts' review of agency actions. As you will read in the next section, the Administrative Procedure Act provides for judicial review of most agency decisions. Agency actions are not automatically subject to judicial review, however, and the courts can deny review under the two theories discussed next.

The Exhaustion Doctrine. The party seeking court review must first exhaust all of his or her administrative remedies under what is called the *exhaustion doctrine.* In other words, the complaining party normally must have gone through the administrative process (from complaint to hearing to final agency order, all of which will be discussed in detail later in the chapter) before seeking court review.

Suppose that an employee who has a disability believes that she has suffered unlawful discrimination in the workplace (see Chapter 22). Under the exhaustion doctrine, before she can file a complaint in court, she must have filed a complaint with the Equal Employment Opportunity Commission (EEOC), and the EEOC must have issued its final ruling.

The Ripeness Doctrine. In addition, under what is known as the *ripeness doctrine,* a court will not review an administrative agency's decision until the case is "ripe for review." Generally, a case is ripe for review if the parties can demonstrate that they have met certain requirements. For example, the party bringing the action must have *standing to sue* the agency (the party must have a direct stake in the outcome of the judicial proceeding, as discussed in Chapter 2), and there must be an *actual controversy* at issue. A court can dismiss the action if the administrative agency has not yet issued a decision or if the party lacks standing.

SECTION 3
THE ADMINISTRATIVE PROCEDURE ACT

All federal agencies must follow specific procedural requirements when fulfilling their three basic functions of rulemaking, enforcement, and adjudication. In this section, we focus on agency rulemaking (enforcement and adjudication will be discussed in a later section of this chapter). Sometimes, Congress specifies certain procedural requirements in an agency's enabling legislation. In the absence of any directives from Congress concerning a particular agency procedure, the Administrative Procedure Act (APA) of 1946[4] applies.

The Arbitrary and Capricious Test

One of Congress's goals in enacting the APA was to provide for more judicial control over administrative agencies. To that end, the APA provides that courts should "hold unlawful and set aside" agency actions found to be "arbitrary, capricious, an abuse of discretion, or otherwise not in accordance with law."[5] Under this standard, parties can challenge regulations as contrary to law or so irrational as to be arbitrary and capricious.

---

3. Pub. L. No. 104-13, May 22, 1995, 109 Stat. 163, amending 44 U.S.C. Sections 3501 *et seq.*

4. 5 U.S.C. Sections 551–706.

5. 5 U.S.C. Section 706(2)(A).

There is no precise definition of what makes a rule arbitrary and capricious, but the standard includes factors such as whether the agency has done any of the following:

1. Failed to provide a rational explanation for its decision.
2. Changed its prior policy without justification.
3. Considered legally inappropriate factors.
4. Entirely failed to consider a relevant factor.
5. Rendered a decision plainly contrary to the evidence.

In the following case, the United States Supreme Court considered the application of the arbitrary and capricious standard.

✳ EXTENDED CASE 6.1 ✳
Federal Communications Commission v. Fox Television Stations, Inc.

Supreme Court of the United States, ___ U.S. ___, 129 S.Ct. 1800, 173 L.Ed.2d 738 (2009).
www.supremecourt.gov/opinions/opinions.aspx[a]

IN THE LANGUAGE OF THE COURT

Justice *SCALIA* delivered the opinion of the Court.
* * * *
The Communications Act of 1934 established a system of limited-term broadcast licenses subject to various "conditions" * * * .

* * * [These conditions include] the indecency ban—the statutory proscription [prohibition] against "utter[ing] any obscene, indecent, or profane language by means of radio communication"—which Congress has instructed the [Federal Communications] Commission to enforce * * * .
* * * *
The Commission first invoked the statutory ban on indecent broadcasts in 1975, declaring a daytime broadcast of George Carlin's "Filthy Words" monologue actionably indecent. At that time, the Commission announced the definition of indecent speech that it uses to this day, prohibiting "language that describes, in terms patently offensive as measured by contemporary community standards for the broadcast medium, sexual or excretory activities or organs, at times of the day when there is a reasonable risk that children may be in the audience."
* * * *

Over a decade later, the Commission emphasized that the "full context" in which particular materials appear is "critically important," but that a few "principal" factors guide the inquiry, such as the "explicitness or graphic nature" of the material, the extent to which the material "dwells on or repeats" the offensive material, and the extent to which the material was presented to "pander," to "titillate," or to "shock."
* * * "Where sexual or excretory references have been made once or have been passing or fleeting in nature, this characteristic has tended to weigh against a finding of indecency."

In 2004, the Commission took one step further by declaring for the first time that a nonliteral (expletive) use of the F- and S-Words could be actionably indecent, even when the word is used only once. The first order to this effect dealt with an NBC broadcast of the Golden Globe Awards, in which the performer Bono [lead singer of the rock group U-2] commented, "This is really, really, f***ing brilliant."
* * * *

The order acknowledged that "prior Commission and staff action have indicated that isolated or fleeting broadcasts of the 'F-Word' * * * are not indecent or would not be acted upon." It explicitly ruled that

"any such interpretation is no longer good law."

[The present case] concerns utterances in two live broadcasts aired by Fox Television Stations, Inc., * * * prior to the Commission's Golden Globes Order. The first occurred during the 2002 Billboard Music Awards, when the singer Cher exclaimed, "I've also had critics for the last 40 years saying that I was on my way out every year. Right. So f*** 'em." The second involved a segment of the 2003 Billboard Music Awards, [when Nicole Richie asked] the audience, "Why do they even call it 'The Simple Life?' Have you ever tried to get cow s*** out of a Prada purse? It's not so f***ing simple."

On March 15, 2006, the Commission released Notices of Apparent Liability for a number of broadcasts that the Commission deemed actionably indecent, including the two described above.
* * * *

* * * In the Commission's view, "granting an automatic exemption for 'isolated or fleeting' expletives unfairly forces viewers (including children)" to take "the first blow" and would allow broadcasters "to air expletives at all hours of a day so long as they did so one at a time."

Fox [appealed] to the Second Circuit [Court of Appeals] for review of the [order] * * * . The Court of

---

a. Under the heading "2008 Term," select "2008 Term Opinions of the Court." When the page opens, scroll down the list to "49" in the left-hand column and click on the case title to access the opinion. The Supreme Court of the United States maintains this Web site.

EXTENDED CASE 6.1 CONTINUED ➥

Appeals reversed the agency's order, finding the Commission's reasoning inadequate under the Administrative Procedure Act. * * * We granted *certiorari*.

* * * *

The Administrative Procedure Act, which sets forth the full extent of judicial authority to review executive agency action for procedural correctness, permits (insofar as relevant here) the setting aside of agency action that is "arbitrary" or "capricious." *Under what we have called this "narrow" standard of review, we insist that an agency "examine the relevant data and articulate a satisfactory explanation for its action." We have made clear, however, that "a court is not to substitute its judgment for that of the agency," and should "uphold a decision of less than ideal clarity if the agency's path may reasonably be discerned."* [Emphasis added.]

In overturning the Commission's judgment, the Court of Appeals here relied in part on Circuit precedent requiring a more substantial explanation for agency action that changes prior policy. The Second Circuit has interpreted the Administrative Procedure Act and our opinion in [a previous case] as requiring agencies to make clear "why the original reasons for adopting the [displaced] rule

or policy are no longer dispositive [a deciding factor]" as well as "why the new rule effectuates the statute as well as or better than the old rule." The Court of Appeals for the District of Columbia Circuit has similarly indicated that a court's standard of review is "heightened somewhat" when an agency reverses course.

We find no basis in the Administrative Procedure Act or in our opinions for a requirement that all agency change be subjected to more searching review. The Act mentions no such heightened standard. [Emphasis added.]

To be sure, the requirement that an agency provide reasoned explanation for its action would ordinarily demand that it display awareness that it *is* changing position. An agency may not, for example, depart from a prior policy *sub silentio* [under silence, without any notice of the change] or simply disregard rules that are still on the books. And of course the agency must show that there are good reasons for the new policy. But it need not demonstrate to a court's satisfaction that the reasons for the new policy are *better* than the reasons for the old one; it suffices that the new policy is permissible under the statute, that there are good reasons for it, and that the agency *believes* it to be better.

* * * *

Judged under the above-described standards, the Commission's new enforcement policy and its order finding the broadcasts actionably indecent were neither arbitrary nor capricious. First, the Commission forthrightly acknowledged that its recent actions have broken new ground, taking account of inconsistent "prior Commission and staff action" and explicitly disavowing them as "no longer good law." * * * There is no doubt that the Commission knew it was making a change. That is why it declined to assess penalties * * *.

Moreover, the agency's reasons for expanding the scope of its enforcement activity were entirely rational. It was certainly reasonable to determine that it made no sense to distinguish between literal and nonliteral uses of offensive words, requiring repetitive use to render only the latter indecent. * * * It is surely rational (if not inescapable) to believe that a safe harbor for single words would "likely lead to more widespread use of the offensive language."

* * * *

The judgment of the United States Court of Appeals for the Second Circuit is reversed, and the case is remanded for further proceedings consistent with this opinion.[b]

---

b. On remand, the U.S. Court of Appeals for the Second Circuit ruled that the FCC's indecency policies were unconstitutionally vague and violated the broadcast networks' First Amendment rights. See *Fox Television Stations, Inc. v. Federal Communications Commission,* 613 F.3d 317 (2010).

 QUESTIONS

1. Today, children are likely exposed to indecent language in various media far more often than they were in the 1970s, when the Federal Communications Commission first began to sanction indecent speech. Does this mean that we need more stringent—or less stringent—regulation of broadcasts? Explain.
2. Technological advances have made it easier for broadcasters to "bleep out" offending words in the programs that they air. Does this development support a more stringent—or less stringent—enforcement policy by the Federal Communications Commission? Explain.

Rulemaking

Today, the major function of an administrative agency is **rulemaking**—the formulation of new regulations, or rules. The APA defines a *rule* as "an agency statement of general or particular applicability and future effect designed to implement,

interpret, or prescribe law and policy."[6] Regulations are sometimes said to be *legislative* because, like statutes, they have a binding effect. Like those who violate statutes, violators of agency rules may be

---

6. 5 U.S.C. Section 551(4).

punished. Because agency rules have such significant legal force, the APA established procedures for agencies to follow in creating rules. Many rules must be adopted using the APA's *notice-and-comment rulemaking* procedure.

Notice-and-comment rulemaking involves three basic steps: notice of the proposed rulemaking, a comment period, and the final rule. The APA recognizes some limited exceptions to these procedural requirements, but they are seldom invoked. If the required procedures are violated, the resulting rule may be invalid.

The impetus for rulemaking may come from various sources, including Congress, the agency itself, or private parties, who may petition an agency to begin a rulemaking (or repeal a rule). For example, environmental groups have petitioned for stricter air-pollution controls to combat emissions that may contribute to global warming.

NOTICE OF THE PROPOSED RULEMAKING

When a federal agency decides to create a new rule, the agency publishes a notice of the proposed rulemaking proceedings in the *Federal Register,* a daily publication of the executive branch that prints government orders, rules, and regulations. The notice states where and when the proceedings will be held, the agency's legal authority for making the rule (usually its enabling legislation), and the terms or subject matter of the proposed rule. The APA requires an agency to make available to the public certain information, such as the key scientific data underlying the proposal. The proposed rule is also often reported by the news media and published in the trade journals of the industries that will be affected by the new rule.

COMMENT PERIOD

After the publication of the notice of the proposed rulemaking proceedings, the agency must allow ample time for persons to comment in writing on the proposed rule. The comment period must be at least thirty days but is often sixty days or longer. An agency can extend the period to allow for more comments or shorten it in emergencies (such as when the Federal Aviation Administration changed airport security procedures after September 11, 2001).

The purpose of this comment period is to give interested parties the opportunity to express their views on the proposed rule in an effort to influence agency policy. Anyone can submit comments. The comments may be in writing or, if a hearing is held, may be given orally. All comments are logged in and become a public record that others can examine.

The agency need not respond to all comments, but it must respond to any significant comments that bear directly on the proposed rule. The agency responds by either modifying its final rule or explaining, in a statement accompanying the final rule, why it did not make any changes. In some circumstances, particularly when the procedure being used in a specific instance is less formal, an agency may accept comments after the comment period is closed. The agency should summarize these *ex parte* (private, "off-the-record") comments in the record for possible review.[7]

THE FINAL RULE

After the agency reviews the comments, it drafts the final rule and publishes it in the *Federal Register.* The final rule must contain a "concise general statement of . . . basis and purpose" that describes the reasoning behind the rule.[8] The final rule may modify the terms of the proposed rule in light of the public comments, but if substantial changes are made, a new proposal and a new opportunity for comment are required. The final rule is later compiled along with the rules and regulations of other federal administrative agencies in the *Code of Federal Regulations.* Final rules have binding legal effect unless the courts later overturn them and for this reason are considered legislative rules. If an agency failed to follow proper rulemaking procedures when it issued the final rule, however, the rule may not be binding.

CASE IN POINT Members of the Hemp Industries Association (HIA) manufacture and sell food products made from hemp seed and oil. These products contain only trace amounts of tetrahydrocannabinols (THC, a component of marijuana) and are nonpsychoactive—that is, they do not affect a person's mind or behavior. In 2001, the U.S. Drug Enforcement Administration (DEA) published an interpretive rule declaring that "any product that contains any amount of THC is a Schedule I controlled substance [a drug whose availability is restricted by law]." Subsequently, without following formal rulemaking procedures, the DEA declared that two legislative rules relating to products containing natural THC were final. These rules effectively

---

7. *Ex parte* is a Latin term meaning "from one party." In the law, it usually refers to proceedings in which only one party to a dispute is present. *Ex parte* communications with judges (or administrative law judges) generally are prohibited. Thus, when agencies accept *ex parte* public comments, they must record them and make them available to others.

8. 5 U.S.C. Section 555(c).

banned the possession and sale of the food products of the HIA's members. The HIA petitioned for court review, arguing that the DEA rules should not have been enforced. A federal appellate court agreed and ruled in favor of the HIA. The DEA should have held hearings on the record concerning the rules, invited public comment, and then issued formal rulings on each finding, conclusion, and exception. Because the DEA did not follow its formal rulemaking procedures, the rules were not enforceable.[9]

Informal Agency Actions

Rather than take the time to conduct notice-and-comment rulemaking, agencies have increasingly been using more informal methods of policymaking, such as issuing interpretive rules and guidance documents. As mentioned previously, *legislative rules* are substantive in that they affect legal rights, whereas *interpretive rules* simply declare policy and do not affect legal rights or obligations. Agencies also issue various other materials, such as guidance documents, which advise the public on the agencies' legal and policy positions.

Informal agency actions are exempt from the APA's requirements because they do not establish legal rights—a party cannot be directly prosecuted for violating an interpretive rule or a guidance document. Nevertheless, an agency's informal action can be of practical importance because it warns regulated entities that the agency may engage in formal rulemaking if they fail to heed the positions taken informally by the agency.

SECTION 4
JUDICIAL DEFERENCE TO AGENCY DECISIONS

When asked to review agency decisions, courts historically granted some deference (significant weight) to the agency's judgment, often citing the agency's great expertise in the subject area of the regulation. This deference seems especially appropriate when applied to an agency's analysis of factual questions, but should it also extend to an agency's interpretation of its own legal authority? In *Chevron U.S.A., Inc. v. Natural Resources Defense Council, Inc.*,[10] the United States Supreme Court held that it should,

thereby creating a standard of broadened deference to agencies on questions of legal interpretation.

The Holding of the *Chevron* Case

At issue in the *Chevron* case was whether the courts should defer to an agency's interpretation of a statute giving it authority to act. The Environmental Protection Agency (EPA) had interpreted the phrase "stationary source" in the Clean Air Act as referring to an entire manufacturing plant, and not to each facility within a plant. The agency's interpretation enabled it to adopt the so-called bubble policy, which allowed companies to offset increases in emissions in part of a plant with decreases elsewhere in the plant—an interpretation that reduced the pollution-control compliance costs faced by manufacturers. An environmental group challenged the legality of the EPA's interpretation.

The Supreme Court held that the courts should defer to an agency's interpretation of *law* as well as fact. The Court found that the agency's interpretation of the statute was reasonable and upheld the bubble policy. The Court's decision in the *Chevron* case created a new standard for courts to use when reviewing agency interpretations of law, which involves the following two questions:

1. Did Congress directly address the issue in dispute in the statute? If so, the statutory language prevails.
2. If the statute is silent or ambiguous, is the agency's interpretation "reasonable"? If it is, a court should uphold the agency's interpretation even if the court would have interpreted the law differently.

When Courts Will Give *Chevron* Deference to Agency Interpretation

The notion that courts should defer to agencies on matters of law was controversial. Under the holding of the *Chevron* case, when the meaning of a particular statute's language is unclear and an agency interprets it, the court must follow the agency's interpretation as long as it is reasonable. This led to considerable discussion and litigation to test the boundaries of the *Chevron* holding. For instance, are courts required to give deference to all agency interpretations or only to those interpretations that result from adjudication or formal rulemaking procedures? Are informal agency interpretations issued through opinion letters and internal memoranda also entitled to deference?

---

9. *Hemp Industries Association v. Drug Enforcement Administration,* 357 F.3d 1012 (9th Cir. 2004).

10. 467 U.S. 837, 104 S.Ct. 2778, 81 L.Ed.2d 694 (1984).

CASE IN POINT The United States has a tariff (tax) schedule that authorizes the U.S. Customs Service to classify and fix the rate of duty on imports. "Ruling letters" set tariff classifications for particular imports. Mead Corporation imported "daily planners," which had been tariff-free for several years. The Customs Service issued a ruling letter reclassifying them as "bound diaries," which were subject to a tariff. Mead brought a lawsuit claiming that the ruling letter should not receive *Chevron* deference because it was not put into effect pursuant to notice-and-comment rulemaking. When the case reached the United States Supreme Court, the Court agreed that the ruling letter was *not* entitled to *Chevron* deference. For agencies to be assured of such judicial deference, they must meet the formal legal standards for notice-and-comment rulemaking.[11]

In the case that follows, an environmental organization brought an action challenging the U.S. Forest Service's decision to issue a special use permit to a business that conducts helicopter-skiing operations in two national forests. As you will read in Chapter 25, the National Environmental Policy Act requires federal agencies to prepare an environmental impact statement (EIS) that considers every significant aspect of the environmental impact of a proposed action. Although the Forest Service prepared an EIS before issuing the use permit, environmental groups claimed that the EIS did not sufficiently analyze increasing recreational pressures in the forests. The groups sought to have the court invalidate the permit. Although the *Chevron* precedent is not specifically mentioned, the court's analysis illustrates the way in which courts review agency decisions.

---

11. *United States v. Mead Corporation,* 533 U.S. 218, 121 S.Ct. 2164, 150 L.Ed.2d 292 (2001).

CASE 6.2
Citizens' Committee to Save Our Canyons v. Krueger

United States Court of Appeals, Tenth Circuit, 513 F.3d 1169 (2008).

BACKGROUND AND FACTS • Under the National Forest Management Act (NFMA), the U.S. Forest Service manages national forests in accordance with forest plans periodically developed for each forest. The plans for two national forests—the Wasatch-Cache and Uinta forests—were initially adopted in 1985 and revised in 2003. The Forest Service interpreted the 1985 forest plans as requiring the forests to allow helicopter skiing, and the plans expressly recognized helicopter skiing as a legitimate use of the national forests. Wasatch Powderbird Guides (WPG) has continuously operated a guided helicopter-skiing business in the Wasatch-Cache and Uinta national forests since 1973. It operates under the authority of special use permits periodically issued by the Forest Service. Citizens' Committee to Save Our Canyons and Utah Environmental Congress (referred to collectively as SOC) are nonprofit organizations whose members use the areas in which WPG operates for nonmotorized uses, such as backcountry skiing, snowshoeing, hiking, and camping. They claimed that their recreational opportunities and experiences were diminished by WPG's operations and argued that the Forest Service failed to comply with relevant laws when issuing WPG's most recent permit. The district court upheld the Forest Service permit, and SOC appealed.

IN THE LANGUAGE OF THE COURT
TYMKOVICH, Circuit Judge.
* * * *

Under the Administrative Procedure Act ("APA"), which governs judicial review of agency actions, * * * we set aside the agency's action * * * if it is "arbitrary, capricious, an abuse of discretion, or otherwise not in accordance with law." We will also set aside an agency action if the agency has failed to follow required procedures.

Our review is highly deferential [respectful of the agency's reasoning]. The duty of a court reviewing agency action under the "arbitrary or capricious" standard is to ascertain whether the agency examined the relevant data and articulated a rational connection between the facts found and the decision made. Furthermore, in reviewing the agency's explanation, the reviewing court must determine whether the agency considered all relevant factors and whether there has been a clear error of judgment. A presumption

CASE 6.2 CONTINUED ➡ of validity attaches to the agency action and the burden of proof rests with the appellants who challenge such action. [Emphasis added.]

* * * *

NFMA requires the Forest Service to "develop, maintain, and, as appropriate, revise land and resource management plans for units of the National Forest System." All permits the Forest Service issues "for the use and occupancy of National Forest System lands shall be consistent with the land management plans."

* * * The EIS examined various options and concluded an acceptable balance between helicopter skiing and other uses could be reached by imposing certain restrictions on WPG's operations. These restrictions reflect no special consideration for WPG's economic viability beyond the goal of providing "a range of diverse, recreational opportunities" including helicopter skiing. The EIS thoroughly explains the Forest Service's approach, and the 2005 permit includes a number of reasonable restrictions on WPG with the goal of allowing both helicopter skiers and other backcountry users to enjoy the national forests. In the end, the Forest Service's permit reflected the "type and level" of heli-skiing it thought appropriately balanced the competing recreational uses in the forests.

Taking the interpretation of the forest plans represented by the EIS as a whole, the EIS and the ultimate permitting decision comply with the Forest Service's interpretation of its forest plans. The Forest Service properly considered how particular options would affect the range of recreational opportunities available in the forests and balanced interests in a way it believed promoted multiple forest uses.

* * * *

In sum, the Forest Service's EIS fully disclosed and considered the impact of its decision to issue a special use permit to WPG. *Our objective is not to "fly speck" the [EIS], but rather, to make a pragmatic judgment whether the [EIS]'s form, content and preparation foster both informed decision-making and informed public participation.* The [National Environmental Policy Act (NEPA)] process in this case, including extensive public comment, considered a variety of options and yielded a number of reasonable restrictions on WPG's operations designed to minimize conflict among forest users. This is all NEPA requires. [Emphasis added.]

DECISION AND REMEDY • *The U.S. Court of Appeals for the Tenth Circuit affirmed the district court's decision that upheld the Forest Service permit allowing WPG to conduct helicopter-skiing operations in two national forests. The Forest Service's EIS properly considered all relevant factors and allowed for public comment. Because the Forest Service's interpretation of the NFMA and NEPA was reasonable, the court found that the permit complied with federal laws.*

WHAT IF THE FACTS WERE DIFFERENT? • *Suppose that the Forest Service had granted WPG a permit for its helicopter-skiing operations on national forest land without preparing an EIS or soliciting public comment. How might that have changed the court's ruling?*

THE ETHICAL DIMENSION • *If it turned out that the helicopter-skiing operation had paid a substantial sum to the Forest Service official who prepared the EIS to influence the official's findings, would the court have been able to consider this fact and invalidate the permit? Why or why not?*

SECTION 5
ENFORCEMENT AND ADJUDICATION

Although rulemaking is the most prominent agency activity, enforcement of the rules is also critical. Often, an agency itself enforces its rules. It identifies alleged violators and pursues civil remedies against them in a proceeding held by the agency rather than in federal court, although the agency's determinations are reviewable in court.

Investigation

After final rules are issued, agencies conduct investigations to monitor compliance with those rules or the requirements of the enabling statute. A typical agency investigation of this kind might begin when a citizen reports a possible violation to the agency. (See this chapter's *Insight into Ethics* feature on the following page for a discussion of how concern about violating regulations has made pharmaceutical companies reluctant to use Twitter and Facebook.)

Many agency rules also require considerable compliance reporting from regulated entities, and such

INSIGHT INTO ETHICS
Should Pharmaceutical Companies Be Allowed to Tweet?

Where do Americans go when they need medical information? More than 60 percent turn to the Internet, and half of those go to social networks, such as Twitter and Facebook, to consult with others about diagnosis and treatments. According to pharmaceutical companies, however, much of the information that potential customers are finding online is incorrect.

Consumers Lack Complete Information on Drugs

Drug companies are, of course, in the business of selling prescription drugs, but they do have an incentive to ensure that consumers have correct information about those drugs. Yet drug manufacturers spend less than 5 percent of their consumer advertising budgets on Internet advertising. (More than 95 percent of the $4 billion that these companies spend on direct consumer advertising goes to traditional outlets, such as newspapers, magazines, and television.)

Similarly, drug companies have little or no presence on sites such as Facebook and Twitter. Why not? They fear that the U.S. Food and Drug Administration (FDA) will retaliate if they do not list all of the potential side effects when they mention their drugs on the Web.

Web site Formats Cannot Show Everything

The FDA requires advertisements for prescription drugs to disclose all of the potential negative side effects. A magazine ad for a prescription drug, for example, typically includes a large block of small print that details potential side effects. Display ads on the Web are not amenable to such lists. So, to avoid violating the FDA's regulations, pharmaceutical companies run only general, disease-related search ads on the Web. Because the ads only rarely mention a drug's brand name, consumers looking for information about a particular drug rarely click on or find such ads.

As a result, consumers have less information about available prescription drugs. For the same reason, drug companies are reluctant to tweet about their drugs. How could they possibly describe all of the potential side effects in only 140 characters?

CRITICAL THINKING

INSIGHT INTO THE E-COMMERCE ENVIRONMENT
Do pharmaceutical companies have an ethical responsibility to correct erroneous information about their products on sites such as Wikipedia?

---

a report may trigger an enforcement investigation. For example, environmental regulators often require reports of emissions, and the Occupational Safety and Health Administration requires companies to report any work-related deaths.

INSPECTIONS Many agencies gather information through on-site inspections. Sometimes, inspecting an office, a factory, or some other business facility is the only way to obtain the evidence needed to prove a regulatory violation. Administrative inspections and tests cover a wide range of activities, including safety inspections of underground coal mines, safety tests of commercial equipment and automobiles, and environmental monitoring of factory emissions. An agency may also ask a firm or individual to submit certain documents or records to the agency for examination. For example, the Federal Trade Commission often asks to inspect corporate records for compliance.

Normally, business firms comply with agency requests to inspect facilities or business records because it is in any firm's interest to maintain a good relationship with regulatory bodies. In some instances, however, such as when a firm thinks an

agency's request is unreasonable and may be detrimental to the firm's interest, the firm may refuse to comply with the request. In such situations, an agency may resort to the use of a subpoena or a search warrant.

SUBPOENAS There are two basic types of subpoenas. The subpoena *ad testificandum* ("to testify") is an ordinary subpoena. It is a writ, or order, compelling a witness to appear at an agency hearing. The subpoena *duces tecum*[12] ("bring it with you") compels an individual or organization to hand over books, papers, records, or documents to the agency. An administrative agency may use either type of subpoena to obtain testimony or documents.

There are limits on the information that an agency can demand. To determine whether an agency is abusing its discretion in its pursuit of information as part of an investigation, a court may consider such factors as the following:

1. *The purpose of the investigation.* An investigation must have a legitimate purpose. Harassment is an

---

12. Pronounced *doo*-suhs *tee*-kum.

example of an improper purpose. An agency may not issue an administrative subpoena to inspect business records if the agency's motive is to harass or pressure the business into settling an unrelated matter.

2. *The relevance of the information being sought.* Information is relevant if it reveals that the law is being violated or if it assures the agency that the law is not being violated.

3. *The specificity of the demand for testimony or documents.* A subpoena must, for example, adequately describe the material being sought.

4. *The burden of the demand on the party from whom the information is sought.* In responding to a request for information, a party must bear the costs of, for example, copying the documents that must be handed over. A business generally is not required to reveal its trade secrets, however.

SEARCHES DURING SITE INSPECTIONS As mentioned, agency investigations often involve on-site inspections. For example, the Environmental Protection Agency (EPA) frequently conducts inspections to enforce environmental laws. The EPA may inspect a site to determine if hazardous wastes are being stored properly or to sample a facility's wastewater to ensure that it complies with the Clean Water Act. Usually, companies do not resist such inspections, although in some circumstances they may do so.

Search Warrant Usually Required. The Fourth Amendment protects against unreasonable searches and seizures by requiring in most instances that a search warrant be obtained before a physical search for evidence is conducted. An agency typically must obtain a search warrant that directs law enforcement officials to search a specific place for a specific item and present it to the agency.

Some Warrantless Searches Legal. Agencies can conduct warrantless searches in several situations. Warrants are not required to conduct searches in certain highly regulated industries. Firms that sell firearms or liquor, for example, are automatically subject to inspections without warrants. Sometimes, a statute permits warrantless searches of certain types of hazardous operations, such as coal mines or liquid propane retailers. A warrantless inspection might also be considered reasonable in emergency situations or when a violation is potentially dangerous to human health or the environment. Finally, if procuring a warrant will defeat the purpose of the inspection (because evidence will be destroyed or concealed, for example), a search undertaken without a warrant may be reasonable. Note also that if a business gives a valid consent to an agency's request for an inspection and search, it has waived its right to object to the lack of a warrant.[13]

Adjudication

After an investigation reveals a suspected violation, an agency may begin to take administrative action against an individual or organization. Most administrative actions are resolved through negotiated settlements at their initial stages, without the need for formal **adjudication** (the process of resolving a dispute by presenting evidence and arguments before a neutral third party decision maker).

NEGOTIATED SETTLEMENTS Depending on the agency, negotiations may take the form of a simple conversation or a series of informal conferences. Whatever form the negotiations take, their purpose is to rectify the problem to the agency's satisfaction and eliminate the need for additional proceedings.

Settlement is an appealing option to firms for two reasons: to avoid appearing uncooperative and to avoid the expense involved in formal adjudication proceedings and in possible later appeals. Settlement is also an attractive option for agencies. To conserve their own resources and avoid formal actions, administrative agencies devote a great deal of effort to giving advice and negotiating solutions to problems.

FORMAL COMPLAINTS If a settlement cannot be reached, the agency may issue a formal complaint against the suspected violator. If the EPA, for example, finds that a factory is polluting groundwater in violation of federal pollution laws, the EPA will issue a complaint against the violator in an effort to bring the plant into compliance with federal regulations. This complaint is a public document, and a press release may accompany it. The factory charged in the complaint will respond by filing an answer to the EPA's allegations. If the factory and the EPA cannot agree on a settlement, the case will be adjudicated.

Agency adjudication may involve a trial-like arbitration procedure before an **administrative law judge (ALJ).** The Administrative Procedure Act (APA) requires that before the hearing takes place, the agency must issue a notice that includes the facts and law on which the complaint is based, the legal authority for the hearing, and its time and place. The administrative adjudication process is described next and illustrated graphically in Exhibit 6–3 on the following page.

---

13. See, for example, *Lakeland Enterprises of Rhinelander, Inc. v. Chao,* 402 F.3d 739 (7th Cir. 2005).

EXHIBIT 6-3 • The Process of Formal Administrative Adjudication

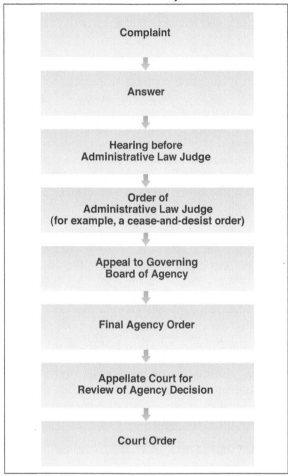

Complaint

↓

Answer

↓

Hearing before Administrative Law Judge

↓

Order of Administrative Law Judge (for example, a cease-and-desist order)

↓

Appeal to Governing Board of Agency

↓

Final Agency Order

↓

Appellate Court for Review of Agency Decision

↓

Court Order

THE ROLE OF THE ADMINISTRATIVE LAW JUDGE The ALJ presides over the hearing and has the power to administer oaths, take testimony, rule on questions of evidence, and make determinations of fact. The law requires an ALJ to be an unbiased adjudicator (judge), even though the ALJ actually works for the agency prosecuting the case (in our example, the EPA). There are no juries in administrative hearings; the ALJ assumes the role of a judge and jury in a trial.

Certain safeguards prevent bias on the part of the ALJ and promote fairness in the proceedings. For example, the APA requires that the ALJ be separate from an agency's investigative and prosecutorial staff. The APA also prohibits *ex parte* (private) communications between the ALJ and any party to an agency proceeding, such as the EPA or the factory. Finally, provisions of the APA protect the ALJ from agency disciplinary actions unless the agency can show good cause for such an action.

HEARING PROCEDURES Hearing procedures vary widely from agency to agency. Administrative agencies generally exercise substantial discretion over the type of procedure that will be used. Frequently, disputes are resolved through informal adjudication proceedings. For example, the parties, their counsel, and the ALJ may simply meet at a table in a conference room to attempt to settle the dispute.

A formal adjudicatory hearing, in contrast, resembles a trial in many respects. Prior to the hearing, the parties are permitted to undertake discovery—involving depositions, interrogatories, and requests for documents or other information, as described in Chapter 2—although the discovery process is not quite as extensive as it would be in a court proceeding. The hearing itself must comply with the procedural requirements of the APA and must also meet the constitutional standards of due process. During the hearing, the parties may give testimony, present other evidence, and cross-examine adverse witnesses. A significant difference between a trial and an administrative agency hearing, though, is that normally much more information, including hearsay (secondhand information), can be introduced as evidence during an administrative hearing. The burden of proof in an enforcement proceeding is placed on the agency.

AGENCY ORDERS Following a hearing, the ALJ renders an **initial order,** or decision, on the case. Either party can appeal the ALJ's decision to the board or commission that governs the agency. If the factory in the example (on page 129 under the "Formal Complaints" heading) is dissatisfied with the ALJ's decision, it can appeal the decision to the EPA. If the factory is dissatisfied with the commission's decision, it can appeal the decision to a federal court of appeals. If no party appeals the case, the ALJ's decision becomes the **final order** of the agency. The ALJ's decision also becomes final if a party appeals and the commission and the court decline to review the case. If a party appeals and the case is reviewed, the final order comes from the commission's decision or (if that decision is appealed to a federal appellate court) that of the reviewing court.

SECTION 6
PUBLIC ACCOUNTABILITY

As a result of growing public concern over the powers exercised by administrative agencies, Congress passed several laws to make agencies more accountable through public scrutiny. Here, we discuss the most significant of these laws.

Freedom of Information Act

Enacted in 1966, the Freedom of Information Act (FOIA)[14] requires the federal government to disclose certain records to any person or entity on written request, even if no reason is given for the request. The FOIA exempts certain types of records, such as those pertaining to national security and those containing information that is confidential or personal.

Under a 1996 amendment to the FOIA, all federal government agencies must make their records available electronically on the Internet and in other electronic formats. Any document an agency creates must be accessible by computer within a year after its creation. Agencies must also provide a clear index to all of their documents.

A request that complies with the FOIA procedures need only contain a reasonably specific description of the information sought. Many agencies now accept requests via e-mail, as well as by fax. The agency has twenty working days to answer a request and must notify the individual if the information sought is being withheld and which exemptions apply. The agency typically charges the person requesting the information a fee for research, copying, and other services.

An agency's failure to comply with a FOIA request can be challenged in a federal district court. The media, industry trade associations, public-interest groups, and even companies seeking information about competitors rely on these FOIA provisions to obtain information from government agencies.

At issue in the following case was whether certain documents requested by reporters fell under an exemption to the FOIA and thus should not be released.

---

14. 5 U.S.C. Section 552.

CASE 6.3
United Technologies Corp. v. U.S. Department of Defense

United States Court of Appeals, District of Columbia Circuit, 601 F.3d 557 (2010).
www.cadc.uscourts.gov/internet/home.nsf[a]

BACKGROUND AND FACTS • Sikorsky Aircraft Corporation makes helicopters, and Pratt and Whitney makes aircraft engines. Both companies are wholly owned by United Technologies Corporation. Both have various foreign and domestic military and civilian customers, and both sell their products to the U.S. Department of Defense (DoD). The Defense Contract Management Agency (DCMA), an agency within the DoD, monitors defense contractors, including Sikorsky and Pratt, to ensure that they satisfy their contractual obligations when providing services and supplies to the DoD. If the DCMA discovers a problem, it notifies the contractor and may issue a Corrective Action Request (CAR) or an audit report to the contractor to remedy the problem. In 2004, a reporter submitted a Freedom of Information Act (FOIA) request to the regional DCMA office for copies of all CARs that had been issued to Sikorsky during the previous year concerning Sikorsky's Black Hawk helicopter. Another reporter requested information, including a CAR and audit-related documents, concerning Pratt's airplane engine center at Middletown, Connecticut. Sikorsky and Pratt argued that the documents were exempt from FOIA disclosure. The DCMA disagreed and ruled that the documents could be disclosed. Sikorsky and Pratt filed separate suits against the DoD in a federal district court, arguing that the decision to release the documents was arbitrary, capricious, and contrary to law under the Administrative Procedure Act. They sought declaratory and injunctive relief preventing the documents' disclosure. The district court granted summary judgment to the DoD in both cases, and Sikorsky and Pratt appealed.

IN THE LANGUAGE OF THE COURT
Karen LeCraft *HENDERSON*, Circuit Judge.
* * * *

Exemption 4 covers "trade secrets and commercial or financial information obtained from a person and privileged or confidential." * * * *For the documents to*

---

a. Select "Opinions" from the options. When the Search page opens, choose "March" and "2010" from the drop-down menus, and click on "Go!" Scroll down the list of search results to the case title and click on the link to the PDF to access the case. The U.S. Court of Appeals for the District of Columbia Circuit maintains this Web site.

CASE CONTINUES ➡

CASE 6.3 CONTINUED ➡ *be exempt from disclosure, their release must be likely to cause the contractors "substantial competitive harm" or "impair the Government's ability to obtain necessary information in the future." [Emphasis added.]*

To qualify [as a "substantial competitive harm"], an identified harm must "flow from the affirmative use of proprietary information by competitors."

* * * *

* * * Sikorsky and Pratt maintain that the documents contain sensitive proprietary information about their quality control processes. Pratt's Director of Quality Military Engines attested that "a competitor with similar expertise could and would use the information to gain insights into the strengths and weaknesses of [Pratt's] quality control system as well as manufacturing techniques and use those insights to revise and improve its own quality control and manufacturing systems." Similarly, Sikorsky asserted that "proprietary information regarding Sikorsky's manufacturing process and procedures" is "inextricably intertwined with the quality control information" included in the CARs and it asserted that "release of this proprietary information would substantially harm Sikorsky's competitive position because its competitors would use this information to their advantage * * *." In response, [the] DCMA simply stated that it had redacted [removed or obscured] all of the sensitive proprietary information and concluded that disclosure of the remaining information was not likely to cause the contractors substantial competitive harm.

We find [the] DCMA's response insufficient. The documents, even as redacted by [the] DCMA, appear to reveal details about Sikorsky's and Pratt's proprietary manufacturing and quality control processes. * * * The documents describe, in part, how the contractors build and inspect helicopters and/or engines. Once disclosed, competitors could, it appears, use the information to improve their own manufacturing and quality control systems, thus making "affirmative use of proprietary information" against which Exemption 4 is meant to guard.

DECISION AND REMEDY • *The federal appellate court concluded that the DCMA had failed to provide a reasoned basis for its conclusion. The court remanded the case to the DCMA to examine the relevant data and give a satisfactory explanation for its decision, if it could, "including a rational connection between the facts found and the choice made."*

THE ETHICAL DIMENSION • *Sikorsky and Pratt also argued that if the documents were released, their competitors would use the documents to discredit them in the eyes of current and potential customers. Would such actions amount to a "substantial competitive harm"? Explain.*

MANAGERIAL IMPLICATIONS • *Businesses that contract with government agencies to provide goods or services can expect to have their processes and procedures monitored by these agencies. This means that proprietary information, including trade secrets, may find its way into various government reports or other documents. To protect this information from competitors, managers in such businesses would be wise to seek counsel as to what types of documents are exempt from disclosure under the FOIA.*

Government in the Sunshine Act

Congress passed the Government in the Sunshine Act,[15] or open meeting law, in 1976. It requires that "every portion of every meeting of an agency" be open to "public observation." The act also requires the establishment of procedures to ensure that the public is provided with adequate advance notice of scheduled meetings and agendas. Like the FOIA, the Sunshine Act contains certain exceptions. Closed meetings are permitted when (1) the subject of the meeting concerns accusing any person of a crime,

(2) an open meeting would frustrate the implementation of agency actions, or (3) the subject of the meeting involves matters relating to future litigation or rulemaking. Courts interpret these exceptions to allow open access whenever possible.

Regulatory Flexibility Act

Concern over the effects of regulation on the efficiency of businesses, particularly smaller ones, led Congress to pass the Regulatory Flexibility Act[16] in

---

15. 5 U.S.C. Section 552b.

16. 5 U.S.C. Sections 601–612.

1980. Under this act, whenever a new regulation will have a "significant impact upon a substantial number of small entities," the agency must conduct a regulatory flexibility analysis. The analysis must measure the cost that the rule would impose on small businesses and must consider less burdensome alternatives. The act also contains provisions to alert small businesses—through advertising in trade journals, for example—about forthcoming regulations. The act reduces some record-keeping burdens for small businesses, especially with regard to hazardous waste management.

Small Business Regulatory Enforcement Fairness Act

The Small Business Regulatory Enforcement Fairness Act (SBREFA) of 1996[17] allows Congress to review new federal regulations for at least sixty days before they take effect. This period gives opponents of the rules time to present their arguments to Congress.

The SBREFA also authorizes the courts to enforce the Regulatory Flexibility Act. This helps to ensure that federal agencies, such as the Internal Revenue Service, will consider ways to reduce the economic impact of new regulations on small businesses. Federal agencies are required to prepare guides that explain in plain English how small businesses can comply with federal regulations.

The SBREFA also set up the National Enforcement Ombudsman at the Small Business Administration to receive comments from small businesses about their dealings with federal agencies. Based on these comments, Regional Small Business Fairness Boards rate the agencies and publicize their findings.

---

17. 5 U.S.C. Sections 801 *et seq.*

REVIEWING
Administrative Law

Assume that the Securities and Exchange Commission (SEC) has a rule that it will enforce statutory provisions prohibiting insider trading only when the insiders make monetary profits for themselves. Then the SEC makes a new rule, declaring that it will now bring enforcement actions against individuals for insider trading even if the individuals did not personally profit from the transactions. In making the new rule, the SEC does not conduct a rulemaking procedure but simply announces its decision. A stockbrokerage firm objects and says that the new rule was unlawfully developed without opportunity for public comment. The brokerage firm challenges the rule in an action that ultimately is reviewed by a federal appellate court. Using the information presented in the chapter, answer the following questions.

1. Is the SEC an executive agency or an independent regulatory agency? Does it matter to the outcome of this dispute? Explain.
2. Suppose that the SEC asserts that it has always had the statutory authority to pursue persons for insider trading regardless of whether they personally profited from the transactions. This is the only argument the SEC makes to justify changing its enforcement rules. Would a court be likely to find that the SEC's action was arbitrary and capricious under the Administrative Procedure Act (APA)? Why or why not?
3. Would a court be likely to give *Chevron* deference to the SEC's interpretation of the law on insider trading? Why or why not?
4. Now assume that a court finds that the new rule is merely "interpretive." What effect would this determination have on whether the SEC had to follow the APA's rulemaking procedures?

⚙ DEBATE THIS: *Because an administrative law judge (ALJ) acts as both judge and jury, there should always be at least three ALJs in each administrative hearing.*

TERMS AND CONCEPTS

adjudication 129

administrative law
judge (ALJ) 129

bureaucracy 120
delegation doctrine 120
enabling legislation 118
final order 130

initial order 130
interpretive rule 120
legislative rule 120

notice-and-comment
rulemaking 123
rulemaking 123

QUESTIONS AND CASE PROBLEMS

6–1. Rulemaking and Adjudication Powers
For decades, the Federal Trade Commission (FTC) resolved fair trade and advertising disputes through individual adjudications. In the 1960s, the FTC began promulgating rules that defined fair and unfair trade practices. In cases involving violations of these rules, the due process rights of participants were more limited and did not include cross-examination. Although anyone charged with violating a rule would receive a full adjudication, the legitimacy of the rule itself could not be challenged in the adjudication. Furthermore, a party charged with violating a rule was almost certain to lose the adjudication. Affected parties complained to a court, arguing that their rights before the FTC were unduly limited by the new rules. What would the court examine to determine whether to uphold the new rules?

6–2. QUESTION WITH SAMPLE ANSWER: Informal Rulemaking.

Assume that the Food and Drug Administration (FDA), using proper procedures, adopts a rule describing its future investigations. This new rule covers all future circumstances in which the FDA wants to regulate food additives. Under the new rule, the FDA is not to regulate food additives without giving food companies an opportunity to cross-examine witnesses. Later, the FDA wants to regulate methylisocyanate, a food additive. The FDA undertakes an informal rulemaking procedure, without cross-examination, and regulates methylisocyanate. Producers protest, saying that the FDA promised them the opportunity for cross-examination. The FDA responds that the Administrative Procedure Act does not require such cross-examination and that it is free to withdraw the promise made in its new rule. If the producers challenge the FDA in court, on what basis would the court rule in their favor?

- **For a sample answer to Question 6–2, go to Appendix F at the end of this text.**

6–3. Arbitrary and Capricious Test Lion Raisins, Inc., is a family-owned, family-operated business that grows raisins and markets them to private enterprises. In the 1990s,

Lion also successfully bid on more than fifteen contracts awarded by the U.S. Department of Agriculture (USDA). In May 1999, a USDA investigation reported that Lion appeared to have falsified inspectors' signatures, listed false moisture content, and changed the grade of raisins on three USDA raisin certificates issued between 1996 and 1998. Lion was subsequently awarded five more USDA contracts. Then, in November 2000, the company was the low bidder on two new USDA contracts for school lunch programs. In January 2001, however, the USDA awarded these contracts to other bidders and, on the basis of the May 1999 report, suspended Lion from participating in government contracts for one year. Lion filed a suit in the U.S. Court of Federal Claims against the USDA, seeking, in part, lost profits on the school lunch contracts on the ground that the USDA's suspension was arbitrary and capricious. What reasoning might the court employ to grant a summary judgment in Lion's favor? [*Lion Raisins, Inc. v. United States,* 51 Fed.Cl. 238 (2001)]

6–4. Investigation Maureen Droge began working for United Air Lines, Inc. (UAL), as a flight attendant in 1990. In 1995, she was assigned to Paris, France, where she became pregnant. Because UAL does not allow its flight attendants to fly during their third trimester of pregnancy, Droge was placed on involuntary leave. She applied for temporary disability benefits through the French social security system, but her request was denied because UAL does not contribute to the French system on behalf of its U.S.-based flight attendants. Droge filed a charge of discrimination with the U.S. Equal Employment Opportunity Commission (EEOC), alleging that UAL had discriminated against her and other Americans. The EEOC issued a subpoena, asking UAL to detail all benefits received by all UAL employees living outside the United States. UAL refused to provide the information, in part, on the grounds that it was irrelevant and compliance would be unduly burdensome. The EEOC filed a suit in a federal district court against UAL. Should the court enforce the subpoena? Why or why not? [*Equal Employment Opportunity Commission v. United Air Lines, Inc.,* 287 F.3d 643 (7th Cir. 2002)]

6–5. Judicial Controls Under federal law, when accepting bids on a contract, an agency must hold "discussions" with all offerors. An agency may ask a single offeror for "clarification" of its proposal, however, without holding "discussions" with the others. Regulations define *clarifications* as "limited exchanges." In March 2001, the U.S. Air Force asked for bids on a contract. The winning contractor would examine, assess, and develop means of integrating national intelligence assets with the U.S. Department of Defense space systems, to enhance the capabilities of the Air Force's Space Warfare Center. Among the bidders were Information Technology and Applications Corp. (ITAC) and RS Information Systems, Inc. (RSIS). The Air Force asked the parties for more information on their subcontractors but did not allow them to change their proposals. Determining that there were weaknesses in ITAC's bid, the Air Force awarded the contract to RSIS. ITAC filed a suit in the U.S. Court of Federal Claims against the government, contending that the postproposal requests to RSIS, and its responses, were improper "discussions." Should the court rule in ITAC's favor? Why or why not? [*Information Technology & Applications Corp. v. United States*, 316 F.3d 1312 (Fed. Cir. 2003)].

6–6. CASE PROBLEM WITH SAMPLE ANSWER: Investigation.

Riverdale Mills Corp. makes plastic-coated steel wire products in Northbridge, Massachusetts. Riverdale uses a water-based cleaning process that generates acidic and alkaline wastewater. To meet federal clean-water requirements, Riverdale has a system within its plant to treat the water. It then flows through a pipe that opens into a manhole-covered test pit outside the plant in full view of Riverdale's employees. Three hundred feet away, the pipe merges into the public sewer system. In October 1997, the Environmental Protection Agency (EPA) sent Justin Pimpare and Daniel Granz to inspect the plant. Without a search warrant and without Riverdale's express consent, the agents took samples from the test pit. Based on the samples, Riverdale and James Knott, the company's owner, were charged with criminal violations of the federal Clean Water Act. The defendants filed a suit in a federal district court against the EPA agents and others, alleging violations of the Fourth Amendment. What right does the Fourth Amendment provide in this context? This right is based on a "reasonable expectation of privacy." Should the agents be held liable? Why or why not? [Riverdale Mills Corp. v. Pimpare, 392 F.3d 55 (1st Cir. 2004)]

- **To view a sample answer for Problem 6–6, go to this book's Web site at www.cengage.com/blaw/cross, select "Chapter 6," and click on "Case Problem with Sample Answer."**

6–7. Rulemaking The Investment Company Act of 1940 prohibits a mutual fund from engaging in certain transactions in which there may be a conflict of interest between the manager of the fund and its shareholders. Under rules issued by the Securities and Exchange Commission (SEC), however, a fund that meets certain conditions may engage in an otherwise prohibited transaction. In June 2004, the SEC added two new conditions. A year later, the SEC reconsidered the new conditions in terms of the costs that they would impose on the funds. Within eight days, and without asking for public input, the SEC readopted the conditions. The Chamber of Commerce of the United States—which is both a mutual fund shareholder and an association with mutual fund managers among its members—asked the U.S. Court of Appeals for the Second Circuit to review the new rules. The Chamber charged, in part, that in readopting the rules, the SEC relied on materials not in the "rulemaking record" without providing an opportunity for public comment. The SEC countered that the information was otherwise "publicly available." In adopting a rule, should an agency consider information that is not part of the rulemaking record? Why or why not? [*Chamber of Commerce of the United States v. Securities and Exchange Commission*, 443 F.3d 890 (D.C.Cir. 2006)]

6–8. Agency Powers A well-documented rise in global temperatures has coincided with a significant increase in the concentration of carbon dioxide in the atmosphere. Some scientists believe that the two trends are related, because when carbon dioxide is released into the atmosphere, it produces a greenhouse effect, trapping solar heat. Under the Clean Air Act (CAA) of 1963, the Environmental Protection Agency (EPA) is authorized to regulate "any" air pollutants "emitted into . . . the ambient air" that in its "judgment cause, or contribute to, air pollution." Calling global warming "the most pressing environmental challenge of our time," a group of private organizations asked the EPA to regulate carbon dioxide and other "greenhouse gas" emissions from new motor vehicles. The EPA refused, stating, among other things, that Congress last amended the CAA in 1990 without authorizing new, binding auto emissions limits. The petitioners—nineteen states, including Massachusetts, and others—asked the U.S. Court of Appeals for the District of Columbia Circuit to review the EPA's denial. Did the EPA have the authority to regulate greenhouse gas emissions from new motor vehicles? If so, was its stated reason for refusing to do so consistent with that authority? Discuss. [*Massachusetts v. Environmental Protection Agency*, 549 U.S. 497, 127 S.Ct. 1438, 167 L.Ed.2d 248 (2007)]

6–9. Judicial Deference Dave Conley, a longtime heavy smoker, was diagnosed with lung cancer. He died two years later. His death certificate stated that the cause of death was cancer, but it also noted other significant conditions that had contributed to his death were a history of cigarette smoking and coal mining. Conley's wife filed for benefits under the Black Lung Benefits Act, which provides for victims of black lung disease caused by coal mining. To qualify for benefits under the act, the exposure to coal dust must be a substantially contributing factor leading to the person's death, which, under the statute, means "hastens death." The U.S. Department of Labor collected Conley's work and medical records. An administrative law judge (ALJ) reviewed the record and took testimony from several physicians about the cause of Conley's death. Only one physician testified that the coal dust was a substantial factor leading to Conley's lung cancer, but he offered no evidence other than his testimony to support his conclusion. The ALJ nevertheless ruled that the coal mining had been a substantial factor that had hastened Conley's death and awarded benefits to Mrs. Conley. Conley's employer appealed to the Benefits Review Board (BRB) for black lung claims. It reversed the ALJ, finding that there was insufficient evidence to hold that coal dust was a substantial factor that triggered Conley's lung cancer. Mrs. Conley appealed to a federal appellate court. Should the federal court defer to the ALJ's decision on the cause of Conley's death? Why or why not? Which decision does the federal appellate court review, the ALJ's conclusions or the BRB's reversal? [*Conley v. National Mines Corp.,* 595 F.3d 297 (6th Cir. 2010)]

6–10. A QUESTION OF ETHICS: Rulemaking.

To ensure highway safety and protect driver health, Congress charged federal agencies with regulating the hours of service of commercial motor vehicle operators. Between 1940 and 2003, the regulations that applied to long-haul truck drivers were mostly unchanged. (Long-haul drivers are those who operate beyond a 150-mile radius of their base.) In 2003, the Federal Motor Carrier Safety Administration (FMSCA) revised the regulations significantly, increasing the number of daily and weekly hours that drivers could work. The agency had not considered the impact of the changes on the health of the drivers, however, and the revisions were overturned. The FMSCA then issued a notice that it would reconsider the revisions and opened them up for public comment. The agency analyzed the costs to the industry and the crash risks due to driver fatigue under different options and concluded that the safety benefits of not allowing more hours were less than the economic costs. In 2005, the agency issued a rule that was nearly identical to the 2003 version. Public Citizen, Inc., and others, including the Owner-Operator Independent Drivers Association, asked the U.S. Court of Appeals for the District of Columbia Circuit to review the 2005 rule as it applied to long-haul drivers. [Owner-Operator Independent Drivers Association, Inc. v. Federal Motor Carrier Safety Administration, 494 F.3d 188 (D.C.Cir. 2007)]

(a) The agency's cost-benefit analysis included new methods that were not disclosed to the public in time for comments. Was this unethical? Should the agency have disclosed the new methodology sooner? Why or why not?

(b) The agency created a graph to show the risk of a crash as a function of the time a driver spent on the job. The graph plotted the first twelve hours of a day individually, but the rest of the time was depicted with an aggregate figure at the seventeenth hour. This made the risk at those hours appear to be lower. Is it unethical for an agency to manipulate data? Explain.

LEGAL RESEARCH EXERCISES ON THE WEB

Go to this text's Web site at **www.cengage.com/blaw/cross**, select "Chapter 6," and click on "Practical Internet Exercises." There you will find the following Internet research exercises that you can perform to learn more about the topics covered in this chapter.

Practical Internet Exercise 6–1: **Legal Perspective**
The Freedom of Information Act

Practical Internet Exercise 6–2: **Management Perspective**
Agency Inspections

CHAPTER 7

✳

Criminal Law and Cyber Crime

The law imposes various sanctions in an effort to ensure that individuals engaged in business in our society can compete and flourish. These sanctions include those imposed by civil law, such as damages for various types of tortious conduct (see Chapter 12), damages for breach of contract (see Chapter 10), and the equitable remedies (see Chapters 1 and 10). Additional sanctions are imposed under criminal law. Indeed, many statutes regulating business provide for criminal as well as civil penalties. Therefore, criminal law joins civil law as an important element in the legal environment of business.

In this chapter, after explaining some essential differences between criminal law and civil law, we look at how crimes are classified and at the elements that must be present for criminal liability to exist. We then examine the various categories of crimes, the defenses that can be raised to avoid criminal liability, and the rules of criminal procedure. We conclude the chapter with a discussion of crimes that occur in cyberspace, which are often called cyber crimes. Generally, *cyber crime* refers more to the way in which particular crimes are committed than to a new category of crimes.

SECTION 1

CIVIL LAW AND CRIMINAL LAW

Recall from Chapter 1 that *civil law* pertains to the duties that exist between persons or between persons and their governments. Criminal law, in contrast, has to do with crime. A **crime** can be defined as a wrong against society proclaimed in a statute and punishable by a fine and/or imprisonment—or, in some cases, death. As mentioned in Chapter 1, because crimes are *offenses against society as a whole,* they are prosecuted by a public official, such as a district attorney (D.A.) or an attorney general (A.G.), not by the victims. Once a crime has been reported, the D.A. typically has the discretion to decide whether to file criminal charges and also determines to what extent to pursue the prosecution or carry out additional investigation.

Major Differences between Civil Law and Criminal Law

Because the state has extensive resources at its disposal when prosecuting criminal cases, there are numerous procedural safeguards to protect the rights of defendants. We look here at one of these safeguards—the higher burden of proof that applies in a criminal case—as well as the harsher sanctions for criminal acts compared with those for civil wrongs. Exhibit 7–1 on the next page summarizes these and other key differences between civil law and criminal law.

BURDEN OF PROOF In a civil case, the plaintiff usually must prove his or her case by a *preponderance of the evidence.* Under this standard, the plaintiff must convince the court that based on the evidence presented by both parties, it is more likely than not that the plaintiff's allegation is true.

EXHIBIT 7–1 • Key Differences between Civil Law and Criminal Law

ISSUE	CIVIL LAW	CRIMINAL LAW
Party Who Brings Suit	The person who suffered harm.	The state.
Wrongful Act	Causing harm to a person or to a person's property.	Violating a statute that prohibits some type of activity.
Burden of Proof	Preponderance of the evidence.	Beyond a reasonable doubt.
Verdict	Three-fourths majority (typically).	Unanimous (almost always).
Remedy	Damages to compensate for the harm or a decree to achieve an equitable result.	Punishment (fine, imprisonment, or death).

In a criminal case, in contrast, the state must prove its case **beyond a reasonable doubt.** If the jury views the evidence in the case as reasonably permitting either a guilty or a not guilty verdict, then the jury's verdict must be not guilty. In other words, the government (prosecutor) must prove beyond a reasonable doubt that the defendant has committed every essential element of the offense with which she or he is charged. If the jurors are not convinced of the defendant's guilt beyond a reasonable doubt, they must find the defendant not guilty. Note also that in a criminal case, the jury's verdict normally must be unanimous—agreed to by all members of the jury—to convict the defendant. (In a civil trial by jury, in contrast, typically only three-fourths of the jurors need to agree.)

CRIMINAL SANCTIONS The sanctions imposed on criminal wrongdoers are also harsher than those that are applied in civil cases. As you will read in Chapter 12, the purpose of tort law is to enable a person harmed by the wrongful act of another to obtain compensation from the wrongdoer, rather than to punish the wrongdoer. In contrast, criminal sanctions are designed to punish those who commit crimes and to deter others from committing similar acts in the future. Criminal sanctions include fines as well as the much harsher penalty of the loss of one's liberty by incarceration in a jail or prison. Most criminal sanctions also involve probation and sometimes require performance of community service, completion of an educational or treatment program, or payment of restitution. The harshest criminal sanction is, of course, the death penalty.

Civil Liability for Criminal Acts

Some torts, such as assault and battery, provide a basis for a criminal prosecution as well as a civil action in tort. Suppose that Jonas is walking down the street, minding his own business, when a person attacks him. In the ensuing struggle, the attacker stabs Jonas several times, seriously injuring him. A police officer restrains and arrests the assailant. In this situation, the assailant may be subject both to criminal prosecution by the state and to a tort lawsuit brought by Jonas to obtain compensation for his injuries. Exhibit 7–2 on the facing page illustrates how the same wrongful act can result in both a civil (tort) action and a criminal action against the wrongdoer.

Classification of Crimes

Depending on their degree of seriousness, crimes are classified as felonies or misdemeanors. **Felonies** are serious crimes punishable by death or by imprisonment for more than one year.[1] Many states also define different degrees of felony offenses and vary the punishment according to the degree.[2] For example, most jurisdictions punish a burglary that involves a forced entry into a home at night more harshly than a burglary that takes place during the day and involves a nonresidential building or structure.

Misdemeanors are less serious crimes, punishable by a fine or by confinement for up to a year. In most jurisdictions, **petty offenses** are considered to be a subset of misdemeanors. Petty offenses are minor violations, such as jaywalking or violations of building codes. Even for petty offenses, however, a

---

1. Some states, such as North Carolina, consider felonies to be punishable by incarceration for at least two years.
2. Although the American Law Institute issued the Model Penal Code in 1962, it is not a uniform code, and each state has developed its own set of laws governing criminal acts. Thus, types of crimes and prescribed punishments may differ from one jurisdiction to another.

EXHIBIT 7-2 • Civil (Tort) Lawsuit and Criminal Prosecution for the Same Act

A person attacks Jonas as he is walking down the street.

PHYSICAL ATTACK AS A <u>TORT</u>

The assailant commits an assault (an intentional, unexcused act that creates in Jonas the reasonable fear of immediate harmful contact) and a battery (intentional harmful contact).

Jonas files a suit against the assailant.

A court orders the assailant to pay Jonas for his injuries.

PHYSICAL ATTACK AS A <u>CRIME</u>

The assailant violates a statute that defines and prohibits the crime of assault ("attempt to commit a violent injury on another") and battery ("commission of an intentional act resulting in injury to another").

The state prosecutes the assailant.

A court orders the assailant to be fined or imprisoned.

guilty party can be put in jail for a few days, fined, or both, depending on state or local law. Whether a crime is a felony or a misdemeanor can determine in which court the case is tried and, in some states, whether the defendant has a right to a jury trial.

SECTION 2
CRIMINAL LIABILITY

Two elements normally must exist for a person to be convicted of a crime: (1) the performance of a prohibited act and (2) a specified state of mind, or intent, on the part of the actor. Additionally, to establish criminal liability, there usually must be a *concurrence* between the act and the intent. In other words, these two elements must occur together.

For example, a woman intends to kill her husband by poisoning him. On the day she plans to do so, she is driving her husband home from work and swerves to avoid hitting a cat crossing the road. As a result, the car crashes into a tree, killing her husband. Even though she had planned to murder her husband, the woman is not guilty of murder in this situation because the two elements did not occur

together. The woman did not intend to kill her husband by driving the car into a tree.

The Criminal Act

Every criminal statute prohibits certain behavior. Most crimes require an act of *commission*—that is, a person must *do* something in order to be accused of a crime. In criminal law, a prohibited act is referred to as the **actus reus**,[3] or guilty act. In some instances, an act of omission can be a crime, but only when a person has a legal duty to perform the omitted act, such as filing a tax return.

The *guilty act* requirement is based on one of the premises of criminal law—that a person should be punished for harm done to society. For a crime to exist, the guilty act must cause some harm to a person or to property. Thinking about killing someone or about stealing a car may be morally wrong, but the thoughts do no harm until they are translated into action. Of course, a person can be punished for *attempting* murder or robbery, but normally only if he or she has taken substantial steps toward the criminal objective.

---

3. Pronounced *ak*-tuhs *ray*-uhs.

State of Mind

A wrongful mental state (*mens rea*)[4] is also typically required to establish criminal liability. The required mental state, or intent, is indicated in the applicable statute or law. Murder, for example, involves the guilty act of killing another human being, and the guilty mental state is the desire, or intent, to take another's life. For theft, the guilty act is the taking of another person's property, and the mental state involves both the awareness that the property belongs to another and the desire to deprive the owner of it.

CRIMINAL NEGLIGENCE OR RECKLESSNESS A court can also find that the required mental state is present when a defendant's acts are reckless or criminally negligent. A defendant is *criminally reckless* if he or she consciously disregards a substantial and unjustifiable risk. *Criminal negligence* involves the mental state in which the defendant deviates from the standard of care that a reasonable person would use under the same circumstances. The defendant is accused of taking an unjustified, substantial, and foreseeable risk that resulted in harm. Under the Model Penal Code, criminal negligence has occurred if the defendant *should have foreseen* the risk, even if she or he was not actually aware of it.[5]

A homicide is classified as *involuntary manslaughter* when it results from an act of criminal negligence and there is no intent to kill. For example, in 2010, Dr. Conrad Murray, the personal physician of pop star Michael Jackson, was charged with involuntary manslaughter after a coroner determined that Jackson's sudden death in 2009 was the result of drug intoxication. Murray had given Jackson propofol, a powerful anesthetic normally used in surgery, as a sleep aid on the night of his death, even though he knew that Jackson had already taken other sedatives.

STRICT LIABILITY AND OVERCRIMINALIZATION In recent years, an increasing number of laws and regulations have imposed criminal sanctions for strict liability crimes—that is, offenses that do not require a wrongful mental state to establish criminal liability. The federal criminal code now lists more than four thousand criminal offenses, many of which do not require a specific mental state. There are also at least ten thousand federal rules that can be enforced through criminal sanctions, and many of these

rules do not require intent. Strict liability crimes are particularly common in environmental laws, laws aimed at combatting illegal drugs, and other laws affecting public health, safety, and welfare. Under federal law, for example, tenants can be evicted from public housing if one of their relatives or guests used illegal drugs—regardless of whether the tenant knew or should have known about the drug activity.[6]

Many states have also enacted laws that punish behavior as criminal without the need to show criminal intent. Under Arizona law, for instance, a hunter who shoots an elk outside the area specified by the permit has committed a crime, regardless of the hunter's intent or knowledge of the law.[7]

Although proponents of such laws argue that they are necessary to protect the public and the environment, critics say laws that criminalize conduct without any required intent have led to *overcriminalization,* or the use of criminal law as the main tool to solve social problems, such as illegal drug use. These critics argue that the removal of the requirement of intent, or malice, from criminal offenses increases the likelihood of people committing crimes unknowingly—and perhaps even innocently. When an honest mistake can lead to a criminal conviction, the idea that crimes are a wrong against society is undermined.

Corporate Criminal Liability

As will be discussed in Chapter 19, a corporation is a legal entity created under the laws of a state. At one time, it was thought that a corporation could not incur criminal liability because, although a corporation is a legal person, it can act only through its agents (corporate directors, officers, and employees). Therefore, the corporate entity itself could not "intend" to commit a crime. Over time, this view has changed. Obviously, corporations cannot be imprisoned, but they can be fined or denied certain legal privileges (such as a license).

LIABILITY OF THE CORPORATE ENTITY Today, corporations normally are liable for the crimes committed by their agents and employees within the course and scope of their employment.[8] For such criminal liability to be imposed, the prosecutor generally must show that the corporation could have

---

4. Pronounced *mehns ray*-uh.
5. Model Penal Code Section 2.02(2)(d).

6. See, for example, *Department of Housing and Urban Development v. Rucker,* 535 U.S. 125, 122 S.Ct. 1230, 152 L.Ed.2d 258 (2002).
7. *State v. Slayton and Remmert,* 1 CA-SA 06-0208 (Ariz.Ct.App. 2007).
8. See Model Penal Code Section 2.07.

prevented the act or that there was authorized consent to, or knowledge of, the act by persons in supervisory positions within the corporation. In addition, corporations can be criminally liable for failing to perform specific duties imposed by law (such as duties under environmental laws or securities laws).

LIABILITY OF THE CORPORATE OFFICERS AND DIRECTORS Corporate directors and officers are personally liable for the crimes they commit, regardless of whether the crimes were committed for their private benefit or on the corporation's behalf. Additionally, corporate directors and officers may be held liable for the actions of employees under their supervision. Under the *responsible corporate officer* doctrine, a court may impose criminal liability on a corporate officer despite whether he or she participated in, directed, or even knew about a given criminal violation.

SECTION 3
TYPES OF CRIMES

Numerous actions are designated as criminal. Federal, state, and local laws provide for the classification and punishment of hundreds of thousands of different criminal acts. Generally, though, criminal acts can be grouped into five broad categories: violent crime (crimes against persons), property crime, public order crime, white-collar crime, and organized crime. Cyber crime—which consists of crimes committed in cyberspace with the use of computers—is, as mentioned earlier in this chapter, less a category of crime than a new way to commit crime. We will examine cyber crime later in this chapter.

Violent Crime

Certain crimes are called *violent crimes,* or crimes against persons, because they cause others to suffer harm or death. Murder is a violent crime. So is sexual assault, or rape. Assault and battery, which will be discussed in Chapter 12 in the context of tort law, are also classified as violent crimes. **Robbery**—defined as the taking of money, personal property, or any other article of value from a person by means of force or fear—is also a violent crime. Typically, states have more severe penalties for *aggravated robbery*—robbery with the use of a deadly weapon.

Each of these violent crimes is further classified by degree, depending on the circumstances surrounding the criminal act. These circumstances include the intent of the person committing the crime, whether a weapon was used, and (for crimes other than murder) the level of pain and suffering experienced by the victim.

Property Crime

The most common type of criminal activity is property crime, in which the goal of the offender is some form of economic gain or the damaging of property. Robbery is a form of property crime, as well as a violent crime, because the offender seeks to gain the property of another. We look here at a number of other crimes that fall within the general category of property crime.

BURGLARY Traditionally, **burglary** was defined as breaking and entering the dwelling of another at night with the intent to commit a felony. Originally, the definition was aimed at protecting an individual's home and its occupants. Most state statutes have eliminated some of the requirements found in the common law definition. The time of day at which the breaking and entering occurs, for example, is usually immaterial. State statutes frequently omit the element of breaking, and some states do not require that the building be a dwelling. When a deadly weapon is used in a burglary, the perpetrator can be charged with *aggravated burglary* and punished more severely.

LARCENY Under the common law, the crime of **larceny** involved the unlawful taking and carrying away of someone else's personal property with the intent to permanently deprive the owner of possession. Put simply, larceny is stealing, or theft. Whereas robbery involves force or fear, larceny does not. Therefore, picking pockets is larceny, not robbery. Similarly, taking an employer's products and supplies home for personal use without permission is larceny. (Note that a person who commits larceny generally can also be sued under tort law because the act of taking possession of another's property involves a trespass to personal property.)

Most states have expanded the definition of property that is subject to larceny statutes. Stealing computer programs may constitute larceny even though the "property" consists of magnetic impulses. The theft of natural gas or Internet and television cable service may also be considered larceny. Trade secrets can be subject to larceny statutes.

The common law distinguished between grand and petit larceny depending on the value of the property taken. Many states have abolished this distinction, but in those that have not, grand larceny (or theft of an item having a value greater than a certain amount) is a felony, and petit larceny is a misdemeanor.

ARSON The willful and malicious burning of a building (and, in some states, personal property) owned by another is the crime of **arson.** At common law, arson applied only to burning down another person's house. The law was designed to protect human life. Today, arson statutes have been extended to cover the destruction of any building, regardless of ownership, by fire or explosion. Every state has a special statute that covers the act of burning a building for the purpose of collecting insurance. (Of course, the insurer need not pay the claim when insurance fraud is proved.)

RECEIVING STOLEN GOODS It is a crime to receive stolen goods. The recipient of such goods need not know the true identity of the owner or the thief. All that is necessary is that the recipient knows or should know that the goods are stolen, which implies an intent to deprive the owner of those goods.

FORGERY The fraudulent making or altering of any writing (including electronic records) in a way that changes the legal rights and liabilities of another is **forgery.** If, without authorization, Severson signs Bennett's name to the back of a check made out to Bennett, Severson is committing forgery. Forgery also includes changing trademarks, falsifying public records, counterfeiting, and altering a legal document.

OBTAINING GOODS BY FALSE PRETENSES It is a criminal act to obtain goods by false pretenses, such as buying groceries with a check knowing that one has insufficient funds to cover it. Purchasing goods with someone else's credit-card number without authorization is another example of obtaining goods by false pretenses. Statutes dealing with such illegal activities vary widely from state to state.

Public Order Crime

Historically, societies have always outlawed activities that are considered contrary to public values and morals. Today, the most common public order crimes include public drunkenness, prostitution, gambling, and illegal drug use. These crimes are sometimes referred to as *victimless crimes* because they normally harm only the offender. From a broader perspective,

however, they are deemed detrimental to society as a whole because they may create an environment that gives rise to property and violent crimes.

White-Collar Crime

Crimes occurring in the business context are popularly referred to as white-collar crimes. Although there is no official definition of **white-collar crime,** the term is commonly used to mean an illegal act or series of acts committed by an individual or business entity using some nonviolent means to obtain a personal or business advantage. Usually, this kind of crime takes place in the course of a legitimate business occupation. Corporate crimes fall into this category. Certain property crimes, such as larceny and forgery, may also be white-collar crimes if they occur within the business context. The crimes discussed next normally occur only in the business context.

EMBEZZLEMENT When a person entrusted with another person's property or funds fraudulently appropriates that property or those funds, **embezzlement** occurs. Typically, embezzlement is carried out by an employee who steals funds. Banks are particularly prone to this problem, but embezzlement can occur in any firm. In a number of businesses, corporate officers or accountants have fraudulently converted funds for their own benefit and then "fixed" the books to cover up their crime. Embezzlement is not larceny because the wrongdoer does not *physically* take the property from the possession of another, and it is not robbery because no force or fear is used.

Embezzlement Takes Many Forms. It does not matter whether the embezzler takes the funds from the victim or from a third person. If the financial officer of a large corporation pockets a certain number of checks from third parties that were given to her to deposit into the corporate account, she is embezzling. Even an employer's failure to remit state withholding taxes collected from employees can constitute embezzlement.

CASE IN POINT Dr. Francis H. George owned and operated a medical practice in Virginia. He employed numerous individuals, including nursing assistants, nurse practitioners, and a pediatrician. George withheld funds from his employees' salaries—funds that represented state income taxes owed to Virginia—and deposited them into a bank account that he used to pay his personal and business expenses. He then failed to file withholding tax returns as required by state law and did not send the withheld funds to the state. He was convicted of embezzlement.[9]

Frequently, an embezzler takes a relatively small amount at one time but does so repeatedly over a long period. This might be done by underreporting income or deposits and embezzling the remaining amount, for example, or by creating fictitious persons or accounts and writing checks to them from the corporate account.

Problems with Prosecution. As a practical matter, an embezzler who returns what has been taken may not be prosecuted because the owner is unwilling to take the time to make a complaint, cooperate with the state's investigative efforts, and appear in court. Also, the owner may not want the crime to become public knowledge. Nevertheless, the intent to return the embezzled property—or its actual return—is not a defense to the crime of embezzlement, as the following case illustrates.

---

9. *George v. Commonwealth of Virginia,* 51 Va.App. 137, 655 S.E.2d 43 (2008).

✳ EXTENDED CASE 7.1 ✳
People v. Sisuphan

Court of Appeal of California, First District, 181 Cal.App.4th 800, 104 Cal.Rptr.3d 654 (2010).

IN THE LANGUAGE OF THE COURT
JENKINS, J. [Judge]
* * * *

As the Director of Finance at Toyota of Marin (the dealership), [Appellant Lou Surivan] Sisuphan managed the financing contracts for vehicle sales and worked with lenders to obtain payment for these transactions. * * * Sisuphan complained repeatedly to management about the performance and attitude of one of the finance managers, Ian McClelland (McClelland). * * * General manager Michael Christian (Christian) opted not to terminate McClelland "because he brought a lot of money into the dealership."

On July 3, 2007, McClelland accepted a large payment from customer Jill Peacock for the vehicle she purchased. Peacock gave him $22,600 in cash and two checks totaling $7,275.51. McClelland prepared a receipt, placed the cash, both checks, and a copy of the receipt in a large manila envelope, and took the envelope to the company safe in Sisuphan's office. McClelland placed the envelope into the hopper at the top of the safe and turned the handle to rotate the hopper and drop its contents down into the safe. The envelope, which was stuffed with a large amount of cash, did not drop all the way down into the safe and became lodged, with a portion "sticking out." McClelland could not retrieve the envelope or push it completely into the safe, so he decided to cut it and transfer the contents to two envelopes. He * * * asked Sisuphan to keep an eye on the envelope while he went to the showroom. While McClelland was gone, Sisuphan "wiggled" the envelope free, extracted it from the safe, and kept it. When McClelland returned, Sisuphan told him "Hey, no problem, [the envelope] dropped into the safe."

Dealership bookkeepers regularly collected payments from the safe and cross-checked these against carbon copies of the receipts in the receipt book. On the morning of July 5, 2007, one of the bookkeepers discovered in this manner that the payment for the Peacock purchase was missing. She placed a post-it note for Sisuphan on the corresponding page of the receipt book, inquiring, "Where's money?" She also notified the controller, the general sales manager, and Christian that a payment was missing. When she asked Sisuphan about the missing payment, "he said they were looking into it."

* * * Christian followed up with the customer, made a police report, and filed a claim with the dealership's insurer. He called all the managers together and told them he would not bring criminal charges if the money was returned within twenty-four hours.

On the evening of July 18, 2007, * * * Sisuphan [went] to Christian's office and admitted that he had taken the money. He claimed he had no intention of stealing it and had taken it to get McClelland fired. He said he had not returned the money during the twenty-four-hour amnesty period because he did not believe Christian's assurance that no punitive action would be taken.

The next day, Christian terminated Sisuphan's employment. He prepared a separation report with a narrative that set out the events relating to the missing money and

EXTENDED CASE CONTINUES ➡

EXTENDED CASE 7.1 CONTINUED ⬇

included a summary of Sisuphan's confession. Sisuphan reviewed and signed the report without making any changes and repaid the entire sum of cash he had taken. * * * However, "the checks were lost [and] not returned." The customer stopped payment on both checks and reissued them.

A week later, the district attorney filed a criminal complaint against Sisuphan, asserting a felony offense of embezzlement by an employee of property valued in excess of $400 * * * . The matter proceeded to a jury trial on April 15, 2008, and the jury returned a guilty verdict. In June 2008, the trial court sentenced Sisuphan to 120 days in custody and three years probation. Sisuphan filed a timely notice of appeal from the judgment of conviction.

* * * *

The trial court excluded evidence that Sisuphan returned the money to the dealership, concluding it was not relevant, because *return of the property is not a defense to embezzlement.* Sisuphan contends that evidence of repayment was relevant to show he lacked fraudulent intent at the time he took the money and asserts, for this reason, that the trial court's ruling violated his Fifth Amendment right to present a defense and "all pertinent evidence of significant value to that defense." [Emphasis added.]

Fraudulent intent is an essential element of embezzlement. Although restoration of the property is not a defense, evidence of repayment may be relevant to the extent it shows that a defendant's intent at the time of the taking was not fraudulent. Such evidence is admissible "only when [a] defendant shows a relevant and probative [tending to prove] link in his subsequent actions from which it might be inferred his original intent was innocent." The question before us, therefore, is whether evidence that Sisuphan returned the money reasonably tends to prove he lacked the requisite intent at the time of the taking. [Emphasis added.]

Section 508 [of the California Penal Code], which sets out the offense of which Sisuphan was convicted, provides: "Every clerk, agent, or servant of any person who fraudulently appropriates to his own use, or secretes with a fraudulent intent to appropriate to his own use, any property of another which has come into his control or care by virtue of his employment * * * is guilty of embezzlement." Sisuphan denies he ever intended "to use the [money] to financially better himself, even temporarily" and contends the evidence he sought to introduce showed "he returned the [money] without having appropriated it to his own use in any way." He argues that this evidence negates fraudulent intent because it supports his claim that he took the money to get McClelland fired and acted "to help his company by drawing attention to the inadequacy and incompetency of an employee." We reject these contentions.

In determining whether Sisuphan's intent was fraudulent at the time of the taking, the issue is not whether he intended to spend the money, but whether he intended to use it for a purpose other than that for which the dealership entrusted it to him. *The offense of embezzlement contemplates a principal's entrustment of property to an agent for certain purposes and the agent's breach of that trust by acting outside his authority in his use of the property.* * * * Sisuphan's undisputed purpose—to get McClelland fired—was beyond the scope of his responsibility and therefore outside the trust afforded him by the dealership. Accordingly, even if the proffered [submitted] evidence shows he took the money for this purpose, it does not tend to prove he lacked fraudulent intent, and the trial court properly excluded this evidence. [Emphasis added.]

* * * *

The judgment is affirmed.

 QUESTIONS

1. Given that Sisuphan returned the cash, was it fair of the dealership's general manager to terminate Sisuphan's employment? Why or why not?
2. Why was Sisuphan convicted of embezzlement instead of larceny? What is the difference between these two crimes?

MAIL AND WIRE FRAUD One of the most potent weapons against white-collar criminals is the Mail Fraud Act of 1990.[10] Under this act, it is a federal crime to use the mails to defraud the public. Illegal use of the mails must involve (1) mailing or causing someone else to mail a writing—something written, printed, or photocopied—for the purpose of executing a scheme to defraud and (2) contemplating or organizing a scheme to defraud by false pretenses. If, for example, Johnson advertises by mail the sale of a cure for cancer that he knows to be fraudulent because it has no medical validity, he can be prosecuted for fraudulent use of the mails.

Federal law also makes it a crime (wire fraud) to use wire, radio, or television transmissions to

---

10. 18 U.S.C. Sections 1341–1342.

defraud.[11] Violators may be fined up to $1,000, imprisoned for up to twenty years, or both. If the violation affects a financial institution, the violator may be fined up to $1 million, imprisoned for up to thirty years, or both.

CASE IN POINT Gabriel Sanchez and Timothy Lyons set up six charities and formed a fund-raising company, North American Acquisitions (NAA), to solicit donations on the charities' behalf through telemarketing. NAA raised more than $6 million, of which less than $5,000 was actually spent on charitable causes. The telemarketers kept 80 percent of the donated funds as commissions, the NAA took 10 percent, and most of the rest of the funds went to Sanchez, who spent it on himself. Lyons and Sanchez were both prosecuted for mail fraud and sentenced to serve fifteen years in prison. They appealed. A federal appellate court affirmed their convictions, ruling that the government can use these antifraud laws to prohibit professional fundraisers from obtaining funds through false pretenses or by making false statements.[12]

Although most fraudulent schemes involve cheating the victim out of tangible property (funds), it can also be a crime to deprive a person of an intangible right to another's honest services. For a discussion of how federal prosecutors are increasingly charging white-collar criminals with "honest-services fraud," and some recent cases on the topic, see this chapter's *Shifting Legal Priorities for Business* feature on the following page.

BRIBERY The crime of bribery involves offering to give something of value to a person in an attempt to influence that person, who usually is (but not always) a public official, to act in a way that serves a private interest. Three types of bribery are considered crimes: bribery of public officials, commercial bribery, and bribery of foreign officials. As an element of the crime of bribery, intent must be present and proved. The bribe itself can be anything the recipient considers to be valuable. Realize that the *crime of bribery occurs when the bribe is offered*—it is not required that the bribe be accepted. *Accepting a bribe* is a separate crime.

Commercial bribery involves corrupt dealings between private persons or businesses. Typically, people make commercial bribes to obtain proprietary information, cover up an inferior product, or secure new business. Industrial espionage sometimes involves commercial bribes. For example, a person in one firm may offer an employee in a competing firm some type of payoff in exchange for trade secrets or pricing schedules. So-called kickbacks, or payoffs for special favors or services, are a form of commercial bribery in some situations.

Bribing foreign officials to obtain favorable business contracts is a crime. This crime was discussed in Chapter 4, along with the Foreign Corrupt Practices Act of 1977, which was passed to curb the use of bribery by U.S. businesspersons in securing foreign contracts.

BANKRUPTCY FRAUD Federal bankruptcy law (see Chapter 15) allows individuals and businesses to be relieved of oppressive debt through bankruptcy proceedings. Numerous white-collar crimes may be committed during the many phases of a bankruptcy action. A creditor, for example, may file a false claim against the debtor, which is a crime. Also, a debtor may fraudulently transfer assets to favored parties before or after the petition for bankruptcy is filed. For instance, a company-owned automobile may be "sold" at a bargain price to a trusted friend or relative. Closely related to the crime of fraudulent transfer of property is the crime of fraudulent concealment of property, such as the hiding of gold coins.

INSIDER TRADING An individual who obtains "inside information" about the plans of a publicly listed corporation can often make stock-trading profits by purchasing or selling corporate securities based on this information. *Insider trading* is a violation of securities law. Basically, securities law prohibits a person who possesses inside information and has a duty not to disclose it to outsiders from trading on that information. He or she may not profit from the purchase or sale of securities based on inside information until the information is made available to the public.

THEFT OF OTHER INTELLECTUAL PROPERTY As will be discussed in Chapter 14, trade secrets constitute a form of intellectual property that for many businesses can be extremely valuable. The Economic Espionage Act of 1996[13] makes the theft of trade secrets a federal crime. The act also makes it a federal crime to buy or possess another person's trade secrets, knowing that the trade secrets were stolen or otherwise acquired without the owner's authorization.

---

11. 18 U.S.C. Section 1343.
12. *United States v. Lyons*, 472 F.3d 1055 (9th Cir. 2007).

13. 18 U.S.C. Sections 1831–1839.

What do former Enron chief executive officer (CEO) Jeffrey Skilling, former Hollinger International CEO Conrad Black, and former Illinois governor Rod Blagojevich have in common? They, along with thousands of other individuals, have been charged under the "honest-services fraud" law. Indeed, 95 percent of the high-profile, white-collar crime cases in recent years have involved individuals who have been charged under this law.

What Is the Honest-Services Fraud Law?

The honest-services fraud law dates back to 1988 and consists of only twenty-eight words. It is known as Section 1346, which refers to the section of Title XVIII of the *United States Code* that defines the offense. The law is broad enough to encompass just about every conceivable white-collar criminal act. Consequently, it has allowed federal prosecutors to attempt to impose criminal penalties on a broad swath of misconduct by public officials and employees, as well as private employees and corporate directors and officers. The key to the law is that it requires individuals to provide the "intangible right of honest services" to their employers. Critics point out that the law is used when the purported crime committed is "fuzzy." When a businessperson is charged with honest-services fraud, there is often a nagging question as to whether the actions involved were truly a crime or just aggressive business behavior.

How Congress Got Involved

Under the U.S. Constitution, the federal government does not have the power to punish fraud directly, but it does have the power to regulate the U.S. mails and interstate commerce. In the 1970s, federal prosecutors started using the federal laws against mail and wire fraud whenever such actions deprived someone of funds or property. Then, a federal prosecutor used the legal theory that a fraudulent action to deprive the public of "honest services" is equivalent to a theft of intangible rights. In 1987, however, the United States Supreme Court rejected this concept of honest services.[a]

Not happy with the Court's ruling, federal prosecutors pleaded with Congress to pass a law. Congress subsequently created a law stating that any scheme to deprive another of honest services will be considered a scheme to defraud. Courts have at times described honest-services fraud as simply the situation in which the public does not get what it wants and deserves— that is, honest, faithful, disinterested services from employees, whether they be public or private.

Interestingly, criminal fraud requires that a victim be cheated out of tangible property, such as money.

Honest-services fraud changes that concept. It involves depriving the victim of an intangible right to another's honest services.

The Law Has Been Applied Widely

Federal prosecutors have used the honest-services fraud law in a variety of situations. In Texas, federal prosecutors successfully brought a charge against three coaches at Baylor University (a private school) for scheming to obtain scholarships for players. In California, federal prosecutors have used the honest-services legal theory to investigate the hierarchy of the Catholic Archdiocese of Los Angeles. Top church officials are being accused of covering up sexual abuse of minors by priests.

The U.S. Supreme Court Decides

In 2010, the United States Supreme Court issued a ruling that could have a major impact on white-collar crime and political fraud cases in the future. The Court ruled that the honest-services fraud law could not be used against Jeffrey Skilling, who had been convicted for his role in the collapse of Enron.[b] According to the Court, honest-services fraud can only be applied in cases that involve bribes and kickbacks. Because there was no evidence that Skilling had solicited or accepted side payments from a third party in exchange for making misrepresentations about the company, he did not commit honest-services fraud.

The Court did not overturn Skilling's conviction, however. Instead, the Court left it up to the lower court to determine whether Skilling's conviction could be upheld on other grounds. In addition, the Court remanded the honest-services fraud conviction of Conrad Black—the newspaper executive who defrauded his media company—for the same reason.[c] In fact, the Court remanded numerous other honest-services fraud cases for reconsideration in light of its decision.

MANAGERIAL IMPLICATIONS

Although the Court did not strike down the entire honest-services fraud law, the justices significantly narrowed its scope to prevent it from being unconstitutionally vague. Federal prosecutors can still prosecute businesspersons and managers who solicit or accept bribes or kickbacks for honest-services fraud, though. There are also many other federal and state laws that criminalize fraud and certain wrongful business conduct.

---

a. *McNally v. United States,* 483 U.S. 350, 107 S.Ct. 2875, 97 L.Ed.2d 292 (1987).

b. *Skilling v. United States,* ___ U.S. ___, 130 S.Ct. 2896, 177 L.Ed.2d 619 (2010). See Case 4.1 on pages 78 and 79.

c. See *Black v. United States,* ___ U.S. ___, 130 S.Ct. 2963, ___ L.Ed.2d ___ (2010).

Violations of the Economic Espionage Act can result in steep penalties: imprisonment for up to ten years and a fine of up to $500,000. A corporation or other organization can be fined up to $5 million. Additionally, the law provides that any property acquired as a result of the violation, such as airplanes and automobiles, and any property used in the commission of the violation, such as computer servers and other electronic devices, is subject to criminal forfeiture—meaning that the government can take the property. A theft of trade secrets conducted via the Internet, for example, could result in the forfeiture of every computer or other device used to commit or facilitate the violation as well as any assets gained.

The unauthorized copying and use of intellectual property, such as books, films, music, and software—commonly known as pirating—is also a crime under federal law. It has been estimated that 35 percent of all business software is pirated, as is nearly 90 percent of downloaded music. In the United States, digital pirates can be criminally prosecuted under the Digital Millennium Copyright Act.[14] An individual who violates the act for purposes of financial gain can be imprisoned for up to five years and fined up to $500,000 on a first offense. The punishment doubles for any subsequent offense.

Organized Crime

White-collar crime takes place within the confines of the legitimate business world. Organized crime, in contrast, operates *illegitimately* by, among other things, providing illegal goods and services. Traditionally, the preferred markets for organized crime have been gambling, prostitution, illegal narcotics, and loan sharking (lending funds at higher-than-legal interest rates), along with more recent ventures into counterfeiting and credit-card scams.

MONEY LAUNDERING The profits from organized crime and illegal activities amount to billions of dollars a year. These profits come from illegal drug transactions and, to a lesser extent, from racketeering, prostitution, and gambling. Under federal law, banks, savings and loan associations, and other financial institutions are required to report currency transactions involving more than $10,000. Consequently, those who engage in illegal activities face difficulties in depositing their cash profits from illegal transactions.

As an alternative to storing cash from illegal transactions in a safe-deposit box, wrongdoers and racketeers have invented ways to launder "dirty" money to make it "clean." This **money laundering** is done through legitimate businesses. For example, Harris, a successful drug dealer, becomes a partner with a restaurateur. Little by little, the restaurant shows increasing profits. As a partner in the restaurant, Harris is able to report the "profits" of the restaurant as legitimate income on which he pays federal and state taxes. He can then spend those funds without worrying that his lifestyle may exceed the level possible with his reported income.

RICO In 1970, in an effort to curb the entry of organized crime into the legitimate business world, Congress passed the Racketeer Influenced and Corrupt Organizations Act (RICO) as part of the Organized Crime Control Act.[15] The statute makes it a federal crime to (1) use income obtained from racketeering activity to purchase any interest in an enterprise, (2) acquire or maintain an interest in an enterprise through racketeering activity, (3) conduct or participate in the affairs of an enterprise through racketeering activity, or (4) conspire to do any of the preceding activities.

The broad language of RICO has allowed it to be applied in cases that have little or nothing to do with organized crime. In fact, today the statute is used to attack white-collar crimes more often than organized crime. In addition, RICO creates civil as well as criminal liability.

Criminal Provisions. RICO incorporates by reference twenty-six separate types of federal crimes and nine types of state felonies, including many business-related crimes, such as bribery, embezzlement, forgery, mail and wire fraud, and securities fraud.[16] To prove a "pattern of racketeering activity" for purposes of RICO, prosecutors must show that the defendant committed at least two of these offenses. Any individual who is found guilty is subject to a fine of up to $25,000 per violation, imprisonment for up to twenty years, or both. Additionally, the statute provides that those who violate RICO may be required to forfeit (give up) any assets, in the form of property or cash, that were acquired as a result of the illegal activity or that were "involved in" or an "instrumentality of" the activity.

---

14. 17 U.S.C. Sections 2301 *et seq.*

15. 18 U.S.C. Sections 1961–1968.

16. See 18 U.S.C. Section 1961(1)(A). The crimes listed in this section include murder, kidnapping, gambling, arson, robbery, bribery, extortion, money laundering, securities fraud, counterfeiting, dealing in obscene matter, dealing in controlled substances (illegal drugs), and a number of others.

Civil Liability. In the event of a RICO violation, the government can seek civil penalties, including the divestiture of a defendant's interest in a business (called forfeiture) or the dissolution of the business. Moreover, in some cases, the statute allows private individuals to sue violators and potentially recover three times their actual losses (treble damages), plus attorneys' fees, for business injuries caused by a violation of the statute. This is perhaps the most controversial aspect of RICO and one that continues to cause debate in the nation's federal courts. The prospect of receiving treble damages in civil RICO lawsuits has given plaintiffs a financial incentive to pursue businesses and employers for violations.

CASE IN POINT Mohawk Industries, Inc., one of the largest carpeting manufacturers in the United States, was sued by a group of its employees for RICO violations. The employees claimed that Mohawk conspired with recruiting agencies to hire illegal immigrants in an effort to keep labor costs low. The employees argued that this pattern of illegal hiring expanded Mohawk's hourly workforce and resulted in lower wages for the plaintiffs. Mohawk filed a motion to dismiss, arguing that its conduct had not violated RICO. In 2006, however, a federal appellate court ruled that the plaintiffs had presented sufficient evidence of racketeering activity for the case to go to trial.[17]

See *Concept Summary 7.1* below for a review of the different types of crimes.

---

17. *Williams v. Mohawk Industries, Inc.,* 465 F.3d 1277 (11th Cir. 2006); *cert.* dismissed, 547 U.S. 516, 126 S.Ct. 2016, 164 L.Ed.2d 776 (2006). For another example, see *Trollinger v. Tyson Foods, Inc.,* 2007 WL 1574275 (E.D.Tenn. 2007).

CONCEPT SUMMARY 7.1
Types of Crimes

Crime Category	Definition and Examples
Violent Crime	1. *Definition*—Crime that causes others to suffer harm or death. 2. *Examples*—Murder, assault and battery, sexual assault (rape), and robbery.
Property Crime	1. *Definition*—Crime in which the goal of the offender is some form of economic gain or the damaging of property; the most common form of crime. 2. *Examples*—Burglary, larceny, arson, receiving stolen goods, forgery, and obtaining goods by false pretenses.
Public Order Crime	1. *Definition*—Crime that is contrary to public values and morals. 2. *Examples*—Public drunkenness, prostitution, gambling, and illegal drug use.
White-Collar Crime	1. *Definition*—An illegal act or series of acts committed by an individual or business entity using some nonviolent means to obtain a personal or business advantage; usually committed in the course of a legitimate occupation. 2. *Examples*—Embezzlement, mail and wire fraud, bribery, bankruptcy fraud, insider trading, and the theft of intellectual property.
Organized Crime	1. *Definition*—A form of crime conducted by groups operating illegitimately to satisfy the public's demand for illegal goods and services (such as gambling and illegal narcotics). 2. *Money laundering*—The establishment of legitimate enterprises through which "dirty" money (obtained through criminal activities, such as illegal drug trafficking) can be "laundered" (made to appear to be legitimate income). 3. *The Racketeer Influenced and Corrupt Organizations Act (RICO) of 1970*—RICO makes it a federal crime to (a) use income obtained from racketeering activity to purchase any interest in an enterprise, (b) acquire or maintain an interest in an enterprise through racketeering activity, (c) conduct or participate in the affairs of an enterprise through racketeering activity, or (d) conspire to do any of the preceding activities. RICO provides for both civil and criminal liability.

DEFENSES TO CRIMINAL LIABILITY

Persons charged with crimes may be relieved of criminal liability if they can show that their criminal actions were justified under the circumstances. In certain situations, the law may also allow a person to be excused from criminal liability because she or he lacks the required mental state. We look at several defenses to criminal liability here.

Note that procedural violations (such as obtaining evidence without a valid search warrant) may also operate as defenses. Evidence obtained in violation of a defendant's constitutional rights may not be admitted in court. If the evidence is suppressed, then there may be no basis for prosecuting the defendant.

Justifiable Use of Force

Probably the best-known defense to criminal liability is **self-defense.** Other situations, however, also justify the use of force: the defense of one's dwelling, the defense of other property, and the prevention of a crime. In all of these situations, it is important to distinguish between deadly and nondeadly force. *Deadly force* is likely to result in death or serious bodily harm. *Nondeadly force* is force that reasonably appears necessary to prevent the imminent use of criminal force.

Generally speaking, people can use the amount of nondeadly force that seems necessary to protect themselves, their dwellings, or other property, or to prevent the commission of a crime. Deadly force can be used in self-defense only when the defender *reasonably believes* that imminent death or grievous bodily harm will otherwise result and has no other means of escaping or avoiding the situation. Deadly force normally can be used to defend a dwelling only if the unlawful entry is violent and the person believes deadly force is necessary to prevent imminent death or great bodily harm. In some jurisdictions, however, deadly force can also be used if the person believes it is necessary to prevent the commission of a felony in the dwelling. Note, too, that many states are expanding the situations in which the use of deadly force can be justified.[18]

Necessity

Sometimes, criminal defendants can be relieved of liability by showing that a criminal act was necessary to prevent an even greater harm. Suppose that Jack Trevor is a convicted felon and, as such, is legally prohibited from possessing a firearm. While he and his wife are in a convenience store, a man draws a gun, points it at the cashier, and demands all the cash in the register. Afraid that the man will start shooting, Trevor grabs the gun and holds onto it until police arrive. In this situation, if Trevor is charged with possession of a firearm, he can assert the defense of **necessity.**

Insanity

A person who suffers from a mental illness may be incapable of the state of mind required to commit a crime. Thus, insanity may be a defense to a criminal charge. Note that an insanity defense does not enable a person to avoid imprisonment. It simply means that if the defendant successfully proves insanity, she or he will be placed in a mental institution.

The courts have had difficulty deciding what the test for legal insanity should be, and psychiatrists as well as lawyers are critical of the tests used. Almost all federal courts and some states use the relatively liberal substantial-capacity test set forth in the Model Penal Code:

> A person is not responsible for criminal conduct if at the time of such conduct as a result of mental disease or defect he or she lacks substantial capacity either to appreciate the wrongfulness of his [or her] conduct or to conform his [or her] conduct to the requirements of the law.

Some states use the *M'Naghten* test,[19] under which a criminal defendant is not responsible if, at the time of the offense, he or she did not know the nature and quality of the act or did not know that the act was wrong. Other states use the irresistible-impulse test. A person operating under an irresistible impulse may know an act is wrong but cannot refrain from doing it. Under any of these tests, proving insanity is extremely difficult. For this reason, the insanity defense is rarely used and usually is not successful.

Mistake

Everyone has heard the saying "Ignorance of the law is no excuse." Ordinarily, ignorance of the law or a mistaken idea about what the law requires is not a valid defense. A *mistake of fact,* however, as opposed to a *mistake of law,* can excuse criminal responsibility if it negates the mental state necessary to commit a crime. If, for example, Oliver Wheaton mistakenly

---

18. See, for example, *State v. Sandoval*, 342 Or. 506, 156 P.3d 60 (2007).

19. A rule derived from *M'Naghten's* Case, 8 Eng.Rep. 718 (1843).

walks off with Julie Tyson's briefcase because he thinks it is his, there is no theft. Theft requires knowledge that the property belongs to another. (If Wheaton's act causes Tyson to incur damages, however, she may sue him in a civil action for trespass to personal property or conversion—torts that will be discussed in Chapter 12.)

Duress

Duress exists when the *wrongful threat* of one person induces another person to perform an act that he or she would not otherwise have performed. In such a situation, duress is said to negate the mental state necessary to commit a crime because the defendant was forced or compelled to commit the act. Duress can be used as a defense to most crimes except murder. Both the definition of duress and the types of crimes that it can excuse vary among the states, however. Generally, to successfully assert duress as a defense, the defendant must reasonably have believed that he or she was in immediate danger, and the jury (or judge) must conclude that the defendant's belief was reasonable.

Entrapment

Entrapment is a defense designed to prevent police officers or other government agents from enticing persons to commit crimes in order to later prosecute them for those crimes. In the typical entrapment case, an undercover agent *suggests* that a crime be committed and somehow pressures or induces an individual to commit it. The agent then arrests the individual for the crime. For entrapment to be considered a defense, both the suggestion and the inducement must take place. The defense is not intended to prevent law enforcement agents from setting a trap for an unwary criminal; rather, its purpose is to prevent them from pushing the individual into a criminal act. The crucial issue is whether the person who committed a crime was predisposed to commit the illegal act or did so only because the agent induced it.

Statute of Limitations

With some exceptions, such as the crime of murder, statutes of limitations apply to crimes just as they do to civil wrongs. In other words, the state must initiate criminal prosecution within a certain number of years. If a criminal action is brought after the statutory time period has expired, the accused person can raise the statute of limitations as a defense. The running of the time period in a statute of limitations may be tolled—that is, suspended or stopped temporarily—if the defendant is a minor or is not in the jurisdiction. When the defendant reaches the age of majority or returns to the jurisdiction, the statute revives, meaning that its time period begins to run or to run again.

Immunity

At times, the state may wish to obtain information from a person accused of a crime. Accused persons are understandably reluctant to give information if it will be used to prosecute them, and they cannot be forced to do so. The privilege against **self-incrimination** is guaranteed by the Fifth Amendment to the U.S. Constitution, which reads, in part, "nor shall [any person] be compelled in any criminal case to be a witness against himself." In cases in which the state wishes to obtain information from a person accused of a crime, the state can grant *immunity* from prosecution or agree to prosecute for a less serious offense in exchange for the information. Once immunity is given, the person has an absolute privilege against self-incrimination and therefore can no longer refuse to testify on Fifth Amendment grounds.

Often, a grant of immunity from prosecution for a serious crime is part of the **plea bargaining** between the defending and prosecuting attorneys. The defendant may be convicted of a lesser offense, while the state uses the defendant's testimony to prosecute accomplices for serious crimes carrying heavy penalties.

▬▬◤ SECTION 5 ◢▬▬
CRIMINAL PROCEDURES

Criminal law brings the force of the state, with all of its resources, to bear against the individual. Criminal procedures are designed to protect the constitutional rights of individuals and to prevent the arbitrary use of power on the part of the government.

The U.S. Constitution provides specific safeguards for those accused of crimes. The United States Supreme Court has ruled that most of these safeguards apply not only in federal court but also in state courts by virtue of the due process clause of the Fourteenth Amendment. These protections include the following:

1. The Fourth Amendment protection from unreasonable searches and seizures.
2. The Fourth Amendment requirement that no warrant for a search or an arrest be issued without probable cause.
3. The Fifth Amendment requirement that no one be deprived of "life, liberty, or property without due process of law."
4. The Fifth Amendment prohibition against **double jeopardy** (trying someone twice for the same criminal offense).[20]
5. The Fifth Amendment requirement that no person be required to be a witness against (incriminate) himself or herself.
6. The Sixth Amendment guarantees of a speedy trial, a trial by jury, a public trial, the right to confront witnesses, and the right to a lawyer at various stages in some proceedings.
7. The Eighth Amendment prohibitions against excessive bail and fines and against cruel and unusual punishment.

---

20. The prohibition against double jeopardy means that once a criminal defendant is found not guilty of a particular crime, the government may not indict that person again and retry him or her for the same crime. The prohibition does not preclude the crime victim from bringing a *civil* suit against that same person to recover damages, however. Additionally, a state's prosecution of a crime will not prevent a separate federal prosecution of the same crime, and vice versa.

The Exclusionary Rule

Under what is known as the **exclusionary rule**, any evidence obtained in violation of the constitutional rights spelled out in the Fourth, Fifth, and Sixth Amendments generally is not admissible at trial. All evidence derived from the illegally obtained evidence is known as the "fruit of the poisonous tree," and such evidence normally must also be excluded from the trial proceedings. For example, if a confession is obtained after an illegal arrest, the arrest is the "poisonous tree," and the confession, if "tainted" by the arrest, is the "fruit."

The purpose of the exclusionary rule is to deter police from conducting warrantless searches and engaging in other misconduct. The rule is sometimes criticized because it can lead to injustice. Many a defendant has "gotten off on a technicality" because law enforcement personnel failed to observe procedural requirements. Even though a defendant may be obviously guilty, if the evidence of that guilt was obtained improperly (without a valid search warrant, for example), it normally cannot be used against the defendant in court.

If a suspect is arrested on the basis of a police officer's mistaken belief that there is an outstanding arrest warrant for that individual, should evidence found during a search incident to the arrest be excluded from the trial? This question arose in the following case.

CASE 7.2
Herring v. United States
Supreme Court of the United States, __ U.S. __ , 129 S.Ct. 695, 172 L.Ed.2d 496 (2009).
www.findlaw.com/casecode/supreme.html[a]

BACKGROUND AND FACTS • The sheriff's office in Dale County, Alabama, maintains copies of arrest warrants in a computer database. When a warrant is recalled, Sharon Morgan, the warrant clerk, enters this information in the database and discards the physical copy of the warrant. In July 2004, Sandy Pope, the warrant clerk in the sheriff's department in neighboring Coffee County, asked Morgan if there were any outstanding arrest warrants for Bennie Herring. Morgan checked her database and told Pope that there was a warrant. Coffee County officers then arrested Herring. A search revealed methamphetamine in his pocket and an illegal gun in his truck. Meanwhile, Morgan discovered that a mistake had been made: the warrant had been recalled. Herring was charged in a federal district court with illegal possession of a gun and drugs. He filed a motion to exclude the evidence on the ground that his arrest had been illegal. The court denied the motion, the U.S. Court of Appeals for the Eleventh Circuit affirmed the denial, and Herring appealed to the United States Supreme Court.

---

a. In the "Browse Supreme Court Opinions" section, click on "2009." On that page, scroll to the name of the case and click on it to access the opinion. FindLaw maintains this Web site.

CASE CONTINUES ➡

CASE 7.2 CONTINUED ➡

IN THE LANGUAGE OF THE COURT
Chief Justice *ROBERTS* delivered the opinion of the Court.
* * * *

* * * We have repeatedly rejected the argument that exclusion [of evidence] is a necessary consequence of a Fourth Amendment violation. Instead we have focused on the efficacy [effectiveness] of the rule in deterring Fourth Amendment violations in the future.

In addition, the benefits of deterrence must outweigh the costs. * * * The principal cost of applying the rule is, of course, letting guilty and possibly dangerous defendants go free.
* * * *

* * * *Evidence should be suppressed only if it can be said that the law enforcement officer had knowledge, or may properly be charged with knowledge, that the search was unconstitutional under the Fourth Amendment.* [Emphasis added.]
* * * *

Indeed, the abuses that gave rise to the exclusionary rule featured *intentional* conduct that was patently unconstitutional. [Emphasis added.]

* * * An error that arises from nonrecurring and attenuated [diluted] negligence is * * * far removed from the core concerns that led us to adopt the rule in the first place.

To trigger the exclusionary rule, police conduct must be sufficiently deliberate that exclusion can meaningfully deter it, and sufficiently culpable [blameworthy] that such deterrence is worth the price paid by the justice system. As laid out in our cases, the exclusionary rule serves to deter deliberate, reckless, or grossly negligent conduct, or in some circumstances recurring or systemic negligence. The error in this case does not rise to that level.
* * * *

* * * [In a previous case, we held that] negligent police miscommunications in the course of acquiring a warrant do not provide a basis to rescind a warrant and render a search or arrest invalid. Here, the miscommunications occurred in a different context—after the warrant had been issued and recalled—but that fact should not require excluding the evidence obtained.
* * * *

We do not suggest that all recordkeeping errors by the police are immune from the exclusionary rule. In this case, however, the conduct at issue was not so objectively culpable as to require exclusion.

DECISION AND REMEDY • *The United States Supreme Court affirmed the lower court's judgment. The exclusionary rule does not apply when a police mistake leading to an unlawful search is the result of an isolated instance of negligence.*

WHAT IF THE FACTS WERE DIFFERENT? • *Suppose that the warrant for Herring's arrest had still been outstanding but had been based on false information. Should the standards applied in this case apply in those circumstances? Explain.*

THE LEGAL ENVIRONMENT DIMENSION • *What does the decision in this case mean for businesses that are subjected to searches by law enforcement personnel?*

The *Miranda* Rule

In regard to criminal procedure, one of the questions many courts faced in the 1950s and 1960s was not whether suspects had constitutional rights—that was not in doubt—but how and when those rights could be exercised. Could the right to be silent (under the Fifth Amendment's protection against self-incrimination) be exercised during pretrial interrogation proceedings or only during the trial?

Were confessions obtained from suspects admissible in court if the suspects had not been advised of their right to remain silent and other constitutional rights?

To clarify these issues, the United States Supreme Court issued a landmark decision in 1966 in *Miranda v. Arizona,* which we present next. Today, the procedural rights required by the Court in this case are familiar to almost every American.

CASE 7.3
Miranda v. Arizona

Supreme Court of the United States, 384 U.S. 436, 86 S.Ct. 1602, 16 L.Ed.2d 694 (1966).

BACKGROUND AND FACTS • On March 13, 1963, Ernesto Miranda was arrested at his home for the kidnapping and rape of an eighteen-year-old woman. Miranda was taken to a Phoenix, Arizona, police station and questioned by two officers. Two hours later, the officers emerged from the interrogation room with a written confession signed by Miranda. A paragraph at the top of the confession stated that the confession had been made voluntarily, without threats or promises of immunity, and "with full knowledge of my legal rights, understanding any statement I make may be used against me." Miranda was at no time advised that he had a right to remain silent and a right to have a lawyer present. The confession was admitted into evidence at the trial, and Miranda was convicted and sentenced to prison for twenty to thirty years. Miranda appealed the decision, claiming that he had not been informed of his constitutional rights. The Supreme Court of Arizona held that Miranda's constitutional rights had not been violated and affirmed his conviction. The *Miranda* case was subsequently reviewed by the United States Supreme Court.

IN THE LANGUAGE OF THE COURT
Mr. Chief Justice *WARREN* delivered the opinion of the Court.

The cases before us raise questions which go to the roots of our concepts of American criminal jurisprudence; the restraints society must observe consistent with the Federal Constitution in prosecuting individuals for crime.

* * * *

At the outset, if a person in custody is to be subjected to interrogation, he must first be informed in clear and unequivocal terms that he has the right to remain silent.

* * * *

The warning of the right to remain silent must be accompanied by the explanation that anything said can and will be used against the individual in court. This warning is needed in order to make him aware not only of the privilege, *but also of the consequences of forgoing it.* * * * [Emphasis added.]

The circumstances surrounding in-custody interrogation can operate very quickly to overbear the will of one merely made aware of his privilege by his interrogators. Therefore the right to have counsel present at the interrogation is indispensable to the protection of the Fifth Amendment privilege under the system we delineate today.

* * * *

In order fully to apprise a person interrogated of the extent of his rights under this system then, it is necessary to warn him not only that he has the right to consult with an attorney, but also that if he is indigent [without funds] a lawyer will be appointed to represent him. * * * The warning of a right to counsel would be hollow if not couched in terms that would convey to the indigent—the person most often subjected to interrogation—the knowledge that he too has a right to have counsel present.

DECISION AND REMEDY • *The United States Supreme Court held that Miranda could not be convicted of the crime on the basis of his confession because his confession was inadmissible as evidence. For any statement made by a defendant to be admissible, the defendant must be informed of certain constitutional rights prior to police interrogation. If the accused waives his or her rights to remain silent and to have counsel present, the government must demonstrate that the waiver was made knowingly, voluntarily, and intelligently.*

IMPACT OF THIS CASE ON TODAY'S LAW • *Despite considerable criticism and later attempts to overrule the* Miranda *decision through legislation, the requirements stated in this case continue to provide the benchmark by which criminal procedures are judged today. Police officers routinely advise suspects of their "*Miranda *rights" on arrest. When Ernesto Miranda himself was later murdered, the suspected murderer was "read his* Miranda *rights."*

CASE CONTINUES ➡

CASE 7.3 CONTINUED ➡ **THE GLOBAL DIMENSION** • *The right to remain silent has long been a legal hallmark in Great Britain as well as in the United States. In 1994, however, the British Parliament passed an act that provides that a criminal defendant's silence may be interpreted as evidence of his or her guilt. British police officers are now required, when making an arrest, to inform the suspect, "You do not have to say anything. But if you do not mention now something which you later use in your defense, the court may decide that your failure to mention it now strengthens the case against you. A record will be made of everything you say, and it may be given in evidence if you are brought to trial." Should U.S. law also change to allow a defendant's silence during questioning to be considered as an indication of guilt? Why or why not?*

Exceptions to the *Miranda* Rule

Although the Supreme Court's decision in the *Miranda* case was controversial, it has survived several attempts by Congress to overrule it.[21] Over time, however, as part of a continuing attempt to balance the rights of accused persons against the rights of society, the Supreme Court has made a number of exceptions to the *Miranda* ruling. For example, the Court has recognized a "public safety" exception, holding that certain statements—such as statements concerning the location of a weapon—are admissible even if the defendant was not given *Miranda* warnings. Additionally, a suspect must unequivocally and assertively ask to exercise her or his right to counsel in order to stop police questioning. Saying, "Maybe I should talk to a lawyer" during an interrogation after being taken into custody is not enough. Police officers are not required to decipher the suspect's intentions in such situations.

Criminal Process

As mentioned earlier in this chapter, a criminal prosecution differs significantly from a civil case in several respects. These differences reflect the desire to safeguard the rights of the individual against the state. Exhibit 7–3 on the facing page summarizes the major steps in processing a criminal case. We now discuss three phases of the criminal process—arrest, indictment or information, and trial—in more detail.

ARREST Before a warrant for arrest can be issued, there must be probable cause to believe that the individual in question has committed a crime. As discussed in Chapter 5, *probable cause* can be defined as a substantial likelihood that the person has committed or is about to commit a crime. Note that probable cause involves a likelihood, not just a possibility. Arrests can be made without a warrant if

there is no time to get one, but the action of the arresting officer is still judged by the standard of probable cause.

INDICTMENT OR INFORMATION Individuals must be formally charged with having committed specific crimes before they can be brought to trial. If issued by a grand jury, such a charge is called an **indictment.**[22] A **grand jury** does not determine the guilt or innocence of an accused party; rather, its function is to hear the state's evidence and to determine whether a reasonable basis (probable cause) exists for believing that a crime has been committed and that a trial ought to be held.

Usually, grand juries are called in cases involving serious crimes, such as murder. For lesser crimes, an individual may be formally charged with a crime by an **information,** or criminal complaint. An information will be issued by a government prosecutor if the prosecutor determines that there is sufficient evidence to justify bringing the individual to trial.

TRIAL At a criminal trial, the accused person does not have to prove anything; the entire burden of proof is on the prosecutor (the state). As discussed at the beginning of this chapter, the burden of proof is higher in a criminal case than in a civil case. The prosecution must show that, based on all the evidence, the defendant's guilt is established *beyond a reasonable doubt*. If there is reasonable doubt as to whether a criminal defendant did, in fact, commit the crime with which she or he has been charged, then the verdict must be "not guilty." Note that giving a verdict of "not guilty" is not the same as stating that the defendant is innocent; it merely means that not enough evidence was properly presented to the court to prove guilt beyond a reasonable doubt.

Courts have complex rules about what types of evidence may be presented and how the evidence may be brought out in criminal cases, especially in jury trials. These rules are designed to ensure that

---

21. *Dickerson v. United States,* 530 U.S. 428, 120 S.Ct. 2326, 147 L.Ed.2d 405 (2000).

22. Pronounced in-*dyte*-ment.

EXHIBIT 7–3 • Major Procedural Steps in a Criminal Case

ARREST
Police officer takes suspect into custody. Most arrests are made without a warrant. After the arrest, the officer searches the suspect, who is then taken to the police station.

BOOKING
At the police station, the suspect is searched again, photographed, fingerprinted, and allowed at least one telephone call. After the booking, charges are reviewed, and if they are not dropped, a complaint is filed and a magistrate (judge) reviews the case for probable cause.

INITIAL APPEARANCE
The defendant appears before the judge, who informs the defendant of the charges and of his or her rights. If the defendant requests a lawyer and cannot afford one, a lawyer is appointed. The judge sets bail (conditions under which a suspect can obtain release pending disposition of the case).

GRAND JURY	**PRELIMINARY HEARING**
A grand jury determines if there is probable cause to believe that the defendant committed the crime. The federal government and about half of the states require grand jury indictments for at least some felonies.	In a court proceeding, a prosecutor presents evidence, and the judge determines if there is probable cause to hold the defendant over for trial.

INDICTMENT	**INFORMATION**
An *indictment* is a written document issued by the grand jury to formally charge the defendant with a crime.	An *information* is a formal criminal charge made by the prosecutor.

ARRAIGNMENT
The defendant is brought before the court, informed of the charges, and asked to enter a plea.

PLEA BARGAIN
A plea bargain is a prosecutor's promise to make concessions (or promise to seek concessions) in return for a defendant's guilty plea. Concessions may include a reduced charge or a lesser sentence.

GUILTY PLEA	**TRIAL**
In many jurisdictions, most cases that reach the arraignment stage do not go to trial but are resolved by a guilty plea, often as a result of a plea bargain. The judge sets the case for sentencing.	Trials can be either jury trials or bench trials. (In a bench trial, there is no jury, and the judge decides questions of fact as well as questions of law.) If the verdict is "guilty," the judge sets a date for the sentencing. Everyone convicted of a crime has the right to an appeal.

evidence presented at trials is relevant, reliable, and not prejudicial toward the defendant.

Federal Sentencing Guidelines

In 1984, Congress passed the Sentencing Reform Act. This act created the U.S. Sentencing Commission, which was charged with the task of standardizing sentences for *federal* crimes. The commission's guidelines, which became effective in 1987, established a range of possible penalties for each federal crime and required the judge to select a sentence from within that range. In other words, the guidelines originally established a mandatory system because judges were not allowed to deviate from the specified sentencing range. Some federal judges felt uneasy about imposing the long prison sentences required by the guidelines on certain criminal defendants, particularly first-time offenders and those convicted in illegal substances cases involving small quantities of drugs.[23]

SHIFT AWAY FROM MANDATORY SENTENCING In 2005, the United States Supreme Court held that certain provisions of the federal sentencing guidelines were unconstitutional.

CASE IN POINT Freddie Booker was arrested with 92.5 grams of crack cocaine in his possession. Booker admitted to police that he had sold an additional 566 grams of crack cocaine, but he was never charged with, or tried for, possession of this additional quantity. Nevertheless, under the federal sentencing guidelines the judge was required to sentence Booker to twenty-two years in prison. The Court ruled that this sentence was unconstitutional because a jury did not find beyond a reasonable doubt that Booker had possessed the additional 566 grams of crack.[24]

Essentially, the Court's ruling changed the federal sentencing guidelines from mandatory to advisory. Depending on the circumstances of the case, a federal trial judge may now depart from the guidelines if she or he believes that it is reasonable to do so.

INCREASED PENALTIES FOR CERTAIN CRIMINAL VIOLATIONS Sentencing guidelines still exist and provide for enhanced punishment for certain types of crimes, including white-collar crimes, violations of the Sarbanes-Oxley Act (discussed in Chapter 4), and violations of securities laws.[25]

In 2009, the Supreme Court considered the sentencing guidelines again and held that a sentencing judge cannot presume that a sentence within the applicable guidelines is reasonable.[26] Before concluding that a particular sentence is reasonable, the court must take into account the various sentencing factors that apply to an individual defendant. When the defendant is a business firm, these factors

include the company's history of past violations, management's cooperation with federal investigators, and the extent to which the firm has undertaken specific programs and procedures to prevent criminal activities by its employees.

SECTION 6
CYBER CRIME

The U.S. Department of Justice broadly defines **computer crime** as any violation of criminal law that involves knowledge of computer technology for its perpetration, investigation, or prosecution. A number of the white-collar crimes discussed earlier in this chapter, such as fraud, embezzlement, and the theft of intellectual property, are now committed with the aid of computers and are thus considered computer crimes.

Many computer crimes fall under the broad label of **cyber crime,** which describes any criminal activity occurring via a computer in the virtual community of the Internet. Most cyber crimes are not "new" crimes. Rather, they are existing crimes in which the Internet is the instrument of wrongdoing. Here we look at several types of activity that constitute cyber crimes against persons or property. Other cyber crimes will be discussed in later chapters as they relate to particular topics, such as banking or consumer law.

Cyber Fraud

As will be explained in Chapter 12, fraud is any misrepresentation knowingly made with the intention of deceiving another and on which a reasonable person would and does rely to her or his detriment. **Cyber fraud,** then, is fraud committed over the Internet. Frauds that were once conducted solely by mail or phone can now be found online, and new technology has led to increasingly creative ways to commit fraud.

Sometimes, Internet fraud is just an electronic version of frauds formerly perpetrated by sending letters. For example, the "Nigerian letter fraud scam" is perhaps the longest-running Internet fraud. In this swindle, con artists send e-mails promising the recipients a percentage if they will send funds to help fictitious officials from the African country transfer millions of nonexistent dollars to Western banks. Some versions of the scam reflect current events. In these updated scams, the e-mails may ask for financial help in retrieving the fortune of a

---

23. See, for example, *United States v. Angelos,* 345 F.Supp.2d 1227 (D. Utah 2004).

24. *United States v. Booker,* 543 U.S. 220, 125 S.Ct. 738, 160 L.Ed.2d 621 (2005).

25. The sentencing guidelines were amended in 2003, as required under the Sarbanes-Oxley Act of 2002, to impose stiffer penalties for corporate securities fraud—see Chapter 29.

26. *Nelson v. United States,* ___ U.S. ___, 129 S.Ct. 890, 172 L.Ed.2d 719 (2009).

loved one or an associate who perished in the conflict in Iraq or Afghanistan or during the earthquake in Haiti.

ONLINE AUCTION FRAUD Online auction fraud, in its most basic form, is a simple process. A person puts up an expensive item for auction, on either a legitimate or a fake auction site, and then refuses to send the product after receiving payment. Or, as a variation, the wrongdoer may provide the purchaser with an item that is worth less than the one offered in the auction. The larger online auction sites, such as eBay, try to protect consumers against such schemes by providing warnings about deceptive sellers or offering various forms of insurance. The nature of the Internet, however, makes it nearly impossible to completely block fraudulent auction activity. Because users can assume multiple identities, it is very difficult to pinpoint fraudulent sellers—they will simply change their screen names with each auction.

ONLINE RETAIL FRAUD Somewhat similar to online auction fraud is online retail fraud, in which consumers pay directly (without bidding) for items that are never delivered. Because most consumers will purchase items only from reputable, well-known sites such as Amazon.com, criminals have had to take advantage of some of the complexities of cyberspace to lure unknowing customers. As with other forms of online fraud, it is difficult to determine the actual extent of online sales fraud, but anecdotal evidence suggests that it is a substantial problem.

CASE IN POINT Jeremy Jaynes grossed more than $750,000 per week selling nonexistent or worthless products such as "penny stock pickers" and "Internet history erasers." By the time he was arrested, he had amassed an estimated $24 million from his various fraudulent schemes.[27]

Cyber Theft

In cyberspace, thieves are not subject to the physical limitations of the "real" world. A thief can steal data stored in a networked computer with Internet access from anywhere on the globe. Only the speed of the connection and the thief's computer equipment limit the quantity of data that can be stolen.

IDENTITY THEFT Not surprisingly, there has been a marked increase in identity theft in recent years. **Identity theft** occurs when the wrongdoer steals a form of identification—such as a name, date of birth, or Social Security number—and uses the information to access the victim's financial resources. This crime existed to a certain extent before the widespread use of the Internet. Thieves would rifle through garbage to find credit-card or bank account numbers and then use those numbers to purchase goods or to withdraw funds from the victims' accounts.

The Internet has provided even easier access to private data. Frequent Web surfers surrender a wealth of information about themselves without knowing it. Many Web sites use "cookies" to collect data on those who visit their sites. The data may include the areas of the site the user visits and the links on which the user clicks. Furthermore, Web browsers often store information such as the consumer's name and e-mail address. Finally, every time a purchase is made online, the item is linked to the purchaser's name, allowing Web retailers to amass a database of who is buying what.

PHISHING A distinct form of identity theft known as **phishing** has added a different wrinkle to the practice. In a phishing attack, the perpetrator "fishes" for financial data and passwords from consumers by posing as a legitimate business, such as a bank or credit-card company. The "phisher" sends an e-mail asking the recipient to update or confirm vital information, often with the threat that an account or some other service will be discontinued if the information is not provided. Once the unsuspecting individual enters the information, the phisher can use it to masquerade as that person or to drain his or her bank or credit account.

VISHING When phishing involves some form of voice communication, the scam is known as **vishing.** In one variation, the consumer receives an e-mail saying that there is a problem with an account and that she or he should call a certain telephone number to resolve the problem. Sometimes, the e-mail even says that a telephone call is being requested so that the recipient will know that this is not a phishing attempt. Of course, the goal is to get the consumer to divulge passwords and account information during the call. In one scheme, e-mails seemingly from the Federal Bureau of Investigation asked recipients to call a special telephone number and provide account information. The perpetrators of vishing scams use Voice over Internet Protocol (VoIP) service, which enables telephone calls to be

---

27. *Jaynes v. Commonwealth of Virginia,* 276 Va.App. 443, 666 S.E.2d 303 (2008).

made over the Internet, because it is inexpensive and enables them to easily hide their identity.

EMPLOYMENT FRAUD   Cyber criminals also look for victims at online job–posting sites. Claiming to be an employment officer in a well-known company, the criminal sends bogus e-mail messages to job seekers. The messages ask the unsuspecting job seekers to reveal enough information to allow for identity theft. As the recession dragged on into 2010 and the unemployment rate continued to rise, opportunities for employment fraud were also on the increase. For example, the job site Monster.com had to ask its 4.5 million users to change their passwords because cyber thieves had broken into its databases and stolen user identities, passwords, and other data. This theft of personal information was one of Britain's largest cyber theft cases.[28]

CREDIT-CARD CRIME ON THE WEB   Credit-card theft was mentioned previously in connection with identity theft. An important point to note, however, is that stolen credit cards are much more likely to hurt merchants and credit-card issuers (such as banks) than consumers. In most situations, the legitimate holders of credit cards are not held responsible for the costs of purchases made with a stolen number (see Chapter 24). That means the financial burden must be borne either by the merchant or by the credit-card company. Most credit-card issuers require merchants to cover the costs—especially if the address to which the goods are sent does not match the billing address of the credit card.

Additionally, companies take risks by storing their online customers' credit-card numbers. In doing so, companies provide quicker service; the consumer can make a purchase by providing a code or clicking on a particular icon without entering a lengthy card number. These electronic warehouses are, however, quite tempting to cyber thieves. Several years ago, for example, an unknown person was able to gain access to computerized records at CardSystems Solutions, a company in Tucson, Arizona, that processes credit-card transactions for small Internet businesses. The breach exposed 40 million credit-card numbers.[29]

Hacking

A **hacker** is someone who uses one computer to break into another. The danger posed by hackers has increased significantly because of **botnets,** or networks of computers that have been appropriated by hackers without the knowledge of their owners. A hacker will secretly install a program on thousands, if not millions, of personal computer "robots," or "bots," that allows him or her to forward transmissions to an even larger number of systems.

MALWARE   Botnets are one of the latest forms of **malware**, a term that refers to any program that is harmful to a computer or, by extension, a computer user. A **worm,** for example, is a software program that is capable of reproducing itself as it spreads from one computer to the next. In 2009, in under three weeks, the computer worm called "Conflicker" spread to more than one million personal computers around the world. It was transmitted to some computers through the use of Facebook and Twitter. This worm also infected servers and devices plugged into infected computers via USB ports, such as iPods and pen drives.

A **virus,** another form of malware, is also able to reproduce itself, but must be attached to an "infested" host file to travel from one computer network to another. For example, hackers are now capable of corrupting banner ads that use Adobe's Flash Player. When an Internet user clicks on the banner ad, a virus is installed. Worms and viruses can be programmed to perform a number of functions, such as prompting host computers to continually "crash" and reboot, or otherwise infect the system.

NEW SERVICE-BASED HACKING AVAILABLE AT LOW COST   A recent trend in business computer applications is the use of "software as a service." Instead of buying software to install on a computer, the user connects to Web-based software. The user can write e-mails, edit spreadsheets, and the like using his or her Web browser. Cyber criminals have adapted this method and now offer "crimeware as a service."

A would-be thief no longer has to be a computer hacker to create a botnet or steal banking information and credit-card numbers. He or she can rent the online services of cyber criminals to do the work on such sites as NeoSploit. The thief can even target individual groups, such as U.S. physicians or British attorneys. The cost of renting a Web site to do the work is only a few cents per target computer.

---

28. John Bingham. "Monster.com Hacking Follows Tradition of Cyber Theft." *Telegraph.co.uk*. 28 January 2009: n.p. Web.

29. The Federal Trade Commission (FTC) brought charges against the company, which ultimately reached a settlement with the FTC.

CYBERTERRORISM Hackers who break into computers without authorization often commit cyber theft, but sometimes their principal aim is to prove how smart they are by gaining access to others' password-protected computers. **Cyberterrorists** are hackers who, rather than trying to gain attention, strive to remain undetected so that they can exploit computers for a serious impact. Just as "real" terrorists destroyed the World Trade Center towers and a portion of the Pentagon on September 11, 2001, cyberterrorists might explode "logic bombs" to shut down central computers. Such activities obviously can pose a danger to national security.

Cyberterrorists as well as hackers may target businesses. The goals of a hacking operation might include a wholesale theft of data, such as a merchant's customer files, or the monitoring of a computer to discover a business firm's plans and transactions. A cyberterrorist might also want to insert false codes or data. For example, the processing control system of a food manufacturer could be changed to alter the levels of ingredients so that consumers of the food would become ill.

A cyberterrorist attack on a major financial institution, such as the New York Stock Exchange or a large bank, could leave securities or money markets in flux and seriously affect the daily lives of millions of citizens. Similarly, any prolonged disruption of computer, cable, satellite, or telecommunications systems due to the actions of expert hackers would have serious repercussions on business operations—and national security—on a global level.

Prosecution of Cyber Crime

The "location" of cyber crime (cyberspace) has raised new issues in the investigation of crimes and the prosecution of offenders. A threshold issue is, of course, jurisdiction. A person who commits an act against a business in California, where the act is a cyber crime, might never have set foot in California but might instead reside in New York, or even in Canada, where the act may not be a crime. If the crime was committed via e-mail, the question arises as to whether the e-mail would constitute sufficient minimum contacts (see Chapter 2) for the victim's state to exercise jurisdiction over the perpetrator.

Identifying the wrongdoer can also be difficult. Cyber criminals do not leave physical traces, such as fingerprints or DNA samples, as evidence of their crimes. Even electronic "footprints" can be hard to find and follow. For example, e-mail may be sent through a remailer, an online service that guarantees that a message cannot be traced to its source.

For these reasons, laws written to protect physical property are often difficult to apply in cyberspace. Nonetheless, governments at both the state and the federal level have taken significant steps toward controlling cyber crime, both by applying existing criminal statutes and by enacting new laws that specifically address wrongs committed in cyberspace.

The Computer Fraud and Abuse Act

Perhaps the most significant federal statute specifically addressing cyber crime is the Counterfeit Access Device and Computer Fraud and Abuse Act of 1984 (commonly known as the Computer Fraud and Abuse Act, or CFAA).[30] Among other things, this act provides that a person who accesses a computer online, without authority, to obtain classified, restricted, or protected data (or attempts to do so) is subject to criminal prosecution. Such data could include financial and credit records, medical records, legal files, military and national security files, and other confidential information in government or private computers. The crime has two elements: accessing a computer without authority and taking the data.

This theft is a felony if it is committed for a commercial purpose or for private financial gain, or if the value of the stolen data (or computer time) exceeds $5,000. Penalties include fines and imprisonment for up to twenty years. A victim of computer theft can also bring a civil suit against the violator to obtain damages, an injunction, and other relief.

---

30. 18 U.S.C. Section 1030.

REVIEWING

Criminal Law and Cyber Crime

Edward Hanousek worked for Pacific & Arctic Railway and Navigation Company (P&A) as a roadmaster of the White Pass & Yukon Railroad in Alaska. Hanousek was responsible "for every detail of the safe and efficient maintenance and construction of track, structures and marine facilities of the entire railroad," including special projects. One project was a rock quarry, known as "6-mile," above the Skagway River. Next to the quarry, and just beneath the surface, ran a high-pressure oil pipeline owned

REVIEWING CONTINUES ▶

REVIEWING

Criminal Law and Cyber Crime, Continued

by Pacific & Arctic Pipeline, Inc., P&A's sister company. When the quarry's backhoe operator punctured the pipeline, an estimated 1,000 to 5,000 gallons of oil were discharged into the river. Hanousek was charged with negligently discharging a harmful quantity of oil into a navigable water of the United States in violation of the criminal provisions of the Clean Water Act (CWA). Using the information presented in the chapter, answer the following questions.

1. Did Hanousek have the required mental state (*mens rea*) to be convicted of a crime? Why or why not?
2. Which theory discussed in the chapter would enable a court to hold Hanousek criminally liable for violating the statute regardless of whether he participated in, directed, or even knew about the specific violation?
3. Could the backhoe operator who punctured the pipeline also be charged with a crime in this situation? Explain.
4. Suppose that at trial, Hanousek argued that he should not be convicted because he was not aware of the requirements of the CWA. Would this defense be successful? Why or why not?

DEBATE THIS: *One legal observer claimed that all Americans may be breaking the law regularly without knowing it because of* overcriminalization, *particularly by the federal government. Should Congress rescind many of the more than four thousand federal crimes now on the books?*

TERMS AND CONCEPTS

actus reus 139
arson 142
beyond a reasonable
   doubt 138
botnet 158
burglary 141
computer crime 156
crime 137
cyber crime 156

cyber fraud 156
cyberterrorist 159
double jeopardy 151
duress 150
embezzlement 142
entrapment 150
exclusionary rule 151
felony 138
forgery 142
grand jury 154
hacker 158

identity theft 157
indictment 154
information 154
larceny 141
malware 158
mens rea 140
misdemeanor 138
money laundering 147
necessity 149
petty offense 138
phishing 157

plea bargaining 150
robbery 141
self-defense 149
self-incrimination 150
virus 158
vishing 157
white-collar crime 142
worm 158

QUESTIONS AND CASE PROBLEMS

7–1. Types of Cyber Crimes The following situations are similar, but each represents a variation of a particular crime. Identify the crime and point out the differences in the variations.

(a) Chen, posing fraudulently as Diamond Credit Card Co., sends an e-mail to Emily, stating that the company has observed suspicious activity in her account and has frozen the account. The e-mail asks her to reregister her credit-card number and password to reopen the account.

(b) Claiming falsely to be Big Buy Retail Finance Co., Conner sends an e-mail to Dino, asking him to confirm or update his personal security information to prevent his Big Buy account from being discontinued.

(c) Felicia posts her résumé on GotWork.com, an online job–posting site, seeking a position in business and managerial finance and accounting. Hayden, who misrepresents himself as an employment officer with International Bank & Commerce Corp., sends her an e-mail asking for more personal information.

7–2. Property Crimes Which, if any, of the following crimes necessarily involves illegal activity on the part of more than one person?

(a) Bribery

(b) Forgery

(c) Embezzlement

(d) Larceny

(e) Receiving stolen property

7–3. QUESTION WITH SAMPLE ANSWER: Cyber Scam.

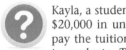

Kayla, a student at Learnwell University, owes $20,000 in unpaid tuition. If Kayla does not pay the tuition, Learnwell will not allow her to graduate. To obtain the funds to pay the debt, she sends e-mail letters to people that she does not personally know asking for financial help to send Milo, her disabled child, to a special school. In reality, Kayla has no children. Is this a crime? If so, which one?

• For a sample answer to Question 7–3, go to Appendix F at the end of this text.

7–4. Exclusionary Rule While Charles McFarland was incarcerated in a state prison, two officers questioned him about his connection to a handgun that had been used to shoot two other officers. McFarland was advised of his rights but was not asked whether he was willing to waive those rights. Instead, to induce McFarland to speak, the officers deceived him into believing that "[n]obody is going to give you charges." McFarland made incriminating admissions and was indicted for possessing a handgun as a convicted felon. Should McFarland's statements be suppressed—that is, not be treated as admissible evidence at trial—because he was not asked whether he was willing to waive his rights prior to making his self-incriminating statements? Why or why not? [*United States v. McFarland,* 424 F.Supp.2d 427 (N.D.N.Y. 2006)]

7–5. White-Collar Crime Helm Instruction Co. in Maumee, Ohio, makes custom electrical control systems. In September 1998, Helm hired Patrick Walsh to work as comptroller. Walsh soon developed a close relationship with Richard Wilhelm, Helm's president, who granted Walsh's request to hire Shari Price as an assistant. Wilhelm was not aware that Walsh and Price were engaged in an extramarital affair. Over the next five years, Walsh and Price spent more than $200,000 of Helm's money on themselves. Among other things, Walsh drew unauthorized checks on Helm's accounts to pay his personal credit cards and issued to Price and himself unauthorized salary increases, overtime payments, and tuition reimbursement payments, altering Helm's records to hide the payments. After an investigation, Helm officials confronted Walsh. He denied the affair with Price, claimed that his unauthorized use of Helm's funds was an "interest-free loan," and argued that it was less of a burden on the company to pay his credit cards than to give him the salary increases to which he felt he was entitled. Did Walsh commit a crime? If so, what crime did he commit? Discuss. [*State v. Walsh,* 113 Ohio App.3d 1515, 866 N.E.2d 513 (6 Dist. 2007)]

7–6. CASE PROBLEM WITH SAMPLE ANSWER: Credit Cards.

Oleksiy Sharapka ordered merchandise online using stolen credit cards. He had the items sent to outlets of Mail Boxes, Etc., and then arranged for someone to deliver the items to his house. He subsequently shipped the goods overseas, primarily to Russia. Sharapka was indicted in a federal district court. At the time of his arrest, government agents found in his possession, among other things, more than three hundred stolen credit-card numbers, including numbers issued by American Express. There was evidence that he had used more than ten of the American Express numbers to buy goods worth between $400,000 and $1 million from at least fourteen vendors. Did Sharapka commit any crimes? If so, who were his victims? Explain. [United States v. Sharapka, *526 F.3d 58 (1st Cir. 2008)]*

• To view a sample answer for Problem 7–6, go to this book's Web site at www.cengage.com/blaw/cross, select "Chapter 7," and click on "Case Problem with Sample Answer."

7–7. Intellectual Property Jiri Klimecek was a member of a group that overrode copyright protection in movies, video games, and software, and made them available for download online. Klimecek bought and installed hardware and software to set up a computer server and paid half of the monthly service charges to connect the server to the Internet. He knew that users around the world could access the server to upload and download copyrighted works. He obtained access to Czech movies and music to make them available. Klimecek was indicted in a federal district court for copyright infringement. He claimed that he did not understand the full scope of the operation. Did Klimecek commit a crime? If so, was he a "minor participant" entitled to a reduced sentence? Explain. [*United States v. Klimecek,* __ F.3d __ (7th Cir. 2009)]

7–8. Fourth Amendment Three police officers, including Maria Trevizo, were on patrol in Tucson, Arizona, near a neighborhood associated with the Crips gang, when they pulled over a car with suspended registration. Each officer talked to one of the three occupants. Trevizo spoke with Lemon Johnson, who was wearing clothing consistent with Crips membership. Visible in his jacket pocket was a police scanner, and he said that he had served time in prison for burglary. Trevizo asked him to get out of the car and patted him down "for officer safety." She found a gun. Johnson was charged in an Arizona state court with illegal possession of a weapon. What standard should apply to an officer's patdown of a passenger during a traffic stop? Should a search warrant be required? Could a search proceed solely on the basis of probable cause? Would a reasonable suspicion short of probable cause be sufficient? Discuss. [*Arizona v. Johnson,* __ U.S. __, 129 S.Ct. 781, 172 L.Ed.2d 694 (2009)]

7–9. Sentencing Guidelines Paul Wilkinson worked for a company that sold fuel to various military bases. He paid an employee of a competitor to provide him with information about bids for contracts for which both companies were bidding. The information enabled Wilkinson to rig the bids and win contracts. When the scam was uncovered, he was indicted for conspiracy to defraud the government, to commit wire fraud, and to steal trade secrets. He pleaded guilty to the charges under a plea arrangement. Given the nature of the offenses, the federal sentencing guidelines provide for a prison term of fifty-one to sixty-three months with no possibility of probation. Due to Wilkinson's cooperation, the prosecution recommended fifty-one months. His attorney argued for a term of ten to sixteen months. The judge sentenced Wilkinson to three years' probation and eight hundred hours of community service, but no prison term. The government appealed, arguing that the sentence was too light in violation of the sentencing guidelines. Can a trial judge give such a light sentence under the sentencing guidelines? Explain your answer. [*United States v. Wilkinson*, 590 F.3d 259 (4th Cir. 2010)]

7–10. A QUESTION OF ETHICS: Identity Theft.

Davis Omole had good grades in high school, played on the football and chess teams, and went on to college. Twenty-year-old Omole was also one of the chief architects of a scheme through which more than one hundred individuals were defrauded. Omole worked at a cell phone store where he stole customers' personal information. He and others used the stolen identities to create one hundred different accounts on eBay, through which they held more than three hundred auctions listing for sale items that they did not own and did not intend to sell—cell phones, plasma televisions, stereos, and more. They collected $90,000 through these auctions. To avoid getting caught, they continuously closed and opened the eBay accounts, activated and deactivated cell phone and e-mail accounts, and changed mailing addresses and post office boxes. Omole, who had previously been convicted in a state court for Internet fraud, was convicted in a federal district court of identity theft and wire fraud. [*United States v. Omole*, 523 F.3d 691 (7th Cir. 2008)]

(a) Before Omole's trial, he sent e-mails to his victims ridiculing them and calling them stupid for having been cheated. During his trial, he displayed contempt for the court. What do these factors show about Omole's ethics?

(b) Under the federal sentencing guidelines, Omole could have been imprisoned for more than eight years, but he received a sentence of only three years, two of which were the mandatory sentence for identity theft. Was this sentence too lenient? Explain.

7–11. VIDEO QUESTION: Criminal Procedures.

Go to this text's Web site at **www.cengage.com/ blaw/cross** and select "Chapter 7." Click on "Video Questions" and view the video titled *Twelve Angry Men*. Then answer the following questions.

(a) The jurors are deliberating on whether to convict the defendant. One juror says that at the beginning of the trial he felt that the defendant was guilty and that "nobody proved otherwise." Does a criminal defendant have to offer evidence of his or her innocence? What must the prosecution show to establish that a defendant is guilty? How does the burden of proof differ in criminal and civil cases?

(b) It is clear that all of the jurors except one (Henry Fonda) believe that the defendant is guilty. How many jurors does it usually take to render a verdict in a criminal case?

(c) When the holdout juror says that under the U.S. Constitution "the defendant does not even have to open his mouth," to which provision is he referring?

(c) Is it wrong for a group of jurors to bully or persuade another juror of the defendant's guilt or innocence? Explain.

LEGAL RESEARCH EXERCISES ON THE WEB

Go to this text's Web site at **www.cengage.com/blaw/cross**, select "Chapter 7," and click on "Practical Internet Exercises." There you will find the following Internet research exercises that you can perform to learn more about the topics covered in this chapter.

Practical Internet Exercise 7–1: **Legal Perspective**
Revisiting *Miranda*

Practical Internet Exercise 7–2: **Management Perspective**
Hackers

Practical Internet Exercise 7–3: **Global Perspective**
Fighting Cyber Crime Worldwide

CHAPTER 8

International Law in a Global Economy

International business transactions are not unique to the modern world. Commerce has always crossed national borders. What is new in our day is the dramatic growth in world trade and the emergence of a global business community. Because exchanges of goods, services, and ideas (intellectual property) on a global level are now routine, students of business law and the legal environment should be familiar with the laws pertaining to international business transactions.

Laws affecting the international legal environment of business include both international law and national law. **International law** can be defined as a body of law—formed as a result of international customs, treaties, and organizations—that governs relations among or between nations. International law may be public, creating standards for the nations themselves; or it may be private, establishing international standards for private transactions that cross national borders. **National law** is the law of a particular nation, such as Brazil, Germany, Japan, or the United States.

In this chapter, we examine how both international law and national law frame business operations in the global context. We also look at some selected areas relating to business activities in a global context, including common types of international business transactions, export and import controls, and the role of trade agreements. We conclude the chapter with a discussion of the application of certain U.S. laws in a transnational setting.

SECTION 1
INTERNATIONAL LAW

The major difference between international law and national law is that government authorities can enforce national law. What government, however, can enforce international law? By definition, a *nation* is a sovereign entity—which means that there is no higher authority to which that nation must submit. If a nation violates an international law and persuasive tactics fail, other countries or international organizations have no recourse except to take coercive actions—from severance of diplomatic relations and boycotts to, as a last resort, war—against the violating nation.

In essence, international law attempts to reconcile the need of each country to be the final authority over its own affairs with the desire of nations to benefit economically from trade and harmonious relations with one another. Sovereign nations can,

and do, voluntarily agree to be governed in certain respects by international law for the purpose of facilitating international trade and commerce, as well as civilized discourse. As a result, a body of international law has evolved. In this section, we examine the primary sources and characteristics of that body of law, as well as some important legal principles and doctrines that have been developed over time to facilitate dealings among nations.

Sources of International Law

Basically, there are three sources of international law: international customs, treaties and international agreements, and international organizations and conferences. We look at each of these sources here.

INTERNATIONAL CUSTOMS One important source of international law consists of the international customs that have evolved among nations in their relations with one another. Article 38(1) of the

Statute of the International Court of Justice refers to an international custom as "evidence of a general practice accepted as law." The legal principles and doctrines that you will read about shortly are rooted in international customs and traditions that have evolved over time in the international arena.

TREATIES AND INTERNATIONAL AGREEMENTS
Treaties and other explicit agreements between or among foreign nations provide another important source of international law. A **treaty** is an agreement or contract between two or more nations that must be authorized and ratified by the supreme power of each nation. Under Article II, Section 2, of the U.S. Constitution, the president has the power "by and with the Advice and Consent of the Senate, to make Treaties, provided two-thirds of the Senators present concur."

A *bilateral* agreement, as the term implies, is an agreement formed by two nations to govern their commercial exchanges or other relations with one another. A *multilateral* agreement is formed by several nations. For example, regional trade associations such as the Andean Common Market, the Association of Southeast Asian Nations, and the European Union are the result of multilateral trade agreements.

INTERNATIONAL ORGANIZATIONS In international law, the term **international organization** generally refers to an organization composed mainly of officials of member nations and usually established by treaty. The United States is a member of more than one hundred multilateral and bilateral organizations, including at least twenty through the United Nations. These organizations adopt resolutions, declarations, and other types of standards that often require nations to behave in a particular manner. The General Assembly of the United Nations, for example, has adopted numerous nonbinding resolutions and declarations that embody principles of international law. Disputes with respect to these resolutions and declarations may be brought before the International Court of Justice. That court, however, normally has authority to settle legal disputes only when nations voluntarily submit to its jurisdiction.

The United Nations Commission on International Trade Law has made considerable progress in establishing uniformity in international law as it relates to trade and commerce. One of the commission's most significant creations to date is the 1980 Convention on Contracts for the International Sale of Goods (CISG). As you will read in Chapter 11, the CISG is similar to Article 2 of the Uniform Commercial Code in that it is designed to settle disputes between parties to sales contracts. It spells out the duties of international buyers and sellers that will apply if the parties have not agreed otherwise in their contracts. The CISG governs only sales contracts between trading partners in nations that have ratified the CISG.

Common Law and Civil Law Systems

Companies operating in foreign nations are subject to the laws of those nations. In addition, international disputes often are resolved through the court systems of foreign nations. Therefore, businesspersons should understand that legal systems around the globe generally are divided into *common law* and *civil law* systems. Exhibit 8–1 on the facing page lists some of the nations that use civil law systems and some that use common law systems.

COMMON LAW SYSTEMS As discussed in Chapter 1, in a *common law* system, the courts independently develop the rules governing certain areas of law, such as torts and contracts. These common law rules apply to all areas not covered by statutory law. Although the common law doctrine of *stare decisis* obligates judges to follow precedential decisions in their jurisdictions, courts may modify or even overturn precedents when deemed necessary.

CIVIL LAW SYSTEMS In contrast to common law countries, most of the European nations, as well as nations in Latin America, Africa, and Asia, base their legal systems on Roman civil law, or "code law." The term *civil law,* as used here, refers not to civil as opposed to criminal law but to *codified* law—an ordered grouping of legal principles enacted into law by a legislature or other governing body.

In a **civil law system**, the primary source of law is a statutory code. Courts interpret the code and apply the rules to individual cases, but courts may not depart from the code and develop their own laws. Judicial precedents are not binding, as they are in a common law system. In theory, the law code sets forth all of the principles needed for the legal system. Trial procedures also differ in civil law systems. Unlike judges in common law systems, judges in civil systems often actively question witnesses.

ISLAMIC LEGAL SYSTEMS A third, less prevalent, legal system is common in Islamic countries, where the law is often influenced by *sharia*, the religious law of Islam. *Sharia* is a comprehensive code of

EXHIBIT 8-1 • The Legal Systems of Selected Nations

CIVIL LAW		COMMON LAW	
Argentina	Indonesia	Australia	Nigeria
Austria	Iran	Bangladesh	Singapore
Brazil	Italy	Canada	United Kingdom
Chile	Japan	Ghana	United States
China	Mexico	India	Zambia
Egypt	Poland	Israel	
Finland	South Korea	Jamaica	
France	Sweden	Kenya	
Germany	Tunisia	Malaysia	
Greece	Venezuela	New Zealand	

principles that governs both the public and the private lives of persons of the Islamic faith, directing many aspects of day-to-day life, including politics, economics, banking, business law, contract law, and social issues. Although *sharia* affects the legal codes of many Muslim countries, the extent of its impact and its interpretation vary widely. In some Middle Eastern nations, aspects of *sharia* have been codified and are enforced by national judicial systems.

International Principles and Doctrines

Over time, a number of legal principles and doctrines have evolved and are employed—to a greater or lesser extent—by the courts of various nations to resolve or reduce conflicts that involve a foreign element. The three important legal principles discussed below are based primarily on courtesy and respect, and are applied in the interests of maintaining harmonious relations among nations.

THE PRINCIPLE OF COMITY Under the principle of **comity,** one nation will defer and give effect to the laws and judicial decrees of another country, as long as they are consistent with the law and public policy of the accommodating nation. For example, a Swedish seller and a U.S. buyer have formed a contract, which the buyer breaches. The seller sues the buyer in a Swedish court, which awards damages. The buyer's assets, however, are in the United States and cannot be reached unless the judgment is enforced by a U.S. court. In this situation, if a U.S. court determines that the procedures and laws applied in the Swedish court are consistent with U.S. national law and policy, the U.S. court will likely defer to, and enforce, the foreign court's judgment.

CASE IN POINT After Karen Goldberg's husband was killed in a terrorist bombing of a bus in Israel, she filed a lawsuit in a federal court in New York against UBS AG, a Switzerland-based global financial services company with many offices in the United States. Goldberg claimed that UBS was liable under the U.S. Anti-Terrorism Act for aiding and abetting the murder of her husband because it provided financial services to the international terrorist organizations responsible for his murder. UBS argued that the case should be transferred to a court in Israel, which would offer a remedy "substantially the same" as the one available in the United States. The court refused to transfer the case, however, because that would require an Israeli court to take evidence and judge the emotional damage suffered by Goldberg, "raising distinct concerns of comity and enforceability." U.S. courts hesitate to impose U.S. law on foreign courts when such law is "an unwarranted intrusion" on the policies governing a foreign nation's judicial system.[1]

One way to understand the principle of comity (and the *act of state doctrine,* which will be discussed shortly) is to consider the relationships among the states in our federal form of government. Each state honors (gives "full faith and credit" to) the contracts, property deeds, wills, and other legal obligations formed in other states, as well as judicial decisions with respect to such obligations. On a global basis, nations similarly attempt to honor judgments rendered in other countries when it is feasible to do so. Of course, in the United States the states are constitutionally required to honor other states' actions, whereas, internationally, nations are not *required* to honor the actions of other nations.

THE ACT OF STATE DOCTRINE The **act of state doctrine** provides that the judicial branch of one country will not examine the validity of public acts

---

1. *Goldberg v. UBS AG,* 690 F.Supp.2d 92 (E.D.N.Y. 2010).

committed by a recognized foreign government within the latter's own territory.

When a Foreign Government Takes Private Property. The act of state doctrine can have important consequences for individuals and firms doing business with, and investing in, other countries. This doctrine is frequently employed in cases involving **expropriation,** which occurs when a government seizes a privately owned business or privately owned goods for a proper public purpose and awards just compensation. When a government seizes private property for an illegal purpose and without just compensation, the taking is referred to as a **confiscation.** The line between these two forms of taking is sometimes blurred because of differing interpretations of what is illegal and what constitutes just compensation.

For example, Flaherty, Inc., a U.S. company, owns a mine in Brazil. The government of Brazil seizes the mine for public use and claims that the profits Flaherty has already realized from the mine constitute just compensation. Flaherty disagrees, but the act of state doctrine may prevent that company's recovery in a U.S. court. Note that in a case alleging that a foreign government has wrongfully taken the plaintiff's property, the defendant government has the burden of proving that the taking was an expropriation, not a confiscation.

Doctrine May Immunize a Foreign Government's Actions. When applicable, both the act of state doctrine and the doctrine of *sovereign immunity,* which we discuss next, tend to shield foreign nations from the jurisdiction of U.S. courts. As a result, firms or individuals who own property overseas generally have little legal protection against government actions in the countries where they operate.

THE DOCTRINE OF SOVEREIGN IMMUNITY When certain conditions are satisfied, the doctrine of **sovereign immunity** exempts foreign nations from the jurisdiction of the U.S. courts. In 1976, Congress codified this rule in the Foreign Sovereign Immunities Act (FSIA).[2] The FSIA exclusively governs the circumstances in which an action may be brought in the United States against a foreign nation, including attempts to attach a foreign nation's property. Because the law is jurisdictional in nature, a plaintiff generally has the burden of showing that a defendant is not entitled to sovereign immunity.

---

2. 28 U.S.C. Sections 1602–1611.

Section 1605 of the FSIA sets forth the major exceptions to the jurisdictional immunity of a foreign state. A foreign state is not immune from the jurisdiction of U.S. courts in the following situations:

1. When the foreign state has waived its immunity either explicitly or by implication.
2. When the foreign state has engaged in commercial activity within the United States or in commercial activity outside the United States that has "a direct effect in the United States."
3. When the foreign state has committed a tort in the United States or has violated certain international laws.

When courts apply the FSIA, questions frequently arise as to whether an entity is a "foreign state" and what constitutes a "commercial activity." Under Section 1603 of the FSIA, a *foreign state* includes both a political subdivision of a foreign state and an instrumentality (department or agency of any branch of a government) of a foreign state. Section 1603 broadly defines a *commercial activity* as a regular course of commercial conduct, transaction, or act that is carried out by a foreign state within the United States. Section 1603, however, does not describe the particulars of what constitutes a commercial activity. Thus, the courts are left to decide whether a particular activity is governmental or commercial in nature.

SECTION 2
DOING BUSINESS INTERNATIONALLY

A U.S. domestic firm can engage in international business transactions in a number of ways. The simplest way is for U.S. firms to **export** their goods and services to foreign markets. Alternatively, a U.S. firm can establish foreign production facilities to be closer to the foreign market or markets in which its products are sold. The advantages may include lower labor costs, fewer government regulations, and lower taxes and trade barriers. A domestic firm can also obtain revenues by licensing its technology to an existing foreign company or by selling franchises to overseas entities.

Exporting

Exporting can take two forms: direct exporting and indirect exporting. In *direct exporting,* a U.S. company signs a sales contract with a foreign purchaser that provides for the conditions of shipment and payment for the goods. (International contracts for the purchase and sale of goods, as well as the use of letters of credit to make payments in international transactions, will be discussed in Chapter 11.) If sufficient business develops in a foreign country, a U.S. company may establish a specialized marketing organization there by appointing a foreign agent or a foreign distributor. This is called *indirect exporting*.

When a U.S. firm wishes to limit its involvement in an international market, it will typically establish an *agency relationship* with a foreign firm (*agency* will be discussed in Chapter 20). The foreign firm then acts as the U.S. firm's agent and can enter contracts in the foreign location on behalf of the principal (the U.S. company).

When a foreign country represents a substantial market, a U.S. firm may wish to appoint a distributor located in that country. The U.S. firm and the distributor enter into a **distribution agreement**—a contract setting out the terms and conditions of the distributorship, such as price, currency of payment, guarantee of supply availability, and method of payment. Disputes concerning distribution agreements may involve jurisdictional or other issues, as well as contract law.

In response to the latest economic recession, the U.S. government has taken a greater interest in the export of goods and services to foreign markets by U.S. companies. For a discussion of a recent federal initiative to encourage exports, see this chapter's *Shifting Legal Priorities for Business* feature on the following page.

Manufacturing Abroad

An alternative to direct or indirect exporting is the establishment of foreign manufacturing facilities. Typically, U.S. firms establish manufacturing plants abroad when they believe that by doing so they will reduce costs—particularly for labor, shipping, and raw materials—and thereby be able to compete more effectively in foreign markets. Foreign firms have done the same in the United States. Sony, Nissan, and other Japanese manufacturers have established U.S. plants to avoid import duties that the U.S. Congress may impose on Japanese products entering this country.

A U.S. firm can conduct manufacturing operations in other countries in several ways. They include licensing, franchising, and investing in a wholly owned subsidiary or a joint venture.

LICENSING A U.S. firm may license a foreign manufacturing company to use its copyrighted, patented, or trademarked intellectual property or trade secrets. Like any other licensing agreement (see Chapter 14), a licensing agreement with a foreign-based firm calls for a payment of royalties on some basis—such as so many cents per unit produced or a certain percentage of profits from units sold in a particular geographic territory. For example, the Coca-Cola Bottling Company licenses firms worldwide to employ (and keep confidential) its secret formula for the syrup used in its soft drink; in return, the company receives a percentage of the income gained from the sale of Coca-Cola by those firms.

The licensing of intellectual property rights benefits all parties to the transaction. The firm that receives the license can take advantage of an established reputation for quality. The firm that grants the license receives income from the foreign sales of its products and also establishes a global reputation. Once a firm's trademark is known worldwide, the demand for other products manufactured or sold by that firm may increase—obviously, an important consideration.

FRANCHISING Franchising is a well-known form of licensing. As you will read in Chapter 17, in a franchise arrangement, the owner of a trademark, trade name, or copyright (the franchisor) licenses another (the franchisee) to use the trademark, trade name, or copyright, under certain conditions or limitations, in the selling of goods or services. In return, the franchisee pays a fee, which is usually based on a percentage of gross or net sales. Examples of international franchises include Holiday Inn and Hertz.

INVESTING IN A WHOLLY OWNED SUBSIDIARY OR A JOINT VENTURE Another way to expand into a foreign market is to establish a wholly owned subsidiary firm in a foreign country. In many European countries, a subsidiary would likely take the form of a *société anonyme* (S.A.), which is similar to a U.S. corporation. In German-speaking nations, it would be called an *Aktiengesellschaft* (A.G.). When a wholly owned subsidiary is established, the parent company, which remains in the United States, retains complete ownership of all of the facilities in the foreign country, as well as total authority and control over all phases of the operation.

A U.S. firm can also expand into international markets through a joint venture. In a joint venture, the U.S. company owns only part of the operation; the rest is owned either by local owners in the foreign country or by another foreign entity. All of the

Although the United States is one of the world's major exporters, exports make up a much smaller share of annual output in the United States than they do in our most important trading partners. In an effort to increase this nation's exports, in 2010 the Obama administration created the National Export Initiative (NEI) with a goal of doubling U.S. exports by 2015. Some commentators believe that another goal of the NEI is to reduce outsourcing—the practice of having manufacturing or other activities performed in lower-wage countries such as China and India. Especially in view of the higher unemployment rate, there is increasing concern that U.S. jobs are being shipped overseas.

The Export Promotion Cabinet

An important component of the NEI is the Export Promotion Cabinet, which reports directly to the president. The cabinet's members include officials from the Departments of Agriculture, Commerce, and State, as well as from the Small Business Administration, the U.S. Export-Import Bank, and the Office of the U.S. Trade Representative. All members must submit detailed plans to the president that outline the steps that they will take to increase U.S. exports.

Increased Efforts to Promote Exports

The U.S. Commerce Department will play a leading role in the NEI and is receiving increased funding to do so. More than three hundred trade experts from the department will serve as advocates for U.S. companies and will help some twenty thousand "client companies" increase their export sales. In addition, the Commerce Department's International Trade Administration will play a more active role in promoting U.S. exports in the emerging high-growth markets of Brazil, China, and India. Finally, the department will identify market opportunities in fast-growing sectors, such as environmental goods and services, biotechnology, and renewable energy.

Increased Export Financing

Under the NEI, the U.S. Export-Import Bank is increasing the financing that it makes available to small and medium-sized businesses by 50 percent. In the initial phase of the NEI, the bank added hundreds of new small-business clients that sell a wide variety of products, from sophisticated polymers to date palm trees and nanotechology-based cosmetics. In addition, the administration has proposed that $30 billion be used to boost lending to small businesses, especially for export purposes.

Removing the Economic Blind Spot

Officials at the Commerce Department believe that in the past the United States has had an economic "blind spot" toward exports. The U.S. government has not placed as much emphasis on exports as the governments of many trading partners, which actively promote their nations' exports. As a result, other countries have been able to slowly chip away at the United States' international competitiveness. One way to improve the situation is to remove barriers that deny U.S. companies fair access to foreign markets. To this end, the government will pursue trade agreements that improve market access for U.S. workers, firms, farmers, and ranchers. In addition, while remaining committed to a rule-based international trading system, the government will continue to combat unfair tariffs and nontariff barriers.

MANAGERIAL IMPLICATIONS

Managers in companies that are now outsourcing or are thinking of doing so may wish to reconsider. Increasingly, the federal government is taking a stance against outsourcing. As long as unemployment remains high in the United States, the emphasis will be on the creation of jobs at home. These efforts will often be backed by subsidies and access to federally supported borrowing initiatives.

---

firms involved in a joint venture share responsibilities, as well as profits and liabilities.

SECTION 3
REGULATION OF SPECIFIC BUSINESS ACTIVITIES

Doing business abroad can affect the economies, foreign policies, domestic politics, and other national interests of the countries involved. For this reason, nations impose laws to restrict or facilitate international business. Controls may also be imposed by international agreements.

Investment Protections

Firms that invest in foreign nations face the risk that the foreign government may expropriate the investment property. Expropriation, as mentioned earlier in this chapter, occurs when property is taken and the owner is paid just compensation for what is taken. This generally does not violate observed principles of international law. Confiscating property without compensation (or without adequate compensation), however, normally violates these principles. Few remedies are available for confiscation of property by a foreign government. Claims are often resolved by lump-sum settlements after negotiations between the United States and the taking nation.

To counter the deterrent effect that the possibility of confiscation may have on potential investors, many countries guarantee compensation to foreign investors if property is taken. A guaranty can be in the form of national constitutional or statutory laws or provisions in international treaties. As further protection for foreign investments, some countries provide insurance for their citizens' investments abroad.

Export Controls

The U.S. Constitution provides in Article I, Section 9, that "No Tax or Duty shall be laid on Articles exported from any State." Thus, Congress cannot impose any export taxes. Congress can, however, use a variety of other devices to restrict or encourage exports. Congress may set export quotas on various items, such as grain being sold abroad. Under the Export Administration Act of 1979,[3] the flow of technologically advanced products and technical data can be restricted.

While restricting certain exports, the United States (and other nations) also use incentives and subsidies to stimulate other exports and thereby

aid domestic businesses. Under the Export Trading Company Act of 1982,[4] for example, U.S. banks are encouraged to invest in export trading companies, which are formed when exporting firms join together to export a line of goods. The Export-Import Bank of the United States provides financial assistance, primarily in the form of credit guaranties given to commercial banks that in turn lend funds to U.S. exporting companies.

Import Controls

All nations have restrictions on imports, and the United States is no exception. Restrictions include strict prohibitions, quotas, and tariffs. Under the Trading with the Enemy Act of 1917,[5] for example, no goods may be imported from nations that have been designated enemies of the United States. Other laws prohibit the importation of illegal drugs, books that urge insurrection against the United States, and agricultural products that pose dangers to domestic crops or animals.

The importation of goods that infringe U.S. patents is also prohibited. The International Trade Commission is the government agency that investigates allegations that imported goods infringe U.S. patents and imposes penalties if necessary. In the following case, the court considered an appeal from a company that had been fined more than $13.5 million for importing certain disposable cameras.

---

3. 50 U.S.C. Sections 2401–2420.

4. 15 U.S.C. Sections 4001, 4003.
5. 12 U.S.C. Section 95a.

CASE 8.1
Fuji Photo Film Co. v. International Trade Commission

United States Court of Appeals, Federal Circuit, 474 F.3d 1281 (2007).

BACKGROUND AND FACTS • Fuji Photo Film Company owns fifteen patents for "lens-fitted film packages" (LFFPs), popularly known as disposable cameras. An LFFP consists of a plastic shell preloaded with film. To develop the film, a consumer gives the LFFP to a film processor and receives back the negatives and prints, but not the shell. Fuji makes and sells LFFPs. Jazz Photo Corporation collected used LFFP shells in the United States, shipped them abroad to insert new film, and imported refurbished shells back into the United States for sale. The International Trade Commission (ITC) determined that Jazz's resale of shells originally sold outside the United States infringed Fuji's patents. In 1999, the ITC issued a cease-and-desist order to stop the imports. While the order was being disputed at the ITC and in the courts, between August 2001 and December 2003 Jazz imported and sold 27 million refurbished LFFPs. Fuji complained to the ITC, which fined Jazz more than $13.5 million. Jack Benun, Jazz's chief operating officer, appealed to the U.S. Court of Appeals for the Federal Circuit.

CASE CONTINUES ➡

CASE 8.1 CONTINUED ➡

IN THE LANGUAGE OF THE COURT
DYK, Circuit Judge.
* * * *

* * * The Commission concluded that 40% of the LFFPs in issue were first sold abroad * * *. This conclusion was supported by substantial evidence. It was based on * * * the identifying numbers printed on the LFFPs and Fuji's production and shipping databases to determine where samples of Fuji-type LFFPs with Jazz packaging (i.e., ones that were refurbished by Jazz) were first sold.

Benun urges that the Commission's decision in this respect was not supported by substantial evidence, primarily arguing that Jazz's so-called informed compliance program required a finding in Jazz's favor. Benun asserts that this program tracked shells from collection through the refurbishment process to sale and insured that only shells collected from the United States were refurbished for sale here. The Commission rejected this argument for two reasons. First, it concluded that the program was too disorganized and incomplete to provide credible evidence that Jazz only refurbished shells collected from the United States. Second, the Commission concluded that at most the program could insure that Jazz only refurbished LFFPs collected from the United States, not LFFPs that were first sold here.

Responding to the second ground, Benun urges that proof that Jazz limited its activities to shells collected in the United States was sufficient * * * because Fuji "infected the pool" of camera shells collected in the United States by taking actions that made it difficult for Jazz and Benun to insure that these shells were from LFFPs first sold here. These actions allegedly included allowing [one company] to import cameras with Japanese writing on them for sale in the United States; allowing [that company] to import spent shells into the United States for recycling; and allowing tourists to bring cameras first sold abroad into the United States for personal use. Under these circumstances, Benun argues that a presumption should arise that shells collected in the United States were first sold here. However, the Commission found that the number of shells falling into these categories was insignificant, and that finding was supported by substantial evidence. Moreover, *there was evidence that Jazz treated substantial numbers of its own shells collected in the United States * * * as having been sold in the United States even though it knew that 90% of these shells were first sold abroad * * **. [Emphasis added.]

In any event, the Commission's first ground—that the program was too incomplete and disorganized to be credible—was supported by substantial evidence. Since there was no suggestion that the incomplete and disorganized nature of the program was due to Fuji's actions, this ground alone was sufficient to justify a conclusion that Benun had not carried his burden to prove [the refurbished LFFPs had been sold first in the United States].

DECISION AND REMEDY • *The U.S. Court of Appeals for the Federal Circuit held that Jazz had violated the cease-and-desist order, affirming this part of the ITC's decision. The court concluded, among other things, that "substantial evidence supports the finding that the majority of the cameras were first sold abroad."*

WHAT IF THE FACTS WERE DIFFERENT? • *Suppose that, after this decision, Jazz fully compensated Fuji for the infringing sales of LFFPs. Would Jazz have acquired the right to refurbish those LFFPs in the future? Explain.*

THE GLOBAL DIMENSION • *How does the prohibition against importing goods that infringe U.S. patents protect those patents outside the United States?*

QUOTAS AND TARIFFS Limits on the amounts of goods that can be imported are known as **quotas.** At one time, the United States had legal quotas on the number of automobiles that could be imported from Japan. Today, Japan "voluntarily" restricts the number of automobiles exported to the United States. **Tariffs** are taxes on imports. A tariff is usually a percentage of the value of the import, but it can be a flat rate per unit (such as per barrel of oil). Tariffs raise the prices of imported goods, causing some consumers to purchase more domestically manufactured goods instead of imports.

Sometimes, countries impose tariffs on goods from a particular nation in retaliation for political acts. For example, in 2009 Mexico imposed tariffs of 10 to 20 percent on ninety products exported from the

United States in retaliation for the Obama administration's cancellation of a cross-border trucking program. The program had been instituted to comply with a provision in the North American Free Trade Agreement (to be discussed shortly) that called for Mexican trucks to eventually be granted full access to U.S. highways. U.S. truck drivers opposed the program, however, and consumer protection groups claimed that the Mexican trucks posed safety issues.

President Barack Obama signed legislation that cut off funding for the program, but asked his trade representative to look into creating a new program for cross-border transportation.

In the following case, an importer provided invoices that understated the value of its imports and resulted in lower tariffs than would have been paid on the full value of the goods. Was this fraud or negligence?

CASE 8.2
United States v. Inn Foods, Inc.

United States Court of Appeals, Federal Circuit, 560 F.3d 1338 (2009).
www.cafc.uscourts.gov[a]

COMPANY PROFILE • Inn Foods, Inc. (www.innfoods.com), was established in 1976 as a subsidiary of the VPS Companies, Inc. Inn Foods imports frozen fruits and vegetables into the United States from sources worldwide. At its plants in California and Texas, the company blends, custom packages, flavors, and seasons vegetables, pasta, potatoes, rice, fruits, and other food products. Each year, Inn Foods sells more than 157 million pounds of food. Its customers include buyers in the food service industry, industrial food markets, and retail food markets at locations around the globe.

BACKGROUND AND FACTS • Between 1987 and 1990, Inn Foods imported frozen produce from six Mexican growers who agreed to issue invoices that understated the value of the produce. For each understated invoice, Inn Foods sent an order confirmation that estimated the produce's actual market value. Inn Foods later remitted the difference to the growers. Through this double-invoicing system, Inn Foods undervalued its purchases by approximately $3.5 million and paid lower tariff taxes as a result. During an investigation by U.S. Customs and Border Protection, Inn Foods' accounting supervisor denied the existence of the double invoices. The federal government filed an action in the U.S. Court of International Trade against Inn Foods. The court held the defendant liable for fraud and assessed the amount of the unpaid taxes—$624,602.55—plus an additional penalty of $7.5 million. Inn Foods appealed, claiming that it had acted negligently, not fraudulently.

IN THE LANGUAGE OF THE COURT
DYK, Circuit Judge.
* * * *

Initially we note that the record fully supports the trade court's determination that Inn Foods knew that the invoice for each shipment of produce was grossly undervalued, and hence false. The Mexican grower sent Inn Foods a copy of the undervalued "factura" invoice; that "factura" invoice was used to value the entries for Customs purposes. There was evidence that the growers specifically informed Inn Foods of the undervaluation. As the trade court noted, for example, a letter * * * from one of the Mexican growers stated that "we ship * * * Broccoli Spears at 0.50/lb" but that "my invoice * * * will read * * * 0.28/lb." Moreover, upon receipt of the undervalued factura, a * * * manager * * * adjusted the prices to reflect the true and higher estimate. This higher amount was entered into Inn Foods's accounting system. Inn Foods then sent an order confirmation to the Mexican grower with the higher price, retaining a copy of both the undervalued and true invoices for its files. *Thus, one invoice served to bring the produce into the United States at a reduced cost and * * * the second to keep accurate accounting records.* [Emphasis added.]

---

a. In the link at the top of the page, click on "Opinions & orders." On that page, click on "2009." In the result, scroll to "2009/3/27" and click on the name of the case to access the opinion. The U.S. Court of Appeals for the Federal Circuit maintains this Web site.

CASE CONTINUES ➡

CASE 8.2 CONTINUED ➡ The existence of the double invoices was also concealed. * * * [For example,] during the initial Customs investigation, Inn Foods's accounting supervisor—with what must have been full knowledge of the falsity of the statement—denied outright the existence of a second invoice reflecting a price higher than the amount reported to Customs. This concealment, too, points strongly to fraudulent intent.

The record also makes clear, and Inn Foods does not contest, that Inn Foods knew the false invoices would be used to enter goods into the United States.

DECISION AND REMEDY • *The U.S. Court of Appeals for the Federal Circuit affirmed the lower court's judgment. The evidence showed that Inn Foods "knowingly entered goods by means of a material false statement."*

WHAT IF THE FACTS WERE DIFFERENT? • *Suppose that after Inn Foods learned of the investigation, the company told U.S. Customs and Border Protection that it was working to correct the "errors" and would "advise" as soon as that happened. Would this have undercut the government's case? Why or why not?*

THE LEGAL ENVIRONMENT DIMENSION • *Inn Foods passed on the cost savings from the lower duties to the growers when it paid them the difference between the understated value of the products and their actual value. Should this in any way absolve Inn Foods of liability for fraud? Explain your answer.*

ANTIDUMPING DUTIES The United States has laws specifically directed at what it sees as unfair international trade practices. **Dumping,** for example, is the sale of imported goods at "less than fair value." *Fair value* is usually determined by the price of those goods in the exporting country. Foreign firms that engage in dumping in the United States hope to undersell U.S. businesses to obtain a larger share of the U.S. market. To prevent this, an extra tariff—known as an *antidumping duty*—may be assessed on the imports.

Two U.S. government agencies are instrumental in imposing antidumping duties: the International Trade Commission (ITC) and the International Trade Administration (ITA). The ITC assesses the effects of dumping on domestic businesses and then makes recommendations to the president concerning temporary import restrictions. The ITA, which is part of the Department of Commerce, decides whether imports were sold at less than fair value. The ITA's determination establishes the amount of antidumping duties, which are set to equal the difference between the price charged in the United States and the price charged in the exporting country. A duty may be retroactive to cover past dumping.

Trade Agreements That Minimize Trade Barriers

Restrictions on imports are also known as *trade barriers*. The elimination of trade barriers is sometimes seen as essential to the world's economic well-being. Most of the world's leading trading nations are members of the World Trade Organization (WTO), which was established in 1995. To minimize trade barriers among nations, each member country of the WTO is required to grant **normal trade relations (NTR) status** (formerly known as *most-favored-nation status*) to other member countries. This means that each member is obligated to treat other members at least as well as it treats the country that receives its most favorable treatment with regard to imports or exports. Various regional trade agreements and associations also help to minimize trade barriers between nations.

THE EUROPEAN UNION (EU) The European Union (EU) arose out of the 1957 Treaty of Rome, which created the Common Market, a free trade zone comprising the nations of Belgium, France, Italy, Luxembourg, the Netherlands, and West Germany. Today, the EU is a single integrated European trading unit made up of twenty-seven European nations.

The EU has its own governing authorities. These include the Council of Ministers, which coordinates economic policies and includes one representative from each nation; a commission, which proposes regulations to the council; and an elected assembly, which oversees the commission. The EU also has its own court, the European Court of Justice, which can review each nation's judicial decisions and is the ultimate authority on EU law.

The EU has gone a long way toward creating a new body of law to govern all of the member nations—although some of its efforts to create uniform laws have been confounded by nationalism. The council and the commission issue regulations, or directives, that define EU law in various areas, such as environmental law, product liability, anticompetitive practices, and corporations. The directives normally are binding on all member countries.

THE NORTH AMERICAN FREE TRADE AGREEMENT (NAFTA) The North American Free Trade Agreement (NAFTA) created a regional trading unit consisting of Canada, Mexico, and the United States. The goal of NAFTA is to eliminate tariffs among these three nations on substantially all goods by reducing the tariffs incrementally over a period of time. NAFTA gives the three countries a competitive advantage by retaining tariffs on goods imported from countries outside the NAFTA trading unit. Additionally, NAFTA provided for the elimination of barriers that traditionally have prevented the cross-border movement of services, such as financial and transportation services. NAFTA also attempts to eliminate citizenship requirements for the licensing of accountants, attorneys, physicians, and other professionals.

THE CENTRAL AMERICA–DOMINICAN REPUBLIC–UNITED STATES FREE TRADE AGREEMENT (CAFTA-DR) The Central America–Dominican Republic–United States Free Trade Agreement (CAFTA-DR) was formed by Costa Rica, the Dominican Republic, El Salvador, Guatemala, Honduras, Nicaragua, and the United States. Its purpose is to reduce trade tariffs and improve market access among all of the signatory nations, including the United States. Legislatures from all seven countries have approved the CAFTA-DR, despite significant opposition in certain nations.

SECTION 4
U.S. LAWS IN A GLOBAL CONTEXT

The internationalization of business raises questions about the extraterritorial application of a nation's laws—that is, the effect of the country's laws outside its boundaries. To what extent do U.S. domestic laws apply to other nations' businesses? To what extent do U.S. domestic laws apply to U.S. firms doing business abroad? Here, we discuss the extraterritorial application of certain U.S. laws, including antitrust laws, tort laws, and laws prohibiting employment discrimination.

U.S. Antitrust Laws

U.S. antitrust laws (to be discussed in Chapters 27 and 28) have a wide application. They may *subject* firms in foreign nations to their provisions, as well as *protect* foreign consumers and competitors from violations committed by U.S. citizens. Section 1 of the Sherman Act—the most important U.S. antitrust law—provides for the extraterritorial effect of the U.S. antitrust laws. The United States is a major proponent of free competition in the global economy. Thus, any conspiracy that has a *substantial effect* on U.S. commerce is within the reach of the Sherman Act. The law applies even if the violation occurs outside the United States, and foreign governments as well as businesses can be sued for violations. Before U.S. courts will exercise jurisdiction and apply antitrust laws, however, it must be shown that the alleged violation had a substantial effect on U.S. commerce.

CASE IN POINT An investigation by the U.S. government revealed that a number of companies that manufactured and sold thermal fax paper on the global market had met in Japan and reached a price-fixing agreement (an agreement to set prices—see Chapter 28). A Florida company that uses thermal fax paper filed a lawsuit against New Oji Paper Company, a Japanese-based manufacturer that had participated in the conspiracy. Although New Oji is based in a foreign nation, it sold fax paper in the United States. Thus, its agreement to sell paper at above-normal prices throughout North America had a *substantial restraining effect* on U.S. commerce. Therefore, the Supreme Court of Florida ruled that it had jurisdiction over New Oji, even though all of the price-fixing activities took place outside the United States.[6]

International Tort Claims

The international application of tort liability is growing in significance and controversy. An increasing number of U.S. plaintiffs are suing foreign (or U.S.) entities for torts that these entities have allegedly committed overseas. Often, these cases involve human rights violations by foreign governments. The Alien Tort Claims Act (ATCA),[7] adopted in 1789, allows even foreign citizens to bring civil suits in U.S. courts for injuries caused by violations of the law of nations or a treaty of the United States.

---

6. *Execu-Tech Business Systems, Inc. v. New Oji Paper Co.,* 752 So.2d 582 (Fla. 2000).
7. 28 U.S.C. Section 1350.

Since 1980, foreign plaintiffs have increasingly used the ATCA to bring actions against companies operating in nations such as Colombia, Ecuador, Egypt, Guatemala, India, Indonesia, Nigeria, and Saudi Arabia. Some of these cases have involved alleged environmental destruction. In addition, mineral companies in Southeast Asia have been sued for collaborating with oppressive government regimes.

The following case involved claims against hundreds of corporations that allegedly "aided and abetted" the government of South Africa in maintaining its apartheid (racially discriminatory) regime.

✳ EXTENDED CASE 8.3 ✳
Khulumani v. Barclay National Bank, Ltd.

United States Court of Appeals, Second Circuit, 504 F.3d 254 (2007).

IN THE LANGUAGE OF THE COURT
PER CURIAM [By the Whole Court].
* * * *
The plaintiffs in this action bring claims under the Alien Tort Claims Act ("ATCA") against approximately fifty corporate defendants and hundreds of "corporate Does" [including Bank of America, N.A.; Barclay National Bank, Ltd.; Citigroup, Inc.; Credit Suisse Group; Deutsche Bank A.G.; General Electric Company; IBM Corporation; and Shell Oil Company]. The plaintiffs argue that these defendants actively and willingly collaborated with the government of South Africa in maintaining a repressive, racially based system known as "apartheid," which restricted the majority black African population in all areas of life while providing benefits for the minority white population.

Three groups of plaintiffs filed ten separate actions in multiple federal district courts asserting these apartheid-related claims. One group, the Khulumani Plaintiffs, filed a complaint against twenty-three domestic and foreign corporations, charging them with various violations of international law. The other two groups, the Ntsebeza and Digwamaje Plaintiffs, brought class action claims on behalf of the "victims of the apartheid related atrocities, human rights' violations, crimes against humanity and unfair [and] discriminatory forced labor practices."

* * * All of the actions [were transferred to a federal district court in] the Southern District of New York * * *. Thirty-one of the fifty-five defendants in the Ntsebeza and Digwamaje actions * * * [and] eighteen of the twenty-three defendants in [the Khulumani] action * * * filed * * * motion[s] to dismiss.

* * * *
Ruling on the defendants' motions to dismiss, the district court held that the plaintiffs failed to establish subject matter jurisdiction under the ATCA. * * * The district court therefore dismissed the plaintiffs' complaints in their entirety. * * * The plaintiffs filed timely notices of appeal [with the U.S. Court of Appeals for the Second Circuit].

* * * *
* * * [This court] vacate[s] the district court's dismissal of the plaintiffs' ATCA claims because the district court erred in holding that aiding and abetting violations of customary international law cannot provide a basis for ATCA jurisdiction. *We hold that * * * a plaintiff may plead a theory of aiding and abetting liability under the ATCA. * * *
* [The majority of the judges on the panel that heard this case agreed on the result but differed on the reasons, which were presented in two concurring opinions. One judge believed that liability on these facts is "well established in international law," citing such examples as the Rome Statute of the International Criminal Court. Another judge stated that grounds existed in such resources of U.S. law as Section 876(b) of the *Restatement (Second) of Torts,* under which liability could be assessed in part for "facilitating the commission of human rights violations by providing the principal tortfeasor with the tools, instrumentalities, or services to commit those violations."] [Emphasis added.]

* * * *
* * * We decline to affirm the dismissal of plaintiffs' ATCA claims on the basis of the prudential concerns[a] raised by the defendants. * * * The Supreme Court [has] identified two different respects in which courts should consider prudential concerns in deciding whether to hear claims brought under the ATCA.[b] First, * * * courts should consider prudential concerns in the context of determining whether to recognize a cause of action under the ATCA. Specifically,

---

a. The term *prudential concerns* refers to the defendants' arguments that the plaintiffs do not have standing to pursue their case in a U.S. court. Here, *prudential* means that the arguments are based on judicially (or legislatively) created principles rather than on the constitutionally based requirements set forth in Article III of the U.S. Constitution.

b. The court is referring to the United States Supreme Court decision in *Sosa v. Alvarez-Machain,* 542 U.S. 692, 124 S.Ct. 2739, 159 L.Ed.2d 718 (2004). In the *Sosa* case, the Court outlined the need for caution in deciding actions under the ATCA and said that the "potential implications for the foreign relations of the United States of recognizing such causes should make courts particularly wary of impinging [encroaching] on the discretion of the Legislative and Executive Branches in managing foreign affairs."

EXTENDED CASE 8.3 CONTINUED ➥

* * * the determination whether a norm is sufficiently definite to support a cause of action should (and, indeed, inevitably must) involve an element of judgment about the practical consequences of making that cause available to litigants in the federal courts. Second, * * * in certain cases, other prudential principles might operate to limit the availability of relief in the federal courts for violations of customary international law.

* * * *

One such principle * * * [is] a policy of case-specific deference to the political branches [of the U.S. government]. *This policy of judicial deference to the Executive Branch on questions of foreign policy has long been established under the prudential justiciability doctrine known as the political question doctrine. Another prudential doctrine that the defendants raise in this case is international comity.* This doctrine * * * asks whether adjudication of the case by a United States court would offend amicable working relationships with a foreign country. [Emphasis added.]

* * * *

We decline to address these case-specific prudential doctrines now and instead remand to the district court to allow it to engage in the first instance in the careful "case-by-case" analysis that questions of this type require.

* * * *

* * * We VACATE the district court's dismissal of the plaintiffs' ATCA claims * * * and REMAND for further proceedings consistent with this opinion.

✴ QUESTIONS

1. What are the ramifications for the defendants of the ruling in this case?
2. How might such "prudential concerns" as the principle of comity affect the eventual outcome?

Antidiscrimination Laws

As will be explained in Chapter 22, federal laws in the United States prohibit discrimination on the basis of race, color, national origin, religion, gender, age, and disability. These laws, as they affect employment relationships, generally apply extraterritorially. Since 1984, for example, the Age Discrimination in Employment Act of 1967 has covered U.S. employees working abroad for U.S. employers. The Americans with Disabilities Act of 1990, which requires employers to accommodate the needs of workers with disabilities, also applies to U.S. nationals working abroad for U.S. firms.

For some time, it was uncertain whether the major U.S. law regulating discriminatory practices in the workplace, Title VII of the Civil Rights Act of 1964, applied extraterritorially. The Civil Rights Act of 1991 addressed this issue. The act provides that Title VII applies extraterritorially to all U.S. employees working for U.S. employers abroad. Generally, U.S. employers must abide by U.S. discrimination laws unless to do so would violate the laws of the country where their workplaces are located. This "foreign laws exception" allows employers to avoid being subjected to conflicting laws.

REVIEWING
International Law in a Global Economy

Robco, Inc., was a Florida arms dealer. The armed forces of Honduras contracted to purchase weapons from Robco over a six-year period. After the government was replaced and a democracy installed, the Honduran government sought to reduce the size of its military, and its relationship with Robco deteriorated. Honduras refused to honor the contract and purchase the inventory of arms, which Robco could sell only at a much lower price. Robco filed a suit in a federal district court in the United States to recover damages for this breach of contract by the government of Honduras. Using the information presented in the chapter, answer the following questions.

REVIEWING CONTINUES ➡

REVIEWING

International Law in a Global Economy, Continued

1. Should the Foreign Sovereign Immunities Act (FSIA) preclude this lawsuit? Why or why not?
2. Does the act of state doctrine bar Robco from seeking to enforce the contract? Explain.
3. Suppose that prior to this lawsuit, the new government of Honduras had enacted a law making it illegal to purchase weapons from foreign arms dealers. What doctrine of deference might lead a U.S. court to dismiss Robco's case in that situation?
4. Now suppose that the U.S. court hears the case and awards damages to Robco, but the government of Honduras has no assets in the United States that can be used to satisfy the judgment. Under which doctrine might Robco be able to collect the damages by asking another nation's court to enforce the U.S. judgment?

⚙ **DEBATE THIS:** *The U.S. federal courts are accepting too many lawsuits initiated by foreigners that concern matters not relevant to this country.*

TERMS AND CONCEPTS

act of state doctrine 165
civil law system 164
comity 165

confiscation 166
distribution agreement 167
dumping 172
export 166
expropriation 166

international law 163
international
 organization 164
national law 163
normal trade relations
 (NTR) status 172

quota 170
sovereign immunity 166
tariff 170
treaty 164

QUESTIONS AND CASE PROBLEMS

8–1. Comity In 1995, France implemented a law that makes the use of the French language mandatory in certain legal documents. Documents relating to securities offerings, such as prospectuses, for example, must be written in French. So must instruction manuals and warranties for goods and services offered for sale in France. Additionally, all agreements entered into with French state or local authorities, with entities controlled by state or local authorities, and with private entities carrying out a public service (such as providing utilities) must be written in French. What kinds of problems might this law pose for U.S. businesspersons who wish to form contracts with French individuals or business firms?

8–2. QUESTION WITH SAMPLE ANSWER: Dumping.

The U.S. pineapple industry alleged that producers of canned pineapple from the Philippines were selling their canned pineapple in the United States for less than its fair market value (dumping). The Philippine producers also exported other products, such as pineapple juice and juice concentrate, which used separate parts of the same fresh pineapple, so they shared raw material costs, according to the producers' own financial records. To determine fair value and anti-dumping duties, the pineapple industry argued that a court should calculate the Philippine producers' cost of production and allocate a portion of the shared fruit costs to the canned fruit. The result of this allocation showed that more than 90 percent of the canned fruit sales were below the cost of production. Is this a reasonable approach to determining the production costs and fair market value of canned pineapple in the United States? Why or why not?

• **For a sample answer to Question 8–2, go to Appendix F at the end of this text.**

8–3. Comity E&L Consulting, Ltd., is a U.S. corporation that sells lumber products in New Jersey, New York, and Pennsylvania. Doman Industries, Ltd., is a Canadian corporation that also sells lumber products, including green hem-fir, a durable product used for home building. Doman supplies more than 95 percent of the green hem-fir for sale in the northeastern United States. In 1990, Doman contracted to sell green hem-fir through E&L, which received monthly payments plus commissions. In 1998, Sherwood Lumber Corp., a New York firm and an E&L competitor, approached E&L about a merger. The negotiations were unsuccessful. According to E&L, Sherwood and Doman then conspired to monopolize the green hem-fir market in the United States. When Doman terminated its contract with E&L, the latter filed a suit in a federal district court against Doman, alleging violations of U.S. antitrust law. Doman filed for bankruptcy in a Canadian court and asked the U.S. court to dismiss E&L's suit, in part, under the principle of comity. What is the principle of comity? On what basis would it apply in this case? What would be the likely result? Discuss. [*E&L Consulting, Ltd. v. Doman Industries, Ltd.,* 360 F.Supp.2d 465 (E.D.N.Y. 2005)]

8–4. Dumping A newspaper printing press system is more than a hundred feet long, stands four or five stories tall, and weighs 2 million pounds. Only about ten of the systems are sold each year in the United States. Because of the size and cost, a newspaper may update its system, rather than replace it, by buying "additions." By the 1990s, Goss International Corp. was the only domestic maker of the equipment in the United States and represented the entire U.S. market. Tokyo Kikai Seisakusho (TKSC), a Japanese corporation, makes the systems in Japan. In the 1990s, TKSC began to compete in the U.S. market, forcing Goss to cut its prices below cost. TKSC's tactics included offering its customers "secret" rebates on prices that were ultimately substantially less than the products' actual market value in Japan. According to TKSC office memos, the goal was to "win completely this survival game" against Goss, the "enemy." Goss filed a suit in a federal district court against TKSC and others, alleging illegal dumping. At what point does a foreign firm's attempt to compete with a domestic manufacturer in the United States become illegal dumping? Was that point reached in this case? Discuss. [*Goss International Corp. v. Man Roland Druckmaschinen Aktiengesellschaft,* 434 F.3d 1081 (8th Cir. 2006)]

8–5. Comity Jan Voda, M.D., a resident of Oklahoma City, Oklahoma, owns three U.S. patents related to guiding catheters for use in interventional cardiology, as well as corresponding foreign patents issued by the European Patent Office, Canada, France, Germany, and Great Britain. Voda filed a suit in a federal district court against Cordis Corp., a U.S. firm, alleging infringement of the U.S. patents under U.S. patent law and of the corresponding foreign patents under the patent law of the various foreign countries. Cordis admitted, "The XB catheters have been sold domestically and internationally since 1994. The XB catheters were manufactured in Miami Lakes, from 1993 to 2001 and have been manufactured in Juarez, Mexico, since 2001." Cordis argued, however, that Voda could not assert infringement claims

under foreign patent law because the court did not have jurisdiction over such claims. Which of the important international legal principles discussed in this chapter would be most likely to apply in this case? How should the court apply it? Explain. [*Voda v. Cordis Corp.,* 476 F.3d 887 (Fed.Cir. 2007)]

8–6. CASE PROBLEM WITH SAMPLE ANSWER: Sovereign Immunity.

When Ferdinand Marcos was president of the Republic of the Philippines, he put assets into a company called Arelma. Its holdings are in New York. A group of plaintiffs, referred to as the Pimentel class, brought a class-action suit in a U.S. district court for human rights violations by Marcos. They won a judgment of $2 billion and sought to attach Arelma's assets to help pay the judgment. At the same time, the Republic of the Philippines established a commission to recover property wrongfully taken by Marcos. A court in the Philippines was convened to determine whether Marcos's property, including Arelma, should be forfeited to the Republic or to other parties. The Philippine government, in opposition to the Pimentel judgment, moved to dismiss the U.S. court proceedings. The district court refused, and the U.S. Court of Appeals for the Ninth Circuit agreed that the Pimentel class should take the assets. The Republic of the Philippines appealed. What are the key international legal issues? [*Republic of the Philippines v. Pimentel,* 553 U.S. 851, 128 S.Ct. 2180, 171 L.Ed.2d 131 (2008)]

• **To view a sample answer for Problem 8–6, go to this book's Web site at www.cengage.com/blaw/cross, select "Chapter 8," and click on "Case Problem with Sample Answer."**

8–7. Dumping Nuclear power plants use low enriched uranium (LEU) as fuel. LEU consists of feed uranium enriched by energy to a certain assay—the percentage of the isotope necessary for a nuclear reaction. The amount of energy is described by an industry standard as a "separative work unit" (SWU). A nuclear utility may buy LEU from an enricher, or the utility may provide an enricher with feed uranium and pay for the SWUs necessary to produce LEU. Under an SWU contract, the LEU returned to the utility may not be exactly the uranium the utility provided. This is because feed uranium is fungible and trades like a commodity (such as wheat or corn), and profitable enrichment requires the constant processing of undifferentiated stock. Foreign enrichers, including Eurodif, S.A., allegedly exported LEU to the United States and sold it for "less than fair value." Did this constitute dumping? Explain. If so, what could be done to prevent it? [*United States v. Eurodif, S.A.,* __ U.S. __, 129 S.Ct. 878, 172 L.Ed.2d 679 (2009)]

8–8. International Agreements and Jurisdiction The plaintiffs in this case were descendants of Holocaust victims who had lived in various countries in Europe. Before the Holocaust, the plaintiffs' ancestors had purchased insurance policies from Assicurazioni Generali, S.P.A., an Italian insurance company. When Generali refused to pay benefits under the policies, the plaintiffs, who were U.S. citizens and the beneficiaries of these policies, sued for breach of the insurance contracts. Due to certain agreements among nations after World War II, such lawsuits could not be filed for many years. In 2000, however, the United States agreed that Germany could establish a foundation—the International Commission on Holocaust-Era Insurance Claims, or ICHEIC—that would compensate victims who had suffered losses at the hands of the Germans during the war. Whenever a German company was sued in a U.S. court based on a Holocaust-era claim, the U.S. government would inform the court that the matter should be referred to the ICHEIC as the exclusive forum and remedy for the resolution. There was no such agreement with Italy, however. The plaintiffs sued the Italy-based Generali in a U.S. district court. The court dismissed the suit, and the plaintiffs appealed. Did the plaintiffs have to take their claim to the ICHEIC rather than sue in a U.S. court? Why or why not? [*In re Assicurazioni Generali, S.P.A.*, 592 F.3d 113 (2d Cir. 2010)]

8–9. A QUESTION OF ETHICS: Sovereign Immunity.

 On December 21, 1988, Pan Am Flight 103 exploded 31,000 feet in the air over Lockerbie, Scotland, killing all 259 passengers and crew on board and 11 people on the ground. Among those killed was Roger Hurst, a U.S. citizen. An investigation determined that a portable radio-cassette player packed in a brown Samsonite suitcase smuggled onto the plane was the source of the explosion. The explosive device was constructed with a digital timer specially made for, and bought by, Libya. Abdel Basset Ali Al-Megrahi, a Libyan government official and an employee of the Libyan Arab Airline (LAA), was convicted by the Scottish High Court of Justiciary on criminal charges that he planned and executed the bombing in association with members of the Jamahiriya Security Organization (JSO) (an agency of the Libyan government that performs security and intelligence functions) or the Libyan military. Members of the victims' families filed a suit in a U.S. district court against the JSO, the LAA, Al-Megrahi, and others. The plaintiffs claimed violations of U.S. federal law, including the Anti-Terrorism Act, and state law, including the intentional infliction of emotional distress. [*Hurst v. Socialist People's Libyan Arab Jamahiriya, 474 F.Supp.2d 19 (D.D.C. 2007)*]

(a) Under what doctrine, codified in which federal statute, might the defendants claim to be immune from the jurisdiction of a U.S. court? Should this law include an exception for "state-sponsored terrorism"? Why or why not?

(b) The defendants agreed to pay $2.7 billion, or $10 million per victim, to settle all claims for "compensatory death damages." The families of eleven victims, including Hurst, were excluded from the settlement because they were "not wrongful death beneficiaries under applicable state law." These plaintiffs continued the suit. The defendants filed a motion to dismiss. Should the motion be granted on the ground that the settlement bars the plaintiffs' claims? Explain.

8–10. SPECIAL CASE ANALYSIS: Alien Torts Claims Act.

Go to Extended Case 8.3, *Khulumani v. Barclay National Bank, Ltd.*, 504 F.3d 254 (2007), on pages 174 and 175. Read the excerpt and answer the following questions:

(a) **Issue:** What was the plaintiffs' claim in this case?

(b) **Rule of Law:** On what U.S. law did the plaintiffs base this claim, and what was the defendants' response?

(c) **Applying the Rule of Law:** How did the trial court respond to the parties' contentions, what was the appellate court's position, and why?

(d) **Conclusion:** Did the court issue an ultimate ruling with respect to the plaintiffs' claim in this case? Explain.

LEGAL RESEARCH EXERCISES ON THE WEB

Go to this text's Web site at **www.cengage.com/blaw/cross**, select "Chapter 8," and click on "Practical Internet Exercises." There you will find the following Internet research exercises that you can perform to learn more about the topics covered in this chapter.

Practical Internet Exercise 8–1:   **Legal Perspective**
                                    The World Trade Organization

Practical Internet Exercise 8–2:   **Management Perspective**
                                    Overseas Business Opportunities

No other areas of law are as dynamic and engender as much controversy as those relating to the public and international environment. All areas of law touch on ethical considerations. But many laws have as their basis practical necessity or commercial need. The law of the public environment, however, concerns issues such as the protection of freedom of speech, the promotion of racial equality, and government regulation of behavior for the public welfare versus individual rights.

The law in the international environment involves such questions as the influence of foreign and international laws, the impact of divergent cultures, and the effect of different legal, political, and economic systems. These issues are in large measure purely ethical in nature. In resolving them, one must rely on basic notions of fairness and justice. Yet conceptions of fairness, justice, and equality differ among individuals and change over time.

Ethical and legal concepts are often closely intertwined. This is because the common law, as it evolved in England and then in America, reflects society's values and customs. This connection between law and ethics is clearly evident in the area of criminal law, which is founded on concepts of right and wrong behavior—although common law concepts governing criminal acts are now expressed in, or replaced by, federal, state, and local criminal statutes. The number of crimes has continued to expand as new ways to commit wrongs have been discovered. In this *Focus on Ethics* feature, we look at the ethical dimensions of selected topics discussed in the preceding chapters, including some issues that are unique to the cyber age.

Free Speech and the Corporation

Free speech is regarded as one of the basic rights of a democratic society. Yet it has never been considered an absolute right. The right of free speech must be balanced against other important rights and the advancement of other important social goals. In that sense, the proper extent of freedom of speech, in its many forms, involves ethical considerations.

Because freedom of speech is not absolute, not all forms of expression are protected. Pornography, for example, is not protected by the First Amendment. Nor are utterances protected that would induce an immediate threat of violence or injury. Even within the context of protected speech, the United States Supreme Court has historically looked to the nature of the speech involved in determining the extent of the protection afforded.

As mentioned in Chapter 5, for example, commercial speech is afforded less protection from government restriction than is noncommercial speech. The lesser degree of protection means in practical terms that it is easier for government to show that the interest it seeks to promote by regulating the speech is more important than protecting the right of speech. But in balancing such conflicting rights and goals, value judgments must be made. For instance, should it make a difference that the speaker is a corporation? Or should the only issue be whether the speech is of a political nature? Is it fair to allow corporations to use their superior economic resources and marketing skills to influence politics? Although it is legal, some argue that it is unethical, particularly when a corporation's decision to allocate funds and influence legislation is motivated by self-interest (profit maximization) rather than by a concern for public welfare.

Global Companies and Censorship Issues—Google China

Doing business on a global level can sometimes involve serious ethical challenges. Consider the ethical firestorm that erupted when Google, Inc., decided to market "Google China" (Google.cn) in 2006. This version of Google's widely used search engine was tailored to the Chinese government's censorship requirements. In China, Web sites that offer pornography, criticism of the government, or information on sensitive topics, such as the Tiananmen Square massacre in 1989, are censored—that is, they cannot be accessed by Web users. Government agencies enforce the censorship and encourage citizens to inform on one another. Thousands of Web sites are shut down each year, and the sites' operators are subject to potential imprisonment.

The Chinese government insists that in restricting access to certain Web sites, it is merely following the lead of other national governments, which also impose controls on information access. As an example, it cites France, which bans access to any Web sites selling or displaying Nazi paraphernalia. The United States itself prohibits the dissemination of certain types of materials, such as child pornography, over the Internet. Furthermore, the U.S. government monitors Web sites and e-mail communications to protect against terrorist threats. How, ask Chinese officials, can other nations point their fingers at China for engaging in a common international practice?

Censorship—The Lesser of Two Evils? Human rights groups came out strongly against Google's decision, maintaining that the company was seeking profits in a lucrative marketplace at the expense of assisting the Chinese Communist Party in suppressing free speech. Google defended its actions by pointing out that its Chinese search engine at least lets users know which sites are being censored. Google China includes the links to censored sites, but when a user tries to access

FOCUS ON ETHICS CONTINUES ➧

a link, the program states that it is not accessible.

Google claimed that its approach was essentially the "lesser of two evils": if U.S. companies did not cooperate with the Chinese government, Chinese residents would have less user-friendly Internet access. Moreover, Google asserted that providing Internet access, even if censored, is a step toward more open access in the future because technology is, in itself, a revolutionary force.

China's Cyberattack and Google's Response

Google's attitude changed in late 2009 when it discovered that its software had been the target of a cyberattack that apparently originated in China. David Drummond, senior vice president of corporate development and Google's chief legal officer, informed the public about the attack in an article on the official Google blog on January 12, 2010. Drummond described the attack as "highly sophisticated" and said that it was not limited to Google—some twenty other large companies were similarly targeted. According to Drummond, a primary goal of the attackers apparently was to access the Gmail accounts of Chinese human rights activists. Google also discovered that the accounts of dozens of human rights advocates in the United States, China, and Europe had routinely been accessed by third parties.

Drummond said that the attacks and the surveillance that the investigation has uncovered have led Google to announce a change in its China policy: "We have decided we are no longer willing to continue censoring our results on Google.cn . . . . We recognize that this may well mean having to shut down Google.cn and potentially our offices in China."[1] In March 2010, Google stopped operating Google.cn and automatically redirected users to its Hong Kong servers at Google.com.hk for search services in Chinese.

Although the Chinese government censors results on Google's Hong Kong servers, it nonetheless found Google's auto-redirect policy unacceptable and threatened to revoke Google's license. In June 2010, Google again revised its policy so that it no longer auto-redirects Chinese users to the Hong Kong servers. Instead, Google directs Chinese users to a Web page at which they must elect to use the Hong Kong servers. In addition, Google reopened Google China to host minimal searches for content that does not require censorship—such as for maps, music, and translation services.

Proponents of human rights applauded Google's efforts to avoid censorship of its search content, but others are not so sure. If Google and similar companies refuse to cooperate with governments that engage in censorship, will this transform the World Wide Web? Will the information highway of the future be forced to stop at national borders?

Ethics and the Administrative Process

In Chapter 5, we noted some of the other constitutional protections that apply in the context of business. We looked in Chapter 6 at how some of those protections apply in the administrative process. As noted in Chapter 6, effective governmental regulation necessitates the gathering of relevant information. Often that information can be obtained only by an on-site inspection of business premises or a firsthand examination of business records. When regulatory needs conflict with constitutional principles, not only are legal issues raised, but ethical ones as well.

Recall that the Fourth Amendment protection from unreasonable searches and seizures applies in the context of business. Within the context of administrative law, this protection has been interpreted as requiring that information sought by a regulatory agency be relevant to the matter under scrutiny. Furthermore, any demand for information must be reasonably specific and not unduly burdensome to the business providing the information.

Regulation and Privacy Rights   Despite acceptance of the need for regulators to gather information, an inherent conflict exists between the regulatory need for information and the individual's right of privacy. Specifically, how much latitude should be afforded to regulators in gathering information and overseeing private activities?

The United States Supreme Court has attempted to resolve the conflict by balancing the regulators' need to know against individual and corporate expectations of freedom from excessive government prying. An important consideration in resolving the conflict is the less intrusive nature of regulatory searches of businesses: most people simply do not have the same degree of concern about protecting places of business as they do about protecting the family dwelling. As a result, the standards for conducting regulatory investigations and searches are different from those that apply when ordinary police investigations and searches are conducted. For example, even though there may be no suspicion of a regulatory violation, an agency may conduct an investigation or search the premises of a business merely to be assured that no violation is occurring. Within industries subject to a history of extensive regulation, searches may be made even without a warrant. Still, though, as noted in Chapter 6, government is restricted in obtaining private information for regulatory purposes only.

---

1. David Drummond. "A New Approach to China." *The Official Google Blog.* 12 January 2010: n.p. Web.

The Ethics of Legal Avoidance In the face of an agency investigation, a business may prevent or delay agency efforts by asserting legal challenges to the nature or manner of the investigation. There remains, however, the question of whether—in an ethical rather than legal sense—a business should challenge any such investigation. We would be expected to challenge an unreasonable search of our homes. Regulatory investigations may be somehow different, though.

Most regulatory investigations have as their objective ensuring compliance with existing regulatory schemes or gathering information for future ones. Such schemes are designed to promote the public welfare. Though individuals may disagree about the effectiveness of the scheme or the individual motives of the regulators, society generally accepts the underlying purpose of the regulation—the promotion of public welfare. In such instances, businesses may have an ethical duty not to use legal means to avoid agency action. Indeed, they may have an ethical duty to aid in regulation by compliance, even though they may have a legal right to delay or avoid it.

International Transactions

Conducting business internationally presents unique challenges including, at times, ethical challenges. This is understandable, given that laws and cultures vary from one country to another. Consider the role of women. In the United States, equal employment opportunity is a fundamental public policy. This policy is clearly expressed in Title VII of the Civil Rights Act of 1964 (to be discussed in Chapter 22), which prohibits discrimination against women in the employment context. Some other countries, however, largely reject any professional role for women. Consequently, U.S. women conducting business transactions in those countries may encounter difficulties. For example,

when the World Bank sent a delegation that included women to negotiate with the Central Bank of Korea, the Koreans were surprised and offended. They thought that the presence of women meant that the negotiations were not being taken seriously.

There are also some important ethical differences among nations. For example, in many foreign nations, gift giving is a common practice between contracting companies or between companies and government officials. To Americans, such gift giving may look suspiciously like an unethical (and possibly illegal) bribe. This cultural difference has been an important source of friction in international business, particularly since the U.S. Congress passed the Foreign Corrupt Practices Act in 1977 (discussed in Chapters 4 and 7). This act prohibits U.S. business firms from offering certain side payments to foreign officials to secure favorable contracts.

DISCUSSION QUESTIONS

1. Do companies, such as Google, that do business on a global level have an ethical duty to foreign citizens not to suppress free speech, or is it acceptable to censor the information that they provide in other nations at the request of a foreign government?

2. The United States banned the pesticide DDT, primarily because of its adverse effects on wildlife. In Asia, however, DDT has been a critical component of the mosquito control necessary to combat malaria. Should the ban in the United States prevent U.S. firms from manufacturing DDT and shipping it to an Asian country, where it could be used to save lives? Why or why not?

3. Should U.S. firms doing business internationally send female employees to foreign nations that reject any role for women in business? Why or why not? How can a U.S. company accommodate the culture of foreign nations and still treat its own employees equally?

UNIT THREE

THE COMMERCIAL ENVIRONMENT

CONTENTS

CHAPTER 9

Contract Formation

The noted legal scholar Roscoe Pound once said that "[t]he social order rests upon the stability and predictability of conduct, of which keeping promises is a large item."[1] Contract law deals with, among other things, the formation and keeping of promises. A **promise** is a person's manifestation of an intent to act or refrain from acting in a specified way.

Like other types of law, contract law reflects our social values, interests, and expectations at a given point in time. It shows, for example, to what extent our society allows people to make promises or commitments that are legally binding. It distinguishes between promises that create only *moral*

obligations (such as a promise to take a friend to lunch) and promises that are legally binding (such as a promise to pay for merchandise purchased).

Common law governs all contracts except when it has been modified or replaced by statutory law, such as the Uniform Commercial Code (UCC),[2] or by administrative agency regulations. Contracts relating to services, real estate, employment, and insurance, for example, generally are governed by the common law of contracts.

Contract law also demonstrates which excuses our society accepts for breaking certain types of promises. In addition, it indicates which promises

are considered to be contrary to public policy—against the interests of society as a whole—and therefore legally invalid. When the person making a promise is a child or is mentally incompetent, for example, a question will arise as to whether the promise should be enforced. Resolving such questions is the essence of contract law.

Contracts for the sale and lease of goods, however, are governed by the UCC—to the extent that the UCC has modified general contract law. The relationship between general contract law and the law governing sales and leases of goods will be explored in detail in Chapter 11. In this chapter's discussion of general contract law, we indicate in footnotes the areas in which the UCC has significantly altered common law contract principles.

---

1. Roscoe Pound. *Jurisprudence.* Vol. 3 (St. Paul, Minn.: West Publishing Co., 1959), p. 162.

2. See Chapters 1 and 11 for further discussions of the significance and coverage of the UCC. Excerpts from the UCC are presented in Appendix C at the end of this book.

SECTION 1
AN OVERVIEW
OF CONTRACT LAW

No aspect of modern life is entirely free of contractual relationships. You acquire rights and obligations, for example, when you borrow funds, when you buy or lease a house, when you obtain insurance, and when you purchase goods or services. Contract law is designed to provide stability and predictability, as well as certainty, for both buyers and sellers in the marketplace.

Contract law deals with, among other things, the formation and enforcement of agreements between parties (in Latin, *pacta sunt servanda*—"agreements shall be kept"). Clearly, many promises are kept because the parties involved feel a moral obligation to keep them or because keeping a promise is in their mutual self-interest. The *promisor* (the person making the promise) and the *promisee* (the person to whom the promise is made) may also decide to honor their agreement for other reasons. In business agreements, the rules of contract law are often followed to avoid potential disputes.

By supplying procedures for enforcing private contractual agreements, contract law provides an essential condition for the existence of a market economy. Without a legal framework of reasonably assured expectations within which to make long-run plans, businesspersons would be able to rely only on the good faith of others. Duty and good faith are usually sufficient to obtain compliance with a promise, but when price changes or adverse economic factors make compliance costly, these elements may not be enough. Contract law is necessary to ensure compliance with a promise or to entitle the innocent party to some form of relief.

The Definition of a Contract

A **contract** is "a promise or a set of promises for the breach of which the law gives a remedy, or the performance of which the law in some way recognizes as a duty."[3] Put simply, a contract is a legally binding agreement between two or more parties who agree to perform or to refrain from performing some act now or in the future. Generally, contract disputes arise when there is a promise of future performance. If the contractual promise is not fulfilled, the party who made it is subject to the sanctions of a court (see Chapter 10). That party may be required to pay damages for failing to perform the contractual promise. In a few instances, the party may be required to perform the promised act.

The Objective Theory of Contracts

In determining whether a contract has been formed, the element of intent is of prime importance. In contract law, intent is determined by what is called the **objective theory of contracts,** not by the personal or subjective intent, or belief, of a party. The theory is that a party's intention to enter into a legally binding agreement, or contract, is judged by outward, objective facts as interpreted by a *reasonable* person, rather than by the party's own secret, subjective intentions. Objective facts include

(1) what the party said when entering into the contract, (2) how the party acted or appeared (intent may be manifested by conduct as well as by oral or written words), and (3) the circumstances surrounding the transaction.

CASE IN POINT Linear Technology Corporation (LTC) makes and sells integrated circuits for use in cell phones and computers. LTC sued its competitor, Micrel, Inc., for patent infringement of a particular chip. In its defense, Micrel claimed that LTC's patent was invalid because LTC had offered to sell the chip commercially before the date on which it could be legally sold. The issue was whether LTC had entered into sales contracts when it solicited input on pricing and accepted distributors' purchase orders using a "will advise" procedure before the critical date. The court ruled that under the objective theory of contracts, no reasonable customer could interpret LTC's requests for information about pricing and potential orders as an offer that could bind LTC to a sale. Therefore, LTC did not violate the ban on sales and could continue its suit against Micrel for patent infringement.[4]

Elements of a Contract

The many topics that will be discussed throughout this chapter concerning contract law require an understanding of the basic elements of a valid contract and the way in which a contract is created. It is also necessary to understand the types of circumstances in which even legally valid contracts will not be enforced.

REQUIREMENTS OF A VALID CONTRACT The following list briefly describes the four requirements that must be met before a valid contract exists. If any of these elements is lacking, no contract will have been formed. (Each requirement will be explained more fully in later sections of this chapter.)

1. *Agreement.* An agreement to form a contract includes an *offer* and an *acceptance.* One party must offer to enter into a legal agreement, and another party must accept the terms of the offer.
2. *Consideration.* Any promises made by the parties to the contract must be supported by legally sufficient and bargained-for *consideration* (something of value received or promised, such as money, to convince a person to make a deal).

---

3. *Restatement (Second) of Contracts,* Section 1. As mentioned in Chapter 1, *Restatements of the Law* are scholarly books that restate the existing common law principles distilled from court opinions as a set of rules on a particular topic. Courts often refer to the *Restatements* for guidance. The *Restatement of the Law of Contracts* was compiled by the American Law Institute in 1932 and is now in its second edition (a third edition is being drafted).

4. *Linear Technology Corp. v. Micrel, Inc.,* 275 F.3d 1040 (Fed.Cir. 2001).

3. *Contractual capacity.* Both parties entering into the contract must have the contractual *capacity* to do so. The law must recognize them as possessing characteristics that qualify them as competent parties.
4. *Legality.* The contract's purpose must be to accomplish some goal that is legal and not against public policy.

DEFENSES TO THE ENFORCEABILITY OF A CONTRACT

Even if all of the requirements listed above are satisfied, a contract may be unenforceable if the following requirements are not met. These requirements typically are raised as defenses to the enforceability of an otherwise valid contract.

1. *Voluntary consent.* The consent of both parties must be voluntary. For example, if a contract was formed as a result of fraud, undue influence, mistake, or duress, the contract may not be enforceable.
2. *Form.* The contract must be in whatever form the law requires. For example, some contracts must be in writing to be enforceable.

SECTION 2
TYPES OF CONTRACTS

There are many types of contracts. In this section, you will learn that contracts can be categorized based on legal distinctions as to formation, performance, and enforceability.

Contract Formation

Contracts can be classified according to how and when they are formed. Exhibit 9–1 below shows three such classifications, and the following subsections explain them in greater detail.

BILATERAL VERSUS UNILATERAL CONTRACTS Every contract involves at least two parties. The *offeror* is the party making the offer. The *offeree* is the party to whom the offer is made. Whether the contract is classified as *bilateral* or *unilateral* depends on what the offeree must do to accept the offer and bind the offeror to a contract.

Bilateral Contracts. If the offeree can accept simply by promising to perform, the contract is a **bilateral contract.** Hence, a bilateral contract is a "promise for a promise." No performance, such as payment of funds or delivery of goods, need take place for a bilateral contract to be formed. The contract comes into existence at the moment the promises are exchanged.

For example, Javier offers to buy Ann's digital camcorder for $200. Javier tells Ann that he will give her the $200 for the camcorder next Friday, when he gets paid. Ann accepts Javier's offer and promises to give him the camcorder when he pays her on Friday. Javier and Ann have formed a bilateral contract.

Unilateral Contracts. If the offer is phrased so that the offeree can accept the offer only by completing the contract performance, the contract is a **unilateral contract.** Hence, a unilateral contract is a "promise for an act." In other words, the time of contract formation in a unilateral contract is not the moment when promises are exchanged but the moment when the contract is *performed.* For example, Reese says to Celia, "If you drive my car from New York to Los Angeles, I'll give you $1,000." Only on Celia's completion of the act—bringing the car to Los Angeles—does she fully accept Reese's offer to pay $1,000. If she chooses not to

EXHIBIT 9–1 • Classifications Based on Contract Formation

CONTRACT FORMATION		
BILATERAL A promise for a promise	**FORMAL** Requires a special form for creation	**EXPRESS** Formed by words
UNILATERAL A promise for an act	**INFORMAL** Requires no special form for creation	**IMPLIED** Formed by the conduct of the parties

accept the offer to drive the car to Los Angeles, there are no legal consequences.

CASE IN POINT Applicants for vacancies in the police department in Providence, Rhode Island, first completed a series of tests. The city then sent the most qualified applicants a letter that said it was "a conditional offer of employment" and informed the applicants that they could attend the police training academy if they passed a medical exam. Meanwhile, a new chief of police revised the selection process and rejected some of those who had received this letter. The rejected applicants sued, claiming that the city had breached its contract. The court held that the letter was a unilateral offer that the plaintiffs had accepted by passing the required medical exam. As a remedy for the breach, the court ordered the city to allow the plaintiffs to attend the police academy.[5]

Contests, lotteries, and other competitions involving prizes are examples of offers to form unilateral contracts. If a person complies with the rules of the contest—such as by submitting the right lottery number at the right place and time—a unilateral contract is formed, binding the organization offering the prize to a contract to perform as promised in

_____

5. *Ardito v. City of Providence*, 263 F.Supp.2d 358 (D.R.I. 2003).

the offer. If the person fails to comply with the contest rules, however, no binding contract is formed. See this chapter's *Insight into Ethics* feature below for a discussion of whether a company can change the advertised prize after the contestants have completed the contest.

Revocation of Offers for Unilateral Contracts.

A problem arises in unilateral contracts when the promisor attempts to *revoke* (cancel) the offer after the promisee has begun performance but before the act has been completed. The promisee can accept the offer only on full performance, and under traditional contract principles an offer may be revoked at any time before the offer is accepted. The present-day view, however, is that an offer to form a unilateral contract becomes irrevocable—cannot be revoked—once performance has begun. Thus, even though the offer has not yet been accepted, the offeror is prohibited from revoking it for a reasonable time period.

For instance, recall the earlier example in which a car is to be driven from New York to Los Angeles. Now suppose that Celia is driving through Nevada and is only a few hundred miles from Los Angeles when Reese calls her on her cell phone and says, "I revoke my offer." Under traditional contract law,

---

INSIGHT INTO ETHICS
Is It Right for a Company to Change the Prize Offered in a Contest?

Courts have historically treated contests as unilateral contracts. Unilateral contracts typically cannot be modified by the offeror after the offeree has begun to perform. But this principle may not apply to contest terms if the company sponsoring the contest reserves the right to cancel the contest or change its terms at any time, as Donna Englert learned to her dismay.

Englert entered the "Quarter Million Dollar Challenge" contest sponsored by Nutritional Sciences, LLC. Contestants were to use Nutritional Sciences' products and training plans for thirteen weeks to lose weight and get fit. A panel of judges would then pick winners in certain categories based on their success in transforming their bodies. When Englert was chosen as female runner-up in her age group, she thought that she would receive the advertised prize of $1,500 cash and $500 worth of Nutritional Sciences' products. Instead, the company sent her a "challenge winner agreement" for $250 cash and $250 worth of products. Englert refused to sign the agreement and filed a lawsuit alleging breach of contract. The state trial court dismissed her claim, and she appealed.

The state appellate court observed that the contestant's compliance with the rules of a contest is necessary to form a binding unilateral contract. Here, the contest rules stipulated that "all winners must agree to the regulations outlined specifically for winners before claiming championship or money." Next to this statement was an asterisk corresponding to a note reserving the right of Nutritional Sciences to cancel the contest or alter its terms at any time. Because of this provision, the court ruled that Nutritional Sciences did not breach the contract when it changed the cash prize from $1,500 to $250.[a]

CRITICAL THINKING

INSIGHT INTO THE SOCIAL ENVIRONMENT
Why would a company that changes its advertised prizes have to worry about its reputation?

_____

a. *Englert v. Nutritional Sciences, LLC,* 2008 WL 4416597 (Ohio App. 2008).

Reese's revocation would terminate the offer. Under the modern view of unilateral contracts, however, Reese will not be able to revoke his offer because Celia has undertaken performance and has driven more than 2,500 miles. In these circumstances, Celia can finish driving to Los Angeles and bind Reese to the contract.

FORMAL VERSUS INFORMAL CONTRACTS Another classification system divides contracts into formal contracts and informal contracts. *Formal contracts* are contracts that require a special form or method of creation (formation) to be enforceable.[6] One example is *letters of credit,* which are frequently used in international sales contracts (see Chapter 8). Letters of credit are agreements to pay contingent on the purchaser's receipt of invoices and *bills of lading* (documents evidencing receipt of, and title to, goods shipped).

Informal contracts (also called *simple contracts*) include all other contracts. No special form is required (except for certain types of contracts that must be in writing), as the contracts are usually based on their substance rather than their form. Typically, businesspersons put their contracts in writing to ensure that there is some proof of a contract's existence should disputes arise.

EXPRESS VERSUS IMPLIED CONTRACTS Contracts may also be categorized as *express* or *implied.* We look here at the differences between these two types of contracts.

Express Contracts. In an **express contract,** the terms of the agreement are fully and explicitly stated in words, oral or written. A signed lease for an apartment or a house is an express written contract. If one classmate calls another on the phone and agrees to buy his textbooks from last semester for $300, an express oral contract has been made.

Implied Contracts. A contract that is implied from the conduct of the parties is called an **implied contract** or an *implied-in-fact contract.* This type of contract differs from an express contract in that the *conduct* of the parties, rather than their words, creates and defines the terms of the contract. (Note that a contract may be a mixture of an express contract and an implied contract. In other words, a contract may contain some express terms, while others are implied.)

CASE IN POINT Lamar Hopkins hired Uhrhahn Construction & Design, Inc., for several projects in building his home. For each project, the parties signed a written contract that was based on a cost estimate and specifications and that required changes to the agreement to be in writing. While the work was in progress, however, Hopkins repeatedly asked Uhrhahn to deviate from the contract specifications, which Uhrhahn did. None of these requests was made in writing. One day, Hopkins asked Uhrhahn to use Durisol blocks instead of the cinder blocks specified in the original contract, indicating that the cost would be the same. Uhrhahn used the Durisol blocks but demanded extra payment when it became clear that the Durisol blocks were more complicated to use. Although Hopkins had paid for the other deviations from the contract that he had orally requested, he refused to pay Uhrhahn for the substitution of the Durisol blocks. Uhrhahn sued for breach of contract. The court found that Hopkins, through his conduct, had waived the provision requiring written contract modification and created an implied contract to pay the extra cost of installing the Durisol blocks.[7]

Implied Contract Requirements. For an implied contract to arise, certain requirements must be met. Normally, if the following conditions exist, a court will hold that an implied contract was formed:

1. The plaintiff furnished some service or property.
2. The plaintiff expected to be paid for that service or property, and the defendant knew or should have known that payment was expected.
3. The defendant had a chance to reject the services or property and did not.

Suppose that you need an accountant to complete your tax return. You notice that there is an accountant's office in your neighborhood. You drop by, explain your problem to an accountant, and learn what fees will be charged. The next day, you return and give the receptionist all of the necessary information and documents. Then you walk out the door without saying anything expressly to the accountant. In this situation, you have entered into an implied contract to pay the accountant the usual and reasonable fees for her services. The contract is implied by your conduct and by hers. She expects to be paid for completing your tax return, and by bringing in the records she will need to do the work, you have implied an intent to pay her.

---

6. See *Restatement (Second) of Contracts,* Section 6, which explains that formal contracts include (1) contracts under seal, (2) recognizances, (3) negotiable instruments, and (4) letters of credit.

7. *Uhrhahn Construction & Design, Inc. v. Hopkins,* 179 P.3d 808 (Utah App. 2008).

Contract Performance

Contracts are also classified according to the degree to which they have been performed. A contract that has been fully performed on both sides is called an **executed contract.** A contract that has not been fully performed by the parties is called an **executory contract.** If one party has fully performed but the other has not, the contract is said to be executed on the one side and executory on the other, but the contract is still classified as executory.

For example, Jackson, Inc., agreed to buy ten tons of coal from the Northern Coal Company. Northern delivered the coal to Jackson's steel mill, where it is being burned. At this point, the contract is executed on the part of Northern and executory on Jackson's part. After Jackson pays Northern, the contract will be executed on both sides.

Contract Enforceability

A *valid contract* has the elements necessary to entitle at least one of the parties to enforce it in court. Those elements, as mentioned earlier, consist of (1) an agreement, including an offer and an acceptance of that offer; (2) support by legally sufficient consideration; (3) parties who have the legal capacity to enter into the contract; and (4) a legal purpose. As you can see in Exhibit 9–2 below, valid contracts may be enforceable, voidable, or unenforceable. Additionally, a contract may be referred to as a *void contract.* We look next at the meaning of the terms *voidable, unenforceable,* and *void* in relation to contract enforceability.

VOIDABLE CONTRACTS A *voidable contract* is a valid contract but one that can be avoided at the option of one or both of the parties. The party having the option can elect either to avoid any duty to perform or to *ratify* (make valid) the contract. If the contract is avoided, both parties are released from it. If it is ratified, both parties must fully perform their respective legal obligations.

Contracts made by minors, mentally incompetent persons, and intoxicated persons may be voidable. For example, contracts made by minors generally are voidable at the option of the minor (with certain exceptions). Additionally, contracts entered into under fraudulent conditions are voidable at the option of the defrauded party. Contracts entered into under legally defined duress or undue influence are also voidable.

UNENFORCEABLE CONTRACTS An *unenforceable contract* is one that cannot be enforced because of certain legal defenses against it. It is not unenforceable because a party failed to satisfy a legal requirement of the contract. Rather, it is a valid contract rendered unenforceable by some statute or law. For example, certain contracts must be in writing, and if they are not, they will not be enforceable except in certain exceptional circumstances.

VOID CONTRACTS A *void contract* is no contract at all. The terms *void* and *contract* are contradictory. A void contract produces no legal obligations on any of the parties. For example, a contract can be void because one of the parties was adjudged by a court

EXHIBIT 9–2 • Enforceable, Voidable, Unenforceable, and Void Contracts

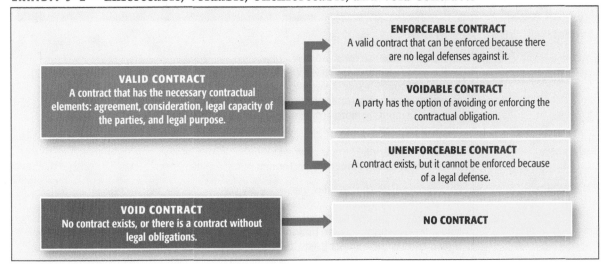

to be legally insane (and thus lacked the legal capacity to enter into a contract) or because the purpose of the contract was illegal.

To review the various types of contracts, see *Concept Summary 9.1* below.

SECTION 3
AGREEMENT

An essential element for contract formation is **agreement**—the parties must agree on the terms of the contract and manifest to each other their *mutual assent* (agreement) to the same bargain. Ordinarily, agreement is evidenced by two events: an *offer* and an *acceptance*. One party offers a certain bargain to another party, who then accepts that bargain. The agreement does not necessarily have to be in writing. Both parties, however, must manifest their assent, or voluntary consent, to the same bargain. Once an agreement is reached, if the other elements of a contract are present (consideration, contractual capacity, and legality—which will be discussed in later sections of this chapter), a valid contract is formed, generally creating enforceable rights and duties between the parties.

Requirements of the Offer

An **offer** is a promise or commitment to do or refrain from doing some specified action in the future. As mentioned earlier, the parties to a contract are the offeror, the one who makes an offer or proposal to another party, and the offeree, the one to whom the offer or proposal is made. Under common law, three elements are necessary for an offer to be effective:

1. The offeror must have a serious intention to become bound by the offer.
2. The terms of the offer must be reasonably certain, or definite, so that the parties and the court can ascertain the terms of the contract.
3. The offer must be communicated to the offeree.

Once an effective offer has been made, the offeree's acceptance of that offer creates a legally binding contract (providing the other essential elements for a valid and enforceable contract are present).

INTENTION The first requirement for an effective offer is a serious intent on the part of the offeror. Serious intent is not determined by the subjective intentions, beliefs, and assumptions of the offeror. Rather, it is determined by what a reasonable person in the offeree's position would conclude that the offeror's words and actions meant. Offers made in obvious anger, jest, or undue excitement do not meet the serious-and-objective-intent test because a reasonable person would realize that a serious offer was not being made. Because these offers are not effective, an offeree's acceptance does not create an agreement.

Suppose that Linda and Dena ride to school each day in Dena's new automobile, which has a market value of $20,000. One cold morning, they get into

CONCEPT SUMMARY 9.1
Types of Contracts

Aspect	Definition
Formation	1. *Bilateral*—A promise for a promise. 2. *Unilateral*—A promise for an act (acceptance is the completed performance of the act). 3. *Formal*—Requires a special form for creation. 4. *Informal*—Requires no special form for creation. 5. *Express*—Formed by words (oral, written, or a combination). 6. *Implied*—Formed by the conduct of the parties.
Performance	1. *Executed*—A fully performed contract. 2. *Executory*—A contract not fully performed.
Enforceability	1. *Enforceable*—The contract has the necessary contractual elements—agreement (offer and acceptance), consideration, legal capacity of the parties, and legal purpose—and there are no legal defenses against it. 2. *Voidable*—One party has the option of avoiding or enforcing the contractual obligation. 3. *Unenforceable*—A contract exists, but it cannot be enforced because of a legal defense. 4. *Void*—No contract exists, or there is a contract without legal obligations.

the car, but Dena cannot get the car started. She yells in anger, "I'll sell this car to anyone for $500!" Linda drops $500 on Dena's lap. A reasonable person—taking into consideration Dena's frustration and the obvious difference in value between the market price of the car and the proposed purchase price—would realize that Dena's offer was not made with serious and objective intent. No agreement was formed.

In the classic case presented next, the court considered whether an offer made "after a few drinks" met the serious-and-objective-intent requirement.

CASE 9.1
Lucy v. Zehmer

Supreme Court of Appeals of Virginia, 196 Va. 493, 84 S.E.2d 516 (1954).

BACKGROUND AND FACTS • W. O. Lucy, the plaintiff, filed a suit against A. H. and Ida Zehmer, the defendants, to compel the Zehmers to transfer title of their property, known as the Ferguson Farm, to the Lucys (W. O. and his wife) for $50,000, as the Zehmers had allegedly agreed to do. Lucy had known A. H. Zehmer for fifteen or twenty years and for the last eight years or so had been anxious to buy the Ferguson Farm from him. One night, Lucy stopped in to visit the Zehmers in the combination restaurant, filling station, and motor court they operated. While there, Lucy tried to buy the Ferguson Farm once again. This time he tried a new approach. According to the trial court transcript, Lucy said to Zehmer, "I bet you wouldn't take $50,000 for that place." Zehmer replied, "Yes, I would too; you wouldn't give fifty." Throughout the evening, the conversation returned to the sale of the Ferguson Farm for $50,000. At the same time, the men continued to drink whiskey and engage in light conversation. Eventually, Lucy enticed Zehmer to write up an agreement to the effect that the Zehmers would sell the Ferguson Farm to Lucy for $50,000 complete. Later, Lucy sued Zehmer to compel him to go through with the sale. Zehmer argued that he had been drunk and that the offer had been made in jest and hence was unenforceable. The trial court agreed with Zehmer, and Lucy appealed.

IN THE LANGUAGE OF THE COURT
BUCHANAN, J. [Justice] delivered the opinion of the court.
* * * *

In his testimony, Zehmer claimed that he "was high as a Georgia pine," and that the transaction "was just a bunch of two doggoned drunks bluffing to see who could talk the biggest and say the most." That claim is inconsistent with his attempt to testify in great detail as to what was said and what was done.
* * * *

The appearance of the contract, the fact that it was under discussion for forty minutes or more before it was signed; Lucy's objection to the first draft because it was written in the singular, and he wanted Mrs. Zehmer to sign it also; the rewriting to meet that objection and the signing by Mrs. Zehmer; the discussion of what was to be included in the sale, the provision for the examination of the title, the completeness of the instrument that was executed, the taking possession of it by Lucy with no request or suggestion by either of the defendants that he give it back, are facts which furnish persuasive evidence that the execution of the contract was a serious business transaction rather than a casual, jesting matter as defendants now contend.
* * * *

In the field of contracts, as generally elsewhere, *we must look to the outward expression of a person as manifesting his intention rather than to his secret and unexpressed intention.* The law imputes to a person an intention corresponding to the reasonable meaning of his words and acts. [Emphasis added.]
* * * *

Whether the writing signed by the defendants and now sought to be enforced by the complainants was the result of a serious offer by Lucy and a serious acceptance by the defendants, or was a serious offer by Lucy and an acceptance in secret jest by the defendants, in either event it constituted a binding contract of sale between the parties.

CASE CONTINUES ➡

CASE 9.1 CONTINUED ➡ **DECISION AND REMEDY** • *The Supreme Court of Appeals of Virginia determined that the writing was an enforceable contract and reversed the ruling of the lower court. The Zehmers were required by court order to follow through with the sale of the Ferguson Farm to the Lucys.*

IMPACT OF THIS CASE ON TODAY'S LAW • *This is a classic case in contract law because it illustrates so clearly the objective theory of contracts with respect to determining whether a serious offer was intended. Today, the courts continue to apply the objective theory of contracts and routinely cite* Lucy v. Zehmer *as a significant precedent in this area.*

WHAT IF THE FACTS WERE DIFFERENT? • *Suppose that the day after Lucy signed the purchase agreement for the farm, he decided that he did not want it after all, and Zehmer sued Lucy to perform the contract. Would this change in the facts alter the court's decision that Lucy and Zehmer had created an enforceable contract? Why or why not?*

The concept of intention can be further clarified through an examination of the types of expressions and statements that are *not* offers. We look at these expressions and statements in the subsections that follow.

Expressions of Opinion. An expression of opinion is not an offer. It does not indicate an intention to enter into a binding agreement.

CASE IN POINT George Hawkins took his son to Edward McGee, a physician, and asked McGee to operate on the son's hand. McGee said that the boy would be in the hospital three or four days and that the hand would *probably* heal a few days later. The son's hand did not heal for a month, but the father did not win a suit for breach of contract. The court held that McGee had not made an offer to heal the son's hand in a few days. He had merely expressed an opinion as to when the hand would heal.[8]

Statements of Future Intent. A statement of an *intention* to do something in the future is not an offer. If Samir says, "I *plan* to sell my stock in Novation, Inc., for $150 per share," no contract is created if John "accepts" and tenders the $150 per share for the stock. Samir has merely expressed his intention to enter into a future contract for the sale of the stock. If John accepts and tenders the $150 per share, no contract is formed because a reasonable person would conclude that Samir was only *thinking about* selling his stock, not *promising* to sell it.

Preliminary Negotiations. A request or invitation to negotiate is not an offer. It only expresses a willingness to discuss the possibility of entering into a contract. Statements such as "Will you sell Blythe Estate?" or "I wouldn't sell my car for less

than $5,000" are examples. A reasonable person in the offeree's position would not conclude that these statements indicated an intention to enter into a binding obligation. Likewise, when the government or private firms require construction work, they invite contractors to submit bids. The *invitation* to submit bids is not an offer, and a contractor does not bind the government or private firm by submitting a bid. (The bids that the contractors submit are offers, however, and the government or private firm can bind the contractor by accepting the bid.)

Advertisements. In general, advertisements (including representations made in mail-order catalogues, price lists, and circulars) are treated not as offers to contract but as invitations to negotiate.[9]

CASE IN POINT An advertisement on the *Science NOW* Web site asked readers to submit "news tips," which the organization would then investigate for possible inclusion in its magazine or on the Web site. Erik Trell, a professor and physician, submitted a manuscript in which he claimed to have solved a famous mathematical problem. When *Science NOW* did not publish the information, Trell filed a lawsuit for breach of contract. He claimed that the *Science NOW* ad was an offer, which he had accepted by submitting his manuscript. The court dismissed Trell's suit, holding that the ad was not an offer, but merely an invitation.[10]

Price lists are another form of invitation to negotiate or trade. A seller's price list is not an offer to sell at that price; it merely invites the buyer to offer to buy at that price. In fact, the seller usually puts "prices subject to change" on the price list. Only in rare circumstances will a price quotation be construed as an offer.

---

8. *Hawkins v. McGee,* 84 N.H. 114, 146 A. 641 (1929).

9. *Restatement (Second) of Contracts,* Section 26, Comment b.

10. *Trell v. American Association for the Advancement of Science,* ___ F.Supp.2d ___ (W.D.N.Y. 2007).

Although most advertisements and the like are treated as invitations to negotiate, this does not mean that an advertisement can never be an offer. On some occasions, courts have construed advertisements to be offers because the ads contained definite terms that invited acceptance (such as an ad offering a reward for the return of a lost dog).

Agreements to Agree. Traditionally, agreements to agree—that is, agreements to agree to the material terms of a contract at some future date—were not considered to be binding contracts. The modern view, however, is that agreements to agree may be enforceable agreements (contracts) if it is clear that the parties intended to be bound by the agreements. In other words, under the modern view the emphasis is on the parties' intent rather than on form.

CASE IN POINT After a person was injured and nearly drowned on a water ride at one of its amusement parks, Six Flags, Inc., filed a lawsuit against the manufacturer that had designed that ride. The defendant-manufacturer claimed that there was no binding contract between the parties, only preliminary negotiations that were never formalized into a construction contract. The court, however, held that a faxed document specifying the details of the water ride, along with the parties' subsequent actions—such as beginning construction and handwriting notes on the fax—was sufficient to show an intent to be bound. Because of the court's finding, the manufacturer was required to provide insurance for the water ride at Six Flags, and its insurer was required to defend Six Flags in the personal-injury lawsuit that arose out of the incident.[11]

Increasingly, the courts are holding that a preliminary agreement constitutes a binding contract if the parties have agreed on all essential terms and no disputed issues remain to be resolved.[12] In contrast, if the parties agree on certain major terms but leave other terms open for further negotiation, a preliminary agreement is binding only in the sense that the parties have committed themselves to negotiate the undecided terms in good faith in an effort to reach a final agreement.

DEFINITENESS OF TERMS The second requirement for an effective offer involves the definiteness of its terms. An offer must have reasonably definite terms so that a court can determine if a breach has occurred and give an appropriate remedy. The specific terms required depend, of course, on the type of contract. Generally, a contract must include the following terms, either expressed in the contract or capable of being reasonably inferred from it:

1. The identification of the parties.
2. The identification of the object or subject matter of the contract (also the quantity, when appropriate), including the work to be performed, with specific identification of such items as goods, services, and land.
3. The consideration to be paid.
4. The time of payment, delivery, or performance.

An offer may invite an acceptance to be worded in such specific terms that the contract is made definite. For example, Marcus Business Machines contacts Best Corporation and offers to sell "from one to ten MacCool copying machines for $1,600 each; state the number desired in acceptance." Best Corporation agrees to buy two copiers. Because the quantity is specified in the acceptance, the terms are definite and the contract is enforceable.

When the parties have clearly manifested an intent to form a contract, courts sometimes are willing to supply a missing term in a contract, especially a sales contract.[13] But a court will not rewrite a contract if the parties' expression of intent is too vague or uncertain to be given any precise meaning.

COMMUNICATION The third requirement for an effective offer is communication—the offer must be communicated to the offeree. Ordinarily, one cannot agree to a bargain without knowing that it exists. For example, Tolson advertises a reward for the return of her lost cat. Dirk, not knowing of the reward, finds the cat and returns it to Tolson. Usually, Dirk cannot recover the reward because an essential element of a reward contract is that the one who claims the reward must have known it was offered. A few states would allow recovery of the reward, but not on contract principles—Dirk would be allowed to recover on the basis that it would be unfair to deny him the reward just because he did not know about it.

The following case illustrates the importance of the communication requirement in contract formation.

---

11. *Six Flags, Inc. v. Steadfast Insurance Co.,* 474 F.Supp.2d 201 (D.Mass. 2007).

12. See, for example, *Basis Technology Corp. v. Amazon.com, Inc.,* 71 Mass.App.Ct. 29, 878 N.E.2d 952 (2008); and *Tractebel Energy Marketing, Inc. v. AEP Power Marketing, Inc.,* 487 F.3d 89 (2d Cir. 2007).

13. See Chapter 11 and UCC 2–204. Note that Article 2 of the UCC specifies different rules relating to the definiteness of terms used in a contract for the sale of goods. In essence, Article 2 modifies general contract law by requiring *less* specificity.

✳ EXTENDED CASE 9.2 ✳
Alexander v. Lafayette Crime Stoppers, Inc.

Court of Appeal of Louisiana, Third District, 28 So.3d 1253 (2010).
www.la3circuit.org/opinions.htm[a]

IN THE LANGUAGE OF THE COURT
AMY, Judge.
* * * *

In the summer of 2002, after several South Louisiana women had been murdered, the Multi Agency Homicide Task Force (Task Force) was established to investigate these murders, believed to be committed by the same individual referred to as the South Louisiana Serial Killer. In April 2003, the Baton Rouge Crime Stoppers (BRCS) began publicizing a reward offer in newspapers, television stations, and billboards around the Baton Rouge area regarding the South Louisiana Serial Killer. A short time later, Lafayette Crime Stoppers (LCS) also publicized a reward offer. Both reward offers provided an expiration date of August 1, 2003.

According to the plaintiffs' petition, on July 9, 2002, Dianne Alexander was attacked in her home in St. Martin Parish. Ms. Alexander's son, Herman Alexander, arrived home during the attack and chased the attacker from the property. Ms. Alexander reported the attack to local police and, later, both Ms. Alexander and her son described the attacker to the St. Martin Sheriff's Department.

According to his investigative report, Lieutenant Boyd, the lead investigator on Ms. Alexander's attack, began to suspect that Ms. Alexander's attacker could be the same man identified as the South Louisiana Serial Killer, after investigators linked the death of a Lafayette woman to the suspected serial killer. In May 2003, Lieutenant Boyd shared information regarding Ms. Alexander's attack with the Lafayette Sheriff's Department, who in turn shared the information with the Task Force.

On May 22, 2003, Ms. Alexander was interviewed by an FBI agent assisting the Task Force. Based upon that interview, a composite sketch was drawn and released to the public on May 23, 2003. Investigators believed the composite sketch matched the description of a possible suspect in an investigation being handled by the Louisiana Attorney General's Office and the Zachary Police Department. On May 25, 2003, a photo lineup was prepared and presented to Ms. Alexander, who identified her attacker as the same man suspected in the Zachary investigation, Derrick Todd Lee.

On or about August 14, 2003, Ms. Alexander contacted LCS and sought to collect the advertised award; however, LCS informed her she was ineligible to receive the award. On February 22, 2006, Ms. Alexander and her son filed a lawsuit against BRCS and LCS, alleging that the defendants owed them $100,000 and $50,000, respectively, for the information they provided to the defendants. The defendants filed motions for summary judgment asserting that a valid contract never existed between the parties. Specifically, the defendants argued that the plaintiffs never provided information to Crime Stoppers via the tipster hotline and thus did not comply with the "form, terms, or conditions required by the Crime Stoppers' offers[.]" The trial court granted the defendants' motions for summary judgment, finding that the offer from Crime Stoppers was conditioned on the information being provided to the defendant entities rather than law enforcement.

The plaintiffs appeal, asserting that there is a genuine issue of material fact that the LCS and BRCS offers contained a requirement that acceptance of the reward must be done through the Crime Stoppers' tipline.
* * * *

The offer made by LCS in a May 14, 2003 press release, reads [in part] as follows:

* * * *

> In order to qualify for the reward, the tipster must provide information which leads to the arrest, DNA match, and the formal filing of charges against a suspect through grand jury indictment or Bill of Information. In addition, the qualifying tip must be received prior to midnight, August 1, 2003.

The offer from BRCS, as published in the *Morning Advocate,* reads [in part] as follows:

> Crime Stoppers, Inc. $100,000 reward for information on the South Louisiana Serial Killer. A $100,000 reward will be given for information leading to the arrest and indictment of the South Louisiana Serial Killer.

Both LCS and BRCS offers were irrevocable offers because they specified a period of time for acceptance. Louisiana Civil Code Article 1934 provides that "acceptance of an irrevocable offer is effective when received by the offeror." *Acceptance is received when it comes into the possession of a person authorized by the offeror to receive it, or when it is deposited in a place the offeror has indicated as the place where communications of that kind are to be deposited for him.* [Emphasis added.]

The plaintiffs argue that there is a genuine issue of material fact as

---

a. Under "2010," click on "February." When that page opens, select "February 3, 2010." When you reach the page for February 3, 2010, scroll down the list to the case title and click on the docket number (CA 09-00927) to access this opinion. The judicial branch of the Louisiana state government maintains this Web site.

EXTENDED CASE 9.2 CONTINUED ➡

to whether they accepted the Crime Stoppers' reward offers; however, the plaintiffs admit that they did not contact either Crime Stopper organization before August 1, 2003. The plaintiffs argue that they accepted the offers by performance when they provided information about the serial killer to law enforcement. Further, the plaintiffs contend that this performance is a customary manner of accepting reward offers from Crime Stopper organization[s].

In the present matter, the plaintiffs' acceptance of the reward offers must have been received by the defendants (offerors) by the time prescribed in the offer (August 1, 2003) in the place where communications of that kind were to be deposited (the phone number cited in the offers). The record contains no evidence indicating the defendants were notified by the plaintiffs in the time and manner indicated in the offer. While the plaintiffs may have provided information related to the arrest or indictment of Derrick Todd Lee to local law enforcement and the Task Force, there is no indication in the offer that either of those parties were the offerors of the reward or persons authorized to receive acceptance on their behalf.

* * * [As to the plaintiffs' argument that providing information to law enforcement is a customary manner of accepting reward offers from Crime Stoppers,] [w]hile acceptance may be valid if customary in similar transactions, according to [Louisiana law], it must be "customary in similar transactions at the time and place the offer is *received*." (Emphasis added [by the court].) As indicated above, there is no evidence in the record that the defendants received any acceptance of the offer. Accordingly, no contract was formed between the parties.

* * * *

For the foregoing reasons, the judgment granting the defendants' motions for summary judgment is affirmed.

QUESTIONS

1. Suppose that the plaintiffs had learned about the reward offer after the killer had already been arrested and indicted due to their assistance but *before* the August 1, 2003, deadline. If they had then called in their information on the tip line, would they have been legally entitled to claim the reward in this circumstance? Explain.
2. The plaintiffs argued that "providing information to law enforcement is a customary manner of accepting reward offers from Crime Stoppers." How did the court respond to this argument?

Termination of the Offer

The communication of an effective offer to an offeree gives the offeree the power to transform the offer into a binding, legal obligation (a contract) by an acceptance. This power of acceptance does not continue forever, though. It can be terminated either by the action of the parties or by operation of law.

TERMINATION BY ACTION OF THE PARTIES An offer can be terminated by the action of the parties in any of three ways: by revocation, by rejection, or by counteroffer.

Revocation of the Offer by the Offeror. The offeror's act of withdrawing (revoking) an offer is known as **revocation.** Unless an offer is irrevocable (discussed shortly), the offeror usually can revoke the offer (even if he or she has promised to keep it open) as long as the revocation is communicated to the offeree before the offeree accepts. Revocation may be accomplished by express repudiation of the offer (for example, with a statement such as "I withdraw my previous offer of October 17") or by performance of acts that are inconsistent with the existence of the offer and are made known to the offeree (for example, selling the offered property to another person in the presence of the offeree).

The general rule followed by most states is that a revocation becomes effective when the offeree or the offeree's *agent* (a person acting on behalf of the offeree) actually receives it. Therefore, a letter of revocation mailed on April 1 and delivered at the offeree's residence or place of business on April 3 becomes effective on April 3.

An offer made to the general public can be revoked in the same manner that the offer was originally communicated. Suppose that an electronics retailer offers a $10,000 reward to anyone providing information leading to the apprehension of the persons who burglarized the store's downtown branch. The offer is published in three local newspapers and four newspapers in neighboring communities. To revoke the offer, the retailer must publish the revocation in all seven of the newspapers in which it published the offer. The revocation is then accessible to the general public, even if some particular offeree does not know about it.

Although most offers are revocable, some can be made irrevocable—that is, they cannot be revoked. Increasingly, courts refuse to allow an offeror to revoke an offer when the offeree has changed position because of *justifiable reliance* on the offer. In some circumstances, "firm offers" made by merchants may also be considered irrevocable—see the discussion of the "merchant's firm offer" in Chapter 11.

Option Contracts. Another form of irrevocable offer is an option contract. An **option contract** is created when an offeror promises to hold an offer open for a specified period of time in return for a payment (consideration) given by the offeree. An option contract takes away the offeror's power to revoke the offer for the period of time specified in the option.

Option contracts are also frequently used in conjunction with the sale or lease of real estate. For example, Tyrell agrees to lease a house from Jackson, the property owner. Included in the lease contract is a clause stating that Tyrell is paying an additional $15,000 for an option to purchase the property within a specified period of time. If Tyrell decides not to purchase the house after the specified period has lapsed, he loses the $15,000, and Jackson is free to sell the property to another buyer.

Rejection of the Offer by the Offeree. If the offeree rejects the offer—by words or by conduct—the offer is terminated. Any subsequent attempt by the offeree to accept will be construed as a new offer, giving the original offeror (now the offeree) the power of acceptance. As with a revocation, a rejection of an offer is effective only when it is actually received by the offeror or the offeror's agent.

Merely inquiring about an offer does not constitute rejection. Suppose that Raymond offers to buy Francie's PlayStation 3 with the stereoscopic 3D update for $300, and Francie responds, "Is that your best offer?" or "Will you pay me $375 for it?" A reasonable person would conclude that Francie did not reject the offer but simply made an inquiry for further consideration of the offer. She can still accept and bind Raymond to the $300 purchase price. When the offeree merely inquires as to the firmness of the offer, there is no reason to presume that he or she intends to reject it.

Counteroffer by the Offeree. A **counteroffer** is a rejection of the original offer and the simultaneous making of a new offer. Suppose that Burke offers to sell his home to Lang for $270,000. Lang responds, "Your price is too high. I'll offer to purchase your house for $250,000." Lang's response is called a counteroffer because it rejects Burke's offer to sell at $270,000 and creates a new offer by Lang to purchase the home at a price of $250,000.

At common law, the **mirror image rule** requires the offeree's acceptance to match the offeror's offer exactly—to mirror the offer. Any change in, or addition to, the terms of the original offer automatically terminates that offer and substitutes the counteroffer. The counteroffer, of course, need not be accepted; but if the original offeror does accept the terms of the counteroffer, a valid contract is created.[14]

TERMINATION BY OPERATION OF LAW The power of the offeree to transform the offer into a binding, legal obligation can be terminated by operation of law through the occurrence of any of the following events:

1. Lapse of time.
2. Destruction of the specific subject matter of the offer.
3. Death or incompetence of the offeror or the offeree.
4. Supervening illegality of the proposed contract.

If the offer states that it will be left open until a particular date, then the offer will terminate at midnight on that day. If the offer states that it will be left open for a number of days, such as ten days, this time period normally begins to run when the offer is actually received by the offeree, not when it is formed or sent. If the offer does not specify a time for acceptance, the offer terminates at the end of a *reasonable* period of time. What constitutes a reasonable period of time depends on the subject matter of the contract, business and market conditions, and other relevant circumstances. An offer to sell farm produce, for example, will terminate sooner than an offer to sell farm equipment because farm produce is perishable and subject to greater fluctuations in market value.

A statute or court decision that makes an offer illegal automatically terminates the offer. For example, Lee offers to lend Kim $10,000 at an annual interest rate of 15 percent. Before Kim can accept the offer, a law is enacted that prohibits interest rates higher than 12 percent. Lee's offer is automatically terminated. (If the statute is enacted after Kim accepts the offer, a valid contract is formed, but the contract may still be unenforceable.)

---

14. The mirror image rule has been greatly modified in regard to sales contracts. Section 2–207 of the UCC provides that a contract is formed if the offeree makes a definite expression of acceptance (such as signing the form in the appropriate location), even though the terms of the acceptance modify or add to the terms of the original offer (see Chapter 11).

Concept Summary 9.2 below provides a review of the ways in which an offer can be terminated.

Acceptance

Acceptance is a voluntary act by the offeree that shows assent (agreement) to the terms of an offer. The offeree's act may consist of words or conduct. The acceptance must be unequivocal and must be communicated to the offeror.

UNEQUIVOCAL ACCEPTANCE To exercise the power of acceptance effectively, the offeree must accept unequivocally. This is the *mirror image rule* previously discussed. If the acceptance is subject to new conditions or if the terms of the acceptance change the original offer, the acceptance may be deemed a counteroffer that implicitly rejects the original offer.

An acceptance may be unequivocal even though the offeree expresses dissatisfaction with the contract. For example, "I accept the offer, but I wish I could have gotten a better price" is an effective acceptance. So, too, is "I accept, but can you shave the price?" In contrast, the statement "I accept the offer but only if I can pay on ninety days' credit" is not an unequivocal acceptance and operates as a counteroffer, rejecting the original offer.

Certain terms, when included in an acceptance, will not change the offer sufficiently to constitute rejection. Suppose that in response to an art dealer's offer to sell a painting, the offeree, Ashton Gibbs, replies, "I accept; please send a written contract." Gibbs is requesting a written contract but is not making it a condition for acceptance. Therefore, the acceptance is effective without the written contract. In contrast, if Gibbs replies, "I accept *if* you send a written contract," the acceptance is expressly conditioned on the request for a writing, and the statement is not an acceptance but a counteroffer. (Notice how important each word is!)[15]

SILENCE AS ACCEPTANCE Ordinarily, silence cannot constitute acceptance, even if the offeror states, "By your silence and inaction, you will be deemed to have accepted this offer." This general rule applies because an offeree should not be obligated to act affirmatively to reject an offer when no consideration has passed to the offeree to impose such a duty.

In some instances, however, the offeree does have a duty to speak. In these situations, her or his

---

15. As noted in Footnote 14, in regard to sales contracts, the UCC provides that an acceptance may still be valid even if some terms are added. The new terms are simply treated as proposed additions to the contract.

CONCEPT SUMMARY 9.2
Methods by Which an Offer Can Be Terminated

By Action of the Parties—

1. *Revocation*—Unless the offer is irrevocable, it can be revoked at any time before acceptance without liability. Revocation is not effective until received by the offeree or the offeree's agent. Some offers, such as a merchant's firm offer and option contracts, are irrevocable. Also, in some situations, an offeree's detrimental reliance or partial performance will cause a court to rule that the offeror cannot revoke the offer.
2. *Rejection*—Accomplished by words or actions that demonstrate a clear intent not to accept the offer; not effective until received by the offeror or the offeror's agent.
3. *Counteroffer*—A rejection of the original offer and the making of a new offer.

By Operation of Law—

1. *Lapse of time*—The offer terminates at the end of the time period specified in the offer or, if no time period is stated in the offer, at the end of a reasonable time period.
2. *Destruction of the subject matter*—When the specific subject matter of the offer is destroyed before the offer is accepted, the offer automatically terminates.
3. *Death or incompetence of the offeror or offeree*—If the offeror or offeree dies or becomes incompetent, this offer terminates (unless the offer is irrevocable).
4. *Supervening illegality*—When a statute or court decision makes the proposed contract illegal, the offer automatically terminates.

silence or inaction will operate as an acceptance. Silence may be an acceptance when an offeree takes the benefit of offered services even though he or she had an opportunity to reject them and knew that they were offered with the expectation of compensation. For example, John is a student who earns extra income by washing store windows. John taps on the window of a store, catches the attention of the store's manager, and points to the window and raises his cleaner, signaling that he will be washing the window. The manager does nothing to stop him. Here, the store manager's silence constitutes an acceptance, and an implied contract is created. The store is bound to pay a reasonable value for John's work. Silence can also operate as acceptance when the offeree has had prior dealings with the offeror.

COMMUNICATION OF ACCEPTANCE In a bilateral contract, communication of acceptance is necessary because acceptance is in the form of a promise (not performance), and the contract is formed when the promise is made (rather than when the act is performed). Communication of acceptance is not necessary if the offer dispenses with the requirement, however, or if the offer can be accepted by silence.

Because a unilateral contract calls for the full performance of some act, acceptance is usually evident, and notification is therefore unnecessary. Nevertheless, exceptions do exist, such as when the offeror requests notice of acceptance or has no way of determining whether the requested act has been performed.

MODE AND TIMELINESS OF ACCEPTANCE In bilateral contracts, acceptance must be timely. Acceptance in a bilateral contract generally is timely if it is made before the offer is terminated. Problems may arise, though, when the parties involved are not dealing face to face. In such situations, the offeree should use an authorized mode of communication.

The Mailbox Rule. Acceptance takes effect, thus completing formation of the contract, at the time the offeree sends or delivers the communication via the mode expressly or impliedly authorized by the offeror. This is the so-called **mailbox rule,** which the majority of courts follow. Under this rule, if the authorized mode of communication is the mail, then an acceptance becomes valid when it is dispatched (placed in the control of the U.S. Postal Service)—*not* when it is received by the offeror. (Note, however, that if the offer stipulates when acceptance will be

effective, then the offer will not be effective until the time specified.)

The mailbox rule does not apply to instantaneous forms of communication, such as when the parties are dealing face to face, by telephone, or by fax. There is still some uncertainty in the courts as to whether e-mail should be considered an instantaneous form of communication to which the mailbox rule does not apply. If the parties have agreed to conduct transactions electronically and if the Uniform Electronic Transactions Act (UETA) applies, then e-mail is considered sent when it either leaves the control of the sender or is received by the recipient. This rule takes the place of the mailbox rule when the UETA applies but essentially allows an e-mail acceptance to become effective when sent (as it would if sent by U.S. mail).

Authorized Means of Acceptance. A means of communicating acceptance can be expressly authorized by the offeror or impliedly authorized by the facts and circumstances surrounding the situation or by law.[16] An acceptance sent by means not expressly or impliedly authorized normally is not effective until it is received by the offeror.

When an offeror specifies how acceptance should be made (for example, by overnight delivery), *express authorization* is said to exist, and the contract is not formed unless the offeree uses that specified mode of acceptance. Moreover, both offeror and offeree are bound in contract the moment this means of acceptance is employed. For example, Shaylee & Perkins, a Massachusetts firm, offers to sell a container of antique furniture to Leaham's Antiques in Colorado. The offer states that Leaham's must accept the offer via FedEx overnight delivery. The acceptance is effective (and a binding contract is formed) the moment that Leaham's gives the overnight envelope containing the acceptance to the FedEx driver.

If the offeror does not expressly authorize a certain mode of acceptance, then acceptance can be made by *any reasonable means.* Courts look at the prevailing business usages and the surrounding circumstances to determine whether the mode of acceptance used was reasonable. Usually, the offeror's choice of a particular means in making the offer implies that the offeree can use the *same* or a *faster* means for acceptance. Thus, if the offer is made via priority mail, it would be reasonable to accept the

---

16. *Restatement (Second) of Contracts,* Section 30, provides that an offer invites acceptance "by any medium reasonable in the circumstances," unless the offer is specific about the means of acceptance.

offer via priority mail or by a faster method, such as by fax or FedEx.

Substitute Method of Acceptance. If the offeror authorizes a particular method of acceptance, but the offeree accepts by a different means, the acceptance may still be effective if the substituted method serves the same purpose as the authorized means. The acceptance is not effective on dispatch, though, and no contract will be formed until the acceptance is received by the offeror. For example, an offer specifies acceptance by FedEx overnight delivery, but the offeree instead accepts by UPS overnight delivery. The substitute method of acceptance will still be effective, but the contract will not be formed until the offeror receives the UPS delivery (rather than the day before, when the letter was given to the carrier).

SECTION 4
CONSIDERATION

The fact that a promise has been made does not mean the promise can or will be enforced. Under common law, a primary basis for the enforcement of promises is consideration. **Consideration** usually is defined as the value (such as cash) given in return for a promise (in a bilateral contract) or in return for a performance (in a unilateral contract).

Often, consideration is broken down into two parts: (1) something of *legally sufficient value* must be given in exchange for the promise, and (2) usually, there must be a *bargained-for exchange*.

Legally Sufficient Value

The "something of legally sufficient value" may consist of (1) a promise to do something that one has no prior legal duty to do, (2) the performance of an action that one is otherwise not obligated to undertake, or (3) the refraining from an action that one has a legal right to undertake (called a *forbearance*). Consideration in bilateral contracts normally consists of a promise in return for a promise, as explained earlier. In contrast, unilateral contracts involve a promise in return for a performance. Suppose that Anita said to her neighbor, "When you finish painting the garage, I will pay you $100." Anita's neighbor paints the garage. The act of painting the garage is the consideration that creates Anita's contractual obligation to pay her neighbor $100.

What if, in return for a promise to pay, a person refrains from pursuing harmful habits (a

forbearance), such as the use of tobacco and alcohol? In most situations, such forbearance constitutes legally sufficient consideration for a promise.[17]

Bargained-for Exchange

The second element of consideration is that it must provide the basis for the bargain struck between the contracting parties. The item of value must be given or promised by the promisor (offeror) in return for the promisee's promise, performance, or promise of performance.

This element of bargained-for exchange distinguishes contracts from gifts. For example, Roberto says to his son, "In consideration of the fact that you are not as wealthy as your brothers, I will pay you $5,000." The fact that the word *consideration* is used does not, by itself, mean that consideration has been given. Indeed, this is not an enforceable promise because the son does not have to do anything in order to receive the promised $5,000. Because the son does not need to give Roberto something of legal value in return for his promise, there is no bargained-for exchange. Rather, Roberto has simply stated his motive for giving his son a gift.

Adequacy of Consideration

Adequacy of consideration involves how much consideration is given. Essentially, it concerns the fairness of the bargain. On the surface, when the items exchanged are of unequal value, fairness would appear to be an issue. A court generally will not question the adequacy of consideration, however, based solely on the comparative value of the things exchanged. Something need not be of direct economic or financial value to be viewed legally sufficient consideration. Under the doctrine of freedom of contract, courts leave it up to the parties to decide what something is worth, and parties are usually free to bargain as they wish. If people could sue merely because they had entered into an unwise contract, the courts would be overloaded with frivolous suits.

Nevertheless, when there is a large disparity in the amount or value of the consideration exchanged, the inadequate consideration may raise a red flag for a court to look more closely at the bargain. This is because shockingly inadequate consideration can indicate that fraud, duress, or undue influence was involved or that the element of bargained-for

---

17. For a classic case holding that a person's promise to refrain from using alcohol and tobacco was sufficient consideration, see *Hamer v. Sidway*, 124 N.Y. 538, 27 N.E. 256 (1891).

exchange was lacking. Judges are troubled about enforcing unequal bargains and generally try to make sure that no defect in a contract's formation negates mutual assent.

Agreements That Lack Consideration

Sometimes, one of the parties (or both parties) to an agreement may think that consideration has been exchanged when in fact it has not. Here, we look at some situations in which the parties' promises or actions do not qualify as contractual consideration.

PREEXISTING DUTY Under most circumstances, a promise to do what one already has a legal duty to do does not constitute legally sufficient consideration. The preexisting legal duty may be imposed by law or may arise out of a previous contract. A sheriff, for example, cannot collect a reward for providing information leading to the capture of a criminal if the sheriff already has a legal duty to capture the criminal.

Likewise, if a party is already bound by contract to perform a certain duty, that duty cannot serve as consideration for a second contract. For example, Bauman-Bache, Inc., begins construction on a seven-story office building and after three months demands an extra $75,000 on its contract. If the extra $75,000 is not paid, the contractor will stop working. The owner of the land, finding no one else to complete the construction, agrees to pay the extra $75,000. The agreement is unenforceable because it is not supported by legally sufficient consideration; Bauman-Bache had a preexisting contractual duty to complete the building.

Unforeseen Difficulties. The rule regarding preexisting duty is meant to prevent extortion and the so-called holdup game. Therefore, when an honest contractor who has contracted with a landowner to construct a building runs into extraordinary difficulties that were totally unforeseen at the time the contract was formed, the courts sometimes allow exceptions to the preexisting duty rule. If a landowner agrees to pay extra compensation to the contractor for overcoming unforeseen difficulties (such as having to use special digging equipment to remove an unforeseen obstacle), the court may refrain from applying the preexisting duty rule and enforce the agreement. When the unforeseen difficulties that give rise to a contract modification are the types of risks ordinarily assumed in business, however, the courts will usually assert the preexisting duty rule.

Rescission and New Contract. The law recognizes that two parties can mutually agree to rescind, or cancel, their contract, at least to the extent that it is executory (still to be carried out). **Rescission**[18] is the unmaking of a contract so as to return the parties to the positions they occupied before the contract was made. Sometimes, parties rescind a contract and make a new contract at the same time. When this occurs, it is often difficult to determine whether there was consideration for the new contract, or whether the parties had a preexisting duty under the previous contract. If a court finds there was a preexisting duty, then the new contract will be invalid because there was no consideration.

PAST CONSIDERATION Promises made in return for actions or events that have already taken place are unenforceable. These promises lack consideration in that the element of bargained-for exchange is missing. In short, a person can bargain for something to take place now or in the future but not for something that has already taken place. Therefore, **past consideration** is no consideration.

Suppose that Elsie, a real estate agent, does her friend Judy a favor by selling Judy's house and not charging a commission. Later, Judy says to Elsie, "In return for your generous act, I will pay you $3,000." This promise involves past consideration. Consequently, a court would not enforce it. Judy is simply creating a situation in which she presents a gift to Elsie.

CASE IN POINT Jamil Blackmon became friends with Allen Iverson when Iverson was a high school student who showed tremendous promise as an athlete. One evening, Blackmon suggested that Iverson use "The Answer" as a nickname in the summer league basketball tournaments. Blackmon said that Iverson would be "The Answer" to all of the National Basketball Association's woes. Later that night, Iverson said that he would give Blackmon 25 percent of any proceeds from the merchandising of products that used "The Answer" as a logo or a slogan. Because Iverson's promise was made in return for past consideration, it was unenforceable. In effect, Iverson stated his intention to give Blackmon a gift.[19]

Promissory Estoppel

Under the doctrine of **promissory estoppel** (also called *detrimental reliance*), a person who has reasonably and substantially relied on the promise of another may be able to obtain some measure of

---

18. Pronounced reh-*sih*-zhen.
19. *Blackmon v. Iverson,* 324 F.Supp.2d 602 (E.D.Pa. 2003).

recovery. This doctrine is applied in a wide variety of contexts in which a promise is otherwise unenforceable, such as when a promise is not supported by consideration. Under this doctrine, a court may enforce an otherwise unenforceable promise to avoid the injustice that would otherwise result. For the doctrine to be applied, the following elements are required:

1. There must be a clear and definite promise.
2. The promisor should have expected that the promisee would rely on the promise.
3. The promisee reasonably relied on the promise by acting or refraining from some act.
4. The promisee's reliance was definite and resulted in substantial detriment.
5. Enforcement of the promise is necessary to avoid injustice.

If these requirements are met, a promise may be enforced even though it is not supported by consideration. In essence, the promisor will be e*stopped* (prevented) from asserting the lack of consideration as a defense.

CASE IN POINT The U.S. Air Force solicited bids for construction of a new building in Anchorage, Alaska. A general contractor, Vern Hickel, contacted eight different subcontractors to find the lowest price on electrical work. Alaska Bussell Electric Company, an electrical subcontractor, told Hickel that it would do the work for $477,498. Hickel reasonably relied on this amount when he submitted his primary bid for the entire project to the Air Force and won the contract. Subsequently, Alaska Bussell realized that it had made a mistake and refused to perform the work for Hickel for $477,498. Hickel had to hire another subcontractor at a substantially higher cost. Under the doctrine of promissory estoppel, Hickel can sue Alaska Bussell for the cost difference because he had detrimentally relied on Alaska Bussell's bid, even though there was no consideration for Alaska Bussell's promise to do the work for $477,498.[20]

SECTION 5
CONTRACTUAL CAPACITY

In addition to agreement and consideration, for a contract to be deemed valid the parties to the contract must have **contractual capacity**—the legal ability to enter into a contractual relationship. Courts generally presume the existence of contractual capacity. In some situations, however, when a person is young, intoxicated, or mentally incompetent, capacity is lacking or may be questionable.

Minors

Today, in almost all states, the *age of majority* (when a person is no longer a minor) for contractual purposes is eighteen years.[21] In addition, some states provide for the termination of minority on marriage. Minority status may also be terminated by a minor's *emancipation,* which occurs when a child's parent or legal guardian relinquishes the legal right to exercise control over the child. Normally, minors who leave home to support themselves are considered emancipated. Several jurisdictions permit minors to petition a court for emancipation themselves. For business purposes, a minor may petition a court to be treated as an adult.

The general rule is that a minor can enter into any contract that an adult can, provided that the contract is not one prohibited by law for minors (for example, the sale of tobacco or alcoholic beverages). A contract entered into by a minor, however, is voidable at the option of that minor, subject to certain exceptions.

The legal avoidance, or setting aside, of a contractual obligation is referred to as *disaffirmance.* To disaffirm, a minor must express his or her intent, through words or conduct, not to be bound to the contract. The minor must disaffirm the entire contract, not merely a portion of it. For example, the minor cannot decide to keep part of the goods purchased under a contract and return the remaining goods.

Intoxication

Intoxication is a condition in which a person's normal capacity to act or think is inhibited by alcohol or some other drug. A contract entered into by an intoxicated person can be either voidable or valid (and thus enforceable). If the person was sufficiently intoxicated to lack mental capacity, then the agreement may be voidable even if the intoxication was purely voluntary. If, despite intoxication, the person understood the legal consequences of the agreement, the contract will be enforceable. For the contract to be voidable, the person must prove that the

---

20. See *Alaska Bussell Electric Co. v. Vern Hickel Construction Co.,* 688 P.2d 576 (1984); also see *Commerce Bancorp, Inc. v. BK International Insurance Brokers, Ltd.,* 490 F.Supp.2d 556 (D.N.J. 2007).

---

21. The age of majority may still be twenty-one for other purposes, such as the purchase and consumption of alcohol.

intoxication impaired her or his reason and judgment so severely that she or he did not comprehend the legal consequences of entering into the contract.

Mental Incompetence

If a court has previously determined that a person is mentally incompetent and has appointed a guardian to represent the individual, any contract made by the mentally incompetent person is *void*—no contract exists. Only the guardian can enter into binding legal obligations on behalf of the mentally incompetent person.

If a court has not previously judged a person to be mentally incompetent, the contract may be *voidable* if the person did not know he or she was entering into the contract or lacked the mental capacity to comprehend its nature, purpose, and consequences. A contract entered into by a mentally incompetent person (whom a court has not previously declared incompetent) may also be *valid* if the person had capacity *at the time the contract was formed*.

SECTION 6
LEGALITY

Legality is the fourth requirement for a valid contract to exist. For a contract to be valid and enforceable, it must be formed for a legal purpose. A contract to do something that is prohibited by federal or state statutory law is illegal and, as such, void from the outset and thus unenforceable. A contract or a clause in a contract can also be illegal even in the absence of a specific statute prohibiting the action promised by the contract. Additionally, a contract to commit a tortious act—such as an agreement to engage in fraudulent misrepresentation (see Chapter 12)—is contrary to public policy and therefore illegal and unenforceable.

Contracts Contrary to Statute

Statutes often set forth rules specifying which terms and clauses may be included in contracts and which are prohibited, as discussed next.

CONTRACTS TO COMMIT A CRIME Any contract to commit a crime is a contract in violation of a statute. Thus, a contract to sell illegal drugs in violation of criminal laws is unenforceable, as is a contract to cover up a corporation's violation of the Sarbanes-Oxley Act (see Chapter 4). Similarly, a contract to smuggle undocumented workers from another country into the United States for an employer is illegal (see

Chapter 23), as is a contract to dump hazardous waste in violation of environmental laws (see Chapter 25). If the object or performance of the contract is rendered illegal by statute *after* the contract has been entered into, the contract is considered to be discharged by law. (See the discussion of impossibility or impracticability of performance in Chapter 10 on page 219.)

USURY Almost every state has a statute that sets the maximum rate of interest that can be charged for different types of transactions, including ordinary loans. A lender who makes a loan at an interest rate above the lawful maximum commits *usury*. Although usurious contracts are illegal, most states simply limit the interest that the lender may collect on the contract to the lawful maximum interest rate in that state. In a few states, the lender can recover the principal amount of the loan but no interest.

GAMBLING Gambling is the creation of risk for the purpose of assuming it. Traditionally, the states have deemed gambling contracts illegal and thus void. All states have statutes that regulate gambling, and many states allow certain forms of gambling, such as horse racing, poker machines, and charity-sponsored bingo. In addition, nearly all states allow state-operated lotteries and gambling on Native American reservations. Even in states that permit certain types of gambling, though, courts often find that gambling contracts are illegal.

CASE IN POINT Casino gambling is legal in Louisiana, as are video poker machines. Nevertheless, Louisiana courts refused to enforce certain contracts relating to the installation of video poker machines. Gaming Venture, Inc. (GVI), had entered into two contracts with Tastee Restaurant Corporation: a licensing agreement and an agreement that authorized GVI to install poker machines in various Tastee locations. When several Tastee restaurants refused to install the machines, GVI sued for breach of contract. The state appellate court held that the two agreements were illegal gambling contracts and therefore void because GVI had failed to get the prior approval of the state video gaming commission.[22]

LICENSING STATUTES All states require members of certain professions—including physicians, lawyers, real estate brokers, accountants, architects, electricians, and stockbrokers—to have licenses. Some licenses are obtained only after extensive schooling and examinations, which indicate to the public that a special skill

---

22. *Gaming Venture, Inc. v. Tastee Restaurant Corp.*, 996 So.2d 515 (La.App. 5 Cir. 2008).

has been acquired. Others require only that the applicant be of good moral character and pay a fee.

Whether a contract with an unlicensed person is legal and enforceable depends on the purpose of the licensing statute. If the statute's purpose is to protect the public from unauthorized practitioners (such as unlicensed attorneys and electricians, for example), then a contract involving an unlicensed practitioner is generally illegal and unenforceable. If the statute's purpose is merely to raise government revenues, however, a contract with an unlicensed person (such as a landscape architect or a massage therapist) may be enforced and the unlicensed practitioner fined.

Contracts Contrary to Public Policy

Although contracts involve private parties, some are not enforceable because of the negative impact they would have on society. Examples include a contract to commit a civil wrong, such as invading another person's privacy (see Chapter 12), and a contract to commit an immoral act, such as selling a child. We look here at other types of business contracts that are often said to be *contrary to public policy.*

CONTRACTS IN RESTRAINT OF TRADE Contracts in restraint of trade (anticompetitive agreements) usually adversely affect the public policy that favors competition in the economy. Typically, such contracts also violate one or more federal or state antitrust statutes.[23] An exception is recognized when the restraint is reasonable and is contained in an ancillary (secondary, or subordinate) clause in a contract. Such restraints often are included in contracts for the sale of an ongoing business and employment contracts.

---

23. Federal statutes include the Sherman Antitrust Act, the Clayton Act, and the Federal Trade Commission Act (see Chapter 27).

Covenants Not to Compete and the Sale of an Ongoing Business. Many contracts involve a type of restraint called a **covenant not to compete,** or a restrictive covenant (promise). A covenant not to compete may be created when a seller agrees not to open a new store in a certain geographic area surrounding the old store. Such an agreement enables the seller to sell, and the purchaser to buy, the goodwill and reputation of an ongoing business without having to worry that the seller will open a competing business a block away. Provided the restrictive covenant is reasonable and is an ancillary part of the sale of an ongoing business, it is enforceable.

Covenants Not to Compete in Employment Contracts. Sometimes, agreements not to compete (also referred to as *noncompete agreements*) are included in employment contracts. People in middle- or upper-level management positions commonly agree not to work for competitors or not to start competing businesses for a specified period of time after termination of employment. Such agreements are legal in most states so long as the specified period of time (of restraint) is not excessive in duration and the geographic restriction is reasonable. What constitutes a reasonable time period may be shorter in the online environment than in conventional employment contracts because the restrictions apply worldwide. To be reasonable, a restriction on competition must protect a legitimate business interest and must not be any greater than necessary to protect that interest.

The contract in the following case provided an exclusive license to open and operate comedy clubs under a certain famous trademark. It included a covenant not to compete. The question was whether the restraint was reasonable.

CASE 9.3
Comedy Club, Inc. v. Improv West Associates

United States Court of Appeals, Ninth Circuit, 553 F.3d 1277 (2009). www.ca9.uscourts.gov[a]

BACKGROUND AND FACTS • Improv West Associates is the founder of the Improv Comedy Club and owner of the "Improv" trademark. Comedy Club, Inc. (CCI), owns and operates restaurants and comedy clubs. Improv West granted CCI an exclusive license to open four Improv clubs per year in

---

a. In the left-hand column, in the "Decisions" pull-down menu, click on "Opinions." On that page, click on "Advanced Search." Type "05-55739" in the "by Case No.:" box, and click on "Search." Then click on the "01/29/2009" link to access the opinion. The U.S. Court of Appeals for the Ninth Circuit maintains this Web site.

CASE CONTINUES ➡

CASE 9.3 CONTINUED ► 2001, 2002, and 2003. Their agreement prohibited CCI from opening any non-Improv comedy clubs "in the contiguous United States" until 2019. When CCI failed to open eight clubs by the end of 2002, Improv West commenced arbitration. The arbitrator's award in 2005 stated that CCI had forfeited its right to open Improv clubs but that the parties' agreement had not terminated and the covenant not to compete was enforceable—CCI could not open any new comedy clubs for its duration. A federal district court confirmed the award, and CCI appealed.

IN THE LANGUAGE OF THE COURT
GOULD, Circuit Judge:
* * * *

The basic outline of what the arbitrator did, terminating an exclusive right to open Improv clubs nationwide, because of contractually inadequate performance contrary to the agreed schedule, while keeping in force the restrictive covenant makes sense in so far as CCI should not have an exclusive license on Improv clubs absent complying with designated performance. And so long as CCI was running some Improv clubs, a restrictive covenant to some degree could protect Improv West from damage caused by improper competition. Because we cannot say that there is no basis in the record for the arbitrator's decision, we hold that the arbitrator's award is not completely irrational.
* * * *

CCI's "business" is operating full-service comedy clubs. CCI currently operates at least seven Improv clubs. As interpreted by the arbitrator, the * * * covenant not to compete applies geographically to the contiguous United States, and does not end until 2019. Thus, the covenant not to compete has dramatic geographic and temporal [time-related] scope. Combined with the arbitrator's ruling that CCI forfeited its rights to use the Improv marks license in any new location, the practical effect of the arbitrator's award * * * is that for more than fourteen years the entire contiguous United States comedy club market, except for CCI's current Improv clubs, is off limits to CCI. This forecloses competition in a substantial share of the comedy club business.
* * * *

* * * *The economic restraint of [this covenant] on competition is too broad to be countenanced [tolerated]* * * . The covenant not to compete must be more narrowly tailored to relate to the areas in which CCI is operating Improv clubs under the license agreement. [Emphasis added.]

However, we do not void the entire * * * covenant not to compete. * * * We weigh CCI's right to operate its business against Improv West's interest to protect and maintain its trademark, trade name and goodwill. This balance tilts in favor of Improv West with regard to counties where CCI is operating an Improv club.

Therefore, we hold that the district court should vacate [set aside] the arbitrator's [award] as to any county where CCI does not currently operate an Improv club, but uphold [the covenant] in those counties where CCI currently operates Improv clubs. Nationwide CCI may open and operate non-Improv comedy clubs in all those counties where it does not currently operate an Improv club. However, CCI may not open or operate any non-Improv clubs in those counties where it currently owns or operates Improv clubs.

DECISION AND REMEDY • *The federal appellate court reversed part of the lower court's confirmation of the award and remanded the case. A covenant not to compete in the comedy club business for fourteen years in forty-eight states is too broad to be enforced.*

THE ETHICAL DIMENSION • *Should companies or any subsidiaries affiliated with CCI be subject to the covenant not to compete? Would it be unethical to impose such a requirement? Discuss.*

THE LEGAL ENVIRONMENT DIMENSION • *Why would a business such as Improv West include a covenant not to compete in such an agreement as the contract at issue in this case? Explain.*

Enforcement Problems. The laws governing the enforceability of covenants not to compete vary significantly from state to state. In some states, such as Texas, such a covenant will not be enforced unless the employee has received some benefit in return for signing the noncompete agreement. This is true even if the covenant is reasonable as to time and area. If the employee receives no benefit, the covenant will be deemed void.

Occasionally, depending on the jurisdiction, courts will *reform* covenants not to compete to make the terms more reasonable and then enforce the reformed covenant. Courts usually resort to contract *reformation* only when necessary to prevent undue burdens or hardships.

UNCONSCIONABLE CONTRACTS A court does not ordinarily look at the fairness or equity of a contract. For example, the courts generally do not inquire into the adequacy of consideration. Persons are assumed to be reasonably intelligent, and the courts will not come to their aid just because they have made an unwise bargain. In certain circumstances, however, bargains are so oppressive that the courts relieve innocent parties of part or all of their duties. Such bargains are deemed **unconscionable** because they are so unscrupulous or grossly unfair as to be "void of conscience."[24] A contract can be unconscionable on either procedural or substantive grounds.

Procedural Unconscionability. *Procedural unconscionability* often involves inconspicuous print, unintelligible language (legalese), or the lack of an opportunity to read the contract or ask questions about its meaning. It can also occur when there is such disparity in bargaining power between the two parties that the weaker party's consent is not voluntary. This type of situation often involves an adhesion contract. An **adhesion contract** is written exclusively by one party (usually, the seller or creditor) and presented to the other (usually, the buyer or borrower) on a take-it-or-leave-it basis. Only those adhesion contracts that unreasonably favor the drafter are unconscionable.[25]

Substantive Unconscionability. *Substantive unconscionability* characterizes those contracts that are oppressive or overly harsh. Courts generally focus on provisions that deprive one party of the benefits of the agreement or leave that party without a remedy for nonperformance by the other. For example, a contract clause that gives the business entity free access to the courts but requires the other party to arbitrate any dispute with the firm may be unconscionable. Contracts drafted by insurance companies and cell phone providers have been struck down as substantively unconscionable when they included provisions that were overly harsh or one sided.[26]

EXCULPATORY CLAUSES Often closely related to the concept of unconscionability are **exculpatory clauses,** which release a party from liability in the event of monetary or physical injury *no matter who is at fault.* Indeed, courts sometimes refuse to enforce such clauses on the ground that they are unconscionable. Exculpatory clauses found in rental agreements for commercial property are frequently held to be contrary to public policy, and such clauses are almost always unenforceable in residential property leases. Courts also usually hold that exculpatory clauses are against public policy in the employment context. Thus, employers frequently cannot enforce exculpatory clauses in contracts with employees or independent contractors (see Chapter 20) to avoid liability for work-related injuries.[27]

Although courts view exculpatory clauses with disfavor, they do enforce such clauses when they do not contravene public policy, are not ambiguous, and do not claim to protect parties from liability for intentional misconduct. Businesses such as health clubs, racetracks, amusement parks, skiing facilities, horse-rental operations, golf-cart concessions, and skydiving organizations frequently use exculpatory clauses to limit their liability for patrons' injuries.

SECTION 7
VOLUNTARY CONSENT

An otherwise valid contract may still be unenforceable if the parties have not genuinely agreed to its terms. As mentioned on page 186, a lack of *voluntary consent* (assent) can be used as a defense to the contract's enforceability.

Voluntary consent may be lacking because of mistakes, fraudulent misrepresentation, undue influence, or duress—in other words, because there is no true "meeting of the minds." Generally, a party who demonstrates that he or she did not truly agree to the terms of a contract can choose either to carry out the contract or to rescind (cancel) it and thus avoid the entire transaction.

---

24. The UCC incorporated the concept of unconscionability in Sections 2–302 and 2A–108. These provisions, which apply to contracts for the sale or lease of goods, will be discussed in Chapter 11.
25. See, for example, *Thibodeau v. Comcast Corp.*, 2006 PA Super. 346, 912 A.2d 874 (2006).
26. See, for example, *Gatton v. T-Mobile USA, Inc.*, 152 Cal.App.4th 571, 61 Cal.Rptr.3d 344 (2007); *Kinkel v. Cingular Wireless, LLC*, 223 Ill.2d 1, 857 N.E.2d 250, 306 Ill.Dec. 157 (2006); and *Aul v. Golden Rule Insurance Co.*, 737 N.W.2d 24 (Wis.App. 2007).
27. See, for example, *Speedway SuperAmerica, LLC v. Erwin*, 250 S.W.3d 339 (2008).

Mistakes

We all make mistakes, so it is not surprising that mistakes are made when contracts are formed. It is important to distinguish between *mistakes of fact* and *mistakes of value or quality.* Only a mistake of fact makes a contract voidable.

MISTAKES OF FACT Mistakes of fact occur in two forms—*bilateral* and *unilateral.* A bilateral, or mutual, mistake is made by both of the contracting parties. A unilateral mistake is made by only *one* of the parties. We look next at these two types of mistakes and illustrate them graphically in Exhibit 9–3 below.

Bilateral (Mutual) Mistakes of Fact.

A bilateral mistake of fact is a "mutual misunderstanding concerning a basic assumption on which the contract was made."[28] When both parties are mistaken about the same material fact, the contract can be rescinded by either party. Normally, the contract is voidable by the adversely affected party. For example, Gilbert contracts to sell Magellan three tracts of undeveloped land for $6 million on the basis of a surveyor's report showing the layout and acreage. After agreeing to the price, the parties discover that the surveyor made an error and that the tracts actually contain 10 percent more acreage than reported. In this situation, Gilbert can seek rescission (cancellation) of the contract based on mutual mistake. The same result—rescission—would occur if both parties had mistakenly believed that the tracts of land were adjoining but they were not.[29]

A word or term in a contract may be subject to more than one reasonable interpretation. If the parties to the contract attach materially different meanings to the term, a court may allow the contract to be rescinded because there has been no true "meeting of the minds."

CASE IN POINT In 1864, Wichelhaus agreed to buy a shipment of Surat cotton from Raffles, "to arrive 'Peerless' from Bombay." There were two ships named *Peerless* sailing from Bombay, India, however. Wichelhaus was referring to the *Peerless* that sailed in October; Raffles meant a different *Peerless* that sailed in December. When Raffles tried to deliver the goods in December, Wichelhaus refused to accept them, and a lawsuit followed. The court held in favor of Wichelhaus, concluding that a mutual mistake had been made because the parties had attached materially different meanings to an essential term of the contract.[30]

Unilateral Mistakes of Fact.

A unilateral mistake occurs when only one of the contracting parties is mistaken about a material fact. Generally, a unilateral mistake does not afford the mistaken party any right to relief from the contract. Normally, the contract is enforceable. For example, DeVinck intends to sell his motor home for $32,500. When he learns that Benson is interested in buying a used motor home, DeVinck faxes Benson an offer to sell the vehicle to him. When typing the fax, however, DeVinck mistakenly keys in the price of $23,500. Benson immediately sends DeVinck a fax accepting

---

28. *Restatement (Second) of Contracts,* Section 152.

29. See, for example, *Rawson v. UMLIC VP, LLC,* 933 So.2d 1206 (Fla.App. 2006).

30. *Raffles v. Wichelhaus,* 159 Eng.Rep. 375 (1864).

EXHIBIT 9-3 • Mistakes of Fact

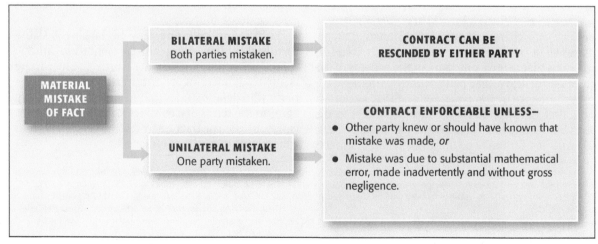

DeVinck's offer. Even though DeVinck intended to sell his motor home for $32,500, his unilateral mistake falls on him. He is bound in contract to sell the motor home to Benson for $23,500.

There are at least two exceptions to this general rule. First, if the *other* party to the contract knows or should have known that a mistake of fact was made, the contract may not be enforceable. In the above example, if Benson knew that DeVinck intended to sell his motor home for $32,500, then DeVinck's unilateral mistake (stating $23,500 in his offer) can render the resulting contract unenforceable.

The second exception arises when a unilateral mistake of fact was due to a mathematical mistake in addition, subtraction, division, or multiplication and was made inadvertently and without gross (extreme) negligence. Of course, in both situations, the mistake must still involve some *material fact*.

MISTAKES OF VALUE If a mistake concerns the future market value or quality of the object of the contract, the mistake is one of *value*, and the contract normally is enforceable. Mistakes of value can be bilateral or unilateral, but either way, they do not serve as a basis for avoiding a contract. For example, Renée buys a violin from Ian for $250. Although the violin is very old, neither party believes that it is particularly valuable. Later, however, an antiques dealer informs the parties that the violin is rare and worth thousands of dollars. Here, both parties were mistaken, but the mistake is a mistake of *value* rather than a mistake of *fact* that would justify contract rescission. This would be true even if, at the time of contracting, only Ian believed that the violin was not particularly valuable (a unilateral mistake) and Renée thought it was rare and worth more than $250.

Fraudulent Misrepresentation

Although fraud is a tort (see Chapter 12), it also affects the authenticity of the innocent party's consent to the contract. When an innocent party is fraudulently induced to enter into a contract, the contract normally can be avoided because that party has not *voluntarily* consented to its terms. Ordinarily, the innocent party can either rescind the contract and be restored to her or his original position or enforce the contract and seek damages for any harms resulting from the fraud.

Generally, fraudulent misrepresentation refers only to misrepresentation that is consciously false and is intended to mislead another. The person making the fraudulent misrepresentation knows or believes that the assertion is false or knows that she

or he does not have a basis (stated or implied) for the assertion. Typically, fraudulent misrepresentation consists of the following elements:

1. A misrepresentation of a material fact must occur.
2. There must be an intent to deceive.
3. The innocent party must justifiably rely on the misrepresentation.

Additionally, to collect damages, a party must have been harmed as a result of the misrepresentation.

The misrepresentation can occur by words or actions, but it must be of a material fact. For example, the statement "This sculpture was created by Michelangelo" is a misrepresentation of fact if another artist sculpted the statue. Misrepresentation also arises when a party takes specific action to conceal a fact that is material to the contract. Therefore, if a seller, by her or his actions, prevents a buyer from learning of some fact that is material to the contract, such behavior constitutes misrepresentation by conduct.

CASE IN POINT Actor Tom Selleck contracted to purchase a horse named Zorro for his daughter from Dolores Cuenca. Cuenca acted as though Zorro was fit to ride in competitions, when in reality the horse suffered from a medical condition. Selleck filed a lawsuit against Cuenca for wrongfully concealing the horse's condition and won. In 2009, a jury awarded Selleck more than $187,000 for Cuenca's misrepresentation by conduct.[31]

Undue Influence

Undue influence arises from special kinds of relationships in which one party can greatly influence another party, thus overcoming that party's free will. A contract entered into under excessive or undue influence lacks voluntary consent and is therefore voidable. Minors and elderly people, for example, are often under the influence of guardians (persons who are legally responsible for another). If a guardian induces a young or elderly ward (a person whom the guardian looks after) to enter into a contract that benefits the guardian, the guardian may have exerted undue influence. Undue influence can arise from a number of fiduciary relationships, such as physician-patient, parent-child, husband-wife, or guardian-ward.

The essential feature of undue influence is that the party being taken advantage of does not, in reality,

---

31. *Selleck v. Cuenca*, Case No. GIN056909, North County of San Diego, California, decided September 9, 2009.

exercise free will in entering into a contract. It is not enough that a person is elderly or suffers from some physical or mental impairment. There must be clear and convincing evidence that the person did not act out of her or his free will. Nonetheless, when a contract enriches the dominant party in a fiduciary relationship, a court will often *presume* that the contract was made under undue influence.

Duress

Agreement to the terms of a contract is not voluntary if one of the parties is *forced* into the agreement. The use of threats to force a party to enter into a contract is referred to as *duress*. In addition, blackmail or extortion to induce consent to a contract constitutes duress. Duress is both a defense to the enforcement of a contract and a ground for the rescission of a contract.

To establish duress, there must be proof of a threat to do something that the threatening party has no right to do. Generally, for duress to occur, the threatened act must be wrongful or illegal and it must render the person incapable of exercising free will. A threat to exercise a legal right, such as the right to sue someone, ordinarily does not constitute duress.

SECTION 8
FORM—
THE STATUTE OF FRAUDS

Another defense to the enforceability of a contract is *form*—that is, some contracts need to be in writing. Every state has a statute, modeled after an old English act, that stipulates what types of contracts must be in writing. Although the statutes vary slightly from state to state, all states require certain types of contracts to be in writing or evidenced by a written (or electronic) memorandum signed by the party against whom enforcement is sought, unless certain exceptions apply. In this text, we refer to these statutes collectively as the **Statute of Frauds.**

The actual name of the Statute of Frauds is misleading because it neither applies to fraud nor invalidates any type of contract. Rather, it denies *enforceability* to certain contracts that do not comply with its requirements. (Note that in some states, an oral contract that would otherwise be unenforceable under the Statute of Frauds may be enforced under the doctrine of promissory estoppel.)

The following types of contracts are said to fall "within" or "under" the Statute of Frauds and therefore require a writing:

1. Contracts involving interests in land.
2. Contracts that cannot by their terms be performed within one year from the day after the date of formation.
3. Collateral, or secondary, contracts, such as promises to answer for the debt or duty of another and promises by the administrator or executor of an estate to pay a debt of the estate personally—that is, out of his or her own pocket.
4. Promises made in consideration of marriage.
5. Under the UCC, contracts for the sale of goods priced at $500 or more.

SECTION 9
THIRD PARTY RIGHTS

Once it has been determined that a valid and legally enforceable contract exists, attention can turn to the rights and duties of the parties to the contract. A contract is a private agreement between the parties who have entered into it, and traditionally these parties alone have rights and liabilities under the contract. This principle is referred to as *privity of contract*. A *third party*—one who is not a direct party to a particular contract—normally does not have rights under that contract.

There are exceptions to the rule of privity of contract. One exception allows a party to a contract to transfer the rights or duties arising from the contract to another person through an *assignment* (of rights) or a *delegation* (of duties). The other exception involves a *third party beneficiary contract*—a contract in which the parties to the contract intend that the contract benefit a third party.

Assignments

In a bilateral contract, the two parties have corresponding rights and duties. One party has a *right* to require the other to perform some task, and the other has a *duty* to perform it. The transfer of contractual *rights* to a third party is known as an **assignment.** Assignments are important because they are involved in many types of business financing.

When rights under a contract are assigned unconditionally, the rights of the *assignor*[32] (the party making the assignment) are extinguished. The third party (the *assignee,*[33] or party receiving the assignment) has a right to demand performance from the other

---

32. Pronounced uh-*sye*-nore.
33. Pronounced uh-*sye*-nee.

original party to the contract. The assignee takes only those rights that the assignor originally had.

As a general rule, all rights can be assigned. Exceptions are made, however, in some circumstances. If a statute expressly prohibits assignment of a particular right, that right cannot be assigned. When a contract is *personal* in nature (such as a contract to be a tutor for a person's children), the rights under the contract cannot be assigned—unless all that remains is a cash payment. A right cannot be assigned if assignment will materially increase or alter the risk or duties of the obligor (the other original party owing performance under the contract). If a contract stipulates that a right cannot be assigned, then *ordinarily* the right cannot be assigned.

There are several exceptions to the rule that a contract can, by its terms, prohibit any assignment of the contract. These exceptions are as follows:

1. A contract cannot prevent an assignment of the right to receive money. This exception exists to encourage the free flow of money and credit in modern business settings.
2. The assignment of rights in real estate often cannot be prohibited, because such a prohibition is contrary to public policy. Prohibitions of this kind are called restraints on *alienation* (transfer of land ownership).
3. The assignment of *negotiable instruments* (which include checks and promissory notes) cannot be prohibited.
4. In a contract for the sale of goods, the right to receive damages for breach of contract or for payment of an account owed may be assigned even though the sales contract prohibits such assignment.

Delegations

Just as a party can transfer rights through an assignment, a party can also transfer duties. The transfer of contractual *duties* to a third party is known as a **delegation.** Normally, a delegation of duties does not relieve the party making the delegation (the *delegator*) of the obligation to perform in the event that the party to whom the duty has been delegated (the *delegatee*) fails to perform. No special form is required to create a valid delegation of duties. As long as the delegator expresses an intention to make the delegation, it is effective; the delegator need not even use the word *delegate*.

As a general rule, any duty can be delegated. Delegation is prohibited, however, in the following circumstances:

1. When special trust has been placed in the obligor.

2. When performance depends on the personal skill or talents of the *obligor* (the person contractually obligated to perform).
3. When performance by a third party will vary materially from that expected by the obligee (the one to whom performance is owed) under the contract.
4. When the contract expressly prohibits delegation.

If a delegation of duties is enforceable, the *obligee* (the one to whom performance is owed) must accept performance from the *delegatee* (the one to whom the duties have been delegated). The obligee can legally refuse performance from the delegatee only if the duty is one that cannot be delegated.

A valid delegation of duties does not relieve the delegator of obligations under the contract. Thus, if the delegatee fails to perform, the delegator is still liable to the obligee.

Third Party Beneficiaries

Another exception to the doctrine of privity of contract exists when the original parties to the contract intend at the time of contracting that the contract performance directly benefit a third person. In this situation, the third person becomes a **third party beneficiary** of the contract. As an **intended beneficiary** of the contract, the third party has legal rights and can sue the promisor directly for breach of the contract.

CASE IN POINT The classic case that gave third party beneficiaries the right to bring a suit directly against a promisor was decided in 1859. The case involved three parties—Holly, Lawrence, and Fox. Holly had borrowed $300 from Lawrence. Shortly thereafter, Holly loaned $300 to Fox, who in return promised Holly that he would pay Holly's debt to Lawrence on the following day. When Lawrence failed to obtain the $300 from Fox, he sued Fox to recover the funds. The court had to decide whether Lawrence could sue Fox directly (rather than suing Holly). The court held that when "a promise [is] made for the benefit of another, he for whose benefit it is made may bring an action for its breach."[34]

The benefit that an **incidental beneficiary** receives from a contract between two parties is unintentional. Because the benefit is *unintentional*, an incidental beneficiary cannot sue to enforce the contract.

---

34. *Lawrence v. Fox*, 20 N.Y. 268 (1859).

REVIEWING
Contract Formation

Mitsui Bank hired Ross Duncan as a branch manager in one of its Southern California locations. At that time, Duncan received an employee handbook informing him that Mitsui would review his performance and salary level annually. In 2008, Mitsui decided to create a new lending program to help financially troubled businesses stay afloat. Duncan was appointed to be the credit development officer (CDO) for the new program and was given a written compensation plan. According to the plan, his compensation would be based on the program's success and would include bonuses and commissions based on the volume of loans and sales. The written plan also stated, "This compensation plan will be reviewed and potentially amended after one year and will be subject to such review and amendment annually thereafter." Duncan's efforts as CDO were successful, and the business-lending program he developed grew to represent 25 percent of Mitsui's business in 2009 and 40 percent in 2010. Nevertheless, Mitsui refused to give Duncan a raise in 2009. In fact, Mitsui amended his compensation plan to reduce his compensation significantly and to change his performance evaluation schedule to every six months. When he had still not received a raise by 2011, Duncan resigned as CDO and filed a lawsuit alleging breach of contract. Using the information presented in the chapter, answer the following questions.

1. What are the four requirements of a valid contract?
2. Did Duncan have a valid contract with Mitsui for employment as CDO? If so, was it a bilateral or a unilateral contract?
3. What are the requirements of an implied contract?
4. Can Duncan establish an implied contract based on the employment manual or the written compensation plan? Why or why not?

DEBATE THIS: *Companies should be able to make or break employment contracts whenever and however they wish.*

TERMS AND CONCEPTS

acceptance 197
adhesion contract 205
agreement 190
assignment 208
bilateral contract 186
consideration 199
contract 185

contractual capacity 201
counteroffer 196
covenant not to compete 203
delegation 209
exculpatory clause 205
executed contract 189
executory contract 189
express contract 188
implied contract 188

incidental beneficiary 209
intended beneficiary 209
mailbox rule 198
mirror image rule 196
objective theory of
  contracts 185
offer 190
option contract 196
past consideration 200

promise 184
promissory estoppel 200
rescission 200
revocation 195
Statute of Frauds 208
third party beneficiary 209
unconscionable 205
unilateral contract 186
voluntary consent 205

QUESTIONS AND CASE PROBLEMS

9–1. Express versus Implied Contracts Everett McCleskey, a local businessperson, is a good friend of Al Miller, the owner of a local candy store. Every day on his lunch hour, McCleskey goes into Miller's candy store and stays about five minutes. After looking at the candy and talking with Miller,

McCleskey usually buys one or two candy bars. One afternoon, McCleskey goes into Miller's candy shop, looks at the candy, and picks up a $1 candy bar. Seeing that Miller is very busy, he waves the candy bar at Miller without saying a word and walks out. Is there a contract? If so, classify it within the categories presented in this chapter.

9–2. QUESTION WITH SAMPLE ANSWER: Implied Contract.

 Janine was hospitalized with severe abdominal pain and placed in an intensive care unit. Her doctor told the hospital personnel to order around-the-clock nursing care for Janine. At the hospital's request, a nursing services firm, Nursing Services Unlimited, provided two weeks of in-hospital care and, after Janine was sent home, an additional two weeks of at-home care. During the at-home period of care, Janine was fully aware that she was receiving the benefit of the nursing services. Nursing Services later billed Janine $4,000 for the nursing care, but Janine refused to pay on the ground that she had never contracted for the services, either orally or in writing. In view of the fact that no express contract was ever formed, can Nursing Services recover the $4,000 from Janine? If so, under what legal theory? Discuss.

- **For a sample answer to Question 9–2, go to Appendix F at the end of this text.**

9–3. Agreement Ball writes to Sullivan and inquires how much Sullivan is asking for a specific forty-acre tract of land Sullivan owns. In a letter received by Ball, Sullivan states, "I will not take less than $60,000 for the forty-acre tract as specified." Ball immediately sends Sullivan a fax stating, "I accept your offer for $60,000 for the forty-acre tract as specified." Discuss whether Ball can hold Sullivan to a contract for the sale of the land.

9–4. Types of Contracts Burger Baby restaurants engaged Air Advertising to fly an advertisement above the Connecticut beaches. The advertisement offered $1,000 to any person who could swim from the Connecticut beaches to Long Island in less than a day. At 10:00 A.M. on October 10, Air Advertising's pilot flew a sign above the Connecticut beaches that read: "Swim across the Sound and Burger Baby pays $1,000." On seeing the sign, Davison dived in. About four hours later, when he was about halfway across the Sound, Air Advertising flew another sign over the Sound that read: "Burger Baby revokes." Davison completed the swim in another six hours. Is there a contract between Davison and Burger Baby? Can Davison recover anything? Why or why not?

9–5. Acceptance Evelyn Kowalchuk, an eighty-eight-year-old widow, and her son, Peter, put their savings into accounts managed by Matthew Stroup. Later, they initiated an arbitration proceeding before the National Association of Securities Dealers (NASD), asserting that Stroup fraudulently or negligently handled their accounts. They asked for an award of $832,000. After the hearing, but before a decision was rendered, Stroup offered to pay the Kowalchuks $285,000, and they e-mailed their acceptance. Stroup signed a settlement agreement and faxed it to the Kowalchuks for their signatures. Meanwhile, the NASD issued an award in the Kowalchuks' favor for $88,788. Stroup immediately told them that he was withdrawing his settlement "offer." When Stroup did not pay according to its terms, the Kowalchuks filed a suit in a New York state court against him for breach of contract. Did these parties have a contract? Why or why not? [*Kowalchuk v. Stroup*, 873 N.Y.S.2d 43 (N.Y.A.D. 1 Dept. 2009)]

9–6. CASE PROBLEM WITH SAMPLE ANSWER: Fraudulent Misrepresentation.

 Ricky and Sherry Wilcox hired Esprit Log and Timber Frame Homes to build a log house, which the Wilcoxes intended to sell. They paid Esprit $125,260 for materials and services. They eventually sold the home for $1,620,000 but sued Esprit due to construction delays. The logs were supposed to arrive at the construction site precut and predrilled, but that did not happen. So it took five extra months to build the house while the logs were cut and drilled one by one. The Wilcoxes claimed that the interest they paid on a loan for the extra construction time cost them about $200,000. The jury agreed and awarded them that much in damages, plus $250,000 in punitive damages and $20,000 in attorneys' fees. Esprit appealed, claiming that the evidence did not support the verdict because the Wilcoxes had sold the house for a good price. Is Esprit's argument credible? Why or why not? How should the court rule? [Esprit Log and Timber Frame Homes, Inc. v. Wilcox, 302 Ga.App. 550, 691 S.E.2d 344 (2010)]

- **To view a sample answer for Problem 9–6, go to this book's Web site at www.cengage.com/blaw/cross, select "Chapter 9," and click on "Case Problem with Sample Answer."**

9–7. Third Party Rights Bruce Albea Contracting, Inc., was the general contractor on a state highway project. Albea and the companies that agreed to guarantee the financial liabilities involved here (called sureties) agreed to be liable for all work on the project. Albea subcontracted with APAC-Southeast, Inc., an asphalt company. The contract stated that it could not be assigned without Albea's consent. Later, Albea and APAC got into a dispute because APAC wanted to be paid more for its asphalt. APAC then sold and assigned its assets, including the contract, to Matthews Contracting Company. Albea was informed of the assignment and did not approve it but allowed Matthews to work. Matthews demanded higher payments for asphalt, and Albea agreed because no other contractor would step in at the original price. Albea suffered a loss on the job and could not pay its bills, so Albea's sureties paid Matthews $2.7 million for work performed. APAC sued Albea and its sureties for $1.2 million for work it had performed before the contract was delegated to Matthews. The trial court granted APAC $1.2 million. On appeal, the defendants argued that APAC had breached the contract by assignment without consent. Did APAC breach the contract with Albea? Did Albea owe APAC anything? Explain your answers. [*Western Surety Co. v. APAC-Southeast, Inc.*, 302 Ga.App. 654, 691 S.E.2d 234 (2010)]

9–8. Offer and Acceptance In 1996, Troy Blackford was gambling at Prairie Meadows Casino when he destroyed a slot machine. After pleading guilty to criminal mischief, Blackford was banned from the casino. In 1998, Blackford was found in the casino, escorted out, and charged with trespass. In 2006, he gambled at the casino again and won $9,387. When Blackford went to collect his winnings, casino employees learned who he was and refused to pay. He sued for breach of contract, contending that he and the casino had an enforceable contract because he had accepted its offer to gamble. The casino argued that it had not made an offer and in fact had banned Blackford from the premises. The trial court held in favor of the casino. The appellate court reversed and ordered a new trial. The casino appealed to the Iowa high court for review. Did the casino make a valid offer to Blackford to gamble and thus create an enforceable contract between them? Explain your answer. [*Blackford v. Prairie Meadows Racetrack and Casino*, 778 N.W.2d 184 (Sup.Ct. Iowa 2010)]

9–9. A QUESTION OF ETHICS: Covenants Not to Compete.

 Retina Consultants, P.C., is a medical practice that specializes in retina eye surgery. This company hired Brendan Coleman as a software engineer in 2000. Prior to his hiring at Retina Consultants, Coleman had created and marketed a software billing program called Clinex. During his stay with Retina Consultants, physicians worked with Coleman to modify his Clinex program to better suit the company's needs. The new program was called Clinex-RE. While employed, Coleman signed an agreement stating that ownership of Clinex remained with Coleman while that of Clinex-RE remained with Retina Consultants. Within the document was the following sentence: "Coleman will not distribute, vend or license to any ophthalmologist or optometrist the Clinex software or any computer application competitive with the Clinex-RE software without the written consent of Retina Consultants." In essence, Coleman agreed to a covenant not to compete (noncompete clause). After quitting his job with Retina Consultants, Coleman attempted to license Clinex and Clinex-RE to other ophthalmologists. He also refused to provide the necessary passwords for Retina Consultants to use Clinex and Clinex-RE. Furthermore, he used the company's

trade secrets and withdrew funds from a company banking account, among other actions. At trial, the court entered a judgment enjoining Coleman from marketing the software that was in competition with the software he had developed for Retina Consultants. The court also obligated Coleman to return the funds taken from the company's bank account. Coleman appealed. [*Coleman v. Retina Consultants, P.C., 286 Ga. 317, 687 S.E.2d 457 (2009)*]

(a) Should the court uphold the noncompete clause? If so, why? If not, why not?

(b) Should the court require Coleman to return the funds he withdrew from the company's accounts? Discuss fully.

(c) Did Coleman's behavior after he left the company influence the court's decision? Explain your answer.

9–10. VIDEO QUESTION: Agreements.

 Go to this text's Web site at **www.cengage.com/ blaw/cross** and select "Chapter 9." Click on "Video Questions" and view the video titled *Real World Legal: Jack's Restaurant, Scene 2.* Then answer the following questions.

(a) In regard to the sale of Jack's Restaurant, Jack (the seller) says that he is going to retain the rights to the restaurant's frozen food line. The buyers, however, thought that their sales agreement included the rights to all of the restaurant's signature dishes—whether fresh or frozen. Did the parties have an "agreement to agree" on the terms of the sale of the restaurant? Why or why not?

(b) Suppose that Jack previously offered to sell the restaurant to these particular buyers and they had all agreed on the price and date for delivery. Would such an offer meet the definiteness requirement, even if no terms pertained to the frozen food line? Explain.

(c) Does Jack's statement that he intended to retain his rights to the frozen food line revoke any earlier offer he may have made to sell the restaurant to these individuals? Why or why not?

(d) Did the buyers unequivocally accept the terms of the offer that Jack expressed in this scene? Explain.

LEGAL RESEARCH EXERCISES ON THE WEB

Go to this text's Web site at **www.cengage.com/blaw/cross**, select "Chapter 9," and click on "Practical Internet Exercises." There you will find the following Internet research exercises that you can perform to learn more about the topics covered in this chapter.

Practical Internet Exercise 9–1: **Legal Perspective**
Contract Terms

Practical Internet Exercise 9–2: **Management Perspective**
Covenants Not to Compete

Practical Internet Exercise 9–3: **Management Perspective**
Offers and Advertisements

CHAPTER 10

Contract Performance, Breach, and Remedies

J ust as rules are necessary to determine when a legally enforceable contract exists, so also are they required to determine when one of the parties can justifiably say, "I have fully performed, so I am now discharged from my obligations under this contract." The legal environment of business requires the identification of some point at which the parties can reasonably know that their duties have ended.

The most common way to **discharge**, or terminate, one's contractual duties is by the **performance** of those duties. For example, a buyer and seller enter into an agreement via e-mail for the sale of a 2011 Lexus for $39,000. This contract will be discharged by performance when the buyer pays $39,000 to the seller and the seller transfers possession of the Lexus to the buyer.

The duty to perform under any contract may be *conditioned* on the occurrence or nonoccurrence of a certain event, or the duty may be *absolute*. In the first part of this chapter, we look at conditions of performance and the degree of performance required to discharge a contract. We also examine some other ways in which a contract can be discharged. In the latter part of this chapter, we look at the remedies available to parties after a contract has been breached.

SECTION 1
DISCHARGE BY PERFORMANCE

The great majority of contracts are discharged by performance. The contract comes to an end when both parties fulfill their respective duties by performing the acts they have promised. Performance can also be accomplished by *tender*. **Tender** is an unconditional offer to perform by a person who is ready, willing, and able to do so. Therefore, a seller who places goods at the disposal of a buyer has tendered delivery and can demand payment. A buyer who offers to pay for goods has tendered payment and can demand delivery of the goods. Once performance has been tendered, the party making the tender has done everything possible to carry out the terms of the contract. If the other party then refuses to perform, the party making the tender can sue for breach of contract.

Conditions

In most contracts, promises of performance are not expressly conditioned or qualified. Instead, they are *absolute promises*. They must be performed, or the parties promising the acts will be in breach of contract. For example, Jerome contracts to sell Alfonso a painting for $10,000. The parties' promises—Jerome's transfer of the painting to Alfonso and Alfonso's payment of $10,000 to Jerome—are unconditional. The payment does not have to be made if the painting is not transferred.

In some situations, however, performance is contingent on the occurrence or nonoccurrence of a certain event. A **condition** is a possible future event, the occurrence or nonoccurrence of which will trigger the performance of a legal obligation or terminate an existing obligation under a contract.[1]

---

1. *The Restatement (Second) of Contracts,* Section 224, defines a *condition* as "an event, not certain to occur, which must occur, unless its nonoccurrence is excused, before performance under a contract becomes due."

If this condition is not satisfied, the obligations of the parties are discharged. Suppose that Alfonso, in the previous example, offers to purchase Jerome's painting only if an independent appraisal indicates that it is worth at least $10,000. Jerome accepts Alfonso's offer. Their obligations (promises) are conditioned on the outcome of the appraisal. Should the condition not be satisfied (for example, if the appraiser deems the value of the painting to be only $5,000), the parties' obligations to each other are discharged and cannot be enforced.

CASE IN POINT Alejandro Alvarado's automobile insurance policy stated that, if involved in an accident, the insured must cooperate with the insurance company in the defense of any claim or lawsuit. When Alvarado was involved in an accident, he notified the insurance company that a negligence lawsuit had been filed against him, but then failed to cooperate in his defense and did not appear in court for the trial. The court entered a judgment against him, which prejudiced the rights of the insurance company. In this situation, a Texas appellate court found that the cooperation clause was a condition to coverage under the policy. Because Alvarado did not cooperate with the insurer, the accident was not covered under the policy, and the company was not liable for the damages awarded.[2]

Types of Performance

There are two basic types of performance—*complete performance* and *substantial performance*. A contract may stipulate that performance must meet the personal satisfaction of either the contracting party or a third party. Such a provision must be considered in determining whether the performance rendered satisfies the contract.

COMPLETE PERFORMANCE When a party performs exactly as agreed, there is no question as to whether the contract has been performed. When a party's performance is perfect, it is said to be complete.

Normally, conditions expressly stated in a contract must be fully satisfied for complete performance to take place. For example, most construction contracts require the builder to meet certain specifications. If the specifications are conditions,

complete performance is required to avoid material breach (*material breach* will be discussed shortly). If the conditions are met, the other party to the contract must then fulfill her or his obligation to pay the builder. If the specifications are not conditions and if the builder, without the other party's permission, fails to comply with the specifications, performance is not complete. What effect does such a failure have on the other party's obligation to pay? The answer is part of the doctrine of substantial performance.

SUBSTANTIAL PERFORMANCE A party who in good faith performs substantially all of the terms of a contract can enforce the contract against the other party under the doctrine of substantial performance. Note that good faith is required. Intentional failure to comply with the terms is a breach of the contract.

Confers Most of the Benefits Promised. Generally, to qualify as substantial, the performance must not vary greatly from the performance promised in the contract, and it must create substantially the same benefits as those promised in the contract. If the omission, variance, or defect in performance is unimportant and can easily be compensated for by awarding damages, a court is likely to hold that the contract has been substantially performed.

Courts decide whether the performance was substantial on a case-by-case basis, examining all of the facts of the particular situation. For example, in a construction contract, a court would look at the intended purpose of the structure and the expense required to bring the structure into complete compliance with the contract. Thus, the exact point at which performance is considered substantial varies.

Entitles the Other Party to Damages. Because substantial performance is not perfect, the other party is entitled to damages to compensate for the failure to comply with the contract. The measure of the damages is the cost to bring the object of the contract into compliance with its terms, if that cost is reasonable under the circumstances. If the cost is unreasonable, the measure of damages is the difference in value between the performance that was rendered and the performance that would have been rendered if the contract had been performed completely.

The following classic case emphasizes that there is no exact formula for deciding when a contract has been substantially performed.

---

2. *Progressive County Mutual Insurance Co. v. Trevino*, 202 S.W.3d 811 (Tex.App.—San Antonio 2006).

☀ EXTENDED CASE 10.1 ☀
Jacob & Youngs v. Kent

Court of Appeals of New York, 230 N.Y. 239, 129 N.E. 889 (1921).

IN THE LANGUAGE OF THE COURT

CARDOZO, J. [Judge]

The plaintiff built a country residence for the defendant at a cost of upwards of $77,000, and now sues to recover a balance of $3,483.46, remaining unpaid. The work of construction ceased in June, 1914, and the defendant then began to occupy the dwelling. There was no complaint of defective performance until March, 1915. One of the specifications for the plumbing work provides that—

> All wrought-iron pipe must be well galvanized, lap welded pipe of the grade known as "standard pipe" of Reading manufacture.

The defendant learned in March, 1915, that some of the pipe, instead of being made in Reading, was the product of other factories. The plaintiff was accordingly directed by the architect to do the work anew. The plumbing was then encased within the walls except in a few places where it had to be exposed. Obedience to the order meant more than the substitution of other pipe. It meant the demolition at great expense of substantial parts of the completed structure. The plaintiff left the work untouched, and asked for a certificate that the final payment was due. Refusal of the certificate was followed by this suit [in a New York state court].

The evidence sustains a finding that the omission of the prescribed brand of pipe was neither fraudulent nor willful. It was the result of the oversight and inattention of the plaintiff's subcontractor. Reading pipe is distinguished from Cohoes pipe and other brands only by the name of the manufacturer stamped

upon it at intervals of between six and seven feet. Even the defendant's architect, though he inspected the pipe upon arrival, failed to notice the discrepancy. The plaintiff tried to show that the brands installed, though made by other manufacturers, were the same in quality, in appearance, in market value, and in cost as the brand stated in the contract—that they were, indeed, the same thing, though manufactured in another place. The evidence was excluded, and a verdict directed for the defendant. The [state intermediate appellate court] reversed, and granted a new trial.

We think the evidence, if admitted, would have supplied some basis for the inference that the defect was insignificant in its relation to the project. The courts never say that one who makes a contract fills the measure of his duty by less than full performance. They do say, however, that *an omission, both trivial and innocent, will sometimes be atoned for by allowance of the resulting damage, and will not always be the breach of a condition* * * * . [Emphasis added.]

* * * Where the line is to be drawn between the important and the trivial cannot be settled by a formula. In the nature of the case precise boundaries are impossible. The same omission may take on one aspect or another according to its setting. Substitution of equivalents may not have the same significance in fields of art on the one side and in those of mere utility on the other. Nowhere will change be tolerated, however, if it is so dominant or pervasive as in any real or substantial measure to frustrate the purpose of the contract. There is no general license to install whatever, in the builder's judgment, may be regarded as "just as good." The question is

one of degree, to be answered, if there is doubt, by the triers of the facts, and, if the inferences are certain, by the judges of the law. *We must weigh the purpose to be served, the desire to be gratified, the excuse for deviation from the letter, the cruelty of enforced adherence. Then only can we tell whether literal fulfillment is to be implied by law as a condition.* [Emphasis added.]

In the circumstances of this case, we think the measure of the allowance is not the cost of replacement, which would be great, but the difference in value, which would be either nominal or nothing. Some of the exposed sections might perhaps have been replaced at moderate expense. The defendant did not limit his demand to them, but treated the plumbing as a unit to be corrected from cellar to roof. In point of fact, the plaintiff never reached the stage at which evidence of the extent of the allowance became necessary. The trial court had excluded evidence that the defect was unsubstantial, and in view of that ruling there was no occasion for the plaintiff to go further with an offer of proof. We think, however, that the offer, if it had been made, would not of necessity have been defective because directed to difference in value. It is true that in most cases the cost of replacement is the measure. The owner is entitled to the money which will permit him to complete, unless the cost of completion is grossly and unfairly out of proportion to the good to be attained. When that is true, the measure is the difference in value. * * * The rule that gives a remedy in cases of substantial performance with compensation for defects of trivial or inappreciable importance has

EXTENDED CASE CONTINUES ➡

EXTENDED CASE 10.1 CONTINUED ⬇

been developed by the courts as an instrument of justice. The measure

of the allowance must be shaped to the same end.

The order should be affirmed, and judgment absolute directed in

favor of the plaintiff upon the stipulation, with costs in all courts.

 QUESTIONS

1. The New York Court of Appeals found that Jacob & Youngs had substantially performed the contract. To what, if any, remedy was Kent entitled?
2. A requirement of substantial performance is good faith. Did Jacob & Youngs substantially perform all of the terms of the contract in good faith? Why or why not?

IMPACT OF THIS CASE ON TODAY'S LAW • *At the time of the* Jacob & Youngs *case, some courts did not apply the doctrine of substantial performance to disputes involving breaches of contract. This landmark decision contributed to a developing trend toward equity and fairness in those circumstances. Today, an unintentional and trivial deviation from the terms of a contract will not prevent its enforcement but will permit an adjustment in the value of its performance.*

PERFORMANCE TO THE SATISFACTION OF ANOTHER
Contracts often state that completed work must personally satisfy one of the parties or a third person. The question then is whether this satisfaction becomes a condition precedent, requiring actual personal satisfaction or approval for discharge, or whether the performance need only satisfy a *reasonable person* (substantial performance).

When the Contract Is Personal. When the subject matter of the contract is *personal,* a contract to be performed to the satisfaction of one of the parties is conditioned, and performance must actually satisfy that party. For example, contracts for portraits, works of art, and tailoring are considered personal. Therefore, only the personal satisfaction of the party fulfills the condition—unless a court finds that the party is expressing dissatisfaction simply to avoid payment or otherwise is not acting in good faith.

Reasonable Person Standard. Most other contracts need to be performed only to the satisfaction of a reasonable person unless they *expressly state otherwise.* When such contracts require performance to the satisfaction of a third party (for example, "to the satisfaction of Robert Ames, the supervising engineer"), the courts are divided. A majority of courts require the work to be satisfactory to a reasonable person, but some courts hold that the personal satisfaction of the third party designated in the contract (Robert Ames, in this example) must be met. Again, the personal judgment must be made honestly, or the condition will be excused.

Material Breach of Contract

A **breach of contract** is the nonperformance of a contractual duty. The breach is *material* when performance is not at least substantial.[3] If there is a material breach, then the nonbreaching party is excused from the performance of contractual duties and can sue for damages resulting from the breach. If the breach is *minor* (not material), the nonbreaching party's duty to perform can sometimes be suspended until the breach has been remedied, but the duty to perform is not entirely excused. Once the minor breach has been cured, the nonbreaching party must resume performance of the contractual obligations.

Any breach entitles the nonbreaching party to sue for damages, but only a material breach discharges the nonbreaching party from the contract. The policy underlying these rules allows contracts to go forward when minor problems occur but allows them to be terminated if major difficulties arise.

CASE IN POINT Su Yong Kim sold an apartment building in Portland, Oregon. At the time of the sale, the building's plumbing violated the city's housing code. Therefore, a clause in the contract stated that the seller (Kim) would correct the violations within eight months. A year later, Kim still had not made the necessary repairs. The buyers stopped making the payments due under the contract, and the dispute ended up in court. The court found that the seller's failure to make the required repairs was a material breach

---

3. *Restatement (Second) of Contracts,* Section 241.

because it defeated the purpose of the contract. The buyers had purchased the building to lease it to tenants, but instead they were losing tenants and being fined by the city due to the substandard plumbing. Because Kim's breach was material, the buyers did not have to continue to perform their obligation to make payments under the contract.[4]

Anticipatory Repudiation

Before either party to a contract has a duty to perform, one of the parties may refuse to carry out his or her contractual obligations. This is called **anticipatory repudiation** of the contract. When an anticipatory repudiation occurs, it is treated as a material breach of the contract, and the nonbreaching party is permitted to bring an action for damages immediately, even though the scheduled time for performance under the contract may still be in the future. Until the nonbreaching party treats an early repudiation as a breach, however, the repudiating party can retract her or his anticipatory repudiation by proper notice and restore the parties to their original obligations.[5]

An anticipatory repudiation is treated as a present, material breach for two reasons. First, the non-breaching party should not be required to remain ready and willing to perform when the other party has already repudiated the contract. Second, the nonbreaching party should have the opportunity to seek a similar contract elsewhere and may have a duty to do so to minimize his or her loss.[6]

Time for Performance

If no time for performance is stated in the contract, a *reasonable time* is implied.[7] If a specific time is stated, the parties must usually perform by that time. Unless time is expressly stated to be vital, however, a delay in performance will not destroy the performing party's right to payment. When time is expressly stated to be "of the essence" or vital, the parties normally must perform within the stated time period because the time element becomes a condition. Even when the contract states that time is of the essence, a court may find that a party who fails to complain about the other party's delay has waived the breach of the time provision.

━━━━━ SECTION 2 ━━━━━

DISCHARGE BY AGREEMENT

Any contract can be discharged by agreement of the parties. The agreement can be contained in the original contract, or the parties can form a new contract for the express purpose of discharging the original contract.

Discharge by Rescission

As mentioned in Chapter 9, *rescission* is the process by which a contract is canceled or terminated and the parties are returned to the positions they occupied before forming it. For **mutual rescission** to take place, the parties must make another agreement that also satisfies the legal requirements for a contract. There must be an *offer*, an *acceptance*, and *consideration*. Ordinarily, if the parties agree to rescind the original contract, their promises not to perform the acts stipulated in the original contract will be legal consideration for the second contract (the rescission).

Agreements to rescind most executory contracts (in which neither party has performed) are enforceable, even if the agreement is made orally and even if the original agreement was in writing. Under the Uniform Commercial Code (UCC), however, agreements to rescind a contract for the sale of goods, regardless of price, must be in writing (or contained in an electronic record) when the contract requires a written rescission.[8] Agreements to rescind contracts involving transfers of realty also must be evidenced by a writing or other record.

When one party has fully performed, an agreement to cancel the original contract normally will *not* be enforceable unless there is additional consideration. Because the performing party has received no consideration for the promise to call off the original bargain, additional consideration is necessary to support a rescission contract.

Discharge by Novation

A contractual obligation may also be discharged through novation. A **novation** occurs when both of the parties to a contract agree to substitute a third

---

4. *Kim v. Park,* 192 Or.App. 365, 86 P.3d 63 (2004).

5. *Restatement (Second) of Contracts,* Section 253; UCC 2–610, 2–611.

6. The doctrine of anticipatory repudiation first arose in the landmark case of *Hochster v. De La Tour,* 2 Ellis and Blackburn Reports 678 (1853), when an English court recognized the delay and expense inherent in a rule requiring a nonbreaching party to wait until the time of performance before suing on an anticipatory repudiation.

7. See UCC 2–204.

8. UCC 2–209(2), (4).

party for one of the original parties. The requirements of a novation are as follows:

1. A previous valid obligation.
2. An agreement by all parties to a new contract.
3. The extinguishing of the old obligation (discharge of the prior party).
4. A new contract that is valid.

For example, Union Corporation contracts to sell its pharmaceutical division to British Pharmaceuticals, Ltd. Before the transfer is completed, Union, British Pharmaceuticals, and a third company, Otis Chemicals, execute a new agreement to transfer all of British Pharmaceuticals' rights and duties in the transaction to Otis Chemicals. As long as the new contract is supported by consideration, the novation will discharge the original contract (between Union and British Pharmaceuticals) and replace it with the new contract (between Union and Otis Chemicals).

A novation expressly or impliedly revokes and discharges a prior contract. The parties involved may expressly state in the new contract that the old contract is now discharged. If the parties do not expressly discharge the old contract, it will be impliedly discharged if the new contract's terms are inconsistent with the old contract's terms. It is this immediate discharge of the prior contract that distinguishes a novation from both an accord and satisfaction, which will be discussed shortly, and an assignment of all rights, which was discussed in Chapter 9.

Discharge by Settlement Agreement

A compromise, or settlement agreement, that arises out of a genuine dispute over the obligations under an existing contract will be recognized at law. Such an agreement will be substituted as a new contract, and it will either expressly or impliedly revoke and discharge the obligations under any prior contract. In contrast to a novation, a settlement agreement does not involve a third party. Rather, the two original parties to the contract form a different agreement to substitute for the original one.

Discharge by Accord and Satisfaction

An *accord* is a contract to perform some act to satisfy an existing contractual duty that is not yet discharged.[9] A *satisfaction* is the performance of the accord agreement. An accord and its satisfaction discharge the original contractual obligation. For a

contract to be discharged by accord and satisfaction, the parties must agree to accept performance that is different from the performance originally promised.

Once the accord has been made, the original obligation is merely suspended. The obligor (the one owing the obligation) can discharge the obligation by performing either the obligation agreed to in the accord or the original obligation. If the obligor refuses to perform the accord, the obligee (the one to whom performance is owed) can bring an action on the original obligation or seek a decree compelling specific performance on the accord.

For example, Frazer has a judgment against Ling for $8,000. Later, both parties agree that the judgment can be satisfied by Ling's transfer of his automobile to Frazer. This agreement to accept the auto in lieu of $8,000 in cash is the accord. If Ling transfers the car to Frazer, the accord is fully performed, and the debt is discharged. If Ling refuses to transfer the car, the accord is breached. Because the original obligation is merely suspended, Frazer can sue Ling to enforce the original judgment for $8,000 in cash or bring an action for breach of the accord.

SECTION 3
DISCHARGE BY OPERATION OF LAW

Under certain circumstances, contractual duties may be discharged by operation of law. These circumstances include material alteration of the contract, the running of the statute of limitations, bankruptcy, and the impossibility or impracticability of performance.

Alteration of the Contract

To discourage parties from altering written contracts, the law operates to allow an innocent party to be discharged when the other party has materially altered a written contract without consent. For example, a party alters a material term of a contract, such as the stated quantity or price, without the knowledge or consent of the other party. In this situation, the party who was unaware of the alteration can treat the contract as discharged or terminated.

Statutes of Limitations

As mentioned earlier in this text, statutes of limitations restrict the period during which a party can sue on a particular cause of action. After the

---

9. *Restatement (Second) of Contracts,* Section 281.

applicable limitations period has passed, a suit can no longer be brought. For example, the limitations period for bringing suits for breach of oral contracts usually is two to three years; for written or otherwise recorded contracts, four to five years; and for recovery of amounts awarded in judgments, ten to twenty years, depending on state law. Lawsuits for breach of a contract for the sale of goods generally must be brought within four years after the cause of action has accrued.[10] By their original agreement, the parties can reduce this four-year period to not less than one year, but they cannot agree to extend it.

Bankruptcy

A proceeding in bankruptcy attempts to allocate the debtors' assets to the creditors in a fair and equitable fashion. Once the assets have been allocated, the debtor receives a **discharge in bankruptcy.** A discharge in bankruptcy will ordinarily bar enforcement of most of the debtor's contracts by the creditors. Partial payment of a debt *after* discharge in bankruptcy will not revive the debt. (Bankruptcy will be discussed in detail in Chapter 15.)

Impossibility or Impracticability of Performance

After a contract has been made, supervening events (such as a fire) may make performance impossible in an objective sense. This is known as **impossibility of performance** and can discharge a contract.[11] Performance may also become so difficult or costly due to some unforeseen event that a court will consider it commercially unfeasible, or impracticable.

OBJECTIVE IMPOSSIBILITY OF PERFORMANCE *Objective impossibility* ("It can't be done") must be distinguished from *subjective impossibility* ("I'm sorry, I simply can't do it"). For example, subjective impossibility occurs when a party cannot deliver goods on time because of freight car shortages or cannot make payment on time because the bank is closed. In effect, in each of these situations the party is saying, "It is impossible for *me* to perform," not "It is impossible for *anyone* to perform." Accordingly, such excuses do not discharge a contract, and the

nonperforming party is normally held in breach of contract.

Note that to justify nonperformance of the contract, the supervening event must have been unforeseeable at the time of the contract's formation. Parties are supposed to consider foreseeable events, such as floods in a flood zone, at the time of contracting and allocate those risks accordingly through insurance and other means. Three basic types of situations, however, may qualify as grounds for the discharge of contractual obligations based on impossibility of performance:[12]

1. *When one of the parties to a personal contract dies or becomes incapacitated prior to performance.* For example, Fred, a famous dancer, contracts with Ethereal Dancing Guild to play a leading role in its new ballet. Before the ballet can be performed, Fred becomes ill and dies. His personal performance was essential to the completion of the contract. Thus, his death discharges the contract and his estate's liability for his nonperformance.

2. *When the specific subject matter of the contract is destroyed.* For example, A-1 Farm Equipment agrees to sell Gudgel the green tractor on its lot and promises to have it ready for Gudgel to pick up on Saturday. On Friday night, however, a truck veers off the nearby highway and smashes into the tractor, destroying it beyond repair. Because the contract was for this specific tractor, A-1's performance is rendered impossible owing to the accident.

3. *When a change in law renders performance illegal.* For example, a contract to build an apartment building becomes impossible to perform when the zoning laws are changed to prohibit the construction of residential rental property at the planned location. A contract to paint a bridge using lead paint becomes impossible when the government passes new regulations forbidding the use of lead paint on bridges.[13]

TEMPORARY IMPOSSIBILITY An occurrence or event that makes performance temporarily impossible operates to suspend performance until the impossibility ceases. Then, ordinarily, the parties must perform the contract as originally planned. If, however, the lapse of time and the change in circumstances surrounding the contract make it substantially more burdensome for the parties to perform the promised

---

10. Section 2–725 of the UCC contains this four-year limitation period. A cause of action in sales contracts generally accrues when the breach occurs, regardless of the aggrieved party's lack of knowledge of the breach. A breach of warranty normally occurs when the seller delivers the goods to the buyer.

11. *Restatement (Second) of Contracts*, Section 261.

12. *Restatement (Second) of Contracts*, Sections 262–266; UCC 2–615.

13. *M.J. Paquet, Inc. v. New Jersey Department of Transportation*, 171 N.J. 378, 794 A.2d 141 (2002).

INSIGHT INTO ETHICS
When Is Impossibility of Performance a Valid Defense?

The doctrine of impossibility of performance is applied only when the parties could not have reasonably foreseen, at the time the contract was formed, the event or events that rendered performance impossible. In some cases, the courts may seem to go too far in holding that the parties should have foreseen certain events or conditions, thus precluding the parties from avoiding contractual obligations under the doctrine of impossibility of performance.

Actually, courts today are more likely to allow parties to raise this defense than courts in the past, which rarely excused parties from performance under this doctrine. Indeed, until the latter part of the nineteenth century, courts were reluctant to discharge a contract even when performance appeared to be impossible. Generally, the courts must balance the freedom of parties to contract (and thereby assume the risks involved) against the injustice that may result when certain contractual obligations are enforced. If the courts allowed parties to raise impossibility of performance as a defense to contractual obligations more often, freedom of contract would suffer.

CRITICAL THINKING
INSIGHT INTO THE SOCIAL ENVIRONMENT
Why might those entering into contracts be worse off in the long run if the courts increasingly accept impossibility of performance as a defense?

---

acts, the contract is discharged.[14] Sometimes, it can be difficult to predict how a court will—or should—rule in a particular situation, as discussed in this chapter's *Insight into Ethics* feature above.

CASE IN POINT Keefe Hurwitz contracted to sell his home in Madisonville, Louisiana, to Wesley and Gwendolyn Payne for a price of $241,500 on August 22, 2005. Four days later, Hurricane Katrina made landfall and caused extensive damage to the house. When Hurwitz refused to pay the cost of the necessary repairs, estimated at $60,000, the Paynes filed a lawsuit to enforce the contract. Hurwitz claimed that Hurricane Katrina had made it impossible for him to perform and had discharged his duties under the contract. The court, however, ruled that Hurricane Katrina had caused only a temporary impossibility. Hurwitz was required to pay for the necessary repairs and to perform the contract as written. In other words, he could not obtain a higher purchase price to offset the cost of the repairs.[15]

COMMERCIAL IMPRACTICABILITY When a supervening event does not render performance objectively impossible but does make it much more difficult or expensive to perform than the parties originally contemplated, the courts may excuse the parties' obligations under the contract. For someone to invoke the doctrine of **commercial impracticability** successfully, however, the anticipated performance must become *extremely* difficult or costly.[16]

The added burden of performance not only must be extreme but also *must not have been known by the parties when the contract was made*. In one classic case, for example, a court held that a contract could be discharged because a party would otherwise have to pay ten times more than the original estimate to excavate a certain amount of gravel.[17] In another case, the court allowed a party to rescind a contract for the sale of land because of a potential problem with contaminated groundwater under the land. The court found that "the potential for substantial and unbargained-for" liability made contract performance economically impracticable.[18]

In the following case, a contract called for an illegal act, although the parties did not know this at the time the contract was formed. Given that the contract could not be performed legally, could performance be excused on the basis of impossibility of performance or commercial impracticability, or was the contract void from the outset? These were the questions before the court.

---

14. For a leading case involving temporary impossibility, see *Autry v. Republic Productions*, 30 Cal.2d 144, 180 P.2d 888 (1947). An actor's contract became temporarily impossible to perform when he was drafted to serve in World War II. After he returned, his duty to perform was discharged because the value of the dollar had declined, making performance substantially burdensome to him.

15. *Payne v. Hurwitz*, 978 So.2d 1000 (La.App. 1st Cir. 2008).

16. *Restatement (Second) of Contracts*, Section 264.

17. *Mineral Park Land Co. v. Howard*, 172 Cal. 289, 156 P. 458 (1916).

18. *Cape-France Enterprises v. Estate of Peed*, 305 Mont. 513, 29 P.3d 1011 (2001).

CASE 10.2
Merry Homes, Inc. v. Chi Hung Luu
Court of Appeals of Texas, Houston, ___ S.W.3d ___ (2010).
www.morelaw.com/verdicts[a]

BACKGROUND AND FACTS • Chi Hung Luu leased premises in Houston, Texas, from Merry Homes, Inc., with the intention of opening a bar and nightclub on the property. The lease provided that Luu could use the premises only for operating a nightclub or bar and for no other purpose. The lease also prohibited Luu from using the premises for, among other things, "any activity that violated any applicable federal, state, or local law." After he signed the lease, Luu submitted an application for a liquor license to the city of Houston. The city denied the application because a city ordinance prohibited the sale of alcoholic beverages where the premises were located, which was fewer than three hundred feet from a public school. The city suggested that Luu take advantage of the "restaurant exception" to the law, which allowed restaurants in such areas to serve alcoholic beverages. Luu considered the restaurant possibility but decided that it would not be financially feasible. When Merry Homes refused to cancel the lease and refund Luu's $6,000 security deposit, Luu brought an action against Merry Homes in a Texas state court. Luu sought a declaratory judgment that the lease was void because it could not be performed legally. Merry Homes counterclaimed for breach of contract and sought to recover eight months of unpaid rent. The trial court declared the lease void, and Merry Homes appealed.

IN THE LANGUAGE OF THE COURT
Jane *BLAND*, Justice.
* * * *
* * * The Texas Alcoholic Beverages Code authorizes counties and cities to adopt regulations prohibiting the sale of alcohol within 300 feet of a public school. The City of Houston has adopted such a regulation.

Although the lease, on its face, does not require violation of the law, the only permissible use of the premises under the lease's terms is impossible and illegal, given the location of the premises relative to a school. As Luu cannot obtain a liquor license and therefore cannot perform under the lease without violating the statute and ordinance, the trial court properly determined that this lease is void for illegality.

Merry Homes [argues] * * * that Luu unconditionally bound himself to perform under the lease, and thus the City of Houston's refusal to grant a liquor license should not excuse his performance, especially because the City's denial is a contingency that Luu should have anticipated.
* * * *
* * * Merry Homes contends that the trial court's decision to declare the lease void cannot be affirmed on the basis of impossibility of performance. Merry Homes relies on Section 10(c) of the lease, which provides that Luu will satisfy himself that the premises can be used for the intended purposes, and thus is bound to perform. *We first note that Section 261 of the [Restatement (Second) of Contracts] only applies to supervening events [events occurring after the contract's formation] that render performance impracticable, not preexisting conditions and events.* The trial court found that the ordinance prohibiting the sale of alcohol on Luu's premises[,] which renders Luu's performance illegal and impracticable[,] existed before the parties executed the lease, and therefore Section 266 of the *Restatement* applies. [Emphasis added.]

Section 266(1) provides:

Where, at the time a contract is made, a party's performance under it is impracticable without his fault because of [a] fact of which he has no reason to know and the nonexistence of which is a basic assumption on which the contract is made, no duty to render that performance arises, unless the language or circumstances indicate the contrary.

---

a. From the "Select a State" menu, select Texas. From the "Select Field to Search" menu, select "Case Caption." Enter "Merry Homes" in the search box and then click "Go." On the page that opens, click on the link to access the court's opinion. Attorney Kent Morlan of Morlan & Associates, P.C., maintains this Web site.

CASE CONTINUES ➡

CASE 10.2 CONTINUED ➧ * * * Although Section 266 excuses performance as impracticable based upon a preexisting condition "of which [the party] has no reason to know," we previously held that "a contract to do a thing which cannot be performed without a violation of the law is void, *whether the parties knew the law or not.*" (Emphasis added [by the court].) The Texas Supreme Court "has long recognized Texas'[s] strong public policy in favor of preserving the freedom of contract." Freedom of contract, however, is not unlimited: "As a rule, parties have the right to contract as they see fit as long as their agreement does not violate the law or public policy." Merry Homes cannot indirectly receive benefits—monthly rental payments—from what the law says it cannot do directly.

DECISION AND REMEDY • *The Court of Appeals of Texas affirmed the trial court's judgment. The lease was void and unenforceable because it could not be performed without violating the law.*

WHAT IF THE FACTS WERE DIFFERENT? • *Suppose that Luu had decided to use the premises for a restaurant, but the wording of the lease had not changed. In this situation, if Luu sought to cancel the lease, would Merry Homes succeed in a suit for breach of contract? Discuss your answer.*

THE ETHICAL DIMENSION • *"Ignorance of the law is no excuse." How does this case affirm that adage?*

FRUSTRATION OF PURPOSE A theory closely allied with the doctrine of commercial impracticability is the doctrine of **frustration of purpose.** In principle, a contract will be discharged if supervening circumstances make it impossible to attain the purpose both parties had in mind when they made the contract. As with commercial impracticability and impossibility, the supervening event must not have been reasonably foreseeable at the time the contract was formed. In contrast to impracticability, which usually involves an event that increases the cost or difficulty of performance, frustration of purpose typically involves an event that decreases the value of what a party receives under the contract.[19]

See Exhibit 10–1 below for a summary of the ways in which a contract can be discharged.

---

19. See, for example, *East Capitol View Community Development Corp., Inc. v. Robinson,* 941 A.2d 1036 (D.C.App. 2008).

EXHIBIT 10–1 • Contract Discharge

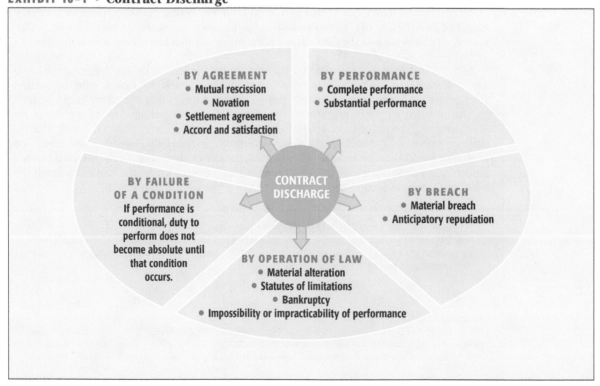

SECTION 4
REMEDIES FOR BREACH OF CONTRACT

When one party breaches a contract, the other party—the nonbreaching party—can choose one or more of several remedies. A *remedy* is the relief provided for an innocent party when the other party has breached the contract. It is the means employed to enforce a right or to redress an injury.

The most common remedies available to a nonbreaching party include damages, rescission and restitution, specific performance, and reformation. As discussed in Chapter 1, a distinction is made between *remedies at law* and *remedies in equity*. Today, the remedy at law normally is monetary damages. Equitable remedies include rescission and restitution, specific performance, and reformation, all of which we will examine. Usually, a court will not award an equitable remedy unless the remedy at law is inadequate. Special legal doctrines and concepts relating to remedies will be discussed in the final pages of this chapter.

Damages

A breach of contract entitles the nonbreaching party to sue for monetary damages. In contract law, damages compensate the nonbreaching party for the loss of the bargain. Often, courts say that innocent parties are to be placed in the position they would have occupied had the contract been fully performed.[20]

Realize at the outset, though, that collecting damages through a court judgment requires litigation, which can be expensive and time consuming. Also keep in mind that court judgments are often difficult to enforce, particularly if the breaching party does not have sufficient assets to pay the damages awarded (as discussed in Chapter 2). For these reasons, most parties settle their lawsuits for damages (or other remedies) prior to trial.

There are four broad categories of damages:

1. Compensatory (to cover direct losses and costs).
2. Consequential (to cover indirect and foreseeable losses).
3. Punitive (to punish and deter wrongdoing).
4. Nominal (to recognize wrongdoing when no monetary loss is shown).

COMPENSATORY DAMAGES Damages that compensate the nonbreaching party for the *loss of the bargain* are known as **compensatory damages.**

These damages compensate the injured party only for damages actually sustained and proved to have arisen directly from the loss of the bargain caused by the breach of contract. They simply replace what was lost because of the wrong or damage and, for this reason, are often said to "make the person whole."

The standard measure of compensatory damages is the difference between the value of the breaching party's promised performance under the contract and the value of her or his actual performance. This amount is reduced by any loss that the injured party has avoided, however.

To illustrate: Wilcox contracts to perform certain services exclusively for Hernandez during the month of March for $4,000. Hernandez cancels the contract and is in breach. Wilcox is able to find another job during the month of March but can earn only $3,000. He can sue Hernandez for breach and recover $1,000 as compensatory damages. Wilcox can also recover from Hernandez the amount that he spent to find the other job. Expenses that are caused directly by a breach of contract—such as those incurred to obtain performance from another source—are known as *incidental damages.*

The measurement of compensatory damages varies by type of contract. Certain types of contracts deserve special mention. They are contracts for the sale of goods, land contracts, and construction contracts.

Sale of Goods. In a contract for the sale of goods, the usual measure of compensatory damages is an amount equal to the difference between the contract price and the market price.[21] For example, Medik Laboratories contracts to buy ten model UTS network servers from Cal Industries for $4,000 each. Cal Industries, however, fails to deliver the ten servers to Medik. The market price of the servers at the time Medik learns of the breach is $4,500. Therefore, Medik's measure of damages is $5,000 (10 × $500), plus any incidental damages (expenses) caused by the breach. When the buyer breaches and the seller has not yet produced the goods, compensatory damages normally equal lost profits on the sale, not the difference between the contract price and the market price.

Sale of Land. Ordinarily, because each parcel of land is unique, the remedy for a seller's breach of a contract for a sale of real estate is specific

---

20. *Restatement (Second) of Contracts*, Section 347.

21. More specifically, the amount is the difference between the contract price and the market price at the time and place at which the goods were to be delivered or tendered. See UCC 2–708, 2–713.

performance—that is, the buyer is awarded the parcel of property for which she or he bargained (*specific performance* will be discussed more fully later in this chapter). When this remedy is unavailable (because the seller has sold the property to someone else, for example) or when the buyer is the party in breach, the measure of damages is typically the difference between the contract price and the market price of the land. The majority of states follow this rule.

A minority of states follow a different rule when the seller breaches the contract and the breach is not deliberate.[22] When the breach was not willful, these states limit the prospective buyer's damages to a refund of any down payment made plus any expenses incurred (such as fees for title searches, attorneys, and escrows). This rule effectively returns purchasers to the positions they occupied prior to the sale, rather than giving them the benefit of the bargain.

Construction Contracts. The measure of damages in a building or construction contract varies depending on which party breaches and when the breach occurs. If the owner breaches *before performance has begun,* the contractor can recover only the profits that would have been made on the contract (that is, the total contract price less the cost of materials and labor). If the owner breaches *during performance,* the contractor can recover the profits plus the costs incurred in partially constructing the building. If the owner breaches *after the construction has been completed,* the contractor can recover the entire contract price, plus interest.

When the construction contractor breaches the contract—either by failing to undertake construction or by stopping work partway through the project—the measure of damages is the cost of completion, which includes reasonable compensation for any delay in performance. If the contractor finishes late, the measure of damages is the loss of use. The rules concerning the measurement of damages in breached construction contracts are summarized in Exhibit 10–2 below.

CONSEQUENTIAL DAMAGES Foreseeable damages that result from a party's breach of contract are called **consequential damages,** or *special damages.* They differ from compensatory damages in that they are caused by special circumstances beyond the contract itself. They flow from the consequences, or results, of a breach.

When a seller fails to deliver goods, knowing that the buyer is planning to use or resell those goods immediately, a court may award consequential damages for the loss of profits from the planned resale. (The buyer will also recover compensatory damages for the difference between the contract price and the market price of the goods.)

PUNITIVE DAMAGES Punitive, or exemplary, damages generally are not recoverable in contract law, even for an intentional breach of contract. Because punitive damages are designed to punish a wrongdoer and set an example to deter similar conduct in the future, they have no legitimate place in contract law. A contract is simply a civil relationship between the parties, so breaching a contract is not a crime; nor does it necessarily harm society (as torts do). Thus, a court will not award punitive damages but will compensate one party for the loss of the bargain—no more and no less.

NOMINAL DAMAGES When no actual damage or financial loss results from a breach of contract and only a technical injury is involved, the court may award **nominal damages** to the innocent party.

---

22. "Deliberate" breaches include the seller's failure to convey (transfer title) the land because the market price has gone up. "Nondeliberate" breaches include the seller's failure to convey the land because of a problem with the title, such as the discovery of an unknown *easement* that gives another a right of use over the property (see Chapter 26).

EXHIBIT 10–2 • Measurement of Damages—Breach of Construction Contracts

PARTY IN BREACH	TIME OF BREACH	MEASUREMENT OF DAMAGES
Owner	Before construction has begun.	Profits (contract price less cost of materials and labor).
Owner	During construction.	Profits, plus costs incurred up to time of breach.
Owner	After construction is completed.	Full contract price, plus interest.
Contractor	Before construction has begun.	Cost in excess of contract price to complete work.
Contractor	Before construction is completed.	Generally, all costs incurred by owner to complete.

Awards of nominal damages are often small, such as one dollar, but they do establish that the defendant acted wrongfully. Most lawsuits for nominal damages are brought as a matter of principle under the theory that a breach has occurred and some damages must be imposed regardless of actual loss.

Assume that Jackson contracts to buy potatoes from Stanley at fifty cents a pound. Stanley breaches the contract and does not deliver the potatoes. In the meantime, the price of potatoes has fallen. Jackson is able to buy them in the open market at half the price he contracted for with Stanley. He is clearly better off because of Stanley's breach. Thus, because Jackson sustained only a technical injury and suffered no monetary loss, he is likely to be awarded only nominal damages if he brings a suit for breach of contract.

Mitigation of Damages

In most situations, when a breach of contract occurs, the innocent injured party is held to a duty to mitigate, or reduce, the damages that he or she suffers. Under this doctrine of **mitigation of damages,** the duty owed depends on the nature of the contract.

For example, some states require a landlord to use reasonable means to find a new tenant if a tenant abandons the premises and fails to pay rent. If an acceptable tenant is found, the landlord is required to lease the premises to this tenant to mitigate the damages recoverable from the former tenant. The former tenant is still liable for the difference between the amount of the rent under the original lease and the rent received from the new tenant. If the landlord has not taken the reasonable steps necessary to find a new tenant, a court will likely reduce any award made by the amount of rent the landlord could have received had such reasonable means been used.

In the majority of states, a person whose employment has been wrongfully terminated owes a duty to mitigate the damages suffered because of the employer's breach of the employment contract. In other words, a wrongfully terminated employee has a duty to take a similar job if one is available. If the employee fails to do this, the damages awarded will be equivalent to the person's salary less the income he or she would have received in a similar job obtained by reasonable means. The employer has the burden of proving that such a job existed and that the employee could have been hired. Normally, the employee is under no duty to take a job of a different type and rank.

Liquidated Damages Provisions

A **liquidated damages** provision in a contract specifies that a certain dollar amount is to be paid in the event of a *future* default or breach of contract. (*Liquidated* means determined, settled, or fixed.) For example, a provision requiring a construction contractor to pay $300 for every day he or she is late in completing the project is a liquidated damages provision.

Liquidated damages provisions are frequently used in construction contracts. They are also common in contracts for the sale of goods.[23] In addition, contracts with entertainers and professional athletes often include liquidated damages provisions. For example, in 2010 a television network settled its contract dispute with *The Tonight Show* host Conan O'Brien for $33 million—somewhat less than the $40 million he would have potentially received in liquidated damages if the dispute had gone to court and he had prevailed.

LIQUIDATED DAMAGES VERSUS PENALTIES Liquidated damages differ from penalties. A **penalty** specifies a certain amount to be paid in the event of a default or breach of contract and is designed to penalize the breaching party. Liquidated damages provisions usually are enforceable. In contrast, if a court finds that a provision calls for a penalty, the agreement as to the amount will not be enforced, and recovery will be limited to actual damages.

ENFORCEABILITY To determine if a particular provision is for liquidated damages or for a penalty, a court asks two questions:
1. When the contract was entered into, was it apparent that damages would be difficult to estimate in the event of a breach?
2. Was the amount set as damages a reasonable estimate and not excessive?

If the answers to both questions are yes, the provision normally will be enforced. If either answer is no, the provision usually will not be enforced.

CASE IN POINT Winthrop Resources Corporation leased nearly $9 million worth of computer equipment to Eaton Hydraulics. When Eaton failed to meet its payment obligations and did not take proper care of the leased equipment, Winthrop filed a lawsuit for breach of the contract. The contract included a liquidated damages provision that valued

---

23. UCC 2–718(1) specifically authorizes the use of liquidated damages provisions.

the computer equipment at more than four times its market value. Eaton challenged the provision, claiming that it called for an unenforceable penalty. According to the court, the amount of actual damages was difficult to ascertain at the time the contract was formed because of the "speculative nature of the value of computers at termination of lease schedules." Therefore, the court ruled that the liquidated damages clause was enforceable and required Eaton to pay nearly $4 million to Winthrop.[24]

Equitable Remedies

Sometimes, damages are an inadequate remedy for a breach of contract so the nonbreaching party asks the court for an equitable remedy. Equitable remedies include rescission and restitution, specific performance, and reformation.

RESCISSION AND RESTITUTION Rescission is essentially an action to undo, or terminate, a contract—to return the contracting parties to the positions they occupied prior to the transaction.[25] When fraud, a mistake, duress, undue influence, misrepresentation, or lack of capacity to contract is present, unilateral rescission is available. Rescission may also be available by statute. The failure of one party to perform entitles the other party to rescind the contract. The rescinding party must give prompt notice to the breaching party.

Generally, to rescind a contract, both parties must make **restitution** to each other by returning goods, property, or funds previously conveyed. If the property or goods can be returned, they must be. If the goods or property have been consumed, restitution must be made in an equivalent dollar amount.

Essentially, restitution involves the plaintiff's recapture of a benefit conferred on the defendant that has unjustly enriched her or him. For example, Katie pays $10,000 to Bob in return for Bob's promise to design a house for her. The next day, Bob calls Katie and tells her that he has taken a position with a large architectural firm in another state and cannot design the house. Katie decides to hire another architect that afternoon. Katie can obtain restitution of the $10,000.

Restitution may be appropriate when a contract is rescinded, but the right to restitution is not limited to rescission cases. For example, restitution might be available when there has been misconduct by a party in a confidential or other special relationship and sometimes even in criminal cases.

SPECIFIC PERFORMANCE The equitable remedy of **specific performance** calls for the performance of the act promised in the contract. This remedy is attractive to a nonbreaching party because it provides the exact bargain promised in the contract. It also avoids some of the problems inherent in a suit for damages, such as collecting a judgment and arranging another contract. In addition, the actual performance may be more valuable than the monetary damages.

Normally, however, specific performance will not be granted unless the party's legal remedy (monetary damages) is inadequate. For this reason, contracts for the sale of goods rarely qualify for specific performance. The legal remedy—monetary damages—is ordinarily adequate in such situations because substantially identical goods can be bought or sold in the market. Only if the goods are unique will a court grant specific performance. For example, paintings, sculptures, or rare books or coins are so unique that monetary damages will not enable a buyer to obtain substantially identical substitutes in the market.

Sale of Land. A court may grant specific performance to a buyer in an action for a breach of contract involving the sale of land. In this situation, the legal remedy of monetary damages may not compensate the buyer adequately because every parcel of land is unique: the same land in the same location obviously cannot be obtained elsewhere. Only when specific performance is unavailable (such as when the seller has sold the property to someone else) will monetary damages be awarded instead.

CASE IN POINT Howard Stainbrook entered into a contract to sell Trent Low forty acres of mostly timbered land for $45,000. Low agreed to pay for a survey of the property and other costs in addition to the price. He gave Stainbrook a check for $1,000 to show his intent to fulfill the contract. One month later, Stainbrook died. His son David became the executor of the estate. After he discovered that the timber on the property was worth more than $100,000, David asked Low to withdraw his offer to buy the forty acres. Low refused and filed a suit against David seeking specific performance of the contract. The court found that because Low had substantially performed his obligations under the contract and

---

24. *Winthrop Resources Corp. v. Eaton Hydraulics, Inc.,* 361 F.3d 465 (8th Cir. 2004).

25. The rescission discussed here is *unilateral* rescission, in which only one party wants to undo the contract. In mutual rescission, both parties agree to undo the contract. Mutual rescission discharges the contract. Unilateral rescission generally is available as a remedy for breach of contract.

offered to perform the rest, he was entitled to specific performance.[26]

Contracts for Personal Services. Personal-service contracts require one party to work personally for another party. Courts generally refuse to grant specific performance of personal-service contracts because to order a party to perform personal services against his or her will amounts to a type of involuntary servitude.[27]

Moreover, the courts do not want to monitor contracts for personal services, which usually require the exercise of personal judgment or talent. For example, if Nicole contracted with a surgeon to perform surgery to remove a tumor on her brain, and he refused, the court would not compel (and she certainly would not want) the surgeon to perform under those circumstances. A court cannot assure meaningful performance in such a situation. If a contract is not deemed personal, the remedy at law of monetary damages may be adequate if substantially identical service (such as lawn mowing) is available from other persons.

REFORMATION **Reformation** is an equitable remedy used when the parties have *imperfectly* expressed their agreement in writing. Reformation allows a court to rewrite the contract to reflect the parties' true intentions.

When Fraud or Mutual Mistake Is Present. Courts order reformation most often when fraud or mutual mistake (for example, a clerical error) is present. Typically, a party seeks reformation so that some other remedy may then be pursued. To illustrate: If Carson contracts to buy a certain parcel of land from Malboa but their contract mistakenly refers to a different parcel of land and not the one being sold, the contract does not reflect the parties' intentions. Accordingly, a court can reform the contract so that it conforms to the parties' intentions and accurately refers to the parcel of land being sold. Carson can then, if necessary, show that Malboa has breached the contract as reformed. She can at that time request an order for specific performance.

In the following case, a court was asked to reform a *deed* (see Chapter 26) eight months after the transaction in which the deed played a principal part.

---

26. *Stainbrook v. Low,* 842 N.E.2d 386 (Ind.App. 2006).
27. Involuntary servitude, or slavery, is contrary to the public policy expressed in the Thirteenth Amendment to the U.S. Constitution. A court can, however, enter an order (injunction) prohibiting a person who breached a personal-service contract from engaging in similar contracts for a period of time in the future.

CASE 10.3
Drake v. Hance
Court of Appeals of North Carolina, 673 S.E.2d 411 (2009).
www.nccourts.org[a]

BACKGROUND AND FACTS • In June 2005, Eric and Debra Hance agreed to buy Garry and Wanda Drake's home in Monroe, North Carolina. The contract described the property as "#15 Legacy Lake." The deed, however, listed "lot 15, Legacy Lake" and "lot 11, Legacy Lake." Lot 15 is the property on which the home sits. Lot 11 is a vacant lot across the street. After the sale, the deed was filed with the appropriate state office. Eight months later, when the Drakes tried to sell lot 11 to a third party, they learned that it had been listed on the Hances' deed. The Drakes told the Hances, who denied that any mistake had been made. Claiming that they had intended to sell only lot 15, the Drakes filed a suit in a North Carolina state court against the Hances. The attorney who closed the sale testified that the deed was drafted improperly. The court reformed it. The Hances appealed.

IN THE LANGUAGE OF THE COURT
CALABRIA, Judge.
* * * *

A deed is a written document that on its face conveys title or an interest in real property. A deed is an integrated document and the parties may not introduce oral or written evidence to contradict its terms.

---

a. In the "Favorites" column, click on "Court Opinions." On that page, in the "Court of Appeals Opinions" section, click on "2009." In the result, scroll to "3 March 2009" and click on the name of the case to access the opinion. The North Carolina Administrative Office of the Courts maintains this Web site.

CASE CONTINUES ➡

However, if a party can show a mutual mistake was made in the execution of a deed, in this case due to the error of the draftsman, parol evidence is competent evidence to show the true intentions of the parties. *If the evidence is strong, cogent, and convincing that the deed, as recorded, did not reflect the agreement between the parties due to a mutual mistake caused by a drafting error, a deed can be reformed.* [Emphasis added.]

In the present case, the closing attorney improperly prepared the deed due to an error in his office. The court found that repeated attempts were made to contact the defendants to correct the error but were unsuccessful. More importantly, the defendants, at that time, did not dispute that an error had been made. The trial court found the closing attorney's testimony "exceptionally persuasive," and we agree.

* * * The evidence of an error by the draftsman was strong, cogent, and convincing. The trial court did not err in reforming the deed based on this evidence.

Competent evidence supports the trial court's findings that the parties contracted for the sale of lot 15 only, and that the attorney erred when drafting the deed that included both lots. The trial court did not err in admitting parol [oral] evidence to determine the intent of the parties, and did not err in reforming the deed when presented evidence of the attorney's mistake.

DECISION AND REMEDY • *The state intermediate appellate court affirmed the lower court's action. The parties had contracted for the sale of only one lot. The deed could be reformed based on the testimony of the party who drafted it.*

THE E-COMMERCE DIMENSION • *Is a mistake such as the one in this case likely to occur when software is used to draft a document? Why or why not?*

THE ETHICAL DIMENSION • *What may have motivated the defendants in this case to assert that there was no mistake in the deed? Discuss.*

Exhibit 10–3 on the facing page graphically summarizes the remedies, including reformation, that are available to the nonbreaching party.

Oral Contracts and Covenants Not to Compete. Courts also frequently reform contracts in two other situations. The first involves two parties who have made a binding oral contract. They further agree to put the oral contract in writing, but in doing so, they make an error in stating the terms. Normally, a court will allow into evidence the correct terms of the oral contract, thereby reforming the written contract.

The second situation occurs when the parties have executed a written covenant not to compete (discussed in Chapter 9 on page 203). If the covenant is for a valid and legitimate purpose (such as the sale of a business) but the area or time restraints of the covenant are unreasonable, some courts will reform the restraints by making them reasonable and will enforce the entire contract as reformed. Other courts, however, will throw out the entire restrictive covenant as illegal.

Election of Remedies

In many cases, a nonbreaching party has several remedies available. When the remedies are inconsistent with one another, the common law of contracts requires the party to choose which remedy to pursue. This is called *election of remedies*.

The purpose of the doctrine of election of remedies is to prevent double recovery. Suppose that McCarthy agrees in writing to sell his land to Tally. Then McCarthy changes his mind and repudiates the contract. Tally can sue for compensatory damages *or* for specific performance. If Tally could seek compensatory damages in addition to specific performance, she would recover twice for the same breach of contract. The doctrine of election of remedies requires Tally to choose the remedy she wants, and it eliminates any possibility of double recovery.

The doctrine has often been applied in a rigid and technical manner, leading to some harsh results. Because of the many problems associated with the doctrine of election of remedies, the UCC expressly rejects it.[28] As will be discussed in Chapter 11, remedies under the UCC are not exclusive but are cumulative in nature and include all the available remedies for breach of contract.

Waiver of Breach

Under certain circumstances, a nonbreaching party may be willing to accept a defective performance of the contract. This knowing relinquishment of a legal

---

28. See UCC 2–703, 2–711.

EXHIBIT 10-3 • Remedies for Breach of Contract

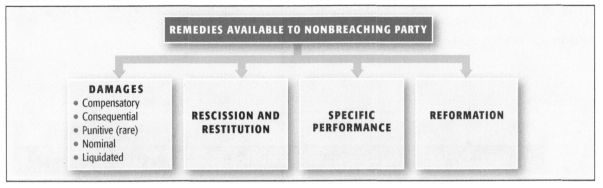

right (that is, the right to require satisfactory and full performance) is called a **waiver.**

CONSEQUENCES OF A WAIVER OF BREACH When a waiver of a breach of contract occurs, the party waiving the breach cannot take any later action on it. In effect, the waiver erases the past breach. The contract continues as if the breach had never occurred. Of course, the waiver of breach of contract extends only to the matter waived and not to the whole contract.

WAIVER OF BREACH AND SUBSEQUENT BREACHES Ordinarily, a waiver by a contracting party will not operate to waive subsequent, additional, or future breaches of contract that are unrelated to the first breach. For example, an owner who waives the right to sue for late completion of a stage of construction does not waive the right to sue for failure to comply with engineering specifications on the same job.

A waiver will be extended to subsequent defective performance, however, if a reasonable person would conclude that similar defective performance in the future will be acceptable. Therefore, a *pattern of conduct* that waives a number of successive breaches will operate as a continued waiver. To change this result, the nonbreaching party should give notice to the breaching party that full performance will be required in the future.

The party who has rendered defective or less-than-full performance remains liable for the damages caused by the breach of contract. In effect, the waiver operates to keep the contract going. The waiver prevents the nonbreaching party from declaring the contract at an end or rescinding the contract. The contract continues, but the nonbreaching party can recover damages caused by the defective or less-than-full performance.

Contract Provisions Limiting Remedies

A contract may include provisions stating that no damages can be recovered for certain types of breaches or that damages will be limited to a maximum amount. The contract may also provide that the only remedy for breach is replacement, repair, or refund of the purchase price. Provisions stating that no damages can be recovered are called *exculpatory clauses* (see Chapter 9 on page 205). Provisions that affect the availability of certain remedies are called *limitation-of-liability clauses.*

Whether a limitation-of-liability clause in a contract will be enforced depends on the type of breach that is excused by the provision. For example, a provision excluding liability for fraudulent or intentional injury will not be enforced. Likewise, a clause excluding liability for illegal acts, acts that are contrary to public policy, or violations of law will not be enforced.

CASE IN POINT Engineering Consulting Services, Ltd. (ECS), contracted with RSN Properties, Inc., a real estate developer, to perform soil studies for $2,200 and render an opinion on the use of septic systems in a particular subdivision being developed. A clause in the contract limited ECS's liability to RSN to the value of the engineering services or the sum of $50,000, whichever was greater. ECS concluded that most of the lots were suitable for septic systems. RSN proceeded with the development in reliance on ECS's conclusions, which turned out to be incorrect. RSN filed a breach of contract lawsuit against ECS and argued that the limitation of liability was against public policy and unenforceable. The court, however, held that the "contract represented a reasonable allocation of risks in an arm's-length business transaction, and did not violate public policy for professional engineering practice." The court therefore enforced the limitation-of-liability clause.[29]

---

29. *RSN Properties, Inc. v. Engineering Consulting Services, Ltd.*, 301 Ga.App. 52, 686 S.E.2d 853 (2009).

A clause that excludes liability for negligence may be enforced in some situations when the parties have roughly equal bargaining positions. If the limitation-of-liability clause is contained in a contract between persons with unequal bargaining power or is part of an adhesion contract, then it may not be enforced.

REVIEWING
Contract Performance, Breach, and Remedies

Kyle Bruno enters a contract with X Entertainment to be a stuntman in a movie. Bruno is widely known as the best motorcycle stuntman in the business, and the movie to be produced, *Xtreme Riders*, has numerous scenes involving high-speed freestyle street-bike stunts. Filming is set to begin August 1 and end by December 1 so that the film can be released the following summer. Both parties to the contract have stipulated that the filming must end on time to capture the profits from the summer movie market. The contract states that Bruno will be paid 10 percent of the net proceeds from the movie for his stunts. The contract also includes a liquidated damages provision, which specifies that if Bruno breaches the contract, he will owe X Entertainment $1 million. In addition, the contract includes a limitation-of-liability clause stating that if Bruno is injured during filming, X Entertainment's liability is limited to nominal damages. Using the information presented in the chapter, answer the following questions.

1. One day, while Bruno is preparing for a difficult stunt, he gets into an argument with the director and refuses to perform any stunts at all. Can X Entertainment seek specific performance of the contract? Why or why not?
2. Suppose that while performing a high-speed wheelie on a motorcycle, Bruno is injured by the intentionally reckless act of an X Entertainment employee. Will a court be likely to enforce the limitation-of-liability clause? Why or why not?
3. What factors would a court consider to determine whether the $1 million liquidated damages provision constitutes valid damages or is a penalty?
4. Suppose that the contract had no liquidated damages provision (or the court refused to enforce it) and X Entertainment breached the contract. The breach caused the release of the film to be delayed until the fall. Could Bruno seek consequential (special) damages for lost profits from the summer movie market in that situation? Explain.

DEBATE THIS: *Courts should always uphold limitation-of-liability clauses, whether or not the two parties to the contract had equal bargaining power.*

TERMS AND CONCEPTS

anticipatory repudiation 217
breach of contract 216
commercial
   impracticability 220
compensatory damages 223

condition 213
consequential damages 224
discharge 213
discharge in bankruptcy 219
frustration of purpose 222
impossibility of
   performance 219

liquidated damages 225
mitigation of damages 225
mutual rescission 217
nominal damages 224
novation 217
performance 213
penalty 225

reformation 227
restitution 226
specific performance 226
tender 213
waiver 229

QUESTIONS AND CASE PROBLEMS

10–1. Conditions The Caplans own a real estate lot, and they contract with Faithful Construction, Inc., to build a house on it for $360,000. The specifications list "all plumbing bowls and fixtures . . . to be Crane brand." The Caplans leave on vacation, and during their absence Faithful is unable to buy and install Crane plumbing fixtures. Instead, Faithful installs Kohler brand fixtures, an equivalent in the industry. On completion of the building contract, the Caplans inspect the work, discover the substitution, and refuse to accept the house, claiming Faithful has breached the conditions set forth in the specifications. Discuss fully the Caplans' claim.

10–2. QUESTION WITH SAMPLE ANSWER: Discharge by Agreement.

Junior owes creditor Iba $1,000, which is due and payable on June 1. Junior has been in a car accident, has missed a great deal of work, and consequently will not have the funds on June 1. Junior's father, Fred, offers to pay Iba $1,100 in four equal installments if Iba will discharge Junior from any further liability on the debt. Iba accepts. Is this transaction a novation or an accord and satisfaction? Explain.

• **For a sample answer to Question 10–2, go to Appendix F at the end of this text.**

10–3. Anticipatory Repudiation ABC Clothiers, Inc., has a contract with Taylor & Sons, a retailer, to deliver one thousand summer suits to Taylor's place of business on or before May 1. On April 1, Taylor senior receives a letter from ABC informing him that ABC will not be able to make the delivery as scheduled. Taylor is very upset, as he had planned a big ad campaign. He wants to file a suit against ABC immediately (on April 2). Taylor's son Tom tells his father that filing a lawsuit is not proper until ABC actually fails to deliver the suits on May 1. Discuss fully who is correct, Taylor or Tom.

10–4. Impossibility of Performance In the following situations, certain events take place after the contracts are formed. Discuss whether each of these contracts is discharged because the events render the contracts impossible to perform.

(a) Jimenez, a famous singer, contracts to perform in your nightclub. He dies prior to performance.

(b) Raglione contracts to sell you her land. Just before title is to be transferred, she dies.

(c) Oppenheim contracts to sell you one thousand bushels of apples from her orchard in the state of Washington. Because of a severe frost, she is unable to deliver the apples.

(d) Maxwell contracts to lease a service station for ten years. His principal income is from the sale of gasoline. Because of an oil embargo by foreign oil-producing nations, gasoline is rationed, cutting sharply into Maxwell's gasoline sales. He cannot make his lease payments.

10–5. Remedies On July 7, 2000, Frances Morelli agreed to sell to Judith Bucklin a house at 126 Lakedell Drive in Warwick, Rhode Island, for $77,000. Bucklin made a deposit on the house. The closing at which the parties would exchange the deed for the price was scheduled for September 1. The agreement did not state that "time is of the essence," but it did provide, in "Paragraph 10," that "[i]f Seller is unable to [convey good, clear, insurable, and marketable title], Buyer shall have the option to: (a) accept such title as Seller is able to convey without abatement or reduction of the Purchase Price, or (b) cancel this Agreement and receive a return of all Deposits." An examination of the public records revealed that the house did not have marketable title. Wishing to be flexible, Bucklin offered Morelli time to resolve the problem, and the closing did not occur as scheduled. Morelli decided "the deal is over" and offered to return the deposit. Bucklin refused and, in mid-October, decided to exercise her option under Paragraph 10(a). She notified Morelli, who did not respond. Bucklin filed a suit in a Rhode Island state court against Morelli. In whose favor should the court rule? Should damages be awarded? If not, what is the appropriate remedy? Why? [*Bucklin v. Morelli*, 912 A.2d 931 (R.I. 2007)]

10–6. CASE PROBLEM WITH SAMPLE ANSWER: Material Breach.

Roger Bannister was the director of technical and product development for Bemis Co. He signed a covenant not to compete that prohibited him from working for a "conflicting organization" for eighteen months following his termination, but required Bemis to pay his salary if he was unable to find a job "consistent with his abilities and education." Bemis terminated Bannister. Mondi Packaging, a Bemis competitor, told him that it would like to offer him a job but could not do so because of the the noncompete agreement. Bemis released Bannister from the agreement with respect to "all other companies than Mondi" and refused to pay his salary. Nine months later, Bannister accepted a position with Bancroft Bag, Inc., another Bemis competitor. He filed a suit in a federal district court against his former employer. Do these facts show a material breach of contract? If so, what is the appropriate remedy? Explain. [Bannister v. Bemis Co., Inc., 556 F.3d 882 (8th Cir. 2009)]

• **To view a sample answer for Problem 10–6, go to this book's Web site at www.cengage.com/blaw/cross, select "Chapter 10," and click on "Case Problem with Sample Answer."**

10–7. Liquidated Damages and Penalties Planned Pethood Plus, Inc., is a veterinarian-owned clinic. It borrowed $389,000 from KeyBank at an interest rate of 9.3 percent per year for ten years. The loan had a "prepayment penalty" clause that clearly stated that if the loan was repaid early, a specific formula would be used to assess a lump-sum payment to extinguish the obligation. The sooner the loan was paid off, the higher the prepayment penalty. After a year, the veterinarians decided to pay off the loan. KeyBank invoked a prepayment penalty of $40,525.92, which was equal to 10.7 percent of the balance due. The veterinarians sued, contending that the prepayment requirement was unenforceable because it was a penalty. The bank countered that the amount was not a penalty but liquidated damages and that the sum was reasonable. The trial court agreed with the bank, and the veterinarians appealed. Was the loan's prepayment charge reasonable, and should it have been enforced? Why or why not? [*Planned Pethood Plus, Inc. v. KeyCorp, Inc.,* 228 P.3d 262 (Colo.App. 2010)]

10–8. Condition Just Homes, LLC (JH), hired Mike Building & Contracting, Inc., to do $1.35 million worth of renovation work on three homes. Community Preservation Corporation (CPC) supervised Mike's work on behalf of JH. The contract stated that in the event of a dispute, JH would have to obtain the project architect's certification to justify terminating Mike. As construction progressed, relations between Mike and CPC worsened. At a certain point in the project, Mike requested partial payment, and CPC recommended that JH not make it. Mike refused to continue work without further payment. JH evicted Mike from the project. Mike sued for breach of contract. JH contended that it had the right to terminate the contract due to CPC's negative reports and Mike's failure to agree with the project's engineer. Mike moved for summary judgment for the amounts owed for work performed, claiming that JH had not fulfilled the condition—that is, JH never obtained the project architect's certification for Mike's termination. Which of the two parties involved breached the contract? Explain your answer. [*Mike Building & Contracting, Inc. v. Just Homes, LLC,* 27 Misc.3d 833, 901 N.Y.S.2d 458 (2010)]

10–9. A QUESTION OF ETHICS: Remedies.

 In 2004, Tamara Cohen, a real estate broker, began showing property in Manhattan to Steven Galistinos, who represented comedian Jerry Seinfeld and his wife, Jessica. According to Cohen, she told Galistinos that her commission would be 5 or 6 percent, and he agreed. According to Galistinos, there was no such agreement. Cohen spoke with Maximillan Sanchez, another broker, about a townhouse owned by Ray and Harriet Mayeri. According to Cohen, Sanchez said that the commission would be 6 percent, which they agreed to split equally. Sanchez later acknowledged that they had agreed to split the fee, but claimed that they had not discussed a specific amount. On a Friday in February 2005, Cohen showed the townhouse to Jessica. According to Cohen, she told Jessica that the commission would be 6 percent, with the Seinfelds paying half, and Jessica agreed. According to Jessica, there was no such conversation. Later that day,

Galistinos asked Cohen to arrange for the Seinfelds to see the premises again. Cohen told Galistinos that her religious beliefs prevented her from showing property on Friday evenings or Saturdays before sundown. She suggested the following Monday or Tuesday, but Galistinos said that Jerry would not be available and asked her to contact Carolyn Liebling, Jerry's business manager. Cohen left Liebling a message. Over the weekend, the Seinfelds toured the building on their own and agreed to buy the property for $3.95 million. Despite repeated attempts, they were unable to contact Cohen. [Cohen v. Seinfeld, 15 Misc.3d 1118(A), 839 N.Y.S.2d 432 (Sup. 2007)]

(a) The contract between the Seinfelds and the Mayeris stated that the sellers would pay Sanchez's fee and the "buyers will pay buyer's real estate broker's fees." The Mayeris paid Sanchez $118,500, which is 3 percent of $3.95 million. The Seinfelds refused to pay Cohen. She filed a suit in a New York state court against them, asserting, among other things, breach of contract. Should the court order the Seinfelds to pay Cohen? If so, is she entitled to a full commission even though she was not available to show the townhouse when the Seinfelds wanted to see it? Explain.

(b) What obligation do parties involved in business deals owe to each other with respect to their religious beliefs? How might the situation in this case have been avoided?

10–10. VIDEO QUESTION: Remedies.

 Go to this text's Web site at **www.cengage.com/blaw/cross** and select "Chapter 10." Click on "Video Questions" and view the video titled *Midnight Run.* Then answer the following questions.

(a) In the video, Eddie (Joe Pantoliano) and Jack (Robert De Niro) negotiate a contract for Jack to find The Duke, a mob accountant who embezzled funds, and bring him back for trial. Does this contract pass the legality requirement discussed in Chapter 9? Why or why not?

(b) Assume that the contract is valid. If Jack breaches the contract by failing to bring in The Duke, what kinds of remedies, if any, can Eddie seek? Explain your answer.

(c) Would the equitable remedy of specific performance be available to either Jack or Eddie in the event of a breach? Why or why not?

LEGAL RESEARCH EXERCISES ON THE WEB

Go to this text's Web site at **www.cengage.com/blaw/cross**, select "Chapter 10," and click on "Practical Internet Exercises." There you will find the following Internet research exercises that you can perform to learn more about the topics covered in this chapter.

Practical Internet Exercise 10–1: **Legal Perspective**
Anticipatory Repudiation

Practical Internet Exercise 10–2: **Management Perspective**
The Duty to Mitigate

Practical Internet Exercise 10–3: **Management Perspective**
Commerical Impracticability

CHAPTER 11

✳ Sales, Leases, and E-Contracts

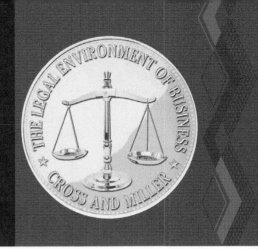

When we turn to contracts for the sale and lease of goods, we move away from common law principles and into the area of statutory law. State statutory law governing sales and lease transactions is based on the Uniform Commercial Code (UCC), which, as mentioned in Chapter 1, has been adopted as law by all of the states.[1] The goal of the UCC is to simplify and streamline commercial transactions, allowing parties to form sales and lease contracts without observing the same degree of formality used in forming other types of contracts.

This chapter opens with a look at the broad scope of Articles 2 and 2A.

---

1. Louisiana has not adopted Articles 2 and 2A, however.

Article 2 of the UCC establishes the requirements to form sales contracts, and we describe how these laws differ from the common law of contracts. Article 2 also stipulates the duties and obligations of parties to sales contracts, although parties normally can agree to different terms than what is stated in the UCC. Article 2A covers similar issues for lease contracts. Because of its importance in commercial transactions, we have included Article 2 in Appendix C of this text.

After an examination of the formation of sales and lease contracts, we consider how Article 2 addresses when title (ownership) passes and who bears the risk of loss, and who can obtain insurance, on goods in the process of being sold. We then look at the performance required in sales and lease contracts and the remedies available if a contract is breached. Also examined are the warranties, both express and implied, that can arise in contracts to sell or lease goods.

The final pages of this chapter cover how traditional laws are being applied to contracts formed online, or *e-contracts*, which often involve sales or leases. Because international sales transactions are increasingly commonplace, we conclude the chapter with an examination of the United Nations Convention on Contracts for the International Sale of Goods, which governs international sales contracts.

SECTION 1
THE SCOPE OF ARTICLE 2—THE SALE OF GOODS

Article 2 of the UCC (as adopted by state statutes) governs **sales contracts,** or contracts for the sale of goods. To facilitate commercial transactions, Article 2 modifies some of the common law contract requirements that were discussed in the previous chapters. To the extent that it has not been modified by the UCC, however, the common law of contracts also applies to sales contracts. For example, the common law requirements for a valid contract—agreement, consideration, capacity, and legality, which were discussed in Chapters 9 and 10—are also applicable to sales contracts. Thus, you should reexamine these common law principles when studying the law of sales.

In general, the rule is that whenever a conflict arises between a common law contract rule and the state statutory law based on the UCC, the UCC controls. In other words, when a UCC provision addresses a certain issue, the UCC rule governs; when the UCC is silent, the common law governs. The relationship between general contract law and the law governing sales of goods is illustrated in Exhibit 11–1 on the following page.

In regard to Article 2, keep two points in mind. First, Article 2 deals with the sale of *goods*. It does not deal with real property (real estate), services, or intangible property such as stocks and bonds. Thus, if the subject matter of a dispute is goods, the UCC governs. If it is real estate or services, the

EXHIBIT 11–1 • The Law Governing Contracts

This exhibit graphically illustrates the relationship between general contract law and statutory law (UCC Articles 2 and 2A) governing contracts for the sale and lease of goods. Sales contracts are not governed exclusively by Article 2 of the UCC but are also governed by general contract law whenever it is relevant and has not been modified by the UCC.

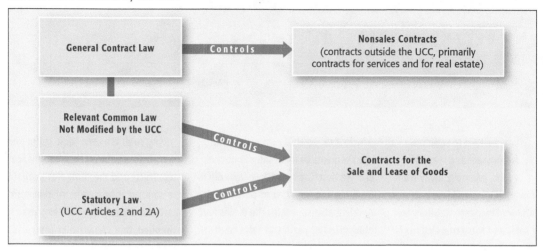

common law applies. Second, in some situations, the rules may vary quite a bit, depending on whether the buyer or the seller is a *merchant*. We look now at how the UCC defines a *sale, goods,* and *merchant status*.

What Is a Sale?

The UCC defines a **sale** as "the passing of title [evidence of ownership rights] from the seller to the buyer for a price" [UCC 2–106(1)]. The price may be payable in cash or in other goods or services.

What Are Goods?

To be characterized as a *good,* an item of property must be *tangible,* and it must be *movable.* **Tangible property** has physical existence—it can be touched or seen. Intangible property—such as corporate stocks and bonds, patents and copyrights, and ordinary contract rights—has only conceptual existence and thus does not come under Article 2. A *movable* item can be carried from place to place. Hence, real estate is excluded from Article 2.

Goods associated with real estate can fall within the scope of Article 2, however [UCC 2–107]. For example, a contract for the sale of minerals, oil, or gas is a contract for the sale of goods if *severance, or separation, is to be made by the seller.* Similarly, a contract for the sale of growing crops or timber to be cut is a contract for the sale of goods *regardless of who severs them.*

In cases involving contracts in which goods and services are combined, the courts generally use the **predominant-factor test** to determine whether a contract is primarily for the sale of goods or for the sale of services. If a court decides that a mixed contract is primarily a goods contract, *any* dispute, even a dispute over the services portion, will be decided under the UCC. For example, an accounting firm contracts to purchase customized software from Micro Systems. The contract states that half of the purchase price is for Micro's professional services and the other half is for the goods (the software). If a court determines that the contract is predominantly for the software, rather than the services to customize the software, the court will hold that the transaction falls under Article 2. Conversely, if the court finds that the services are predominant, it will hold that the transaction is not governed by the UCC.

Who Is a Merchant?

Article 2 governs the sale of goods in general. It applies to sales transactions between all buyers and sellers. In a limited number of instances, though, the UCC presumes that special business standards ought to be imposed because of merchants' relatively high degree of commercial expertise.[2] Such standards

---

2. The provisions that apply only to merchants deal principally with the Statute of Frauds, firm offers, confirmatory memoranda, warranties, and contract modification. These special rules reflect expedient business practices commonly known to merchants in the commercial setting. They will be discussed later in this chapter.

do not apply to the casual or inexperienced seller or buyer (consumer). Section 2–104 sets forth three ways in which merchant status can arise:

1. A merchant is a person who *deals in goods of the kind* involved in the sales contract. Thus, a retailer, a wholesaler, or a manufacturer is a merchant of the goods sold in his or her business. A merchant for one type of goods is not necessarily a merchant for another type. For example, a sporting goods retailer is a merchant when selling tennis rackets but not when selling a used computer.

2. A merchant is a person who, by occupation, holds himself or herself out as having knowledge and skill unique to the practices or goods involved in the transaction. This broad definition may include banks or universities as merchants.

3. A person who *employs a merchant as a broker, agent, or other intermediary* has the status of merchant in that transaction. Hence, if an art collector hires a broker to purchase or sell art for her, the collector is considered a merchant in the transaction.

In summary, a person is a **merchant** when she or he, acting in a mercantile capacity, possesses or uses an expertise specifically related to the goods being sold. This basic distinction is not always clearcut. For example, state courts appear to be split on whether farmers should be considered merchants.

SECTION 2
THE SCOPE OF ARTICLE 2A—LEASES

In the past few decades, leases of personal property (goods) have become increasingly common. Consumers and business firms lease automobiles, industrial equipment, items for use in the home (such as floor polishers), and many other types of goods. Article 2A of the UCC was created to fill the need for uniform guidelines in this area.

Article 2A covers any transaction that creates a lease of goods or a sublease of goods [UCC 2A–102, 2A–103(1)(k)]. Article 2A is essentially a repetition of Article 2, except that it applies to leases of goods rather than sales of goods and thus varies to reflect differences between sales and lease transactions. (Note that Article 2A is not concerned with leases of real property, such as land or buildings.)

Article 2A defines a **lease agreement** as a lessor and lessee's bargain with respect to the lease of goods, as found in their language and as implied by

other circumstances [UCC 2A–103(1)(k)]. A **lessor** is one who transfers the right to the possession and use of goods under a lease [UCC 2A–103(1)(p)]. A **lessee** is one who acquires the right to the possession and use of goods under a lease [UCC 2A–103(1)(o)]. In other words, the lessee is the party who is leasing the goods from the lessor. Article 2A applies to all types of leases of goods. Special rules apply to certain types of leases, however, including consumer leases and finance leases.

SECTION 3
THE FORMATION OF SALES AND LEASE CONTRACTS

In regard to the formation of sales and lease contracts, the UCC modifies the common law in several ways, as discussed in the subsections that follow. Remember, though, that parties to sales contracts are basically free to establish whatever terms they wish. The UCC comes into play when the parties either fail to provide certain terms in their contract or wish to change the effect of the UCC's terms in the contract's application. The UCC makes this very clear time and again by its use of such phrases as "unless the parties otherwise agree" and "absent a contrary agreement by the parties."

Offer

In general contract law, the moment a definite offer is met by an unqualified acceptance, a binding contract is formed. In commercial sales transactions, the verbal exchanges, correspondence, and actions of the parties may not reveal exactly when a binding contractual obligation arises. The UCC states that an agreement sufficient to constitute a contract can exist even if the moment of its making is undetermined [UCC 2–204(2), 2A–204(2)].

OPEN TERMS According to general contract law, an offer must be definite enough for the parties (and the courts) to ascertain its essential terms when it is accepted. In contrast, the UCC states that a sales or lease contract will not fail for indefiniteness even if one or more terms are left open as long as (1) the parties intended to make a contract and (2) there is a reasonably certain basis for the court to grant an appropriate remedy [UCC 2–204(3), 2A–204(3)].

Relative to the common law of contracts, the UCC has radically lessened the requirement of definiteness of terms. Keep in mind, though, that if too many terms are left open, a court may find that the parties did not intend to form a contract.

Open Price Term. If the parties have not agreed on a price, the court will determine a "reasonable price at the time for delivery" [UCC 2–305(1)]. If either the buyer or the seller is to determine the price, the price is to be fixed in good faith [UCC 2–305(2)]. Under the UCC, *good faith* means honesty in fact and the observance of reasonable commercial standards of fair dealing in the trade [UCC 2–103(1)(b)]. The concepts of *good faith* and *commercial reasonableness* permeate the UCC. For a discussion of how sellers might charge slightly higher prices for goods in the interest of promoting "fair trade," see this chapter's *Shifting Legal Priorities for Business* feature on the facing page.

Sometimes, the price fails to be fixed (specified) through the fault of one of the parties. In that situation, the other party can treat the contract as canceled or specify a reasonable price. For example, Perez and Merrick enter into a contract for the sale of goods and agree that Perez will determine the price. Perez refuses to specify the price. Merrick can either treat the contract as canceled or set a reasonable price [UCC 2–305(3)].

Open Payment Term. When the parties do not specify payment terms, payment is due at the time and place at which the buyer is to receive the goods [UCC 2–310(a)]. The buyer can tender payment using any commercially normal or acceptable means, such as a check or credit card. If the seller demands payment in cash, however, the buyer must be given a reasonable time to obtain it [UCC 2–511(2)]. This is especially important when the contract states a definite and final time for performance.

Open Delivery Term. When no delivery terms are specified, the buyer normally takes delivery at the seller's place of business [UCC 2–308(a)]. If the seller has no place of business, the seller's residence is used. When goods are located in some other place and both parties know it, delivery is made there. If the time for shipment or delivery is not clearly specified in the sales contract, then the court will infer a "reasonable" time for performance [UCC 2–309(1)].

Open Quantity Term. Normally, if the parties do not specify a quantity, a court will have no basis for determining a remedy. This is because there is almost no way to determine objectively what is a reasonable quantity of goods for someone to purchase (whereas a court can objectively determine a reasonable price for particular goods by looking at the market). The UCC recognizes two exceptions in requirements and output contracts [UCC 2–306(1)].

In a **requirements contract,** the buyer agrees to purchase and the seller agrees to sell all or up to a stated amount of what the buyer *needs* or *requires*. There is implicit consideration in a requirements contract because the buyer gives up the right to buy from any other seller, and this forfeited right creates a legal detriment. Requirements contracts are common in the business world and normally are enforceable. If, however, the buyer promises to purchase only if he or she *wishes* to do so, or if the buyer reserves the right to buy the goods from someone other than the seller, the promise lacks consideration and is unenforceable by either party.[3]

In an **output contract,** the seller agrees to sell and the buyer agrees to buy all or up to a stated amount of what the seller *produces*. Again, because the seller essentially forfeits the right to sell goods to another buyer, there is implicit consideration in an output contract.

The UCC imposes a *good faith limitation* on requirements and output contracts. The quantity under such contracts is the amount of requirements or the amount of output that occurs during a *normal* production period. The actual quantity purchased or sold cannot be unreasonably disproportionate to normal or comparable prior requirements or output [UCC 2–306].

MERCHANT'S FIRM OFFER Under regular contract principles, an offer can be revoked at any time before acceptance. The major common law exception is an *option contract* (discussed in Chapter 9 on page 196), in which the offeree pays consideration for the offeror's irrevocable promise to keep the offer open for a stated period. The UCC creates a second exception, which applies only to firm offers for the sale or lease of goods made by a merchant (regardless of whether or not the offeree is a merchant).

A **firm offer** arises when a merchant-offeror gives *assurances in a signed writing* that the offer will remain open. The merchant's firm offer is irrevocable without the necessity of consideration[4] for

---

3. See, for example, *In re Anchor Glass Container Corp.,* 345 Bankr. 765 (M.D.Fla. 2006).
4. If the offeree pays consideration, then an option contract (not a merchant's firm offer) is formed.

Sales contracts, whether domestic or international, involve the transfer of a quantity of goods at a price. But sales contracts can do more than that. Thanks to the Fair Trade movement, they can also benefit poor farmers in developing countries and promote environmentally sustainable farming practices.

What Is the Fair Trade Movement?

The origins of the Fair Trade movement can be traced to an effort in Europe almost fifty years ago to provide relief to refugees and other poor communities by selling their handicrafts. But the movement only began to expand in the 1980s when the "Fair Trade" label was developed in the Netherlands to identify coffee produced under certain conditions. Today, Fairtrade Labeling Organizations International determines minimum "fair" prices that ensure that small producers can earn a living wage. Products obtained at these prices can bear the Fair Trade label. Retailers can still charge any price they wish, but because they pay more for products with the Fair Trade label, they usually pass these costs on to consumers in the form of slightly higher prices.

TransFair U.S.A. founder Paul Rice describes the Fair Trade movement this way: "Fair Trade creates the opportunity for businesses to increase their profits through socially responsible business practices, for consumers to vote with every purchase for a more equitable world, and for farmers to view themselves not as an anonymous cog in the world market, but as a valuable contributor to a global society."

The Principles of Fair Trade

Under the Fair Trade system, low-income farmers and artisans in developing countries form alliances with importers and marketers in Western Europe and North America. Participants must agree to certain basic principles:

- Producers must receive a stable minimum price for their products.
- Forced or child labor will not be used.
- Production methods must be environmentally friendly.

When these standards are met, international certification bodies allow the products to carry a Fair Trade logo, such as the well-known label borne by some coffee imported into the United States.

Emphasis on Environmental Sustainability

As mentioned, only producers who agree to use environmentally sustainable farming methods can sell their products through the Fair Trade system. The farmers must agree to preserve valuable ecosystems for future generations. The use of harmful chemicals and genetically modified organisms is strictly prohibited.

According to Paulette Stenzel, professor of international business law at the Eli Broad College of Business at Michigan State University, "Fair Trade is simply one way of carrying out business, which takes into account all aspects of sustainability, especially of the producers." Stenzel argues that businesses must take responsibility for environmental and socioeconomic outcomes that are directly related to their activities: "Today, many companies realize that sustainability efforts must be based on the triple bottom line of economy, social equity, and environment."

MANAGERIAL IMPLICATIONS

Today, Fair Trade certification is available in the United States for coffee, cocoa and chocolate, tea and herbs, fresh fruit, sugar, rice, and vanilla. As more consumers become aware of the movement, sales of Fair Trade products are likely to grow. Collaboration between Fair Trade producers and retail outlets in the United States is a key aspect of the movement. Marketing managers at large retail companies may find that their bottom lines will improve if they seek products bearing the Fair Trade label for their customers.

---

the stated period or, if no definite period is stated, a reasonable period (neither to exceed three months) [UCC 2–205, 2A–205].

To illustrate: Osaka, a used-car dealer, writes a letter to Bennett on January 1, stating, "I have a used 2010 Suzuki on the lot that I'll sell you for $20,500 any time between now and January 31." By January 18, Osaka has heard nothing from Bennett, so he sells the Suzuki to another person. On January 23, Bennett tenders $20,500 to Osaka and asks for the car. When Osaka tells him the car has already been sold, Bennett claims that Osaka has breached a valid contract. Bennett is right. Osaka is a merchant of used cars and assured Bennett in a signed writing that he would keep his offer open until the end of January. Thus, Bennett's acceptance on January 23 created a contract, which Osaka breached.

Acceptance

Acceptance of an offer to buy, sell, or lease goods generally may be made in any reasonable manner and by any reasonable means. When the offeror does not specify a means of acceptance, the UCC provides that acceptance can be made by any means of communication that is reasonable under the circumstances [UCC 2–206(1), 2A–206(1)]. The UCC permits an offeree to accept an offer to buy goods "either by a prompt *promise* to ship or by the prompt or current shipment of conforming or nonconforming goods" [UCC 2–206(1)(b)]. Conforming goods are goods that accord with the contract's terms; nonconforming goods do not.

SHIPMENT OF NONCONFORMING GOODS The seller's prompt shipment of nonconforming goods constitutes both an *acceptance* (a contract) and a *breach* of that contract. This rule does not apply if the seller **seasonably** (within a reasonable amount of time) notifies the buyer that the nonconforming shipment is offered only as an *accommodation,* or as a favor. The notice of accommodation must clearly indicate to the buyer that the shipment does not constitute an acceptance and that therefore no contract has been formed.

Assume that Barton orders one thousand black fans from Stroh. Stroh ships one thousand blue fans to Barton, notifying Barton that these are sent as an accommodation because Stroh has only blue fans in stock. The shipment of blue fans is not an acceptance but a counteroffer. A contract will be formed only if Barton accepts the blue fans. If, however, Stroh ships one thousand blue fans instead of black *without* notifying Barton that the goods are being shipped as an accommodation, Stroh's shipment acts as both an acceptance of Barton's offer and a breach of the resulting contract. Barton may sue Stroh for any appropriate damages.

COMMUNICATION OF ACCEPTANCE Under the common law, a unilateral offer can be accepted by beginning performance (unless the offeror would not otherwise know about it). The UCC is more stringent than the common law in this regard because it requires notification. Under the UCC, if the offeror is not notified within a reasonable time that the offeree has accepted the contract by beginning performance, then the offeror can treat the offer as having lapsed before acceptance [UCC 2–206(2), 2A–206(2)].

ADDITIONAL TERMS Recall that under the common law, the mirror image rule requires that the terms of the acceptance exactly match those of the offer (see Chapter 9 on page 196). The UCC dispenses with the mirror image rule. Generally, the UCC takes the position that if the offeree's response indicates a *definite* acceptance of the offer, a contract is formed,

even if the acceptance includes terms additional to or different from those contained in the offer [UCC 2–207(1)]. If one (or both) of the parties is a *nonmerchant,* the contract is formed according to the terms of the original offer and not according to the additional terms of the acceptance [UCC 2–207(2)].

Rules When Both Parties Are Merchants. The drafters of the UCC created a special rule for merchants to avoid the "battle of the forms," which occurs when two merchants exchange separate standard forms containing different contract terms. Under UCC 2–207(2), in contracts *between merchants,* the additional terms *automatically* become part of the contract *unless* one of the following conditions arises:

1. The original offer expressly limited acceptance to its terms.
2. The new or changed terms materially alter the contract.
3. The offeror objects to the new or changed terms within a reasonable period of time.

Generally, if the modification does not involve any unreasonable element of surprise or hardship for the offeror, a court will hold that the modification did not materially alter the contract. Courts also consider the parties' prior dealings when determining whether an alteration is material.

Rule for Striking Additional Terms. The UCC provides yet another option for dealing with conflicting terms in the parties' writings. Section 2–207(3) states that conduct by both parties that recognizes the existence of a contract is sufficient to establish a contract for sale even though the writings of the parties do not otherwise establish a contract. In this situation, the terms of the particular contract will consist of those terms on which the writings of the parties agree. In a dispute over contract terms, this provision allows a court simply to strike from the contract those terms on which the parties do not agree.

Suppose that SMT Marketing orders goods over the phone from Brigg Sales, Inc., which ships the goods to SMT with an acknowledgment form (confirming the order). SMT accepts and pays for the goods. The parties' writings do not establish a contract, but there is no question that a contract exists. If a dispute arises over the terms, such as the extent of any warranties, UCC 2–207(3) provides the governing rule.

Consideration

The common law rule that a contract requires consideration also applies to sales and lease contracts.

Unlike the common law, however, the UCC does not require a contract modification to be supported by new consideration. The UCC states that an agreement modifying a contract for the sale or lease of goods "needs no consideration to be binding" [UCC 2–209(1), 2A–208(1)].

Of course, any contract modification must be made in good faith [UCC 1–304]. For example, Allied, Inc., agrees to lease a new recreational vehicle (RV) to Diane Lee for a stated monthly payment. Subsequently, a sudden shift in the market makes it difficult for Allied to lease the new RV to Lee at the contract price without suffering a loss. Allied tells Lee of the situation, and she agrees to pay an additional sum for the lease of the RV. Later, Lee reconsiders and refuses to pay more than the original price. Under the UCC, Lee's promise to modify the contract needs no consideration to be binding. Hence, she is bound by the modified contract.

In this example, a shift in the market is a *good faith* reason for contract modification. What if there really was no shift in the market, however, and Allied knew that Lee needed the RV immediately but refused to deliver it unless Lee agreed to pay an additional amount? This attempt at extortion through modification without a legitimate commercial reason would be ineffective because it would violate the duty of good faith. Allied would not be permitted to enforce the higher price.

The Statute of Frauds

As discussed in Chapter 9, the Statute of Frauds requires that certain types of contracts, to be enforceable, must be in writing or be evidenced by a written memorandum or record. The UCC contains Statute of Frauds provisions covering sales and lease contracts. Under these provisions, sales contracts for goods priced at $500 or more and lease contracts requiring total payments of $1,000 or more must be in writing to be enforceable [UCC 2–201(1), 2A–201(1)]. (These low threshold amounts may eventually be raised.)

The UCC has also greatly relaxed the requirements for the sufficiency of a writing to satisfy the Statute of Frauds. A writing or a memorandum will be sufficient as long as it indicates that the parties intended to form a contract and as long as it is signed by the party (or agent of the party) against whom enforcement is sought. The contract normally will not be enforceable beyond the quantity of goods shown in the writing, however. All other terms can be proved in court by oral testimony. For leases, the writing must reasonably identify and describe the goods leased and the lease term.

SPECIAL RULES FOR CONTRACTS BETWEEN MERCHANTS Once again, the UCC provides a special rule for merchants in sales transactions (there is no corresponding rule that applies to leases under Article 2A). Merchants can satisfy the Statute of Frauds if, after the parties have agreed orally, one of the merchants sends a signed written confirmation to the other merchant within a reasonable time.

The communication must indicate the terms of the agreement, and the merchant receiving the confirmation must have reason to know of its contents. Generally, courts hold that it is sufficient if a merchant sends an e-mail confirmation of the agreement.[5] Unless the merchant who receives the confirmation gives written notice of objection to its contents within ten days after receipt, the writing is sufficient against the receiving merchant, even though she or he has not signed it [UCC 2–201(2)].

For example, Alfonso is a merchant-buyer in Cleveland. He contracts over the telephone to purchase $6,000 worth of spare aircraft parts from Goldstein, a merchant-seller in New York City. Two days later, Goldstein sends a written and signed confirmation detailing the terms of the oral contract, and Alfonso subsequently receives it. If Alfonso does not notify Goldstein in writing of his objection to the contents of the confirmation within ten days of receipt, Alfonso cannot raise the Statute of Frauds as a defense against the enforcement of the oral contract.

EXCEPTIONS The UCC defines three exceptions to the writing requirements of the Statute of Frauds under which an oral contract will be enforceable [UCC 2–201(3), 2A–201(4)].

Specially Manufactured Goods. An oral contract is enforceable if (1) it is for goods that are *specially manufactured* for a particular buyer or specially manufactured or obtained for a particular lessee, (2) these goods are *not suitable for resale or lease* to others in the ordinary course of the seller's or lessor's business, and (3) the seller or lessor has *substantially started to manufacture* the goods or has made commitments for the manufacture or procurement of the goods. In these situations, once the seller or lessor has taken action, the buyer or lessee cannot repudiate the agreement claiming the Statute of Frauds as a defense.

Admissions. An oral contract for the sale or lease of goods is enforceable if the party against whom

---

5. See, for example, *Bazak International Corp. v. Tarrant Apparel Group,* 378 F.Supp.2d 377 (S.D.N.Y. 2005); and *Great White Bear, LLC v. Mervyns, LLC,* 2007 WL 1295747 (S.D.N.Y. 2007).

enforcement is sought admits in pleadings, testimony, or other court proceedings that a sales or lease contract was made. In this situation, the contract will be enforceable even though it was oral, but enforceability will be limited to the quantity of goods admitted.

For example, Lane and Salazar negotiate an agreement over the telephone. Lane requests a delivery price for five hundred gallons of gasoline and a separate price for seven hundred gallons of gasoline. Salazar replies that the price would be the same, $3.10 per gallon. Lane orally orders five hundred gallons. Salazar honestly believes that Lane ordered seven hundred gallons and tenders that amount. Lane refuses the shipment. Lane admits that an oral contract was made, but only for five hundred gallons. Because Lane admits the existence of the oral contract, Lane cannot plead the Statute of Frauds as a defense. The contract is enforceable, however, only to the extent of the quantity admitted (five hundred gallons).

Is it possible to admit to a contract in court and also assert the Statute of Frauds as a defense? That was the position of the one of the parties in the following case.

CASE 11.1
Glacial Plains Cooperative v. Lindgren

Court of Appeals of Minnesota, 759 N.W.2d 661 (2009).
www.lawlibrary.state.mn.us/archive[a]

COMPANY PROFILE • Glacial Plains Cooperative is a locally owned agricultural cooperative based in west central Minnesota. Glacial Plains employs fifty to one hundred workers, who supply grain marketing, seed, energy, feed, and agronomy products and services. Recent annual sales have averaged between $50 million and $100 million. The cooperative also offers short-term, low-interest loans and other financial products to its members. Glacial Plains' motto is "Solid Performance and Returning Cash to Member Owners."

BACKGROUND AND FACTS • Gerald Lindgren, a farmer, agreed by phone to sell grain to Glacial Plains Cooperative. They reached four agreements: two for the delivery of 9,000 and 10,000 bushels of soybeans in the fall of 2006, one for the delivery of 65,000 bushels of corn in the same season, and one for the sale of 30,000 bushels of corn in the fall of 2007. Glacial Plains sent Lindgren four written—but unsigned—contracts. Lindgren made the soybean deliveries and part of the first corn delivery, but sold the rest of his corn to another dealer. Glacial Plains bought corn elsewhere, paying a higher price, and filed a suit in a Minnesota state court against Lindgren for breach of contract. During a deposition and in papers filed with the court, Lindgren acknowledged his oral agreements with Glacial Plains and admitted that he did not fully perform. He argued, nonetheless, that the agreements were unenforceable because they were not signed. The court denied Lindgren's defense. He appealed.

IN THE LANGUAGE OF THE COURT
KLAPHAKE, Judge.
   * * * *

Appellant argues that the oral corn agreements are not enforceable because they violate the Statute of Frauds. Minnesota's version of the UCC provides that a contract for the sale of goods for the price of $500 or more is not enforceable "unless there is some writing sufficient to indicate that a contract for sale has been made between the parties and signed by the party against whom enforcement is sought."

Respondent argues that the oral agreements fall within * * * the admission exception.

The admission exception to the code's statute of frauds is found in [Minnesota Statutes Section 36.2-201(3)(b), Minnesota's version of UCC 2–201(3)(b)], which provides that even when there is no signed writing sufficient to satisfy the writing requirement, *the Statute of Frauds will not act to abolish the contract "if the party against whom enforcement is sought admits in pleading,*

---

a. In the "Court of Appeals Opinions" box, click on "Index by Release Date." On that page, in the "Published" column in the "2009" section, select "January–March." In the result, scroll to "January 27, 2009" and click on the docket number of the case to access the opinion. The Minnesota State Law Library maintains this Web site.

CASE 11.1 CONTINUED ➡ *testimony or otherwise in court that a contract for sale was made."* The exception was created to reduce the risk of fraud: Where the making of a contract is admitted in court, no additional writing is necessary for protection against fraud, and the contract becomes enforceable notwithstanding the provisions of the statute of frauds. [Emphasis added.]

Appellant has made such an admission here. During his deposition and in his summary judgment papers, appellant acknowledged that he made two oral agreements in April 2006 for the sale of corn to be delivered in 2006 and 2007, and that he operated under the assumption that he was obligated under these agreements throughout the summer of 2006. He further admitted that he * * * decided [the unsigned contracts] were unenforceable, and stopped performing on the 2006 corn contract and never performed on the 2007 corn agreement. * * * Based on these admissions by appellant, we conclude that the admission exception applies here, removing the agreement from the UCC statute of frauds.

* * * Meeting the Minnesota Statute of Frauds does not prove the terms of the contract; meeting the Statute of Frauds simply removes the defense and allows a jury to determine the issue of whether the parties entered into an agreement and its terms.

DECISION AND REMEDY • *The state intermediate appellate court affirmed the lower court's decision. The appellate court remanded the case for a determination of the terms of the contracts.*

WHAT IF THE FACTS WERE DIFFERENT? • *Suppose that Lindgren had admitted to a lesser quantity than he had orally promised to Glacial Plains but that other proof of the true terms was available. What might have been the result? Explain your answer.*

THE LEGAL ENVIRONMENT DIMENSION • *Lindgren entered into an agreement in the spring of 2006 to deliver corn to Great Plains in the fall of 2007. Should the court have denied the enforcement of this agreement under the one-year rule? Explain.*

Partial Performance. An oral contract for the sale or lease of goods is enforceable if payment has been made and accepted or goods have been received and accepted. This is the "partial performance" exception. The oral contract will be enforced at least to the extent that performance *actually* took place.

CASE IN POINT Quality Pork International formed an oral contract with Rupari Food Services, Inc., which buys and sells food products to retail operations. Quality was to ship three orders of pork to Star Food Processing, Inc., and Rupari was to pay for the products. Quality shipped the pork to Star and sent invoices to Rupari. Rupari billed Star for all three orders but paid Quality only for the first two. Quality filed a suit against Rupari to recover $44,051.98, the cost of the third order. Rupari argued that because the parties did not have a written agreement, there was no enforceable contract. The court held that even though Rupari had not signed a written contract or purchase order, it had accepted the goods and partially performed the contract by paying for the first two shipments. Rupari's conduct was sufficient to prove the existence of a contract, and the court required Rupari to pay for the last shipment.[6]

The exceptions just discussed and other ways in which sales law differs from general contract law are summarized in Exhibit 11–2 on the next page.

SECTION 4
TITLE, RISK, AND INSURABLE INTEREST

Before the creation of the UCC, *title*—the right of ownership—was the central concept in sales law, controlling all issues of rights and remedies of the parties to a sales contract. There were numerous problems with this concept, however. For example, it was frequently difficult to determine when title actually passed from the seller to the buyer, and therefore it was also difficult to predict which party a court would decide had title at the time of a loss. Because of such problems, the UCC divorced the question of title as completely as possible from the question of the rights and obligations of buyers, sellers, and third parties (such as subsequent purchasers, creditors, or the tax collector). In most situations, the UCC has replaced the concept of title with three other concepts: identification, risk of loss, and insurable interest.

---

6. *Quality Pork International v. Rupari Food Services, Inc.,* 267 Neb. 474, 675 N.W.2d 642 (2004).

EXHIBIT 11-2 • Major Differences between Contract Law and Sales Law

	CONTRACT LAW	SALES LAW
Contract Terms	Contract must contain all material terms.	Open terms are acceptable if parties intended to form a contract, but the contract is not enforceable beyond quantity term.
Acceptance	Mirror image rule applies. If additional terms are added in acceptance, a counteroffer is created.	Additional terms will not negate acceptance unless acceptance is expressly conditioned on assent to the additional terms.
Contract Modification	Modification requires consideration.	Modification does not require consideration.
Irrevocable Offers	Option contracts (with consideration).	Merchants' firm offers (without consideration).
Statute of Frauds Requirements	All material terms must be included in the writing.	Writing is required only for sale of goods priced at $500 or more, but the contract is not enforceable beyond the quantity specified. Merchants can satisfy the writing by a confirmation evidencing their agreement. *Exceptions:* 1. Specially manufactured goods. 2. Admissions by party against whom enforcement is sought. 3. Partial performance.

In lease contracts, of course, the lessor-owner of the goods retains title. Hence, the UCC's provisions relating to passage of title do not apply to leased goods. Other concepts discussed in this section, though, including identification, risk of loss, and insurable interest, relate to lease contracts as well as to sales contracts.

Identification

Before any interest in specific goods can pass from the seller or lessor to the buyer or lessee, the goods must be (1) in existence and (2) identified as the specific goods designated in the contract [UCC 2–105(2)]. **Identification** takes place when specific goods are designated as the subject matter of a sales or lease contract. Title and risk of loss cannot pass to the buyer from the seller unless the goods are identified to the contract. (As mentioned, title to leased goods remains with the lessor—or, if the owner is a third party, with that party.)

Identification is significant because it gives the buyer or lessee the right to insure (or to have an insurable interest in) the goods and the right to recover from third parties who damage the goods. Once the goods are in existence, the parties can agree in their contract on when identification will take place. If they do not so specify, the UCC will determine when identification takes place [UCC 2–501(1), 2A–217].

EXISTING GOODS If the contract calls for the sale or lease of specific and ascertained goods that are already in existence, identification takes place at the time the contract is made. For example, Litco, LLC, contracts to purchase or lease a fleet of five cars by their vehicle identification numbers (VINs). Because the cars are identified by their VINs, identification has taken place, and Litco acquires an insurable interest in them at the time of contracting.

Goods that are part of a larger mass are identified when the goods are marked, shipped, or somehow designated by the seller or lessor as the particular goods to pass under the contract. Suppose that a buyer orders 10,000 pairs of men's jeans from a lot that contains 90,000 articles of clothing for men, women, and children. Until the seller separates the 10,000 pairs of jeans from the other items, title and risk of loss remain with the seller.

FUTURE GOODS Any goods that are not in existence at the time of contracting are known as future goods. If a sale or lease involves unborn animals to be born within twelve months after contracting, identification takes place when the animals are conceived. If a sale involves crops that are to be harvested within twelve months (or the next harvest season occurring after contracting, whichever is longer), identification takes place when the crops are planted. Otherwise, identification takes place when the crops begin to grow. In a sale or lease of any other future goods, identification occurs when the goods are shipped, marked, or otherwise designated by the seller or lessor as the goods to which the contract refers.

CASE IN POINT Gordon Bonner signed a contract with Ronnie Carman to build a forty-six-foot motorboat for $278,950. The contract required progress payments but did not contain any specific provisions regarding delivery (which, as you will read shortly, can determine when title to the goods passes to the buyer). After nearly three years, with the boat still not completed, Carman filed for bankruptcy. The bankruptcy trustee wanted to sell the unfinished boat to pay Carman's creditors, but Bonner claimed that the boat—which was still on Carman's business premises—was his. The court held that under the UCC, the boat constituted future goods because it did not exist at the time the contract was signed. In addition, title had not passed to Bonner, because the boat had not been identified to the contract—for example, by listing its hull number in the contract or by later marking or designating it as Bonner's. Therefore, the bankruptcy trustee could sell it and distribute the funds to Carman's creditors.[7]

When Title Passes

Once goods exist and are identified, the provisions of UCC 2–401 apply to the passage of title. In nearly all subsections of UCC 2–401, the words "unless otherwise explicitly agreed" appear, meaning that any explicit understanding between the buyer and the seller determines when title passes. Without an explicit agreement to the contrary, *title passes to the buyer at the time and the place the seller performs by delivering the goods* [UCC 2–401(2)]. For example, if a person buys cattle at a livestock auction, title will pass when the cattle are physically delivered to him or her (unless, of course, the parties agree otherwise).

SHIPMENT AND DESTINATION CONTRACTS Unless otherwise agreed, delivery arrangements can determine when title passes from the seller to the buyer. In a **shipment contract,** the seller is required or authorized to ship goods by carrier, such as a trucking company. Under a shipment contract, the seller is required only to deliver the goods into the hands of a carrier, and title passes to the buyer at the time and place of shipment [UCC 2–401(2)(a)]. Generally,

a contract is assumed to be a shipment contract if nothing to the contrary is stated in the contract.

In a **destination contract,** the seller is required to deliver the goods to a particular destination, usually directly to the buyer, but sometimes to another party designated by the buyer. Title passes to the buyer when the goods are *tendered* at that destination [UCC 2–401(2)(b)]. As you will read later in this chapter, *tender of delivery* occurs when the seller places or holds conforming goods at the buyer's disposal (with any necessary notice), enabling the buyer to take possession [UCC 2–503(1)].

DELIVERY WITHOUT MOVEMENT OF THE GOODS Sometimes, a sales contract does not call for the seller to ship or deliver the goods (such as when the buyer is to pick up the goods). In that situation, the passage of title depends on whether the seller must deliver a **document of title,** such as a bill of lading or a warehouse receipt, to the buyer. A *bill of lading* is a receipt for goods that is signed by a carrier and serves as a contract for the transportation of the goods. A *warehouse receipt* is a receipt issued by a warehouser for goods stored in a warehouse.

When a document of title is required, title passes to the buyer *when and where the document is delivered.* Thus, if the goods are stored in a warehouse, title passes to the buyer when the appropriate documents are delivered to the buyer. The goods never move. In fact, the buyer can choose to leave the goods at the same warehouse for a period of time, and the buyer's title to those goods will be unaffected.

When no document of title is required, and delivery is made without moving the goods, title passes at the time and place the sales contract is made, if the goods have already been identified. If the goods have not been identified, title does not pass until identification occurs. Suppose that Juarez sells lumber to Bodan. They agree that Bodan will pick up the lumber at the yard. If the lumber has been identified (segregated, marked, or in any other way distinguished from all other lumber), title passes to Bodan when the contract is signed. If the lumber is still in large storage bins at the mill, title does not pass to Bodan until the particular pieces of lumber to be sold under this contract are identified [UCC 2–401(3)].

Risk of Loss

Under the UCC, risk of loss does not necessarily pass with title. When risk of loss passes from a seller or lessor to a buyer or lessee is generally determined by the contract between the parties.

---

7. *In re Carman,* 399 Bankr. 158 (D.Md. 2009). For another case in which a boat was held to be future goods, see *Gonsalves v. Montgomery,* 2006 WL 2711540 (N.D.Cal. 2006).

Sometimes, the contract states expressly when the risk of loss passes. At other times, it does not, and a court must interpret the existing terms to ascertain whether the risk has passed. When no provision in the contract indicates when risk passes, the UCC provides special rules, based on delivery terms, to guide the courts.

DELIVERY WITH MOVEMENT OF THE GOODS—CARRIER CASES When the contract involves movement of the goods through a common carrier but does not specify when risk of loss passes, the courts first look for specific delivery terms in the contract. The terms that have traditionally been used in contracts are listed and defined in Exhibit 11–3 below. *Unless the parties agree otherwise,* these terms will determine which party will pay the costs of delivering the goods and who will bear the risk of loss. If the contract does not include these terms, then the courts must decide whether the contract is a shipment or a destination contract.

Shipment Contracts. In a shipment contract, the seller or lessor is required or authorized to ship goods by carrier, but is not required to deliver them to a particular destination. The risk of loss in a shipment contract passes to the buyer or lessee when the goods are delivered to the carrier [UCC 2–509(1)(a), 2A–219(2)(a)].

For example, a seller in Texas sells five hundred cases of grapefruit to a buyer in New York, F.O.B. Houston (free on board in Houston, which means that the buyer pays the transportation charges from Houston). The contract authorizes shipment by carrier. It does not require that the seller tender the grapefruit in New York. Risk passes to the buyer when conforming goods are properly placed in the possession of the carrier. If the goods are damaged in transit, the loss is the buyer's. (Actually, buyers have recourse against carriers, subject to certain limitations, and they may insure the goods from the time the goods leave the seller.)

Destination Contracts. In a destination contract, the risk of loss passes to the buyer or lessee when the goods are tendered to the buyer or lessee at the specified destination [UCC 2–509(1)(b), 2A–219(2)(b)]. In the preceding example involving the cases of grapefruit, if the contract had been a destination contract, F.O.B. New York, risk of loss during transit to New York would have been the seller's. Risk of loss would not have passed to the buyer until the carrier tendered the goods to the buyer in New York.

Whether a contract is a shipment contract or a destination contract can have significant consequences for the parties. When an agreement is ambiguous as to whether it is a shipment or a destination contract, courts normally will presume that it is a shipment contract. The parties must use clear and explicit language to overcome this presumption and create a destination contract.

DELIVERY WITHOUT MOVEMENT OF THE GOODS The UCC also addresses situations in which the contract does not require the goods to be shipped or moved. Frequently, the buyer or lessee is to pick up the goods from the seller or lessor, or the goods are to be held by a bailee. A *bailment* is a temporary delivery of personal property, without passage of title, into the care

EXHIBIT 11–3 • Contract Terms—Definitions
The contract terms listed and defined in this exhibit help to determine which party will bear the costs of delivery and when risk of loss will pass from the seller to the buyer.

F.O.B. (free on board)—Indicates that the selling price of goods includes transportation costs to the specific F.O.B. place named in the contract. The seller pays the expenses and carries the risk of loss to the F.O.B. place named [UCC 2–319(1)]. If the named place is the place from which the goods are shipped (for example, the seller's city or place of business), the contract is a shipment contract. If the named place is the place to which the goods are to be shipped (for example, the buyer's city or place of business), the contract is a destination contract.
F.A.S. (free alongside ship)—Requires that the seller, at his or her own expense and risk, deliver the goods alongside the vessel in the manner usual in that port or on a dock designated and provided by the buyer [UCC 2–319(2)]. An F.A.S. contract is essentially an F.O.B. contract for ships.
C.I.F. or **C.&F.** (cost, insurance, and freight or just cost and freight)—Requires, among other things, that the seller "put the goods in possession of a carrier" before risk passes to the buyer [UCC 2–320(2)]. (These are basically pricing terms, and the contracts remain shipment contracts, not destination contracts.)
Delivery ex-ship (delivery from the carrying vessel)—Means that risk of loss does not pass to the buyer until the goods are properly unloaded from the ship or other carrier [UCC 2–322].

of another, called a *bailee*. Under the UCC, a bailee is a party who—by a bill of lading, warehouse receipt, or other document of title—acknowledges possession of goods and/or contracts to deliver them. For example, a warehousing company or a trucking company may be a bailee.

Goods Held by the Seller. When the seller keeps the goods for pickup, a document of title usually is not used. If the seller is not a merchant, the risk of loss to goods held by the seller passes to the buyer on *tender of delivery* [UCC 2–509(3)]. This means that the seller bears the risk of loss until he or she makes the goods available to the buyer and notifies the buyer that the goods are ready to be picked up. If the seller is a merchant, risk of loss to goods held by the seller passes to the buyer when the buyer *actually takes physical possession of the goods* [UCC 2–509(3)]. In other words, the merchant bears the risk of loss between the time the contract is formed and the time the buyer picks up the goods.

CASE IN POINT Henry Ganno purchased a twelve-foot beam at a lumberyard, and an employee at the lumberyard loaded it onto Ganno's truck. A sign at the lumberyard stated that the store did not secure loads for customers, but Ganno did not tie down or otherwise secure the beam to his truck. After he drove onto the highway, the beam fell out of his truck. While he was trying to retrieve the beam, he was struck by another vehicle and injured. Ganno sued the lumberyard for negligence, but the court held that Ganno—not the lumberyard—bore the risk of loss and injury after he left the lumberyard's premises. Once the truck was loaded, the risk of loss passed to Ganno under the UCC because he had taken physical possession of the goods.[8]

With respect to leases, the risk of loss passes to the lessee on the lessee's receipt of the goods if the lessor is a merchant. Otherwise, the risk passes to the lessee on tender of delivery [UCC 2A–219(2)(c)].

Goods Held by a Bailee. When a bailee is holding goods that are to be delivered under a contract without being moved, the goods are usually represented by a document of title, such as a bill of lading or a warehouse receipt.[9] Risk of loss passes to the buyer when (1) the buyer receives a negotiable document of title for the goods, (2) the bailee acknowledges the buyer's right to possess the goods, or (3) the buyer receives a nonnegotiable document of title or a writing (record) directing the bailee to hand over the goods *and* the buyer has had a *reasonable time* to present the document to the bailee and demand the goods. Obviously, if the bailee refuses to honor the document, the risk of loss remains with the seller [UCC 2–503(4)(b), 2–509(2)].

With respect to leases, if goods held by a bailee are to be delivered without being moved, the risk of loss passes to the lessee on acknowledgment by the bailee of the lessee's right to possession of the goods [UCC 2A–219(2)(b)].

BREACH OF A SALES OR LEASE CONTRACT When a sales or lease contract is breached, the transfer of risk operates differently depending on which party breaches. Generally, the party in breach bears the risk of loss. Therefore, if the seller delivers goods that are so nonconforming that the buyer has the right to reject them, the risk of loss remains with the seller. The risk of loss does not pass to the buyer until the defects are *cured*—that is, until the goods are repaired, replaced, or discounted in price by the seller—or until the buyer accepts the goods in spite of their defects (thus waiving the right to reject) [UCC 2–510(1)]. Article 2A provides a similar rule for leases [UCC 2A–220(1)(a)].

When a buyer or lessee breaches a contract, the risk of loss *immediately shifts* to the buyer or lessee. This rule has three important limitations [UCC 2–510(3), 2A–220(2)]:

1. The seller or lessor must already have identified the contract goods.
2. The buyer or lessee bears the risk for only a *commercially reasonable time* after the seller or lessor has learned of the breach.
3. The buyer or lessee is liable only to the extent of any deficiency in the seller's or lessor's insurance coverage.

Insurable Interest

Parties to sales and lease contracts often obtain insurance coverage to protect against damage, loss, or destruction of goods. Any party purchasing insurance, however, must have a sufficient interest in the insured item to obtain a valid policy. Insurance laws—not the UCC—determine sufficiency. The UCC is helpful, though, because it contains certain rules regarding insurable interests in goods.

---

8. *Ganno v. Lanoga Corp.*, 119 Wash.App. 310, 80 P.3d 180 (2003).
9. A negotiable document of title actually stands for the goods it covers, so any transfer of the goods requires the surrender of the document. In contrast, a nonnegotiable document of title merely serves as evidence of the goods' existence.

A buyer or lessee has an **insurable interest** in *identified goods*. The moment the contract goods are identified by the seller or lessor, the buyer or lessee has a special property interest that allows the buyer or lessee to obtain the necessary insurance coverage for those goods, even before the risk of loss has passed [UCC 2–501(1), 2A–218(1)]. Identification can be made at any time and in any manner agreed to by the parties. If the parties do not explicitly agree on identification in their contract, then the UCC provisions on identification that were previously discussed in this chapter apply.

A seller has an insurable interest in goods as long as he or she retains title to the goods. Even after title passes to a buyer, a seller who has a security interest in the goods (a right to secure payment) still has an insurable interest and can insure the goods [UCC 2–501(2)]. Thus, both the buyer and the seller can have an insurable interest in identical goods at the same time. Of course, the buyer or seller must sustain an actual loss to have the right to recover from an insurance company. In regard to leases, the lessor retains an insurable interest in leased goods unless the lessee exercises an option to buy, in which event the risk of loss passes to the lessee [UCC 2A–218(3)].

SECTION 5
PERFORMANCE OF SALES AND LEASE CONTRACTS

The performance that is required of the parties under a sales or lease contract consists of the duties and obligations each party has under the terms of the contract. The basic obligation of the seller or lessor is to transfer and deliver the goods as stated in the contract, and the basic duty of the buyer or lessee is to accept and pay for the goods.

Keep in mind that "duties and obligations" under the terms of the contract include those specified by the agreement, by custom, and by the UCC. Thus, parties to a sales or lease contract may be bound not only by terms they expressly agreed on, but also by terms implied by custom, such as a customary method of weighing or measuring particular goods. In addition, the UCC sometimes imposes terms on parties to a sales contract, such as the requirement that a seller find a substitute carrier to deliver goods to the buyer if the agreed-on carrier becomes unavailable. In this section, we examine the basic performance obligations of the parties under a sales or lease contract.

The UCC's Good Faith Provision

The obligations of good faith and commercial reasonableness underlie every sales and lease contract. The UCC's good faith provision, which can never be disclaimed, reads as follows: "Every contract or duty within this Act imposes an obligation of good faith in its performance or enforcement" [UCC 1–304]. *Good faith* means honesty in fact. For a merchant, it means honesty in fact and the observance of reasonable commercial standards of fair dealing in the trade [UCC 2–103(1)(b)]. In other words, merchants are held to a higher standard of performance or duty than are nonmerchants.

Obligations of the Seller or Lessor

As stated, the basic duty of the seller or lessor is to deliver the goods called for under the contract to the buyer or lessee. Goods that conform to the contract description in every way are called **conforming goods.** To fulfill the contract, the seller or lessor must either deliver or tender delivery of conforming goods to the buyer or lessee. **Tender of delivery** occurs when the seller or lessor makes conforming goods available to the buyer or lessee and gives the buyer or lessee whatever notification is reasonably necessary to enable the buyer or lessee to take delivery [UCC 2–503(1), 2A–508(1)].

Tender must occur at a *reasonable hour* and in a *reasonable manner*. For example, a seller cannot call the buyer at 2:00 A.M. and say, "The goods are ready. I'll give you twenty minutes to get them." Unless the parties have agreed otherwise, the goods must be tendered for delivery at a reasonable hour and kept available for a reasonable period of time to enable the buyer to take possession of them [UCC 2–503(1)(a)]. Normally, all goods called for by a contract must be tendered in a single delivery—unless the parties have agreed that the goods may be delivered in several lots or *installments* [UCC 2–307, 2–612, 2A–510].

PLACE OF DELIVERY The buyer and seller (or lessor and lessee) may agree that the goods will be delivered to a particular destination where the buyer or lessee will take possession. If the contract does not designate the place of delivery, then the goods must be made available to the buyer at the *seller's place of business* or, if the seller has none, the *seller's residence*

[UCC 2–308(a)]. If, at the time of contracting, the parties know that the goods identified to the contract are located somewhere other than the seller's business, then the *location of the goods* is the place for their delivery [UCC 2–308(b)].

THE PERFECT TENDER RULE The seller or lessor has an obligation to ship or tender *conforming goods,* which the buyer or lessee is then obligated to accept and pay for according to the terms of the contract [UCC 2–507]. Under the common law, the seller was obligated to deliver goods that conformed with the terms of the contract in every detail. This was called the **perfect tender rule.** The UCC preserves the perfect tender doctrine by stating that if goods or tender of delivery fails *in any respect* to conform to the contract, the buyer or lessee has the right to accept the goods, reject the entire shipment, or accept part and reject part [UCC 2–601, 2A–509].

For example, a lessor contracts to lease fifty Comclear monitors to be delivered at the lessee's place of business on or before October 1. On September 28, the lessor discovers that it has only thirty Comclear monitors in inventory but will have another twenty Comclear monitors within the next two weeks. The lessor tenders delivery of the thirty Comclear monitors on October 1, with the promise that the other monitors will be delivered within two weeks. Because the lessor has failed to make a perfect tender of fifty Comclear monitors, the lessee has the right to reject the entire shipment and hold the lessor in breach.

Because of the rigidity of the perfect tender rule, several exceptions to the rule have been created. Some of these exceptions are discussed next.

Cure. The UCC does not specifically define the term **cure,** but it refers to the right of the seller or lessor to repair, adjust, or replace defective or nonconforming goods [UCC 2–508, 2A–513]. When any delivery is rejected because of nonconforming goods and the time for performance has not yet expired, the seller or lessor can attempt to "cure" the defect *within the contract time for performance* [UCC 2–508(1), 2A–513(1)]. To do so, the seller or lessor must seasonably (timely) notify the buyer or lessee of the intention to cure. Once the time for performance under the contract has expired, the seller or lessor can still exercise the right to cure if he or she has *reasonable grounds to believe that the nonconforming tender will be acceptable to the buyer or lessee* [UCC 2–508(2), 2A–513(2)].

The right to cure substantially restricts the right of the buyer or lessee to reject goods. For example, if a lessee refuses a tender of goods as nonconforming

but does not disclose the nature of the defect to the lessor, the lessee cannot later assert the defect as a defense if the defect is one that the lessor could have cured. Generally, buyers and lessees must act in good faith and state specific reasons for refusing to accept goods [UCC 2–605, 2A–514].

Substitution of Carriers. When an agreed-on manner of delivery (such as the use of a particular carrier to transport the goods) becomes impracticable or unavailable through no fault of either party, but a commercially reasonable substitute is available, this substitute performance is sufficient tender to the buyer and must be used [UCC 2–614(1)]. Note that the seller normally is responsible for any additional shipping costs, unless contrary arrangements have been made in the sales contract.

Commercial Impracticability. As discussed in Chapter 10 on page 220, occurrences unforeseen by either party when a contract was made may make performance commercially impracticable. When this occurs, the perfect tender rule no longer applies. According to UCC 2–615(a) and 2A–405(a), a delay in delivery or nondelivery in whole or in part is not a breach if performance has been made impracticable "by the occurrence of a contingency the nonoccurrence of which was a basic assumption on which the contract was made." The seller or lessor must, however, notify the buyer or lessee as soon as practicable that there will be a delay or nondelivery.

The doctrine of commercial impracticability does not extend to problems that could have been foreseen. An increase in cost resulting from inflation, for instance, does not in and of itself excuse performance, as this kind of foreseeable risk is ordinarily assumed by a seller or lessor conducting business.[10] The nonoccurrence of the contingency must have been a basic assumption on which the contract was made [UCC 2–615, 2A–405].

CASE IN POINT By contract, Hoosier Energy Rural Electric Cooperative was required to make lease payments to John Hancock Life Insurance Company for sixty-three years. The lease payments were guaranteed by Ambac Assurance Corporation, but when the latest global financial crisis struck, Ambac's credit rating was downgraded. This meant that Hoosier would have to pay $120 million to John Hancock or find another guarantor within a very short

---

10. For a classic case on this issue, see *Maple Farms, Inc. v. City School District of Elmira,* 76 Misc.2d 1080, 352 N.Y.S.2d 784 (1974).

time. Hoosier went to court, claiming commercial impracticability. Hoosier argued that the obstacles it faced in finding another guarantor were a result of the credit crisis and could not have been guarded against. The court agreed and issued an injunction that prevented John Hancock from obtaining the $120 million, even though Hoosier had agreed to the payment when it entered into the contract.[11]

Destruction of Identified Goods. Sometimes, an unexpected event, such as a fire, totally destroys goods through no fault of either party and before risk passes to the buyer or lessee. In such a situation, *if the goods were identified at the time the contract was formed,* the parties are excused from performance [UCC 2–613, 2A–221]. If the goods are only partially destroyed, however, the buyer or lessee can inspect them and either treat the contract as void or accept the damaged goods with a reduction in the contract price.

Assurance and Cooperation. Two other exceptions to the perfect tender doctrine apply equally to both parties to sales and lease contracts: the right of assurance and the duty of cooperation.

The UCC provides that if one of the parties to a contract has "reasonable grounds" to believe that the other party will not perform as contracted, she or he may *in writing* "demand adequate assurance of due performance" from the other party. Until such assurance is received, she or he may "suspend" further performance without liability. What constitutes "reasonable grounds" is determined by commercial standards. If such assurances are not forthcoming within a reasonable time (not to exceed thirty days), the failure to respond may be treated as a *repudiation* of the contract [UCC 2–609, 2A–401].

CASE IN POINT Two companies that made road-surfacing materials, Koch Materials and Shore Slurry Seal, Inc., entered into a contract. Koch obtained a license to use Novachip, a special material made by Shore, and Shore agreed to buy all of its asphalt from Koch for the next seven years. A few years into the contract term, Shore notified Koch that it was planning to sell its assets to Asphalt Paving Systems, Inc. Koch demanded assurances that Asphalt Paving would continue the deal, but Shore refused to provide assurances. The court held that Koch could

treat Shore's failure to give assurances as a repudiation and sue Shore for breach of contract.[12]

Sometimes, the performance of one party depends on the cooperation of the other. The UCC provides that when such cooperation is not forthcoming, the other party can suspend his or her own performance without liability and hold the uncooperative party in breach or proceed to perform the contract in any reasonable manner [UCC 2–311(3)].

Obligations of the Buyer or Lessee

Once the seller or lessor has adequately tendered delivery, the buyer or lessee is obligated to accept the goods and pay for them according to the terms of the contract.

PAYMENT In the absence of any specific agreements, the buyer or lessee must make payment at the time and place the goods are *received* [UCC 2–310(a), 2A–516(1)]. When a sale is made on credit, the buyer is obliged to pay according to the specified credit terms (for example, 60, 90, or 120 days), not when the goods are received. The credit period usually begins on the *date of shipment* [UCC 2–310(d)]. Under a lease contract, a lessee must make the lease payment that was specified in the contract [UCC 2A–516(1)].

Payment can be made by any means agreed on between the parties—cash or any other method generally acceptable in the commercial world. If the seller demands cash when the buyer offers a check, credit card, or the like, the seller must permit the buyer reasonable time to obtain legal tender [UCC 2–511].

RIGHT OF INSPECTION Unless the parties otherwise agree, or for C.O.D. (collect on delivery) transactions, the buyer or lessee has an absolute right to inspect the goods before making payment. This right allows the buyer or lessee to verify that the goods tendered or delivered conform to the contract. Inspection can take place at any reasonable place and time and in any reasonable manner. If the goods are not as ordered, the buyer or lessee has no duty to pay. *An opportunity for inspection is therefore a condition precedent to the right of the seller or lessor to enforce payment* [UCC 2–513(1), 2A–515(1)].

The following case focuses on the buyer's right to inspect the goods before acceptance, as well as the buyer's right to reject nonconforming goods.

---

11. *Hoosier Energy Rural Electric Cooperative, Inc. v. John Hancock Life Insurance Co.,* 588 F.Supp.2d 919 (S.D.Ind. 2008).

12. *Koch Materials Co. v. Shore Slurry Seal, Inc.,* 205 F.Supp.2d 324 (D.N.J. 2002).

✴ EXTENDED CASE 11.2 ✴
Romero v. Scoggin-Dickey Chevrolet-Buick, Inc.

Court of Appeals of Texas, Amarillo, ___ S.W.3d ___ (2010).
www.7thcoa.courts.state.tx.us[a]

IN THE LANGUAGE OF THE COURT
Patrick A. *PIRTLE*,
Justice.
* * * *

* * * Jessie Romero went to the Scoggin-Dickey Chevrolet-Buick, Inc., dealership in Lubbock, Texas, and sought to purchase a 2006 Silverado pickup from Fred Morales. Romero proposed to purchase the pickup by assigning the dealership the factory rebates, supplying two trade-in vehicles (a 2003 Mitsubishi Montero SP and a 2002 Chevrolet Silverado pickup), and paying the cash difference. At the time of the negotiations, Romero did not have the proposed trade-in vehicles on the lot for inspection by Scoggin-Dickey.

After negotiating a value for the trade-in vehicles, Romero and Morales signed a contract order wherein Scoggin-Dickey agreed to sell Romero the 2006 Silverado pickup for $21,888. In return, Romero agreed to trade in two vehicles having a combined net value of $15,000, assign factory rebates totaling $3,000, and pay $4,333.52 in cash.

Romero paid the cash, assigned the rebates, and took possession of the 2006 Silverado pickup. At that time, Romero did not deliver the trade-in vehicles to Scoggin-Dickey, nor did Scoggin-Dickey transfer title to the 2006 Silverado pickup to Romero. Subsequently, Romero showed Morales the location of the [Mitsubishi] Montero. After several weeks passed, Romero informed Morales that the 2002 Silverado pickup was located at a body shop. The pickup was not in running condition and was eventually towed by wrecker to Scoggin-Dickey.

After inspecting the trade-in vehicles, Scoggin-Dickey determined the Montero and 2002 Silverado pickup had little, or no, commercial value. Thereafter, Scoggin-Dickey took back the 2006 Silverado pickup and made two settlement offers to Romero pertaining to a partial refund of his down payment. Romero rejected the offers and filed suit.

* * * The trial court concluded, as a matter of law, that Scoggin-Dickey had a right to inspect the trade-in vehicles under [the Texas Code's equivalent to UCC Section 2–513] and, upon inspection, had validly exercised their right to reject the vehicles tendered by Romero.

* * * *

* * * Romero [argued on appeal, among other things, that] Scoggin-Dickey had no legal right to inspect and/or reject the trade-in vehicles after the contract order was executed[.]

* * * *

* * * *Unless the parties agree otherwise, a buyer has a right to inspect goods identified to a contract for sale at any reasonable place and time and in any reasonable manner prior to payment or acceptance of the goods. This is an implied condition in all contracts for sale.* Moreover, if the goods are nonconforming, the buyer also has "an absolute right to reject." Thus, the trial court correctly held, as a matter of law, that Scoggin-Dickey had a right to inspect Romero's trade-in vehicles to verify ownership, make, model, and value, even after the contract order was executed. If the trade-in vehicles did not conform to their description in the contract order, Scoggin-Dickey had a right to reject any nonconforming vehicle. [Emphasis added.]

* * * Execution of the contract order did not constitute a "sale" because there was no present transfer of ownership of the 2006 Silverado pickup to Romero or a transfer of ownership of the two trade-in vehicles in full payment of the purchase price to Scoggin-Dickey. Rather, the contract order was a *contract for sale*, [that is,] "a contract to sell goods at a future time"; or conditional sale. * * * Under these facts, the trial court could conclude that the parties intended that vehicle ownership pass in the future when the balance of the purchase price was paid to Scoggin-Dickey, [that is, when] Romero tendered two trade-in vehicles conforming to their description in the contract order.

* * * *

The trial court's judgment is affirmed.

---

a. In the right-hand column, under "Case Information," select "Opinion Search." When that page opens, fill out the "Case Number" boxes with "09," "0086," and "CV." In the "Date Written" box, enter "2/9/2010." Next, in the "Opinion Text" box, type "Romero." Then click on "Search." On the next page, select "View Opinion" to read the case. The Texas Seventh Court of Appeals in Amarillo, Texas, maintains this Web site.

QUESTIONS

1. Why didn't the "contract order" signed by the parties constitute a binding contract for the sale of goods?
2. According to the court, "Romero and Scoggin-Dickey were both buyers and sellers." What did the court mean by this statement?

ACCEPTANCE Once the buyer or lessee has had a reasonable opportunity to inspect the goods, the buyer or lessee can demonstrate acceptance of the delivered goods by words or conduct. A buyer or lessee who indicates to the seller or lessor that either the goods are conforming or he or she will retain them in spite of their nonconformity has accepted the goods [UCC 2–606(1)(a), 2A–515(1)(a)]. Acceptance of the goods is presumed when the buyer or lessee *fails to reject* the goods within a reasonable period of time [UCC 2–602(1), 2–606(1)(b), 2A–515(1)(b)].

In sales contracts, if the buyer *performs any act inconsistent with the seller's ownership,* then the buyer will be deemed to have accepted the goods. For example, any use or resale of the goods—except for the limited purpose of testing or inspecting the goods—generally constitutes an acceptance [UCC 2–606(1)(c)].

If some of the goods delivered do not conform to the contract and the seller or lessor has failed to cure, the buyer or lessee can make a *partial* acceptance [UCC 2–601(c), 2A–509(1)]. A buyer or lessee cannot accept less than a single commercial unit, however [UCC 2–105(6), 2A–103(1)(c)]. A commercial unit can be a single article (such as a machine), a set of articles (such as a suite of furniture), a quantity (such as a bale, a gross, or a carload), or any other unit treated in the trade as a single whole.

Anticipatory Repudiation

What if, before the time for contract performance, one party clearly communicates to the other the intention *not* to perform? Such an action is a breach of the contract by *anticipatory repudiation.* When anticipatory repudiation occurs, the nonbreaching party has a choice of two responses: (1) treat the repudiation as a final breach by pursuing a remedy or (2) wait to see if the repudiating party will decide to honor the contract despite the avowed intention to renege [UCC 2–610, 2A–402]. In either situation, the nonbreaching party may suspend performance.

The UCC permits the breaching party to "retract" his or her repudiation (subject to some limitations). This can be done by any method that clearly indicates the party's intent to perform. Once retraction is made, the rights of the repudiating party under the contract are reinstated.

REMEDIES FOR BREACH OF SALES AND LEASE CONTRACTS

Sometimes, circumstances make it difficult for a person to carry out the performance promised in a contract, in which case the contract may be breached. When a breach occurs, the aggrieved party looks for remedies. These remedies range from retaining the goods to requiring the breaching party's performance under the contract. The general purpose of these remedies is to put the aggrieved party "in as good a position as if the other party had fully performed." Remedies under the UCC are *cumulative* in nature. In other words, an innocent party to a breached sales or lease contract is not limited to one, exclusive remedy. (Of course, a party still may not recover twice for the same harm.)

Remedies of the Seller or Lessor

When the buyer or lessee is in breach, the seller or lessor has numerous remedies under the UCC. Generally, the remedies available to the seller or lessor depend on the circumstances existing at the time of the breach. The most pertinent considerations are which party has possession of the goods, whether the goods are in transit, and whether the buyer or lessee has rejected or accepted the goods.

WHEN THE GOODS ARE IN THE POSSESSION OF THE SELLER OR LESSOR Under the UCC, if the buyer or lessee breaches the contract before the goods have been delivered, the seller or lessor has the right to pursue the following remedies:

1. Cancel (rescind) the contract.
2. Resell the goods and sue to recover damages.
3. Sue to recover the purchase price or lease payments due.
4. Sue to recover damages for the buyer's nonacceptance of goods.

The Right to Cancel the Contract. If the buyer or lessee breaches the contract, the seller or lessor can choose to simply cancel the contract [UCC 2–703(f), 2A–523(1)(a)]. The seller or lessor must notify the buyer or lessee of the cancellation, and at that point all remaining obligations of the seller or lessor are discharged. The buyer or lessee is not discharged from all remaining obligations, however. He or she is in breach, and the seller or lessor can pursue remedies available under the UCC for breach.

The Right to Withhold Delivery. In general, sellers and lessors can withhold delivery or discontinue performance of their obligations under sales or lease contracts when the buyers or lessees are in breach. This is true whether a buyer or lessee has wrongfully rejected or revoked acceptance of contract goods (which will be discussed later in this chapter), failed to make a payment, or repudiated the contract [UCC 2–703(a), 2A–523(1)(c)]. The seller or lessor can also refuse to deliver the goods to a buyer or lessee who is insolvent (unable to pay debts as they become due) unless the buyer or lessee pays in cash [UCC 2–702(1), 2A–525(1)].

The Right to Resell or Dispose of the Goods. When a buyer or lessee breaches or repudiates the contract while the seller or lessor is in possession of the goods, the seller or lessor can resell or dispose of the goods. The seller can retain any profits made as a result of the sale and can hold the buyer or lessee liable for any loss [UCC 2–703(d), 2–706(1), 2A–523(1)(e), 2A–527(1)]. The seller must give the original buyer reasonable notice of the resale, unless the goods are perishable.

The Right to Recover the Purchase Price or Lease Payments Due. Under the UCC, an unpaid seller or lessor can bring an action to recover the purchase price or the payments due under the lease contract, plus incidental damages [UCC 2–709(1), 2A–529(1)]. If a seller or lessor is unable to resell or dispose of the goods and sues for the contract price or lease payments due, the goods must be held for the buyer or lessee. The seller or lessor can resell the goods at any time prior to collecting the judgment from the buyer or lessee. If the goods are resold, the net proceeds from the sale must be credited to the buyer or lessee because of the duty to mitigate damages.

The Right to Recover Damages for the Buyer's Nonacceptance. If a buyer or lessee repudiates a contract or wrongfully refuses to accept the goods, a seller or lessor can bring an action to recover the damages sustained. Ordinarily, the amount of damages equals the difference between the contract price or lease payments and the market price or lease payments at the time and place of tender of the goods, plus incidental damages [UCC 2–708(1),

2A–528(1)]. When the ordinary measure of damages is inadequate to put the seller or lessor in as good a position as the buyer's or lessee's performance would have, the UCC provides an alternative. In that situation, the proper measure of damages is the lost profits of the seller or lessor, including a reasonable allowance for overhead and other expenses [UCC 2–708(2), 2A–528(2)].

WHEN THE GOODS ARE IN TRANSIT When the seller or lessor has delivered the goods to a carrier or a bailee but the buyer or lessee has not yet received them, the goods are said to be *in transit*. If, while the goods are in transit, the seller or lessor learns that the buyer or lessee is insolvent, the seller or lessor can stop the carrier or bailee from delivering the goods, regardless of the quantity of goods shipped. To stop delivery, the seller or lessor must *timely notify* the carrier or other bailee that the goods are to be returned or held for the seller or lessor. If the buyer or lessee is in breach but is not insolvent, the seller or lessor can stop the goods in transit only if the quantity shipped is at least a carload, a truckload, a planeload, or a larger shipment [UCC 2–705(1), 2A–526(1)].

WHEN THE GOODS ARE IN THE POSSESSION OF THE BUYER OR LESSEE When the buyer or lessee has breached a sales or lease contract and the goods are in his or her possession, the seller or lessor can sue to recover the purchase price of the goods or the lease payments due, plus incidental damages [UCC 2–709(1), 2A–529(1)]. A seller may also have a right to reclaim the goods from the buyer in some instances, such as when the buyer received the goods on credit. If a lessee is in default (fails to make payments that are due, for example), the lessor may reclaim the leased goods that are in the lessee's possession [UCC 2A–525(2)].

Remedies of the Buyer or Lessee

When the seller or lessor breaches the contract, the buyer or lessee has numerous remedies available under the UCC. Like the remedies available to sellers and lessors, the remedies available to buyers and lessees depend on the circumstances existing at the time of the breach.

WHEN THE SELLER OR LESSOR REFUSES TO DELIVER THE GOODS If the seller or lessor refuses to deliver the goods to the buyer or lessee, the basic remedies available to the buyer or lessee include the right to:

1. Cancel the contract.
2. Recover goods that have been paid for if the seller or lessor is insolvent.
3. Sue to obtain specific performance if the goods are unique or if damages are an inadequate remedy.
4. Buy other goods (obtain *cover*—discussed next) and recover damages from the seller.
5. Sue to obtain identified goods held by a third party (*replevy* goods—discussed shortly).
6. Sue to recover damages.

The Right of Cover. In certain situations, buyers and lessees can protect themselves by obtaining **cover**—that is, by buying or leasing substitute goods for those that were due under the contract. This option is available when the seller or lessor repudiates the contract or fails to deliver the goods. (Cover is also available when a buyer or lessee has rightfully rejected goods or revoked acceptance.)

In obtaining cover, the buyer or lessee must act in good faith and without unreasonable delay [UCC 2–712, 2A–518]. After purchasing or leasing substitute goods, the buyer or lessee can recover from the seller or lessor the difference between the cost of cover and the contract price (or lease payments), plus incidental and consequential damages, less the expenses (such as delivery costs) that were saved as a result of the breach [UCC 2–712, 2–715, 2A–518]. *Consequential damages* are any losses suffered by the buyer or lessee that the seller or lessor had reason to know about at the time of contract formation. Consequential damages can also include any injury to the buyer's or lessee's person or property proximately resulting from the contract's breach [UCC 2–715(2), 2A–520(2)].

Buyers and lessees are not required to cover, and failure to do so will not bar them from using any other remedies available under the UCC. A buyer or lessee who fails to cover, however, risks collecting a lower amount of consequential damages. A court may reduce the consequential damages by the amount of the loss that could have been avoided had the buyer or lessee purchased or leased substitute goods.

The Right to Replevy Goods. Buyers and lessees also have the right to replevy goods. **Replevin**[13] is an action to recover identified goods in the hands of a party who is unlawfully withholding them. Under the UCC, a buyer or lessee can replevy goods identified to the contract if the seller or lessor has repudiated or breached the contract. To maintain an action

to replevy goods, buyers and lessees must usually show that they were unable to cover for the goods after making a reasonable effort [UCC 2–716(3), 2A–521(3)].

The Right to Recover Damages. If a seller or lessor repudiates the contract or fails to deliver the goods, the buyer or lessee can sue for damages. The measure of recovery is the difference between the contract price (or lease payments) and the market price of the goods (or lease payments that could be obtained for the goods) at the time the buyer (or lessee) *learned* of the breach. The market price or market lease payments are determined at the place where the seller or lessor was supposed to deliver the goods. The buyer or lessee can also recover incidental and consequential damages less the expenses that were saved as a result of the breach [UCC 2–713, 2A–519].

Consider an example. Schilling orders ten thousand bushels of wheat from Valdone for $7.00 per bushel, with delivery due on June 14 and payment due on June 20. Valdone does not deliver on June 14. On June 14, the market price of wheat is $7.50 per bushel. Schilling chooses to do without the wheat. He sues Valdone for damages for nondelivery. Schilling can recover $0.50 × 10,000, or $5,000, plus any expenses the breach has caused him. The measure of damages is the market price on the day Schilling was to have received delivery less the contract price. (Any expenses Schilling saved by the breach would be deducted from the damages.)

WHEN THE SELLER OR LESSOR DELIVERS NONCONFORMING GOODS When the seller or lessor delivers nonconforming goods, the buyer or lessee has several remedies available under the UCC.

The Right to Reject the Goods. If either the goods or the tender of the goods by the seller or lessor fails to conform to the contract in any respect, the buyer or lessee can reject all of the goods or any commercial unit of the goods [UCC 2–601, 2A–509]. If the buyer or lessee rejects the goods, she or he may then obtain cover or cancel the contract, and may seek damages just as if the seller or lessor had refused to deliver the goods (see the earlier discussion of these remedies).

CASE IN POINT Jorge Jauregui contracted to buy a new Kawai RX5 piano for $24,282 from Bobb's Piano Sales & Service, Inc. When the piano was delivered with "unacceptable damage," Jauregui rejected it and filed a lawsuit for breach of contract.

---

13. Pronounced ruh-*pleh*-vun, derived from the Old French word *plevir*, meaning "to pledge."

The court ruled that Bobb's had breached the contract by delivering nonconforming goods. Jauregui was entitled to damages equal to the contract price with interest, plus the sales tax, delivery charge, and attorneys' fees.[14]

The buyer or lessee must reject the goods within a reasonable amount of time after delivery or tender of delivery and must seasonally (timely) notify the seller or lessor [UCC 2–602(1), 2A–509(2)]. If the buyer or lessee fails to reject the goods within a reasonable amount of time, acceptance will be presumed. The buyer or lessee must also designate defects that are ascertainable by reasonable inspection. Failure to do so precludes the buyer or lessee from using such defects to justify rejection or to establish breach when the seller or lessor could have cured the defects if they had been disclosed seasonally [UCC 2–605, 2A–514]. A merchant buyer or lessee has a good faith obligation to follow any reasonable instructions received from the seller or lessor with respect to the goods [UCC 2–603, 2A–511].

Revocation of Acceptance. Acceptance of the goods precludes the buyer or lessee from exercising the right of rejection, but it does not necessarily prevent the buyer or lessee from pursuing other remedies. In certain circumstances, a buyer or lessee is permitted to *revoke* his or her acceptance of the goods. Acceptance of a lot or a commercial unit can be revoked if the nonconformity *substantially* impairs the value of the lot or unit *and* if one of the following factors is present:

1. Acceptance was predicated on the reasonable assumption that the nonconformity would be cured, and it has not been cured within a reasonable period of time [UCC 2–608(1)(a), 2A–517(1)(a)].
2. The buyer or lessee did not discover the nonconformity before acceptance, either because it was difficult to discover before acceptance or because assurances made by the seller or lessor that the goods were conforming kept the buyer or lessee from inspecting the goods [UCC 2–608(1)(b), 2A–517(1)(b)].

Revocation of acceptance is not effective until notice is given to the seller or lessor. Notice must occur within a reasonable time after the buyer or lessee either discovers or *should have discovered* the grounds for revocation.

The Right to Recover Damages for Accepted Goods. A buyer or lessee who has accepted nonconforming goods may also keep the goods and recover for any loss "resulting in the ordinary course of events . . . as determined in any manner which is reasonable" [UCC 2–714(1), 2A–519(3)]. To do so, the buyer or lessee must notify the seller or lessor of the breach within a reasonable time after the defect was or should have been discovered.

CASE IN POINT James Fitl attended a sports-card show in San Francisco, California, where he met Mark Strek, an exhibitor at the show. Fitl bought a 1952 Mickey Mantle Topps baseball card for $17,750 from Strek, who had represented that the card was in near-mint condition. Strek delivered it to Fitl in Nebraska, and Fitl placed it in a safe-deposit box. Two years later, Fitl sent the card to Professional Sports Authenticators (PSA), a sports-card grading service. PSA told Fitl that the card was ungradable because it had been discolored and doctored. Fitl complained to Strek, who refused to refund the purchase price because of the amount of time that had gone by. Fitl then filed a lawsuit, and the court awarded him $17,750, plus his court costs. Strek appealed. The Nebraska Supreme Court affirmed Fitl's right to recover damages. The court held that Fitl had reasonably relied on Strek's representation that the card was "authentic," which it was not, and that Fitl had given Strek timely notice of the card's defects when they were discovered.[15]

Additional Provisions Affecting Remedies

The parties to a sales or lease contract can vary their respective rights and obligations by contractual agreement. For example, a seller and buyer can expressly provide for remedies in addition to those provided in the UCC. The parties can also specify remedies in lieu of those provided in the UCC, or they can change the measure of damages. As under the common law of contracts, they may also include clauses in their contracts providing for liquidated damages in the event of a breach or a delay in performance (see Chapter 10 on page 225).

Additionally, a seller can stipulate that the buyer's only remedy on the seller's breach will be repair or replacement of the item, or the seller can limit the buyer's remedy to return of the goods and refund of the purchase price. In sales and lease contracts, an

---

14. *Jauregui v. Bobb's Piano Sales & Service, Inc.*, 922 So.2d 303 (Fla. App. 2006).

15. *Fitl v. Strek*, 269 Neb. 51, 690 N.W.2d 605 (2005).

agreed-on remedy is in addition to those provided in the UCC unless the parties expressly agree that the remedy is exclusive of all others [UCC 2–719(1), 2A–503(1), (2)].

SECTION 7
SALES AND LEASE WARRANTIES

Warranty is an age-old concept. In sales and lease law, a warranty is an assurance or guarantee by the seller or lessor of certain facts concerning the goods being sold or leased. The UCC has numerous rules governing product warranties as they occur in sales and lease contracts.

Because a warranty imposes a duty on the seller or lessor, a breach of warranty is a breach of the seller's or lessor's promise. Assuming that the parties have not agreed to limit or modify the remedies available, if the seller or lessor breaches a warranty, the buyer or lessee can sue to recover damages from the seller or lessor. Under some circumstances, a breach of warranty can allow the buyer or lessee to cancel the agreement.

Warranties of Title

Under the UCC, three types of title warranties—*good title, no liens,* and *no infringements*—can automatically arise in sales and lease contracts [UCC 2–312, 2A–211]. Normally, a seller or lessor can disclaim or modify these title warranties only by including *specific language* in the contract. For example, sellers may assert that they are transferring only such rights, title, and interest as they have in the goods.

In most sales, sellers warrant that they have good and valid title to the goods sold and that the transfer of the title is rightful [UCC 2–312(1)(a)]. A second warranty of title protects buyers and lessees who are *unaware* of any encumbrances (claims, charges, or liabilities—usually called *liens*[16]) against goods at the time the contract is made [UCC 2–312(1)(b), 2A–211(1)]. This warranty protects buyers who, for example, unknowingly purchase goods that are subject to a creditor's security interest (a *security interest* is an interest in the goods that secures payment or performance of an obligation—see Chapter 15). If a creditor legally repossesses the goods from a buyer *who had no actual knowledge of the security interest,* the buyer can recover from the seller for breach of warranty. (A

buyer who has *actual knowledge of a security interest* has no recourse against a seller.) Article 2A affords similar protection for lessees [UCC 2A–211(1)].

Finally, when the seller or lessor is a merchant, he or she automatically warrants that the buyer or lessee takes the good *free of infringements.* In other words, a merchant promises that the goods delivered are free from any copyright, trademark, or patent claims of a third person [UCC 2–312(3), 2A–211(2)].

Express Warranties

A seller or lessor can create an **express warranty** by making representations concerning the quality, condition, description, or performance potential of the goods. Under UCC 2–313 and 2A–210, express warranties arise when a seller or lessor indicates any of the following:

1. That the goods conform to any *affirmation* (a declaration that something is true) *of fact* or *promise* that the seller or lessor makes to the buyer or lessee about the goods. Such affirmations or promises are usually made during the bargaining process. Statements such as "these drill bits will *easily* penetrate stainless steel—and without dulling" are express warranties.
2. That the goods conform to any *description* of them. For example, a label that reads "Crate contains one 150-horsepower diesel engine" or a contract that calls for the delivery of a "wool coat" creates an express warranty that the content of the goods sold conforms to the description.
3. That the goods conform to any *sample or model* of the goods shown to the buyer or lessee.

Express warranties can be found in a seller's or lessor's advertisement, brochure, or promotional materials, in addition to being made orally or in an express warranty provision in a sales or lease contract.

BASIS OF THE BARGAIN To create an express warranty, a seller or lessor does not have to use formal words such as *warrant* or *guarantee.* It is only necessary that a reasonable buyer or lessee would regard the representation as being part of the basis of the bargain [UCC 2–313(2), 2A–210(2)]. Just what constitutes the basis of the bargain is hard to say. The UCC does not define the concept, and it is a question of fact in each case whether a representation was made at such a time and in such a way that it induced the buyer or lessee to enter into the contract. Therefore, if an express warranty is not intended, the marketing agent or salesperson should not promise too much.

---

16. Pronounced *leens.* Liens will be discussed in Chapter 15.

STATEMENTS OF OPINION AND VALUE Only statements of fact create express warranties. A seller or lessor who makes a statement that merely relates to the value or worth of the goods, or states an opinion about or recommends the goods, does not create an express warranty [UCC 2–313(2), 2A–210(2)].

Suppose that a seller claims that "this is the best used car to come along in years; it has four new tires and a 250-horsepower engine just rebuilt this year." The seller has made several *affirmations of fact* that can create a warranty: The automobile has an engine; it has a 250-horsepower engine; the engine was rebuilt this year; there are four tires on the automobile; and the tires are new.

The seller's *opinion* that the vehicle is "the best used car to come along in years," however, is known as "puffery" and creates no warranty. (**Puffery** is an expression of opinion by a seller or lessor that is not made as a representation of fact.) It is not always easy to determine whether a statement constitutes an express warranty or puffery. The reasonableness of the buyer's or lessee's reliance appears to be the controlling criterion in many cases.

CASE IN POINT A tobacco farmer read an advertisement for Chlor-O-Pic, a chemical fumigant, which stated that, if applied as directed, Chlor-O-Pic would give "season-long control with application in fall, winter, or spring" against black shank disease, a fungal disease that destroys tobacco crops. The farmer bought Chlor-O-Pic and applied it as directed to his tobacco crop. Nonetheless, the crop developed black shank disease. The farmer sued the manufacturer of Chlor-O-Pic, arguing that he had purchased the product in reliance on a "strong promise" of "season-long control." The court found that the manufacturer's strong promise had created an express warranty and that the farmer was entitled to the value of the damaged crop.[17]

Implied Warranties

An **implied warranty** is one that *the law derives* by inference from the nature of the transaction or the relative situations or circumstances of the parties. Under the UCC, merchants impliedly warrant that the goods they sell or lease are merchantable and, in certain circumstances, fit for a particular purpose. In addition, an implied warranty may arise from a course of dealing or usage of trade. We examine these three types of implied warranties in the following subsections.

IMPLIED WARRANTY OF MERCHANTABILITY Every sale or lease of goods made by a merchant who deals in goods of the kind sold or leased automatically gives rise to an **implied warranty of merchantability** [UCC 2–314, 2A–212]. Thus, a merchant who is in the business of selling ski equipment makes an implied warranty of merchantability every time he sells a pair of skis. A neighbor selling her skis at a garage sale does not (because she is not in the business of selling goods of this type).

Merchantable Goods. To be *merchantable*, goods must be "reasonably fit for the ordinary purposes for which such goods are used." They must be of at least average, fair, or medium-grade quality. The quality must be comparable to quality that will pass without objection in the trade or market for goods of the same description. To be merchantable, the goods must also be adequately packaged and labeled, and they must conform to the promises or affirmations of fact made on the container or label, if any. Of course, merchants are not absolute insurers against *all* accidents arising in connection with the goods. For example, a bar of soap is not unmerchantable merely because a user could slip and fall by stepping on it.

CASE IN POINT Darrell Shoop bought a Dodge Dakota truck that had been manufactured by DaimlerChrysler Corporation. Almost immediately, he had problems with the truck. During the first eighteen months, the engine, suspension, steering, transmission, and other components required repairs twelve times, including at least five times for the same defect, which remained uncorrected. Shoop eventually traded in the truck and filed a lawsuit against DaimlerChrysler for breach of the implied warranty of merchantability. The court held that Shoop could maintain an action against DaimlerChrysler and use the fact that the truck had required a significant number of repairs as evidence that it was unmerchantable.[18]

Merchantable Food. The UCC treats the serving of food or drink to be consumed on or off the premises as a sale of goods subject to the implied warranty of merchantability [UCC 2–314(1)]. "Merchantable" food is food that is fit to eat on the basis of consumer expectations. For example, the courts assume

---

17. *Triple E, Inc. v. Hendrix & Dail, Inc.,* 344 S.C. 186, 543 S.E.2d 245 (2001). See also *Nomo Agroindustrial Sa De CV v. Enza Zaden North America, Inc.,* 492 F.Supp.2d 1175 (D.Ariz. 2007).

18. *Shoop v. DaimlerChrysler Corp.,* 371 Ill.App.3d 1058, 864 N.E.2d 785, 309 Ill.Dec. 544 (2007).

that consumers should reasonably expect to find on occasion bones in fish fillets, cherry pits in cherry pie, a nutshell in a package of shelled nuts, and the like—because such substances are natural to the ingredients or the finished food product. In contrast, consumers would not reasonably expect to find an inchworm in a can of peas or a piece of glass in a soft drink—because these substances are *not* natural to the food product.

In the following classic case, the court had to determine whether one should reasonably expect to find a fish bone in fish chowder.

CASE 11.3
Webster v. Blue Ship Tea Room, Inc.

Supreme Judicial Court of Massachusetts, 347 Mass. 421, 198 N.E.2d 309 (1964).

BACKGROUND AND FACTS • Blue Ship Tea Room, Inc., was located in Boston in an old building overlooking the ocean. Webster, who had been born and raised in New England, went to the restaurant and ordered fish chowder. The chowder was milky in color. After three or four spoonfuls, she felt something lodged in her throat. As a result, she underwent two esophagoscopies; in the second esophagoscopy, a fish bone was found and removed. Webster filed a suit against the restaurant in a Massachusetts state court for breach of the implied warranty of merchantability. The jury rendered a verdict for Webster, and the restaurant appealed to the state's highest court.

IN THE LANGUAGE OF THE COURT
REARDON, Justice.

[The plaintiff] ordered a cup of fish chowder. Presently, there was set before her "a small bowl of fish chowder." * * * After 3 or 4 [spoonfuls] she was aware that something had lodged in her throat because she "couldn't swallow and couldn't clear her throat by gulping and she could feel it." This misadventure led to two esophagoscopies [procedures in which a telescope-like instrument is used to look into the throat] at the Massachusetts General Hospital, in the second of which, on April 27, 1959, a fish bone was found and removed. The sequence of events produced injury to the plaintiff which was not insubstantial.

We must decide whether a fish bone lurking in a fish chowder, about the ingredients of which there is no other complaint, constitutes a breach of implied warranty under applicable provisions of the Uniform Commercial Code * * *. As the judge put it in his charge [jury instruction], "Was the fish chowder fit to be eaten and wholesome? * * * Nobody is claiming that the fish itself wasn't wholesome. * * * But the bone of contention here—I don't mean that for a pun—but was this fish bone a foreign substance that made the fish chowder unwholesome or not fit to be eaten?"

* * * *

[We think that it] is not too much to say that a person sitting down in New England to consume a good New England fish chowder embarks on a gustatory [taste-related] adventure which may entail the removal of some fish bones from his bowl as he proceeds. We are not inclined to tamper with age-old recipes by any amendment reflecting the plaintiff's view of the effect of the Uniform Commercial Code upon them. We are aware of the heavy body of case law involving foreign substances in food, but we sense a strong distinction between them and those relative to unwholesomeness of the food itself, [such as] tainted mackerel, and a fish bone in a fish chowder. * * * We consider that the joys of life in New England include the ready availability of fresh fish chowder. We should be prepared to cope with the hazards of fish bones, the occasional presence of which in chowders is, it seems to us, to be anticipated, and which, in the light of a hallowed tradition, do not impair their fitness or merchantability.

DECISION AND REMEDY • *The Supreme Judicial Court of Massachusetts "sympathized with a plaintiff who has suffered a peculiarly New England injury" but entered a judgment for the defendant, Blue Ship Tea Room. A fish bone in fish chowder is not a breach of the implied warranty of merchantability.*

IMPACT OF THIS CASE ON TODAY'S LAW • *This classic case, phrased in memorable language, was an early application of the UCC's implied warranty of merchantability to food products. The case established the rule that consumers should expect to find, on occasion, elements of food products that are natural to the product (such as fish bones in fish chowder). Courts today still apply this rule.*

THE E-COMMERCE DIMENSION • *If Webster had made the chowder herself from a recipe that she had found on the Internet, could she have successfully brought an action against its author for a breach of the implied warranty of merchantability? Explain.*

IMPLIED WARRANTY OF FITNESS FOR A PARTICULAR PURPOSE The **implied warranty of fitness for a particular purpose** arises when *any* seller or lessor (merchant or nonmerchant) knows the particular purpose for which a buyer or lessee will use the goods *and* knows that the buyer or lessee is relying on the skill and judgment of the seller or lessor to select suitable goods [UCC 2–315, 2A–213].

Goods can be merchantable but unfit for a particular purpose. For example, you need a gallon of paint to match the color of your living room walls—a light shade somewhere between coral and peach. You take a sample to your local hardware store and request a gallon of paint of that color. Instead, you are given a gallon of bright blue paint. Here, the salesperson has not breached any warranty of implied merchantability—the bright blue paint is of high quality and suitable for interior walls—but she or he has breached an implied warranty of fitness for a particular purpose.

A seller or lessor need not have actual knowledge of the buyer's or lessee's particular purpose. It is sufficient if a seller or lessor "has reason to know" the purpose. For an implied warranty to be created, however, the buyer or lessee must have *relied* on the skill or judgment of the seller or lessor in selecting or furnishing suitable goods. Moreover, the seller or lessor must have reason to know that the buyer or lessee is relying on her or his judgment or skill.

WARRANTIES IMPLIED FROM PRIOR DEALINGS OR TRADE CUSTOM Implied warranties can also arise (or be excluded or modified) as a result of course of dealing or usage of trade [UCC 2–314(3), 2A–212(3)]. In the absence of evidence to the contrary, when both parties to a sales or lease contract have knowledge of a well-recognized trade custom, the courts will infer that both parties intended for that custom to apply to their contract. For instance, if the industrywide custom is to lubricate a new car before it is delivered and a dealer fails to do so, the dealer

can be held liable to a buyer for damages resulting from the breach of an implied warranty. (This would also be negligence on the part of the dealer—see Chapter 12.)

SECTION 8
E-CONTRACTS

Numerous contracts are formed online. Electronic contracts, or **e-contracts,** must meet the same basic requirements (agreement, consideration, contractual capacity, and legality) as paper contracts. Disputes concerning e-contracts, however, tend to center on contract terms and whether the parties voluntarily agreed to those terms.

Online contracts may be formed not only for the sale of goods and services but also for *licensing.* The "sale" of software generally involves a license, or a right to use the software, rather than the passage of title (ownership rights) from the seller to the buyer. For example, Galynn wants to obtain software that will allow her to work on spreadsheets on her BlackBerry. She goes online and purchases GridMagic. During the transaction, she has to click on several on-screen "I agree" boxes to indicate that she understands that she is purchasing only the right to use the software and will not obtain any ownership rights. After she agrees to these terms (the licensing agreement), she can download the software.

As you read through the following subsections, keep in mind that although we typically refer to the offeror and the offeree as a *seller* and a *buyer,* in many online transactions these parties would be more accurately described as a *licensor* and a *licensee.*

Online Offers

Sellers doing business via the Internet can protect themselves against contract disputes and legal liability by creating offers that clearly spell out the terms that will govern their transactions if the offers are accepted. All important terms should be conspicuous and easy to view.

DISPLAYING THE OFFER The seller's Web site should include a hypertext link to a page containing the full contract so that potential buyers are made aware of the terms to which they are assenting. The contract generally must be displayed online in a readable format, such as a twelve-point typeface. All provisions should be reasonably clear. Suppose that Netquip sells a variety of heavy equipment, such as trucks and trailers, on its Web site. Because Netquip's pricing schedule is very complex, the schedule must be fully provided and explained on the Web site. In addition, the terms of the sale (such as any warranties and the refund policy) must be fully disclosed.

PROVISIONS TO INCLUDE An important rule to keep in mind is that the offeror (the seller) controls the offer and thus the resulting contract. The seller should therefore anticipate the terms he or she wants to include in a contract and provide for them in the offer. In some instances, a standardized contract form may suffice. At a minimum, an online offer should include the following provisions:

1. *Acceptance of terms.* A clause that clearly indicates what constitutes the buyer's agreement to the terms of the offer, such as a box containing the words "I accept" that the buyer can click. (Mechanisms for accepting online offers will be discussed in detail later in the chapter.)
2. *Payment.* A provision specifying how payment for the goods (including any applicable taxes) must be made.
3. *Return policy.* A statement of the seller's refund and return policies.
4. *Disclaimer.* Disclaimers of liability for certain uses of the goods. For example, an online seller of business forms may add a disclaimer that the seller does not accept responsibility for the buyer's reliance on the forms rather than on an attorney's advice.
5. *Limitation on remedies.* A provision specifying the remedies available to the buyer if the goods are found to be defective or if the contract is otherwise breached. Any limitation of remedies should be clearly spelled out.
6. *Privacy policy.* A statement indicating how the seller will use the information gathered about the buyer.
7. *Dispute resolution.* Provisions relating to dispute settlement, such as an arbitration clause or a forum-selection clause. An arbitration clause specifies

that any dispute arising under the contract will be arbitrated in a designated forum. A **forum-selection clause** indicates the forum, or location (such as a court or jurisdiction), in which contract disputes will be resolved. A forum-selection clause will help to avert future jurisdictional problems and to ensure that the seller will not be required to appear in court in a distant state.

CASE IN POINT Before advertisers can place ads through Google, Inc., they must agree to certain terms that are displayed in an online window. These terms include a forum-selection clause, which provides that any dispute is to be "adjudicated in Santa Clara County, California." Lawrence Feldman, who advertised through Google, complained that he was overcharged and filed a lawsuit against Google in a federal district court in Pennsylvania. The court held that Feldman had agreed to the forum-selection clause in Google's online contract and transferred the case to a court in Santa Clara County.[19]

Some online contracts might also include a **choice-of-law clause** in which the parties specify that any dispute arising out of the contract will be settled in accordance with the law of a particular jurisdiction, such as a state or country. Choice-of-law clauses are particularly common in international contracts, but they may also appear in e-contracts to specify which state's laws will govern in the United States.

Online Acceptances

The *Restatement (Second) of Contracts,* which, as noted earlier, is a compilation of common law contract principles, states that parties may agree to a contract "by written or spoken words or by other action or by failure to act."[20] Section 2–204 of the UCC states that any contract for the sale of goods "may be made in any manner sufficient to show agreement, including conduct by both parties which recognizes the existence of such a contract."

CLICK-ON AGREEMENTS The courts have used the *Restatement* and UCC provisions to conclude that a binding contract can be created by conduct, including the act of clicking on a box indicating "I accept" or "I agree" to accept an online offer. The agreement resulting from such an acceptance is often called a **click-on agreement** (sometimes referred to as a *click-on license* or *click-wrap agreement*).

---

19. *Feldman v. Google, Inc.,* 513 F.Supp.2d 229 (E.D.Pa. 2007).
20. *Restatement (Second) of Contracts,* Section 19.

Generally, the law does not require that the parties have read all of the terms in a contract for it to be effective. Therefore, clicking on a box that states "I agree" to certain terms can be enough. The terms may be contained on a Web site through which the buyer is obtaining goods or services, or they may appear on a computer screen when software is loaded from a CD-ROM or DVD or downloaded from the Internet.

SHRINK-WRAP AGREEMENTS With a **shrink-wrap agreement** (or *shrink-wrap license*), the terms are expressed inside the box in which the goods are packaged. (The term *shrink-wrap* refers to the plastic that covers the box.) Usually, the party who opens the box is told that she or he agrees to the terms by keeping whatever is in the box. Similarly, when a purchaser opens a software package, he or she agrees to abide by the terms of the limited license agreement. In most instances, a shrink-wrap agreement is not between a retailer and a buyer, but between the manufacturer of the hardware or software and the ultimate buyer-user of the product. The terms generally concern warranties, remedies, and other issues associated with the use of the product.

In some cases, the courts have enforced the terms of shrink-wrap agreements in the same way as the terms of other contracts. These courts have reasoned that by including the terms with the product, the seller proposed a contract. Thus, a buyer's failure to object to terms contained within a shrink-wrapped software package may constitute an acceptance of the terms by conduct.

Nevertheless, the courts have sometimes refused to enforce certain terms included in shrink-wrap agreements because the buyers did not expressly consent to them. One factor that courts consider important is whether the parties formed their contract before or after the seller communicated the terms of the shrink-wrap agreement to the buyer. If a buyer orders a product over the telephone, for instance, and is not informed of an arbitration clause or forum-selection clause at that time, a court may conclude that those terms were not part of the contract.

BROWSE-WRAP TERMS Like the terms of click-on agreements, **browse-wrap terms** can occur in transactions conducted over the Internet. Unlike click-on agreements, however, browse-wrap terms do not require Internet users to assent to the terms before, say, downloading or using certain software. In other words, a person can install the software without clicking "I agree" to the terms of a license. Browse-wrap terms are often unenforceable because they do not satisfy the agreement requirement of contract formation.

CASE IN POINT Netscape Communications Corporation provided free downloadable software called "SmartDownload" on its Web site to those who indicated, by clicking on a designated box, that they wished to obtain it. On the Web site's download page was a reference to a license agreement that the user could view only by scrolling to the next screen. In other words, the user did not have to agree to the terms of the license before downloading the software. One of the terms required all disputes to be submitted to arbitration in California. When a group of users filed a lawsuit against Netscape in New York, the court held that the arbitration clause in the browse-wrap license agreement was unenforceable because users were not required to indicate their assent to the agreement.[21]

E-Signatures

Today, numerous technologies exist that allow electronic documents to be signed. For example, a digitized signature, or **e-signature,** is a graphical image of a handwritten signature, often created using a digital pen and pad, such as an ePad, and special software.

Although most states have laws governing e-signatures, these laws are not uniform. Some states—California is a notable example—prohibit many types of documents from being signed with e-signatures, whereas other states are more permissive.

To create more uniformity among the states, the National Conference of Commissioners on Uniform State Laws and the American Law Institute created the Uniform Electronic Transactions Act (UETA). To date, the UETA has been adopted, at least in part, by forty-eight states. Among other things, the UETA declares that a signature may not be denied legal effect or enforceability solely because it is in electronic form. The UETA does not apply to a transaction unless each of the parties has previously agreed to conduct transactions by electronic means. The agreement need not be explicit, however. It can be implied by the conduct of the parties and the surrounding circumstances.[22]

In addition, the federal government enacted the Electronic Signatures in Global and National Commerce Act (E-SIGN Act),[23] which provides that no contract, record, or signature may be "denied legal effect" solely because it is in electronic form. In other words, under this law, an electronic signature is

---

21. *Specht v. Netscape Communications Corp.,* 306 F.3d 17 (2d Cir. 2002). Also see *Jesmer v. Retail Magic, Inc.,* 863 N.Y.S.2d 737 (2008).
22. UETA 5(b), and Comment 4B.
23. 15 U.S.C. Sections 7001 *et seq.*

as valid as a signature on paper, and an e-document can be as enforceable as a paper one.

SECTION 9
INTERNATIONAL SALES CONTRACTS

International sales contracts between firms or individuals located in different countries may be governed by the 1980 United Nations Convention on Contracts for the International Sale of Goods (CISG). The CISG governs international contracts only if the countries of the parties to the contract have ratified the CISG and if the parties have not agreed that some other law will govern their contract. As of 2010, the CISG had been adopted by seventy countries, including the United States, Canada, Mexico, some Central and South American countries, China, Japan, and most European nations. That means that the CISG is the uniform international sales law of countries that account for more than two-thirds of all global trade.

Applicability of the CISG

Essentially, the CISG is to international sales contracts what Article 2 of the UCC is to domestic sales contracts. Whenever the parties to international transactions have failed to specify in writing the precise terms of a contract, the CISG will be applied. Unlike the UCC, however, the CISG does not apply to consumer sales. Neither the UCC nor the CISG applies to contracts for services.

Businesspersons must take special care when drafting international sales contracts to avoid problems caused by distance, including language differences and differences in national laws. For instance, a choice-of-language clause designates the official language by which the contract will be interpreted in the event of a dispute. The appendix following this chapter (pages 264–267) shows an actual international sales contract used by Starbucks Coffee Company. The contract illustrates many of the special terms and clauses that typically are contained in international contracts for the sale of goods.

A Comparison of CISG and UCC Provisions

The provisions of the CISG, although similar for the most part to those of the UCC, differ from them in some respects. Major differences exist between the CISG and the UCC in regard to the mirror image rule and irrevocable offers, for example.

Under the UCC, a definite expression of acceptance that contains additional terms can still result in the formation of a contract, unless the additional terms are conditioned on the consent of the offeror. In other words, the UCC does away with the mirror image rule (see page 196) in domestic sales contracts. Under the CISG, however, if the acceptance contains additional terms that materially alter the contract, no contract will be formed. Thus, if an additional term relates to payment, quality, quantity, price, or the settlement of disputes, the CISG considers the added term a material alteration. In effect, then, the CISG requires that the terms of the acceptance mirror those of the offer.

The UCC provides that a merchant's firm offer is irrevocable, even without consideration, if the merchant gives assurances in a signed writing. In contrast, under Article 16(2) of the CISG, an offer can become irrevocable without a signed writing if the offeror simply states orally that the offer is irrevocable or if the offeree reasonably relies on the offer as being irrevocable.

Remedies for Breach

The CISG provides international sellers and buyers with remedies very similar to those available under the UCC. Article 74 of the CISG provides for monetary damages, including foreseeable consequential damages, on a contract's breach. As under the UCC, the measure of damages normally is the difference between the contract price and the market price of the goods. The CISG also allows for specific performance as a remedy under Article 28.

REVIEWING
Sales, Leases, and E-Contracts

Guy Holcomb owns and operates Oasis Goodtime Emporium, an adult entertainment establishment. Holcomb wanted to create an adult Internet system for Oasis that would offer customers adult theme videos and "live" chat room programs using performers at the club. On May 10, Holcomb

REVIEWING

Sales, Leases, and E-Contracts, Continued

signed a work order authorizing Thomas Consulting Group (TCG) "to deliver a working prototype of a customer chat system, demonstrating the integration of live video and chatting in a Web browser." In exchange for creating the prototype, Holcomb agreed to pay TCG $64,697. On May 20, Holcomb signed an additional work order in the amount of $12,943 for TCG to install a customized firewall system. The work orders stated that Holcomb would make monthly installment payments to TCG, and both parties expected the work would be finished by September. Due to unforeseen problems largely attributable to system configuration and software incompatibility, the project required more time than anticipated. By the end of the summer, the Web site was still not ready, and Holcomb had fallen behind in his payments to TCG. TCG threatened to cease work and file a suit for breach of contract unless the bill was paid. Rather than make further payments, Holcomb wanted to abandon the Web site project. Using the information presented in the chapter, answer the following questions.

1. Would a court be likely to decide that the transaction between Holcomb and TCG was covered by the Uniform Commercial Code (UCC)? Why or why not?
2. Would a court be likely to consider Holcomb a merchant under the UCC? Why or why not?
3. Did the parties have a valid contract under the UCC? Were any terms left open in the contract? If so, which terms? How would a court deal with open terms?
4. Suppose that Holcomb and TCG meet in October in an attempt to resolve their problems. At that time, the parties reach an oral agreement that TCG will continue to work without demanding full payment of the past due amounts and Holcomb will pay TCG $5,000 per week. Assuming the contract falls under the UCC, is the oral agreement enforceable? Why or why not?

DEBATE THIS: *The UCC should require the same degree of definiteness of terms, especially with respect to price and quantity, as contract law does.*

TERMS AND CONCEPTS

	e-signature 259	insurable interest 246	replevin 252
	express warranty 254	lease agreement 235	requirements contract 236
browse-wrap terms 259	firm offer 236	lessee 235	sale 234
choice-of-law clause 258	forum-selection clause 258	lessor 235	sales contract 233
click-on agreement 258	identification 242	merchant 235	seasonably 238
conforming goods 246	implied warranty 255	output contract 236	shipment contract 243
cover 252	implied warranty of fitness	perfect tender rule 247	shrink-wrap agreement 259
cure 247	for a particular	predominant-factor	tangible property 234
destination contract 243	purpose 257	test 234	tender of delivery 246
document of title 243	implied warranty of	puffery 255	
e-contract 257	merchantability 255		

QUESTIONS AND CASE PROBLEMS

11–1. Additional Terms Strike offers to sell Bailey one thousand shirts for a stated price. The offer declares that shipment will be made by the Dependable Truck Line. Bailey replies, "I accept your offer for one thousand shirts at the price quoted. Delivery to be by Yellow Express Truck Line." Both Strike and Bailey are merchants. Three weeks later, Strike ships the shirts by the Dependable Truck Line, and Bailey refuses shipment. Strike sues for breach of contract. Bailey claims (a) that there never was a contract because the reply, which included a modification of carriers, did not constitute an acceptance and (b) that even if there had been a contract, Strike would have been in breach owing to having shipped the shirts by Dependable, contrary to the contract terms. Discuss fully Bailey's claims.

11–2. QUESTION WITH SAMPLE ANSWER: Online Acceptance.

Anne is a reporter for *Daily Business Journal*, a print publication consulted by investors and other businesspersons. She often uses the Internet to perform research for the articles that she writes for the publication. While visiting the Web site of Cyberspace Investments Corp., Anne reads a pop-up window that states, "Our business newsletter, *E-Commerce Weekly*, is available at a one-year subscription rate of $5 per issue. To subscribe, enter your e-mail address below and click 'SUBSCRIBE.' By subscribing, you agree to the terms of the subscriber's agreement. To read this agreement, click 'AGREEMENT.'" Anne enters her e-mail address, but does not click on "AGREEMENT" to read the terms. Has Anne entered into an enforceable contract to pay for *E-Commerce Weekly?* Explain.

- **For a sample answer to Question 11–2, go to Appendix F at the end of this text.**

11–3. Anticipatory Repudiation Topken has contracted to sell Lorwin five hundred washing machines of a certain model at list price. Topken is to ship the goods on or before December 1. Topken produces one thousand washing machines of this model but has not yet prepared Lorwin's shipment. On November 1, Lorwin repudiates the contract. Discuss the remedies available to Topken.

11–4. Shipment and Destination Contracts In 2003, Karen Pearson and Steve and Tara Carlson agreed to buy a 2004 Dynasty recreational vehicle (RV) from DeMartini's RV Sales in Grass Valley, California. On September 29, Pearson, the Carlsons, and DeMartini's signed a contract providing that "seller agrees to deliver the vehicle to you on the date this contract is signed." The buyers made a payment of $145,000 on the total price of $356,416 the next day, when they also signed a form acknowledging that the RV had been inspected and accepted. They agreed to return later to have the RV transported out of state for delivery (to avoid paying state sales tax on the purchase). On October 7, Steve Carlson returned to DeMartini's to ride with the seller's driver to Nevada to consummate the out-of-state delivery. When the RV developed problems, Pearson and the Carlsons filed a suit in a federal district court against the RV's manufacturer, Monaco Coach Corp., alleging, in part, breach of warranty under state law. The applicable statute is expressly limited to goods sold in California. Monaco argued that this RV had been sold in Nevada. How does the Uniform Commercial Code (UCC) define a sale? What does the UCC provide with respect to the passage of title? How do these provisions apply here? Discuss. [*Carlson v. Monaco Coach Corp.*, 486 F.Supp.2d 1127 (E.D.Cal. 2007)]

11–5. Additional Terms Continental Insurance Co. issued a policy to cover shipments by Oakley Fertilizer, Inc. Oakley agreed to ship three thousand tons of fertilizer by barge from New Orleans, Louisiana, to Ameropa North America in Caruthersville, Missouri. Oakley sent Ameropa a contract form that set out these terms and stated that title and risk would pass to the buyer after the seller was paid for the goods. Ameropa e-mailed a different form that set out the same essential terms but stated that title and risk of loss would pass to the buyer when the goods were loaded onto the barges in New Orleans. The cargo was loaded onto barges but had not yet been delivered when it was damaged in Hurricane Katrina. Oakley filed a claim for the loss with Continental but was denied coverage. Oakley filed a suit in a Missouri state court against the insurer. Continental argued that title and risk passed to Ameropa before the damage as specified in the buyer's form under Section 2–207(3) of the Uniform Commercial Code because the parties did not have a valid contract under UCC 2–207(1). Apply UCC 2–207 on additional terms in an acceptance to these facts. Is Continental correct? Explain. [*Oakley Fertilizer, Inc. v. Continental Insurance Co.*, 276 S.W.3d 342 (Mo. App.E.D. 2009)]

11–6. CASE PROBLEM WITH SAMPLE ANSWER: Obligations of the Seller.

Flint Hills Resources, LP, a refiner of crude oil, agreed to buy "approximately 1,000 barrels per day" of Mexican natural gas condensate from JAG Energy, Inc., an oil broker. Four months into the contract, Pemex, the only authorized seller of freshly extracted Mexican condensate, warned Flint Hills that some companies might be selling stolen Mexican condensate. Fearing potential criminal liability, Flint Hills refused to accept more deliveries from JAG without proof of the title to its product. JAG promised to forward documents showing its chain of title. After several weeks, when JAG did not produce the documents, Flint Hills canceled their agreement. JAG filed a suit in a federal district court against Flint Hills, alleging breach of contract. Did Flint Hills have a right to demand assurance of JAG's title to its product? If so, did Flint Hills act reasonably in exercising that right? Explain. [Flint Hills Resources LP v. JAG Energy, Inc., 559 F.3d 373 (5th Cir. 2009)]

- **To view a sample answer for Problem 11–6, go to this book's Web site at www.cengage.com/blaw/cross, select "Chapter 11," and click on "Case Problem with Sample Answer."**

11–7. Breach and Damages Before Chad DeRosier could build a house on his undeveloped property, he needed to have some fill dirt deposited on the land. Utility Systems of America, Inc., was doing roadwork nearby, and DeRosier asked Utility if it would like to deposit extra fill dirt on his property. Utility said it would, and DeRosier obtained the necessary permit. The permit was for 1,500 cubic yards of fill dirt, the amount that DeRosier needed. DeRosier gave Utility a copy of the permit. Later, DeRosier found 6,500 cubic yards of fill dirt on his land and had to have 5,000 cubic yards of it removed. Utility denied responsibility but said that it would remove the fill dirt for $9,500. DeRosier filed a suit against Utility and hired another company to remove the fill dirt and to do certain foundation work. He paid $46,629 to that contractor. The district court held that Utility had breached its contract and ordered it to pay DeRosier $22,829 in general damages and $8,000 in consequential damages. Utility appealed. In view of the fact that Utility charged nothing for the fill dirt, did a breach of contract occur? If a breach occurred, should the damages be greater than $9,500? Can consequential damages be justified? Discuss. [*DeRosier v. Utility Systems of America, Inc.*, 780 N.W.2d 1 (Minn.App. 2010)]

11–8. A QUESTION OF ETHICS: Revocation.

Scotwood Industries, Inc., sells calcium chloride flake for use in ice melt products. Between July and September 2004, Scotwood delivered thirty-seven shipments of flake to Frank Miller & Sons, Inc. After each delivery, Scotwood billed Miller, which paid thirty-five of the invoices and processed 30 to 50 percent of the flake. In August, Miller began complaining about the product's quality. Scotwood assured Miller that it would remedy the situation. Finally, in October, Miller told Scotwood, "This is totally unacceptable. We are willing to discuss Scotwood picking up the material." Miller claimed that the flake was substantially defective because it was chunked. Calcium chloride maintains its purity for

up to five years, but if it is exposed to and absorbs moisture, it chunks and becomes unusable. In response to Scotwood's suit to collect payment on the unpaid invoices, Miller filed a counterclaim in a federal district court for breach of contract, seeking to recover based on revocation of acceptance, among other things. [Scotwood Industries, Inc. v. Frank Miller & Sons, Inc., *435 F.Supp.2d 1160* (D.Kan. 2006)]

(a) What is revocation of acceptance? How does a buyer effectively exercise this option? Do the facts in this case support this theory as a ground for Miller to recover damages? Why or why not?

(b) Is there an ethical basis for allowing a buyer to revoke acceptance of goods and recover damages? If so, is there an ethical limit to this right? Discuss.

11–9. VIDEO QUESTION: Warranties.

Go to this text's Web site at **www.cengage.com/ blaw/cross** and select "Chapter 11." Click on "Video Questions" and view the video titled *Matilda*. Then answer the following questions.

(a) What warranties of title arise in the sales of used cars by dealers?

(b) In the video, a father (Danny DeVito) uses a tool to turn back the numbers on a vehicle's odometer. When he sells this car, if he tells the buyer the mileage is only 60,000 knowing that it is really 120,000, has he breached an express warranty? If the seller did not make any oral statements about the car's mileage, could the buyer claim an express warranty existed? Explain.

(c) What would a person who buys the car in the video have to show to prove that the seller breached the implied warranty of merchantability?

LEGAL RESEARCH EXERCISES ON THE WEB

Go to this text's Web site at **www.cengage.com/blaw/cross**, select "Chapter 11," and click on "Practical Internet Exercises." There you will find the following Internet research exercises that you can perform to learn more about the topics covered in this chapter.

Practical Internet Exercise 11–1: **Legal Perspective**
                                    Is It a Contract?

Practical Internet Exercise 11–2: **Management Perspective**
                                    A Checklist for Sales Contracts

(1)

OVERLAND COFFEE IMPORT CONTRACT
OF THE
GREEN COFFEE ASSOCIATION
OF
NEW YORK CITY, INC.*

(2)

Contract Seller's No.: __504617__
Buyer's No.: __P9264__
Date: __10/11/12__

(3) SOLD BY: __XYZ Co.__
TO: __Starbucks__

QUANTITY: __Five Hundred__ (500) Tons of __Bags__ __Mexican__ coffee
weighing about __152.117 lbs.__ per bag.

(4) PACKAGING: Coffee must be packed in clean sound bags of uniform size made of sisal, henequen, jute, burlap, or similar woven material, without inner lining or outer covering of any material properly sewn by hand and/or machine. Bulk shipments are allowed if agreed by mutual consent of Buyer and Seller.

(5) DESCRIPTION: __High grown Mexican Altura__

PRICE: At __Ten/$10.00 dollars__ U.S. Currency, per __lb.__ net, (U.S. Funds)
Upon delivery in Bonded Public Warehouse at __Laredo, TX__
(City and State)

(6) PAYMENT: __Cash against warehouse receipts__

Bill and tender to DATE when all import requirements and governmental regulations have been satisfied, and coffee delivered or discharged (as per contract terms). Seller is obliged to give the Buyer two (2) calendar days free time in Bonded Public Warehouse following but not including date of tender.

(7) ARRIVAL: During __December__ via __truck__
(Period) (Method of Transportation)
from __Mexico__ for arrival at __Laredo, TX, USA__
(Country of Exportation) (Country of Importation)
Partial shipments permitted.

(8) ADVICE OF ARRIVAL: Advice of arrival with warehouse name and location, together with the quantity, description, marks and place of entry, must be transmitted directly, or through Seller's Agent/Broker, to the Buyer or his Agent/ Broker. Advice will be given as soon as known but not later than the fifth business day following arrival at the named warehouse. Such advice may be given verbally with written confirmation to be sent the same day.

(9) WEIGHTS: (1) DELIVERED WEIGHTS: Coffee covered by this contract is to be weighed at location named in tender. Actual tare to be allowed.
(2) SHIPPING WEIGHTS: Coffee covered by this contract is sold on shipping weights. Any loss in weight exceeding __1/2__ percent at location named in tender is for account of Seller at contract price.
(3) Coffee is to be weighed within fifteen (15) calendar days after tender. Weighing expenses, if any, for account of __Seller__ (Seller or Buyer)

(10) MARKINGS: Bags to be branded in English with the name of Country of Origin and otherwise to comply with laws and regulations of the Country of Importation, in effect at the time of entry, governing marking of import merchandise. Any expense incurred by failure to comply with these regulations to be borne by Exporter/Seller.

(11) RULINGS: The "Rulings on Coffee Contracts" of the Green Coffee Association of New York City, Inc., in effect on the date this contract is made, is incorporated for all purposes as a part of this agreement, and together herewith, constitute the entire contract. No variation or addition hereto shall be valid unless signed by the parties to the contract.
Seller guarantees that the terms printed on the reverse hereof, which by reference are made a part hereof, are identical with the terms as printed in By-Laws and Rules of the Green Coffee Association of New York City, Inc., heretofore adopted.
Exceptions to this guarantee are:

ACCEPTED:
__XYZ Co.__

COMMISSION TO BE PAID BY:
__Seller__

(12) BY _____*DM*_____ Seller
Agent

__Starbucks__
BY _____ Buyer
Agent

__ABC Brokerage__ Broker(s)

(13) When this contract is executed by a person acting for another, such person hereby represents that he is fully authorized to commit his principal.

* Reprinted with permission of The Green Coffee Association of New York City, Inc.

An Example of a Contract for the International Sale of Coffee

① This is a contract for a sale of coffee to be *imported* internationally. If the parties have their principal places of business located in different countries, the contract may be subject to the United Nations Convention on Contracts for the International Sale of Goods (CISG). If the parties' principal places of business are located in the United States, the contract may be subject to the Uniform Commercial Code (UCC).

② Quantity is one of the most important terms to include in a contract. Without it, a court may not be able to enforce the contract.

③ Weight per unit (bag) can be exactly stated or approximately stated. If it is not so stated, usage of trade in international contracts determines standards of weight.

④ Packaging requirements can be conditions for acceptance and payment. Bulk shipments are not permitted without the consent of the buyer.

⑤ A description of the coffee and the "Markings" constitute express warranties. International contracts rely more heavily on descriptions and models or samples.

⑥ Under the UCC, parties may enter into a valid contract even though the price is not set. Under the CISG, a contract must provide for an exact determination of the price.

⑦ The terms of payment may take one of two forms: credit or cash. Credit terms can be complicated. A cash term can be simple, and payment can be made by any means acceptable in the ordinary course of business (for example, a personal check or a letter of credit). If the seller insists on actual cash, the buyer must be given a reasonable time to get it.

⑧ *Tender* means the seller has placed goods that conform to the contract at the buyer's disposition. This contract requires that the coffee meet all import regulations and that it be ready for pickup by the buyer at a "Bonded Public Warehouse." (A *bonded warehouse* is a place in which goods can be stored without payment of taxes until the goods are removed.)

⑨ The delivery date is significant because, if it is not met, the buyer may hold the seller in breach of the contract. Under this contract, the seller is given a "period" within which to deliver the goods, instead of a specific day. The seller is also given some time to rectify goods that do not pass inspection (see the "Guarantee" clause on page two of the contract).

⑩ As part of a proper tender, the seller (or its agent) must inform the buyer (or its agent) when the goods have arrived at their destination. The responsibilities of agents are set out in Chapter 20.

⑪ In some contracts, delivered and shipped weights can be important. During shipping, some loss can be attributed to the type of goods (spoilage of fresh produce, for example) or to the transportation itself. A seller and buyer can agree on the extent to which either of them will bear such losses.

⑫ Documents are often incorporated in a contract by reference, because including them word for word can make a contract difficult to read. If the document is later revised, the entire contract might have to be reworked. Documents that are typically incorporated by reference include detailed payment and delivery terms, special provisions, and sets of rules, codes, and standards.

⑬ In international sales transactions, and for domestic deals involving certain products, brokers are used to form the contracts. When so used, the brokers are entitled to a commission. See Chapter 20.

(Continued)

An Example of a Contract for the International Sale of Coffee

TERMS AND CONDITIONS

ARBITRATION: All controversies relating to, in connection with, or arising out of this contract, its modification, making or the authority or obligations of the signatories hereto, and whether involving the principals, agents, brokers, or others who actually subscribe hereto, shall be settled by arbitration in accordance with the "Rules of Arbitration" of the Green Coffee Association of New York City, Inc., as they exist at the time of the arbitration (including provisions as to payment of fees and expenses). Arbitration is the sole remedy hereunder, and it shall be held in accordance with the law of New York State, and judgment of any award may be entered in the courts of that State, or in any other court of competent jurisdiction. All notices or judicial service in reference to arbitration or enforcement shall be deemed given if transmitted as required by the aforesaid rules.

GUARANTEE: (a) If all or any of the coffee is refused admission into the country of importation by reason of any violation of governmental laws or acts, which violation existed at the time the coffee arrived at Bonded Public Warehouse, seller is required, as to the amount not admitted and as soon as possible, to deliver replacement coffee in conformity to all terms and conditions of this contract, excepting only the Arrival terms, but not later than thirty (30) days after the date of the violation notice. Any payment made and expenses incurred for any coffee denied entry shall be refunded within ten (10) calendar days of denial of entry, and payment shall be made for the replacement delivery in accordance with the terms of this contract. Consequently, if Buyer removes the coffee from the Bonded Public Warehouse, Seller's responsibility as to such portion hereunder ceases.
(b) Contracts containing the overstamp "No Pass-No Sale" on the face of the contract shall be interpreted to mean: If any or all of the coffee is not admitted into the country of Importation in its original condition by reason of failure to meet requirements of the government's laws or Acts, the contract shall be deemed null and void as to that portion of the coffee which is not admitted in its original condition. Any payment made and expenses incurred for any coffee denied entry shall be refunded within ten (10) calendar days of denial of entry.

CONTINGENCY: This contract is not contingent upon any other contract.

CLAIMS: Coffee shall be considered accepted as to quality unless within *fifteen* (15) calendar days after delivery at Bonded Public Warehouse or within *fifteen* (15) calendar days after all Government clearances have been received, whichever is later, either:
(a) Claims are settled by the parties hereto, or,
(b) Arbitration proceedings have been filed by one of the parties in accordance with the provisions hereof.
(c) If neither (a) nor (b) has been done in the stated period or if any portion of the coffee has been removed from the Bonded Public Warehouse before representative sealed samples have been drawn by the Green Coffee Association of New York City, Inc., in accordance with its rules, Seller's responsibility for quality claims ceases for that portion so removed.
(d) Any question of quality submitted to arbitration shall be a matter of allowance only, unless otherwise provided in the contract.

DELIVERY: (a) No more than three (3) chops may be tendered for each lot of 250 bags.
(b) Each chop of coffee tendered is to be uniform in grade and appearance. All expense necessary to make coffee uniform shall be for account of seller.
(c) Notice of arrival and/or sampling order constitutes a tender, and must be given not later than the fifth business day following arrival at Bonded Public Warehouse stated on the contract.

INSURANCE: Seller is responsible for any loss or damage, or both, until Delivery and Discharge of coffee at the Bonded Public Warehouse in the Country of Importation.

All Insurance Risks, costs and responsibility are for Seller's Account until Delivery and Discharge of coffee at the Bonded Public Warehouse in the Country of Importation.

Buyer's insurance responsibility begins from the day of importation or from the day of tender, whichever is later.

FREIGHT: Seller to provide and pay for all transportation and related expenses to the Bonded Public Warehouse in the Country of Importation.

EXPORT DUTIES/TAXES: Exporter is to pay all Export taxes, duties or other fees or charges, if any, levied because of exportation.

IMPORT DUTIES/TAXES: Any Duty or Tax whatsoever, imposed by the government or any authority of the Country of Importation, shall be borne by the Importer/Buyer.

INSOLVENCY OR FINANCIAL FAILURE OF BUYER OR SELLER: If, at any time before the contract is fully executed, either party hereto shall meet with creditors because of inability generally to make payment of obligations when due, or shall suspend such payments, fail to meet his general trade obligations in the regular course of business, shall file a petition in bankruptcy or, for an arrangement, shall become insolvent, or commit an act of bankruptcy, then the other party may at his option, expressed in writing, declare the aforesaid to constitute a breach and default of this contract, and may, in addition to other remedies, decline to deliver further or make payment or may sell or purchase for the defaulter's account, and may collect damage for any injury or loss, or shall account for the profit, if any, occasioned by such sale or purchase.

This clause is subject to the provisions of (11 USC 365 (e) 1) if invoked.

BREACH OR DEFAULT OF CONTRACT: In the event either party hereto fails to perform, or breaches or repudiates this agreement, the other party shall subject to the specific provisions of this contract be entitled to the remedies and relief provided for by the Uniform Commercial Code of the State of New York. The computation and ascertainment of damages, or the determination of any other dispute as to relief, shall be made by the arbitrators in accordance with the Arbitration Clause herein.

Consequential damages shall not, however, be allowed.

An Example of a Contract for the International Sale of Coffee

14 Arbitration is the settling of a dispute by submitting it to a disinterested party (other than a court), which renders a decision. The procedures and costs can be provided for in an arbitration clause or incorporated through other documents. To enforce an award rendered in an arbitration, the winning party can "enter" (submit) the award in a court "of competent jurisdiction." For a general discussion of arbitration and other forms of dispute resolution (other than courts), see Chapter 3.

15 When goods are imported internationally, they must meet certain import requirements before being released to the buyer. Because of this, buyers frequently want a guaranty clause that covers the goods not admitted into the country and that either requires the seller to replace the goods within a stated time or allows the contract for those goods not admitted to be void. See Chapter 10.

16 In the "Claims" clause, the parties agree that the buyer has a certain time within which to reject the goods. The right to reject is a right by law and does not need to be stated in a contract. If the buyer does not exercise the right within the time specified in the contract, the goods will be considered accepted.

17 Many international contracts include definitions of terms so that the parties understand what they mean. Some terms are used in a particular industry in a specific way. Here, the word *chop* refers to a unit of like-grade coffee beans. The buyer has a right to inspect ("sample") the coffee. If the coffee does not conform to the contract, the seller must correct the nonconformity.

18 The "Delivery," "Insurance," and "Freight" clauses, with the "Arrival" clause on page one of the contract, indicate that this is a destination contract. The seller has the obligation to deliver the goods to the destination, not simply deliver them into the hands of a carrier. Under this contract, the destination is a "Bonded Public Warehouse" in a specific location. The seller bears the risk of loss until the goods are delivered at their destination. Typically, the seller will have bought insurance to cover the risk.

19 Delivery terms are commonly placed in all sales contracts. Such terms determine who pays freight and other costs and, in the absence of an agreement specifying otherwise, who bears the risk of loss. International contracts may use these delivery terms, or they may use INCOTERMS, which are published by the International Chamber of Commerce. For example, the INCOTERM DDP (delivered duty paid) requires the seller to arrange shipment, obtain and pay for import or export permits, and get the goods through customs to a named destination.

20 Exported and imported goods are subject to duties, taxes, and other charges imposed by the governments of the countries involved. International contracts spell out who is responsible for these charges.

21 This clause protects a party if the other party should become financially unable to fulfill the obligations under the contract. Thus, if the seller cannot afford to deliver, or the buyer cannot afford to pay, for the stated reasons, the other party can consider the contract breached. This right is subject to "11 USC 365(e)(1)," which refers to a specific provision of the U.S. Bankruptcy Code dealing with executory contracts. Bankruptcy provisions are covered in Chapter 15.

22 In the "Breach or Default of Contract" clause, the parties agreed that the remedies under this contract are the remedies (except for consequential damages) provided by the UCC, as in effect in the state of New York. The amount and "ascertainment" of damages, as well as other disputes about relief, are to be determined by arbitration. Arbitration is discussed in Chapter 3.

23 Three clauses frequently included in international contracts are omitted here. There is no choice-of-language clause designating the official language to be used in interpreting the contract terms. There is no choice-of-forum clause designating the place in which disputes will be litigated, except for arbitration (law of New York State). Finally, there is no *force majeure* clause relieving the sellers or buyers from nonperformance due to events beyond their control.

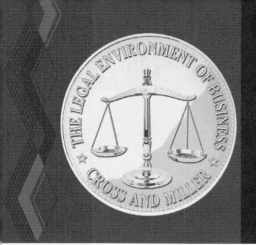

CHAPTER 12

✳ Torts and Cyber Torts

Part of doing business today— and, indeed, part of everyday life—is the risk of being involved in a lawsuit. The list of circumstances in which businesspersons can be sued is long and varied. A customer who is injured by a security guard at a business establishment, for example, may attempt to sue the business owner, claiming that the security guard's conduct was wrongful. Any time that one party's allegedly wrongful conduct causes injury to another, an action may arise under the law of *torts* (the word *tort* is French for "wrong"). Through tort law, society compensates those who have suffered injuries as a result of the wrongful conduct of others.

Many of the lawsuits brought by or against business firms are based on the tort theories discussed in this chapter, which covers intentional and unintentional torts. *Intentional torts* arise from intentional acts, whereas *unintentional torts (negligence)* often result from carelessness (as when an employee at a store knocks over a display case, injuring a customer). In addition, this chapter discusses how tort law applies to wrongful actions in the online environment. Tort theories also come into play in the context of product liability (liability for defective products), which will be discussed in detail in Chapter 13.

SECTION 1
THE BASIS OF TORT LAW

Two notions serve as the basis of all **torts:** wrongs and compensation. Tort law is designed to compensate those who have suffered a loss or injury due to another person's wrongful act. In a tort action, one person or group brings a lawsuit against another person or group to obtain compensation (monetary damages) or other relief for the harm suffered.

The Purpose of Tort Law

The basic purpose of tort law is to provide remedies for the invasion of various *protected interests*. Society recognizes an interest in personal physical safety, and tort law provides remedies for acts that cause physical injury or that interfere with physical security and freedom of movement. Society recognizes an interest in protecting property, and tort law provides remedies for acts that cause destruction of or damage to property. Society also recognizes an interest in protecting certain intangible interests, such as personal privacy, family relations, reputation, and dignity, and tort law provides remedies for invasion of these interests.

Damages Available in Tort Actions

Because the purpose of tort law is to compensate the injured party for the damage suffered, it is important to have an understanding of the types of damages that plaintiffs seek in tort actions.

COMPENSATORY DAMAGES **Compensatory damages** are intended to compensate or reimburse a plaintiff for actual losses—that is, to make the plaintiff whole and put her or him in the same position that she or he would have been in had the tort not occurred. Compensatory damages awards in tort cases are often broken down into *special damages* and *general damages*.

Special damages compensate the plaintiff for quantifiable monetary losses, such as medical expenses, lost wages and benefits (now and in the future), extra costs, the loss of irreplaceable items, and the costs of repairing or replacing damaged property.

CASE IN POINT Seaway Marine Transport operates the *Enterprise,* a large cargo ship, which has twenty-two hatches for storing coal. When the *Enterprise* positioned itself to receive a load of coal on the shores of Lake Erie in Ohio, it struck a land-based coal-loading machine operated by Bessemer & Lake Erie Railroad Company. A federal court found Seaway liable for negligence and awarded $522,000 in special damages to compensate Bessemer for the cost of repairing the damage to the loading boom.[1]

General damages compensate individuals (not companies) for the nonmonetary aspects of the harm suffered, such as pain and suffering. A court might award general damages for physical or emotional pain and suffering, loss of companionship, loss of consortium (losing the emotional and physical benefits of a spousal relationship), disfigurement, loss of reputation, or loss or impairment of mental or physical capacity.

PUNITIVE DAMAGES Occasionally, the courts may award **punitive damages** in tort cases to punish the wrongdoer and deter others from similar wrongdoing. Punitive damages are appropriate only when the defendant's conduct was particularly egregious or reprehensible. Usually, this means that punitive damages are available mainly in intentional tort actions and only rarely in negligence lawsuits (as will be discussed later in this chapter). They may be awarded, however, in suits involving *gross negligence,* which can be defined as an intentional failure to perform a manifest duty in reckless disregard of the consequences of such a failure for the life or property of another.

Courts exercise great restraint in granting punitive damages to plaintiffs in tort actions because punitive damages are subject to the limitations imposed by the due process clause of the U.S. Constitution (see Chapter 5). The United States Supreme Court has held that to the extent an award of punitive damages is grossly excessive, it furthers no legitimate purpose and violates due process requirements.[2] Consequently, an appellate court will sometimes reduce the amount of punitive damages awarded to a plaintiff on the ground that it is excessive and thereby violates the due process clause.[3]

Tort Reform

Critics of the current tort law system contend that it encourages trivial and unfounded lawsuits, which clog the courts, and that it is unnecessarily costly. In particular, they say, damages awards are often excessive and bear little relationship to the actual damage suffered. Such large awards encourage plaintiffs and their lawyers to bring frivolous suits. The result, in the critics' view, is a system that disproportionately rewards a few plaintiffs while imposing a "tort tax" on business and society as a whole. Furthermore, the tax manifests itself in other ways. Because physicians, hospitals, and pharmaceutical companies are worried about medical malpractice suits, they have changed their behavior. Physicians, for example, order more tests than necessary, adding to the nation's health-care costs.

The federal government and a number of states have begun to take some steps toward tort reform. At the federal level, the Class Action Fairness Act (CAFA) of 2005[4] shifted jurisdiction over large interstate tort and product liability class-action lawsuits from the state courts to the federal courts. The intent was to prevent plaintiffs' attorneys from *forum shopping*—looking for a state court known to be sympathetic to their clients' cause and predisposed to award large damages in class-action suits, even though the case might have only a tenuous connection to that jurisdiction.

At the state level, more than half of the states have placed caps ranging from $250,000 to $750,000 on noneconomic (general) damages (for example, pain and suffering), especially in medical malpractice suits. More than thirty states have limited punitive damages, with some imposing outright bans.

SECTION 2
INTENTIONAL TORTS AGAINST PERSONS

An **intentional tort,** as the term implies, requires intent. The **tortfeasor** (the one committing the tort) must intend to commit an act, the consequences of which interfere with the personal or business interests of another in a way not permitted by law. An evil or harmful motive is not required—in fact, the actor may even have a beneficial motive for committing what turns out to be a tortious act. In tort law, *intent* means only that the actor intended the consequences of his or her act or knew with substantial

---

1. *Bessemer & Lake Erie Railroad Co. v. Seaway Marine Transport,* 596 F.3d 357 (6th Cir. 2010).

2. *State Farm Mutual Automobile Insurance Co. v. Campbell,* 538 U.S. 408, 123 S.Ct. 1513, 155 L.Ed.2d 585 (2003).

3. See, for example, *Buell-Wilson v. Ford Motor Co.,* 160 Cal.App.4th 1107, 73 Cal.Rptr.3d 277 (2008).

4. 28 U.S.C. Sections 1711–1715, 1453.

certainty that specific consequences would result from the act. The law generally assumes that individuals intend the *normal* consequences of their actions. Thus, forcefully pushing another—even if done in jest and without any evil motive—is an intentional tort (if injury results), because the object of a strong push can ordinarily be expected to be abruptly displaced.

Intentional torts against persons include assault and battery, false imprisonment, infliction of emotional distress, defamation, invasion of privacy, appropriation, fraudulent misrepresentation, and torts related to misuse of litigation. We discuss these torts in the following subsections.

Assault and Battery

An **assault** is any intentional and unexcused threat of immediate harmful or offensive contact, including words or acts that create in another person a reasonable apprehension of harmful contact. An assault can be completed even if there is no actual contact with the plaintiff, provided that the defendant's conduct creates a reasonable apprehension of imminent harm in the plaintiff. Tort law aims to protect individuals from having to expect harmful or offensive contact.

The *completion* of the act that caused the apprehension, if it results in harm to the plaintiff, is a **battery,** which is defined as an unexcused and harmful or offensive physical contact *intentionally* performed. For example, Ivan threatens Jean with a gun, then shoots her. The pointing of the gun at Jean is an assault; the firing of the gun (if the bullet hits Jean) is a battery. The contact can be harmful, or it can be merely offensive (such as an unwelcome kiss). Physical injury need not occur. The contact can involve any part of the body or anything attached to it—for example, a hat or other item of clothing, a purse, or a chair in which one is sitting. Whether the contact is offensive is determined by the *reasonable person standard.*[5] The contact can be made by the defendant or by some force that the defendant sets in motion—for example, a thrown rock or poisoned food.

If the plaintiff shows that there was contact, and the jury (or judge, if there is no jury) agrees that the contact was offensive, then the plaintiff has a right to compensation. A plaintiff may be compensated for the emotional harm or loss of reputation resulting from a battery, as well as for physical harm. A defendant may raise a number of legally recognized *defenses* (reasons why the plaintiff should not obtain damages) that justify his or her conduct, including self-defense and defense of others.

False Imprisonment

False imprisonment is the intentional confinement or restraint of another person's activities without justification. False imprisonment interferes with the freedom to move without restraint. The confinement can be accomplished through the use of physical barriers, physical restraint, or threats of physical force. Moral pressure does not constitute false imprisonment. It is essential that the person being restrained not agree to the restraint.

Businesspersons often face suits for false imprisonment after they have attempted to confine a suspected shoplifter for questioning. Under the "privilege to detain" granted to merchants in most states, a merchant can use *reasonable force* to detain or delay persons suspected of shoplifting and hold them for the police. Although laws vary from state to state, most states require that any detention be conducted in a *reasonable* manner and for only a *reasonable* length of time. Undue force or unreasonable detention can lead to liability for the business.

Intentional Infliction of Emotional Distress

The tort of *intentional infliction of emotional distress* is an intentional act that amounts to extreme and outrageous conduct resulting in severe emotional distress to another. To be **actionable** (capable of serving as the ground for a lawsuit), the act must be extreme and outrageous to the point that it exceeds the bounds of decency accepted by society.

CASE IN POINT Michael Perkins, an off-duty police officer, went to Wal-Mart to purchase a few items, including a $20 ink cartridge. The cashier, Alicia Jackson, was an acquaintance and apparently scanned the cartridge but then voided it out, so he was not charged for it. Soon after, Wal-Mart's theft prevention staff discovered that Jackson had been involved in an illegal "under-ringing" scheme for some time. In this scheme, a cashier either fails to "ring up" (charge for) merchandise or scans an item and then voids the transaction. (This allows the cashier's friends to obtain merchandise for free.) Elijah Wilson, the police officer who questioned Jackson, disliked Perkins and, after learning of Perkins's connection to the case, encouraged her to implicate him in the criminal scheme, which she did. Despite claiming no knowledge of the

---

5. The *reasonable person standard* is an "objective" test of how a reasonable person would have acted under the same circumstances. See the subsection entitled "The Duty of Care and Its Breach" later in this chapter on pages 280–282.

scheme, Perkins was disciplined at work and charged with a crime. He was later acquitted. The court held that Perkins might be able to prove an intentional infliction of emotional distress claim against Wilson.[6]

Courts in most jurisdictions are wary of emotional distress claims and confine them to situations involving truly outrageous behavior. Acts that cause indignity or annoyance alone usually are not sufficient, but repeated annoyances (such as those experienced by a person who is being stalked), coupled with threats, are enough. When the outrageous conduct consists of speech about a public figure, the First Amendment's guarantee of freedom of speech also limits emotional distress claims.

CASE IN POINT *Hustler* magazine once printed a false advertisement that showed a picture of the late Reverend Jerry Falwell and described him as having lost his virginity to his mother in an outhouse while he was drunk. Falwell sued the magazine for intentional infliction of emotional distress and won, but the United States Supreme Court overturned the decision. The Court held that creators of parodies of public figures are protected under the First Amendment from intentional infliction of emotional distress claims.[7] (The Court used the same standards that apply to public figures in defamation lawsuits, discussed next.)

Defamation

As discussed in Chapter 5, the freedom of speech guaranteed by the First Amendment is not absolute. In interpreting the First Amendment, the courts must balance the vital guarantee of free speech against other pervasive and strong social interests, including society's interest in preventing and redressing attacks on reputation.

Defamation of character involves wrongfully hurting a person's good reputation. The law imposes a general duty on all persons to refrain from making false, defamatory *statements of fact* about others. Breaching this duty in writing or other permanent form (such as a digital recording) involves the tort of **libel.** Breaching this duty orally involves the tort of **slander.** The tort of defamation also arises when a false statement of fact

is made about a person's product, business, or legal ownership rights to property.

Often at issue in defamation lawsuits (including online defamation, which will be discussed later in this chapter) is whether the defendant made a statement of fact or a *statement of opinion*. Statements of opinion normally are not actionable because they are protected under the First Amendment. In other words, making a negative statement about another person is not defamation unless the statement is false and represents something as a fact (for example, "Lane cheats on his taxes") rather than a personal opinion (for example, "Lane is a jerk").

THE PUBLICATION REQUIREMENT The basis of the tort of defamation is the publication of a statement or statements that hold an individual up to contempt, ridicule, or hatred. *Publication* here means that the defamatory statements are communicated (either intentionally or accidentally) to persons other than the defamed party. If Rodriques writes Andrews a private letter falsely accusing him of embezzling funds, the action does not constitute libel. If Peters falsely states that Gordon is dishonest and incompetent when no one else is around, the action does not constitute slander. In neither case was the message communicated to a third party.

The courts usually have held that even dictating a letter to a secretary constitutes publication, although the publication may be privileged (a concept that will be explained shortly). Moreover, if a third party merely overhears defamatory statements by chance, the courts usually hold that this also constitutes publication. Defamatory statements made via the Internet are actionable as well. Note also that any individual who repeats or republishes defamatory statements normally is liable even if that person reveals the source of the statements.

DAMAGES FOR LIBEL Once a defendant's liability for libel is established, general damages are presumed as a matter of law. General damages are designed to compensate the plaintiff for nonspecific harms such as disgrace or dishonor in the eyes of the community, humiliation, injured reputation, and emotional distress—harms that are difficult to measure. In other words, to recover damages in a libel case, the plaintiff need not prove that he or she was actually injured in any way as a result of the libelous statement.

DAMAGES FOR SLANDER In contrast to cases alleging libel, in a case alleging slander the plaintiff must

---

6. *Perkins v. Wal-Mart Stores, Inc.,* ___ So.3d ___, 2010 WL 610627 (Miss.App. 2010).
7. *Hustler Magazine, Inc. v. Falwell,* 485 U.S. 46, 108 S.Ct. 876, 99 L.Ed.2d 41 (1988). For another example of how the courts protect parody, see *Busch v. Viacom International, Inc.,* 477 F.Supp.2d 764 (N.D.Tex. 2007), involving a false endorsement of televangelist Pat Robertson's diet shake.

prove special damages to establish the defendant's liability. The plaintiff must show that the slanderous statement caused her or him to suffer actual economic or monetary losses. Unless this initial hurdle of proving special damages is overcome, a plaintiff alleging slander normally cannot go forward with the suit and recover any damages. This requirement is imposed in slander cases because oral statements have a temporary quality. In contrast, a libelous (written) statement has the quality of permanence, can be circulated widely, and usually results from some degree of deliberation on the part of the author.

Exceptions to the burden of proving special damages in cases alleging slander are made for certain types of slanderous statements. If a false statement constitutes "slander *per se,*" no proof of special damages is required for it to be actionable. In most states, the following four types of utterances are considered to be slander *per se:*

1. A statement that another has a particular type of disease (historically, leprosy and sexually transmitted diseases, but now also including allegations of mental illness).
2. A statement that another has committed improprieties while engaging in a profession or trade.
3. A statement that another has committed or has been imprisoned for a serious crime.
4. A statement that a person (usually only an unmarried person and sometimes only a woman) is unchaste or has engaged in serious sexual misconduct.

DEFENSES TO DEFAMATION Truth normally is an absolute defense against a defamation charge. In other words, if a defendant in a defamation case can prove that the allegedly defamatory statements of fact were true, normally no tort has been committed. Other defenses to defamation may exist if the speech is *privileged* or concerns a public figure. Note that the majority of defamation actions are filed in state courts, and state laws differ somewhat in the defenses they allow, such as privilege (discussed next).

Privileged Speech. In some circumstances, a person will not be liable for defamatory statements because she or he enjoys a **privilege,** or immunity. With respect to defamation, privileged communications are of two types: absolute and qualified.[8] Only in judicial proceedings and certain government proceedings is an *absolute privilege* granted. For example,

statements made by attorneys and judges in the courtroom during a trial are absolutely privileged. So are statements made by government officials during legislative debate, even if the legislators make such statements maliciously—that is, knowing them to be untrue. An absolute privilege is granted in these situations because judicial and government personnel deal with matters that are so much in the public interest that the parties involved should be able to speak out fully and freely and without restriction.

In other situations, a person will not be liable for defamatory statements because he or she has a *qualified,* or *conditional, privilege.* An employer's statements in written evaluations of employees, for example, are protected by qualified privilege. Generally, if the statements are made in good faith and the publication is limited to those who have a legitimate interest in the communication, the statements fall within the area of qualified privilege. The concept of conditional privilege rests on the common law assumption that in some situations, the right to know or speak is equal in importance to the right not to be defamed. If a communication is conditionally privileged, a plaintiff can recover damages only by showing that the privilege was abused.

Public Figures. Public officials who exercise substantial governmental power and any persons in the public limelight are considered **public figures**. In general, public figures are considered "fair game," and false and defamatory statements about them that are published in the media will not constitute defamation unless the statements are made with **actual malice.** To be made with actual malice, a statement must be made *with either knowledge of its falsity or a reckless disregard of the truth.*[9]

Statements made about public figures, especially when they are communicated via a public medium, usually are related to matters of general public interest. Some public figures, such as politicians, are people who substantially affect all of us. Furthermore, public figures generally have some access to a public medium for answering disparaging falsehoods about themselves; private individuals do not. For these reasons, public figures have a greater burden of proof in defamation cases (they must prove actual malice) than do private individuals.

CASE IN POINT Lynne Spears, the mother of pop star Britney Spears, wrote a book in which she

---

8. Note that the term *privileged communication* in this context is not the same as privileged communication between a professional, such as an attorney, and his or her client.

9. *New York Times Co. v. Sullivan,* 376 U.S. 254, 84 S.Ct. 710, 11 L.Ed.2d 686 (1964). As mentioned earlier, the First Amendment protects the creator of a parody from liability for defamation of a public figure.

claimed that Sam Lutfi, Britney's former business manager, contributed to a mental breakdown that Britney experienced in 2008. Among other things, the book stated that Lutfi hid psychiatric drugs in Britney's food, disabled her cars and phones, and stole funds from her bank accounts. Lutfi filed a lawsuit for defamation and asserted that Lynne's statements were untrue, disparaging, and made with actual malice. A Los Angeles trial court found that Lutfi was a public figure and had alleged enough evidence in his complaint for the case to go forward to trial. Lynne has appealed that ruling. If the case goes to trial, a central issue will be whether Lynne believed in the truth of her statements or made them with reckless disregard for the truth.[10]

Invasion of Privacy

A person has a right to solitude and freedom from prying public eyes—in other words, to privacy. As mentioned in Chapter 5, the courts have held that certain amendments to the U.S. Constitution imply a right to privacy. Some state constitutions explicitly provide for privacy rights, as do a number of federal and state statutes. Tort law also safeguards these rights through the tort of *invasion of privacy*. Generally, to successfully sue for an invasion of privacy, a person must have a reasonable expectation of privacy, and the invasion must be highly offensive. Four acts can qualify as invasions of privacy:

1. *Appropriation of identity.* Under the common law, using a person's name, picture, or other likeness for commercial purposes without permission is a tortious invasion of privacy. Most states today have also enacted statutes prohibiting *appropriation* (discussed further in the next subsection).
2. *Intrusion into an individual's affairs or seclusion.* For example, invading someone's home or searching someone's personal computer without authorization is an invasion of privacy. This tort has been held to extend to eavesdropping by wiretap, unauthorized scanning of a bank account, compulsory blood testing, and window peeping. One court found that a man who had repeatedly followed a woman (the wife of his girlfriend's former husband), photographed her, and made obscene gestures at her had intruded into her privacy.[11]
3. *False light.* The publication of information that places a person in a false light is another category

of invasion of privacy. This could be a story attributing to someone ideas not held or actions not taken by that person. (The publication of such a story could involve the tort of defamation as well.)
4. *Public disclosure of private facts.* This type of invasion of privacy occurs when a person publicly discloses private facts about an individual that an ordinary person would find objectionable or embarrassing. A newspaper account of a private citizen's sex life or financial affairs could be an actionable invasion of privacy, even if the information revealed is true, because it is not of public concern.

Appropriation

The use of another person's name, likeness, or other identifying characteristic, without permission and for the benefit of the user, constitutes the tort of **appropriation** (sometimes referred to as the *right of publicity*). Under the law, an individual's right to privacy normally includes the right to the exclusive use of his or her identity.

CASE IN POINT In one early case, Vanna White, the hostess of the popular *Wheel of Fortune* game show, brought a case against Samsung Electronics America, Inc. Without White's permission, Samsung had included in an advertisement a robotic image dressed in a wig, gown, and jewelry, in a setting that resembled the *Wheel of Fortune* set, in a stance for which White is famous. The court ruled in White's favor, holding that the tort of appropriation does not require the use of a celebrity's name or actual likeness. The court stated that Samsung's robot ad left "little doubt" as to the identity of the celebrity that the ad was meant to depict.[12]

DEGREE OF LIKENESS Courts may differ as to the degree of likeness that is required to impose liability for the tort of appropriation. This is particularly true when the plaintiff is claiming appropriation based on a depiction in an animated film or video game.

CASE IN POINT The Naked Cowboy, Robert Burck, has been a street entertainer in New York City's Times Square for more than ten years. He performs for tourists wearing only a white cowboy hat, white cowboy boots, and white underwear and carrying a guitar strategically placed to give the illusion of nudity. Burck has become a well-known persona,

---

10. *Lutfi v. Spears,* No. BC 406904 (Sup.Ct.—Los Angeles, Dept. 23, July 7, 2009).
11. *Anderson v. Mergenhagen,* 283 Ga.App. 546, 642 S.E.2d 105 (2007).
12. *White v. Samsung Electronics America, Inc.,* 971 F.2d 1395 (9th Cir. 1992).

appearing in television shows, movies, and video games, and has licensed his name and likeness to certain companies, including Chevrolet. When Mars, Inc., the maker of M&Ms candy, began using a video on billboards in Times Square that depicted a blue M&M dressed exactly like The Naked Cowboy, Burck sued for appropriation. The court held that Mars's creation of a cartoon character dressed in The Naked Cowboy's signature costume did not amount to appropriation by use of Burck's "portrait or picture."[13]

RIGHT OF PUBLICITY AS A PROPERTY RIGHT As mentioned, in many states the common law tort of appropriation has become known as the right of publicity.[14] Rather than being aimed at protecting a person's right to be left alone (privacy), this right aims to protect an individual's pecuniary (financial) interest in the commercial exploitation of his or her identity. In other words, this right allows public figures, celebrities, and entertainers to sue anyone who uses their images for commercial benefit without their permission.

Cases involving the right of publicity generally turn on whether the use was commercial. For instance, if a television news program reports on a celebrity and shows an image of the person, the use likely would not be classified as commercial. In contrast, including the celebrity's image on a poster without his or her permission would be a commercial use.

Because the right of publicity is similar to a property right, most states have concluded that the right is inheritable and survives the death of the person who held the right. Normally, though, the person must provide for the passage of the right to another in her or his will.

Fraudulent Misrepresentation

A misrepresentation leads another to believe in a condition that is different from the condition that actually exists. This is often accomplished through a false or an incorrect statement. Although persons sometimes make misrepresentations accidentally because they are unaware of the existing facts, the tort of **fraudulent misrepresentation,** or *fraud,* involves *intentional* deceit for personal gain. The tort includes several elements:

1. A misrepresentation of material facts or conditions with knowledge that they are false or with reckless disregard for the truth.
2. An intent to induce another party to rely on the misrepresentation.
3. A justifiable reliance on the misrepresentation by the deceived party.
4. Damages suffered as a result of that reliance.
5. A causal connection between the misrepresentation and the injury suffered.

For fraud to occur, more than mere *puffery,* or seller's talk, must be involved. Fraud exists only when a person represents as a fact something he or she knows is untrue. For example, it is fraud to claim that the roof of a building does not leak when one knows that it does. Facts are objectively ascertainable, whereas seller's talk—such as "I am the best accountant in town"—is not, because the speaker is representing a subjective view.

Normally, the tort of fraudulent misrepresentation occurs only when there is reliance on a *statement of fact.* Sometimes, however, reliance on a *statement of opinion* may involve the tort of fraudulent misrepresentation if the individual making the statement of opinion has superior knowledge of the subject matter. For example, when a lawyer makes a statement of opinion about the law in a state in which the lawyer is licensed to practice, a court would construe reliance on the statement to be equivalent to reliance on a statement of fact.

Abusive or Frivolous Litigation

Persons or businesses generally have a right to sue when they have been injured. In recent years, however, an increasing number of meritless lawsuits have been filed simply to harass the defendants. Defending oneself in any legal proceeding can be costly, time consuming, and emotionally draining. Tort law recognizes that people have a right not to be sued without a legally just and proper reason. It therefore protects individuals from the misuse of litigation. Torts related to abusive litigation include malicious prosecution and abuse of process.

If the party that initiated a lawsuit did so out of malice and without probable cause (a legitimate legal reason), and ended up losing that suit, the party can be sued for *malicious prosecution.* In some states, the plaintiff (who was the defendant in the

---

13. Note that Burck was allowed to continue his lawsuit against Mars for violation of trademark law—see Chapter 14. *Burck v. Mars, Inc.,* 571 F.Supp.2d 446 (S.D.N.Y. 2008). See also *Kirby v. Sega of America, Inc.,* 144 Cal.App.4th 47, 50 Cal.Rptr.3d 607 (2006).

14. See, for example, California Civil Code Sections 3344 and 3344.1.

first proceeding) must also prove injury other than the normal costs of litigation, such as lost profits.

Abuse of process can apply to any person using a legal process against another in an improper manner or to accomplish a purpose for which the process was not designed. The key difference between the torts of abuse of process and malicious prosecution is the level of proof. Abuse of process does not require the plaintiff to prove malice or show that the defendant (who was previously the plaintiff) lost in a prior legal proceeding.[15] In addition, abuse of process is not limited to prior litigation. It can be based on the wrongful use of subpoenas, court orders to attach or seize real property, or other types of formal legal process.

Concept Summary 12.1 below reviews intentional torts against persons.

---

15. *Palmer v. Diaz,* 214 P.3d 546 (Colo.App. 2009); and *Bernhard-Thomas Building Systems, LLC v. Duncan,* 918 A.2d 889 (Conn. App. 2007).

BUSINESS TORTS

Most torts can occur in any context, but a few torts, referred to as **business torts,** apply only to wrongful interferences with the business rights of others. Business torts generally fall into two categories—interference with a contractual relationship and interference with a business relationship.

Wrongful Interference with a Contractual Relationship

Three elements are necessary for *wrongful interference with a contractual relationship* to occur:

1. A valid, enforceable contract must exist between two parties.
2. A third party must know that this contract exists.
3. This third party must *intentionally induce* a party to the contract to breach the contract.

CONCEPT SUMMARY 12.1
Intentional Torts against Persons

Name of Tort	Description
Assault and Battery	Any unexcused and intentional act that causes another person to be apprehensive of immediate harm is an assault. An assault resulting in physical contact is a battery.
False Imprisonment	An intentional confinement or restraint of another person's movement without justification.
Intentional Infliction of Emotional Distress	An intentional act that amounts to extreme and outrageous conduct resulting in severe emotional distress to another.
Defamation (Libel or Slander)	A false statement of fact, not made under privilege, that is communicated to a third person and that causes damage to a person's reputation. For public figures, the plaintiff must also prove that the statement was made with actual malice.
Invasion of Privacy	Publishing or otherwise making known or using information relating to a person's private life and affairs, with which the public has no legitimate concern, without that person's permission or approval.
Appropriation	The use of another person's name, likeness, or other identifying characteristic without permission and for the benefit of the user.
Fraudulent Misrepresentation (Fraud)	A false representation made by one party, through misstatement of facts or through conduct, with the intention of deceiving another and on which the other reasonably relies to his or her detriment.
Abusive or Frivolous Litigation	The filing of a lawsuit without legitimate grounds and with malice. Alternatively, the use of a legal process in an improper manner.

CASE IN POINT A landmark case in this area involved an opera singer, Joanna Wagner, who was under contract to sing for a man named Lumley for a specified period of years. A man named Gye, who knew of this contract, nonetheless "enticed" Wagner to refuse to carry out the agreement, and Wagner began to sing for Gye. Gye's action constituted a tort because it interfered with the contractual relationship between Wagner and Lumley. (Of course, Wagner's refusal to carry out the agreement also entitled Lumley to sue Wagner for breach of contract.)[16]

The body of tort law relating to wrongful interference with a contractual relationship has increased greatly in recent years. In principle, any lawful contract can be the basis for an action of this type. The contract could be between a firm and its employees or a firm and its customers. Sometimes, a competitor of a firm draws away one of the firm's key employees. Only if the original employer can show that the competitor knew of the contract's existence, and intentionally induced the breach, can damages be recovered from the competitor.

Wrongful Interference with a Business Relationship

Businesspersons devise countless schemes to attract customers. They are prohibited, however, from unreasonably interfering with another's business in their attempts to gain a greater share of the market.

There is a difference between *competitive practices* and *predatory behavior*—actions undertaken with the intention of unlawfully driving competitors completely out of the market. Attempting to attract customers in general is a legitimate business practice, whereas specifically targeting the customers of a competitor is more likely to be predatory. For example, the mall contains two athletic shoe stores: Joe's and Sprint. Joe's cannot station an employee at the entrance to Sprint to divert customers to Joe's by telling them that Joe's will beat Sprint's prices. Doing this would constitute the tort of wrongful interference with a business relationship because it would interfere with a prospective economic advantage. Such behavior is commonly considered to be an unfair trade practice. If this type of activity were permitted, Joe's would reap the benefits of Sprint's advertising.

Although state laws vary on wrongful interference with a business relationship, generally a plaintiff must

prove that the defendant used predatory methods to intentionally harm an established business relationship or prospective economic advantage. The plaintiff must also prove that the defendant's interference caused the plaintiff to suffer economic harm.

Defenses to Wrongful Interference

A person will not be liable for the tort of wrongful interference with a contractual or business relationship if it can be shown that the interference was justified or permissible. Bona fide competitive behavior is a permissible interference, even if it results in the breaking of a contract.

For example, if Jerrod's Meats advertises so effectively that it induces Sam's Restaurant to break its contract with Burke's Meat Company, Burke's will be unable to recover against Jerrod's on a wrongful interference theory. After all, the public policy that favors free competition through advertising outweighs any possible instability that such competitive activity might cause in contractual relations. Although luring customers away from a competitor through aggressive marketing and advertising strategies obviously interferes with the competitor's relationship with its customers, courts typically allow such activities in the spirit of competition.

SECTION 4
INTENTIONAL TORTS AGAINST PROPERTY

Intentional torts against property include trespass to land, trespass to personal property, conversion, and disparagement of property. These torts are wrongful actions that interfere with individuals' legally recognized rights with regard to their land or personal property. The law distinguishes real property from personal property (see Chapter 26). *Real property* is land and things permanently attached to the land. *Personal property* consists of all other items, which are basically movable. Thus, a house and lot are real property, whereas the furniture inside a house is personal property. Cash and securities are also personal property.

Trespass to Land

The tort of **trespass to land** occurs any time a person, without permission, enters onto, above, or below the surface of land that is owned by another; causes anything to enter onto the land; or remains

---

16. *Lumley v. Gye,* 118 Eng.Rep. 749 (1853).

on the land or permits anything to remain on it. Actual harm to the land is not an essential element of this tort because the tort is designed to protect the right of an owner to exclusive possession. Common types of trespass to land include walking or driving on another's land; shooting a gun over another's land; throwing rocks at or spraying water on a building that belongs to someone else; building a dam across a river, thereby causing water to back up on someone else's land; and constructing one's building so that it extends onto an adjoining landowner's property.

TRESPASS CRITERIA, RIGHTS, AND DUTIES Before a person can be a trespasser, the real property owner (or other person in actual and exclusive possession of the property, such as a person who is leasing the property) must establish that person as a trespasser. For example, "posted" trespass signs expressly establish as a trespasser a person who ignores these signs and enters onto the property. Any person who enters onto another's property to commit an illegal act (such as a thief entering a lumberyard at night to steal lumber) is established impliedly as a trespasser, without posted signs.

At common law, a trespasser is liable for damages caused to the property and generally cannot hold the owner liable for injuries that the trespasser sustains on the premises. This common law rule is being abandoned in many jurisdictions, however, in favor of a *reasonable duty of care* rule that varies depending on the status of the parties. For example, a landowner may have a duty to post a notice that guard dogs patrol the property. Also, under the "attractive nuisance" doctrine, a landowner may be held liable for injuries sustained by young children on the landowner's property if the children were attracted to the premises by some object, such as a swimming pool or an abandoned building. Finally, an owner can remove a trespasser from the premises—or detain a trespasser on the premises for a reasonable time—through the use of reasonable force without being liable for assault, battery, or false imprisonment.

DEFENSES AGAINST TRESPASS TO LAND Trespass to land involves wrongful interference with another person's real property rights. If it can be shown that the trespass was warranted, however, as when a trespasser enters to assist someone in danger, a defense exists. Another defense exists when the trespasser can show that he or she had a license to come onto the land. A *licensee* is one who is invited (or allowed to enter) onto the property of another for the licensee's benefit. A person who enters another's

property to read an electric meter, for example, is a licensee. When you purchase a ticket to attend a movie or sporting event, you are licensed to go onto the property of another to view that movie or event. Note that licenses to enter onto another's property are *revocable* by the property owner. If a property owner asks an electric meter reader to leave and she or he refuses to do so, the meter reader at that point becomes a trespasser.

Trespass to Personal Property

Whenever any individual wrongfully takes or harms the personal property of another or otherwise interferes with the lawful owner's possession and enjoyment of personal property, **trespass to personal property** occurs. This tort may also be called *trespass to chattels* or *trespass to personalty*.[17] In this context, harm means not only destruction of the property, but also anything that diminishes its value, condition, or quality. Trespass to personal property involves intentional meddling with a possessory interest (one arising from possession), including barring an owner's access to personal property. If Kelly takes Ryan's business law book as a practical joke and hides it so that Ryan is unable to find it for several days before the final examination, Kelly has engaged in a trespass to personal property.

If it can be shown that trespass to personal property was warranted, then a complete defense exists. Most states, for example, allow automobile repair shops to hold a customer's car (under what is called an *artisan's lien*—see Chapter 15) when the customer refuses to pay for repairs already completed.

Conversion

Whenever a person wrongfully possesses or uses the personal property of another without permission, the tort of **conversion** occurs. Any act that deprives an owner of personal property or of the use of that property without that owner's permission and without just cause can be conversion. Even the taking of electronic records and data may form the basis of a common law conversion claim.

Often, when conversion occurs, a trespass to personal property also occurs because the original taking of the personal property from the owner was a trespass, and wrongfully retaining it is conversion. Conversion is the civil side of crimes related to theft, but it is not limited to theft. Even when

---

17. Pronounced *per*-sun-ul-tee.

the rightful owner consented to the initial taking of the property, so no theft or trespass occurred, a failure to return the property may still be conversion. For example, Chen borrows Mark's iPad to use while traveling home from school for the holidays. When Chen returns to school, Mark asks for his iPad back, but Chen says that he gave it to his little brother for Christmas. In this situation, Mark can sue Chen for conversion, and Chen will have to either return the iPad or pay damages equal to its value.

Note that conversion can occur even when a person mistakenly believed that she or he was entitled to the goods. In other words, good intentions are not a defense against conversion. Someone who buys stolen goods, for example, has committed the tort of conversion even if he or she did not know the goods were stolen. If the true owner brings a tort action against the buyer, the buyer must either return the property to the owner or pay the owner the full value of the property (despite having already paid the purchase price to the thief).

The following case involved a university's conversion of the fruits of a professor's work—property created and accumulated over several years. The question before the court was how to make a fair estimate of the property's value.

CASE 12.1
Trustees of University of District of Columbia v. Vossoughi
District of Columbia Court of Appeals, 963 A.2d 1162 (2009).

BACKGROUND AND FACTS • Jafar Vossoughi is an expert in applied mechanics and experimental biomechanics, which encompasses the testing of mechanical theories and the creation and use of experimental devices for biomechanical research. In the 1990s, while teaching at the University of the District of Columbia (UDC), Vossoughi set up a laboratory to conduct research. When his employment contract expired, he remained on campus and continued his research. In 2000, without Vossoughi's knowledge, UDC cleaned out the laboratory and threw away most of its contents. Vossoughi filed a suit in a District of Columbia court against UDC, seeking damages for the loss of his course materials, unpublished research data, unique scientific instruments, and other items. He personally testified as to the "replacement cost." A jury found UDC liable for conversion (the wrongful taking of someone's personal property) and awarded Vossoughi $1.65 million. UDC appealed.

IN THE LANGUAGE OF THE COURT
GLICKMAN, Associate Judge:
* * * *

The usual and traditional measure of damages for conversion of property is the fair market value of the property at the time of the conversion. * * * But fair market value is not always the test. Sometimes fair market value cannot be determined, or would be inadequate, as when, for example, the article destroyed was unique or possessed qualities the special nature of which could only be appreciated by the owner. Accordingly, *for purposes of awarding adequate compensation for the destruction of property, value means exchange value or the value to the owner if this is greater than the exchange value.* In general, therefore, a person tortiously deprived of property is entitled to damages based upon its special value to him if that is greater than its market value. Where the lost property in such cases is replaceable, it is appropriate to measure damages for its loss by the cost of replacement. [Emphasis added.]

* * * Dr. Vossoughi's course materials, unpublished research and fabricated instruments * * * had great use value to Dr. Vossoughi but no comparable (if any) market value.
* * * *

* * * Dr. Vossoughi based his estimates of the value of the property on the time it would take him to replicate it. This was a conceptually reasonable approach * * *. UDC complains of the vagueness of Dr. Vossoughi's testimony: for example, his estimates were rough approximations, and he did not specify exactly how he valued his or others' time * * *. But our cases have held that an owner is qualified to estimate the value of his property based on his familiarity with its quality and condition * * *. In this case, Dr. Vossoughi certainly had the requisite [necessary] familiarity, and given his experience as a fabricator of instruments, a teacher, a researcher, and a grant recipient, he also had considerable expertise to draw on. His opinions

CASE 12.1 CONTINUED ➡ clearly were informed ones. There is nothing to show that his estimates were unrealistic; on the contrary, they were corroborated [substantiated] by [Vossoughi's expert witnesses] Dr. Conway and Dr. Saha.

UDC further argues that Dr. Vossoughi's valuation of his course materials was flawed in [two] respects. First, Dr. Vossoughi admitted his course materials were not salable ("Nobody would buy somebody else's [teaching] notes. It's useless [except] for that particular class."). But * * * the absence of an exchange value does not mean the course materials had no compensable use value to Dr. Vossoughi. Second, Dr. Vossoughi acknowledged having been compensated by * * * UDC from his teaching salary to prepare the course materials and teach the courses. But this fact does not diminish the value of his course materials to Dr. Vossoughi; if anything, it confirms their value.

DECISION AND REMEDY • *The District of Columbia Court of Appeals affirmed the award. Vossoughi's evidence was "not speculative and unreliable." His lost property was difficult to value, but the evidence allowed the jury to make a fair estimate of its worth.*

THE LEGAL ENVIRONMENT DIMENSION • *Should plaintiffs be required to prove the amount of their damages with certainty and exactitude? Why or why not?*

THE ETHICAL DIMENSION • *Did Vossoughi have an ethical duty to reduce the amount of his damages by, for example, retrieving from the trash as much of his property as he could? Discuss.*

Disparagement of Property

Disparagement of property occurs when economically injurious falsehoods are made about another's product or property rather than about another's reputation (as in the tort of defamation). *Disparagement of property* is a general term for torts that can be more specifically referred to as *slander of quality* or *slander of title*.

SLANDER OF QUALITY The publication of false information about another's product, alleging that it is not what its seller claims, constitutes the tort of **slander of quality,** or **trade libel.** To establish trade libel, the plaintiff must prove that the improper publication caused a third person to refrain from dealing with the plaintiff and that the plaintiff sustained economic damages (such as lost profits) as a result.

An improper publication may be both a slander of quality and a defamation of character. For example, a statement that disparages the quality of a product may also, by implication, disparage the character of a person who would sell such a product.

SLANDER OF TITLE When a publication falsely denies or casts doubt on another's legal ownership of property, resulting in financial loss to the property's owner, the tort of **slander of title** occurs. Usually, this is an intentional tort in which someone knowingly publishes an untrue statement about another's ownership of certain property with the intent of discouraging a third person from dealing with the person slandered. For example, it would be difficult for a car dealer to attract customers after competitors published a notice that the dealer's stock consisted of stolen automobiles.

See *Concept Summary 12.2* on the following page for a review of intentional torts against property.

SECTION 5
NEGLIGENCE

Negligence suits are probably the most prevalent type of lawsuits brought against businesses today. The tort of **negligence** occurs when someone suffers injury because of another's failure to live up to a required *duty of care*. In contrast to intentional torts, in torts involving negligence, the tortfeasor neither wishes to bring about the consequences of the act nor believes that they will occur. The actor's conduct merely creates a risk of such consequences. If no risk is created, there is no negligence. Moreover, the risk must be foreseeable—that is, it must be such that a reasonable person engaging in the same activity would anticipate the risk and guard against it. In determining what is reasonable conduct, courts consider the nature of the possible harm. Creating a very slight risk of a dangerous explosion might be unreasonable, whereas creating a distinct possibility of someone's burning his or her fingers on a stove might be reasonable.

Many of the intentional torts discussed earlier in this chapter constitute negligence if the element of

CONCEPT SUMMARY 12.2
Intentional Torts against Property

Name of Tort	Description
Trespass to Land	The invasion of another's real property without consent or privilege. Once a person is expressly or impliedly established as a trespasser, the property owner has specific rights, which may include the right to detain or remove the trespasser.
Trespass to Personal Property	The intentional interference with an owner's right to use, possess, or enjoy his or her personal property without the owner's consent.
Conversion	The wrongful possession or use of another person's personal property without just cause.
Disparagement of Property	Any economically injurious falsehood that is made about another's product or property; an inclusive term for the torts of *slander of quality* and *slander of title*.

intent is missing (or cannot be proved). Suppose that Juarez walks up to Maya and intentionally shoves her. Maya falls and breaks her arm as a result. In this situation, Juarez committed an intentional tort (battery). If Juarez carelessly bumps into Maya, however, and she falls and breaks her arm as a result, Juarez's action constitutes negligence. In either situation, Juarez has committed a tort.

To succeed in a negligence action, the plaintiff must prove each of the following:

1. *Duty.* That the defendant owed a duty of care to the plaintiff.
2. *Breach.* That the defendant breached that duty.
3. *Causation.* That the defendant's breach caused the plaintiff's injury.
4. *Damages.* That the plaintiff suffered a legally recognizable injury.

We discuss each of these four elements of negligence on the following pages.

The Duty of Care and Its Breach

Central to the tort of negligence is the concept of a **duty of care.** This concept arises from the notion that if we are to live in society with other people, some actions can be tolerated and some cannot, and some actions are reasonable and some are not. The basic principle underlying the duty of care is that people are free to act as they please so long as their actions do not infringe on the interests of others.

When someone fails to comply with the duty to exercise reasonable care, a potentially tortious act may have been committed. Failure to live up to a standard of care may be an act (accidentally setting fire to a building) or an omission (neglecting to put out a campfire). It may be a careless act or a carefully performed but nevertheless dangerous act that results in injury. Courts consider the nature of the act (whether it is outrageous or commonplace), the manner in which the act is performed (heedlessly versus cautiously), and the nature of the injury (whether it is serious or slight) in determining whether the duty of care has been breached.

CASE IN POINT Stella Liebeck, an eighty-year-old woman, purchased a cup of coffee at a McDonald's drive-through window. As she removed the lid, Liebeck held the cup between her legs and accidentally spilled the coffee on herself, causing third degree burns. She was hospitalized for eight days and underwent skin grafts but suffered permanent scars. At trial, evidence showed that McDonald's required its restaurants to serve their coffee at 180 to 190 degrees Fahrenheit—10 to 30 degrees hotter than competitors' restaurants. At that temperature, the coffee would cause third-degree burns in two to seven seconds. Based on this evidence, a jury found that McDonald's had breached its duty of care and awarded Liebeck a famously large amount of compensatory and punitive damages.[18]

---

18. *Liebeck v. McDonald's Restaurants,* No. D-202-CV 9302419, 1995 WL 360309 (N.M. Dist.Ct. 1994). The jury awarded $200,000 in compensatory damages and $2.7 million in punitive damages, which the court reduced to $480,000 ($680,000 total). The parties appealed, but then entered into an out-of-court settlement for an undisclosed amount less than $600,000. See also *Boyle v. Christensen,* 219 P.3d 58 (Utah App. 2009).

THE REASONABLE PERSON STANDARD Tort law measures duty by the **reasonable person standard.** In determining whether a duty of care has been breached, for example, the courts ask how a reasonable person would have acted in the same circumstances. The reasonable person standard is said to be (though in an absolute sense it cannot be) objective. It is not necessarily how a particular person *would* act. It is society's judgment of how an ordinarily prudent person *should* act. If the so-called reasonable person existed, he or she would be careful, conscientious, even tempered, and honest. That individuals are required to exercise a reasonable standard of care in their activities is a pervasive concept in business law, and many of the issues dealt with in subsequent chapters of this text have to do with this duty.

In negligence cases, the degree of care to be exercised varies, depending on the defendant's occupation or profession, her or his relationship with the plaintiff, and other factors. Generally, whether an action constitutes a breach of the duty of care is determined on a case-by-case basis. The outcome depends on how the judge (or jury, if it is a jury trial) decides a reasonable person in the position of the defendant would have acted in the particular circumstances of the case. In the following subsections, we examine the degree of care typically expected of landowners and professionals.

THE DUTY OF LANDOWNERS Landowners are expected to exercise reasonable care to protect individuals coming onto their property from harm. In some jurisdictions, landowners may even have a duty to protect trespassers against certain risks. Landowners who rent or lease premises to tenants are expected to exercise reasonable care to ensure that the tenants and their guests are not harmed in common areas, such as stairways, entryways, and laundry rooms.

Landowners who rent or lease premises to tenants also have a duty to supply correct information to tenants. If they breach this duty, landowners can be held liable for negligent misrepresentation. Unlike intentional misrepresentation, or fraud, negligent misrepresentation requires only that the person making the statement or omission did not have a reasonable basis for believing its truthfulness.

The Duty to Warn Business Invitees of Risks. Retailers and other firms that explicitly or implicitly invite persons to come onto their premises are usually charged with a duty to exercise reasonable care to protect these **business invitees.** For example, if you entered a supermarket, slipped on a wet floor,

and sustained injuries as a result, the owner of the supermarket would be liable for damages if, when you slipped, there was no sign warning that the floor was wet. A court would hold that the business owner was negligent because the owner failed to exercise a reasonable degree of care in protecting the store's customers against foreseeable risks about which the owner knew or *should have known.* That a patron might slip on the wet floor and be injured as a result was a foreseeable risk. The owner should have taken care to avoid this risk and warned the customer of it (by posting a sign or setting out orange cones, for example).

The landowner also has a duty to discover and remove any hidden dangers that might injure a customer or other invitee. Store owners have a duty to protect customers from slipping and injuring themselves on merchandise that has fallen off the shelves, for example. Thus, the owners of business premises should evaluate and frequently reassess potential hazards on the property to ensure the safety of business invitees.

Obvious Risks Provide an Exception. Some risks, of course, are so obvious that an owner need not warn of them. For example, a business owner does not need to warn customers to open a door before attempting to walk through it. Other risks, however, even though they may seem obvious to a business owner, may not be so in the eyes of another, such as a child. In addition, even if a risk is obvious, that does not necessarily excuse a business owner from the duty to protect customers from foreseeable harm.

CASE IN POINT Giorgio's Grill in Hollywood, Florida, is a restaurant that becomes a nightclub after certain hours. At those times, as the manager of Giorgio's knew, the staff and customers traditionally threw paper napkins into the air as the music played. The napkins landed on the floor, but no one picked them up. One night, Jane Izquierdo went to Giorgio's. She had been to the club on prior occasions and knew about the napkin-throwing tradition. Not long after arriving, Izquierdo slipped and fell, breaking her leg. She required surgery and three months of recovery in a wheelchair. She sued Giorgio's for negligence, but lost at trial because a jury found that the risk of slipping on the napkins was obvious. A state appellate court reversed the lower court's decision, however. The court held that the obviousness of a risk does not discharge a business owner's duty to maintain the premises in a safe condition (although it does discharge the duty to warn).[19]

19. *Izquierdo v. Gyroscope, Inc.*, 946 So.2d 115 (Fla.App. 2007).

THE DUTY OF PROFESSIONALS If an individual has knowledge or skill superior to that of an ordinary person, the individual's conduct must be consistent with that status. Professionals—including physicians, dentists, architects, engineers, accountants, and lawyers, among others—are required to have a standard minimum level of special knowledge and ability. Therefore, in determining what constitutes reasonable care in the case of professionals, the law takes their training and expertise into account. Thus, an accountant's conduct is judged not by the reasonable person standard, but by the reasonable accountant standard.

If a professional violates his or her duty of care toward a client, the client may bring a suit against the professional, alleging **malpractice,** which is essentially professional negligence. For example, a patient might sue a physician for *medical malpractice.* A client might sue an attorney for *legal malpractice.*

NO DUTY TO RESCUE Although the law requires individuals to act reasonably and responsibly in their relations with one another, a person will not be considered negligent for failing to come to the aid of a stranger in peril. For example, assume that you are walking down a city street and see a pedestrian about to step directly in front of an oncoming bus. You realize that the person has not seen the bus and is unaware of the danger. Do you have a legal duty to warn that individual? No. Although most people would probably concede that, in this situation, the observer has an *ethical* duty to warn, tort law does not impose a general duty to rescue others in peril.

People involved in special relationships, however, have been held to have a duty to rescue other parties within the relationship. A person has a duty to rescue his or her child or spouse if either is in danger, for example. Other special relationships, such as those between teachers and students or hiking and hunting partners, may also give rise to a duty to rescue. In addition, if a person who has no duty to rescue undertakes to rescue another, then the rescuer is charged with a duty to follow through with due care in the rescue attempt. Most states also have laws that require motorists involved in an automobile accident to stop and render aid. Failure to do so is both a tort and a crime.

Causation

Another element necessary to a negligence action is *causation*. If a person breaches a duty of care and someone suffers injury, the person's act must have caused the harm for it to constitute the tort of negligence. In deciding whether the requirement of causation is met, the court must address two questions, which we discuss next.

IS THERE CAUSATION IN FACT? Did the injury occur because of the defendant's act, or would it have occurred anyway? If the injury would not have occurred without the defendant's act, then there is causation in fact. **Causation in fact** usually can be determined by use of the *but for* test: "but for" the wrongful act, the injury would not have occurred. This test determines whether there was an actual cause-and-effect relationship between the act and the injury suffered. In theory, causation in fact is limitless. One could claim, for example, that "but for" the creation of the world, a particular injury would not have occurred. Thus, as a practical matter, the law has to establish limits, and it does so through the concept of proximate cause.

WAS THE ACT THE PROXIMATE, OR LEGAL, CAUSE OF THE INJURY? Proximate cause, or *legal cause,* exists when the connection between an act and an injury is strong enough to justify imposing liability. Proximate cause asks whether the injuries sustained were foreseeable or too remotely connected to the incident to trigger liability. Judges use proximate cause to limit the scope of the defendant's liability to a subset of the total number of potential plaintiffs that might have been harmed by the defendant's actions.

Consider an example. Ackerman carelessly leaves a campfire burning. The fire not only burns down the forest but also sets off an explosion in a nearby chemical plant that spills chemicals into a river, killing all the fish for a hundred miles downstream and ruining the economy of a tourist resort. Should Ackerman be liable to the resort owners? To the tourists whose vacations were ruined? These are questions of proximate cause that a court must decide.

Both of these causation questions must be answered in the affirmative for liability in tort to arise. If a defendant's action constitutes causation in fact but a court decides that the action is not the proximate cause of the plaintiff's injury, the causation requirement has not been met—and the defendant normally will not be liable to the plaintiff.

Questions of proximate cause are linked to the concept of foreseeability because it would be unfair to impose liability on a defendant unless the defendant's actions created a foreseeable risk of injury. Probably the most cited case on the concept of foreseeability and proximate cause is the *Palsgraf* case, which is presented next.

CASE 12.2
Palsgraf v. Long Island Railroad Co.
Court of Appeals of New York, 248 N.Y. 339, 162 N.E. 99 (1928).

BACKGROUND AND FACTS • The plaintiff, Helen Palsgraf, was waiting for a train on a station platform. A man carrying a package was rushing to catch a train that was moving away from a platform across the tracks from Palsgraf. As the man attempted to jump aboard the moving train, he seemed unsteady and about to fall. A railroad guard on the car reached forward to grab him, and another guard on the platform pushed him from behind to help him board the train. In the process, the man's package, which (unknown to the railroad guards) contained fireworks, fell on the railroad tracks and exploded. There was nothing about the package to indicate its contents. The repercussions of the explosion caused scales at the other end of the train platform to fall on Palsgraf, causing injuries for which she sued the railroad company. At the trial, the jury found that the railroad guards had been negligent in their conduct. The railroad company appealed. The appellate court affirmed the trial court's judgment, and the railroad company appealed to New York's highest state court.

IN THE LANGUAGE OF THE COURT
CARDOZO, C.J. [Chief Justice]
* * * *

 The conduct of the defendant's guard, if a wrong in its relation to the holder of the package, was not a wrong in its relation to the plaintiff, standing far away. Relatively to her it was not negligence at all.
* * * *

 * * * What the plaintiff must show is "a wrong" to herself; i.e., a violation of her own right, and not merely a wrong to someone else[.] * * * *The risk reasonably to be perceived defines the duty to be obeyed[.]* * * * Here, by concession, there was nothing in the situation to suggest to the most cautious mind that the parcel wrapped in newspaper would spread wreckage through the station. If the guard had thrown it down knowingly and willfully, he would not have threatened the plaintiff's safety, so far as appearances could warn him. His conduct would not have involved, even then, an unreasonable probability of invasion of her bodily security. Liability can be no greater where the act is inadvertent. [Emphasis added.]

 * * * One who seeks redress at law does not make out a cause of action by showing without more that there has been damage to his person. If the harm was not willful, he must show that the act as to him had possibilities of danger so many and apparent as to entitle him to be protected against the doing of it though the harm was unintended. * * * The victim does not sue * * * to vindicate an interest invaded in the person of another. * * * He sues for breach of a duty owing to himself.

 * * * [To rule otherwise] would entail liability for any and all consequences, however novel or extraordinary.

DECISION AND REMEDY • *Palsgraf's complaint was dismissed. The railroad had not been negligent toward her because injury to her was not foreseeable. Had the owner of the fireworks been harmed, and had he filed suit, there could well have been a different result.*

IMPACT OF THIS CASE ON TODAY'S LAW • *The* Palsgraf *case established foreseeability as the test for proximate cause. Today, the courts continue to apply this test in determining proximate cause—and thus tort liability for injuries. Generally, if the victim or the consequences of a harm done were unforeseeable, there is no proximate cause. Note, though, that in the online environment, distinctions based on physical proximity, such as that used by the court in this case, are largely inapplicable.*

THE GLOBAL DIMENSION • *The concept of proximate cause is common among nations around the globe, but its application differs from country to country. What would be the advantages and disadvantages of a universal principle of proximate cause applied everywhere by all courts in all relevant cases? Discuss.*

The Injury Requirement and Damages

For a tort to have been committed, the plaintiff must have suffered a *legally recognizable* injury. To recover damages (receive compensation), the plaintiff must have suffered some loss, harm, wrong, or invasion of a protected interest. Essentially, the purpose of tort law is to compensate for legally recognized harms and injuries resulting from wrongful acts. If no harm or injury results from a given negligent action, there is nothing to compensate— and no tort exists.

For example, if you carelessly bump into a passerby, who stumbles and falls as a result, you may be liable in tort if the passerby is injured in the fall. If the person is unharmed, however, there normally can be no suit for damages because no injury was suffered.

Compensatory damages are the norm in negligence cases. Occasionally, though, a court will award punitive damages if the defendant's conduct was *grossly negligent,* meaning that the defendant intentionally failed to perform a duty with reckless disregard of the consequences to others.

SECTION 6
DEFENSES TO NEGLIGENCE

Defendants often defend against negligence claims by asserting that the plaintiffs have failed to prove the existence of one or more of the required elements for negligence. Additionally, there are three basic *affirmative* defenses in negligence cases (defenses that a defendant can use to avoid liability even if the facts are as the plaintiff states): *assumption of risk, superseding cause,* and *contributory and comparative negligence.*

Note that when a state has enacted a law that places a cap on the amount of noneconomic damages that can be awarded, this law can be similar to a defense because it limits the plaintiff's recovery. This chapter's *Insight into Ethics* feature on page 287 discusses some effects of such limitations on damages.

Assumption of Risk

A plaintiff who voluntarily enters into a risky situation, knowing about the risk involved, will not be allowed to recover. This is the defense of **assumption of risk.** The requirements of this defense are (1) knowledge of the risk and (2) voluntary assumption of the risk. This defense frequently is asserted when the plaintiff was injured during recreational activities that involve known risk, such as skiing and skydiving. Note that assumption of risk can apply not only to participants in sporting events, but also to spectators and bystanders who are injured while attending those events.

CASE IN POINT Delinda Taylor, who was a Seattle Mariners fan, took her sons to see a Mariners baseball game. They arrived early so that they could watch the players warm up and get their autographs. Taylor was standing by her seat near the foul line watching Mariners' pitcher Freddie Garcia throwing the ball with another player. When she looked away from the field, an errant ball got past Garcia and struck Taylor in the face, causing serious injuries. She filed a negligence lawsuit against the Mariners (Baseball Club of Seattle) to recover for her injuries. The Mariners asserted the defense of assumption of risk. The court ruled that Taylor was familiar with baseball and that she knew about and had voluntarily assumed the risk of getting hit by a thrown baseball.[20]

EXPRESS OR IMPLIED ASSUMPTION OF RISK The risk can be assumed by express agreement, or the assumption of risk can be implied by the plaintiff's knowledge of the risk and subsequent conduct. For example, a driver, Bryan Stewart, knows that there is a risk of being killed or injured in a crash whenever he enters a race. Therefore, a court will deem that Stewart has assumed the risk of racing. Of course, a person does not assume a risk different from or greater than the risk normally carried by the activity. Thus, Stewart does not assume the risk that the banking in the curves of the racetrack will give way during the race because of a construction defect.

In the following case, the plaintiff was driving a beverage cart on a golf course during a golfing event. Does this mean that she was a "participant" in the sport and thus assumed the risk of being hit by a golf ball? That was the issue before the court.

---

20. *Taylor v. Baseball Club of Seattle, LP,* 132 Wash.App. 32, 130 P.3d 835 (2006); see also *Allred v. Capital Area Soccer League, Inc.,* 669 S.E.2d 777 (N.C.App. 2008).

✳ EXTENDED CASE 12.3 ✳
Pfenning v. Lineman

Court of Appeals of Indiana, 922 N.E.2d 45 (2010).
Indianalawblog.com/archives/ind_appct_decisions[a]

IN THE LANGUAGE OF THE COURT
DARDEN, Judge.
* * * *

* * * Whitey's [31 Club], a bar, sponsored a golf scramble at the Elks' golf course in Marion, [Indiana,] on August 19, 2006. * * * Jerry Jones * * * signed up to drive a beverage cart.

The morning of the scramble, Jones invited [his] then-sixteen-year-old [granddaughter, Cassie] Pfenning, to ride in a beverage cart with him during the tournament. With her mother's permission, Pfenning agreed to join Jones.

Upon arriving at the golf course, Jones retrieved a beverage cart for his and Pfenning's use * * * . The cart had a large cooler in the back for drinks but no roof or windshield. Pfenning received no instructions regarding how or where to operate the cart; she was unfamiliar with golf etiquette and had been to a golf course only once before in 1997.

Prior to the start of the scramble, Jones decided to join one of the teams playing in the scramble as it was short a player. He therefore left Pfenning with his sister, Lottie Kendall. Kendall and Pfenning drove the beverage cart together for a short period of time until Kendall also decided to play in a foursome. Christie Edwards, a Whitey's employee, therefore took Kendall's place in the beverage cart. Pfenning drove the cart, and Edwards dispensed the beverages to the scramble's participants.

Approximately three hours into the tournament, [Joseph] Lineman, a participant in the scramble, hit a drive from the sixteenth hole's tee. * * * Pfenning, who was driving the beverage cart on a cart path near the eighteenth hole, did not hear any warning regarding the ball's approach. After traveling more than two hundred feet, the ball struck Pfenning in the mouth, causing injuries to her mouth, jaw, and teeth.

On February 7, 2007, Pfenning filed a complaint against the Defendants [Lineman, Whitey's, the Elks Club, and others]. She alleged [that the defendants were negligent in failing to exercise reasonable care for her safety while on the golf course.]
* * * *

[Pfenning also alleged that] as a direct and proximate result of the Defendants' negligent conduct, [she] suffered painful and permanent injuries and incurred significant medical and dental expenses. Several of [her] teeth were destroyed and her teeth remain missing and/or disfigured.

[Pfenning also alleged that] as a direct and proximate result of the Defendants' negligent conduct, [Pfenning] suffered mental and emotional pain and anguish. As a direct and proximate result of the Defendants' negligent conduct, [her] ability to function as a whole person has been impaired. The quality of [her] life has been significantly diminished as a result of the Defendants' negligent conduct.
* * * *

* * * The trial court [granted] the Defendants' motions for summary judgment.

* * * *

Pfenning asserts that the trial court erred in granting summary judgment in favor of the Defendants. She argues that the Defendants owed her a duty to prevent her from being injured and were negligent in breaching that duty.
* * * *

This court had consistently held that *"there is no duty from one participant in a sports activity to another to prevent injury resulting from an inherent risk of the sport."* [Emphasis added.]
* * * *

Here, Pfenning maintains that she was not a participant in the golf scramble because "she was not playing; she was not watching the event; she was not signed up on a team; nor was she doing anything related to the activity of golf." Thus, she argues that the Defendants owed her a duty to prevent her injury. We disagree.

Pfenning's presence on the golf course was due to the fact there was a golf scramble; she had agreed to function as a driver or rider in a beverage cart provided for the golf scramble; and she performed this function and assisted in providing beverages to players in the golf scramble. If not for the golf scramble, Pfenning would not have been on the golf course the day of the incident. Although not a player herself, she clearly was "part of the sporting event * * * involved[.]"
* * * *

Pfenning, however, also seems to argue that she could not have consented to the inherent risks of golf as "she knew nothing about golf and could not appreciate any

---

a. Scroll down the page to the link given under "February 12, 2010." When the next page opens, click on the case name to access the opinion. The Indiana Law Blog maintains this Web site.

EXTENDED CASE CONTINUES ▶

EXTENDED CASE 12.3 CONTINUED ⬇

risk involved with being near a golf course." We find this argument unavailing [failing to achieve the desired result].

* * * *

Even if we were to assume that Pfenning arrived at the golf course utterly ignorant of the game, the undisputed facts show that Pfenning had been participating in the golf scramble event for approximately

three hours prior to being struck by the golf ball. Over this extended time period, she had been delivering beverages to foursomes during play. We find that this supports an inference that Pfenning was aware of the inherent risks of golf; namely, that it involves players hitting golf balls long distances and that some, if not many, of these balls invariably fail to land where intended

Given Pfenning's status as a participant in the golf scramble, with

its inherent risks, we find that the Defendants did not owe her a duty.

* * * *

Finding no issues of material fact and that the Defendants are entitled to summary judgment as a matter of law, we conclude that the trial court properly granted summary judgment in favor of the Defendants.

Affirmed.

QUESTIONS

1. Should the courts distinguish between different levels of participation in a sporting event when determining liability? Explain.
2. Suppose that Pfenning had been riding in the beverage cart with her grandfather when she was struck by the golf ball. In that situation, would the outcome of this case have been any different? Why or why not?

WHEN COURTS DO NOT APPLY ASSUMPTION OF RISK Courts do not apply the assumption of risk doctrine in emergency situations. Nor does this doctrine apply when a statute protects a class of people from harm and a member of the class is injured by the harm. For instance, because federal and state statutes protect employees from harmful working conditions, employees do not assume the risks associated with the workplace. An employee who is injured generally will be compensated regardless of fault under state workers' compensation statutes (see Chapter 21).

Superseding Cause

An unforeseeable intervening event may break the causal connection between a wrongful act and an injury to another. If so, the intervening event acts as a **superseding cause**—that is, it relieves a defendant of liability for injuries caused by the intervening event. For example, Derrick, while riding his bicycle, negligently hits Julie, who is walking on the sidewalk. As a result of the impact, Julie falls and fractures her hip. While she is waiting for help to arrive, a small aircraft crashes nearby and explodes, and some of the fiery debris hits her, causing her to sustain severe burns. Derrick will be liable for the damages related to Julie's fractured hip, but normally he will not be liable for the injuries caused by the plane crash—because the risk of a plane crashing nearby and injuring Julie was not foreseeable.

Contributory and Comparative Negligence

All individuals are expected to exercise a reasonable degree of care in looking out for themselves. In the past, under the common law doctrine of **contributory negligence,** a plaintiff who was also negligent (failed to exercise a reasonable degree of care) could not recover anything from the defendant. Under this rule, no matter how insignificant the plaintiff's negligence was relative to the defendant's negligence, the plaintiff would be precluded from recovering any damages. Today, only a few jurisdictions still hold to this doctrine.

In most states, the doctrine of contributory negligence has been replaced by a **comparative negligence** standard. The comparative negligence standard enables both the plaintiff's and the defendant's negligence to be computed and the liability for damages distributed accordingly. The plaintiff's financial recovery may be reduced, or even prohibited, depending on whether the state has a pure or modified comparative negligence system.

"PURE" COMPARATIVE NEGLIGENCE STATES Some jurisdictions, including California and New York, have adopted a "pure" form of comparative negligence that allows the plaintiff to recover damages

INSIGHT INTO ETHICS
Some Consequences of Caps on Medical Malpractice Awards

As part of the effort to curb excessive tort litigation, many states have enacted limits on the amount of general noneconomic damages that can be awarded. (Noneconomic damages include damages for pain and suffering, emotional distress, inconvenience, physical impairment, disfigurement, and the like.) Some states also specifically limit damage awards in medical malpractice (professional negligence) cases.

Limitations on Damages

Although placing such caps on damage awards may seem a logical way to reduce the number of negligence cases filed, it raises issues of fairness. Why should a plaintiff who loses a limb, for example, not be able to obtain adequate monetary damages for the mental anguish associated with such an injury? The limits also encourage plaintiffs' attorneys to find ways to avoid these caps, such as by suing other defendants (including nurses and additional health-care professionals) to whom the caps do not apply.

More than half of the states now limit damage awards in medical malpractice cases. For example, California caps noneconomic damages in medical malpractice cases at $250,000—even if the plaintiff dies.[a] States hope that these limitations will reduce the frequency and severity of malpractice claims and thereby reduce health-care expenditures, although there is no definitive scientific evidence showing that damages caps lower health-care costs.[b]

Michigan Nurse Sued for Negligence

As an example of how ethical issues can result from placing caps on medical malpractice claims, consider what happened in one Michigan case. A fifty-two-year-old Michigan farmer developed a blood clot in his leg and underwent emergency surgery at a hospital to remove it. After the surgery, a health-care professional removed the epidural catheter (a tube that enables painkillers to pass into the space surrounding the spinal cord). Eleven minutes later, a nurse came in and gave him a blood thinner called Heparin. According to the standard of care for this procedure, Heparin should not be given until at least one hour after the epidural catheter has been removed to ensure that the catheter site has sufficient time to coagulate and stop bleeding.

In this situation, the Heparin was given too soon and was given continuously for the next twenty-four hours. As a result, the patient experienced bleeding into the epidural space under his skin, and pressure built up in his spinal column. The hospital physicians and nurses failed to recognize the problem, and he was left with a permanent spinal cord injury and paralysis. Because of Michigan's cap on malpractice awards,[c] though, the negligent physician and the hospital responsible for his lifelong injuries were able to settle the claims against them for the legislatively mandated maximum of $717,000 for pain and suffering (and $1.1 million in economic damages).

CRITICAL THINKING

INSIGHT INTO THE SOCIAL ENVIRONMENT
If plaintiffs can still collect significant amounts of economic damages, will the limits on noneconomic damages be effective at reducing the number of negligence lawsuits filed? Why or why not?

a. See California Civil Code Section 3333.2.
b. Fred J. Hellinger and William E. Encinosa. "The Impact of State Laws Limiting Malpractice Damage Awards on Health Care Expenditures." *American Journal of Public Health.* August 2006: 1375–1381.

c. Michigan Compiled Laws Section 600.1483.

---

even if her or his fault is greater than that of the defendant. Under a pure comparative negligence system, a judge or jury assigns a percentage of fault to each responsible party and then apportions the damages award accordingly.

In states with such systems, even if the plaintiff's percentage of fault is very large, he or she will still be entitled to collect a share of damages from the other responsible party or parties. For example, Jill sustains injuries when her car is struck by Carson's truck. She files a lawsuit. At trial, the jury

determines that Jill was also negligent and that Carson was only 20 percent at fault for the accident that caused Jill's injuries. Because they live in a pure comparative negligence state, Jill is entitled to recover 20 percent of the damages she sustained from Carson.

MODIFIED COMPARATIVE FAULT STATES Most jurisdictions in the United States have adopted a modified comparative fault system under which plaintiffs who are largely responsible for their own injuries are not allowed to recover damages. There are two variations of modified comparative fault systems: those that follow a "50 percent rule" and those that follow a "51 percent rule."

Under the 50 percent rule, the plaintiff in a negligence action recovers nothing if she or he was 50 percent or more at fault. Thus, an injured party can recover only if it is determined that his or her responsibility for the injury is 49 percent or less. If the injured party's level of fault reaches 50 percent, he or she cannot recover *any* damages.

Under the 51 percent rule, the plaintiff in a negligence action recovers nothing if she or he was responsible for *more than half* (51 percent or more) of the accident. Thus, if the plaintiff was 50 percent at fault in causing the injury, then she or he can still recover, but once the plaintiff's level of fault reaches 51 percent, recovery is barred.

SECTION 7
SPECIAL NEGLIGENCE DOCTRINES AND STATUTES

A number of special doctrines and statutes relating to negligence are also important to a plaintiff's liability. We examine a few of them here.

Res Ipsa Loquitur

Generally, in lawsuits involving negligence, the plaintiff has the burden of proving that the defendant was negligent. In certain situations, however, the courts may presume that negligence has occurred, in which case the burden of proof rests on the defendant—that is, the defendant must prove that he or she was *not* negligent. The presumption of the defendant's negligence is known as the doctrine of **res ipsa loquitur**,[21] which translates as "the facts speak for themselves." This doctrine is applied only when the event creating the damage or injury is one that ordinarily does not occur in the absence of negligence.

CASE IN POINT Mary Gubbins underwent abdominal surgery and, following the surgery, suffered nerve damage in her spine near the area of the operation. She was unable to walk or stand for months, and even though she regained some use of her legs through physical therapy, her mobility was impaired and she experienced pain. In her subsequent negligence lawsuit, Gubbins asserted *res ipsa loquitur*, because the

injury never would have occurred in the absence of the surgeon's negligence.[22]

For the doctrine of *res ipsa loquitur* to apply, the event must have been within the defendant's power to control and not due to any voluntary action or contribution on the part of the plaintiff.

Negligence *Per Se*

Certain conduct, whether it consists of an action or a failure to act, may be treated as **negligence *per se*** ("in or of itself"). Negligence *per se* may occur if an individual violates a statute or an ordinance providing for a criminal penalty and that violation causes another to be injured. The statute must be designed to prevent the type of injury that the plaintiff suffered, and it must clearly set out what standard of conduct is expected, when and where it is expected, and of whom it is expected. The standard of conduct required by the statute is the duty that the defendant owes to the plaintiff, and a violation of the statute is the breach of that duty.

CASE IN POINT A Delaware statute states that anyone "who operates a motor vehicle and who fails to give full time and attention to the operation of the vehicle" is guilty of inattentive driving. Michael Moore was cited for inattentive driving after he collided with Debra Wright's car when he backed a truck out of a parking space. Moore paid the ticket, which meant that he pleaded guilty to violating the statute. The day after the accident, Wright began having back pain, which eventually required surgery. She sued Moore for damages, alleging negligence *per se*. The Delaware Supreme Court ruled that the inattentive driving statute sets forth a sufficiently specific standard of conduct to warrant application of negligence *per se*.[23]

"Danger Invites Rescue" Doctrine

Sometimes, a person who is trying to avoid harm—such as an individual who swerves to avoid a head-on collision with a drunk driver—ends up causing harm to another (such as a cyclist riding in the bike lane) as a result. In those situations, the original wrongdoer (the drunk driver in this scenario) is liable to anyone who is injured, even if the injury actually resulted from another person's attempt to escape harm. The "danger invites rescue" doctrine extends the same protection to a person who is trying to rescue another from harm—the original

---

21. Pronounced *rayz ihp-suh low-kwuh-tuhr*.

22. See, for example, *Gubbins v. Hurson*, 885 A.2d 269 (D.C. 2005).
23. *Wright v. Moore*, 931 A.2d 405 (Del.Supr. 2007).

wrongdoer is liable for injuries to the individual attempting a rescue.

Under the "danger invites rescue" doctrine, a person who is injured while going to someone else's rescue can sue the person who caused the dangerous situation. The idea is that the rescuer should not be held liable for any damages because he or she did not cause the danger and because danger invites rescue. For example, Ludlam drives down a street and fails to see a stop sign because he is trying to end a squabble between his two young children in the car's backseat. Salter, on the curb near the stop sign, realizes that Ludlam is about to hit a pedestrian walking across the street at the intersection. Salter runs into the street to push the pedestrian out of the way, and Ludlam's vehicle hits Salter instead. Ludlam will be liable for Salter's injury as the rescuer, as well as for any injuries the other pedestrian (or any bystanders) may have sustained.

Special Negligence Statutes

A number of states have enacted statutes prescribing duties and responsibilities in certain circumstances. For example, most states now have what are called **Good Samaritan statutes.**[24] Under these statutes, someone who is aided voluntarily by another cannot turn around and sue the "Good Samaritan" for negligence. These laws were passed largely to protect physicians and medical personnel who volunteer their services in emergency situations to those in need, such as individuals hurt in car accidents. Indeed, the California Supreme Court has interpreted that state's Good Samaritan statute to mean that a person who renders nonmedical aid is not immune from liability.[25] Thus, only medical personnel and persons rendering medical aid in emergencies are protected in California.

Many states have also passed **dram shop acts,**[26] under which a tavern owner or bartender may be held liable for injuries caused by a person who became intoxicated while drinking at the bar or who was already intoxicated when served by the bartender. Some states' statutes also impose liability

on *social hosts* (persons hosting parties) for injuries caused by guests who became intoxicated at the hosts' homes. Under these statutes, it is unnecessary to prove that the tavern owner, bartender, or social host was negligent. Thus, if Jane hosts a Super Bowl party at which Brett, a minor, sneaks alcoholic drinks, Jane is potentially liable for damages resulting from Brett's drunk driving after the party.

SECTION 8
CYBER TORTS

Torts can also be committed in the online environment. Torts committed via the Internet are often called **cyber torts.** Over the years, the courts have had to decide how to apply traditional tort law to torts committed in cyberspace. To date, most cyber torts have involved defamation, so this discussion will focus on how the traditional tort law concerning defamation is being adapted to apply to online defamation.

Identifying the Author of Online Defamation

An initial issue raised by online defamation was simply discovering who was committing it. In the real world, identifying the author of a defamatory remark generally is an easy matter, but suppose that a business firm has discovered that defamatory statements about its policies and products are being posted in an online forum. Such forums allow anyone—customers, employees, or crackpots—to complain about a firm that they dislike while remaining anonymous.

Therefore, a threshold barrier to anyone who seeks to bring an action for online defamation is discovering the identity of the person who posted the defamatory message. An Internet service provider (ISP)—a company that provides connections to the Internet—can disclose personal information about its customers only when ordered to do so by a court. Consequently, businesses and individuals are increasingly bringing lawsuits against "John Does" (John Doe, Jane Doe, and the like are fictitious names used in lawsuits when the identity of a party is not known or when a party wishes to conceal his or her name for privacy reasons). Then, using the authority of the courts, the plaintiffs can obtain from the ISPs the identity of the persons responsible for the defamatory messages.

Liability of Internet Service Providers

Recall from the discussion of defamation earlier in this chapter that one who repeats or otherwise

---

24. These laws derive their name from the Good Samaritan story in the Bible. In the story, a traveler who had been robbed and beaten lay along the roadside, ignored by those passing by. Eventually, a man from the region of Samaria (the "Good Samaritan") stopped to render assistance to the injured person.

25. *Van Horn v. Watson,* 45 Cal.4th 322, 197 P.3d 164, 86 Cal. Rptr.3d 350 (2008).

26. Historically, a dram was a small unit of liquid, and distilled spirits (strong alcoholic liquor) were sold in drams. Thus, a dram shop was a place where liquor was sold in drams.

republishes a defamatory statement is subject to liability as if he or she had originally published it. Thus, newspapers, magazines, and television and radio stations may be subject to liability for defamatory content that they publish or broadcast, even though the content was prepared or created by others. Applying this rule to cyberspace, however, raises an important issue: Should ISPs be regarded as publishers and therefore be held liable for defamatory messages that are posted by their users in online forums or other arenas?

Before 1996, the courts grappled with this question. Then Congress passed the Communications Decency Act (CDA), which states that "[n]o provider or user of an interactive computer service shall be treated as the publisher or speaker of any information provided by another information content provider."[27] Thus, under the CDA, ISPs generally are treated differently from publishers in print and other media and are not liable for publishing defamatory statements that come from a third party.

CASE IN POINT Four teenagers and their parents brought a negligence action against the social networking site MySpace, Inc. All of the minors were females who had been sexually assaulted by adult men whom they had met on MySpace. They claimed that MySpace was negligent by failing to implement reasonable, basic safety precautions with regard to protecting young children from sexual predators. The court, however, held that MySpace was entitled to immunity under the CDA. MySpace could not be held liable for creating or failing to limit the content on its Web site that was provided by third party users (the four teenagers and the men who had assaulted them).[28]

The Spread of Spam

Businesses and individuals alike are targets of **spam.** Spam refers to the unsolicited "junk e-mails" that flood virtual mailboxes with advertisements, solicitations, and other messages.[29] Considered relatively harmless in the early days of the Internet's popularity, by 2010 spam accounted for roughly 75 percent of all e-mails.

STATE REGULATION OF SPAM In an attempt to combat spam, thirty-six states have enacted laws that prohibit or regulate its use. Many state laws that regulate spam require the senders of e-mail ads to instruct the recipients on how they can "opt out" of further e-mail ads from the same sources. For instance, in some states an unsolicited e-mail ad must include a toll-free phone number or return e-mail address through which the recipient can contact the sender to request that no more ads be e-mailed. Responding to complaints from overwhelmed constituents, a number of jurisdictions have started to pass antispamming laws.

THE FEDERAL CAN-SPAM ACT In 2003, Congress enacted the Controlling the Assault of Non-Solicited Pornography and Marketing (CAN-SPAM) Act. The legislation applies to any "commercial electronic mail messages" that are sent to promote a commercial product or service. Significantly, the statute preempts state antispam laws except for those provisions in state laws that prohibit false and deceptive e-mailing practices.

Generally, the act permits the sending of unsolicited commercial e-mail but prohibits certain types of spamming activities, including the use of a false return address and the use of false, misleading, or deceptive information when sending e-mail. The statute also prohibits the use of "dictionary attacks"—sending messages to randomly generated e-mail addresses—and the "harvesting" of e-mail addresses from Web sites through the use of specialized software.

CASE IN POINT In 2007, federal officials arrested Robert Alan Soloway, who was known as the "Spam King" and considered one of the world's most prolific spammers. Soloway had been using *botnets* (networks of software robots, or bots, that run automatically) to send out hundreds of millions of unwanted e-mails. He was charged under anti–identity theft laws for the appropriation of other people's domain names, among other crimes. Soloway pleaded guilty to mail fraud, spam, and failure to pay taxes.[30]

Arresting prolific spammers, however, has done little to curb spam, which continues to flow at a rate of 70 billion messages per day.

THE U.S. SAFE WEB ACT After the CAN-SPAM Act of 2003 prohibited false and deceptive e-mails originating in the United States, spamming from servers located in other nations increased. These cross-

---

27. 47 U.S.C. Section 230.

28. *Doe II v. MySpace, Inc.,* 175 Cal.App.4th 561, 96 Cal.Rptr.3d 148 (2009).

29. The term *spam* is said to come from a Monty Python song with the lyrics, "Spam spam spam spam, spam spam spam spam, lovely spam, wonderful spam." Like these lyrics, spam online is often considered to be a repetition of worthless text.

30. "'Spam King of Seattle' Soloway pleads guilty." *SC Magazine.* 17 March 2008: n.p. Web.

border spammers generally were able to escape detection and legal sanctions because the Federal Trade Commission (FTC) lacked the authority to investigate foreign spamming.

Congress sought to rectify the situation by enacting the U.S. Safe Web Act of 2006 (also known as the Undertaking Spam, Spyware, and Fraud Enforcement with Enforcers Beyond Borders Act). The act allows the FTC to cooperate and share information with foreign agencies in investigating and prosecuting those involved in spamming, spyware, and various Internet frauds and deceptions. It also provides ISPs with a "safe harbor" (immunity from liability) for supplying information to the FTC concerning possible unfair or deceptive conduct in foreign jurisdictions.

REVIEWING
Torts and Cyber Torts

Elaine Sweeney went to Ragged Mountain Ski Resort in New Hampshire with a friend. Elaine went snow tubing down a snow-tube run designed exclusively for snow tubers. There were no Ragged Mountain employees present in the snow-tube area to instruct Elaine on the proper use of a snow tube. On her fourth run down the trail, Elaine crossed over the center line between snow-tube lanes, collided with another snow tuber, and was injured. Elaine filed a negligence action against Ragged Mountain seeking compensation for the injuries that she sustained. Two years earlier, the New Hampshire state legislature had enacted a statute that prohibited a person who participates in the sport of skiing from suing a ski-area operator for injuries caused by the risks inherent in skiing. Using the information presented in the chapter, answer the following questions.

1. What defense will Ragged Mountain probably assert?
2. The central question in this case is whether the state statute establishing that skiers assume the risks inherent in the sport bars Elaine's suit. What would your decision be on this issue? Why?
3. Suppose that the court concludes that the statute applies only to skiing and not to snow tubing. Will Elaine's lawsuit be successful? Explain.
4. Now suppose that the jury concludes that Elaine was partly at fault for the accident. Under what theory might her damages be reduced in proportion to the degree to which her actions contributed to the accident and her resulting injuries?

DEBATE THIS: *Each time a state legislature enacts a law that applies the assumption of risk doctrine to a particular sport, participants in that sport suffer.*

TERMS AND CONCEPTS

actionable 270
actual malice 272
appropriation 273
assault 270
assumption of risk 284
battery 270
business invitee 281
business tort 275
causation in fact 282
comparative negligence 286

compensatory damages 268
contributory negligence 286
conversion 277
cyber tort 289
defamation 271
disparagement of
  property 279
dram shop act 289
duty of care 280
fraudulent
  misrepresentation 274
Good Samaritan statute 289

intentional tort 269
libel 271
malpractice 282
negligence 279
negligence *per se* 288
privilege 272
proximate cause 282
public figure 272
punitive damages 269
reasonable person
  standard 281
res ipsa loquitur 288

slander 271
slander of quality 279
slander of title 279
spam 290
superseding cause 286
tort 268
tortfeasor 269
trade libel 279
trespass to land 276
trespass to personal
  property 277

QUESTIONS AND CASE PROBLEMS

12–1. Negligence Shannon's physician gives her some pain medication and tells her not to drive after she takes it, as the medication induces drowsiness. In spite of the doctor's warning, Shannon decides to drive to the store while on the medication. Owing to her lack of alertness, she fails to stop at a traffic light and crashes into another vehicle, causing a passenger in that vehicle to be injured. Is Shannon liable for the tort of negligence? Explain fully.

12–2. QUESTION WITH SAMPLE ANSWER: Wrongful Interference.

Lothar owns a bakery. He has been trying to obtain a long-term contract with the owner of Martha's Tea Salons for some time. Lothar starts a local advertising campaign on radio and television and in the newspaper. This advertising campaign is so persuasive that Martha decides to break the contract she has had with Harley's Bakery so that she can patronize Lothar's bakery. Is Lothar liable to Harley's Bakery for the tort of wrongful interference with a contractual relationship? Is Martha liable for this tort? Discuss your answers.

- **For a sample answer to Question 12–2, go to Appendix F at the end of this text.**

12–3. Intentional Torts against Property Gerrit is a former employee of ABC Auto Repair Co. He enters ABC's repair shop, claiming that the company owes him $800 in back wages. Gerrit argues with ABC's general manager, Steward, and Steward orders him off the property. Gerrit refuses to leave, and Steward tells two mechanics to throw him off the property. Gerrit runs to his truck, but on the way, he grabs some tools valued at $800; then he drives away. Gerrit refuses to return the tools.
- (a) Discuss whether Gerrit has committed any torts.
- (b) If the mechanics had thrown Gerrit off the property, would ABC be guilty of assault and battery? Explain.

12–4. Emotional Distress Between 1996 and 1998, Donna Swanson received several anonymous, handwritten letters that, among other things, accused her husband Alan of infidelity. In 1998, John Grisham, Jr., the author of *The Firm* and many other best-selling novels, received an anonymous letter that appeared to have been written by the same person. Grisham and the Swansons suspected Katherine Almy, who soon filed a suit in a Virginia state court against them, alleging, among other things, intentional infliction of emotional distress. According to Almy, Grisham had said that he "really, really wanted to make [her] suffer for writing those letters," and the three devised a scheme to falsely accuse her. They gave David Liebman, a handwriting analyst, samples of Almy's handwriting. These included copies of confidential documents from her children's files at St. Anne's–Belfield School in Charlottesville, Virginia, where Alan Swanson

taught and Grisham served on the board of directors. In Almy's view, Grisham influenced Liebman to report that Almy might have written the letters and misrepresented this report as conclusive, which led the police to confront Almy. She claimed that she then suffered severe emotional distress and depression, causing "a complete disintegration of virtually every aspect of her life" and requiring her "to undergo extensive therapy." In response, the defendants asked the court to dismiss the complaint for failure to state a claim. Should the court grant this request? Explain. [*Almy v. Grisham,* 273 Va. 68, 639 S.E.2d 182 (2007)]

12–5. Negligence Mitsubishi Motors North America, Inc., operates an auto plant in Normal, Illinois. In 2003, TNT Logistics Corp. coordinated deliveries of auto parts to the plant, and DeKeyser Express, Inc., transported the parts. On January 21, TNT told DeKeyser to transport three pallets of parts from Trelleborg YSH, Inc., to the plant. DeKeyser dispatched its driver, Lola Camp. At Trelleborg's loading dock, Camp noticed that the pallets would fit inside the trailer only if they were stacked. Camp was concerned that the load might shift during transport. DeKeyser dispatcher Ken Kasprzak and TNT supervisor Alan Marten told her that she would not be liable for any damage. Trelleborg loaded the pallets, and Camp drove to TNT's dock in Normal. When she opened the trailer door, the top pallet slipped. As Camp tried to close the door to prevent the pallet from falling, she injured her shoulder and arm. She filed a suit against TNT and Trelleborg, claiming negligence. What is their defense? Discuss. [*Camp v. TNT Logistics Corp.,* 553 F.3d 502 (7th Cir. 2009)]

12–6. CASE PROBLEM WITH SAMPLE ANSWER: Negligence and Multiparty Liability.

Alice Banks was injured when a chair she was sitting on at an Elks club collapsed. As a result of her injury, Dr. Robert Boyce performed the surgery on her back, fusing certain vertebrae. However, Boyce fused the wrong vertebrae and then had to perform a second surgery to correct the error. Then, during rehabilitation at a nursing home, Banks developed a serious staph infection that required additional surgeries and extensive care and treatment. She sued the Elks club and Boyce for negligence. The Elks club and Boyce filed motions against each other and also sued the nursing home. After complicated holdings by lower courts, the Tennessee Supreme Court reviewed the matter. Did the Elks club have primary liability for all of the injuries suffered by Banks after the initial accident, or did each defendant alone contribute to Banks's injuries? Explain. [Banks v. Elks Club Pride of Tennessee, *301 S.W.3d 214 (Sup. Ct.Tenn. 2010)]*

- **To view a sample answer for Problem 12–6, go to this book's Web site at www.cengage.com/blaw/cross, select "Chapter 12," and click on "Case Problem with Sample Answer."**

12–7. Libel and Invasion of Privacy The *Northwest Herald,* a newspaper in Illinois, regularly received e-mail reports from area police departments about criminal arrests. The paper published the information, which is proper because the reports are public records. One day, the *Herald* received an e-mail stating that Carolene Eubanks had been charged with theft and obstruction of justice. The paper put that information into an issue that was to be published four days later. Several hours after the original e-mail had been received, the police issued another e-mail, explaining that Eubanks had not been charged with anything; the correct name was Barbara Bradshaw. Due to a long weekend, no one at the *Herald* noticed the e-mail until after the paper had been published. The following day, five days after the e-mails had been received, the paper published a correction. Eubanks sued the *Herald* for libel and for invasion of privacy. Does Eubanks have a good case for either tort? Why or why not? [*Eubanks v. Northwest Herald Newspapers,* 922 N.E.2d 1196 (App.Ct.Ill. 2010)]

12–8. A QUESTION OF ETHICS: Dram Shop Acts.

 Donald and Gloria Bowden hosted a late after-noon cookout at their home in South Carolina, inviting mostly business acquaintances. Justin Parks, who was nineteen years old, attended the party. Alcoholic beverages were available to all of the guests, even those who, like Parks, were not minors but were under-age. Parks consumed alcohol at the party and left with other guests. One of these guests detained Parks at the guest's home to give Parks time to "sober up." Parks then drove himself from this guest's home and was killed in a one-car accident. At the time of death, he had a blood alcohol content of 0.291 percent, which exceeded the state's limit for driving a motor vehicle. Linda Marcum, Parks's mother, filed a suit in a South Carolina state court against the Bowdens and others, alleging that they were negligent. [Marcum v. Bowden, *372 S.C. 452, 643 S.E.2d 85 (2007)]*

(a) Considering the principles discussed in this chapter, what are arguments in favor of, and against, hold-ing social hosts liable in this situation? Explain.

(b) The states vary widely in assessing liability and imposing sanctions in the circumstances described

in this problem. In other words, justice is not equal for parents and other social hosts who serve alcoholic beverages to underage individuals. Why is that?

12–9. VIDEO QUESTION: Negligence.

 Go to this text's Web site at **www.cengage.com/ blaw/cross** and select "Chapter 12." Click on "Video Questions" and view the video titled *Jaws.* Then answer the following questions.

(a) In the video, the mayor (Murray Hamilton) and a few other men try to persuade Chief Brody (Roy Scheider) not to close the town's beaches. If Brody keeps the beaches open and a swimmer is injured or killed because he failed to warn swimmers about the potential shark danger, has Brody committed the tort of negligence? Explain.

(b) Can Chief Brody be held liable for any injuries or deaths to swimmers under the doctrine of strict liability? Why or why not?

(c) Suppose that Chief Brody goes against the mayor's instructions and warns townspeople to stay off the beach. Nevertheless, several swimmers do not heed his warning and are injured as a result. What defense or defenses could Brody raise under these circumstances if he is sued for negligence?

12–10. SPECIAL CASE ANALYSIS: Assumption of Risk.

Go to Extended Case 12.3, *Pfenning v. Lineman,* 922 N.E.2d 45 (2010), on pages 285 and 286. Read the excerpt and answer the following questions.

(a) **Issue:** The focus in this case was the application of the doctrine of assumption of risk to whom and in what circumstances?

(b) **Rule of Law:** What are the requirements for an injured person to be held liable for his or her injury under the doctrine of assumption of risk?

(c) **Applying the Rule of Law:** How did the court evaluate the facts in this case to assess liability under the doctrine of assumption of risk?

(d) **Conclusion:** Among the parties involved in this case, who was held liable for the plaintiff's injury and why?

LEGAL RESEARCH EXERCISES ON THE WEB

Go to this text's Web site at **www.cengage.com/blaw/cross**, select "Chapter 12," and click on "Practical Internet Exercises." There you will find the following Internet research exercises that you can perform to learn more about the topics covered in this chapter.

Practical Internet Exercise 12–1: **Legal Perspective**
Online Defamation

Practical Internet Exercise 12–2: **Management Perspective**
Legal and Illegal Uses of Spam

CHAPTER 13

✳

Strict Liability
and Product Liability

The intentional torts and negligence discussed in Chapter 12 involve acts that depart from a reasonable standard of care and cause injuries. In this chapter, we look at another category of tort—**strict liability**, or *liability without fault.* Under the doctrine of strict liability, a person who engages in certain activities can be held responsible for any harm that results to others, even if the person used the utmost care.

We open this chapter with an examination of this doctrine and then look at an area of tort law of particular importance to businesspersons—product liability. **Product liability** refers to the liability incurred by manufacturers and sellers of products when product defects cause injury or property damage to consumers, users, or **bystanders** (people in the vicinity of the product when it fails).

<hr>

SECTION 1
STRICT LIABILITY

The modern concept of strict liability traces its origins, in part, to the 1868 English case of *Rylands v. Fletcher.*[1] In the coal-mining area of Lancashire, England, the Rylands, who were mill owners, had constructed a reservoir on their land. Water from the reservoir broke through a filled-in shaft of an abandoned coal mine nearby and flooded the connecting passageways in an active coal mine owned by Fletcher. Fletcher sued the Rylands, and the court held that the defendants (the Rylands) were liable, even though the circumstances did not fit within existing tort liability theories. The court held that a "person who for his own purposes brings on his land and collects and keeps there anything likely to do mischief if it escapes . . . is *prima facie*[2] answerable for all the damage which is the natural consequence of its escape."

British courts liberally applied the doctrine that emerged from the *Rylands* case. Initially, few U.S. courts accepted this doctrine, presumably because the courts were worried about its effect on the expansion of American business. Today, however, the doctrine of strict liability is the norm rather than the exception.

Abnormally Dangerous Activities

Strict liability for damages proximately caused by an abnormally dangerous, or ultrahazardous, activity is one application of strict liability. Courts apply the doctrine of strict liability in these situations because of the extreme risk of the activity. Abnormally dangerous activities are those that involve a high risk of serious harm to persons or property that cannot be completely guarded against by the exercise of reasonable care—activities such as blasting or storing explosives. Even if blasting with dynamite is performed with all reasonable care, there is still a risk of injury. When that risk is balanced against the potential for harm, it seems reasonable to ask the person engaged in the activity to pay for injuries caused by that activity. Although no fault exists, there is still

---

1. 3 L.R.–E & I App. [Law Reports, English & Irish Appeal Cases] (H.L. [House of Lords] 1868).
2. *Prima facie* is Latin for "at first sight." Legally, it refers to a fact that is presumed to be true unless contradicted by evidence.

responsibility because of the dangerous nature of the undertaking.

Other Applications of Strict Liability

Persons who keep wild animals are strictly liable for any harm inflicted by the animals. The basis for applying strict liability is that wild animals, should they escape from confinement, pose a serious risk of harm to people in the vicinity. An owner of domestic animals (such as dogs, cats, cows, or sheep) may be strictly liable for harm caused by those animals if the owner knew, or should have known, that the animals were dangerous or had a propensity to harm others.

A significant application of strict liability is in the area of product liability—liability of manufacturers and sellers for harmful or defective products. Liability here is a matter of social policy and is based on two factors: (1) the manufacturing company can better bear the cost of injury because it can spread the cost throughout society by increasing prices of goods, and (2) the manufacturing company is making a profit from its activities and therefore should bear the cost of injury as an operating expense. We discuss product liability throughout the remainder of this chapter.

SECTION 2
PRODUCT LIABILITY

Those who make, sell, or lease goods can be held liable for physical harm or property damage caused by those goods to a consumer, user, or bystander. This is called *product liability*. Product liability may be based on warranty theories, as well as on the theories of negligence, misrepresentation, and strict liability. Note that multiple theories of liability can be, and often are, asserted in the same case. We look here at product liability based on negligence and on misrepresentation.

Product Liability Based on Negligence

In Chapter 12, *negligence* was defined as the failure to exercise the degree of care that a reasonable, prudent person would have exercised under the circumstances. If a manufacturer fails to exercise "due care" to make a product safe, a person who is injured by the product may sue the manufacturer for negligence.

DUE CARE MUST BE EXERCISED Due care must be exercised in designing the product, selecting the

materials, using the appropriate production process, assembling and testing the product, and placing adequate warnings on the label informing the user of dangers of which an ordinary person might not be aware. The duty of care also extends to the inspection and testing of any purchased components that are used in the product sold by the manufacturer.

PRIVITY OF CONTRACT IS NOT REQUIRED A product liability action based on negligence does not require the injured plaintiff and the negligent defendant-manufacturer to be in *privity of contract* (see Chapter 9 on page 208). In other words, the plaintiff and the defendant need not be directly involved in a contractual relationship with one another. Thus, any person who is injured by a product may bring a negligence suit even though he or she was not the one who actually purchased the product. A manufacturer, seller, or lessor is liable for failure to exercise due care to *any person* who sustains an injury proximately caused by a negligently made (defective) product. Relative to the long history of the common law, this exception to the privity requirement is a fairly recent development—it dates to the early part of the twentieth century.[3]

Product Liability Based on Misrepresentation

When a user or consumer is injured as a result of a manufacturer's or seller's fraudulent misrepresentation, the basis of liability may be the tort of fraud. In this situation, the misrepresentation must have been made knowingly or with reckless disregard for the facts. The intentional mislabeling of packaged cosmetics, for instance, or the intentional concealment of a product's defects constitutes fraudulent misrepresentation. The misrepresentation must be of a material fact, and the seller must have intended to induce the buyer's reliance on the misrepresentation. Misrepresentation on a label or advertisement is enough to show an intent to induce the reliance of anyone who may use the product. In addition, the buyer must have relied on the misrepresentation.

SECTION 3
STRICT PRODUCT LIABILITY

As discussed, under the doctrine of *strict liability*, people may be liable for the results of their acts regardless of their intentions or their exercise of reasonable

---

3. A landmark case in this respect is *MacPherson v. Buick Motor Co.,* 217 N.Y. 382, 111 N.E. 1050 (1916).

care. In addition, liability does not depend on privity of contract. The injured party does not have to be the buyer or a third party beneficiary (see Chapter 9), as required under sales law warranties. In the 1960s, courts applied the doctrine of strict liability in several landmark cases involving manufactured goods, and it has since become a common method of holding manufacturers liable.

Strict Product Liability and Public Policy

The law imposes strict product liability as a matter of public policy. This public policy rests on the threefold assumption that (1) consumers should be protected against unsafe products; (2) manufacturers and distributors should not escape liability for faulty products simply because they are not in privity of contract with the ultimate user of those products; and (3) manufacturers, sellers, and lessors of products are in a better position to bear the costs associated with injuries caused by their products—costs that they can ultimately pass on to all consumers in the form of higher prices.

California was the first state to impose strict product liability in tort on manufacturers. In a landmark decision, *Greenman v. Yuba Power Products, Inc.,*[4] the California Supreme Court set out the reason for applying tort law rather than contract law (including laws governing warranties) in cases involving consumers who were injured by defective products. According to the *Greenman* court, the "purpose of such liability is to [e]nsure that the costs of injuries resulting from defective products are borne by the manufacturers . . . rather than by the injured persons who are powerless to protect themselves." Today, the majority of states recognize strict product liability, although some state courts limit its application to situations involving personal injuries (rather than property damage).

The Requirements for Strict Product Liability

The courts often look to the *Restatements of the Law* for guidance, even though the *Restatements* are not binding authorities. Section 402A of the *Restatement (Second) of Torts,* which was originally issued in 1964, has become a widely accepted statement of how the doctrine of strict liability should be applied to sellers of goods (including manufacturers, processors, assemblers, packagers, bottlers, wholesalers, distributors, retailers, and lessors).

The bases for an action in strict liability that are set forth in Section 402A of the *Restatement (Second) of Torts* can be summarized as a series of six requirements. Depending on the jurisdiction, if the following six requirements are met, a manufacturer's liability to an injured party can be almost unlimited:

1. The product must be in a *defective condition* when the defendant sells it.
2. The defendant normally must be engaged in the *business of selling* (or otherwise distributing) that product.
3. The product must be *unreasonably dangerous* to the user or consumer because of its defective condition (in most states).
4. The plaintiff must incur *physical harm* to self or property by use or consumption of the product.
5. The defective condition must be the *proximate cause* of the injury or damage.
6. The *goods must not have been substantially changed* from the time the product was sold to the time the injury was sustained.

PROVING A DEFECTIVE CONDITION Under these requirements, in any action against a manufacturer, seller, or lessor, the plaintiff need not show why or in what manner the product became defective. The plaintiff does, however, have to prove that the product was defective at the time it left the hands of the seller or lessor and that this defective condition made it "unreasonably dangerous" to the user or consumer. Unless evidence can be presented to support the conclusion that the product was defective when it was sold or leased, the plaintiff will not succeed. If the product was delivered in a safe condition and subsequent mishandling made it harmful to the user, the seller or lessor normally is not strictly liable.

IDENTIFYING UNREASONABLY DANGEROUS PRODUCTS The *Restatement* recognizes that many products cannot be made entirely safe for all uses; thus, sellers or lessors are liable only for products that are *unreasonably* dangerous. A court could consider a product so defective as to be an **unreasonably dangerous product** in either of the following situations:

1. The product was dangerous beyond the expectation of the ordinary consumer.
2. A less dangerous alternative was *economically* feasible for the manufacturer, but the manufacturer failed to produce it.

---

4. 59 Cal.2d 57, 377 P.2d 897, 27 Cal.Rptr. 697 (1962).

As will be discussed next, a product may be unreasonably dangerous due to a flaw in the manufacturing process, a faulty design, or an inadequate warning.

Product Defects

Because Section 402A of the *Restatement (Second) of Torts* did not clearly define such terms as *defective* and *unreasonably dangerous,* these terms have been subject to different interpretations by different courts. In 1997, to address these concerns, the American Law Institute issued the *Restatement (Third) of Torts: Products Liability.* This *Restatement* defines the three types of product defects that have traditionally been recognized in product liability law—manufacturing defects, design defects, and inadequate warnings.

MANUFACTURING DEFECTS According to Section 2(a) of the *Restatement (Third) of Torts,* a product "contains a manufacturing defect when the product departs from its intended design even though all possible care was exercised in the preparation and marketing of the product." Basically, a manufacturing defect is a departure from a product's design specifications that results in products that are physically flawed, damaged, or incorrectly assembled. A glass bottle that is made too thin and explodes in a consumer's face is an example of a product with a manufacturing defect.

Usually, such defects occur when a manufacturer fails to assemble, test, or adequately check the quality of a product. Liability is imposed on the manufacturer (and on the wholesaler and retailer) regardless of whether the manufacturer's quality control efforts were "reasonable." The idea behind holding defendants strictly liable for manufacturing defects is to encourage greater investment in product safety and stringent quality control standards. Cases involving allegations of a manufacturing defect are often decided based on the opinions and testimony of experts.

CASE IN POINT While Kevin Schmude was standing on an eight-foot ladder that he had purchased, it collapsed and he was seriously injured. He filed a lawsuit against the ladder's maker, Tricam Industries, Inc., based on a manufacturing defect. Experts testified that the preexisting holes in the ladder's top cap did not properly line up with the holes in the rear right rail and backing plate. As a result of the misalignment, the rivet at the rear legs of the ladder was more likely to fail. A jury concluded that this manufacturing defect made the ladder unreasonably dangerous and awarded Schmude more than $677,000 in damages.[5]

DESIGN DEFECTS Unlike a product with a manufacturing defect, a product with a design defect is made in conformity with the manufacturer's design specifications but nevertheless results in injury to the user because the design itself was faulty. A product "is defective in design when the foreseeable risks of harm posed by the product could have been reduced or avoided by the adoption of a reasonable alternative design by the seller or other distributor, or a predecessor in the commercial chain of distribution, and the omission of the alternative design renders the product not reasonably safe."[6]

For example, after a massive recall of Toyota vehicles in 2009 due to problems with purportedly unintended acceleration, owners of recalled cars filed numerous product liability lawsuits against Toyota. Some of these lawsuits claimed that the Japanese automaker negligently manufactured the cars or made fraudulent misrepresentations concerning the electronic throttle control system used in the cars. In 2010, Toyota admitted that there was in fact a design defect that caused some Prius models to have brake problems.

Test for Design Defects. To successfully assert a design defect, a plaintiff has to show that a reasonable alternative design was available and that the defendant's failure to adopt the alternative design rendered the product not reasonably safe. In other words, a manufacturer or other defendant is liable only when the harm was reasonably preventable.

Factors to Be Considered. According to the *Restatement,* a court can consider a broad range of factors, including the magnitude and probability of the foreseeable risks as well as the relative advantages and disadvantages of the product as it was designed and as it could have been designed. Basically, most courts engage in a risk-utility analysis, determining whether the risk of harm from the product as designed outweighs its utility to the user and to the public.

In the following case, a smoker who developed lung cancer sued a cigarette manufacturer, claiming that there was a defect in the design of its cigarettes. The jury instruction given by the trial court and quoted by the appellate court shows the numerous factors that judges and juries consider in determining design defects.

---

5. *Schmude v. Tricam Industries, Inc.,* 550 F.Supp.2d 846 (E.D.Wis. 2008).
6. *Restatement (Third) of Torts: Products Liability,* Section 2(b).

CASE 13.1

Bullock v. Philip Morris USA, Inc.

Court of Appeal of California, Second District, Division 3, 159 Cal.App.4th 655, 71 Cal.Rptr.3d 775 (2008).
www.courtinfo.ca.gov/courts/courtsofappeal[a]

COMPANY PROFILE • Philip Morris started as a tobacco products shop in London in 1847. Philip Morris & Co., Ltd., was incorporated in New York in 1902. It introduced the famous Marlboro cigarette in 1924. From 1954 on, it established itself on a worldwide basis. It is the largest seller of cigarettes in the United States and, along with other cigarette makers, has been the object of numerous lawsuits.

BACKGROUND AND FACTS • Jodie Bullock smoked cigarettes manufactured by Philip Morris for forty-five years from 1956, when she was seventeen years old, until she was diagnosed with lung cancer in 2001. By the late 1950s, scientists in the United States had proved that cigarette smoking caused lung cancer. Nonetheless, Philip Morris issued full-page announcements stating there was no proof that cigarette smoking caused cancer and that "numerous scientists" questioned "the validity of the statistics themselves." Philip Morris's chief executive officer, Joseph Cullman III, stated on the television news program *Face the Nation* (CBS, January 3, 1971), "We do not believe that cigarettes are hazardous; we don't accept that." Jodie Bullock sued Philip Morris in April 2001, seeking to recover damages for personal injuries based on product liability, among other claims. At trial, the jury found that there was a defect in the design of the cigarettes and that they were negligently designed. It awarded Bullock $850,000 in compensatory damages, including $100,000 in noneconomic damages for pain and suffering, and later awarded her $28 billion in punitive damages. Philip Morris appealed.

IN THE LANGUAGE OF THE COURT
CROSKEY, J. [Judge]

* * * *

Philip Morris heavily advertised its cigarettes on television in the 1950's and 1960's, until the federal government banned cigarette advertising on television in 1970. Television advertising had a particularly strong influence on youths under the age of 18, for whom there was a positive correlation between television viewing time and the incidence of smoking. Philip Morris's print advertisements for Marlboro and other cigarette brands in 1956, when Bullock began smoking at the age of 17, and generally in the years from 1954 to 1969, depicted handsome men and glamorous young women. Some advertisements featured slogans such as "Loved for Gentleness" and "'The gentlest cigarette you can smoke.'"

* * * *

Philip Morris contends (1) the evidence failed to establish a design defect under the risk-benefit test because there is no substantial evidence that a safer alternative cigarette design was available, that the failure to use a safer design was a cause of Bullock's lung cancer, or that Bullock would have smoked a safer cigarette if it were available; (2) the evidence failed to establish a design defect under the consumer expectations test or liability based on a failure to warn because there is no substantial evidence that the ordinary consumer was unaware of the dangers of cigarette smoking.

* * * *

A product is defective in design for purposes of tort liability if the benefits of the design do not outweigh the risk of danger inherent in the design, or if the product, used in an intended or reasonably foreseeable manner, has failed to perform as safely as an ordinary consumer would expect. [Emphasis added.]

Philip Morris challenges the finding of liability for design defect based on a risk-benefit theory by challenging the sufficiency of the evidence that a safer alternative design existed and the sufficiency of the evidence that its failure to use a safer alternative design caused Bullock's injuries. Philip Morris's argument is based on the premise that a plaintiff alleging a design defect based on a risk-benefit theory must prove that the defendant could have used a safer alternative design. The jury, however, was not so instructed. The court instructed the jury to

---
a. To access this court opinion, click on "Opinions 2nd District" and then click on recent "Published Opinions." Go to "January 30, 2008," and click on the name of the case.

CASE 13.1 CONTINUED ➡ determine whether the benefits of the design outweighed the risks by considering several factors, but did not instruct that any single factor was essential:

"In determining whether the benefits of the design outweigh its risks, you should consider, among other things, the gravity of the danger posed by the design, the likelihood that the danger would cause damage, the existence or nonexistence of warnings, the time of the manufacture, the financial cost of an improved design, and the adverse consequences to the product and the consumer that would result from an alternate design."

* * * We review the sufficiency of the evidence to support a verdict under the law stated in the instructions given, rather than under some other law on which the jury was not instructed.

* * * Accordingly, we conclude that Philip Morris has shown no error with respect to the finding of liability for a design defect based on the risk-benefit test.

• **DECISION AND REMEDY** • *The Court of Appeal of California for the Second District affirmed the trial court's judgment as to the finding of liability. Philip Morris failed to show any error with respect to its liability for product liability based on a design defect.*

• **WHAT IF THE FACTS WERE DIFFERENT?** • *Assume that Philip Morris had never publicly denied the scientific link between smoking and lung cancer. In other words, the company simply sold cigarettes without saying anything about the medical consequences of smoking. Do you think the jury award would have been the same? If yes, how?*

• **THE ETHICAL DIMENSION** • *Under what circumstances, if any, could Philip Morris have justified its continuing campaign to discredit the scientific arguments that linked smoking with lung cancer?*

INADEQUATE WARNINGS A product may also be deemed defective because of inadequate instructions or warnings. A product will be considered defective "when the foreseeable risks of harm posed by the product could have been reduced or avoided by the provision of reasonable instructions or warnings by the seller or other distributor, or a predecessor in the commercial chain of distribution, and the omission of the instructions or warnings renders the product not reasonably safe."[7]

Important factors for a court to consider include the risks of a product, the "content and comprehensibility" and "intensity of expression" of warnings and instructions, and the "characteristics of expected user groups."[8] Courts apply a "reasonableness" test to determine if the warnings adequately alert consumers to the product's risks. For example, children will likely respond readily to bright, bold, simple warning labels, whereas educated adults might need more detailed information.

An action alleging that a product is defective due to an inadequate label can be based on state law. (For a discussion of a case involving a state law that required warning labels on violent video games, see this chapter's *Insight into Ethics* feature on page 301.) Can a state-law claim still be asserted if a federal agency approved the label? That was the question in the following case.

---

7. *Restatement (Third) of Torts: Products Liability,* Section 2(c).

8. *Restatement (Third) of Torts: Products Liability,* Section 2, Comment h.

CASE 13.2
Wyeth v. Levine

Supreme Court of the United States, __ U.S. __, 129 S.Ct. 1187, 173 L.Ed.2d 51 (2009).
www.findlaw.com/casecode/supreme.html[a]

BACKGROUND AND FACTS • Diane Levine, a professional guitar player and pianist, visited Plainfield Health Center in Vermont for treatment of a migraine headache. A physician's assistant gave her Phenergan (an antihistamine used to treat nausea) with a syringe—the intravenous-push (IV-push) method. The drug's label, which the U.S. Food and Drug Administration (FDA) had approved, did not warn

---

a. In the "Browse Supreme Court Opinions" section, click on "2009." On that page, scroll to the name of the case and click on it to access the opinion. FindLaw maintains this Web site.

CASE CONTINUES ➡

CASE 13.2 CONTINUED ➡ that this method was more risky than the IV-drip method. Phenergan entered Levine's artery and, because the drug is corrosive, led to gangrene and the amputation of her forearm. She filed a suit in a Vermont state court against Wyeth, the drug's manufacturer, alleging that the label's warning was inadequate. Levine was awarded damages of $7.4 million. The Vermont Supreme Court affirmed the result. Wyeth appealed.

IN THE LANGUAGE OF THE COURT
Justice *STEVENS* delivered the opinion of the Court.
* * * *

Wyeth first argues that Levine's state-law claims are pre-empted because it is impossible for it to comply with both the state-law duties underlying those claims and its federal labeling duties. * * * Generally speaking, a manufacturer may only change a drug label after the FDA approves a supplemental application. There is, however, an FDA regulation that permits a manufacturer to make certain changes to its label before receiving the agency's approval. Among other things, this * * * regulation provides that if a manufacturer is changing a label to "add or strengthen a contraindication, warning, precaution, or adverse reaction" * * * , it may make the labeling change upon filing its supplemental application with the FDA; it need not wait for FDA approval.
* * * *

* * * *The* * * *regulation permitted Wyeth to unilaterally strengthen its warning, and the mere fact that the FDA approved Phenergan's label does not establish that it would have prohibited such a change.* [Emphasis added.]
* * * *

Wyeth also argues that requiring it to comply with a state-law duty to provide a stronger warning about IV-push administration would obstruct the purposes and objectives of federal drug labeling regulation.

* * * The most glaring problem with this argument is that all evidence of Congress' purposes is to the contrary. Building on its 1906 Act, Congress enacted the [Food, Drug and Cosmetic Act (FDCA) in 1938—see Chapter 24] to bolster consumer protection against harmful products. Congress did not provide a federal remedy for consumers harmed by unsafe or ineffective drugs in the 1938 statute or in any subsequent amendment. Evidently, it determined that widely available state rights of action provided appropriate relief for injured consumers. It may also have recognized that state-law remedies further consumer protection by motivating manufacturers to produce safe and effective drugs and to give adequate warnings.

If Congress thought state-law suits posed an obstacle to its objectives, it surely would have enacted an express pre-emption provision at some point during the FDCA's 70-year history. * * * Its silence on the issue, coupled with its certain awareness of the prevalence of state tort litigation, is powerful evidence that Congress did not intend FDA oversight to be the exclusive means of ensuring drug safety and effectiveness.

DECISION AND REMEDY • *The United States Supreme Court affirmed the lower court's decision. The FDA's approval of Phenergan's label did not preempt Levine's claim against the drug's manufacturer.*

WHAT IF THE FACTS WERE DIFFERENT? • *Suppose that the Phenergan label had contained a stronger warning against the IV-push method without explicitly stating that the method should not be used. Would the result in Levine's case have been the same? Discuss.*

THE LEGAL ENVIRONMENT DIMENSION • *In a 2006 preamble to a regulation, for the first time the FDA expressed the opinion that state-law actions "threaten [the] FDA's statutorily prescribed role as the expert Federal agency responsible for evaluating and regulating drugs." What might have motivated this dramatic change in the agency's traditional position?*

Obvious Risks. There is no duty to warn about risks that are obvious or commonly known. Warnings about such risks do not add to the safety of a product and could even detract from it by making other warnings seem less significant. As will be discussed later in the chapter, the obviousness of a risk and a user's decision

to proceed in the face of that risk may be a defense in a product liability suit based on an inadequate warning.

CASE IN POINT Sixteen-year-old Gary Crosswhite attempted to do a back flip on a trampoline in his backyard and accidentally landed on his head and

INSIGHT INTO ETHICS
Warning Labels for Video Games

The video game industry uses a voluntary rating system that includes six age-specific labels. Should video game makers also be required to attach labels to their games that warn parents of excessive violence? When California legislated this requirement, video software dealers sued.

The act defined a violent video game as one in which "the range of options available to a player includes killing, maiming, dismembering, or sexually assaulting an image of a human being." While agreeing that some video games are unquestionably violent by everyday standards, the trial court pointed out, as did the federal court that heard the appeal, that many video games are based on popular novels or motion pictures and have complex plot lines. Accordingly, the court found that the definition of a violent video game was unconstitutionally vague and thus violated the First Amendment's guarantee of freedom of speech. The court also noted the existence of the voluntary rating system.

The state appealed, but the U.S. Court of Appeals for the Ninth Circuit also found that the statute's definition of a violent video game was unconstitutionally broad.[a] The appeals court noted that other federal circuit courts had already ruled against extending restrictions on sex-based content to restrictions on violence in video games.[b]

CRITICAL THINKING

INSIGHT INTO THE SOCIAL ENVIRONMENT
Why would some legislators believe that the six-part voluntary labeling system for video games is not sufficient to protect minors?

---

a. *Video Software Dealers Association v. Schwarzenegger*, 556 F.3d 950 (9th Cir. 2009).
b. See, for example, *Interactive Digital Software Association v. St. Louis County*, 329 F.3d 954 (8th Cir. 2003).

---

neck. The fall fractured his spine and resulted in paraplegia. Crosswhite filed a strict product liability lawsuit against the manufacturer, in which he claimed that the trampoline was defective because of inadequate warnings and instructions. The court found that there were nine warning labels affixed to the trampoline, an instruction manual with safety warnings, and a placard attached to the entrance that advised users not to do flips. These warnings were sufficient to make the risks obvious and insulate the manufacturer from liability for Crosswhite's injuries.[9]

Note that risks that may seem obvious to some users will not be obvious to all users, especially when the users are likely to be children. A young child may not be able to read or understand warning labels or comprehend the risk of certain activities. Therefore, if a child is permanently injured by diving into a shallow, aboveground pool, the manufacturer cannot escape liability simply by having a warning label on the box in which the pool was shipped. To avoid liability, the manufacturer would have to prove that the warnings it provided were adequate to make the risk of injury obvious to a young child using the pool.[10]

Foreseeable Misuses. Generally, a seller must warn those who purchase its product of the harm

that can result from the foreseeable misuse of the product as well. The key is the foreseeability of the misuse. Sellers are not required to take precautions against every conceivable misuse of a product, just those that are foreseeable.

Market-Share Liability

Ordinarily, in all product liability claims, a plaintiff must prove that the defective product that caused his or her injury was the product of a specific defendant. In a few situations, however, courts have dropped this requirement when plaintiffs could not prove which of many distributors of a harmful product supplied the particular product that caused the injuries.

CASE IN POINT John Smith, a resident of Hawaii, was a hemophiliac. Because of his condition, Smith received injections of a blood protein known as antihemophiliac factor (AHF) concentrate. Smith later tested positive for the acquired immune deficiency syndrome (AIDS) virus. Because it was not known which manufacturer was responsible for the particular AHF received by Smith, the court held that all of the manufacturers of AHF could be held liable under the theory of **market-share liability.**[11]

---

9. *Crosswhite v. Jumpking, Inc.*, 411 F.Supp.2d 1228 (D.Or. 2006).
10. See, for example, *Bunch v. Hoffinger Industries, Inc.*, 123 Cal. App.4th 1278, 20 Cal.Rptr.3d 780 (2004).

11. *Smith v. Cutter Biological, Inc.*, 72 Haw. 416, 823 P.2d 717 (1991). See also *Sutowski v. Eli Lilly & Co.*, 82 Ohio St.3d 347, 696 N.E.2d 187 (1998); and *In re Methyl Tertiary Butyl Ether ("MTBE") Products Liability Litigation*, 447 F.Supp.2d 289 (S.D.N.Y. 2006).

Courts in many jurisdictions do not recognize this theory of liability because they believe that it deviates too significantly from traditional legal principles.[12] In jurisdictions that do recognize market-share liability, it is usually applied in cases involving drugs or chemicals, when it is difficult or impossible to determine which company made a particular product.

Other Applications of Strict Product Liability

Almost all courts extend the strict liability of manufacturers and other sellers to injured bystanders. Thus, if a defective forklift that will not go into reverse injures a passerby, that individual can sue the manufacturer for product liability (and possibly bring a negligence action against the forklift operator as well).

Strict product liability also applies to suppliers of component parts. For example, suppose that General Motors buys brake pads from a subcontractor and puts them in Chevrolets without changing their composition. If those pads are defective, both the supplier of the brake pads and General Motors will be held strictly liable for the injuries caused by the defects.

SECTION 4
DEFENSES TO PRODUCT LIABILITY

Defendants in product liability suits can raise a number of defenses. One defense, of course, is to show that there is no basis for the plaintiff's claim.

For example, in a product liability case based on negligence, if a defendant can show that the plaintiff has *not* met the requirements (such as causation) for an action in negligence, generally the defendant will not be liable. Similarly, in a case involving strict product liability, a defendant can claim that the plaintiff failed to meet one of the requirements. For example, if the defendant establishes that the goods were altered after they were sold, normally the defendant will not be held liable.[13] Defendants may also assert the defenses discussed next.

Assumption of Risk

Assumption of risk can sometimes be used as a defense in a product liability action. To establish such a defense, the defendant must show that (1) the plaintiff knew and appreciated the risk created by the product defect, and (2) the plaintiff voluntarily assumed the risk, even though it was unreasonable to do so. For example, if a buyer failed to heed a seller's product recall, the buyer may be deemed to have assumed the risk of the product defect that the seller offered to cure. (See pages 284–286 for a more detailed discussion of assumption of risk.)

In the following case, an injured user of a tanning booth had signed an exculpatory clause stating that she was using the booth at her own risk and that she released the manufacturer, among others, from any liability for any injuries. The issue before the court was whether an exculpatory clause can relieve a manufacturer from strict product liability.

---

12. For the Illinois Supreme Court's position on market-share liability, see *Smith v. Eli Lilly & Co.*, 137 Ill.2d 222, 560 N.E.2d 324 (1990). Pennsylvania law also does not recognize market-share liability. See *Bortell v. Eli Lilly & Co.*, 406 F.Supp.2d 1 (D.D.C. 2005).

13. See, for example, *Edmondson v. Macclesfield L-P Gas Co.*, 642 S.E.2d 265 (N.C.App. 2007); and *Pichardo v. C. S. Brown Co.*, 35 A.D.3d 303, 827 N.Y.S.2d 131 (N.Y.App. 2006).

✳ EXTENDED CASE 13.3 ✳
Boles v. Sun Ergoline, Inc.
Supreme Court of Colorado, 223 P.3d 724 (2010).
www.cobar.org/ors.cfm[a]

IN THE LANGUAGE OF THE COURT
Justice *COATS* delivered the opinion of the court.
* * * *
Savannah Boles brought suit against

Sun Ergoline, Inc., asserting a strict products liability claim for personal injury. Sun Ergoline moved for summary judgment, countering that Boles's claim was barred by a release she signed prior to using its product. The trial court agreed and granted Sun Ergoline's motion on the basis

of the following undisputed facts.

Executive Tans operated an upright tanning booth manufactured by Sun Ergoline. Prior to using the booth, Boles signed a release form provided by Executive Tans that contained the following exculpatory agreement: "I have read

---

a. Under the heading "Opinions," select "Colorado Supreme Court Opinions." When that page opens, select "February 8, 2010" from the list of dates under the heading "Cases published announced on." When that page appears, scroll down the page to the case title and click on the link to view the opinion. The Colorado Bar Association maintains this Web site.

EXTENDED CASE 13.3 CONTINUED ⬇

the instructions for proper use of the tanning facilities and do so at my own risk and hereby release the owners, operators, franchiser, or manufacturers, from any damage or harm that I might incur due to use of the facilities." After entering the booth, several of Boles's fingers came in contact with an exhaust fan located at the top of the booth, partially amputating them.

On direct appeal, the court of appeals affirmed. * * * [It found] that the language of the release was broad enough to include any damage or harm that might occur due to Boles's use of the facilities [and] * * * found no violation of public policy.

We granted Boles's petition for a writ of *certiorari* [a request by the losing party asking the higher court to hear the case] challenging the court of appeals' determination that the exculpatory agreement barred her strict products liability claim.

* * * *

"Strict products liability" has been described as a "term of art that reflects the judgment that products liability is a discrete area of tort law which borrows from both negligence and warranty" but "is not fully congruent with classical tort or contract law." Rather than resting on negligence principles, it "is premised on the concept of enterprise liability for casting a defective product into the stream of commerce." *In strict products liability, the focus is on the nature of the product rather than the conduct of either the manufacturer or the person injured.* [Emphasis added.]

As such, strict products liability evolved to accommodate, and is driven by, public policy considerations surrounding the relationship between manufacturers and consumers in general, rather than any particular transaction or contract for sale. In addition to the typical inaccessibility of information and inequality of bargaining power inherent in any disclaimer or ordinary consumer's agreement to release a manufacturer, a claim for strict products liability is also premised on a number of public policy considerations that would be flatly thwarted [prevented] by legitimizing such disclaimers or exculpatory agreements. Not least among these is the deliberate provision of economic incentives for manufacturers to improve product safety and take advantage of their unique "position to spread the risk of loss among all who use the product."

* * * The *Second Restatement of Torts* clearly indicates that exculpatory agreements between a manufacturer and an end-user can have no effect. * * * The *Third Restatement* would even more emphatically prohibit "contractual exculpations" from barring or reducing otherwise valid products liability claims for personal injuries by ordinary consumers against sellers or distributors of new products.

There appears to be virtually universal agreement on this point among the other jurisdictions considering the question.

* * * An agreement releasing a manufacturer from strict products liability for personal injury, in exchange for nothing more than an individual consumer's right to have or use the product, necessarily violates the public policy of this jurisdiction and is void.

* * * *

Because the lower courts erred * * * in finding the exculpatory agreement in this case enforceable, the judgment of the court of appeals is reversed with directions to remand for further proceedings consistent with this opinion.

QUESTIONS

1. What did the court mean when it stated that strict product liability laws are "not fully congruent" with classical tort law?
2. Why would the enforcement of the exculpatory clause in this case conflict with the rationale underlying strict product liability?

Product Misuse

Similar to the defense of voluntary assumption of risk is that of **product misuse,** which occurs when a product is used for a purpose for which it was not intended. Here, in contrast to assumption of risk, the injured party *does not know that the product is dangerous for a particular use.* The courts have severely limited this defense, however. Even if the injured party does not know about the inherent danger of using the product in a wrong way, if the misuse is reasonably foreseeable the seller must take measures to guard against it.

CASE IN POINT Five-year-old Cheyenne Saleena Stark was riding in the backseat of her parents' Ford Taurus. Cheyenne was using a three-point seatbelt designed by Ford and was not sitting in a booster seat when the car was involved in a collision. As a result of the accident, she suffered a spinal cord injury and was paralyzed from the waist down. The family filed a lawsuit against Ford alleging that the "film spool" in the vehicle's seatbelt was defectively designed. Ford claimed that Cheyenne had misused the seatbelt by wearing the shoulder belt behind her back and argued that Cheyenne would not have been so seriously injured had she been wearing the seatbelt correctly. The court, however, ruled that Ford could not assert product misuse as a defense. Cheyenne was too young to be negligent, and it is reasonably foreseeable that a child would wear a seatbelt incorrectly without understanding the risks. Therefore, even if some of Cheyenne's injuries resulted from the improper use of her seatbelt, the manufacturer could not avoid liability.[14]

Comparative Negligence (Fault)

Developments in the area of comparative negligence, or fault (discussed in Chapter 12), have also affected the doctrine of strict liability. In the past, the plaintiff's conduct was never a defense to liability for a defective product. Today, courts in many jurisdictions will consider the negligent or intentional actions of both the plaintiff and the defendant when apportioning liability and damages.[15] This means that a defendant may be able to limit at least some of its liability if it can show that the plaintiff's misuse of the product contributed to his or her injuries. When proved, comparative negligence differs from other defenses in that it does not completely absolve the defendant of liability, but it can reduce the total amount of damages that will be awarded to the plaintiff. Note that some jurisdictions allow only intentional conduct to affect a plaintiff's recovery, whereas other states allow ordinary negligence to be used as a defense to product liability.

CASE IN POINT Dan Smith, a mechanic, was not wearing a hard hat at work when he was asked to start the diesel engine of an air compressor. Because the compressor was an older model, he had to prop open a door to start it. When the engine started, the door fell from its position and hit Smith's head. The injury caused him to suffer from seizures. Smith sued the manufacturer, claiming that the engine was defectively designed. The manufacturer contended that Smith had been negligent by failing to wear a hard hat and propping open the door in an unsafe manner. Although Smith argued that ordinary

negligence could not be used as a defense in product liability cases, the court ruled that defendants can use the plaintiff's ordinary negligence to reduce their liability proportionately.[16]

Commonly Known Dangers

The dangers associated with certain products (such as matches and sharp knives) are so commonly known that, as already mentioned, manufacturers need not warn users of those dangers. If a defendant succeeds in convincing the court that a plaintiff's injury resulted from a *commonly known danger,* the defendant will not be liable.

CASE IN POINT Marguerite Jamieson was injured when an elastic exercise rope slipped off her foot and struck her in the eye, causing a detachment of the retina. Jamieson claimed that the manufacturer should be liable because it had failed to warn users that the exerciser might slip off a foot in such a manner. The court stated that to hold the manufacturer liable in these circumstances "would go beyond the reasonable dictates of justice in fixing the liabilities of manufacturers." After all, stated the court, "almost every physical object can be inherently dangerous or potentially dangerous in a sense. . . . A manufacturer cannot manufacture a knife that will not cut or a hammer that will not mash a thumb or a stove that will not burn a finger. The law does not require [manufacturers] to warn of such common dangers."[17]

Knowledgeable User

A related defense is the *knowledgeable user* defense. If a particular danger (such as electrical shock) is or should be commonly known by particular users of a product (such as electricians), the manufacturer need not warn these users of the danger.

CASE IN POINT The parents of teenagers who had become overweight and developed health problems filed a product liability suit against McDonald's. The teenagers claimed that the fast-food chain had failed to warn customers of the adverse health effects of eating its food. The court rejected this claim, however, based on the knowledgeable user defense. The court found that it is well known that the food at McDonald's contains high levels of cholesterol, fat, salt, and sugar and is therefore unhealthful. The court's opinion, which thwarted future lawsuits against fast-food restaurants,

---

14. *Stark ex rel. Jacobsen v. Ford Motor Co.,* 693 S.E.2d 253 (N.C.App. 2010).
15. See, for example, *State Farm Insurance Companies v. Premier Manufactured Systems, Inc.,* 213 Ariz. 419, 142 P.3d 1232 (2006); and *Industrial Risk Insurers v. American Engineering Testing, Inc.,* 318 Wis.2d 148, 769 N.W.2d 82 (Wis.App. 2009).

16. *Smith v. Ingersoll-Rand Co.,* 14 P.3d 990 (Alaska 2000).
17. *Jamieson v. Woodward & Lothrop,* 247 F.2d 23 (D.C.Cir. 1957).

stated: "If consumers know (or reasonably should know) the potential ill health effects of eating at McDonald's, they cannot blame McDonald's if they, nonetheless, choose to satiate their appetite with a surfeit [excess] of supersized McDonald's products."[18]

Statutes of Limitations and Repose

As previously discussed, statutes of limitations restrict the time within which an action may be brought. The statute of limitations for product liability cases varies according to state law, and unlike warranty claims, product liability claims are not

---

18. *Pelman v. McDonald's Corp.*, 237 F.Supp.2d 512 (S.D.N.Y. 2003).

subject to the UCC's limitation period. Usually, the injured party must bring a product liability claim within two to four years. Often, the running of the prescribed period is *tolled* (that is, suspended) until the party suffering an injury has discovered it or should have discovered it. To ensure that sellers and manufacturers will not be left vulnerable to lawsuits indefinitely, many states have passed laws, called **statutes of repose,** that place *outer* time limits on product liability actions. For example, a statute of repose may require that claims be brought within twelve years from the date of sale or manufacture of the defective product. If the plaintiff does not bring an action before the prescribed period expires, the seller cannot be held liable.

REVIEWING
Strict Liability and Product Liability

Shalene Kolchek bought a Great Lakes spa from Val Porter, a dealer who was selling spas at the state fair. Kolchek signed an installment contract; then Porter and Kolchek arranged for the spa to be delivered and installed for her the next day. Three months later, Kolchek left her six-year-old daughter, Litisha, alone in the spa. While exploring the spa's hydromassage jets, Litisha stuck her index finger into one of the jet holes and was unable to remove her finger from the jet. Litisha yanked hard, injuring her finger, then panicked and screamed for help. Kolchek was unable to remove Litisha's finger, and the local police and rescue team were called to assist. After a three-hour operation that included draining the spa, sawing out a section of the spa's plastic molding, and slicing the jet casing, Litisha's finger was freed. Following this procedure, the spa was no longer functional. Litisha was taken to the local emergency room, where she was told that a bone in her finger was broken in two places. Using the information presented in the chapter, answer the following questions.

1. Under which theory or theories of product liability can Kolchek sue to recover for Litisha's injuries? Could Kolchek sue Porter or Great Lakes?
2. Would privity of contract be required for Kolchek to succeed in a product liability action against Great Lakes?
3. For an action in strict product liability against Great Lakes, what six requirements must Kolchek meet?
4. What defenses to product liability might Porter or Great Lakes be able to assert?

DEBATE THIS: *All liability suits against tobacco companies for lung cancer should be thrown out of court now and forever.*

TERMS AND CONCEPTS

bystander 294

market-share liability 301
product liability 294
product misuse 303

statute of repose 305
strict liability 294

unreasonably dangerous
product 296

QUESTIONS AND CASE PROBLEMS

13–1. Product Liability Chen buys a television set manufactured by Quality TV Appliance, Inc. She is going on vacation, so she takes the set to her mother's house for her mother to use. Because the set is defective, it explodes, causing her mother to be seriously injured. Chen's mother sues Quality to obtain compensation for her injury and for the damage to her house. Under what theory or theories discussed in this chapter might Chen's mother recover damages from Quality? Explain.

13–2. QUESTION WITH SAMPLE ANSWER: Product Liability.

Jason Clark, an experienced hunter, bought a paintball gun. Clark practiced with the gun and knew how to screw in the carbon dioxide cartridge, pump the gun, and use its safety and trigger. Although Clark was aware that he could purchase protective eyewear, he chose not to buy it. Clark had taken gun safety courses and understood that it was "common sense" not to shoot anyone in the face. Clark's friend, Chris Wright, also owned a paintball gun and was similarly familiar with the gun's use and its risks. Clark, Wright, and their friends played a game that involved shooting paintballs at cars whose occupants also had the guns. One night, while Clark and Wright were cruising with their guns, Wright shot at Clark's car, but hit Clark in the eye. Clark filed a product liability lawsuit against the manufacturer of Wright's paintball gun to recover for the injury. Clark claimed that the gun was defectively designed. During the trial, Wright testified that his gun "never malfunctioned." In whose favor should the court rule? Why?

• **For a sample answer to Question 13–2, go to Appendix F at the end of this text.**

13–3. Strict Liability Danny and Marion Klein were injured when part of a fireworks display went astray and exploded near them. They sued Pyrodyne Corp., the pyrotechnic company that had been hired to set up and discharge the fireworks, alleging, among other things, that the company should be strictly liable for damages caused by the fireworks display. Will the court agree with the Kleins? What factors will the court consider in making its decision? Discuss fully.

13–4. Inadequate Warnings A water pipe burst, flooding a company's switchboard and tripping the switchboard circuit breakers. Company employees assigned to reactivate the switchboard included an electrical technician with twelve years of on-the-job training, a licensed electrician, and an electrical engineer who had studied power engineering in college and had twenty years of experience. The employees attempted to switch one of the circuit breakers back on without testing for short circuits, which they later admitted they knew how to do and should have done. The circuit breaker failed to

engage but ignited an explosive fire. The company sued the supplier of the circuit breakers for damages, alleging that the supplier had failed to give adequate warnings and instructions regarding the circuit breakers. How might the supplier defend against this claim? Discuss.

13–5. Defenses to Product Liability Baxter manufactures electric hair dryers. Julie purchases a Baxter dryer from her local Ace Drugstore. Cox, a friend and guest in Julie's home, has taken a shower and wants to dry her hair. Julie tells Cox to use the new Baxter hair dryer that she has just purchased. As Cox plugs in the dryer, sparks fly out from the motor, and sparks continue to fly as she operates it. Despite this, Cox begins drying her hair. Suddenly, the entire dryer ignites into flames, severely burning Cox's scalp. Cox sues Baxter on the basis of negligence and strict liability in tort. Baxter admits that the dryer was defective but denies liability, particularly because Cox was not the person who purchased the dryer. In other words, Cox had no contractual relationship with Baxter. Discuss the validity of Baxter's defense. Are there any other defenses that Baxter might assert to avoid liability? Discuss fully.

13–6. Design Defects Mary Jane Boerner began smoking in 1945 at the age of fifteen. For a short time, she smoked Lucky Strikes (a brand of cigarettes) before switching to the Pall Mall brand, which she smoked until she quit altogether in 1981. Pall Malls had higher levels of carcinogenic tar than other cigarettes and lacked effective filters, which would have reduced the amount of tar inhaled into the lungs. In 1996, Mary Jane developed lung cancer. She and her husband, Henry Boerner, filed a suit in a federal district court against Brown & Williamson Tobacco Co., the maker of Pall Malls. The Boerners claimed, among other things, that Pall Malls contained a design defect. Mary Jane died in 1999. According to Dr. Peter Marvin, her treating physician, she died from the effects of cigarette smoke. Henry continued the suit, offering evidence that Pall Malls featured a filter that actually increased the amount of tar taken into the body. When is a product defective in design? Does this product meet the requirements? Why or why not? [*Boerner v. Brown & Williamson Tobacco Co.*, 394 F.3d 594 (8th Cir. 2005)]

13–7. CASE PROBLEM WITH SAMPLE ANSWER: Product Liability.

Bret D'Auguste was an experienced skier when he rented equipment to ski at Hunter Mountain Ski Bowl, Inc., owned by Shanty Hollow Corp., in New York. The adjustable retention/release value for the bindings on the rented equipment was set at a level that, according to skiing industry standards, was too low— meaning that the skis would be released too easily—given D'Auguste's height, weight, and ability. When D'Auguste entered a "double black diamond," or extremely difficult, trail, he noticed immediately that the surface consisted of ice

and almost no snow. He tried to exit the steeply declining trail by making a sharp right turn, but in the attempt, his left ski snapped off. D'Auguste lost his balance, fell, and slid down the mountain, striking his face and head against a fence along the trail. According to a report by a rental shop employee, one of the bindings on D'Auguste's skis had a "cracked heel housing." D'Auguste filed a suit in a New York state court against Shanty Hollow and others, including the bindings' manufacturer, on a theory of strict product liability. The manufacturer filed a motion for summary judgment. On what basis might the court grant the motion? On what basis might the court deny the motion? How should the court rule? Explain. [D'Auguste v. Shanty Hollow Corp., 26 A.D.3d 403, 809 N.Y.S.2d 555 (2 Dept. 2006)]

- **To view a sample answer for Problem 13–7, go to this book's Web site at www.cengage.com/blaw/cross, select "Chapter 13," and click on "Case Problem with Sample Answer."**

13–8. Defenses to Product Liability Terry Kunkle and VanBuren High hosted a Christmas party in Berkeley County, South Carolina. Guests had drinks and hors d'oeuvres at a residence and adjourned to dinner in a barn across a public road. Brandon Stroud ferried the guests to the barn in a golf car made by Textron, Inc. The golf car was not equipped with lights, and Textron did not warn against its use on public roads at night. South Carolina does not require golf cars to be equipped with lights, but does ban their operation on public roads at night. As Stroud attempted to cross the road at 8:30 P.M., his golf car was struck by a vehicle driven by Joseph Thornley. Stroud was killed. His estate filed a suit in a South Carolina state court against Textron, alleging strict product liability and product liability based on negligence. The estate claimed that the golf car was defective and unreasonably dangerous. What might Textron assert in its defense? Explain. [*Moore v. Barony House Restaurant, LLC*, 382 S.C. 35, 674 S.E.2d 500 (S.C.App. 2009)]

13–9. Product Liability Yun Tung Chow tried to unclog a floor drain in the kitchen of the restaurant where he worked. He used a drain cleaner called Lewis Red Devil Lye that contained crystalline sodium hydroxide. The product label said to wear eye protection, to put one tablespoon of lye directly into the drain, and to keep one's face away from the drain because there could be dangerous backsplash. Without eye protection, Chow mixed three tablespoons of lye in a can and poured that mixture down the drain while bending over it. Liquid splashed back into his face, causing injury. He brought a product liability suit based on inadequate warnings and design defect. The trial court granted summary judgment to the manufacturer, and Chow appealed. An expert for Chow stated that the product was defective because it had a tendency to back-splash. Is that a convincing argument? Why or why not? [*Yun Tung Chow v. Reckitt & Coleman, Inc.*, 69 A.D.3d 413, 891 N.Y.S.2d 402 (N.Y.A.D. 1 Dept. 2010)]

13–10. A QUESTION OF ETHICS: Dangerous Products.

 Susan Calles lived with her four daughters, Amanda, age eleven, Victoria, age five, and Jenna and Jillian, age three. In March 1998, Calles bought an Aim N Flame utility lighter, which she stored on the top shelf of her kitchen cabinet. A trigger can ignite the Aim N Flame after an "ON/OFF" switch is slid to the "on" position. On the night of March 31, Calles and Victoria left to get videos. Jenna and Jillian were in bed, and Amanda was watching television. Calles returned to find fire trucks and emergency vehicles around her home. Robert Finn, a fire investigator, determined that Jenna had started a fire using the lighter. Jillian suffered smoke inhalation, was hospitalized, and died on April 21. Calles filed a suit in an Illinois state court against Scripto-Tokai Corp., which distributed the Aim N Flame, and others. In her suit, which was grounded, in part, in strict liability claims, Calles alleged that the lighter was an "unreasonably dangerous product." Scripto filed a motion for summary judgment. [Calles v. Scripto-Tokai Corp., 224 Ill.2d 247, 864 N.E.2d 249, 309 Ill.Dec. 383 (2007)]

(a) A product is unreasonably dangerous when it is dangerous beyond the expectation of the ordinary consumer. Whose expectation—Calles's or Jenna's—applies? Does the lighter pass this test? Explain.

(b) Calles presented evidence as to the likelihood and seriousness of injury from lighters that do not have child-safety devices. Scripto argued that the Aim N Flame is an alternative source of fire and is safer than a match. Calles admitted that she knew the dangers presented by lighters in the hands of children. Scripto admitted that it had been a defendant in several suits for injuries under similar circumstances. How should the court rule? Why?

LEGAL RESEARCH EXERCISES ON THE WEB

Go to this text's Web site at **www.cengage.com/blaw/cross**, select "Chapter 13," and click on "Practical Internet Exercises." There you will find the following Internet research exercises that you can perform to learn more about the topics covered in this chapter.

Practical Internet Exercise 13–1: **Legal Perspective**
Product Liability Litigation

Practical Internet Exercise 13–2: **Management Perspective**
The Duty to Warn

CHAPTER 14

Intellectual Property and Internet Law

O f significant concern to businesspersons is the need to protect their rights in intellectual property, which in today's world may exceed the value of physical property, such as machines and buildings. **Intellectual property** is any property that results from intellectual, creative processes—that is to say, the products of an individual's mind. Although it is an abstract term for an abstract concept, intellectual property is nonetheless familiar to almost everyone. The information contained in books and computer files is intellec-

tual property. The software you use, the movies you see, and the music you listen to are all forms of intellectual property.

The need to protect creative works was recognized by the framers of the U.S. Constitution more than two hundred years ago: Article I, Section 8, of the U.S. Constitution authorized Congress "[t]o promote the Progress of Science and useful Arts, by securing for limited Times to Authors and Inventors the exclusive Right to their respective Writings and Discoveries." Laws protecting patents, trademarks,

and copyrights are explicitly designed to protect and reward inventive and artistic creativity.

In today's global economy, however, protecting intellectual property in one country is no longer sufficient. Therefore, the United States participates in international agreements to secure ownership rights in intellectual property in other nations. We discuss some of these international agreements at the end of this chapter.

SECTION 1
TRADEMARKS AND RELATED PROPERTY

A **trademark** is a distinctive mark, motto, device, or implement that a manufacturer stamps, prints, or otherwise affixes to the goods it produces so that they can be identified on the market and their origins made known. In other words, a trademark is a source indicator. At common law, the person who

used a symbol or mark to identify a business or product was protected in the use of that trademark. Clearly, by using another's trademark, a business could lead consumers to believe that its goods were made by the other business. The law seeks to avoid this kind of confusion. In this section, we examine various aspects of the law governing trademarks.

In the following classic case concerning Coca-Cola, the defendants argued that the Coca-Cola trademark was entitled to no protection under the law because the term did not accurately represent the product.

CASE 14.1
The Coca-Cola Co. v. The Koke Co. of America

Supreme Court of the United States, 254 U.S. 143, 41 S.Ct. 113, 65 L.Ed. 189 (1920).
www.findlaw.com/casecode/supreme.html[a]

COMPANY PROFILE • John Pemberton, an Atlanta pharmacist, invented a caramel-colored, carbonated soft drink in 1886. His bookkeeper, Frank Robinson, named the beverage Coca-Cola after two of the ingredients, coca leaves and kola nuts. Asa Candler bought the Coca-Cola Company (www.thecoca-colacompany.com) in 1891, and within seven years, he had made the soft drink available throughout the United States, as well as in parts of Canada and Mexico. Candler continued to sell Coke aggressively and to open up new markets, reaching Europe before 1910. In doing so, however, he attracted numerous competitors, some of which tried to capitalize directly on the Coke name.

BACKGROUND AND FACTS • The Coca-Cola Company sought to enjoin (prevent) the Koke Company of America and other beverage companies from, among other things, using the word *Koke* for their products. The Koke Company of America and other beverage companies contended that the Coca-Cola trademark was a fraudulent representation and that Coca-Cola was therefore not entitled to any help from the courts. The Koke Company and the other defendants alleged that the Coca-Cola Company, by its use of the Coca-Cola name, represented that the beverage contained cocaine (from coca leaves), which it no longer did. The trial court granted the injunction against the Koke Company, but the appellate court reversed the lower court's ruling. Coca-Cola then appealed to the United States Supreme Court.

IN THE LANGUAGE OF THE COURT
Mr. Justice *HOLMES* delivered the opinion of the Court.
* * * *

* * * Before 1900 the beginning of [Coca-Cola's] good will was more or less helped by the presence of cocaine, a drug that, like alcohol or caffeine or opium, may be described as a deadly poison or as a valuable [pharmaceutical item, depending on the speaker's purposes]. The amount seems to have been very small,[b] but it may have been enough to begin a bad habit and after the Food and Drug Act of June 30, 1906, if not earlier, long before this suit was brought, it was eliminated from the plaintiff's compound.

* * * Since 1900 the sales have increased at a very great rate corresponding to a like increase in advertising. The name now characterizes a beverage to be had at almost any soda fountain. It means a single thing coming from a single source, and well known to the community. It hardly would be too much to say that the drink characterizes the name as much as the name the drink. In other words *Coca-Cola probably means to most persons the plaintiff's familiar product to be had everywhere rather than a compound of particular substances.* * * * Before this suit was brought the plaintiff had advertised to the public that it must not expect and would not find cocaine, and had eliminated everything tending to suggest cocaine effects except the name and the picture of [coca] leaves and nuts, which probably conveyed little or nothing to most who saw it. It appears to us that it would be going too far to deny the plaintiff relief against a palpable [readily evident] fraud because possibly here and there an ignorant person might call for the drink with the hope for incipient cocaine intoxication. The plaintiff's position must be judged by the facts as they were when the suit was begun, not by the facts of a different condition and an earlier time. [Emphasis added.]

DECISION AND REMEDY • *The district court's injunction was allowed to stand. The competing beverage companies were enjoined from calling their products Koke.*

---

a. This is the "U.S. Supreme Court Opinions" page within the Web site of the "FindLaw Internet Legal Resources" database. This page provides several options for accessing an opinion. Because you know the citation for this case, you can go to the "Citation Search" box, type in the appropriate volume and page numbers for the *United States Reports* ("254" and "143," respectively, for the *Coca-Cola* case), and click on "Search."

b. In reality, until 1903 the amount of active cocaine in each bottle of Coke was equivalent to one "line" of cocaine.

CASE CONTINUES ➡

CASE 14.1 CONTINUED ▶ **IMPACT OF THIS CASE ON TODAY'S LAW** • *In this early case, the United States Supreme Court made it clear that trademarks and trade names (and nicknames for those marks and names, such as the nickname "Coke" for "Coca-Cola") that are in common use receive protection under the common law. This holding is significant historically because it is the predecessor to the federal statute later passed to protect trademark rights—the Lanham Act of 1946, to be discussed next. In many ways, this act represented a codification of common law principles governing trademarks.*

WHAT IF THE FACTS WERE DIFFERENT? • *Suppose that Coca-Cola had been trying to make the public believe that its product contained cocaine. Would the result in this case likely have been different? Why or why not?*

Statutory Protection of Trademarks

Statutory protection of trademarks and related property is provided at the federal level by the Lanham Act of 1946.[1] The Lanham Act was enacted, in part, to protect manufacturers from losing business to rival companies that used confusingly similar trademarks. The Lanham Act incorporates the common law of trademarks and provides remedies for owners of trademarks who wish to enforce their claims in federal court. Many states also have trademark statutes.

TRADEMARK DILUTION Before 1995, federal trademark law prohibited only the unauthorized use of the same mark on competing—or on noncompeting but "related"—goods or services. Protection was given only when the unauthorized use would likely confuse consumers as to the origin of those goods and services. In 1995, Congress amended the Lanham Act by passing the Federal Trademark Dilution Act,[2] which allowed trademark owners to bring suits in federal court for trademark **dilution.** Trademark dilution laws protect "distinctive" or "famous" trademarks (such as Jergens, McDonald's, Dell, and Apple) from certain unauthorized uses even when the use is on noncompeting goods or is unlikely to confuse. More than half of the states have also enacted trademark dilution laws.

SIMILAR MARKS MAY CONSTITUTE TRADEMARK DILUTION A famous mark may be diluted not only by the use of an *identical* mark but also by the use of a *similar* mark.[3] A similar mark is more likely to lessen the value of a famous mark when the companies using the marks provide related goods or compete against each other in the same market.

CASE IN POINT Samantha Lundberg operated "Sambuck's Coffeehouse," a small business in Astoria, Oregon, even though she knew that "Starbucks" is one of the largest coffee chains in the nation. When Starbucks Corporation filed a dilution lawsuit, the federal court ruled that use of the "Sambuck's" mark constituted trademark dilution because it created confusion for consumers. Not only was there a "high degree" of similarity between the marks, but also both companies provided coffee-related services and marketed their services through "stand-alone" retail stores. Therefore, the use of the similar mark (Sambuck's) reduced the value of the famous mark (Starbucks).[4]

Trademark Registration

Trademarks may be registered with the state or with the federal government. To register for protection under federal trademark law, a person must file an application with the U.S. Patent and Trademark Office in Washington, D.C. Under current law, a mark can be registered (1) if it is currently in commerce or (2) if the applicant intends to put it into commerce within six months.

In special circumstances, the six-month period can be extended by thirty months, giving the applicant a total of three years from the date of notice of trademark approval to make use of the mark and file the required use statement. Registration is postponed until the mark is actually used. Nonetheless, during this waiting period, any applicant can legally protect his or her trademark against a third party who previously has neither used the mark nor filed an application for it. Registration is renewable between the fifth and sixth years after the initial registration and every ten years thereafter (every twenty years for those trademarks registered before 1990).

---

1. 15 U.S.C. Sections 1051–1128.
2. 15 U.S.C. Section 1125.
3. See *Moseley v. V Secret Catalogue, Inc.,* 537 U.S. 418, 123 S.Ct. 1115, 155 L.Ed.2d 1 (2003).

---

4. *Starbucks Corp. v. Lundberg,* 2005 WL 3183858 (D.Or. 2005).

Trademark Infringement

Registration of a trademark with the U.S. Patent and Trademark Office gives notice on a nationwide basis that the trademark belongs exclusively to the registrant. The registrant is also allowed to use the symbol ® to indicate that the mark has been registered. Whenever that trademark is copied to a substantial degree or used in its entirety by another, intentionally or unintentionally, the trademark has been *infringed* (used without authorization).

When a trademark has been infringed, the owner of the mark has a cause of action against the infringer. To succeed in a trademark infringement action, the owner must show that the defendant's use of the mark created a likelihood of confusion about the origin of the defendant's goods or services. The owner need not prove that the infringer acted intentionally or that the trademark was registered (although registration does provide proof of the date of inception of the trademark's use).

The most commonly granted remedy for trademark infringement is an *injunction* to prevent further infringement. Under the Lanham Act, a trademark owner that successfully proves infringement can recover actual damages, plus the profits that the infringer wrongfully received from the unauthorized use of the mark. A court can also order the destruction of any goods bearing the unauthorized trademark. In some situations, the trademark owner may also be able to recover attorneys' fees.

Distinctiveness of Mark

A trademark must be sufficiently distinct to enable consumers to identify the manufacturer of the goods easily and to distinguish between those goods and competing products.

STRONG MARKS Fanciful, arbitrary, or suggestive trademarks are generally considered to be the most distinctive (strongest) trademarks. Marks that are fanciful, arbitrary, or suggestive are protected as inherently distinctive without demonstrating secondary meaning. These marks receive automatic protection because they serve to identify a particular product's source, as opposed to describing the product itself.

Fanciful and Arbitrary Trademarks. Fanciful trademarks are inherently distinctive and include invented words, such as "Xerox" for one manufacturer's copiers and "Kodak" for another company's photographic products. Arbitrary trademarks are those that use common words in an uncommon way that is nondescriptive, such as "Dutch Boy" as a name for paint. Even a single letter used in a particular style can be an arbitrary trademark.

CASE IN POINT Sports entertainment company ESPN sued Quiksilver, Inc., a maker of surfer clothing, alleging trademark infringement. ESPN claimed that Quiksilver's clothing had used the stylized "X" mark that ESPN uses in connection with the "X Games," a competition focusing on extreme action sports. Quiksilver filed counterclaims for trademark infringement and dilution, arguing that it had a long history of using the stylized X on its products. ESPN created the X Games in the mid-1990s, and Quiksilver has been using the X mark since 1994. ESPN, which has trademark applications pending for the stylized X, asked the court to dismiss Quiksilver's counterclaims. A federal district court ruled that the X on Quiksilver's clothing is clearly an arbitrary mark. Noting that "the two Xs are similar enough that a consumer might well confuse them," the court refused to dismiss Quiksilver's claims and allowed the dispute to go to trial.[5]

Suggestive Trademarks. Suggestive trademarks suggest something about a product's nature, quality, or characteristics, without describing the product directly. These marks require imagination on the part of the consumer to identify the characteristic. For example, "Dairy Queen" suggests an association between its products and milk, but it does not directly describe ice cream. "Blu-ray" is a suggestive mark that is associated with the high-quality, high-definition video contained on a particular optical data storage disc. Although blue-violet lasers are used to read blu-ray discs, the term *blu-ray* does not directly describe the disc.

SECONDARY MEANING Descriptive terms, geographic terms, and personal names are not inherently distinctive and do not receive protection under the law until they acquire a secondary meaning. A secondary meaning may arise when customers begin to associate a specific term or phrase (such as *London Fog*) with specific trademarked items (coats with "London Fog" labels) made by a particular company.

CASE IN POINT Frosty Treats, Inc., sells frozen desserts out of ice cream trucks. The video game series Twisted Metal depicts an ice cream truck with

---

5. *ESPN, Inc. v. Quiksilver, Inc.*, 586 F.Supp.2d 219 (S.D.N.Y. 2008).

a clown character on it that is similar to the clowns on Frosty Treats' trucks. In the last game of the series, the truck bears the label "Frosty Treats." Frosty sued the video game maker for trademark infringement, but the court held that "Frosty Treats" is a descriptive term and is not protected by trademark law unless it has acquired a secondary meaning. To establish secondary meaning, Frosty Treats would have had to show that the public recognized its trademark and associated it with a single source. Because Frosty Treats failed to do so, the court entered a judgment in favor of the video game producer.[6]

Once a secondary meaning is attached to a term or name, a trademark is considered distinctive and is protected. Even a color can qualify for trademark protection, as did the color schemes used by some state university sports teams, including Ohio State University and Louisiana State University.[7]

GENERIC TERMS Generic terms that refer to an entire class of products, such as *bicycle* and *computer,* receive no protection, even if they acquire secondary meanings.[8] A particularly thorny problem arises when a trademark acquires generic use. For example, *aspirin* and *thermos* were originally the names of trademarked products, but today the words are used generically. Other trademarks that have acquired generic use are *escalator, trampoline, raisin bran, dry ice, lanolin, linoleum, nylon,* and *corn flakes.*

Service, Certification, and Collective Marks

A **service mark** is essentially a trademark that is used to distinguish the *services* (rather than the products) of one person or company from those of another. For example, each airline has a particular mark or symbol associated with its name. Titles and character names used in radio and television are frequently registered as service marks.

Other marks protected by law include certification marks and collective marks. A **certification mark** is used by one or more persons, other than the owner, to certify the region, materials, mode of manufacture, quality, or other characteristic of specific goods or services. When used by members of a

cooperative, association, or other organization, it is referred to as a **collective mark.** Examples of certification marks are the phrases "Good Housekeeping Seal of Approval" and "UL Tested." Collective marks appear at the ends of motion picture credits to indicate the various associations and organizations that participated in the making of the films. The union marks found on the tags of certain products are also collective marks.

Trade Dress

The term **trade dress** refers to the image and overall appearance of a product. Trade dress is a broad concept and can include either all or part of the total image or overall impression created by a product or its packaging. For example, the distinctive decor, menu, layout, and style of service of a particular restaurant may be regarded as trade dress. Trade dress can also include the layout and appearance of a catalogue, the use of a lighthouse as part of the design of a golf hole, the fish shape of a cracker, or the G-shaped design of a Gucci watch.

Basically, trade dress is subject to the same protection as trademarks. In cases involving trade dress infringement, as in trademark infringement cases, a major consideration is whether consumers are likely to be confused by the allegedly infringing use.

Counterfeit Goods

Counterfeit goods copy or otherwise imitate trademarked goods, but they are not the genuine trademarked goods. The importation of goods that bear counterfeit (fake) trademarks poses a growing problem for U.S. businesses, consumers, and law enforcement. In addition to the negative financial effects on legitimate businesses, certain counterfeit goods, such as pharmaceuticals and nutritional supplements, can present serious public health risks. It is estimated that nearly 7 percent of the goods imported into the United States from abroad are counterfeit.

THE STOP COUNTERFEITING IN MANUFACTURED GOODS ACT The Stop Counterfeiting in Manufactured Goods Act[9] (SCMGA) was enacted to combat counterfeit goods. The act makes it a crime to traffic intentionally in or attempt to traffic in counterfeit goods or services, or to knowingly use a counterfeit mark on or in connection with goods

---

6. *Frosty Treats, Inc. v. Sony Computer Entertainment America, Inc.,* 426 F.3d 1001 (8th Cir. 2005).

7. *Board of Supervisors of Louisiana State University v. Smack Apparel Co.,* 438 F.Supp.2d 653 (E.D.La. 2006).

8. See, for example, *America Online, Inc. v. AT&T Corp.,* 243 F.3d 812 (4th Cir. 2001).

9. Pub. L. No. 109-181 (2006), which amended 18 U.S.C. Sections 2318–2320.

or services. Before this act, the law did not prohibit the creation or shipment of counterfeit labels that were not attached to any product. Therefore, counterfeiters would make labels and packaging bearing another's trademark, ship the labels to another location, and then affix them to an inferior product to deceive buyers. The SCMGA closed this loophole by making it a crime to knowingly traffic in counterfeit labels, stickers, packaging, and the like, regardless of whether the item is attached to any goods.

COUNTERFEITING PENALTIES Persons found guilty of violating the SCMGA may be fined up to $2 million or imprisoned for up to ten years (or more if they are repeat offenders). If a court finds that the statute was violated, it must order the defendant to forfeit the counterfeit products (which are then destroyed), as well as any property used in the commission of the crime. The defendant must also pay restitution to the trademark holder or victim in an amount equal to the victim's actual loss.

CASE IN POINT Wajdi Beydoun pleaded guilty to conspiring to import cigarette-rolling papers from Mexico that were falsely marked as "Zig-Zags" and selling them in the United States. The court sentenced Beydoun to prison and ordered him to pay $566,267 in restitution. On appeal, the court affirmed the prison sentence but reversed the restitution because the amount exceeded the actual loss suffered by the legitimate sellers of Zig-Zag rolling papers.[10]

Trade Names

Trademarks apply to *products.* The term **trade name** is used to indicate part or all of a business's name, whether the business is a sole proprietorship, a partnership, or a corporation. Generally, a trade name is directly related to a business and its goodwill. A trade name may be protected as a trademark if the trade name is also the name of the company's trademarked product—for example, Coca-Cola. Unless it is also used as a trademark or service mark, a trade name cannot be registered with the federal government. Trade names are protected under the common law, but only if they are unusual or fancifully used. The word *Safeway,* for example, was sufficiently fanciful to obtain protection as a trade name for a grocery chain.

SECTION 2
CYBER MARKS

In cyberspace, trademarks are sometimes referred to as **cyber marks.** We turn now to a discussion of how new laws and the courts address trademark-related issues in cyberspace.

Domain Names

As e-commerce expanded worldwide, one issue that emerged involved the rights of a trademark owner to use the mark as part of a domain name. A **domain name** is part of an Internet address—for example, "westlaw.com." Every domain name ends with a generic top level domain (TLD), which is the part of the name to the right of the period that indicates the type of entity that operates the site. For example, *com* is an abbreviation for *commercial,* and *edu* is short for *education.*

The second level domain (SLD)—the part of the name to the left of the period—is chosen by the business entity or individual registering the domain name. Competition for SLDs among firms with similar names and products has led to numerous disputes. By using an identical or similar domain name, parties have attempted to profit from a competitor's goodwill, sell pornography, offer for sale another party's domain name, or otherwise infringe on others' trademarks.

The Internet Corporation for Assigned Names and Numbers (ICANN), a nonprofit corporation, oversees the distribution of domain names and operates an online arbitration system. Due to numerous complaints, ICANN completely overhauled the domain name distribution system and began using a new system in 2009. One of the goals of the new system is to alleviate the problem of *cybersquatting.* **Cybersquatting** occurs when a person registers a domain name that is the same as, or confusingly similar to, the trademark of another and then offers to sell the domain name back to the trademark owner.

Anticybersquatting Legislation

During the 1990s, cybersquatting led to so much litigation that Congress passed the Anticybersquatting Consumer Protection Act (ACPA) of 1999,[11] which amended the Lanham Act—the federal law

---

10. *United States v. Beydoun,* 469 F.3d 102 (5th Cir. 2006).

11. 15 U.S.C. Section 1129.

protecting trademarks discussed earlier. The ACPA makes it illegal for a person to "register, traffic in, or use" a domain name (1) if the name is identical or confusingly similar to the trademark of another and (2) if the one registering, trafficking in, or using the domain name has a "bad faith intent" to profit from that trademark.

THE ONGOING PROBLEM OF CYBERSQUATTING The ACPA was intended to stamp out cybersquatting, but the practice continues to present a problem for businesses today, largely because more TLDs are available and many more companies are registering domain names. Domain name registrars have also proliferated. They charge a fee to businesses and individuals to register new names and to renew annual registrations (often through automated software). Many of these companies also buy and sell expired domain names. All domain name registrars are supposed to relay information about these transactions to ICANN and other companies that keep a master list of domain names. This information is not always transmitted, however. The speed at which domain names change hands and the difficulty in tracking mass automated registrations have created an environment where cybersquatting can flourish.

TYPOSQUATTING Cybersquatters have also developed new tactics, such as **typosquatting,** or registering a name that is a misspelling of a popular brand, such as hotmai.com or myspac.com. Because many Internet users are not perfect typists, Web pages using these misspelled names receive a lot of traffic. More traffic generally means increased profit (advertisers often pay Web sites based on the number of unique visits, or hits), which in turn provides incentive for more cybersquatters. Also, if the misspelling is significant, the trademark owner may have difficulty proving that the name is identical or confusingly similar to the trademark of another as the ACPA requires.

Cybersquatting is costly for businesses, which must attempt to register all variations of a name to protect their domain name rights from would-be cybersquatters and typosquatters. Large corporations may have to register thousands of domain names across the globe just to protect their basic brands and trademarks.

APPLICABILITY AND SANCTIONS OF THE ACPA The ACPA applies to all domain name registrations of trademarks. Successful plaintiffs in suits brought under the act can collect actual damages and profits, or they can elect to receive statutory damages ranging from $1,000 to $100,000.

Although some successful lawsuits have been brought under the ACPA, plaintiffs may encounter roadblocks. Some domain name registrars offer privacy services that hide the true owners of Web sites, making it difficult for trademark owners to identify cybersquatters. Thus, before a trademark owner can bring a suit, he or she has to ask the court for a subpoena to discover the identity of the owner of the infringing Web site. Because of the high costs of court proceedings, discovery, and even arbitration, many disputes over cybersquatting are settled out of court.

Meta Tags

Search engines compile their results by looking through a Web site's key-word field. **Meta tags,** or key words, may be inserted into this field to increase the likelihood that a site will be included in search engine results, even though the site may have nothing to do with the inserted words. Using this same technique, one site may appropriate the key words of other sites with more frequent hits so that the appropriating site will appear in the same search engine results as the more popular sites. Using another's trademark in a meta tag without the owner's permission, however, normally constitutes trademark infringement. Some uses of another's trademark as a meta tag may be permissible if the use is reasonably necessary and does not suggest that the owner authorized or sponsored the use.

CASE IN POINT Terri Welles, a former model who had been "Playmate of the Year" in *Playboy* magazine, established a Web site that used the terms *Playboy* and *Playmate* as meta tags. Playboy Enterprises, Inc. (PEI), which publishes *Playboy,* filed a suit seeking to prevent Welles from using these meta tags. The court determined that Welles's use of PEI's meta tags to direct users to her Web site was permissible because it did not suggest sponsorship and there were no descriptive substitutes for the terms *Playboy* and *Playmate.*[12]

Dilution in the Online World

As discussed earlier, trademark *dilution* occurs when a trademark is used, without authorization, in a way that diminishes the distinctive quality of the mark. Unlike trademark infringement, a claim of dilution

---

12. *Playboy Enterprises, Inc. v. Welles,* 279 F.3d 796 (9th Cir. 2002). See also *Canfield v. Health Communications, Inc.,* 2008 WL 961318 (C.D.Cal. 2008).

does not require proof that consumers are likely to be confused by a connection between the unauthorized use and the mark. For this reason, the products involved need not be similar.

CASE IN POINT In the first case alleging dilution on the Web, a court precluded the use of "candyland.com" as the URL for an adult site. The lawsuit was brought by the company that manufactures the Candyland children's game and owns the "Candyland" mark. Although consumers were not likely to connect candyland.com with the children's game, the court reasoned that the sexually explicit adult site would dilute the value of the "Candyland" mark.[13]

Licensing

One way to avoid litigation and still make use of another's trademark or other form of intellectual property is to obtain a license to do so. A **license** in this context is essentially an agreement, or contract, permitting the use of a trademark, copyright, patent, or trade secret for certain purposes. The party that owns the intellectual property rights and issues the license is the *licensor,* and the party obtaining the license is the *licensee.*

A license grants only the rights expressly described in the license agreement. A licensor might, for example, allow the licensee to use the trademark as part of its company name, or as part of its domain name, but not otherwise use the mark on any products or services. Disputes frequently arise over licensing agreements, particularly when the license involves Internet uses.

CASE IN POINT Perry Ellis International (PEI) owns the "Perry Ellis America" registered trademark (the PEA trademark), which is distinctive and known worldwide as a mark of quality apparel. In 2006, PEI granted URI Corporation an exclusive license to manufacture and distribute footwear using the PEA trademark in Mexico. The agreement required URI to comply with numerous conditions regarding the manufacturing and distribution of the licensed footwear and to sell the shoes only in certain (listed) high-quality stores. URI was not permitted to authorize any other party to use the PEA trademark. Despite this explicit licensing agreement, PEI discovered that footwear bearing its PEA trademark was being sold in discount stores in Mexico. PEI terminated the agreement and filed a lawsuit in a federal district court against URI. PEI was awarded more than $1 million in damages.[14]

Software creators typically license, rather than sell, their software to others. Software licensing agreements frequently include restrictions that prohibit licensees from sharing the software and using it to create similar software. Restrictive licenses enable creators to retain greater control over proprietary software and may offer more protection than intellectual property laws.

SECTION 3
PATENTS

A **patent** is a grant from the government that gives an inventor the right to exclude others from making, using, or selling his or her invention for a period of twenty years from the date of filing the application for a patent. Patents for designs, as opposed to those for inventions, are given for a fourteen-year period. The applicant must demonstrate to the satisfaction of the U.S. Patent and Trademark Office that the invention, discovery, process, or design is novel, useful, and not obvious in light of current technology.

In contrast to patent law in many other countries, in the United States the first person to invent a product or process gets the patent rights rather than the first person to file for a patent on that product or process. Because it can be difficult to prove who invented an item first, however, the first person to file an application is often deemed the first to invent (unless the inventor has detailed prior research notes or other evidence). An inventor can publish the invention or offer it for sale before filing a patent application but must apply for a patent within one year of doing so or forfeit the patent rights.

The period of patent protection begins on the date the patent application is filed, rather than when the patent is issued, which may sometimes be years later. After the patent period ends (either fourteen or twenty years later), the product or process enters the public domain, and anyone can make, sell, or use the invention without paying the patent holder.

Searchable Patent Databases

A significant development relating to patents is the availability online of the world's patent databases. The Web site of the U.S. Patent and Trademark Office

---

13. *Hasbro, Inc. v. Internet Entertainment Group, Ltd.,* 1996 WL 84853 (W.D.Wash. 1996).

14. *Perry Ellis International, Inc. v. URI Corporation,* 2007 WL 3047143 (S.D.Fla. 2007).

(www.uspto.gov) provides searchable databases covering U.S. patents granted since 1976. The Web site of the European Patent Office (www.epo.org) provides online access to 50 million patent documents in more than seventy nations through a searchable network of databases. Businesses use these searchable databases in many ways. Because patents are valuable assets, businesses may need to perform patent searches to list or inventory their assets. Patent searches may also be conducted to study trends and patterns in a specific technology or to gather information about competitors in the industry.

What Is Patentable?

Under federal law, "[w]hoever invents or discovers any new and useful process, machine, manufacture, or composition of matter, or any new and useful improvement thereof, may obtain a patent therefor, subject to the conditions and requirements of

this title."[15] Thus, to be patentable, the item must be novel and not obvious.

In sum, almost anything is patentable, except (1) the laws of nature, (2) natural phenomena, and (3) abstract ideas (including algorithms[16]). Even artistic methods, certain works of art, and the structure of storylines are patentable, provided that they are novel and not obvious. Plants that are reproduced asexually (by means other than from seed), such as hybrid or genetically engineered plants, are patentable in the United States, as are genetically engineered (or cloned) microorganisms and animals.

In the following case, the focus was on the application of the test for proving whether a patent claim was "obvious."

---

15. 35 U.S.C. Section 101.
16. An *algorithm* is a step-by-step procedure, formula, or set of instructions for accomplishing a specific task—such as the set of rules used by a search engine to rank the listings contained within its index in response to a particular query.

✳ EXTENDED CASE 14.2 ✳
KSR International Co. v. Teleflex, Inc.

Supreme Court of the United States, 550 U.S. 398, 127 S.Ct. 1727, 167 L.Ed.2d 705 (2007).

IN THE LANGUAGE OF THE COURT
Justice *KENNEDY* delivered the opinion of the Court.

Teleflex Incorporated * * * sued KSR International Company [in a federal district court] for patent infringement. The patent at issue is entitled "Adjustable Pedal Assembly With Electronic Throttle Control." The patentee is Steven J. Engelgau, and the patent is referred to as "the Engelgau patent." Teleflex holds the exclusive license to the patent.

Claim 4 of the Engelgau patent describes a mechanism for combining an electronic sensor with an adjustable automobile pedal so the pedal's position can be transmitted to a computer that controls the throttle in the vehicle's engine. [KSR designed a pedal assembly for General Motors Corporation (GMC)

to use in its Chevrolet and GMC light trucks.] When Teleflex accused KSR of infringing the Engelgau patent * * *, KSR countered that claim 4 was invalid * * * because its subject matter was obvious.

* * * *

Seeking to resolve the question of obviousness with * * * uniformity and consistency, [the courts have] employed an approach referred to by the parties as the "teaching, suggestion, or motivation" test (TSM test), under which a patent claim is only proved obvious if some motivation or suggestion to combine the prior art teachings can be found in the prior art, the nature of the problem, or the knowledge of a person having ordinary skill in the art. KSR challenges that test, or at least its application in this case.

* * * *

* * * Important for this case are two adjustable pedals disclosed in [other patents]. The Asano patent

reveals a support structure that houses the pedal so that even when the pedal location is adjusted relative to the driver, one of the pedal's pivot points stays fixed. * * * The Redding patent reveals a different, sliding mechanism where both the pedal and the pivot point are adjusted.

[Also important for this case are two] patents involving electronic pedal sensors for computer-controlled throttles. These inventions * * * taught that it was preferable to detect the pedal's position in the pedal assembly, not in the engine. The [Smith] patent disclosed a pedal with an electronic sensor on a pivot point in the pedal assembly.

* * * *

* * * The [Rixon patent] discloses an adjustable pedal assembly with an electronic sensor for detecting the pedal's position.

* * * *

EXTENDED CASE 14.2 CONTINUED ◆

The District Court granted summary judgment in KSR's favor.

* * * *

* * * The court compared the teachings of the prior art to the claims of Engelgau. It found "little difference." [The] Asano [patent] taught everything contained in claim 4 except the use of a sensor to detect the pedal's position and transmit it to the computer controlling the throttle. That additional aspect was revealed in sources such as * * * sensors [previously] used by Chevrolet.

* * * The District Court [also] held KSR had satisfied the [TSM] test. It reasoned (1) the state of the industry would lead inevitably to combinations of electronic sensors and adjustable pedals, (2) Rixon provided the basis for these developments, and (3) Smith taught a solution to the wire chafing problems in Rixon, namely locating the sensor on the fixed structure of the pedal.

* * * *

* * * [The U.S.] Court of Appeals [for the Federal Circuit] reversed. It ruled the District Court had not been strict enough in applying the [TSM] test, having failed to make "finding[s] as to the specific understanding or principle within the knowledge of a skilled artisan that would have motivated one with no knowledge of [the] invention * * * to attach an electronic control to the support bracket of the Asano assembly."

Here, the Court of Appeals found, the Asano pedal was designed to solve the "constant ratio problem"—that is, to ensure that the force required to depress the pedal is the same no matter how the pedal is adjusted—whereas Engelgau sought to provide a simpler, smaller, cheaper adjustable electronic pedal. As for Rixon, the court explained, that pedal suffered from the problem of wire chafing but was not designed to solve it. In the court's view Rixon did not teach anything helpful to Engelgau's purpose. Smith, in turn, did not relate to adjustable pedals and did not "necessarily go to the issue of motivation to attach the electronic control on the support bracket of the pedal assembly."

* * * *

We begin by rejecting the rigid approach of the Court of Appeals. Throughout this Court's engagement with the question of obviousness, our cases have set forth an expansive and flexible approach inconsistent with the way the Court of Appeals applied its TSM test here.

* * * *For over a half century, the Court has held that a patent for a combination which only unites old elements with no change in their respective functions * * * obviously withdraws what is already known into the field of its monopoly and diminishes the resources available to skillful [persons]. * * * [Emphasis added.]*

* * * *

* * * If a technique has been used to improve one device, and a person of ordinary skill in the art would recognize that it would improve similar devices in the same way, using the technique is obvious unless its actual application is beyond his or her skill.

* * * *

The first error of the Court of Appeals in this case was to * * * [hold] that courts and patent examiners should look only to the problem the patentee was trying to solve.

The second error of the Court of Appeals lay in its assumption that a person of ordinary skill attempting to solve a problem will be led only to those elements of prior art designed to solve the same problem.

* * * *

When we apply the standards we have explained to the instant facts, claim 4 must be found obvious. * * * We see little difference between the teachings of Asano and Smith and the adjustable electronic pedal disclosed in claim 4 of the Engelgau patent. A person having ordinary skill in the art could have combined Asano with a pedal position sensor in a fashion encompassed by claim 4, and would have seen the benefits of doing so.

* * * *

* * * The judgment of the Court of Appeals is reversed, and the case remanded for further proceedings consistent with this opinion.

 QUESTIONS

1. Suppose that a person of ordinary skill creates an item by implementing a predictable variation of another's patented invention. Does the Court's opinion indicate that the item is likely or unlikely to be patentable? Discuss.
2. Based on the Court's reasoning, what other factors should be considered in determining the obviousness of a patent?

PATENTS FOR SOFTWARE At one time, it was difficult for developers and manufacturers of software to obtain patent protection because many software products simply automate procedures that can be performed manually. In other words, it was thought that computer programs did not meet the "novel" and "not obvious" requirements previously mentioned. Also, the basis for software is often a mathematical equation or formula, which is not patentable. In 1981, however, the United States

Supreme Court opened the way for software products to receive patents when it held that it is possible to obtain a patent for a *process* that incorporates a computer program.[17]

PATENTS FOR BUSINESS PROCESSES In a landmark case, *State Street Bank & Trust Co. v. Signature Financial Group, Inc.,*[18] a federal appellate court ruled that business processes were patentable. After the decision in the *State Street* case, numerous technology firms applied for and received patents on business processes or methods. Walker Digital obtained a business process patent for its "Dutch auction" system, which allows Priceline.com users to name their own price for airline tickets and hotels. Amazon.com patented its "one-click" online payment system.

In 2008, however, the court that had decided the *State Street* case made it significantly more difficult to obtain patents for business processes when it reversed its earlier decision and invalidated "pure" business process patents.

CASE IN POINT Two individuals applied to patent a process that used transactions to hedge the risk in commodity trading. The U.S. Patent and Trademark Office denied their application because it was not limited to a machine and did not describe any methods for working out which transactions to perform. The applicants appealed. After soliciting input from numerous interest groups, the U.S. Court of Appeals for the Federal Circuit established a new test for business process patents. Under this test, a business process patent is valid only if it is tied to a particular machine or apparatus or transforms a particular article into a different state or object. Because the process in question failed to meet the machine-or-transformation test, the court upheld the denial of a patent.[19]

Patent Infringement

If a firm makes, uses, or sells another's patented design, product, or process without the patent owner's permission, that firm commits the tort of patent infringement. Patent infringement may occur even though the patent owner has not put the patented product into commerce. Patent infringement may also occur even though not all features or parts of a product are copied. (With respect to a patented process, however, all steps or their equivalent must be copied for infringement to exist.)

Note that, as a general rule, under U.S. law no patent infringement occurs when a patented product is made and sold in another country. The United States Supreme Court has narrowly construed patent infringement as it applies to exported software.

CASE IN POINT AT&T Corporation holds a patent on a device used to digitally encode, compress, and process recorded speech. AT&T brought an infringement case against Microsoft Corporation, which admitted that its Windows operating system incorporated software code that infringed on AT&T's patent. The case reached the United States Supreme Court on the question of whether Microsoft's liability extended to computers made in another country. The Court held that it did not. Microsoft was liable only for infringement in the United States and not for the Windows-based computers produced in foreign locations. The Court reasoned that Microsoft had not "supplied" the software for the computers but had only electronically transmitted a master copy, which the foreign manufacturers then copied and loaded onto the computers.[20]

Remedies for Patent Infringement

If a patent is infringed, the patent holder may sue for relief in federal court. The patent holder can seek an injunction against the infringer and can also request damages for royalties and lost profits. In some cases, the court may grant the winning party reimbursement for attorneys' fees and costs. If the court determines that the infringement was willful, the court can triple the amount of damages awarded (treble damages).

In the past, permanent injunctions were routinely granted to prevent future infringement. In 2006, however, the United States Supreme Court ruled that patent holders are not automatically entitled to a permanent injunction against future infringing activities—the courts have discretion to decide whether equity requires it. According to the Court, a patent holder must prove that it has suffered irreparable injury and that the public interest would not be disserved by a permanent injunction.[21] This decision gives courts discretion to decide what is equitable in the circumstances and allows them to

17. *Diamond v. Diehr,* 450 U.S. 175, 101 S.Ct. 1048, 67 L.Ed.2d 155 (1981).
18. 149 F.3d 1368 (Fed.Cir. 1998).
19. *In re Bilski,* 545 F.3d 943 (Fed.Cir. 2008).

20. *Microsoft Corp. v. AT&T Corp.,* 550 U.S. 437, 127 S.Ct. 1746, 167 L.Ed.2d 737 (2007).
21. *eBay, Inc. v. MercExchange, LLC,* 547 U.S. 388, 126 S.Ct. 1837, 164 L.Ed.2d 641 (2006).

consider what is in the public interest rather than just the interests of the parties.

CASE IN POINT In the first case applying this rule, a court found that although Microsoft had infringed on the patent of a small software company, the latter was not entitled to an injunction. According to the court, the small company was not irreparably harmed and could be adequately compensated by damages. Also, the public might suffer negative effects from an injunction because the infringement involved part of Microsoft's widely used Office suite software.[22]

SECTION 4
COPYRIGHTS

A **copyright** is an intangible property right granted by federal statute to the author or originator of a literary or artistic production of a specified type. The Copyright Act of 1976,[23] as amended, governs copyrights. Works created after January 1, 1978, are automatically given statutory copyright protection for the life of the author plus 70 years. For copyrights owned by publishing houses, the copyright expires 95 years from the date of publication or 120 years from the date of creation, whichever comes first. For works by more than one author, the copyright expires 70 years after the death of the last surviving author.[24]

Copyrights can be registered with the U.S. Copyright Office in Washington, D.C. A copyright owner no longer needs to place the symbol © or the term *Copr.* or *Copyright* on the work to have the work protected against infringement. Chances are that if somebody created it, somebody owns it.

What Is Protected Expression?

Works that are copyrightable include books, records, films, artworks, architectural plans, menus, music videos, product packaging, and computer software. To be protected, a work must be "fixed in a durable medium" from which it can be perceived, reproduced, or communicated. Protection is automatic. Registration is not required.

To obtain protection under the Copyright Act, a work must be original and fall into one of the following categories:

1. Literary works (including newspaper and magazine articles, computer and training manuals, catalogues, brochures, and print advertisements).
2. Musical works and accompanying words (including advertising jingles).
3. Dramatic works and accompanying music.
4. Pantomimes and choreographic works (including ballets and other forms of dance).
5. Pictorial, graphic, and sculptural works (including cartoons, maps, posters, statues, and even stuffed animals).
6. Motion pictures and other audiovisual works (including multimedia works).
7. Sound recordings.
8. Architectural works.

SECTION 102 EXCLUSIONS It is not possible to copyright an *idea*. Section 102 of the Copyright Act specifically excludes copyright protection for any "idea, procedure, process, system, method of operation, concept, principle, or discovery, regardless of the form in which it is described, explained, illustrated, or embodied." Thus, anyone can freely use the underlying ideas or principles embodied in a work. What is copyrightable is the particular way in which an idea is expressed. Whenever an idea and an expression are inseparable, the expression cannot be copyrighted. Generally, anything that is not an original expression will not qualify for copyright protection. Facts widely known to the public are not copyrightable. Page numbers are not copyrightable because they follow a sequence known to everyone. Mathematical calculations are not copyrightable.

COMPILATIONS OF FACTS Unlike ideas, *compilations of facts* are copyrightable. Under Section 103 of the Copyright Act, a compilation is "a work formed by the collection and assembling of preexisting materials or data that are selected, coordinated, or arranged in such a way that the resulting work as a whole constitutes an original work of authorship." The key requirement in the copyrightability of a compilation is originality. If the facts are selected, coordinated, or arranged in an original way, they can qualify for copyright protection. Therefore, the White Pages of a telephone directory do not qualify for copyright protection because the facts (names, addresses, and telephone numbers) are listed in alphabetical order

---

22. *Z4 Technologies, Inc. v. Microsoft Corp.*, 434 F.Supp.2d 437 (E.D.Tex. 2006).
23. 17 U.S.C. Sections 101 *et seq.*
24. These time periods reflect the extensions of the length of copyright protection enacted by Congress in the Copyright Term Extension Act of 1998, 17 U.S.C.A. Section 302. The United States Supreme Court upheld the constitutionality of the act in 2003. See *Eldred v. Ashcroft*, 537 U.S. 186, 123 S.Ct. 769, 154 L.Ed.2d 683 (2003).

rather than being selected, coordinated, or arranged in an original way. The Yellow Pages of a telephone directory, in contrast, may be copyrightable, provided the information is selected, coordinated, or arranged in an original way. Similarly, a compilation of information about yachts listed for sale has qualified for copyright protection.[25]

Copyright Infringement

Whenever the form or expression of an idea is copied, an infringement of copyright has occurred. The reproduction does not have to be exactly the same as the original, nor does it have to reproduce the original in its entirety. If a substantial part of the original is reproduced, the copyright has been infringed.

REMEDIES FOR COPYRIGHT INFRINGEMENT Those who infringe copyrights may be liable for damages or criminal penalties. These range from actual damages or statutory damages, imposed at the court's discretion, to criminal proceedings for willful violations. Actual damages are based on the harm caused to the copyright holder by the infringement, while statutory damages, not to exceed $150,000, are provided for under the Copyright Act. Criminal proceedings may result in fines and/or imprisonment. A court can also issue a permanent injunction against a defendant when the court deems it necessary to prevent future copyright infringement.

CASE IN POINT Rusty Carroll operated an online term paper business, R2C2, Inc., that offered up to 300,000 research papers for sale at nine different Web sites. Individuals whose work was posted on these Web sites without their permission filed a lawsuit against Carroll for copyright infringement. A federal district court in Illinois ruled that an injunction was proper because the plaintiffs had shown that they had suffered irreparable harm and that monetary damages were inadequate to compensate them. Because Carroll had repeatedly failed to comply with court orders regarding discovery, the court found that the copyright infringement was likely to continue unless an injunction was issued. The court therefore issued a permanent injunction prohibiting Carroll and R2C2 from selling any term paper without sworn documentary evidence that the paper's author had given permission.[26]

THE "FAIR USE" EXCEPTION An exception to liability for copyright infringement is made under the "fair use" doctrine. In certain circumstances, a person or organization can reproduce copyrighted material without paying royalties (fees paid to the copyright holder for the privilege of reproducing the copyrighted material). Section 107 of the Copyright Act provides as follows:

> [T]he fair use of a copyrighted work, including such use by reproduction in copies or phonorecords or by any other means specified by [Section 106 of the Copyright Act], for purposes such as criticism, comment, news reporting, teaching (including multiple copies for classroom use), scholarship, or research, is not an infringement of copyright. In determining whether the use made of a work in any particular case is a fair use the factors to be considered shall include–
>
> (1) the purpose and character of the use, including whether such use is of a commercial nature or is for nonprofit educational purposes;
> (2) the nature of the copyrighted work;
> (3) the amount and substantiality of the portion used in relation to the copyrighted work as a whole; and
> (4) the effect of the use upon the potential market for or value of the copyrighted work.

WHAT IS FAIR USE? Because these guidelines are very broad, the courts determine whether a particular use is fair on a case-by-case basis. Thus, even if a person who reproduces copyrighted material believes the fair use exception applies, that person may still be committing a violation. In determining whether a use is fair, courts have often considered the fourth factor to be the most important.

CASE IN POINT The owner of copyrighted music, BMG Music Publishing, granted a license to Leadsinger, Inc., a manufacturer of karaoke devices. The license gave Leadsinger permission to reproduce the sound recordings, but not to reprint the song lyrics, which appeared at the bottom of a TV screen when the karaoke device was used. BMG demanded that Leadsinger pay a "lyric reprint" fee and a "synchronization" fee. Leadsinger refused to pay, claiming that its use of the lyrics was educational and thus did not constitute copyright infringement under the fair use exception. A federal appellate court disagreed. The court held that Leadsinger's display of the lyrics was not a fair use because it would have a negative effect on the value of the copyrighted work.[27]

---

25. *BUC International Corp. v. International Yacht Council, Ltd.,* 489 F.3d 1129 (11th Cir. 2007).

26. *Weidner v. Carroll,* No. 06-782-DRH, U.S. District Court for the Southern District of Illinois, January 21, 2010.

27. *Leadsinger, Inc. v. BMG Music Publishing,* 512 F.3d 522 (9th Cir. 2008).

Copyright Protection for Software

In 1980, Congress passed the Computer Software Copyright Act, which amended the Copyright Act of 1976 to include computer programs in the list of creative works protected by federal copyright law.[28] Generally, the courts have extended copyright protection to those parts of a computer program that can be read by humans, such as the "high-level" language of a source code, and to the binary-language object code, which is readable only by the computer. Additionally, such elements as the overall structure, sequence, and organization of a program have been deemed copyrightable. Not all aspects of software are protected, however. For the most part, courts have not extended copyright protection to the "look and feel"—the general appearance, command structure, video images, menus, windows, and other screen displays—of computer programs.

SECTION 5
COPYRIGHTS IN DIGITAL INFORMATION

Copyright law is probably the most important form of intellectual property protection on the Internet. This is because much of the material on the Internet (including software and database information) is copyrighted, and in order to transfer that material online, it must be "copied." Generally, whenever a party downloads software or music into a computer's random access memory, or RAM, without authorization, a copyright is infringed. Technology has vastly increased the potential for copyright infringement.

CASE IN POINT A musical group used only a few seconds from the guitar solo of another group's copyrighted sound recording, without permission, while recording a rap song that was included in the sound track of a movie. Nevertheless, a federal appellate court held that digitally sampling a copyrighted sound recording of any length constitutes copyright infringement.[29]

Initially, criminal penalties for copyright violations could be imposed only if unauthorized copies were exchanged for financial gain. Yet much piracy of copyrighted materials online was "altruistic" in nature; unauthorized copies were made simply to be shared with others. Then, Congress amended the law and extended criminal liability for the piracy of copyrighted materials to persons who exchange unauthorized copies of copyrighted works without realizing a profit.

Digital Millennium Copyright Act

In 1998, Congress passed further legislation to protect copyright holders—the Digital Millennium Copyright Act (DMCA).[30] The DMCA gave significant protection to owners of copyrights in digital information.[31] Among other things, the act established civil and criminal penalties for anyone who circumvents (bypasses) encryption software or other technological antipiracy protection. Also prohibited are the manufacture, import, sale, and distribution of devices or services for circumvention.

The DMCA provides for exceptions to fit the needs of libraries, scientists, universities, and others. In general, the law does not restrict the "fair use" of circumvention methods for educational and other noncommercial purposes. For example, circumvention is allowed to test computer security, to conduct encryption research, to protect personal privacy, and to enable parents to monitor their children's use of the Internet. The exceptions are to be reconsidered every three years.

The DMCA also limits the liability of Internet service providers (ISPs). Under the act, an ISP is not liable for copyright infringement by its customer *unless* the ISP is aware of the subscriber's violation. An ISP may be held liable only if it fails to take action to shut down the subscriber after learning of the violation. A copyright holder must act promptly, however, by pursuing a claim in court, or the subscriber has the right to be restored to online access.

MP3 and File-Sharing Technology

Soon after the Internet became popular, a few enterprising programmers created software to compress large data files, particularly those associated with music. The best-known compression and decompression system is MP3, which enables music fans to download songs or entire CDs onto their computers or onto portable listening devices, such as iPods or iPhones. The MP3 system also made it possible for music fans to access other music fans' files by engaging in file-sharing via the Internet.

---

28. Pub. L. No. 96-517 (1980), amending 17 U.S.C. Sections 101, 117.
29. *Bridgeport Music, Inc. v. Dimension Films,* 410 F.3d 792 (6th Cir. 2005).
30. 17 U.S.C. Sections 512, 1201–1205, 1301–1332; and 28 U.S.C. Section 4001.
31. This act implemented the World Intellectual Property Organization Copyright Treaty of 1996, which will be discussed later in this chapter on page 326.

File-sharing is accomplished through **peer-to-peer (P2P) networking.** The concept is simple. Rather than going through a central Web server, P2P networking uses numerous personal computers (PCs) that are connected to the Internet. Individuals on the same network can access files stored on one another's PCs through a **distributed network.** Parts of the network may be distributed all over the country or the world, which offers an unlimited number of uses. Persons scattered throughout the country or the world can work together on the same project by using file-sharing programs.

A newer method of sharing files via the Internet is **cloud computing,** which is essentially a subscription-based or pay-per-use service that extends a computer's software or storage capabilities. Cloud computing can deliver a single application through a browser to multiple users, or it might be a utility program to pool resources and provide data storage and virtual servers that can be accessed on demand. Amazon, Facebook, Google, IBM, and Sun Microsystems are using and developing more cloud computing services.

SHARING STORED MUSIC FILES When file-sharing is used to download others' stored music files, copyright issues arise. Recording artists and their labels stand to lose large amounts of royalties and revenues if relatively few CDs are purchased and then made available on distributed networks, from which anyone can get them for free.

CASE IN POINT The issue of file-sharing infringement has been the subject of an ongoing debate since the highly publicized case of *A&M Records, Inc. v. Napster, Inc.*[32] Napster, Inc., operated a Web site with free software that enabled users to copy and transfer MP3 files via the Internet. When firms in the recording industry sued Napster, the court held that Napster was liable for contributory and vicarious[33] (indirect) copyright infringement because it had assisted others in obtaining unauthorized copies of copyrighted music.

In the following case, a group of recording companies sued an Internet user who had downloaded a number of copyrighted songs from the Internet. The user then shared the audio files with others via a P2P network. One of the issues before the court was whether the user was an "innocent infringer"—that is, whether she was innocent of copyright infringement because she was unaware that the works were copyrighted.

---

32. 239 F.3d 1004 (9th Cir. 2001).

33. *Vicarious (indirect) liability* exists when one person is subject to liability for another's actions. A common example occurs in the employment context, when an employer is held vicariously liable by third parties for torts committed by employees in the course of their employment.

CASE 14.3
Maverick Recording Co. v. Harper

United States Court of Appeals, Fifth Circuit, 598 F.3d 193 (2010).
www.ca5.uscourts.gov/Opinions/aspx[a]

COMPANY PROFILE • Recording star Madonna, others in the music business, and Time Warner created Maverick Records in 1992. Initially, the company saw great success with Alanis Morissette, The Prodigy, Candlebox, and the Deftones. It also created the sound track for the movie *The Matrix*. In a dispute over management of the company, Madonna and another co-owner were bought out. Today, Maverick is a wholly owned subsidiary of Warner Music Group.

BACKGROUND AND FACTS • Maverick Recording Company and several other music-recording firms (the plaintiffs) hired MediaSentry to investigate the infringement of their copyrights over the Internet. During its investigation, MediaSentry discovered that Whitney Harper was using a file-sharing program to share digital audio files with other users of a peer-to-peer network. The shared audio files included a number of the plaintiffs' copyrighted works. The plaintiffs brought an action in a federal court against Harper for copyright infringement. They sought $750 per infringed work, the minimum amount of damages set forth in Section 504(c)(1) of the Copyright Act. Harper asserted that her infringement was "innocent" and that therefore Section 504(c)(2) of the Copyright Act should apply. That section provides that when an infringer was not aware, and had no reason to believe, that

---

a. In the box titled "and/or Title contains text," type in "Maverick." On the page that opens, click on the docket number beside the case title to access the opinion. The U.S. Court of Appeals for the Fifth Circuit maintains this Web site.

CASE 14.3 CONTINUED ➡ his or her acts constituted copyright infringement, "the court in its discretion may reduce the award of statutory damages to a sum of not less than $200." The trial court granted summary judgment for the plaintiffs on the issue of copyright infringement and enjoined Harper from further downloading and sharing of copyrighted works. The court, however, awarded the plaintiffs only $200 per infringed work. Both parties appealed. Harper claimed that there was insufficient evidence of copyright infringement. The plaintiffs argued that the district court had erred by failing to rule out the innocent infringer defense as a matter of law.

IN THE LANGUAGE OF THE COURT
Edith Brown *CLEMENT,* Circuit Judge:
* * * *

The uncontroverted [undisputed] evidence is more than sufficient to compel a finding that Harper had downloaded the files: there was no evidence from which a fact-finder could draw a reasonable inference that Harper had *not* downloaded them or that they were something other than audio files. * * * The district court properly rejected Harper's argument that the evidence of infringement was insufficient.

* * * *

* * * The district court held that there was a genuine issue of material fact as to whether Harper was an innocent infringer. * * * Harper averred [asserted] in an affidavit that she did not understand the nature of file-sharing programs and that she believed that listening to music from file-sharing networks was akin to listening to a noninfringing Internet radio station. The district court ruled that this assertion created a triable [capable of being tried before a judge or a jury] issue as to whether Harper's infringement was "innocent" under [Section 504(c)(2) of the Copyright Act].

* * * We hold that the defense was unavailable to her as a matter of law. *The innocent infringer defense is limited by [Section 402(d) of the Copyright Act]: with one exception not relevant here, when a proper copyright notice "appears on the published * * * phonorecords to which a defendant * * * had access, then no weight shall be given to such a defendant's interposition of a defense based on innocent infringement in mitigation of actual or statutory damages."* [Emphasis added.]

The district court acknowledged that Plaintiffs provided proper notice on each of the published phonorecords from which the audio files were taken. * * * Harper contended only that she was too young and naive to understand that the copyrights on published music applied to downloaded music.

These arguments are insufficient to defeat the interposition [interference] of the [Section 402(d)] limitation on the innocent infringer defense. Harper's reliance on her own understanding of copyright law—or lack thereof—is irrelevant in the context of [Section 402(d)]. *The plain language of the statute shows that the infringer's knowledge or intent does not affect its application. Lack of legal sophistication cannot overcome a properly asserted [Section 402(d)] limitation to the innocent infringer defense.* [Emphasis added.]

* * * *

In short, the district court found a genuine issue of fact as to whether Harper intended to infringe Plaintiffs' copyrights, but that issue was not material: [Section 402(d)] forecloses, as a matter of law, Harper's innocent infringer defense. Because the defense does not apply, Plaintiffs are entitled to statutory damages. And because Plaintiffs requested the minimum statutory damages under [Section 504(c)(1)], Harper's culpability is not an issue and there are no issues left for trial. Plaintiffs must be awarded statutory damages of $750 per infringed work.

DECISION AND REMEDY • *The U.S. Court of Appeals for the Fifth Circuit affirmed the trial court's finding of copyright liability, reversed its finding that the innocent infringer defense presented an issue for trial, and remanded the case for further proceedings consistent with the court's opinion. The appellate court concluded that the district court had erred by awarding damages of $200 per infringement because Harper was not an innocent infringer.*

THE ETHICAL DIMENSION • *In this and other cases involving similar rulings, the courts have held that when the published phonorecordings from which audio files were taken contained copyright notices, the innocent infringer defense does not apply. It is irrelevant that the notice is not provided in the online file. Is this fair? Explain.*

CASE CONTINUES ➡

CASE 14.3 CONTINUED ▶ **MANAGERIAL IMPLICATIONS** • *Owners and managers of firms in the business of recording and distributing music face a constant challenge in protecting their copyrights. This is particularly true for audio files in the online environment, where Internet users can easily download a copyrighted song and make it available to P2P file-sharing networks. Among other things, this means that recording companies must be ever vigilant in searching the Web to find infringing uses of works distributed online. Today, it is not uncommon for companies to hire antipiracy firms to investigate the illegal downloading of their copyrighted materials.*

THE EVOLUTION OF FILE-SHARING TECHNOLOGIES
After the *Napster* decision, the recording industry filed and won numerous lawsuits against companies that distribute online file-sharing software. Other companies then developed technologies that allow P2P network users to share stored music files, without paying a fee, more quickly and efficiently than ever. Software such as Morpheus, KaZaA, and LimeWire, for example, provides users with an interface that is similar to a Web browser.[34] When a user performs a search, the software locates a list of peers that have the file available for downloading.

Because of the automated procedures, the companies do not maintain a central index and are unable to determine whether users are exchanging copyrighted files. Nevertheless, the United States Supreme Court has held that companies that distribute file-sharing software intending that it be used to violate copyright laws can be liable for users' copyright infringement.

CASE IN POINT In *Metro-Goldwyn-Mayer Studios, Inc. v. Grokster, Ltd.,*[35] music and film industry organizations sued Grokster, Ltd., and StreamCast Networks, Inc., for contributory and vicarious copyright infringement. The Supreme Court held that anyone who distributes file-sharing software "with the object of promoting its use to infringe copyright, as shown by clear expression or other affirmative steps taken to foster infringement, . . . is liable for the resulting acts of infringement by third parties."

DVDS AND FILE-SHARING File-sharing also creates problems for the motion picture industry, which has lost significant amounts of revenue as a result

of pirated DVDs. Nearly one-third of the people in the United States—many of them young men—have illegally copied a movie onto a DVD in violation of copyright laws.[36] Numerous Web sites offer software that facilitates the illegal copying of movies, such as BitTorrent, which enables users to download high-quality files from the Internet.

CASE IN POINT TorrentSpy, a popular BitTorrent indexing Web site, enabled users to locate and exchange files. The Motion Picture Association of America (MPAA) and Columbia Pictures Industries brought a lawsuit against the operators of TorrentSpy for facilitating copyright infringement. The MPAA also claimed that the operators had destroyed evidence that would reveal the identity of individual infringers. The operators had ignored a court order to keep server logs of the Internet addresses of people who facilitated the trading of files via the site. Because TorrentSpy's operators had willfully destroyed evidence, a federal court found in favor of the MPAA and ordered the defendants to pay a judgment of $111 million.[37]

◢◣ SECTION 6 ◢◣
TRADE SECRETS

The law of trade secrets protects some business processes and information that are not, or cannot be, patented, copyrighted, or trademarked against appropriation by competitors. A **trade secret** is basically information of commercial value. Trade secrets may include customer lists, plans, research

---

34. In 2005, KaZaA entered into a settlement agreement with four major music companies that had alleged copyright infringement. KaZaA agreed to offer only legitimate, fee-based music downloads. Note also that although the publisher of Morpheus is no longer in business, the software is still available.

35. 545 U.S. 913, 125 S.Ct. 2764, 162 L.Ed.2d 781 (2005). Grokster, Ltd., later settled this dispute out of court and stopped distributing its software.

36. Chris Tribbey. "Report: DVD Piracy Is Growing." *Home Media Magazine.* 7 May 2009.

37. *Columbia Pictures Industries v. Bunnell,* 2007 WL 4877701 (C.D.Cal. 2007). The final judgment awarding damages and issuing a permanent injunction was filed on May 5, 2008 (No. 2:06-CV-01093-FMC-JCx). See David Kravets. "TorrentSpy Dinged $111 Million in MPAA Lawsuit." *Wired.com.* 7 May 2008: n.p. Web.

and development, pricing information, marketing methods, production techniques, and generally anything that makes an individual company unique and that would have value to a competitor.

Unlike copyright and trademark protection, protection of trade secrets extends both to ideas and to their expression. (For this reason, and because a trade secret involves no registration or filing requirements, trade secret protection may be well suited for software.) Of course, the secret formula, method, or other information must be disclosed to some persons, particularly to key employees. Businesses generally attempt to protect their trade secrets by having all employees who use a process or information agree in their contracts, or in confidentiality agreements, never to divulge it.[38]

State and Federal Law on Trade Secrets

Under Section 757 of the *Restatement of Torts,* those who disclose or use another's trade secret, without authorization, are liable to that other party if (1) they discovered the secret by improper means or (2) their disclosure or use constitutes a breach of a duty owed to the other party. The theft of confidential business data by industrial espionage, as when a business taps into a competitor's computer, is a theft of trade secrets without any contractual violation and is actionable in itself.

Trade secrets were protected under the common law, but the protection provided varied from state to state. Today, most states' laws are based on the Uniform Trade Secrets Act,[39] which has been adopted in forty-seven states. Additionally, in 1996 Congress passed the Economic Espionage Act,[40] which made the theft of trade secrets a federal crime. We examined the provisions and significance of this act in Chapter 7, in the context of crimes related to business.

Trade Secrets in Cyberspace

Computer technology is undercutting many business firms' ability to protect their confidential information, including trade secrets.[41] For example, a dishonest employee could e-mail trade secrets in a company's computer to a competitor or a future employer. If e-mail is not an option, the employee might walk out with the information on a flash pen drive.

For a comprehensive summary of trade secrets and the other forms of intellectual property discussed in this chapter, see Exhibit 14–1 on the following page.

◢◤◢ SECTION 7 ◢◤◢
INTERNATIONAL PROTECTION FOR INTELLECTUAL PROPERTY

For many years, the United States has been a party to various international agreements relating to intellectual property rights. For example, the Paris Convention of 1883, to which about 172 countries are signatory, allows parties in one country to file for patent and trademark protection in any of the other member countries. Other international agreements in this area include the Berne Convention; the Trade-Related Aspects of Intellectual Property Rights, or, more simply, the TRIPS agreement; and the Madrid Protocol. To learn about a new international treaty being negotiated that will affect international property rights, see this chapter's *Shifting Legal Priorities for Business* feature on page 327.

The Berne Convention

Under the Berne Convention of 1886 (an international copyright agreement), as amended, if a U.S. citizen writes a book, every country that has signed the convention must recognize the U.S. author's copyright in the book. Also, if a citizen of a country that has not signed the convention first publishes a book in one of the 170 countries that have signed, all other countries that have signed the convention must recognize that author's copyright. Copyright notice is not needed to gain protection under the Berne Convention for works published after March 1, 1989.

The laws of many countries, as well as international laws, are being updated to reflect changes

---

38. See, for example, *Verigy US, Inc. v. Mayder,* 2008 WL 564634 (N.D.Cal. 2008); and *Gleeson v. Preferred Sourcing, LLC,* 883 N.E.2d 164 (Ind.App. 2008).

39. The Uniform Trade Secrets Act, as drafted by the National Conference of Commissioners on Uniform State Laws, (NCCUSL), can be found at www.nccusl.org. As with all uniform laws, each state has codified the law within its own state statutory code.

40. 18 U.S.C. Sections 1831–1839.

41. Note that in at least one case, a court has held that customers' e-mail addresses may constitute trade secrets. See *T-N-T Motorsports, Inc. v. Hennessey Motorsports, Inc.,* 965 S.W.2d 18 (Tex.App.—Houston 1998); rehearing overruled (1998); petition dismissed (1998).

EXHIBIT 14-1 • Forms of Intellectual Property

FORM	DEFINITION	HOW ACQUIRED	DURATION	REMEDY FOR INFRINGEMENT
Patent	A grant from the government that gives an inventor exclusive rights to an invention.	By filing a patent application with the U.S. Patent and Trademark Office and receiving its approval.	Twenty years from the date of the application; for design patents, fourteen years.	Monetary damages, including royalties and lost profits, *plus* attorneys' fees. Damages may be tripled for intentional infringements.
Copyright	The right of an author or originator of a literary or artistic work, or other production that falls within a specified category, to have the exclusive use of that work for a given period of time.	Automatic (once the work or creation is put in tangible form). Only the *expression* of an idea (and not the idea itself) can be protected by copyright.	For authors: the life of the author, plus 70 years. For publishers: 95 years after the date of publication or 120 years after creation.	Actual damages plus profits received by the party who infringed *or* statutory damages under the Copyright Act, *plus* costs and attorneys' fees in either situation.
Trademark (Service Mark and Trade Dress)	Any distinctive word, name, symbol, or device (image or appearance), or combination thereof, that an entity uses to distinguish its goods or services from those of others. The owner has the exclusive right to use that mark or trade dress.	1. At common law, ownership created by use of the mark. 2. Registration with the appropriate federal or state office gives notice and is permitted if the mark is currently in use or will be within the next six months.	Unlimited, as long as it is in use. To continue notice by registration, the owner must renew by filing between the fifth and sixth years, and thereafter, every ten years.	1. Injunction prohibiting the future use of the mark. 2. Actual damages *plus* profits received by the party who infringed (can be increased under the Lanham Act). 3. Destruction of articles that infringed. 4. *Plus* costs and attorneys' fees.
Trade Secret	Any information that a business possesses and that gives the business an advantage over competitors (including formulas, lists, patterns, plans, processes, and programs).	Through the originality and development of the information and processes that constitute the business secret and are unknown to others.	Unlimited, so long as not revealed to others. Once revealed to others, it is no longer a trade secret.	Monetary damages for misappropriation (the Uniform Trade Secrets Act also permits punitive damages if willful), *plus* costs and attorneys' fees.

in technology and the expansion of the Internet. Copyright holders and other owners of intellectual property generally agree that changes in the law are needed to stop the increasing international piracy of their property. The World Intellectual Property Organization (WIPO) Copyright Treaty of 1996, a special agreement under the Berne Convention, attempts to update international law governing copyright protection to include more safeguards against copyright infringement via the Internet. The United States signed the WIPO treaty in 1996 and implemented its terms in the Digital Millennium Copyright Act of 1998, which was discussed earlier in this chapter on page 321.

This convention and other international agreements have given some protection to intellectual property on a worldwide level. None of them, however, has been as significant and far reaching in scope as the agreement discussed next.

The TRIPS Agreement

Representatives from more than one hundred nations signed the TRIPS agreement in 1994. The agreement established, for the first time, standards for the international protection of intellectual property rights, including patents, trademarks, and copyrights for movies, computer programs, books, and music. The TRIPS agreement provides that each member country of the World Trade Organization must include in its domestic laws broad intellectual property rights and effective remedies (including civil and criminal penalties) for violations of those rights.

NO DISCRIMINATION AGAINST FOREIGN INTELLECTUAL PROPERTY OWNERS Generally, the TRIPS agreement forbids member nations from discriminating against foreign owners of intellectual property rights (in the administration, regulation, or adjudication of such rights). In other words, a member nation cannot give its own nationals (citizens) favorable treatment without offering the same treatment to nationals of all other member countries. For instance, if a U.S. software manufacturer brings a suit for the infringement of intellectual property rights under Germany's national laws, the U.S. manufacturer is entitled to receive the same treatment as a German manufacturer because Germany is a member of the agreement. Each member nation must also ensure that legal procedures are available for parties who wish to bring actions for infringement of intellectual property rights. Additionally, a related document established a mechanism for settling disputes among member nations.

TYPES OF COVERED INTELLECTUAL PROPERTY Particular provisions of the TRIPS agreement relate to patent, trademark, and copyright protection for intellectual property. The agreement specifically provides copyright protection for computer programs by stating that compilations of data, databases, and other materials are "intellectual creations" and are to be protected as copyrightable works. Other provisions relate to trade secrets and the rental of computer programs and cinematographic works.

The Madrid Protocol

In the past, one of the difficulties in protecting U.S. trademarks internationally was the time and expense required to apply for trademark registration in foreign countries. The filing fees and procedures for trademark registration vary significantly among individual countries. The Madrid Protocol, which was signed into law in 2003, may help to resolve these problems. The Madrid Protocol is an international treaty that has been signed by seventy-nine countries. Under its provisions, a U.S. company wishing to register its trademark abroad can submit a single application and designate other member countries in which the company would like to register its mark. The treaty is designed to reduce the costs of international trademark protection by more than 60 percent, according to proponents.

Although the Madrid Protocol may simplify and reduce the cost of trademark registration in foreign countries, it remains to be seen whether it will provide significant benefits to trademark owners. Even with a similar registration process, there is still a question as to whether member countries will enforce the law and protect the mark. Moreover, the cost savings of using the Madrid Protocol may be negated by its requirement that a trademark owner use local agents in the applicable jurisdiction if problems arise.

REVIEWING

Intellectual Property and Internet Law

Two computer science majors, Trent and Xavier, have an idea for a new video game, which they propose to call "Hallowed." They form a business and begin developing their idea. Several months later, Trent and Xavier run into a problem with their design and consult with a friend, Brad, who is an expert in designing computer source codes. After the software is completed but before Hallowed is marketed, a video game called Halo 2 is released for both the Xbox and the Playstation 3 systems. Halo 2 uses source codes similar to those of Hallowed and imitates Hallowed's overall look and feel, although not all the features are alike. Using the information presented in the chapter, answer the following questions.

1. Would the name *Hallowed* receive protection as a trademark or as trade dress? Explain.
2. If Trent and Xavier had obtained a business process patent on Hallowed, would the release of Halo 2 have infringed on their patent? Why or why not?
3. Based only on the facts described above, could Trent and Xavier sue the makers of Halo 2 for copyright infringement? Why or why not?
4. Suppose that Trent and Xavier discover that Brad took the idea of Hallowed and sold it to the company that produced Halo 2. Which type of intellectual property issue does this raise?

⚙ **DEBATE THIS:** *Congress has amended copyright law several times. Copyright holders now have protection for many decades. Was Congress right in extending these copyright time periods? Why or why not?*

TERMS AND CONCEPTS

certification mark 312
cloud computing 322
collective mark 312
copyright 319

cyber mark 313
cybersquatting 313
dilution 310
distributed network 322
domain name 313
intellectual property 308

license 315
meta tag 314
patent 315
peer-to-peer (P2P)
    networking 322
service mark 312

trade dress 312
trade name 313
trade secret 324
trademark 308
typosquatting 314

QUESTIONS AND CASE PROBLEMS

14–1. Fair Use Professor Wise is teaching a summer seminar in business torts at State University. Several times during the course, he makes copies of relevant sections from business law texts and distributes them to his students. Wise does not realize that the daughter of one of the textbook authors is a member of his seminar. She tells her father about Wise's copying activities, which have taken place without her father's or his publisher's permission. Her father sues Wise for copyright infringement. Wise claims protection under the fair use doctrine. Who will prevail? Explain.

14–2. QUESTION WITH SAMPLE ANSWER: Copyright Infringement.

 In which of the following situations would a court likely hold Ursula liable for copyright infringement?

(a) Ursula goes to the library and photocopies ten pages from a scholarly journal relating to a topic on which she is writing a term paper.

(b) Ursula makes blouses, dresses, and other clothes and sells them in her small shop. She advertises some of the outfits as Guest items, hoping that customers might mistakenly assume that they were made by Guess, the well-known clothing manufacturer.

(c) Ursula teaches Latin American history at a small university. She has a digital video recorder and frequently records television programs relating to Latin America and puts them on DVDs. She then takes the DVDs to her classroom so that her students can watch them.

• **For a sample answer to Question 14–2, go to Appendix F at the end of this text.**

14–3. Trademark Infringement Sync Computers, Inc., makes computer-related products under the brand name "Sync," which the company registers as a trademark. Without Sync's permission, E-Product Corp. embeds the Sync mark in E-Product's Web site, in black type on a blue background. This tag causes the E-Product site to be returned at the top of the list of results on a search engine query for "Sync." Does E-Product's use of the Sync mark as a meta tag without Sync's permission constitute trademark infringement? Explain.

14–4. Patent Infringement As a cattle rancher in Nebraska, Gerald Gohl used handheld searchlights to find and help calving animals (animals giving birth) in harsh blizzard conditions. Gohl thought that it would be more helpful to have a portable searchlight mounted on the outside of a vehicle and remotely controlled. He and Al Gebhardt developed and patented practical applications of this idea—the Golight and the wireless, remote-controlled Radio Ray, which could rotate 360 degrees—and formed Golight, Inc., to make and market these products. In 1997, Wal-Mart Stores, Inc., began selling a portable, wireless, remote-controlled searchlight that was identical to the Radio Ray except for a stop piece that prevented the light from rotating more than 351 degrees. Golight sent Wal-Mart a letter claiming that its device infringed Golight's patent. Wal-Mart sold its remaining inventory of the devices and stopped carrying the product. Golight filed a suit in a federal district court against Wal-Mart, alleging patent infringement. How should the court rule? Explain. [*Golight, Inc. v. Wal-Mart Stores, Inc.,* 355 F.3d 1327 (Fed.Cir. 2004)]

14–5. Trade Secrets Briefing.com offers Internet-based analyses of investment opportunities to investors. Richard Green is the company's president. One of Briefing.com's competitors is StreetAccount, LLC (limited liability

company), whose owners include Gregory Jones and Cynthia Dietzmann. Jones worked for Briefing.com for six years until he quit in March 2003 and was a member of its board of directors until April 2003. Dietzmann worked for Briefing.com for seven years until she quit in March 2003. As Briefing.com employees, Jones and Dietzmann had access to confidential business data. For instance, Dietzmann developed a list of contacts through which Briefing.com obtained market information to display online. When Dietzmann quit, she did not return all of the contact information to the company. Briefing.com and Green filed a suit in a federal district court against Jones, Dietzmann, and StreetAccount, alleging that they had appropriated these data and other "trade secrets" to form a competing business. What are trade secrets? Why are they protected? Under what circumstances is a party liable at common law for their appropriation? How should these principles apply in this case? [*Briefing.com v. Jones,* 2006 WY 16, 126 P.3d 928 (2006)]

14–6. CASE PROBLEM WITH SAMPLE ANSWER: Trademarks.

 In 1969, Jack Masquelier, a professor of pharmacology, discovered a chemical antioxidant made from the bark of a French pine tree. The substance supposedly assists in nutritional distribution and blood circulation. Horphag Research, Ltd., began to sell the product under the name Pycnogenol, which Horphag registered as a trademark in 1993. Pycnogenol became one of the fifteen best-selling herbal supplements in the United States. In 1999, through the Web site www.healthierlife.com, *Larry Garcia began to sell Masquelier's Original OPCs, a supplement derived from grape pits. Claiming that this product was the "true Pycnogenol," Garcia used the mark as a meta tag and a generic term, attributing the results of research on Horphag's product to Masquelier's and altering quotations from scientific literature to substitute the name of Masquelier's product for Horphag's. Customers who purchased Garcia's product contacted Horphag about it, only to learn that they had not bought Horphag's product. Others called Horphag to ask whether Garcia "was selling . . . real Pycnogenol." Horphag filed a suit in a federal district court against Garcia, alleging, among other things, that he was diluting Horphag's mark. What is trademark dilution? Did it occur here? Explain.* [*Horphag Research, Ltd. v. Garcia,* 475 F.3d 1029 (9th Cir. 2007)]

• **To view a sample answer for Problem 14–6, go to this book's Web site at** www.cengage.com/blaw/cross, **select "Chapter 14," and click on "Case Problem with Sample Answer."**

14–7. Copyright Redwin Wilchcombe is a musician and music producer. In 2002, Wilchcombe met Jonathan Smith, known as Lil Jon, a member of Lil Jon & The East Side Boyz (LJESB). Lil Jon and LJESB are under contract to give TeeVee Toons, Inc. (TVT), all rights to LJESB's recordings and Lil Jon's songs. Wilchcombe composed, performed, and recorded a song titled *Tha Weedman* at Lil Jon's request, based on his idea, and with his suggestions for LJESB's album *Kings of Crunk*. They did not discuss payment and Wilchcombe was not paid, but he was given credit on the album as a producer. By 2005, the album had sold 2 million copies. Wilchcombe filed a suit in a federal district court against TVT and the others, alleging copyright infringement. The defendants asserted that they had a license to use the song. Wilchcombe argued that he had never granted a license to anyone. Do these facts indicate that the defendants had a license to use Wilchcombe's song? If so, what does that mean for Wilchcombe's cause? Explain. [*Wilchcombe v. TeeVee Toons, Inc.*, 555 F.3d 949 (11th Cir. 2009)]

14–8. Trade Secrets Peggy Hamilton was a major shareholder in Carbon Processing and Reclamation (CPR), LLC. After a dispute, she sold her interest in the company and signed a confidentiality agreement not to divulge company business to anyone. A year later, when William Jones, the owner of CPR, left on a trip, he let an employee, Jesse Edwards, drive his company car. There were boxes containing some detailed company records in the car. Edwards and his wife, Channon, were in the middle of a divorce, and she suspected him of hiding financial information from her. When Channon saw the boxes in the car her husband was driving, she got a car key from Hamilton, who still had one from when she was an owner. Channon used the key to get into the boxes of company information. Jones then sued Hamilton for breach of the confidentiality agreement, contending that allowing Channon to have access to the files was assisting in the theft of trade secrets. The trial court dismissed the claim, but Jones appealed. Could Hamilton's actions be the basis for a claim of trade secret violation? What factors should be taken into consideration? [*Jones v. Hamilton*, ___ So.3d ___ (Ala.Civ.App. 2010)]

14–9. A QUESTION OF ETHICS: Copyright Infringement.

Custom Copies, Inc., in Gainesville, Florida, is a copy shop that, on request, reproduces and distributes, for profit, material published and owned by others. One of the copy shop's primary activities is the preparation and sale of coursepacks, which contain compilations of readings for college courses. For a particular coursepack, a teacher selects the readings and delivers a syllabus to the copy shop, which obtains the materials from a library, copies them, and then binds and sells the copies. Blackwell Publishing, Inc., in Malden, Massachusetts, publishes books and journals in medicine and other fields and owns the copyrights to these publications. Blackwell and others filed a suit in a federal district court against Custom Copies, alleging copyright infringement for its "routine and systematic reproduction of materials from plaintiffs' publications, without seeking permission," to compile coursepacks for classes at the University of Florida. The plaintiffs asked the court to issue an injunction and award them damages, as well the profit from the infringement. The defendant filed a motion to dismiss the complaint. [Blackwell Publishing, Inc. v. Custom Copies, Inc., ___ F.Supp.2d ___ (N.D.Fla. 2007)]

(a) Custom Copies argued, in part, that creating and selling did not "distribute" the coursepacks. Does a copy shop violate copyright law if it only copies materials for coursepacks? Does the copying fall under the "fair use" exception? Should the court grant the defendant's motion? Why or why not?

(b) What is the potential impact if copies of a book or journal are created and sold without the permission of, and the payment of royalties or a fee to, the copyright owner? Explain.

14–10. VIDEO QUESTION: Protecting Ideas.

Go to this text's Web site at **www.cengage.com/blaw/cross** and select "Chapter 14." Click on "Video Questions" and view the video titled *The Jerk.* Then answer the following questions.

(a) In the video, Navin (Steve Martin) creates a special handle for Mr. Fox's (Bill Macy's) glasses. Can Navin obtain a patent or a copyright protecting his invention? Explain your answer.

(b) Suppose that after Navin legally protects his idea, Fox steals it and decides to develop it for himself, without Navin's permission. Has Fox committed infringement? If so, what kind—trademark, patent, or copyright?

(c) Suppose that after Navin legally protects his idea, he realizes he doesn't have the funds to mass-produce the glasses' special handle. Navin therefore agrees to allow Fox to manufacture the product. Has Navin granted Fox a license? Explain.

(d) Assume that Navin is able to manufacture his invention. What might Navin do to ensure that his product is identifiable and can be distinguished from other products on the market?

LEGAL RESEARCH EXERCISES ON THE WEB

Go to this text's Web site at **www.cengage.com/blaw/cross**, select "Chapter 14," and click on "Practical Internet Exercises." There you will find the following Internet research exercises that you can perform to learn more about the topics covered in this chapter.

Practical Internet Exercise 14–1: **Legal Perspective**
Unwarranted Legal Threats

Practical Internet Exercise 14–2: **Management Perspective**
Protecting Intellectual Property across Borders

Practical Internet Exercise 14–3: **Technological Perspective**
File-Sharing

CHAPTER 15

Creditor-Debtor Relations and Bankruptcy

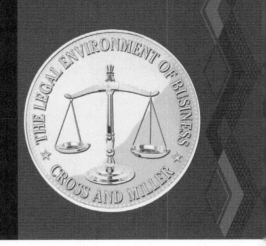

Normally, creditors have no problem collecting the debts owed to them. When disputes arise over the amount owed, however, or when the debtor simply cannot or will not pay, what happens? What remedies are available to creditors when a debtor defaults—that is, fails to pay as promised?

In this chapter, we first focus on some basic laws that assist the creditor and debtor in resolving their dispute without resorting to bankruptcy or mortgage foreclosure (see Chapter 16). We then examine the process of bankruptcy as a last resort in resolving creditor-debtor problems. We look at the different types

of relief available to debtors under federal bankruptcy law and discuss the basic bankruptcy procedures required for specific types of relief. Our discussion specifically includes changes that resulted from the Bankruptcy Reform Act of 2005.

SECTION 1
LAWS ASSISTING CREDITORS

Both the common law and statutory laws create various rights and remedies for creditors. We discuss some of these rights and remedies—including liens, garnishment, and creditors' composition agreements—next.

Liens

A **lien** is an encumbrance on (claim against) property to satisfy a debt or protect a claim for the payment of a debt. As mentioned, liens may arise under the common law (usually by possession of the property) or under statutory law. Statutory liens include *mechanic's liens,* whereas *artisan's liens* were recognized at common law. *Judicial liens* are those that represent a creditor's efforts to collect on a debt before or after a judgment is entered by a court.

Liens are a very important tool for creditors because they generally take priority over other claims against the same property. In fact, mechanic's and artisan's liens normally take priority over creditors who have a *perfected security interest* in the property. (A *security interest* is an interest in a debtor's personal property—called collateral—that a seller, lender, or other creditor takes to secure payment of a debt or performance of an obligation. A creditor who has *perfected* a security interest, as specified by Article 9 of the Uniform Commercial Code—by filing a financing statement, for example—usually prevails against other parties with an interest in the same property, except for certain lienholders.)

MECHANIC'S LIENS When a person contracts for labor, services, or materials to be furnished for the purpose of making improvements on real property but does not immediately pay for the improvements, the creditor can place a **mechanic's lien** on the property. This creates a special type of creditor-debtor relationship in which the real estate itself becomes security for the debt.

For example, a painter agrees to paint a house for a homeowner for an agreed-on price to cover labor and materials. If the homeowner refuses to pay or pays only a portion of the charges, a mechanic's lien against the property can be created. The painter is then a lienholder, and the real property is encumbered (burdened) with the mechanic's lien for the amount owed. If the homeowner does not pay the lien, the property can be sold to satisfy the debt. Notice of the *foreclosure* (the process by which the creditor deprives the debtor of his or her property—see Chapter 16) and sale must be given to the debtor in advance, however.

Note that state law governs the procedures that must be followed to create a mechanic's (or other statutory) lien. Generally, the lienholder must file a written notice of lien against the particular property involved. The notice of lien must be filed within a specific time period, measured from the last date on which materials or labor was provided (usually within 60 to 120 days). If the property owner fails to pay the debt, the lienholder is entitled to foreclose on the real estate on which the work or materials were provided and to sell it to satisfy the debt. The sale proceeds are used to pay the debt and the costs of the legal proceedings; the surplus, if any, is paid to the former owner.

ARTISAN'S LIENS An **artisan's lien** is a device created at common law through which a creditor can recover payment from a debtor for labor and materials furnished in the repair of personal property. In contrast to a mechanic's lien, an artisan's lien is *possessory*. This means that the lienholder ordinarily must have retained possession of the property and have expressly or impliedly agreed to provide the services on a cash, not a credit, basis. The lien remains in existence as long as the lienholder maintains possession, and the lien is terminated once possession is *voluntarily* surrendered—unless the surrender is only temporary. As mentioned, artisan's liens usually take priority over other creditors' claims to the same property.

CASE IN POINT Erie Power Technologies, Inc., hired Shaw Group to design and fabricate steam generators for Erie's power plant. Erie delivered the necessary materials for the development of the generators and made several payments to Shaw as the work progressed. Shaw completed the fabrication of the materials in its possession, but Erie made no further payments and filed for bankruptcy. Under the bankruptcy reorganization plan (which will be discussed later in this chapter), Erie was required to pay Shaw $320,000 for completing the generators. Erie then filed a lawsuit to recover that payment, claiming that those funds should have gone to other secured creditors who had priority over Shaw. The court held that Shaw had a common law artisan's lien on the goods that it possessed and had added value to them. Because the artisan's lien took priority over the claims of other secured creditors, the court granted a summary judgment in favor of Shaw.[1]

Modern statutes permit the holder of an artisan's lien to foreclose and sell the property subject to the lien to satisfy the debt. As with a mechanic's lien, the lienholder is required to give notice to the owner of the property prior to foreclosure and sale. The sale proceeds are used to pay the debt and the costs of the legal proceedings, and the surplus, if any, is paid to the former owner.

JUDICIAL LIENS When a debt is past due, a creditor can bring a legal action against the debtor to collect the debt. If the creditor is successful in the action, the court awards the creditor a judgment against the debtor (usually for the amount of the debt plus any interest and legal costs incurred in obtaining the judgment). Frequently, however, the creditor is unable to collect the awarded amount.

To ensure that a judgment in the creditor's favor will be collectible, the creditor is permitted to request that certain nonexempt property of the debtor be seized to satisfy the debt. (As will be discussed later in this chapter, some kinds of property are exempt from attachment by creditors.) A court's order to seize the debtor's property is known as a *writ of attachment* if it is issued prior to a judgment in the creditor's favor. If the order is issued after a judgment, it is referred to as a *writ of execution.*

Writ of Attachment. In the context of judicial liens, **attachment** refers to a court-ordered seizure and taking into custody of property prior to the securing of a judgment for a past-due debt. Normally, attachment is a *prejudgment* remedy, occurring either at the time a lawsuit is filed or immediately afterwards. To attach before a judgment, a creditor must comply with the specific state's statutory restrictions and requirements. The due process clause of the Fourteenth Amendment to the U.S. Constitution also applies and requires that the debtor be given notice and an opportunity to be heard (see Chapter 5).

The creditor must have an enforceable right to payment of the debt under law and must follow certain procedures. Otherwise, the creditor can be liable for damages for wrongful attachment. Typically, the creditor must file with the court an *affidavit* (a written statement, made under oath) stating that the debtor has failed to pay and indicating the statutory grounds under which attachment is sought. The creditor must also post a bond to cover at least the court costs, the value of the property attached, and the value of the loss of use of that property suffered by the debtor. When the court is satisfied that all the requirements have been met, it issues a **writ of attachment,** which directs the sheriff or other officer to seize nonexempt property. If the creditor

---

1. *In re Erie Power Technologies, Inc.,* 364 Bankr. 896 (W.D.Pa. 2007).

prevails at trial, the seized property can be sold to satisfy the judgment.

Writ of Execution. If a creditor obtains a judgment against the debtor and the debtor will not or cannot pay the judgment, the creditor is entitled to go back to the court and request a **writ of execution.** A writ of execution is an order that directs the sheriff to seize (levy) and sell any of the debtor's nonexempt real or personal property that is within the court's geographic jurisdiction (usually the county in which the courthouse is located).

The proceeds of the sale are used to pay the judgment, accrued interest, and costs of the sale. Any excess is paid to the debtor. The debtor can pay the judgment and redeem the nonexempt property at any time before the sale takes place. (Because of exemption laws and bankruptcy laws, however, many judgments are uncollectible.)

Garnishment

An order for **garnishment** permits a creditor to collect a debt by seizing property of the debtor that is held by a third party. In a garnishment proceeding, the third party—the person or entity on whom the garnishment judgment is served—is called the *garnishee.* Typically, the garnishee is the debtor's employer, and the creditor is seeking a judgment so that part of the debtor's usual paycheck will be paid to the creditor. In some situations, however, the garnishee is a third party that holds funds belonging to the debtor (such as a bank) or has possession of, or exercises control over, funds or other types of property owned by the debtor. A creditor can garnish almost all types of property, including tax refunds, pensions, and trust funds—so long as the property is not exempt from garnishment and is in the possession of a third party.

State law governs garnishment actions, so the specific procedures vary from state to state. According to the laws in many states, the judgment creditor needs to obtain only one order of garnishment, which will then apply continuously to the judgment debtor's weekly wages until the entire debt is paid. Garnishment can be a prejudgment remedy, requiring a hearing before a court, but it is most often a postjudgment remedy.

Both federal and state laws limit the amount that can be taken from a debtor's weekly take-home pay through garnishment proceedings.[2] Federal law provides a minimal framework to protect debtors

from losing all their income to pay judgment debts.[3] State laws also provide dollar exemptions, and these amounts are often larger than those provided by federal law. Under federal law, an employer cannot dismiss an employee because his or her wages are being garnished.

Creditors' Composition Agreements

Creditors may contract with the debtor for discharge of the debtor's liquidated debts (debts that are definite, or fixed, in amount) on payment of a sum less than that owed. These agreements are referred to as **creditors' composition agreements** (or *composition agreements*) and usually are held to be enforceable unless they are formed under duress.

Concept Summary 15.1 on the top of the following page provides a synopsis of the remedies available to creditors.

────▰▰▰ SECTION 2 ▰▰▰────
SURETYSHIP AND GUARANTY

When a third person promises to pay a debt owed by another in the event that the debtor does not pay, either a *suretyship* or a *guaranty* relationship is created. Exhibit 15–1 on the bottom of the next page illustrates these relationships. The third person's creditworthiness becomes the security for the debt owed. At common law, there were significant differences in the liability of a surety and that of a guarantor, as discussed in the following subsections. Today, however, the distinctions outlined here have been abolished in some states.

Suretyship

A contract of strict **suretyship** is a promise made by a third person to be responsible for the debtor's obligation. It is an express contract between the **surety** (the third party) and the creditor. In the strictest sense, the surety is primarily liable for the debt of the principal. This means that the creditor can demand payment from the surety from the moment the debt is due and that the creditor need not exhaust all legal remedies against the principal debtor before holding the surety responsible for payment.

---

2. A few states (for example, Texas) do not permit garnishment of wages by private parties except under a child-support order.

3. For example, the federal Consumer Credit Protection Act, 15 U.S.C. Sections 1601–1693r, provides that a debtor can retain either 75 percent of his or her disposable earnings per week or an amount equivalent to thirty hours of work paid at federal minimum wage rates, whichever is greater.

CONCEPT SUMMARY 15.1
Remedies Available to Creditors

Remedy	Description

Liens	1. *Mechanic's lien*—A lien placed on an owner's real estate for labor, services, or materials furnished for improvements made to the realty.
	2. *Artisan's lien*—A lien placed on an owner's personal property for labor performed or value added to that property.
	3. *Judicial liens*—
	  a. Writ of attachment—A court-ordered seizure of property prior to a court's final determination of the creditor's rights to the property. Creditors must strictly comply with applicable state statutes to obtain a writ of attachment.
	  b. Writ of execution—A court order directing the sheriff to seize (levy) and sell a debtor's nonexempt real or personal property to satisfy a court's judgment in the creditor's favor.

Garnishment	A collection remedy that allows the creditor to attach a debtor's funds (such as wages owed or bank accounts) and property that are held by a third person.
Creditors' Composition Agreement	A contract between a debtor and her or his creditors by which the debtor's debts are discharged by payment of a sum less than the amount that is actually owed.

For example, Roberto Delmar wants to borrow from the bank to buy a used car. Because Roberto is still in college, the bank will not lend him the funds unless his father, José Delmar, who has dealt with the bank before, will cosign the note (add his signature to the note, thereby becoming a surety and thus jointly liable for payment of the debt). When José Delmar cosigns the note, he becomes primarily liable to the bank. On the note's due date, the bank can seek payment from either Roberto or José Delmar, or both jointly.

Guaranty

With a suretyship arrangement, the surety is *primarily* liable for the debtor's obligation. With a guaranty

EXHIBIT 15–1 • Suretyship and Guaranty Parties
In a suretyship or guaranty arrangement, a third party promises to be responsible for a debtor's obligations. A third party who agrees to be responsible for the debt even if the primary debtor does not default is known as a surety. A third party who agrees to be *secondarily* responsible for the debt—that is, responsible only if the primary debtor defaults—is known as a guarantor.

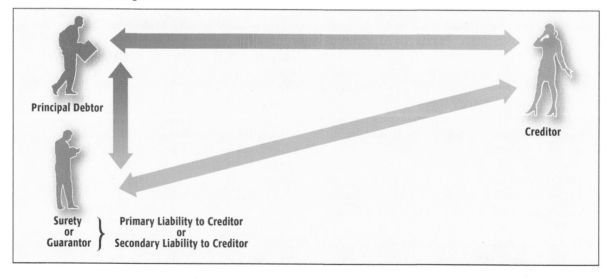

arrangement, the **guarantor**—the third person making the guaranty—is *secondarily* liable. The guarantor can be required to pay the obligation *only after the principal debtor defaults,* and usually only after the creditor has made an attempt to collect from the debtor. The guaranty contract terms determine the extent and time of the guarantor's liability.

For example, a corporation, BX Enterprises, needs to borrow to meet its payroll. The bank is skeptical about the creditworthiness of BX and requires Dawson, its president, who is a wealthy businessperson and owner of 70 percent of BX Enterprises, to sign an agreement making herself personally liable for payment if BX does not pay off the loan. As a guarantor of the loan, Dawson cannot be held liable until BX Enterprises is in default.

Under the Statute of Frauds, a guaranty contract between the guarantor and the creditor must be in writing (recorded) to be enforceable unless the *main purpose* exception applies.[4] At common law, a suretyship agreement did not need to be in writing to be enforceable, and oral surety agreements were sufficient. Today, however, some states require a writing (or electronic record) to enforce a suretyship.

In the following case, a guarantor claimed that she did not understand the full extent of her liability under a guaranty agreement at the time she signed it. Did her alleged ignorance of the terms of the agreement excuse her from liability for the debt after the primary debtor's default? That was the issue before the court.

---

4. Briefly, the main purpose exception provides that if the main purpose of the guaranty agreement is to benefit the guarantor, then the contract need not be in writing to be enforceable.

✳ EXTENDED CASE 15.1 ✳
Overseas Private Investment Corp. v. Kim

New York Supreme Court, Appellate Division, 69 A.D.3d 1185, 895 N.Y.S.2d 217 (2010).
www.courts.state.ny.us/decisions/index.shtml[a]

IN THE LANGUAGE OF THE COURT
KAVANAGH, J. [Justice]

* * * *

In February 2005, defendant Nam Koo Kim (hereinafter the husband), as sole owner of Majestic Group Korea, Ltd., entered into a loan agreement on behalf of the company with plaintiff [the Overseas Private Investment Corporation] to borrow $1,500,000 for the purposes of financing a "Ruby Tuesday's" restaurant in South Korea. The husband and his wife, defendant Hee Sun Kim (hereinafter the wife), issued personal guaranties for the loan. In October 2005, Majestic defaulted on the loan and a restructured loan and assumption agreement was executed by the parties and included a promissory note by the husband to pay plaintiff $1,517,000 in the event of a default. Once again, the wife agreed to personally guaranty the terms of the note and signed a written commitment to that effect. When the borrowers defaulted on the restructured loan, plaintiff, as was its right under the agreement, accelerated payments of the promissory note and commenced this action seeking recovery of the amount due under the note, together with interest and counsel fees. Plaintiff moved for summary judgment, and [the trial court granted the plaintiff's motion].

* * * *

* * * Defendants argue that a question of fact has been created as to the scope of the wife's guaranty and the Supreme Court [trial court] erred by granting plaintiff summary judgment. We do not agree.

A party is entitled to a judgment on a guaranty of a note if it proves that there has been a default on the payment of a promissory note and the party against whom judgment has been sought has executed a valid guaranty warranting the payment of the amount due under that note.

In her defense, the wife argues that when she signed the guaranty she was only provided with the last page of the agreement and claims to have been told that her liability under the guaranty was limited to the value of her real property interest in Virginia. However, she admits that she did not participate in the negotiations that led up to the issuance of the promissory note and that it was her husband who asked her to sign the guaranty agreement. While the husband echoes the wife's claim that she signed the guaranty agreement without seeing the entire document, he does not deny that, at the time, he was in possession of the entire agreement. In addition, he provides no confirmation of his wife's assertion that when she signed the guaranty agreement she was told that her legal obligation was limited to the value of her real estate interest in Virginia. In addition, the terms of the guaranty are clear on its face and specifically provide

---

a. In the left-hand column of the page, select "3rd Dept." under the heading "Appellate Decisions." When the next page opens, select "January 2010" from the drop-down menu in the upper-left corner, and then click on "Decisions" in the January 21 calendar box. Scroll down the list to the case title to access its opinion. The New York Supreme Court maintains this Web site.

EXTENDED CASE CONTINUES ➡

EXTENDED CASE 15.1 CONTINUED ⬇

that the wife has guaranteed full payment of the promissory note. In fact, immediately above the wife's signature is an acknowledgment to the effect that she "has received a copy of this Restructured Loan Deferral Letter, agrees to all terms and conditions hereof, and confirms that the Personal Guaranty is, and remains, in full force and effect." In

short, the wife's contention that it was her understanding that she was providing a limited commitment in regard to the payment of the promissory note is belied [contradicted] by what is clearly set forth in the document and, *"in the absence of fraud, duress or some other wrongful act by a party to a contract, a signer of an agreement is deemed to be conclusively bound by its terms whether or not he or she read it."* The wife—who by her

own admission had no contact with plaintiff in regard to this transaction—has presented no documentary evidence to support the conclusion that plaintiff used duress or fraud to procure her signature on this document. As such, she is bound by the terms of her guaranty. [Emphasis added.]

* * * *

ORDERED that the order is affirmed, with costs.

 QUESTIONS

1. If the guaranty agreement had not been in writing, would the agreement have been enforceable? Explain.
2. A guarantor can be required to pay a debt only after the principal debtor defaults. Which party was the principal debtor in this case?

Actions Releasing the Surety and the Guarantor

The actions that release the surety from an obligation are basically the same as those that discharge the guarantor. Making any material modification to the terms of the original contract—without the consent of the surety or guarantor—discharges the surety or guarantor's obligation. The extent to which the surety or guarantor is discharged depends on whether he or she was compensated, and to what extent he or she suffered a loss from the modification. For example, a father who receives no consideration in return for acting as a surety on his daughter's loan will be completely discharged if the loan contract is modified without his consent.

In addition, if a creditor surrenders the collateral to the debtor or impairs the collateral without the consent of the surety or guarantor, these acts can reduce the obligation of the surety or guarantor. Naturally, any payment of the principal obligation by the debtor or by another person on the debtor's behalf discharges the surety or guarantor from the obligation. Even if the creditor refused to accept payment of the principal debt when it was tendered, the obligation of the surety or guarantor can be discharged (if the creditor knew about the suretyship or guaranty).

Defenses of the Surety and the Guarantor

Generally, the surety or guarantor can also assert any of the defenses available to the principal debtor to avoid liability on the obligation to the creditor. A few exceptions do exist, however. The surety or guarantor cannot assert the principal debtor's incapacity

or bankruptcy as a defense, nor can the surety assert the statute of limitations as a defense.

Obviously, a surety or guarantor may also have his or her own defenses—for example, incapacity or bankruptcy. If the creditor fraudulently induced the person to act as a surety or guarantor on the debt, the surety or guarantor can assert fraud as a defense. In most states, the creditor has a legal duty to inform the surety, before the formation of the suretyship contract, of material facts known by the creditor that would substantially increase the surety's risk. Failure to so inform may constitute fraud and renders the suretyship obligation voidable.

Rights of the Surety and the Guarantor

When the surety or guarantor pays the debt owed to the creditor, he or she acquires certain rights, as discussed next.

THE RIGHT OF SUBROGATION The surety or guarantor has the legal **right of subrogation.** Simply stated, this means that any right that the creditor had against the debtor now becomes the right of the surety or guarantor. Included are creditor rights in bankruptcy, rights to collateral possessed by the creditor, and rights to judgments obtained by the creditor. In short, the surety or guarantor now stands in the shoes of the creditor and may pursue any remedies that were available to the creditor against the debtor.

CASE IN POINT Guerrero Brothers, Inc. (GBI), contracted with the Public School System (PSS) to build a high school. Century Insurance Company (CIC) agreed to provide GBI with the required payment and performance bonds on the project. Thus, CIC acted as a surety of GBI's performance and promised to finish the project if GBI defaulted. Four years after construction began, PSS terminated GBI's contract for default, and CIC fulfilled GBI's obligations by finishing construction of the school. Numerous disputes arose, and litigation ensued. Ultimately, PSS agreed to pay GBI $500,000 in contract funds. CIC then filed an action against GBI and PSS to recover the $867,867.16 it claimed PSS owed it for finishing the school. The court found that CIC, as a performing surety, was entitled to the remaining contract funds through the right of subrogation. It had performed GBI's obligations and therefore stepped into GBI's shoes and had the right to obtain payment from PSS.[5]

THE RIGHT OF REIMBURSEMENT The surety or guarantor has a **right of reimbursement** from the debtor. Basically, the surety or guarantor is entitled to receive from the debtor all outlays made on behalf of the arrangement. Such outlays can include expenses incurred as well as the actual amount of the debt paid to the creditor.

THE RIGHT OF CONTRIBUTION Two or more sureties are called **co-sureties.** When a co-surety pays more than her or his proportionate share on a debtor's default, she or he is entitled to recover from the other co-sureties the amount paid above that surety's obligation. This is the **right of contribution.** Generally, a co-surety's liability either is determined by agreement or, in the absence of agreement, is set at the maximum liability under the suretyship contract.

For example, assume that two co-sureties are obligated under a suretyship contract to guarantee the debt of a debtor. Together, the sureties' maximum liability is $25,000. Surety A's maximum liability is $15,000, and Surety B's is $10,000. The debtor owes $10,000 and is in default. Surety A pays the creditor the entire $10,000. In the absence of agreement, Surety A can recover $4,000 from Surety B ($10,000/$25,000 × $10,000 = $4,000, Surety B's obligation).

———— **SECTION 3** ————
PROTECTION FOR DEBTORS

The law protects debtors as well as creditors. Certain property of the debtor, for example, is exempt under state law from creditors' actions. Consumer

protection statutes (see Chapter 24) also protect debtors' rights. Of course, bankruptcy laws, which will be discussed shortly, are designed specifically to assist debtors in need of help.

In most states, certain types of real and personal property are exempt from execution or attachment. State exemption statutes usually include both real and personal property.

Exempted Real Property

Probably the most familiar exemption for real property is the **homestead exemption.** Each state permits the debtor to retain the family home, either in its entirety or up to a specified dollar amount, free from the claims of unsecured creditors or trustees in bankruptcy. (Note that federal bankruptcy law now places a cap on the amount that debtors filing bankruptcy can claim is exempt under their state's homestead exemption. [See page 345]).

For example, Beere owes Veltman $40,000. The debt is the subject of a lawsuit, and the court awards Veltman a judgment of $40,000 against Beere. Beere's homestead is valued at $50,000, and the homestead exemption is $25,000. There are no outstanding mortgages or other liens on his homestead. To satisfy the judgment debt, Beere's family home is sold at public auction for $45,000. The proceeds of the sale are distributed as follows:

1. Beere is given $25,000 as his homestead exemption.
2. Veltman is paid $20,000 toward the judgment debt, leaving a $20,000 deficiency judgment (that is, "leftover debt") that can be satisfied from any other nonexempt property (personal or real) that Beere may own, if permitted by state law.

In a few states, statutes allow the homestead exemption only if the judgment debtor has a family. If a judgment debtor does not have a family, a creditor may be entitled to collect the full amount realized from the sale of the debtor's home. In addition, note that the homestead exemption interacts with other areas of law and can sometimes operate to cancel out a portion of a lien on a debtor's real property.

CASE IN POINT Antonio Stanley purchased a modular home from Yates Mobile Services Corporation. When Stanley failed to pay the purchase price of the home, Yates obtained a judicial lien against Stanley's property in the amount of $165,138.05. Stanley then filed for bankruptcy and asserted the homestead exemption. The court found that Stanley was entitled to avoid the lien to the extent that it impaired

---

5. *Century Insurance Co. v. Guerrero Brothers, Inc.*, 2010 WL 997112 (N.Mariana Islands 2010).

his exemption. Using a bankruptcy law formula, the court determined that the total impairment was $143,639.05 and that Stanley could avoid paying this amount to Yates. Thus, Yates was left with a judicial lien on Stanley's home in the amount of $21,499.[6]

Exempted Personal Property

Personal property that is most often exempt from satisfaction of judgment debts includes the following:

1. Household furniture up to a specified dollar amount.
2. Clothing and certain personal possessions, such as family pictures or a Bible.
3. A vehicle (or vehicles) for transportation (at least up to a specified dollar amount).
4. Certain classified animals, usually livestock but including pets.
5. Equipment that the debtor uses in a business or trade, such as tools or professional instruments, up to a specified dollar amount.

SECTION 4
BANKRUPTCY LAW

Bankruptcy law in the United States has two goals—to protect a debtor by giving him or her a fresh start, free from creditors' claims, and to provide a fair means of distributing a debtor's assets to creditors. Bankruptcy law is federal law, but state laws on secured transactions, liens, judgments, and exemptions also play a role in federal bankruptcy proceedings.

Bankruptcy law (called the Bankruptcy Code, or simply, the Code) prior to 2005 was based on the Bankruptcy Reform Act of 1978, as amended. In 2005, Congress enacted bankruptcy reform legislation that significantly overhauled certain provisions of the Bankruptcy Code for the first time in twenty-five years.[7] One of the major goals of this legislation was to require more consumers to pay as many of their debts as they possibly could, instead of having those debts fully extinguished in bankruptcy.

Bankruptcy Courts

Bankruptcy proceedings are held in federal bankruptcy courts, which are under the authority of U.S. district courts, and rulings by bankruptcy courts can be appealed to the district courts. A bankruptcy court

holds proceedings that are required to administer the estate of the debtor in bankruptcy. (The *estate* consists of the debtor's assets, as will be discussed shortly.) A bankruptcy court can conduct a jury trial if the appropriate district court has authorized it and if the parties to the bankruptcy consent to a jury trial.

Types of Bankruptcy Relief

The Bankruptcy Code is contained in Title 11 of the *United States Code* (U.S.C.) and has eight "chapters." Chapters 1, 3, and 5 of the Code include general definitional provisions, as well as provisions governing case administration, creditors, the debtor, and the estate. These three chapters of the Code normally apply to all types of bankruptcies.

Four chapters of the Code set forth the most important types of relief that debtors can seek.

1. Chapter 7 provides for **liquidation proceedings** (the selling of all nonexempt assets and the distribution of the proceeds to the debtor's creditors).
2. Chapter 11 governs reorganizations.
3. Chapter 12 (for family farmers and family fishermen) and Chapter 13 (for individuals) provide for adjustment of the debts of parties with regular incomes.[8]

Note that a debtor (except for a municipality) need not be insolvent[9] to file for bankruptcy relief under the Code. Anyone obligated to a creditor can declare bankruptcy.

Special Requirements for Consumer-Debtors

A **consumer-debtor** is a debtor whose debts result primarily from the purchase of goods for personal, family, or household use. To ensure that a consumer-debtor is aware of the types of relief available, the Code requires that the clerk of the court give all consumer-debtors written notice of the general purpose, benefits, and costs of each chapter under which they might proceed. In addition, the clerk must provide consumer-debtors with information on the types of services available from credit counseling agencies.

---

6. *In re Stanley,* __ Bankr. __, 2010 WL 2103441 (M.D.N.C. 2010).
7. The full title of the act is the Bankruptcy Abuse Prevention and Consumer Protection Act of 2005, Pub. L. No. 109-8, 119 Stat. 23 (April 20, 2005).

8. There are no Chapters 2, 4, 6, 8, or 10 in Title 11. Such "gaps" are not uncommon in the *United States Code.* They occur because, when a statute is enacted, chapter numbers (or other subdivisional unit numbers) are sometimes reserved for future use. A gap may also appear if a law has been repealed.
9. The inability to pay debts as they come due is known as *equitable* insolvency. A *balance-sheet* insolvency, which exists when a debtor's liabilities exceed assets, is not used as the test for filing for relief. Thus, it is possible for debtors to petition voluntarily for bankruptcy even though their assets far exceed their liabilities. This situation may occur when a debtor's cash-flow problems become severe.

In practice, most of these steps are handled by an attorney, not by court clerks.

SECTION 5
LIQUIDATION PROCEEDINGS

Liquidation under Chapter 7 of the Bankruptcy Code is probably the most familiar type of bankruptcy proceeding and is often referred to as an *ordinary,* or *straight, bankruptcy*. Put simply, a debtor in a liquidation bankruptcy turns all assets over to a **bankruptcy trustee,** a person appointed by the court to manage the debtor's funds. The trustee sells the nonexempt assets and distributes the proceeds to creditors. With certain exceptions, the remaining debts are then **discharged** (extinguished), and the debtor is relieved of the obligation to pay the debts.

Any "person"—defined as including individuals, partnerships, and corporations[10]—may be a debtor in a liquidation proceeding. A husband and wife may file jointly for bankruptcy under a single petition. Insurance companies, banks, savings and loan associations, investment companies licensed by the Small Business Administration, and credit unions *cannot* be debtors in a liquidation bankruptcy, however. Other chapters of the Code or other federal or state statutes apply to them.

A straight bankruptcy can be commenced by the filing of either a voluntary or an involuntary **petition in bankruptcy**—the document that is filed with a bankruptcy court to initiate bankruptcy proceedings. If a debtor files the petition, the bankruptcy is voluntary. If one or more creditors file a petition to force the debtor into bankruptcy, the bankruptcy is involuntary. We discuss both voluntary and involuntary bankruptcy proceedings under Chapter 7 in the following subsections.

Voluntary Bankruptcy

To bring a voluntary petition in bankruptcy, the debtor files official forms designated for that purpose in the bankruptcy court. Current bankruptcy law specifies that before debtors can file a petition, they must receive credit counseling from an approved nonprofit agency within the 180-day period preceding the date of filing. Debtors filing a Chapter 7 petition must include a certificate proving that they have received individual or group counseling from an approved agency within the last 180 days (roughly six months).

A consumer-debtor who is filing for liquidation bankruptcy must confirm the accuracy of the petition's contents. The debtor must also state in the petition, at the time of filing, that he or she understands the relief available under other chapters of the Code and has chosen to proceed under Chapter 7. Attorneys representing the consumer-debtors must file an affidavit stating that they have informed the debtors of the relief available under each chapter of the Code. In addition, the attorneys must reasonably attempt to verify the accuracy of the consumer-debtors' petitions and schedules (described below). Failure to do so is considered perjury.

CHAPTER 7 SCHEDULES The voluntary petition must contain the following schedules:

1. A list of both secured and unsecured creditors, their addresses, and the amount of debt owed to each.
2. A statement of the financial affairs of the debtor.
3. A list of all property owned by the debtor, including property that the debtor claims is exempt.
4. A list of current income and expenses.
5. A certificate of credit counseling (as discussed previously).
6. Proof of payments received from employers within sixty days prior to the filing of the petition.
7. A statement of the amount of monthly income, itemized to show how the amount is calculated.
8. A copy of the debtor's federal income tax return for the most recent year ending immediately before the filing of the petition.

The official forms must be completed accurately, sworn to under oath, and signed by the debtor. To conceal assets or knowingly supply false information on these schedules is a crime under the bankruptcy laws.

With the exception of tax returns, failure to file the required schedules within forty-five days after the filing of the petition (unless an extension of up to forty-five days is granted) will result in an automatic dismissal of the petition. The debtor has up to seven days before the date of the first creditors' meeting to provide a copy of the most recent tax returns to the trustee.

TAX RETURNS DURING BANKRUPTCY In addition, a debtor may be required to file a tax return at the end of each tax year while the case is pending and to provide a copy to the court. This may be done at the request of the court or of the **U.S. trustee**—a government official who performs administrative tasks that a bankruptcy judge would otherwise have to perform, including supervising the work of the bankruptcy trustee. Any *party in interest* (a party,

---

10. The definition of *corporation* includes unincorporated companies and associations. It also covers labor unions.

such as a creditor, who has a valid interest in the outcome of the proceedings) may make this request as well. Debtors may also be required to file tax returns during Chapter 11 and 13 bankruptcies.

SUBSTANTIAL ABUSE AND THE MEANS TEST In the past, a bankruptcy court could dismiss a Chapter 7 petition for relief (discharge of debts) if the use of Chapter 7 would constitute a "substantial abuse" of bankruptcy law. Today, the law provides a *means test* to determine a debtor's eligibility for Chapter 7. The purpose of the test is to keep upper-income people from abusing the bankruptcy process by filing for Chapter 7, as was thought to have happened in the past. The test forces more people to file for Chapter 13 bankruptcy rather than have their debts discharged under Chapter 7. Exhibit 15–2 below outlines the essential features of the means test, but there are exceptions that apply in a small number of cases.

The Basic Formula. A debtor wishing to file for bankruptcy must complete the means test to determine whether she or he qualifies for Chapter 7. The debtor's average monthly income in recent months is compared with the median income in the geographic area in which the person lives. (The U.S. Trustee Program provides these data at its Web site.) If the debtor's income is below the median income, the debtor usually is allowed to file for Chapter 7

bankruptcy, as there is no presumption of bankruptcy abuse.

Applying the Means Test to Future Disposable Income. If the debtor's income is above the median income, then further calculations must be made to determine whether the person will have sufficient disposable income in the future to repay at least some of his or her unsecured debts. *Disposable income* is calculated by subtracting living expenses and secured debt payments, such as mortgage payments, from monthly income. In making this calculation, the debtor's recent monthly income is presumed to continue for the next sixty months. Living expenses are the amounts allowed under formulas used by the Internal Revenue Service (IRS). The IRS allowances include modest allocations for food, clothing, housing, utilities, transportation (including a car payment), health care, and other necessities. (The U.S. Trustee Program's Web site also provides these amounts.) The allowances do not include expenditures for items such as cell phones and cable television service.

Once future disposable income has been estimated, that amount is used to determine whether the debtor will have income that could be applied to unsecured debts. To a large extent, this process follows the prior law on substantial abuse. The court may also consider the debtor's bad faith or other circumstances indicating abuse.

EXHIBIT 15–2 • The Means Test to Determine Chapter 7 Eligibility

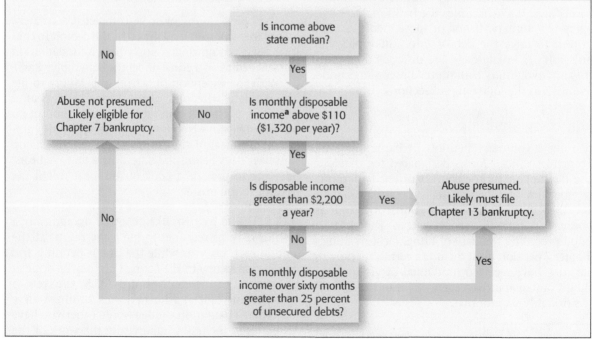

a. Income minus living expenses and secured debt payments equals *disposable income.*

ADDITIONAL GROUNDS FOR DISMISSAL As noted, a debtor's voluntary petition for Chapter 7 relief may be dismissed for substantial abuse or for failing to provide the necessary documents (such as schedules and tax returns) within the specified time. In addition, a motion to dismiss a Chapter 7 filing might be granted in two other situations. First, if the debtor has been convicted of a violent crime or a drug-trafficking offense, the victim can file a motion to dismiss the voluntary petition. Second, if the debtor fails to pay post-petition domestic-support obligations (which include child and spousal support), the court may dismiss the debtor's petition.

ORDER FOR RELIEF If the voluntary petition for bankruptcy is found to be proper, the filing of the petition will itself constitute an **order for relief.** (An order for relief is a court's grant of assistance to a petitioner.) Once a consumer-debtor's voluntary petition has been filed, the trustee and creditors must be given notice of the order for relief by mail not more than twenty days after entry of the order.

Involuntary Bankruptcy

An involuntary bankruptcy occurs when the debtor's creditors force the debtor into bankruptcy proceedings.[11] For an involuntary action to be filed, the following requirements must be met: If the debtor has twelve or more creditors, three or more of these creditors having unsecured claims totaling at least $14,425 must join in the petition. If a debtor has fewer than twelve creditors, one or more creditors having a claim totaling $14,425 or more may file.[12]

If the debtor challenges the involuntary petition, a hearing will be held, and the bankruptcy court will enter an order for relief if it finds either of the following:

---

11. An involuntary case cannot be filed against a charitable institution or a farmer (an individual or business that receives more than 50 percent of gross income from farming operations).
12. 11 U.S.C. Section 303. The amounts stated are in accordance with those computed on April 1, 2010.

1. The debtor is not paying debts as they come due.
2. A general receiver, assignee, or custodian took possession of, or was appointed to take charge of, substantially all of the debtor's property within 120 days before the filing of the petition.

If the court grants an order for relief, the debtor will be required to supply the same information in the bankruptcy schedules as in a voluntary bankruptcy.

An involuntary petition should not be used as an everyday debt-collection device, and the Code provides penalties for the filing of frivolous petitions against debtors. Petitioning creditors may be required to pay the costs and attorneys' fees incurred by the debtor in defending against the petition. If the petition was filed in bad faith, damages can be awarded for injury to the debtor's reputation.

Automatic Stay

The moment a petition, either voluntary or involuntary, is filed, an **automatic stay,** or suspension, of almost all actions by creditors against the debtor or the debtor's property normally goes into effect. In other words, once a petition has been filed, creditors cannot contact the debtor by phone or mail or start any legal proceedings to recover debts or to repossess property. (In some circumstances, a secured creditor or other party in interest may petition the bankruptcy court for relief from the automatic stay, as will be discussed shortly.)

The Code provides that if a creditor *knowingly* violates the automatic stay (a willful violation), any injured party, including the debtor, is entitled to recover actual damages, costs, and attorneys' fees, and may be awarded punitive damages as well. Until the bankruptcy proceeding is closed or dismissed, the automatic stay prohibits a creditor from taking any act to collect, assess, or recover a claim against the debtor that arose before the filing of the petition.

Did a university's refusal to provide a transcript unless a debt was paid constitute an act in violation of the automatic stay? That was the issue in the following case.

CASE 15.2
In re Kuehn

United States Court of Appeals, Seventh Circuit, 563 F.3d 289 (2009).
www.ca7.uscourts.gov[a]

BACKGROUND AND FACTS • Stefanie Kuehn, an art teacher, obtained a master's degree at Cardinal Stritch University in Wisconsin. But when Kuehn asked for a transcript—which was required to

---

a. In the left-hand column, click on "Opinions." On that page, in the "Case Number:" boxes, type "07" and "3954" and click on "List Case(s)." In the result, click on the appropriate link to access the opinion.

CASE CONTINUES ▶

CASE 15.2 CONTINUED ➡ receive an increase in salary from her school district—the university refused because she owed more than $6,000 in tuition. Kuehn offered to pay the nominal transcript fee but not the tuition. She then filed a petition in a federal bankruptcy court, listing the university as her only creditor. While the case was pending, she again asked for a transcript. The university once more refused unless she paid the tuition. Kuehn complained to the court, which ordered the university to provide a transcript. A federal district court affirmed the order. The university appealed.

IN THE LANGUAGE OF THE COURT
EASTERBROOK, Chief Judge.
* * * *

* * * *[If] providing a transcript is an implicit part of the educational contract, covered by the fee for the course hours, [then] Kuehn * * * has a contract or property right for which she has already paid.* (Well, she hasn't paid, but her obligation to do so has been [stayed by the bankruptcy petition] so it comes to the same thing.) The University cannot charge Kuehn extra if the fee for instruction covers transcripts, too. Then the University's refusal to certify a transcript of Kuehn's grades would be an act to collect the discharged debt and would violate * * * the automatic stay. [Emphasis added.]

Well, then, does Kuehn have a property interest because a certified transcript is part of the package of goods and services that a college offers in exchange for tuition? Property interests are created and defined by state law unless a federal law requires a different result. Nothing in the Bankruptcy Code creates or alters property rights in grades or the right to receive a transcript. Other federal law addresses privacy concerns but not property interests. What remain are state statutes and common law.

* * * *

Wisconsin courts have not considered whether a student has a contract or property right to receive a transcript. No Wisconsin statute is on point. *Under Wisconsin common law, property rights may arise from custom and usage. Universities have consistently provided transcripts at or around cost.* A transcript currently sets students back $4 at Cardinal Stritch University, $3 at Harvard University, and nothing at the University of Chicago if delivered electronically (otherwise $12). Fees at other universities are similar. We could not find any case in any court where a university had asserted that it could charge a student more than cost for a transcript, and, as far as we can tell, no university has ever tried to profit by charging a fee based on the transcript's effect on a student's future income. [Emphasis added.]

* * * *

Kuehn's property right might be limited to her grades, * * * and not include a right to receive a transcript from the University certifying those grades. But the custom of universities has been to provide certified transcripts, and for good reason. Intangible grades are worthless without proof. Kuehn's school district increases compensation only after it receives a certified transcript. Other employers have similar policies. * * * A right to receive a certified copy of a transcript is essential to a meaningful property right in grades.

* * * *

* * * We conclude that Kuehn has a state-law right to receive a certified copy of her transcript. The University's refusal to honor that right until Kuehn paid her back tuition was an act to collect a debt and thereby violated the automatic stay.

DECISION AND REMEDY • *The U.S. Court of Appeals for the Seventh Circuit affirmed the lower court's order. Kuehn had a right to a copy of her transcript, and the university's refusal to honor that right until she paid her tuition was an act to collect a debt in violation of the automatic stay.*

WHAT IF THE FACTS WERE DIFFERENT? • *Suppose that instead of offering to pay for a transcript, Kuehn had tried to obtain one on credit. Would the university's refusal to provide one on that basis have led to the same result? Why or why not?*

THE ETHICAL DIMENSION • *Some might say that higher education institutions should be able to use all methods possible to collect unpaid tuition, including withholding certified grade transcripts. What ethical issues would this approach raise?*

THE ADEQUATE PROTECTION DOCTRINE Underlying the Code's automatic-stay provision for a secured creditor is a concept known as *adequate protection*. The **adequate protection doctrine,** among other things, protects secured creditors from losing their security as a result of the automatic stay. The bankruptcy court can provide adequate protection by requiring the debtor or trustee to make periodic cash payments or a one-time cash payment (or to provide additional collateral or replacement liens) to the extent that the stay may actually cause the value of the property to decrease.

EXCEPTIONS TO THE AUTOMATIC STAY The Code provides several exceptions to the automatic stay. Collection efforts can continue for domestic-support obligations, which include any debt owed to or recoverable by a spouse, a former spouse, a child of the debtor, that child's parent or guardian, or a governmental unit. In addition, proceedings against the debtor related to divorce, child custody or visitation, domestic violence, and support enforcement are not stayed. Also excepted are investigations by a securities regulatory agency (see Chapter 29) and certain statutory liens for property taxes.

LIMITATIONS ON THE AUTOMATIC STAY A secured creditor or other party in interest can petition the bankruptcy court for relief from the automatic stay. If a creditor or other party requests relief from the stay, the stay will automatically terminate sixty days after the request, unless the court grants an extension or the parties agree otherwise. Also, the automatic stay on secured debts, such as a financed automobile, will terminate thirty days after the petition is filed if the debtor filed a bankruptcy petition that was dismissed within the prior year. Any party in interest can request that the court extend the stay by showing that the filing is in good faith.

If the debtor had two or more bankruptcy petitions dismissed during the prior year, the Code presumes bad faith, and the automatic stay does *not* go into effect until the court determines that the petition was filed in good faith. In addition, the automatic stay on secured property terminates forty-five days after the creditors' meeting (to be discussed shortly) unless the debtor redeems or reaffirms certain debts (*reaffirmation* will be discussed later in this chapter). In other words, the debtor cannot keep the secured property, even if she or he continues to make payments on it, without reinstating the rights of the secured party to collect on the debt.

Bankruptcy Estate

On the commencement of a liquidation proceeding under Chapter 7, a *bankruptcy estate* (sometimes called an *estate in property*) is created. This task is performed by the bankruptcy trustee, as described next. The estate consists of all the debtor's interests in property currently held, wherever located. It also includes *community property*—that is, property jointly owned by a husband and wife in certain states—property transferred in a transaction voidable by the trustee, proceeds and profits from the property of the estate, and certain after-acquired property. Interests in certain property—such as gifts, inheritances, property settlements (from a divorce), and life insurance death proceeds—to which the debtor becomes entitled *within 180 days after filing* may also become part of the estate. Withholdings for employee benefit plan contributions are excluded from the estate.

Generally, though, the filing of a bankruptcy petition fixes a dividing line: property acquired prior to the filing of the petition becomes property of the estate, and property acquired after the filing of the petition (except as just noted) remains the debtor's.

The Bankruptcy Trustee

Promptly after the order for relief in the liquidation proceeding has been entered, a trustee is appointed. The basic duty of the trustee is to collect and reduce to cash the property in the bankruptcy estate that is not exempt. (Exemptions will be discussed later in the chapter.) The trustee is held accountable for administering the debtor's estate to preserve the interests of both the debtor and unsecured creditors. To enable the trustee to accomplish this duty, the Code gives the trustee certain powers, stated in both general and specific terms. These powers must be exercised within two years of the order for relief.

DUTIES FOR MEANS TESTING The trustee is required to promptly review all materials filed by the debtor to determine if there is substantial abuse. Within ten days after the first meeting of the creditors (held soon after the order for relief is granted, as discussed later), the trustee must file a statement indicating whether the case is presumed to be an abuse under the means test. When there is a presumption of abuse, the trustee must either file a motion to dismiss the petition (or convert it to a Chapter 13 case) or file a statement setting forth the reasons why a motion would not be appropriate.

THE TRUSTEE'S POWERS The trustee has the power to require persons holding the debtor's property at the time the petition is filed to deliver the property to the trustee.[13] To enable the trustee to implement this power, the Code provides that the trustee has rights *equivalent* to those of certain other parties, such as a creditor who has a judicial lien. This power of a trustee, which is equivalent to that of a lien creditor, is known as *strong-arm power*.

In addition, the trustee has specific *powers of avoidance*—that is, the trustee can set aside (avoid) a sale or other transfer of the debtor's property, taking it back as a part of the debtor's estate. These powers include voidable rights available to the debtor, preferences, and fraudulent transfers by the debtor. Each is discussed in more detail below. In addition, a trustee can avoid certain statutory liens (creditors' claims against the debtor's property).

The debtor shares most of the trustee's avoidance powers. Thus, if the trustee does not take action to enforce one of the rights just mentioned, the debtor in a liquidation bankruptcy can enforce that right.

VOIDABLE RIGHTS A trustee steps into the shoes of the debtor. Thus, any reason that a debtor can use to obtain the return of her or his property can be used by the trustee as well. These grounds include fraud, duress, incapacity, and mutual mistake.

For example, Ben sells his boat to Tara. Tara gives Ben a check, knowing that she has insufficient funds in her bank account to cover the check. Tara has committed fraud. Ben has the right to avoid that transfer and recover the boat from Tara. If Ben files for bankruptcy relief under Chapter 7, the trustee can exercise the same right to recover the boat from Tara, and the boat becomes a part of the debtor's estate.

PREFERENCES A debtor is not permitted to transfer property or to make a payment that favors—or gives a **preference** to—one creditor over others. The trustee is allowed to recover payments made both voluntarily and involuntarily to one creditor in preference over another.

To have made a preferential payment that can be recovered, an *insolvent* debtor must have transferred property, for a *preexisting* debt, within *ninety days* prior to the filing of the bankruptcy petition. The transfer must have given the creditor more than the creditor would have received as a result of the bankruptcy proceedings. The Code presumes that a debtor is insolvent during the ninety-day period before filing a petition.

If a **preferred creditor** (one who has received a preferential transfer from the debtor) has sold the property to an innocent third party, the trustee cannot recover the property from the innocent party. The trustee generally can force the preferred creditor to pay the value of the property, however.

Preferences to Insiders. Sometimes, the creditor receiving the preference is an **insider**—an individual, a partner, a partnership, a corporation, or an officer or a director of a corporation (or a relative of one of these) who has a close relationship with the debtor. In this situation, the avoidance power of the trustee is extended to transfers made within *one year* before filing. (If the transfer was fraudulent, as will be discussed shortly, the trustee can avoid transfers made within *two years* before filing.) Note, however, that if the transfer occurred before the ninety-day period, the trustee is required to prove that the debtor was insolvent at the time it occurred or that the transfer was made to or for the benefit of an insider.

What Constitutes a Preference? Not all transfers are preferences. To be a preference, the transfer must be made for something other than current consideration. Most courts generally assume that payment for services rendered *within fifteen days* before the payment is not a preference. If a creditor receives payment in the ordinary course of business from an individual or business debtor, such as payment of last month's cell phone bill, the bankruptcy trustee cannot recover the payment.

To be recoverable, a preference must be a transfer for an antecedent (preexisting) debt, such as a year-old landscaping bill. In addition, the Code permits a consumer-debtor to transfer any property to a creditor up to a total value of $5,850 without the transfer's constituting a preference. Payment of domestic-support debts does not constitute a preference.

FRAUDULENT TRANSFERS The trustee may avoid fraudulent transfers or obligations if they (1) were made within two years of the filing of the petition, or (2) were made with actual intent to hinder, delay, or defraud a creditor. For example, a debtor who is thinking about petitioning for bankruptcy sells her gold jewelry, worth $10,000, to a friend for $500. The friend agrees that in the future he will "sell" the collection back to the debtor for the same amount. This is a fraudulent transfer that the trustee can undo.

---

13. Usually, though, the trustee takes constructive, rather than actual, possession of the debtor's property. For example, to obtain control of a debtor's business inventory, a trustee might change the locks on the doors to the business and hire a security guard.

Transfers made for less than reasonably equivalent consideration are also vulnerable if the debtor thereby became insolvent or was left engaged in business with an unreasonably small amount of capital. When a fraudulent transfer is made outside the Code's two-year limit, creditors may seek alternative relief under state laws. Some state laws may allow creditors to recover for transfers made up to three years before the filing of a petition. Courts have even held that severance payments—that is, compensation paid to an employee who is fired—can constitute a fraudulent transfer under the Code.[14]

Exemptions

As just described, the trustee takes control over the debtor's property in a Chapter 7 bankruptcy, but an individual debtor is entitled to exempt (exclude) certain property from the bankruptcy. The Bankruptcy Code exempts the following property:[15]

1. Up to $21,625 in equity in the debtor's residence and burial plot (the homestead exemption).
2. Interest in a motor vehicle up to $3,450.
3. Interest, up to $550 for a particular item, in household goods and furnishings, wearing apparel, appliances, books, animals, crops, and musical instruments (the aggregate total of all items is limited to $11,525).
4. Interest in jewelry up to $1,450.
5. Interest in any other property up to $1,150, plus any unused part of the $21,625 homestead exemption up to $10,825.
6. Interest in any tools of the debtor's trade up to $2,175.
7. A life insurance contract owned by the debtor (other than a credit life insurance contract).
8. Certain interests in accrued dividends and interest under, or loan value of, life insurance contracts owned by the debtor, not to exceed $11,525.
9. Professionally prescribed health aids.
10. The right to receive Social Security and certain welfare benefits, alimony and support, certain retirement funds and pensions, and education savings accounts held for specific periods of time.
11. The right to receive certain personal-injury and other awards up to $21,625.

Individual states have the power to pass legislation precluding debtors from using the federal exemptions within the state. A majority of the states have done this. In those states, debtors may use only state, not federal, exemptions. In the rest of the states, an individual debtor (or a husband and wife filing jointly) may choose either the exemptions provided under state law or the federal exemptions.

The Homestead Exemption

The 2005 reforms significantly changed the law for those debtors seeking to use state homestead exemption statutes. In six states, including Florida and Texas, homestead exemptions allowed debtors petitioning for bankruptcy to shield *unlimited* amounts of equity in their homes from creditors. The Bankruptcy Code now places limits on the amount that can be claimed as exempt in bankruptcy. In addition, a debtor must have lived in a state for two years before filing the bankruptcy petition to use the state homestead exemption (prior law required only six months).

In general, if the debtor acquired the homestead within three and a half years preceding the date of filing, the maximum equity exempted is $146,450, even if state law would permit a higher amount. Note, however, that a debtor who has violated securities laws, been convicted of a felony, or engaged in certain other intentional misconduct may not be able to claim the exemption.

Creditors' Meeting and Claims

Within a reasonable time after the order for relief has been granted (not less than twenty days or more than forty days), the trustee must call a meeting of the creditors listed in the schedules filed by the debtor. The bankruptcy judge does not attend this meeting. The debtor is required to attend (unless excused by the court) and to submit to examination under oath by the creditors and the trustee. At the meeting, the debtor is questioned under oath to ensure that he or she is aware of the potential consequences of bankruptcy and of relief available under the different chapters of the Bankruptcy Code.

To be entitled to receive a portion of the debtor's estate, each creditor normally files a *proof of claim* with the bankruptcy court clerk within ninety days of the creditors' meeting.[16] The proof of claim

---

14. See, for example, *In the Matter of TransTexas Gas Corp.*, 597 F.3d 298 (5th Cir. 2010).
15. The dollar amounts stated in the Bankruptcy Code are adjusted automatically every three years on April 1 based on changes in the Consumer Price Index. The adjusted amounts are rounded to the nearest $25. The amounts stated are in accordance with those computed on April 1, 2010.

---

16. This ninety-day rule applies in Chapter 12 and Chapter 13 bankruptcies as well.

lists the creditor's name and address, as well as the amount that the creditor asserts is owed to the creditor by the debtor. A creditor need not file a proof of claim if the debtor's schedules list the creditor's claim as liquidated (exactly determined) and the creditor does not dispute the amount of the claim. A proof of claim is necessary if there is any dispute concerning the claim.

Distribution of Property

In the next step in a Chapter 7 bankruptcy, the trustee distributes the bankruptcy estate to the creditors. In the distribution of the debtor's estate, secured creditors take priority over unsecured creditors. The Code provides that a consumer-debtor, within thirty days of filing a liquidation petition or before the date of the first meeting of the creditors (whichever is first), must file with the clerk a statement of intention with respect to the secured collateral. The statement must indicate whether the debtor will retain the collateral or surrender the collateral to the secured party. Also, if applicable, the debtor must specify whether the collateral will be claimed as exempt property and whether the debtor intends to redeem the property or reaffirm the debt secured by the collateral. The trustee is obligated to enforce the debtor's statement within forty-five days after it is filed.

In a bankruptcy case in which the debtor has no assets (called a "no-asset case"), creditors are notified of the debtor's petition for bankruptcy but are instructed not to file a claim. In no-asset cases, the unsecured creditors will receive no payment, and most, if not all, of these debts will be discharged.

DISTRIBUTION TO SECURED CREDITORS As discussed earlier, secured creditors are creditors who received an interest in collateral to secure a debtor's payment or performance. If the collateral is surrendered to the secured party, the secured creditor can enforce the security interest either by accepting the property in full satisfaction of the debt or by selling the collateral and using the proceeds to pay off the debt. Thus, the secured party has priority over unsecured parties as to the proceeds from the disposition of the collateral. Should the collateral be insufficient to cover the secured debt owed, the secured creditor becomes an unsecured creditor for the difference.

DISTRIBUTION TO UNSECURED CREDITORS Bankruptcy law establishes an order of priority for classes of debts owed to *unsecured* creditors, and they are

paid in the order of their priority. Each class must be fully paid before the next class is entitled to any of the remaining proceeds. If there are insufficient proceeds to pay fully all the creditors in a class, the proceeds are distributed *proportionately* to the creditors in that class, and classes lower in priority receive nothing. In almost all Chapter 7 bankruptcies, the funds will be insufficient to pay all creditors. The order of priority among classes of unsecured creditors is as follows (some of these classes involve cases against bankrupt businesses):

1. Claims for domestic-support obligations, such as child support and alimony.
2. Administrative expenses, including court costs, trustee fees, and attorneys' fees.
3. In an involuntary bankruptcy, expenses incurred by the debtor in the ordinary course of business.
4. Unpaid wages, salaries, and commissions earned within ninety days of the filing of the petition; the amount is capped for each claimant.
5. Unsecured claims for contributions to be made to employee benefit plans. The amount is capped for each claimant.
6. Consumer deposits given to the debtor before the petition was filed. The amount is capped for each claimant.
7. Certain taxes and penalties owed to government units, such as income and property taxes.
8. Claims for death or personal injury resulting from the unlawful operation of a motor vehicle.
9. Claims of general creditors.

If any amount remains after the priority classes of creditors have been satisfied, it is turned over to the debtor.

Discharge

From the debtor's point of view, the primary purpose of liquidation is to obtain a fresh start through a discharge of debts. Certain debts, however, are not dischargeable in bankruptcy. Also, certain debtors may not qualify to have all debts discharged in bankruptcy. These situations are discussed next.

EXCEPTIONS TO DISCHARGE Discharge of a debt may be denied because of the nature of the claim or the conduct of the debtor. Claims that are not dischargeable in bankruptcy include the following:

1. Claims for back taxes accruing within two years prior to bankruptcy.
2. Claims for amounts borrowed by the debtor to pay federal taxes or any nondischargeable taxes

(such as federal and state income taxes, employ-ment taxes, and property taxes).

3. Claims against property or funds obtained by the debtor under false pretenses or by false representations.

4. Claims by creditors who were not notified of the bankruptcy. These claims did not appear on the schedules the debtor was required to file.

5. Claims based on fraud[17] or misuse of funds by the debtor while acting in a fiduciary capacity or claims involving the debtor's embezzlement or larceny.

6. Domestic-support obligations and property set-tlements as provided for in a separation agree-ment or divorce decree.

7. Claims for amounts due on a retirement ac-count loan.

8. Claims based on willful or malicious conduct by the debtor toward another or the property of another.

9. Certain government fines and penalties.

10. Certain student loans or obligations to repay funds received as an educational benefit, schol-arship, or stipend—unless payment of the loans imposes an undue hardship on the debtor and the debtor's dependents. (For an example of what constitutes undue hardship, see the *Case in Point* feature that follows this list.)

11. Consumer debts of more than $600 for lux-ury goods or services owed to a single creditor incurred within ninety days of the order for relief.

12. Cash advances totaling more than $875 that are extensions of open-end consumer credit obtained by the debtor within seventy days of the order for relief.

13. Judgments against a debtor as a result of the debtor's operation of a motor vehicle while intoxicated.

14. Fees or assessments arising from property in a homeowners' association, as long as the debtor retained an interest in the property.

15. Taxes with respect to which the debtor failed to provide required or requested tax documents.

CASE IN POINT Keldric Mosley incurred student loans while attending Alcorn State University and then joined the U.S. Army Reserve Officers' Training

Corps. He was injured during training and resigned from the Corps because of medical problems related to his injuries. Mosley worked briefly for several employers, but depressed and physically limited by his injuries, he was unable to keep any of the jobs. A federal bankruptcy court granted him a dis-charge under Chapter 7, but it did not include the student loans. By 2004, Mosley was homeless and had a monthly income of $210 in disability bene-fits, but he still owed $45,000 in student loans. He asked the bankruptcy court to reopen his case and discharge his student loans based on undue hard-ship. The court held that Mosley's medical prob-lems, lack of skills, and "dire living conditions" made it unlikely that he would be able to hold a job and repay the loans. The court therefore discharged the debt, reasoning that Mosley could not main-tain a minimal standard of living if forced to repay the loans.[18]

OBJECTIONS TO DISCHARGE In addition to the exceptions to discharge previously discussed, a bank-ruptcy court may also deny the discharge based on the debtor's conduct. In such a situation, the assets of the debtor are still distributed to the creditors, but the debtor remains liable for the unpaid portion of all claims. Grounds for a denial of discharge of the debtor include the following:

1. The debtor's concealment or destruction of prop-erty with the intent to hinder, delay, or defraud a creditor.

2. The debtor's fraudulent concealment or destruc-tion of financial records.

3. The grant of a discharge to the debtor within eight years before the petition was filed.

4. The debtor's failure to complete the required con-sumer education course.

5. Proceedings in which the debtor could be found guilty of a felony (basically, a court may not dis-charge any debt until the completion of felony proceedings against the debtor).

EFFECT OF A DISCHARGE The primary effect of a dis-charge is to void, or set aside, any judgment on a discharged debt and prohibit any action to collect a discharged debt. A discharge does not affect the lia-bility of a co-debtor. (For a discussion of how some debts that were discharged in bankruptcy have still appeared on debtors' credit reports, see this chapter's *Insight into Ethics* feature on the following page.)

---

17. Even if a debtor who is sued for fraud settles the lawsuit, the United States Supreme Court has held that the amount due under the settlement agreement may not be discharged in bankruptcy because of the underlying fraud. See *Archer v. Warner*, 538 U.S. 314, 123 S.Ct. 1462, 155 L.Ed.2d 454 (2003).

18. *In re Mosley*, 494 F.3d 1320 (11th Cir. 2007).

INSIGHT INTO ETHICS
The Debt That Never Goes Away

When a bankruptcy judge discharges certain debts, they are no longer supposed to appear on debtors' credit reports. Nonetheless, many credit-card companies and other creditors have been keeping debts active even after they have been discharged in bankruptcy. Not surprisingly, some aggressive entrepreneurs have found a way to profit from this practice. Companies with names such as eCast Settlement and Max Recovery purchase discharged debt obligations at pennies on the dollar. Then they pursue the debtors and pressure them to pay the debts even though they have been discharged. Some of these companies have been successful enough to become publicly traded on the New York Stock Exchange.

The fact that discharged debt does not have a zero dollar value indicates that some consumers have been repaying these debts. As the number of bankruptcies rose during the latest recession, the market price of fully discharged Chapter 7 debt actually increased—to about seven cents on the dollar.

One federal district court judge, though, has had enough. In a class-action lawsuit, plaintiffs claimed that credit reporting agencies had violated the federal Fair Credit Reporting Act (see Chapter 24) by failing to follow reasonable procedures that ensured accurate reporting of debts discharged in Chapter 7 bankruptcies. The court agreed and ordered the agencies to revise their procedures.[a] Today, credit agencies must automatically report all prebankruptcy debt as "discharged," unless the debt is nondischargable. Although the purchasers of discharged debt may still attempt to pressure consumers into paying debts that they do not owe, the change in the credit bureaus' procedures may give consumers additional help in their efforts to rebuild their lives after bankruptcy.

CRITICAL THINKING

INSIGHT INTO THE ECONOMIC ENVIRONMENT
About six years ago, one could buy debt that had been discharged in bankruptcy for less than five cents on the dollar. Why has the price increased to seven cents on the dollar?

a. *White v. Experian Information Solutions,* No. 05-CV-1-70 DOC (C.D.Cal. 2008).

On petition by the trustee or a creditor, the bankruptcy court can, within one year, revoke the discharge decree if it is discovered that the debtor acted fraudulently or dishonestly during the bankruptcy proceedings. The revocation renders the discharge void, allowing creditors not satisfied by the distribution of the debtor's estate to proceed with their claims against the debtor.

Reaffirmation of Debt

An agreement to pay a debt dischargeable in bankruptcy is called a **reaffirmation agreement.** A debtor may wish to pay a debt—for example, a debt owed to a family member, physician, bank, or some other creditor—even though the debt could be discharged in bankruptcy.

To be enforceable, reaffirmation agreements must be made before the debtor is granted a discharge. The agreement must be signed and filed with the court. Court approval is required unless the debtor is represented by an attorney during the negotiation of the reaffirmation and submits the proper documents and certifications. Even when the debtor is represented by an attorney, court approval may be required if it appears that the reaffirmation will result in undue hardship on the debtor. When court approval is required, a separate hearing will take place. The court will approve the reaffirmation only if it finds that the agreement will not result in undue hardship to the debtor and that the reaffirmation is consistent with the debtor's best interests.

To discourage creditors from engaging in abusive reaffirmation practices, the law provides specific language for disclosures that must be given to debtors entering into reaffirmation agreements. Among other things, these disclosures explain that the debtor is not required to reaffirm any debt, but that liens on secured property, such as mortgages and cars, will remain in effect even if the debt is not reaffirmed.

The reaffirmation agreement must disclose the amount of the debt reaffirmed, the rate of interest, the date payments begin, and the right to rescind. The disclosures also caution the debtor: "Only agree to reaffirm a debt if it is in your best interest. Be sure you can afford the payments you agree to make." The original disclosure documents must be signed by the debtor, certified by the debtor's attorney, and filed with the court at the same time as the reaffirmation agreement. A reaffirmation agreement that is not accompanied by the original signed disclosures will not be effective.

<hr>
SECTION 6
REORGANIZATIONS
<hr>

The type of bankruptcy proceeding most commonly used by corporate debtors is the Chapter 11 *reorganization.* In a reorganization, the creditors and the debtor formulate a plan under which the debtor pays a portion of the debts and is discharged of the remainder. The debtor is allowed to continue in business. Although this type of bankruptcy is generally a corporate reorganization, any debtor (except a stockbroker or a commodities broker) who is eligible for Chapter 7 relief is eligible for relief under Chapter 11. Railroads are also eligible.

In 1994, Congress established a "fast-track" Chapter 11 procedure for small-business debtors whose liabilities do not exceed $2.19 million and who do not own or manage real estate. The fast track enables a debtor to avoid the appointment of a creditors' committee and also shortens the filing periods and relaxes certain other requirements. Because the process is shorter and simpler, it is less costly.

The same principles that govern the filing of a liquidation (Chapter 7) petition apply to reorganization (Chapter 11) proceedings. The case may be brought either voluntarily or involuntarily. The automatic-stay provisions and adequate protection doctrine apply in reorganizations as well. An exception from the automatic stay is triggered if the debtor files for bankruptcy again within two years and new grounds for dismissal (such as substantial abuse) or conversion of the case are established.

Workouts

In some instances, to avoid bankruptcy proceedings, creditors may prefer private, negotiated adjustments of creditor-debtor relations, also known as **workouts.** Often, these out-of-court workouts are much more flexible and thus more conducive to a speedy settlement. Speed is critical because delay is one of the most costly elements in any bankruptcy proceeding. Another advantage of workouts is that they avoid the various administrative costs of bankruptcy proceedings.

Creditors' Best Interests

After a petition for Chapter 11 bankruptcy has been filed, a bankruptcy court, after notice and a hearing, can dismiss or suspend all proceedings at any time if dismissal or suspension would better serve the interests of the creditors. The Bankruptcy Code also allows a court, after notice and a hearing, to dismiss a case under reorganization "for cause." Cause includes the absence of a reasonable likelihood of rehabilitation, the inability to effect a plan, and an unreasonable delay by the debtor that is prejudicial to (may harm the interests of) creditors.[19]

Debtor in Possession

On entry of the order for relief, the debtor generally continues to operate the business as a **debtor in possession (DIP).** The court, however, may appoint a trustee (often referred to as a *receiver*) to operate the debtor's business if gross mismanagement of the business is shown or if appointing a trustee is in the best interests of the estate.

The DIP's role is similar to that of a trustee in a liquidation. The DIP is entitled to avoid preferential payments made to creditors and fraudulent transfers of assets. The DIP has the power to decide whether to cancel or assume obligations under prepetition executory contracts (those that are not yet performed) or unexpired leases. The DIP can also exercise a trustee's strong-arm powers.

Creditors' Committees

As soon as practicable after the entry of the order for relief, a creditors' committee of unsecured creditors is appointed.[20] This committee often is composed of the biggest suppliers to the business. The committee may consult with the trustee or the DIP concerning the administration of the case or the formulation of the plan. Additional creditors' committees may be appointed to represent special interest creditors.

Generally, no orders affecting the estate will be entered without the consent of the committee or after a hearing in which the judge is informed of the committee's position. As mentioned earlier, businesses with debts of less than $2.19 million that do not own or manage real estate can avoid creditors' committees. In these cases, orders can be entered without a committee's consent.

<hr>

19. See 11 U.S.C. Section 1112(b). Debtors are not prohibited from filing successive petitions, however. A debtor whose petition is dismissed, for example, can file a new Chapter 11 petition (which may be granted unless it is filed in bad faith).

20. If the debtor has filed a reorganization plan accepted by the creditors, the trustee may decide not to call a meeting of the creditors.

The Reorganization Plan

A reorganization plan to rehabilitate the debtor is a plan to conserve and administer the debtor's assets in the hope of an eventual return to successful operation and solvency. The plan must be fair and equitable and must do the following:

1. Designate classes of claims and interests.
2. Specify the treatment to be afforded the classes. (The plan must provide the same treatment for all claims in a particular class.)
3. Provide an adequate means for execution. (Individual debtors are required to utilize post-petition assets as necessary to execute the plan.)
4. Provide for payment of tax claims over a five-year period.

FILING THE PLAN Only the debtor may file a plan within the first 120 days after the date of the order for relief. This period may be extended, but not beyond eighteen months from the date of the order for relief. If the debtor does not meet the 120-day deadline or obtain an extension, and if the debtor fails to procure the required creditor consent (discussed below) within 180 days, any party may propose a plan. The plan need not provide for full repayment to unsecured creditors. Instead, creditors receive a percentage of each dollar owed to them by the debtor. If a small-business debtor chooses to avoid a creditors' committee, the time for the debtor's filing is 180 days.

ACCEPTANCE AND CONFIRMATION OF THE PLAN Once the plan has been developed, it is submitted to each class of creditors for acceptance. For the plan to be adopted, each class that is adversely affected by the plan must accept it. A class has accepted the plan when a majority of the creditors, representing two-thirds of the amount of the total claim, vote to approve it. Confirmation is conditioned on the debtor's certification that all postpetition domestic-support obligations have been paid in full.

Even when all classes of creditors accept the plan, the court may refuse to confirm it if it is not "in the best interests of the creditors." The plan can also be modified on the request of the debtor, the trustee, the U.S. trustee, or a holder of an unsecured claim. If an unsecured creditor objects to the plan, specific rules apply to the value of property to be distributed under the plan. Tax claims must be paid over a five-year period.

Even if only one class of creditors has accepted the plan, the court may still confirm the plan under the Code's so-called **cram-down provision.** In other words, the court may confirm the plan over the objections of a class of creditors. Before the court can exercise this right of cram-down confirmation, it must be demonstrated that the plan does not discriminate unfairly against any creditors and is fair and equitable.

DISCHARGE The plan is binding on confirmation; however, the law provides that confirmation of a plan does not discharge an individual debtor. *For individual debtors, the plan must be completed before discharge will be granted,* unless the court orders otherwise. For all other debtors, the court may order discharge at any time after the plan is confirmed. At this time, the debtor is given a reorganization discharge from all claims not protected under the plan. This discharge does not apply to any claims that would be denied discharge under liquidation.

SECTION 7
BANKRUPTCY RELIEF UNDER CHAPTER 13 AND CHAPTER 12

In addition to bankruptcy relief through liquidation and reorganization, the Code also provides for individuals' repayment plans (Chapter 13) and family-farmer and family-fisherman debt adjustments (Chapter 12).

Chapter 13—Individuals' Repayment Plans

Chapter 13 of the Code provides for "Adjustment of Debts of an Individual with Regular Income." Individuals (not partnerships or corporations) with regular income who owe fixed (liquidated) unsecured debts of less than $360,475 or fixed secured debts of less than $1,081,400 may take advantage of bankruptcy repayment plans. Among those eligible are salaried employees; sole proprietors; and individuals who live on welfare, Social Security, fixed pensions, or investment income. Many small-business debtors have a choice of filing under either Chapter 11 or Chapter 13. Repayment plans offer some advantages because they are less expensive and less complicated than reorganization or liquidation proceedings.

FILING THE PETITION A Chapter 13 repayment plan case can be initiated only by the debtor's filing of a voluntary petition or by court conversion of a Chapter 7 petition (because of a finding of substantial abuse under the means test, for example). Certain liquidation and reorganization cases may be converted to repayment plan cases with the consent of the debtor.[21] A trustee, who will make payments under the plan, must be appointed. On the filing of a repayment plan petition, the automatic stay previously discussed takes effect. Although the stay applies to all or part of the debtor's consumer debt, it does not apply to any business debt incurred by the debtor or to any domestic-support obligations.

GOOD FAITH REQUIREMENT The Bankruptcy Code imposes the requirement of good faith on a debtor at both the time of the filing of the petition and the time of the filing of the plan. The Code does not define good faith, but if the circumstances on the whole indicate bad faith, a court can dismiss a debtor's Chapter 13 petition.

CASE IN POINT Roger and Pauline Buis bought an air show business, including a helicopter. They decorated the helicopter as "Otto the Clown" and operated the business as Otto Airshows. Several years later, a competitor won a defamation lawsuit against the Buises and Otto Airshows. The Buises then stopped doing business as Otto Airshows and formed a new firm, Prop and Rotor Aviation, Inc., to which they leased the Otto equipment. Within a month, they filed a bankruptcy petition under Chapter 13. The plan and the schedules failed to mention the lawsuit, the equipment lease, and several other items. The court therefore dismissed the Buises' petition due to bad faith. The debtors had not included all of their assets and liabilities on their initial petition, and they had timed its filing to avoid payment on the defamation judgment.[22]

PLAN PROVISIONS A plan of rehabilitation by repayment must provide for the following:

1. The turning over to the trustee of such future earnings or income of the debtor as is necessary for execution of the plan.
2. Full payment through deferred cash payments of all claims entitled to priority, such as taxes.[23]
3. Identical treatment of all claims within a particular class. (The Code permits the debtor to list co-debtors, such as guarantors or sureties, as a separate class.)

The repayment plan may provide either for payment of all obligations in full or for payment of a lesser amount. The length of the payment plan can be three or five years, depending on the debtor's family income. If the debtor's family income is greater than the median family income in the relevant geographic area under the means test, the term of the proposed plan must be for five years.[24] The term may not exceed five years.

The debtor must begin making payments under the proposed plan within thirty days after the plan has been *filed* and must continue to make "timely" payments from her or his disposable income. Failure of the debtor to make timely payments or to commence payments within the thirty-day period will allow the court to convert the case to a liquidation bankruptcy or to dismiss the petition.

CONFIRMATION OF THE PLAN After the plan is filed, the court holds a confirmation hearing, at which interested parties (such as creditors) may object to the plan. The hearing must be held at least twenty days, but no more than forty-five days, after the meeting of the creditors. The debtor must have filed all prepetition tax returns and paid all postpetition domestic-support obligations before a court will confirm any plan. The court will confirm a plan with respect to each claim of a secured creditor under any of the following circumstances:

1. If the secured creditors have accepted the plan.
2. If the plan provides that secured creditors retain their liens until there is payment in full or until the debtor receives a discharge.
3. If the debtor surrenders the property securing the claims to the creditors.

In addition, for a motor vehicle purchased within 910 days before the petition is filed, the plan must provide that a creditor who extended credit for part or all of the purchase price retains its lien until the entire debt is paid.

DISCHARGE After the debtor has completed all payments, the court grants a discharge of all debts provided for by the repayment plan. Except for allowed claims not provided for by the plan, certain long-term debts provided for by the plan, certain tax claims, payments on retirement accounts, and claims for domestic-support obligations, all other debts are dischargeable. Under prior law, a discharge

---

21. A Chapter 13 repayment plan may be converted to a Chapter 7 liquidation at the request of the debtor or, under certain circumstances, by a creditor "for cause." A Chapter 13 case may be converted to a Chapter 11 case after a hearing.
22. *In re Buis,* 337 Bankr. 243 (N.D.Fla. 2006).
23. As with a Chapter 11 reorganization plan, full repayment of all claims is not always required.
24. See 11 U.S.C. Section 1322(d) for details on when the court will find that the Chapter 13 plan should extend to a five-year period.

of debts under a Chapter 13 repayment plan was sometimes referred to as a "superdischarge" because it allowed the discharge of fraudulently incurred debt and claims resulting from malicious or willful injury. The 2005 reforms, however, deleted most of the "superdischarge" provisions, especially for debts based on fraud or taxes. Today, debts related to injury or property damage caused while driving under the influence of alcohol or drugs are also nondischargeable.

CASE IN POINT James Ellett owed $18,000 in personal income taxes to the state of California at the time he petitioned for Chapter 13 bankruptcy. Ellett listed the debt in his petition but misstated the last digit of his Social Security number (SSN). Because of this error, the California Franchise Tax Board (FTB) did not receive any notice of Ellett's bankruptcy and never filed a proof of claim or received

any distribution through his repayment plan. After Ellett completed the repayment plan and received a discharge, the FTB attempted to collect the tax debt. Ellett filed a lawsuit seeking a court declaration that the debt to the FTB had been discharged. The court ruled against him, and he appealed. A federal appellate court concluded that because of Ellett's negligence in listing an erroneous SSN on his bankruptcy petition, the FTB had never been notified of his bankruptcy. Thus, the tax debt was not discharged.[25]

In the following case, the issue before the United States Supreme Court was whether the discharge of certain student loan debt had been rendered void by a legal error on the part of the bankruptcy court.

---

25. *Ellett v. Stanislaus,* 506 F.3d 774 (9th Cir. 2007). (Stanislaus was the name of the director of the Franchise Tax Board.)

CASE 15.3
United Student Aid Funds, Inc. v. Espinosa

Supreme Court of the United States, ___ U.S. ___, 130 S.Ct. 1367, 176 L.Ed.2d 158 (2010).
www.supremecourt.gov[a]

BACKGROUND AND FACTS • Francisco Espinosa filed a petition for an individual repayment plan under Chapter 13 of the Bankruptcy Code. The plan proposed that Espinosa would repay only the principal of his student loan debt and that the interest on the loan would be discharged once the principal was repaid. Under Chapter 13, a student loan cannot be discharged unless the bankruptcy court finds that payment of the debt would constitute an undue hardship for the debtor. Despite this requirement, no undue hardship hearing was requested by Espinosa, by the court, or by United Student Aid Funds, Inc. (United), the creditor. United received notice of the plan but did not object to it. In addition, United failed to file an appeal after the bankruptcy court subsequently confirmed the plan. Years later, however, United filed a motion under Federal Rule of Civil Procedure 60(b)(4) asking the bankruptcy court to rule that its order confirming the plan was void because the order was issued in violation of the laws and rules governing bankruptcy. The court denied the petition and ordered United to cease its collection efforts. United appealed to the U.S. District Court for the District of Arizona, which reversed the bankruptcy court's ruling. On further appeal, the U.S. Court of Appeals for the Ninth Circuit reversed the district court's judgment. United appealed to the United States Supreme Court.

IN THE LANGUAGE OF THE COURT
Justice *THOMAS* delivered the opinion of the Court.
* * * *

A discharge under Chapter 13 "is broader than the discharge received in any other chapter." Chapter 13 nevertheless restricts or prohibits entirely the discharge of certain types of debts. As relevant here, [Section] 1328(a) [of the Bankruptcy Code] provides that when a debtor has completed the repayments required by a confirmed plan,

---

a. In the left-hand column, select "Opinions" and click on "Latest Slip Opinions." When that page opens, scroll down the list to the date 3/23/10 and click on the case title to access the case. The Supreme Court of the United States maintains this Web site.

CASE 15.3 CONTINUED ➡ a bankruptcy court "shall grant the debtor a discharge of all debts provided for by the plan or disallowed under Section 502 of this title, except," *inter alia* [among others], "any debt * * * of the kind specified in [Section] 523(a)(8). [That section], in turn, specifies certain student loan debts "unless excepting such debt from discharge * * * would impose an undue hardship on the debtor and the debtor's dependents." * * * *[The] Bankruptcy Rules require a party seeking to determine the dischargeability of a student loan debt to commence an adversary proceeding by serving a summons and complaint on affected creditors.* We must decide whether the Bankruptcy Court's order confirming Espinosa's plan is "void" under Federal Rule of Civil Procedure 60(b)(4) because the Bankruptcy Court confirmed the plan without complying with these requirements. [Emphasis added.]

The Bankruptcy Court's order confirming Espinosa's proposed plan was a final judgment, from which United did not appeal. * * * Rule 60(b)(4)—the provision under which United brought this motion—authorizes the court to relieve a party from a final judgment if "the judgment is void."

* * * *

"A judgment is not void * * * simply because it is or may have been erroneous." Similarly, a motion under Rule 60(b)(4) is not a substitute for a timely appeal. Instead, Rule 60(b)(4) applies only in the rare instance where a judgment is premised either on a certain type of jurisdictional error or on a violation of due process that deprives a party of notice or the opportunity to be heard.

* * * *

Unable to demonstrate a jurisdictional error or a due process violation, United and the Government, as *amicus* [friend of the court], urge us to expand the universe of judgment defects that support Rule 60(b)(4) relief. Specifically, they contend that the Bankruptcy Court's confirmation order is void because the court lacked statutory authority to confirm Espinosa's plan absent a finding of undue hardship.

* * * *

*Given the Code's clear * * * requirement for an undue hardship determination, the Bankruptcy Court's failure to find undue hardship before confirming Espinosa's plan was a legal error. But the order remains enforceable and binding on United because United had notice of the error and failed to object or timely appeal.* [Emphasis added.]

United's response—that it had no obligation to object to Espinosa's plan until Espinosa served it with the summons and complaint the Bankruptcy Rules require—is unavailing [fails to achieve the desired result]. Rule 60(b)(4) does not provide a license for litigants to sleep on their rights. United had actual notice of the filing of Espinosa's plan, its contents, and the Bankruptcy Court's subsequent confirmation of the plan. In addition, United filed a proof of claim regarding Espinosa's student loan debt, thereby submitting itself to the Bankruptcy Court's jurisdiction with respect to that claim. United therefore forfeited its arguments regarding the validity of service or the adequacy of the Bankruptcy Court's procedures by failing to raise a timely objection in that court.

DECISION AND REMEDY • *The United States Supreme Court affirmed the judgment of the U.S. Court of Appeals for the Ninth Circuit. The bankruptcy court's order confirming Espinosa's Chapter 13 repayment plan was not void, and the student loan debt was thus discharged.*

THE ETHICAL DIMENSION • *At one point, United argued that if the Court failed to declare the bankruptcy court's order void, it would encourage dishonest debtors to abuse the Chapter 13 process. How might such abuse occur? Discuss whether the possibility of such abuse should affect the Court's decision.*

MANAGERIAL IMPLICATIONS • *Business owners and managers should be aware that courts generally have little sympathy for those who "sleep on their rights." In this case, the creditor could have objected to the plan, but it did not. The creditor also could have appealed the confirmation order, but it did not. Only years later did the creditor seek to have the confirmation order declared void. To protect their rights, businesspersons should take care, if a client or other debtor petitions for bankruptcy relief, to respond to any notices received from the debtor or the bankruptcy court in a timely fashion.*

Chapter 12—Family Farmers and Fishermen

In 1986, to help relieve economic pressure on small farmers, Congress created Chapter 12 of the Bankruptcy Code. In 2005, Congress extended this protection to family fishermen, modified its provisions somewhat, and made it a permanent chapter in the Bankruptcy Code (previously, the statutes authorizing Chapter 12 had to be periodically renewed by Congress).

For purposes of Chapter 12, a *family farmer* is one whose gross income is at least 50 percent farm dependent and whose debts are at least 50 percent farm related. The total debt for a family farmer must not exceed $3,792,650. A partnership or closely held corporation (see Chapter 19) at least 50 percent owned by the farm family can also qualify as a family farmer.[26]

A *family fisherman* is defined as one whose gross income is at least 50 percent dependent on commercial fishing operations[27] and whose debts are at least 80 percent related to commercial fishing. The total debt for a family fisherman must not exceed $1,757,475. As with family farmers, a partnership or closely held corporation can also qualify.

FILING THE PETITION The procedure for filing a family-farmer or family-fisherman bankruptcy plan is very similar to the procedure for filing a repayment plan under Chapter 13. The debtor must file a plan not later than ninety days after the order for relief. The filing of the petition acts as an automatic stay against creditors' and co-obligors' actions against the estate.

A farmer or fisherman who has already filed a reorganization or repayment plan may convert it to a Chapter 12 plan. The debtor may also convert a Chapter 12 plan to a liquidation plan.

CONTENT AND CONFIRMATION OF THE PLAN The content of a plan under Chapter 12 is basically the same as that of a Chapter 13 repayment plan. Generally, the plan must be confirmed or denied within forty-five days of filing.

Court confirmation of the plan is the same as for a repayment plan. The plan must provide for payment of secured debts at the value of the collateral. If the secured debt exceeds the value of the collateral, the remaining debt is unsecured. For unsecured debtors, the plan must be confirmed if either (1) the value of the property to be distributed under the plan equals the amount of the claim or (2) the plan provides that all of the debtor's disposable income to be received in a three-year period (or longer, by court approval) will be applied to making payments. Disposable income is all income received less amounts needed to support the farmer or fisherman and his or her family and to continue the farming or commercial fishing operation. Completion of payments under the plan discharges all debts provided for by the plan.

See *Concept Summary 15.2* below and on the facing page for a comparison of bankruptcy procedures under Chapters 7, 11, 12, and 13.

---

26. Note that for a corporation or partnership to qualify under Chapter 12, at least 80 percent of the value of the firm's assets must consist of assets related to the farming operation.
27. Commercial fishing operations include catching, harvesting, or raising fish, shrimp, lobsters, urchins, seaweed, shellfish, or other aquatic species or products.

CONCEPT SUMMARY 15.2
Forms of Bankruptcy Relief Compared

Issue	Chapter 7	Chapter 11	Chapters 12 and 13
Purpose	Liquidation	Reorganization	Adjustment
Who Can Petition	Debtor (voluntary) or creditors (involuntary).	Debtor (voluntary) or creditors (involuntary).	Debtor (voluntary) only.
Who Can Be a Debtor	Any "person" (including partnerships, corporations, and municipalities) except railroads, insurance companies, banks, savings and loan	Any debtor eligible for Chapter 7 relief; railroads are also eligible. Individuals have specific rules and limitations.	*Chapter 12*—Any family farmer (one whose gross income is at least 50 percent farm dependent and whose debts are at least 50 percent farm related) or family fisherman (one whose gross income is at

CONCEPT SUMMARY 15.2

Forms of Bankruptcy Relief Compared, Continued

Issue	Chapter 7	Chapter 11	Chapters 12 and 13
Purpose	Liquidation	Reorganization	Adjustment
Who Can Be a Debtor–Continued	institutions, investment companies licensed by the Small Business Administration, and credit unions. Farmers and charitable institutions cannot be involuntarily petitioned. If the court finds the petition to be a substantial abuse of the use of Chapter 7, the debtor may be required to convert to a Chapter 13 repayment plan.		least 50 percent dependent on commercial fishing operations and whose debts are at least 80 percent related to commercial fishing) or any partnership or closely held corporation at least 50 percent owned by a family farmer or fisherman, when total debt does not exceed a specified amount ($3,792,650 for farmers and $1,757,475 for fishermen). *Chapter 13*—Any individual (not partnerships or corporations) with regular income who owes fixed (liquidated) unsecured debts of less than $360,475 or fixed secured debts of less than $1,081,400.
Procedure Leading to Discharge	Nonexempt property is sold, and the proceeds are distributed (in order) to priority groups. Dischargeable debts are terminated.	Plan is submitted; if it is approved and followed, debts are discharged.	Plan is submitted and must be approved if the value of the property to be distributed equals the amount of the claims or if the debtor turns over disposable income for a three-year or five-year period; if the plan is followed, debts are discharged.
Advantages	On liquidation and distribution, most debts are discharged, and the debtor has an opportunity for a fresh start.	Debtor continues in business. Creditors can accept the plan, or it can be "crammed down" on them. The plan allows for the reorganization and liquidation of debts over the plan period.	Debtor continues in business or in possession of assets. If the plan is approved, most debts are discharged after the plan period.

REVIEWING

Creditor-Debtor Relations and Bankruptcy

Three months ago, Janet Hart's husband of twenty years died of cancer. Although he had medical insurance, he left Janet with outstanding medical bills of more than $50,000. Janet has worked at the local library for the past ten years, earning $1,500 per month. Since her husband's death, Janet also receives $1,500 in Social Security benefits and $1,100 in life insurance proceeds every month, for a total monthly income of $4,300. After she pays the mortgage payment of $1,500 and the amounts due

REVIEWING CONTINUES ➡

REVIEWING

Creditor-Debtor Relations and Bankruptcy, Continued

on other debts, Janet has barely enough left to buy groceries for her family (she has two teen-age daughters at home). She decides to file for Chapter 7 bankruptcy, hoping for a fresh start. Using the information presented in the chapter, answer the following questions.

1. What must Janet do *before* filing a petition for relief under Chapter 7?
2. How much time does Janet have after filing the bankruptcy petition to submit the required schedules? What happens if Janet does not meet the deadline?
3. Assume that Janet files a petition under Chapter 7. Further assume that the median family income in the geographic area in which Janet lives is $49,300. What steps would a court take to determine whether Janet's petition is presumed to be "substantial abuse" using the means test?
4. Suppose that the court determines that no *presumption* of substantial abuse applies in Janet's case. Nevertheless, the court finds that Janet does have the ability to pay at least a portion of the medical bills out of her disposable income. What would the court likely order in that situation?

● DEBATE THIS: *Rather than being allowed to file Chapter 7 bankruptcy petitions, individuals and couples should always be forced to make an effort to pay off their debts through Chapter 13.*

TERMS AND CONCEPTS

adequate protection
   doctrine 343
artisan's lien 332
attachment 332
automatic stay 341
bankruptcy trustee 339
consumer-debtor 338
co-surety 337

cram-down provision 350
creditors' composition
   agreement 333
debtor in
   possession (DIP) 349
discharge 339
garnishment 333
guarantor 335
homestead exemption 337
insider 344

lien 331
liquidation proceedings 338
mechanic's lien 331
order for relief 341
petition in bankruptcy 339
preference 344
preferred creditor 344
reaffirmation
   agreement 348
right of contribution 337

right of reimbursement 337
right of subrogation 336
surety 333
suretyship 333
U.S. trustee 339
workout 349
writ of attachment 332
writ of execution 333

QUESTIONS AND CASE PROBLEMS

15–1. Voluntary versus Involuntary Bankruptcy
Burke has been a rancher all her life, raising cattle and crops. Her ranch is valued at $500,000, almost all of which is exempt under state law. Burke has eight creditors and a total indebtedness of $70,000. Two of her largest creditors are Oman ($30,000 owed) and Sneed ($25,000 owed). The other six creditors have claims of less than $5,000 each. A drought has ruined all of Burke's crops and forced her to sell many of her cattle at a loss. She cannot pay off her creditors.

(a) Under the Bankruptcy Code, can Burke, with a $500,000 ranch, voluntarily petition herself into bankruptcy? Explain.

(b) Could either Oman or Sneed force Burke into involuntary bankruptcy? Explain.

15–2. QUESTION WITH SAMPLE ANSWER: Preferences.

Peaslee is not known for his business sense. He started a greenhouse and nursery business two years ago, and because of his lack of experience, he soon was in debt to a number of creditors. On February 1, Peaslee borrowed $5,000 from his father to pay some of these creditors. On May 1, Peaslee paid back the $5,000, depleting his working capital. One creditor, the Cool Springs Nursery Supply Corp., had extended credit to Peaslee on numerous purchases.

Cool Springs pressured Peaslee for payment, and on July 1, Peaslee paid Cool Springs half the amount owed. On September 1, Peaslee voluntarily petitioned himself into bankruptcy. The trustee in bankruptcy claims that both Peaslee's father and Cool Springs must turn over to the debtor's estate the amounts Peaslee paid to them. Discuss fully the trustee's claims.

- **For a sample answer to Question 15–2, go to Appendix F at the end of this text.**

15–3. Mechanic's Lien Grant is the owner of a relatively old home valued at $45,000. He notices that the bathtubs and fixtures are leaking and need to be replaced. He contracts with Jane's Plumbing to replace the bathtubs and fixtures. Jane replaces them, and on June 1 she submits her bill of $4,000 to Grant. Because of financial difficulties, Grant does not pay the bill. Grant's only asset is his home, but his state's homestead exemption is $40,000. Discuss fully Jane's remedies in this situation.

15–4. Discharge in Bankruptcy Rhonda Schroeder married Gennady Shvartsshteyn (Gene) in 1997. Gene worked at Royal Courier and Air Domestic Connect in Illinois, where Melissa Winyard also worked in 1999 and 2000. During this time, Gene and Winyard had an affair. A year after leaving Royal, Winyard filed a petition in a federal bankruptcy court under Chapter 7 and was granted a discharge of her debts. Sometime later, in a letter to Schroeder who had learned of the affair, Winyard wrote, "I never intentionally wanted any of this to happen. I never wanted to disrupt your marriage." Schroeder obtained a divorce and, in 2005, filed a suit in an Illinois state court against Winyard, alleging "alienation of affection." Schroeder claimed that there had been "mutual love and affection" in her marriage until Winyard engaged in conduct intended to alienate her husband's affection. Schroeder charged that Winyard "caused him to have sexual intercourse with her," resulting in "the destruction of the marital relationship." Winyard filed a motion for summary judgment on the ground that any liability on her part had been discharged in her bankruptcy. Is there an exception to discharge for "willful and malicious conduct"? If so, does Schroeder's claim qualify? Discuss. [*Schroeder v. Winyard,* 375 Ill.App.3d 358, 873 N.E.2d 35, 313 Ill.Dec. 740 (2 Dist. 2007)]

15–5. Attachment In 2004 and 2005, Kent Avery, on behalf of his law firm—the Law Office of Kent Avery, LLC—contracted with Marlin Broadcasting, LLC, to air commercials on WCCC-FM, 106.9 "The Rock." Avery, who was the sole member of his firm, helped to create the ads, which solicited direct contact with "defense attorney Kent Avery," featured his voice, and repeated his name and experience to make potential clients familiar with him. When WCCC was not paid for the broadcasts, Marlin filed a suit in a Connecticut state court against Avery and his firm, alleging an outstanding balance of $35,250. Pending the court's hearing of the suit, Marlin filed a request for a writ of attachment. Marlin offered in

evidence the parties' contracts, the ads' transcripts, and WCCC's invoices. Avery contended that he could not be held personally liable for the cost of the ads. Marlin countered that the ads unjustly enriched Avery by conferring a personal benefit on him to Marlin's detriment. What is the purpose of attachment? What must a creditor prove to obtain a writ of attachment? Did Marlin meet this test? Explain. [*Marlin Broadcasting, LLC v. Law Office of Kent Avery, LLC,* 101 Conn.App. 638, 922 A.2d 1131 (2007)]

15–6. CASE PROBLEM WITH SAMPLE ANSWER: Discharge in Bankruptcy.

Cathy Coleman took out loans to complete her college education. After graduation, Coleman was irregularly employed as a teacher before filing a petition in a federal bankruptcy court under Chapter 13. The court confirmed a five-year plan under which Coleman was required to commit all of her disposable income to paying the student loans. Less than a year later, she was laid off. Still owing more than $100,000 to Educational Credit Management Corp., Coleman asked the court to discharge the debt on the ground that it would be undue hardship for her to pay it. Under Chapter 13, when is a debtor normally entitled to a discharge? Are student loans dischargeable? If not, is "undue hardship" a legitimate ground for an exception? With respect to a debtor, what is the goal of bankruptcy? With these facts and principles in mind, what argument could be made in support of Coleman's request? [In re Coleman, 560 F.3d 1000 (9th Cir. 2009)]

- **To view a sample answer for Problem 15–6, go to this book's Web site at www.cengage.com/blaw/cross, select "Chapter 15," and click on "Case Problem with Sample Answer."**

15–7. Liens Autolign Manufacturing Group, Inc., was a plastic injection molder that made parts for the auto industry. Because of a fire at its plant, Autolign subcontracted its work to several other companies to produce parts for its customers. Autolign provided the subcontractors with molds it owned so that they could produce the exact parts needed. The subcontractors produced the parts for Autolign, which it then sold to automakers. Shortly afterward, Autolign ceased operations. The subcontractors sued Autolign for breach of contract, claiming that they were never paid for the parts that they had produced for Autolign. The subcontractors asserted a statutory "molder's lien" on the molds in their possession. A molder's lien is similar to an artisan's lien in that it is possessory, but was established by a Michigan statute rather than common law. One of Autolign's creditors, Wamco 34, Ltd., argued that the molds were its property because the molds were used to secure repayment of a debt that Autolign owed to Wamco. The trial court held that Wamco was a secured creditor and that its interest had priority over the plaintiffs' lien in the molds. The subcontractors appealed. Which party had the superior claim? Explain your answer. [*Delta Engineered Plastics, LLC v. Autolign Manufacturing Group, Inc.,* 286 Mich.App. 115, 777 N.W.2d 502 (2010)]

15–8. Discharge in Bankruptcy Caroline McAfee loaned $400,000 to Carter Oaks Crossing. Joseph Harman, president of Carter Oaks Crossing, signed a promissory note providing that the company would repay the amount with interest in installments beginning in 1999 and ending by 2006. Harman signed a personal guaranty for the note. Carter Oaks Crossing defaulted on the note, so McAfee sued Harman for payment under the guaranty. Harman moved for summary judgment on the ground that McAfee's claim against him had been discharged in his Chapter 7 bankruptcy case, filed after 1999 but before the default on the note. The guaranty was not listed among Harman's debts in the bankruptcy filing. Would the obligation under the guaranty have been discharged in bankruptcy, as Harman claimed? Why or why not? [*Harman v. McAfee*, 302 Ga.App. 698, 691 S.E.2d 586 (2010)]

15–9. A QUESTION OF ETHICS: Guaranty.

73-75 Main Avenue, LLC, agreed to lease a portion of the commercial property at 73 Main Avenue, Norwalk, Connecticut, to PP Door Enterprise, Inc. Nan Zhang, as manager of PP Door, signed the lease agreement. The lessor required the principal officers of PP Door to execute personal guaranties. In addition, the principal officers agreed to provide the lessor with credit information. Apparently, both the lessor and the principals of PP Door signed the lease and guaranty agreements that were sent to PP Door's office. When PP Door failed to make monthly payments, 73-75 Main Avenue filed a suit against PP Door and its owner, Ping Ying Li. At trial, Li testified that she was the sole owner of PP Door but denied that Zhang was its manager. She also denied signing the guaranty agreement. She claimed that she had signed the credit authorization form because Zhang had told her he was too young to have good credit. Li claimed to have no knowledge of the lease agreement. She did admit, however, that she had paid the rent. She claimed that Zhang had been in a car accident and had asked her to help pay his bills, including the rent at 73 Main Avenue. Li further testified that she did not see the name PP Door on the storefront of the leased location. [73-75 Main Avenue, LLC v. PP Door Enterprise, Inc., 120 Conn.App. 150, 991 A.2d 650 (2010)]

(a) Li argued that she was not liable on the lease agreement because Zhang was not authorized to bind her to the lease. Do the facts support Li? Why or why not?

(b) Li claimed that the guaranty for rent was not enforceable against her. Why might the court agree?

15–10. VIDEO QUESTION: Bankruptcy.

Go to this text's Web site at **www.cengage.com/blaw/cross** and select "Chapter 15." Click on "Video Questions" and view the video titled *Field of Dreams*. Then answer the following questions.

(a) Before this scene, the movie makes clear that Ray (Kevin Costner) is unable to pay his bills, but he has not filed a voluntary petition for bankruptcy. What would be required for Ray's creditors to force him into an involuntary bankruptcy?

(b) If Ray did file a voluntary petition for a Chapter 7 bankruptcy, what exemptions might protect him from "losing everything" and being evicted as the man indicated in this scene? How much equity in the farm home could Ray claim as exempt if he filed the petition?

(c) What are the requirements for Ray to qualify as a family farmer under Chapter 12 of the Bankruptcy Code?

(d) How would the results of a Chapter 12 bankruptcy differ from those of a Chapter 7 bankruptcy for Ray?

LEGAL RESEARCH EXERCISES ON THE WEB

Go to this text's Web site at **www.cengage.com/blaw/cross**, select "Chapter 15," and click on "Practical Internet Exercises." There you will find the following Internet research exercises that you can perform to learn more about the topics covered in this chapter.

Practical Internet Exercise 15–1: **Legal Perspective**
Debtor-Creditor Relations

Practical Internet Exercise 15–2: **Management Perspective**
Bankruptcy Alternatives

CHAPTER 16

Mortgages and Foreclosures after the Recession

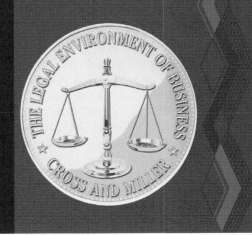

During the early years of the twenty-first century, the United States experienced one of the biggest real estate bubbles in its history as prices of homes in many areas increased at unprecedented rates. The bubble started to shrink in 2006 and was still deflating in 2011. As a result of the collapse of the housing market and the financial crisis that accompanied it, the United States and much of the rest of the world suffered through what is now called the Great Recession. Although the recession may be over by the time you read this, the real estate market is still in turmoil in countless areas. Many people have lost their homes to foreclosure because they could not make the payments; others can afford the payments but choose not to because they owe more on the properties than those properties are worth.

This chapter examines the rights and obligations that apply to homeowners and their lenders. This chapter begins with a discussion of *mortgages*—the loans that lenders provide to enable borrowers to purchase real property (*real property* will be discussed in Chapter 26). Next, we examine the laws that protect borrowers when they obtain mortgages. This chapter concludes with a discussion of the options that lenders and homeowners have when homeowners cannot continue to make their mortgage payments.

SECTION 1
MORTGAGES

When individuals purchase real property, they typically borrow funds from a financial institution for part or all of the purchase price. A **mortgage** is a written instrument that gives the creditor (the *mortgagee*) an interest in, or lien on, the property being acquired by the debtor (the *mortgagor*) as security for the debt's payment. Here, we look first at the different types of mortgages, including some new varieties that helped to inflate the housing bubble. Then we consider some of the ways that creditors protect their interest in the property and examine some of the more important provisions in a typical mortgage document.

Types of Mortgages

Mortgage loans are contracts, and as such, they come in a variety of forms. Lenders offer various types of mortgages to meet the needs of different borrowers. In recent decades, the expansion of home ownership became a political goal, and lenders were encouraged to become more creative in devising new types of mortgages. In many instances, these new mortgages were aimed at borrowers who could not qualify for traditional mortgages and lacked the funds to make a **down payment** (the part of the purchase price that is paid up front in cash).

In general, these mortgages, which include some adjustable-rate mortgages, interest-only mortgages, and balloon mortgages, feature a low initial interest rate. Often, the borrower hopes to refinance—pay off the original mortgage and obtain a new one at more favorable terms—within a few years. When the housing bubble burst and house prices began to decline, however, refinancing became more difficult than many borrowers had anticipated.

FIXED-RATE MORTGAGES *Fixed-rate mortgages* are the simplest mortgage loans. A **fixed-rate mortgage** is a standard mortgage with a fixed, or unchanging, rate of interest. Payments on the loan remain the same for the duration of the mortgage, which ranges from fifteen to forty years. Lenders determine the interest rate based on a variety of factors, including the borrower's credit history, credit score, income, and debts. Today, for a borrower to qualify for a standard fixed-rate mortgage loan, lenders typically require that the monthly mortgage payment (including principal, interest, taxes, and insurance) not exceed 28 percent of the person's gross income.

ADJUSTABLE-RATE MORTGAGES The rate of interest paid by the borrower changes periodically with an **adjustable-rate mortgage (ARM).** Typically, the initial interest rate for an ARM is set at a relatively low fixed rate for a specified period, such as a year or three years. After that time, the interest rate adjusts annually or by some other period, such as biannually or monthly. ARMs generally are described in terms of the initial fixed period and the adjustment period. For example, if the interest rate is fixed for three years and then adjusts annually, the mortgage is called a 3/1 ARM; if the rate adjusts annually after five years, the mortgage is a 5/1 ARM.

The interest rate adjustment is calculated by adding a certain number of percentage points (called the margin) to an index rate (one of various governmental interest rates). The margin and index rate are specified in the mortgage loan documents. For example, Greta and Marcus obtain a 3/1 ARM to purchase a home. After three years, when the first adjustment is to be made, the index rate is 6 percent. If the margin specified in the loan documents is 3 percentage points, the fully indexed interest rate for the ARM would be 9 percent. Most ARMs, however, have lifetime interest rate caps that limit the amount that the rate can rise over the duration of the loan.

Some ARMs also have caps that stipulate the maximum increase that can occur at any particular adjustment period. In the Greta and Marcus example above, if the initial interest rate was 5 percent and the loan stipulated that the rate could rise no more than 3 percentage points in one adjustment period, the interest rate after three years would increase to 8 percent, not 9 percent, because of the cap. Note that the interest rate could be adjusted downward as well as upward; if the index rate was 1 percent, the adjusted rate would potentially fall to 4 percent, although some ARMs also limit the amount that the rate can fall.

INTEREST-ONLY (IO) MORTGAGES With an **interest-only (IO) mortgage,** the borrower can choose to pay only the interest portion of the monthly payments and forgo paying any of the principal for a specified period of time. (IO loans can be for fixed-rate or adjustable-rate mortgages.) This IO payment usually is available for three to ten years. After the IO payment option is exhausted, the borrower's payment increases to include payments on the principal.

SUBPRIME MORTGAGES During the late 1990s and the first decade of the 2000s, *subprime lending* increased significantly. A **subprime mortgage** is a loan made to a borrower who does not qualify for a standard mortgage. Often, such borrowers have poor credit scores or high current *debt-to-income ratios*—that is, the total amount owed as a percentage of current after-tax income. Subprime mortgages are riskier than traditional mortgages and have a higher default rate. Consequently, lenders charge a higher interest rate for subprime loans. Subprime mortgages can be fixed-rate, adjustable-rate, or IO loans. Subprime lending allows many people who could not otherwise purchase real property to do so, but at a higher risk to the lender.

BALLOON MORTGAGES Similar to an ARM, a **balloon mortgage** starts with low payments for a specified period, usually seven to ten years. At the end of that period, a large balloon payment for the entire balance of the mortgage loan is due. Because the balloon payment is often very large, many borrowers refinance when this payment is due. A potential disadvantage is that the lender will set the interest rate of the refinanced loan at whatever the market dictates at that time. As a result, the payments may be higher than they would have been if the buyer had initially obtained a fixed-rate mortgage instead of a balloon mortgage.

HYBRID AND REVERSE MORTGAGES A variety of other less common mortgages are also available. One example is a **hybrid mortgage** (also called a *two-step mortgage*), which starts as a fixed-rate mortgage and then converts into an ARM.

With a **reverse mortgage,** instead of borrowing funds from a bank to buy a home, existing homeowners take cash for the equity in their home. The mortgage does not need to be repaid until the home is sold or the owner dies. Reverse mortgages are geared toward older borrowers (over the age of sixty-two) who have substantial equity in their homes. By converting a portion of that equity into cash, the homeowners can supplement their retirement income.

Home Equity Loans

Home equity refers to the portion of a home's value that is "paid off." For example, if Susanna has a home valued at $200,000 and owes the bank $120,000 on her mortgage, she has 40 percent equity in her house ($80,000/$200,000 = 40 percent). With a **home equity loan,** a bank accepts the borrower's equity as *collateral,* which can be seized if the loan is not repaid on time. If Susanna takes out a $30,000 home equity loan, the amount is added to the amount of her mortgage ($30,000 + $120,000 = $150,000), so she now has only $50,000 (25 percent) equity in her $200,000 home.

Borrowers often take out home equity loans to obtain funds to renovate the property itself. Others obtain home equity loans to pay off debt, such as credit-card debt, that carries a higher interest rate than they will pay on the home equity loan. This strategy can lead to problems, however, if the borrower cannot keep up the payments. Many Americans who lost their homes during the Great Recession were able to pay their original mortgage loans, but not their home equity loans. From the lender's perspective, a home equity loan is riskier than a mortgage loan because home equity loans are *subordinated,* which means that they take a lower priority in any proceeding that occurs if the homeowner fails to make the payments on the primary mortgage.

Creditor Protection

When creditors grant mortgages, they are advancing a significant amount of funds for a number of years. Consequently, creditors take a number of steps to protect their interest. One precaution is to require debtors to obtain private mortgage insurance if they do not make a down payment of at least 20 percent of the purchase price. For example, if a borrower makes a down payment of only 5 percent of the purchase price, the creditor might require insurance covering 15 percent of the cost. Then, if the debtor defaults, the creditor repossesses the house and receives reimbursement from the insurer for the covered portion of the loan.

In addition, the creditor will record the mortgage with the appropriate office in the county where the property is located. Recording ensures that the creditor is officially on record as holding an interest in the property. A lender that fails to record a mortgage could find itself in the position of an unsecured creditor.

Mortgages normally are lengthy documents that include a number of provisions. Many of these provisions are aimed at protecting the creditor's investment.

STATUTE OF FRAUDS Because a mortgage involves a transfer of real property, it must be in writing to comply with the Statute of Frauds (see page 208 in Chapter 9). Most mortgages today are highly formal documents that follow similar formats, but a mortgage is not required to follow any particular form. Indeed, as long as the mortgage satisfies the Statute of Frauds, it generally will be effective.

IMPORTANT MORTGAGE PROVISIONS Mortgage documents ordinarily contain all or most of the following terms:

1. *The terms of the underlying loan.* These include the loan amount, the interest rate, the period of repayment, and other important financial terms, such as the margin and index rate for an ARM. Many lenders include a **prepayment penalty clause,** which requires the borrower to pay a penalty if the mortgage is repaid in full within a certain period. A prepayment penalty helps to protect the lender should the borrower refinance within a short time after obtaining a mortgage.
2. *Provisions relating to the maintenance of the property.* Because the mortgage conveys an interest in the property to the lender, the lender will require the borrower to maintain the property in such a way that the lender's investment is protected.
3. *A statement obligating the borrower to maintain* **homeowners' insurance** (*also known as* hazard insurance) *on the property.* This type of insurance protects the lender's interest in the event of a loss due to certain hazards, such as fire or storm damages.
4. *A list of the nonloan financial obligations to be borne by the borrower.* For example, the borrower typically is required to pay all property taxes, assessments, and other claims against the property.
5. *A provision requiring that the borrower pay certain obligations.* For example, a borrower may be required to pay some or all of the taxes, insurance, assessments, or other expenses associated with the property in advance or through the lender. In this way, the lender is assured that the funds for these expenses will be available when the bills come due.

Although a record number of homeowners have failed to keep up with their mortgage payments in recent years, courts have continued to enforce the terms of plainly written financing documents. In today's more protective environment, borrowers cannot avoid the clear meaning of terms in financing documents, even when the effect may be harsh.

---------- **SECTION 2** ----------
REAL ESTATE FINANCING LAW

During the real estate boom in the first decade of the 2000s, some lenders were less than honest with borrowers about the loan terms they were signing. As a result, many individuals failed to understand how much the monthly payments on ARMs, interest-only mortgages, and other exotic types of loans might increase. In addition, fees and penalties often were not properly disclosed. In an effort to provide more protection for borrowers, Congress and the Federal Reserve Board have instituted a number of new requirements, mostly in the form of required disclosures. Here, we examine some of the more important statutes that provide protection for borrowers. First, though, we look at some of the practices that led to the enactment of these statutes.

Predatory Lending and Other Improper Practices

The general term *predatory lending* is often used to describe situations in which borrowers are the victims of loan terms or lending procedures that are excessive, deceptive, or not properly disclosed. Predatory lending typically occurs during the loan origination process. It includes a number of practices ranging from failure to disclose terms to providing misleading information to outright dishonesty.

Two specific types of improper practices are often at the core of a violation. *Steering and targeting* occurs when the lender manipulates a borrower into accepting a loan product that benefits the lender but is not the best loan for the borrower. For example, a lender may steer a borrower toward an ARM, even though the buyer qualifies for a fixed-rate mortgage. *Loan flipping* occurs when a lender convinces a homeowner to refinance soon after obtaining a mortgage. Such early refinancing rarely benefits the homeowner and may, in fact, result in prepayment penalties.

The Truth-in-Lending Act (TILA)

The Truth-in-Lending Act (TILA) of 1968[1] requires lenders to disclose the terms of a loan in clear, readily understandable language so that borrowers can make rational choices. (We will discuss the TILA in more detail in Chapter 24 in the context of consumer law.) With respect to real estate transactions, the TILA applies only to residential loans.

REQUIRED DISCLOSURES   The major terms that must be disclosed under the TILA include the loan principal; the interest rate at which the loan is made; the **annual percentage rate,** or **APR** (the actual cost of the loan on a yearly basis); and all fees and costs associated with the loan. The TILA requires that these disclosures be made on standardized forms and based on uniform formulas of calculation. Certain types of loans—including ARMs, reverse mortgages, open-ended home equity loans, and high-interest loans—have specially tailored disclosure requirements. The Mortgage Disclosure Improvement Act (MDIA) of 2008[2] amended the TILA to strengthen the disclosures required for ARMs, which, as mentioned earlier, played a leading role in the recent real estate meltdown.

PROHIBITIONS AND REQUIREMENTS   The TILA prohibits certain lender abuses and creates certain borrower rights. Among the prohibited practices is the charging of prepayment penalties on most subprime mortgages and home equity loans.

The TILA also addresses other unfair, abusive, or deceptive home mortgage–lending practices. For example, lenders may not coerce an **appraiser** (an individual who specializes in determining the value of specified real or personal property) into misstating the value of a property on which a loan is to be issued. Also, a loan cannot be advertised as a fixed-rate loan if, in fact, its rate or payment amounts will change.

Right to Rescind.   A mortgage cannot be finalized until at least seven days after a borrower has received the TILA paperwork. Even if all required disclosures are provided, the TILA gives the borrower the right to rescind (cancel) a mortgage within three business days. According to the 2008 amendments, Sunday is the only day of the week that is not a business day. If the lender fails to provide material TILA disclosures, including the three-day right to rescind, the rescission period lasts up to three years.

---

1. 15 U.S.C. Sections 1601–1693r.

2. The Mortgage Disclosure Improvement Act is contained in Sections 2501 through 2503 of the Housing and Economic Recovery Act of 2008, Pub. L. No. 110-289, enacted on July 30, 2008. Congress then amended its provisions as part of the Emergency Economic Stabilization Act of 2008 (also known as the Bailout Bill), Pub. L. No. 110-343, enacted on October 3, 2008.

Written Representations. The TILA requirements apply to the written materials the lender provides, not to any oral representations. If a lender provides the required TILA disclosures, a borrower who fails to read the relevant documents cannot claim fraud, even if the lender orally misrepresented the terms of the loan.

CASE IN POINT Patricia Ostolaza and José Diaz owned a home on which they had two mortgage loans and a home equity line of credit provided by Bank of America. Anthony Falcone called them and said that he could refinance their mortgages in a manner that would reduce their monthly payments. Falcone said that he represented Bank of America when in fact he represented Countrywide Home Loans, Inc. At the closing of the new loan, the homeowners were given all of the relevant documents, including the TILA disclosure statement. The documents accurately stated the monthly payment under the new loan, which was higher than the couple's original payments. The homeowners later filed a lawsuit against Falcone and Countrywide Bank, alleging fraud. The trial court dismissed the suit, and the appellate court upheld the dismissal because the homeowners had been given the opportunity to read all of the relevant documents, but had not done so.[3]

Protection for High-Cost Mortgage Loan Recipients

In the last twenty years, lenders have provided many high-cost and high-fee mortgage products to people who could not easily obtain credit under other loan programs. These loans are commonly known as HOEPA loans, named after the Home Ownership and Equity Protection Act (HOEPA) of 1994,[4] which amended the TILA to create this special category of loans. The rules pertaining to HOEPA loans are contained in Section 32 of *Regulation Z*, enacted by the Federal Reserve Board to implement the TILA (see Chapter 24).

A loan can qualify for protection under HOEPA either because it carries a high rate of interest or because it entails high fees for the borrower. HOEPA applies if the APR disclosed for the loan exceeds the interest rates of **Treasury securities** (or bonds) of comparable maturity by more than 8 percentage points for a first mortgage and 10 percentage points for a second mortgage. HOEPA can also apply when the total fees paid by the consumer exceed 8 percent of the loan amount or a set dollar amount (based on changes in the Consumer Price Index), whichever is larger.

SPECIAL CONSUMER PROTECTIONS If a loan qualifies for HOEPA protection, the consumer must receive several disclosures in addition to those required by the TILA. The lender must disclose the APR, the regular payment amount, and any required balloon payments. For loans with a variable rate of interest, the lender must disclose that the rate and monthly payments may increase and state the potential maximum monthly payment. These disclosures must be provided at least three business days before the loan is finalized.

In addition, the lender must provide a written notice stating that the consumer need not complete the loan simply because he or she received the disclosures or signed the loan application. Borrowers must also be informed that they could lose their home (and all funds invested in it) if they default on the loan.

HOEPA also prohibits lenders from engaging in certain practices, such as requiring balloon payments for loans with terms of five years or less. Loans that result in negative amortization are also prohibited. **Negative amortization** occurs when the monthly payments are insufficient to cover the interest due on the loan. The difference is then added to the principal, so the balance owed on the loan increases over time.

REMEDIES AND LIABILITIES For HOEPA violations, consumers can obtain damages in an amount equal to all finance charges and fees paid if the lender's failure to disclose is deemed material. Any failure to comply with HOEPA provisions also extends the borrower's right to rescind the loan for up to three years.

Whether a particular loan is covered by HOEPA and thus is entitled to the statute's significant protections can have important ramifications because it can determine whether a lender can foreclose on a loan. In the following case, a consumer challenged the foreclosure of her home by claiming that the bank had not met all of the requirements under HOEPA.

---

3. *Ostolaza-Diaz v. Countrywide Bank, N.A.*, 2010 WL 95145 (4th Cir. 2010).

4. 15 U.S.C. Sections 1637 and 1647.

CASE 16.1
Bank of New York v. Parnell

Court of Appeal of Louisiana, Fifth Circuit, 32 So.3d 877 (2010).
www.fifthcircuit.org/Opinions.aspx[a]

BACKGROUND AND FACTS • Kathleen Parnell executed a promissory note and mortgage in favor of EquiCredit Corporation of America on May 9, 2001. Later that year, EquiCredit assigned its rights to the Bank of New York. On June 19, 2003, Parnell's attorney wrote a letter to the Bank of New York on behalf of Parnell providing a notice of rescission. The letter stated that rescission was proper because the loan was governed by the Home Ownership and Equity Protection Act (HOEPA) and that EquiCredit had failed to deliver required material disclosures. These disclosures included documents stating that Parnell did not need to enter into the loan and that she could lose her home as a result of entering into the loan. The bank responded that the loan was not large enough to trigger HOEPA disclosures but that, in any event, Parnell had received full and accurate disclosures. Later, the bank filed a petition alleging that Parnell was in default and that it was accelerating the payments due under the mortgage. Subsequently, the trial judge directed the sheriff to seize and sell the property secured by the mortgage. Parnell filed a petition to stop the seizure and sale. The bank filed a motion for summary judgment in its favor, which the court granted. Parnell appealed.

IN THE LANGUAGE OF THE COURT
Fredericka Homberg *WICKER,* Judge.
* * * *

Congress enacted the Truth in Lending Act to assure a meaningful disclosure of credit terms so that the consumer will be able to compare more readily the various credit terms available to him and avoid the uninformed use of credit, and to protect the consumer against inaccurate and unfair credit billing and credit card practices. Accordingly, *the Act requires creditors to provide borrowers with clear and accurate disclosures of terms dealing with things like finance charges, annual percentage rates of interest, and the borrower's rights. A creditor's failure to comply with these disclosure requirements may result in actual and statutory damages.* Additionally, if a creditor fails to provide a consumer with material disclosures when the loan is secured by the consumer's "principal dwelling," the consumer has "the right to rescind the transaction until midnight of the third business day following the consummation of the transaction or the delivery of the information and rescission forms required * * * whichever is later." If the required material disclosures are not delivered, the rescission period expires "three years after the date of consummation [completion] of the transaction or upon the sale of the property, whichever occurs first." [Emphasis added.]

The Truth in Lending Act as amended by HOEPA and Regulation Z of the Federal Reserve Board provides that when a consumer loan violates the Act, the consumer is entitled to rescind the loan, to recover monies and other property given to the creditor, and to [cancel] any mortgages made in connection with the loan.

* * * *

TILA was enacted in 1968 to aid the unsophisticated consumer so that he would not be easily misled as to the total costs of financing. Consequently, it is not surprising that courts have held that TILA, as a remedial statute which is designed to balance the scales, [and] "thought to be weighed in favor of lenders," is to be liberally construed in favor of borrowers. Nonetheless, finding that TILA's protections were still inadequate, Congress added the protections and requirements of the Home Ownership and Equity Protection Act ("HOEPA") in 1994. HOEPA was designed to address the problem of "reverse redlining," that is, the targeting of persons for "credit on unfair terms" based on their income, race, or ethnicity. In an attempt to even the playing field, Congress enacted HOEPA to ensure that consumers understand the terms of such loans and are protected from high pressure sales tactics[.] * * * The legislation requires creditors making High Cost Mortgages to provide a special, streamlined High Cost Mortgage

---

a. Select "Search by Case Number" in the list of options. When that page opens, enter "09" and "439" in the two boxes for the case number. When the case title appears in the box below, click on the Adobe Reader icon to view the case. The Louisiana court system maintains this Web site.

CASE 16.1 CONTINUED ➡ disclosure three days before consummation of the transaction. The bill also prohibits High Cost Mortgages from including certain terms such as prepayment penalties and balloon payments that have proven particularly problematic.

Accordingly, we find that the trial judge erred in granting summary judgment insofar as the HOEPA claim.

DECISION AND REMEDY • *The appellate court overturned the lower court's grant of summary judgment and sent the case back to the lower court for a full trial on the issue.*

THE LEGAL ENVIRONMENT DIMENSION • *The Truth-in-Lending Act, HOEPA, and other consumer protection laws exist to protect purchasers from unscrupulous lenders or sellers. As consumers become better informed about these issues, will these laws still be needed? Discuss.*

WHAT IF THE FACTS WERE DIFFERENT? • *If the lender had been dealing with a borrower who was a professor of finance at Harvard, would the appellate judge have ruled the same way? Why or why not?*

Protection for Higher-Priced Mortgage Loans

In 2008, the Federal Reserve Board enacted an amendment to Regulation Z that created a second category of expensive loans, called Higher-Priced Mortgage Loans (HPMLs). Only mortgages secured by a consumer's principal home qualify to receive the HPML designation.

REQUIREMENTS TO QUALIFY To be an HPML, a mortgage must have an APR that exceeds the *average prime offer rate* for a comparable transaction by 1.5 percentage points or more if the loan is a first lien on a dwelling. (The **average prime offer rate** is the rate offered to the best-qualified borrowers as established by a survey of lenders.) If the loan is secured by a subordinate lien on a home, then the APR must exceed the average prime offer rate by 3.5 percentage points or more in order to be considered an HPML.

Mortgages excluded from coverage include those for the initial construction of a home, temporary or *bridge loans* that are one year or shorter in duration, home equity lines of credit, and reverse mortgages. (**Bridge loans** are short-term loans that allow a buyer to make a down payment on a new home before selling her or his current home.)

SPECIAL PROTECTIONS FOR CONSUMERS As with a HOEPA loan, consumers receiving an HPML receive additional protections. First, lenders cannot make an HPML based on the value of the consumer's home without verifying the consumer's ability to repay the loan. This verification is typically accomplished through review of the consumer's financial records such as tax returns, bank account statements, and payroll records. The creditor must also verify the consumer's other credit obligations.

Second, prepayment penalties are severely restricted for HPMLs. Prepayment penalties are allowed only if they are limited to two years, and they will not even apply if the source of the prepayment funds is a refinancing by the creditor or the creditor's affiliate. Additionally, lenders must establish *escrow accounts* for borrowers' payments for homeowners' insurance and property taxes for all first mortgages. (An escrow account holds funds to be paid to a third party—see Chapter 26.) Finally, lenders cannot structure a loan specifically to evade the HPML protections.

SECTION 3
FORECLOSURES

If a homeowner **defaults,** or fails to make mortgage payments, the lender has the right to foreclose on the mortgaged property. **Foreclosure** is a process that allows a lender to legally repossess and auction off the property that is securing a loan.[5] Foreclosure is expensive and time consuming, however, and generally benefits neither the borrowers, who lose their homes, nor the lenders, which face the prospect of losses on their loans. Therefore, various methods to avoid foreclosure have been developed. We look first at some of these methods and then turn to the foreclosure process itself.

How to Avoid Foreclosure

In the past, especially during the Great Depression of the 1930s, a number of alternatives to foreclosure

---

5. Lenders other than those holding a first mortgage on a property may also foreclose. For example, a roofing company holding a mechanic's lien for the unpaid cost of a new roof can foreclose on the property.

have been developed. More recently, as foreclosures have become more common than at any time since the Great Depression, Congress has intervened to aid in the modification of mortgage loans.

FORBEARANCE AND WORKOUT AGREEMENTS The first preforeclosure option a borrower has is called forbearance. **Forbearance** is the postponement, for a limited time, of part or all of the payments on a loan in jeopardy of foreclosure. Such payment waivers had their origins in the Great Depression. A lender grants forbearance when it expects that, during the forbearance period, the borrower can solve the problem by securing a new job, selling the property, or finding another acceptable solution.

When a borrower fails to make payments as required, the lender may attempt to negotiate a workout. As noted in Chapter 15, a *workout* is a voluntary process to cure the default in some fashion. The parties may even create a formal **workout agreement**—a written document that describes the rights and responsibilities of the parties as they try to resolve the default without proceeding to foreclosure. In such an agreement, the lender will likely agree to delay seeking foreclosure or other legal rights. In exchange, the borrower may agree to provide financial information to the lender on which a workout might be constructed. Whether a workout is possible or preferable to foreclosure depends on many factors, including the value of the property, the amount of the unpaid principal, the market in which the property will be sold, the relationship of the lender and the borrower, and the financial condition of the borrower.

HOUSING AND URBAN DEVELOPMENT ASSISTANCE A lender may be able to work with the borrower to obtain an interest-free loan from the U.S. Department of Housing and Urban Development (HUD) to bring the mortgage current. HUD assistance may be available if the loan is at least four months (but not more than twelve months) delinquent, if the property is not in foreclosure, and if the borrower is able to make full mortgage payments. When the lender files a claim, HUD pays the lender the amount necessary to make the mortgage current. The borrower executes a note to HUD, and a lien for the second loan is placed on the property. The promissory note is interest free and comes due if the property is sold.

SHORT SALES When an owner is unable to make mortgage payments, a lender may agree to a **short sale**—that is, a sale of the property for less than the balance of the mortgage loan. Typically, the borrower

has to show some hardship, such as the loss of job, a decline in the value of the home, a divorce, or a death in the household. In a short sale, the borrower sells the real property with the permission of the lender, often for an amount less than the balance due on the mortgage loan. The lender receives the proceeds of the sale, and the borrower still owes the balance of the debt to the lender, unless the lender specifically agrees to forgive the remaining debt. In 2007, Congress passed the Mortgage Forgiveness Debt Relief Act,[6] which eliminated income taxes on the forgiven debt. (Ordinarily, forgiven debt must be reported as income that is subject to federal income tax.)

A short sale can offer several advantages. Although the borrower's credit rating is affected, the negative impact is less than it would be with a foreclosure, which generally remains on the borrower's credit report for seven years.[7] The short sale process also avoids the expense of foreclosure for the lender and the trauma of being evicted from the home for the homeowner. But because the lender often has approval rights in a short sale, the sale process can take much longer than a standard real estate transaction. In addition, although the parties' losses are mitigated, the borrower still loses her or his home.

SALE AND LEASEBACK In some situations, the homeowner may be able to sell the property to an investor who is looking for an income property. The owner sells the property to the investor and then leases it back at an amount that is less than the monthly mortgage payment. The owner-seller uses the proceeds of the sale to pay off the mortgage and still has the use and possession of the property. In some circumstances, this strategy can also be used to raise capital when there is no risk of loss of the property.

HOME AFFORDABLE MODIFICATION PROGRAM In 2009, the U.S. Treasury Department launched the Home Affordable Modification Program (HAMP) to encourage private lenders to modify mortgages so as to lower the monthly payments of borrowers who are in default. The program may share in the costs of modifying the loan and provides incentives to lenders based on successful loan modification. A series of steps must be taken to determine debtor eligibility, the appropriate method for reducing the mortgage burden, and the possibility of forbearance of part of the mortgage loan.

---

6. Pub. L. No. 110-142, December 7, 2007.
7. Credit reporting agencies also claim that a foreclosure looks much worse on a credit report than a bankruptcy.

Determination If a Homeowner Qualifies.
HAMP modifications are not available for every mortgage. To qualify, the loan must have originated on or before January 1, 2009, the home must be occupied by the owner, and the unpaid balance may not exceed $729,750 for a single-unit property.[8] The homeowner must be facing financial hardship and be either more than sixty days late on mortgage payments or at risk of imminent default. Homeowners are required to verify their hardship through appropriate documentation.

In addition, the home must be the homeowner's primary residence. Investor-owned homes, vacant homes, and condemned properties are not eligible under the program. Borrowers in active litigation related to their mortgage may take advantage of the program without waiving their legal rights.

Steps Taken to Alleviate the Mortgage Burden.
The purpose of HAMP is not to force lenders to forgive all high-risk mortgages, but rather to reduce monthly mortgage payments to a level that the homeowner can reasonably pay. The goal is to reduce the debtor's mortgage payment to 31 percent of his or her gross monthly income.

The loan is then restructured by adding any delinquencies (such as accrued interest, past-due taxes, or unpaid insurance premiums) to the principal amount. This increases the number of payments but eliminates the delinquencies by spreading them over the life of the loan. Once the loan is restructured, lenders try to incrementally lower the mortgage interest rate to a level at which the payments are less than 31 percent of the debtor's income. If the lender cannot reach the 31 percent target by lowering the interest rate to 2 percent, then the lender can **reamortize** the loan (change the way the payments are configured), extending the schedule of payments for up to forty years.

Borrowers who qualify under HAMP then begin a ninety-day trial period to determine their ability to make three modified monthly mortgage payments. If they succeed, the lender offers them permanent modifications.

VOLUNTARY CONVEYANCE Under some circumstances, the parties might benefit from a **deed in lieu of foreclosure,** by which the property is conveyed (transferred) to the lender in satisfaction of the mortgage. A property that is worth close to the outstanding loan principal and on which no other loans have been taken might be the subject of such a conveyance.

Although the lender faces the risk that it may ultimately sell the property for less than the loan amount, the lender avoids the time, risk, and expense of foreclosure litigation. The borrower who gives the property to the lender without a fight also avoids the foreclosure process and may preserve a better credit rating than if he or she had been forced to give up the property involuntarily.

FRIENDLY FORECLOSURE Another way for the parties to avoid a contested foreclosure is to engage in a friendly foreclosure. In such a transaction, the borrower in default agrees to submit to the court's jurisdiction, to waive any defenses as well as the right to appeal, and to cooperate with the lender. This process takes longer than a voluntary conveyance, but all of the parties have greater certainty as to the finality of the transaction with respect to others who might have a financial interest in the property.

PREPACKAGED BANKRUPTCY Bankruptcy allows a borrower to escape payment of some debts (see Chapter 15). A prepackaged bankruptcy allows a debtor to negotiate terms with all of her or his creditors in advance. The package of agreements is then submitted to the bankruptcy court for approval. This approach to bankruptcy will likely save considerable time and expense for all parties involved, although the creditors are also likely to receive less than full payment on their particular debts.

The Foreclosure Procedure

If all efforts to find another solution fail, the lender will proceed to foreclosure—a process that dates back to English law. A formal foreclosure is necessary to extinguish the borrower's *equitable right of redemption* (discussed later). Generally, two types of foreclosure are used in the United States: **judicial foreclosure** and **power of sale foreclosure.** In a judicial foreclosure, which is available in all states, a court supervises the process. In a power of sale foreclosure, the lender is allowed to foreclose on and sell the property without judicial supervision. Only a few states permit power of sale foreclosures because borrowers have less protection when a court does not supervise the process.

ACCELERATION CLAUSES In a strict foreclosure, the lender may seek only the amount of the missed payments, not the entire loan amount. Therefore, lenders often include an *acceleration clause* in their loan documents. An **acceleration clause** allows

---

8. Higher limits are allowed for properties with two to four units.

the lender to call the entire loan due—even if only one payment is late or missed. Thus, with an acceleration clause, the lender can foreclose only once on the entire amount of the loan rather than having to foreclosure on smaller amounts over a period of time as each payment is missed.

NOTICE OF DEFAULT AND OF SALE To initiate a foreclosure, a lender must record a **notice of default** with the appropriate county office. The borrower is then on notice of a possible foreclosure and can take steps to pay the loan and cure the default. If the loan is not paid within a reasonable time (usually three months), the borrower will receive a **notice of sale.** In addition, the notice of sale usually is posted on the property, recorded with the county, and announced in the newspaper.

The property is then sold in an auction on the courthouse steps at the time and location indicated in the notice of sale. The buyer generally has to pay cash within twenty-four hours for the property. If the procedures are not followed precisely, the parties may have to resort to litigation to establish clear ownership of the property. The following case illustrates how the notice requirements work.

✳ EXTENDED CASE 16.2 ✳
Mitchell v. Valteau

Court of Appeal of Louisiana, Fourth Circuit, 30 So.3d 1108 (2010).
www.la4th.org/Opinions.aspx[a]

IN THE LANGUAGE OF THE COURT
Patricia Rivet *MURRAY,* Judge.
* * * *

On April 30, 2001, Dr. Mitchell borrowed $143,724 to purchase a house and the lot on which it was located * * * (the "Property"). [The loan] * * * was secured by a mortgage on the Property. * * * The mortgage contained [a clause] providing for the acceleration of the amount secured and the sale of the property in the event of a default on the loan.

In 2006, Dr. Mitchell defaulted on her mortgage payments. On December 15, 2006, [the lending bank] commenced an executory proceeding * * *. The trial court ordered the issuance of a writ of seizure and sale.

On January 23, 2007, Dr. Mitchell was served personally with the notice of seizure, which stated that a sheriff's sale was tentatively scheduled for November 2, 2007.

Subsequently, * * * Dr. Mitchell and [the bank] entered into a [repayment agreement that postponed the seizure and sale of the property while the agreement was in place]. * * * Although Dr. Mitchell made a few (about two) payments, she was unable to comply with the payment terms of the repayment agreement.

On July 19, 2007, the trial court ordered that the original petition be amended and that an amended writ of seizure be issued. On September 7, 2007, the sheriff issued an amended notice of seizure. * * * The sheriff attempted to serve Dr. Mitchell at her residence on seven occasions. Because the sheriff was unable to serve Dr. Mitchell, [the court appointed a receiver who] accepted service on Dr. Mitchell's behalf.

On January 3, 2008, the Property was sold at a sheriff's sale * * *.
* * * *

On April 11, 2008, Dr. Mitchell filed a Petition to Annul Executory Proceedings and Judicial Sale, and for Damages for Wrongful Seizure

[against Sheriff Paul Valteau, Jr., the lending bank, and others].

On November 18, 2008, [the bank] filed a motion for summary judgment. Following a hearing, the trial court granted the motion and rendered judgment dismissing all the parties. [Dr. Mitchell appealed.]
* * * *

A creditor seeking to enforce a mortgage or privilege on property by executory process must file a petition praying for the seizure and sale of the property affected by the mortgage or privilege. * * * In this case, [the bank] filed a petition for executor process and attached thereto authentic evidence satisfying all three requirements for obtaining an order of seizure and sale: a copy of the note, mortgage agreement, and a certified copy of the assignment of the mortgage note to it. * * * It is undisputed that Dr. Mitchell was served with the initial notice of seizure. Dr. Mitchell, however, contends that the sheriff also was required to serve her with the amended notice of seizure from

---

a. From the search mode choices, select "Search Cases by Published Date" and in the "Sort By" drop-down menu, select "Date Published." Then select "Click for Calendar." Using the arrow at the top of the calendar, go to January 2010, then click on "27." Scroll through the list at the bottom of the page to the case title and click on "Download" to access the opinion. The Louisiana court system maintains this Web site.

EXTENDED CASE 16.2 CONTINUED

which her property was seized and sold. [Emphasis added.]

Resolution of the issue of whether service of the amended notice of seizure was required turns on construction of several * * * statutory provisions. La. C.C.P. Art. [Louisiana Code of Civil Procedure Article] 2721 provides that the sheriff must serve upon the defendant "a written notice of the seizure of the property. ["] La. C.C.P. Art. 2293(B) also provides that the sheriff shall serve "a notice of seizure."

* * * *

Construing La. R.S. [Louisiana Revised Statutes] 13:3852 and La. C.C.P. Art. 2293(B) * * * [a prior court] rejected a debtor's argument that she was entitled to a second notice of seizure when the first sale was delayed.

* * * [There,] the court * * * reasoned that the debtor had defaulted under the terms of the mortgage and that the creditor had validly exercised its right to have the property seized and sold in accord with the executor process provisions. * * * The court further reasoned that read together La. C.C.P. Art 2293(B)—which requires service of "a written notice of seizure of the property"—and La. R.S. 13:3852—which requires [that] the notice include "the date of the first scheduled sale of the property"—mandate that "upon seizure of their property, a defendant receive a written notice that informs them of the first scheduled sale date." * * * The court still further reasoned that there was no Louisiana authority for requiring a creditor to provide a debtor with notice of a rescheduled judicial sale.

The situation in this case is analogous to the situation presented in the [referenced] case. Dr. Mitchell defaulted on her loan agreement and [the bank] established its right to proceed by executory process to seize and sell the Property. Dr. Mitchell was served with a notice of seizure. Thereafter, she entered into the repayment agreement, [which] expressly provided that the executor proceeding would be placed on hold for the time the repayment agreement was in place. The agreement also provided for the resumption of the foreclosure in the event of a default in its terms, which Dr. Mitchell acknowledged occurred. When the executory proceeding was resumed, there was no obligation to serve Dr. Mitchell with another notice of seizure.

* * * We thus find the trial court correctly concluded that there was no requirement that Dr. Mitchell be served with the amended notice of seizure.

QUESTIONS

1. What are the purposes of the notice provisions in the Louisiana code? Did this court stay true to those purposes? Explain your answer.
2. How might the lender have avoided the dispute in this case?

DEFICIENCY JUDGMENTS If any equity remains after the foreclosed property is sold, the borrower is often able to keep the difference between the sale price and the mortgage amount. If the sale amount is not enough to cover the loan amount, the lender can ask a court for a *deficiency judgment* (a judgment against the borrower for the amount of debt remaining unpaid after the collateral is sold). A deficiency judgment requires the borrower to make up the difference to the lender over time. (Note that some states do not allow deficiency judgments for mortgaged residential real estate.)

Redemption Rights

Borrowers in every state have the right to purchase the property after default by paying the full amount of the debt, plus any interest and costs that have accrued, before the foreclosure sale. This is referred to as the buyer's **equitable right of redemption.**

Equitable redemption allows a defaulting borrower to gain title and regain possession of a property.[9] The idea behind equitable redemption is that it is only fair, or equitable, for the borrower to have a chance to regain possession after default. Although many critics question the utility of this right, all states still allow for an equitable right of redemption.

Some states have passed laws that entitle a borrower to repurchase property even *after* a judicial foreclosure.[10] This is called a **statutory right of redemption,** and it may be exercised even if the property was purchased at auction by a third party. Generally, the borrower may exercise this right for up to one year from the time the house is sold at a

---

9. Note that a foreclosure proceeding is the legal means by which a lender terminates the borrower's equitable right of redemption.
10. This right of redemption is not available after a power of sale foreclosure.

foreclosure sale.[11] The borrower[12] must pay the price at which the house was sold at the foreclosure sale (the redemption price), plus taxes, interest, and assessments, as opposed to the balance owed on the foreclosed loan.

---

11. Some states do not allow a borrower to waive the statutory right of redemption. This means that a buyer at auction must wait one year to obtain title to, and possession of, a foreclosed property.
12. Some states also allow the spouse of a defaulting borrower or creditors holding liens on the property to purchase the property under the statutory right of redemption.

Some states allow the borrower to retain possession of the property after the foreclosure sale until the statutory redemption period ends. If the borrower does not exercise the right of redemption, the new buyer receives title to and possession of the property. The statutes creating this right were enacted to drive up sale prices at foreclosure auctions on the theory that third parties would offer prices too high for defaulting borrowers to afford. Instead, in many states, the statutory right of redemption has created a strong disincentive for potential buyers to tie up their funds in an uncertain transaction.

REVIEWING
Mortgages and Foreclosures after the Recession

Al and Betty Smith's home is valued at $200,000. They have paid off their mortgage and own the house outright—that is, they have 100 percent home equity. They lost most of their savings when the stock market declined during the Great Recession. Now they want to start a new business and need funds, so they decide to obtain a home equity loan. They borrow $150,000 for ten years at an interest rate of 12 percent. On the date they take out the loan, a ten-year Treasury bond is yielding 3 percent. The Smiths pay a total of $10,000 in fees to Alpha Bank. The Smiths are not given any notice that they can lose their home if they do not meet their obligations under the loan. Two weeks after completing the loan, the Smiths change their minds and want to rescind the loan.

1. Is the Smiths' loan covered by the Truth-in-Lending Act as amended by the Home Ownership and Equity Protection Act? Why or why not?
2. Do the Smiths have a right to rescind the loan two weeks after the fact, or are they too late? Explain.
3. Assume now that Alpha Bank gave the Smiths all of the required notices before the loan was completed. If all other facts remain the same, do the Smiths have a right to rescind? Discuss your answer.
4. Suppose now that the Smiths never rescind the loan and that they default four years later while still owing Alpha Bank $120,000. The bank forecloses and raises only $110,000 when the house is sold at auction. If the state where the Smiths live follows the majority rule, can Alpha Bank seek the remaining $10,000 from the Smiths?

DEBATE THIS: *Federal legislation enacted in the past few years has unfairly benefited homeowners who should not have bought such expensive houses and taken on so much debt.*

TERMS AND CONCEPTS

acceleration clause 367

adjustable-rate
  mortgage (ARM) 360

annual percentage
  rate (APR) 362

appraiser 362

average prime offer
  rate 365

balloon mortgage 360

bridge loan 365

deed in lieu of
  foreclosure 367

default 365

down payment 359

equitable right of
  redemption 369

fixed-rate mortgage 359

forbearance 366

foreclosure 365

home equity loan 361

homeowners' insurance 361

hybrid mortgage 360

interest-only
  (IO) mortgage 360

judicial foreclosure 367

mortgage 359

negative amortization 363	prepayment penalty	statutory right of	Treasury securities 363
notice of default 368	clause 361	redemption 369	workout agreement 366
notice of sale 368	reamortize 367	subprime mortgage 360	
power of sale	reverse mortgage 360		
foreclosure 367	short sale 366		

QUESTIONS AND CASE PROBLEMS

16–1. Disclosure Requirements Rancho Mortgage, Inc., is planning a new advertising campaign designed to attract homebuyers in a difficult economic environment. Rancho wants to promote its new loan product, which offers a fixed interest rate for the first five years and then switches to a variable rate of interest. Rancho believes that Spanish-speaking homebuyers have been underserved in recent years, and it wants to direct its ads to that market. What must Rancho say (and not say) in its advertising campaigns about the structure of the loan product, and in what language? What language should Rancho use in its Truth-in-Lending disclosures? Why?

16–2. QUESTION WITH SAMPLE ANSWER: Real Estate Financing.

Jane Lane refinanced her mortgage with Central Equity, Inc. Central Equity split the transaction into two separate loan documents with separate Truth-in-Lending disclosure statements and settlement statements. Two years later, Lane sought to exercise her right to rescission under the Home Ownership and Equity Protection Act (HOEPA), but Central Equity refused. Central Equity responded that the original transactions comprised two separate loan transactions and because neither loan imposed sufficient fees and costs to trigger HOEPA, its protections did not apply. Lane claims that if the costs and fees were combined into a single transaction (which Lane expected the loan to be), they would surpass the HOEPA threshold and trigger its protections. In turn, because Central Equity did not provide the necessary disclosures under HOEPA, Lane argues that she can properly rescind under its provisions. Is Lane correct? Does loan splitting allow the lender to count each loan transaction with a borrower separately for HOEPA purposes? Why or why not?

• **For a sample answer to Question 16–2, go to Appendix F at the end of this text.**

16–3. Lender's Options In 2008, Frank relocated and purchased a home in a beautiful mountain town. The home was five years old, and Frank purchased it for $450,000. He paid $90,000 as a down payment and financed the remaining $360,000 of the purchase price with a loan from Bank of Town. Frank signed mortgage documents that gave Bank of Town a mortgage interest in the home. Frank made payments on the loan for three years. But the housing market declined significantly, and Frank's home is now valued at only $265,000. The balance due on his loan is $354,000. In addition to the decline in housing prices, the economy has slowed, and the booming business that Frank started when he bought the home has experienced a decrease in revenues. It seems inevitable that Frank will not be able to make his mortgage payments. Discuss Bank of Town's options in this situation.

16–4. Home Ownership and Equity Protection Act Michael and Edith Jones owned a home that went into foreclosure. During this time, they were contacted by a representative of Rees-Max, whose notice read: "There are only a few months to go in your redemption period! Your options to save the equity in your home are fading. Call me immediately for a no-bull, no-obligation assessment of your situation. Even if you have been 'promised' by a mortgage broker or investor that they will help, CALL ME . . . ." The Joneses contacted Rees-Max, and they entered into a sale and leaseback transaction. Rees-Max would purchase the property from the Joneses, the Joneses would lease the property for a few months, and then the Joneses would purchase the property back from Rees-Max on a contract. The property was appraised at $278,000 and purchased by Rees-Max for $214,000, with more than $30,000 in fees. The Joneses disputed these fees, and Rees-Max moved to evict them. The agreement did not use the terms *debt, security,* or *mortgage,* and the documents stated that no security interest was granted. Does this transaction constitute a mortgage that would receive protection under the Truth-in-Lending Act and the Home Ownership and Equity Protection Act? Why or why not? [*Jones v. Rees-Max, LLC,* 514 F.Supp.2d 1139 (D.Minn. 2007)]

16–5. Right of Rescission George and Mona Antanuos obtained a mortgage loan secured with rental property from the First National Bank of Arizona. At the closing, they received from the bank a "Notice of Right to Cancel," informing them of their three-day rescission period under the Truth-in-Lending Act (TILA). The following day, according to the Antanuoses, they informed the lender via fax that they wished to exercise their right to rescind. The lender refused to rescind the agreement. George and Mona sued the bank. In federal court, the Antanuoses did not dispute that a consumer's right to rescind under the TILA applies only to the consumer's original dwelling and that they had used their commercial property as a security interest. Instead, the Antanuoses argued that the bank was prohibited from denying them the rescission right because they relied to their detriment on the bank's disclosure, which would have been required under the TILA. Would the court be convinced? Explain. [*Antanuos v. First National Bank of Arizona*, 508 F.Supp.2d 466 (E.D.Va. 2007)]

16–6. Mortgage Foreclosure In January 2003, Gary Ryder and Washington Mutual Bank, F.A., executed a note in which Ryder promised to pay $2,450,000, plus interest at a rate that could vary from month to month. The amount of the first payment was $10,933. The note was to be paid in full by February 1, 2033. A mortgage on Ryder's real property at 345 Round Hill Road in Greenwich, Connecticut, in favor of the bank secured his obligations under the note. The note and mortgage required that he pay the taxes on the property, which he did not do in 2004 and 2005. The bank notified him that he was in default and, when he failed to act, paid $50,095.92 in taxes, penalties, interest, and fees. Other disputes arose between the parties, and Ryder filed a suit in a federal district court against the bank, alleging, in part, breach of contract. He charged, among other things, that some of his timely payments were not processed and were subjected to incorrect late fees, forcing him to make excessive payments and ultimately resulting in "non-payment by Ryder." The bank filed a counterclaim, seeking to foreclose on the mortgage. What should a creditor be required to prove to foreclose on mortgaged property? What would be a debtor's most effective defense? Which party in this case is likely to prevail on the bank's counterclaim? Why? [*Ryder v. Washington Mutual Bank, F.A.*, 501 F.Supp.2d 311 (D.Conn. 2007)]

16–7. CASE PROBLEM WITH SAMPLE ANSWER: Wrongful Foreclosure.

 After a series of bankruptcies and foreclosures, Wells Fargo Home Mortgage, the mortgagee, foreclosed on the debtors' home and purchased it for $33,500. The debtors then filed a complaint against Wells Fargo and certain related entities, claiming wrongful foreclosure and breach of contract. The debtors sought damages, specific performance, and other remedies. The dispute grew out of a loan note for $51,300 that the plaintiffs had executed with Southern Atlantic Financial Services, Inc. In exchange for that loan, the plaintiffs gave Southern Atlantic a security interest in their home. Southern Atlantic transferred its interest in the property and the note to GE Capital Mortgage Services, Inc. On September 30, 2000, Wells Fargo Home Mortgage started servicing this loan for GE. Wells Fargo acquired the loan from GE on December 1, 2004. When the plaintiffs did not make all of the required payments, Wells Fargo sought relief from a stay to file a foreclosure because the debtors were in arrears on the mortgage. The parties agreed that Wells Fargo could have relief from the stay if the debtors failed to make all future payments. Claiming default, Wells Fargo then filed a foreclosure and bought the property at the sale. The debtors filed a complaint

alleging that the price paid was shockingly insufficient and constituted wrongful foreclosure and a breach of fiduciary duty. Under what circumstances is a foreclosure sale unfair? Does a property foreclosure sale have to realize the market price? The amount owed on the note? Discuss. [*In re Sharpe*, 425 Bankr. 620 (N.D.Ala. 2010)]

- • **To view a sample answer for Problem 16–7, go to this book's Web site at www.cengage.com/blaw/cross, select "Chapter 16," and click on "Case Problem with Sample Answer."**

16–8. Foreclosure on Mortgage and Liens LaSalle Bank loaned $8 million to Cypress Creek to build an apartment complex. The loan was secured by a mortgage. Cypress Creek hired contractors to provide concrete work, plumbing, carpentry, and other construction services. Cypress Creek went bankrupt, owing LaSalle $3 million. The contractors recorded mechanic's liens when they did not get paid for their work. The property was sold to LaSalle at a sheriff's sale for $1.3 million. The contractors claimed that they should be paid the amounts they were owed out of the $1.3 million and that the mechanic's liens should be satisfied before any funds were distributed to LaSalle for its mortgage. The trial court distributed the $1.3 million primarily to LaSalle, with only a small fraction going to the contractors. Do the liens come before the mortgage in priority of payment? Discuss. [*LaSalle Bank v. Cypress Creek*, 925 N.E.2d 233 (Ill.App.3d 2010)]

16–9. A QUESTION OF ETHICS: Predatory Lending.

 Peter Sutton owned a home that was subject to two mortgages, but his only source of income was a $1,080 monthly Social Security benefit. In an effort to reduce his mortgage payments, which exceeded $1,400 per month, he sought a refinancing loan through an Apex Mortgage Services mortgage broker. According to Sutton, the broker led him to believe that he could receive, from Countrywide Home Loans, Inc., a refinancing loan with payments of $428 per month. The broker, however, ultimately arranged for Sutton to receive an adjustable-rate loan from Countrywide; the loan required monthly payments that started at more than $1,000 per month and were subject to further increases. Sutton also alleged that the broker reported his monthly income as four times the actual amount and failed to inform Sutton about the existence of a prepayment penalty. Sutton signed forms stating that he agreed to the terms of the loan arranged by the broker. He claimed, however, that he did not understand the terms of the loan until after the closing. As compensation for brokering Sutton's loan, Countrywide paid Apex $7,270, which included a yield-spread premium of $4,710. (A yield-spread premium is a form of compensation paid to a broker by a lender for providing a borrower with a loan that carries an interest rate above the lender's par rate.) Sutton sued the broker and lender claiming violations of federal law. [*Sutton v. Countrywide Home Loans, Inc.*, ___ F.3d ___ (11th Cir. 2009)]

(a) Who is ethically responsible for Sutton's predicament? To what extent does Sutton have a duty to read and understand what he signs? Discuss.

(b) Sutton argued that because the broker provided services that were of no value to Sutton, the broker should not receive the yield-spread premium. Do you agree? Why or why not?

(c) Did Countrywide, the lender, have any ethical obligation to monitor the activities of the broker?

Would the result have been different if Countrywide had intervened before the documents were signed? Explain.

LEGAL RESEARCH EXERCISES ON THE WEB

Go to this text's Web site at **www.cengage.com/blaw/cross**, select "Chapter 16," and click on "Practical Internet Exercises." There you will find the following Internet research exercises that you can perform to learn more about the topics covered in this chapter.

Practical Internet Exercise 16–1: Legal Perspective
Federal Loan Modification Program

Practical Internet Exercise 16–2: Management Perspective
Understanding the Truth-in-Lending Act

Many aspects of the commercial environment lend themselves to ethical analysis. Businesspersons certainly face ethical questions when they deal with the application of black-letter law to contracts. (*Black-letter law* is an informal term for the principles of law that courts usually accept or that are embodied in statutes.) Courts, for example, generally will not inquire into the adequacy of the consideration given in a contract. In other words, a court will not reevaluate a contract to determine whether what each party gave is equivalent to what that party received.

Ethical questions are also at the core of many principles of the law of sales. Many of the provisions of the Uniform Commercial Code (UCC), such as good faith and commercial reasonableness, though designed to meet the practical needs of business dealings, express ethical standards as well. Product liability also involves ethics. Many of the principles of product liability are based on principles designed to aid individuals injured, without extensive inquiry into issues of fault.

The areas of law covered in the previous unit constitute an important part of the legal environment of business. In each of these areas, new legal (and ethical) challenges have emerged as a result of developments in technology. In this *Focus on Ethics* feature, we look at the ethical dimensions of selected topics discussed in the preceding chapters, including some issues that are unique to the cyber age.

Freedom of Contract and Freedom from Contract

Generally, as you read in Chapter 4, a responsible business manager will evaluate a business transaction on the basis of three criteria—legality, profitability, and ethics. But what does acting ethically mean in the area of contracts? If you enter into a contract with an individual who fails to look after her or his own interests, is that your fault? Should you be doing something about it? If the contract happens to be to your advantage and to the other party's detriment, do you have a responsibility to correct the situation?

The answer to the question just raised is not simple. On the one hand, a common ethical assumption in our society is that individuals should be held responsible for the consequences of their own actions, including their contractual promises. This principle is expressed in the legal concept of freedom of contract. On the other hand, another common assumption in our society is that individuals should not harm one another by their actions. This is the basis of both tort law and criminal law.

In the area of contract law, ethical behavior often involves balancing these principles. In the above example, if you purchased the car and your neighbor later learned its true value and sued you for the difference, very likely no court of law would find that the contract should be rescinded. At times, however, courts will hold that the principle of freedom *of* contract should give way to the principle of freedom *from* contract, a doctrine based on the assumption that people should not be harmed by the actions of others. We look next at some examples of situations in which parties to contracts may be excused from performance under their contracts to prevent injustice.

Unconscionability The doctrine of unconscionability is a good example of how the law attempts to enforce ethical behavior. Under this doctrine, a contract may be deemed to be so unfair to one party as to be unenforceable—even though that party voluntarily agreed to the contract's terms. Unconscionable action, like unethical action, defies precise definition. Information about the particular facts and specific circumstances surrounding the contract is essential. For example, a court might find that a contract made with a marginally literate consumer was unfair and unenforceable but might uphold the same contract made with a major business firm.

Section 2–302 of the Uniform Commercial Code, which incorporates the common law concept of unconscionability, similarly does not define the concept with any precision. Rather, it leaves it to the courts to determine when a contract is so one sided and unfair to one party as to be unconscionable and thus unenforceable.

Usually, courts will do all that they can to save contracts rather than render them unenforceable. Only in extreme situations, as when a contract or clause is so one sided as to "shock the conscience" of the court, will a court hold a contract or contractual clause unconscionable.

Exculpatory Clauses In some situations, courts have also refused to enforce exculpatory clauses on the ground that they are unconscionable or contrary to public policy. An *exculpatory clause* attempts to excuse a party from liability in the event of monetary or physical injury, no matter who is at fault. In some situations, such clauses are upheld. Generally, the law permits parties to assume, by express agreement, the risks inherent in certain activities. For example, a health club can require its members to sign a clause releasing the club from any liability for injuries the members might incur while using the club's equipment and facilities. Likewise, an exculpatory clause releasing a ski resort from liability for skiing accidents would likely be enforced.[1] In such situations, exculpatory clauses make it possible for a firm's owner to stay in business—by

---

1. *Myers v. Lutsen Mountains Corp.*, 587 F.3d 891 (8th Cir. 2009).

shifting some of the liability risks from the business to the customer.

Nonetheless, some jurisdictions take a dubious view of exculpatory clauses, particularly when the agreement is between parties with unequal bargaining power, such as a landlord and a tenant or an employer and an employee. Frequently, courts will hold that an exculpatory clause that attempts to exempt an employer from *all* liability for negligence toward its employees is against public policy and thus void.[2] The courts reason that disparity in bargaining power and economic necessity force the employee to accept the employer's terms. Also, if a plaintiff can prove that an exculpatory clause is ambiguous, the courts generally will not enforce the clause.[3]

Covenants Not to Compete

In today's complicated, technological business world, knowledge learned on the job, including trade secrets, has become a valuable commodity. To prevent this knowledge from falling into the hands of competitors, more and more employers are requiring their employees to sign covenants not to compete. The increasing number of lawsuits over noncompete clauses in employment contracts has caused many courts to reconsider the reasonableness of these covenants. Jurisdictions vary in their approach to covenants not to compete.

Many jurisdictions will enforce noncompete covenants in the employment context if (1) the limitations placed on an employee are reasonable as to time and geographic area, and (2) the limitations do not impose a greater restraint than necessary to protect the goodwill or other business interests of the employer.[4] In a number of jurisdictions, if a court finds that a restraint in a noncompete covenant is not reasonable in light of the circumstances, it will reform the unreasonable provision and then enforce it. For example, a court might rewrite an unreasonable restriction by reducing the time period during which a former employee cannot compete from three years to one year and then enforce the reformed agreement.[5]

Other jurisdictions are not so "employer friendly" and refuse to enforce unreasonable covenants. Under California law, covenants not to compete are illegal, as are a number of other types of agreements that have a similar effect.[6] Other western states also tend to regard noncompete covenants with suspicion. For example, the Washington Supreme Court has refused to reform noncompete covenants that are unreasonable and lacking in consideration.[7] Courts in Arizona and Texas have reached similar conclusions.[8] One of the reasons that the courts usually look closely at such covenants and evaluate them on a case-by-case basis is the strong public policy favoring competition in this country.

Good Faith and Commercial Reasonableness

The concepts of good faith and commercial reasonableness permeate the UCC and help to prevent unethical behavior by businesspersons. These two key concepts are read into every contract and impose certain duties on all parties. Additionally, reasonability in the formation, performance, and termination of contracts underlies almost all of the UCC's provisions.

As an example, consider the UCC's approach to open terms. Section 2–311(1) states that when a term is to be specified by one of the parties, "any such specification must be made in good faith and within limits set by commercial reasonableness." The requirement of commercial reasonableness means that the term subsequently supplied by one party should not come as a surprise to the other. The party filling in the missing term may not take advantage of the opportunity to add a term that will be beneficial to himself or herself (and detrimental to the other party) and then demand a contractual performance that the other party totally failed to anticipate. Under the UCC, the party filling in the missing term is not allowed to deviate from what is commercially reasonable in the context of the transaction. Courts frequently look to course of dealing, usage of trade, and the surrounding circumstances in determining what is commercially reasonable in a given situation.

Good Faith in Output and Requirements Contracts
The obligation of good faith is particularly important in so-called output and requirements contracts.

---

2. See, for example, *City of Santa Barbara v. Superior Court,* 62 Cal. Rptr.3d 527, 161 P.3d 1095 (2007); and *Health Net of California, Inc. v. Department of Health Services,* 113 Cal.App.4th 224, 6 Cal. Rptr.3d 235 (2003).

3. See, for example, *Tatman v. Space Coast Kennel Club, Inc.,* 27 So.3d 108 (Fla.App. 5 Dist. 2010).

4. See *Drummond American, LLC v. Share Corp.,* ___ F.Supp.2d ___ (E.D.Tex. 2010); and *TEKsystems, Inc. v. Bolton,* ___ F.Supp.2d ___ (D.Md. 2010).

5. See, for example, *Estee Lauder Companies v. Batra,* 430 F.Supp.2d 158 (S.D.N.Y. 2006); *National Café Services, Ltd. v. Podaras,* 148 S.W.3d 194 (Tex.App.—Waco 2004); *Pathfinder Communications Corp. v. Macy,* 795 N.E.2d 1103 (Ind.App. 2003); and *Health Care Enterprises, Inc. v. Levy,* 715 So.2d 341 (Fla.App.4th 1998).

6. For a discussion of these agreements, including "no hire" agreements (which prevent employees who have left a firm from hiring other employees from the firm to work in a competing business), see *Thomas Weisel Partners, LLC v. BNP Paribas,* ___ F.Supp.2d ___ (N.D.Cal. 2010).

7. See, for example, *Labriola v. Pollard Group, Inc.,* 152 Wash.2d 828, 100 P.3d 791 (2004).

8. *Bandera Drilling Co., Inc. v. Sledge Drilling Corp.,* 293 S.W.3d 867 (Tex.App.—Eastland 2009); and *Varsity Gold, Inc. v. Porzio,* 202 Ariz. 355, 45 P.3d 352 (2002).

FOCUS ON ETHICS CONTINUES ➧

UCC 2–306 states that "quantity" in these contracts "means such actual output or requirements as may occur in good faith." For example, assume that the market price of the goods subject to a requirements contract rises rapidly and dramatically because of an extreme shortage of materials necessary to their production. The buyer could claim that her needs are equivalent to the seller's entire output. Then, after buying all of the seller's output at the contract price (which is substantially below the market price), the buyer could turn around and sell the goods that she does not need at the higher market price. Under the UCC, this type of unethical behavior is prohibited, even though the buyer in this instance has not technically breached the contract.

Commercial Reasonableness   Under the UCC, the concept of good faith is closely linked to commercial reasonableness. All commercial actions—including the performance and enforcement of contract obligations—must display commercial reasonableness. A merchant is expected to act in a reasonable manner according to reasonable commercial customs. The reliance of the UCC's drafters on commercial customs, or usage of trade, as a guideline to reasonable behavior in a given trade or industry indicates the importance of commercial reasonableness in sales law.

The concept of commercial reasonableness is clearly expressed in the doctrine of commercial impracticability. Under this doctrine, which is related to the common law doctrine of impossibility of performance, a party's nonperformance of a contractual obligation may be excused when, because of unforeseen circumstances, performance of the contract becomes impracticable. The courts make clear, however, that performance will not be excused under this doctrine unless the nonperforming party has made every reasonable effort to fulfill his or her obligations.

Pharmacies and the Duty of Care

A significant issue that has surfaced in recent years has to do with whether pharmacies should have a duty of care to third parties. In other words, should pharmacies that dispense mind-altering drugs to known drug abusers be liable to third parties who are injured as a result of the drug users' actions?

The *Sanchez* Case   This question came to the fore in a case heard by the Nevada Supreme Court in 2009. The case involved a woman, Patricia Copening, who, while under the influence of the psychotropic drug hydrocodone, caused a car accident that killed Gregory Sanchez, Jr., and seriously injured another person. Copening was arrested and spent nine months in jail.

The families of Sanchez and the injured person sued Copening and, among others, several pharmacies that had filled her prescriptions. These pharmacies had all been notified earlier by the Nevada Prescription Controlled Substance Abuse Prevention Task Force that Copening had obtained approximately 4,500 hydrocodone pills at thirteen different pharmacies between May 2002 and May 2003. The families argued that this notification had created a duty of care on the part of the pharmacies and that they had breached this duty by filling Copening's prescriptions. The trial court disagreed and granted summary judgment for the defendant pharmacies. On appeal, the Nevada Supreme Court affirmed the trial court's decision—the pharmacists owed no duty to third parties.[9]

The Controversy Continues   The Nevada Supreme Court's opinion did little to stem the controversy over this issue. For those who argue that such a duty should be imposed, however, Nevada's high court did hold out some hope. In a footnote to the opinion, the court noted that at the time of the accident in 2004, the task force had never advised pharmacies what, if anything, they should do with the information they received about potential drug abusers. In 2006, however, the Nevada Board of Pharmacy amended its regulations to add detailed instructions on what pharmacists should do in similar situations. The court stated that this change in the regulations "may have created a special relationship that could justify imposing a duty in favor of third parties."

Those who argue against such a duty include, of course, pharmacists and pharmacies. According to Jesse Vivian, a professor in the Department of Pharmacy Practice at Wayne State University in Detroit, had the court held that pharmacies owe a specific duty to protect the general public from the actions of drug-abusing patients, this would have created a zone of risk that would be impossible to define. Such a decision would open the door to unimaginable claims against pharmacies.

Trademark Protection versus Free Speech Rights

Another legal issue involving questions of fairness pits the rights of trademark owners against the right to free speech. The issue is whether a company's ownership rights in a trademark used as a domain name outweigh the free speech rights of others who use a similar domain name to criticize or parody the company. A common tactic of those critical of a company's goods or services is to add the word *sucks* or *stinks* (or some

---

9. *Sanchez v. Wal-Mart Stores, Inc.*, 221 P.3d 1276 (Nev. 2009).

other disparaging term) to the trademark owner's domain name.

A number of companies have sued the owners of such sites for trademark infringement in the hope that a court or an arbitrating panel will order the site owner to cease using the domain name. To date, though, companies have had little success pursuing this alternative. After all, one of the primary reasons trademarks are protected under U.S. law is to prevent customers from becoming confused about the origin of the goods for sale—and a "sucks" site certainly does not create such confusion.

Furthermore, U.S. courts and arbitrators give extensive protection to free speech rights, including the right to express opinions about companies and their products.[10] Even international arbitration panels, when hearing disputes between U.S. parties, give U.S. constitutional law protecting speech significant weight. Consider a case brought before an arbitrating panel of the WIPO (World Intellectual Property Organization) Arbitration and Mediation Center in 2009. In that case, a Web site was created to parody the Sutherland Institute, a Utah public-policy think tank using the domain name sutherlandinstitute.org. The parodying site's Web site was at sutherlandinstitute.com, and its home page closely resembled that of the Sutherland Institute. Even though the parodying site's domain name and parts of its Web site were confusingly similar to those of the Sutherland Institute, the WIPO panelists refused to transfer the domain name to the institute. The panelists stated that they "would not rule that the domain name was used in bad faith because the two organizations were from the United States and the U.S. Constitution protects the right to free speech."[11]

Trade Secrets versus Free Speech Rights

Another ongoing issue with ethical dimensions involves the point at which free speech rights come into conflict with the right of copyright holders to protect their property by using encryption technology. This issue came before the California Supreme Court in the case of *DVD Copy Control Association v. Bunner.*[12] Trade associations in the movie industry sued an

Internet Web site operator who had posted the code of a computer program that cracked technology used to encrypt DVDs. This posed a significant threat to the movie industry because, by using the code-cracking software, users would be able to duplicate the copyrighted movies stored on the DVDs.

In their suit, the trade associations claimed that the Web site operator had misappropriated trade secrets. The defendant argued that software programs designed to break encryption programs were a form of constitutionally protected speech. When the case reached the California Supreme Court, the court held that although the First Amendment applies to computer code, computer code is not a form of "pure speech," and the courts can therefore protect it to a lesser extent. The court reinstated a trial court order that enjoined (prevented) the Web site operator from continuing to post the code.

Ethics and Bankruptcy

The first goal of bankruptcy law is to provide relief and protection to debtors. Society generally has concluded that everyone should be given the chance to start over. But how far should society go in allowing debtors to avoid obligations that they voluntarily incurred?

Consider the concept of bankruptcy from the point of view of the creditor. The creditor has extended a transfer of purchasing power from herself or himself to the debtor. That transfer of purchasing power represents a transfer of an asset for an asset. The debtor obtains the asset of funds, goods, or services, and the creditor obtains the asset of a *secured* or *unsecured* legal obligation to repay. Once the debtor is in bankruptcy, voluntarily or involuntarily, the asset that the creditor owns most often has a diminished value. Indeed, in many circumstances, that asset has no value. Yet the easier it becomes for debtors to discharge their debts under bankruptcy laws, the greater will be the incentive for debtors to use such laws to avoid paying amounts that are legally owed.

Clearly, bankruptcy law is a balancing act between providing a second chance for debtors and ensuring that creditors are given reasonable protection. Among other things, when the number of bankruptcies increases, creditors incur higher risks in making loans—because bankruptcy shifts the cost of the debt from the debtor to the creditor. To compensate for these higher risks, creditors may increase the interest rates charged to everyone, require additional security (collateral), or become more selective in granting credit. Thus, with more lenient bankruptcy laws, debtors who find themselves in bankruptcy will be better off, but debtors who will never be in bankruptcy will be worse off.

---

10. Many businesses have concluded that the best approach is to register such insulting domain names before the cybergripers themselves can register them.

11. *Sutherland Institute v. Continuative, LLC,* WIPO Arbitration and Mediation Center, Case No. D2009-0893.

12. 31 Cal.4th 864, 4 Cal.Rptr.3d 69 (2003). See also *O'Grady v. Superior Court,* 139 Cal.App.4th 1423, 44 Cal.Rptr.3d 72 (2006), in which a state appellate court distinguished the situation from the *Bunner* case and held that Apple Computer could prevent an online publisher from disclosing confidential information about a product that the company had not yet released.

FOCUS ON ETHICS CONTINUES ➡

Consequences of Bankruptcy

Under bankruptcy law, filing for personal bankruptcy (particularly under Chapter 7) is difficult. Although the stigma attached to bankruptcy today is less than it once was, bankruptcy is never easy for debtors. Many debtors feel a sense of shame and failure when they petition for bankruptcy. After all, bankruptcy is a matter of public record, and there is no way to avoid a certain amount of publicity. In one case, for example, a couple who filed for Chapter 7 bankruptcy wanted to use their attorney's mailing address in another town on their bankruptcy schedules in an effort to prevent an elderly parent and one of their employers from learning about the bankruptcy. The court, however, held that debtors are not entitled to be protected from publicity surrounding the filing of their cases.[13]

A court in another case held that the public interest in information involving a particular bankruptcy debtor (Gitto Global Corporation) was important enough to justify disclosing a previously sealed report from a bankruptcy examiner. In essence, the court gave the media access to the bankruptcy examiner's report on the misconduct of more than 120 individuals at the debtor company.[14]

Bankruptcy also has other consequences for debtors, including blemished credit ratings for up to ten years and higher interest charges for new debts, such as those incurred through the purchase of cars or homes. Some private employers may even refuse to hire a job applicant who has filed for bankruptcy. The courts provide little relief for applicants who are denied a job for this reason.[15]

Thus, bankruptcy can have adverse effects for both debtors and creditors. Because of the consequences of bankruptcy, debtors do not always get the fresh start promised by bankruptcy law. At the same time, creditors rarely are able to recover all that is owed them once a debtor petitions for bankruptcy.

DISCUSSION QUESTIONS

1. In determining whether an exculpatory clause should be enforced, why does it matter whether the contract containing the clause involves essential services (such as transportation) or nonessential services (such as skiing or other leisure-time activities)?

2. Employers often include covenants not to compete in employment contracts to protect their trade secrets. What effect, if any, will the growth in e-commerce have on the reasonability of covenants not to compete?

3. How can a court objectively measure good faith and commercial reasonableness?

4. Generally, do you believe that the law has struck a fair balance between the rights of intellectual property owners and the rights of the public?

5. Is it unethical to avoid paying one's debts by going into bankruptcy? Does a person have a moral responsibility to pay his or her debts? Discuss.

---

13. *In the Matter of Laws,* 223 Bankr. 714 (D.Neb. 1998).
14. *In re Gitto Global Corp.,* 422 F.3d 1 (D.Mass. 2005).

---

15. See, for example, *In re Potter,* 354 Bankr. 301 (D.Ala. 2006); and *In re Stinson,* 285 Bankr. 239 (W.D.Va. 2002).

UNIT FOUR

THE
BUSINESS
ENVIRONMENT

CONTENTS

CHAPTER 17

Sole Proprietorships, Franchises, and Partnerships

Anyone who starts a business must first decide which form of business organization will be most appropriate for the new endeavor. In making this decision, the **entrepreneur** (one who initiates and assumes the financial risk of a new enterprise) needs to consider a number of factors, especially (1) ease of creation, (2) the liability of the owners, (3) tax considerations, and (4) the need for capital. In studying this unit, keep these factors in mind as you read about the various business organizational forms available

to entrepreneurs. You may also find it helpful to refer to Exhibit 19–3 on pages 442 and 443, which compares the major business forms in use today with respect to these and other factors.

Traditionally, entrepreneurs have relied on three major business forms—the sole proprietorship, the partnership, and the corporation. In this chapter, we examine the sole proprietorship and the traditional (general) partnership. We also look at franchises, which are widely used today. The franchise is not actually a separate organizational form. Rather,

it is a contractual arrangement, and the parties to a franchise contract may use any one of several organizational forms. For example, the parties may be a sole proprietor and a corporation or two corporations.

In Chapter 18, we will look at the limited liability company, a relatively new and increasingly popular form of business enterprise, and some newer variations on partnerships. The third major traditional form—the corporation—will be discussed in Chapter 19.

SECTION 1
SOLE PROPRIETORSHIPS

The simplest form of business organization is a **sole proprietorship.** In this form, the owner is the business. Thus, anyone who does business without creating a separate business organization has a sole proprietorship. More than two-thirds of all U.S. businesses are sole proprietorships. They are usually small enterprises—about 99 percent of the sole proprietorships in the United States have revenues of less than $1 million per year. Sole proprietors can own and manage any type of business from an informal, home-office undertaking to a large restaurant or construction firm.

Advantages of the Sole Proprietorship

A major advantage of the sole proprietorship is that the proprietor owns the entire business and receives

all of the profits (because she or he assumes all of the risk). In addition, starting a sole proprietorship is often easier and less costly than starting any other kind of business, as few legal formalities are required.[1] No documents need to be filed with the government to start a sole proprietorship (though a state business license may be required to operate certain types of businesses).

This form of business organization also offers more flexibility than does a partnership or a corporation. The sole proprietor is free to make any decision he or she wishes concerning the business—such as whom to hire, when to take a vacation, and what kind of business to pursue. In addition, the proprietor can sell or transfer all or part of the business to another party at any time and does not need approval from anyone else (as would be required

---

1. Although starting a sole proprietorship involves fewer legal formalities than other business organizational forms, even small sole proprietorships may need to comply with zoning requirements, obtain licenses, and the like.

from partners in a partnership or normally from shareholders in a corporation).

A sole proprietor pays only personal income taxes (including Social Security and Medicare taxes) on the business's profits, which are reported as personal income on the proprietor's personal income tax return. Sole proprietors are also allowed to establish certain retirement accounts that are tax-exempt until the funds are withdrawn, usually after age fifty-nine and a half.

Disadvantages of the Sole Proprietorship

The major disadvantage of the sole proprietorship is that the proprietor alone bears the burden of any losses or liabilities incurred by the business enterprise. In other words, the sole proprietor has unlimited liability, or legal responsibility, for all obligations that arise in doing business. Any lawsuit against the business or its employees can lead to unlimited personal liability for the owner of a sole proprietorship. Creditors can go after the owner's personal assets to satisfy any business debts. This unlimited liability is a major factor to be considered in choosing a business form.

CASE IN POINT Garden City Boxing Club, Inc. (GCB), owned the exclusive right to broadcast via closed-circuit television several prizefights, including a match between Oscar De La Hoya and Fernando Vargas. GCB sold the right to receive the broadcasts to bars and other commercial venues, which cannot legally broadcast these programs to patrons without authorization. José Melendez ordered a satellite television system (DISH) to be installed by Antenas Enterprises, a sole proprietorship. Although the Antenas employee installed the satellite system at a restaurant called Mundelein Burrito, he incorrectly identified the account as being residential rather than commercial. Mundelein's patrons watched the De La Hoya–Vargas match, as well as three other fights, for which the restaurant paid only the residential rate to DISH and nothing to GCB. GCB filed a suit against Luis Dominguez, the sole proprietor of Antenas, to collect the unpaid fee. The court issued a summary judgment in GCB's favor and held Dominguez personally liable for the amount of Mundelein's fee, plus damages and attorneys' fees.[2]

The sole proprietorship also has the disadvantage of lacking continuity on the death of the proprietor.

---

2. *Garden City Boxing Club, Inc. v. Dominguez,* ___ F.Supp.2d ___ (2006).

When the owner dies, so does the business—it is automatically dissolved. Another disadvantage is that in raising capital, the proprietor is limited to his or her personal funds and any personal loans that he or she can obtain.

SECTION 2
FRANCHISES

Instead of setting up a sole proprietorship to market their own products or services, many entrepreneurs opt to purchase a franchise. A **franchise** is an arrangement in which the owner of a trademark, a trade name, or a copyright licenses others to use the trademark, trade name, or copyright in the selling of goods or services. A **franchisee** (a purchaser of a franchise) generally is legally independent of the **franchisor** (the seller of the franchise). At the same time, the franchise is economically dependent on the franchisor's integrated business system.

In other words, a franchisee can operate as an independent businessperson but still obtain the advantages of a regional or national organization. Today, franchising companies and their franchisees account for a significant portion of all retail sales in this country. Well-known franchises include McDonald's, 7-Eleven, and Holiday Inn. Franchising has also become a popular way for businesses to expand their operations internationally because franchisees can operate abroad without violating the legal restrictions that many nations impose on foreign ownership of businesses.

Types of Franchises

Many different kinds of businesses now sell franchises, and numerous types of franchises are available. Generally, though, franchises fall into one of three classifications: distributorships, chain-style business operations, and manufacturing arrangements.

DISTRIBUTORSHIP In a *distributorship*, a manufacturer (the franchisor) licenses a dealer (the franchisee) to sell its product. Often, a distributorship covers an exclusive territory. An example is an automobile dealership or a beer distributorship, such as a distributorship for Anheuser-Busch products.

CHAIN-STYLE BUSINESS OPERATION In a *chain-style business operation*, a franchise operates under a franchisor's trade name and is identified as a member of a select group of dealers that engage in the franchisor's business. The franchisee is generally required to follow standardized or prescribed methods of operation. Often, the franchisor insists that the franchisee maintain certain standards of performance. In addition, the franchisee may be required to obtain materials and supplies exclusively from the franchisor. McDonald's and most other fast-food chains are examples of this type of franchise. Chain-style franchises are also common in service-related businesses, including real estate brokerage firms, such as Century 21, and tax-preparation services, such as H&R Block, Inc.

MANUFACTURING ARRANGEMENT In a *manufacturing,* or *processing-plant, arrangement,* the franchisor transmits to the franchisee the essential ingredients or formula to make a particular product. The franchisee then markets the product either at wholesale or at retail in accordance with the franchisor's standards. Examples of this type of franchise include Coca-Cola and other soft-drink bottling companies.

Laws Governing Franchising

Because a franchise relationship is primarily a contractual relationship, it is governed by contract law. If the franchise exists primarily for the sale of products manufactured by the franchisor, the law governing sales contracts as expressed in Article 2 of the Uniform Commercial Code applies (see Chapter 11). Additionally, the federal government and most states have enacted laws governing certain aspects of franchising. Generally, these laws are designed to protect prospective franchisees from dishonest franchisors and to prevent franchisors from terminating franchises without good cause.

FEDERAL REGULATION OF FRANCHISES The federal government regulates franchising through laws that apply to specific industries and through the Franchise Rule, created by the Federal Trade Commission (FTC).

Industry-Specific Standards. Congress has enacted laws that protect franchisees in certain industries, such as automobile dealerships and service stations. These laws protect the franchisee from unreasonable demands and bad faith terminations of the franchise by the franchisor. If an automobile manufacturer–franchisor terminates a franchise because of a dealer-franchisee's failure to comply with unreasonable demands (for example, failure to attain an unrealistically high sales quota), the manufacturer may be liable for

damages.[3] Similarly, federal law prescribes the conditions under which a franchisor of service stations can terminate the franchise.[4] Federal antitrust laws (see Chapters 27 and 28) also apply in certain circumstances to prohibit certain types of anticompetitive agreements.

The Franchise Rule. The FTC's Franchise Rule requires franchisors to disclose certain material facts that a prospective franchisee needs in order to make an informed decision concerning the purchase of a franchise.[5] The rule was designed to enable potential franchisees to weigh the risks and benefits of an investment. The rule requires the franchisor to make numerous written disclosures to prospective franchisees, but franchisors can provide online disclosure documents as long as they meet certain requirements. Prospective franchisees must be able to download or save all electronic disclosure documents.

Under the Franchise Rule, all representations made to a prospective franchisee must have a reasonable basis. If a franchisor provides projected earnings figures, the franchisor must indicate whether the figures are based on actual data or hypothetical examples. (The rule does not require franchisors to provide potential earnings figures, however, as discussed in the *Insight into Ethics* feature.) If a franchisor makes sales or earnings projections based on actual data for a specific franchise location, the franchisor must disclose the number and percentage of its existing franchises that have achieved this result.

Franchisors are required to explain termination, cancellation, and renewal provisions of the franchise contract to potential franchisees before the agreement is signed. In addition, a franchisor must provide disclosures concerning any lawsuits that it has filed against franchisees and settlement agreements that it has entered into with them. Those who violate the Franchise Rule are subject to substantial civil penalties, and the FTC can sue on behalf of injured parties to recover damages.

STATE PROTECTION FOR FRANCHISEES State legislation varies but often is aimed at protecting franchisees from unfair practices and bad faith terminations by franchisors. Approximately fifteen states have laws similar to the federal rules that

---

3. Automobile Dealers' Franchise Act of 1965, also known as the Automobile Dealers' Day in Court Act, 15 U.S.C. Sections 1221 *et seq.*
4. Petroleum Marketing Practices Act (PMPA) of 1979, 15 U.S.C. Sections 2801 *et seq.* See Extended Case 17.2 on pages 386 and 388.
5. 16 C.F.R. Section 436.1.

INSIGHT INTO ETHICS
Information on Potential Earnings Provided by Franchisors

Entrepreneurs who are thinking about investing in a franchise almost invariably ask, "How much will I make?" Surprisingly, the law does not require franchisors to provide any estimate of, or actual data on, the earnings potential of a franchise. Franchisors can voluntarily choose to provide earnings data on their uniform disclosure documents but are not required to do so. If franchisors do make earnings claims, as mentioned in the text, they must indicate whether these figures are actual or hypothetical, follow specific rules, and have a reasonable basis for these claims. About 75 percent of franchisors choose not to provide information about earnings potential.

The failure of the FTC's Franchise Rule to require disclosure of earnings potential has led to many complaints from franchisees. After all, some franchisees invest their life savings in franchises that ultimately fail because of unrealistic earnings expectations. Moreover, the franchisee may be legally responsible to continue operating and paying the franchisor even when the business is not turning a profit.

For instance, Thomas Anderson asked the franchisor, Rocky Mountain Chocolate Factory, Inc. (RMCF), and five of its franchisees for earnings information before he entered into a franchise agreement, but he did not receive any data. When his chocolate franchise failed to become profitable, Anderson and his partner were ordered by a court to pay $33,109 in past due royalties and interest to RMCF (plus court costs and expenses).[a]

CRITICAL THINKING
INSIGHT INTO THE BUSINESS ENVIRONMENT
If the law required franchisors to provide estimates of potential earnings, would there be more or less growth in the number of franchises? Explain your answer.

a. *Rocky Mountain Chocolate Factory, Inc. v. SDMS, Inc.*, 2009 WL 579516 (D.Colo. 2009).

---

require franchisors to provide presale disclosures to prospective franchisees.[6]

Some state laws also require that a disclosure document (known as the Franchise Disclosure Document, or FDD) be registered or filed with a state official. State laws may also require that a franchisor submit advertising aimed at prospective franchisees to the state for approval. To protect franchisees, a state law might require the disclosure of information such as the actual costs of operation, recurring expenses, and profits earned, along with facts substantiating these figures. State deceptive trade practices acts (see Chapter 24) may also apply and prohibit certain types of actions on the part of franchisors. To protect franchisees against arbitrary or bad faith terminations, state law may prohibit termination without "good cause" or require that certain procedures be followed in terminating a franchising relationship.

CASE IN POINT FMS, Inc., entered into a franchise agreement with Samsung Construction Equipment North America to become an authorized dealership for the sale of Samsung-brand equipment. Volvo Construction Equipment North America, Inc.,

purchased Samsung's business and eventually modified and rebranded the construction equipment so that it could be sold under its own name. When Volvo canceled FMS's franchise agreement, FMS filed a lawsuit alleging that Volvo, among other things, had violated Maine's franchise law, which prohibits termination of a franchise without "good cause." A federal appellate court, however, found that because Volvo was no longer manufacturing the Samsung-brand equipment, it did have good cause to terminate FMS's franchise. Although the statute would have prevented Volvo from terminating the FMS franchise as to the Samsung-brand equipment, the statute did not apply to the rebranded equipment.[7]

The Franchise Contract

The franchise relationship is defined by a contract between the franchisor and the franchisee. The franchise contract specifies the terms and conditions of the franchise and spells out the rights and duties of the franchisor and the franchisee. If either party fails to perform its contractual duties, that party may be subject to a lawsuit for breach of contract. Furthermore, if a franchisee is induced to enter into a

---

6. These states include California, Hawaii, Illinois, Indiana, Maryland, Michigan, Minnesota, New York, North Dakota, Oregon, Rhode Island, South Dakota, Virginia, Washington, and Wisconsin.

7. *FMS, Inc. v. Volvo Construction Equipment North America, Inc.*, 557 F.3d 758 (7th Cir. 2009).

franchise contract by the franchisor's fraudulent misrepresentation, the franchisor may be liable for damages. Generally, statutes and the case law governing franchising tend to emphasize the importance of good faith and fair dealing in franchise relationships.

Because each type of franchise relationship has its own characteristics, it is difficult to describe the broad range of details a franchising contract may include. We look next at some of the major issues that typically are addressed in a franchise contract.

PAYMENT FOR THE FRANCHISE The franchisee ordinarily pays an initial fee or lump-sum price for the franchise license (the privilege of being granted a franchise). This fee is separate from the various products that the franchisee purchases from or through the franchisor. In some industries, the franchisor relies heavily on the initial sale of the franchise for realizing a profit. In other industries, the continued dealing between the parties brings profit to both. In most situations, the franchisor receives a stated percentage of the annual (or monthly) sales or annual volume of business done by the franchisee. The franchise agreement may also require the franchisee to pay a percentage of the franchisor's advertising costs and certain administrative expenses.

BUSINESS PREMISES The franchise agreement may specify whether the premises for the business must be leased or purchased outright. Sometimes, a building must be constructed to meet the terms of the agreement. Certainly, the agreement will specify whether the franchisor or the franchisee is responsible for supplying equipment and furnishings for the premises.

LOCATION OF THE FRANCHISE Typically, the franchisor determines the territory to be served. Some franchise contracts give the franchisee exclusive rights, or "territorial rights," to a certain geographic area. Other franchise contracts, while defining the territory allotted to a particular franchise, either specifically state that the franchise is nonexclusive or are silent on the issue of territorial rights.

Many franchise cases involve disputes over territorial rights, and the implied covenant of good faith and fair dealing often comes into play in this area of franchising. If the franchise contract does not grant the franchisee exclusive territorial rights and the franchisor allows a competing franchise to be established nearby, the franchisee may suffer a significant loss in profits. In this situation, a court may hold that the franchisor's actions breached an implied covenant of good faith and fair dealing.

BUSINESS ORGANIZATION As part of the franchise agreement, the franchisor may require that the business use a particular organizational form and capital structure. The franchise agreement may also set out standards of operation in such aspects of the business as sales quotas, quality, and record keeping. Additionally, a franchisor may retain stringent control over the training of personnel involved in the operation and over administrative aspects of the business.

QUALITY CONTROL The day-to-day operation of the franchise business normally is left up to the franchisee. Nonetheless, the franchise agreement may provide for some degree of supervision and control by the franchisor so that it can protect the franchise's name and reputation. When the franchise prepares a product, such as food, or provides a service, such as motel accommodations, the contract often states that the franchisor will establish certain standards for the facility. Typically, the contract will state that the franchisor is permitted to make periodic inspections to ensure that the standards are being maintained.

As a general rule, the validity of a provision permitting the franchisor to establish and enforce certain quality standards is unquestioned. Because the franchisor has a legitimate interest in maintaining the quality of the product or service to protect its name and reputation, it can exercise greater control in this area than would otherwise be tolerated. If a franchisor exercises too much control over the operations of its franchisees, however, the franchisor risks potential liability under agency law for the tortious acts of the franchisees' employees (see Chapter 20).

PRICING ARRANGEMENTS Franchises provide the franchisor with an outlet for the firm's goods and services. Depending on the nature of the business, the franchisor may require the franchisee to purchase certain supplies from the franchisor at an established price.[8] A franchisor cannot, however, set the prices at which the franchisee will resell the goods because such price setting may be a violation of state or federal antitrust laws, or both. A franchisor can suggest retail prices but cannot mandate them.

Franchise Termination

The duration of the franchise is a matter to be determined between the parties. Generally, a franchise relationship starts with a short trial period, such as a year, so that the franchisee and the franchisor

---

8. Although a franchisor can require franchisees to purchase supplies from it, requiring a franchisee to purchase exclusively from the franchisor may violate federal antitrust laws (see Chapters 27 and 28).

can determine whether they want to stay in business with one another. Usually, the franchise agreement specifies that termination must be "for cause," such as the death or disability of the franchisee, insolvency of the franchisee, breach of the franchise agreement, or failure to meet specified sales quotas. Most franchise contracts provide that notice of termination must be given. If no set time for termination is specified, then a reasonable time, with notice, is implied. A franchisee must be given reasonable time to wind up the business—that is, to do the

accounting and return the copyright or trademark or any other property of the franchisor.

A franchise agreement may grant the franchisee the opportunity to cure an ordinary, curable breach within a certain period of time after notice to enable the franchisee to postpone, or even avoid, the termination of the contract. Could a franchisee's conduct so seriously undermine the basis of the agreement that the franchisor could cancel the contract despite a notice-and-cure provision? That was the issue in the following case.

CASE 17.1

LJL Transportation, Inc. v. Pilot Air Freight Corp.

Supreme Court of Pennsylvania, 599 Pa. 546, 962 A.2d 639 (2009).
www.courts.state.pa.us/T/SupremeCourt[a]

BACKGROUND AND FACTS • Pilot Air Freight Corporation moves freight through a network of company-owned and company-franchised locations at airports and other sites. Franchisees included LJL Transportation, Inc., which is owned by Louis Pektor and Leo Decker. The franchise agreement required LJL to assign all shipments to the Pilot network. The agreement also provided that "Pilot shall allow Franchisee an opportunity to cure a default within ninety (90) days of receipt of written notice." After eight years as a Pilot franchisee, LJL began to divert shipments to Northeast Transportation, a competing service owned by Pektor and Decker. On learning of the diversions, Pilot terminated the franchise agreement. LJL filed a suit in a Pennsylvania state court against Pilot, alleging breach of contract and asserting a right to cure. The court issued a summary judgment in Pilot's favor, and a state intermediate appellate court affirmed. LJL appealed.

IN THE LANGUAGE OF THE COURT
Justice *TODD.*
* * * *
* * * There is no Pennsylvania case law directly governing the resolution of the particular question presented in this appeal * * *. Courts from other jurisdictions appear to be in accord that * * * a termination clause affording the right to notice and cure is * * * a cumulative remedy which does not bar the non-breaching party from exercising other remedies available to it in the event of a breach by the other party going directly to the heart of the contract, and destroying the fundamental trust upon which the contractual relationship is built.
* * * *
* * * [This] view [is] consistent with the law * * * regarding the effect of material breaches, and likewise consistent with the policy * * * requiring good faith and honesty in the performance and enforcement of contractual relations.
* * * *
* * * *Self-dealing is the antithesis [exact opposite] of that [policy] and it violates the relationship of trust necessarily underlying such agreements.* [Emphasis added.]
*The franchisee's breach of its implied duty of honesty and fidelity [goes] to the heart of the contract. Merely requiring the franchisee to retroactively undo its wrongdoing * * * would not be an adequate remedy.* [Emphasis added.]
* * * *

---

a. In the "Conducting Business with the Court" section, click on "Supreme Court Opinions." On that page, in the "Caption" box, type "LJL"; in the "Month" pull-down menu, select "January"; in the "Year" pull-down menu, choose "2009"; and click on "Search." In the result, click on the link to access the opinion. The Unified Judicial System of Pennsylvania maintains this Web site.

CASE CONTINUES ➡

CASE 17.1 CONTINUED ➡   * * * Consequently, we have no difficulty in concluding that when there is a breach of contract going directly to the essence of the contract, which is so exceedingly grave as to irreparably damage the trust between the contracting parties, the non-breaching party may terminate the contract without notice * * * . Requiring such notice before termination under such circumstances would be a useless gesture, as such a breach may not reasonably be cured. Such a breach is so fundamentally destructive, it understandably and inevitably causes the trust which is the bedrock foundation and veritable lifeblood of the parties' contractual relationship to essentially evaporate. We find our law does not require a non-breaching party to prolong a contractual relationship under such circumstances.

DECISION AND REMEDY • *The Pennsylvania Supreme Court affirmed the lower court's judgment. A franchise agreement may be terminated immediately when there is a material breach of the contract so serious it goes directly to the heart and essence of the contract, rendering the breach incurable.*

THE ETHICAL DIMENSION • *From an ethical perspective, if LJL had been allowed to invoke the right-to-cure provision, could it have undone its wrongdoing so that the franchise relationship could have continued? Why or why not?*

WHAT IF THE FACTS WERE DIFFERENT? • *Suppose that Pilot had terminated its franchise agreement simply because it no longer wished to be bound. Would refusing to allow LJL to invoke the right-to-cure provision in that circumstance have been valid?*

WRONGFUL TERMINATION Because a franchisor's termination of a franchise often has adverse consequences for the franchisee, much franchise litigation involves claims of wrongful termination. Generally, the termination provisions of contracts are more favorable to the franchisor than to the franchisee. This means that the franchisee, who normally invests a substantial amount of time and financial resources in making the franchise operation successful, may receive little or nothing for the business on termination. The franchisor owns the trademark and hence the business. It is in this area that statutory and case law become important. The federal and state laws discussed earlier attempt, among other things, to protect franchisees from the arbitrary or unfair termination of their franchises by the franchisors.

In the following case, a group of service-station franchisees claimed that their franchisor had violated the Petroleum Marketing Practices Act (PMPA) of 1979, which limits the circumstances in which petroleum franchisors may terminate a franchise. The franchisees contended that changes in the rental provisions of the franchise contract had effectively increased their fuel costs, thereby "constructively" (in effect) terminating the franchises. The franchisees, however, had continued to operate their service stations. Under the PMPA, must a franchisee abandon its franchise in order to recover for constructive termination? That was the issue facing the United States Supreme Court.

✳ EXTENDED CASE 17.2 ✳
Mac's Shell Service, Inc. v. Shell Oil Products Co.

Supreme Court of the United States, ___U.S.___, 130 S.Ct. 1251, 176 L.Ed.2d 36 (2010).
www.supremecourt.gov[a]

IN THE LANGUAGE OF THE COURT
Justice *ALITO* delivered the opinion of the Court.
* * * *
   This litigation involves a dispute between Shell Oil Company (Shell), a petroleum franchisor, and several Shell franchisees in Massachusetts. Pursuant to their franchise agreements with Shell, each franchisee was required to pay Shell monthly rent for use of the service-station premises. For many years, Shell offered the franchisees a rent subsidy that reduced the monthly rent by a set amount for every gallon of motor fuel a franchisee sold above a specified threshold. Shell renewed the subsidy annually

---

a. Select "Opinions" under "Supreme Court Documents" in the left column. On the page that opens, under "Current Term," select "Latest Slip Opinions." In the list of cases that appears, scroll down to "30" and click on the case title to access the opinion. The United States Supreme Court maintains this Web site.

through notices that "explicitly provided for cancellation [of the rent subsidy] with thirty days' notice." Nonetheless, Shell representatives made various oral representations to the franchisees "that the subsidy or something like it would always exist."

In 1998, Shell joined with two other oil companies to create Motiva Enterprises LLC (Motiva), a joint venture that combined the companies' petroleum-marketing operations in the eastern United States. Shell assigned to Motiva its rights and obligations under the relevant franchise agreements. * * * Effective January 1, 2000, Motiva ended the volume-based rent subsidy, thus increasing the franchisees' rent.

In July 2001, sixty-three Shell franchisees (hereinafter dealers) filed suit against Shell and Motiva in Federal District Court. Their complaint alleged that Motiva's discontinuation of the rent subsidy constituted a breach of contract under state law. Additionally, the dealers asserted [a claim] under the PMPA [Petroleum Marketing Practices Act]. * * * They maintained that Shell and Motiva, by eliminating the rent subsidy, had "constructively terminated" their franchises in violation of the Act.

After a two-week trial involving eight of the dealers, the jury found against Shell and Motiva on all claims. Both before and after the jury's verdict, Shell and Motiva moved for judgment as a matter of law on the dealers' [PMPA claim]. They argued that they could not be found liable for constructive termination under the Act because none of the dealers had abandoned their franchises in response to Motiva's elimination of the rent subsidy— something Shell and Motiva said was a necessary element of any constructive termination claim. * * * The District Court denied [the motion], and Shell and Motiva appealed. [The U.S. Court of Appeals

for the First Circuit affirmed the district court's judgment, and Shell and Motiva appealed to the United States Supreme Court.]

* * * *

The * * * question we are asked to decide is whether a service-station franchisee may recover for constructive termination under the PMPA when the franchisor's allegedly wrongful conduct did not force the franchisee to abandon its franchise. *For the reasons that follow, we conclude that a necessary element of any constructive termination claim under the Act is that the franchisor's conduct forced an end to the franchisee's use of the franchisor's trademark, purchase of the franchisor's fuel, or occupation of the franchisor's service station.* [Emphasis added.]

When given its ordinary meaning, the text of the PMPA prohibits only that franchisor conduct that has the effect of ending a franchise. As relevant here, the Act provides that "no franchisor * * * may * * * terminate any franchise," except for an enumerated reason and after providing written notice.

The word "terminate" ordinarily means "put an end to." * * * The object of the verb "terminate" is the noun "franchise," a term the Act defines as "any contract" for the provision of one (or more) of the three elements of a typical petroleum franchise. Thus, when given its ordinary meaning, the Act is violated only if an agreement for the use of a trademark, purchase of motor fuel, or lease of a premises is "put [to] an end" * * * . Conduct that does not force an end to the franchise, in contrast, is not prohibited by the Act's plain terms.

* * * *

Requiring franchisees to abandon their franchises before claiming constructive termination is also consistent with the general understanding of the doctrine of constructive termination. As applied in analogous legal contexts—both now and at the time Congress enacted the PMPA—*a plaintiff must actually*

sever a particular legal relationship in order to maintain a claim for constructive termination. For example, courts have long recognized a theory of constructive discharge in the field of employment law. Similarly, landlord-tenant law has long recognized the concept of constructive eviction. The general rule under that doctrine is that a tenant must actually move out in order to claim constructive eviction. [Emphasis added.]

As generally understood in these and other contexts, a termination is deemed "constructive" because it is the plaintiff, rather than the defendant, who formally puts an end to the particular legal relationship— not because there is no end to the relationship at all. There is no reason why a different understanding should apply to constructive termination claims under the PMPA. At the time when it enacted the statute, Congress presumably was aware of how courts applied the doctrine of constructive termination in these analogous legal contexts. And in the absence of any contrary evidence, we think it reasonable to interpret the Act in a way that is consistent with this well-established body of law.

* * * *

We therefore hold that a necessary element of any constructive termination claim under the PMPA is that the complained-of conduct forced an end to the franchisee's use of the franchisor's trademark, purchase of the franchisor's fuel, or occupation of the franchisor's service station. Because none of the dealers in this litigation abandoned any element of their franchise operations in response to Motiva's elimination of the rent subsidy, they cannot maintain a constructive termination claim on the basis of that conduct.

* * * *

The judgment of the Court of Appeals is reversed * * * . The cases are remanded for further proceedings consistent with this opinion.

It is so ordered.

EXTENDED CASE CONTINUES ➡

EXTENDED CASE 17.2 CONTINUED ⬇

QUESTIONS

1. The PMPA regulates only the circumstances in which service-station franchisors may terminate a franchise or decline to renew a franchise relationship. Are there any reasons why Congress might have limited the scope of the PMPA to just these two aspects of franchising? Explain.

2. Suppose that some of the service-station franchisees, on the expiration of their contracts with Shell, signed a renewal agreement with Motiva, even though the franchisees believed that the rental terms of the new agreement were unacceptable. Given the Court's reasoning on the issue of constructive termination, would the franchisees have been likely to succeed in a suit against the franchisor for "constructive nonrenewal" of the franchise agreement? Why or why not?

THE IMPORTANCE OF GOOD FAITH AND FAIR DEALING Generally, both statutory law and case law emphasize the importance of good faith and fair dealing in terminating a franchise relationship. In determining whether a franchisor has acted in good faith when terminating a franchise agreement, the courts usually try to balance the rights of both parties. If a court perceives that a franchisor has arbitrarily or unfairly terminated a franchise, the franchisee will be provided with a remedy for wrongful termination. If a franchisor's decision to terminate a franchise was made in the normal course of the franchisor's business operations, however, and reasonable notice of termination was given to the franchisee, in most instances a court will not consider the termination wrongful.

CASE IN POINT Chapin Miller acquired Chic Miller's Chevrolet, a General Motors Corporation (GM) dealership. Chic Miller's entered into lending agreements, commonly known as floor plan financing, to enable it to buy new vehicles from GM. At first, the dealership had floor plan financing through GM, but then it switched to Chase Manhattan Bank. In 2002, Chase declined to provide further financing, and Chic Miller's was unable to obtain a loan from any other lender, including GM. Under the franchise's "Dealer Sales and Service Agreement," GM could terminate a dealership for "Failure of Dealer to maintain the line of credit." In March 2003, GM terminated Chic Miller's franchise. Chic Miller's claimed that GM had failed to act in good faith in terminating the franchise, but the court held in GM's favor. GM had good cause to terminate the dealership because Chic Miller's failed to maintain floor plan financing, which was a material requirement under the franchise agreement.[9]

---

9. *Chic Miller's Chevrolet, Inc. v. General Motors, Inc.*, 352 F.Supp.2d 251 (D.Conn. 2005).

SECTION 3
PARTNERSHIPS

A traditional **partnership** arises from an agreement, express or implied, between two or more persons to carry on a business for profit. Partners are co-owners of the business and have joint control over its operation and the right to share in its profits.

Traditional partnerships are governed both by common law concepts (in particular, those relating to agency) and by statutory law. As in so many other areas of business law, the National Conference of Commissioners on Uniform State Laws has drafted uniform laws for partnerships, and these have been widely adopted by the states.

Agency Concepts and Partnership Law

When two or more persons agree to do business as partners, they enter into a special relationship with one another. To an extent, their relationship is similar to an agency relationship because each partner is deemed to be the agent of the other partners and of the partnership. The agency concepts that you will read about in Chapter 20 thus apply—specifically, the imputation of knowledge of, and responsibility for, acts carried out within the scope of the partnership relationship. In their relationships with one another, partners, like agents, are bound by fiduciary ties.

In one important way, however, partnership law is distinct from agency law. In a partnership, two or more persons agree to commit some or all of their funds or other assets, labor, and skills to a business with the understanding that profits and losses will be shared. Thus, each partner has an ownership interest in the firm. In a nonpartnership agency relationship, the agent usually does not have an ownership interest in the business, nor is he or she obligated to bear a portion of ordinary business losses.

The Uniform Partnership Act

The Uniform Partnership Act (UPA) governs the operation of partnerships *in the absence of express agreement* and has done much to reduce controversies in the law relating to partnerships. Except for Louisiana, all of the states, as well as the District of Columbia, have adopted the UPA. A majority of the states have enacted the most recent version of the UPA to provide limited liability for partners in a limited liability partnership.[10]

Parties sometimes find themselves in conflict over whether their business enterprise is a legal partnership. The UPA defines a partnership as "an association of two or more persons to carry on as co-owners a business for profit" [UPA 101(6)]. Note that the UPA's definition of *person* includes corporations, so a corporation can be a partner in a partnership [UPA 101(10)]. The *intent* to associate is a key element of a partnership, and one cannot join a partnership unless all other partners consent [UPA 401(i)].

When Does a Partnership Exist?

In resolving disputes over whether a partnership exists, courts usually look for the following three essential elements, which are implicit in the UPA's definition of a traditional (general) partnership:

1. A sharing of profits or losses.
2. A joint ownership of the business.
3. An equal right to be involved in the management of the business.

If the evidence in a particular case is insufficient to establish all three factors, the UPA provides a set of guidelines to be used. For example, the sharing of profits and losses from a business creates a presumption that a partnership exists. No presumption is made, however, if the profits were received as payment of any of the following [UPA 202(c)(3)]:

1. A debt by installments or interest on a loan.
2. Wages of an employee or for the services of an independent contractor.
3. Rent to a landlord.
4. An annuity to a surviving spouse or representative of a deceased partner.
5. A sale of the **goodwill** (the valuable reputation of a business viewed as an intangible asset) of a business or property.

To illustrate: A debtor owes a creditor $5,000 on an unsecured debt. To repay the debt, the debtor agrees to pay (and the creditor, to accept) 10 percent of the debtor's monthly business profits until the loan with interest has been paid. Although the creditor is sharing profits from the business, the debtor and creditor are not presumed to be partners.

Joint Property Ownership and Partnership Status

Joint ownership of property does not in and of itself create a partnership. In fact, the sharing of gross returns and even profits from such ownership "does not by itself establish a partnership" [UPA 202(c)(1) and (2)].[11] Suppose that MacPherson and Bunker jointly own a piece of farmland and lease it to a farmer for a share of the profits from the farming operation in lieu of set rental payments. This arrangement normally would not make MacPherson, Bunker, and the farmer partners.

Note, though, that while the sharing of profits from ownership of property does not prove the existence of a partnership, sharing *both profits and losses* usually does. For example, two sisters, Zoe and Cienna, buy a restaurant together, open a joint bank account from which they pay for supplies and expenses, and share the proceeds (and losses) that the restaurant generates. Zoe manages the restaurant and Cienna handles the bookkeeping. After eight years, Cienna stops keeping the books and does no other work for the restaurant. Zoe claims that she and Cienna did not establish a partnership. In this situation, a court would find that a partnership existed because the sisters shared management responsibilities, had a joint account, and shared the profits and losses of the restaurant equally.

Entity versus Aggregate

At common law, a partnership was treated only as an aggregate of individuals and never as a separate legal entity. Thus, at common law a lawsuit could never be brought by or against the firm in its own name; each individual partner had to sue or be sued.

Today, in contrast, a majority of the states follow the UPA and treat a partnership as an entity for most purposes. For example, a partnership usually can sue or be sued, collect judgments, and have all accounting procedures in the name of the partnership entity

---

10. At the time this book went to press, more than two-thirds of the states, as well as the District of Columbia, Puerto Rico, and the U.S. Virgin Islands, had adopted the UPA with the 1997 amendments.

11. See, for example, *In re Estate of Ivanchak*, 169 Ohio App.3d 140, 862 N.E.2d 151 (2006).

[UPA 201, 307(a)]. As an entity, a partnership may hold the title to real or personal property in its name rather than in the names of the individual partners. Additionally, federal procedural laws permit the partnership to be treated as an entity in suits in federal courts and bankruptcy proceedings.

Tax Treatment of Partnerships

Modern law does treat a partnership as an aggregate of the individual partners rather than a separate legal entity in one situation—for federal income tax purposes. The partnership is a pass-through entity and not a taxpaying entity. A **pass-through entity** is a business entity that has no tax liability; the entity's income is passed through to the owners of the entity, who pay taxes on it. Thus, the income or losses the partnership incurs are "passed through" the entity framework and attributed to the partners on their individual tax returns. The partnership itself pays no taxes and is responsible only for filing an **information return** with the Internal Revenue Service. A partner's profit from the partnership (whether distributed or not) is taxed as individual income to the individual partner.

Partnership Formation

As a general rule, agreements to form a partnership can be *oral, written,* or *implied by conduct.* Some partnership agreements, however, must be in writing (or an electronic record) to be legally enforceable under the Statute of Frauds (see Chapter 9 for details). For example, a partnership agreement that authorizes the partners to deal in transfers of real property must be evidenced by a sufficient writing (or record).

THE PARTNERSHIP AGREEMENT A partnership agreement, also known as **articles of partnership,** can include almost any terms that the parties wish, unless they are illegal or contrary to public policy or statute [UPA 103]. The terms commonly included in a partnership agreement are listed in Exhibit 17–1 below.

DURATION OF THE PARTNERSHIP The partnership agreement can specify the duration of the partnership by stating that it will continue until a designated date or until the completion of a particular project. This is called a *partnership for a term.* Generally, withdrawal from a partnership for a term prematurely

EXHIBIT 17–1 • **Terms Commonly Included in a Partnership Agreement**

TERM	DESCRIPTION
Basic Structure	• Name of the partnership. • Names of the partners. • Location of the business and the state law under which the partnership is organized. • Purpose of the partnership. • Duration of the partnership.
Capital Contributions	• Amount of capital that each partner is contributing. • The agreed-on value of any real or personal property that is contributed instead of cash. • How gains and losses on contributed capital will be allocated and whether contributions will earn interest.
Sharing of Profits and Losses	• Percentage of the profits and losses of the business that each partner will receive. • When distributions of profit will be made and how net profit will be calculated.
Management and Control	• How management responsibilities will be divided among the partners. • Name(s) of the managing partner or partners and whether other partners have voting rights.
Accounting and Partnership Records	• Name of the bank in which the partnership will maintain its business and checking accounts. • Statement that an accounting of partnership records will be maintained and that any partner, or her or his agent, can review these records at any time. • The dates of the partnership's fiscal year (if used) and when the annual audit of the books will take place.
Dissociation and Dissolution	• Events that will cause the dissociation of a partner or dissolve the partnership, such as the retirement, death, or incapacity of any partner. • How partnership property will be valued and apportioned on dissociation and dissolution. • Whether an arbitrator will determine the value of partnership property on dissociation and dissolution and whether that determination will be binding.
Arbitration	• Whether arbitration is required for any dispute relating to the partnership agreement.

(before the expiration date) constitutes a breach of the agreement, and the responsible partner can be held liable for any resulting losses [UPA 602(b)(2)].

If no fixed duration is specified, the partnership is a *partnership at will.* Any partner can dissolve this type of partnership at any time without violating the agreement and without incurring liability for losses to other partners that result from the termination.

PARTNERSHIP BY ESTOPPEL Occasionally, persons who are not partners nevertheless hold themselves out as partners and make representations that third parties rely on in dealing with them. In such a situation, a court may conclude that a **partnership by estoppel** exists and impose liability—but not partnership *rights*—on the alleged partner or partners. Similarly, a partnership by estoppel may be imposed when a partner represents, expressly or impliedly, that a nonpartner is a member of the firm. Whenever a third person has reasonably and detrimentally relied on the representation that a nonpartner was part of the partnership, a partnership by estoppel is deemed to exist. When this occurs, the nonpartner is regarded as an agent whose acts are binding on the partnership [UPA 308].

CASE IN POINT Gary Chavers operated Chavers Welding and Construction (CWC). Gary's two sons began to work in the business after graduating from high school. CWC contracted with Epsco, Inc., to provide payroll services for CWC. Epsco extended credit to CWC, which the Chaverses represented was a partnership. When CWC's account was more than $80,000 delinquent, Epsco sued to recover payment. The father filed for bankruptcy, and his obligation to Epsco was discharged. The sons claimed that their father owned CWC as a sole proprietor and that they were not partners in the business. The court, however, held that the sons were liable for CWC's debts based on partnership by estoppel. Because the Chaverses had represented to Epsco that CWC was a partnership and Epsco had relied on this representation when extending credit, the sons were prevented from claiming that no partnership existed.[12]

Rights of Partners

The rights and duties of partners are governed largely by the specific terms of their partnership agreement. In the absence of provisions to the contrary in the partnership agreement, the law imposes the rights discussed here and the duties that will be discussed in the next subsections. The character and nature of the partnership business generally influence the application of these rights and duties. The rights of partners in a partnership relate to the following areas: management, interest in the partnership, compensation, inspection of books, accounting, and property.

MANAGEMENT In a traditional partnership, all partners have equal rights in managing the partnership [UPA 401(f)]. Unless the partners agree otherwise, each partner has one vote in management matters *regardless of the proportional size of his or her interest in the firm.* In a large partnership, partners often agree to delegate daily management responsibilities to a management committee made up of one or more of the partners.

The majority rule controls decisions on ordinary matters connected with partnership business, unless otherwise specified in the agreement. Decisions that significantly affect the nature of the partnership or that are outside the ordinary course of the partnership business, however, require the *unanimous* consent of the partners [UPA 301(2), 401(i), 401(j)].

Unanimous consent is likely to be required for a decision to undertake any of the following actions:

1. To alter the essential nature of the firm's business as expressed in the partnership agreement or to alter the capital structure of the partnership.
2. To admit new partners or engage in a completely new business.
3. To assign partnership property to a trust for the benefit of creditors.
4. To dispose of the partnership's *goodwill* (defined on page 389).
5. To confess judgment against the partnership or to submit partnership claims to arbitration. (A **confession of judgment** is an act by a debtor that permits a judgment to be entered against him or her by a creditor, for an agreed sum, without the institution of legal proceedings.)
6. To undertake any act that would make further conduct of partnership business impossible.
7. To amend the terms of the partnership agreement.

INTEREST IN THE PARTNERSHIP Each partner is entitled to the proportion of business profits and losses that is specified in the partnership agreement. If the agreement does not apportion profits (indicate how the profits will be shared), the UPA provides that profits will be shared equally. If the agreement

---

12. *Chavers v. Epsco, Inc.*, 352 Ark. 65, 98 S.W.3d 421 (2003).

does not apportion losses, losses will be shared in the same ratio as profits [UPA 401(b)].

For example, Rico and Brett form a partnership. The partnership agreement provides for capital contributions of $60,000 from Rico and $40,000 from Brett, but it is silent as to how they will share profits or losses. In this situation, they will share both profits and losses equally. If their partnership agreement had provided that they would share profits in the same ratio as capital contributions, however, 60 percent of the profits would go to Rico, and 40 percent would go to Brett. If this agreement was silent as to losses, losses would be shared in the same ratio as profits (60 percent and 40 percent, respectively).

Compensation. Devoting time, skill, and energy to partnership business is a partner's duty and generally is not a compensable service. Rather, as mentioned, a partner's income from the partnership takes the form of a distribution of profits according to the partner's share in the business. Partners can, of course, agree otherwise. For example, the managing partner of a law firm often receives a salary—in addition to her or his share of profits—for performing special administrative or managerial duties.

Inspection of the Books. Partnership books and records must be kept accessible to all partners. Each partner has the right to receive (and the corresponding duty to produce) full and complete information concerning the conduct of all aspects of partnership business [UPA 403]. Each firm retains books for recording and securing such information. Partners contribute the information, and a bookkeeper typically has the duty to preserve it. The books must be kept at the firm's principal business office (unless the partners agree otherwise). Every partner, whether active or inactive, is entitled to inspect all books and records on demand and can make copies of the materials.

Accounting of Partnership Assets or Profits. An accounting of partnership assets or profits is required to determine the value of each partner's share in the partnership. An accounting can be performed voluntarily, or it can be compelled by court order. Under UPA 405(b), a partner has the right to bring an action for an accounting during the term of the partnership, as well as on the partnership's dissolution and winding up.

Property Rights. Property acquired *by* a partnership is the property of the partnership and not of the partners individually [UPA 203]. Partnership property includes all property that was originally contributed to the partnership and anything later purchased by the partnership or in the partnership's name (except in rare circumstances) [UPA 204]. A partner may use or possess partnership property only on behalf of the partnership [UPA 401(g)]. A partner is *not* a co-owner of partnership property and has no right to sell, mortgage, or transfer partnership property to another [UPA 501].

In other words, partnership property is owned by the partnership as an entity and not by the individual partners. Thus, a creditor of an individual partner cannot seek to use partnership property to satisfy the partner's debt. Such a creditor can, however, petition a court for a **charging order** to attach the individual partner's *interest* in the partnership (her or his proportionate share of the profits and losses and right to receive distributions) to satisfy the partner's obligation [UPA 502]. A partner can also assign her or his right to a share of the partnership profits to another to satisfy a debt.

Duties and Liabilities of Partners

The duties and liabilities of partners that we examine here are basically derived from agency law. Each partner is an agent of every other partner and acts as both a principal and an agent in any business transaction within the scope of the partnership agreement. Each partner is also a general agent of the partnership in carrying out the usual business of the firm "or business of the kind carried on by the partnership" [UPA 301(1)]. Thus, every act of a partner concerning partnership business and "business of the kind" and every contract signed in the partnership's name bind the firm.

FIDUCIARY DUTIES The fiduciary duties that a partner owes to the partnership and the other partners are the duty of care and the duty of loyalty [UPA 404(a)]. Under the UPA, a partner's *duty of care* is limited to refraining from "grossly negligent or reckless conduct, intentional misconduct, or a knowing violation of law" [UPA 404(c)]. A partner is not liable to the partnership for simple negligence or honest errors in judgment in conducting partnership business.

Duty of Loyalty. The *duty of loyalty* requires a partner to account to the partnership for "any property, profit, or benefit" derived by the partner in the conduct of the partnership's business or from the use of its property. A partner must also refrain from competing with the partnership in business or dealing with the firm as an adverse party [UPA 404(b)]. The duty of loyalty can be breached by self-dealing, misusing partnership property, disclosing trade secrets, or usurping a partnership business opportunity. The following case is a classic example.

CASE 17.3
Meinhard v. Salmon

Court of Appeals of New York, 249 N.Y. 458, 164 N.E. 545 (1928).
www.nycourts.gov/reporter/Index.htm[a]

BACKGROUND AND FACTS • Walter Salmon negotiated a twenty-year lease for the Hotel Bristol in New York City. To pay for the conversion of the building into shops and offices, Salmon entered into an agreement with Morton Meinhard to assume half of the cost. They agreed to share the profits and losses from the *joint venture*,[b] but Salmon was to have the sole power to manage the building. Less than four months before the end of the lease term, the building's owner, Elbridge Gerry, approached Salmon about a project to raze the converted structure, clear five adjacent lots, and construct a single building across the whole property. Salmon agreed and signed a new lease in the name of his own business, Midpoint Realty Company, without telling Meinhard. When Meinhard learned of the deal, he filed a suit in a New York state court against Salmon. The court ruled in Meinhard's favor, and Salmon appealed.

IN THE LANGUAGE OF THE COURT
CARDOZO, C.J. [Chief Justice]
* * * *

Joint adventurers, like copartners, owe to one another, while the enterprise continues, the duty of the finest loyalty. Many forms of conduct permissible in a work-a-day world for those acting at arm's length are forbidden to those bound by fiduciary ties. * * * Not honesty alone, but the punctilio [strictness in observance of details] of an honor the most sensitive, is then the standard of behavior. As to this there has developed a tradition that is unbending and inveterate [entrenched]. Uncompromising rigidity has been the attitude of courts * * * when petitioned to undermine the rule of undivided loyalty.

* * * The trouble about [Salmon's] conduct is that he excluded his coadventurer from any chance to compete, from any chance to enjoy the opportunity for benefit.

* * * The very fact that Salmon was in control with exclusive powers of direction charged him the more obviously with the duty of disclosure, [because] only through disclosure could opportunity be equalized.

* * * Authority is, of course, abundant that one partner may not appropriate to his own use a renewal of a lease, though its term is to begin at the expiration of the partnership. The lease at hand with its many changes is not strictly a renewal. Even so, the standard of loyalty for those in trust relations is without the fixed divisions of a graduated scale. * * * *A man obtaining [an]* * * * *opportunity* * * * *by the position he occupies as a partner is bound by his obligation to his copartners in such dealings not to separate his interest from theirs, but, if he acquires any benefit, to communicate it to them. Certain it is also that there may be no abuse of special opportunities growing out of a special trust as manager or agent.* [Emphasis added.]

* * * Very likely [Salmon] assumed in all good faith that with the approaching end of the venture he might ignore his coadventurer and take the extension for himself. He had given to the enterprise time and labor as well as money. He had made it a success. Meinhard, who had given money, but neither time nor labor, had already been richly paid. * * * [But] Salmon had put himself in a position in which thought of self was to be renounced, however hard the abnegation [self-denial]. He was much more than a coadventurer. He was a managing coadventurer. For him and for those like him the rule of undivided loyalty is relentless.

DECISION AND REMEDY • *The Court of Appeals of New York held that Salmon had breached his fiduciary duty by failing to inform Meinhard of the business opportunity and secretly taking advantage of it himself.*

---

a. In the links at the bottom of the page, click on "Archives." In the result, scroll to the name of the case and click on it to access the opinion. The New York State Law Reporting Bureau maintains this Web site.

b. An organization created by two or more persons in contemplation of a limited activity or a single transaction. This special business form is similar to a partnership in many respects.

CASE CONTINUES ➤

CASE 17.3 CONTINUED ➡ **IMPACT OF THIS CASE ON TODAY'S LAW** • *This landmark case involved a joint venture, not a partnership. At the time, a member of a joint venture had only the duty to refrain from actively subverting the rights of the other members. The decision in this case imposed the highest standard of loyalty on joint-venture members. The duty is now the same in both joint ventures and partnerships. The eloquent language in this case that describes the standard of loyalty is frequently quoted approvingly by courts in cases involving partnerships.*

WHAT IF THE FACTS WERE DIFFERENT? • *Suppose that Salmon had disclosed Gerry's proposal to Meinhard, who had said that he was not interested. Would the result in this case have been different? Explain.*

Breach and Waiver of Fiduciary Duties. A partner's fiduciary duties may not be waived or eliminated in the partnership agreement, and in fulfilling them each partner must act consistently with the obligation of good faith and fair dealing [UPA 103(b), 404(d)]. The agreement can specify acts that the partners agree will violate a fiduciary duty.

Note that a partner may pursue his or her own interests without automatically violating these duties [UPA 404(e)]. The key is whether the partner has disclosed the interest to the other partners. For example, a partner who owns a shopping mall may vote against a partnership proposal to open a competing mall, provided that the partner has fully disclosed her interest in the existing shopping mall to the other partners at the firm. A partner cannot make secret profits or put self-interest before his or her duty to the interest of the partnership, however.

AUTHORITY OF PARTNERS The UPA affirms general principles of agency law that pertain to a partner's authority to bind a partnership in contract. A partner may also subject the partnership to tort liability under agency principles. When a partner is carrying on partnership business or business of the kind with third parties in the usual way, apparent authority exists, and both the partner and the firm share liability.

The partnership will not be liable, however, if the third parties *know* that the partner has no such authority. For example, Patricia, a partner in a law firm, applies for a bank loan on behalf of the partnership without authorization from the other partners. If the bank manager knows that Patricia has no authority to do so and nonetheless grants the loan, Patricia will be personally bound, but the partnership will not be liable.

A partnership may file in a designated state office a "statement of partnership authority" to limit a partner's capacity to act as the firm's agent or transfer property on its behalf [UPA 105, 303]. Any such limit on a partner's authority, however, normally does not affect a third party who does not know about the statement (except in real estate transactions when the statement has been recorded with the appropriate state office—see Chapter 26).

The agency concepts relating to apparent authority, actual authority, and ratification that will be discussed in Chapter 20 also apply to partnerships. The extent of *implied authority* generally is broader for partners than for ordinary agents, however.

The Scope of Implied Powers. The character and scope of the partnership business and the customary nature of the particular business operation determine the implied powers of partners. For example, a *trading partnership* is a business that has goods in inventory and makes profits buying and selling those goods. A partner in a trading partnership has a wide range of implied powers, such as to advertise products, hire employees, and extend the firm's credit by issuing or signing checks.

In an ordinary partnership, the partners can exercise all implied powers reasonably necessary and customary to carry on that particular business. Some customarily implied powers include the authority to make warranties on goods in the sales business and the power to enter into contracts consistent with the firm's regular course of business. Most partners also have the implied authority to make admissions and representations concerning partnership affairs. A partner might also have the implied power to convey (transfer) real property in the firm's name when such conveyances are part of the ordinary course of partnership business.

Authorized versus Unauthorized Actions. If a partner acts within the scope of authority, the partnership is legally bound to honor the partner's commitments to third parties. For example, a partner's authority to sell partnership products carries with it the implied authority to transfer title and to make usual warranties. Hence, in a partnership that operates a retail tire store, any partner negotiating a contract with a customer for the sale of a set of tires can specify that "each tire will be warranted for normal wear for 40,000 miles." This same partner, however, does not have the authority to sell office equipment, fixtures, or the partnership's retail facility without the consent of all of the other partners.

In addition, because partnerships are formed to generate profits, a partner generally does not have the authority to make charitable contributions without the consent of the other partners. Such actions are not binding on the partnership unless they are ratified by all of the other partners.

LIABILITY OF PARTNERS One significant disadvantage associated with a traditional partnership is that the partners are *personally* liable for the debts of the partnership. Moreover, in most states, the liability is essentially unlimited because the acts of one partner in the ordinary course of business subject the other partners to personal liability [UPA 305]. The following subsections explain the rules on a partner's liability.

Joint Liability. At one time, each partner in a partnership generally was jointly liable for the partnership's obligations. **Joint liability** means that a third party must sue all of the partners as a group, but each partner can be held liable for the full amount.[13] If a third party sued a partner on a contractual debt, the lawsuit had to name all of the partners as defendants to seek partnership assets to pay any judgment. With joint liability, the partnership's assets must be exhausted before creditors can reach the partners' individual assets.[14]

Joint and Several Liability. In the majority of the states, under UPA 306(a), partners are both jointly and severally (separately, or individually) liable for all partnership obligations, including contracts, torts, and breaches of trust. **Joint and several liability** means that a third party has the option of suing all of the partners together (jointly) or one or more of the partners separately (severally). This is true even if a partner did not participate in,

ratify, or know about whatever it was that gave rise to the cause of action. Normally, though, the partnership's assets must be exhausted before a creditor can enforce a judgment against a partner's separate assets [UPA 307(d)].

A judgment against one partner severally (separately) does not extinguish the others' liability. Those not sued in the first action normally may be sued subsequently, unless the court in the first action held that the partnership was in no way liable. If a plaintiff is successful in a suit against a partner or partners, he or she may collect on the judgment only against the assets of those partners named as defendants. A partner who commits a tort may be required to indemnify (reimburse) the partnership for any damages it pays—unless the tort was committed in the ordinary course of the partnership's business.

CASE IN POINT Nicole Moren was a partner in Jax Restaurant. After work one day, Moren was called back to the restaurant to help in the kitchen. She brought her two-year-old-son, Remington, and put him on the kitchen counter. While she was making pizzas, Remington reached into the dough press. His hand was crushed, causing permanent injuries. Through his father, Remington filed a suit against the partnership for negligence. The partnership filed a complaint against Moren, arguing that it was entitled to indemnity (compensation or reimbursement) from Moren for her negligence. The court held in favor of Moren and ordered the partnership to pay damages to Remington. Moren was not required to indemnify the partnership because her negligence occurred in the ordinary course of the partnership's business.[15]

Liability of Incoming Partners. A partner newly admitted to an existing partnership is not personally liable for any partnership obligation incurred before the person became a partner [UPA 306(b)]. In other words, the new partner's liability to existing creditors of the partnership is limited to her or his capital contribution to the firm.

For example, Smartclub, an existing partnership with four members, admits a new partner, Alex Jaff. He contributes $100,000 to the partnership. Smartclub has debts amounting to $600,000 at the time Jaff joins the firm. Although Jaff's capital contribution of $100,000 can be used to satisfy Smartclub's obligations, Jaff is not personally liable for partnership debts that were incurred before he became a partner. Thus, his personal assets cannot

---

13. Under the previous version of the UPA, which is still in effect in a few states, partners were subject to joint liability on partnership debts and contracts, excluding partnership debts arising from torts. States that still follow the previous version of the UPA include Connecticut, West Virginia, and Wyoming. In these states, the partners are subject to *joint liability* on contracts and to *joint and several liability* (discussed next) on debts arising from torts.

14. For a case applying joint liability to a partnership, see *Shar's Cars, LLC v. Elder,* 97 P.3d 724 (Utah App. 2004).

15. *Moren v. Jax Restaurant,* 679 N.W.2d 165 (Minn.App. 2004).

be used to satisfy the partnership's preexisting debt. If, however, the managing partner at Smartclub borrows funds for the partnership after Jaff becomes a partner, Jaff will be personally liable for those amounts, along with all other partners.

Dissociation of a Partner

Dissociation occurs when a partner ceases to be associated in the carrying on of the partnership business. Although a partner always has the *power* to dissociate from the firm, he or she may not have the *right* to dissociate. Dissociation normally entitles the partner to have his or her interest purchased by the partnership, and terminates his or her actual authority to act for the partnership and to participate with the partners in running the business. After that, the partnership continues to do business without the dissociated partner.

EVENTS THAT CAUSE DISSOCIATION Under UPA 601, a partner can be dissociated from a partnership in any of the following ways:

1. By the partner's voluntarily giving notice of an "express will to withdraw." (Note that when a partner gives notice of her or his intent to withdraw, the remaining partners must decide whether to continue or give up the partnership business. If they do not agree to continue the partnership, the voluntary dissociation of a partner will dissolve the firm [UPA 801(1)].)
2. By the occurrence of an event specified in the partnership agreement.
3. By a unanimous vote of the other partners under certain circumstances, such as when a partner transfers substantially all of her or his interest in the partnership, or when it becomes unlawful to carry on partnership business with that partner.
4. By order of a court or arbitrator if the partner has engaged in wrongful conduct that affects the partnership business, breached the partnership agreement or violated a duty owed to the partnership or the other partners, or engaged in conduct that makes it "not reasonably practicable to carry on the business in partnership with the partner" [UPA 601(5)].
5. By the partner's declaring bankruptcy, assigning his or her interest in the partnership for the benefit of creditors, or becoming physically or mentally incapacitated, or by the partner's death. Note that although the bankruptcy or death of a partner represents that partner's "dissociation" from the partnership, it is not an *automatic* ground for

the partnership's dissolution (*dissolution* will be discussed shortly).

WRONGFUL DISSOCIATION As mentioned, a partner has the power to dissociate from a partnership at any time, but if she or he lacks the right to dissociate, then the dissociation is considered wrongful under the law [UPA 602]. When a partner's dissociation breaches a partnership agreement, for instance, it is wrongful. Suppose that a partnership agreement states that it is a breach of the agreement for any partner to assign partnership property to a creditor without the consent of the other partners. If Janis, a partner, makes such an assignment, she has not only breached the agreement but has also wrongfully dissociated from the partnership. Similarly, if a partner refuses to perform duties required by the partnership agreement—such as accounting for profits earned from the use of partnership property—this breach can be treated as a wrongful dissociation.

A partner who wrongfully dissociates is liable to the partnership and to the other partners for damages caused by the dissociation. This liability is in addition to any other obligation of the partner to the partnership or to the other partners. Thus, a wrongfully dissociating partner is liable to the partnership not only for any damages caused by breach of the partnership agreement, but also for costs incurred to replace the partner's expertise or to obtain new financing.

EFFECTS OF DISSOCIATION Dissociation (rightful or wrongful) terminates some of the rights of the dissociated partner, requires that the partnership purchase his or her interest, and alters the liability of the parties to third parties.

Rights and Duties. On a partner's dissociation, his or her right to participate in the management and conduct of the partnership business terminates [UPA 603]. The partner's duty of loyalty also ends. A partner's duty of care continues only with respect to events that occurred before dissociation, unless the partner participates in winding up the partnership's business (which will be discussed shortly). For example, Debbie Pearson is a partner who is leaving an accounting firm, Bubb & Pearson. Pearson can immediately compete with the firm for new clients. She must exercise care in completing ongoing client transactions, however, and must account to the firm for any fees received from the old clients based on those transactions.

After a partner's dissociation, his or her interest in the partnership must be purchased according to the rules in UPA 701. The **buyout price** is based on the amount that would have been distributed to the partner if the partnership had been wound up on the date of dissociation. Offset against the price are amounts owed by the partner to the partnership, including damages for wrongful dissociation.

CASE IN POINT In 1978, Wilbur and Dee Warnick and their son Randall bought a ranch for $335,000 and formed a partnership to operate it. The partners' initial capital contributions totaled $60,000, of which Randall paid 34 percent. Over the next twenty years, each partner contributed funds to the operation and received cash distributions from the partnership. In 1999, Randall dissociated from the partnership. When the parties could not agree on a buyout price, Randall filed a lawsuit. The court awarded Randall $115,783.13—the amount of his cash contributions, plus 34 percent of the increase in the value of the partnership's assets above all partners' cash contributions. Randall's parents appealed, arguing that $50,000 should be deducted from the appraised value of the assets for the estimated expenses of selling them. The court affirmed the buyout price, however, because "purely hypothetical costs of sale are not a required deduction in valuing partnership assets" to determine a buyout price.[16]

Liability to Third Parties. For two years after a partner dissociates from a continuing partnership, the partnership may be bound by the acts of the dissociated partner based on apparent authority [UPA 702]. In other words, the partnership may be liable to a third party with whom a dissociated partner enters into a transaction if the third party reasonably believed that the dissociated partner was still a partner. Similarly, a dissociated partner may be liable for partnership obligations entered into during a two-year period following dissociation [UPA 703].

To avoid this possible liability, a partnership should notify its creditors, customers, and clients of a partner's dissociation. In addition, either the partnership or the dissociated partner can file a statement of dissociation in the appropriate state office to limit the dissociated partner's authority to ninety days after the filing [UPA 704]. Filing this statement helps to minimize the firm's potential liability for the former partner and vice versa.

Partnership Termination

The same events that cause dissociation can result in the end of the partnership if the remaining partners no longer wish to (or are unable to) continue the partnership business. Only certain departures of a partner will end the partnership, though, and generally the partnership can continue if the remaining partners consent [UPA 801].

The termination of a partnership is referred to as **dissolution,** which essentially means the commencement of the winding up process. **Winding up** is the actual process of collecting, liquidating, and distributing the partnership assets.[17] Here, we discuss the dissolution and winding up of partnership business.

DISSOLUTION Dissolution of a partnership generally can be brought about by acts of the partners, by operation of law, or by judicial decree [UPA 801]. Any partnership (including one for a fixed term) can be dissolved by the partners' agreement. Similarly, if the partnership agreement states that it will dissolve on a certain event, such as a partner's death or bankruptcy, then the occurrence of that event will dissolve the partnership. A partnership for a fixed term or a particular undertaking is dissolved by operation of law at the expiration of the term or on the completion of the undertaking.

Any event that makes it unlawful for the partnership to continue its business will result in dissolution [UPA 801(4)]. Under the UPA, a court may order dissolution when it becomes obviously impractical for the firm to continue—for example, if the business can only be operated at a loss [UPA 801(5)]. Note, however, that even when one partner has brought a court action seeking to dissolve a partnership, the partnership continues to exist until it is legally dissolved by the court or by the parties' agreement.

CASE IN POINT Ellin Curley and Lawrence Kaiser were married when they formed a general partnership, K&K Associates. Later, Curley and Kaiser were divorced and entered into an amended partnership agreement that stated that Curley owned 80 percent of the firm and Kaiser owned 20 percent. K&K invested part of its capital, but the investment suffered losses. When Kaiser refused to pay his share of the losses, Curley filed a suit for breach of contract and requested judicial dissolution of K&K. While

---

16. *Warnick v. Warnick,* 2006 WY 58, 133 P.3d 997 (2006).

17. Although "winding down" would seem to describe more accurately the process of settling accounts and liquidating the assets of a partnership, English and U.S. statutory and case law have traditionally used "winding up" to denote this final stage of a partnership's existence.

the lawsuit was pending, Kaiser died, and his new wife was substituted as the defendant. A provision in the amended agreement stated that if Kaiser died while still a partner, K&K would terminate, and the value of Kaiser's ownership interest in the closing capital account would be zero. The defense argued that this provision was not enforceable because the partnership no longer existed. The court ruled that although the dissolution process had begun, the partnership still existed when Kaiser died. Therefore, the provision in the amended agreement effectively terminated the partnership and reduced the value of Kaiser's interest to zero.[18]

WINDING UP AND DISTRIBUTION OF ASSETS After dissolution, the partnership continues for the limited purpose of the winding up process.[19] The partners cannot create new obligations on behalf of the partnership. They have authority only to complete transactions begun but not finished at the time of dissolution and to wind up the business of the partnership [UPA 803, 804(1)].

Winding up includes collecting and preserving partnership assets, discharging liabilities (paying debts), and accounting to each partner for the value of his or her interest in the partnership. Partners continue to have fiduciary duties to one another and to the firm during this process. UPA 401(h) provides that a partner is entitled to compensation for services in winding up partnership affairs (and reimbursement for expenses incurred in the process) above and apart from his or her share in the partnership profits.

Both creditors of the partnership and creditors of the individual partners can make claims on the partnership's assets. In general, partnership creditors share proportionately with the partners' individual creditors in the partners' assets, which include their interests in the partnership. A partnership's assets are distributed according to the following priorities [UPA 807]:

1. Payment of debts, including those owed to partner and nonpartner creditors.
2. Return of capital contributions and distribution of profits to partners.

If the partnership's liabilities are greater than its assets, the partners bear the losses—in the absence of a contrary agreement—in the same proportion in which they shared the profits (rather than, for example, in proportion to their contributions to the partnership's capital).

PARTNERSHIP BUY-SELL AGREEMENTS Before entering into a partnership, partners should agree on how the assets will be valued and divided in the event that the partnership dissolves. A **buy-sell agreement**, sometimes called simply a *buyout agreement*, provides for one or more partners to buy out the other or others, should the situation warrant. Agreeing beforehand on who buys what, under what circumstances, and, if possible, at what price may eliminate costly negotiations or litigation later. Alternatively, the agreement may specify that one or more partners will determine the value of the interest being sold and that the other or others will decide whether to buy or sell.

Under UPA 701(a), if a partner's dissociation does not result in a dissolution of the partnership, a buyout of the partner's interest is mandatory. The UPA contains an extensive set of buyout rules that apply when the partners do not have a buyout agreement. Basically, a withdrawing partner receives the same amount through a buyout that he or she would receive if the business were winding up [UPA 701(b)].

---

18. *Curley v. Kaiser,* 112 Conn.App. 213, 962 A.2d 167 (2009).
19. Note that at any time after dissolution but before winding up is completed, all of the partners may decide to continue the partnership business and waive the right to have the business wound up [UPA 802].

REVIEWING
Sole Proprietorships, Franchises, and Partnerships

Carlos Del Rey decided to open a Mexican fast-food restaurant and signed a franchise contract with a national chain called La Grande Enchilada. The contract required the franchisee to strictly follow the franchisor's operating manual and stated that failure to do so would be grounds for terminating the franchise contract. The manual set forth detailed operating procedures and safety standards, and provided that a La Grande Enchilada representative would inspect the restaurant monthly to ensure compliance. Nine months after Del Rey began operating his restaurant, a spark from the grill ignited an oily towel in

REVIEWING

Sole Proprietorships, Franchises, and Partnerships, Continued

the kitchen. No one was injured, but by the time firefighters were able to put out the fire, the kitchen had sustained extensive damage. The cook told the fire department that the towel was "about two feet from the grill" when it caught fire. This was in compliance with the franchisor's manual that required towels be placed at least one foot from the grills. Nevertheless, the next day La Grande Enchilada notified Del Rey that his franchise would terminate in thirty days for failure to follow the prescribed safety procedures. Using the information presented in the chapter, answer the following questions.

1. What type of franchise was Del Rey's La Grande Enchilada restaurant?
2. If Del Rey operates the restaurant as a sole proprietorship, then who bears the loss for the damaged kitchen? Explain.
3. Assume that Del Rey files a lawsuit against La Grande Enchilada, claiming that his franchise was wrongfully terminated. What is the main factor that a court would consider in determining whether the franchise was wrongfully terminated?
4. Would a court be likely to rule that La Grande Enchilada had good cause to terminate Del Rey's franchise in this situation? Why or why not?

⊛ DEBATE THIS: *A partnership should automatically end when one partner dissociates from the firm.*

TERMS AND CONCEPTS

	confession of judgment 391	franchisor 381	partnership 388
	dissociation 396	goodwill 389	partnership by estoppel 391
articles of partnership 390	dissolution 397	information return 390	pass-through entity 390
buyout price 397	entrepreneur 380	joint and several	sole proprietorship 380
buy-sell agreement 398	franchise 381	liability 395	winding up 397
charging order 392	franchisee 381	joint liability 395	

QUESTIONS AND CASE PROBLEMS

17–1. Franchising Maria, Pablo, and Vicky are recent college graduates who would like to go into business for themselves. They are considering purchasing a franchise. If they enter into a franchising arrangement, they would have the support of a large company that could answer any questions they might have. Also, a firm that has been in business for many years would be experienced in dealing with some of the problems that novice businesspersons might encounter. These and other attributes of franchises can lessen some of the risks of the marketplace. What other aspects of franchising—positive and negative—should Maria, Pablo, and Vicky consider before committing themselves to a particular franchise?

17–2. QUESTION WITH SAMPLE ANSWER: Control of a Franchise.

National Foods, Inc., sells franchises to its fast-food restaurants, known as Chicky-D's. Under the franchise agreement, franchisees agree to hire and train employees strictly according to Chicky-D's standards. Chicky-D's regional supervisors are required to approve all job candidates before they are hired and all general policies affecting those employees. Chicky-D's reserves the right to terminate a franchise for violating the franchisor's rules. In practice, however, Chicky-D's regional supervisors routinely approve new employees and individual franchisees' policies. After several incidents of racist comments and conduct by Tim, a recently hired assistant manager at a Chicky-D's, Sharon, a counterperson at the restaurant, resigns. Sharon files a suit in a federal district court against National. National files a motion for summary judgment, arguing that it is not liable for harassment by franchise employees. Will the court grant National's motion? Why or why not?

- **For a sample answer to Question 17–2, go to Appendix F at the end of this text.**

17–3. Partnership Formation Daniel is the owner of a chain of shoe stores. He hires Rubya to be the manager of a new store, which is to open in Grand Rapids, Michigan. Daniel, by written contract, agrees to pay Rubya a monthly salary and 20 percent of the profits. Without Daniel's knowledge, Rubya represents himself to Classen as Daniel's partner and shows Classen the agreement to share profits. Classen extends credit to Rubya. Rubya defaults. Discuss whether Classen can hold Daniel liable as a partner.

17–4. Sole Proprietorship James Ferguson operates Jim's 11#E Auto Sales in Jonesborough, Tennessee, as a sole proprietorship. In 1999, Consumers Insurance Co. issued a policy to "Jim Ferguson, Jim's 11#E Auto Sales" covering "Owned 'Autos' Only." *Auto* was defined to include "a land motor vehicle," which was not further explained in the policy. Coverage extended to damage caused by the owner or driver of an underinsured motor vehicle. In 2000, Ferguson bought and titled in his own name a 1976 Harley-Davidson motorcycle, intending to repair and sell the cycle through his dealership. In October 2001, while riding the motorcycle, Ferguson was struck by an auto driven by John Jenkins. Ferguson filed a suit in a Tennessee state court against Jenkins, who was underinsured with respect to Ferguson's medical bills, and Consumers. The insurer argued, among other things, that because the motorcycle was bought and titled in Ferguson's own name, and he was riding it at the time of the accident, it was his personal vehicle and thus was not covered under the dealership's policy. What is the relationship between a sole proprietor and a sole proprietorship? How might this status affect the court's decision in this case? [*Ferguson v. Jenkins*, 204 S.W.3d 779 (Tenn.App. 2006)]

17–5. Partnership Dissolution Nine minority partners each owned one-half of 1 percent of J&J Celcom, a partnership with AT&T, which owned the rest. AT&T, using its majority power, voted to buy out the minority partners. It offered each partner a price that was slightly higher than the price provided by a third party's appraisal. Some of the partners accepted the offer, but others did not. AT&T then voted to dissolve the partnership, forcing the remaining minority partners to accept the appraisal price. Those partners sued. The trial court held for AT&T, and the minority partners appealed. The appeals court held that the price offered was the fair market price, but certified the following question to Washington State's highest court: "Does a controlling partner violate the duty of loyalty to the partnership or to dissenting minority partners where the controlling partner causes the partnership to sell all its assets" to another party? How should the Washington Supreme Court answer this question? Why? [*J&J Celcom v. AT&T Wireless Services, Inc.*, 162 Wash.2d 102, 169 P.3d 823 (Sup.Ct. 2007)]

17–6. CASE PROBLEM WITH SAMPLE ANSWER: Franchise Termination.

Walid Elkhatib, a Palestinian Arab, emigrated to the United States in 1971 and became a U.S. citizen. Eight years later, Elkhatib bought a Dunkin' Donuts, Inc., franchise in Bellwood, Illinois. Dunkin' Donuts began offering breakfast sandwiches with bacon, ham, or sausage through its franchises in 1984, but Elkhatib refused to sell these items at his store on the ground that his religion forbade the handling of pork. In 1995, Elkhatib opened a second franchise in Berkeley, Illinois, at which he also refused to sell pork products. The next year, at both locations, Elkhatib began selling meatless sandwiches. In 1998, Elkhatib opened a third franchise in Westchester, Illinois. When he proposed to relocate this franchise, Dunkin' Donuts refused to approve the new location and added that it would not renew any of his franchise agreements because he did not carry the full sandwich line. Elkhatib filed a suit in a federal district court against Dunkin' Donuts and others. The defendants filed a motion for summary judgment. Did Dunkin' Donuts act in good faith in its relationship with Elkhatib? Explain. [Elkhatib v. Dunkin' Donuts, Inc., 493 F.3d 827 (7th Cir. 2007)]

- **To view a sample answer for Problem 17–6, go to this book's Web site at www.cengage.com/blaw/cross, select "Chapter 17," and click on "Case Problem with Sample Answer."**

17–7. Sole Proprietorship Julie Anne Gaskill is an oral and maxillofacial surgeon in Bowling Green, Kentucky. Her medical practice is a sole proprietorship that consists of Gaskill as the sole surgeon and an office staff. She sees every patient, exercises all professional judgment and skill, and manages the business. When Gaskill and her spouse, John Robbins, initiated divorce proceedings in a Kentucky state court, her accountant estimated the value of the practice at $221,610, excluding goodwill. Robbins's accountant estimated the value at $669,075, including goodwill. (Goodwill is the ability or reputation of a business to draw customers, get them to return, and contribute to future profitability.) How can a sole proprietor's reputation, skill, and relationships with customers be valued? Could these qualities be divided into "personal" and "enterprise" goodwill, with some goodwill associated with the business and some solely due to the personal qualities of the proprietor? If so, what might comprise each type? Is this an effective method for valuing Gaskill's practice? Discuss. [*Gaskill v. Robbins*, 282 S.W.3d 306 (Ky. 2009)]

17–8. Partnership Dissolution George Chaney and William Dickerson were partners in Bowen's Mill Landing, which purchased a large piece of land in the 1980s. The partners had planned to develop the property, but nothing was ever done. Chaney died in 1990, and his wife inherited his interest. When she died in 2004, her two sons, John and Dewey Lynch, inherited the half-interest in the partnership.

Dickerson died in 1995, and his daughter, Billie Thompson, inherited his half-interest. In 2006, the Lynches filed a petition for partition, asking that a commission be appointed to make a fair division of the land, giving the Lynches half and Thompson half. In 2007, the commission reported on how to divide the land into two parts. Thompson objected that the land belonged to Bowen's Mill Landing and could not be divided. The trial court ordered Thompson to "effectuate the dissolution of any partnership entity and . . . to wind up the business and affairs of any partnership" so that the land could be divided. Thompson appealed. Can the court order the partnership to dissolve? Why or why not? [*Thompson v. Lynch*, 990 A.2d 432 (Sup.Ct.Del. 2010)]

17–9. Franchise Disclosure Peaberry Coffee, Inc., owned and operated about twenty company stores in the Denver area. The company began a franchise program and prepared a disclosure document as required by the Federal Trade Commission (FTC). Peaberry sold ten franchises, and each franchisee received a disclosure document. Later, when the franchises did not do well, the franchisees sued Peaberry, claiming that its FTC disclosure document had been fraudulent. Specifically, the franchisees claimed that Peaberry had not disclosed that most of the company stores were unprofitable and that its parent company had suffered significant financial losses over the years. In addition, the trial court found that an article in the *Denver Business Journal*—in which an executive had said that Peaberry was profitable—was fraudulent. This article had been included in the franchisees' information packets. The district court dismissed the franchisees' complaint, noting that the FTC disclosure document had contained an exculpatory clause (see Chapter 9 on page 205). This clause said that the buyers should not rely on any material that was not in the franchise contract itself. The franchisees appealed. Can a franchisor disclaim the relevance of the information it provides to franchisees? Why or why not? [*Colorado Coffee Bean, LLC v. Peaberry Coffee, Inc.*, ___ P.3d ___ (Colo.App. 2010)]

17–10. A QUESTION OF ETHICS: Wrongful Dissociation.

Elliot Willensky and Beverly Moran formed a partnership to renovate and "flip" (resell) some property. According to their agreement, Moran would finance the purchase and renovation of the property, and Willensky would provide labor and oversight of the renovation work. Moran would be reimbursed from the profits of the sale, and the remainder of the profits would be divided evenly. Any losses would also be divided evenly. Moran paid $240,000 for a house and planned to spend $60,000 for its renovation. The parties agreed that the renovation would be completed in six months. Willensky lived in the house during the renovation. More than a year later, the project still was not completed, and the cost was much more than the $60,000 originally planned. Willensky often failed to communicate with Moran, and when she learned that her funds were nearly exhausted and the house nowhere near completion, she became worried. She told Willensky that he would have to pay rent and utility bills if he wished to continue to live in the house. Shortly thereafter, Willensky left for Florida due to a family emergency, saying that he would return as soon as he could. He never returned, however, and Moran lost touch with him. Moran took over the project and discovered that Willensky had left numerous bills unpaid, spent money on excessive or unnecessary items, and misappropriated funds for his personal use. After completing the project, paying all expenses relating to the renovation (in all, the renovation costs came to $311,222), and selling the property, Moran brought an action in a Tennessee state court to dissolve the partnership and to recover damages from Willensky for breach of contract and wrongful dissociation from the partnership. [Moran v. Willensky, ___ S.W.3d ___ (Tenn.Ct.App. 2010)]

(a) Moran alleged that Willensky had wrongfully dissociated from the partnership. When did this dissociation occur? Why was his dissociation wrongful?

(b) Which of Willensky's actions simply represent unethical behavior or bad management, and which constitute a breach of the agreement?

LEGAL RESEARCH EXERCISES ON THE WEB

Go to this text's Web site at **www.cengage.com/blaw/cross**, select "Chapter 17," and click on "Practical Internet Exercises." There you will find the following Internet research exercises that you can perform to learn more about the topics covered in this chapter.

Practical Internet Exercise 17–1: **Legal Perspective**
Liability of Dissociated Partners

Practical Internet Exercise 17–2: **Economic Perspective**
Taxation of Partnerships

Practical Internet Exercise 17–3: **Management Perspective**
Franchises

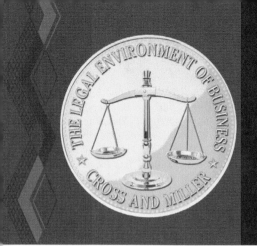

CHAPTER 18

✹
Limited Liability Companies and Limited Partnerships

In the previous chapter, we examined sole proprietorships, franchises, and traditional partnerships. Here, we examine a relatively new form of business organization called the *limited liability company* (LLC). LLCs are becoming an organizational form of choice among businesspersons—a trend encouraged by state statutes permitting their use. We

also examine business forms designed to limit the liability of partners.

This chapter begins with a discussion of the important aspects of an LLC, including its formation, jurisdictional requirements, and the advantages and disadvantages of choosing to do business as an LLC. This is followed by an examination of its management

and operation options. We then look at a similar type of entity that is also relatively new—the *limited liability partnership* (LLP). This chapter concludes with a discussion of the *limited partnership* (LP), a special type of partnership in which some of the partners have limited liability, and the *limited liability limited partnership* (LLLP).

SECTION 1
THE LIMITED LIABILITY COMPANY

A **limited liability company (LLC)** is a hybrid form that combines the limited liability aspects of the corporation and the tax advantages of a partnership. These business forms are governed by state LLC statutes. These laws vary, of course, from state to state. In an attempt to create more uniformity among the states in this respect, in 1995 the National Conference of Commissioners on Uniform State Laws issued the Uniform Limited Liability Company Act (ULLCA), but less than one-fifth of the states adopted it. Some provisions are common to most state statutes, however, and we base our discussion of LLCs in this section on these common elements.

In 1977, Wyoming became the first state to pass legislation authorizing the creation of an LLC. Although LLCs emerged in the United States in the latter half of the 1900s, they have been used for more than a century in other foreign jurisdictions, including several European and South American nations. For example, the South American *limitada* is a form of business organization that operates

more or less as a partnership but provides limited liability for the owners. Japan has the *godo kaisha*, a limited liability type of business organization that is similar to an LLC.

Taxation of the LLC

In the United States, after Wyoming's adoption of an LLC statute, it still was unclear how the Internal Revenue Service (IRS) would treat the LLC for tax purposes. In 1988, however, the IRS ruled that Wyoming LLCs would be taxed as partnerships instead of corporations, providing that certain requirements were met. Before this ruling, only one additional state—Florida, in 1982—had authorized LLCs. The 1988 ruling encouraged other states to enact LLC statutes, and in less than a decade, all states had done so.

In 1997, IRS rules also encouraged more widespread use of LLCs in the business world. Under these rules, any unincorporated business with more than one owner is automatically taxed as a partnership unless it indicates otherwise on its tax form or fits into one of the exceptions. The exceptions involve publicly traded companies, companies formed under a state incorporation statute, and certain foreign-owned companies. If a business chooses to be taxed as a corporation, it can indicate this preference by checking a box on its tax form.

Part of the impetus behind creating LLCs in this country is that foreign investors are allowed to become LLC members. Thus, in an era increasingly characterized by global business efforts and investments, the LLC offers U.S. firms and potential investors from other countries flexibility and the opportunity for limited liability and increased tax benefits.

The Nature of the LLC

LLCs share many characteristics with corporations. Like corporations, LLCs are creatures of state statute. In other words, they must be formed and operated in compliance with state law. Like the shareholders of a corporation, the owners of an LLC, who are called **members,** enjoy limited liability [ULLCA 303].[1] Thus, if the LLC is sued for wrongful discharge, for example, its individual members, managers, and agents cannot be held liable based solely on their status in the LLC.[2]

Similar to corporations, LLCs are legal entities apart from their owners. As a legal person, the LLC can sue or be sued, enter into contracts, and hold title to property [ULLCA 201]. The terminology used to describe LLCs formed in other states or nations is also similar to that used in corporate law. For example, an LLC formed in one state but doing business in another state is referred to in the second state as a *foreign LLC.*

---

1. Members of an LLC can also bring derivative actions, which you will read about in Chapter 19, on behalf of the LLC [ULLCA 101]. As with a corporate shareholder's derivative suit, any damages recovered go to the LLC, not to the members personally.
2. See, for example, *McFarland v. Virginia Retirement Services of Chesterfield, LLC,* 477 F.Supp.2d 727 (2007).

The Formation of the LLC

As mentioned, LLCs are creatures of statute and thus must follow state statutory requirements. To form an LLC, **articles of organization** must be filed with a central state agency—usually the secretary of state's office [ULLCA 202].[3] Typically, the articles are required to include such information as the name of the business, its principal address, the name and address of a registered agent, the names of the owners, and information on how the LLC will be managed [ULLCA 203]. The business's name must include the words *Limited Liability Company* or the initials *LLC* [ULLCA 105(a)]. Although a majority of the states permit one-member LLCs, some states require at least two members.

Businesspersons sometimes enter into contracts on behalf of a business organization that is not yet formed. As you will read in Chapter 19, persons who are forming a corporation may enter into contracts during the process of incorporation but before the corporation becomes a legal entity. These contracts are referred to as *preincorporation contracts.* Once the corporation is formed and adopts the preincorporation contracts (by means of a *novation,* discussed in Chapter 10), it can enforce the contract terms.

In the following case, the question was whether the same principle extends to LLCs. A person in the process of forming an LLC entered into a preorganization contract under which the LLC would be obligated to purchase a hotel. Once the LLC legally existed, the owners of the hotel refused to sell the property to the LLC, claiming that the contract was unenforceable.

---

3. In addition to requiring articles of organization to be filed, a few states require that a notice of the intention to form an LLC be published in a local newspaper.

CASE 18.1
02 Development, LLC v. 607 South Park, LLC
Court of Appeal of California, Second District, 159 Cal.App.4th 609, 71 Cal.Rptr.3d 608 (2008).

BACKGROUND AND FACTS • In 2004, 607 South Park, LLC, entered into a written agreement to sell Park Plaza Hotel to 607 Park View Associates, Ltd., for $8.7 million. The general partner of 607 Park View Associates was Creative Environments of Hollywood, Inc. In 2005, Creative Environments assigned the rights to the hotel purchase to another company, 02 Development, LLC. At the time, 02 Development did not yet exist; it was legally created several months later. When 607 South Park subsequently refused to sell the hotel, 02 Development sued 607 South Park for breach of the hotel purchase agreement. 607 South Park moved for summary judgment, arguing that no enforceable contract

CASE CONTINUES ➡

CASE 18.1 CONTINUED ➧ existed because at the time of the assignment, 02 Development did not yet legally exist. Furthermore, 607 South Park argued that 02 Development suffered no damages because it was "not ready, willing, and able to fund the purchase of the hotel." The trial court granted the motion and entered judgment in favor of 607 South Park. 02 Development appealed.

IN THE LANGUAGE OF THE COURT
ROTHSCHILD, J. [Judge]
 * * * *

It is hornbook law [black letter, or well-established, law] that a corporation can enforce preincorporation contracts made in its behalf, as long as the corporation "has adopted the contract or otherwise succeeded to it." * * * California law does not deviate from that well-established norm. *607 South Park does not argue that limited liability companies should be treated differently from corporations in this respect, and we are aware of no authority that would support such a position.* 607 South Park's first ground for its summary judgment motion—that there is no enforceable contract between 607 South Park and 02 Development because 02 Development did not exist when the assignment agreement was executed—therefore fails as a matter of law. [Emphasis added.]

607 South Park's principal contention to the contrary is that a nonexistent business entity cannot be a party to a contract. The contention is true but irrelevant. *When the assignment agreement was executed, 02 Development did not exist, so it was not then a party to the agreement. But once 02 Development came into existence, it could enforce any pre-organization contract made in its behalf, such as the assignment agreement, if it adopted or ratified it.* [Emphasis added.]
 * * * *

In the trial court, 607 South Park contended that in order to prove causation, 02 Development would have to prove either that it had the $8.7 million necessary to fund the transaction or that it had legally binding commitments from third parties to provide the necessary funding.* * * 607 South Park disavows [this contention] on appeal.

Instead, 607 South Park now argues that its motion was based on the proposition that 02 Development "must present admissible evidence that it would have been financially able to close the transaction." But 607 South Park's evidence in support of its motion showed only that 02 Development had neither the $8.7 million to fund the transaction nor legally binding commitments from third parties to provide the funding. *607 South Park presented no evidence that 02 Development would have been unable to arrange for the necessary funding to close the transaction on time if 607 South Park had given it the opportunity instead of repudiating the contract in advance.* Because 607 South Park introduced no evidence to support an argument based on the proposition of law that 607 South Park is now advocating, the burden of production never shifted to 02 Development to present contrary evidence. For all of these reasons, the trial court erred when it granted 607 South Park's motion for summary judgment. [Emphasis added.]

DECISION AND REMEDY • *The California intermediate appellate court reversed the judgment and directed the trial court to enter an order denying 607 South Park's motion for summary judgment. According to the appellate court, limited liability companies should be treated the same as corporations with respect to preorganization contracts.*

THE LEGAL ENVIRONMENT DIMENSION • *Why did the appellate court dismiss 607 South Park's argument that 02 Development should be required to prove that it had funding commitments for $8.7 million?*

THE ETHICAL DIMENSION • *What might have been some of the reasons that 607 South Park refused to sell the property to 02 Development?*

Jurisdictional Requirements

One of the significant differences between LLCs and corporations involves federal jurisdictional requirements. Under the federal jurisdiction statute, a corporation is deemed to be a citizen of the state where it is incorporated and maintains its principal place of business. The statute does not mention the state citizenship of partnerships, LLCs, and other unincorporated associations, but the courts have tended to regard these entities as citizens of every state in which their members are citizens.

The state citizenship of an LLC may come into play when a party sues the LLC based on diversity of citizenship. Remember from Chapter 2 that when parties to a lawsuit are from different states and the amount in controversy exceeds $75,000, a federal court can exercise diversity jurisdiction. *Total* diversity of citizenship must exist, however.

Suppose that Jen Fong, a citizen of New York, wishes to bring a suit against Skycel, an LLC formed under the laws of Connecticut. One of Skycel's members also lives in New York. Fong will not be able to bring a suit against Skycel in federal court on the basis of diversity jurisdiction because the defendant LLC is also a citizen of New York. The same would be true if Fong was bringing a suit against multiple defendants and one of the defendants lived in New York.

Advantages of the LLC

The LLC offers many advantages to businesspersons, which is why this form of business organization has become increasingly popular.

LIMITED LIABILITY A key advantage of the LLC is that the liability of members is limited to the amount of their investments. Although the LLC as an entity can be held liable for any loss or injury caused by the wrongful acts or omissions of its members, the members themselves typically are not personally liable.

As you will read in Chapter 19 on page 427, the courts on occasion make an exception to the limited liability of shareholders. In certain circumstances, a court will *pierce the corporate veil* and hold a shareholder personally liable for a corporate obligation. Sometimes, the corporate veil is pierced when a corporation is deemed to be merely an "alter ego" of the shareholder-owner (see Chapter 19 on page 429). A court may apply the alter-ego theory when a shareholder mixes (commingles) personal and corporate funds together or fails to observe required corporate formalities.

Whether the alter-ego theory should be applied to an LLC was at issue in the following case.

✳ EXTENDED CASE 18.2 ✳
ORX Resources, Inc. v. MBW Exploration, LLC

Court of Appeal of Louisiana, Fourth Circuit, 32 So.3d 931 (2010).
www.la4th.org[a]

IN THE LANGUAGE OF THE COURT
Charles R. *JONES*, Judge.
* * * *

On January 16, 2003, ORX [Resources, Inc.,] entered into the "Clovelly Purchase Agreement" with Coastline Oil & Gas, Inc. Pursuant to this Agreement, ORX purchased certain oil, gas and mineral leases/interests in a tract of land located in Lafourche Parish, known as the "Clovelly Prospect." ORX partnered with other entities, including MBW [Exploration, LLC], to share in the expense and potential profits of the

venture to explore and develop the Clovelly Prospect. The partnering parties entered into a Joint Operating Agreement ("JOA") and the Clovelly Prospect Participation Agreement ("Participation Agreement"). Mr. [Mark] Washauer signed these documents in October of 2003 and December of 2004, respectively, on behalf of MBW, in his capacity as a "Managing Member." However, MBW did not come into existence until July of 2005, when its articles of organization were filed with the Louisiana Secretary of State.

The JOA provided that ORX was to serve as the "Operator" drilling a

well within the Clovelly Prospect. It further provided that the nonoperating working interest partners, like MBW, would pay their proportionate share of the costs in exchange for a corresponding working interest ownership share in the Clovelly Prospect. The drilled well was governed by the Participation Agreement, which provided that MBW had a working interest in the Clovelly Prospect whereby MBW would share in 2.5% of the costs incurred, and would gain a proportionate share of the returns, if any, produced by the well.

Later, ORX submitted an Authorization for Expenditure

---

a. In the "Case Searching Options" area of the screen, select "Opinions." When the search page opens, select "Search Case Year and Number" and then enter "2009" in the "Case Year" box and "0662" in the "Case Number" box. When the search result appears at the bottom of the screen, click on "Download Opinion." The Louisiana Court of Appeal for the Fourth Circuit maintains this Web site.

EXTENDED CASE CONTINUES ➡

EXTENDED CASE 18.2 CONTINUED ⬇

("AFE") to MBW for approval, which Mr. Washauer signed in his own name. Additionally, he paid MBW's participation fee with a check drawn from the account of another entity, MBW Properties, LLC.

In 2006, ORX, as the well Operator, began planning the Allain LeBreton Well No. 2 in the Clovelly Prospect ("the Well"), which was the "initial well" called for in the Participation Agreement. * * * Mr. Washauer paid the full amount of MBW's share of an ORX cash call invoice of $59,325 with a personal check.

The well proved to be unsuccessful, and was ultimately plugged. MBW's unpaid share of expenses for said project amounted to $84,220.01, for which ORX demanded payment via correspondence, but to no avail. As a result, ORX filed suit for breach of contract against both MBW and Mr. Washauer ("the Appellants").

* * * [The trial court—a state district court—determined that Washauer operated MBW as his alter ego and allowed ORX to pierce the veil of the LLC. The court granted summary judgment in favor of ORX, holding that Washauer and MBW were liable, jointly and severally, to ORX in the amount of $84,220.01.]

The Appellants timely filed [an] appeal from this judgment.

* * * *

We first address whether the district court erred in ruling that the alter ego theory of the corporate veil piercing applied to Louisiana limited liability companies.

* * * *

The provisions of La. R.S. [Louisiana Revised Statutes] 12:1320(D) provide for the piercing of an LLC's veil when the situation so warrants.

* * * *

* * * *Piercing the veil of an LLC is justified to prevent the use of the LLC form to defraud creditors.* Under our * * * review, we find that the district court did not err in determining that the alter ego theory of corporate veil piercing applies to a Louisiana limited liability company, under the facts of this case, where it appears that Mr. Washauer used MBW as a shell and tried to avoid paying a legitimate debt of the LLC. [Emphasis added.]

* * * *

The Louisiana Supreme Court has identified *five nonexclusive factors to be used in determining whether to apply the alter ego doctrine: [commingling of corporate and shareholder funds; failure to follow statutory formalities for incorporating and transacting corporate affairs;*

undercapitalization; failure to provide separate bank accounts and bookkeeping records; and failure to hold regular shareholder and director meetings]. [Emphasis added.]

* * * *

In applying [these] factors, * * * we find that Mr. Washauer's activities on behalf of MBW do merit the piercing of the veil of this LLC. Commingling of the LLC's funds occurred with the funds of Mr. Washauer and a separate company of his. This commingling occurred because MBW was undercapitalized and did not have a separate bank account to transact its own affairs. Furthermore, at the time MBW began contracting with ORX, it was not yet recognized as an LLC by the Louisiana Secretary of State. Lastly, while LLCs are not bound by corporate laws to hold regular meetings, the fact that MBW has not had a meeting in over a year further evidences that Mr. Washauer was operating MBW at his leisure and direction. Thus, we find that the district court did not err in determining that MBW was being operated as the alter ego of Mr. Washauer under the [above-mentioned] factors, and therefore, he can be held personally liable jointly and solidarily [severally] with MBW.

For the foregoing reasons, * * * the judgment of the district court is affirmed * * * .

 QUESTIONS

1. One of the advantages of the LLC is that its members enjoy limited personal liability for the company's obligations. In view of this fact, does the possibility that a court may hold an LLC member personally liable for the LLC's debts reduce the utility of the LLC form of business organization? Explain.

2. What does "jointly and solidarily" (jointly and severally) mean in terms of liability? Would ORX prefer that Washauer and MBW be held personally liable jointly and severally, rather than that Washauer alone be held personally liable? Explain.

FLEXIBILITY IN TAXATION Another advantage of the LLC is its flexibility in regard to taxation. An LLC that has *two or more members* can choose to be taxed as either a partnership or a corporation. As will be discussed in Chapter 19, a corporate entity must pay income taxes on its profits, and the shareholders pay personal income taxes on profits distributed as

dividends. An LLC that wants to distribute profits to its members may prefer to be taxed as a partnership to avoid the "double taxation" that is characteristic of the corporate entity.

Unless an LLC indicates that it wishes to be taxed as a corporation, the IRS automatically taxes it as a partnership. This means that the LLC, as an entity, pays no taxes. Rather, as in a partnership, profits are "passed through" the LLC to the members, who then personally pay taxes on the profits. If an LLC's members want to reinvest profits in the business rather than distribute the profits to members, however, they may prefer to be taxed as a corporation. Corporate income tax rates may be lower than personal tax rates. Part of the attractiveness of the LLC is this flexibility with respect to taxation.

An LLC that has only *one member* cannot be taxed as a partnership. For federal income tax purposes, one-member LLCs are automatically taxed as sole proprietorships unless they indicate that they wish to be taxed as corporations. With respect to state taxes, most states follow the IRS rules.

MANAGEMENT AND FOREIGN INVESTORS Another advantage of the LLC for businesspersons is the flexibility it offers in terms of business operations and management—as will be discussed shortly. Because foreign investors can participate in an LLC, the LLC form of business is attractive as a way to encourage investment.

Disadvantages of the LLC

The main disadvantage of the LLC is that state LLC statutes are not uniform. Therefore, businesses that operate in more than one state may not receive consistent treatment in these states. Generally, most states apply to a foreign LLC (an LLC formed in another state) the law of the state where the LLC was formed. Nonetheless, difficulties can arise when one state's court must interpret and apply another state's laws.

SECTION 2
MANAGEMENT AND OPERATION OF AN LLC

As mentioned, an advantage of the LLC form of business is the flexibility it offers in terms of management and operation. Here, we discuss management options, the operating agreement, and general operating procedures of LLCs.

Management of an LLC

Basically, LLC members have two options for managing the firm. It can be either a "member-managed" LLC or a "manager-managed" LLC. Most state LLC statutes and the ULLCA provide that unless the articles of organization specify otherwise, an LLC is assumed to be member managed [ULLCA 203(a)(6)].

In a *member-managed* LLC, all of the members participate in management, and decisions are made by majority vote [ULLCA 404(a)]. In a *manager-managed* LLC, the members designate a group of persons to manage the firm. The management group may consist of only members, both members and nonmembers, or only nonmembers.

Under the ULLCA, managers in a manager-managed LLC owe fiduciary duties (the duty of loyalty and the duty of care) to the LLC and its members—just as corporate directors and officers owe fiduciary duties to the corporation and its shareholders [ULLCA 409(a), 409(h)]. But because not all states have adopted the ULLCA, some state statutes provide that managers owe fiduciary duties only to the LLC and not to the LLC's members. Although to whom the duty is owed may seem insignificant at first glance, it can have a dramatic effect on the outcome of litigation. See this chapter's *Insight into Ethics* feature on the following page for further discussion of this issue.

The LLC Operating Agreement

The members of an LLC can decide how to operate the various aspects of the business by forming an **operating agreement** [ULLCA 103(a)]. Operating agreements typically contain provisions relating to management, how profits will be divided, the transfer of membership interests, whether the LLC will be dissolved on the death or departure of a member, and other important issues.

A WRITING IS PREFERRED In many states, an operating agreement is not required for an LLC to exist, and if there is one, it need not be in writing. Generally, though, LLC members should protect their interests by creating a written operating agreement. As with any business, disputes may arise over any number of issues. If there is no agreement covering the topic under dispute, such as how profits will be divided, the state LLC statute will govern the outcome. For example, most LLC statutes provide that if the members have not specified how profits will be divided, they will be divided equally among the members.

PARTNERSHIP LAW MAY APPLY When an issue, such as the authority of individual members, is not covered by an operating agreement or by an LLC statute, the courts often apply principles of partnership law. These principles can give the members broad authority to bind the LLC unless the operating agreement provides otherwise.

INSIGHT INTO ETHICS
Fiduciary Duties of LLC Managers

Fiduciary duties, such as the duty of loyalty and the duty of care, have an ethical component because they require a person to act honestly and faithfully toward another. In states that have adopted the ULLCA, the managers of a manager-managed LLC owe fiduciary duties to the members and thus basically are required to behave ethically toward them. In other states, however, the LLC statutes may not include such a requirement. Consequently, even when a manager has acted unfairly and unethically toward members, the members may not be able to sue the manager for a breach of fiduciary duties.

In North Carolina and Virginia, for example, the LLC statutes do not explicitly create fiduciary duties to members. Instead, the statutes require that a manager exercise good business judgment in the best interests of the company. Because the statutes are silent on the manager's duty to members, in 2009 courts in those two states held that a manager-member owed fiduciary duties only to the LLC and not to the other members.[a] In contrast, in two other cases decided in 2009, courts in Idaho and Kentucky held that a manager-member owed fiduciary duties to the LLC's other members and that the members could sue the manager for breaching fiduciary duties.[b]

CRITICAL THINKING
INSIGHT INTO THE ETHICAL ENVIRONMENT
Why wouldn't a manager always owe a fiduciary duty to the members of an LLC?

---

a. *Remora Investments, LLC v. Orr,* 277 Va. 316, 673 S.E.2d 845 (2009), applying Virginia Code Sections 13.1–1024.1; and *Kaplan v. O.K. Technologies, LLC,* 675 S.E.2d 133 (N.C.App. 2009), applying North Carolina General Statutes Section 57C-3-22(b).

b. *Bushi v. Sage Health Care, LLC,* 146 Idaho 764, 203 P.3d 694 (2009), applying Idaho Code Sections 30-6-101 *et seq.;* and *Patmon v. Hobbs,* 280 S.W.3d 589 (Ky.App. 2009), applying Kentucky Revised Statutes Section 275.170.

CASE IN POINT Clifford Kuhn, Jr., and Joseph Tumminelli formed Touch of Class Limousine Service as an LLC. They did not create a written operating agreement but orally agreed that Kuhn would provide the financial backing and that Tumminelli would manage the day-to-day operations. Tumminelli embezzled $283,000 from the company after cashing customers' checks at Quick Cash, Inc., a local check-cashing service. Kuhn sued Tumminelli and Quick Cash to recover the embezzled funds. He argued that Quick Cash was liable because Tumminelli did not have the authority to cash the company's checks. The court, however, held that in the absence of a written operating agreement to the contrary, a member of an LLC, like a partner in a partnership, has the authority to cash a firm's checks.[4]

General Operating Procedures

An LLC's operating agreement can also include provisions governing decision-making procedures. For instance, the agreement can set forth procedures for choosing or removing managers. Although most LLC statutes are silent on this issue, the ULLCA provides that members may choose and remove managers by majority vote [ULLCA 404(b)(3)].

The members are also free to include in the agreement provisions designating when and for what purposes they will hold formal members' meetings. Most state LLC statutes have no provisions regarding members' meetings, which is in contrast to most state laws governing corporations, as you will read in Chapter 19.

Members may also specify in their agreement how voting rights will be apportioned. If they do not, LLC statutes in most states provide that voting rights are apportioned according to each member's capital contributions.[5] Some states provide that, in the absence of an agreement to the contrary, each member has one vote.

SECTION 3
DISSOCIATION AND DISSOLUTION OF AN LLC

Recall from Chapter 17 that in the context of partnerships, *dissociation* occurs when a partner ceases to be associated in the carrying on of the partnership business. The same concept applies to LLCs. A member

---

4. *Kuhn v. Tumminelli,* 366 N.J.Super. 431, 841 A.2d 496 (2004).

5. In contrast, partners in a partnership generally have equal rights in management and equal voting rights unless they specify otherwise in their partnership agreement (see Chapter 17).

of an LLC has the *power* to dissociate from the LLC at any time, but he or she may not have the *right* to dissociate. Under the ULLCA, the events that trigger a member's dissociation from an LLC are similar to the events causing a partner to be dissociated under the Uniform Partnership Act (UPA). These include voluntary withdrawal, expulsion by other members or by court order, bankruptcy, incompetence, and death. Generally, even if a member dies or otherwise dissociates from an LLC, the other members may continue to carry on the LLC business, unless the operating agreement provides otherwise.

Effect of Dissociation

When a member dissociates from an LLC, he or she loses the right to participate in management and the right to act as an agent for the LLC. The member's duty of loyalty to the LLC also terminates, and the duty of care continues only with respect to events that occurred before dissociation. Generally, the dissociated member also has a right to have his or her interest in the LLC bought out by the other members. The LLC's operating agreement may contain provisions establishing a buyout price, but if it does not, the member's interest is usually purchased at a fair value. In states that have adopted the ULLCA, the LLC must purchase the interest at fair value within 120 days after the dissociation.

If the member's dissociation violates the LLC's operating agreement, it is considered legally wrongful, and the dissociated member can be held liable for damages caused by the dissociation. Suppose that Chadwick and Barrow are members in an LLC. Chadwick manages the accounts, and Barrow, who has many connections in the community and is a skilled investor, brings in the business. If Barrow wrongfully dissociates from the LLC, the LLC's business will suffer, and Chadwick can hold Barrow liable for the loss of business resulting from her withdrawal.

Dissolution

Regardless of whether a member's dissociation was wrongful or rightful, normally the dissociated member has no right to force the LLC to dissolve. The remaining members can opt either to continue or to dissolve the business. Members can also stipulate in their operating agreement that certain events will cause dissolution, or they can agree that they have the power to dissolve the LLC by vote. As with partnerships, a court can order an LLC to be dissolved in certain circumstances, such as when the members have engaged in illegal or oppressive conduct, or when it is no longer feasible to carry on the business.

When an LLC is dissolved, any members who did not wrongfully dissociate may participate in the winding up process. To wind up the business, members must collect, liquidate, and distribute the LLC's assets. Members may preserve the assets for a reasonable time to optimize their return, and they continue to have the authority to perform reasonable acts in conjunction with winding up. In other words, the LLC will be bound by the reasonable acts of its members during the winding up process. Once all of the LLC's assets have been sold, the proceeds are distributed to pay off debts to creditors first (including debts owed to members who are creditors of the LLC). The members' capital contributions are returned next, and any remaining amounts are then distributed to members in equal shares or according to their operating agreement.

SECTION 4
LIMITED LIABILITY PARTNERSHIPS

The **limited liability partnership (LLP)** is a hybrid form of business designed mostly for professionals who normally do business as partners in a partnership. The first state to enact an LLP statute was Texas, in 1991. Other states quickly followed suit, and by 1997, almost all of the states had enacted LLP statutes.

The major advantage of the LLP is that it allows a partnership to continue as a pass-through entity for tax purposes but limits the personal liability of the partners. The LLP is especially attractive for two categories of businesses: professional service firms and family businesses. In fact, all of the "Big Four" accounting firms—the four largest international accountancy and professional services firms—are organized as LLPs, including Ernst & Young, LLP, and PricewaterhouseCoopers, LLP.

Formation of an LLP

LLPs must be formed and operated in compliance with state statutes, which may include provisions of the UPA. The appropriate form must be filed with a central state agency, usually the secretary of state's office, and the business's name must include either "Limited Liability Partnership" or "LLP" [UPA 1001, 1002]. In addition, an LLP must file an annual report with the state to remain qualified as an LLP in that state [UPA 1003].

In most states, it is relatively easy to convert a traditional partnership into an LLP because the firm's basic organizational structure remains the same. Additionally, all of the statutory and common law rules governing partnerships still apply (apart from those modified by the LLP statute). Normally, LLP statutes are simply amendments to a state's already existing partnership law.

Liability in an LLP

An LLP allows professionals, such as attorneys and accountants, to avoid personal liability for the malpractice of other partners. A partner in an LLP is still liable for her or his own wrongful acts, such as negligence, however. Also liable is the partner who supervised the individual who committed a wrongful act. (This generally is true for all types of partners and partnerships, not just LLPs.)

Although LLP statutes vary from state to state, generally each state statute limits the liability of partners in some way. For example, Delaware law protects each innocent partner from the "debts and obligations of the partnership arising from negligence, wrongful acts, or misconduct." The UPA more broadly exempts partners from personal liability for any partnership obligation, "whether arising in contract, tort, or otherwise" [UPA 306(c)]. Although the language of these statutes may seem to apply specifically to attorneys, almost any group of professionals can organize as an LLP.

LIABILITY FROM STATE TO STATE When an LLP formed in one state wants to do business in another state, it may be required to register in the second state—for example, by filing a statement of foreign qualification [UPA 1102]. Because state LLP statutes are not uniform, a question sometimes arises as to which law applies if the LLP statutes in the two states provide different liability protection. Most states apply the law of the state in which the LLP was formed, even when the firm does business in another state, which is also the rule under UPA 1101.

SHARING LIABILITY AMONG PARTNERS When more than one partner in an LLP is negligent, there is a question as to how liability should be shared. Some states provide for proportionate liability—that is, for separate determinations of the negligence of the partners. For example, accountants Don and Jane are partners in an LLP, with Don supervising Jane. Jane negligently fails to file a tax return for one of their clients, Centaur Tools. Centaur files a suit against Don and Jane. Under a proportionate liability statute,

Don will be liable for no more than his portion of the responsibility for the missed tax deadline. In a state that does not allow for proportionate liability, Don can be held liable for the entire loss.

SECTION 5
LIMITED PARTNERSHIPS

We now look at a business organizational form that limits the liability of *some* of its owners—the **limited partnership (LP)**. LPs originated in medieval Europe and have been in existence in the United States since the early 1800s. In many ways, LPs are like the traditional partnerships discussed in Chapter 17, but they differ from traditional partnerships in several ways. For this reason, they are sometimes referred to as *special partnerships*.

A limited partnership consists of at least one *general partner* and one or more *limited partners*. A **general partner** assumes management responsibility for the partnership and has full responsibility for the partnership and for all its debts. A **limited partner** contributes cash or other property and owns an interest in the firm but does not undertake any management responsibilities and is not personally liable for partnership debts beyond the amount of his or her investment. A limited partner can forfeit limited liability by taking part in the management of the business. A comparison of traditional (general) partnerships and limited partnerships appears in Exhibit 18–1 on the facing page.[6]

Until 1976, the law governing limited partnerships in all states except Louisiana was the Uniform Limited Partnership Act (ULPA). Since 1976, most states and the District of Columbia have adopted the revised version of the ULPA, known as the Revised Uniform Limited Partnership Act (RULPA). Because the RULPA is the dominant law governing limited partnerships in the United States, we refer to it in the following discussion. Note, however, that amendments to make the RULPA more flexible were proposed to the states in 2001, and fifteen states have adopted the 2001 version of this law.

Formation of an LP

In contrast to the informal, private, and voluntary agreement that usually suffices for a general

---

6. Under the UPA, a general partnership can be converted into a limited partnership and vice versa [UPA 902, 903]. The UPA also provides for the merger of a general partnership with one or more general or limited partnerships [UPA 905].

EXHIBIT 18-1 • A Comparison of Traditional and Limited Partnerships

CHARACTERISTIC	TRADITIONAL PARTNERSHIP (UPA)	LIMITED PARTNERSHIP (RULPA)
Creation	By agreement of two or more persons to carry on a business as co-owners for profit.	By agreement of two or more persons to carry on a business as co-owners for profit. Must include one or more general partners and one or more limited partners. Filing of a certificate with the secretary of state is required.
Sharing of Profits and Losses	By agreement; or, in the absence of agreement, profits are shared equally by the partners, and losses are shared in the same ratio as profits.	Profits are shared as required in the certificate agreement, and losses are shared likewise, up to the amount of the limited partners' capital contributions. In the absence of a provision in the certificate agreement, profits and losses are shared on the basis of percentages of capital contributions.
Liability	Unlimited personal liability of all partners.	Unlimited personal liability of all general partners; limited partners liable only to the extent of their capital contributions.
Capital Contribution	No minimum or mandatory amount; set by agreement.	Set by agreement.
Management	By agreement; or, in the absence of agreement, all partners have an equal voice.	Only the general partner (or the general partners). Limited partners have no voice or else are subject to liability as general partners (but only if a third party has reason to believe that the limited partner is a general partner). A limited partner may act as an agent or employee of the partnership and vote on amending the certificate or on the sale or dissolution of the partnership.
Duration	Terminated by agreement of the partners, but can continue to do business even when a partner dissociates from the partnership.	Terminated by agreement in the certificate or by retirement, death, or mental incompetence of a general partner in the absence of the right of the other general partners to continue the partnership. Death of a limited partner does not terminate the partnership, unless he or she is the only remaining limited partner.
Distribution of Assets on Liquidation– Order of Priorities	1. Payment of debts, including those owed to partner and nonpartner creditors. 2. Return of capital contributions and distribution of profit to partners.	1. Outside creditors and partner creditors. 2. Partners and former partners entitled to distributions of partnership assets. 3. Unless otherwise agreed, return of capital contributions and distribution of profit to partners.

partnership, the formation of an LP is a public and formal proceeding that must follow statutory requirements. A limited partnership must have at least one general partner and one limited partner, as mentioned previously. Additionally, the partners must sign a **certificate of limited partnership**, which requires information such as the name, mailing address, and capital contribution of each general and limited partner. (The information required is similar to that found in a corporation's *articles of incorporation*—see Chapter 19.) The certificate must

be filed with the designated state official—under the RULPA, the secretary of state. The certificate is usually open to public inspection.

Liabilities of Partners in an LP

General partners, unlike limited partners, are personally liable to the partnership's creditors. Thus, at least one general partner is necessary in a limited partnership so that someone has personal liability. This policy can be circumvented in states that allow a corporation to be the general partner in a partnership. Because the corporation has limited liability by virtue of corporation statutes, if a corporation is the general partner, no one in the limited partnership has personal liability.

The liability of a limited partner, as mentioned, is limited to the capital that she or he contributes or agrees to contribute to the partnership [RULPA 502]. Limited partners enjoy this limited liability only so long as they do not participate in management [RULPA 303]. A limited partner who participates in management will be just as liable as a general partner to any creditor who transacts business with the limited partnership and believes, based on the limited partner's conduct, that the limited partner is a general partner [RULPA 303]. It is not always clear how much review and advisement a limited partner can engage in before being exposed to liability, though.

Rights and Duties in an LP

With the exception of the right to participate in management, limited partners have essentially the same rights as general partners. Limited partners have a right of access to the partnership's books and to information regarding partnership business. On dissolution of the partnership, limited partners are entitled to a return of their contributions in accordance with the partnership certificate [RULPA 201(a)(10)]. They can also assign their interests subject to the certificate [RULPA 702, 704] and can sue an outside party on behalf of the firm if the general partners with authority to do so have refused to file suit [RULPA 1001].

General and limited partners also owe each other a fiduciary duty to exercise good faith in transactions related to the partnership. Can this duty be waived through a provision in the partnership agreement? That was the issue in the following case.

CASE 18.3
1515 North Wells, LP v. 1513 North Wells, LLC

Appellate Court of Illinois, First District, 392 Ill.App.3d 863, 913 N.E.2d 1 (2009).

BACKGROUND AND FACTS • Thomas Bracken (owner of 1513 North Wells, LLC), Mark Sutherland, and Alex Pearsall were limited partners in 1515 North Wells, LP. Sutherland and Pearsall's company, SP Development Corporation, was 1515's general partner. The partnership was formed to build a condominium with residential and commercial space. SP chose another Sutherland and Pearsall company, Sutherland and Pearsall Development, to be the general contractor for the 1515 project. Meanwhile, Bracken borrowed $250,000 from 1515. When he did not repay the loan, 1515 filed a suit in an Illinois state court to collect. In response, Bracken filed a claim that included SP Development Corporation, alleging breach of fiduciary duty. The court ordered Bracken to repay the loan and SP to pay Bracken $900,000. SP appealed, arguing that a provision in 1515's partnership agreement, which allowed all partners to engage in "whatever activities they choose," effectively "relaxed" SP's fiduciary duty.

IN THE LANGUAGE OF THE COURT
Justice *CAHILL* delivered the opinion of the court:
* * * *
* * * Paragraph 1.7 of the limited partnership agreement * * * provided:

The General Partner and each Limited Partner may, notwithstanding this Agreement, engage in whatever activities they choose, whether the same are competitive with the Partnership or otherwise, without having or incurring any obligation to offer any interest in such activities to the Partnership or any Partner.

* * * *

The general partner argues that paragraph 1.7 did in fact relax the parties' fiduciary duties to each other.
* * * *

A fiduciary relationship exists between partners and each is bound to exercise the utmost good faith in all dealings and transactions related to the partnership. To state a claim for breach of fiduciary duty, a plaintiff must establish (1) a fiduciary duty on the part of the defendant, (2) the defendant's breach of that duty, and (3) damages that were proximately caused by the defendant's breach.

CASE 18.3 CONTINUED ➡ *Under Section 103(b)(3) of the Uniform Partnership Act, a partnership agreement may not "eliminate or reduce a partner's fiduciary duties."* Language in an agreement that allows the partners discretion in certain areas does not metamorphose [transform] the document into an unrestricted license to engage in self-dealing at the expense of those to whom the managing partner owes such a duty. *There is no authority for the proposition that there can be* a priori *waiver of fiduciary duties in a partnership.* Nor is the practice of imposing purported advance waivers of fiduciary duties in limited partnership enterprises to be given judicial recognition. [Emphasis added.]

Here, there was ample evidence to support the [trial] court's finding of a breach of fiduciary duty, including the "cost plus fee" contract that the general partner awarded to the general contractor and the profits from condominium upgrades that went to the general contractor, not to the limited partnership. Paragraph 1.7 of the limited partnership agreement did not immunize the partners against liability for breach of fiduciary duty.

DECISION AND REMEDY • *The state intermediate appellate court affirmed the lower court's judgment. A partnership agreement cannot "contract away" the fiduciary duty that a general partner owes to limited partners.*

WHAT IF THE FACTS WERE DIFFERENT? • *Suppose that instead of choosing Sutherland and Pearsall Development to be the general contractor, SP had selected a party with no connection to any of 1515's partners. Is it likely that the result in this case would have been different? Why or why not?*

THE ETHICAL DIMENSION • *Did any of the parties involved in this case commit an ethical violation? Discuss.*

Dissociation and Dissolution

A general partner has the power to voluntarily dissociate, or withdraw, from a limited partnership unless the partnership agreement specifies otherwise. A limited partner theoretically can withdraw from the partnership by giving six months' notice unless the partnership agreement specifies a term, as most do. Also, some states have passed laws prohibiting the withdrawal of limited partners.

In a limited partnership, a general partner's voluntary dissociation from the firm normally will lead to dissolution *unless* all partners agree to continue the business. Similarly, the bankruptcy, retirement, death, or mental incompetence of a general partner will cause the dissociation of that partner and the dissolution of the limited partnership unless the other members agree to continue the firm [RULPA 801]. Bankruptcy of a limited partner, however, does not dissolve the partnership unless it causes the bankruptcy of the firm. Death or an assignment of the interest of a limited partner does not dissolve a limited partnership [RULPA 702, 704, 705]. A limited partnership can be dissolved by court decree [RULPA 802].

On dissolution, creditors' claims, including those of partners who are creditors, take first priority. After that, partners and former partners receive unpaid distributions of partnership assets and, except as otherwise agreed, amounts representing returns of their contributions and amounts proportionate to their shares of the distributions [RULPA 804].

CASE IN POINT Actor Kevin Costner was a limited partner in Midnight Star Enterprises, LP, which consisted of a casino, bar, and restaurant in Deadwood, South Dakota. Another firm owned by Costner was the general partner in Midnight Star, and Carla and Francis Caneva were limited partners. The Canevas owned a small part of Midnight Star and were its managers until the relationship among the partners soured. The general partner filed a petition to dissolve the partnership and hired an accountant, who determined the firm's fair market value to be $3.1 million. The Canevas solicited a competitor's offer to buy the business for $6.2 million and convinced the trial court to rule that this was the appropriate amount. Costner and his firm (the general partner) appealed. They argued that a limited partner should not be able to force the sale of the firm when the other partners wished to continue the business. The South Dakota Supreme Court agreed. The LP did not have to be sold on the open market on dissolution. The court also concluded that the correct value of the business was the accountant's figure. Thus, Costner and the general partner could buy out the Canevas' interest in Midnight Star and continue operating the business.[7]

---

7. *In re Dissolution of Midnight Star Enterprises, LP,* 2006 SD 98, 724 N.W.2d 334 (2006).

Limited Liability Limited Partnerships

A **limited liability limited partnership (LLLP)** is a type of limited partnership. An LLLP differs from a limited partnership in that a general partner in an LLLP has the same liability as a limited partner in a limited partnership. In other words, the liability of all partners is limited to the amount of their investments in the firm.

A few states provide expressly for LLLPs.[8] In states that do not provide for LLLPs but do allow for limited partnerships and limited liability partnerships, a limited partnership should probably still be able to register with the state as an LLLP.

---

8. See, for example, Colorado Revised Statutes Annotated Section 7-62-109. Other states that provide expressly for limited liability limited partnerships include Delaware, Florida, Georgia, Kentucky, Maryland, Nevada, Texas, and Virginia.

REVIEWING

Limited Liability Companies and Limited Partnerships

The city of Papagos, Arizona, had a deteriorating bridge in need of repair on a prominent public roadway. The city posted notices seeking proposals for an artistic bridge design and reconstruction. Davidson Masonry, LLC, which was owned and managed by Carl Davidson and his wife, Marilyn Rowe, decided to submit a bid to create a decorative concrete structure that incorporated artistic metalwork. They contacted Shana Lafayette, a local sculptor who specialized in large-scale metal creations, to help them design the bridge. The city selected their bridge design and awarded them the contract for a commission of $184,000. Davidson Masonry and Lafayette then entered into an agreement to work together on the bridge project. Davidson Masonry agreed to install and pay for concrete and structural work, and Lafayette agreed to install the metalwork at her expense. They agreed that overall profits would be split, with 25 percent going to Lafayette and 75 percent going to Davidson Masonry. Lafayette designed numerous metal sculptures of salmon that were incorporated into colorful decorative concrete forms designed by Rowe, while Davidson performed the structural engineering. The group worked together successfully until the completion of the project. Using the information presented in the chapter, answer the following questions.

1. Would Davidson Masonry automatically be taxed as a partnership or a corporation?
2. Is Davidson Masonry member managed or manager managed?
3. Suppose that during construction, Lafayette had entered into an agreement to rent space in a warehouse that was close to the bridge so that she could work on her sculptures near the site where they would eventually be installed. She entered into the contract without the knowledge or consent of Davidson Masonry. In this situation, would a court be likely to hold that Davidson Masonry was bound by the contract that Lafayette entered? Why or why not?
4. Now suppose that Rowe has an argument with her husband and wants to withdraw from being a member of Davidson Masonry. What is the term for such a withdrawal, and what effect would it have on the LLC?

⚙ **DEBATE THIS:** *Because LLCs are essentially just partnerships with limited liability for members, all partnership laws should apply.*

TERMS AND CONCEPTS

articles of organization 403
certificate of limited
  partnership 411

general partner 410
limited liability
  company (LLC) 402
limited liability limited
  partnership (LLLP) 414

limited liability
  partnership (LLP) 409
limited partner 410
limited partnership (LP) 410

member 403
operating agreement 407

QUESTIONS AND CASE PROBLEMS

18–1. Limited Liability Companies John, Lesa, and Tabir form a limited liability company. John contributes 60 percent of the capital, and Lesa and Tabir each contribute 20 percent. Nothing is decided about how profits will be divided. John assumes that he will be entitled to 60 percent of the profits, in accordance with his contribution. Lesa and Tabir, however, assume that the profits will be divided equally. A dispute over the profits arises, and ultimately a court has to decide the issue. What law will the court apply? In most states, what will result? How could this dispute have been avoided in the first place? Discuss fully.

18–2. QUESTION WITH SAMPLE ANSWER: Partnership Dissolution.

Dorinda, Luis, and Elizabeth form a limited partnership. Dorinda is a general partner, and Luis and Elizabeth are limited partners. Consider the separate events below, and discuss fully whether each event constitutes a dissolution of the limited partnership.

(a) Luis assigns his partnership interest to Ashley.
(b) Elizabeth is petitioned into involuntary bankruptcy.
(c) Dorinda dies.

- **For a sample answer to Question 18–2, go to Appendix F at the end of this text.**

18–3. Diversity Jurisdiction and Limited Liability Companies Joe, a resident of New Jersey, wants to open a restaurant. He asks Kay, his friend, an experienced attorney and a New Yorker, for her business and legal advice in exchange for a 20 percent ownership interest in the restaurant. Kay helps Joe negotiate a lease for the restaurant premises and advises Joe to organize the business as a limited liability company (LLC). Joe forms Café Olé, LLC, and with Kay's help, obtains financing. Then, the night before the restaurant opens, Joe tells Kay that he is "cutting her out of the deal." The restaurant proves to be a success. Kay wants to file a suit in a federal district court against Joe and the LLC. Can a federal court exercise jurisdiction over the parties based on diversity of citizenship? Explain.

18–4. Fiduciary Duties Westbury Properties, Inc., and others (collectively, the Westbury group) owned, managed, and developed real property. Jerry Stoker and the Stoker Group, Inc. (the Stokers), also developed real property. The Westbury group entered into agreements with the Stokers concerning a large tract of property in Houston County, Georgia. The parties formed limited liability companies (LLCs), including Bellemeade, LLC (the LLC group), to develop various parcels of the tract for residential purposes. The operating agreements provided that "no Member shall be accountable to the [LLC] or to any other Member with respect to [any other] business or activity even if the business or activity competes with the [LLC's] business." The Westbury group entered into agreements with other parties to develop additional parcels

within the tract in competition with the LLC group. The Stokers filed a suit in a Georgia state court against the Westbury group, alleging, among other things, breach of fiduciary duty. What duties do the members of an LLC owe to each other? Under what principle might the terms of an operating agreement alter these duties? In whose favor should the court rule? Discuss. [*Stoker v. Bellemeade, LLC,* 272 Ga.App. 817, 615 S.E.2d 1 (2005)]

18–5. Limited Liability Companies A "Certificate of Formation" (CF) for Grupo Dos Chiles, LLC, was filed with the Delaware secretary of state in February 2000. The CF named Jamie Rivera as the "initial member." The next month, Jamie's mother, Yolanda Martinez, and Alfred Shriver, who had a personal relationship with Martinez at the time, signed an "LLC Agreement" for Grupo, naming themselves "managing partners." Grupo's business was the operation of Dancing Peppers Cantina, a restaurant in Alexandria, Virginia. Identifying themselves as Grupo's owners, Shriver and Martinez borrowed funds from Advanceme, Inc., a restaurant lender. In June 2003, Grupo lost its LLC status in Delaware for failing to pay state taxes, and by the end of July, Martinez and Shriver had ended their relationship. Shriver filed a suit in a Virginia state court against Martinez to wind up Grupo's affairs. Meanwhile, without consulting Shriver, Martinez paid Grupo's back taxes. Shriver filed a suit in a Delaware state court against Martinez, asking the court to dissolve the firm. What effect did the LLC agreement have on the CF? Did Martinez's unilateral act reestablish Grupo's LLC status? Should the Delaware court grant Shriver's request? Why or why not? [*In re Grupo Dos Chiles, LLC,* __ A.2d __ (Del.Ch. 2006)]

18–6. Limited Liability Companies A limited liability company (LLC) sold a Manhattan apartment building that it owned. The owners of 25 percent of the membership interests in the LLC filed a lawsuit on behalf of the LLC—called a derivative suit—claiming that those in majority control of the LLC had sold the building for less than its market value and had personally profited from the deal. The trial court dismissed the suit, holding that the plaintiffs individually could not bring a derivative suit "to redress wrongs suffered by the corporation" because such actions were permitted only for corporations and could not be brought for an LLC. An intermediate appellate court reversed, holding that derivative suits on behalf of LLCs are permitted. That decision was appealed. A key problem for the court was that the state law governing LLCs did not address the issue. How should such matters logically be resolved? Are the minority owners in an LLC at the mercy of the decisions of the majority owners? Explain. [*Tzolis v. Wolff,* 10 N.Y.3d 100, 884 N.E.2d 1005 (2008)]

18–7. CASE PROBLEM WITH SAMPLE ANSWER: Limited Partnership.

James Carpenter contracted with Austin Estates, LP, to buy property in Texas. Carpenter asked Sandra McBeth to invest in the deal. He admitted

that a dispute had arisen with the city of Austin over water for the property, but he assured her that it would not be a significant obstacle. McBeth agreed to invest $800,000 to hold open the option to buy the property. She became a limited partner in StoneLake Ranch, LP. Carpenter acted as the firm's general partner. Despite his assurances to McBeth, the purchase was delayed due to the water dispute. Unable to complete the purchase in a timely manner, Carpenter paid the $800,000 to Austin Estates without notifying McBeth. Later, Carpenter and others—excluding McBeth—bought the property and sold it at a profit. McBeth filed a suit in a Texas state court against Carpenter. What is the nature of the fiduciary duty that a general partner owes a limited partner? Did Carpenter breach that duty in this case? Explain. [McBeth v. Carpenter, 565 F.3d 171 (5th Cir. 2009)]

• To view a sample answer for Problem 18–7, go to this book's Web site at www.cengage.com/blaw/cross, select "Chapter 18," and click on "Case Problem with Sample Answer."

18–8. LLC Dissolution Walter Van Houten and John King formed 1545 Ocean Avenue, LLC, with each managing 50 percent of the business. Its purpose was to renovate an existing building and construct a new commercial building. Van Houten and King quarreled over many aspects of the work on the properties. King claimed that Van Houten paid the contractors too much for the work performed. As the projects neared completion, King demanded that the LLC be dissolved and that Van Houten agree to a buyout. Because the parties could not agree on a buyout, King sued for dissolution. The trial court enjoined (prevented) further work on the projects until the dispute was settled. As the ground for dissolution, King cited the fights over management decisions. There was no claim of fraud or frustration of purpose. The trial court ordered that the LLC be dissolved, and Van Houten appealed. Should either of the owners be forced to dissolve the LLC before the completion of its purpose—that is, before the building projects are finished? Explain. [*In re 1545 Ocean Avenue, LLC*, 893 N.Y.S.2d 590 (N.Y.A.D. 2 Dept. 2010)]

18–9. A QUESTION OF ETHICS: Limited Liability Companies.

 Blushing Brides, LLC, a publisher of wedding planning magazines in Columbus, Ohio, opened an account with Gray Printing Co. in July 2000.

On behalf of Blushing Brides, Louis Zacks, the firm's member-manager, signed a credit agreement that identified the firm as the "purchaser" and required payment within thirty days. Despite the agreement, Blushing Brides typically took up to six months to pay the full amount for its orders. Gray printed and shipped 10,000 copies of a fall/winter 2001 issue for Blushing Brides but had not been paid when the firm ordered 15,000 copies of a spring/summer 2002 issue. Gray refused to print the new order without an assurance of payment. On May 22, Zacks signed a promissory note payable to Gray within thirty days for $14,778, plus interest at 6 percent per year. Gray printed the new order but by October had been paid only $7,500. Gray filed a suit in an Ohio state court against Blushing Brides and Zacks to collect the balance. [Gray Printing Co. v. Blushing Brides, LLC, __ N.E.2d __ (Ohio App. 10 Dist. 2006)]

(a) Under what circumstances is a member of an LLC liable for the firm's debts? In this case, is Zacks personally liable under the credit agreement for the unpaid amount on Blushing Brides' account? Did Zacks's promissory note affect the parties' liability on the account? Explain.

(b) Should a member of an LLC assume an ethical responsibility to meet the obligations of the firm? Discuss.

(c) Gray shipped only 10,000 copies of the spring/summer 2002 issue of *Blushing Brides'* magazine, waiting for the publisher to identify a destination for the other 5,000 copies. The magazine had a retail price of $4.50 per copy. Did Gray have a legal or ethical duty to "mitigate the damages" by attempting to sell or otherwise distribute these copies itself? Why or why not?

18–10. SPECIAL CASE ANALYSIS: Limited Liability Companies.
Go to Extended Case 18.2, *ORX Resources, Inc. v. MBW Exploration, LLC*, 32 So.3d 931 (2010) on pages 405 and 406. Read the excerpt and answer the following questions.

(a) **Issue:** What was the main issue in this case?

(b) **Rule of Law:** What rule of law did the court apply?

(c) **Applying the Rule of Law:** Describe how the court applied the rule of law to the facts of this case.

(d) **Conclusion:** What was the court's conclusion?

LEGAL RESEARCH EXERCISES ON THE WEB

Go to this text's Web site at **www.cengage.com/blaw/cross**, select "Chapter 18," and click on "Practical Internet Exercises." There you will find the following Internet research exercises that you can perform to learn more about the topics covered in this chapter.

Practical Internet Exercise 18–1: **Legal Perspective**
Limited Liability Companies

Practical Internet Exercise 18–2: **Management Perspective**
Limited Partnerships and Limited Liability Partnerships

CHAPTER 19
✴
Corporations

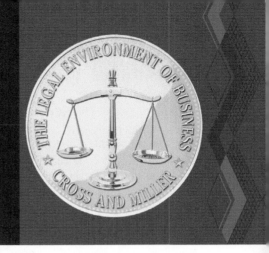

The corporation is a creature of statute. It is an artificial being, existing only in law and neither tangible nor visible. Its existence generally depends on state law, although some corporations, especially public organizations, are created under federal law. Each state has its own body of corporate law, and these laws are not entirely uniform.

The Model Business Corporation Act (MBCA) is a codification of modern corporation law that has been influential in shaping state corporation statutes. Today, the majority of state statutes are guided by the most recent version of the MBCA, often referred to as the Revised Model Business Corporation Act (RMBCA). (Excerpts from the RMBCA are included on the Web site that accompanies this text.) Keep in mind, however, that corporation laws vary considerably, even among states that have used the MBCA or the RMBCA as a basis for their statutes, and several states do not follow either act. Consequently, individual state corporation laws should be relied on to determine corporate law, rather than the MBCA or RMBCA.

In this chapter, we examine the nature of the corporate form of business enterprise and the various classifications of corporations, followed by a discussion of the formation of today's corporation and its powers. We then consider the roles of corporate directors, officers, and shareholders.

SECTION 1
THE NATURE AND CLASSIFICATION OF CORPORATIONS

A corporation is a legal entity created and recognized by state law. This business entity can have one or more owners (called shareholders), and it operates under a name distinct from the names of its owners. The owners may be individuals, or *natural persons* (as opposed to the artificial *legal person* of the corporation), or other businesses. Although the corporation substitutes itself for its shareholders when conducting corporate business and incurring liability, its authority to act and the liability for its actions are separate and apart from the individuals who own it.

A corporation is recognized as a "person," and it enjoys many of the same rights and privileges under state and federal law that U.S. citizens enjoy. For example, corporations possess the same right of access to the courts as citizens and can sue or be sued. The constitutional guarantees of due process, free speech, and freedom from unreasonable searches and seizures also apply to corporations.

Corporate Personnel

In a corporation, the responsibility for the overall management of the firm is entrusted to a *board of directors*, whose members are elected by the shareholders. The board of directors makes the policy decisions and hires *corporate officers* and other employees to run the daily business operations of the corporation.

When an individual purchases a share of stock in a corporation, that person becomes a shareholder and an owner of the corporation. Unlike the partners in a partnership, the body of shareholders can change constantly without affecting the continued existence of the corporation. A shareholder can sue the corporation, and the corporation can sue a shareholder. Additionally, under certain circumstances, a shareholder can sue on behalf of a corporation, as will be discussed later in this chapter.

The Limited Liability of Shareholders

One of the key advantages of the corporate form is the limited liability of its owners. Normally, corporate shareholders are not personally liable for the obligations of the corporation beyond the extent of their investments. In certain limited situations, however, a court can *pierce the corporate veil* (see page 427) and impose liability on shareholders for the corporation's obligations. Additionally, creditors often will not extend credit to small companies unless the shareholders assume personal liability, as guarantors, for corporate obligations.

Corporate Earnings and Taxation

When a corporation earns profits, it can either distribute them to its shareholders in the form of *dividends* (see page 440) or retain the profits. These **retained earnings,** if invested properly, will yield higher corporate profits in the future and thus cause the price of the company's stock to rise. Individual shareholders can then reap the benefits of these retained earnings in the capital gains that they receive when they sell their stock.

CORPORATE TAXATION Whether a corporation retains its profits or passes them on to the shareholders as dividends, those profits are subject to income tax by various levels of government. Failure to pay taxes can lead to severe consequences. The state can suspend the entity's corporate status until the taxes are paid or even dissolve the corporation for failing to pay taxes.

Another important aspect of corporate taxation is that corporate profits can be subject to double taxation. The company pays tax on its profits, and then if the profits are passed on to the shareholders as dividends, the shareholders must also pay income tax on them (unless the dividends represent distributions of capital). The corporation normally does not receive a tax deduction for dividends it distributes. This double-taxation feature is one of the major disadvantages of the corporate form.

A taxation issue of increasing importance to corporations is whether they are required to collect state sales taxes on goods or services sold to consumers via the Internet. See this chapter's *Shifting Legal Priorities for Business* feature on the facing page for a discussion of this issue.

HOLDING COMPANIES Some U.S. corporations use holding companies to reduce or defer their U.S. income taxes. At its simplest, a **holding company** (sometimes referred to as a *parent company*) is a company whose business activity consists of holding shares in another company. Typically, the holding company is established in a low-tax or no-tax offshore jurisdiction, such as the Cayman Islands, Dubai, Hong Kong, Luxembourg, Monaco, or Panama.

Sometimes, a U.S. corporation sets up a holding company in a low-tax offshore environment and then transfers its cash, bonds, stocks, and other investments to the holding company. Generally, any profits received by the holding company on these investments are taxed at the rate of the offshore jurisdiction where the company is registered (not at the rates applicable to the corporation or its shareholders in their country of residence). Thus, deposits of cash, for example, may earn interest that is taxed at only a minimal rate. Once the profits are brought "onshore," though, they are taxed at the federal corporate income tax rate, and any payments received by the shareholders are also taxable at the full U.S. rates.

In the federal government's 2011 budget, the Obama administration proposed measures that would restrict multinational companies from deferring the payment of taxes on profits earned overseas.

Torts and Criminal Acts

A corporation is liable for the torts committed by its agents or officers within the course and scope of their employment. This principle applies to a corporation exactly as it applies to agency relationships (see Chapter 20). It follows the doctrine of *respondeat superior.*

Under modern criminal law, a corporation may also be held liable for the criminal acts of its agents and employees, provided the punishment is one that can be applied to the corporation. Although corporations cannot be imprisoned, they can be fined. (Of course, corporate directors and officers can be imprisoned, and many have been in recent years.) In addition, under sentencing guidelines for crimes committed by corporate employees (white-collar crimes), corporate lawbreakers can face fines amounting to hundreds of millions of dollars.[1]

CASE IN POINT Brian Gauthier worked as a dump truck driver for Angelo Todesca Corporation. Although the truck was missing its back-up alarm that automatically sounded when the truck was put

---

1. Note that the Sarbanes-Oxley Act of 2002 (see Chapter 4) stiffened the penalties for certain types of corporate crime and ordered the U.S. Sentencing Commission to revise the sentencing guidelines accordingly.

Governments at the state and federal levels have long debated whether states should be able to collect sales taxes on online sales to their residents. State governments claim that their inability to tax online sales has caused them to lose billions of dollars in sales tax revenue. The issue has taken on new urgency as the states search desperately for revenue in the wake of the economic recession that began in late 2007.

Supreme Court Precedent Requires Physical Presence

In 1992, the United States Supreme Court ruled that no individual state can compel an out-of-state business that lacks a substantial physical presence (such as a warehouse, office, or retail store) within that state to collect and remit state taxes.[a] The Court recognized that Congress has the power to pass legislation requiring out-of-state corporations to collect and remit state sales taxes, but Congress so far has chosen not to tax Internet transactions.

In fact, Congress temporarily prohibited the states from taxing Internet sales, and that ban was extended until 2014.[b] Thus, only online retailers that also have a physical presence within a state must collect state taxes on any Web sales made to residents of that state. (Otherwise, state residents are required to self-report their purchases and pay so-called use taxes to the state, which rarely occurs.)

New York Changed Its Definition of Physical Presence

In an effort to collect taxes on Internet sales made by out-of-state corporations, New York changed its tax laws in 2008 to redefine *physical presence.* Under the new law, if an online retailer pays any party within the state to solicit business for its products, that retailer has a physical presence in the state and must collect state taxes.[c] For example, Amazon.com, the largest U.S. online retailer, pays thousands of associates in New York to post ads that link to Amazon's Web site. Consequently, the law requires Amazon to collect tax on any sales to New York residents.

Both Amazon and Overstock.com, a Utah corporation, filed lawsuits in 2009 claiming that the new law was unconstitutional. A New York court dismissed Amazon's case, finding that the law provided a sufficient basis for requiring collection of New York taxes. As long as the seller has a substantial connection with the state, the taxes need not derive from in-state activity. The court also observed that "out-of-state sellers can shield themselves from a tax-collection obligation by altogether prohibiting in-state solicitation activities . . . on their behalf."[d] As a result, Amazon now collects and pays state sales taxes on shipments to New York.

Overstock also lost its lawsuit but has filed an appeal.[e] In the meantime, to avoid having to collect the sales tax, Overstock canceled agreements with its New York affiliates that were being paid to direct traffic to its Web site. In 2009 and 2010, Amazon ended its arrangements with affiliates in Colorado, North Carolina, and Rhode Island for the same reason. Fifteen other states, including California, Illinois, Iowa, Maryland, New Mexico, Vermont, and Virginia, are now considering passing laws similar to New York's.

MANAGERIAL IMPLICATIONS

Most states and municipal governments continue to struggle with budgets, so they will continue to seek additional sources of revenues. These governments will pass more laws to try to capture taxes from commercial activities on the Internet. Therefore, managers whose companies sell goods or services on the Internet must keep track of what lawmakers are planning in this contentious area.

a. See *Quill Corp. v. North Dakota,* 504 U.S. 298, 112 S.Ct. 1904, 119 L.Ed.2d 91 (1992).

b. Internet Tax Freedom Act, Pub. L. No. 105-277; 47 U.S.C. Section 151 note (1998); extended to 2014 by Pub. L. No. 110-108.

c. New York Tax Law Section 1101(b)(8)(vi).

d. *Amazon.com, LLC v. New York State Department of Taxation and Finance,* 23 Misc.3d 418, 877 N.Y.S.2d 842 (2009).

e. *Overstock.com, Inc. v. New York State Department of Taxation and Finance,* 2009 WL 1259061 (2009).

---

into reverse, Angelo allowed Gauthier to continue driving the truck. At a worksite, when Gauthier backed up to dump the truck's load, he struck and killed a police officer who was facing away from the truck. The state charged Angelo and Gauthier with the crime of vehicular homicide. Angelo argued that a corporation could not be guilty of vehicular homicide because it cannot operate a vehicle. The court ruled that if an employee commits a crime "while engaged in corporate business that the employee has been authorized to conduct," the corporation can be held liable for the crime. Hence, the court held that Angelo was liable for Gauthier's negligent operation of its truck, which resulted in a person's death.[2]

---

2. *Commonwealth v. Angelo Todesca Corp.,* 446 Mass. 128, 842 N.E.2d 930 (2006).

Classification of Corporations

Corporations can be classified in several ways. The classification of a corporation normally depends on its location, purpose, and ownership characteristics, as described in the following subsections.

DOMESTIC, FOREIGN, AND ALIEN CORPORATIONS A corporation is referred to as a **domestic corporation** by its home state (the state in which it incorporates). A corporation formed in one state but doing business in another is referred to in the second state as a **foreign corporation.** A corporation formed in another country (say, Mexico) but doing business in the United States is referred to in the United States as an **alien corporation.**

A corporation does not have an automatic right to do business in a state other than its state of incorporation. In some instances, it must obtain a *certificate of authority* in any state in which it plans to do business. Once the certificate has been issued, the corporation generally can exercise in that state all of the powers conferred on it by its home state. If a foreign corporation does business in a state without obtaining a certificate of authority, the state can impose substantial fines and sanctions on the corporation, and sometimes even on its officers, directors, or agents.

Note that most state statutes specify certain activities that are not considered "doing business" within the state, such as participating in lawsuits and holding meetings. Normally, a foreign corporation can conduct isolated business transactions (but not repeated transactions) within a state without obtaining a certificate of authority to do business there.

PUBLIC AND PRIVATE CORPORATIONS A **public corporation** is a corporation formed by the government to meet some political or governmental purpose. Cities and towns that incorporate are common examples. In addition, many federal government organizations, such as the U.S. Postal Service, the Tennessee Valley Authority, and AMTRAK, are public corporations. Note that a public corporation is not the same as a *publicly held* corporation. A **publicly held corporation** (often called a *public company*) is any corporation whose shares are publicly traded in a securities market, such as the New York Stock Exchange or NASDAQ (an electronic stock exchange founded by the National Association of Securities Dealers).

In contrast to public corporations, private corporations (such as publicly held companies) are created either wholly or in part for private benefit (for profit). Most corporations are private. Although they may serve a public purpose, as a public electric or gas utility does, they are owned by private persons rather than by the government.

NONPROFIT CORPORATIONS Corporations formed for purposes other than making a profit are called *nonprofit* or *not-for-profit* corporations. Private hospitals, educational institutions, charities, and religious organizations, for example, are frequently organized as nonprofit corporations. The nonprofit corporation is a convenient form of organization that allows various groups to own property and to form contracts without exposing the individual members to personal liability.

CLOSELY HELD CORPORATIONS Most corporate enterprises in the United States fall into the category of closely held corporations (sometimes called *close corporations*). A **closely held corporation** is one whose shares are not publicly traded. In fact, there is no trading market for the shares. The shares are often held by family members or by a relatively small group of persons. Usually, the members of the small group constituting a closely held corporation are personally known to each other. Closely held corporations are also sometimes referred to as *privately held* corporations.

In practice, a closely held corporation is often operated like a partnership. Some states have enacted special statutory provisions that apply to these corporations and allow them to depart significantly from certain formalities required by traditional corporation law.[3]

Additionally, a provision in the RMBCA gives a closely held corporation considerable flexibility in determining its rules of operation [RMBCA 7.32]. If all of a corporation's shareholders agree in writing, the corporation can operate without directors, bylaws, annual or special shareholders' or directors' meetings, stock certificates, or formal records of shareholders' or directors' decisions.[4]

Management of Closely Held Corporations. A closely held corporation has a single shareholder or a tightly knit group of shareholders, who usually hold the positions of directors and officers. Management of a closely held corporation resembles that of a sole proprietorship or a partnership. As a corporation, however, the firm must meet all specific legal requirements set forth in state statutes.

---

3. For example, in some states (such as Maryland), a closely held corporation need not have a board of directors.
4. Shareholders cannot agree, however, to eliminate certain rights of shareholders, such as the right to inspect corporate books and records or the right to bring *derivative actions* (lawsuits on behalf of the corporation—see page 441).

To prevent a majority shareholder from dominating a closely held corporation, the company may require that more than a simple majority of the directors approve any action taken by the board. Typically, this would apply only to extraordinary actions, such as changing the amount of dividends or dismissing an employee-shareholder, and not to ordinary business decisions.

Transfer of Shares in Closely Held Corporations.

By definition, a closely held corporation has a small number of shareholders. Thus, the transfer of one shareholder's shares to someone else can cause serious management problems. The other shareholders may find themselves required to share control with someone they do not know or like. To avoid this situation, the corporation could restrict the transferability of shares to outside persons. Shareholders could be required to offer their shares to the closely held corporation or other shareholders before selling them to an outside purchaser.

Control of a closely held corporation can also be stabilized through the use of a *shareholder agreement.* A shareholder agreement can provide that when one of the original shareholders dies, her or his shares of stock in the corporation will be divided in such a way that the proportionate holdings of the survivors, and thus their proportionate control, will be maintained. Agreements between shareholders can also restrict the transfer of a closely held corporation's stock in other ways.

CASE IN POINT The Kearns-Tribune Corporation, a closely held corporation owned by the Kearns-McCarthey family, owned *The Salt Lake Tribune.* In 1997, the family sold the corporation to cable company Tele-Communications, Inc. (TCI). As part of the agreement, the family received an option to repurchase the assets of *The Tribune* at a later date. After TCI merged with AT&T Corporation, giving AT&T control over Kearns-Tribune, the family attempted to exercise the option to repurchase *The Tribune.* The court denied the request, however, because Kearns-Tribune had previously signed another agreement with Deseret News to form the Newspaper Agency Corporation (NAC), with Kearns-Tribune and Deseret News each owning 50 percent of NAC. Under that contract, the shareholders agreed to prohibit the transfer of ownership of NAC stock. Therefore, the stock transfer restriction was an obstacle to the family's claim for specific performance of the option.[5]

---

5. *Salt Lake Tribune Publishing Co. v. AT&T Corp.,* 320 F.3d 1081 (10th Cir. 2003).

Misappropriation of Funds in Closely Held Corporations.

Sometimes, a majority shareholder in a closely held corporation takes advantage of his or her position and misappropriates company funds. In such situations, the normal remedy for the injured minority shareholders is to have their shares appraised and to be paid the fair market value for them.

S CORPORATIONS A closely held corporation that meets the qualifying requirements specified in Subchapter S of the Internal Revenue Code can choose to operate as an **S corporation.** If a corporation has S corporation status, it can avoid the imposition of income taxes at the corporate level while retaining many of the advantages of a corporation, particularly limited liability.

Qualification Requirements.

Among the numerous requirements for S corporation status, the following are the most important:

1. The corporation must be a domestic corporation.
2. The corporation must not be a member of an affiliated group of corporations.
3. The shareholders of the corporation must be individuals, estates, or certain trusts and tax-exempt organizations.
4. The corporation must have no more than one hundred shareholders.
5. The corporation must have only one class of stock, although all shareholders do not need to have the same voting rights.
6. No shareholder of the corporation may be a nonresident alien.

Benefits.

For tax purposes, an S corporation is treated differently than a regular corporation. An S corporation is taxed like a partnership, so the corporate income passes through to the shareholders, who pay personal income tax on it. This treatment enables the S corporation to avoid double taxation (see page 418).

In addition, the shareholders' tax brackets may be lower than the tax bracket that the corporation would have been in if the tax had been imposed at the corporate level. The resulting tax saving is particularly attractive when the corporation wants to accumulate earnings for some future business purpose. If the corporation has losses, the S election allows the shareholders to use the losses to offset other income. Nevertheless, because the limited liability company and the limited liability partnership (see Chapter 18) offer similar tax advantages and greater flexibility, the S corporation has lost some of its appeal.

PROFESSIONAL CORPORATIONS Professionals such as physicians, lawyers, dentists, and accountants can incorporate. Professional corporations are typically identified by the letters *P.C.* (professional corporation), *S.C.* (service corporation), or *P.A.* (professional association).

In general, the laws governing the formation and operation of professional corporations are similar to those governing ordinary business corporations. There are some differences in terms of liability, however. For liability purposes, some courts treat a professional corporation somewhat like a partnership and hold each professional liable for any malpractice committed within the scope of the business by the others in the firm. With the exception of malpractice or a breach of duty to clients or patients, a shareholder in a professional corporation generally cannot be held liable for the torts committed by other professionals at the firm.

SECTION 2
CORPORATE FORMATION

Up to this point, we have discussed some of the general characteristics of corporations. We now examine the process by which corporations come into existence. Incorporating a business is much simpler today than it was twenty years ago. In fact, many states allow businesses to incorporate online.

One of the more common reasons for creating a corporation is the need for additional capital to finance expansion. Many Fortune 500 companies started as sole proprietorships or partnerships and then converted to corporate entities. Incorporation may be the best choice for an expanding business organization because a corporation can obtain more capital by issuing shares of stock.

Promotional Activities

In the past, preliminary steps were taken to organize and promote the business prior to incorporating. Contracts were made with investors and others on behalf of the future corporation. Today, however, due to the relative ease of forming a corporation in most states, persons incorporating their business rarely, if ever, engage in preliminary promotional activities.

Nevertheless, it is important for businesspersons to understand that they are personally liable for all preincorporation contracts made with investors, accountants, or others on behalf of the future corporation. A promoter may limit her or his potential liability in an initial promotional contract with a third party by including a provision that makes the corporation, once formed, assume liability under the contract. If the contract does not include such a provision, the promoter's personal liability continues. A promoter will remain personally liable for the preincorporation contract until the corporation assumes liability through a *novation* (a contract to substitute a third party in the place of one of the original contracting parties—see Chapter 10). A newly formed corporation is not liable for any preincorporation contract unless it has expressly agreed to its terms (in the initial contract or the novation).

Incorporation Procedures

Exact procedures for incorporation differ among states, but the basic steps are as follows: (1) select a state of incorporation, (2) secure the corporate name, (3) prepare the articles of incorporation, and (4) file the articles of incorporation with the secretary of state. These steps are discussed in more detail in the following subsections.

SELECT THE STATE OF INCORPORATION The first step in the incorporation process is to select a state in which to incorporate. Because state laws differ, individuals may look for the states that offer the most advantageous tax or incorporation provisions. Another consideration is the fee that a particular state charges to incorporate as well as the annual fees and the fees for specific transactions (such as stock transfers).

Delaware has historically had the least restrictive laws, along with provisions that favor corporate management. Consequently, many corporations, including a number of the largest, have incorporated there. Delaware's statutes permit firms to incorporate in that state and conduct business and locate their operating headquarters elsewhere. Most other states now permit this as well. Generally, though, closely held corporations, particularly those of a professional nature, incorporate in the state where their principal shareholders live and work. For reasons of convenience and cost, businesses often choose to incorporate in the state in which most of the corporation's business will be conducted.

SECURE THE CORPORATE NAME The choice of a corporate name is subject to state approval to ensure against duplication or deception. State statutes usually require that the secretary of state run a check on the proposed name in the state of incorporation. Some states require that the persons incorporating a firm, at their own expense, run a check on the proposed name, which can often be accomplished via Internet-based services. Once cleared, a name can be reserved for a short time, for a fee, pending the completion of the articles of incorporation.

Must Include Words That Disclose Corporate Status.

All states require the corporation name to include the word *Corporation (Corp.), Incorporated (Inc.), Company (Co.),* or *Limited (Ltd.).* A firm's failure to disclose its corporate status through the use of one of these terms or abbreviations can result in the individual who signed a contract for the corporation being held personally liable (as an undisclosed principal—see Chapter 20).

Cannot Infringe on Another's Trademark Rights.

A new corporation's name cannot be the same as (or deceptively similar to) the name of an existing corporation doing business within the state (see Chapter 14). Suppose that an existing corporation is named Digital Synergy, Inc. The state will not likely allow a new corporation to use the name Digital Synergy Company. That name is deceptively similar to the first and could cause confusion. This similar name could also transfer part of the goodwill established by the first corporate user to the second, thus infringing on the first company's trademark rights.

If those incorporating a firm contemplate doing business in other states—or over the Internet—they will also need to check existing corporate names in those states to avoid liability for trademark infringement. A related issue concerns the new firm's Internet domain name. Because the firm will want to use its name as a domain name, those incorporating the firm will need to make sure that the name is available by checking the ICANN database of domain names.

PREPARE THE ARTICLES OF INCORPORATION The primary document needed to incorporate a business is the **articles of incorporation.** The articles include basic information about the corporation and serve as a primary source of authority for its future organization and business functions. The person or persons who execute (sign) the articles are called *incorporators*. Generally, the articles of incorporation *must* include the following information [RMBCA 2.02].

1. The name of the corporation.
2. The number of shares the corporation is authorized to issue.

3. The name and street address of the corporation's initial registered agent and registered office.
4. The name and address of each incorporator.

In addition, the articles *may* set forth other information, such as the names and addresses of the initial members of the board of directors, the duration and purpose of the corporation, a par value for shares of the corporation, and any other information pertinent to the rights and duties of the corporation's shareholders and directors. Articles of incorporation vary widely depending on the jurisdiction and the size and type of the corporation. Frequently, the articles do not provide much detail about the firm's operations, which are spelled out in the company's **bylaws** (internal rules of management adopted by the corporation at its first organizational meeting).

Shares of the Corporation.

The articles must specify the number of shares of stock the corporation is authorized to issue [RMBCA 2.02(a)]. For instance, a company might state that the aggregate number of shares that the corporation has the authority to issue is five thousand. Large corporations often state a par value for each share, such as $.20 per share, and specify the various types or classes of stock authorized for issuance (see the discussion of *common* and *preferred stock* later in this chapter). Sometimes, the articles set forth the capital structure of the corporation and other relevant information concerning equity, shares, and credit. To allow for the raising of additional capital in the future, the articles of incorporation often authorize many more shares of stock than will initially be issued. This avoids the cumbersome and sometimes complicated task of amending the articles of incorporation at a later date.

Registered Office and Agent.

The corporation must indicate the location and street address of its registered office within the state. Usually, the registered office is also the principal office of the corporation. The corporation must also give the name and address of a specific person who has been designated as an *agent* and who can receive legal documents (such as orders to appear in court) on behalf of the corporation.

Incorporators.

Each incorporator must be listed by name and address. The incorporators need not have any interest at all in the corporation, and sometimes signing the articles is their only duty. Many states do not have residency or age requirements for incorporators. In some states, only one incorporator is needed, but other states require as many as three. Incorporators frequently participate in the first organizational meeting of the corporation.

Duration and Purpose. A corporation has perpetual existence unless the articles state otherwise. The RMBCA does not require a specific statement of purpose to be included in the articles. A corporation can be formed for any lawful purpose. Some incorporators include a general statement of purpose "to engage in any lawful act or activity," while others specify the intended business activities (such as "to engage in the production and sale of agricultural products"). The trend is toward allowing corporate articles to state that the corporation is organized for "any legal business," with no mention of specifics, to avoid the need for future amendments to the corporate articles [RMBCA 2.02(b)(2)(i), 3.01]. (Stating that a corporation is organized for any legal business also might avoid potential *ultra vires* issues, as will be discussed later in this chapter.)

Internal Organization. The articles can describe the corporation's internal management structure, although this usually is included in the bylaws adopted after the corporation is formed. The articles of incorporation commence the corporation. The bylaws are formed after commencement by the board of directors. Bylaws cannot conflict with the incorporation statute or the articles of incorporation [RMBCA 2.06].

Under the RMBCA, shareholders may amend or repeal the bylaws. The board of directors may also amend or repeal the bylaws unless the articles of incorporation or provisions of the incorporation statute reserve this power to the shareholders exclusively [RMBCA 10.20]. The bylaws typically describe such matters as voting requirements for shareholders, the election of the board of directors, and the methods of replacing directors. Bylaws also frequently outline the manner and time of holding shareholders' and board meetings (see page 431).

FILE THE ARTICLES WITH THE STATE Once the articles of incorporation have been prepared and signed by the incorporators, they are sent to the appropriate state official, usually the secretary of state, along with the required filing fee. In most states, the secretary of state then stamps the articles "Filed" and returns a copy of the articles to the incorporators. Once this occurs, the corporation officially exists. (Note that some states issue a *certificate of incorporation,* or *corporate charter,* which is similar to articles of incorporation, representing the state's authorization for the corporation to conduct business.[6] This procedure was typical under the unrevised MBCA.)

First Organizational Meeting to Adopt Bylaws

After incorporation, the first organizational meeting must be held. Usually, the most important function of this meeting is the adoption of bylaws, which, as mentioned, are the internal rules of management for the corporation. If the articles of incorporation named the initial board of directors, then the directors, by majority vote, call the meeting to adopt the bylaws and complete the company's organization. If the articles did not name the directors (as is typical), then the incorporators hold the meeting to elect the directors, adopt bylaws, and complete the routine business of incorporation (authorizing the issuance of shares and hiring employees, for example). The business transacted depends on the requirements of the state's corporation statute, the nature of the corporation, the provisions made in the articles, and the desires of the incorporators.

Improper Incorporation

The procedures for incorporation are very specific. If they are not followed precisely, others may be able to challenge the existence of the corporation. Errors in incorporation procedures can become important when, for example, a third party who is attempting to enforce a contract or bring a suit for a tort injury learns of them.

***DE JURE* AND *DE FACTO* CORPORATIONS** If a corporation has substantially complied with all conditions precedent to incorporation, the corporation is said to have *de jure* (rightful and lawful) existence. In most states and under RMBCA 2.03(b), the secretary of state's filing of the articles of incorporation is conclusive proof that all mandatory statutory provisions have been met [RMBCA 2.03(b)].

Sometimes, the incorporators fail to comply with all statutory mandates. If the defect is minor, such as an incorrect address listed on the articles of incorporation, most courts will overlook the defect and find that a corporation (*de jure*) exists. If the defect is substantial, however, such as a corporation's failure to hold an organizational meeting to adopt bylaws, the outcome will vary depending on the court. Some states, including Mississippi, New York, Ohio, and Oklahoma, still recognize the common law doctrine of *de facto* corporation.[7] In those states, the courts will treat a corporation as a legal corporation despite the defect in its formation if the following three requirements are met:

---

6. Under some circumstances, such as when a corporation fails to pay taxes, a state can revoke the firm's corporate charter or status as a corporation.

7. See, for example, *In re Hausman,* 13 N.Y.3d 408, 921 N.E.2d 191, 893 N.Y.S.2d 499 (2009).

1. A state statute exists under which the corporation can be validly incorporated.
2. The parties have made a good faith attempt to comply with the statute.
3. The parties have already undertaken to do business as a corporation.

Many state courts, however, have interpreted their states' version of the RMBCA as abolishing the common law doctrine of *de facto* corporations. These states include Alaska, Arizona, the District of Columbia, New Mexico, Minnesota, Oregon, South Dakota, Tennessee, Utah, and Washington. In those states, if there is a substantial defect in complying with the incorporation statute, the corporation does not legally exist, and the incorporators are personally liable.

CORPORATION BY ESTOPPEL If a business holds itself out to others as being a corporation but has made no attempt to incorporate, the firm may be estopped (prevented) from denying corporate status in a lawsuit by a third party. This doctrine of corporation by estoppel is most commonly applied when a third party contracts with an entity that claims to be a corporation but has not filed articles of incorporation—or contracts with a person claiming to be an agent of a corporation that does not in fact exist. When justice requires, courts in some states will treat an alleged corporation as if it were an actual corporation for the purpose of determining rights and liabilities in particular circumstances.[8] Recognition of corporate status does not extend beyond the resolution of the problem at hand.

In the following case, a party sought to avoid liability on a contract with a firm that had not yet filed its articles of incorporation. Could the party escape liability on the ground that the corporation did not exist at the time of the contract?

---

8. Some states have expressly rejected the common law theory of corporation by estoppel, finding that it is inconsistent with their statutory law, whereas other states have abolished only the doctrines of *de facto* and *de jure* corporations. See, for example, *Stone v. Jetmar Properties, LLC,* 733 N.W.2d 480 (Minn.App. 2007).

CASE 19.1

Brown v. W. P. Media, Inc.

Supreme Court of Alabama, 17 So.3d 1167 (2009).

BACKGROUND AND FACTS • In 2001, W. P. Media, Inc., and Alabama MBA, Inc., agreed to form a joint venture—to be called Alabaster Wireless MBA, LLC—to provide wireless Internet services to consumers. W. P. Media was to create a wireless network and provide ongoing technical support. Alabama MBA was to contribute capital of $79,300, and W. P. Media was to contribute "proprietary technology" in the same amount. Hugh Brown signed the parties' contract on Alabama MBA's behalf as the chair of its board. At the time, however, Alabama MBA's articles of incorporation had not yet been filed. Brown filed the articles of incorporation in 2002. Later, Brown and Alabama MBA filed a suit in an Alabama state court, alleging that W. P. Media had breached their contract by not building the wireless network. The court issued a summary judgment in the defendant's favor. The plaintiffs appealed.

IN THE LANGUAGE OF THE COURT
SMITH, Justice.
* * * *
Corporate action may * * * be established under principles of estoppel, whether or not an entity or organization qualifies as a de facto corporation. The doctrine is based on conduct by a party that recognizes an organization as a corporation or an express or implied representation by a corporation that it is a corporation. In the first instance, estoppel cannot apply to one who has not dealt with the organization or in any way recognized it as having corporate existence, or who has participated in holding it out as a corporation. In the second instance, where a party has contracted or otherwise dealt with an organization, believing it to be a corporation, there may have been no holding out of corporate status by the organization. *In either instance, estoppel arises from the contract or course of dealing by the parties and is applicable in a suit by the party dealing with the organization, as well as in a suit by the organization.* [Emphasis added.]

CASE CONTINUES ▶

CASE 19.1 CONTINUED ➡ Alabama MBA * * * argues that because W. P. Media treated Alabama MBA as a corporation, W. P. Media is now estopped from denying Alabama MBA's corporate existence.
* * * *

W. P. Media entered into a contractual relationship with Alabama MBA to operate Alabaster Wireless. The operating agreement identified Alabama MBA as a corporation, was executed in Alabama MBA's corporate name, and was signed by Brown as Alabama MBA's "chairman of the board." W. P. Media further concedes * * * that Alabama MBA and Brown had essentially "represented" that Alabama MBA was "a viable, legal corporation" and that W. P. Media had "no reason to doubt" those representations. Although Alabama MBA had not yet filed articles of incorporation at the time the operating agreement was executed in 2001, the articles of incorporation were subsequently filed in 2002. * * * At no time during the venture did W. P. Media challenge the validity of the operating agreement until after it was sued for breaching the operating agreement. Under the facts of this case, we hold that W. P. Media's actions of entering into a contract with Alabama MBA and participating with Alabama MBA in the joint venture before and after Alabama MBA's articles of incorporation were filed estop W. P. Media from denying Alabama MBA's corporate existence for purposes of challenging the validity of the operating agreement.

DECISION AND REMEDY • *The Alabama Supreme Court reversed the lower court's judgment and remanded the case. Under the principle of corporation by estoppel, W. P. Media could not deny Alabama MBA's corporate existence.*

THE LEGAL ENVIRONMENT DIMENSION • *Did Alabama MBA exist as a de facto corporation when it entered into the contract with W. P. Media? Why or why not?*

WHAT IF THE FACTS WERE DIFFERENT? • *Would the result in this case have been different if the parties' contract to build and operate a wireless network had been negotiated and agreed to entirely online? Discuss.*

SECTION 3
CORPORATE POWERS

Under modern law, a corporation generally can engage in any act and enter into any contract available to a natural person in order to accomplish the purposes for which it was formed. When a corporation is created, the express and implied powers necessary to achieve its purpose also come into existence.

Express Powers

The express powers of a corporation are found in its articles of incorporation, in the law of the state of incorporation, and in the state and federal constitutions. State statutes often give corporations a wide variety of powers, allowing a corporation to issue stocks and bonds, execute contracts and negotiable instruments, buy and sell (or lease) property, pay employee benefits, and make charitable contributions.

Corporate bylaws and the resolutions of the corporation's board of directors also grant or restrict certain powers. Because state corporation statutes frequently provide default rules that apply if the company's bylaws are silent on an issue, it is important that the bylaws set forth the specific operating rules of the corporation. In addition, after the bylaws are adopted, the corporation's board of directors will pass resolutions that also grant or restrict corporate powers.

The following order of priority is used if a conflict arises among the various documents involving a corporation:

1. The U.S. Constitution.
2. State constitutions.
3. State statutes.
4. The articles of incorporation.
5. Bylaws.
6. Resolutions of the board of directors.

Implied Powers

Certain implied powers arise when a corporation is created. Unless expressly prohibited by a constitution, a statute, or the articles of incorporation, the corporation has the implied power to perform all acts reasonably appropriate and necessary to accomplish its corporate purposes. For this reason, a corporation has the implied power to borrow funds within certain limits, lend funds, and extend credit to those with whom it has a legal or contractual relationship.

To borrow funds, the corporation acts through its board of directors to authorize the loan. Most often, the president or chief executive officer of the corporation will execute the necessary papers on behalf of the corporation. Corporate officers such as these have the implied power to bind the corporation in matters directly connected with the *ordinary* business affairs of the enterprise. There is a limit to what a corporate officer can do, though. A corporate officer does not have the authority to bind the corporation to an action that will greatly affect the corporate purpose or undertaking, such as the sale of substantial corporate assets.

Ultra Vires Doctrine

The term **ultra vires** means "beyond the power." In corporate law, acts of a corporation that are beyond its express or implied powers are *ultra vires* acts. Under Section 3.04 of the RMBCA, shareholders can seek an injunction from a court to prevent the corporation from engaging in *ultra vires* acts. The attorney general in the state of incorporation can also bring an action to obtain an injunction against *ultra vires* transactions or to institute dissolution proceedings against the corporation on the basis of *ultra vires* acts. The corporation or its shareholders (on behalf of the corporation) can seek damages from the officers and directors who were responsible for the *ultra vires* acts.

In the past, most cases dealing with *ultra vires* acts involved contracts made for unauthorized purposes. Now, however, most private corporations are organized for "any legal business" and do not state a specific purpose, so the *ultra vires* doctrine has declined in importance in recent years. Today, cases that allege *ultra vires* acts usually involve nonprofit corporations or municipal (public) corporations.

CASE IN POINT Four men formed a nonprofit corporation to create the Armenian Genocide Museum & Memorial (AGM&M). The bylaws appointed them as trustees (similar to corporate directors) for life. One of the trustees, Gerard L. Cafesjian, became the chair and president of AGM&M. Eventually, the relationship among the trustees deteriorated, and Cafesjian resigned. The corporation then brought a suit claiming that Cafesjian had engaged in numerous *ultra vires* acts, self-dealing, and mismanagement. Among other things, although the bylaws required an 80 percent affirmative vote of the trustees to take

action, Cafesjian had taken many actions without the board's approval. He had also entered into contracts for real estate transactions in which he had a personal interest. Because Cafesjian had taken actions that exceeded his authority and had failed to follow the rules set forth in the bylaws for board meetings, the court ruled that the corporation could go forward with its suit.[9]

SECTION 4
PIERCING THE CORPORATE VEIL

Occasionally, the owners use a corporate entity to perpetrate a fraud, circumvent the law, or in some other way accomplish an illegitimate objective. In these situations, the courts will ignore the corporate structure and **pierce the corporate veil,** exposing the shareholders to personal liability [RMBCA 2.04].

Generally, when the corporate privilege is abused for personal benefit, the courts will require the owners to assume personal liability to creditors for the corporation's debts. The courts will also impose personal liability when the corporate business is treated so carelessly that the corporation and the controlling shareholders are no longer separate entities. In short, when the facts show that great injustice would result from the use of a corporation to avoid individual responsibility, a court will look behind the corporate structure to the individual shareholders.

Factors That Lead Courts to Pierce the Corporate Veil

The following are some of the factors that frequently cause the courts to pierce the corporate veil:

1. A party is tricked or misled into dealing with the corporation rather than the individual.
2. The corporation is set up never to make a profit or always to be insolvent, or it is too "thinly" capitalized—that is, it has insufficient capital at the time it is formed to meet its prospective debts or potential liabilities.
3. The corporation is formed to evade an existing legal obligation.
4. Statutory corporate formalities, such as holding required corporation meetings, are not followed.
5. Personal and corporate interests are mixed together, or **commingled,** to the extent that the corporation has no separate identity.

9. *Armenian Assembly of America, Inc. v. Cafesjian,* 692 F.Supp.2d 20 (D.C. 2010).

Although state corporation codes usually do not prohibit a shareholder from lending funds to her or his corporation, courts will scrutinize the transaction closely if the loan comes from an officer, director, or majority shareholder. Loans from persons who control the corporation must be made in good faith and for fair value.

A Potential Problem for Closely Held Corporations

The potential for corporate assets to be used for personal benefit is especially great in a closely held corporation, in which the shares are held by a single person or by only a few individuals, usually family members. In such a situation, the separate status of the corporate entity and the sole shareholder (or family-member shareholders) must be carefully preserved. Certain practices invite trouble for the one-person or family-owned corporation: the commingling of corporate and personal funds, the failure to hold board of directors' meetings and record the minutes, and the shareholders' continuous personal use of corporate property (for example, vehicles).

In the following case, a creditor asked the court to pierce the corporate veil and hold the sole shareholder-owner of the debtor corporation personally liable for a corporate debt.

✳ EXTENDED CASE 19.2 ✳
Schultz v. General Electric Healthcare Financial Services

Court of Appeals of Kentucky, ____ S.W.3d ____ (2010).

IN THE LANGUAGE OF THE COURT
STUMBO, Judge.
* * * *

[Thomas] Schultz was the president and sole shareholder/owner of Intra-Med [Services, Inc.], a Kentucky corporation that performed medical diagnostic imaging services, such as MRIs and CT scans. GE [General Electric Healthcare Financial Services, Inc.; General Electric Company; and General Electric Capital Corporation] entered into a contract to lease certain medical equipment to Intra-Med. In 2004, Intra-Med defaulted on the contract by failing to make the required lease payments to GE.

On July 8, 2004, GE filed a complaint against Intra-Med in Jefferson Circuit Court. On November 15, 2004, the court entered a judgment on the pleadings in favor of GE for over $4.7 million. GE was able to collect approximately $700,000 of the judgment.

While collecting on its judgment, GE learned of certain documents that Intra-Med had produced in discovery in another lawsuit. Those documents revealed that Mr. Schultz had used Intra-Med assets for his own purposes. For example, Mr. Schultz bought multiple pieces of property for himself using Intra-Med funds and when some of this property was later sold, Mr. Schultz kept the proceeds. GE intervened in this other lawsuit and filed a third-party complaint against Mr. Schultz seeking to pierce the corporate veil and hold him personally liable for the judgment against Intra-Med.

On April 17, 2007, GE filed a motion for partial judgment on the pleadings in which it requested a partial judgment in the amount of $1,150,000. This was allegedly the amount of Intra-Med funds which Schultz used improperly.

On August 10, 2007, the trial court held that Mr. Schultz's admissions in his answer to GE's third-party complaint support the conclusion that Schultz improperly used Intra-Med's funds. It also held that none of Mr. Schultz's affirmative defenses would preclude an entry of judgment against him. However, the court found that Mr. Schultz might have been entitled to receive some payments from Intra-Med because he personally loaned the company $700,000. Because of this possibility, the court denied GE's motion.

GE next filed a motion in which it stated it would settle for $450,000, the difference between $1,150,000 and the claimed $700,000 loan. GE also stipulated that it would voluntarily dismiss its remaining claims against Mr. Schultz if the court entered the $450,000 judgment. The court ultimately granted the motion on September 10, 2007. Mr. Schultz filed a motion to alter or amend, but it was denied. This appeal followed.

* * * *

Mr. Schultz admitted several facts in his answer to GE's third-party complaint. The relevant admitted facts are: on November 15, 2004, GE was awarded a judgment in the amount of $4,746,921.80, plus interest, against Intra-Med; Mr. Schultz had knowledge of the GE judgment on or after November 15, 2005; on or about December of 1998, Mr. Schultz, individually, purchased real property located at 7405 New LaGrange Road, Louisville, KY 40242, using Intra-Med funds; Intra-Med did not receive any of the proceeds from the subsequent sale of the New LaGrange Road property in March of 2004; on or about October of 2000, Mr. Schultz, individually, purchased and improved real property located at 8700 Dixie

Highway, Louisville, KY 40258, using Intra-Med funds; after entry of the GE judgment, Mr. Schultz sold the Dixie Highway property, which had been purchased and renovated by Mr. Schultz with Intra-Med funds, for $850,000; Intra-Med did not receive any of the proceeds from the sale of the Dixie Highway property; on or about May 24, 2001, Mr. Schultz, individually, purchased a marina slip for $23,000 with Intra-Med funds; and Intra-Med did not receive any of the proceeds from the subsequent sale of the marina slip. It is from these admitted facts that GE moved for a judgment on the pleadings.

"Three basic theories have been utilized to hold the shareholders of a corporation responsible for corporate liabilities. These have been labeled (1) the instrumentality theory; (2) the alter ego theory;

and (3) the equity formulation." GE focused on the instrumentality theory in its motion.

Under the instrumentality theory three elements must be established in order to warrant a piercing of the corporate veil: (1) that the corporation was a mere instrumentality of the shareholder; (2) that the shareholder exercised control over the corporation in such a way as to defraud or to harm the plaintiff; and (3) that a refusal to disregard the corporate entity would subject the plaintiff to unjust loss. The courts adopting this test have been virtually unanimous in requiring that these three elements co-exist before the corporate veil will be pierced. [Emphasis added.]

* * * *

The admitted facts * * * support the finding that the corporate veil should be pierced under the instrumentality theory. Mr. Schultz treated the corporation as a mere instrumentality by using corporate

funds for his own individual purposes to purchase real estate and a boat slip. The admitted facts also demonstrate that Mr. Schultz harmed GE by using corporate funds as his own even after GE obtained a monetary judgment against Intra-Med. Money that could have been used to satisfy that judgment was used by Mr. Schultz for his own purposes. Finally, not piercing the corporate veil would subject GE to an unjust loss. As previously stated, money that could have been used to satisfy GE's judgment against Intra-Med was removed from the company and used elsewhere. GE has only been able to recover around $700,000 from a $4.7 million judgment. Piercing the corporate veil appears to be the only method for GE to recover its judgment.

* * * *

For the foregoing reasons we affirm the trial court's judgment on the pleadings.

 QUESTIONS

1. Schultz argued that even if the corporate veil should be pierced, the $450,000 judgment against him was too much and should be reduced. How might the court have responded to this argument?
2. Suppose that Schultz had turned over the proceeds from the sale of his properties to his corporation, Intra-Med, and used them to pay part or all of GE's judgment. In this situation, if the funds were insufficient to cover the debt, would the court have pierced the corporate veil to obtain the balance from Schultz personally? Explain.

The Alter-Ego Theory

Sometimes, courts pierce the corporate veil under the theory that the corporation was not operated as a separate entity, but was just another side (or alter ego) of the individual or group who actually controlled the corporation. This is called the alter-ego theory. The theory is applied when a corporation is so dominated and controlled by an individual or group that the separate identities of the person (or group) and the corporation are no longer distinct. Courts use the alter-ego theory to avoid injustice or fraud that would result if wrongdoers were allowed to hide behind the protection of limited liability.

CASE IN POINT Harvey and Barbara Jacobson owned Aqua Clear Technologies, Inc., which installed and serviced home water-softening systems. The Jacobsons consistently took funds out of the business for their personal expenses, including

payments for their home, cars, health-insurance premiums, and credit cards. Three weeks after Aqua filed a bankruptcy petition, Harvey formed another corporation called Discount Water Services, Inc. Discount appropriated Aqua's equipment and inventory (without buying it) and continued to service water-softening systems for Aqua's customers, even using the same phone number. The trustee appointed to Aqua's bankruptcy case sought to recover Aqua's assets on the ground that Discount was Aqua's alter ego. The court ruled that Discount was simply a continuation of Aqua's business (its alter ego) under a new name, and therefore held Discount liable for the claims (totaling $108,732.64) asserted against Aqua in bankruptcy.[10]

---

10. *In re Aqua Clear Technologies, Inc.*, 361 Bankr. 567 (S.D.Fla. 2007).

DIRECTORS AND OFFICERS

Corporate directors, officers, and shareholders all play different roles within the corporate entity. Sometimes, actions that may benefit the corporation as a whole do not coincide with the separate interests of the individuals making up the corporation. In such situations, it is important to know the rights and duties of all participants in the corporate enterprise and the ways in which conflicts among corporate participants are resolved.

Roles of Directors

The board of directors is the ultimate authority in every corporation. Directors have responsibility for all policymaking decisions necessary to the management of all corporate affairs. Additionally, the directors must act as a body in carrying out routine corporate business. The board selects and removes the corporate officers, determines the capital structure of the corporation, and declares dividends. Each director has one vote, and customarily the majority rules. The general areas of responsibility of the board of directors are shown in Exhibit 19–1 below.

Directors are sometimes inappropriately characterized as *agents* because they act on behalf of the corporation. No individual director, however, can act as an agent to bind the corporation. As a group, directors collectively control the corporation in a way that no agent is able to control a principal. In addition, although directors occupy positions of trust and control over the corporation, they are not *trustees* because they do not hold title to property for the use and benefit of others.

Few qualifications are required for directors. Only a handful of states impose minimum age and residency requirements. A director may be a shareholder, but that is not necessary (unless the articles of incorporation or bylaws require ownership interest).

ELECTION OF DIRECTORS Subject to statutory limitations, the number of directors is set forth in the corporation's articles or bylaws. Historically, the minimum number of directors has been three, but today many states permit fewer. Normally, the incorporators appoint the first board of directors at the time the corporation is created, or the directors are named in the articles of incorporation. The initial board serves until the first annual shareholders' meeting. Subsequent directors are elected by a majority vote of the shareholders.

A director usually serves for a term of one year—from annual meeting to annual meeting. Most state statutes permit longer and staggered terms. A common practice is to elect one-third of the board members each year for a three-year term. In this way, there is greater management continuity.

Removal of Directors. A director can be removed *for cause*—that is, for failing to perform a required duty—either as specified in the articles or bylaws or by shareholder action. The board of directors may also have the power to remove a director for cause, subject to shareholder review. In most states, a director cannot be removed without cause unless the shareholders have reserved the right to do so at the time of election.

Vacancies on the Board. Vacancies occur on the board if a director dies or resigns or when a new position is created through amendment of the articles or bylaws. In these situations, either the shareholders or the board itself can fill the vacant position, depending on state law or on the provisions of the

EXHIBIT 19–1 • Directors' Management Responsibilities

RESPONSIBILITIES	EXAMPLES
Authorize Major Corporate Policy Decisions	• Oversee major contract negotiations and management-labor negotiations. • Initiate negotiations on the sale or lease of corporate assets outside the regular course of business. • Decide whether to pursue new product lines or business opportunities.
Select and Remove Corporate Officers and Other Managerial Employees, and Determine Their Compensation	• Search for and hire corporate executives and determine the elements of their compensation packages, including stock options. • Supervise managerial employees and make decisions regarding their termination.
Make Financial Decisions	• Make decisions regarding the issuance of authorized shares and bonds. • Decide when to declare dividends to be paid to shareholders.

bylaws. Note, however, that even when an election appears to be authorized by the bylaws, a court can invalidate the results if the directors were attempting to manipulate the election in order to reduce the shareholders' influence.

CASE IN POINT The bylaws of Liquid Audio, Inc., authorized a board of five directors, with two directors to be elected each year. Another company offered to buy all of Liquid Audio's stock, but the board rejected this offer. Fearing that the shareholders would elect new directors who would allow the sale, the directors amended the bylaws to increase the number of directors to seven, thereby diminishing the shareholders' influence in the upcoming election. When the shareholders challenged the election, the court ruled that the directors' action was illegal because they had attempted to diminish the shareholders' right to vote effectively in an election of directors.[11]

COMPENSATION OF DIRECTORS In the past, corporate directors rarely were compensated, but today they are often paid at least nominal sums and may receive more substantial compensation in large corporations because of the time, work, effort, and especially risk involved. Most states permit the corporate articles or bylaws to authorize compensation for directors. In fact, the RMBCA states that unless the articles or bylaws provide otherwise, the board itself may set the directors' compensation [RMBCA 8.11]. Directors also gain through indirect benefits, such as business contacts and prestige, and other rewards, such as stock options.

In many corporations, directors are also chief corporate officers (president or chief executive officer, for example) and receive compensation in their managerial positions. A director who is also an officer of the corporation is referred to as an **inside director,** whereas a director who does not hold a management position is an **outside director.** Typically, a corporation's board of directors includes both inside and outside directors.

BOARD OF DIRECTORS' MEETINGS The board of directors conducts business by holding formal meetings with recorded minutes. The dates of regular meetings are usually established in the articles or bylaws or by board resolution, and ordinarily no further notice is required. Special meetings can be called, with notice sent to all directors. Today, most states allow directors to participate in board of directors' meetings from remote locations via telephone or Web conferencing, provided that all the directors can simultaneously hear each other during the meeting [RMBCA 8.20].

Normally, a majority of the board of directors must be present to constitute a *quorum* [RMBCA 8.24]. (A **quorum** is the minimum number of members of a body of officials or other group that must be present for business to be validly transacted.) Modern incorporation statutes, however, generally permit the articles of incorporation or bylaws to set a quorum at more or less than a majority.[12]

Once a quorum is present, the directors transact business and vote on issues affecting the corporation. Each director present at the meeting has one vote.[13] Ordinary matters generally require a simple majority vote; certain extraordinary issues may require a greater-than-majority vote. In other words, the affirmative vote of a majority of the directors present at a meeting binds the board of directors with regard to most decisions.

RIGHTS OF DIRECTORS A corporate director must have certain rights to function properly in that position. The *right to participation* means that directors are entitled to participate in all board of directors' meetings and have a right to be notified of these meetings. Because the dates of regular board meetings are usually specified in the bylaws, no notice of these meetings is required. If special meetings are called, however, notice is required unless waived by the director [RMBCA 8.23].

A director also has a *right of inspection,* which means that each director can access the corporation's books and records, facilities, and premises. Inspection rights are essential for directors to make informed decisions and to exercise the necessary supervision over corporate officers and employees. This right of inspection is almost absolute and cannot be restricted (by the articles, bylaws, or any act of the board of directors).

When a director becomes involved in litigation by virtue of her or his position or actions, the director may also have a *right to indemnification* (reimbursement) for the legal costs, fees, and damages incurred. Most states allow corporations to indemnify and

---

11. *MM Companies, Inc. v. Liquid Audio, Inc.,* 813 A.2d 1118 (Del. Sup.Ct. 2003).

12. See, for example, Delaware Code Annotated Title 8, Section 141(b), and New York Business Corporation Law Section 707. Both these state statutes allow corporations to set a quorum at less than a majority, but not less than one-third of the directors.

13. The one exception is in Louisiana, which allows a director to vote by proxy under certain circumstances.

purchase liability insurance for corporate directors [RMBCA 8.51].

COMMITTEES OF THE BOARD OF DIRECTORS When a board of directors has a large number of members and must deal with myriad complex business issues, meetings can become unwieldy. Therefore, the boards of large, publicly held corporations typically create committees, appoint directors to serve on individual committees, and delegate certain tasks to these committees. Committees focus on individual subjects and increase the efficiency of the board. The most common types of committees are discussed next.

Executive Committee. The board members often elect an executive committee to handle interim management decisions between board meetings. The committee is limited to making management decisions about ordinary business matters and conducting preliminary investigations into proposals. It cannot declare dividends, authorize the issuance of shares, amend the bylaws, or initiate any actions that require shareholder approval.

Audit Committee. The audit committee is responsible for the selection, compensation, and oversight of the independent public accountants who audit the corporation's financial records. The Sarbanes-Oxley Act of 2002 (see Chapter 4) requires all publicly held corporations to have an audit committee.

Nominating Committee. The nominating committee chooses the candidates for the board of directors that management wishes to submit to the shareholders in the next election. The committee can nominate but cannot select directors to fill vacancies on the board (because only the shareholders can elect directors) [RMBCA 8.25].

Compensation Committee. The compensation committee reviews and decides the salaries, bonuses, stock options, and other benefits that are given to the corporation's top executives. The committee may also determine the compensation of directors.

Litigation Committee. This committee decides whether the corporation should pursue requests by shareholders to file a lawsuit against some party that has allegedly harmed the corporation. The committee members investigate the allegations and weigh the costs and benefits of litigation.

In addition to appointing committees, the board of directors can also delegate some of its functions to corporate officers. In doing so, the board is not relieved of its overall responsibility for directing the affairs of the corporation. Instead, corporate officers and managerial personnel are empowered to make decisions relating to ordinary, daily corporate activities within well-defined guidelines.

Corporate Officers and Executives

The board of directors hires officers and other executive employees. At a minimum, most corporations have a president, one or more vice presidents, a secretary, and a treasurer. In most states, an individual can hold more than one office, such as president and secretary, and can be both an officer and a director of the corporation. In addition to carrying out the duties articulated in the bylaws, corporate and managerial officers act as agents of the corporation, and the ordinary rules of agency (as will be discussed in Chapter 20) normally apply to their employment.

Corporate officers and other high-level managers are employees of the company, so their rights are defined by employment contracts. Nevertheless, the board of directors normally can remove a corporate officer at any time with or without cause. If the directors remove an officer in violation of the terms of an employment contract, however, the corporation may be liable for breach of contract.

The duties of corporate officers are similar to those of directors because both groups are involved in decision making and are in similar positions of control. Hence, officers and directors are viewed as having the same fiduciary duties of care and loyalty in their conduct of corporate affairs, a subject to which we now turn.

Duties and Liabilities of Directors and Officers

Directors and officers are deemed to be fiduciaries of the corporation because their relationship with the corporation and its shareholders is one of trust and confidence. As fiduciaries, directors and officers owe ethical—and legal—duties to the corporation and the shareholders as a whole. These fiduciary duties include the duty of care and the duty of loyalty.

DUTY OF CARE Directors and officers must exercise due care in performing their duties. The standard of *due care* has been variously described in judicial decisions and codified in many state corporation codes. Generally, a director or officer is required to act in good faith, to exercise the care that an ordinarily prudent (careful) person would exercise in similar circumstances, and to do what she or he believes is in the best interests of the corporation [RMBCA 8.30(a), 8.42(a)]. Directors and officers whose failure to exercise due care results in harm to the corporation or its shareholders can be held liable for negligence (unless the *business judgment rule* applies, as will be discussed shortly).

Duty to Make Informed Decisions. Directors and officers are expected to be informed on corporate matters and to conduct a reasonable investigation of the situation before making a decision. This means that they must do what is necessary to keep adequately informed: attend meetings and presentations, ask for information from those who have it, read reports, and review other written materials. In other words, directors and officers must investigate, study, and discuss matters and evaluate alternatives before making a decision. They cannot decide on the spur of the moment without adequate research.

Although directors and officers are expected to act in accordance with their own knowledge and training, they are also normally entitled to rely on information given to them by certain other persons. Most states and Section 8.30(b) of the RMBCA allow a director to make decisions in reliance on information furnished by competent officers or employees, professionals such as attorneys and accountants, and committees of the board of directors (on which the director does not serve). The reliance must be in good faith, of course, to insulate a director from liability if the information later proves to be inaccurate or unreliable.

Duty to Exercise Reasonable Supervision. Directors are also expected to exercise a reasonable amount of supervision when they delegate work to corporate officers and employees. Suppose that Dale, a corporate bank director, fails to attend any board of directors' meetings for five years. In addition, Dale never inspects any of the corporate books or records and generally fails to supervise the activities of the bank president and the loan committee. Meanwhile, Brennan, the bank president, who is a corporate officer, makes various improper loans and permits large overdrafts. In this situation, Dale (the corporate director) can be held liable to the corporation for losses resulting from the unsupervised actions of the bank president and the loan committee.

Dissenting Directors. Directors are expected to attend board of directors' meetings, and their votes should be entered into the minutes. Sometimes, an individual director disagrees with the majority's vote (which becomes an act of the board of directors). Unless a dissent is entered in the minutes, the director is presumed to have assented. If a decision later leads to the directors being held liable for mismanagement, dissenting directors are rarely held individually liable to the corporation. For this reason, a director who is absent from a given meeting sometimes registers a dissent with the secretary of the board regarding actions taken at the meeting.

THE BUSINESS JUDGMENT RULE Directors and officers are expected to exercise due care and to use their best judgment in guiding corporate management, but they are not insurers of business success. Under the **business judgment rule,** a corporate director or officer will not be liable to the corporation or to its shareholders for honest mistakes of judgment and bad business decisions. Courts give significant deference to the decisions of corporate directors and officers, and consider the reasonableness of a decision at the time it was made, without the benefit of hindsight. Thus, corporate decision makers are not subjected to second-guessing by shareholders or others in the corporation.

The business judgment rule will apply as long as the following occurred:

1. The director or officer took reasonable steps to become informed about the matter.
2. He or she had a rational basis for the decision.
3. There was no conflict of interest between the director or officer's personal interest and that of the corporation.

In fact, unless there is evidence of bad faith, fraud, or a clear breach of fiduciary duties, most courts will apply the rule and protect directors and officers who make bad business decisions from liability for those choices. Consequently, if there is a reasonable basis for a business decision, a court is unlikely to interfere with that decision, even if the corporation suffers as a result. Note also that as a practical matter, corporate officers face liability more often than directors under this rule because they work at the corporation every day, whereas directors meet once a month or less.

DUTY OF LOYALTY *Loyalty* can be defined as faithfulness to one's obligations and duties. In the corporate context, the duty of loyalty requires directors and officers to subordinate their personal interests to the welfare of the corporation. For instance, a director should not oppose a transaction that is in the corporation's best interest simply because pursuing it may cost the director her or his position. Directors cannot use corporate funds or confidential corporate information for personal advantage and must refrain from self-dealing. Cases dealing with the duty of loyalty typically involve one or more of the following:

1. Competing with the corporation.
2. Usurping (taking personal advantage of) a corporate opportunity.
3. Having an interest that conflicts with that of the corporation.

4. Using information that is not available to the public to make a profit trading securities (see *insider trading* on page 635 in Chapter 29).
5. Authorizing a corporate transaction that is detrimental to minority shareholders.
6. Selling control over the corporation.

The following classic case illustrates the conflict that can arise between a corporate official's personal interest and his or her duty of loyalty.

CASE 19.3
Guth v. Loft, Inc.
Supreme Court of Delaware, 23 Del.Ch. 255, 5 A.2d 503 (1939).

BACKGROUND AND FACTS • Loft, Inc., made and sold candies, syrups, beverages, and food from its offices and plant in Long Island City, New York. Loft operated 115 retail outlets in several states and also sold its products wholesale. Charles Guth was Loft's president. Guth and his family owned Grace Company, which made syrups for soft drinks in a plant in Baltimore, Maryland. Coca-Cola Company supplied Loft with cola syrup. Unhappy with what he felt was Coca-Cola's high price, Guth entered into an agreement with Roy Megargel to acquire the trademark and formula for Pepsi-Cola and form Pepsi-Cola Corporation. Neither Guth nor Megargel could finance the new venture, however, and Grace was insolvent. Without the knowledge of Loft's board, Guth used Loft's capital, credit, facilities, and employees to further the Pepsi enterprise. At Guth's direction, Loft made the concentrate for the syrup, which was sent to Grace to add sugar and water. Loft charged Grace for the concentrate but allowed forty months' credit. Grace charged Pepsi for the syrup but also granted substantial credit. Grace sold the syrup to Pepsi's customers, including Loft, which paid on delivery or within thirty days. Loft also paid for Pepsi's advertising. Finally, losing profits at its stores as a result of switching from Coca-Cola, Loft filed a suit in a Delaware state court against Guth, Grace, and Pepsi, seeking their Pepsi stock and an accounting. The court entered a judgment in the plaintiff's favor. The defendants appealed to the Delaware Supreme Court.

IN THE LANGUAGE OF THE COURT
LAYTON, Chief Justice, delivering the opinion of the court:
* * * *
    Corporate officers and directors are not permitted to use their position of trust and confidence to further their private interests. * * * They stand in a fiduciary relation to the corporation and its stockholders. A public policy, existing through the years, and derived from a profound knowledge of human characteristics and motives, has established *a rule that demands of a corporate officer or director, peremptorily [not open for debate] and inexorably [unavoidably], the most scrupulous observance of his duty, not only affirmatively to protect the interests of the corporation committed to his charge, but also to refrain from doing anything that would work injury to the corporation* * * *. The rule that requires an undivided and unselfish loyalty to the corporation demands that there shall be no conflict between duty and self-interest. [Emphasis added.]
    * * * *
    * * * *If there is presented to a corporate officer or director a business opportunity which the corporation is financially able to undertake [that] is* * * * *in the line of the corporation's business and is of practical advantage to it* * * * *and, by embracing the opportunity, the self-interest of the officer or director will be brought into conflict with that of his corporation, the law will not permit him to seize the opportunity for himself.* * * * In such circumstances, * * * the corporation may elect to claim

CASE 19.3 CONTINUED ▶ all of the benefits of the transaction for itself, and the law will impress a trust in favor of the corporation upon the property, interests and profits so acquired. [Emphasis added.]

     * * * *

     * * * The appellants contend that no conflict of interest between Guth and Loft resulted from his acquirement and exploitation of the Pepsi-Cola opportunity [and] that the acquisition did not place Guth in competition with Loft * * *. [In this case, however,] Guth was Loft, and Guth was Pepsi. He absolutely controlled Loft. His authority over Pepsi was supreme. As Pepsi, he created and controlled the supply of Pepsi-Cola syrup, and he determined the price and the terms. What he offered, as Pepsi, he had the power, as Loft, to accept. Upon any consideration of human characteristics and motives, he created a conflict between self-interest and duty. He made himself the judge in his own cause. * * * Moreover, a reasonable probability of injury to Loft resulted from the situation forced upon it. Guth was in the same position to impose his terms upon Loft as had been the Coca-Cola Company.

     * * * The facts and circumstances demonstrate that Guth's appropriation of the Pepsi-Cola opportunity to himself placed him in a competitive position with Loft with respect to a commodity essential to it, thereby rendering his personal interests incompatible with the superior interests of his corporation; and this situation was accomplished, not openly and with his own resources, but secretly and with the money and facilities of the corporation which was committed to his protection.

DECISION AND REMEDY • *The Delaware Supreme Court upheld the judgment of the lower court. The state supreme court was "convinced that the opportunity to acquire the Pepsi-Cola trademark and formula, goodwill and business belonged to [Loft], and that Guth, as its President, had no right to appropriate the opportunity to himself."*

IMPACT OF THIS CASE ON TODAY'S LAW • *This early Delaware decision was one of the first to set forth a test for determining when a corporate officer or director has breached the duty of loyalty. The test has two basic parts—whether the opportunity was reasonably related to the corporation's line of business, and whether the corporation was financially able to undertake the opportunity. The court also considered whether the corporation had an interest or expectancy in the opportunity and recognized that when the corporation had "no interest or expectancy, the officer or director is entitled to treat the opportunity as his own."*

WHAT IF THE FACTS WERE DIFFERENT? • *Suppose that Loft's board of directors had approved Pepsi-Cola's use of its personnel and equipment. Would the court's decision have been different? Discuss.*

DISCLOSURE OF POTENTIAL CONFLICTS OF INTEREST
Corporate directors often have many business affiliations, and a director may sit on the board of more than one corporation. Of course, directors are precluded from entering into or supporting businesses that operate in direct competition with corporations on whose boards they serve. Their fiduciary duty requires them to make a full disclosure of any potential conflicts of interest that might arise in any corporate transaction [RMBCA 8.60].

Sometimes, a corporation enters into a contract or engages in a transaction in which an officer or director has a personal interest. The director or officer must make a *full disclosure* of the nature of the conflicting interest and all facts pertinent to the transaction, and must abstain from voting on the proposed transaction.

For example, Ballo Corporation needs office space. Stephanie Colson, one of its five directors, owns the building adjoining the corporation's headquarters. Colson can negotiate a lease for the space to Ballo if she fully discloses her conflicting interest and any facts known to her about the proposed transaction to Ballo and the other four directors. If the lease arrangement is fair and reasonable, Colson abstains from voting on it, and the other members of the corporation's board of directors unanimously approve it, the contract is valid. The rule is one of reason. Otherwise, directors would be prevented from ever having financial dealings with the corporations they serve.

LIABILITY OF DIRECTORS AND OFFICERS Directors and officers are exposed to liability on many fronts. They can be held liable for negligence in certain circumstances, as previously discussed. They may also be held liable for the crimes and torts committed by themselves or by corporate employees under their supervision.

Additionally, if shareholders perceive that the corporate directors are not acting in the best interests of the corporation, they may sue the directors, in what is called a *shareholder's derivative suit,* on behalf of the corporation. (This type of action will be discussed later in this chapter, in the context of shareholders' rights.) Directors and officers can also be held personally liable under a number of statutes, such as statutes enacted to protect consumers or the environment (see Chapters 24 and 25).

See *Concept Summary 19.1* below for a review of the duties and liabilities of directors and officers.

SECTION 6
SHAREHOLDERS

The acquisition of a share of stock makes a person an owner and a shareholder in a corporation. Shareholders thus own the corporation. Although they have no legal title to corporate property, such as buildings and equipment, they do have an equitable (ownership) interest in the firm.

As a general rule, shareholders have no responsibility for the daily management of the corporation,

although they are ultimately responsible for choosing the board of directors, which does have such control. Ordinarily, corporate officers and other employees owe no direct duty to individual shareholders (unless some contract or special relationship exists between them in addition to the corporate relationship). Their duty is to act in the best interests of the corporation and its shareholder-owners *as a whole.* In turn, as you will read later in this chapter, controlling shareholders owe a fiduciary duty to minority shareholders.

Shareholders' Powers

Shareholders' powers may be established in the articles of incorporation and under the state's general corporation law. Shareholders must approve fundamental changes affecting the corporation before the changes can be implemented. Hence, shareholder approval normally is required to amend the articles of incorporation or bylaws, to conduct a merger or dissolve the corporation, and to sell all or substantially all of the corporation's assets. Some of these powers are subject to prior board approval. Shareholder approval may also be requested (though it is not required) for certain other actions, such as to approve an independent auditor.

CONCEPT SUMMARY 19.1
Duties and Liabilities of Directors and Officers

Aspect	Description
Duties of Directors and Officers	1. *Duty of care*—Directors and officers are obligated to act in good faith, to use prudent business judgment in the conduct of corporate affairs, and to act in the corporation's best interests. If a director or officer fails to exercise this duty of care, he or she may be answerable to the corporation and to the shareholders for breaching the duty. The *business judgment rule* immunizes a director from liability for a corporate decision as long as it was within the power of the corporation and the authority of the director to make and was an informed, reasonable, and loyal decision. 2. *Duty of loyalty*—Directors and officers have a fiduciary duty to subordinate their own interests to those of the corporation in matters relating to the corporation. 3. *Conflicts of interest*—To fulfill their duty of loyalty, directors and officers must make a full disclosure of any potential conflicts between their personal interests and those of the corporation.
Liability of Directors and Officers	Corporate directors and officers are personally liable for their own torts and crimes (when not protected under the business judgment rule). Additionally, they may be held personally liable for the torts and crimes committed by corporate personnel under their direct supervision. They may also be held personally liable for violating certain statutes, such as environmental and consumer protection laws, and can sometimes be sued by shareholders for mismanaging the corporation.

Shareholders also have the power to vote to elect or remove members of the board of directors. As described earlier, the first board of directors is either named in the articles of incorporation or chosen by the incorporators to serve until the first shareholders' meeting. From that time on, selection and retention of directors are exclusively shareholder functions.

Directors usually serve their full terms; if the shareholders judge them unsatisfactory, they are simply not reelected. Shareholders have the inherent power, however, to remove a director from office *for cause* (breach of duty or misconduct) by a majority vote.[14] As noted earlier in this chapter, some state statutes (and some articles of incorporation) permit removal of directors without cause by the vote of a majority of the shareholders entitled to vote.[15]

Shareholders' Meetings

Shareholders' meetings must occur at least annually. In addition, special meetings can be called to deal with urgent matters.

A corporation must notify its shareholders of the date, time, and place of an annual or special shareholders' meeting at least ten days, but not more than sixty days, before the meeting date [RMBCA 7.05].[16] (The date and time of the annual meeting can be specified in the bylaws.) Notice of a special meeting must include a statement of the purpose of the meeting, and business transacted at the meeting is limited to that purpose.

PROXIES It usually is not practical for owners of only a few shares of stock of publicly traded corporations to attend a shareholders' meeting. Therefore, the law allows stockholders to appoint another person as their agent to vote their shares at the meeting. The signed appointment form or electronic transmission authorizing an agent to vote the shares is called a **proxy** (from the Latin *procurare,* meaning "to manage or take care of").

Management often solicits proxies, but any person can do so to concentrate voting power. Groups of shareholders have used proxies as a device for taking over a corporation. Proxies normally are revocable (can be withdrawn), unless they are specifically designated as irrevocable and coupled with an interest (such as when the person receiving the proxies from shareholders has agreed to buy their shares). Under RMBCA 7.22(c), proxies are valid for eleven months, unless the proxy agreement mandates a longer period.

SHAREHOLDER PROPOSALS When shareholders want to change a company policy, they can put their ideas up for a shareholder vote. They do this by submitting a shareholder proposal to the board of directors and asking the board to include the proposal in the proxy materials that are sent to all shareholders before meetings.

The Securities and Exchange Commission (SEC), which regulates the purchase and sale of securities (see Chapter 29), has special provisions relating to proxies and shareholder proposals. SEC Rule 14a-8 provides that all shareholders who own stock worth at least $1,000 are eligible to submit proposals for inclusion in corporate proxy materials. The corporation is required to include information on whatever proposals will be considered at the shareholders' meeting along with proxy materials. Only those proposals that relate to significant policy considerations, not ordinary business operations, must be included.

Under the SEC's e-proxy rules,[17] all public companies must post their proxy materials on the Internet and notify shareholders how to find that information. Although the law requires proxy materials to be posted online, public companies may still choose among several options—including paper documents or a DVD sent by mail—for actually delivering the materials to shareholders.

Shareholder Voting

Shareholders exercise ownership control through the power of their votes. Corporate business matters are presented in the form of resolutions, which shareholders vote to approve or disapprove. Unless there is a provision to the contrary, each common shareholder is entitled to one vote per share, although certain voting techniques enhance the power of the shareholder's vote. The articles of incorporation can

14. A director can often demand court review of removal for cause, however.
15. Most states allow *cumulative voting* (on page 438) for directors. If cumulative voting is authorized, a director may not be removed if the number of votes against removal would be sufficient to elect a director under cumulative voting. See, for example, California Corporations Code Section 303A. See also Section 8.08(c) of the RMBCA.
16. The shareholder can waive the requirement of notice by signing a waiver form [RMBCA 7.06]. A shareholder who does not receive notice but who learns of the meeting and attends without protesting the lack of notice is said to have waived notice by such conduct.
17. 17 C.F.R. Parts 240, 249, and 274.

exclude or limit voting rights, particularly for certain classes of shares. For example, owners of preferred shares are usually denied the right to vote [RMBCA 7.21]. If a state statute requires specific voting procedures, the corporation's articles or bylaws must be consistent with the statute.

QUORUM REQUIREMENTS For shareholders to act during a meeting, a quorum must be present. Generally, a quorum exists when shareholders holding more than 50 percent of the outstanding shares are present, but state laws often permit the articles of incorporation to set higher or lower quorum requirements. In some states, obtaining the unanimous written consent of shareholders is a permissible alternative to holding a shareholders' meeting [RMBCA 7.25].

Once a quorum is present, voting can proceed. A straight majority vote of the shares represented at the meeting is usually required to pass resolutions. Assume that Novo Pictures, Inc., has 10,000 outstanding shares of voting stock. Its articles of incorporation set the quorum at 50 percent of outstanding shares and provide that a majority vote of the shares present is necessary to pass ordinary matters. Therefore, for this firm, at the shareholders' meeting, a quorum of stockholders representing 5,000 outstanding shares must be present to conduct business, and a vote of at least 2,501 of those shares is needed to pass ordinary resolutions. Thus, if 6,000 shares are represented, a vote of 3,001 will be necessary.

At times, more than a simple majority vote will be required either by statute or by the articles of incorporation. Extraordinary corporate matters, such as a merger, a consolidation, or dissolution of the corporation, require a higher percentage of all corporate shares entitled to vote, not just a majority of those present at that particular meeting [RMBCA 7.27].

VOTING LISTS The RMBCA requires a corporation to maintain an alphabetical voting list of shareholders. The corporation prepares the voting list before each shareholders' meeting. Ordinarily, only persons whose names appear on the corporation's stockholder records as owners are entitled to vote. The voting list contains the name and address of each shareholder as shown on the corporate records on a given cutoff date, or *record date*. (Under RMBCA 7.07, the bylaws or board of directors may fix a record date that is as much as seventy days before the meeting.) The voting list also includes the number of voting shares held by each owner. The list is usually kept at the corporate headquarters and must be made available for shareholder inspection [RMBCA 7.20].

CUMULATIVE VOTING Most states permit, and many require, shareholders to elect directors by *cumulative voting,* a voting method designed to allow minority shareholders to be represented on the board of directors.[18] With cumulative voting, each shareholder is entitled to a total number of votes equal to the number of board members to be elected multiplied by the number of voting shares that the shareholder owns. The shareholder can cast all of these votes for one candidate or split them among several nominees for director. All nominees stand for election at the same time. When cumulative voting is not required by statute or under the articles, the entire board can be elected by a majority of shares at a shareholders' meeting.

Suppose that a corporation has 10,000 shares issued and outstanding. The minority shareholders hold 3,000 shares, and the majority shareholders hold the other 7,000 shares. Three members of the board are to be elected. The majority shareholders' nominees are Alvarez, Beasley, and Caravel. The minority shareholders' nominee is Dovrik. Can Dovrik be elected to the board by the minority shareholders?

If cumulative voting is allowed, the answer is yes. The minority shareholders have 9,000 votes among them (the number of directors to be elected times the number of shares, or $3 \times 3,000 = 9,000$ votes). All of these votes can be cast to elect Dovrik. The majority shareholders have 21,000 votes ($3 \times 7,000 = 21,000$ votes), but these votes must be distributed among their three nominees. The result of cumulative voting is that no matter how the majority shareholders cast their 21,000 votes, they will not be able to elect all three directors if the minority shareholders cast all of their 9,000 votes for Dovrik, as illustrated in Exhibit 19–2 on the facing page.

OTHER VOTING TECHNIQUES A group of shareholders can agree in writing prior to a shareholders' meeting, in a *shareholder voting agreement,* to vote their shares together in a specified manner. Such agreements usually are held to be valid and enforceable. A shareholder can also appoint a voting agent and vote by proxy, as mentioned previously.

Another technique is for shareholders to enter into a *voting trust.* A **voting trust** is an agreement (a trust contract) under which a shareholder assigns the right to vote his or her shares to a trustee, usually for a specified period of time. The trustee is then

---

18. See, for example, California Corporations Code Section 708. Some states, such as Nebraska, require cumulative voting in their state constitutions. Under RMBCA 7.28, no cumulative voting rights exist unless the articles of incorporation so provide.

EXHIBIT 19-2 • Results of Cumulative Voting

BALLOT	MAJORITY SHAREHOLDER VOTES			MINORITY SHAREHOLDER VOTES	DIRECTORS ELECTED
	Alvarez	*Beasley*	*Caravel*	*Dovrik*	
1	10,000	10,000	1,000	9,000	Alvarez, Beasley, Dovrik
2	9,001	9,000	2,999	9,000	Alvarez, Beasley, Dovrik
3	6,000	7,000	8,000	9,000	Beasley, Caravel, Dovrik

responsible for voting the shares on behalf of all the shareholders in the trust. The shareholder retains all rights of ownership (for example, the right to receive dividend payments) except the power to vote the shares [RMBCA 7.30].

Although shareholders are free to make voting agreements among themselves and with management, corporate managers must be careful that such agreements do not constitute a breach of their fiduciary duties. Agreements regarding voting must be in the corporation's best interests, or the corporate officers and directors can be sued.

CASE IN POINT Several shareholders of Cryo-Cell International, Inc., mounted a proxy contest in an effort to replace the board of directors. Another stockholder, Andrew Filipowski, agreed to support management in exchange for being included in management's slate of directors. The company's chief executive officer, Mercedes Walton, secretly promised Filipowski that if management's slate won, the board of directors would add another board seat to be filled by a Filipowski designee. After management won the election, Walton prepared to add Filipowski's designee to the board. When the dissident shareholders challenged the election results, the court held that the board's actions and Walton's secret agreement constituted serious breaches of fiduciary duty that tainted the election. The court therefore ordered a new election to be held.[19]

Rights of Shareholders

Shareholders possess numerous rights. A significant right—the right to vote their shares—has already been discussed. We look at some additional rights of shareholders in the following subsections.

STOCK CERTIFICATES In the past, corporations commonly issued **stock certificates** that evidenced ownership of a specified number of shares in the corporation. Today, however, most shares of stock are uncertificated—that is, no actual, physical stock certificates are issued [RMBCA 6.26]. Instead, the corporation keeps an official record of its shareholders

---

19. *Portnoy v. Cryo-Cell International, Inc.*, 940 A.2d 43 (Del.Ch. 2008).

and may send each of them a letter or other notice that contains the pertinent information that formerly was included on the face of stock certificates.

Stock is intangible personal property, and the ownership right has always existed independently of any stock certificate. Thus, if a stock certificate was lost or destroyed, ownership was not destroyed with it. A new certificate could be issued to replace the one that was lost or destroyed. Notice of shareholders' meetings, dividends, and operational and financial reports are all distributed according to the recorded ownership listed in the corporation's books, not on the basis of possession of a certificate.

PREEMPTIVE RIGHTS Sometimes, the articles of incorporation grant preemptive rights to shareholders. With **preemptive rights**, a shareholder receives a preference over all other purchasers to subscribe to or purchase a prorated share of a new issue of stock. In other words, the shareholder can purchase a percentage of the new shares that is equal to his or her current percentage of ownership in the corporation.

Under RMBCA 6.30, preemptive rights do not exist unless provided for in the articles of incorporation. Preemptive rights allow each shareholder to maintain her or his proportionate control, voting power, or financial interest in the corporation. Generally, preemptive rights apply only to additional, newly issued stock sold for cash, and the preemptive rights must be exercised within a specified time period, which usually is thirty days.

Preemptive rights are most important in closely held corporations because each shareholder owns a relatively small number of shares but controls a substantial interest in the corporation. Without preemptive rights, it would be possible for a shareholder to lose his or her proportionate control over the firm.

STOCK WARRANTS **Stock warrants** are rights to buy stock at a stated price by a specified date that are given by the company. Usually, when preemptive rights exist and a corporation is issuing additional shares, it gives its shareholders stock warrants. Warrants are often publicly traded on securities exchanges.

DIVIDENDS A **dividend** is a distribution of corporate profits or income *ordered by the directors* and paid to the shareholders in proportion to their respective shares in the corporation. Dividends can be paid in cash, property, stock of the corporation that is paying the dividends, or stock of other corporations.[20]

State laws vary, but each state determines the general circumstances and legal requirements under which dividends are paid. State laws also control the sources of revenue to be used. Only certain funds are legally available for paying dividends. Once declared, a cash dividend becomes a corporate debt enforceable at law like any other debt. Depending on state law, dividends may be paid from the following sources:

1. *Retained earnings.* All states allow dividends to be paid from the undistributed net profits earned by the corporation, including capital gains from the sale of fixed assets.
2. *Net profits.* A few states allow dividends to be issued from current net profits without regard to deficits in prior years.
3. *Surplus.* A number of states allow dividends to be paid out of any kind of surplus.

Illegal Dividends. Sometimes, dividends are improperly paid from an unauthorized account, or their payment causes the corporation to become insolvent. Generally, shareholders must return illegal dividends only if they knew that the dividends were illegal when the payment was received (or if the dividends were paid when the corporation was insolvent). Whenever dividends are illegal or improper, the board of directors can be held personally liable for the amount of the payment.

Failure to Declare a Dividend. When directors fail to declare a dividend, shareholders can ask a court to compel the directors to meet and declare a dividend. To succeed, the shareholders must show that the directors have acted so unreasonably in withholding the dividend that their conduct is an abuse of their discretion.

Often, a corporation accumulates large cash reserves for a legitimate corporate purpose, such as expansion or research. The mere fact that the firm has sufficient earnings or surplus available to pay a dividend normally is not enough to compel the directors to distribute funds that, in the board's opinion, should not be distributed. The courts are reluctant to interfere with corporate operations and will not compel directors to declare dividends unless abuse of discretion is clearly shown.

INSPECTION RIGHTS Shareholders in a corporation enjoy both common law and statutory inspection rights. The RMBCA provides that every shareholder is entitled to examine specified corporate records, including voting lists [RMBCA 7.20, 16.02]. The shareholder's right of inspection is limited, however, to the inspection and copying of corporate books and records for a *proper purpose,* and the request to inspect must be made in advance. The shareholder may inspect in person, or an attorney, accountant, or other authorized assistant can do so as the shareholder's agent.

The power of inspection is fraught with potential abuses, and the corporation is allowed to protect itself from them. For example, a shareholder can properly be denied access to corporate records to prevent harassment or to protect trade secrets or other confidential corporate information. Some states require that a shareholder must have held her or his shares for a minimum period of time immediately preceding the demand to inspect or must hold a minimum number of outstanding shares. A shareholder who is denied the right of inspection can seek a court order to compel the inspection.

CASE IN POINT Craig Johnson was the sole officer and director and the majority shareholder of Distributed Solutions, Inc. (DSI), which provided consulting services, including payroll services. Jeffrey Hagen was a minority shareholder. Johnson sold DSI's payroll services to himself and set up another payroll services company. Although DSI revenues had been $739,034 and $934,532 the two previous years, the following year all of DSI's assets were sold. Johnson told Hagen that he was dissolving the firm because it conducted no business and had no future prospects. Hagen asked to inspect the corporate records so that he could determine DSI's financial condition, the value of its stock, and whether any misconduct had occurred. When there was no response, Hagen filed a lawsuit to compel the inspection. An Illinois appellate court found that Hagen had shown a proper purpose and allowed him access to DSI's records.[21]

TRANSFER OF SHARES Corporate stock represents an ownership right in intangible personal property. The law generally recognizes the right of an owner to transfer property to another person unless there are valid restrictions on its transferability. When shares are transferred, a new entry is made in the corporate stock book to indicate the new owner. Until the corporation is notified and the entry is complete, all rights—including voting rights, notice of shareholders' meetings,

---

20. On one occasion, a distillery declared and paid a dividend in bonded whiskey.

21. *Hagen v. Distributed Solutions, Inc.,* 328 Ill.App.3d 132, 764 N.E.2d 1141, 262 Ill.Dec. 24 (1 Dist. 2002).

and the right to dividend distributions—remain with the current record owner.

RIGHTS ON DISSOLUTION When a corporation is dissolved and its outstanding debts and the claims of its creditors have been satisfied, the remaining assets are distributed to the shareholders in proportion to the percentage of shares owned by each shareholder. The articles of incorporation may provide that certain classes of preferred stock will be given priority. If no class of stock has been given preference in the distribution of assets, all of the stockholders share the remaining assets.

THE SHAREHOLDER'S DERIVATIVE SUIT When the corporation is harmed by the actions of a third party, the directors can bring a lawsuit in the name of the corporation against that party. If the corporate directors fail to bring a lawsuit, shareholders can do so "derivatively" in what is known as a **shareholder's derivative suit.** Before shareholders can bring a derivative suit, they must submit a written demand to the corporation, asking the board of directors to take appropriate action [RMBCA 7.40]. The directors then have ninety days in which to act. Only if they refuse to do so can the derivative suit go forward.

The right of shareholders to bring a derivative action is especially important when the wrong suffered by the corporation results from the actions of the corporate directors and officers—because they, for obvious reasons, would probably be unwilling to take any action against themselves. Nevertheless, a court will dismiss a derivative suit if a majority of the directors or an independent panel determines in good faith that the lawsuit is not in the best interests of the corporation [RMBCA 7.44].

When shareholders bring a derivative suit, they are not pursuing rights or benefits for themselves personally but are acting as guardians of the corporate entity. Therefore, if the suit is successful, any damages recovered normally go into the corporation's treasury, not to the shareholders personally.

Liabilities of Shareholders

One of the hallmarks of the corporate form of organization is that shareholders are not personally liable for the debts of the corporation. If the corporation fails, the shareholders can lose their investments, but that generally is the limit of their liability. As previously discussed, in certain instances of fraud, undercapitalization, or careless observance of corporate formalities, a court will pierce the corporate veil and hold the shareholders

individually liable. But these situations are the exception, not the rule.

A shareholder also can be personally liable in certain other rare instances. One relates to illegal dividends, which were discussed previously. Another relates to watered stock. Still another concerns the fiduciary duty that majority shareholders owe to minority shareholders.

WATERED STOCK When a corporation issues shares for less than their fair market value, the shares are referred to as **watered stock.**[22] Usually, the shareholder who receives watered stock must pay the difference to the corporation (the shareholder is personally liable). In some states, the shareholder who receives watered stock may be liable to creditors of the corporation for unpaid corporate debts.

For example, during the formation of a corporation, Gomez, one of the incorporators, transfers his property, Sunset Beach, to the corporation for 10,000 shares of stock at a par value of $100 per share for a total price of $1 million. After the property is transferred and the shares are issued, Sunset Beach is carried on the corporate books at a value of $1 million. On appraisal, it is discovered that the market value of the property at the time of transfer was only $500,000. The shares issued to Gomez are therefore watered stock, and he is liable to the corporation for the difference between the value of the shares and the value of the property.

BREACH OF FIDUCIARY DUTY In some instances, a majority shareholder is regarded as having a fiduciary duty to the corporation and to the minority shareholders. This duty occurs when a single shareholder (or a few shareholders acting in concert) owns a sufficient number of shares to exercise *de facto* (actual) control over the corporation. In these situations, the majority shareholder owes a fiduciary duty to the minority shareholders.

When a majority shareholder breaches her or his fiduciary duty to a minority shareholder, the minority shareholder can sue for damages. A breach of fiduciary duties by those who control a closely held corporation normally constitutes what is known as *oppressive conduct.* A common example of a breach of fiduciary duty occurs when the majority shareholders "freeze out" the minority shareholders and exclude them from certain benefits of participating in the firm.

---

22. The phrase *watered stock* was originally used to describe cattle that were kept thirsty during a long drive and then were allowed to drink large quantities of water just before their sale. The increased weight of the watered stock allowed the seller to reap a higher profit.

MAJOR BUSINESS FORMS COMPARED

As mentioned in Chapter 17, when deciding which form of business organization to choose, business-persons normally consider several factors. These factors include the ease of creation, the liability of the owners, tax considerations, and the ability to raise capital. Each major form of business organization offers distinct advantages and disadvantages with respect to these and other factors.

Exhibit 19–3 below and on the facing page summarizes the essential advantages and disadvantages of each of the forms of business organization discussed in Unit Four.

EXHIBIT 19–3 • Major Forms of Business Compared

CHARACTERISTIC	SOLE PROPRIETORSHIP	PARTNERSHIP	CORPORATION
Method of Creation	Created at will by owner.	Created by agreement of the parties.	Authorized by the state under the state's corporation law.
Legal Position	Not a separate entity; owner is the business.	A traditional partnership is a separate legal entity in most states.	Always a legal entity separate and distinct from its owners—a legal fiction for the purposes of owning property and being a party to litigation.
Liability	Unlimited liability.	Unlimited liability.	Limited liability of shareholders—shareholders are not liable for the debts of the corporation.
Duration	Determined by owner; automatically dissolved on owner's death.	Terminated by agreement of the partners, but can continue to do business even when a partner dissociates from the partnership.	Can have perpetual existence.
Transferability of Interest	Interest can be transferred, but individual's proprietorship then ends.	Although partnership interest can be assigned, assignee does not have full rights of a partner.	Shares of stock can be transferred.
Management	Completely at owner's discretion.	Each partner has a direct and equal voice in management unless expressly agreed otherwise in the partnership agreement.	Shareholders elect directors, who set policy and appoint officers.
Taxation	Owner pays personal taxes on business income.	Each partner pays pro rata share of income taxes on net profits, whether or not they are distributed.	Double taxation—corporation pays income tax on net profits, with no deduction for dividends, and shareholders pay income tax on disbursed dividends they receive.
Organizational Fees, Annual License Fees, and Annual Reports	None or minimal.	None or minimal.	All required.
Transaction of Business in Other States	Generally no limitation.	Generally no limitation.[a]	Normally must qualify to do business and obtain certificate of authority.

a. A few states have enacted statutes requiring that foreign partnerships qualify to do business within the state.

EXHIBIT 19-3 • Major Forms of Business Compared—Continued

CHARACTERISTIC	LIMITED PARTNERSHIP	LIMITED LIABILITY COMPANY	LIMITED LIABILITY PARTNERSHIP
Method of Creation	Created by agreement to carry on a business for profit. At least one party must be a general partner and the other(s) limited partner(s). Certificate of limited partnership is filed. Charter must be issued by the state.	Created by an agreement of the member-owners of the company. Articles of organization are filed. Charter must be issued by the state.	Created by agreement of the partners. A statement of qualification for the limited liability partnership is filed.
Legal Position	Treated as a legal entity.	Treated as a legal entity.	Generally, treated same as a traditional partnership.
Liability	Unlimited liability of all general partners; limited partners are liable only to the extent of their capital contributions.	Member-owners' liability is limited to the amount of their capital contributions or investments.	Varies, but under the Uniform Partnership Act, liability of a partner for acts committed by other partners is limited.
Duration	By agreement in certificate, or by termination of the last general partner (retirement, death, and the like) or last limited partner.	Unless a single-member LLC, can have perpetual existence (same as a corporation).	Remains in existence until cancellation or revocation.
Transferability of Interest	Interest can be assigned (same as in a traditional partnership), but if assignee becomes a member with consent of other partners, certificate must be amended.	Member interests are freely transferable.	Interest can be assigned same as in a traditional partnership.
Management	General partners have equal voice or by agreement. Limited partners may not retain limited liability if they actively participate in management.	Member-owners can fully participate in management or can designate a group of persons to manage on behalf of the members.	Same as in a traditional partnership.
Taxation	Generally taxed as a partnership.	LLC is not taxed, and members are taxed personally on profits "passed through" the LLC.	Same as in a traditional partnership.
Organizational Fees, Annual License Fees, and Annual Reports	Organizational fee required; others not usually required.	Organizational fee required; others vary with states.	Fees are set by each state for filing statements of qualification, statements of foreign qualification, and annual reports.
Transaction of Business in Other States	Generally no limitation.	Generally no limitation, but may vary depending on state.	Must file a statement of foreign qualification before doing business in another state.

REVIEWING
Corporations

David Brock is on the board of directors of Firm Body Fitness, Inc., which owns a string of fitness clubs in New Mexico. Brock owns 15 percent of the Firm Body stock and is also employed as a tanning technician at one of the fitness clubs. After the January financial report showed that Firm Body's tanning division was operating at a substantial net loss, the board of directors, led by Marty Levinson, discussed the possibility of terminating the tanning operations. Brock successfully convinced a majority of the board that the tanning division was necessary to market the clubs' overall fitness package. By April, the tanning division's financial losses had risen. The board hired a business analyst, who conducted surveys and determined that the tanning operations did not significantly increase membership. A shareholder, Diego Peñada, discovered that Brock owned stock in Sunglow, Inc., the company from which Firm Body purchased its tanning equipment. Peñada notified Levinson, who privately reprimanded Brock. Shortly thereafter, Brock and Mandy Vail, who owned 37 percent of the Firm Body stock and also held shares of Sunglow, voted to replace Levinson on the board of directors. Using the information presented in the chapter, answer the following questions.

1. What duties did Brock, as a director, owe to Firm Body?
2. Does the fact that Brock owned shares in Sunglow establish a conflict of interest? Why or why not?
3. Suppose that Firm Body brought an action against Brock claiming that he had breached the duty of loyalty by not disclosing his interest in Sunglow to the other directors. What theory might Brock use in his defense?
4. Now suppose that Firm Body did not bring an action against Brock. What type of lawsuit might Peñada be able to bring based on these facts?

DEBATE THIS: *Because most shareholders never bother to vote for directors, shareholders have no real control over corporations.*

TERMS AND CONCEPTS

alien corporation 420
articles of incorporation 423
business judgment rule 433
bylaws 423
closely held corporation 420
commingle 427

dividend 440
domestic corporation 420
foreign corporation 420
holding company 418
inside director 431
outside director 431
pierce the corporate veil 427
preemptive rights 439

proxy 437
public corporation 420
publicly held
 corporation 420
quorum 431
retained earnings 418
S corporation 421

shareholder's derivative
 suit 441
stock certificate 439
stock warrant 439
ultra vires 427
voting trust 438
watered stock 441

QUESTIONS AND CASE PROBLEMS

19–1. Incorporation Jonathan, Gary, and Ricardo are active members of a partnership called Swim City. The partnership manufactures, sells, and installs outdoor swimming pools in the states of Arkansas and Texas. The partners want to continue to be active in management and to expand the business into other states as well. They are also concerned about rather large recent judgments entered against swimming

pool companies throughout the United States. Based on these facts only, discuss whether the partnership should incorporate.

19–2. QUESTION WITH SAMPLE ANSWER: Liability of Directors.

AstroStar, Inc., has approximately five hundred shareholders. Its board of directors consists of three members (Eckhart, Dolan, and

Macero). At a regular board meeting, the board selects Galiard as president of the corporation by a two-to-one vote, with Eckhart dissenting. The minutes of the meeting do not register Eckhart's dissenting vote. Later, an audit reveals that Galiard is a former convict and has embezzled $500,000 from the corporation that is not covered by insurance. Can the corporation hold directors Eckhart, Dolan, and Macero personally liable? Discuss.

• **For a sample answer to Question 19–2, go to Appendix F at the end of this text.**

19–3. Conflicts of Interest Oxy Corp. is negotiating with Wick Construction Co. for renovation of Oxy's corporate headquarters. Wick, the owner of Wick Construction Co., is also one of the five members of Oxy's board of directors. The contract terms are standard for this type of contract. Wick has previously informed two of the other directors of his interest in the construction company. Oxy's board approves the contract by a three-to-two vote, with Wick voting with the majority. Discuss whether this contract is binding on the corporation.

19–4. Duties of Majority Shareholders Steve and Marie Venturini were involved in the operation of Steve's Sizzling Steakhouse in Carlstadt, New Jersey, from the day their parents opened it in the 1930s. By the 1980s, Steve, Marie, and her husband, Joe, were running it. The business was a corporation with Steve and Marie each owning half of the stock. Steve died in 2001, leaving his stock in equal shares to his sons Steve and Gregg. Son Steve had never worked there. Gregg had done occasional maintenance work until his father's death. Despite their lack of participation, the sons were paid more than $750 per week each. In 2002, Marie's son Blaise, who had obtained a college degree in restaurant management while working part-time at the steakhouse, took over its management. When his cousins became threatening, he denied them access to the business and its books. Marie refused Gregg and Steve's offer of about $1.4 million for her stock in the restaurant, and they refused her offer of about $800,000 for theirs. They filed a suit in a New Jersey state court against her, claiming, among other things, a breach of fiduciary duty. Should the court order the aunt to buy out the nephews or the nephews to buy out the aunt, or neither? Why? [*Venturini v. Steve's Steakhouse, Inc.,* __ N.J.Super. __, __ A.2d __ (Ch.Div. 2006)]

19–5. Role of Directors The board of directors of Necanicum Investment Co., a property management corporation in Oregon, meets on a regular basis. Necanicum paid the directors $6,000 each in the third quarter of 2003. It did not report the payments as part of its payroll and did not pay unemployment tax on the payments. The Oregon Employment Department contended that the company owed $700 in unemployment taxes on the payments to the directors. Necanicum protested. The administrative law judge (ALJ) for the Employment Department held that the company owed the taxes because directors' fees are the same as wages for unemployment tax purposes.

Necanicum appealed, but the court of appeals affirmed the ALJ's ruling. The company appealed again. Are payments to directors the same as wages for tax purposes? Why or why not? [*Necanicum Investment Co. v. Employment Department,* 345 Or. 138, 190 P.3d 368 (2008)]

19–6. Duties of Directors and Officers First Niles Financial, Inc., is a company whose sole business is to own and operate a bank, Home Federal Savings and Loan Association of Niles, Ohio. First Niles's directors included bank officers William Stephens, Daniel Csontos, and Lawrence Safarek; James Kramer, president of an air-conditioning company that serviced the bank; and Ralph Zuzolo, whose law firm served the bank and whose title company participated in most of its real estate deals. First Niles's board put the bank up for sale and received three bids. Farmers National Bank Corp. stated that it would not retain the board. Cortland Bancorp indicated that it would terminate the directors but consider them for future service. First Financial Corp. said nothing about the directors. The board did not pursue Farmers' offer, failed to timely respond to Cortland's request, and rejected First Financial's bid. Leonard Gantler and other First Niles shareholders filed a suit in a Delaware state court against Stephens and the others. What duties do directors and officers owe to a corporation and its shareholders? How might those duties have been breached here? Discuss. [*Gantler v. Stephens,* 965 A.2d 695 (Del. Sup.Ct. 2009)]

19–7. CASE PROBLEM WITH SAMPLE ANSWER: Piercing the Corporate Veil.

Smith Services, Inc., was a corporation solely owned by Tony Smith. Bear, Inc., owned and operated Laker Express, a fueling station in Kentucky. Smith charged fuel to an account at Laker Express and owed approximately $35,000. There was no written agreement indicating who was liable on the account in the event of default, but all invoices had been issued to Smith Services. Smith later dissolved Smith Services and continued to run his business as a sole proprietorship. When Laker Express sued Smith Services to collect on the debt, there were no assets in the corporation. Laker Express sued Tony Smith personally and asked the court to pierce the corporate veil, claiming that Smith was engaged in fraud and was using the corporate form only to protect himself. The trial court dismissed the case, and Laker Express appealed. Should the court pierce the corporate veil and hold Smith personally liable for the unpaid corporate debt? Why or why not? Or should Laker Express have been more careful when dealing with clients? Explain. [*Bear, Inc. v. Smith,* 303 S.W.3d 137 (Ky.App. 2010)]

• **To view a sample answer for Problem 19–7, go to this book's Web site at www.cengage.com/blaw/cross, select "Chapter 19," and click on "Case Problem with Sample Answer."**

19–8. Fiduciary Duty of Officers Designer Surfaces, Inc., supplied countertops to homeowners who shopped at stores such as Lowe's and Costco. The homeowners paid the store, which then contracted with Designer to fabricate and install the countertops. Designer bought materials from Arizona Tile, LLC, on an open account. Designer's only known corporate officers were Howard Berger and John McCarthy. Designer became insolvent and could not pay Arizona Tile for all the materials it had purchased, including materials for which Designer had already received payment from the retail stores. Arizona Tile sued Designer and won a default judgment, but the company had no funds. Arizona Tile then sued Berger and McCarthy personally for diverting company funds that Designer had received in trust for payment to Arizona Tile. Arizona Tile argued that the use of the funds for other purposes was a breach of fiduciary duty. Berger and McCarthy argued that corporate law imposed neither a fiduciary duty on corporate officers nor personal liability for breach of a duty to suppliers of materials. Which argument is more credible and why? [*Arizona Tile, LLC v. Berger*, 223 Ariz. 491, 224 P.3d 988 (Ariz.App. 2010)]

19–9. A QUESTION OF ETHICS: Improper Incorporation.

Mike Lyons incorporated Lyons Concrete, Inc., in Montana, but did not file its first annual report, so the state involuntarily dissolved the firm in 1996. Unaware of the dissolution, Lyons continued to do business as Lyons Concrete. In 2003, he signed a written contract with William Weimar to form and pour a certain amount of concrete on Weimar's property in Lake County for $19,810. Weimar was in a rush to complete the entire project, and he and Lyons orally agreed to additional work on a time-and-materials basis. When scheduling conflicts arose, Weimar had his own employees set some of the forms, which proved deficient. Weimar also directed Lyons to pour concrete in the rain, which undercut its quality. In mid-project, Lyons submitted an invoice for $14,389, which Weimar paid. After the work was complete, Lyons sent Weimar an invoice for $25,731, but Weimar refused to pay, claiming that the $14,389 covered everything. To recover the unpaid amount, Lyons filed a mechanic's lien as "Mike Lyons d/b/a Lyons Concrete, Inc." against Weimar's property. Weimar filed a suit in a Montana state court to strike the lien, and Lyons filed a counterclaim to reassert it. [Weimar v. Lyons, *338 Mont. 242, 164 P.3d 922 (2007)]*

(a) Before the trial, Weimar asked for a change of venue on the ground that a sign on the courthouse lawn advertised "Lyons Concrete." How might the sign affect a trial on the parties' dispute? Should the court grant this request? Why or why not?

(b) Weimar asked the court to dismiss the counterclaim on the ground that the state had dissolved Lyons Concrete in 1996. Lyons immediately filed new articles of incorporation for "Lyons Concrete, Inc." Under what doctrine might the court rule that Weimar could not deny the existence of Lyons Concrete? What ethical values underlie this doctrine? Should the court make this ruling? Explain.

(c) At the trial, Weimar argued, in part, that there was no "fixed price" contract between the parties and that even if there were, the poor quality of the work, which required repairs, amounted to a breach, excusing Weimar's further performance. Should the court rule in Weimar's favor on this basis? Why or why not?

19–10. VIDEO QUESTION: Corporation versus LLC.

Go to this text's Web site at **www.cengage.com/blaw/cross** and select "Chapter 19." Click on "Video Questions" and view the video titled *Corporation or LLC: Which Is Better?* Then answer the following questions.

(a) Compare the liability that Anna and Caleb would be exposed to as shareholders/owners of a corporation versus as members of an LLC.

(b) How does the taxation of corporations and LLCs differ?

(c) Given that Anna and Caleb conduct their business (Wizard Internet) over the Internet, can you think of any drawbacks to forming an LLC? Discuss fully.

(d) If you were in Anna and Caleb's position, would you choose to create a corporation or an LLC? Why?

LEGAL RESEARCH EXERCISES ON THE WEB

Go to this text's Web site at **www.cengage.com/blaw/cross**, select "Chapter 19," and click on "Practical Internet Exercises." There you will find the following Internet research exercises that you can perform to learn more about the topics covered in this chapter.

Practical Internet Exercise 19–1: **Legal Perspective**
Liability of Directors and Officers

Practical Internet Exercise 19–2: **Management Perspective**
Online Incorporation

In Chapter 4, we examined the importance of ethical standards in the business context. We also offered suggestions on how business decision makers can create an ethical workplace. Here, we look at selected areas in which the relationships within specific business organizational forms may raise ethical issues.

Fiduciary Duties of All Partners and Corporate Directors

The law of agency, which will be outlined in Chapter 20, permeates nearly all relationships within any partnership or corporation. An important duty that arises in the law of agency, and applies to all partners and corporate directors, officers, and management personnel, is the duty of loyalty. As caretakers of the shareholders' wealth, corporate directors and officers also have a fiduciary duty to exercise care when making decisions affecting the corporate enterprise.

The Duty of Loyalty   Every individual has his or her own personal interests, which may at times conflict with the interests of the partnership or corporation with which he or she is affiliated. In particular, a partner or a corporate director may face a conflict between personal interests and the interests of the business entity. Corporate officers and directors may find themselves in a position to acquire assets that would also benefit the corporation if acquired in the corporation's name. If an officer does purchase the asset without offering the opportunity to the corporation, however, she or he may be liable for usurping a corporate opportunity.[1]

Most courts also hold that a corporate officer or director has a fiduciary duty to disclose improper conduct to the corporation. The Supreme Court of Arkansas weighed in on this issue in 2007. Thomas Coughlin was a top executive in theft prevention at Wal-Mart who held several other high-level positions prior to becoming a member of the corporation's board of directors. He retired in 2005 and entered into a retirement agreement and release of claims with Wal-Mart under which he was to receive millions of dollars in benefits over the years.

Then Wal-Mart discovered that Coughlin, before his retirement, had abused his position of authority and conspired with subordinates to misappropriate hundreds of thousands of dollars in property and cash through various fraudulent schemes. Wal-Mart filed a lawsuit alleging that Coughlin had breached his fiduciary duty of loyalty by failing to disclose his misconduct before entering a self-dealing contract. Ultimately, the state's highest court agreed and held that the director's fiduciary duty obligated him to divulge material facts of *past* fraud to the corporation before entering the contract. The court stated, "We are persuaded, in addition, that the majority view is correct, which is that the failure of a fiduciary to disclose material facts of his fraudulent conduct to his corporation prior to entering into a self-dealing contract with that corporation will void that contract."[2]

The Duty of Care   In addition to the duty of loyalty, every corporate director or officer owes a duty of care. *Due care* means that officers and directors must keep themselves informed and make businesslike judgments. Officers have a duty to disclose material information that shareholders need for competent decision making. Some courts have even suggested that corporate directors have a duty to detect and "ferret out" wrongdoing within the corporation.[3] In fact, a number of courts applying Delaware law have recognized that directors may be held liable for failing to exercise proper oversight.[4] For example, in 2009 a Delaware court held that shareholders of Citigroup, Inc., could sue the directors and officers for failure to exercise due care to adequately protect the corporation from exposure to the subprime lending market.[5] Corporate law also creates other structures to protect shareholder interests, such as the right to inspect books and records.

Although traditionally the duty of care did not require directors to monitor the behavior of corporate employees to detect and prevent wrongdoing, the tide may be changing. Since the corporate sentencing guidelines were issued in 1991, courts have had the power to impose substantial penalties on corporations and corporate directors for criminal wrongdoing. The guidelines allow these penalties to be mitigated, though, if a company can show that it has an effective compliance program in place to detect and prevent wrongdoing by corporate personnel. Since the Sarbanes-Oxley Act of 2002 required the sentencing commission to revise these guidelines, the penalties for white-collar crimes, such as federal mail and wire fraud, have increased dramatically.

---

1. For a landmark case on this issue, see *Guth v. Loft, Inc.*, 5 A.2d 503 (Del. 1939), presented as Case 19.3 on pages 434 and 435.

2. *Wal-Mart Stores, Inc. v. Coughlin*, 369 Ark. 365, 255 S.W.3d 424 (2007); also see *Blankenship v. USA Truck, Inc.*, 601 F.3d 852 (8th Cir. 2010) interpreting Arkansas law by applying the *Wal-Mart* case.

3. *In re Caremark International, Inc. Derivative Litigation*, 698 A.2d 959 (Del.Ch. 1996); also *Forsythe v. ESC Fund Management Co. (U.S.), Inc.*, 2007 WL 2982247 (Del.Ch. 2007).

4. See, for example, *McCall v. Scott*, 239 F.3d 808 (6th Cir. 2001); *Guttman v. Huang*, 823 A.2d 492 (Del.Ch. 2003); *Landy v. D'Alessandro*, 316 F.Supp.2d 49 (D.Mass. 2004); and *Miller v. U.S. Foodservice, Inc.*, 361 F.Supp.2d 470 (D.Md. 2005).

5. *In re Citigroup, Inc., Shareholder Derivative Litigation*, 964 A.2d 106 (Del.Ch. 2009).

FOCUS ON ETHICS CONTINUES ➡

Fiduciary Duties to Creditors   It is a long-standing principle that corporate directors ordinarily owe fiduciary duties only to a corporation's shareholders. Directors who favor the interests of other corporate "stakeholders," such as creditors, over those of the shareholders have been held liable for breaching these duties. The picture changes, however, when a corporation approaches insolvency. At this point, the shareholders' equity interests in the corporation may be worthless, while the interests of creditors become paramount. In this situation, do the fiduciary duties of loyalty and care extend to the corporation's creditors as well as to the shareholders? The answer to this question, according to some courts, is yes. In a leading case on this issue, a Delaware court noted that "the possibility of insolvency can do curious things to incentives, exposing creditors to risks of opportunistic behavior and creating complexities for directors." The court held that when a corporation is on the brink of insolvency, the directors assume a fiduciary duty to other stakeholders that sustain the corporate entity, including creditors.[6] When a corporation is insolvent, courts often require directors to consider the best interests of the whole corporate enterprise—including all its constituent groups—and not to give preference to the interests of any one group.[7]

---

6. *Credit Lyonnais Bank Nederland N.V. v. Pathe Communications Corp.,* 1991 WL 277613 (Del.Ch. 1991). See also *Production Resources Group, LLC v. NCT Group, Inc.,* 863 A.2d 772 (Del.Ch. 2004); and *In re Amcast Industrial Corp.,* 365 Bankr. 91 (S.D. Ohio 2007).

7. See *Berg & Berg Enterprises, LLC v. Boyle,* 178 Cal.App.4th 1020, 100 Cal.Rptr.3d 875 (2009).

Franchise Relationships

Franchise relationships can create significant ethical issues. One issue has to do with the franchisor's quality control over the franchisee's activities. On the one hand, if the franchisor ignores the problem of quality control, the reputation of the franchisor's business may suffer. On the other hand, if a franchisor's control over the operations of the franchisee is too extensive, the franchisor may be liable for the torts of the franchisee's employees under agency theory (see Chapter 20). Even when an independent business entity purchases a franchise and the franchise agreement specifies that no agency relationship exists, the courts may find otherwise.

DISCUSSION QUESTIONS

1. Do you agree that when a corporation is approaching insolvency, the directors' fiduciary obligations should extend to the corporation's creditors as well as to the shareholders? In this situation, should the fiduciary duties owed to creditors take priority over the duties to shareholders? Why or why not?

2. As explained, if a franchisor exercises "too much control" over a franchisee's business operations, a court may deem the franchisor to be liable as an employer for the torts committed by the franchisee's employees. How can holding franchisors liable in such circumstances be squared with the doctrine of *freedom of contract* (see pages 199 and 374)?

UNIT FIVE

THE EMPLOYMENT ENVIRONMENT

CONTENTS

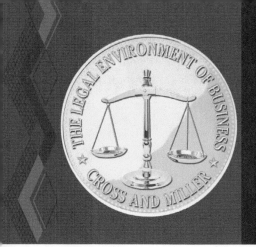

CHAPTER 20
✸
Agency

One of the more common, important, and pervasive legal relationships is that of **agency.** In an agency relationship involving two parties, one of the parties, called the *agent,* agrees to represent or act for the other, called the *principal.* The principal has the right to control the agent's conduct in matters entrusted to the agent. By using agents, a principal can conduct multiple business operations simultaneously in various locations. Thus, for example, contracts that bind the principal can be made at different places with different persons at the same time.

A familiar example of an agent is a corporate officer who serves in a representative capacity for the owners of the corporation. In this capacity, the officer has the authority to bind the principal (the corporation) to a contract. In fact, agency law is essential to the existence and operation of a corporate entity because only through its agents can a corporation function and enter into contracts.

Most employees are also considered to be agents of their employers. Thus, some of the concepts of employment law that you will learn about in Chapters 21 and 22 are based on agency law. Indeed, agency relationships permeate the business world. For that reason, an understanding of the law of agency is crucial to understanding business law.

SECTION 1
AGENCY RELATIONSHIPS

Section 1(1) of the *Restatement (Third) of Agency*[1] defines *agency* as "the fiduciary relation [that] results from the manifestation of consent by one person to another that the other shall act in his [or her] behalf and subject to his [or her] control, and consent by the other so to act." In other words, in a principal-agent relationship, the parties have agreed that the agent will act *on behalf and instead of* the principal in negotiating and transacting business with third parties.

The term **fiduciary** is at the heart of agency law. This term can be used both as a noun and as an adjective. When used as a noun, it refers to a person having a duty created by his or her undertaking to act primarily for another's benefit in matters connected with the undertaking. When used as an adjective, as

in the phrase *fiduciary relationship,* it means that the relationship involves trust and confidence.

Agency relationships commonly exist between employers and employees. Agency relationships may sometimes also exist between employers and independent contractors who are hired to perform special tasks or services.

Employer-Employee Relationships

Normally, all employees who deal with third parties are deemed to be agents. A salesperson in a department store, for instance, is an agent of the store's owner (the principal) and acts on the owner's behalf. Any sale of goods made by the salesperson to a customer is binding on the principal. Similarly, most representations of fact made by the salesperson with respect to the goods sold are binding on the principal.

Because employees who deal with third parties generally are deemed to be agents of their employers, agency law and employment law overlap considerably. Agency relationships, though, can exist outside an employer-employee relationship, and

---

1. The *Restatement (Third) of Agency* is an authoritative summary of the law of agency and is often referred to by judges in their decisions and opinions.

thus agency law has a broader reach than employment law does.

Employment laws (state and federal) apply only to the employer-employee relationship. Statutes governing Social Security, withholding taxes, workers' compensation, unemployment compensation, workplace safety, employment discrimination, and other aspects of employment (see Chapters 21 and 22) are applicable only when an employer-employee relationship exists. *These laws do not apply to an independent contractor.*

Employer–Independent Contractor Relationships

Independent contractors are not employees because, by definition, those who hire them have no control over the details of their work performance. Section 2 of the *Restatement (Third) of Agency* defines an **independent contractor** as follows:

> [An independent contractor is] a person who contracts with another to do something for him [or her] but who is not controlled by the other nor subject to the other's right to control with respect to his [or her] physical conduct in the performance of the undertaking. He [or she] may or may not be an agent.

Building contractors and subcontractors are independent contractors; a property owner who hires a contractor and subcontractors to complete a project does not control the details of the way they perform their work. Truck drivers who own their vehicles and hire out on a per-job basis are independent contractors, but truck drivers who drive company trucks on a regular basis usually are employees.

The relationship between a principal and an independent contractor may or may not involve an agency relationship. To illustrate: An owner of real estate who hires a real estate broker to negotiate the sale of her property not only has contracted with an independent contractor (the real estate broker) but also has established an agency relationship for the specific purpose of selling the property. Another example is an insurance agent, who is both an independent contractor and an agent of the insurance company for which he or she sells policies. (Note that an insurance *broker,* in contrast, normally is an agent of the person obtaining insurance and not of the insurance company.)

Determination of Employee Status

The courts are frequently asked to determine whether a particular worker is an employee or an independent contractor. How a court decides this issue can have a significant effect on the rights and liabilities of the parties. For example, employers are required to pay certain taxes, such as Social Security and unemployment taxes, for employees but not for independent contractors.

CRITERIA USED BY THE COURTS In deciding whether a worker is categorized as an employee or an independent contractor, courts often consider the following questions:

1. How much control does the employer exercise over the details of the work? (If the employer exercises considerable control over the details of the work and the day-to-day activities of the worker, this indicates employee status. This is perhaps the most important factor weighed by the courts in determining employee status.)
2. Is the worker engaged in an occupation or business distinct from that of the employer? (If so, this points to independent-contractor, not employee, status.)
3. Is the work usually done under the employer's direction or by a specialist without supervision? (If the work is usually done under the employer's direction, this indicates employee status.)
4. Does the employer supply the tools at the place of work? (If so, this indicates employee status.)
5. For how long is the person employed? (If the person is employed for a long period of time, this indicates employee status.)
6. What is the method of payment—by time period or at the completion of the job? (Payment by time period, such as once every two weeks or once a month, indicates employee status.)
7. What degree of skill is required of the worker? (If a great degree of skill is required, this may indicate that the person is an independent contractor hired for a specialized job and not an employee.)

Sometimes, workers may benefit from having employee status—for tax purposes and to be protected under certain employment laws, for example. As mentioned earlier, federal statutes governing employment discrimination apply only when an employer-employee relationship exists. Protection under employment-discrimination statutes provides a significant incentive for workers to claim that they are employees rather than independent contractors.

CASE IN POINT A Puerto Rican television station, WIPR, contracted with Victoria Lis Alberty-Vélez to co-host a television show. Alberty-Vélez signed a new contract for every new episode, each of which required her to work a certain number of days. She was under no other commitment to work for WIPR and was free to pursue other opportunities during the weeks between filming. WIPR did not withhold any taxes from the lump-sum amount it paid her for each contract. When Alberty-Vélez became pregnant, WIPR stopped contracting with her. She filed a lawsuit claiming that WIPR was discriminating against her in violation of federal employment-discrimination laws, but the court found in favor of WIPR. Because the parties had structured their relationship through the use of repeated fixed-length contracts and had described the woman as an independent contractor on tax documents, she could not maintain an employment-discrimination suit.[2]

CRITERIA USED BY THE IRS The Internal Revenue Service (IRS) has established its own criteria for determining whether a worker is an independent contractor or an employee. Although the IRS once considered twenty factors in determining a worker's status, guidelines today encourage IRS examiners to look closely at just one of those factors—the degree of control the business exercises over the worker.

The IRS tends to scrutinize closely a firm's classification of its workers, because, as mentioned, employers can avoid certain tax liabilities by hiring independent contractors instead of employees. Even when a firm has classified a worker as an independent contractor, the IRS may decide that the worker is actually an employee. In that situation, the employer will be responsible for paying any applicable Social Security, withholding, and unemployment taxes. Microsoft Corporation, for example, was once ordered to pay back payroll taxes for hundreds of temporary workers who had contractually agreed to work for Microsoft as independent contractors.[3]

EMPLOYEE STATUS AND "WORKS FOR HIRE" Under the Copyright Act of 1976, any copyrighted work created by an employee within the scope of her or his employment at the request of the employer is a "work for hire," and the employer owns the copyright to the work. In contrast, when an employer hires an independent contractor—a freelance artist, writer, or computer programmer, for example—the independent contractor normally owns the copyright. In this situation, the employer can own the copyright only if the parties agree in writing that the

work is a "work for hire" and the work falls into one of nine specific categories, including audiovisual and other works.

CASE IN POINT Artisan House, Inc., hired professional photographer Steven H. Lindner, owner of SHL Imaging, Inc., to take pictures of its products for the creation of color slides to be used by Artisan's sales force. Lindner controlled his own work and carefully chose the lighting and angles used in the photographs. When Lindner later discovered that Artisan had published the photographs in a catalogue and brochures without his permission, he had SHL register the photographs with the copyright office and file a lawsuit for copyright infringement. Artisan claimed that its publication of the photographs was authorized because they were works for hire. The court, however, decided that SHL was an independent contractor and owned the copyright to the photographs. SHL had only given Artisan permission (a license) to provide the photographs to its sales reps, not to reproduce them in other publications. Because Artisan had used the photographs in an unauthorized manner, the court ruled that Artisan was liable for copyright infringement.[4]

SECTION 2
FORMATION OF THE AGENCY RELATIONSHIP

Agency relationships normally are *consensual*—that is, they come about by voluntary consent and agreement between the parties. Generally, the agreement need not be in writing,[5] and consideration is not required.

A person must have contractual capacity to be a principal.[6] Those who cannot legally enter into contracts directly should not be allowed to do so indirectly through an agent. Any person can be an agent, however, regardless of whether he or she has the capacity to contract (including minors).

An agency relationship can be created for any legal purpose. An agency relationship created for a

---

2. *Alberty-Vélez v. Corporación de Puerto Rico para la Difusión Pública,* 361 F.3d 1 (1st Cir. 2004).

3. *Vizcaino v. U.S. District Court for the Western District of Washington,* 173 F.3d 713 (9th Cir. 1999).

4. *SHL Imaging, Inc. v. Artisan House, Inc.,* 117 F.Supp.2d 301 (S.D.N.Y. 2000).

5. There are two main exceptions to the statement that agency agreements need not be in writing. An agency agreement must be in writing (1) whenever the agent is empowered to enter into a contract that the Statute of Frauds requires to be in writing and (2) whenever an agent is given power of attorney.

6. Note that some states allow a minor to be a principal. When a minor is permitted to be a principal, any resulting contracts will be voidable by the minor principal but *not* by an adult third party.

purpose that is illegal or contrary to public policy is unenforceable. If Archer (as principal) contracts with Burke (as agent) to sell illegal narcotics, the agency relationship is unenforceable because selling illegal narcotics is a felony and is contrary to public policy. It is also illegal for physicians and other licensed professionals to employ unlicensed agents to perform professional actions.

An agency relationship can arise in four ways: by agreement of the parties, by ratification, by estoppel, and by operation of law. We look here at each of these possibilities.

Agency by Agreement

Most agency relationships are based on an express or implied agreement that the agent will act for the principal and that the principal agrees to have the agent so act. An agency agreement can take the form of an express written contract or be created by an oral agreement. For example, Henry asks Grace, a gardener, to contract with others for the care of his lawn on a regular basis. If Grace agrees, an agency relationship exists between Henry and Grace for the lawn care.

An agency agreement can also be implied by conduct. For example, a hotel expressly allows only Hans Cooper to park cars, but Hans has no employment contract there. The hotel's manager tells Hans when to work, as well as where and how to park the cars. The hotel's conduct manifests a willingness to have Hans park its customers' cars, and Hans can infer from the hotel's conduct that he has authority to act as a parking valet. Thus, there is an implied agreement that Hans is an agent of the hotel and provides valet parking services for hotel guests.

At issue in the following case was whether an agency relationship arose when a man, who was being hospitalized, asked his wife to sign the admissions papers for him.

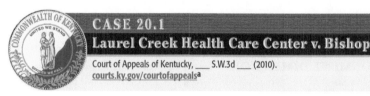

CASE 20.1
Laurel Creek Health Care Center v. Bishop

Court of Appeals of Kentucky, ___ S.W.3d ___ (2010).
courts.ky.gov/courtofappeals[a]

BACKGROUND AND FACTS • Gilbert Bishop was admitted to Laurel Creek Health Care Center suffering from various physical ailments. During an examination, Bishop told Laurel Creek staff that he could not use his hands well enough to write or hold a pencil, but he was otherwise found to be mentally competent. Bishop's sister, Rachel Combs, testified that when she arrived at the facility, she offered to sign the admissions forms, but Laurel Creek employees told her that it was their policy to have the patient's spouse sign the admissions papers if the patient was unable to do so. Combs also testified that Bishop asked her to get his wife, Anna, so that she could sign his admissions papers. Combs then brought Anna to the hospital, and Anna signed the admissions paperwork, which contained a provision for mandatory arbitration. Subsequently, Bishop went into cardiopulmonary arrest and died. Following his death, Bishop's family brought an action in a Kentucky state court against Laurel Creek for negligence. Laurel Creek asked the trial court to order the parties to proceed to arbitration in accordance with the mandatory arbitration provision contained in the admissions paperwork signed by Anna. The trial court denied the request on the ground that Anna was not Bishop's agent and had no legal authority to make decisions for him. Laurel Creek appealed.

IN THE LANGUAGE OF THE COURT
LAMBERT, Judge.
* * * *

Laurel Creek first argues that this is a case of actual agency and that Anna Bishop had actual authority as Gilbert's agent to sign the admissions paperwork and is therefore bound by the arbitration agreement therein.

---

a. Select "Searchable Opinions" from the "Related Content" list on the right side of the screen. On the page that opens, under "Select Search Category," choose "Court of Appeals Opinions (1996+)"; then enter "2009-CA-001055" in the "Enter Search Request" box and click on "Search." In the "Search Results" list, select the highlighted link to access the case. The Kentucky Court of Appeals maintains this Web site.

CASE CONTINUES ▶

* * * *

We agree with Laurel Creek that Gilbert created an actual agency relationship between him and his wife. According to his sister, Rachel, Gilbert specifically asked that his wife be brought to the nursing home so that she could sign the admissions documents for him, and Anna acted upon that delegation of authority and signed the admissions papers. This is consistent with the creation of actual authority as described in the *Restatement (Third) of Agency*, [Section] 2.01, Comment c (2006). The Restatement explains the rationale for the creation of actual agency in three steps. *First, "the principal manifests assent to be affected by the agent's action."* In the instant case, Gilbert asked that Anna come to the hospital to sign the papers for him. *Second, "the agent's actions establish the agent's consent to act on the principal's behalf."* Here, Anna signed all the admissions papers per her husband's request and therefore consented to act on Gilbert's behalf. *Third, by acting within such authority, the agent affects the principal's legal relations with third parties.* Clearly here, Anna's actions affected Gilbert's relations with Laurel Creek, a third party. [Emphasis added.]

* * * *

* * * The evidence indicates that Gilbert indicated to Laurel Creek that he was physically incapable of signing the documents but was of sound mental capacity and wanted his wife to sign the documents on his behalf. When Gilbert communicated this to his sister, and the sister brought Anna in to sign the documents, Gilbert created an agency relationship upon which Laurel Creek relied.

DECISION AND REMEDY • *The Kentucky Court of Appeals reversed the trial court's judgment and remanded the case for further proceedings consistent with its opinion. An actual agency relationship between Bishop and his wife, Anna, had been formed, and the trial court had erred when it found otherwise.*

THE ECONOMIC DIMENSION • *Which party benefited from the court's ruling? Why?*

THE LEGAL ENVIRONMENT DIMENSION • *Laurel Creek argued that even if there was no actual agency relationship, an implied agency relationship existed. Is this argument valid? Why or why not?*

Agency by Ratification

On occasion, a person who is in fact not an agent (or who is an agent acting outside the scope of her or his authority) may make a contract on behalf of another (a principal). If the principal affirms that contract by word or by action, an agency relationship is created by *ratification*. Ratification involves a question of intent, and intent can be expressed by either words or conduct. The basic requirements for ratification will be discussed later in this chapter.

Agency by Estoppel

When a principal causes a third person to believe that another person is the principal's agent, and the third person acts to his or her detriment in reasonable reliance on that belief, the principal is "estopped to deny" (prevented from denying) the agency relationship. In such a situation, the principal's actions have created the *appearance* of an agency that does not in fact exist. The third person must prove that he or she *reasonably* believed that an agency relationship existed, however.[7] Facts and circumstances must show that an ordinary, prudent person familiar with business practice and custom would have been justified in concluding that the agent had authority.

CASE IN POINT Marsha and Jerry Wiedmaier owned Wiedmaier, Inc., a corporation that operated a truck stop. Their son, Michael, did not own any interest in the corporation but had worked at the truck stop as a fuel operator. Michael decided to form his own business called Extreme Diecast, LLC. To obtain a line of credit with Motorsport Marketing, Inc., which sells racing memorabilia, Michael asked his mother to sign the credit application form. After Marsha had signed as "Secretary-Owner" of Wiedmaier, Inc., Michael added his name to the list of corporate owners and faxed the form to Motorsport. Later, when Michael stopped making payments on the merchandise he had ordered, Motorsport sued Wiedmaier, Inc., for the unpaid

---

7. These concepts also apply when a person who is in fact an agent undertakes an action that is beyond the scope of her or his authority, as will be discussed later in this chapter.

balance. The court ruled that Michael was an apparent agent of Wiedmaier, Inc., because the credit application had caused Motorsport to reasonably believe that Michael was acting as Wiedmaier's agent in ordering merchandise.[8]

Note that the acts or declarations of a purported *agent* in and of themselves do not create an agency by estoppel. Rather, it is the deeds or statements of the *principal* that create an agency by estoppel. Thus, in the *Case in Point* feature just discussed, if Marsha Wiedmaier had not signed the credit application on behalf of the principal-corporation, then Motorsport would not have been justified in believing that Michael was Wiedmaier's agent.

Agency by Operation of Law

The courts may find an agency relationship in the absence of a formal agreement in other situations as well. This may occur in family relationships, such as when one spouse purchases certain basic necessaries and charges them to the other spouse's account. The courts often rule that a spouse is liable for payment for the necessaries because of either a social policy or a legal duty to supply necessaries to family members.

Agency by operation of law may also occur in emergency situations, when the agent is unable to contact the principal and the agent's failure to act outside the scope of her or his authority would cause the principal substantial loss. For example, a railroad engineer may contract on behalf of his or her employer for medical care for an injured motorist hit by the train.

---

8. *Motorsport Marketing, Inc. v. Wiedmaier, Inc.,* 195 S.W.3d 492 (Mo. App. 2006).

Concept Summary 20.1 below reviews the various ways that agencies are formed.

SECTION 3
DUTIES AND RIGHTS OF AGENTS AND PRINCIPALS

Once the principal-agent relationship has been created, both parties have duties that govern their conduct. As discussed previously, the principal-agent relationship is *fiduciary*—based on trust. In a fiduciary relationship, each party owes the other the duty to act with the utmost good faith. In this section, we examine the various duties of agents and principals.

Agent's Duties to the Principal

Generally, the agent owes the principal five duties—performance, notification, loyalty, obedience, and accounting.

PERFORMANCE An implied condition in every agency contract is the agent's agreement to use reasonable diligence and skill in performing the work. When an agent fails to perform his or her duties, liability for breach of contract may result. The degree of skill or care required of an agent is usually that expected of a reasonable person under similar circumstances. Generally, this is interpreted to mean ordinary care. If an agent has represented herself or himself as possessing special skills, however, the agent is expected to exercise the degree of skill claimed. Failure to do so constitutes a breach of the agent's duty.

CONCEPT SUMMARY 20.1
Formation of the Agency Relationship

Method of Formation	Description
By Agreement	The agency relationship is formed through express consent (oral or written) or implied by conduct.
By Ratification	The principal either by act or by agreement ratifies the conduct of a person who is not in fact an agent.
By Estoppel	The principal causes a third person to believe that another person is the principal's agent, and the third person acts to his or her detriment in reasonable reliance on that belief.
By Operation of Law	The agency relationship is based on a social or legal duty (such as the need to support family members) or formed in emergency situations when the agent is unable to contact the principal and failure to act outside the scope of the agent's authority would cause the principal substantial loss.

Not all agency relationships are based on contract. In some situations, an agent acts gratuitously—that is, without payment. A gratuitous agent cannot be liable for breach of contract, as there is no contract. He or she is subject only to tort liability. Once a gratuitous agent has begun to act in an agency capacity, he or she has the duty to continue to perform in that capacity in an acceptable manner and is subject to the same standards of care and duty to perform as other agents.

For example, Bower's friend Alcott is a real estate broker. Alcott offers to sell Bower's farm at no charge. If Alcott never attempts to sell the farm, Bower has no legal cause of action to force her to do so. If Alcott does find a buyer, however, but negligently fails to follow through with the sales contract, causing the buyer to seek other property, then Bower can sue Alcott for negligence.

NOTIFICATION An agent is required to notify the principal of all matters that come to her or his attention concerning the subject matter of the agency. This is the *duty of notification,* or the duty to inform. Suppose that Perez, an artist, is about to negotiate a contract to sell a series of paintings to Barber's Art Gallery for $25,000. Perez's agent learns that Barber is insolvent and will be unable to pay for the paintings. The agent has a duty to inform Perez of Barber's insolvency because it is relevant to the subject matter of the agency, which is the sale of Perez's paintings. Generally, the law assumes that the principal is aware of any information acquired by the agent that is relevant to the agency—regardless of whether the agent actually passes on this information to the principal. It is a basic tenet of agency law that notice to the agent is notice to the principal.

LOYALTY Loyalty is one of the most fundamental duties in a fiduciary relationship. Basically, the agent has the duty to act *solely for the benefit of his or her* *principal* and not in the interest of the agent or a third party. For example, an agent cannot represent two principals in the same transaction unless both know of the dual capacity and consent to it. The duty of loyalty also means that any information or knowledge acquired through the agency relationship is confidential. It is a breach of loyalty to disclose such information either during the agency relationship or after its termination. Typical examples of confidential information are trade secrets and customer lists compiled by the principal.

In short, the agent's loyalty must be undivided. The agent's actions must be strictly for the benefit of the principal and must not result in any secret profit for the agent.

CASE IN POINT Don Cousins contracted with Leo Hodgins, a real estate agent, to negotiate the purchase of an office building. While working for Cousins, Hodgins discovered that the property owner would sell the building only as a package deal with another parcel. Hodgins then formed a company to buy the two properties and resell the building to Cousins. When Cousins discovered these actions, he filed a lawsuit alleging that Hodgins had breached his fiduciary duties. The court ruled in Cousins's favor. As a real estate agent, Hodgins had a duty to communicate all offers to his principal and not to secretly purchase the property and then resell it to his principal. Hodgins was required to act in Cousins's best interests and could only become the purchaser in this situation with Cousins's knowledge and approval.[9]

In the following case, an employer alleged that a former employee had breached his duty of loyalty by planning a competing business while still working for the employer.

---

9. *Cousins v. Realty Ventures, Inc.,* 844 So.2d 860 (La.App. 5 Cir. 2003).

✴ EXTENDED CASE 20.2 ✴
Taser International, Inc. v. Ward

Court of Appeals of Arizona, Division 1, 224 Ariz. 389, 231 P.3d 921 (2010).

IN THE LANGUAGE OF THE COURT
PORTLEY, Judge.
* * * *
    Taser International develops and manu-
factures electronic control devices, commonly called stun guns, and accessories for electronic control devices, including a personal video and audio recording device called TASER CAM. Taser sells its products
to the military, law enforcement, corrections, private security, and the general public.

    [Steve] Ward was employed full-time with Taser from January 1, 2004, to July 24, 2007, and served as Taser's vice president of marketing during the time relevant to this appeal. He was an at-will employee,[a] and he did not sign any employment contract, non-compete agreement, or non-disclosure agreement.

* * * *

In December 2006, Ward began exploring whether he could personally develop the concept of an eyeglass-mounted camera. He sought legal advice about whether he could permissibly develop such a camera independent of Taser, and hired patent counsel to conduct a patent search on the idea.

Between April 2007 and his resignation approximately four months later, Ward shifted his exploration to the concept of a clip-on camera device, after learning that the eyeglass-mounted concept was already patent protected. He directed patent counsel to conduct a patent search on the modified idea. He communicated with JAM-Proactive, a product development company, about the design and development of a clip-on camera device, and he received a detailed product development proposal from JAM-Proactive on June 12, 2007. Prior to his resignation, Ward planned to leave Taser to form a new business, and completed substantial work on a business plan to develop, market, and sell a clip-on camera device.

Ward resigned on July 24, 2007. * * * He formed Vievu LLC on August 23, 2007, and Vievu now markets a clip-on camera device to general consumers and law enforcement. Ten months after Ward resigned, Taser announced the AXON, a product that provides an audio-video record of an incident from the visual perspective of the person involved.

[Taser filed a suit against Ward in an Arizona state court alleging, among other things, that Ward had breached his duty of loyalty to Taser.

Taser moved for summary judgment in its favor, which the court granted. Ward appealed.]

* * * *

"In Arizona, an employee/agent owes his or her employer/principal a fiduciary duty. *It is too plain to need discussion that an agent is under the duty to act with entire good faith and loyalty for the furtherance of the interests of his principal in all matters concerning or affecting the subject of his agency, and if he fails to do so, he is responsible to his principal for any loss resulting therefrom.*" [Emphasis added.]

One aspect of this broad principle is that an employee is precluded from actively competing with his or her employer during the period of employment.

Although an employee may not compete prior to termination, "[the employee] may take action [during employment], not otherwise wrongful, to prepare for competition following termination of the agency relationship." Preparation cannot take the form of "acts in direct competition with the employer's business."

The line separating mere preparation from active competition may be difficult to discern in some cases, and we must "focus on the nature of the defendant's preparations to compete." [Emphasis added.]

* * * *

It is undisputed that, prior to his resignation, Ward did not solicit or recruit any Taser employees, distributors, customers, or vendors; he did not buy, sell, or incorporate any business; he did not acquire office space or other general business services; he did not contact or enter into any agreements with suppliers or manufacturers for his proposed clip-on camera; and he did not sell any products. However, Ward did begin developing a business plan, counseled with several attorneys, explored and abandoned the concept of an eyeglass-mounted camera device, and engaged, to

some extent, in the exploration and development of a clip-on camera device.

Ward argues that his pre-termination activities did not constitute active competition but were merely lawful preparation for a future business venture. Taser contends, however, that "this case is not about just investigating computer software, acquiring a line of credit, securing office space, or getting prices on telephones * * * [but] about developing a rival design during employment, knowing full well TASER has sold such a device and continues to develop a second-generation product."

Upon review, we agree with Ward that certain of his pre-termination activities are qualitatively different than "direct competition" and cannot form the basis for liability.

* * * *

However, assuming Taser was engaged in the research and development of a recording device during Ward's employment, assuming Ward knew or should have known of those efforts, and assuming Taser's device would compete with Ward's concept, substantial design and development efforts by Ward during his employment would constitute direct competition with the business activities of Taser and would violate his duty of loyalty. In the context of a business which engages in research, design, development, manufacture, and marketing of products, we cannot limit "competition" to just actual sales of competing products.

Summary judgment on this theory is nevertheless improper because a genuine issue of material fact exists as to the extent of Ward's pre-termination design and development efforts.

* * * *

For the foregoing reasons, we reverse the grant of summary judgment entered in favor of Taser * * * and remand for further proceedings.

---

a. *Employment at will* is a common law doctrine under which either party may terminate an employment relationship at any time for any reason, unless a contract specifies otherwise.

EXTENDED CASE CONTINUES ➜

EXTENDED CASE 20.2 CONTINUED ▼

1. Why was it unclear whether Ward's pretermination actions constituted direct competition with his employer or were mere planning activities?
2. Suppose that Ward's planning and development efforts were focused on a product that in no way would compete with Taser's products. Would such efforts have breached his duty of loyalty to Taser in any way? Explain fully.

OBEDIENCE When acting on behalf of the principal, an agent has a duty to follow all lawful and clearly stated instructions of the principal. Any deviation from such instructions is a violation of this duty. During emergency situations, however, when the principal cannot be consulted, the agent may deviate from the instructions without violating this duty. Whenever instructions are not clearly stated, the agent can fulfill the duty of obedience by acting in good faith and in a manner reasonable under the circumstances.

ACCOUNTING Unless an agent and a principal agree otherwise, the agent has a duty to keep and make available to the principal an account of all property and funds received and paid out on behalf of the principal. This includes gifts from third parties in connection with the agency. For example, a gift from a customer to a salesperson for prompt deliveries made by the salesperson's firm, in the absence of a company policy to the contrary, belongs to the firm.

The agent has a duty to maintain separate accounts for the principal's funds and the agent's personal funds, and the agent must not intermingle the funds in these accounts. Whenever a licensed professional (such as an attorney) violates this duty to account, he or she may be subject to disciplinary proceedings carried out by the appropriate regulatory institution (such as the state bar association) in addition to being liable to the principal (the professional's client) for failure to account.

Principal's Duties to the Agent

The principal also has certain duties to the agent. These duties relate to compensation, reimbursement and indemnification, cooperation, and safe working conditions.

COMPENSATION In general, when a principal requests certain services from an agent, the agent reasonably expects payment. The principal therefore has a duty to pay the agent for services rendered. For example, when an accountant or an attorney is asked to act as an agent, an agreement to compensate the agent for this service is implied. The principal also has a duty to pay that compensation in a timely manner. Unless the agency relationship is gratuitous and the agent does not act in exchange for payment, the principal must pay the agreed-on value for the agent's services. If no amount has been expressly agreed on, then the principal owes the agent the customary compensation for such services.

REIMBURSEMENT AND INDEMNIFICATION Whenever an agent disburses funds to fulfill the request of the principal or to pay for necessary expenses in the course of reasonable performance of her or his agency duties, the principal has the duty to reimburse the agent for these payments.[10] Agents cannot recover for expenses incurred by their own misconduct or negligence, though.

Subject to the terms of the agency agreement, the principal has the duty to *indemnify* (compensate) an agent for liabilities incurred because of authorized and lawful acts and transactions. For example, if the agent, on the principal's behalf, forms a contract with a third party, and the principal fails to perform the contract, the third party may sue the agent for damages. In this situation, the principal is obligated to compensate the agent for any costs incurred by the agent as a result of the principal's failure to perform the contract.

Additionally, the principal must indemnify the agent for the value of benefits that the agent confers on the principal. The amount of indemnification usually is specified in the agency contract. If it is not, the courts will look to the nature of the business and the type of loss to determine the amount. Note that this rule applies to acts by gratuitous agents as well.

COOPERATION A principal has a duty to cooperate with the agent and to assist the agent in performing

---

10. This principle applies to acts by gratuitous agents as well. If a finder of a dog that becomes sick takes the dog to a veterinarian and pays the required fees for the veterinarian's services, the gratuitous agent is entitled to be reimbursed for those fees by the owner of the dog.

his or her duties. The principal must do nothing to prevent that performance. For example, when a principal grants an agent an exclusive territory, it creates an *exclusive agency,* in which the principal cannot compete with the agent or appoint or allow another agent to compete. If the principal does so, it violates the exclusive agency, and the principal is exposed to liability for the agent's lost profits. Suppose that Akers (the principal) creates an exclusive agency by granting Johnson (the agent) a territory within which only Johnson may sell Akers's products. If Akers begins to sell the products himself within Johnson's territory or permits another agent to do so, Akers has violated the exclusive agency and can be held liable for Johnson's lost profits.

SAFE WORKING CONDITIONS The common law requires the principal to provide safe working premises, equipment, and conditions for all agents and employees. The principal has a duty to inspect working areas and to warn agents and employees about any unsafe situations. When the agent is an employee, the employer's liability is frequently covered by state workers' compensation insurance, and federal and state statutes often require the employer to meet certain safety standards (see Chapter 21).

Rights and Remedies of Agents and Principals

In general, for every duty of the principal, the agent has a corresponding right, and vice versa. An agent also has the right to perform agency duties without interference by the principal. When one party to the agency relationship violates his or her duty to the other party, the remedies available to the non-breaching party arise out of contract and tort law. These remedies include monetary damages, termination of the agency relationship, an injunction, and required accountings.

────── SECTION 4 *──────*
SCOPE OF AGENT'S AUTHORITY

The liability of a principal to third parties with whom an agent contracts depends on whether the agent had the authority to enter into legally binding contracts on the principal's behalf. An agent's authority can be either *actual* (express or implied) or *apparent.* If an agent contracts outside the scope of

his or her authority, the principal may still become liable by ratifying the contract.

Express Authority

Express authority is authority declared in clear, direct, and definite terms. Express authority can be given orally or in writing.

THE EQUAL DIGNITY RULE In most states, the **equal dignity rule** requires that if the contract being executed is or must be in writing, then the agent's authority must also be in writing. Failure to comply with the equal dignity rule can make a contract voidable *at the option of the principal.* The law regards the contract at that point as a mere offer. If the principal decides to accept the offer, the acceptance must be ratified, or affirmed, in writing.

For example, Paloma (the principal) orally asks Austin (the agent) to sell a ranch that Paloma owns. Austin finds a buyer and signs a sales contract (a contract for an interest in realty must be in writing) on behalf of Paloma to sell the ranch. The buyer cannot enforce the contract unless Paloma subsequently ratifies Austin's agency status in writing. Once the contract is ratified, either party can enforce rights under the contract.

Modern business practice allows exceptions to the equal dignity rule. An executive officer of a corporation normally is not required to obtain written authority from the corporation to conduct *ordinary* business transactions. The equal dignity rule also does not apply when the agent acts in the presence of the principal or when the agent's act of signing is merely perfunctory (token or customary). Thus, if Healy (the principal) negotiates a contract but is called out of town the day it is to be signed and orally authorizes Santini to sign, the oral authorization is sufficient.

POWER OF ATTORNEY Giving an agent a **power of attorney** confers express authority.[11] The power of attorney is a written document and is usually notarized. (A document is notarized when a **notary public**—a public official authorized to attest to the authenticity of signatures—signs and dates the document and imprints it with her or his seal of authority.) Most states have statutory provisions for creating a power of attorney. A power of attorney can be special (permitting the agent to perform specified acts only), or it can be general (permitting the agent to transact all business for

---

11. An agent who holds a power of attorney is called an *attorney-in-fact* for the principal. The holder does not have to be an attorney-at-law (and often is not).

the principal). Because of the extensive authority granted to an agent by a general power of attorney (see Exhibit 20–1 below), it should be used with great caution and usually only in exceptional circumstances. Ordinarily, a power of attorney terminates on the incapacity or death of the person giving the power.[12]

_____

12. A *durable* power of attorney, however, continues to be effective despite the principal's incapacity. An elderly person, for example, might grant a durable power of attorney to provide for the handling of property and investments or specific health-care needs should he or she become incompetent.

Implied Authority

An agent has the **implied authority** to do what is reasonably necessary to carry out express authority and accomplish the objectives of the agency. Authority can also be implied by custom or inferred from the position the agent occupies. For example, Archer is employed by Packard Grocery to manage one of its stores. Packard has not expressly stated that Archer has authority to contract with third persons. Nevertheless, authority to manage a business implies authority to do what is reasonably required (as is customary or can be inferred from a manager's position) to operate

EXHIBIT 20–1 • A Sample General Power of Attorney

GENERAL POWER OF ATTORNEY

Know All Men by These Presents:

That I, _____ , hereinafter referred to as PRINCIPAL, in the County of _____

State of _____ , do(es) appoint _____ as my true and lawful attorney.

In principal's name, and for principal's use and benefit, said attorney is authorized hereby;

(1) To demand, sue for, collect, and receive all money, debts, accounts, legacies, bequests, interest, dividends, annuities, and demands as are now or shall hereafter become due, payable, or belonging to principal, and take all lawful means, for the recovery thereof and to compromise the same and give discharges for the same;
(2) To buy and sell land, make contracts of every kind relative to land, any interest therein or the possession thereof, and to take possession and exercise control over the use thereof;
(3) To buy, sell, mortgage, hypothecate, assign, transfer, and in any manner deal with goods, wares and merchandise, choses in action, certificates or shares of capital stock, and other property in possession or in action, and to make, do, and transact all and every kind of business of whatever nature;
(4) To execute, acknowledge, and deliver contracts of sale, escrow instructions, deeds, leases including leases for minerals and hydrocarbon substances and assignments of leases, covenants, agreements and assignments of agreements, mortgages and assignments of mortgages, conveyances in trust, to secure indebtedness or other obligations, and assign the beneficial interest thereunder, subordinations of liens or encumbrances, bills of lading, receipts, evidences of debt, releases, bonds, notes, bills, requests to reconvey deeds of trust, partial or full judgments, satisfactions of mortgages, and other debts, and other written instruments of whatever kind and nature, all upon such terms and conditions as said attorney shall approve.

GIVING AND GRANTING to said attorney full power and authority to do all and every act and thing whatsoever requisite and necessary to be done relative to any of the foregoing as fully to all intents and purposes as principal might or could do if personally present.

All that said attorney shall lawfully do or cause to be done under the authority of this power of attorney is expressly approved.

Dated: _____   /s/_____

State of _____   } SS.
    County of _____
On _____ , before me, the undersigned, a Notary Public in and for said
State, personally appeared _____

known to me to be the person _____ whose name _____ subscribed
to the within instrument and acknowledged that _____ executed the same.

Witness my hand and official seal.   (Seal) _____
                                                          Notary Public in and for said State.

the business. This includes forming contracts to hire employees, to buy merchandise and equipment, and to advertise the products sold in the store.

In general, implied authority is authority customarily associated with the position occupied by the agent or authority that can be inferred from the express authority given to the agent to perform fully his or her duties. For example, an agent has authority to solicit orders for goods sold by the principal. The agent, however, does not carry any goods with him when soliciting orders and thus generally would not have the authority to collect payments for the goods. The test is whether it was reasonable for the agent to believe that she or he had the authority to enter into the contract in question.

Also note that an agent's implied authority cannot contradict his or her express authority. Thus, if a principal has limited an agent's authority—by forbidding a manager to enter into contracts to hire additional workers, for example—then the fact that managers customarily would have such authority is irrelevant.

Apparent Authority

Actual authority (express or implied) arises from what the principal makes clear *to the agent*. Apparent authority, in contrast, arises from what the principal causes a third party to believe. An agent has **apparent authority** when the principal, by either word or action, causes a *third party* reasonably to believe that the agent has authority to act, even though the agent has no express or implied authority.

Apparent authority usually comes into existence through a principal's pattern of conduct over time. For example, Ashley is a traveling salesperson with the authority to solicit orders for a principal's goods. Because she does not carry any goods with her, she normally would not have the implied authority to collect payments from customers on behalf of the principal. Suppose that she does accept payments from Cabo Enterprises, however, and submits them to the principal's accounting department for processing. If the principal does nothing to stop Ashley from continuing this practice, a pattern develops over time, and the principal confers apparent authority on Ashley to accept payments from Cabo.

In the following case, an employee misappropriated more than $1 million from her employer by using his credit card without authorization over a number of years. The issue before the court was whether the employee had apparent authority to use the card.

CASE 20.3
Azur v. Chase Bank, USA

United States Court of Appeals, Third Circuit, 601 F.3d 212 (2010).
www.ca3.uscourts.gov[a]

BACKGROUND AND FACTS • ATM Corporation of America, Inc. (ATM), manages settlement services for large national lenders. Francis Azur, the founder of ATM, served as its president and chief executive officer until September 2007, when ATM was sold. In July 1997, ATM hired Michelle Vanek to be Azur's personal assistant. Vanek's responsibilities included opening Azur's personal bills, preparing and presenting checks for Azur to sign, balancing Azur's checking and savings accounts, and reviewing his credit-card and bank statements. Vanek also had access to Azur's credit-card number so that she could make purchases for him. Over a period of seven years, Vanek withdrew unauthorized cash advances of between $200 and $700, typically twice a day, from Azur's credit-card account with Chase Bank, USA. The fraudulent charges were reflected on at least sixty-five monthly billing statements sent by Chase to Azur, and Vanek paid the bills by either writing checks and forging Azur's signature or making online payments from Azur's checking account. In all, Vanek misappropriated more than $1 million from Azur. When Azur discovered Vanek's fraudulent scheme in 2006, he terminated her employment and closed the Chase account. Azur sued Chase, seeking reimbursement of the fraudulent charges under Section 1643 of the Truth-in-Lending Act, or TILA.[b] A magistrate judge concluded that Azur's claim failed because Vanek

a. Under "Opinions and Oral Arguments," select "Search for Opinions." When the search page appears, type "Azur" in the search box and click on "Go." When the case information appears at the bottom of the search page, click on the highlighted link to the PDF to access the case. The U.S. Court of Appeals for the Third Circuit maintains this Web site.

b. Among other things, the TILA protects holders of credit cards from liability for the fraudulent use of their credit cards. (See Chapter 24 for a detailed discussion of this consumer-protection statute.)

CASE CONTINUES ▶

CASE 20.3 CONTINUED ⟶ had apparent authority to use Azur's credit card. The trial court—a U.S. district court—agreed and granted Chase's motion for summary judgment on this issue. Azur appealed.

IN THE LANGUAGE OF THE COURT
FISHER, Circuit Judge.
* * * *

* * * [Section 1643 of the TILA] provides that "[a] cardholder shall be liable for the unauthorized use of a credit card" in certain circumstances. The term *"unauthorized use" is defined as the "use of a credit card by a person other than the cardholder who does not have actual, implied, or apparent authority for such use and from which the cardholder receives no benefit."* [Emphasis added.]

To determine whether apparent authority exists, we turn to applicable state agency law. * * * Citing the *Restatement (Second) of Agency*, the Pennsylvania Supreme Court has explained as follows:

> Apparent authority is power to bind a principal which the principal has not actually granted but which he leads persons with whom his agent deals to believe that he has granted. Persons with whom the agent deals can reasonably believe that the agent has power to bind his principal if, for instance, the principal knowingly permits the agent to exercise such power or if the principal holds the agent out as possessing such power.

* * * *

* * * A cardholder may, in certain circumstances, vest a fraudulent user with the apparent authority to use a credit card by enabling the continuous payment of the credit card charges over a period of time.

Here, Azur's negligent omissions led Chase to reasonably believe that the fraudulent charges were authorized. Although Azur may not have been aware that Vanek was using the Chase credit card, or even that the Chase credit card account existed, Azur knew that he had a Dollar Bank checking account, and he did not review his Dollar Bank statements or exercise any other oversight over Vanek, his employee. * * * Had Azur occasionally reviewed his statements, Azur would have likely noticed that checks had been written to Chase. Because Chase reasonably believed that a prudent business person would oversee his employees in such a manner, Chase reasonably relied on the continuous payment of the fraudulent charges.

DECISION AND REMEDY • *The U.S. Court of Appeals for the Third Circuit affirmed the trial court's judgment, holding that Azur had vested Vanek with apparent authority to use the Chase credit card.*

THE ETHICAL DIMENSION • *The TILA essentially is a consumer-protection law. How does allowing a credit-card company to avoid liability—if a card user has apparent authority to use the card—protect consumers?*

MANAGERIAL IMPLICATIONS • *Business owners and managers should take precautions to avoid being held liable, under a theory of apparent authority, for unauthorized credit-card charges made by their employees. Any employee who has access to the employer's credit-card number, credit-card statements, bank accounts, and other financial data should be carefully supervised. The employer should periodically review bank statements and credit-card payments to ensure that no checks have been forged and that all payments to credit-card companies are for authorized charges.*

Emergency Powers

When an unforeseen emergency demands action by the agent to protect or preserve the property and rights of the principal, but the agent is unable to communicate with the principal, the agent has emergency power. For example, Fulsom is an engineer for Pacific Drilling Company. While Fulsom is acting within the scope of his employment, he is severely injured in an accident at an oil rig many miles from home. Acosta, the rig supervisor, directs Thompson, a physician, to give medical aid to Fulsom and to charge Pacific for the medical services. Acosta, an agent, has no express or implied authority to bind the principal, Pacific Drilling, for Thompson's medical services. Because of the emergency situation, however, the law recognizes Acosta as having authority to act appropriately under the circumstances.

Ratification

Ratification occurs when the principal affirms, or accepts responsibility for, an agent's *unauthorized* act. When ratification occurs, the principal is bound to the agent's act, and the act is treated as if it had been authorized by the principal *from the outset.* Ratification can be either express or implied.

If the principal does not ratify the contract, the principal is not bound, and the third party's agreement with the agent is viewed as merely an unaccepted offer. Because the third party's agreement is an unaccepted offer, the third party can revoke it at any time, without liability, before the principal ratifies the contract. The agent, however, may be liable to the third party for misrepresenting her or his authority.

The requirements for ratification can be summarized as follows:

1. The agent must have acted on behalf of an identified principal who subsequently ratifies the action.
2. The principal must know all of the material facts involved in the transaction. If a principal ratifies a contract without knowing all of the facts, the principal can rescind (cancel) the contract.[13]
3. The principal must affirm the agent's act in its entirety.
4. The principal must have the legal capacity to authorize the transaction at the time the agent engages in the act and at the time the principal ratifies. The third party must also have the legal capacity to engage in the transaction.
5. The principal's affirmation (ratification) must occur before the third party withdraws from the transaction.
6. The principal must observe the same formalities when ratifying the act as would have been required to authorize it initially.

SECTION 5
LIABILITY FOR CONTRACTS

Liability for contracts formed by an agent depends on how the principal is classified and on whether the actions of the agent were authorized or unauthorized. Principals are classified as disclosed, unidentified, or undisclosed.[14]

A **disclosed principal** is a principal whose identity is known by the third party at the time the contract is made by the agent. An **unidentified principal** is a principal whose identity is not known by the third party, but the third party knows that the agent is or may be acting for a principal at the time the contract is made. An **undisclosed principal** is a principal whose identity is totally unknown by the third party, and the third party has no knowledge that the agent is acting in an agency capacity at the time the contract is made.

Authorized Acts

If an agent acts within the scope of her or his authority, normally the principal is obligated to perform the contract regardless of whether the principal was disclosed, unidentified, or undisclosed. Whether the agent may also be held liable under the contract, however, depends on the disclosed, unidentified, or undisclosed status of the principal.

DISCLOSED OR UNIDENTIFIED PRINCIPAL A disclosed or unidentified principal is liable to a third party for a contract made by the agent. If the principal is disclosed, the agent has no contractual liability for the nonperformance of the principal or the third party. If the principal is unidentified, in most states the agent is also treated as a party to the contract, and the third party can hold the agent liable for contractual nonperformance.[15]

CASE IN POINT Walgreens leased commercial property at a mall owned by Kedzie Plaza Associates to operate a drugstore. A property management company, Taxman Corporation, signed the lease on behalf of the principal, Kedzie. The lease required the landlord to keep the sidewalks free of snow and ice, so Taxman, on behalf of Kedzie, contracted with another company to remove ice and snow from the sidewalks surrounding the Walgreens store. When a Walgreens employee slipped on ice outside the store and was injured, she sued Taxman, among others, for negligence. Because the principal's identity (Kedzie) was fully disclosed in the snow-removal contract, however, the court ruled that the agent, Taxman, could not be held liable. Taxman did not assume a contractual obligation to remove the snow but merely retained a contractor to do so on behalf of the owner.[16]

---

13. If the third party has changed position in reliance on the apparent contract, however, the principal can rescind but must reimburse the third party for any costs.
14. *Restatement (Third) of Agency,* Section 1.04 (2).

15. *Restatement (Third) of Agency,* Section 6.02.
16. *McBride v. Taxman Corp.,* 327 Ill.App.3d 992, 765 N.E.2d 51 (2002).

UNDISCLOSED PRINCIPAL When neither the fact of an agency relationship nor the identity of the principal is disclosed, the undisclosed principal is bound to perform just as if the principal had been fully disclosed at the time the contract was made.

When a principal's identity is undisclosed and the agent is forced to pay the third party, the agent is entitled to be *indemnified* (compensated) by the principal. The principal has a duty to perform, even though his or her identity is undisclosed, and failure to perform makes the principal ultimately liable. Once the undisclosed principal's identity is revealed, the third party generally can elect to hold either the principal or the agent liable on the contract.

Conversely, the undisclosed principal can require the third party to fulfill the contract, *unless* (1) the undisclosed principal was expressly excluded as a party in the written contract; (2) the contract is a negotiable instrument signed by the agent with no indication of signing in a representative capacity;[17] or (3) the performance of the agent is personal to the contract, allowing the third party to refuse the principal's performance.

Unauthorized Acts

If an agent has no authority but nevertheless contracts with a third party, the principal cannot be held liable on the contract. It does not matter whether the principal was disclosed, unidentified, or undisclosed. The person who acted as an agent is liable, however. For example, Updike signs a contract for the purchase of a truck, purportedly acting as an agent under authority granted by Parker. In fact, Parker has not given Updike any such authority. Parker refuses to pay for the truck, claiming that Updike had no authority to purchase it. The seller of the truck is entitled to hold Updike liable for payment.

If an agent for a disclosed or unidentified principal contracts with a third party without authorization, the third party who relied on the agency status can also hold the agent liable for breaching the *implied warranty of authority*. The agent's liability here is based on the third party's reliance on the agent's purported authority, not on the breach of the contract itself.[18] For example, Pinnell, a reclusive

artist, hires Auber to solicit offers for particular paintings from various galleries, but does not authorize her to enter into sales agreements. Olaf, a gallery owner, offers to buy two of Pinnell's paintings for an upcoming show. If Auber draws up a sales contract with Olaf, she impliedly warrants that she has the authority to enter into sales contracts on behalf of Pinnell. If Pinnell does not agree to ratify Auber's sales contract, Olaf cannot hold Pinnell liable, but he can hold Auber liable for breaching the implied warranty of authority.

Note that if the third party knows at the time the contract is made that the agent does not have authority, then the agent is not liable. Similarly, if the agent expressed to the third party *uncertainty* as to the extent of her or his authority, the agent is not personally liable.

Actions by E-Agents

Although in the past standard agency principles applied only to *human* agents, today these same agency principles also apply to e-agents. An electronic agent, or **e-agent,** is a semiautonomous computer program that is capable of executing specific tasks. E-agents used in e-commerce include software that can search through many databases and retrieve only relevant information for the user.

The Uniform Electronic Transactions Act (UETA), which was discussed on pages 459 to 460 in Chapter 11, sets forth provisions relating to the principal's liability for the actions of e-agents. According to Section 15 of the UETA, e-agents can enter into binding agreements on behalf of their principals—at least, in those states that have adopted the act. Thus, if consumers place an order over the Internet, and the company (principal) takes the order via an e-agent, the company cannot later claim that it did not receive the order.

The UETA also stipulates that if an e-agent does not provide an opportunity to prevent errors at the time of the transaction, the other party to the transaction can avoid the transaction. Therefore, if an e-agent fails to provide an on-screen confirmation of a purchase or sale, the other party can avoid the effect of any errors. For example, Bigelow wants to purchase three copies of three different books (a total of nine items). The e-agent mistakenly records an order for thirty-three of a single book and does not provide an on-screen verification of the order. If thirty-three books are then sent to Bigelow, he can avoid the contract to purchase them.

---

17. Under the Uniform Commercial Code (UCC), only the agent is liable if the instrument neither names the principal nor shows that the agent signed in a representative capacity [UCC 3–402(b)(2)].

18. The agent is not liable on the contract, because the agent was never intended personally to be a party to the contract.

LIABILITY FOR TORTS AND CRIMES

Obviously, any person, including an agent, is liable for his or her own torts and crimes. Whether a principal can also be held liable for an agent's torts and crimes depends on several factors, which we examine here. In some situations, a principal may be held liable not only for the torts of an agent, but also for torts committed by an independent contractor.

Principal's Tortious Conduct

A principal who acts through an agent may be liable for harm resulting from the principal's own negligence or recklessness. Therefore, a principal may be liable if he or she gives improper instructions, authorizes the use of improper materials or tools, or establishes improper rules that result in the agent's committing a tort. For instance, Peter knows that Audrey's driver's license has been suspended but nevertheless tells her to use the company truck to deliver some equipment to a customer. If someone is injured as a result, Peter will be liable for his own negligence in instructing Audrey to drive without a valid license.

Principal's Authorization of Agent's Tortious Conduct

Similarly, a principal who authorizes an agent to commit a tort may be liable to persons or property injured thereby, because the act is considered to be the principal's. For example, Pagani directs his agent, Atkin, to cut the corn on specific acreage, which neither of them has the right to do. The harvest is therefore a trespass (a tort), and Pagani is liable to the owner of the corn.

Note that an agent acting at the principal's direction can be liable as a *tortfeasor* (one who commits a wrong, or tort), along with the principal, for committing the tortious act even if the agent was unaware that the act was wrong. Assume in the above example that Atkin, the agent, did not know that Pagani lacked the right to harvest the corn. Atkin can still be held liable to the owner of the field for damages, along with Pagani, the principal.

Liability for Agent's Misrepresentation

A principal is exposed to tort liability whenever a third person sustains a loss due to the agent's misrepresentation. The principal's liability depends on whether the agent was actually or apparently authorized to make representations and whether the representations were made within the scope of the agency. The principal is always directly responsible for an agent's misrepresentation made within the scope of the agent's authority.

Suppose that Ainsley is a demonstrator for Pavlovich's products. Pavlovich sends Ainsley to a home show to demonstrate the products and to answer questions from consumers. Pavlovich has given Ainsley authority to make statements about the products. If Ainsley makes only true representations, all is fine. But if he makes false claims, Pavlovich will be liable for any injuries or damages sustained by third parties in reliance on Ainsley's false representations.

APPARENT IMPLIED AUTHORITY When a principal has placed an agent in a position of apparent authority—making it possible for the agent to defraud a third party—the principal may also be liable for the agent's fraudulent acts. For example, partners in a partnership (see Chapter 17) generally have the apparent implied authority to act as agents on behalf of the firm. Thus, if one of the partners commits a tort or a crime, the partnership itself—and often the other partners personally—can be held liable for the loss.

CASE IN POINT Selheimer & Company, a securities broker-dealer that operated as a partnership, provided various financial services. The managing partner, Perry Selheimer, embezzled funds that clients had turned over to the firm for investment. After Selheimer was convicted, other partners in the firm claimed that they were not liable for losses resulting from his illegal activities. The court, however, held that Selheimer had apparent implied authority to act in the ordinary course of the partnership's business. Thus, the firm, as principal, was liable, and under the law of partnerships, the personal assets of the individual partners could be used to cover the firm's liability.[19]

INNOCENT MISREPRESENTATION Tort liability based on fraud requires proof that a material misstatement was made knowingly and with the intent to deceive. An agent's *innocent* mistakes occurring in a contract transaction or involving a warranty contained in the contract can provide grounds for the third party's rescission of the contract and the award of damages.

---

19. *In re Selheimer & Co.*, 319 Bankr. 395 (E.D.Pa. 2005).

Moreover, justice dictates that when a principal knows that an agent is not accurately advised of facts but does not correct either the agent's or the third party's impressions, the principal is directly responsible to the third party for resulting damages. The point is that the principal is always directly responsible for an agent's misrepresentation made within the scope of authority.

Liability for Agent's Negligence

Under the doctrine of **respondeat superior**,[20] the principal-employer is liable for any harm caused to a third party by an agent-employee within the scope of employment. This doctrine imposes **vicarious liability,** or indirect liability, on the employer—that is, liability without regard to the personal fault of the employer for torts committed by an employee in the course or scope of employment. Third parties injured through the negligence of an employee can sue either that employee or the employer, if the employee's negligent conduct occurred while the employee was acting within the scope of employment.

RATIONALE UNDERLYING THE DOCTRINE OF RESPONDEAT SUPERIOR At early common law, a servant (employee) was viewed as the master's (employer's) property. The master was deemed to have absolute control over the servant's acts and was held strictly liable for them, no matter how carefully the master supervised the servant. The rationale for the doctrine of *respondeat superior* is based on the social duty that requires every person to manage his or her affairs, whether accomplished by the person or through agents, so as not to injure another. Liability is imposed on employers because they are deemed to be in a better financial position to bear the loss. The superior financial position carries with it the duty to be responsible for damages.

Generally, public policy requires that an injured person be afforded effective relief, and a business enterprise is usually better able to provide that relief than is an individual employee. Employers normally carry liability insurance to cover any damages awarded as a result of such lawsuits. They are also able to spread the cost of risk over the entire business enterprise.

The doctrine of *respondeat superior,* which the courts have applied for nearly two centuries,

continues to have practical implications in all situations involving principal-agent (employer-employee) relationships. Today, the small-town grocer with one clerk and the multinational corporation with thousands of employees are equally subject to the doctrinal demand of "let the master respond." (Keep this principle in mind when you read through Chapters 21 through 23.)

THE SCOPE OF EMPLOYMENT The key to determining whether a principal may be liable for the torts of an agent under the doctrine of *respondeat superior* is whether the torts are committed within the scope of the agency or employment. The *Restatement (Third) of Agency,* Section 7.07(2) states:

> An employee acts within the scope of employment when performing work assigned by the employer or engaging in a course of conduct subject to the employer's control. An employee's act is not within the scope of employment when it occurs within the independent course of conduct not intended by the employee to serve any purpose of the employer.

In other words, an employee who is driving a UPS truck and delivering shipments is acting within the scope of her employment. When that same employee drives home in her own vehicle after work, she is no longer acting within the scope of her employment.

THE DISTINCTION BETWEEN A "DETOUR" AND A "FROLIC" A useful insight into the concept of "scope of employment" may be gained from Judge Baron Parke's classic distinction between a "detour" and a "frolic" in the case of *Joel v. Morison* (1834).[21] In this case, the English court held that if a servant merely took a detour from his master's business, the master would be responsible. If, however, the servant was on a "frolic of his own" and not in any way "on his master's business," the master would not be liable.

Consider an example. Mandel, a traveling salesperson, while driving his employer's vehicle to call on a customer, decides to stop at the post office—which is one block off his route—to mail a personal letter. As Mandel approaches the post office, he negligently runs into a parked vehicle owned by Chan. In this situation, because Mandel's detour from the employer's business is not substantial, he is still acting within the scope of employment, and

---

20. Pronounced ree-*spahn*-dee-uht soo-*peer*-ee-your. The doctrine of *respondeat superior* applies not only to employer-employee relationships but also to other principal-agent relationships in which the principal has the right of control over the agent.

21. 6 Car. & P. 501, 172 Eng.Rep. 1338 (1834).

the employer is liable. The result would be different, though, if Mandel had decided to pick up a few friends for cocktails in another city and in the process had negligently run the vehicle into Chan's. In that circumstance, the departure from the employer's business would be substantial, and the employer normally would not be liable to Chan for damages. Mandel would be considered to have been on a "frolic" of his own.

NOTICE OF DANGEROUS CONDITIONS The employer is charged with knowledge of any dangerous conditions discovered by an employee and pertinent to the employment situation. Suppose that Brad, a maintenance employee in an apartment building, notices a lead pipe protruding from the ground in the building's courtyard. Brad neglects either to fix the pipe or to inform his employer of the danger. John trips on the pipe and is injured. The employer is charged with knowledge of the dangerous condition regardless of whether Brad actually informed the employer. That knowledge is imputed to the employer by virtue of the employment relationship.

BORROWED SERVANTS Employers sometimes lend the services of their employees to other employers. Suppose that an employer leases ground-moving equipment to another employer and sends along an employee to operate the machinery. Who is liable for injuries caused by the employee's negligent actions on the job site?

Liability turns on *which employer had the primary right to control* the employee at the time the injuries occurred. Generally, the employer who rents out the equipment is presumed to retain control over her or his employee. If the rental is for a relatively long period of time, however, control may be deemed to pass to the employer who is renting the equipment and presumably controlling and directing the employee.

Liability for Agent's Intentional Torts

Most intentional torts that employees commit have no relation to their employment; thus, their employers will not be held liable. Nevertheless, under the doctrine of *respondeat superior,* the employer can be liable for intentional torts of the employee that are committed within the course and scope of employment, just as the employer is liable for negligence. For example, an employer is liable when an employee (such as a "bouncer"

at a nightclub or a security guard at a department store) commits the tort of assault and battery or false imprisonment while acting within the scope of employment.

In addition, an employer who knows or should know that an employee has a propensity for committing tortious acts is liable for the employee's acts even if they would not ordinarily be considered within the scope of employment. For example, if an employer hires a bouncer knowing that he has a history of arrests for criminal assault and battery, the employer may be liable if the employee viciously attacks a patron in the parking lot after hours.

An employer is also liable for permitting an employee to engage in reckless actions that can injure others. For example, an employer observes an employee smoking while filling containerized trucks with highly flammable liquids. Failure to stop the employee will cause the employer to be liable for any injuries that result if a truck explodes. Needless to say, most employers purchase liability insurance to cover their potential liability for employee conduct in many situations.

Liability for Independent Contractor's Torts

Generally, an employer is not liable for physical harm caused to a third person by the negligent act of an independent contractor in the performance of the contract. This is because the employer does not have *the right to control* the details of an independent contractor's performance. Courts make an exception to this rule when the contract involves unusually hazardous activities, such as blasting operations, the transportation of highly volatile chemicals, or the use of poisonous gases. In these situations, an employer cannot be shielded from liability merely by using an independent contractor. Strict liability is imposed on the employer-principal as a matter of law. Also, in some states, strict liability may be imposed by statute.

Liability for Agent's Crimes

An agent is liable for his or her own crimes. A principal or employer is not liable for an agent's or employee's crime simply because the agent or employee committed the crime while otherwise acting within the scope of authority or employment. An exception to this rule is made when the principal or employer participated in the crime by conspiracy or other action. In some jurisdictions, under specific statutes, a principal may be liable if an agent, in the course and scope of employment, violates regulations such as those governing sanitation, prices, weights, and the sale of liquor.

SECTION 7
TERMINATION OF AN AGENCY

Agency law is similar to contract law in that both an agency and a contract may be terminated by an act of the parties or by operation of law. Once the relationship between the principal and the agent has ended, the agent no longer has the right (*actual* authority) to bind the principal. For an agent's *apparent* authority to be terminated, though, third persons may also need to be notified that the agency has been terminated.

Termination by Act of the Parties

An agency relationship may be terminated by act of the parties in any of the following ways:

1. *Lapse of time.* When an agency agreement specifies the time period during which the agency relationship will exist, the agency ends when that time period expires. For example, Akers signs an agreement of agency with Janz "beginning January 1, 2012, and ending December 31, 2014." The agency is automatically terminated on December 31, 2014. If no definite time is stated, then the agency continues for a reasonable time and can be terminated at will by either party. What constitutes a reasonable time depends on the circumstances and the nature of the agency relationship.

2. *Purpose achieved.* If an agent is employed to accomplish a particular objective, such as the purchase of breeding stock for a cattle rancher, the agency automatically ends after the cattle have been purchased. If more than one agent is employed to accomplish the same purpose, such as the sale of real estate, the first agent to complete the sale automatically terminates the agency relationship for all the others.

3. *Occurrence of a specific event.* When an agency relationship is to terminate on the happening of a certain event, the agency automatically ends when the event occurs. For example, if Posner appoints Rubik to handle her business affairs while she is away, the agency automatically terminates when Posner returns.

4. *Mutual agreement.* The parties to an agency can cancel (rescind) their contract by mutually agreeing to terminate the agency relationship, whether the agency contract is in writing or whether it is for a specific duration.

5. *Termination by one party.* As a *general* rule, either party can terminate the agency relationship—because agency is a consensual relationship, and thus neither party can be compelled to continue in the relationship. The agent's act is said to be a *renunciation* of authority. The principal's act is a *revocation* of authority. Although both parties may have the *power* to terminate the agency, they may not possess the *right* to terminate and therefore may be liable for breach of contract, or *wrongful termination.*

WRONGFUL TERMINATION Wrongful termination can subject the canceling party to a lawsuit for breach of contract. For example, Rawlins has a one-year employment contract with Munro to act as agent in return for $65,000. Although Munro has the *power* to discharge Rawlins before the contract period expires, if he does so, he can be sued for breaching the contract because he had no *right* to terminate the agency.

Even in an agency at will—that is, an agency that either party may terminate at any time—the principal who wishes to terminate must give the agent *reasonable* notice. The notice must be at least sufficient to allow the agent to recoup his or her expenses and, in some situations, to make a normal profit.

AGENCY COUPLED WITH AN INTEREST A special rule applies in an *agency coupled with an interest.* This type of agency is not an agency in the usual sense because it is created for the agent's benefit instead of for the principal's benefit. For example, Julie borrows $5,000 from Rob, giving Rob some of her jewelry and signing a letter authorizing him to sell the jewelry as her agent if she fails to repay the loan. After Julie receives the $5,000 from Rob, she attempts to revoke his authority to sell the jewelry as her agent. Julie will not succeed in this attempt because a principal cannot revoke an agency created for the agent's benefit.

An agency coupled with an interest should not be confused with a situation in which the agent merely derives proceeds or profits from the sale of the subject matter. For example, an agent who merely receives a commission from the sale of real property does not have a beneficial interest in the property itself.

NOTICE OF TERMINATION When an agency has been terminated by act of the parties, it is the principal's duty to inform any third parties who know of the existence of the agency that it has been terminated (notice of the termination may be given by others, however).

Although an agent's actual authority ends when the agency is terminated, an agent's *apparent authority* continues until the third party receives notice (from any source) that such authority has been terminated. If the principal knows that a third party has dealt with the agent, the principal is expected to notify that person *directly*. For third parties who have heard about the agency but have not yet dealt with the agent, *constructive notice* is sufficient.[22]

No particular form is required for notice of termination of the principal-agent relationship to be effective. The principal can personally notify the agent, or the agent can learn of the termination through some other means. For example, Manning bids on a shipment of steel, and Stone is hired as an agent to arrange transportation for the shipment. When Stone learns that Manning has lost the bid, Stone's authority to make the transportation arrangement terminates. If the agent's authority is written, however, normally it must be revoked in writing (unless the written document contains an expiration date).

Termination by Operation of Law

Certain events terminate agency authority automatically because their occurrence makes it impossible for the agent to perform or improbable that the principal would continue to want performance. We look at these events here. Note that when an agency terminates by operation of law, there is no duty to notify third persons—unless the agent's authority is coupled with an interest.

1. *Death or insanity.* The general rule is that the death or insanity of either the principal or the agent automatically and immediately terminates an ordinary agency relationship.[23] Knowledge of the death or insanity is not required.

2. *Impossibility.* When the specific subject matter of an agency is destroyed or lost, the agency terminates. For example, Gonzalez employs Arnez to sell Gonzalez's house. Prior to any sale, the house is destroyed by fire. Arnez's agency and authority to sell the house terminate. Similarly, when it is impossible for the agent to perform the agency lawfully because of a change in the law, the agency terminates.

3. *Changed circumstances.* When an event occurs that has such an unusual effect on the subject matter of the agency that the agent can reasonably infer that the principal will not want the agency to continue, the agency terminates. Suppose that Baird hires Joslen to sell a tract of land for $40,000. Subsequently, Joslen learns that there is oil under the land and that the land is therefore worth $1 million. The agency and Joslen's authority to sell the land for $40,000 are terminated.

4. *Bankruptcy.* If either the principal or the agent petitions for bankruptcy, the agency is *usually* terminated. In certain circumstances, such as when the agent's financial status is irrelevant to the purpose of the agency, the agency relationship may continue. *Insolvency* (the inability to pay debts when they come due or when liabilities exceed assets), as distinguished from bankruptcy, does not necessarily terminate the relationship.

5. *War.* When the principal's country and the agent's country are at war with each other, the agency is terminated. In this situation, the agency is automatically suspended or terminated because there is no way to enforce the legal rights and obligations of the parties.

See *Concept Summary 20.2* on the following page for a synopsis of the rules governing the termination of an agency.

---

22. With *constructive notice* of a fact, knowledge of the fact is imputed by law to a person if he or she could have discovered the fact by proper diligence. Constructive notice is often accomplished by publication in a newspaper.

23. An exception to this rule exists in the bank-customer relationship. A bank, as agent, can continue to exercise specific types of authority even after the customer's death or insanity, and can continue to pay checks drawn by the customer for ten days after death.

CONCEPT SUMMARY 20.2
Termination of an Agency

Method of Termination	Rules	Termination of Agent's Authority
Act of the Parties		
1. Lapse of time.	Automatic at end of the stated time.	
2. Purpose achieved.	Automatic on the completion of the purpose.	**Notice to Third Parties Required—**
3. Occurrence of a specific event.	Normally automatic on the happening of the event.	1. Direct to those who have dealt with agency.
4. Mutual agreement.	Mutual consent required.	2. Constructive to all others.
5. At the option of one party (revocation, if by principal; renunciation, if by agent).	Either party normally has a right to terminate the agency but may lack the power to do so; wrongful termination can lead to liability for breach of contract.	
Operation of Law		
1. Death or insanity.	Automatic on the death or insanity of either the principal or the agent (except when the agency is coupled with an interest).	
2. Impossibility—destruction of the specific subject matter.	Applies any time the agency cannot be performed because of an event beyond the parties' control.	**No Notice Required—** Automatic on the happening of the event.
3. Changed circumstances.	Events so unusual that it would be inequitable to allow the agency to continue to exist.	
4. Bankruptcy.	Bankruptcy petition (not mere insolvency) usually terminates the agency.	
5. War between principal's country and agent's country.	Automatically suspends or terminates agency—no way to enforce legal rights.	

REVIEWING
Agency

Lynne Meyer, on her way to a business meeting and in a hurry, stopped at a Buy-Mart store for a new pair of nylons to wear to the meeting. There was a long line at one of the checkout counters, but a cashier, Valerie Watts, opened another counter and began loading the cash drawer. Meyer told Watts that she was in a hurry and asked Watts to work faster. Instead, Watts, only slowed her pace. At this point, Meyer hit Watts. It is not clear whether Meyer hit Watts intentionally or, in an attempt to retrieve the nylons, hit her inadvertently. In response, Watts grabbed Meyer by the hair and hit her repeatedly in the back of the head, while Meyer screamed for help. Management personnel separated the two women and questioned them about the incident. Watts was immediately fired for violating the store's no-fighting policy. Meyer subsequently sued Buy-Mart, alleging that the store was liable for the tort (assault and battery) committed by its employee. Using the information presented in the chapter, answer the following questions.

REVIEWING

Agency, Continued

1. Under what doctrine discussed in this chapter might Buy-Mart be held liable for the tort committed by Watts?
2. What is the key factor in determining whether Buy-Mart is liable under this doctrine?
3. How is Buy-Mart's potential liability affected by whether Watts's behavior constituted an intentional tort or negligence?
4. Suppose that when Watts applied for the job at Buy-Mart, she disclosed in her application that she had previously been convicted of felony assault and battery. Nevertheless, Buy-Mart hired Watts as a cashier. How might this fact affect Buy-Mart's liability for Watts's actions?

DEBATE THIS: *The doctrine of* respondeat superior *should be modified to make agents solely liable for some of their tortious acts.*

TERMS AND CONCEPTS

	e-agent 464	independent contractor 451	undisclosed principal 463

agency 450

apparent authority 461

disclosed principal 463

e-agent 464

equal dignity rule 459

express authority 459

fiduciary 450

implied authority 460

independent contractor 451

notary public 459

power of attorney 459

ratification 463

respondeat superior 466

undisclosed principal 463

unidentified principal 463

vicarious liability 466

QUESTIONS AND CASE PROBLEMS

20–1. Agency Formation Paul Gett is a well-known, wealthy financial expert living in the city of Torris. Adam Wade, Gett's friend, tells Timothy Brown that he is Gett's agent for the purchase of rare coins. Wade even shows Brown a local newspaper clipping mentioning Gett's interest in coin collecting. Brown, knowing of Wade's friendship with Gett, contracts with Wade to sell a rare coin to Gett valued at $25,000. Wade takes the coin and disappears with it. On the payment due date, Brown seeks to collect from Gett, claiming that Wade's agency made Gett liable. Gett does not deny that Wade was a friend, but he claims that Wade was never his agent. Discuss fully whether an agency was in existence at the time the contract for the rare coin was made.

20–2. QUESTION WITH SAMPLE ANSWER: Duty of Loyalty.

Peter hires Alice as an agent to sell a piece of property he owns. The price is to be at least $30,000. Alice discovers that the fair market value of Peter's property is actually at least

$45,000 and could be higher because a shopping mall is going to be built nearby. Alice forms a real estate partnership with her cousin Carl, and she prepares for Peter's signature a contract for the sale of the property to Carl for $32,000. Peter signs the contract. Just before closing and passage of title, Peter learns about the shopping mall and the increased fair market value of his property. Peter refuses to deed the property to Carl. Carl claims that Alice, as agent, solicited a price above that agreed on when the agency was created and that the contract is therefore binding and enforceable. Discuss fully whether Peter is bound to this contract.

- **For a sample answer to Question 20–2, go to Appendix F at the end of this text.**

20–3. Ratification by Principal Springer was a political candidate running for Congress. He was operating on a tight budget and instructed his campaign staff not to purchase any campaign materials without his explicit authorization. In spite of these instructions, one of his campaign workers ordered Dubychek Printing Co. to print some promotional materials for Springer's campaign. When the printed materials arrived, Springer did not return them but instead used them during his campaign. When Springer failed to pay for the materials, Dubychek sued for recovery of the price. Springer contended that he was not liable on the sales contract because he had not authorized his agent to purchase the printing services. Dubychek argued that the campaign worker was Springer's agent and that the worker had authority to make the printing contract. Additionally, Dubychek claimed that even if the purchase was unauthorized, Springer's use of the materials constituted ratification of his agent's unauthorized purchase. Is Dubychek correct? Explain.

20-4. Agent's Duties to Principal In July 2001, John Warren viewed a condominium in Woodland Hills, California, as a potential buyer. Hildegard Merrill was the agent for the seller. Because Warren's credit rating was poor, Merrill told him he needed a co-borrower to obtain a mortgage at a reasonable rate. Merrill said that her daughter Charmaine would "go on title" until the loan and sale were complete if Warren would pay her $10,000. Merrill also offered to defer her commission on the sale as a loan to Warren so that he could make a 20 percent down payment on the property. He agreed to both plans. Merrill applied for and secured the mortgage in Charmaine's name alone by misrepresenting her daughter's address, business, and income. To close the sale, Merrill had Warren remove his name from the title to the property. In October, Warren moved into the condominium, repaid Merrill the amount of her deferred commission, and began paying the mortgage. Within a few months, Merrill had Warren evicted. Warren filed a suit in a California state court against Merrill and Charmaine. Who among these parties was in an agency relationship? What is the basic duty that an agent owes a principal? Was the duty breached here? Explain. [*Warren v. Merrill*, 143 Cal.App.4th 96, 49 Cal.Rptr.3d 122 (2 Dist. 2006)]

20-5. Apparent Authority Lee Dennegar and Mark Knutson lived in Dennegar's house in Raritan, New Jersey. Dennegar paid the mortgage and other household expenses. With Dennegar's consent, Knutson managed their household's financial affairs and the "general office functions concerned with maintaining the house." Dennegar allowed Knutson to handle the mail and "to do with it as he chose." Knutson wrote checks for Dennegar to sign, although Knutson signed Dennegar's name to many of the checks with Dennegar's consent. AT&T Universal issued a credit card in Dennegar's name in February 2001. Monthly statements were mailed to Dennegar's house, and payments were sometimes made on those statements. Knutson died in June 2003. The unpaid charges on the card of $14,752.93 were assigned to New Century Financial Services, Inc. New Century filed a suit in a New Jersey state court against Dennegar to collect the unpaid amount. Dennegar claimed that he never applied for or used the card and knew nothing about it. Under what theory could Dennegar be liable

for the charges? Explain. [*New Century Financial Services, Inc. v. Dennegar*, 394 N.J.Super. 595, 928 A.2d 48 (A.D. 2007)]

20-6. Agent's Duties to Principal Su Ru Chen owned the Lucky Duck Fortune Cookie Factory in Everett, Massachusetts, which made Chinese-style fortune cookies for restaurants. In November 2001, Chen listed the business for sale with Bob Sun, a real estate broker, for $35,000. Sun's daughter Frances and her fiancé, Chiu Chung Chan, decided that Chan would buy the business. Acting as a broker on Chen's (the seller's) behalf, Frances asked about the Lucky Duck's finances. Chen said that each month the business sold at least 1,000 boxes of cookies at a $2,000 profit. Frances negotiated a price of $23,000, which Chan (her fiancé) paid. When Chan began to operate the Lucky Duck, it became clear that the demand for the cookies was actually about 500 boxes per month—a rate at which the business would suffer losses. Less than two months later, the factory closed. Chan filed a suit in a Massachusetts state court against Chen, alleging fraud, among other things. Chan's proof included Frances's testimony as to what Chen had said to her. Chen objected to the admission of this testimony. What is the basis for this objection? Should the court admit the testimony? Why or why not? [*Chan v. Chen*, 70 Mass.App.Ct. 79, 872 N.E.2d 1153 (2007)]

20-7. CASE PROBLEM WITH SAMPLE ANSWER: Undisclosed Principal.

 *Homeowners Jim and Lisa Criss hired Kevin and Cathie Pappas, doing business as Outside Creations, to undertake a landscaping project. Kevin signed the parties' contract as "Outside Creations Rep." The Crisses made payments on the contract with checks payable to Kevin, who deposited them in his personal account—there was no Outside Creations account. Later, alleging breach of contract, the Crisses filed a suit in a Georgia state court against the Pappases. The defendants contended that they could not be liable because the contract was not with them personally. They claimed that they were the agents of Forever Green Landscaping and Irrigation, Inc., which had been operating under the name "Outside Creations" at the time of the contract and had since filed for bankruptcy. The Crisses pointed out that the name "Forever Green" was not in the contract. Can the Pappases be liable on this contract? Why or why not? [*Pappas v. Criss*, 296 Ga.App. 803, 676 S.E.2d 21 (2009)]*

- **To view a sample answer for Problem 20-7, go to this book's Web site at www.cengage.com/blaw/cross, select "Chapter 20," and click on "Case Problem with Sample Answer."**

20-8. Agency by Ratification Wesley Hall, an independent contractor managing property for Acree Investments, Ltd., lost control of a fire he had set to clear ten acres of Acree land. The runaway fire burned seventy-eight acres of Earl Barrs's property. Russell Acree, one of the owners of Acree Investments, had previously owned the ten acres, but he had put it into the company and was no longer the principal owner. Hall had worked for Russell Acree in the past and had told the state forestry department that he was burning the land for Acree. Barrs sued Russell Acree for the acts of his agent, Hall. In his suit, Barrs noted that Hall had been an employee of Russell Acree, Hall had talked about burning the land "for Acree," Russell Acree had apologized to Barrs for the fire, and Acree Investments had not been identified as the principal property owner until Barrs had filed his lawsuit. Barrs argued that those facts were sufficient to create an agency by ratification to impose liability on Russell Acree. Was Barrs's agency by ratification claim valid? Why or why not? [*Barrs v. Acree*, 691 S.E.2d 575 (Ga.App. 2010)]

20–9. Liability Based on Actual or Apparent Authority Summerall Electric Co. and other subcontractors were hired by National Church Services, Inc. (NCS), which was the general contractor on a construction project for the Church of God at Southaven. As work progressed, payments from NCS to the subcontractors were late and eventually stopped altogether. The church had paid NCS in full for the entire project beforehand, but apparently NCS had mismanaged the project. When payments from NCS stopped, the subcontractors filed *mechanic's liens* (see page 331 in Chapter 15) for the value of the work they had performed but for which they had not been paid. The subcontractors sued the church, contending that it was liable for the payments because NCS was its agent on the basis of either actual or apparent authority. Was NCS an agent for the church, thereby making the church liable to the subcontractors? Explain your reasoning. [*Summerall Electric Co. v. Church of God at Southaven*, 25 So.3d 1090 (App.Miss. 2010)]

20–10. A QUESTION OF ETHICS: Power of Attorney.

Warren Davis lived with Renee Brandt in a house that Davis owned in Virginia Beach, Virginia. At Davis's request, attorney Leigh Ansell prepared, and Davis acknowledged, a durable power of attorney appointing Ansell to act as Davis's attorney-in-fact. Ansell was authorized to sign "any . . . instrument of . . . deposit" and "any contract . . . relating to . . . personal property." Ansell could act "in any circumstances as fully and effectively as I could do as part of my normal, everyday business affairs if acting personally." A few days later, at Davis's direction, Ansell prepared, and Davis signed, a will that gave Brandt the right to occupy, rent-free, the house in which she and Davis lived "so long as she lives in the premises." The will's other chief beneficiaries were Davis's daughters, Sharon Jones and Jody Clark. According to Ansell, Davis intended to "take care of [Brandt] outside of this will" and asked Ansell to designate Brandt the beneficiary "payable on death" of Davis's $250,000 certificate of deposit (CD). The CD had no other named beneficiary. Less than two months later, Davis died. A suit between Brandt and Davis's daughters ensued in a Virginia state court. [Jones v. Brandt, 274 Va. 131, 645 S.E.2d 312 (2007)]

(a) Should the language in a power of attorney be interpreted broadly or strictly? Why?

(b) In this case, did Ansell have the authority under the power of attorney to change the beneficiary of Davis's CD? Explain.

(c) Ansell advised Davis by letter that he had complied with the instruction to designate Brandt the beneficiary of the CD. Davis made no objection. Based on these facts, what theory might apply to validate the designation?

LEGAL RESEARCH EXERCISES ON THE WEB

Go to this text's Web site at **www.cengage.com/blaw/cross**, select "Chapter 20," and click on "Practical Internet Exercises." There you will find the following Internet research exercises that you can perform to learn more about the topics covered in this chapter.

Practical Internet Exercise 20–1: **Legal Perspective**
Liability in Agency Relationships

Practical Internet Exercise 20–2: **Management Perspective**
Problems with Using Independent Contractors

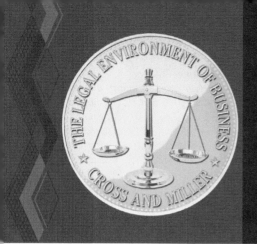

CHAPTER 21
❋
Employment
Relationships

Until the early 1900s, most employer-employee relationships were governed by the common law. Even today, under the common law *employment-at-will doctrine*, private employers are generally free to hire and fire workers at will, unless doing so violates an employee's contractual or statutory rights. Now, however, there are numerous statutes and administrative agency regulations that regulate the workplace. Thus, to a large extent, statutory law has displaced common law doctrines.

In this chapter, we look at the most significant laws regulating employment relationships. We deal with other important laws regulating the workplace—those that prohibit employment discrimination, restrict immigration, and regulate labor unions—in Chapters 22 and 23.

SECTION 1
EMPLOYMENT AT WILL

Traditionally, employment relationships have generally been governed by the common law doctrine of **employment at will.** Under this doctrine, either party may terminate the employment relationship at any time and for any reason, unless doing so would violate the provisions of an employment contract or a statute. The majority of U.S. workers continue to have the legal status of "employees at will." In other words, this common law doctrine is still in widespread use, and only one state (Montana) does not apply the doctrine.

Nonetheless, as mentioned in the chapter introduction, federal and state statutes governing employment relationships prevent the doctrine from being applied in a number of circumstances. Today, an employer is not permitted to fire an employee if doing so would violate a federal or state employment statute, such as one prohibiting employment termination for discriminatory reasons (see Chapter 22). Note that the distinction made under agency law (see Chapter 20) between employee status and independent-contractor status is important here. The employment laws that will be discussed in this chapter and in Chapter 22 apply only to the employer-employee relationship. They do not apply to independent contractors.

Exceptions to the Employment-at-Will Doctrine

Under the employment-at-will doctrine, as mentioned, an employer may hire and fire employees at will (regardless of the employees' performance) without liability, unless the decision violates the terms of an employment contract or statutory law. Because of the harsh effects of the employment-at-will doctrine for employees, courts have carved out various exceptions to this doctrine. These exceptions are based on contract theory, tort theory, and public policy.

EXCEPTIONS BASED ON CONTRACT THEORY Some courts have held that an *implied* employment contract exists between the employer and the employee. If the employee is fired outside the terms of the implied contract, he or she may succeed in an action for breach of contract even though no written employment contract exists. For example, an employer's manual or personnel bulletin may state that, as a matter of policy, workers will be dismissed only for good cause. If the employee is aware of this policy and continues to work for the employer, a court may find that there is an implied contract based on the terms stated in the manual or bulletin. Generally, the key consideration in determining whether an employment manual creates an implied contractual obligation is the employee's reasonable expectations.

Courts in a few states have gone further and held that all employment contracts contain an implied covenant of good faith. This means that both sides promise to abide by the contract in good faith. If an employer fires an employee for an arbitrary or unjustified reason, the employee can claim that the covenant of good faith was breached and the contract violated.

Increasingly, employers and their employees are negotiating the terms of employment contracts via e-mail and other forms of electronic communication. See this chapter's *Shifting Legal Priorities for Business* feature on page 477 for a discussion of whether the promises that employers make to employees in e-mail exchanges are enforceable in court.

In the following case, an employment contract that explicitly stated that the employment was "at will" also contained provisions relating to the contract's renewal under certain circumstances. Was this an at-will contract, or was the employer bound by the renewal provisions? That was the issue before the court.

CASE 21.1
Ellis v. BlueSky Charter School

Court of Appeals of Minnesota, ___ N.W.2d ___ (2010).
www.lawlibrary.state.mn.us/archive/index.html[a]

BACKGROUND AND FACTS • In November 2008, Thomas Ellis signed an employment agreement with BlueSky Charter School, which provided that Ellis was to serve as the school director for the 2008–2009 school year. The title of the agreement stated the dates July 1, 2008 through June 30, 2009. The first sentence of the agreement stated that it was "a general at will agreement," with the phrase *at will agreement* set in bold type. The agreement also provided that "positions [would] automatically renew for one year after one year of service unless specific actions [were] taken by the board before April 15th of each year." It defined the work year as "220 days from July 1 to June 30." At a meeting of the school's board of directors on May 7, 2009, the school terminated Ellis's contract. Ellis filed an action against the school in a Minnesota state court, alleging that the school had breached the employment contract. Ellis argued that because his contract was terminated after April 15, 2009, the school was obligated to employ him for the remainder of the 2008–2009 school year and through the 2009–2010 school year. He sought damages for pay that he was owed as of May 2009 and thereafter, through the school year ending in 2010. He also sought future damages for lost benefits and the decreased value of retirement benefits, as well as severance pay and other amounts associated with termination. The trial court held for the school, and Ellis appealed.

IN THE LANGUAGE OF THE COURT
CRIPPEN, Judge.
* * * *

In Minnesota, an employment contract of indefinite duration is generally interpreted to be a contract for employment at will, which may be terminated at any time without cause. Conversely, an employment agreement for a fixed term is generally interpreted as terminable only for cause. Express language may override these general rules of interpretation. [Emphasis added.]

The employment agreement of the parties unambiguously declared "at will" employment. Without qualification or limitation, the first line of the agreement states that it is a "general at will agreement covering the [listed] positions." The words "at will agreement" are the only terms that appear in bold type in the text of the contract.

---

a. In the box titled "Court of Appeals Opinions," select "Index by Docket Number." When that page appears, click on the link in the right-hand column to "Docket No. 09-." On the page that opens, scroll down the list to Docket No. A09-1205 and click on the highlighted link to access the case. The Minnesota State Appellate Courts Archive maintains this Web site.

CASE CONTINUES ▶

CASE 21.1 CONTINUED ➡ * * * *

The agreement refers to a work year from July 1, 2008 to June 30, 2009. * * * [Ellis] argues that these references establish a fixed-term contract. Although the contract is not expressly declared an agreement for a set term, the references to start and end dates, standing alone, would likely be sufficient to establish a term contract terminable only for cause. But * * * the general rule for construing indefinite contracts is overcome by express terms in a contract. The plain language of the "at will" phrase overrides the general rule for construing a fixed-term contact, expressly replacing any implication that might have been drawn from the reference to start and end dates.

DECISION AND REMEDY • *The Minnesota appellate court affirmed the decision of the lower court, ruling that Ellis was not entitled to recover damages based on a breach of his employment contract because his position was "at will."*

THE LEGAL ENVIRONMENT DIMENSION • *In contract law, an ambiguous contract is to be construed against the drafter—because the drafter of the contract was responsible for the ambiguity. Should the contract between Ellis and the school be deemed an ambiguous contract? Explain.*

THE ETHICAL DIMENSION • *Is the at-will employment tradition fair to employees? Why or why not?*

EXCEPTIONS BASED ON TORT THEORY In some situations, the discharge of an employee may give rise to an action for wrongful discharge under tort theories. Abusive discharge procedures may result in a lawsuit for intentional infliction of emotional distress or defamation. In addition, some courts have permitted workers to sue their employers under the tort theory of fraud. Under this theory, an employer may be held liable for making false promises to a prospective employee if the person detrimentally relies on the employer's representations by taking the job.

Suppose that an employer induces a prospective employee to leave a lucrative position and move to another state by offering "a long-term job with a thriving business." In fact, the employer is having significant financial problems. Furthermore, the employer is planning a merger that will result in the elimination of the position offered to the prospective employee. If the person takes the job in reliance on the employer's representations and is laid off shortly thereafter, he or she may be able to bring an action against the employer for fraud.[1]

EXCEPTIONS BASED ON PUBLIC POLICY Most often, a common law exception to the employment-at-will doctrine is made on the basis of public policy. Courts may apply this exception when an employer fires a worker for reasons that violate a fundamental public policy of the jurisdiction. Generally, the courts require

that the public policy involved be expressed clearly in the statutory law governing the jurisdiction.

For example, employers with fifty or more employees are required by the federal Family and Medical Leave Act (FMLA—see page 481) to give employees up to twelve weeks of unpaid family or medical leave per year. Mila's employer has only forty employees and thus is not covered by the law. Nonetheless, if Mila is fired from her job because she takes three weeks of unpaid family leave to help her son through a difficult surgery, a court may deem that the employer's actions violated the public policy expressed in the FMLA.

An exception may also be made when an employee "blows the whistle" on an employer's wrongdoing. **Whistleblowing** occurs when an employee tells government authorities, upper-level managers, or the media that her or his employer is engaged in some unsafe or illegal activity. Whistleblowers on occasion have been protected from wrongful discharge for reasons of public policy.[2] Normally, however, whistleblowers seek protection from retaliatory discharge under federal and state statutory laws, such as the Whistleblower Protection Act of 1989.[3]

Wrongful Discharge

Whenever an employer discharges an employee in violation of an employment contract or a statutory law protecting employees, the employee may

---

1. See, for example, *Helmer v. Bingham Toyota Isuzu,* 129 Cal. App.4th 1121, 29 Cal.Rptr.3d 136 (2005).

2. See, for example, *Wendeln v. The Beatrice Manor, Inc.,* 271 Neb. 373, 712 N.W.2d 226 (2006).

3. 5 U.S.C. Section 1201.

Today, e-mail is used in nearly every aspect of the employment environment—from workplace communications to negotiations of contracts with employees. As you learned in Chapter 9, under the one-year rule of the Statute of Frauds, most employment contracts must be in writing. But electronic communications, including e-mail, instant messages, text messages, and even Twitter, can be used as evidence to show that a contract existed or that the parties modified their contract.

Moreover, although many employment contracts include traditional integration clauses stating that the contract can be modified only by a signed writing, such a clause may not necessarily prevent e-mail modifications. Under the federal E-Sign Act and the Uniform Electronic Transactions Act, what constitutes a signed writing has changed. A court cannot refuse to enforce a contract solely because it is contained in an electronic record, and a name typed at the end of an e-mail can be a signature.

E-Mail Evidence That an Employment Contract Existed

The court applied this rule in a recent case. Robert Moroni negotiated a deal to provide consulting services for Medco Health Solutions, Inc., a third party administrator of prescription-drug plans. Medco sent Moroni an e-mail setting forth the details of the parties' agreement. Moroni e-mailed a counteroffer, proposing that he would work on Medco's projects two days a week for thirteen months, in exchange for $17,000 per month ($204,000 annually), plus travel expenses. Medco accepted via e-mail, and Moroni began performing the contract, but Medco refused to pay him. Moroni sued for breach of contract. Medco argued that no enforceable contract existed and that the e-mail exchange showed only an agreement to agree. The court, however, ruled that the e-mail amounted to an agreement to the essential terms of an employment contract.[a]

E-Mail Modifications of an Employment Contract

In another case, Arthur Stevens sold his public relations firm in New York to Publicis, S.A., a French global communications company. (*S.A.* stands for *Société Anonyme,* the French equivalent of a U.S. corporation.) The sale involved two contracts: a stock purchase agreement (SPA) and an employment contract. Stevens received an initial payment of more than $3 million under the SPA and stood to receive additional payments of up to $4 million over the next three years, depending on the new company's earnings. The employment contract allowed Stevens to stay on as chief executive officer (CEO) of the new company for three years and contained an integration clause that required any modification to be in a signed writing.

Within six months of the sale, however, the new company had lost $900,000 and was not meeting revenue and profit targets. Stevens was removed as CEO and given the option of leaving the firm or staying to develop new business. An agent of Publicis then e-mailed Stevens another option, giving him specific information on the responsibilities he could assume. Within a day, Stevens sent an e-mail stating, "I accept your proposal with total enthusiasm and excitement." The message also said that he was "psyched" about his new position. Nevertheless, Stevens later sued Publicis, claiming that it had breached the terms of his original employment contract by not keeping him on as CEO. The court, however, held that in the e-mail exchanges, Stevens had accepted the proposed modification of his employment contract in a signed writing. Because the e-mail modification was binding, Stevens could not sue Publicis.[b]

MANAGERIAL IMPLICATIONS

Communication with potential and actual employees via Twitter, instant messaging, Facebook, MySpace, and e-mail has become common. Managers must understand that a court may review the entire thread of such communications and determine that the exchange is sufficient to create an agreement about the essential terms of a contract. Thus, any form of online communication about a job or a modification of an employment agreement must be treated as if it were part of actual contract negotiations.

a. *Moroni v. Medco Health Solutions, Inc.,* 2008 WL 3539476 (E.D.Mich. 2008).

b. *Stevens v. Publicis, S.A.,* 50 A.D.3d 253, 854 N.Y.S.2d 690 (1 Dept. 2008).

bring an action for **wrongful discharge.** Even if an employer's actions do not violate any express employment contract or statute, the employer may still be subject to liability under a common law doctrine, such as a tort theory or agency. For example, if an employer discharges a female employee and publicly discloses private facts about her sex life to her co-workers, the employee could bring a wrongful discharge suit based on an invasion of privacy (see Chapter 12).

SECTION 2
WAGE AND HOUR LAWS

In the 1930s, Congress enacted several laws regulating the wages and working hours of employees. In 1931, Congress passed the Davis-Bacon Act,[4] which requires contractors and subcontractors working on federal government construction projects to pay "prevailing wages" to their employees. In 1936, the Walsh-Healey Act[5] was passed. This act requires that a minimum wage, as well as overtime pay at 1.5 times regular pay rates, be paid to employees of manufacturers or suppliers entering into contracts with agencies of the federal government.

In 1938, Congress passed the Fair Labor Standards Act (FLSA).[6] This act extended wage-hour requirements to cover all employers engaged in interstate commerce or in the production of goods for interstate commerce, plus selected other types of businesses. Here, we examine the FLSA's provisions in regard to child labor, minimum wages, and overtime.

Child Labor

The FLSA prohibits oppressive child labor. Children under fourteen years of age are allowed to do certain types of work, such as deliver newspapers, work for their parents, and be employed in the entertainment and (with some exceptions) agricultural areas. Children who are fourteen or fifteen years of age are allowed to work, but not in hazardous occupations. There are also numerous restrictions on how many hours per day and per week children can work.

Working times and hours are not restricted for persons between the ages of sixteen and eighteen, but they cannot be employed in hazardous jobs or in jobs detrimental to their health and well-being. None of these restrictions apply to those over the age of eighteen.

Minimum Wages

The FLSA provides that a **minimum wage** of $7.25 per hour must be paid to employees in covered industries. Congress periodically revises this minimum wage. Additionally, many states have minimum wage laws. When the state minimum wage is greater than the federal minimum wage, the employee is entitled to the higher wage.

When an employee receives tips while on the job, special rules apply. The employer is only required to pay $2.13 an hour in direct wages—but only if that amount, plus the tips received, equals at least the federal minimum wage ($7.25 per hour). If an employee's tips combined with the employer's direct wages of at least $2.13 an hour do not equal the federal minimum hourly wage, the employer must make up the difference. The FLSA does not prevent employers, who are paying at least the federal minimum hourly wage, from taking employee tips and making another arrangement for tip distribution. Under the FLSA, employers who customarily furnish food or lodging to employees can deduct the reasonable cost of those services from the employees' wages.

Overtime Provisions and Exemptions

Under the FLSA, any employee who works more than forty hours per week must be paid no less than 1.5 times her or his regular pay for all hours over forty. Note that the FLSA overtime provisions apply only after an employee has worked more than forty hours per *week*. Thus, employees who work for ten hours a day, four days per week, are not entitled to overtime pay, because they do not work more than forty hours per week.

Certain employees—usually administrative, executive, and professional employees, as well as outside salespersons and computer programmers—are exempt from the FLSA's overtime provisions. Employers are not required to pay overtime wages to exempt employees. An employer can voluntarily pay overtime to ineligible employees but cannot waive or reduce the overtime requirements of the FLSA.

An executive employee is one whose primary duty is management. An employee's primary duty is determined by what he or she does that is of principal value to the employer, not by how much time the employee spends doing particular tasks. An employer cannot deny overtime wages to an employee based only on the employee's job title, however, and must be able to show that the employee's primary duty qualifies her or him for an exemption.[7]

CASE IN POINT Starbucks hired Kevin Keevican as a barista to wait on customers, operate the cash register, make drinks, and clean the equipment. Eventually, he was promoted to manager. As manager, Keevican worked seventy hours a week for $650 to $800, a 10 to 20 percent bonus,

---

4. 40 U.S.C. Sections 276a–276a-5.
5. 41 U.S.C. Sections 35–45.
6. 29 U.S.C. Sections 201–260.

7. See, for example, *Slusser v. Vantage Builders, Inc.,* 576 F.Supp.2d 1207 (D.N.M. 2008).

and fringe benefits, such as paid sick leave, which were not available to baristas. Keevican quit and, along with other former managers, filed a claim against Starbucks for unpaid overtime. The managers admitted that they had performed many managerial tasks, but argued that they had spent 70 to 80 percent of their time on barista chores and thus were not executive employees. The court, however, found that each manager was "the single highest-ranking employee in his [or her] particular store and was responsible on site for that store's day-to-day overall operations." Therefore, each manager's primary duty was managerial, and Starbucks was not required to pay overtime.[8]

The exemptions from the overtime-pay requirement do not apply to manual laborers or to licensed nurses, police, firefighters, and other public-safety workers. White-collar workers who earn more than $100,000 per year, computer programmers, dental hygienists, and insurance adjusters are typically exempt, though they must also meet certain other criteria.

In the following case, the issue before the court was whether an employee of a pharmaceutical company was an administrative employee and therefore exempt from the overtime requirements of the FLSA.

---

8. *Mims v. Starbucks Corp.*, 2007 WL 10369 (S.D.Tex. 2007).

✳ EXTENDED CASE 21.2 ✳
Smith v. Johnson and Johnson

United States Court of Appeals, Third Circuit, 593 F.3d 280 (2010).
www.ca3.uscourts.gov[a]

IN THE LANGUAGE OF THE COURT

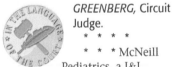

GREENBERG, Circuit Judge.

* * * *

* * * McNeill Pediatrics, a J&J [Johnson and Johnson] wholly owned subsidiary, employed [Patty Lee] Smith in the position of Senior Professional Sales Representative. In essence, Smith's position required her to travel to various doctors' offices and hospitals where she extolled the benefit of J&J's pharmaceutical drug Concerta to the prescribing doctors. * * * Smith, however, did not sell Concerta (a controlled substance) directly to the doctors, as such sales are prohibited by law.

J&J gave Smith a list of target doctors that it created and told her to complete an average of ten visits per day, visiting every doctor on her target list at least once each quarter. To schedule visits with reluctant

doctors, Smith had to be inventive and cultivate relationships with the doctor's staff, an endeavor in which she found that coffee and donuts were useful tools. J&J left the itinerary and order of Smith's visits to the target doctors to her discretion. * * * J&J gave her a budget for these visits and she could use the money in the budget to take the doctors to lunch or to sponsor seminars.

* * * *

In Smith's deposition she made it clear that she appreciated the freedom and responsibility that her position provided. Though a supervisor accompanied Smith during the doctor visits on a few days each quarter, by her own calculation Smith was unsupervised 95% of the time. As Smith explained during her deposition, "it was really up to me to run the territory the way I wanted to. And it was not a micromanaged type of job. I had pretty much the ability to work it the way I wanted to work it." According to Smith's

job description, she was required to plan and prioritize her responsibilities in a manner that maximized business results. J&J witnesses testified (and J&J documents confirmed) that Smith was the "expert" on her own territory and was supposed to develop a strategic plan to achieve higher sales.

* * * *

Smith earned a base salary of $66,000 but was not paid overtime, though J&J, at its discretion, could award her a bonus.

Smith filed suit seeking overtime pay under the Fair Labor Standards Act ("FLSA"). * * * J&J moved for summary judgment, arguing that she was not entitled to overtime pay under the FLSA because she was exempt from that statute under * * * the "administrative employee" exemption. [The court granted J&J's motion, and Smith appealed.]

* * * *

Under the FLSA, employees who work more than 40 hours per week

---

a. In the "Opinions and Oral Arguments" box, select "Opinion Archives." When that page opens, select "February" in the list under "2010 Decision." Scroll down the list of "Precedential" cases in the left-hand column and click on the highlighted case title to access the opinion. The U.S. Court of Appeals for the Third Circuit maintains this Web site.

EXTENDED CASE CONTINUES ➡

EXTENDED CASE 21.2 CONTINUED ⬇

are entitled to overtime pay unless they fall within one of the FLSA's exemptions. * * * The District Court held that the administrative employee exemption applied to Smith, so we focus on the regulations describing that exemption.

Under the administrative employee exemption, anyone employed in a bona fide administrative capacity is exempt from the FLSA's overtime requirements. The Secretary [of Labor] has defined an administrative employee as someone:

(1) Compensated on a salary or fee basis at a rate of not less than $455 per week * * * *exclusive of board, lodging or other facilities;*

(2) Whose primary duty is the performance of office or non-manual work directly related to the management or general business operations of the

employer or the employer's customers; and

(3) Whose primary duty includes the exercise of discretion and independent judgment with respect to matters of significance. [Emphasis added.]

The parties agree that Smith's salary qualifies her for the administrative employee exemption, but dispute her qualification for that exemption under the remaining two sections.

We find that the administrative employee exemption applies to Smith. While testifying at her deposition Smith elaborated on the independent and managerial qualities that her position required. Her non-manual position required her to form a strategic plan designed to maximize sales in her territory. We think that this requirement satisfied the "directly related to the

management or general business operations of the employer" provision of the administrative employee exemption because it involved a high level of planning and foresight, and the strategic plan that Smith developed guided the execution of her remaining duties.

When we turn to the "exercise of discretion and independent judgment with respect to matters of significance" requirement, we note that Smith executed nearly all of her duties without direct oversight. In fact, she described herself as the manager of her own business who could run her own territory as she saw fit. Given these descriptions, we conclude that Smith was subject to the administrative employee exemption.

* * * *

The District Court's order * * * will be affirmed * * *.

QUESTIONS

1. Is it unfair to exempt employees to deprive them of overtime wages? Why or why not?
2. J&J argued that Smith was exempt under either the administrative employee exemption or the outside salesperson exemption. The district court found, though, that Smith did not qualify for the outside salesperson exemption. What single fact might have made Smith ineligible for the outside salesperson exemption?

SECTION 3

LAYOFFS

During the latest economic recession in the United States, mass layoffs of workers resulted in high unemployment rates. Later in this chapter, we will discuss unemployment insurance, which helps some workers manage financially until they can find another job. In this section, we discuss the laws pertaining to employee layoffs, an area that is increasingly the subject of litigation.

The Worker Adjustment and Retraining Notification Act

Since 1988, the Worker Adjustment and Retraining Notification Act,[9] or the WARN Act, has required large businesses to provide sixty days' notice before implementing a mass layoff or closing a plant that

employs more than fifty full-time workers. This federal law applies to employers with at least one hundred full-time employees. It is intended to give workers advance notice so that they can start looking for a new job while they are still employed.

The WARN Act defines the term *mass layoff* as a reduction in force that, during any thirty-day period, results in an employment loss of either:

1. At least 33 percent of the full-time employees at a single job site and at least fifty employees; or
2. At least five hundred full-time employees.

An *employment loss* is defined as a layoff that exceeds six months or a reduction in hours of work of more than 50 percent during each month of any six-month period.

NOTIFICATION REQUIREMENTS The WARN Act requires that advance notice of the layoff be sent to the affected workers *or* their representative (if the workers are members of a labor union), as well as to state and local government authorities. The state

---

9. 29 U.S.C. Sections 2101 *et seq.*

and local authorities are notified so that they can provide resources, such as job training, to displaced workers. Employers must also provide notice to part-time and seasonal employees who are being laid off, even though these workers do not count in determining whether the act's provisions are triggered. Note also that even companies that are planning to file for bankruptcy normally must provide notice under the WARN Act before implementing a mass layoff. Nevertheless, employers can sometimes avoid the WARN notice requirements by staggering layoffs over many months or various locations.

REMEDIES FOR VIOLATIONS An employer that orders a mass layoff or plant closing in violation of the WARN Act can be fined up to $500 for each day of the violation. Employees can recover back pay for each day of the violation (up to sixty days), plus reasonable attorneys' fees. An employee can also recover benefits under an employee benefit plan, including the cost of medical expenses that would have been covered by the plan. (Employees who are laid off may also claim that the layoff was discriminatory in violation of the laws described in Chapter 22 if it disproportionately affects members of a protected class, such as minorities or women.)

State Laws Requiring Layoff Notices

Many states also have statutes requiring employers to provide notice before initiating mass layoffs, and these laws may have different and even stricter requirements than the WARN Act. In New York, for instance, companies with fifty or more employees must provide ninety days' notice before any layoff that affects twenty-five or more full-time employees. The law in Illinois applies to companies with seventy-five or more employees and requires sixty days' advance notice of any layoff that affects twenty-five or more full-time employees at one plant or two hundred and fifty employees.

SECTION 4
FAMILY AND MEDICAL LEAVE

In 1993, Congress passed the Family and Medical Leave Act (FMLA)[10] to allow employees to take time off work for family or medical reasons. A majority of the states also have legislation allowing for a leave from employment for family or medical reasons, and many employers maintain private family-leave plans for their workers. The FMLA does not supersede any state or local law that provides more generous family- or medical-leave protection. In 2009, significant changes to the FMLA created new categories of leave for military caregivers and for qualifying exigencies that arise due to military service.

Coverage and Application

The FMLA requires employers who have fifty or more employees to provide an employee with up to twelve weeks of unpaid family or medical leave during any twelve-month period. The FMLA expressly covers private and public (government) employees who have worked 1,250 hours for their employers for at least a year.[11] An employee may take *family leave* to care for a newborn baby or a child recently placed for adoption or foster care.[12] An employee can take *medical leave* when the employee or the employee's spouse, child, or parent has a serious health condition requiring care.

In addition, an employee caring for a family member with a serious injury or illness incurred as a result of military duty can now take up to twenty-six weeks of *military caregiver leave* within a twelve-month period.[13] An employee can also take up to twelve weeks of *qualifying exigency leave* to handle specified nonmedical emergencies when a spouse, parent, or child is on, or called to, active military duty.[14]

Benefits and Protections

When an employee takes FMLA leave, the employer must continue the worker's health-care coverage on the same terms as if the employee had continued to work. On returning from FMLA leave, most employees must be restored to their original position or to a comparable position (with nearly equivalent pay and benefits, for example). An important exception allows the employer to avoid reinstating a *key employee*—defined as an employee whose pay falls within the top 10 percent of the firm's workforce.

---

10. 29 U.S.C. Sections 2601, 2611–2619, 2651–2654.

11. Note that changes to the FMLA rules allow certain employees who have taken a break from their employment to qualify for FMLA leave if they worked a total of twelve months during the previous seven years. See 29 C.F.R. Section 825.110(b)(1-2).
12. The foster care must be state sanctioned for such an arrangement to fall within the coverage of the FMLA.
13. 29 C.F.R. Section 825.200.
14. 29 C.F.R. Section 825.126.

Employees suffering from addiction to drugs or alcohol pose a special problem under the FMLA. Under what circumstances do days off resulting from the addiction, as opposed to days off for medical treatment in a medical facility, count as part of protected leave? That issue was addressed in the following case.

CASE 21.3
Darst v. Interstate Brands Corp.

United States Court of Appeals, Seventh Circuit, 512 F.3d 903 (2008).

BACKGROUND AND FACTS • Krzysztof Chalimoniuk worked for Interstate Brands Corporation (IBC) for fifteen years before he was fired for excessive absenteeism. Chalimoniuk, an alcoholic, sought treatment for his condition. He requested leave under the Family and Medical Leave Act (FMLA) from July 29 to August 14, 2000, to deal with the problem. From August 4 to 11, he was hospitalized for treatment of alcohol dependence and withdrawal. When he failed to return to work on August 15, he was fired for being absent. IBC noted that he was also absent from July 29 to August 3, when he was not hospitalized, and those days were counted as improper absences because he had already exceeded the number of days he could miss under the company's leave policy. Chalimoniuk sued, contending that IBC had violated his FMLA rights. During the course of litigation, Chalimoniuk filed for bankruptcy, and his claim against IBC became part of the bankruptcy estate. Richard Darst, as trustee for the estate, continued to prosecute the claim. The district court granted summary judgment in favor of IBC. Darst appealed.

IN THE LANGUAGE OF THE COURT
ROEVNER, Circuit Judge.
* * * *
The substantive law at issue is the FMLA. Under the FMLA, eligible employees are entitled to up to twelve weeks of unpaid leave per year for absence due to, among other things, a "Serious Health Condition" that renders the employee unable to perform the functions of his or her job. To ensure the entitlement, the FMLA makes it "unlawful for any employer to interfere with, restrain, or deny the exercise of or the attempt to exercise, any right provided." When an employee alleges a deprivation of the substantive guarantees of the FMLA, the employee must establish, by a preponderance of the evidence, an entitlement to the disputed leave. Because the district court resolved the case on a motion for summary judgment, Chalimoniuk need only raise a genuine issue of material fact regarding his entitlement to FMLA leave on the relevant dates.

A Serious Health Condition is defined as an illness, injury, impairment, or physical or mental condition that involves either (1) inpatient care in a hospital, hospice, or residential medical facility; or (2) continuing treatment by a health care provider. Although the statute itself does not specifically address whether alcoholism [and] substance abuse constitute serious health conditions, Department of Labor regulations that implement the statute provide the answer. *As we noted above, substance abuse may be a Serious Health Condition under certain conditions but FMLA leave may be taken only for treatment for substance abuse. On the other hand, absence because of the employee's use of the substance, rather than for treatment, does not qualify for FMLA leave. Under this regulation, Chalimoniuk was entitled to FMLA leave only for treatment for substance abuse.* Because of the final sentence in the regulation, the parties argue over whether Chalimoniuk was intoxicated on July 31, August 2 or August 3, but we will assume for the purposes of summary judgment that he was not intoxicated on those days. Even if he was sober on those days, however, he has provided no explanation for his absence that would excuse the absence under IBC's point system except that he was in treatment for alcoholism. [Emphasis added.]
* * * *
Dr. Pfeifer [Chalimoniuk's physician] confirmed that Chalimoniuk received inpatient treatment at [the hospital] from August 4 until August 11. He produced no records and had no recollection of treating Chalimoniuk prior to that time. Chalimoniuk provided an affidavit from Dr. Pfeifer stating the doctor's belief that "treatment" for alcoholism begins when the patient takes the first step towards seeking professional help. According to Dr. Pfeifer, this includes the first

CASE 21.3 CONTINUED ▶ phone call to the health care provider seeking evaluation, treatment or referral. Based on his training and experience as a medical doctor, Dr. Pfeifer averred [asserted] that Chalimoniuk's treatment therefore began on July 29, when he first contacted his physician's office. *Under the FMLA, however, "treatment" is a defined term that does not include actions such as calling to make an appointment. Treatment would include examinations to determine if a serious health condition exists and evaluation of the condition.* But Chalimoniuk has produced no evidence that he was being examined or evaluated on July 29, August 2 or August 3. Treatment does not include "any activities that can be initiated without a visit to a health care provider." Chalimoniuk complains that memories have faded since the time of his termination, that his doctors could have testified regarding his treatment on those days if he had known closer to the time that the company was challenging the fact of treatment on the days in question. But Chalimoniuk knew as of August 15, days after his treatment ended, that the company was denying him FMLA leave for all of the days he was absent except the period of his hospitalization. He had ample opportunities to preserve any relevant evidence. Thus, because Chalimoniuk has produced no evidence that he received any treatment as that term is defined by the FMLA on the days in question, he was not entitled to FMLA leave on those dates. Because he had exceeded the number of points allowable under IBC's absenteeism policy, the defendants were free to terminate his employment without running afoul of the FMLA. [Emphasis added.]

DECISION AND REMEDY • *The appeals court affirmed that Chalimoniuk's employer did not violate his FMLA leave by dismissing him for excessive absences. FMLA leave covered the days he was receiving medical treatment, not the days he missed work prior to or after the treatment.*

THE ETHICAL DIMENSION • *Did IBC take unfair advantage of the "letter of the law" by not granting Chalimoniuk a little more leave time? After all, he was, in fact, dealing with his problem. Explain your answer.*

THE LEGAL ENVIRONMENT DIMENSION • *Although IBC won this case, defending against the lawsuit was costly. How can employers avoid such litigation?*

Employer Violations

An employer that violates the FMLA can be required to provide various remedies, including (1) damages for lost wages and benefits, denied compensation, and actual monetary losses (such as the cost of providing for care of a family member) up to an amount equivalent to the employee's wages for twelve weeks; (2) job reinstatement; and (3) promotion, if a promotion was denied.

In addition, a successful plaintiff is entitled to court costs and attorneys' fees. If bad faith on the part of the employer is shown, the plaintiff may also receive two times the amount of damages awarded by the judge or jury. Supervisors can also be held personally liable, as employers, for violations of the act.

Employers generally are required to notify employees when an absence will be counted against leave authorized under the act. If an employer fails to provide such notice, and the employee consequently is damaged because he or she did not receive notice, the employer may be sanctioned.[15]

SECTION 5
WORKER HEALTH AND SAFETY

Under the common law, employees who were injured on the job had to file lawsuits against their employers to obtain recovery. Today, numerous state and federal statutes protect employees from the risk of accidental injury, death, or disease resulting from their employment. This section discusses the primary federal statute governing health and safety in the workplace, along with state workers' compensation acts.

The Occupational Safety and Health Act

At the federal level, the primary legislation protecting employees' health and safety is the Occupational Safety and Health Act of 1970,[16] which is administered by the Occupational Safety and Health Administration (OSHA). Congress passed this act in an attempt to

---

15. *Ragsdale v. Wolverine World Wide, Inc.,* 535 U.S. 81, 122 S.Ct. 1155, 152 L.Ed.2d 167 (2002).

16. 29 U.S.C. Sections 553, 651–678.

ensure safe and healthful working conditions for practically every employee in the country.

REQUIREMENTS The act imposes a general duty on employers to keep workplaces safe. To this end, OSHA has established specific safety standards that employers must follow depending on the industry. For instance, OSHA regulations require the use of safety guards on certain mechanical equipment and set maximum levels of exposure to substances in the workplace that may be harmful to a worker's health. The act also requires that employers post certain notices in the workplace, perform prescribed record-keeping, and submit specific reports.

For instance, employers with eleven or more employees are required to keep occupational injury and illness records for each employee. Each record must be made available for inspection when requested by an OSHA compliance officer. Whenever a work-related injury or disease occurs, employers must make reports directly to OSHA. If an employee dies or five or more employees are hospitalized because of a work-related incident, the employer must notify the U.S. Department of Labor within forty-eight hours. A company that fails to do so will be fined. Following the incident, a complete inspection of the premises is mandatory.

ENFORCEMENT PROCEDURES AND VIOLATIONS OSHA compliance officers may enter and inspect the facilities of any establishment covered by the Occupational Safety and Health Act. Employees may also file complaints of violations. Under the act, an employer cannot discharge an employee who files a complaint or who, in good faith, refuses to work in a high-risk area if bodily harm or death might result.

Criminal penalties for willful violation of the Occupational Safety and Health Act are limited. Employers may also be prosecuted under state laws, however. In other words, the act does not preempt state and local criminal laws.

State Workers' Compensation Laws

State **workers' compensation laws** establish an administrative procedure for compensating workers injured on the job. Instead of suing, an injured worker files a claim with the administrative agency or board that administers local workers' compensation claims.

Most workers' compensation statutes are similar. No state covers all employees. Typically, domestic workers, agricultural workers, temporary employees, and employees of common carriers (companies that provide transportation services to the public) are excluded, but minors are covered. Usually, the statutes allow employers to purchase insurance from a private insurer or a state fund to pay workers' compensation benefits in the event of a claim. Most states also allow employers to be *self-insured*—that is, employers that show an ability to pay claims do not need to buy insurance.

WORKERS' COMPENSATION REQUIREMENTS In general, the only requirements to recover benefits under state workers' compensation laws are:

1. The existence of an employment relationship.
2. An *accidental* injury that *occurred on the job or in the course of employment,* regardless of fault. (If an employee is injured while commuting to or from work, the injury usually will not be considered to have occurred on the job or in the course of employment and hence will not be covered.)

An injured employee must notify her or his employer promptly (usually within thirty days of the accident). Generally, an employee must also file a workers' compensation claim with the appropriate state agency or board within a certain period (sixty days to two years) from the time the injury is first noticed, rather than from the time of the accident.

WORKERS' COMPENSATION AND LITIGATION An employee who accepts workers' compensation benefits is prohibited from suing for injuries caused by the employer's negligence. By barring lawsuits for negligence, workers' compensation laws also prevent employers from raising common law defenses to negligence, such as contributory negligence or assumption of risk, to avoid liability. A worker may sue an employer who *intentionally* injures the worker, however.

SECTION 6
INCOME SECURITY

Federal and state governments participate in insurance programs designed to protect employees and their families from the financial impact of retirement, disability, death, hospitalization, and unemployment. The key federal law on this subject is the Social Security Act of 1935.[17]

---

17. 42 U.S.C. Sections 301–1397e.

Social Security

The Social Security Act of 1935 provides for old-age (retirement), survivors', and disability insurance. The act is therefore often referred to as OASDI. Both employers and employees must "contribute" under the Federal Insurance Contributions Act (FICA)[18] to help pay for benefits that will partially make up for the employees' loss of income on retirement.

The basis for the employee's and the employer's contribution is the employee's annual wage base— the maximum amount of the employee's wages that is subject to the tax. The employer withholds the employee's FICA contribution from the employee's wages and then matches this contribution. The annual wage base is adjusted each year as needed to take into account the rising cost of living. In 2010, employers were required to withhold 6.2 percent of each employee's wages, up to a maximum wage base of $106,800, and to match this contribution.

Retired workers are eligible to receive monthly payments from the Social Security Administration, which administers the Social Security Act. Social Security benefits are fixed by statute but increase automatically with increases in the cost of living.

Medicare

Medicare, a federal government health-insurance program, is administered by the Social Security Administration for people sixty-five years of age and older and for some under age sixty-five who are disabled. It originally had two parts, one pertaining to hospital costs and the other to nonhospital medical costs, such as visits to physicians' offices. Medicare now offers additional coverage options and a prescription-drug plan. People who have Medicare hospital insurance can obtain additional federal medical insurance if they pay small monthly premiums, which increase as the cost of medical care rises.

As with Social Security, both the employer and the employee contribute to Medicare, but the programs differ in that there is no cap on the amount of wages subject to the Medicare tax. In 2010, both the employer and the employee were required to pay 1.45 percent of *all* wages and salaries to finance Medicare. Thus, for Social Security and Medicare together, in 2010 the employer and employee each paid 7.65 percent of the first $106,800 of income (6.2 percent for Social Security + 1.45 percent for Medicare), for a combined total of 15.3 percent. In addition, all wages and salaries above $106,800 were taxed at a combined (employer and employee) rate of 2.9 percent for Medicare.[19] Self-employed persons pay both the employer and the employee portions of the Social Security and Medicare taxes (15.3 percent of income up to $106,800 and 2.9 percent of income above that amount in 2010).

Private Pension Plans

The major federal statute regulating employee retirement plans set up by employers is the Employee Retirement Income Security Act (ERISA) of 1974.[20] This act empowers a branch of the U.S. Department of Labor to enforce its provisions governing employers who have private pension funds for their employees. ERISA created the Pension Benefit Guaranty Corporation (PBGC), an independent federal agency, to provide timely and uninterrupted payment of voluntary private pension benefits. The pension plans pay annual insurance premiums (at set rates adjusted for inflation) to the PBGC, which then pays benefits to participants in the event that a plan is unable to do so. Under the Pension Protection Act of 2006,[21] the director of the PBGC is appointed by the president and confirmed by the Senate.

ERISA does not require an employer to establish a pension plan. When a plan exists, however, ERISA provides standards for its management. A key provision of ERISA concerns vesting. **Vesting** gives an employee a legal right to receive pension benefits at some future date when she or he stops working. Before ERISA was enacted, some employees who had worked for companies for as long as thirty years received no pension benefits when their employment terminated because those benefits had not vested. ERISA establishes complex vesting rules. Generally, however, all of an employee's contributions to a pension plan vest immediately, and the employee's rights to the employer's contributions vest after five years of employment.

In an attempt to prevent mismanagement of pension funds, ERISA has established rules on how they must be invested. Managers must choose

---

18. 26 U.S.C. Sections 3101–3125.

19. Note that as a result of the 2010 health-care reform legislation (the Health Care and Education Reconciliation Act of 2010, H.R. 4872), not only are Medicare tax rates expected to rise, but also the applicable compensation base will expand to include more than just salary incomes. For instance, starting in 2012, there will be a 3.8 percent Medicare payroll tax on investment income for families making more than $250,000 per year.

20. 29 U.S.C. Sections 1001 *et seq.*

21. The Pension Protection Act amended 26 U.S.C. Sections 430–432, 436, 4966, 4967, 6039I, 6050U, 6050V, 6695A, 6720B, 7443B; and 29 U.S.C. Sections 1082–1085, 1202a.

investments cautiously and must diversify the plan's investments to minimize the risk of large losses. ERISA also includes detailed record-keeping and reporting requirements.

Unemployment Compensation

To ease the financial impact of unemployment, the United States has a system of unemployment insurance. The Federal Unemployment Tax Act (FUTA) of 1935[22] created a state-administered system that provides unemployment compensation to eligible individuals. Under this system, employers pay into a fund, and the proceeds are paid out to qualified unemployed workers. The FUTA and state laws require employers that fall under the provisions of the act to pay unemployment taxes at regular intervals.

To be eligible for unemployment compensation, a worker must be willing and able to work. Workers who have been fired for misconduct or who have voluntarily left their jobs are not eligible for benefits. In the past, workers had to actively seek employment to continue receiving benefits. Due to the high unemployment rates after the Great Recession, however, President Barack Obama announced measures that allow jobless persons to retain their unemployment benefits while pursuing additional education and training (rather than seeking employment).

COBRA

For workers whose jobs have been terminated—and who are thus no longer eligible for group health-insurance plans—federal law also provides a right to continued health-care coverage. The Consolidated Omnibus Budget Reconciliation Act (COBRA) of 1985[23] prohibits an employer from eliminating a worker's medical, optical, or dental insurance on the voluntary or involuntary termination of the worker's employment.

Employers, with some exceptions, must inform employees of COBRA's provisions when they face termination or a reduction of hours that would affect their eligibility for coverage under the plan. Only workers fired for gross misconduct are excluded from protection.

PROCEDURES A worker has sixty days (beginning with the date that the group coverage would stop) to decide whether to continue with the employer's group insurance plan. If the worker chooses to discontinue the coverage, then the employer has no further obligation. If the worker chooses to continue coverage, though, the employer is obligated to keep the policy active for up to eighteen months (twenty-nine months if the worker is disabled). The coverage provided must be the same as that enjoyed by the worker prior to the termination or reduction of work. If family members were originally included, for instance, COBRA prohibits their exclusion.

PAYMENT The worker does not receive the insurance coverage for free. Generally, an employer can require the employee to pay all of the premiums, plus a 2 percent administrative charge. In 2009, however, the law was changed to provide for certain workers who involuntarily lost their jobs.[24] These employees can be charged no more than 35 percent of the premiums. The employer receives a tax credit as reimbursement for the remaining 65 percent of the premiums.

If the worker fails to pay the required premiums (or if the employer completely eliminates its group benefit plan), the employer is relieved of further responsibility. (The employer is also relieved of the obligation if the worker becomes eligible for Medicare or obtains coverage under another health plan, such as a spouse's or new employer's plan.) An employer that does not comply with COBRA risks substantial penalties, such as a tax of up to 10 percent of the annual cost of the group plan or $500,000, whichever is less.

Employer-Sponsored Group Health Plans

The Health Insurance Portability and Accountability Act (HIPAA),[25] which was discussed in Chapter 5 in the context of its privacy protections, contains provisions that affect employer-sponsored group health plans. HIPAA does not require employers to provide health insurance, but it does establish requirements for those that do provide such coverage. For instance, HIPAA strictly limits an employer's ability to exclude coverage for *preexisting conditions*. It also requires employers to give credit to employees for previous health coverage (including COBRA coverage) to decrease any waiting period before their coverage becomes effective.

---

24. These changes were made by the American Recovery and Reinvestment Act (Stimulus Bill) of 2009, Pub. L. No. 111-5, 123 Stat. 115 (February 17, 2009). The provisions for workers who involuntarily lost their jobs were originally set to end in 2009 but were later extended through November 2010.

25. 29 U.S.C. Sections 1181 *et seq.*

In addition, HIPAA restricts the manner in which covered employers collect, use, and disclose the health information of employees and their families. Employers must train employees, designate privacy officials, and distribute privacy notices to ensure that employees' health information is not disclosed to unauthorized parties. Failure to comply with HIPAA regulations can result in civil penalties of up to $100 per person per violation (with a cap of $25,000 per year). The employer is also subject to criminal prosecution for certain types of HIPAA violations and can face up to $250,000 in criminal fines and imprisonment for up to ten years if convicted.

SECTION 7
EMPLOYEE PRIVACY RIGHTS

In the last thirty years, concerns about the privacy rights of employees have arisen in response to the sometimes invasive tactics used by employers to monitor and screen workers. Perhaps the greatest privacy concern in today's employment arena has to do with electronic monitoring of employees' activities.

Electronic Monitoring

According to the American Management Association, more than two-thirds of employers engage in some form of electronic monitoring of their employees. This surveillance may include monitoring employees' e-mails, blogs, instant messages, tweets, Internet use, and computer files; video-recording employee job performance; and recording and reviewing telephone conversations, voice mail, and text messages.

Various specially designed software products have made it easier for an employer to track employees' Internet use, including the specific Web sites visited and the time spent surfing the Web. Indeed, inappropriate Web surfing seems to be a primary concern for employers. More than 75 percent of them are monitoring workers' Web connections. Filtering software, which was discussed in Chapter 5, can be used to prevent access to certain Web sites, such as sites containing sexually explicit images. Private employers are generally free to use filtering software to block access to certain Web sites because the First Amendment's protection of free speech prevents only *government employers* from restraining speech by blocking Web sites.

EMPLOYEE PRIVACY PROTECTION Recall from Chapter 5 that the United States Supreme Court has inferred a personal right to privacy from the constitutional guarantees provided by the First, Third, Fourth, Fifth, and Ninth Amendments to the Constitution. Tort law (see Chapter 12), state constitutions, and a number of state and federal statutes also provide for privacy rights.

When determining whether an employer should be held liable for violating an employee's privacy rights, the courts generally weigh the employer's interests against the employee's reasonable expectation of privacy. Normally, if employees are informed that their communications are being monitored, they cannot reasonably expect those communications to be private. If employees are not informed that certain communications are being monitored, however, the employer may be held liable for invading their privacy. For this reason, most employers that engage in electronic monitoring notify their employees about the monitoring.

Nevertheless, establishing a general privacy policy may not sufficiently protect an employer who monitors other forms of communications that the policy fails to mention. Similarly, notifying employees that their e-mails may be monitored may not protect an employer who monitors text messages. Courts also look at other factors when deciding if the employee had a reasonable expectation of privacy. For instance, if the employer provided the e-mail system or blog that the employee used for communications, a court will typically hold that the employee did not have a reasonable expectation of privacy.

ELECTRONIC COMMUNICATIONS PRIVACY ACT The major statute governing electronic monitoring by employers is the Electronic Communications Privacy Act (ECPA) of 1986.[26] This act amended existing federal wiretapping law to cover electronic forms of communications, such as communications via cell phones and e-mail. The ECPA prohibits the intentional interception of any wire or electronic communication or the intentional disclosure or use of the information obtained by the interception. Excluded from coverage are any electronic communications through devices that are "furnished to the subscriber or user by a provider of wire or electronic communication service" and that are being used by the subscriber or user, or by the provider of the service, "in the ordinary course of its business."

This "business-extension exception" to the ECPA allows an employer to monitor employees' electronic communications in the ordinary course of business.

---

26. 18 U.S.C. Sections 2510–2521.

It does not, however, permit an employer to monitor employees' personal communications. Nevertheless, under another exception to the ECPA, an employer may avoid liability if the employees consent to having their electronic communications intercepted by the employer. Thus, by simply requiring employees to sign forms indicating that they consent to such monitoring, an employer can avoid liability for monitoring employees' personal communications.

STORED COMMUNICATIONS Part of the ECPA is known as the Stored Communications Act (SCA).[27] The SCA prohibits intentional and unauthorized access to *stored* electronic communications and sets forth criminal and civil sanctions for violators. A person can violate the SCA by intentionally accessing a stored electronic communication or by intentionally exceeding the authorization given to access the communication. To prove a violation, however, an individual must show that the other party (for example, an employer) lacked the authority to access the stored communication. Proving this lack of authority may be difficult at times, especially when an employer provided the electronic communication device.

CASE IN POINT Jeff Quon, a police sergeant for Ontario, California, was issued a pager with wireless text-messaging services provided by Arch Wireless Operating Company. Although the city had a general policy that employees should not use work computers, Internet, and e-mail for personal matters, it did not expressly mention the pagers or text messaging. On several occasions, Quon paid the city overage charges for exceeding the limit on text messages. Without Quon's knowledge, his supervisors obtained transcripts of his stored text messages from Arch Wireless to determine whether any of the texts were personal. When Quon learned that the city had read his personal texts, he filed a lawsuit against the city and Arch Wireless for violating his privacy rights. A federal appellate court ruled that Quon had a reasonable expectation of privacy in his text messages that were temporarily stored by Arch Wireless, a third party provider. Therefore, Arch Wireless should not have provided transcripts to the city without his authorization. On appeal, the United States Supreme Court reversed that ruling, finding that the search of Quon's text messages was reasonable. Because the police department had a written policy, which Quon admitted that

he understood applied to the pagers, he should have had no reasonable expectation of privacy.[28]

Other Types of Monitoring

In addition to monitoring their employees' online activities, employers also engage in other types of employee screening and monitoring practices. The practices discussed next often have been challenged as violations of employee privacy rights.

LIE-DETECTOR TESTS At one time, many employers required employees or job applicants to take polygraph examinations (lie-detector tests). In 1988, Congress passed the Employee Polygraph Protection Act,[29] which generally prohibits employers from requiring or causing employees or job applicants to take lie-detector tests or suggesting or requesting that they do so. The act also restricts employers' ability to use or ask about the results of any lie-detector test or to take any negative employment action based on the results.

Employers excepted from these prohibitions include federal, state, and local government employers; certain security service firms; and companies manufacturing and distributing controlled substances. Other employers may use polygraph tests when investigating losses attributable to theft, including embezzlement and the theft of trade secrets.

DRUG TESTING In the interest of public safety and to reduce unnecessary costs, many employers, including the government, require their employees to submit to drug testing. Government (public) employers, of course, are constrained in drug testing by the Fourth Amendment to the U.S. Constitution, which prohibits unreasonable searches and seizures (see Chapter 5). Drug testing of public employees is allowed by statute for transportation workers and is normally upheld by the courts when drug use in a particular job may threaten public safety. Also, when there is a reasonable basis for suspecting public employees of drug use, courts often find that drug testing does not violate the Fourth Amendment.

The Fourth Amendment does not apply to drug testing conducted by private employers. Hence, the privacy rights and drug testing of private-sector employees are governed by state law, which varies from state to state. Many states have statutes that allow drug testing by private employers but put restrictions on when and how the testing may be

27. 18 U.S.C. Sections 2701–2711.

28. *City of Ontario, California v. Quon,* __ U.S. __, 130 S.Ct. 2619, 177 L.Ed.2d 216 (2010).

29. 29 U.S.C. Sections 2001 *et seq.*

performed. A collective bargaining agreement (as will be discussed in Chapter 23) may also provide protection against drug testing (or authorize drug testing under certain conditions). The permissibility of a private employee's drug test often hinges on whether the employer's testing was reasonable. Random drug tests and even "zero-tolerance" policies (which deny a "second chance" to employees who test positive for drugs) have been held to be reasonable.[30]

GENETIC TESTING A serious privacy issue arose when some employers began conducting genetic testing of employees or prospective employees in an effort to identify individuals who might develop significant health problems in the future. To date, however, only a few cases involving this issue have come before the courts.

CASE IN POINT Lawrence Berkeley Laboratory screened prospective employees for the gene that causes sickle-cell anemia, although the applicants were not informed of this. When the prospective employees subsequently sued the laboratory, a federal appellate court held that they had a cause of action for violation of their privacy rights. The case was later settled for $2.2 million.[31]

In 2008, to prevent the improper use of genetic information by employers and health insurance providers, Congress passed the Genetic Information Nondiscrimination Act (GINA).[32] Under GINA, employers cannot make decisions about hiring, firing, job placement, or promotion based on the results of genetic testing. GINA also prohibits group health plans and insurers from denying coverage or charging higher premiums based solely on a genetic predisposition to develop a disease in the future.

---

30. See *CITGO Asphalt Refining Co. v. Paper, Allied-Industrial, Chemical, and Energy Workers International Union Local No. 2–991*, 385 F.3d 809 (3d Cir. 2004).

31. *Norman-Bloodsaw v. Lawrence Berkeley Laboratory*, 135 F.3d 1260 (9th Cir. 1998).
32. 26 U.S.C. Section 9834; 42 U.S.C. Sections 300gg-53, 1320d-9, 2000ff-1 to 2000ff-11.

REVIEWING
Employment Relationships

Rick Saldona began working as a traveling salesperson for Aimer Winery in 1988. Sales constituted 90 percent of Saldona's work time. Saldona worked an average of fifty hours per week but received no overtime pay. In June 2011, Saldona's new supervisor, Caesar Braxton, claimed that Saldona had been inflating his reported sales calls and required Saldona to submit to a polygraph test. Saldona reported Braxton to the U.S. Department of Labor, which prohibited Aimer from requiring Saldona to take a polygraph test for this purpose. In August 2011, Saldona's wife, Venita, fell from a ladder and sustained a head injury while employed as a full-time agricultural harvester. Saldona delivered to Aimer's Human Resources Department a letter from his wife's physician indicating that she would need daily care for several months, and Saldona took leave until December 2011. Aimer had sixty-three employees at that time. When Saldona returned to Aimer, he was informed that his position had been eliminated because his sales territory had been combined with an adjacent territory. Using the information presented in the chapter, answer the following questions.

1. Would Saldona have been legally entitled to receive overtime pay at a higher rate? Why or why not?
2. What is the maximum length of time Saldona would have been allowed to take leave to care for his injured spouse?
3. Under what circumstances would Aimer have been allowed to require an employee to take a polygraph test?
4. Would Aimer likely be able to avoid reinstating Saldona under the *key employee* exception? Why or why not?

⊛ DEBATE THIS: *The U.S. labor market is highly competitive, so state and federal laws that require overtime pay are unnecessary and should be abolished.*

TERMS AND CONCEPTS

minimum wage 478

vesting 485

employment at will 474

whistleblowing 476

workers' compensation laws 484

wrongful discharge 477

QUESTIONS AND CASE PROBLEMS

21–1. Hours and Wages Calzoni Boating Co. is an interstate business engaged in manufacturing and selling boats. The company has five hundred nonunion employees. Representatives of these employees are requesting a four-day, ten-hours-per-day workweek, and Calzoni is concerned that this would require paying time and a half after eight hours per day. Which federal act is Calzoni thinking of that might require this? Will the act in fact require paying time and a half for all hours worked over eight hours per day if the employees' proposal is accepted? Explain.

21–2. QUESTION WITH SAMPLE ANSWER: Wrongful Discharge.

 Denton and Carlo were employed at an appliance plant. Their job required them to perform occasional maintenance work while standing on wire mesh twenty feet above the plant floor. Other employees had fallen through the mesh, and one of them had been killed by the fall. When their supervisor told them to perform tasks that would likely involve walking on the mesh, Denton and Carlo refused because they feared they might suffer bodily injury or death. Because they refused to do the requested work, the two employees were fired from their jobs. Was their discharge wrongful? If so, under what federal employment law? To what federal agency or department should they turn for assistance?

- **For a sample answer to Question 21–2, go to Appendix F at the end of this text.**

21–3. Hours and Wages Tradesmen International, Inc., leases skilled tradespersons (field employees) to construction contractors. To receive a job offer through Tradesmen, applicants must either complete an Occupational Safety and Health Administration ten-hour general construction safety course or commit to registering for the course within sixty days and completing it within a reasonable time. The class instruction has no effect on the trade skills of any field employee. The classes are held outside regular working hours. Employees perform no work in the class and are not compensated for the time spent in the class. Elaine Chao, the U.S. secretary of labor, filed a suit in a federal district court against Tradesmen for failing to pay overtime compensation to those who attend

the class. Does Tradesmen's practice—requiring the class as a prerequisite to employment but not paying applicants to attend it—violate the Fair Labor Standards Act? Explain. [*Chao v. Tradesmen International, Inc.,* 310 F.3d 904 (6th Cir. 2002)]

21–4. Workers' Compensation Laws The Touch of Class Lounge is in a suburban shopping plaza, or strip mall, in Omaha, Nebraska. Patricia Bauer, the Lounge's owner, does not own the parking lot, which is provided for the common use of all of the businesses in the plaza. Stephanie Zoucha was a bartender at the Lounge. Her duties ended when she locked the door after closing. On June 4, 2001, at 1:15 A.M., Zoucha closed the bar and locked the door from the inside. An hour later, she walked to her car in the parking lot, where she was struck with "[l]ike a tire iron on the back of my head." Zoucha sustained a skull fracture and other injuries, including significant cognitive damage (impairment of speech and thought formation). Her purse, containing her tip money, was stolen. She identified her attacker as William Nunez, who had been in the Lounge earlier that night. Zoucha filed a petition in a Nebraska state court to obtain workers' compensation. What are the requirements for receiving workers' compensation? Should Zoucha's request be granted or denied? Why? [*Zoucha v. Touch of Class Lounge,* 269 Neb. 89, 690 N.W.2d 610 (2005)]

21–5. CASE PROBLEM WITH SAMPLE ANSWER: Family and Medical Leave Act.

Jennifer Willis worked for Coca Cola Enterprises, Inc. (CCE), in Louisiana as a senior account manager. On a Monday in May 2003, Willis called her supervisor to tell him that she was sick and would not be able to work that day. She also said that she was pregnant, but she did not say she was sick because of the pregnancy. On Tuesday, she called to ask where to report to work and was told that she could not return without a doctor's release. She said that she had a doctor's appointment on "Wednesday," which her supervisor understood to be the next day. Willis meant the following Wednesday. For more than a week, Willis did not contact CCE. When she returned to work, she was told that she had violated CCE's "No Call/No Show" policy. Under this policy "an employee absent from work for three consecutive days without notifying the supervi-

sor during that period will be considered to have voluntarily resigned." She was fired. Willis filed a suit in a federal district court against CCE under the Family and Medical Leave Act (FMLA). To be eligible for FMLA leave, an employee must inform an employer of the reason for the leave. Did Willis meet this requirement? Did CCE's response to Willis's absence violate the FMLA? Explain. [Willis v. Coca Cola Enterprises, Inc., 445 F.3d 413 (5th Cir. 2006)]

- **To view a sample answer for Problem 21–5, go to this book's Web site at www.cengage.com/blaw/cross, select "Chapter 21," and click on "Case Problem with Sample Answer."**

21–6. Unemployment Insurance Mary Garas, a chemist, sought work in Missouri through Kelly Services, Inc. Kelly is a staffing agency that places individuals in jobs of varying duration with other companies. Through Kelly, Garas worked at Merial Co. from April 2005 to February 2006. After the assignment ended, Garas asked Kelly for more work. Meanwhile, she filed a claim for unemployment benefits with the Missouri Division of Employment Security (DES). In March, Kelly recruiter Rebecca Cockrum told Garas about a temporary assignment with Celsis Laboratory. Garas said that she would prefer a "more stable position," but later asked Cockrum to submit her résumé to Celsis. Before the employer responded, Kelly told the DES that Garas had refused suitable work. Under a Missouri state statute, a claim for unemployment benefits must be denied if "the claimant failed without good cause . . . to accept suitable work when offered the claimant . . . by an employer by whom the individual was formerly employed." The DES denied Garas's claim for benefits. She filed an appeal with a state court. Was the DES's denial right or wrong? Why? [Garas v. Kelly Services, Inc., 211 S.W.3d 149 (Mo. App.E.D. 2007)]

21–7. Vesting The United Auto Workers (UAW) represents workers at Caterpillar, Inc., and negotiates labor contracts on their behalf. A 1988 labor agreement provided lifetime no-cost medical benefits for retirees but did not state when the employees' rights to those benefits vested. This agreement expired in 1991. Caterpillar and the UAW did not reach a new agreement until 1998. Under the new agreement, retiree medical benefits were subject to certain limits, and retirees were to be responsible for paying some of the costs. Workers who retired during the period when no agreement was in force filed a suit in a federal district court to obtain benefits under the 1988 agreement. Review the Employee Retirement Income Security Act vesting rules for private pension plans on page 485. What is the most plausible application of those rules to these facts? Why? [Winnett v. Caterpillar, Inc., 553 F.3d 1000 (6th Cir. 2009)]

21–8. Minimum Wage Misty Cumbie worked as a waitress at Vita Café in Portland, Oregon. The café was owned and operated by Woody Woo, Inc. Woody Woo paid its servers an hourly wage that was higher than the state's minimum wage, but the servers were required to contribute their tips to a "tip pool." Approximately one-third of the tip-pool funds went to the servers, and the rest was distributed to the kitchen staff that otherwise rarely received tips for their service. Cumbie sued Woody Woo, alleging that the tip-pooling arrangement violated the minimum wage provisions of the Fair Labor Standards Act (FLSA). The district court dismissed the suit for failure to state a claim. Cumbie appealed. Did Woody Woo's tip-pooling policy violate the FLSA rights of the servers? Explain your answer. [*Cumbie v. Woody Woo, Inc.*, 596 F.3d 577 (9th Cir. 2010)]

21–9. A QUESTION OF ETHICS: Workers' Compensation Law.

In 1999, after working for Atchison Leather Products, Inc., in Kansas for ten years, Beverly Tull began to complain of hand, wrist, and shoulder pain. Atchison recommended that she contact a certain physician, who in April 2000 diagnosed the condition as carpal tunnel syndrome "severe enough" for surgery. In August, Tull filed a claim with the state workers' compensation board. Because Atchison changed workers' compensation insurance companies every year, a dispute arose as to which company should pay Tull's claim. Fearing liability, no insurer would authorize treatment, and Tull was forced to delay surgery until December. The board granted her temporary total disability benefits for the subsequent six weeks that she missed work. On April 23, 2002, Berger Co. bought Atchison. The new employer adjusted Tull's work so that it was less demanding and stressful, but she continued to suffer pain. In July, a physician diagnosed her condition as permanent. The board granted her permanent partial disability benefits. By May 2005, the bickering over the financial responsibility for Tull's claim involved five insurers—four of which had each covered Atchison for a single year and one of which covered Berger. [Tull v. Atchison Leather Products, Inc., 37 Kan.App.2d 87, 150 P.3d 316 (2007)]

(a) When an injured employee files a claim for workers' compensation, a proceeding is held to assess the injury and determine the amount of compensation. Should a dispute between insurers over the payment of the claim be resolved in the same proceeding? Why or why not?

(b) The board designated April 23, 2002, as the date of Tull's injury. What is the reason for determining the date of a worker's injury? Should the board in this case have selected this date or a different date? Why?

(c) How should the board assess liability for the payment of Tull's medical expenses and disability benefits? Would it be appropriate to impose joint and several liability on the insurers (holding each of them responsible for the full amount of damages), or should the individual liability of each of them be determined? Explain.

21–10. VIDEO QUESTION: Employment at Will.

Go to this text's Web site at **www.cengage.com/ blaw/cross** and select "Chapter 21." Click on "Video Questions" and view the video titled *Employment at Will.* Then answer the following questions.

(a) In the video, Laura asserts that she can fire Ray "for any reason; for no reason." Is this true? Explain your answer.

(b) What exceptions to the employment-at-will doctrine are discussed in the chapter? Does Ray's situation fit any of these exceptions?

(c) Would Ray be protected from wrongful discharge under whistleblowing statutes? Why or why not?

(d) Assume that you are the employer in this scenario. What arguments can you make that Ray should not be able to sue for wrongful discharge in this situation?

LEGAL RESEARCH EXERCISES ON THE WEB

Go to this text's Web site at **www.cengage.com/blaw/cross**, select "Chapter 21," and click on "Practical Internet Exercises." There you will find the following Internet research exercises that you can perform to learn more about the topics covered in this chapter.

Practical Internet Exercise 21–1: **Legal Perspective**
Workers' Compensation

Practical Internet Exercise 21–2: **Management Perspective**
Workplace Monitoring and Surveillance

CHAPTER 22

Employment Discrimination

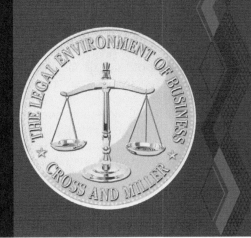

Out of the 1950s and 1960s civil rights movement to end racial and other forms of discrimination grew a body of law protecting employees against discrimination in the workplace. This protective legislation further eroded the employment-at-will doctrine, which was discussed in Chapter 21. In the past several decades, judicial decisions, administrative agency actions, and legislation have restricted the ability of both employers and unions to discriminate against workers on the basis of race, color, religion, national origin, gender, age, or disability. A class of

persons defined by one or more of these criteria is known as a **protected class**.

Several federal statutes prohibit **employment discrimination** against members of protected classes. The most important statute is Title VII of the Civil Rights Act of 1964.[1] Title VII prohibits employment discrimination on the basis of race, color, religion, national origin, and gender. The Age Discrimination in Employment Act of 1967[2] and the Americans with Disabilities Act of 1990[3]

1. 42 U.S.C. Sections 2000e–2000e-17.
2. 29 U.S.C. Sections 621–634.
3. 42 U.S.C. Sections 12102–12118.

prohibit discrimination on the basis of age and disability, respectively. As was discussed in Chapter 8, the protections afforded under these laws also extend to U.S. citizens who are working abroad for U.S. firms or for companies that are controlled by U.S. firms.

This chapter focuses on the kinds of discrimination prohibited by these federal statutes. Note, however, that discrimination against employees on the basis of any of the above-mentioned criteria may also violate state human rights statutes or other state laws prohibiting discrimination.

SECTION 1
TITLE VII OF THE CIVIL RIGHTS ACT OF 1964

Title VII of the Civil Rights Act of 1964 and its amendments prohibit job discrimination against employees, applicants, and union members on the basis of race, color, national origin, religion, and gender at any stage of employment. It prohibits discrimination in the hiring process, as well as in discipline procedures, discharge, promotion, and benefits. Title VII applies to employers with fifteen or more employees, labor unions with fifteen or more members, labor unions that operate hiring halls (to which members go regularly to be assigned jobs as they become available), employment agencies, and state and local governing units or agencies.

The United States Supreme Court has also ruled that an employer with fewer than fifteen employees

is not automatically shielded from a lawsuit filed under Title VII.[4] A special section of the act prohibits discrimination in most federal government employment. When Title VII applies to the employer, any employee—including an undocumented (alien) worker—can bring an action for employment discrimination.

The Equal Employment Opportunity Commission

The Equal Employment Opportunity Commission (EEOC) monitors compliance with Title VII. A victim of alleged discrimination must first file a claim with the EEOC before a lawsuit can be brought against the employer. The EEOC may investigate the dispute and attempt to obtain the parties' voluntary consent

4. *Arbaugh v. Y&H Corp.*, 546 U.S. 500, 126 S.Ct. 1235, 163 L.Ed.2d 1097 (2006).

to an out-of-court settlement. If a voluntary agreement cannot be reached, the EEOC may file a suit against the employer on the employee's behalf.

The EEOC does not investigate every claim of employment discrimination. Generally, it takes only "priority cases," such as cases that affect many workers and cases involving retaliatory discharge (firing an employee in retaliation for submitting a claim with the EEOC). If the EEOC decides not to investigate a claim, the victim may bring his or her own lawsuit against the employer.

Intentional and Unintentional Discrimination

Title VII of the Civil Rights Act of 1964 prohibits both intentional and unintentional discrimination.

INTENTIONAL DISCRIMINATION Intentional discrimination by an employer against an employee is known as **disparate-treatment discrimination.** Because intent may sometimes be difficult to prove, courts have established certain procedures for resolving disparate-treatment cases. Suppose that a woman applies for employment with a construction firm and is rejected. If she sues on the basis of disparate-treatment discrimination in hiring, she must show that (1) she is a member of a protected class, (2) she applied and was qualified for the job in question, (3) she was rejected by the employer, and (4) the employer continued to seek applicants for the position or filled the position with a person not in a protected class.

If the woman can meet these relatively easy requirements, she has made out a *prima facie* **case** of illegal discrimination. Making out a *prima facie* case of discrimination means that the plaintiff has met her initial burden of proof and will win unless the employer can present a legally acceptable defense. (Defenses to claims of employment discrimination will be discussed later in this chapter.) The burden then shifts to the employer-defendant, who must articulate a legal reason for not hiring the plaintiff. For example, the employer might say that the plaintiff was not hired because she lacked sufficient experience or training. To prevail, the plaintiff must then show that the employer's reason is a *pretext* (not the true reason) and that discriminatory intent actually motivated the employer's decision.

UNINTENTIONAL DISCRIMINATION Employers often use interviews and tests to choose from among a large number of applicants for job openings. Minimum educational requirements are also common. Some employer practices, such as those involving educational requirements, may have an unintended discriminatory impact on a protected class. **Disparate-impact discrimination** occurs when a protected group of people is adversely affected by an employer's practices, procedures, or tests, even though they do not appear to be discriminatory.

In a disparate-impact discrimination case, the complaining party must first use one of two statistical methods to show that the employer's practices, procedures, or tests are discriminatory in effect. Under the *pool of applicants* test, a plaintiff can prove a disparate impact by showing that the percentage of the protected class in the employer's workforce does not reflect the percentage of that group in the pool of qualified individuals available in the local labor market. Alternatively, a plaintiff can prove disparate impact by comparing the *selection rates* of members of a protected class with the selection rates of nonmembers, regardless of the relative percentages of the two groups in the employer's workforce. Under EEOC guidelines, a selection rate for a protected class that is less than four-fifths, or 80 percent, of the rate for the group with the highest rate of hiring generally will be regarded as evidence of disparate impact.

Once a disparate impact has been proved using one of these methods, the plaintiff must show a causal link between the employer's practice and the discriminatory effect. This establishes a *prima facie* case, and the burden of proof then shifts to the employer to show that the practices or procedures in question were justified.

Discrimination Based on Race, Color, and National Origin

Title VII prohibits employers from discriminating against employees or job applicants on the basis of race, color, or national origin. Although there has been some uncertainty in the federal courts about what constitutes race versus national origin discrimination, race is interpreted broadly to apply to the ancestry or ethnic characteristics of a group of persons, such as Native Americans. The national origin provisions make it unlawful to discriminate against persons based on their birth in another country, such as Iraq or the Philippines, or their ancestry or culture, such as Hispanic.

If an employer's standards or policies for selecting or promoting employees have a discriminatory effect on employees or job applicants in these protected classes, then a presumption of illegal discrimination arises. To avoid liability, the employer must then show that its standards or policies have a substantial, demonstrable relationship to realistic qualifications for the job in question.

CASE IN POINT Jiann Min Chang was an instructor at Alabama Agricultural and Mechanical University (AAMU). When AAMU terminated his employment, Chang filed a lawsuit claiming discrimination based on national origin. Chang established a *prima facie* case because he (1) was a member of a protected class, (2) was qualified for the job, (3) suffered an adverse employment action, and (4) was replaced by someone outside his protected class (a non-Asian instructor). When the burden of proof shifted to the employer, however, AAMU showed that Chang had argued with a university vice president and refused to comply with her instructions. The court ruled that the university had not renewed Chang's contract for a legitimate reason—insubordination—and therefore was not liable for unlawful discrimination.[5]

REVERSE DISCRIMINATION Note that Title VII also protects against *reverse discrimination*—that is, discrimination against majority group individuals, such as white males. For example, if an African American woman fired several white men from their management positions at a school district, the district could be held liable for reverse discrimination unless it had articulated a legitimate, nondiscriminatory reason for its actions.[6]

In 2009, the United States Supreme Court issued a decision that will have a significant impact on disparate-impact and reverse discrimination litigation. Employers may find the application of the ruling somewhat confusing, however, because the Court found that an employer had engaged in reverse discrimination when it discarded test results in an attempt to avoid unlawful discrimination.

CASE IN POINT The fire department in New Haven, Connecticut, administered a test to determine which firefighters were eligible for promotions. No African Americans and only two Hispanic firefighters passed the test. Fearing that it would be sued for racial discrimination if it used the test results for promotions, the city refused to certify (and basically discarded) the results. The white firefighters (and one Hispanic) who had passed the test then sued the city, claiming reverse discrimination. The lower courts found in favor of the city, but the United States Supreme Court reversed. The Court held that the city's race-conscious, discriminatory actions were not justified. An employer can engage in intentional discrimination to remedy unintentional discrimination only if the employer has "a strong basis in evidence" to believe that it will be successfully sued for disparate-impact discrimination. Mere fear of litigation was not a sufficient reason for the city to discard its test results. The city subsequently promoted all the firefighters involved in the lawsuit.[7]

POTENTIAL SECTION 1981 CLAIMS Victims of racial or ethnic discrimination may also have a cause of action under 42 U.S.C. Section 1981. This section, which was enacted as part of the Civil Rights Act of 1866 to protect the rights of freed slaves, prohibits discrimination on the basis of race or ethnicity in the formation or enforcement of contracts. Because employment is often a contractual relationship, Section 1981 can provide an alternative basis for a plaintiff's action and is potentially advantageous because it does not place a cap on damages.

Discrimination Based on Religion

Title VII of the Civil Rights Act of 1964 also prohibits government employers, private employers, and unions from discriminating against persons because of their religion. Employers cannot treat their employees more or less favorably based on their religious beliefs or practices and cannot require employees to participate in any religious activity (or forbid them from participating in one).

If an employee's religion prohibits her or him from working on a certain day of the week or at a certain type of job, the employer must make a reasonable attempt to accommodate these religious requirements. Employers must reasonably accommodate an employee's sincerely held religious belief even if the belief is not based on the doctrines of a traditionally recognized religion, such as Christianity or Judaism, or denomination, such as Baptist.

Discrimination Based on Gender

Under Title VII, as well as under other federal acts (including the Equal Pay Act of 1963, which is

---

5. *Jiann Min Chang v. Alabama Agricultural and Mechanical University,* 2009 WL 3403180 (11th Cir. 2009).

6. See, for example, *Johnston v. School District of Philadelphia,* 2006 WL 999966 (E.D.Pa. 2006).

7. *Ricci v. DeStefano,* ___ U.S. ___, 129 S.Ct. 2658, 174 L.Ed.2d 490 (2009).

discussed next), employers are forbidden from discriminating against employees on the basis of gender. Employers are prohibited from classifying jobs as male or female and from advertising in help-wanted columns that are designated male or female unless the employer can prove that the gender of the applicant is essential to the job. Employers also cannot have separate male and female seniority lists or refuse to promote employees based on their gender.

Generally, to succeed in a suit for gender discrimination, a plaintiff must demonstrate that gender was a determining factor in the employer's decision to hire, fire, or promote him or her. Typically, this involves looking at all of the surrounding circumstances.

CASE IN POINT The EEOC filed a lawsuit against a plastics manufacturer, Polycon Industries, Inc. The EEOC alleged that the company had reserved higher-paying production jobs for male employees and refused to promote female workers to these jobs because of their gender. The EEOC decided to pursue the case when it received complaints from women who had applied for production jobs but had never even been interviewed.[8]

The Pregnancy Discrimination Act of 1978,[9] which amended Title VII, expanded the definition of gender discrimination to include discrimination based on pregnancy. Women affected by pregnancy, childbirth, or related medical conditions must be treated—for all employment-related purposes, including the receipt of benefits under employee benefit programs—the same as other persons not so affected but similar in ability to work.

EQUAL PAY ACT The Equal Pay Act of 1963[10] prohibits employers from engaging in gender-based wage discrimination. For the act's equal pay requirements to apply, the male and female employees must work at the same establishment doing similar work. The work need not be identical, provided that it involves substantial equality in skill, effort, responsibility, and working conditions. To determine whether the Equal Pay Act has been violated, a court will look at the primary duties of the two jobs, focusing on the job content rather than the job description.[11] If the court finds that the wage differential is based on a permissible practice, such as a seniority or merit system, it does not violate the Equal Pay Act.

2009 EQUAL PAY LEGISLATION More than four decades after the Equal Pay Act was enacted, there is still a significant gap between the wages earned by male and female employees in the United States. Women typically earn about three-quarters of what men earn. This continuing disparity prompted Congress to pass the Paycheck Fairness Act of 2009, which closed some loopholes in the Equal Pay Act that allowed employers to justify wage discrimination if it was based on any factor other than gender. The Paycheck Fairness Act clarifies the defenses that employers may offer and prohibits the use of gender-based differentials in assessing an employee's education, training, or experience. The act also provides additional remedies for wage discrimination, including compensatory and punitive damages, which are available as remedies for discrimination based on race and national origin.

In another 2009 action, Congress responded to a 2007 decision by the United States Supreme Court that required a plaintiff alleging wage discrimination to file a complaint within 180 days of the decision that set the discriminatory pay.[12] Congress rejected this limit when it enacted the Lilly Ledbetter Fair Pay Act of 2009.[13] The act makes discriminatory wages actionable under federal law regardless of when the discrimination began. Each time a person is paid discriminatory wages, benefits, or other compensation, a cause of action arises (and the plaintiff has 180 days from that date to file a complaint). In other words, if a plaintiff continues to work for the employer while receiving discriminatory wages, the time period for filing a complaint is basically unlimited.

Constructive Discharge

The majority of Title VII complaints involve unlawful discrimination in decisions to hire or fire employees. In some situations, however, employees who leave their jobs voluntarily can claim that they were "constructively discharged" by the employer. **Constructive discharge** occurs when the employer causes the employee's working conditions to be so intolerable that a reasonable person in the employee's position would feel compelled to quit.

---

8. Case No. 2:09-cv-00141-RL-PRC, filed in the U.S. District Court for the Northern District of Indiana, Hammond Division.

9. 42 U.S.C. Section 2000e(k).

10. 29 U.S.C. Section 206(d).

11. For an illustration of the factors courts consider in wage-discrimination claims under the Equal Pay Act, see *Beck-Wilson v. Principi,* 441 F.3d 353 (6th Cir. 2006).

12. *Ledbetter v. Goodyear Tire Co.,* 550 U.S. 618, 127 S.Ct. 2162, 167 L.Ed.2d 982 (2007).

13. Pub. L. No. 111-2, 123 Stat. 5 (January 5, 2009), amending 42 U.S.C. Section 2000e-5[e].

PROVING CONSTRUCTIVE DISCHARGE The plaintiff must present objective proof of intolerable working conditions, which the employer knew or had reason to know about yet failed to correct within a reasonable time period. Courts generally also require the employee to show causation—that the employer's unlawful discrimination caused the working conditions to be intolerable. Put a different way, the employee's resignation must be a foreseeable result of the employer's discriminatory action. Although courts weigh the facts on a case-by-case basis, employee demotion is one of the most frequently cited reasons for a finding of constructive discharge, particularly when the employee was subjected to humiliation.

For example, Khalil's employer humiliates him by informing him in front of his co-workers that he is being demoted to an inferior position. Khalil's co-workers then continually insult, harass, and make derogatory remarks to him about his national origin (he is from Iraq). The employer is aware of this discriminatory treatment but does nothing to remedy the situation, despite repeated complaints from Khalil. After several months, Khalil quits his job and files a Title VII claim. In this situation, Khalil would likely have sufficient evidence to maintain an action for constructive discharge in violation of Title VII.

APPLIES TO ALL TITLE VII DISCRIMINATION Note that constructive discharge is a theory that plaintiffs can use to establish any type of discrimination claims under Title VII, including race, color, national origin, religion, gender, pregnancy, and sexual harassment. Constructive discharge has also been successfully used in situations that involve discrimination based on age or disability (both of which will be discussed later in this chapter). Constructive discharge is most commonly asserted in cases involving sexual harassment, however.

When constructive discharge is claimed, the employee can pursue damages for loss of income, including back pay. These damages ordinarily are not available to an employee who left a job voluntarily.

Sexual Harassment

Title VII also protects employees against **sexual harassment** in the workplace. Sexual harassment can take two forms: *quid pro quo* harassment and hostile-environment harassment. *Quid pro quo* is a Latin phrase that is often translated as "something in exchange for something else." *Quid pro quo* harassment occurs when sexual favors are demanded in return for job opportunities, promotions, salary

increases, or other benefits. According to the United States Supreme Court, hostile-environment harassment occurs when "the workplace is permeated with discriminatory intimidation, ridicule, and insult, that is sufficiently severe or pervasive to alter the conditions of the victim's employment and create an abusive working environment."[14]

The courts determine whether the sexually offensive conduct was sufficiently severe or pervasive to create a hostile environment on a case-by-case basis. Typically, a single incident of sexually offensive conduct is not enough to permeate the work environment (although there have been exceptions when the conduct was particularly objectionable).[15] Note also that if the employee who is alleging sexual harassment has signed an employment contract containing an arbitration clause (see Chapter 3), she or he will most likely be required to arbitrate the claim.[16]

HARASSMENT BY SUPERVISORS For an employer to be held liable for a supervisor's sexual harassment, the supervisor normally must have taken *a tangible employment action* against the employee. A **tangible employment action** is a significant change in employment status or benefits, such as when an employee is fired, refused a promotion, demoted, or reassigned to a position with significantly different responsibilities. Only a supervisor, or another person acting with the authority of the employer, can cause this sort of harm. A co-worker cannot dock another employee's pay, demote her or him, or set conditions for continued employment, for example. A constructive discharge also qualifies as a tangible employment action.[17]

THE *ELLERTH/FARAGHER* AFFIRMATIVE DEFENSE In 1998, the United States Supreme Court issued several important rulings that have had a lasting impact on cases involving alleged sexual harassment by supervisors.[18] The Court held that an employer (a city) was liable for a supervisor's harassment of employees even though the employer was unaware of the

---

14. *Harris v. Forklift Systems,* 510 U.S. 17, 114 S.Ct. 367, 126 L.Ed.2d 295 (1993). See also *Baker v. Via Christi Regional Medical Center,* 491 F.Supp.2d 1040 (D.Kan. 2007).
15. See, for example, *Pomales v. Celulares Telefonica, Inc.,* 447 F.3d 79 (1st Cir. 2006); and *Fontanez-Nunez v. Janssen Ortho, LLC,* 447 F.3d 50 (1st Cir. 2006).
16. See, for example, *EEOC v. Cheesecake Factory, Inc.,* 2009 WL 1259359 (D.Ariz. 2009).
17. See, for example, *Pennsylvania State Police v. Suders,* 542 U.S. 129, 124 S.Ct. 2342, 159 L.Ed.2d 204 (2004).
18. *Burlington Industries, Inc. v. Ellerth,* 524 U.S. 742, 118 S.Ct. 2257, 141 L.Ed.2d 633 (1998); and *Faragher v. City of Boca Raton,* 524 U.S. 775, 118 S.Ct. 2275, 141 L.Ed.2d 662 (1998).

behavior. Although the city had a written policy against sexual harassment, it had not distributed the policy to its employees and had not established any complaint procedures for employees who felt that they had been sexually harassed. In another case, the Court held that an employer can be liable for a supervisor's sexual harassment even though the employee does not suffer adverse job consequences.

The Court's decisions in these cases established what has become known as the *Ellerth/Faragher* affirmative defense to charges of sexual harassment. The defense has two elements:

1. The employer must have taken reasonable care to prevent and promptly correct any sexually harassing behavior (by establishing effective harassment policies and complaint procedures, for example).
2. The plaintiff-employee must have unreasonably failed to take advantage of preventive or corrective opportunities provided by the employer to avoid harm.

An employer that can prove both elements will not be liable for a supervisor's harassment.

RETALIATION BY EMPLOYERS Employers sometimes retaliate against employees who complain about sexual harassment or other Title VII violations. Retaliation can take many forms. An employer might demote or fire the person, or otherwise change the terms, conditions, and benefits of employment. Title VII prohibits retaliation, and employees can sue their employers when it occurs. In a *retaliation claim,* an individual asserts that she or he has suffered a harm as a result of making a charge, testifying, or participating in a Title VII investigation or proceeding. In a 2009 decision, the United States Supreme Court held that Title VII's retaliation protection extends to an employee who speaks out about discrimination not on her or his own initiative, but in answering questions during an employer's internal investigation of another employee's complaint.[19]

At one time, the courts disagreed as to whether the plaintiff had to show that the challenged action adversely affected the terms or conditions of *employment* to prove retaliation. In the following case, the United States Supreme Court resolved the question of whether Title VII's ban on retaliation covers acts that are not job related.

---

19. *Crawford v. Metropolitan Government of Nashville and Davidson County, Tennessee,* __ U.S. __, 129 S.Ct. 846, 172 L.Ed.2d 650 (2009).

✳ EXTENDED CASE 22.1 ✳
Burlington Northern and Santa Fe Railroad Co. v. White

Supreme Court of the United States, 548 U.S. 53, 126 S.Ct. 2405, 165 L.Ed.2d 345 (2006).

IN THE LANGUAGE OF THE COURT
Justice *BREYER* delivered the opinion of the Court.
 * * * *
 * * * Sheila White [was] the only woman working in the Maintenance of Way department at [Burlington Northern & Santa Fe Railway Company's] Tennessee Yard.

In September 1997, White complained to Burlington officials that her * * * supervisor, Bill Joiner, had repeatedly told her that women should not be working in the Maintenance of Way department. [Joiner was disciplined. White was reassigned from forklift duty to "track laborer" tasks.]
 * * * *
 On October 10, White filed a complaint with the Equal Employment Opportunity Commission (EEOC * * *).

[In December, White's supervisor, Percy Sharkey, complained to Burlington officials that White had been insubordinate. She was suspended without pay but reinstated after an investigation and awarded back pay for the period of the suspension. White filed a second charge with the EEOC.]
 * * * *
 * * * [Later,] White filed this Title VII action against Burlington in federal [district] court. * * * She claimed that Burlington's actions—(1) changing her job responsibilities, and (2) suspending her * * * without pay—amounted to unlawful retaliation in violation of Title VII. A jury found in White's favor * * * [and] awarded her $43,500 in * * * damages * * * .

 * * * [On appeal, the U.S. Court of Appeals for the Sixth Circuit held that Title VII's antiretaliation ban is limited to acts that adversely affect the terms, conditions, or benefits of employment, and] affirmed the District Court's judgment in White's favor on both retaliation claims. [Burlington appealed to the United States Supreme Court.]

EXTENDED CASE 22.1 CONTINUED ⬇

* * * *

* * * The language of the [antidiscrimination] provision differs from that of the anti-retaliation provision in important ways.

The * * * words in the [antidiscrimination] provision—"hire," "discharge," "compensation, terms, conditions, or privileges of employment," "employment opportunities," and "status as an employee"—explicitly limit the scope of that provision to actions that affect employment or alter the conditions of the workplace. No such limiting words appear in the anti-retaliation provision.

* * * The two provisions differ not only in language but in purpose as well. The anti-discrimination provision seeks a workplace where individuals are not discriminated against because of their racial, ethnic, religious, or gender-based status. *The anti-retaliation provision seeks to secure that primary objective by preventing* an employer from interfering (through retaliation) with an employee's efforts to secure or advance enforcement of the Act's basic guarantees. The [antidiscrimination] provision seeks to prevent injury to individuals based on who they are, i.e., their status. *The anti-retaliation provision seeks to prevent harm to individuals based on what they do, i.e., their conduct.* [Emphasis added.]

To secure the first objective, Congress did not need to prohibit anything other than employment-related discrimination.

But one cannot secure the second objective by focusing only upon employer actions and harm that concern employment and the workplace. * * * *An employer can effectively retaliate against an employee by taking actions not directly related to his employment or by causing him harm outside the workplace.* * * * [Emphasis added.]

* * * *

* * * We conclude that * * * the anti-retaliation provision extends beyond workplace-related or employment-related retaliatory acts * * *.

* * * *

* * * A plaintiff must show that a reasonable employee would have found the challenged action materially adverse, which in this context means it well might have dissuaded a reasonable worker from making or supporting a charge of discrimination.

* * * *

* * * [In this case,] the track labor duties were by all accounts more arduous and dirtier; * * * the forklift operator position required more qualifications, which is an indication of prestige; and * * * the forklift operator position was objectively considered a better job and the male employees resented White for occupying it. Based on this record, a jury could reasonably conclude that the reassignment of responsibilities would have been materially adverse to a reasonable employee.

* * * *

For these reasons, the judgment of the Court of Appeals is affirmed.

 QUESTIONS

1. Why did the Court evaluate the language of Title VII's antidiscrimination and antiretaliation provisions?
2. What was the Court's interpretation of those provisions?

HARASSMENT BY CO-WORKERS AND OTHERS When the harassment of co-workers, rather than supervisors, creates a hostile working environment, an employee may still have a cause of action against the employer. Normally, though, the employer will be held liable only if it knew or should have known about the harassment and failed to take immediate remedial action.

Occasionally, a court may also hold an employer liable for harassment by *nonemployees* if the employer knew about the harassment and failed to take corrective action. Suppose that Gordon, who owns and manages a Great Bites restaurant, knows that one of his regular customers, Dean, repeatedly harasses Sharon, a waitress. If Gordon does nothing and permits the harassment to continue, he may be liable under Title VII even though Dean is not an employee of the restaurant.

CASE IN POINT Kathleen Torres-Negrón, a sales representative at Merck & Company, Inc., was temporarily assigned to work in Mexico at Merck-Mexico (a subsidiary of Merck). She claimed that she was being sexually harassed and informed the supervisor in Mexico. When she filed a lawsuit, Merck argued that it should not be liable because the alleged harassers were employed by Merck-Mexico and not by the U.S.-based Merck. Although the trial court granted a summary judgment in Merck's favor, an appellate court held that there was a sufficient issue of fact as to whether Merck and Merck-Mexico could be considered a single employer for purposes of a Title VII claim. Thus, the court ruled that there was enough evidence of Merck's control over the alleged harassers for the employee to take her case to a jury.[20]

SAME-GENDER HARASSMENT In 1998, in the landmark case *Oncale v. Sundowner Offshore Services, Inc.*,[21] the Supreme Court held that Title VII protection extends to situations in which individuals are sexually harassed by members of the same gender. It can be difficult, though, to prove that the harassment in same-gender cases is "based on sex." When the victim is homosexual, some courts have found that the harasser's conduct does not qualify as sexual harassment under Title VII because it was based on the employee's sexual orientation, not on his or her "sex."[22] It is easier to establish a case of same-gender harassment when the harasser is homosexual.[23]

Although federal law (Title VII) does not prohibit discrimination or harassment based on a person's sexual orientation, a growing number of states have enacted laws that prohibit sexual orientation discrimination in private employment.[24] Many companies have also voluntarily established nondiscrimination policies that include sexual orientation.

Online Harassment

Employees' online activities can create a hostile working environment in many ways. Racial jokes, ethnic slurs, or other comments contained in e-mail, text or instant messages, and blog posts can become the basis for a claim of hostile-environment harassment or other forms of discrimination. A worker who regularly sees sexually explicit images on a co-worker's computer screen may find the images offensive and claim that they create a hostile working environment.[25] Nevertheless, employers may be able to avoid liability for online harassment by taking prompt remedial action.

CASE IN POINT While working at WorldCom Corporation, Angela Daniels received racially harassing e-mailed jokes from another employee. Shortly afterward, the company issued a warning to the offending employee about the proper use of the e-mail system and held two meetings to discuss company policy on the use of the system. In Daniels's suit against WorldCom for racial discrimination, a federal district court concluded that the employer was not liable for its employee's racially harassing e-mails because the employer took prompt remedial action.[26]

Remedies under Title VII

Employer liability under Title VII may be extensive. If the plaintiff successfully proves that unlawful discrimination occurred, he or she may be awarded reinstatement, back pay, retroactive promotions, and damages. Compensatory damages are available only in cases of intentional discrimination. Punitive damages may be recovered against a private employer only if the employer acted with malice or reckless indifference to an individual's rights. The statute limits the total amount of compensatory and punitive damages that plaintiffs can recover from specific employers (ranging from $50,000 from employers with one hundred or fewer employees to $300,000 from employers with more than five hundred employees).

SECTION 2

DISCRIMINATION BASED ON AGE

Age discrimination is potentially the most widespread form of discrimination, because anyone—regardless of race, color, national origin, or gender—could be a victim at some point in life. The Age Discrimination in Employment Act (ADEA) of 1967, as amended, prohibits employment discrimination on the basis of age against individuals forty years of age or older. The act also prohibits mandatory retirement for nonmanagerial workers. The United States Supreme Court has made it clear that the text and the legislative history of the ADEA show that it was meant to protect relatively older workers from discrimination that gives an unfair advantage to the relatively young. For the act to apply, an employer must have twenty or more employees, and the employer's business activities must affect interstate commerce. The EEOC administers the ADEA, but the act also permits private causes of action against employers for age discrimination.

---

20. *Torres-Negrón v. Merck & Company, Inc.*, 488 F.3d 34 (1st Cir. 2007).

21. 523 U.S. 75, 118 S.Ct. 998, 140 L.Ed.2d 207 (1998).

22. See, for example, *McCown v. St. John's Health System*, 349 F.3d 540 (8th Cir. 2003); and *Rene v. MGM Grand Hotel, Inc.*, 305 F.3d 1061 (9th Cir. 2002).

23. See, for example, *Tepperwien v. Entergy Nuclear Operations, Inc.*, 606 F.Supp.2d 427 (S.D.N.Y. 2009).

24. See, for example, 775 Illinois Compiled Statutes 5/1–103.

25. See, for example, *Doe v. XYC Corp.*, 382 N.J.Super. 122 (App. Div. 2005).

26. *Daniels v. WorldCom Corp.*, 1998 WL 91261 (N.D.Tex. 1998). See also *Musgrove v. Mobil Oil Corp.*, 2003 WL 21653125 (N.D.Tex. 2003).

Procedures under the ADEA

The burden-shifting procedure under the ADEA differs from the procedure under Title VII as a result of a United States Supreme Court decision, which dramatically changed the burden of proof in age discrimination cases.[27] As explained earlier, if the plaintiff in a Title VII case can show that the employer was motivated, at least in part, by unlawful discrimination, the burden of proof shifts to the employer to articulate a legitimate nondiscriminatory reason for the challenged action. Thus, in cases in which the employer has a "mixed motive" for discharging an employee, the employer has the burden of proving its reason was legitimate.

Under the ADEA, in contrast, a plaintiff must show that the unlawful discrimination was not just *a* reason but *the* reason for the adverse employment action. In other words, the employee has the burden of persuasion to establish *but for* causation—that is, that age discrimination was, in fact, the reason for the adverse decision. Thus, to establish a *prima facie* case, the plaintiff must show that she or he (1) was a member of the protected age group, (2) was qualified for the position from which she or he was discharged, and (3) was discharged because of age discrimination. Then the burden shifts to the employer. If the employer offers a legitimate reason for its action, then the plaintiff must show that the stated reason is only a pretext for the employer's decision. The following case illustrates this process.

---

27. *Gross v. FBL Financial Services, Inc.,* ___ U.S. ___, 129 S.Ct. 2343, 174 L.Ed.2d 119 (2009).

CASE 22.2
Mora v. Jackson Memorial Foundation, Inc.

United States Court of Appeals, Eleventh Circuit, 597 F.3d 1201 (2010).
www.ca11.uscourts.gov/opinions/search.php[a]

BACKGROUND AND FACTS • Josephine Mora was sixty-two years old when she was fired from her job as a fund-raiser for Jackson Memorial Foundation, Inc. Mora's supervisor had become dissatisfied with Mora's work and recommended that she be fired. The foundation's chief executive officer, Mr. Rodriguez, agreed. Later, though, Rodriguez decided to give Mora a different position in his office "where he could observe her more closely." Mora worked with Rodriguez for a month, and more errors and issues with professionalism supposedly arose. Mora contended that when Rodriguez fired her, he told her, "I need someone younger I can pay less." A former employee stated that she had heard this conversation, adding that she heard Rodriguez say to Mora, "You are very old, you are very inept. What you should be doing is taking care of old people. They really need you. I need somebody younger that I can pay less and I can control." Another former employee stated that Rodriguez explained to her and another employee that Mora was "too old to be working here anyway." Rodriguez denied that he had made these statements, and one of the employees substantiated Rodriguez's version of events. Mora sued the foundation in a federal district court for wrongful termination under the Age Discrimination in Employment Act (ADEA). The foundation moved for summary judgment, arguing that regardless of the discrimination issue, Mora still would have been terminated for poor job performance. The district court granted the motion, and Mora appealed.

IN THE LANGUAGE OF THE COURT
PER CURIAM [By the Whole Court].
* * * *

After Plaintiff [Mora] appealed, the Supreme Court, in *Gross v. FBL Financial Services, Inc.,*[b] clarified the nature of ADEA claims. The Supreme Court concluded that ADEA claims are not subject to the burden-shifting protocol set forth for Title VII suits in

---

a. In the box titled "Search by Case Number or Docket Number," enter "08-16113"—the case docket number. In the search results, click on the link to the docket number to access the opinion. The U.S. Court of Appeals for the Eleventh Circuit maintains this Web site.

b. ___U.S.___, 129 S.Ct. 2343, 174 L.Ed.2d 119 (2009).

CASE CONTINUES ➡

CASE 22.2 CONTINUED ⬥ *Price Waterhouse v. Hopkins.*[c] The ADEA requires that "age [be] the reason that the employer decided to act." *Because an ADEA plaintiff must establish "but for" causality, no "same decision" affirmative defense [the argument that the same decision—to fire someone, for example—would have been made regardless of the alleged discrimination] can exist: the employer either acted "because of" the plaintiff's age or it did not.* [Emphasis added.]

Because the Supreme Court has excluded the whole idea of a "mixed motive" ADEA claim—and the corresponding "same decision" defense—we need not consider the district court's analysis of Defendant's [the foundation's] affirmative defense. Instead, * * * we look to determine whether a material factual question exists on this record about whether Defendant discriminated against her. We say "Yes."

* * * *

A plaintiff in an ADEA claim may "establish a claim of illegal age discrimination through either direct evidence or circumstantial evidence." Plaintiff's testimony that Rodriguez fired her because she was "too old" was substantiated by the affidavits of two other employees of Defendant. Rodriguez and Quevedo [another employee] testified that no such comments were made * * *.

The resolution of this case depends on whose account of the pertinent conversations a jury would credit. We conclude that a reasonable juror could accept that Rodriguez made the discriminatory-sounding remarks and that the remarks are sufficient evidence of a discriminatory motive which was the "but for" cause of Plaintiff's dismissal. Summary judgment for Defendant was therefore incorrect.

We have considered cases factually similar to Plaintiff's. In [one case], we concluded that statements from a county official who "didn't want to hire any old pilots" were direct evidence of discrimination * * *. In [another case], we likewise concluded that an employer's statement that he wanted "aggressive, young men like himself to be promoted" was circumstantial evidence of discrimination.

While these cases were litigated under the now-defunct ADEA mixed motive theory, they remain instructive. Plaintiff's situation is similar. A reasonable juror could find that Rodriguez's statements should be taken at face value and that he fired Plaintiff because of her age.

DECISION AND REMEDY • *The U.S. Court of Appeals for the Eleventh Circuit vacated (set aside) the decision of the trial court and remanded the case for further proceedings. Because there was a "disputed question of material fact" as to whether the plaintiff had been fired because of her age, the defendant was not entitled to summary judgment.*

THE ETHICAL DIMENSION • *Is the court's decision in this case fair to employers? Why or why not?*

MANAGERIAL IMPLICATIONS • *Business owners and supervisory personnel should be careful to avoid statements regarding an employee's age that may sound discriminatory. If the employee later has to be dismissed due to poor performance, comments about his or her age may become the basis for an age discrimination lawsuit.*

---

c. 490 U.S. 228, 109 S.Ct. 1775, 104 L.Ed.2d 268 (1989).

Replacing Older Workers with Younger Workers

Numerous age discrimination cases have been brought against employers who, to cut costs, replaced older, higher-salaried employees with younger, lower-salaried workers. Whether a firing is discriminatory or simply part of a rational business decision to prune the company's ranks is not always clear. Companies typically defend a decision to discharge a worker by asserting that the worker could no longer perform her or his duties or that the worker's skills were no longer needed.

A plaintiff must prove only that the discharge was motivated by age bias. The plaintiff does not need to prove that she or he was replaced by a person "outside the protected class" (under the age of forty years), as long as the replacement worker is younger than the plaintiff.[28] The issue in all ADEA cases is whether age discrimination has, in fact, occurred, regardless of the age of the replacement worker. Nevertheless, the bigger the age gap, the more likely the plaintiff is to succeed in showing age discrimination.

When an older worker who is laid off as part of a restructuring subsequently files a suit against the company for age discrimination, he or she must present evidence that the layoff was motivated by age bias. Relevant evidence that will be allowed at trial might include testimony from other employees or former employees concerning the company's attitudes toward the workers' ages.[29]

State Employees Not Covered by the ADEA

Generally, the states are immune under the Eleventh Amendment from lawsuits brought by private individuals in federal court—unless a state consents to the suit. This immunity stems from the United States Supreme Court's interpretation of the Eleventh Amendment (the text of this amendment is included in Appendix B).

CASE IN POINT In two cases, professors and librarians contended that their employers—two Florida state universities—denied them salary increases and other benefits because they were getting old and their successors could be hired at a lower cost. The universities claimed that as agencies of a sovereign state, they could not be sued without the state's consent. The cases ultimately reached the United States Supreme Court, which held that the Eleventh Amendment bars private parties from suing state employers for violations of the ADEA.[30]

State immunity under the Eleventh Amendment is not absolute, as the Court explained in 2004. In some situations, such as when fundamental rights are at stake, Congress has the power to abrogate (abolish) state immunity to private suits through legislation that unequivocally shows Congress's intent to subject states to private suits.[31] Generally, though, the Court has found that state employers are immune from private suits brought by employees under the ADEA (for age discrimination), the

Americans with Disabilities Act (for disability-based discrimination),[32] and the Fair Labor Standards Act.[33] As explained in Chapter 21, state employers are not immune from the requirements of the Family and Medical Leave Act.[34]

SECTION 3
DISCRIMINATION BASED ON DISABILITY

The Americans with Disabilities Act (ADA) of 1990 is designed to eliminate discriminatory employment practices that prevent otherwise qualified workers with disabilities from fully participating in the national labor force. The ADA prohibits disability-based discrimination in all workplaces with fifteen or more workers (with the exception of state government employers, who are generally immune under the Eleventh Amendment, as was just discussed). Basically, the ADA requires that employers "reasonably accommodate" the needs of persons with disabilities unless to do so would cause the employer to suffer an "undue hardship." In 2008, Congress enacted the ADA Amendments Act,[35] which broadened the coverage of the ADA's protections, as discussed shortly.

Procedures under the ADA

To prevail on a claim under the ADA, a plaintiff must show that he or she (1) has a disability, (2) is otherwise qualified for the employment in question, and (3) was excluded from the employment solely because of the disability. As in Title VII cases, the plaintiff must pursue his or her claim through the EEOC before filing an action in court for a violation of the ADA. The EEOC may decide to investigate and perhaps even sue the employer on behalf of the employee. The EEOC can bring a suit on behalf of the employee under the ADA even if the employee signed an arbitration agreement with the employer.[36]

---

28. *O'Connor v. Consolidated Coin Caterers Corp.,* 517 U.S. 308, 116 S.Ct. 1307, 134 L.Ed.2d 433 (1996).

29. See, for example, *Sprint/United Management Co. v. Mendelsohn,* 552 U.S. 379, 128 S.Ct. 1140, 170 L.Ed.2d 1 (2008).

30. *Kimel v. Florida Board of Regents,* 528 U.S. 62, 120 S.Ct. 631, 145 L.Ed.2d 522 (2000).

31. *Tennessee v. Lane,* 541 U.S. 509, 124 S.Ct. 1978, 158 L.Ed.2d 820 (2004).

32. *Board of Trustees of the University of Alabama v. Garrett,* 531 U.S. 356, 121 S.Ct. 955, 148 L.Ed.2d 866 (2001).

33. *Alden v. Maine,* 527 U.S. 706, 119 S.Ct. 2240, 144 L.Ed.2d 636 (1999).

34. *Nevada Department of Human Resources v. Hibbs,* 538 U.S. 721, 123 S.Ct. 1972, 155 L.Ed.2d 953 (2003).

35. 42 U.S.C. Sections 12103 and 12205a.

36. This was the Supreme Court's ruling in *EEOC v. Waffle House, Inc.,* 534 U.S. 279, 122 S.Ct. 754, 151 L.Ed.2d 755 (2002).

If the EEOC decides not to sue, then the employee may do so. Plaintiffs in lawsuits brought under the ADA may seek many of the same remedies that are available under Title VII. These include reinstatement, back pay, a limited amount of compensatory and punitive damages (for intentional discrimination), and certain other forms of relief. Repeat violators may be ordered to pay fines of up to $100,000.

What Is a Disability?

The ADA broadly defines *persons with disabilities* as persons with physical or mental impairments that "substantially limit" their everyday activities. More specifically, the ADA defines a *disability* as "(1) a physical or mental impairment that substantially limits one or more of the major life activities of such individuals; (2) a record of such impairment; or (3) being regarded as having such an impairment."

Health conditions that have been considered disabilities under federal law include blindness, alcoholism, heart disease, cancer, muscular dystrophy, cerebral palsy, paraplegia, diabetes, acquired immune deficiency syndrome (AIDS), testing positive for the human immunodeficiency virus (HIV, the virus that causes AIDS), and morbid obesity (which exists when an individual's weight is two times the normal weight for his or her height). The ADA excludes from coverage certain conditions, such as kleptomania (the obsessive desire to steal).

AN INITIAL NARROW INTERPRETATION Although the ADA's definition of disability is broad, United States Supreme Court rulings from 1999 to 2007 interpreted that definition narrowly and made it harder for

employees to establish a disability under the act. In 1999, the Supreme Court held that severe myopia, or nearsightedness, which can be corrected with lenses, does not qualify as a disability under the ADA.[37] In 2002, the Supreme Court held that repetitive-stress injuries (such as carpal tunnel syndrome) ordinarily do not constitute a disability under the ADA.[38] After that ruling, the courts began focusing on how the person functioned when using corrective devices or taking medication, not on how the person functioned without these measures.[39]

2008 AMENDMENTS BROADEN DEFINITION In response to the Supreme Court's limiting decisions, Congress decided to amend the ADA in 2008. Basically, the amendments reverse the Court's restrictive interpretation of disability under the ADA and prohibit employers from considering mitigating measures or medications when determining if an individual has a disability. As a result, disability is now determined on a case-by-case basis.

A condition may fit the definition of disability in one set of circumstances, but not in another. What makes the difference in an individual situation? The court in the following case answered that question.

---

37. *Sutton v. United Airlines, Inc.*, 527 U.S. 471, 119 S.Ct. 2139, 144 L.Ed.2d 450 (1999).
38. *Toyota Motor Manufacturing, Kentucky, Inc. v. Williams*, 534 U.S. 184, 122 S.Ct. 681, 151 L.Ed.2d 615 (2002). This case was invalidated by the 2008 amendments to the ADA.
39. See, for example, *Orr v. Wal-mart Stores, Inc.*, 297 F.3d 720 (8th Cir. 2002).

CASE 22.3
Rohr v. Salt River Project Agricultural Improvement and Power District

United States Court of Appeals, Ninth Circuit, 555 F.3d 850 (2009).
www.ca9.uscourts.gov[a]

BACKGROUND AND FACTS • Diabetes is a chronic disease associated with an increased risk of heart disease, stroke, high blood pressure, blindness, kidney disease, nervous system disease, and amputations, among other things. Larry Rohr has type 2 diabetes, which results from the body's failure to use insulin properly. He tires quickly and suffers from high blood pressure, deteriorating vision, and loss of feeling in his hands and feet. Insulin injections, other medicine, blood tests, and a strict diet are fixtures of his daily life. If he fails to follow this regimen, his blood sugar rises to a level that aggravates his disease. At the time of his diagnosis, he was a welding metallurgy specialist for the Salt River Project Agricultural Improvement and Power District, which provides utility services to homes in Arizona. Due to the effort required to manage his diabetes, particularly his strict diet schedule, Rohr's physician forbade

---

a. In the left-hand column, click on "Decisions" and then on "Opinions." When that page opens, click on "Advanced Search." In the "by Case No.:" box, type "06-16527" and click on "Search." In the result, click on the case title to access the opinion.

CASE 22.3 CONTINUED ▶ his assignment to tasks involving overnight, out-of-town travel. Salt River told Rohr that this would prevent him from performing the essential functions of his job, such as responding to power outages. Rohr was asked to transfer, apply for disability benefits, or take early retirement. He filed a suit in a federal district court against Salt River, alleging discrimination. The court issued a summary judgment in the employer's favor. Rohr appealed.

IN THE LANGUAGE OF THE COURT
BAER, Senior District Judge:
* * * *

The ADA defines "disability," in pertinent part, as "a physical or mental impairment that substantially limits one or more of the major life activities of such individual." Diabetes is a "physical impairment" because it affects the digestive, hemic [blood] and endocrine systems, and eating is a "major life activity." Whether Rohr's diabetes substantially limits his eating is an individualized inquiry. *Once an impairment is found, the issue is whether Rohr's diabetes substantially limits his activity of eating.* [Emphasis added.]
* * * *

To determine whether an insulin-dependent type 2 diabetic like Rohr is substantially limited in his eating, we must compare the condition, manner or duration under which he can eat as compared to the condition, manner or duration under which the average person in the general population can eat.
* * * *

Finally, we must consider not only whether the symptoms of Rohr's diabetes substantially limit one of his major life activities, but also whether his efforts to mitigate [diminish] the disease constitute a substantial limitation.
* * * *

* * * For people like Rohr, who must treat their diabetes with insulin, the failure to take insulin will result in severe problems and eventually death. Insulin injections themselves can be dangerous. * * * It is difficult to determine how much insulin to take, as the necessary amount varies depending on the food and activity level. * * * To obtain the appropriate balance, Rohr must test his blood glucose levels * * * numerous times a day.

If daily insulin injections alone more or less stabilized Rohr's blood sugar levels, such that any limitation imposed on his diet would be minor, then Rohr's major life activity of eating might not be substantially limited. However, [there are] substantial limitations on his eating in spite of his medicine and insulin. He must snack regularly, plan his daily schedule around his diet, avoid skipping meals and eat immediately when he feels dizzy or light-headed. * * * Straying from a diet for more than one or two meals is not a cause for medical concern for most people, and skipping a meal, or eating a large one, does not expose them to the risk of fainting. * * * For Rohr, the effort required to control his diet is itself substantially limiting.

DECISION AND REMEDY • *The U.S. Court of Appeals for the Ninth Circuit vacated the lower court's judgment and remanded the case for trial. Diabetes satisfies the ADA's definition of "disability" if it significantly restricts an individual's eating.*

THE E-COMMERCE DIMENSION • *If Rohr could have monitored his condition and regimen through a cell phone or other portable Internet connection, would the result in this case likely have been affected? Explain.*

THE LEGAL ENVIRONMENT DIMENSION • *Salt River argued that type 1 diabetes is harder to control than Rohr's type 2 diabetes. Assuming this is true, would it support a conclusion that Rohr does not suffer from a disability? Why or why not?*

Reasonable Accommodation

The ADA does not require that employers accommodate the needs of job applicants or employees with disabilities who are not otherwise qualified for the work. If a job applicant or an employee with a disability, with reasonable accommodation, can perform essential job functions, however, the employer must make the accommodation. Required modifications may include installing ramps for a wheelchair, establishing flexible working hours, creating or modifying job assignments, and designing or improving training materials and procedures.

Generally, employers should give primary consideration to employees' preferences in deciding what accommodations should be made.

UNDUE HARDSHIP Employers who do not accommodate the needs of persons with disabilities must demonstrate that the accommodations would cause *undue hardship* in terms of being significantly difficult or expensive for the employer. Usually, the courts decide whether an accommodation constitutes an undue hardship on a case-by-case basis.

For example, Bryan Lockhart, who uses a wheelchair, works for a cell phone company that provides parking for its employees. Lockhart informs the company supervisors that the parking spaces are so narrow that he is unable to extend the ramp on his van that allows him to get in and out of the vehicle. Lockhart therefore requests that the company reasonably accommodate his needs by paying a monthly fee for him to use a larger parking space in an adjacent lot. In this situation, a court would likely find that it would not be an undue hardship for the employer to pay for additional parking for Lockhart.

JOB APPLICATIONS AND PHYSICAL EXAMS Employers must modify their job-application and selection process so that those with disabilities can compete for jobs with those who do not have disabilities. For instance, a job announcement might be modified to allow job applicants to respond by e-mail or letter, as well as by telephone, so that it does not discriminate against potential applicants with hearing impairments.

Employers are restricted in the kinds of questions they may ask on job-application forms and during preemployment interviews. In addition, employers cannot require persons with disabilities to submit to preemployment physicals unless such exams are required of all other applicants. An employer can condition an offer of employment on the applicant's successfully passing a medical examination, but can only disqualify the applicant if the medical problems discovered would make it impossible for the applicant to perform the job. For example, when filling the position of delivery truck driver, a company cannot screen out all applicants who are unable to meet the U.S. Department of Transportation's hearing standard. The company would first have to prove that drivers who are deaf are not qualified to perform the essential job function of driving safely and pose a higher risk of accidents than drivers who are not deaf.[40]

SUBSTANCE ABUSERS Drug addiction is considered a disability under the ADA because it is a substantially limiting impairment. Those who are actually using illegal drugs are not protected by the act, however. The ADA protects only persons with *former* drug addictions—those who have completed or are now in a supervised drug-rehabilitation program. Individuals who have used drugs casually in the past are not protected under the act. They are not considered addicts and therefore do not have a disability (addiction).

People suffering from alcoholism are protected by the ADA. Employers cannot legally discriminate against employees simply because they suffer from alcoholism. Of course, employers have the right to prohibit the use of alcohol in the workplace and can require that employees not be under the influence of alcohol while working. Employers can also fire or refuse to hire a person who is an alcoholic if he or she poses a substantial risk of harm either to himself or herself or to others and the risk cannot be reduced by reasonable accommodation.

HEALTH-INSURANCE PLANS Workers with disabilities must be given equal access to any health insurance provided to other employees. Nevertheless, an employer can put a limit, or cap, on health-care payments under its group health policy as long as the cap is applied equally to all insured employees and does not discriminate on the basis of disability. Whenever a group health-care plan makes a disability-based distinction in its benefits, the plan violates the ADA (unless the employer can justify its actions under the business necessity defense, as will be discussed later in this chapter).

Association Discrimination

The ADA contains an "association provision" that protects qualified individuals from employment discrimination based on an identified disability of a person with whom the qualified individual is known to have a relationship or an association.[41] The purpose of this provision is to prevent employers from taking adverse employment actions based on stereotypes or assumptions about individuals who associate with people who have disabilities. An employer cannot, for instance, refuse to hire the parent of a child with a disability based on the assumption that the person will miss work too often or be unreliable.

To establish a *prima facie* case of association discrimination under the ADA, the plaintiff must show that she or he (1) was qualified for the job, (2) was subjected to an adverse employment action, and

---

40. See, for example, *Bates v. United Parcel Service, Inc.,* 465 F.3d 1069 (9th Cir. 2006).

41. 42 U.S.C. Section 12112(b)(4).

(3) was known by her or his employer to have a relative or an associate with a disability.

CASE IN POINT Randall Francin had worked at Mosby, Inc., for twelve years before his wife was diagnosed with amyotrophic lateral sclerosis (Lou Gehrig's disease). He discussed his rights for leave under the Family and Medical Leave Act (see Chapter 21) with a company representative. Early in 2004, Francin received a "merit award increase" in salary and subsequently discussed his wife's illness with his supervisor. In September 2004, Francin was fired. Francin filed a lawsuit claiming that Mosby had discriminated against him because of his association with a person with a disability. Although the trial court granted a summary judgment for Mosby, the appellate court found that there was sufficient evidence that Francin's wife's illness was a contributing factor to his termination for the case to go to trial. Thus, summary judgment was inappropriate.[42]

SECTION 4
DEFENSES TO EMPLOYMENT DISCRIMINATION

The first line of defense for an employer charged with employment discrimination is to assert that the plaintiff has failed to meet his or her initial burden of proving that discrimination occurred. As noted, plaintiffs bringing cases under the ADEA may find it difficult to meet this initial burden because they must prove that age discrimination was, in fact, the reason for their employer's decision to discharge them.

Once a plaintiff succeeds in proving that discrimination occurred, then the burden shifts to the employer to justify the discriminatory practice. Often, employers attempt to justify the discrimination by claiming that it was the result of a business necessity, a bona fide occupational qualification, or a seniority system. Alternatively, they may assert that employee misconduct should limit their liability. In some situations, as noted earlier, an effective antiharassment policy and prompt remedial action when harassment occurs may shield employers from liability for sexual harassment under Title VII.

Business Necessity

An employer may defend against a claim of disparate-impact (unintentional) discrimination by asserting that a practice that has a discriminatory effect is a **business necessity.** If requiring a high school diploma, for example, is shown to have a discriminatory effect, an employer might argue that a high school education is necessary for workers to perform the job at a required level of competence. If the employer can demonstrate to the court's satisfaction that a definite connection exists between a high school education and job performance, then the employer normally will succeed in this business necessity defense.

Bona Fide Occupational Qualification

Another defense applies when discrimination against a protected class is essential to a job—that is, when a particular trait is a **bona fide occupational qualification (BFOQ).** Race, color, and national origin, however, can never be BFOQs.

Generally, courts have restricted the BFOQ defense to instances in which the employee's gender or religion is essential to the job. For example, a women's clothing store might legitimately hire only female salespersons if part of a salesperson's job involves assisting clients in the store's dressing rooms. Similarly, the Federal Aviation Administration can legitimately impose age limits for airline pilots—but an airline cannot impose weight limits only on female flight attendants.

Seniority Systems

An employer with a history of discrimination may have no members of protected classes in upper-level positions. Even if the employer now seeks to be unbiased, it may face a lawsuit from members of protected classes claiming that they should be promoted ahead of schedule to compensate for past discrimination. If no present intent to discriminate is shown, however, and if promotions or other job benefits are distributed according to a fair **seniority system** (in which workers with more years of service are promoted first or laid off last), the employer normally has a good defense against the suit.

According to the United States Supreme Court, this defense may also apply to claims of discrimination under the ADA. A baggage handler who had injured his back requested an assignment to a mailroom position at U.S. Airways, Inc. The airline refused to give the employee the position because another employee had seniority. The Court sided with U.S. Airways. If an employee with a disability requests an accommodation that conflicts with an employer's seniority system, the accommodation generally will not be considered "reasonable" under the ADA.[43]

---

42. *Francin v. Mosby, Inc.,* 248 S.W.3d 619 (Mo. 2008).

43. *U.S. Airways, Inc. v. Barnett,* 535 U.S. 391, 122 S.Ct. 1516, 152 L.Ed.2d 589 (2002).

After-Acquired Evidence of Employee Misconduct

In some situations, employers have attempted to avoid liability for employment discrimination on the basis of "after-acquired evidence"—that is, evidence that the employer discovers after a lawsuit is filed—of an employee's misconduct. Suppose that an employer fires a worker, who then sues the employer for employment discrimination. During pretrial investigation, the employer learns that the employee made material misrepresentations on his employment application—misrepresentations that, had the employer known about them, would have served as a ground to fire the individual. Can this after-acquired evidence be used as a defense?

According to the United States Supreme Court, after-acquired evidence of wrongdoing cannot be used to shield an employer entirely from liability for employment discrimination. It may, however, be used to limit the amount of damages for which the employer is liable.[44]

SECTION 5
AFFIRMATIVE ACTION

Federal statutes and regulations providing for equal opportunity in the workplace were designed to reduce or eliminate discriminatory practices with respect to hiring, retaining, and promoting employees. **Affirmative action** programs go a step further and attempt to "make up" for past patterns of discrimination by giving members of protected classes preferential treatment in hiring or promotion. During the 1960s, all federal and state government agencies, private companies that contracted to do business with the federal government, and institutions that received federal funding were required to implement affirmative action policies.

Title VII of the Civil Rights Act of 1964 neither requires nor prohibits affirmative action. Thus, most private companies and organizations have not been required to implement affirmative action policies, though many have done so voluntarily. Affirmative action programs have been controversial, however, particularly when they result in reverse discrimination against members of a majority group, such as white males.

Constitutionality of Affirmative Action Programs

Because of their inherently discriminatory nature, affirmative action programs may violate the equal protection clause of the Fourteenth Amendment to the U.S. Constitution. The United States Supreme Court has held that any federal, state, or local government affirmative action program that uses racial or ethnic classifications as the basis for making decisions is subject to strict scrutiny by the courts.[45] Recall from Chapter 5 that strict scrutiny is the highest standard, which means that most programs do not survive a court's analysis under this test.

Today, an affirmative action program normally is constitutional only if it attempts to remedy past discrimination and does not make use of quotas or preferences. Furthermore, once such a program has succeeded in the goal of remedying past discrimination, it must be changed or dropped.

Affirmative Action in Schools

Most of the affirmative action cases that have reached the United States Supreme Court in the last twenty years have involved university admissions programs and schools, rather than business employers. Generally, the Court has found that a school admissions policy that *automatically* awards minority group applicants a specified number of points violates the equal protection clause.[46] A school can, however, "consider race or ethnicity more flexibly as a 'plus' factor in the context of individualized consideration of each and every applicant."[47] In other words, it is unconstitutional for schools to apply a mechanical formula that gives "diversity bonuses" based on race or ethnicity.

CASE IN POINT In 2007, the Supreme Court ruled on two cases involving the use of racial classifications to assign students to schools. Two school districts (in Seattle, Washington, and Jefferson County, Kentucky) had adopted student assignment plans that relied on race to determine which schools certain children would attend. The Seattle plan classified children as "white" or "nonwhite" and used the racial classifications as a "tiebreaker" to determine which school students would attend. The Jefferson

---

44. *McKennon v. Nashville Banner Publishing Co.,* 513 U.S. 352, 115 S.Ct. 879, 130 L.Ed.2d 852 (1995). See also *EEOC v. Dial Corp.,* 469 F.3d 735 (8th Cir. 2006).

45. See the landmark decision in *Adarand Constructors, Inc. v. Peña,* 515 U.S. 200, 115 S.Ct. 2097, 132 L.Ed.2d 158 (1995).
46. *Gratz v. Bollinger,* 539 U.S. 244, 123 S.Ct. 2411, 156 L.Ed.2d 257 (2003).
47. *Grutter v. Bollinger,* 539 U.S. 306, 123 S.Ct. 2325, 156 L.Ed.2d 304 (2003).

County plan classified students as "black" or "other" to assign them to schools. When parents claimed that the racial preferences violated the equal protection clause, the Court held that the school districts had failed to show that the use of racial classifications was necessary to achieve their stated goal of racial diversity. Hence, the Court found that both districts' affirmative action programs were unconstitutional.[48]

---

48. The Court consolidated the two cases and issued one opinion for both. See, *Parents Involved in Community Schools v. Seattle School District No. 1*, 551 U.S. 701, 127 S.Ct. 2738, 168 L.Ed.2d 508 (2007).

REVIEWING

Employment Discrimination

Amaani Lyle, an African American woman, was hired by Warner Brothers Television Productions to be a scriptwriters' assistant for the writers of *Friends,* a popular, adult-oriented television series. One of her essential job duties was to type detailed notes for the scriptwriters during brainstorming sessions in which they discussed jokes, dialogue, and story lines. The writers then combed through Lyle's notes after the meetings for script material. During these meetings, the three male scriptwriters told lewd and vulgar jokes and made sexually explicit comments and gestures. They often talked about their personal sexual experiences and fantasies, and some of these conversations were then used in episodes of *Friends.*

During the meetings, Lyle never complained that she found the writers' conduct offensive. After four months, Lyle was fired because she could not type fast enough to keep up with the writers' conversations during the meetings. She filed a suit against Warner Brothers, alleging sexual harassment and claiming that her termination was based on racial discrimination. Using the information presented in the chapter, answer the following questions.

1. Would Lyle's claim of racial discrimination be for intentional (disparate-treatment) or unintentional (disparate-impact) discrimination? Explain.
2. Can Lyle establish a *prima facie* case of racial discrimination? Why or why not?
3. When Lyle was hired, she was told that typing speed was extremely important to the position. At the time, she maintained that she could type eighty words per minute, so she was not given a typing test. It later turned out that Lyle could type only fifty words per minute. What impact might typing speed have on Lyle's lawsuit?
4. Lyle's sexual-harassment claim is based on the hostile working environment created by the writers' sexually offensive conduct at meetings that she was required to attend. The writers, however, argue that their behavior was essential to the "creative process" of writing for *Friends,* a show that routinely contained sexual innuendos and adult humor. Which defense discussed in the chapter might Warner Brothers assert using this argument?

DEBATE THIS: *Members of minority groups and women have made enough economic progress in the last several decades that they no longer need special legislation to protect them.*

TERMS AND CONCEPTS

affirmative action 508
bona fide occupational
   qualification (BFOQ) 507
business necessity 507

constructive discharge 496
disparate-impact
   discrimination 494
disparate-treatment
   discrimination 494

employment
   discrimination 493
prima facie case 494
protected class 493
seniority system 507

sexual harassment 497
tangible employment
   action 497

QUESTIONS AND CASE PROBLEMS

22-1. Title VII Violations Discuss fully whether either of the following actions would constitute a violation of Title VII of the 1964 Civil Rights Act, as amended:

(a) Tennington, Inc., is a consulting firm and has ten employees. These employees travel on consulting jobs in seven states. Tennington has an employment record of hiring only white males.

(b) Novo Films is making a movie about Africa and needs to employ approximately one hundred extras for this picture. To hire these extras, Novo advertises in all major newspapers in Southern California. The ad states that only African Americans need apply.

22-2. QUESTION WITH SAMPLE ANSWER: Religious Discrimination.

When Kayla Caldwell got a job as a cashier at a Costco store, she wore multiple pierced earrings and had four tattoos, but she had no facial piercings. Over the next two years, Caldwell engaged in various forms of body modification, including facial piercing and cutting. Then Costco revised its dress code to prohibit all facial jewelry, except earrings. Caldwell was told that she would have to remove her facial jewelry. She asked for a complete exemption from the code, asserting that she was a member of the Church of Body Modification and that eyebrow piercing was part of her religion. She was told to remove the jewelry, cover it, or go home. She went home and was later discharged for her absence. Based on these facts, will Caldwell be successful in a lawsuit against Costco for religious discrimination in violation of Title VII? Does an employer have an obligation to accommodate its employees' religious practices? If so, to what extent?

• **For a sample answer to Question 22-2, go to Appendix F at the end of this text.**

22-3. Discrimination Based on Gender For twenty years, Darlene Jespersen worked as a bartender at Harrah's Casino in Reno, Nevada. In 2000, Harrah's implemented a "Personal Best" program that included new grooming standards. Among other requirements, women were told to wear makeup "applied neatly in complimentary colors." Jespersen, who never wore makeup off the job, felt so uncomfortable wearing it on the job that it interfered with her ability to perform. Unwilling to wear makeup and not qualifying for another position at Harrah's with similar compensation, Jespersen quit her job. She filed a suit in a federal district court against Harrah's Operating Co., the casino's owner, alleging that the makeup policy discriminated against women in violation of Title VII of the Civil Rights Act of 1964. Harrah's argued that any burdens under the new program fell equally on both genders, citing the "Personal Best" short-hair standard that applied only to men. Jespersen responded by describing her personal reaction to the makeup policy and emphasizing her exemplary record during her tenure at Harrah's. In whose favor should the court rule? Why? [*Jespersen v. Harrah's Operating Co.*, 444 F.3d 1104 (9th Cir. 2006)]

22-4. Discrimination Based on Disability Cerebral palsy limits Steven Bradley's use of his legs. He uses forearm crutches for short-distance walks and a wheelchair for longer distances. Standing for more than ten or fifteen minutes is difficult. With support, however, Bradley can climb stairs and get on and off a stool. His condition also restricts the use of his fourth finger to, for example, type, but it does not limit his ability to write—he completed two years of college. His grip strength is normal, and he can lift heavy objects. In 2001, Bradley applied for a "greeter" or "cashier" position at a Wal-Mart Stores, Inc., Supercenter in Richmond, Missouri. The job description stated, "No experience or qualification is required." Bradley indicated that he was available for full- or part-time work from 4:00 P.M. to 10:00 P.M. any evening. His employment history showed that he currently worked as a proofreader and that he had previously worked as an administrator. His application was rejected, according to Janet Daugherty, the personnel manager, based on his "work history" and the "direct threat" that he posed to the safety of himself and others. Bradley claimed, however, that the store refused to hire him due to his disability. What steps must Bradley follow to pursue his claim? What does he need to show to prevail? Is he likely to meet these requirements? Discuss. [*EEOC v. Wal-Mart Stores, Inc.*, 477 F.3d 561 (8th Cir. 2007)]

22-5. Defenses to Employment Discrimination The Milwaukee County Juvenile Detention Center established a new policy that required each unit of the facility to be staffed at all times by at least one officer of the same gender as the detainees housed at a unit. The purpose of the policy, administrators said, was to reduce the likelihood of sexual abuse of juveniles by officers of the other gender. Because there were many more male units in the center than female units, the policy had the effect of reducing the number of shifts available for women officers and increasing the number of shifts for men. Two female officers sued for gender discrimination. The district court held for the county, finding that the policy of assignment was based on a bona fide occupational qualification (BFOQ) and so was not illegal gender discrimination. The officers appealed. What would be evidence that the county had a valid BFOQ? [*Henry v. Milwaukee County*, 539 F.3d 573 (7th Cir. 2008)]

22-6. CASE PROBLEM WITH SAMPLE ANSWER: Sexual Harassment.

The Metropolitan Government of Nashville and Davidson County, Tennessee (Metro), began looking into rumors of sexual harassment by the Metro School District's employee relations director, Gene Hughes. Veronica Frazier, a Metro human resources officer,

asked Vicky Crawford, a Metro employee, whether she had witnessed "inappropriate behavior" by Hughes. Crawford described several instances of sexually harassing behavior. Two other employees also reported being sexually harassed by Hughes. Metro took no action against Hughes, but soon after completing the investigation, Metro accused Crawford of embezzlement and fired her. The two other employees were also fired. Crawford filed a suit in a federal district court against Metro, claiming retaliation under Title VII. What arguments can be made that Crawford's situation does or does not qualify as a retaliation claim under Title VII? Discuss. [Crawford v. Metropolitan Government of Nashville and Davidson County, Tennessee, __ U.S. __, 129 S.Ct. 846, 172 L.Ed.2d 650 (2009)]

- To view a sample answer for Problem 22–6, go to this book's Web site at www.cengage.com/blaw/cross, select "Chapter 22," and click on "Case Problem with Sample Answer."

22–7. Discrimination Based on Gender Brenda Lewis had been employed for two years at Heartland Inns of America, LLC, and gradually worked her way up the management ladder. Lewis, who described herself as a tomboy, was commended for her good work. When she moved to a different Heartland hotel, the director of operations, Barbara Cullinan, told one of the owners that Lewis was not a "good fit" for the front desk because she was not feminine enough. Cullinan told various people that the hotel wanted "pretty" girls at the front desk. Cullinan then informed Lewis that her hiring had not been done properly and that she would need to undergo another interview. Soon after the interview, Cullinan fired Lewis. The reason given in a letter was that Lewis was hostile during the interview. Lewis sued Heartland for gender discrimination based on unlawful gender stereotyping. The district court dismissed the suit. Lewis appealed. Does her claim fall under Title VII's prohibition against discrimination based on gender? Why or why not? [Lewis v. Heartland Inns of America, LLC, 591 F.3d 1033 (8th Cir. 2010)]

22–8. A QUESTION OF ETHICS: Discrimination Based on Disability.

 Titan Distribution, Inc., employed Quintak, Inc., to run its tire mounting and distribution operation in Des Moines, Iowa. Robert Chalfant worked for Quintak as a second shift supervisor at Titan. He suffered a heart attack in 1992 and underwent heart bypass surgery in 1997. He also had arthritis. In July 2002, Titan decided to fire Quintak. Chalfant applied to work at Titan. On his application, he described himself as disabled. After a physical exam, Titan's physician concluded that Chalfant could work in his current capacity, and he was notified that he would be hired. Despite the notice, Nadis Barucic, a Titan employee, wrote "not pass px" at the top of Chalfant's application, and he was not hired. He took a job with AMPCO Systems, a parking ramp management company. This work involved walking up to five miles a day and lifting more weight than he had at Titan. In September, Titan eliminated its second shift. Chalfant filed a suit in a federal district court

against Titan, in part, under the Americans with Disabilities Act (ADA). Titan argued that it had not hired Chalfant because he did not pass the physical, but no one—including Barucic—could explain why she had written "not pass px" on his application. Later, Titan claimed that Chalfant was not hired because the entire second shift was going to be eliminated. [Chalfant v. Titan Distribution, Inc., 475 F.3d 982 (8th Cir. 2007)]

(a) What must Chalfant establish to make his case under the ADA? Can he meet these requirements? Explain.

(b) In employment-discrimination cases, punitive damages can be appropriate when an employer acts with malice or reckless indifference toward an employee's protected rights. Would an award of punitive damages to Chalfant be appropriate in this case? Discuss.

22–9. VIDEO QUESTION: Employment Discrimination.

 Go to this text's Web site at www.cengage.com/blaw/cross and select "Chapter 22." Click on "Video Questions" and view the video titled *Mary Tyler Moore*. Then answer the following questions.

(a) In the video, Mr. Grant (Ed Asner) asks Mary (Mary Tyler Moore) some personal questions during a job interview, including why she is not married and what religion she practices. He also tells her that he "figured he'd hire a man." Can Mary make out a *prima facie* case of gender or religious discrimination based on these questions? Why or why not?

(b) Can Mary prove a *prima facie* case of age discrimination because Mr. Grant asked her age during the interview and then implied that she was "hedging" about her age? What would she need to prove under the Age Discrimination in Employment Act?

(c) How does the fact that Mr. Grant hired Mary as an associate producer affect her ability to establish a case of employment discrimination?

(d) Mr. Grant says that he will hire Mary to see if it works out but fire her if he does not like her or if she does not like him at the end of this trial period. Can he do that? Explain. If he fired Mary a few weeks later, would this affect Mary's ability to sue for employment discrimination? Why or why not?

22–10. SPECIAL CASE ANALYSIS: Sexual Harassment.
Go to Extended Case 22.1, *Burlington Northern and Santa Fe Railway Co. v. White*, 548 U.S. 53, 126 S.Ct. 2405, 165 L.Ed.2d 345 (2006), on pages 498 and 499. Read the excerpt and answer the following questions.

(a) **Issue:** What was the plaintiff's complaint, the defendant's response, and the chief legal dispute between them?

(b) **Rule of Law:** Which provisions of Title VII did the Court consider, and which rule of statutory interpretation governed the Court's consideration?

(c) **Applying the Rule of Law:** How did the Court interpret these provisions, and how did that interpretation apply to the circumstances in this case?

(d) **Conclusion:** Based on its application of the principles in this case, what did the Court conclude?

LEGAL RESEARCH EXERCISES ON THE WEB

Go to this text's Web site at **www.cengage.com/blaw/cross**, select "Chapter 22," and click on "Practical Internet Exercises." There you will find the following Internet research exercises that you can perform to learn more about the topics covered in this chapter.

Practical Internet Exercise 22–1: **Legal Perspective**
Americans with Disabilities

Practical Internet Exercise 22–2: **Management Perspective**
Equal Employment Opportunity

Practical Internet Exercise 22–3: **Social Perspective**
Religious and National Origin Discrimination

CHAPTER 23

Immigration and Labor Law

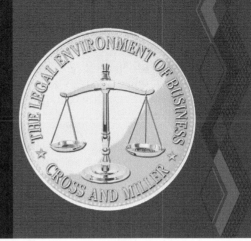

During the nineteenth century, two separate forces began to affect the employment environment in the United States—a rise in immigration and the Industrial Revolution. Both led to significant changes in the legal environment of the workplace, which we will examine in this chapter. Legislation was enacted to prohibit employers from hiring illegal immigrants. Immigration law has evolved over the years into a myriad of complex rules that employers need to follow when hiring foreign-born workers.

During the Industrial Revolution, fewer Americans were self-employed than ever before, and employers generally set the terms of employment. Moreover, with increasing industrialization, the size of workplaces and the number of on-the-job hazards increased. Workers came to believe that to counter the power and freedom of their employers and to protect themselves, they needed to organize into unions. But at that time, employers discouraged—sometimes forcibly—collective activities such as unions. Beginning in 1932, Congress enacted a number of statutes that generally increased employees' rights. At the heart of these rights is the right to join unions and engage in *collective bargaining* with management to negotiate working conditions, salaries, and benefits for a group of workers.

This chapter begins with a discussion of immigration law and its importance to today's business owners and employers. We then describe labor laws and examine the process of unionizing a company. We also discuss collective bargaining, strikes, lockouts, and the labor practices that are considered unfair under federal law. This chapter closes with a brief discussion of the rights of nonunion employees.

SECTION 1
IMMIGRATION LAW

The United States did not have any laws restricting immigration until the late nineteenth century when there was a huge surge in the number of persons who emigrated from China and Europe. In recent years, immigration law has become an area of increasing concern for businesses as the number of immigrants—especially illegal immigrants from Mexico—to the United States has grown. An estimated 11 to 12 million illegal immigrants now live in the United States. The great majority of these people came to find jobs, but U.S. employers face serious penalties if they hire illegal immigrants. Thus, an understanding of U.S. immigration laws has become increasingly important for businesses. Today, the most important laws affecting the employment relationship are the Immigration Reform and Control Act (IRCA) of 1986[1] and the Immigration Act of 1990.[2]

The Immigration Reform and Control Act

When the IRCA was enacted in 1986, it provided amnesty to certain groups of illegal aliens living in the United States at the time. It also established a system that sanctions employers that hire illegal immigrants who lack work authorization. The IRCA makes it illegal to hire, recruit, or refer for a fee someone not authorized to work in this country. Through Immigration and Customs Enforcement

---

1. 29 U.S.C. Section 1802.
2. This act amended various provisions of the Immigration and Nationality Act of 1952, 8 U.S.C. Sections 1101 *et seq.*

officers, the federal government conducts random compliance audits and engages in enforcement actions against employers who hire illegal immigrants.

I-9 EMPLOYMENT VERIFICATION To comply with IRCA requirements, an employer must perform **I-9 verifications** for new hires, including those hired as "contractors" or "day workers" if they work under the employer's direct supervision. The employer must complete Form I-9, Employment Eligibility Verification, which is available from U.S. Citizenship and Immigration Services,[3] for each worker within three days of his or her commencement of employment. The three-day period allows the employer to check the form's accuracy and to review and verify documents establishing the prospective worker's identity and eligibility for employment in the United States.

The employer must attest, under penalty of perjury, that an employee produced documents establishing his or her identity and legal employability. Acceptable documents include a U.S. passport establishing the person's citizenship or a document authorizing a foreign citizen to work in the United States, such as a permanent resident card or an *Alien Registration Receipt* (discussed on page 516).

Note that most legal actions alleging violations of I-9 rules are brought against employees. An employee must state on the I-9 form that she or he is a U.S. citizen or otherwise authorized to work in the United States. If the employee enters false information on the form or presents false documentation, the employer can fire the worker, who then may be subject to deportation.

The IRCA prohibits "knowing" violations, including situations in which an employer "should have known" that the worker was unauthorized. Good faith is a defense under the statute, and employers are legally entitled to rely on a document authorizing a person to work that reasonably appears on its face to be genuine, even if it is later established to be counterfeit.

ENFORCEMENT The IRCA rules are enforced by U.S. Immigration and Customs Enforcement (ICE), a federal agency that was established in 2003 as the largest investigative arm of the U.S. Department of Homeland Security. ICE has a general inspection program that conducts random compliance audits.

Other audits may occur if the agency receives a written complaint alleging that an employer has committed violations. Government inspections include a review of an employer's file of I-9 forms. The government does not need a subpoena or a warrant to conduct such an inspection.

The federal government increased its enforcement actions significantly during the George W. Bush administration. The largest workplace raid in U.S. history took place at an Iowa meatpacking plant in 2008 and resulted in the detention of nearly four hundred illegal workers. The Obama administration, in contrast, prefers that ICE conduct audits of employer records, rather than workplace raids, to investigate suspected immigration violations. This enforcement strategy focuses more on sanctioning employers for violations and forcing them to fire illegal immigrants than it does on arresting and deporting the illegal workers. Nevertheless, workplace raids still occur. For example, twenty-nine people were taken into custody as the result of an ICE raid at a Baltimore restaurant in 2010.

Administrative Actions. If an investigation reveals a possible violation, ICE will bring an administrative action and issue a Notice of Intent to Fine, which sets out the charges against the employer. The employer has a right to a hearing on the enforcement action if it files a request within thirty days. This hearing is conducted before an administrative law judge (ALJ—see Chapter 6), and the employer has a right to counsel and to discovery (see Chapter 2). A typical defense in such actions is good faith or substantial compliance with the documentation provisions.

Criminal Actions. ICE can seek criminal punishment for acts such as harboring an alien or illegally inducing illegal immigration. For example, in 2008 eight employees of George's Processing, Inc., were indicted by a Missouri federal jury after an ICE raid resulted in the arrest of many illegal aliens at the plant. Evidence suggested that a human resources manager helped applicants complete their I-9 forms with knowledge that they had fraudulently obtained identity documents. The potential penalty for this crime is ten years in prison without parole.

A company may present a defense demonstrating that the employee alleged to be in violation was truly an independent contractor rather than an employee and therefore not subject to the I-9 requirements. Even for independent contractors, though, a party's actual knowledge that a worker was unauthorized is illegal. Ultimately, the ALJ reviewing the case makes

---

3. U.S. Citizenship and Immigration Services is a federal agency that is part of the U.S. Department of Homeland Security.

a ruling and assesses penalties if he or she finds a violation. This hearing may be appealed administratively or to a federal court.

Individuals who believe they have suffered as a result of illegal hiring have no direct cause of action to sue an employer under current law. They may sue under the Racketeer Influenced and Corrupt Organizations Act (RICO), though, using the violations as a predicate illegal act.[4] The following case illustrates such an action.

---

4. RICO was discussed in Chapter 7.

CASE 23.1
Trollinger v. Tyson Foods, Inc.

United States District Court, Eastern District of Tennessee, ___ F.Supp.2d ___ (2007).

BACKGROUND AND FACTS • Tyson Foods, Inc., is one of the nation's largest poultry processors, with more than 100,000 employees. One of its plants is located in Shelbyville, Tennessee. In December 2001, Tyson was indicted for conspiring to smuggle illegal aliens into the country and employ them. Soon after the indictment was filed, four former workers at the Shelbyville facility filed this action against Tyson under the Racketeer Influenced and Corrupt Organizations Act (RICO), alleging that Tyson engaged in an illegal scheme to depress wages by hiring illegal immigrants. Tyson moved to dismiss the complaint.

IN THE LANGUAGE OF THE COURT
COLLIER, J. [Judge]
* * * *

* * * * The Complaint alleges Defendants engaged in a long-term pattern and practice of violating [the Immigration Reform and Control Act]. * * * . The Complaint states Tyson signs Employment Eligibility Verification Forms (I-9 forms) in mass quantities before any documents are inspected, more than three days after new hires have been employed, and based on a review of copies of documents rather than reviewing the original documents. The Complaint further alleges Tyson prohibits its employees from taking into account obvious facts which indicate that documents do not relate to the people tendering them; rehires persons whom it previously hired under different names, usually after a short absence; hires workers who appear decades younger than the pictures on their stolen identity documents; uses temporary employment placement services to hire illegal immigrants and then "loan" them to Tyson for a fee; and gives employees leave to "get good documents" after Tyson learns the initial documents submitted by the illegal alien actually belong to someone else.
* * * *

In the context of the present illegal immigration problem in the United States, it is widely, if not universally, known that illegal immigration from Mexico is done in substantial part through smuggling. It is also of note that Tyson's processing plants are all located in areas where the predominant illegal alien population is from Mexico. *This knowledge along with the above allegations satisfies the requirement that the Complaint alleges Defendants had a subjective belief that large numbers of its illegal alien employees had been brought into the United States illegally.* [Emphasis added.]

DECISION AND REMEDY • *The court denied Tyson's motion to dismiss the complaint.*

WHAT IF THE FACTS WERE DIFFERENT? • *Assume that Tyson's human resources managers were acting on their own, in clear violation of that company's written employment policy. Would the judge have ruled differently? Why or why not?*

THE GLOBAL DIMENSION • *Many businesses in U.S. communities near the border with Mexico rely on the purchasing power of immigrants, both legal and illegal. What incentives, if any, do these businesses have to help enforce U.S. immigration laws?*

PENALTIES An employer who violates the law by hiring an unauthorized alien is subject to substantial penalties. The employer can be fined up to $2,200 for each unauthorized employee for a first offense, $5,000 per employee for a second offense, and up to $11,000 for subsequent offenses. Employers who have engaged in a "pattern or practice of violations" are subject to criminal penalties, which include additional fines and imprisonment for up to ten years. A company may also be barred from future government contracts for violations.

In determining the penalty, ICE considers the seriousness of the violation (such as intentional falsification of documents) and the employer's past compliance. ICE regulations also identify factors that will mitigate or aggravate the penalty under certain circumstances, such as whether the employer cooperated in the investigation or is a small business.

ANTI-DISCRIMINATION PROVISIONS The passage of the Immigration Reform and Control Act (IRCA) led to concerns about discrimination based on national origin. Some employers reportedly refused to hire Latinos out of concern for violating the statute. Amendments to the act established prohibitions on unfair immigration-related employment practices. The IRCA now provides that it is an unfair immigration-related practice for an employer to discriminate against any individual (other than an unauthorized alien) with respect to hiring or discharging the individual from employment.[5] Companies must exercise reasonable care to evaluate the required I-9 documents in a fair and consistent manner. They may not require greater proof from some prospective employees or reject apparently sufficient documentation of work authorization or citizenship.

A prospective employee who believes that he or she has been subject to discrimination may file a charge with the Office of Special Counsel (OSC) for Immigration Related Unfair Employment Practices. The OSC investigates the charge and may file a complaint with an ALJ if it finds the complaint has merit. If the OSC fails to file such a complaint within 120 days, the private party may bring a private action for discrimination. The standards and procedures for evaluating the action parallel those of Title VII of the Civil Rights Act, which was discussed in Chapter 22.

The Immigration Act

U.S. immigration laws have long included provisions that permit businesses to hire foreign workers with special qualifications when there are not enough qualified workers available in the United States. The Immigration Act of 1990 placed caps on the number of visas (entry permits) that can be issued to immigrants each year.

Most temporary visas are set aside for workers who can be characterized as "persons of extraordinary ability," professionals holding advanced degrees, or other skilled workers and professionals. To hire such an individual, an employer must submit a petition to U.S. Citizenship and Immigration Services, which determines whether the job candidate meets the legal standards. Each visa is for a specific job, and there are legal limits on the employee's ability to switch jobs once he or she is in the United States.

I-551 ALIEN REGISTRATION RECEIPTS A company seeking to hire a noncitizen worker may do so if the worker is self-authorized. This means that the worker either is a lawful permanent resident or has a valid temporary Employment Authorization Document. A lawful permanent resident can prove his or her status to an employer by presenting an **I-551 Alien Registration Receipt,** known as a green card, or a properly stamped foreign passport.

Many immigrant workers are not already self-authorized, and an employer that wishes to hire them may obtain labor certification, or green cards, for them. To gain authorization for hiring a foreign worker, the employer must show that no U.S. worker is qualified, willing, and able to take the job.[6] Approximately fifty thousand new green cards are issued each year. A green card can be obtained only for a person who is being hired for a permanent, full-time position. (A separate authorization system provides for the temporary entry and hiring of non-immigrant visa workers.)

THE H-1B VISA PROGRAM The most common and controversial visa program today is the H-1B visa system. To obtain an H1-B visa, the potential employee must be qualified in a "specialty occupation," which is defined as involving highly specialized knowledge and the attainment of a bachelor's or higher degree or its equivalent. The recipients of these visas

---

5. 8 U.S.C. Section 1324b.

6. The most relevant regulations can be found at 20 C.F.R. 655 (for temporary employment) and 20 C.F.R. (for permanent employment).

include many high-tech workers, such as computer programmers and electronics specialists. Individuals with H-1B visas can stay in the United States for three to six years and work only for the sponsoring employer.

LABOR CERTIFICATION Before an employer can submit an H-1B application, it must file a Labor Certification application on a form known as ETA 9035. The employer must agree to provide a wage level at least equal to the wages offered to other individuals with similar experience and qualifications, and must attest that the hiring will not adversely affect other workers similarly employed. The employer is required to inform U.S. workers of the intent to hire a foreign worker by posting the form. The U.S. Department of Labor reviews the applications and may reject them for omissions or inaccuracies.

H-2, O, L, AND E VISAS Other specialty temporary visas are available for other categories of employees. H-2 visas provide for workers performing agricultural labor of a seasonal nature. O visas provide entry for persons who have "extraordinary ability in the sciences, arts, education, business or athletics which has been demonstrated by sustained national or international acclaim." L visas allow a company's foreign managers or executives to work inside the United States. E visas permit the entry of certain foreign investors or entrepreneurs.

SECTION 2
FEDERAL LABOR LAWS

Federal labor laws governing union-employer relations have developed considerably since the first law was enacted in 1932. Initially, the laws were concerned with protecting the rights and interests of workers. Subsequent legislation placed some restraints on unions and granted rights to employers. We look here at four major federal statutes regulating union-employer relations.

Norris-LaGuardia Act

Congress protected peaceful strikes, picketing, and boycotts in 1932 in the Norris-LaGuardia Act.[7] The statute restricted the power of federal courts to issue injunctions against unions engaged in peaceful strikes. In effect, this act declared a national policy permitting employees to organize.

National Labor Relations Act

One of the foremost statutes regulating labor is the National Labor Relations Act (NLRA) of 1935.[8] This act established the rights of employees to engage in collective bargaining and to strike. The act also specifically defined a number of employer practices as unfair to labor:

1. Interference with the efforts of employees to form, join, or assist labor organizations or to engage in concerted activities for their mutual aid or protection.
2. An employer's domination of a labor organization or contribution of financial or other support to it.
3. Discrimination in the hiring of or the awarding of tenure to employees for reason of union affiliation.
4. Discrimination against employees for filing charges under the act or giving testimony under the act.
5. Refusal to bargain collectively with the duly designated representative of the employees.

THE NATIONAL LABOR RELATIONS BOARD To ensure that employees' rights would be protected, the NLRA established the National Labor Relations Board (NLRB). The NLRB has the authority to investigate employees' charges of unfair labor practices and to file complaints against employers in response to these charges. When violations are found, the NLRB may also issue a **cease-and-desist order**—an order compelling the employer to stop engaging in unfair practices. Cease-and-desist orders can be enforced by a federal appellate court, if necessary. Disputes over alleged unfair labor practices are first decided by the NLRB and may then be appealed to a federal court.

Under the NLRA, employers and unions have a duty to bargain in good faith. Bargaining over certain subjects is mandatory, and a party's refusal to bargain over these subjects is an unfair labor practice that can be reported to the NLRB. In one case, for example, an employer was required to bargain with the union over the use of hidden video surveillance cameras.[9]

WORKERS PROTECTED BY THE NLRA To be protected under the NLRA, an individual must be an employee

---

7. 29 U.S.C. Sections 101–110, 113–115.

8. 20 U.S.C. Sections 151–169.
9. *National Steel Corp. v. NLRB*, 324 F.3d 928 (7th Cir. 2003).

or a job applicant (otherwise, the NLRA's ban on discrimination in regard to hiring would mean little). Additionally, the United States Supreme Court has held that individuals who are hired by a union to organize a company (union organizers) are to be considered employees of the company for NLRA purposes.[10]

Labor-Management Relations Act

The Labor-Management Relations Act (LMRA) of 1947[11] was passed to proscribe certain unfair union practices, such as the *closed shop*. A **closed shop** is a firm that requires union membership as a condition of employment. Although the act made the closed shop illegal, it preserved the legality of the union shop. A **union shop** is a firm that does not require union membership as a prerequisite for employment but can, and usually does, require that workers join the union after a specified amount of time on the job.

The LMRA also prohibited unions from refusing to bargain with employers, engaging in certain types of picketing, and *featherbedding* (causing employers to hire more employees than necessary). In addition, the act allowed individual states to pass their own **right-to-work laws**—laws making it illegal for union membership to be required for *continued* employment in any establishment. Thus, union shops are technically illegal in the twenty-two states that have right-to-work laws.

Labor-Management Reporting and Disclosure Act

The Labor-Management Reporting and Disclosure Act (LMRDA) of 1959[12] established an employee bill of rights and reporting requirements for union activities. The act strictly regulates unions' internal business procedures, including elections. For example, the LMRDA requires unions to hold regularly scheduled elections of officers using secret ballots. Former convicts are prohibited from holding union office. Moreover, union officials are accountable for union property and funds. Members have the right to attend and to participate in union meetings, to nominate officers, and to vote in most union proceedings.

The act also outlawed *hot-cargo agreements*, in which employers voluntarily agree with unions not to handle, use, or deal in goods of other employers produced by nonunion employees. The act made all such boycotts illegal.

Coverage and Procedures

Coverage of federal labor laws is broad and extends to all employers whose business activity either involves or affects interstate commerce. Some workers are specifically excluded from these laws. Railroads and airlines are not covered by the NLRA but are covered by a separate act, the Railway Labor Act, which closely parallels the NLRA. Other types of workers, such as agricultural workers and domestic servants, are excluded from the NLRA and have no coverage under separate legislation.

When a union or employee believes that an employer has violated federal labor law (or vice versa), a charge is filed with a regional office of the NLRB. The form for an employee to use to file an unfair labor practice charge against an employer is shown in Exhibit 23–1 on the facing page. The charge is investigated, and if it is found worthy, the regional director files a complaint. An ALJ initially hears the complaint and rules on it. The board reviews the ALJ's findings and decision. If the NLRB finds a violation, it may issue remedial orders (such as requiring the rehiring of discharged workers). The NLRB decision may be appealed to a U.S. court of appeals.

▬▬▬▬◤ **SECTION 3** ◢▬▬▬▬
THE DECISION TO FORM OR SELECT A UNION

The key starting point for labor relations law is the decision by a company's employees to form a union, which is usually referred to as their *bargaining representative*. In workplaces that have no union, workers bargain individually with the employer. If the workers decide that they want the added power of collective union representation, they must follow certain steps to have the union certified. The employer will often resist these efforts to unionize.

Preliminary Organizing

Suppose that a national union, such as the Communication Workers of America (CWA), wants to organize workers who produce semiconductor chips. The union would visit a manufacturing plant

---

10. *NLRB v. Town & Country Electric, Inc.*, 516 U.S. 85, 116 S.Ct. 450, 133 L.Ed.2d 371 (1995).

11. 29 U.S.C. Sections 141 *et seq.*

12. 29 U.S.C. Sections 401 *et seq.*

EXHIBIT 23-1 • Unfair Labor Practice Complaint Form

FORM EXEMPT UNDER 44 U.S.C 3512

FORM NLRB-501
(9-07)

UNITED STATES OF AMERICA
NATIONAL LABOR RELATIONS BOARD
CHARGE AGAINST EMPLOYER

DO NOT WRITE IN THIS SPACE

Case	Date Filed
	/ /

INSTRUCTIONS:
File an original together with four copies and a copy for each additional charged party named in item 1 with NLRB Regional Director for the region in which the alleged unfair labor practice occurred or is occurring.

1. EMPLOYER AGAINST WHOM CHARGE IS BROUGHT

a. Name of Employer

b. Number of workers employed

c. Address *(Street, city, state, and ZIP code)*

d. Employer Representative

e. Telephone No.
( ) -

Fax No.
( ) -

f. Type of Establishment *(factory, mine, wholesaler, etc.)*

g. Identify principal product or service

h. The above-named employer has engaged in and is engaging in unfair labor practices within the meaning of section 8(a), subsections (1) and *(list subsections)* _____ of the National Labor Relations Act, and these unfair labor practices are practices affecting commerce within the meaning of the Act, or these unfair labor practices are unfair practices affecting commerce within the meaning of the Act and the Postal Reorganization Act.

2. Basis of the Charge *(set forth a clear and concise statement of the facts constituting the alleged unfair labor practices)*

3. Full name of party filing charge *(if labor organization, give full name, including local name and number)*

4a. Address *(Street and number, city, state, and ZIP code)*

4b. Telephone No.
( ) -

Fax No.
( ) -

5. Full name of national or international labor organization of which it is an affiliate or constituent unit *(to be filled in when charge is filed by a labor organization)*

6. DECLARATION
I declare that I have read the above charge and that the statements are true to the best of my knowledge and belief.

By _____
(signature of representative or person making charge)

_____
(Print/type name and title or office, if any)

Address _____

(fax) ( ) -

( ) -
(Telephone No.)

/ /
(date)

WILLFUL FALSE STATEMENTS ON THIS CHARGE CAN BE PUNISHED BY FINE AND IMPRISONMENT (U.S. CODE, TITLE 18, SECTION 1001)

PRIVACY ACT STATEMENT

Solicitation of the information on this form is authorized by the National Labor Relations Act (NLRA), 29 U.S.C. § 151 *et seq.* The principal use of the information is to assist the National Labor Relations Board (NLRB) in processing unfair labor practice and related proceedings or litigation. The routine uses for the information are fully set forth in the Federal Register, 71 Fed. Reg. 74942-43 (Dec. 13, 2006). The NLRB will further explain these uses upon request. Disclosure of this information to the NLRB is voluntary; however, failure to supply the information will cause the NLRB to decline to invoke its processes.

of a company—SemiCo, in this example. If some SemiCo workers are interested in joining the union, they must begin organizing. An essential part of the process is to decide exactly which workers will be covered in the planned union. Will all manufacturing workers be covered or just those engaged in a single stage in the manufacturing process?

The first step in forming a union is to get the relevant workers to sign **authorization cards.** These cards usually state that the worker desires to have a certain union, such as the CWA, represent the workforce. If a majority of the workers sign authorization cards, the organizers can present the cards to the employer and ask for formal recognition of the union. The employer is not required to recognize the union at this point, but it may do so voluntarily on a showing of majority support. (Under pro-union legislation that has been proposed in the U.S. Congress, the employer would be required to recognize the union as soon as a majority of the workers had signed authorization cards—without holding an election, as described next.[13])

If the employer refuses to voluntarily recognize the union after a majority of the workers sign authorization cards—or if fewer than 50 percent of the workers sign authorization cards—the union organizers can petition the NLRB for an election. For an election to be held, the NLRB requires that unionizers demonstrate that at least 30 percent of the workers to be represented support a union or an election on unionization.

Appropriate Bargaining Unit

The NLRB considers the employees' petition as a basis for calling an election. In addition to a sufficient showing of interest in unionization, the proposed union must represent an **appropriate bargaining unit.**

Not every group of workers can form together into a single union. One key requirement of an appropriate bargaining unit is a *mutuality of interest* among all the workers to be represented. Groups of workers with significantly conflicting interests may not be represented in a single union.

JOB SIMILARITY One factor in determining the mutuality of interest is the *similarity of the jobs* of

---

13. If the proposed Employee Free Choice Act (or Card Check Bill) becomes law, some of the information on the following pages may change.

all the workers to be unionized. The NLRB considers factors such as similar levels of skill and qualifications, similar levels of wages and benefits, and similar working conditions. If represented workers have vastly different working conditions, they are unlikely to have the mutuality of interest necessary to bargain as a single unit with their employer.

One issue of job similarity has involved companies that employ both general industrial workers and craft workers (those with specialized skills, such as electricians). On many occasions, the NLRB has found that industrial and craft workers should be represented by different unions, although this is not an absolute rule.

WORK-SITE PROXIMITY A second factor in determining the appropriate bargaining unit is *geographical.* If workers at only a single manufacturing plant are to be unionized, the geographical factor is not a problem. Even if the workers desire to join a national union, such as the CWA, they can join together in a single "local" division of that union. Geographical disparity may become a problem if a union is attempting to join workers at many different manufacturing sites together into a single union.

NONMANAGEMENT EMPLOYEES A third factor to be considered is the rule against unionization of *management* employees. Labor laws differentiate between labor and management and preclude members of management from being part of a union. There is no clear-cut definition of *management*, but supervisors are considered management and may not be included in worker unions. A supervisor is an individual who has the discretionary authority, as a representative of the employer, to make such decisions as hiring, suspending, promoting, firing, and disciplining other workers. Professional employees, including legal and medical personnel, may be considered labor rather than management.

SECTION 4
UNION ELECTION

Labor law provides for an election to determine whether employees choose to be represented by a union and, if so, which union. The NLRB supervises this election and ensures secret voting and voter eligibility. The election is usually held about a month after the NLRB orders the vote (although this interval may be much longer if management disputes the composition of an appropriate bargaining unit). If the election is a fair one, and if the proposed union receives majority support (more than 50 percent of the votes), the board certifies the union as the bargaining representative. Otherwise, the board will not certify the union.

Sometimes, a plant with an existing union may attempt to *decertify* (de-unionize) the union. Although this action may be encouraged by management, it must be conducted by the employees. This action also requires a petition to the NLRB, with a showing of 30 percent employee support and no certification within the past year. The NLRB may grant this petition and call for a decertification election.

Union Election Campaigns

Union organizers may campaign among workers to solicit votes for unionization. Many disputes arise between labor and management during election campaigns. Generally, the employer retains great control over unionizing activities that take place on company property and company time. For example, management may prohibit all solicitation and distribution of pamphlets on company property as long as it has a legitimate business reason for doing so (such as to ensure safety or to prevent interference with business). The employer may also reasonably limit the times and places where solicitation occurs—such as limiting it to the lunchroom during breaks. The employer may also deny all outsiders access to the workplace. All of these actions are lawful.

The key restriction on management is the *nondiscrimination* rule. An employer may prohibit all solicitation during work time or in certain places but may not *selectively* prohibit union solicitation during work time. If the employer permits political candidates to campaign on the employer's premises, for example, it also must permit union solicitation.

Suppose that a union is seeking to organize clerks at a department store owned by Amanti Enterprises. Amanti can prohibit all union solicitation in areas of the store open to the public because the unionizing activities could interfere with the store's business. It can also restrict union-related activities to coffee breaks and lunch hours. Amanti cannot, however, allow solicitation for charitable causes during work hours or in the public part of the store if it prohibits union-related solicitation.

Management Election Campaigns

An employer may also campaign against the union (or for decertification of an existing union) among its workers. The NLRB carefully monitors campaign tactics, however. Management can call all workers together during work time and make a speech against unionization. It need not give union supporters an equal opportunity for rebuttal. The NLRB does restrict what management may say in such a speech, however.

NO THREATS In campaigning against the union, the employer may not make threats of reprisals if employees vote to unionize. Employers must be very careful on this issue. For example, suppose an employer says, "Our competitor's plant in town became unionized, and half the workers lost their jobs." The NLRB might consider this to be a veiled threat and therefore unfair.

"LABORATORY CONDITIONS" Obviously, management and union election campaigns are not like national political campaigns, when a political party can make almost any claim. The NLRB tries to maintain "laboratory conditions" for a fair election that is unaffected by pressure. In establishing such conditions, the board considers the totality of circumstances in the campaign. The NLRB is especially concerned about promises (or threats) made by the employer at the last minute, immediately before the election. If the employer issued threats or engaged in other unfair labor practices, the NLRB may certify the union, even though it lost the election. Alternatively, the NLRB may ask a court to order a new election.

During a campaign, employers cannot undertake certain types of surveillance of workers or even create the impression of observing workers to identify union sympathizers. Not all management tactics will be deemed illegal, however.

In the following case, the question was whether managers' brief interruptions of unionizing activities constituted illegal surveillance in violation of the National Labor Relations Act.

✳ EXTENDED CASE 23.2 ✳
**Local Joint Executive Board of Las Vegas v.
National Labor Relations Board**

United States Court of Appeals, Ninth Circuit, 515 F.3d 942 (2008).

IN THE LANGUAGE OF THE COURT

CALLAHAN, Circuit Judge: Local Joint Executive Board of Las Vegas, the Culinary Workers Unions Local 226, and the Bartenders Unions Local 165, AFL-CIO [American Federation of Labor and Congress of Industrial Organizations] ("the Unions"), petition this court for review of a decision by the National Labor Relations Board ("the Board") reversing the Administrative Law Judge's ("ALJ") conclusion that agents of Aladdin Gaming, LLC ("the Company")[,] engaged in illegal surveillance in violation of Section 8(a)(1) of the National Labor Relations Act ("NLRA" or "the Act"). We deny the Unions' petition for review.

The Company operates a hotel and casino in Las Vegas, Nevada. On May 30, 2003, the Unions began an open campaign to organize the housekeeping, food, and beverage departments. * * * The issue in this appeal is whether two incidents where human resources managers [Ms. Sapien and Ms. Briand] interrupted employees who were discussing union cards in an open dining room constitute unlawful surveillance under Section 8(a)(1) [of the National Labor Relations Act (NLRA)].

* * * *

Section 8(a)(1) of the NLRA states that "[i]t shall be an unfair labor practice for an employer (1) to interfere with, restrain, or coerce employees in the exercise of the rights guaranteed in section 157 of this title." The Board has interpreted Section 8(a)(1) to make observation of union activity unlawful, "if the observation goes beyond casual and becomes unduly intrusive." * * *

"The test for determining whether an employer engages in unlawful surveillance or whether it creates the impression of surveillance is an objective one and involves the determination of whether the employer's conduct, under the circumstances, was such as would tend to interfere with, restrain or coerce employees in the exercise of the rights guaranteed under Section 7 of the [National Labor Relations] Act."

The NLRB refined the objective test for surveillance by announcing that, "[i]ndicia of coerciveness include the duration of the observation, the employer's distance from its employees while observing them, and whether the employer engaged in other coercive behavior during its observation." We determine that this three-factor test is "rational and consistent" with the NLRA, and accordingly, we defer to the Board's interpretation of when surveillance becomes coercive and the application of the test to these facts. By announcing factors to consider when deciding when otherwise lawful observation becomes coercive, the Board exercised its "primary power of interpretation and application of the Act" granted by Congress.

In addition, the NLRB found that the views expressed by [human resources managers] Ms. Sapien and Ms. Briand were protected under Section 8(c) of the NLRA. "Section 8(c) of the Act specifically prohibits [the Board] from finding that an uncoercive speech, whenever delivered by the employer, constitutes an unfair labor practice." The Supreme Court has stated that "an employer's free speech right to communicate his views to his employees is firmly established and cannot be infringed by a union or the Board." "Thus, *an employer is free to communicate to*

his employees any of his general views about unionism or any of his specific views about a particular union, so long as the communications do not contain 'a threat of reprisal or force or promise of benefit.'" Of course, "any assessment of the precise scope of employer expression . . . must be made in the context of its labor relations setting. Thus, an employer's rights cannot outweigh the equal rights of the employees to associate freely, as those rights are embodied in Section 7 and protected by [the NLRA]." [Emphasis added.]

There is no evidence that either Ms. Sapien or Ms. Briand used threats, force, or promises of benefits that would strip their speech of the protections of Section 8(c). Ms. Sapien attempted to give the buffet servers additional facts to consider before signing the union cards. Ms. Briand told Ms. Felix [an employee] that Ms. Bueno [another employee] should not sign a union card without fully understanding the consequences and provided her opinion that the union may not be able to deliver on its promises. Ms. Felix voluntarily translated Ms. Briand's comments for Ms. Bueno. After Ms. Felix explained the translation, Ms. Briand left.

The unions do not contend that the observations of organizing activity by Ms. Sapien or Ms. Briand were unlawful by themselves. The unions argue that the interruption of protected union activity, even to express opinions protected by Section 8(c), makes the otherwise lawful observation unlawful.

We defer to the Board's conclusion that Ms. Sapien's and Ms. Briand's brief, spontaneous interruptions were not coercive because it is "rational and consistent" with the Act. Applying its new three-factor test, the Board reasonably

EXTENDED CASE 23.2 CONTINUED ❧

determined that where the duration of the observation was short and the employer's behavior was not out of the ordinary, verbally interrupting organizing activity does not necessarily violate [the NLRA]. The Board's creation of a three-factor test for unlawful surveillance is "reasonably defensible." * * * Therefore, the petition for review is DENIED.

 QUESTIONS

1. Why did the administrative law judge originally rule that the two brief verbal interventions by the company's human resources managers were in violation of the National Labor Relations Act?
2. Would the result in this case have been different if there had been two dozen similar incidents? If so, how?

SECTION 5
COLLECTIVE BARGAINING

If a fair election is held and the union wins, the NLRB will certify the union as the *exclusive bargaining representative* of the workers. Unions may provide a variety of services to their members, but the central legal right of a union is to serve as the sole representative of the group of workers in bargaining with the employer over the workers' rights.

The concept of bargaining is at the heart of the federal labor laws. When a union is officially recognized, it may make a demand to bargain with the employer. The union then sits at the table opposite the representatives of management to negotiate contracts for its workers. The terms of employment that result from the negotiations apply to all workers in the bargaining unit, even those who do not choose to belong to the union. This process is known as **collective bargaining.** Such bargaining is like most other business negotiations, and each side uses its economic power to pressure or persuade the other side to grant concessions.

Bargaining does not mean that one side must give in to the other or that compromises must be made. It does mean that a demand must be taken seriously and considered as part of a package to be negotiated. Most important, both sides must bargain in "good faith."

Subjects of Bargaining

A common issue in collective bargaining concerns the subjects over which the parties can bargain. The law makes certain subjects mandatory for collective bargaining. These topics cannot be "taken off the table" unilaterally but must be discussed and bargained over.

TERMS AND CONDITIONS OF EMPLOYMENT The NLRA provides that employers may bargain with workers over wages, hours of work, and other terms and conditions of employment. These are broad terms that cover many employment issues. Suppose that a union wants a contract provision granting all workers four weeks of paid vacation. The company need not give in to this demand but must at least consider it and bargain over it.

Many other employment issues are also considered appropriate subjects for collective bargaining. These include safety rules, insurance coverage, pension and other employee benefit plans, procedures for employee discipline, procedures for employee grievances against the company, and even the price of food sold in the company cafeteria.

CLOSING OR RELOCATING A PLANT Management need not bargain with a union over the decision to close a particular facility. Similarly, management need not bargain over a decision to relocate a plant if the move involves a basic change in the nature of the employer's operation. Management may choose to bargain over such decisions, however, to obtain concessions on other bargaining subjects.

Management must bargain over the economic consequences of such decisions. Thus, issues such as **severance pay** (compensation for the termination of employment) in the event of a plant shutdown are appropriate for collective bargaining. Also, if a relocation does *not* involve a basic change in the nature of an operation, management must bargain over the decision unless it can show that (1) the work performed at the new location varies significantly from the work performed at the former plant; (2) the work performed at the former plant is to be discontinued entirely and not moved to the new location; (3) the move involves a change in the scope and direction of the enterprise; or (4) labor costs were not a factor in the decision; or even if labor costs were a factor, the union could not have offered concessions that would have changed the decision to relocate.

Good Faith Bargaining

Parties engaged in collective bargaining often claim that the other side is not bargaining in good faith, as required by labor law. Although good faith is a matter of subjective intent, a party's actions are used to evaluate the finding of good or bad faith in bargaining.

Obviously, the employer must be willing to meet with union representatives. Excessive delaying tactics may be proof of bad faith, as is insistence on obviously unreasonable contract terms. Suppose that a company makes a single overall contract offer on a take-it-or-leave-it basis and refuses to consider modifications of individual terms. This also is considered bad faith bargaining.

Examples of other actions that have been found to constitute bad faith bargaining include the following:

1. Engaging in a campaign among workers to undermine the union.
2. Constantly shifting positions on disputed contract terms.
3. Sending representatives who lack authority to commit the company to a contract.

If an employer (or a union) refuses to bargain in good faith without justification, it has committed an unfair labor practice, and the other party may petition the NLRB for an order requiring good faith bargaining. Except in extreme situations, the NLRB does not have authority to require a party to accede to any specific contract terms. The NLRB may require a party to reimburse the other side for its litigation expenses.

SECTION 6
STRIKES AND LOCKOUTS

The law does not require parties to reach a contract agreement in collective bargaining. Even when parties have bargained in good faith, they may be unable to reach a final agreement. When extensive collective bargaining has been conducted and the parties still cannot agree, an impasse has been reached.

When bargaining has reached an impasse, the union may call a strike against the employer to pressure it into making concessions. A **strike** occurs when the unionized workers leave their jobs and refuse to work. The workers also typically picket the business, standing outside the facility with signs that complain of management's unfairness. A strike is an extreme action. Striking workers lose their right to be paid, and management loses production and may lose customers, if it cannot fill their orders. Labor law regulates the circumstances and conduct of strikes.

A union may strike when the employer has engaged in unfair labor practices, but most strikes are "economic strikes," which are initiated because the union wants a better contract. For example, in 2010 the union representing workers at the Disneyland Hotel organized a hunger strike to draw attention to a prolonged contract dispute over workers' health-care benefits and workloads. After two years of negotiations with the hotel, the workers still had no signed contract for health-care benefits.

The Right to Strike

The right to strike is guaranteed by the NLRA, within limits. Strike activities, such as picketing, are protected by the free speech guarantee of the First Amendment to the U.S. Constitution. Persons who are not employees have a right to participate in picketing an employer. The NLRA also gives workers the right to refuse to cross a picket line of fellow workers who are engaged in a lawful strike. Employers are permitted to hire replacement workers to substitute for the striking workers.

Illegal Strikes

An otherwise lawful strike may become illegal because of the conduct of the strikers. Violent strikes (including the threat of violence) are illegal. The use of violence against management employees or substitute workers is illegal. Certain forms of "massed picketing" are also illegal. If the strikers form a barrier and deny management or other nonunion workers access to the plant, the strike is illegal. Similarly, "sit-down" strikes, in which employees simply stay in the plant without working, are illegal.

SECONDARY BOYCOTTS A strike directed against someone other than the strikers' employer, such as the companies that sell materials to the employer, is a **secondary boycott.** Suppose that the unionized workers of SemiCo (our hypothetical semiconductor company) go out on strike. To increase their economic leverage, the workers picket the leading suppliers and customers of SemiCo in an attempt to hurt the company's business. SemiCo is considered the primary employer, and its suppliers and customers are considered secondary employers. Picketing of the suppliers or customers is a secondary boycott, which was made illegal by the Taft-Hartley Act.

Common Situs Picketing. A controversy may arise in a strike when both the primary employer and a secondary employer occupy the same job site. In this situation, it may be difficult to distinguish between lawful picketing of the primary employer and an unlawful strike against a secondary employer. The law permits a union to picket a site occupied by both primary and secondary employers, an act called **common situs picketing.** If evidence indicates that the strike is directed against the secondary employer, however, it may become illegal. For example, a threatening letter about the strike sent by the union to the secondary employer may show that the picketing includes an illegal secondary boycott.

Hot-Cargo Agreements. When employers voluntarily agree with unions not to handle, use, or deal in nonunion-produced goods of other employers, it is known as a **hot-cargo agreement.** This particular type of secondary boycott was *not* made illegal by the Taft-Hartley Act, because that act only prevented unions from inducing *employees* to strike or otherwise acting to force employers not to handle these goods. The Landrum-Griffin Act addressed this problem:

> It shall be [an] unfair labor practice for any labor organization and any employer to enter into any contract or any agreement . . . whereby such employer . . . agrees to refrain from handling, using, selling, transporting or otherwise dealing in any of the products of any other employer, or to cease doing business with any other person.

Hot-cargo agreements are therefore illegal. Parties injured by an illegal hot-cargo agreement or other secondary boycott may sue the union for damages.

A union may legally urge consumer boycotts of the primary employer, even at the site of a secondary employer. Suppose that a union is on strike against SemiCo, which manufactures semiconductors that are bought by Intellect, Inc., a distributor of electronic components. Intellect sells SemiCo's semiconductors to computer manufacturers. The striking workers can urge the manufacturers not to buy SemiCo's products. The workers cannot urge a total boycott of Intellect, as that would constitute a secondary boycott.

WILDCAT STRIKES A **wildcat strike** occurs when a minority group of workers, perhaps dissatisfied with a union's representation, calls its own strike. The union is the exclusive bargaining representative of a group of workers, and only the union can call a strike. A wildcat strike, unauthorized by the certified union, is illegal.

STRIKES THAT THREATEN NATIONAL HEALTH OR SAFETY The law also places some restrictions on—but does not prohibit—strikes that threaten national health or safety. The Taft-Hartley Act provides time to encourage the settlement of these disputes, called the cooling-off period. This eighty-day cooling-off period allows federal courts to issue injunctions against strikes that would create a national emergency. The president of the United States can obtain a court injunction that will last for eighty days, and presidents have occasionally used this provision. During these eighty days, the president and other government officials can work with the employer and the union to produce a settlement and avoid a strike that may cause a national emergency.

STRIKES THAT CONTRAVENE NO-STRIKE CLAUSES A strike may also be illegal if it contravenes a *no-strike clause.* The previous collective bargaining agreement between a union and an employer may have contained a clause in which the union agreed not to strike (a **no-strike clause**). The law permits the employer to enforce this no-strike clause and obtain an injunction against the strike in some circumstances.

Replacement Workers

Suppose that SemiCo's workers go out on strike. SemiCo is not required to shut down its operations but may find substitute workers to replace the strikers, if possible. These substitute workers are often called "scabs" by union supporters. An employer may even give the replacement workers permanent positions with the company.

Even the National Football League (NFL), when struck by the players in 1987, found replacements to play for the NFL teams. Although some scoffed at the ability of the replacement players, the tactic was largely successful for management, as the strike was called off after only three weeks. An employer can even use an employment agency to recruit replacement workers.

The Rights of Strikers after a Strike Ends

An important issue concerns the rights of strikers after a strike ends. In a typical economic strike, the employer has a right to hire permanent replacements during the strike and need not terminate the replacement workers when the economic strikers seek to return to work. In other words, striking workers are not guaranteed the right to return to their jobs after the strike if satisfactory replacement workers have been found.

If the employer has not hired replacement workers to fill the strikers' positions then the employer must rehire the economic strikers to fill any vacancies. Employers may not discriminate against former economic strikers, and those who are rehired retain their seniority rights. Different rules apply when a union strikes because the employer has engaged in unfair labor practices. In this situation, the employer may still hire replacements but must give the strikers back their jobs once the strike is over.

Lockouts

Lockouts are the employer's counterpart to the worker's right to strike. A **lockout** occurs when the employer shuts down to prevent employees from working. Lockouts usually are used when the employer believes that a strike is imminent. Lockouts may be a legal employer response.

CASE IN POINT In a leading United States Supreme Court case on this issue, a union and an employer had reached a stalemate in collective bargaining. The employer feared that the union would delay a strike until the busy season and thereby cause the employer to suffer more greatly from the strike. The employer called a lockout before the busy season to

deny the union this leverage, and the Court held that this action was legal.[14]

Some lockouts are illegal, however. An employer may not use a lockout as a tool to break the union and pressure employees into decertification. Consequently, an employer must show some economic justification for instituting a lockout.

SECTION 7
UNFAIR LABOR PRACTICES

The preceding sections have discussed unfair labor practices involved in the significant acts of union elections, collective bargaining, and strikes. Many unfair labor practices may occur within the normal working relationship as well. The most important of these practices are discussed in the following sections and listed in Exhibit 23–2 below.

Employer's Refusal to Recognize the Union and to Negotiate

As discussed, once a union has been certified as the exclusive representative of a bargaining unit, an employer must recognize and bargain in good faith with the union over issues affecting all employees who are within the bargaining unit. Failure to do so is an unfair labor practice. Because the National Labor Relations Act embraces a policy of majority rule, certification of the union as the bargaining unit's representative binds *all* of the employees in that bargaining unit. Thus, the union must fairly represent all the members of the bargaining unit.

Certification does not mean that a union will continue indefinitely as the exclusive representative of the bargaining unit. If the union loses the majority

---

14. *American Ship Building Co. v. NLRB*, 380 U.S. 300, 85 S.Ct. 955, 13 L.Ed.2d 855 (1965).

EXHIBIT 23–2 • Basic Unfair Labor Practices

EMPLOYERS *It is unfair to . . .*	UNIONS *It is unfair to . . .*
1. Refuse to recognize a union and refuse to bargain in good faith.	1. Refuse to bargain in good faith.
2. Interfere with, restrain, or coerce employees in their efforts to form a union and bargain collectively.	2. Picket to coerce unionization without the support of a majority of the employees.
3. Dominate a union.	3. Demand the hiring of unnecessary excess workers.
4. Discriminate against union workers.	4. Discriminate against nonunion workers.
5. Punish employees for engaging in concerted activity.	5. Agree to participate in a secondary boycott.
	6. Engage in an illegal strike.
	7. Charge excessive membership fees.

support of those it represents, an employer is not obligated to continue recognition of, or negotiation with, the union. As a practical matter, a newly elected representative needs time to establish itself among the workers and to begin to formulate and implement its programs. Therefore, as a matter of labor policy, a union is immune from attack by employers and from repudiation by the employees for a period of one year after certification. During this period, it is *presumed* that the union enjoys majority support among the employees; the employer cannot refuse to deal with the union as the employees' exclusive representative, even if the employees prefer not to be represented by that union.

Beyond the one-year period, the presumption of majority support continues, but it is *rebuttable*. An employer may rebut (attempt to refute) the presumption with objective evidence that a majority of employees do not wish to be represented by the union. If the evidence is sufficient to support a *good faith belief* that the union no longer enjoys majority support among the employees, the employer may refuse to continue to recognize and negotiate with the union.[15]

Employer's Interference in Union Activities

The NLRA declares it to be an unfair labor practice for an employer to interfere with, restrain, or coerce employees in the exercise of their rights to form a union and bargain collectively. Unlawful employer interference may take a variety of forms.

Courts have found it an unfair labor practice for an employer to make threats that may interfere with an employee's decision to join a union. Even asking employees about their views on the union may be considered coercive. Employees responding to such questioning must be able to remain anonymous and must receive assurances against employer reprisals. Employers also may not prohibit certain forms of union activity in the workplace. If an employee has a grievance with the company, the employer cannot prevent the union's participation in support of the employee, for example.

If an employer has unlawfully interfered with the operation of a union, the NLRB or a reviewing court may issue a cease-and-desist order halting the practice. The company typically is required to post the order on a bulletin board and renounce its past unlawful conduct.

Employer's Domination of a Union

In the early days of unionization, employers fought back by forming employer-sponsored unions to represent employees. These "company unions" were seldom more than the puppets of management. The NLRA outlawed company unions and any other form of employer domination of workers' unions.

Under the law against employer domination, an employer can have no say in which employees belong to the union or which employees serve as union officers. Nor may supervisors or other management personnel participate in union meetings.

Company actions that support a union may be considered improper potential domination. For this reason, a company cannot give union workers pay for time spent on union activities, because this is considered undue support for the union. The company may not provide financial aid to a union and may not solicit workers to join a union.

Employer's Discrimination against Union Employees

The NLRA prohibits employers from discriminating against workers because they are union officers or are otherwise associated with a union. When workers must be laid off, the company cannot consider union participation as a criterion for deciding whom to fire.

The provisions prohibiting discrimination also apply to hiring decisions. Suppose that certain employees of SemiCo are represented by a union, but the company is attempting to weaken the union's strength. The company is prohibited from requiring potential new hires to guarantee that they will not join the union.

Discriminatory punishment of union members or officers can be difficult to prove. The company will claim to have good reasons for its action. The NLRB has specified a series of factors to be considered in determining whether an action had an unlawful, discriminatory motivation. These factors include giving inconsistent reasons for the action, applying rules inconsistently and more strictly against union members, failing to give an expected warning prior

---

15. An employer cannot agree to a collective bargaining agreement and later refuse to abide by it, however, on the ground of a good faith belief that the union did not have majority support when the agreement was negotiated. See *Auciello Iron Works, Inc. v. NLRB*, 517 U.S. 781, 116 S.Ct. 1754, 135 L.Ed.2d 64 (1996).

to discharge or other discipline, and acting contrary to worker seniority.

The decision to close a facility cannot be made with a discriminatory motive. If a company has several facilities and only one is unionized, the company cannot shut down the union plant simply because of the union. The company could shut down the union plant if it were demonstrably less efficient than the other facilities, however.

Union's Unfair Labor Practices

Certain union activities are declared to be unfair labor practices by the Taft-Hartley Act. Secondary boycotts and illegal strikes, discussed earlier, are examples of such union unfair labor practices.

COERCION Another significant union unfair labor practice is coercion or restraint on an employee's decision to participate in or refrain from participating in union activities. Obviously, it is unlawful for a union to threaten an employee or a family with violence for failure to join the union. The law's prohibition includes economic coercion as well. Suppose that a union official declares, "We have a lot of power here; you had better join the union, or you may lose your job." This threat is an unfair labor practice.

The NLRA provides unions with the authority to regulate their own internal affairs, which includes disciplining union members. This discipline cannot be used in an improperly coercive fashion, however. For example, Stan Kowalski is a union member who feels that the union is no longer providing proper representation for employees at his workplace. He starts a campaign to decertify the union. The union may expel Kowalski from membership, but it may not fine or otherwise discipline the worker.

DISCRIMINATION Another significant union unfair labor practice is discrimination. A union may not discriminate against workers because they refuse to join. This provision also prohibits a union from using its influence to cause an employer to discriminate against workers who refuse to join the union. A union cannot force an employer to deny promotions to workers who fail to join the union.

OTHER UNFAIR PRACTICES Other union unfair labor practices include demanding the hiring of unnecessary workers, participating in picketing to coerce unionization without majority employee support, and refusing to engage in good faith bargaining with employer representatives.

Unions are allowed to bargain for certain "union security clauses" in contracts. Although closed shops are illegal, a union can bargain for a provision that requires workers to contribute to the union within thirty days after they are hired. This is typically called an *agency shop,* or *union shop, clause.*

The union shop clause can compel workers to begin paying dues to the certified union but cannot require the worker to "join" the union. Dues payment can be required to prevent workers from taking the benefits of union bargaining without contributing to the union's efforts. The clause cannot require workers to contribute their efforts to the union, however, or to go out on strike.

Even a requirement of dues payment has its limits. Excessive initiation fees or dues may be illegal. Unions often use their revenues to contribute to causes or to lobby politicians. A nonunion employee subject to an agency shop clause who must pay dues cannot be required to contribute to this sort of union expenditure.

SECTION 8
RIGHTS OF NONUNION EMPLOYEES

Most labor law involves the formation of unions and associated rights. Even nonunion employees have some similar rights, however. Most workers do not belong to unions, so this issue is significant. The NLRA protects concerted employee action, for example, and does not limit its protection to certified unions.

Concerted Activity

Data from the NLRB indicate that growing numbers of nonunion employees are challenging employer barriers to their **concerted action.** Protected concerted action is that taken by employees for their mutual benefit regarding wages, hours, or terms and conditions of employment.

Even an action by a *single* employee may be protected concerted activity, if that action is taken for the benefit of other employees and if the employee has at least discussed the action with other approving workers. If only a single worker engages in a protest or walkout, the employer will not be liable for an unfair labor practice if it fires the worker unless the employer is aware that this protest or walkout is concerted activity taken with the assent of other workers.

In the following case, an employer discharged an employee for "complaining." The employee claimed that this "complaining" constituted concerted activity on behalf of herself and other employees.

CASE 23.3
National Labor Relations Board v. Hotel Employees and Restaurant Employees International Union Local 26, AFL-CIO

United States Court of Appeals, First Circuit, 446 F.3d 200 (2006).
www.ca1.uscourts.gov[a]

BACKGROUND AND FACTS • The Hotel Employees and Restaurant Employees International Union, Local 26, AFL-CIO (the Union), represents 5,800 hotel workers in Boston, Massachusetts. In 1997, the Union hired Janice Loux as its president. In September 1998, Loux hired Emma Johnson as a researcher. In June 1999, the Logan Airport Ramada Inn near Boston announced that it would be closing and all employees would be discharged. Hilton Hotels Corporation would reopen the hotel, but the discharged employees would not be given a right of reemployment. Loux scheduled a leafleting campaign against Hilton. Each Union employee was to leaflet in a two-hour shift at times varying from day to day, in addition to other job duties. During the campaign, Johnson repeatedly asked Loux to allow employees to switch shifts. Loux refused. On August 6, the Union reached an agreement with Hilton and the leafleting stopped. Less than two weeks later, Loux fired Johnson for "complaining about the Hilton campaign." Johnson filed an unfair labor practice charge with the National Labor Relations Board (NLRB) against the Union. The NLRB concluded that the Union discharged Johnson "because of her protected concerted activity." The Union petitioned the U.S. Court of Appeals for the First Circuit for review.

IN THE LANGUAGE OF THE COURT
BOWMAN, Senior Circuit Judge.
* * * *
* * * The Union argues that Johnson did not engage in concerted activity, but rather engaged in self-motivated complaining about her schedule.

To qualify as concerted activity, conduct need not take place in a union setting and it is not necessary that a collective bargaining agreement be in effect. It is sufficient that the complaining employee intends or contemplates, as an end result, group activity which will also benefit some other employees. We recognize that even a conversation can constitute concerted activity, but to qualify as such, it must appear at the very least that it was engaged in with the object of initiating or inducing or preparing for group action or that it had some relation to group action in the interest of the employees. [Emphasis added.]

We conclude * * * that Johnson engaged in concerted activity. * * * Johnson polled co-employees about their desire to switch shifts and/or work only one day per weekend, she informed co-employees that she would present her ideas to Loux at a staff meeting, and she later presented her ideas that would benefit all employees to Loux. Johnson also gave Loux alternative weekend schedules that either would have granted employees one weekend day off per week or at least ensured that the employees did not work in the middle of both weekend days. Some employees supported Johnson's ideas. * * * *Johnson's conduct related to group action that would have benefited the Union's employees such that it constituted concerted activity.* [Emphasis added.]
* * * *

[Next] we ask whether * * * Loux discharged Johnson because she engaged in protected concerted activity. * * * After Loux announced that the leafletting campaign could last up to four months, that employees could not take any vacations until it was concluded, and that employees would work seven days per week during the campaign, Johnson began to discuss schedule changes openly with co-employees. Johnson then advocated to Loux on behalf of the employees for the ability to switch shifts or be allowed to work four-hour shifts on one weekend day so that they could enjoy one day off per week.

---

a. In the right-hand column, click on "Opinions." When that page opens, in the "Opinion Number begins with" box, type "05-1924" and click on "Submit Search." From the result, in the "Click for Opinion" column, click on the link to read the case. The U.S. Court of Appeals for the First Circuit maintains this Web site.

CASE CONTINUES ➡

CASE 23.3 CONTINUED ➡   * * * Loux knew about this activity [and] * * * Loux's motivation for discharging Johnson was rooted in Johnson's protesting the leafletting schedule. For instance, * * * Johnson's [job performance was rated in May 1999] as very good * * *. Soon after, in July 1999, Loux initiated the leafletting campaign against the Hilton and Johnson began voicing complaints about the leafletting schedule. That is when Loux became extremely critical of Johnson's performance and attitude. * * * Johnson was discharged because she complained about the Hilton campaign. * * * Thus, we conclude * * * that *a motivating factor in the Union's discharge of Johnson was her protected concerted activity.* [Emphasis added.]

* * * *

The Union admits that Johnson's poor attitude during the leafletting activities was a reason for her discharge. * * * This criticism is inextricably related to the fact that Johnson made herself a pest in Loux's eyes by continually complaining about the * * * leafletting schedule. * * * Johnson may have been an irritant to Loux because she was challenging the schedule; but that irritating activity by Johnson is protected by * * * the NLRA.

DECISION AND REMEDY • *The U.S. Court of Appeals for the First Circuit denied the Union's petition for review. The court affirmed the NLRB's conclusion that the Union was liable for discharging Johnson. "A consistent theme runs through the . . . testimony and supports the . . . finding that Johnson's protected concerted activity motivated Loux to discharge her."*

THE LEGAL ENVIRONMENT DIMENSION • *Would Emma Johnson have been able to file a wrongful discharge claim (discussed in Chapter 22) against Hilton Hotels based on these facts? Discuss.*

THE ETHICAL DIMENSION • *Should an employee's complaints be considered protected "concerted" activity? Is the holding of this case fair to the employer? Why or why not?*

Safety

A common circumstance for nonunion activity is concern over workplace safety. The Labor-Management Relations Act authorizes an employee to walk off the job if he or she has a good faith belief that the working conditions are abnormally dangerous. The employer cannot lawfully discharge the employee under these conditions.

Suppose that Knight Company operates a plant building mobile homes. A large ventilation fan at the plant blows dust and abrasive materials into the faces of workers. The workers have complained, but Knight Company has done nothing. The workers finally refuse to work until the fan is modified, and Knight fires them. The NLRB will find that the walkout is a protected activity and can command Knight to rehire the workers with back pay.

To be protected under federal labor law, a safety walkout must be *concerted* activity. If a single worker walks out over a safety complaint, other workers must be affected by the safety issue for the walkout to be protected under the LMRA.

REVIEWING
Immigration and Labor Law

In April 2010, several employees of Javatech, Inc., a computer hardware developer with 250 employees, formed the Javatech Employees Union (JEU). In June, the National Labor Relations Board (NLRB) conducted an election that showed that a majority of Javatech employees supported the union. JEU began bargaining with management over wages and benefits. In January 2011, Javatech management offered JEU a 1 percent annual wage increase to all employees with no other changes in employment benefits. JEU countered by requesting a 3 percent wage increase and an employee health-insurance package. Javatech management responded that the 1 percent wage increase was the company's only offer. JEU petitioned the NLRB for an order requesting good faith bargaining. After meeting

REVIEWING

Immigration and Labor Law, Continued

with an NLRB representative, Javatech management still refused to consider modifying its position. JEU leaders then became embroiled in a dispute about whether JEU should accept this offer or go on strike. New union leaders were elected in July 2011, and the employer refused to meet with the new JEU representatives, claiming that the union no longer had majority support from employees. In August 2011, a group of seven Javatech engineers began feeling ill while working with a new adhesive used in creating motherboards. The seven engineers discussed going on strike without union support. Before reaching agreement, one of the engineers, Rosa Molina, became dizzy while working with the adhesive and walked out of the workplace. Using the information presented in the chapter, answer the following questions.

1. How many of Javatech's 250 employees must have signed authorization cards to allow JEU to petition the NLRB for an election?
2. What must Javatech change in its collective bargaining negotiations to demonstrate that it is bargaining in good faith with JEU, as required by labor law?
3. Could the seven engineers legally call a strike? What would this be called?
4. Would Molina's safety walkout be protected under the Labor-Management Relations Act?

DEBATE THIS: *The U.S. labor market is highly competitive, so state and federal laws that require overtime pay are unnecessary and should be abolished.*

TERMS AND CONCEPTS

appropriate bargaining
    unit 520
authorization card 520
cease-and-desist order 517
closed shop 518

collective bargaining 523
common situs picketing 525
concerted action 528
hot-cargo agreement 525
I-551 Alien Registration
    Receipt 516

I-9 verification 514
lockout 526
no-strike clause 525
right-to-work law 518
secondary boycott 524
severance pay 523

strike 524
union shop 518
wildcat strike 525

QUESTIONS AND CASE PROBLEMS

23–1. Union Recognition A group of employees at the Briarwood Furniture Co.'s manufacturing plant were interested in joining a union. A representative of the American Federation of Labor and Congress of Industrial Organizations (AFL-CIO) told the group that her union was prepared to represent the workers and suggested that the group begin organizing by obtaining authorization cards from their fellow employees. After obtaining 252 authorization cards from among Briarwood's 500 nonmanagement employees, the organizers requested that the company recognize the AFL-CIO as the official representative of the employees. The company refused. Has the company violated federal labor laws? What should the organizers do?

23–2. Appropriate Bargaining Unit The Briarwood Furniture Co., discussed in the preceding problem, employs 400 unskilled workers and 100 skilled workers in its plant. The unskilled workers operate the industrial machinery used in processing Briarwood's line of standardized plastic office furniture. The skilled workers, who work in an entirely separate part of the plant, are experienced artisans who craft Briarwood's line of expensive wood furniture products. Do you see any problems with a single union's representing all the workers at the Briarwood plant? Explain. Would your answers to Question 23–1 change if you knew that fifty-one of the authorization cards had been signed by the skilled workers, with the remainder signed by the unskilled workers? Explain.

23-3. QUESTION WITH SAMPLE ANSWER: Union Election.

 Consolidated Stores is undergoing a unionization campaign. Prior to the election, management says that the union is unnecessary to protect workers. Management also provides bonuses and wage increases to the workers during this period. The employees reject the union. Union organizers protest that the wage increases during the election campaign unfairly prejudiced the vote. Should these wage increases be regarded as an unfair labor practice? Discuss.

- **For a sample answer to Question 23-3, go to Appendix F at the end of this text.**

23-4. Strikes SimpCo was engaged in ongoing negotiations over a new labor contract with the union representing the company's employees. As the deadline for expiration of the old labor contract drew near, several employees who were involved in union activities were disciplined for being late to work. The union claimed that other employees had not been dealt with as harshly and that the company was discriminating on the basis of union activity. When the negotiations failed to prove fruitful and the old contract expired, the union called a strike. The company claimed that the action was an economic strike to press the union's demands for higher wages. The union contended that the action was an unfair labor practice strike because of the alleged discrimination. What importance does the distinction have for the striking workers and the company?

23-5. Unfair Labor Practice The New York Department of Education's e-mail policy prohibits the use of the e-mail system for unofficial purposes, except that officials of the New York Public Employees Federation (PEF), the union representing state employees, can use the system for some limited communications, including the scheduling of union meetings and activities. In 1998, Michael Darcy, an elected PEF official, began sending mass, union-related e-mails to employees, including a summary of a union delegates' convention, a union newsletter, a criticism of proposed state legislation, and a criticism of the state governor and the Governor's Office of Employee Relations. Richard Cate, the department's chief operating officer, met with Darcy and reiterated the department's e-mail policy. When Darcy refused to stop his use of the e-mail system, Cate terminated his access to it. Darcy filed a complaint with the New York Public Employment Relations Board, alleging an unfair labor practice. Do the circumstances support Cate's action? Why or why not? [*Benson v. Cuevas*, 293 A.D.2d 927, 741 N.Y.S.2d 310 (3 Dept. 2002)]

23-6. Collective Bargaining Verizon New York, Inc. (VNY), provides telecommunications services. VNY and the Communications Workers of America (CWA) are parties to collective bargaining agreements covering installation and maintenance employees. At one time, VNY supported annual blood drives. VNY, CWA, and charitable organizations jointly set dates, arranged appointments, and adjusted work schedules for the drives. For each drive, about a thousand employees, including managers, spent up to four hours traveling to a donor site, giving blood, recovering, and returning to their jobs. Employees received full pay for the time. In 2001, VNY told CWA that it would no longer allow employees to participate "on Company time," claiming that it had experienced problems meeting customer requests for service during the drives. CWA filed a complaint with the National Labor Relations Board (NLRB), asking that VNY be ordered to bargain over the decision. Did VNY commit an unfair labor practice? Should the NLRB grant CWA's request? Why or why not? [*Verizon New York, Inc. v. National Labor Relations Board*, 360 F.3d 206 (D.C. Cir. 2004)]

23-7. Collective Bargaining Ceridian Corp. provides employment services to other companies. One of its divisions offers counseling to its customers' employees through a call-in center in Eagan, Minnesota. Under Ceridian's "Personal Days Off" (PDO) policy, employees can use a certain amount of paid time off each year for whatever purpose they wish, but unpaid leave is not available. Employees who take time off in excess of their PDO are subject to discipline, including discharge. In June 2003, the National Labor Relations Board (NLRB) certified Service Employees International Union 113 as the exclusive collective bargaining representative for 130 employees at the call-in center. The union assembled a six-employee team to negotiate a collective bargaining agreement. Ceridian refused to meet with the team during nonworking hours or to grant the members unpaid leave to attend bargaining sessions during working hours, but required them to use their PDO instead. The union filed an unfair-labor-practice charge with the NLRB against Ceridian, alleging that the employer impermissibly interfered with its employees' choice of bargaining representatives. Did Ceridian commit an unfair labor practice? Explain. [*Ceridian Corp. v. National Labor Relations Board*, 435 F.3d 352 (D.C.Cir. 2006)]

23-8. CASE PROBLEM WITH SAMPLE ANSWER: Immigration.

 Nicole Tipton and Sadik Seferi owned and operated a restaurant in Iowa. Acting on a tip from the local police, agents of Immigration and Customs Enforcement executed search warrants at the restaurant and at an apartment where some restaurant workers lived. The agents discovered six undocumented aliens working at the restaurant and living together. When the I-9 forms for the restaurant's employees were reviewed, none were found for the six aliens. They were paid in cash, while other employees were paid by check. The jury found Tipton and Seferi guilty of hiring and harboring illegal

aliens. *Both were given prison terms. The defendants challenged the conviction, contending that they did not violate the law because they did not know that the workers were unauthorized aliens. Was that argument credible? Why or why not?* [United States v. Tipton, *518 F.3d 591 (8th Cir. 2008)]*

• **To view a sample answer for Problem 23–8, go to this book's Web site at www.cengage.com/blaw/cross, select "Chapter 23," and click on "Case Problem with Sample Answer."**

23–9. Unfair Labor Practices The Laborers' International Union of North America, Local 578, and Shaw Stone & Webster Construction, Inc., were parties to a collective bargaining agreement that covered workers at the company. The agreement contained a union-security provision that required all company employees who were represented by the union to join the union. If an employee failed to join or pay union dues, the union would request that the employee be fired. After Sebedeo Lopez went to work for Shaw Stone, he failed to pay his union initiation fee and monthly dues. Lopez's shop steward told him to pay these fees, although the amount owed was unclear. He was also told that the union was pressing the company to fire him. Lopez agreed to pay the fees and left a money order for $200 at the union's office, but the union claimed that it did not find the money order. Lopez promised to pay another $215 in a few days, but the union demanded his immediate dismissal. Shaw Stone fired him on the spot. Lopez complained to the National Labor Relations Board (NLRB), which brought unfair labor practice charges against the union. An administrative law judge ruled against the union, and the NLRB agreed. The union appealed. Was the union guilty of unfair labor practices under the National Labor Relations Act by having Lopez fired? Why or why not? [*Laborers' International Union of North America, Local 578 v. National Labor Relations Board*, 594 F.3d 732 (10th Cir. 2010)]

23–10. A QUESTION OF ETHICS: Immigration Work Status.

Mohammad Hashmi, a citizen of Pakistan, entered the United States in 2002 on a student visa. Two years later, when he applied for a job at CompuCredit, he completed an I-9 form and checked the box to indicate that he was "a citizen or national of the United States." Soon after submitting that form, he married a U.S. citizen. Several months later, the federal immigration services claimed that Hashmi had misrepresented himself as a U.S. citizen. Hashmi contended that he had not misrepresented himself. At an administrative hearing, he testified that when he filled out the I-9 form he believed that he was a "national of the United States" because he was legally in the country under a student visa and was going to marry a U.S. citizen. He requested that his immigration status be adjusted to account for the fact that he was employed and married to an American. The immigration judge rejected that request and found that Hashmi had made a false claim on the I-9 form. He ruled that Hashmi was "inadmissible" to the United States and that his legal status in the country could not be amended because of his marriage or employment. Hashmi appealed. [Hashmi v. Mukasey, *533 F.3d 700 (8th Cir. 2008)]*

(a) Was it reasonable for Hashmi to think that he was a U.S. national? What if his misunderstanding was due to the fact that he was not proficient in the English language?

(b) Should Hashmi's visa status be changed because of his marriage and employment? Why or why not? How should the appellate court rule in this case?

(c) Should the court consider what happens to Hashmi's wife if he is denied legal status? In general, should the law consider the interests of family members when determining a person's immigration status? Explain.

LEGAL RESEARCH EXERCISES ON THE WEB

Go to this text's Web site at **www.cengage.com/blaw/cross**, select "Chapter 23," and click on "Practical Internet Exercises." There you will find the following Internet research exercises that you can perform to learn more about the topics covered in this chapter.

Practical Internet Exercise 23–1: Legal Perspective
The National Labor Relations Board

Practical Internet Exercise 23–2: Management Perspective
Mail Policies and Union Activity

Practical Internet Exercise 23–3: Historical Perspective
Labor Unions and Labor Law

Ethical principles—and challenging ethical issues—pervade the areas of agency and employment. As you read in Chapter 20, when one person agrees to act on behalf of another, as an agent does in an agency relationship, that person assumes certain ethical responsibilities. Similarly, the principal also assumes certain ethical duties. In essence, agency law gives legal force to the ethical duties arising in an agency relationship. Although agency law also focuses on the rights of agents and principals, those rights are framed by the concept of duty—that is, an agent's duty becomes a right for the principal, and vice versa. Significantly, many of the duties of the principal and agent are negotiable when they form their contract. In forming a contract, the principal and the agent can extend or abridge many of the ordinary duties owed in such a relationship.

Employees who deal with third parties are also deemed to be agents and thus share the ethical (and legal) duties imposed under agency law. In the employment context, however, it is not always possible for an employee to negotiate favorable employment terms. Often, an employee who is offered a job must either accept the job on the employer's terms or look elsewhere for a position. Although numerous federal and state statutes protect employees, in some situations employees still have little recourse against their employers. At the same time, employers complain that statutes regulating employment relationships impose so many requirements that they find it hard to exercise a reasonable amount of control over their workplaces.

The Agent's Duty to the Principal

The very nature of the principal-agent relationship is one of trust. Because of the nature of this relationship, which we call a fiduciary relationship, an agent is considered to owe certain duties to the principal. These duties include being loyal and obedient, informing the principal of important facts concerning the agency, accounting to the principal for property or funds received, and performing with reasonable diligence and skill.

Thus, ethical conduct would prevent an agent from representing two principals in the same transaction, making a secret profit from the agency relationship, or failing to disclose the agent's interest in property being purchased by the principal. The expected ethical conduct of the agent has evolved into rules that, if breached, cause the agent to be held legally liable.

Does an Agent Also Have a Duty to Society? A question that sometimes arises is whether an agent's obligation extends beyond the duty to the principal and includes a duty to society as well. Consider, for example, the situation faced by an employee who knows that her employer is engaging in an unethical—or even illegal—practice, such as marketing an unsafe product. Does the employee's duty to the principal include keeping silent about this practice, which may harm users of the product? Does the employee have a duty to protect consumers by disclosing this information to the public, even if she loses her job as a result? Some scholars have argued that many of the greatest evils in the past thirty years have been accomplished in the name of duty to the principal.

Does an Agent's Breach of Loyalty Terminate the Agent's Authority? Suppose that an employee-agent who is authorized to access company trade secrets contained in computer files takes those secrets to a competitor for whom the employee is about to begin working. Clearly, in this situation the agent has violated the ethical—and legal—duty of loyalty to the principal. Does this breach of loyalty mean that the employee's act of accessing the trade secrets was unauthorized? The question has significant implications because if the act was unauthorized, the employee will be subject to state and federal laws prohibiting unauthorized access to computer information and data. If the act was authorized, the employee will not be subject to such laws.

To date, most courts have ruled that an agent's authority continues, even though there was a breach of loyalty. In one case, for example, three employees of Lockheed Martin Corporation copied confidential information and trade secrets from Lockheed's computer network onto compact discs and BlackBerries. Lockheed had authorized the employee-agents to access these files but was understandably upset when the three resigned and went to work for a competitor, taking the trade secrets with them. Lockheed sued the former agents under the Computer Fraud and Abuse Act (discussed in Chapter 12), arguing that they had accessed the data without authorization. The federal district court, however, held that the individuals did have authorization to access the computer network and did not lose this authorization when they breached the duty of loyalty. Therefore, the court dismissed the case.[1]

The Principal's Duty to the Agent

Just as agents owe certain duties to their principals, so do principals owe duties to their agents, such as compensation and reimbursement for job-related expenses. Principals also owe their agents a duty of cooperation. One might expect principals to cooperate

---

1. *Lockheed Martin Corp. v. Speed,* 2006 WL 2683058 (M.D.Fla. 2006). See also *Cenveo Corp. v. CelumSolutions Software GMBH & Co. KG,* 504 F.Supp.2d 574 (D.Minn. 2007).

with their agents out of self-interest, but this does not always happen.

Suppose that a principal hires an agent on commission to sell a building, and the agent puts considerable time and expense into finding a buyer. If the principal changes his mind and decides to retain the building, he may try to prevent the agent from completing the sale. Is such action ethical? Does it violate the principal's duty of cooperation? What alternatives would the principal have?

Although a principal is legally obligated to fulfill certain duties to the agent, these duties do not include any specific duty of loyalty. Some argue that employers' failure to be loyal to their employees has resulted in a reduction in employee loyalty to employers. After all, they maintain, why should an employee be loyal to an employer's interests over the years when the employee knows that the employer has no corresponding legal duty to be loyal to the employee's interests? Employers who do show a sense of loyalty toward their employees—for example, by not laying off longtime, faithful employees when business is slow or when those employees could be replaced by younger workers at lower cost—base that loyalty primarily on ethical, not legal, considerations.

Respondeat Superior

Agency relationships have ethical ramifications for third parties as well as for agents and principals. A legal concept that addresses the effect of agency relationships on third parties is the doctrine of *respondeat superior*. This doctrine raises a significant ethical question: Why should innocent employers be required to assume responsibility for the tortious, or wrongful, actions of their agent-employees? The answer has to do with the courts' perception that when one of two innocent parties must suffer a loss, the party in the better position to prevent that loss should bear the burden. In an employment relationship, for example, the employer has more control over the employee's behavior than a third party to the relationship does.

Another reason for retaining the doctrine of *respondeat superior* in our laws is that the employer is assumed to be better able to pay any damages incurred by a third party. One of our society's shared beliefs is that an injured party should be afforded the most effective relief possible. Thus, even though an employer may be absolutely innocent, the employer has "deeper pockets" than the employee and will be more likely to have the funds necessary to make the injured party whole.

Immigration Reform

Unauthorized (illegal) workers make up 5 percent of the total U.S. workforce and 12 percent of the workers in the construction industry. The federal government during the Bush administration significantly stepped up enforcement actions (raids) to combat the growing number of illegal immigrants. The raids targeted workers in many industries, including food processing and packaging firms, contractors (landscape, cleaning, and janitorial services), construction firms, temporary employment services, and fast-food restaurants. Often, the unauthorized workers were performing jobs that no one else wanted because the jobs paid low wages or involved substandard conditions.

As a result of these raids, many immigrant workers were detained and deported, their families were torn apart, the businesses for which they worked were disrupted, and some managers faced prison terms. The impact of these raids on immigrants—in a nation founded by immigrants—has led many U.S. citizens to believe that reforming the immigration laws is a moral imperative. Many believe that it is unethical to imprison and deport these impoverished and unrepresented workers—who often were already being exploited by their U.S. employers.

When President Barack Obama took office, he promised to reform immigration law. His goals were to decrease bureaucracy, increase efficiency, and boost the number of immigrant workers with legal status in the United States in an effort to keep families together and meet employers' needs for workers. Although the number of workplace raids has decreased, the Obama administration's policies have not resulted in more favorable treatment of immigrant workers. For example, in September 2009, American Apparel, a U.S.-based clothing company, laid off more than 1,600 workers in Los Angeles rather than face fines for employing undocumented workers.[2]

Problems with I-9 Verification

Verifying a person's eligibility to work in the United States can be a complicated and costly process for employers. The most recent I-9 form (see Chapter 23) specifies the documents that an employer may accept to verify employment eligibility and identification. At the same time, it is illegal for an employer to discriminate against foreign-born workers by requiring them to provide a driver's license or Social Security card to prove their identity. If an employer relies on the documents a worker provides to prove identity and eligibility (such as a school photo identification card) and these documents later prove to be fraudulent or invalid, the employer can be sanctioned for hiring a

---

2. "Immigration Reforms: How a Broken System Breaks Communities," *Making Contact*, a production of the National Radio Project, January 26, 2010.

FOCUS ON ETHICS CONTINUES ▶

person that the employer "should have known" was unauthorized. Thus, employers are forced to choose between violating antidiscrimination laws and risking sanctions for violating immigration laws. It is an ethical dilemma with no easy answer.

Discrimination against Transgender Persons

Although some states have laws that specifically ban discrimination based on gender identity, most courts have held that federal law (Title VII, discussed in Chapter 22) does *not* protect transgender persons from discrimination. This situation may be changing, however, now that one federal court has extended Title VII protection against gender discrimination to transsexuals. Diane Schroer (previously David Schroer) was born male but always identified with the female gender. Schroer, who has master's degrees in history and international relations, served twenty-five years in the military and was a commander of special forces. After retiring with top-secret clearance, Schroer applied for a terrorism specialist position at the Library of Congress. At the job interview, Schroer dressed as a man and received the highest interview score of all eighteen candidates. The selection committee unanimously voted to offer the job to Schroer.

Schroer then met with her future supervisor and explained that she had been diagnosed with gender identity disorder and was planning to have sex reassignment surgery. The next day, the Library of Congress withdrew its offer to hire Schroer. When Schroer sued alleging gender discrimination, the Library claimed that it had withdrawn its offer because Schroer was untrustworthy and would be unable to receive the needed security clearance. The court, however, found that these reasons were pretexts (excuses) and ruled in favor of Schroer. The court held that the Library had refused to hire Schroer because her appearance and background did not comport with the selection committee's stereotypes about how women and men should act and appear. The court concluded that the revocation of the job offer violated Title VII; it was discrimination "because of sex," even though Title VII does not include transsexuals as a protected class. In 2009, Schroer was awarded nearly $500,000 in back pay and damages.[3]

DISCUSSION QUESTIONS

1. How much obedience and loyalty does an agent-employee owe to an employer? What if the employer engages in an activity—or requests that the employee engage in an activity—that violates the employee's ethical standards but does not violate any public policy or law? In such a situation, does an employee's duty to abide by her or his own ethical standards override the employee's duty of loyalty to the employer?

2. When an agent acts in violation of his or her ethical or legal duty to the principal, should that action terminate the agent's authority to act on behalf of the principal? Why or why not?

3. If an agent-employee injures a third party during the course of employment, under the doctrine of *respondeat superior,* the employer may be held liable for the employee's action even though the employer did not authorize the action and was not even aware of it. Is it fair to hold the employer liable in this situation? Would it be more equitable if the employee alone was held liable for his or her tortious (legally wrongful) actions to third parties, even when the actions were committed within the scope of employment?

4. How should immigration law be reformed? Does the United States have any ethical duties to undocumented (illegal) aliens who come here to work? How can the law be fair and balance the rights of immigrants, their families, the companies that employ them, and U.S. citizens?

5. Should the law prohibit discrimination against transgender persons? Why or why not?

---

3. *Schroer v. Billington,* 577 F.Supp.2d 293 (D.D.C. 2008).

UNIT SIX

THE REGULATORY ENVIRONMENT

CONTENTS

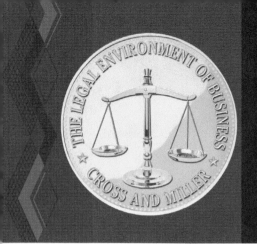

CHAPTER 24

✳ Consumer Protection

All statutes, agency rules, and common law judicial decisions that serve to protect the interests of consumers are classified as **consumer law**. Traditionally, in disputes involving consumers, it was assumed that the freedom to contract carried with it the obligation to live by the deal made. Over time, this attitude has changed considerably. Today, myriad federal and state laws protect consumers from unfair trade practices, unsafe products,

discriminatory or unreasonable credit requirements, and other problems related to consumer transactions. Nearly every agency and department of the federal government has an office of consumer affairs, and most states have one or more such offices to help consumers. Also, typically the attorney general's office assists consumers at the state level.

In this chapter, we examine some of the major laws and regulations protecting consumers. Because of the

wide variation among state consumer protection laws, our primary focus in this chapter is on federal legislation. Realize, though, that state laws often provide more sweeping and significant protections for the consumer than do federal laws. Exhibit 24–1 below indicates many of the areas of consumer law that are regulated by federal statutes.

EXHIBIT 24–1 • Selected Areas of Consumer Law Regulated by Statutes

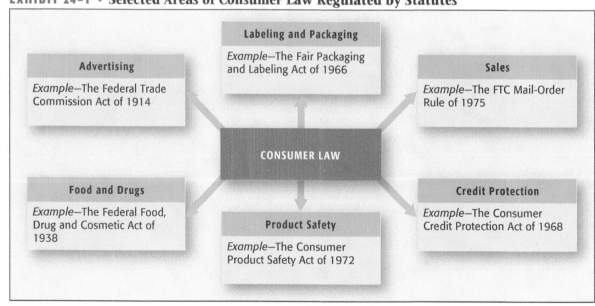

SECTION 1
DECEPTIVE ADVERTISING

One of the earliest federal consumer protection laws—and still one of the more important—was the Federal Trade Commission Act of 1914 (mentioned in Chapter 6).[1] The act created the Federal Trade Commission (FTC) to carry out the broadly stated goal of preventing unfair and deceptive trade practices, including deceptive advertising.[2]

Generally, **deceptive advertising** occurs if a reasonable consumer would be misled by the advertising claim. Vague generalities and obvious exaggerations are permissible. These claims are known as *puffery*. When a claim takes on the appearance of literal authenticity, however, it may create problems. Advertising that *appears* to be based on factual evidence but in fact is not reasonably supported by some evidence will be deemed deceptive.

Some advertisements contain "half-truths," meaning that the presented information is true but incomplete and therefore leads consumers to a false conclusion. For example, the maker of Campbell's soups advertised that "most" Campbell's soups are low in fat and cholesterol and thus helpful in fighting heart disease. What the ad did not say was that many Campbell's soups are high in sodium, and high-sodium diets may increase the risk of heart disease. Hence, the FTC ruled that Campbell's claims were deceptive. Advertising that contains an endorsement by a celebrity may be deemed deceptive if the celebrity does not actually use the product.

Even before the FTC brought the following case, *Wired* magazine had already put the product in question on its list of the top ten "snake oil gadgets."

---

1. 15 U.S.C. Sections 41–58.
2. 15 U.S.C. Section 45.

CASE 24.1
Federal Trade Commission v. QT, Inc.
United States Court of Appeals, Seventh Circuit, 512 F.3d 858 (2008).
www.ca7.uscourts.gov[a]

BACKGROUND AND FACTS • QT, Inc., heavily promoted the Q-Ray Ionized Bracelet on television infomercials and on its Web site. In its promotions, the company claimed that the bracelet offered immediate and significant or complete pain relief and could cure chronic pain. At trial, the U.S. district court labeled all such claims fraudulent; forbade further promotional claims; and ordered the company to pay $16 million, plus interest, into a fund to be distributed to customers. QT appealed to the U.S. Court of Appeals for the Seventh Circuit.

IN THE LANGUAGE OF THE COURT
EASTERBROOK, Chief Judge.

* * * According to the district court's findings, almost everything that defendants have said about the bracelet is false. Here are some highlights:

- Defendants promoted the bracelet as a miraculous cure for chronic pain, but it has no therapeutic effect.
- Defendants told consumers that claims of "immediate, significant or complete pain relief" had been "test-proven"; they hadn't.
  * * * *
- Defendants represented that the therapeutic effect wears off in a year or two, despite knowing that the bracelet's properties do not change. This assertion is designed to lead customers to buy new bracelets. Likewise the false statement that the bracelet has a "memory cycle specific to each individual wearer" so that only the bracelet's original wearer can experience pain relief is designed to increase sales by eliminating the second-hand market and "explaining" the otherwise-embarrassing fact that the buyer's friends and neighbors can't perceive any effect.

---

a. Click on "Opinions" in the left-hand column. In the boxes for the case number, type "07" and "1662," and then click on "List Case(s)." Follow the links to access the opinion. The U.S. Court of Appeals for the Seventh Circuit maintains this Web site.

CASE CONTINUES ▶

CASE 24.1 CONTINUED ➡ The magistrate judge [the judge presiding over the trial] did not commit a clear error, or abuse his discretion, in concluding that the defendants set out to bilk unsophisticated persons who found themselves in pain from arthritis and other chronic conditions.

   * * * *The Federal Trade Commission Act forbids false and misleading statements, and a statement that is plausible but has not been tested in the most reliable way cannot be condemned out of hand.* [Emphasis added.]

   * * * For the Q-Ray Ionized Bracelet, * * * all statements about how the product works—Q-Rays, ionization, enhancing the flow of bio-energy, and the like—are blather [nonsense]. Defendants might as well have said: "Beneficent creatures from the 17th Dimension use this bracelet as a beacon to locate people who need pain relief, and whisk them off to their home-world every night to provide help in ways unknown to our science."

   * * * *Proof is what separates an effect new to science from a swindle.* Defendants themselves told customers that the bracelet's efficacy had been "test-proven"; * * * but defendants have no proof of the Q-Ray Ionized Bracelet's efficacy. The "tests" on which they relied were bunk. * * * What remain are testimonials, which are not a form of proof * * *. That's why the "testimonial" of someone who keeps elephants off the streets of a large city by snapping his fingers is the basis of a joke rather than proof of cause and effect. [Emphasis added.]

   * * * *

   Physicians know how to treat pain. Why pay $200 for a Q-Ray Ionized Bracelet when you can get relief from an aspirin tablet that costs [one cent]?

DECISION AND REMEDY • *The federal appellate court affirmed the district court's decision. QT, Inc., was required to stop its deceptive advertising and to pay the $16 million, plus interest, so that its customers could be reimbursed.*

WHAT IF THE FACTS WERE DIFFERENT? • *Assume that the defendant had actually conducted scientific studies, but they were inconclusive. How might the judge have ruled in that situation?*

THE ETHICAL DIMENSION • *Most people have seen infomercials. Does the fact that QT used infomercials to make fraudulent promotional claims mean that all products "pitched" on television are suspect? Why or why not?*

Bait-and-Switch Advertising

The FTC has issued rules that govern specific advertising techniques. One of the most important rules is contained in the FTC's "Guides Against Bait Advertising,"[3] issued in 1968. The rule seeks to prevent **bait-and-switch advertising**—that is, advertising a very low price for a particular item that will likely be unavailable to the consumer, who will then be encouraged to purchase a more expensive item. The low price is the "bait" to lure the consumer into the store. The salesperson is instructed to "switch" the consumer to a different, more expensive item. Under the FTC guidelines, bait-and-switch advertising occurs if the seller refuses to show the advertised item, fails to have a reasonable quantity of the item in stock, fails to promise to deliver the advertised item within a reasonable time, or discourages employees from selling the item.

Online Deceptive Advertising

Deceptive advertising can occur in the online environment as well. The FTC actively monitors online advertising and has identified hundreds of Web sites that have made false or deceptive claims for products ranging from medical treatments for various diseases to exercise equipment and weight-loss aids.

The FTC has issued guidelines to help online businesses comply with existing laws prohibiting deceptive advertising.[4] These guidelines include three basic requirements:

1. All ads—both online and offline—must be truthful and not misleading.
2. The claims made in an ad must be substantiated; that is, advertisers must have evidence to back up their claims.
3. Ads cannot be unfair, which the FTC defines as "likely to cause substantial consumer injury that

---

3. 16 C.F.R. Part 238.

4. "Advertising and Marketing on the Internet: Rules of the Road." *www.ftc.com.* September 2000: n.p. Web.

consumers could not reasonably avoid and that is not outweighed by the benefit to consumers or competition."

The guidelines also call for "clear and conspicuous" disclosure of any qualifying or limiting information. The overall impression of the ad is important in meeting this requirement. The FTC suggests that advertisers should assume that consumers will not read an entire Web page. Therefore, to satisfy the "clear and conspicuous" requirement, the disclosure should be placed as close as possible to the claim being qualified or be included within the claim itself. If such placement is not feasible, the next-best location is on a section of the page to which a consumer can easily scroll. Generally, hyperlinks to a disclosure are recommended only for lengthy disclosures or for disclosures that must be repeated in several locations on the Web page.

FTC Actions against Deceptive Advertising

The FTC receives complaints from many sources, including competitors of alleged violators, consumers, consumer organizations, trade associations, Better Business Bureaus, government organizations, and state and local officials. When the agency receives numerous and widespread complaints about a particular problem, it will investigate.

THE COMPLAINT ORDER If the FTC concludes that a given advertisement is unfair or deceptive, it drafts a formal complaint, which is sent to the alleged offender. The company may agree to settle the complaint without further proceedings. If not, the FTC can conduct a hearing in which the company can present its defense (see Chapter 6).

THE CEASE-AND-DESIST ORDER If the FTC succeeds in proving that an advertisement is unfair or deceptive, it usually issues a *cease-and-desist order* (see page 517) requiring the company to stop the challenged advertising. In some circumstances, it may also impose a sanction known as **counteradvertising,** which requires the company to advertise anew—in print, on the Internet, on radio, and on television—to inform the public about the earlier misinformation. The FTC sometimes institutes a **multiple product order,** which requires a firm to cease and desist from false advertising in regard to all of its products, not just the product that was the subject of the original action. When a company's deceptive ad leads to wrongful payments by consumers, the FTC may seek other remedies, including restitution.

CASE IN POINT Verity International, Ltd., billed phone-line subscribers who accessed certain online pornography sites at the rate for international calls to Madagascar. When consumers complained about the charges, Verity told them that the charges were valid and had to be paid, or the consumers would face further collection activity. A federal appellate court held that this representation of "uncontestability" was deceptive and a violation of the FTC Act. The court ordered Verity to pay nearly $18 million in restitution to consumers.[5]

Telemarketing and Fax Advertising

The Telephone Consumer Protection Act (TCPA)[6] prohibits telephone solicitation using an automatic telephone dialing system or a prerecorded voice. In addition, most states have statutes regulating telephone solicitation. The TCPA also makes it illegal to transmit ads via fax without first obtaining the recipient's permission. (Similar issues have arisen with respect to junk e-mail, called *spam*—see page 290.)

The Federal Communications Commission (FCC) enforces the act. The FCC imposes substantial fines ($11,000 each day) on companies that violate the junk fax provisions of the act and has even fined one company as much as $5.4 million.[7] The TCPA also gives consumers a right to sue for either $500 for each violation of the act or for the actual monetary losses resulting from a violation, whichever is greater. If a court finds that a defendant willfully or knowingly violated the act, the court has the discretion to treble (triple) the amount of damages awarded.

The Telemarketing and Consumer Fraud and Abuse Prevention Act of 1994[8] directed the FTC to establish rules governing telemarketing and to bring actions against fraudulent telemarketers. The FTC's Telemarketing Sales Rule (TSR)[9] requires a telemarketer to identify the seller's name, describe the product being sold, and disclose all material facts related to the sale (such as the total cost of the goods being sold). The TSR makes it illegal for telemarketers to misrepresent information or facts about their goods

---

5. *Federal Trade Commission v. Verity International, Ltd.,* 443 F.3d 48 (2d Cir. 2006).
6. 47 U.S.C. Sections 227 *et seq.*
7. See *Missouri ex rel. Nixon v. American Blast Fax, Inc.,* 323 F.3d 649 (8th Cir. 2003); *cert.* denied, 540 U.S. 1104, 124 S.Ct. 1043, 157 L.Ed.2d 888 (2004).
8. 15 U.S.C. Sections 6101–6108.
9. 15 U.S.C. Sections 1331–1341.

or services. A telemarketer must also remove a consumer's name from its list of potential contacts if the customer so requests. An amendment to the TSR established the national Do Not Call Registry. Telemarketers must refrain from calling those consumers who have placed their names on the list. Significantly, the TSR applies to any offer made to consumers in the United States—even if the offer comes from a foreign firm. Thus, the TSR helps to protect consumers from illegal cross-border telemarketing operations.

SECTION 2
LABELING AND PACKAGING LAWS

A number of federal and state laws deal specifically with the information given on labels and packages. In general, labels must be accurate, and they must use words that are easily understood by the ordinary consumer. For example, a box of cereal cannot be labeled "giant" if that would exaggerate the amount of cereal contained in the box.

In some instances, labels must specify the raw materials used in the product, such as the percentage of cotton, nylon, or other fiber used in a garment. In other instances, the product must carry a warning. Cigarette packages and advertising, for example, must include one of several warnings about the health hazards associated with smoking.[10]

Federal Statutes

Numerous federal laws regulate the labeling and packaging of products. These include the Wool Products Labeling Act of 1939,[11] the Fur Products Labeling Act of 1951,[12] the Flammable Fabrics Act of 1953,[13] and the Fair Packaging and Labeling Act of 1966.[14] The Comprehensive Smokeless Tobacco Health Education Act of 1986[15] requires producers, packagers, and importers of smokeless tobacco to include one of several warnings about the use of smokeless tobacco on the labels of their products.

The Energy Policy and Conservation Act of 1975[16] requires automakers to attach an information label to every new car. This label must include the Environmental Protection Agency's fuel economy estimate for the vehicle. In the following case, the buyer of a new car complained that the vehicle had failed to achieve the fuel economy estimate advertised in the automaker's brochure and listed on the label.

---

10. 15 U.S.C. Sections 1331–1341.
11. 15 U.S.C. Section 68.
12. 15 U.S.C. Section 69.
13. 15 U.S.C. Section 1191.
14. 15 U.S.C. Sections 1451 *et seq.*
15. 15 U.S.C. Sections 4501–4508.
16. 49 U.S.C. Section 32908(b)(1).

CASE 24.2
Paduano v. American Honda Motor Co.

California Court of Appeal, Fourth District, 169 Cal.App.4th 1453, 88 Cal.Rptr.3d 90 (2009).

BACKGROUND AND FACTS • In 2004, Gaetano Paduano bought a new Honda Civic Hybrid in California. The information label on the car stated that the fuel economy estimates from the Environmental Protection Agency (EPA) were forty-seven miles per gallon (mpg) and forty-eight mpg for city and highway driving, respectively. Honda's sales brochure added, "Just drive the Hybrid like you would a conventional car and save on fuel bills." Paduano soon became frustrated with the car's fuel economy, which was less than half of the EPA's estimate. When American Honda Motor Company refused to repurchase the vehicle, Paduano filed a suit in a California state court against the automaker, alleging deceptive advertising in violation of the state's Consumer Legal Remedies Act and Unfair Competition Law. Honda argued that the federal Energy Policy and Conservation Act (EPCA), which prescribed the EPA's fuel economy estimate, preempted Paduano's claims (preemption was discussed in Chapter 5 on page 102). The court issued a summary judgment in Honda's favor. Paduano appealed to a state intermediate appellate court.

IN THE LANGUAGE OF THE COURT
AARON, J. [Judge]
* * * *

The basic rules of preemption are not in dispute: *Under the supremacy clause of the United States Constitution, Congress has the power to preempt state law concerning matters that lie within the authority of Congress. In determining whether federal law preempts state*

CASE 24.2 CONTINUED ▶ *law, a court's task is to discern congressional intent.* Congress's express intent in this regard will be found when Congress explicitly states that it is preempting state authority. [Emphasis added.]

* * * *

Honda * * * argues that [the EPCA] prevents Paduano from pursuing his * * * claims. That provision states in pertinent part,

> When a requirement under [the EPCA] is in effect, a State or a political subdivision of a State may adopt or enforce a law or regulation on disclosure of fuel economy or fuel operating costs for an automobile covered by [the EPCA] only if the law or regulation is identical to that requirement.

* * * Honda goes on to assert that "Paduano's deceptive advertising and misrepresentation claims would impose *non* identical disclosure requirements."

Contrary to Honda's characterization * * * , Paduano's claims are based on statements Honda made in its advertising brochure to the effect that one may drive a Civic Hybrid in the same manner as one would a conventional car, and need not do anything "special," in order to achieve the beneficial fuel economy of the EPA estimates. * * * Paduano is challenging * * * Honda's * * * commentary in which it alludes to those estimates in a manner that may give consumers the misimpression that they will be able to achieve mileage close to the EPA estimates while driving a Honda hybrid in the same manner as they would a conventional vehicle. Paduano does not seek to require Honda to provide "additional alleged facts" regarding the Civic Hybrid's fuel economy, as Honda suggests, but rather, seeks to prevent Honda from making misleading claims about how easy it is to achieve better fuel economy. Contrary to Honda's assertions, if Paduano were to prevail on his claims, Honda would not have to do anything differently with regard to its disclosure of the EPA mileage estimates.

* * * *

* * * Allowing states to regulate false advertising and unfair business practices may further the goals of the EPCA, and we reject Honda's claim.

DECISION AND REMEDY • *The state intermediate appellate court concluded that federal law did not preempt Paduano's claims concerning Honda's advertising. The court reversed the judgment and remanded the case.*

THE ETHICAL DIMENSION • *Suppose that the defendant automaker had opposed this action solely to avoid paying for a car that had proved to be a "lemon." Would this have been unethical? Explain.*

THE LEGAL ENVIRONMENT DIMENSION • *What does the interpretation of the law in this case suggest to businesspersons who sell products labeled with statements mandated by federal or state law?*

Food Labeling

Because the quality and safety of food are so important to consumers, several statutes deal specifically with food labeling. The Fair Packaging and Labeling Act requires that food product labels identify (1) the product; (2) the net quantity of the contents and, if the number of servings is stated, the size of a serving; (3) the manufacturer; and (4) the packager or distributor. The act includes additional requirements concerning descriptions on packages, savings claims, components of nonfood products, and standards for the partial filling of packages.

Food products must bear labels detailing the nutritional content, including the number of calories and the amounts of various nutrients that the food contains. The Nutrition Labeling and Education Act of 1990[17] requires food labels to provide standard nutrition facts (including the amount and type of fat that the food contains) and regulates the use of such terms as *fresh* and *low fat*. The U.S. Food and Drug Administration (FDA) and the U.S. Department of Agriculture are the primary agencies that issue regulations on food labeling. These rules are published in the *Federal Register* and updated annually.

New rules that became effective in 2009 require the labels on fresh meats, vegetables, and fruits to indicate where the food originated so that consumers can know whether their food was imported. See

---

17. 21 U.S.C. Section 343.1.

Tucked into the 2,700-page health-care reform bill that President Obama signed into law in March 2010 was a provision aimed at combating the problem of obesity in the United States. The provision requires all restaurant chains with twenty or more locations to post the caloric content of the foods on their menus so that customers will know how many calories they are eating.[a] The hope is that customers, armed with this information, will consider the number of calories when they make their food choices. The new federal law will supersede all state and local laws already in existence.

What the Law Does and Does Not Cover

The law now directs the U.S. Food and Drug Administration (FDA) to create a new national standard for menu labeling and to establish specific regulations supporting that standard—a task that will take at least a year. Nevertheless, the outlines of the new requirement are clear. Any restaurant to which the law applies will have to post the caloric content of the foods listed on its standard menu, menu boards, or menu lists for drive-thru windows. Signs will also have to be posted near salad bars and buffets, providing information on the foods offered there. Exempt from the rules are condiments, daily specials, and foods offered for only a limited period (less than sixty days). In addition, restaurants will be required to post standard guidelines on the number of calories that an average person requires daily so that customers can

determine what portion of a day's calories a particular food choice will provide.

The law applies to foods offered through vending machines. The foods most affected will be those that do not list the number of calories on the front of the package.

The Law Will Spur Innovations

Restaurant chains affected by the new law will likely be forced to innovate as customers discover how many calories some of their favorite foods contain. Some customers, for example, may be surprised to learn that a Big Mac hamburger from McDonald's provides 540 calories—more than a quarter of the 2,000 calories needed by an average adult each day. The restaurant chains will have to create lower-calorie foods that taste as good as their high-calorie popular items. Some chains are already doing just that. Dunkin' Donuts has launched a lower-calorie DDSmart option. KFC now offers grilled chicken, and Starbucks has switched to lower-fat milk for espresso-based drinks.

MANAGERIAL IMPLICATIONS

Although the new requirements currently apply only to restaurant chains with twenty or more locations, managers in other restaurant situations can anticipate that calorie-posting requirements will eventually affect them. The FDA may even decide to impose criminal penalties on those who violate the calorie-posting requirements. Therefore, managers throughout the food-services industry should start thinking now about how they are going to comply with any calorie-posting requirements in the future. It is always less costly to introduce change gradually than all at once.

---

a. See Section 4205 of the Patient Protection and Affordable Care Act, H.R. 3590, passed by Congress on March 21, 2010 (also see the Health Care and Education Reconciliation Act of 2010, H.R. 4872).

---

this chapter's *Shifting Legal Priorities for Business* feature above for a discussion of a new requirement imposed on restaurant chains by the health-care legislation enacted in 2010.

SECTION 3
SALES

A number of statutes protect consumers by requiring the disclosure of certain terms in sales transactions and providing rules governing unsolicited merchandise and various forms of sales, such as door-to-door

sales, mail-order sales, and referral sales. The FTC has regulatory authority in this area, as do other federal agencies. The Federal Reserve Board of Governors, for example, has issued **Regulation Z**,[18] which governs credit provisions associated with sales contracts, as will be discussed later in this chapter. Many states and the FTC have **"cooling-off" laws** that permit the buyers of goods sold door to door to cancel their contracts within three business days. The FTC rule further requires that consumers be notified in Spanish of this right if the oral negotiations for the sale were in that language.

---

18. 12 C.F.R. Sections 226.1–226.30.

Telephone and Mail-Order Sales

The FTC Mail or Telephone Order Merchandise Rule of 1993 amended the FTC Mail-Order Rule of 1975.[19] The rule provides specific protections for consumers who purchase goods over the phone, through the mail, online via computer, or by fax machine. Among other things, the rule requires merchants to ship orders within the time promised in their catalogues or advertisements and to notify consumers when orders cannot be shipped on time. The rule also requires merchants to issue a refund within a specified period of time when a consumer cancels an order.

In addition, under the Postal Reorganization Act of 1970,[20] a consumer who receives *unsolicited* merchandise sent by U.S. mail can keep it, throw it away, or dispose of it in any manner that she or he sees fit. The recipient will not be obligated to the sender.

Online Sales

The FTC and other federal agencies have brought numerous enforcement actions against those who perpetrate online fraud (see the discussion of wire fraud in Chapter 7). Nonetheless, protecting consumers from fraudulent and deceptive sales practices conducted via the Internet has proved to be a challenging task. The number of consumers who have fallen prey to Internet fraud has actually grown in recent years. Faced with economic recession, job losses, mounting debt, and dwindling savings, many consumers are looking for any source of income. Complaints to the FTC about sales of fraudulent business opportunities, such as work-at-home offers and real estate systems, nearly doubled from 2008 to 2009, and nearly tripled in the first six months of 2010.

────────── SECTION 4 ──────────
CREDIT PROTECTION

Credit protection is one of the more important aspects of consumer protection legislation. Nearly 80 percent of U.S. consumers have credit cards, and most carry a balance on these cards, which amounts to about $2.5 trillion of debt nationwide. In 2010, Congress established a new agency, the Consumer Financial Protection Bureau, which is dedicated to overseeing the practices of banks, mortgage lenders, and credit-card companies.[21] We discuss significant consumer credit protection legislation next.

The Truth-in-Lending Act

A key statute regulating the credit and credit-card industries is Title I of the Consumer Credit Protection Act,[22] which is commonly referred to as the Truth-in-Lending Act (TILA). The TILA has been amended several times, most recently in 2009, when Congress passed sweeping reforms to strengthen its consumer protections.[23]

The TILA is basically a *disclosure law*. It is administered by the Federal Reserve Board and requires sellers and lenders to disclose credit terms or loan terms so that individuals can shop around for the best financing arrangements. TILA requirements apply only to persons who, in the ordinary course of business, lend funds, sell on credit, or arrange for the extension of credit. Thus, sales or loans made between two consumers do not come under the protection of the act. Additionally, this law protects only debtors who are natural persons (as opposed to the artificial "person" of a corporation). It does not extend to other legal entities.

DISCLOSURE REQUIREMENTS The disclosure requirements are contained in Regulation Z. If the contracting parties are subject to the TILA, the requirements of Regulation Z apply to any transaction involving an installment sales contract that calls for payment to be made in more than four installments. Transactions subject to Regulation Z typically include installment loans, retail and installment sales, car loans, home-improvement loans, and certain real estate loans if the amount of financing is less than $25,000.

Under the provisions of the TILA, all of the terms of a credit instrument must be clearly and conspicuously disclosed. A lender must disclose the annual percentage rate (APR), finance charge, amount financed, and total payments (the sum of the amount loaned, plus any fees, finance charges, and interest at the end of the loan). The TILA provides for contract rescission (cancellation) if a creditor

---

19. 16 C.F.R. Sections 435.1–435.2.
20. 39 U.S.C. Section 3009.

21. Title 10 of the Restoring American Financial Stability Act of 2010, S.B. 3217, April 15, 2010.
22. 15 U.S.C. Sections 1601–1693r.
23. The TILA was amended in 1980 by the Truth-in-Lending Simplification and Reform Act. It was significantly amended again in 2009 by the Credit Card Accountability, Responsibility, and Disclosure Act of 2009, Pub. L. No. 111-24, 123 Stat. 1734, enacting 15 U.S.C. Sections 1616, 1651, 1665c–1665e, 1666b, 1666i-1, 1666i-2, and 1693l-1, and 16 U.S.C. Section 1a-7b, as well as amending many other provisions of the TILA.

fails to follow *exactly* the procedures required by the act.[24]

EQUAL CREDIT OPPORTUNITY In 1974, Congress enacted the Equal Credit Opportunity Act (ECOA)[25] as an amendment to the TILA. The ECOA prohibits the denial of credit solely on the basis of race, religion, national origin, color, gender, marital status, or age. The act also prohibits credit discrimination on the basis of whether an individual receives certain forms of income, such as public-assistance benefits.

Under the ECOA, a creditor may not require the signature of an applicant's spouse, except as a joint applicant, on a credit instrument if the applicant qualifies under the creditor's standards of creditworthiness for the amount and terms of the credit request.

CASE IN POINT Tonja, an African American, applied for financing with a used-car dealer. The dealer looked at Tonja's credit report and, without submitting the application to the lender, decided that she would not qualify. Instead of informing Tonja that she did not qualify, the dealer told her that she needed a cosigner on the loan to purchase the car. She filed a complaint. According to a federal appellate court, the dealer qualified as a creditor in this situation because the dealer unilaterally denied the credit and thus could be held liable under the ECOA.[26]

CREDIT-CARD RULES The TILA also contains provisions regarding credit cards. One provision limits the liability of a cardholder to $50 per card for unauthorized charges made before the creditor is notified that the card has been lost. If a consumer receives an *unsolicited* credit card in the mail that is later stolen, the company that issued the card cannot charge the consumer for any unauthorized charges. Another provision requires credit-card companies to disclose the balance computation method that is used to determine the outstanding balance and to state when finance charges begin to accrue. Other provisions set forth procedures for resolving billing disputes with the credit-card company. These procedures are used if, for example, a cardholder thinks that an error has occurred in billing or wishes to withhold payment for a faulty product purchased by credit card.

ADDITIONAL CREDIT-CARD PROTECTION In 2009, President Barack Obama signed into law amendments to the credit-card protections of the TILA. The most significant provisions of the new rules impose the following requirements on credit-card companies:

1. A company may not retroactively increase the interest rates on existing card balances, unless the account is sixty days delinquent.
2. A company must provide forty-five days' advance notice to consumers before changing the credit-card terms.
3. Monthly bills must be sent to cardholders twenty-one days before the due date.
4. The interest rate charged on a customer's credit-card balance may not be increased except in specific situations, such as when a promotional rate ends.
5. A company may not charge over-limit fees except in specified situations.
6. When the customer has balances at different interest rates, payments in excess of the minimum amount due must be applied first to the balance with the highest rate (for example, a higher interest rate is commonly charged for cash advances).
7. A company may not compute finance charges based on the previous billing cycle (a practice known as double-cycle billing, which hurts consumers because they are charged interest for the previous cycle even though they have paid the bill in full).

CONSUMER LEASES The Consumer Leasing Act (CLA) of 1988[27] amended the TILA to provide protection for consumers who lease automobiles and other goods. The CLA applies to those who lease or arrange to lease consumer goods in the ordinary course of their business. The act applies only if the goods are priced at $25,000 or less and if the lease term exceeds four months. The CLA and its implementing regulation, Regulation M,[28] require lessors to disclose in writing (or by electronic record) all of the material terms of the lease.

The Fair Credit Reporting Act

The Fair Credit Reporting Act (FCRA)[29] protects consumers against inaccurate credit reporting and requires that lenders and other creditors report correct, relevant, and up-to-date information. The act

---

24. Note, however, that amendments to the TILA enacted in 1995 prevent borrowers from rescinding loans because of minor clerical errors in closing documents [15 U.S.C. Sections 1605, 1631, 1635, 1640, and 1641].
25. 15 U.S.C. Sections 1691–1691f.
26. *Treadway v. Gateway Chevrolet Oldsmobile, Inc.,* 362 F.3d 971 (7th Cir. 2004).

27. 15 U.S.C. Sections 1667–1667e.
28. 12 C.F.R. Part 213.
29. 15 U.S.C. Sections 1681–1681t.

provides that consumer credit reporting agencies may issue credit reports to users only for specified purposes, including the extension of credit, the issuance of insurance policies, and compliance with a court order, and in response to a consumer's request for a copy of his or her own credit report.

CONSUMER NOTIFICATION AND INACCURATE INFORMATION Any time a consumer is denied credit or insurance on the basis of her or his credit report, the consumer must be notified of that fact and of the name and address of the credit reporting agency that issued the report. The same notice must be sent to consumers who are charged more than others ordinarily would be for credit or insurance because of their credit reports.

Under the FCRA, consumers may request the source of any information used by the credit agency, as well as the identity of anyone who has received an agency's report. Consumers are also permitted to access the information about them contained in a credit reporting agency's files. If a consumer discovers that an agency's files contain inaccurate information, he or she should report the problem to the agency. On the consumer's written request, the agency must conduct a systematic examination of its records. Any unverifiable or erroneous information must be deleted within a reasonable period of time.

REMEDIES FOR VIOLATIONS A credit reporting agency that fails to comply with the act is liable for actual damages, plus additional damages not to exceed $1,000 and attorneys' fees.[30] Creditors and other companies that use information from credit reporting agencies may also be liable for violations of the FCRA. In 2007, the United States Supreme Court held that an insurance company's failure to notify new customers that they were paying higher insurance rates as a result of their credit scores was a *willful* violation of the FCRA.[31]

CASE IN POINT Rex Saunders obtained an auto loan from Branch Banking & Trust Company of Virginia (BB&T), which failed to give Saunders a payment coupon book and rebuffed his attempts to make payments on the loan. In fact, BB&T told him that it had not extended a loan to him. Eventually, BB&T discovered its mistake and demanded full payment, plus interest and penalties. When payment was not immediately forthcoming, BB&T declared that Saunders was in default. It then repossessed the car and forwarded adverse credit information about Saunders to credit reporting agencies, without noting that Saunders disputed the information. Saunders filed a lawsuit alleging violations of the FCRA and was awarded $80,000 in punitive damages. An appellate court found that the damages award was reasonable, given BB&T's willful violation.[32]

The Fair and Accurate Credit Transactions Act

In an effort to combat identity theft (discussed in Chapter 7), Congress passed the Fair and Accurate Credit Transactions (FACT) Act of 2003.[33] The act established a national fraud alert system so that consumers who suspect that they have been or may be victimized by identity theft can place an alert on their credit files. The act also requires the major credit reporting agencies to provide consumers with free copies of their own credit reports every twelve months.

Another provision requires account numbers on credit-card receipts to be truncated (shortened) so that merchants, employees, or others who may have access to the receipts do not have the consumers' names and full credit-card numbers. The act further mandates that financial institutions work with the FTC to identify "red flag" indicators of identity theft and to develop rules for the disposal of sensitive credit information.

The FACT Act gives consumers who have been victimized by identity theft some assistance in rebuilding their credit reputations. For example, credit reporting agencies must stop reporting allegedly fraudulent account information once the consumer establishes that identify theft has occurred. Business owners and creditors are required to provide consumers with copies of any records that can help the consumer prove that a particular account or transaction is fraudulent (records showing that a fraudulent signature was used in the creation of an account, for example). In addition, the act allows consumers to report the accounts affected by identity theft directly to creditors in order to help prevent the spread of erroneous credit information.

---

30. 15 U.S.C. Section 1681n.

31. *Safeco Insurance. Co. of America v. Burr,* 551 U.S. 47, 127 S.Ct. 2201, 167 L.Ed.2d 1045 (2007).

32. *Saunders v. Branch Banking & Trust Co. of Virginia,* 526 F.3d 142 (4th Cir. 2008).

33. Pub. L. No. 108-159, 117 Stat. 1952 (December 4, 2003).

The Fair Debt Collection Practices Act

In 1977, Congress enacted the Fair Debt Collection Practices Act (FDCPA)[34] in an attempt to curb perceived abuses by collection agencies. The act applies only to specialized debt-collection agencies and attorneys who regularly attempt to collect debts on behalf of someone else, usually for a percentage of the amount owed. Creditors attempting to collect debts are not covered by the act unless, by misrepresenting themselves, they cause debtors to believe they are collection agencies.

PROHIBITED DEBT-COLLECTION TACTICS Under the FDCPA, a collection agency may not do any of the following:

1. Contact the debtor at the debtor's place of employment if the debtor's employer objects.
2. Contact the debtor at inconvenient or unusual times (for example, at three o'clock in the morning) or at any time, if the debtor is being represented by an attorney.
3. Contact third parties other than the debtor's parents, spouse, or financial adviser about payment of a debt unless a court authorizes such action.
4. Harass or intimidate the debtor (by using abusive language or threatening violence, for example) or make false or misleading statements (such as posing as a police officer).

5. Communicate with the debtor at any time after receiving notice that the debtor is refusing to pay the debt, except to advise the debtor of further action to be taken by the collection agency.

NOTIFICATION AND BONA FIDE ERRORS The FDCPA also requires a collection agency to include a **validation notice** whenever it initially contacts a debtor for payment of a debt or within five days of that initial contact. The notice must state that the debtor has thirty days in which to dispute the debt and to request a written verification of the debt from the collection agency. A debt collector who fails to comply with the act is liable for actual damages, plus additional damages not to exceed $1,000[35] and attorneys' fees.

Debt collectors who violate the act are exempt from liability if they can show that the violation was not intentional and "resulted from a bona fide error notwithstanding the maintenance of procedures reasonably adapted to avoid any such error." The "bona fide error" defense typically has been applied to mistakes of fact or clerical errors. Should the defense also apply to mistakes of law? In other words, if a debt collector violates the act because of a mistaken interpretation of the legal requirements of the FDCPA, can the debt collector avoid liability under the act? That was the issue in the following case.

---

34. 15 U.S.C. Section 1692.

35. According to the U.S. Court of Appeals for the Sixth Circuit, the $1,000 limit on damages applies to each lawsuit, not to each violation. See *Wright v. Finance Service of Norwalk, Inc.,* 22 F.3d 647 (6th Cir. 1994).

※ EXTENDED CASE 24.3 ※
Jerman v. Carlisle, McNellie, Rini, Kramer & Ulrich, LPA

Supreme Court of the United States, ___ U.S. ___, 130 S.Ct. 1605, 176 L.Ed.2d 519 (2010).

IN THE LANGUAGE OF THE COURT
Justice *SOTOMAYOR* delivered the opinion of the Court.
* * * *
Respondents in this case are a law firm, Carlisle, McNellie, Rini, Kramer & Ulrich, L.P.A., [Legal Professional Association], and one of its attorneys, Adrienne S. Foster (collectively Carlisle). In April 2006, Carlisle filed a complaint in Ohio

state court on behalf of a client, Countrywide Home Loans, Inc. Carlisle sought foreclosure of a mortgage held by Countrywide in real property owned by petitioner Karen L. Jerman. The complaint included a "Notice," later served on Jerman, stating that the mortgage debt would be assumed to be valid unless Jerman disputed it in writing. Jerman's lawyer sent a letter disputing the debt, and Carlisle sought verification from Countrywide. When Countrywide

acknowledged that Jerman had, in fact, already paid the debt in full, Carlisle withdrew the foreclosure lawsuit.

Jerman then filed her own lawsuit seeking * * * damages under the FDCPA [Fair Debt Collection Practices Act], contending that Carlisle violated [the act] by stating that her debt would be assumed valid unless she disputed it in writing. While acknowledging a division of authority on the

EXTENDED CASE 24.3 CONTINUED ▶

question, the District Court held that Carlisle had violated [the act] by requiring Jerman to dispute the debt in writing. The court ultimately granted summary judgment to Carlisle, however, concluding that Section 1692k(c) [of the FDCPA] shielded it from liability because the violation was not intentional, resulted from a bona fide error, and occurred despite the maintenance of procedures reasonably adapted to avoid any such error. The Court of Appeals for the Sixth Circuit affirmed. Acknowledging that the Courts of Appeals are divided regarding the scope of the bona fide error defense, and that the "majority view is that the defense is available for clerical and factual errors only," the Sixth Circuit nonetheless held that Section 1692k(c) extends to "mistakes of law."

* * * *

The parties disagree about whether a "violation" resulting from a debt collector's misinterpretation of the legal requirements of the FDCPA can ever be "not intentional" under 1692k(c). Jerman contends that when a debt collector intentionally commits the act giving rise to the violation (here, sending a notice that included the "in writing" language), a misunderstanding about what the Act requires cannot render the violation "not intentional," given the general rule that mistake or ignorance of law is no defense. Carlisle and the dissent, in contrast, argue that nothing in the statutory text excludes legal errors from the category of "bona fide error[s]" covered by 1692k(c) and note that the Act refers not to an unintentional "act" but rather an unintentional "violation." The latter

term, they contend, evinces [makes clear] Congress' intent to impose liability only when a party knows its conduct is unlawful. Carlisle urges us, therefore, to read 1692k(c) to encompass "all types of error," including mistakes of law.

We decline to adopt the expansive reading of Section 1692k(c) that Carlisle proposes. *We have long recognized the "common maxim, familiar to all minds, that ignorance of the law will not excuse any person, either civilly or criminally." Our law is therefore no stranger to the possibility that an act may be "intentional" for purposes of civil liability, even if the actor lacked actual knowledge that her conduct violated the law.* [Emphasis added.]

* * * When Congress has intended to provide a mistake-of-law defense to civil liability, it has often done so more explicitly than here. In particular, the FTC [Federal Trade Commission] Act's administrative-penalty provisions—which * * * Congress expressly incorporated into the FDCPA—apply only when a debt collector acts with "actual knowledge or knowledge fairly implied on the basis of objective circumstances" that its action was "prohibited by [the FDCPA]." Given the absence of similar language in Section 1692k(c), it is a fair inference that Congress chose to permit injured consumers to recover actual damages, costs, fees, and modest statutory damages for "intentional" conduct, including violations resulting from mistaken interpretation of the FDCPA, while reserving the more onerous penalties of the FTC Act for debt collectors whose intentional actions also reflected "knowledge fairly implied on the basis of objective circumstances" that the conduct was prohibited.

* * * *

We draw additional support for the conclusion that bona fide errors in Section 1692k(c) do not include mistaken interpretations of the FDCPA from the requirement that a debt collector maintain "procedures reasonably adapted to avoid any such error." The dictionary defines "procedure" as "a series of steps followed in a regular orderly definite way." In that light, the statutory phrase is more naturally read to apply to processes that have mechanical or other such "regular orderly" steps to avoid mistakes—for instance, the kind of internal controls a debt collector might adopt to ensure its employees do not communicate with consumers at the wrong time of day or make false representations as to the amount of a debt. * * * We do not dispute that some entities may maintain procedures to avoid legal errors. But legal reasoning is not a mechanical or strictly linear process. For this reason, we find * * * that the broad statutory requirement of procedures reasonably designed to avoid "any" bona fide error indicates that the relevant procedures are ones that help to avoid errors like clerical or factual mistakes. Such procedures are more likely to avoid error than those applicable to legal reasoning, particularly in the context of a comprehensive and complex federal statute such as the FDCPA that imposes open-ended prohibitions on, *inter alia* [among other things], "false, deceptive," or "unfair" practices.

* * * *

For the reasons discussed above, the judgment of the United States Court of Appeals for the Sixth Circuit is reversed, and the case is remanded for further proceedings consistent with this opinion.

 QUESTIONS

1. One of the concerns raised by Carlisle was that if attorneys could be held liable for their reasonable misinterpretations of the FDCPA's requirements, there would be a "flood of lawsuits" against creditors' attorneys by plaintiffs seeking damages and attorneys' fees. Should this concern have any bearing on the outcome of this case? Why or why not?
2. Jerman's attorneys contended that if the Court agreed with Carlisle's argument (that the bona fide error defense included errors in legal interpretation), ethical debt collectors would be placed at a disadvantage. Why would this be?

Garnishment of Wages

Despite the increasing number of protections afforded debtors, creditors are not without means of securing payment on debts. One of these is the right to garnish a debtor's wages after the debt has gone unpaid for a prolonged period. Recall from Chapter 15 that in a garnishment process, a creditor directly attaches, or seizes, a portion of the debtor's assets (such as wages) that are in the possession of a third party (such as an employer).

State law governs the garnishment process, but the law varies among the states as to how easily garnishment can be obtained. Indeed, a few states, such as Texas, prohibit garnishment of wages except for child support and court-approved spousal maintenance. Constitutional due process and federal legislation under the TILA also provide certain protections against abuse.[36] In general, the debtor is entitled to notice and an opportunity to be heard. Moreover, wages cannot be garnished beyond 25 percent of the debtor's after-tax earnings, and the garnishment must leave the debtor with at least a specified minimum income.

SECTION 5

CONSUMER HEALTH AND SAFETY

The laws discussed earlier regarding the labeling and packaging of products are intended to promote consumer health and safety. Nevertheless, there is a significant distinction between regulating the information dispensed about a product and regulating the actual content of the product. The classic example is tobacco products. Producers of tobacco products are required to warn consumers about the hazards associated with the use of their products, but the sale of tobacco products has not been subjected to significant restrictions or banned outright, despite the obvious dangers to health.[37] Here, we examine various laws that regulate the actual products made available to consumers.

The Federal Food, Drug and Cosmetic Act

The first federal legislation regulating food and drugs was enacted in 1906 as the Pure Food and Drugs Act.

That law, as amended in 1938, exists today as the Federal Food, Drug and Cosmetic Act (FFDCA).[38] The act protects consumers against adulterated and misbranded foods and drugs. As to foods, in its present form, the act establishes food standards, specifies safe levels of potentially hazardous food additives, and sets classifications of foods and food advertising. Most of these statutory requirements are monitored and enforced by the Food and Drug Administration (FDA).

The FFDCA also charges the FDA with the responsibility of ensuring that drugs are safe and effective before they are marketed to the public. Because the FDA must ensure the safety of new medications, there is always a delay before drugs are available to the public, and this sometimes leads to controversy.

CASE IN POINT A group of terminally ill patients claimed that they were entitled, under the U.S. Constitution, to access experimental drugs before the FDA completed its clinical tests. The court, however, found that the FDA's policy of limiting access to drugs undergoing tests was rationally related to protecting patients from potentially unsafe drugs. Therefore, the court held that terminally ill patients do not have a fundamental constitutional right of access to experimental drugs.[39]

The Consumer Product Safety Act

As early as 1953, Congress began enacting laws to protect consumers from specific classes of unsafe products, such as highly flammable clothing or materials. Then, in 1972, Congress enacted the Consumer Product Safety Act,[40] which created the first comprehensive scheme of regulation over matters of consumer safety. The act also established the Consumer Product Safety Commission (CPSC), which has far-reaching authority over consumer safety.

THE CPSC'S AUTHORITY The CPSC conducts research on the safety of individual consumer products and maintains a clearinghouse on the risks associated with various products. The Consumer Product Safety Act authorizes the CPSC to:

1. Set safety standards for consumer products.
2. Ban the manufacture and sale of any product that the commission believes poses an "unreasonable risk" to consumers. (Products banned by the CPSC have included various types of fireworks,

---

36. 15 U.S.C. Sections 1671–1677.
37. We are ignoring recent civil litigation concerning the liability of tobacco product manufacturers for injuries that arise from the use of tobacco. See, for example, *Philip Morris USA v. Williams*, 549 U.S. 346, 127 S.Ct. 1057, 166 L.Ed.2d 940 (2007).

38. 21 U.S.C. Sections 301–393.
39. *Abigail Alliance for Better Access to Developmental Drugs v. von Eschenbach*, 495 F.3d 695 (D.C.Cir. 2007).
40. 15 U.S.C. Sections 2051–2083.

cribs, and toys, as well as many products containing asbestos or vinyl chloride.)

3. Remove from the market any products it believes to be imminently hazardous. The CPSC's authority is sufficiently broad to allow it to ban any product that it believes poses an "unreasonable risk" to consumers. The CPSC frequently works in conjunction with manufacturers to voluntarily recall defective products from stores.

4. Require manufacturers to report on any products already sold or intended for sale if the products have proved to be hazardous.

5. Administer other product-safety legislation, including the Child Protection and Toy Safety Act of 1969[41] and the Federal Hazardous Substances Act of 1960.[42]

NOTIFICATION REQUIREMENTS The Consumer Product Safety Act requires the distributors of consumer products to notify the CPSC immediately if they receive information that a product "contains a defect which . . . creates a substantial risk to the public" or "an unreasonable risk of serious injury or death."

CASE IN POINT A company that sold juicers received twenty-three letters from customers complaining that during operation the juicer had suddenly exploded, sending pieces of glass and razor-sharp metal across the room. Nevertheless, the company waited more than six months before notifying the CPSC. In a case filed by the federal government, the court held that a company is required to report a problem to the CPSC within twenty-four hours after receiving information about a threat. Even if it must investigate the allegations, the company should not take more than ten days to verify the information and report the problem. The court found that the company had violated the law and ordered it to pay damages.[43]

---

41. 15 U.S.C. Section 1262(e).
42. 15 U.S.C. Sections 1261–1273.

43. *United States v. Mirama Enterprises, Inc.,* 185 F.Supp.2d 1148 (S.D.Cal. 2002).

REVIEWING
Consumer Protection

Leota Sage saw a local motorcycle dealer's newspaper advertisement offering a MetroRider EZ electric scooter for $1,699. When she went to the dealership, however, she learned that the EZ model had been sold out. The salesperson told Sage that he still had the higher-end MetroRider FX model in stock for $2,199 and would sell her one for $1,999. Sage was disappointed but decided to purchase the FX model. When Sage said that she wished to purchase the scooter on credit, she was directed to the dealer's credit department. As she filled out the credit forms, the clerk told Sage, who is an Asian American, that she would need a cosigner to obtain a loan. Sage could not understand why she would need a cosigner and asked to speak to the store manager. The manager apologized, told her that the clerk was mistaken, and said that he would "speak to" the clerk about that. The manager completed Sage's credit application, and Sage then rode the scooter home. Seven months later, Sage received a letter from the manufacturer informing her that a flaw had been discovered in the scooter's braking system and that the model had been recalled. Using the information presented in the chapter, answer the following questions.

1. Did the dealer engage in deceptive advertising? Why or why not?
2. Suppose that Sage had ordered the scooter through the dealer's Web site but that the dealer had been unable to deliver it by the date promised. What would the FTC have required the merchant to do in that situation?
3. Assuming that the clerk required a cosigner based on Sage's race or gender, what act prohibits such credit discrimination?
4. What organization has the authority to ban the sale of scooters based on safety concerns?

DEBATE THIS: *Laws against bait-and-switch advertising should be abolished because no consumer is ever forced to buy anything.*

TERMS AND CONCEPTS

bait-and-switch
  advertising 540

consumer law 538
"cooling-off" laws 544
counteradvertising 541

deceptive advertising 539
multiple product orders 541

Regulation Z 544
validation notice 548

QUESTIONS AND CASE PROBLEMS

24–1. Unsolicited Merchandise Andrew, a resident of California, received an advertising circular in the U.S. mail announcing a new line of regional cookbooks distributed by the Every-Kind Cookbook Co. Andrew didn't want any books and threw the circular away. Two days later, Andrew received in the mail an introductory cookbook entitled *Lower Mongolian Regional Cookbook,* as announced in the circular, on a "trial basis" from Every-Kind. Andrew was not interested but did not go to the trouble to return the cookbook. Every-Kind demanded payment of $20.95 for the *Lower Mongolian Regional Cookbook.* Discuss whether Andrew can be required to pay for the book.

24–2. Credit-Card Rules Maria Ochoa receives two new credit cards on May 1. She has solicited one of them from Midtown Department Store, and the other arrives unsolicited from High-Flying Airlines. During the month of May, Ochoa makes numerous credit-card purchases from Midtown Department Store, but she does not use the High-Flying Airlines card. On May 31, a burglar breaks into Ochoa's home and steals both credit cards, along with other items. Ochoa notifies the Midtown Department Store of the theft on June 2, but she fails to notify High-Flying Airlines. Using the Midtown credit card, the burglar makes a $500 purchase on June 1 and a $200 purchase on June 3. The burglar then charges a vacation flight on the High-Flying Airlines card for $1,000 on June 5. Ochoa receives the bills for these charges and refuses to pay them. Discuss Ochoa's liability for the charges.

24–3. QUESTION WITH SAMPLE ANSWER: Sales.

On June 28, a salesperson for Renowned Books called on the Gonchars at their home. After a very persuasive sales pitch by the agent, the Gonchars agreed in writing to purchase a twenty-volume set of historical encyclopedias from Renowned Books for a total of $299. A down payment of $35 was required, with the remainder of the cost to be paid in monthly payments over a one-year period. Two days later, the Gonchars, having second thoughts, contacted the book company and stated that they had decided to rescind the contract. Renowned Books said this would be impossible. Did Renowned Books violate

any consumer law by not allowing the Gonchars to rescind their contract? Explain.

• **For a sample answer to Question 24–3, go to Appendix F at the end of this text.**

24–4. Fair Credit Reporting Act Source One Associates, Inc., is based in Poughquag, New York. Peter Easton, Source One's president, is responsible for its daily operations. Between 1995 and 1997, Source One received requests from persons in Massachusetts seeking financial information about individuals and businesses. To obtain this information, Easton first obtained the targeted individuals' credit reports through Equifax Consumer Information Services by claiming that the reports would be used only in connection with credit transactions involving the consumers. From the reports, Easton identified financial institutions at which the targeted individuals held accounts. He then called the institutions to learn the account balances by impersonating either officers of the institutions or the account holders. The information was then provided to Source One's customers for a fee. Easton did not know why the customers wanted the information. The state ("commonwealth") of Massachusetts filed a suit in a Massachusetts state court against Source One and Easton, alleging, among other things, violations of the Fair Credit Reporting Act (FCRA). Did the defendants violate the FCRA? Explain. [*Commonwealth v. Source One Associates, Inc.,* 436 Mass. 118, 763 N.E.2d 42 (2002)]

24–5. Food Labeling One of the products that McDonald's Corp. sells is the Happy Meal®, which consists of a McDonald's food entree, a small order of french fries, a small drink, and a toy. In the early 1990s, McDonald's began to aim its Happy Meal marketing at children aged one to three. In 1995, McDonald's began making nutritional information for its food products available in documents known as "McDonald's Nutrition Facts." Each document lists each food item that the restaurant serves and provides a nutritional breakdown, but the Happy Meal is not included. Marc Cohen filed a suit in an Illinois state court against McDonald's, alleging, among other things, that the defendant had violated a state law prohibiting consumer fraud and deceptive business practices by failing to adhere to the Nutrition Labeling and Education Act (NLEA) of 1990. The NLEA sets out different requirements for products specifically intended for children under the age of four—generally, the products' labels cannot declare the percent of daily value of nutritional components. Would this requirement be readily understood by a consumer who is not familiar with nutritional standards? Why or why not? Should a state court impose such regulations? Explain. [*Cohen v. McDonald's Corp.*, 347 Ill.App.3d 627, 808 N.E.2d 1, 283 Ill.Dec. 451 (1 Dist. 2004)]

24–6. Debt Collection 55th Management Corp. in New York City owns residential property that it leases to various tenants. In June 2000, claiming that one of the tenants, Leslie Goldman, owed more than $13,000 in back rent, 55th retained Jeffrey Cohen, an attorney, to initiate nonpayment proceedings. Cohen filed a petition in a New York state court against Goldman, seeking recovery of the unpaid rent and at least $3,000 in attorneys' fees. After receiving notice of the petition, Goldman filed a suit in a federal district court against Cohen. Goldman contended that the notice of the petition constituted an initial contact that, under the Fair Debt Collection Practices Act (FDCPA), required a validation notice. Because Cohen did not give Goldman a validation notice at the time, or within five days, of the notice of the petition, Goldman argued that Cohen was in violation of the FDCPA. Should the filing of a suit in a state court be considered "communication," requiring a debt collector to provide a validation notice under the FDCPA? Why or why not? [*Goldman v. Cohen*, 445 F.3d 152 (2d Cir. 2006)]

24–7. CASE PROBLEM WITH SAMPLE ANSWER: Food Labeling.

The Nutrition Labeling and Education Act (NLEA) requires packaged food to have a "Nutrition Facts" panel that sets out "nutrition information," including "the total number of calories" per serving. Restaurants are exempt from this requirement. The NLEA also regulates nutritional content claims, such as "low sodium," that a purveyor might choose to add to a label. The NLEA permits a state or city to require restaurants to disclose nutrition information about the food they serve, but expressly preempts state or local attempts to regulate nutritional content claims. New York City Health Code Section 81.50 requires 10 percent of the restaurants in the city, including McDonald's, Burger King, and KFC, to post calorie content information on their menus. The New York State Restaurant Association (NYSRA) filed a suit in a federal district court, contending that the NLEA preempts Section 81.50. (Under the U.S. Constitution, state or local laws that conflict with federal laws are preempted.) Is the NYSRA correct? Explain. [New York State Restaurant Association v. New York City Board of Health, 556 F.3d 114 (2d Cir. 2009)]

- **To view a sample answer for Problem 24–7, go to this book's Web site at www.cengage.com/blaw/cross, select "Chapter 24," and click on "Case Problem with Sample Answer."**

24–8. Deceptive Advertising Brian Cleary and Rita Burke filed a suit against the major cigarette maker Philip Morris USA, Inc., seeking class-action status for a claim of deceptive advertising. Cleary and Burke claimed that "light" cigarettes, such as Marlboro Lights, were advertised as safer than regular cigarettes, even though the health effects are the same. They contended that the tobacco companies concealed the true nature of light cigarettes. Philip Morris correctly claimed that it was authorized by the government to advertise cigarettes, including light cigarettes. Assuming that is true, should the plaintiffs still be able to bring a deceptive advertising claim against the tobacco company? Why or why not? [*Cleary v. Philip Morris USA, Inc.*, 683 F.Supp.2d 730 (N.D.Ill. 2010)]

24–9. A QUESTION OF ETHICS: Debt-Collection Practices.

After graduating from law school—and serving time in prison for attempting to collect debts by posing as an FBI agent—Barry Sussman theorized that if a debt-collection business collected only debts that it owned as a result of buying checks written on accounts with insufficient funds (NSF checks), it would not be subject to the Federal Debt Collection Practices Act (FDCPA). Sussman formed Check Investors, Inc., to act on his theory. Check Investors bought more than 2.2 million NSF checks, with an estimated face value of about $348 million, for pennies on the dollar. Check Investors added a fee of $125 or $130 (more than the legal limit in most states) to the face amount of each check and aggressively pursued its drawer to collect. The firm's employees were told to accuse drawers of being criminals and to threaten them with arrest and prosecution. The threats were false. Check Investors never took steps to initiate a prosecution. The employees contacted the drawers' family members and used "saturation phoning"—phoning a drawer numerous times in a short period. They used abusive language, referring to drawers as "deadbeats," "retards," "thieves," and "idiots." Between January 2000 and January 2003, Check Investors netted more than $10.2 million from its efforts. [Federal Trade Commission v. Check Investors, Inc., 502 F.3d 159 (3d Cir. 2007)]

(a) The Federal Trade Commission filed a suit in a federal district court against Check Investors and others, alleging, in part, violations of the FDCPA. Was Check Investors a "debt collector," collecting "debts," within the meaning of the FDCPA? If so, did its methods violate the FDCPA? Were its practices unethical? What might Check Investors argue in its defense? Discuss.

(b) Are "deadbeats" the primary beneficiaries of laws such as the FDCPA? If not, how would you characterize debtors who default on their obligations?

24–10. VIDEO QUESTION: Deceptive Advertising.

Go to this text's Web site at **www.cengage.com/blaw/cross** and select "Chapter 24." Click on "Video Questions" and view the video titled *Advertising Communication Law: Bait and Switch.* Then answer the following questions.

(a) Is the auto dealership's advertisement for the truck in the video deceptive? Why or why not?

(b) Is the advertisement for the truck an offer to which the dealership is bound? Does it matter if Betty detrimentally relied on the advertisement?

(c) Is Tony committed to buying Betty's trade-in truck for $3,000 because that is what he told her over the phone?

LEGAL RESEARCH EXERCISES ON THE WEB

Go to this text's Web site at **www.cengage.com/blaw/cross**, select "Chapter 24," and click on "Practical Internet Exercises." There you will find the following Internet research exercises that you can perform to learn more about the topics covered in this chapter.

Practical Internet Exercise 24–1: **Legal Perspective**
The Food and Drug Administration

Practical Internet Exercise 24–2: **Management Perspective**
Internet Advertising and Marketing

CHAPTER 25
✳
Environmental Law

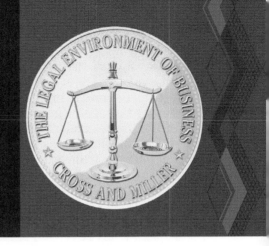

Concern over the degradation of the environment has increased over time in response to the environmental effects of population growth, urbanization, and industrialization. Environmental protection is not without a price, however. For many businesses, the costs of complying with environmental regulations are high, and for some they may seem too high. A constant tension exists between the desire to increase profits and productivity and the need to protect the environment.

In this chapter, we discuss **environmental law**, which consists of all laws and regulations designed to protect and preserve our environmental resources. To a great extent, environmental law consists of statutes passed by federal, state, or local governments and regulations issued by administrative agencies. Before examining statutory and regulatory environmental laws, however, we look at the remedies against environmental pollution that are available under the common law.

SECTION 1
COMMON LAW ACTIONS

Common law remedies against environmental pollution originated centuries ago in England. Those responsible for operations that created dirt, smoke, noxious odors, noise, or toxic substances were sometimes held liable under common law theories of nuisance or negligence. Today, injured individuals continue to rely on the common law to obtain damages and injunctions against business polluters.

Nuisance

Under the common law doctrine of **nuisance,** persons may be held liable if they use their property in a manner that unreasonably interferes with others' rights to use or enjoy their own property. Courts typically balance the harm caused by the pollution against the costs of stopping it. Courts have often denied injunctive relief on the ground that the hardships that would be imposed on the polluter and on the community are greater than the hardships suffered by the plaintiff. For example, a factory that causes neighboring landowners to suffer from smoke, soot, and vibrations may be left in operation if it is the core of the local economy. The injured parties may be awarded only monetary damages, which may include compensation for the decline in the value of their property caused by the factory's operation.

A property owner may be given relief from pollution if he or she can identify a distinct harm separate from that affecting the general public. This harm is referred to as a "private" nuisance. Under the common law, individuals were denied standing (access to the courts—see Chapter 2) unless they suffered a harm distinct from the harm suffered by the public at large. Some states still require this. A public authority (such as a state's attorney general), however, can sue to stop a "public" nuisance.

Negligence and Strict Liability

An injured party may sue a business polluter in tort under the negligence and strict liability theories discussed in Chapters 12 and 13. The basis for a negligence action is a business's alleged failure to use reasonable care toward a party whose injury was foreseeable and was caused by the lack of reasonable care. For example, employees might sue an employer whose failure to use proper pollution controls contaminated the air, causing the employees to suffer respiratory illnesses. Lawsuits for personal injuries caused by exposure to a toxic substance, such as asbestos, radiation, or hazardous waste, have given rise to a growing body of tort law known as **toxic torts.**

Businesses that engage in ultrahazardous activities—such as the transportation of radioactive materials—are strictly liable for any injuries the activities cause. In a strict liability action, the injured party does not have to prove that the business failed to exercise reasonable care.

SECTION 2
FEDERAL, STATE, AND LOCAL REGULATIONS

All levels of government in the United States regulate some aspect of the environment. In this section, we look at some of the ways in which the federal, state, and local governments control business activities and land use in the interests of environmental preservation and protection.

State and Local Regulations

In addition to the federal regulations to be discussed shortly, many states have enacted laws to protect the environment. State laws may restrict a business's discharge of chemicals into the air or water or regulate its disposal of toxic wastes. States may also regulate the disposal or recycling of other wastes, including glass, metal, plastic containers, and paper. Additionally, states may restrict emissions from motor vehicles.

City, county, and other local governments also regulate some aspects of the environment. For instance, local zoning laws may be designed to inhibit or regulate the growth of cities and suburbs or to protect the natural environment. In the interest of safeguarding the environment, such laws may prohibit certain land uses. Even when zoning laws permit a business's proposed development, the proposal may have to be altered to lessen the development's impact on the environment. In addition, cities and counties may impose rules regulating methods of waste removal, the appearance of buildings, the maximum noise level, and other aspects of the local environment.

State and local regulatory agencies also play a significant role in implementing federal environmental legislation. Typically, the federal government relies on state and local governments to enforce federal environmental statutes and regulations such as those regulating air quality.

Federal Regulations

Congress has passed a number of statutes to control the impact of human activities on the environment. Exhibit 25–1 on the facing page lists and summarizes the major federal environmental statutes discussed in this chapter. Most of these statutes are designed to address pollution in the air, water, or land. Some of the laws specifically regulate toxic chemicals, including pesticides, herbicides, and hazardous wastes.

ENVIRONMENTAL REGULATORY AGENCIES The primary federal agency regulating environmental law is the Environmental Protection Agency (EPA), which was created in 1970 to coordinate federal environmental responsibilities. Other federal agencies with authority for regulating specific environmental matters include the Department of the Interior, the Department of Defense, the Department of Labor, the Food and Drug Administration, and the Nuclear Regulatory Commission. All federal agencies must take environmental factors into consideration when making significant decisions. In addition, as mentioned, state and local agencies play an important role in enforcing federal environmental legislation.

Most federal environmental laws provide that citizens can sue to enforce environmental regulations if government agencies fail to do so—or to limit enforcement actions if agencies go too far in their actions. Typically, a threshold hurdle in such suits is meeting the requirements for standing to sue (see page 34 in Chapter 2).

ENVIRONMENTAL IMPACT STATEMENTS The National Environmental Policy Act of 1969[1] requires that an **environmental impact statement (EIS)** be prepared for every major federal action that significantly affects the quality of the environment. An EIS must analyze (1) the impact on the environment that the action will have, (2) any adverse effects on the environment and alternative actions that might be taken, and (3) irreversible effects the action might generate.

An action qualifies as "major" if it involves a substantial commitment of resources (monetary or otherwise). An action is "federal" if a federal agency has the power to control it. Development of a ski resort by a private developer on federal land, for example, may require an EIS. Construction or operation of a nuclear plant, which requires a federal permit, or creation of a dam as part of a federal project requires an EIS. If an agency decides that an EIS is

---

1. 42 U.S.C. Sections 4321–4370d.

EXHIBIT 25-1 • Major Federal Environmental Statutes

POPULAR NAME	PURPOSE	STATUTE REFERENCE
Rivers and Harbors Appropriations Act (1899)	To prohibit ships and manufacturers from discharging and depositing refuse in navigable waterways.	33 U.S.C. Sections 401–418.
Federal Insecticide, Fungicide, and Rodenticide Act (1947)	To control the use of pesticides and herbicides.	7 U.S.C. Sections 136–136y.
Federal Water Pollution Control Act (1948)	To eliminate the discharge of pollutants from major sources into navigable waters.	33 U.S.C. Sections 1251–1387.
Clean Air Act (1963, 1970)	To control air pollution from mobile and stationary sources.	42 U.S.C. Sections 7401–7671q.
National Environmental Policy Act (1969)	To limit environmental harm from federal government activities.	42 U.S.C. Sections 4321–4370d.
Ocean Dumping Act (1972)	To prohibit the dumping of radiological, chemical, and biological warfare agents and high-level radioactive waste into the ocean.	16 U.S.C. Sections 1401–1445.
Endangered Species Act (1973)	To protect species that are threatened with extinction.	16 U.S.C. Sections 1531–1544.
Safe Drinking Water Act (1974)	To regulate pollutants in public drinking water systems.	42 U.S.C. Sections 300f–300j-25.
Resource Conservation and Recovery Act (1976)	To establish standards for hazardous waste disposal.	42 U.S.C. Sections 6901–6986.
Toxic Substances Control Act (1976)	To regulate toxic chemicals and chemical compounds.	15 U.S.C. Sections 2601–2692.
Comprehensive Environmental Response, Compensation, and Liability Act (1980)	To regulate the clean-up of hazardous waste–disposal sites.	42 U.S.C. Sections 9601–9675.
Oil Pollution Act (1990)	To establish liability for the clean-up of navigable waters after oil-spill disasters.	33 U.S.C. Sections 2701–2761.
Small Business Liability Relief and Brownfields Revitalization Act (2002)	To allow developers who comply with state voluntary clean-up programs to avoid federal liability for the properties that they decontaminate and develop.	42 U.S.C. Section 9628.

unnecessary, it must issue a statement supporting this conclusion. Private citizens, consumer interest groups, businesses, and others often use EISs as a means to challenge agency actions that they believe improperly threaten the environment.

SECTION 3
AIR POLLUTION

Federal involvement with air pollution goes back to the 1950s and 1960s, when Congress authorized funds for air-pollution research. In 1963, the federal government passed the Clean Air Act[2] to address multistate air pollution and provide assistance to the states. Later amendments to the act, especially those enacted in 1970, provide the basis for issuing regulations to control air pollution. The Clean Air Act covers both mobile sources (such as automobiles and other vehicles) and stationary sources (such as electric utilities and industrial plants) of pollution.

Mobile Sources

Regulations governing air pollution from automobiles and other mobile sources specify pollution standards and establish time schedules for meeting the standards. For example, 1990 amendments to the Clean Air Act required automobile manufacturers to cut new automobiles' exhaust emissions of nitrogen oxide by 60 percent and emissions of

2. 42 U.S.C. Sections 7401–7671q.

hydrocarbons and carbon monoxide by 35 percent by 1998. Beginning with 2004 models, the rules also applied to sport-utility vehicles (SUVs) and light trucks. The EPA periodically updates the pollution standards in light of new developments and data, reducing the amount of emissions allowed.

In 2009, the Obama administration announced a long-term goal of reducing emissions, including those from cars and SUVs, by 80 percent by 2050. In 2010, the administration ordered the EPA to develop national standards regulating fuel economy and emissions for medium- and heavy-duty trucks starting with 2014 models.

A growing concern among many scientists and others around the world is that greenhouse gases, such as carbon dioxide (CO_2), are contributing to global warming. The Clean Air Act, as amended, however, does not specifically mention CO_2 emissions. Therefore, up until 2009, the EPA did not regulate CO_2 emissions from motor vehicles.

CASE IN POINT In 2007, environmental groups and several states, including Massachusetts, sued the EPA in an effort to force the agency to regulate CO_2 emissions. When the case reached the United States Supreme Court, the EPA argued that the plaintiffs lacked standing because global warming has widespread effects and thus an individual plaintiff could not show the particularized harm required for standing. Furthermore, the agency maintained, it did not have authority under the Clean Air Act to address global climate change and regulate CO_2. The Court, however, ruled that Massachusetts had standing because its coastline, including state-owned lands, faced an imminent threat from rising sea levels caused by global warming. The Court also held that the Clean Air Act's broad definition of air pollutant gives the EPA authority to regulate CO_2 and requires

the EPA to regulate any air pollutants that might "endanger public health or welfare." Accordingly, the Court ordered the EPA to determine whether CO_2 was a pollutant that endangered public health.[3] (In 2009, the EPA concluded that greenhouse gases, including CO_2 emissions, do constitute a public danger.)

Stationary Sources

The Clean Air Act also authorizes the EPA to establish air-quality standards for stationary sources (such as manufacturing plants) but recognizes that the primary responsibility for implementing these standards rests with state and local governments. The standards are aimed at controlling hazardous air pollutants—those likely to cause death or a serious, irreversible, or incapacitating condition such as cancer or neurological or reproductive damage.

LISTING OF HAZARDOUS AIR POLLUTANTS The Clean Air Act requires the EPA to list all hazardous air pollutants (HAPs) on a prioritized schedule. In all, nearly two hundred substances—including asbestos, benzene, beryllium, cadmium, and vinyl chloride—have been classified as hazardous. They are emitted from stationary sources by a variety of business activities, including smelting (melting ore to produce metal), dry cleaning, house painting, and commercial baking.

Mercury was added to the list of hazardous substances in 2000. The EPA attempted nonetheless to remove mercury from its list of designated HAPs emitted from steam-generating electricity plants. New Jersey and others challenged this delisting in the following case.

3. *Massachusetts v. Environmental Protection Agency,* 549 U.S. 497, 127 S.Ct. 1438, 167 L.Ed.2d 248 (2007).

CASE 25.1
State of New Jersey v. Environmental Protection Agency

United States Court of Appeals, District of Columbia Circuit, 517 F.3d 574 (2008).
www.cadc.uscourts.gov/bin/opinions/allopinions.asp[a]

BACKGROUND AND FACTS • The Environmental Protection Agency (EPA) published a rule—the Delisting Rule—that had the effect of removing from its regulation the emissions of mercury from steam-generating electricity plants that used coal or oil as their energy sources. This Delisting Rule ran counter to the EPA's own conclusions at the end of 2000 that it was "appropriate and necessary"

a. Select "February" and "2008" from the drop-down menus for "Month" and "Year" and click on "Go!" Scroll down to case number "05-1097" and click on the link to access the opinion. The U.S. Court of Appeals for the District of Columbia maintains this Web site.

CASE 25.1 CONTINUED ➧ to regulate mercury emissions. At that time, the agency placed mercury on its list of hazardous air pollutants (HAPs) to be monitored at electricity-generating sites. Later, however, the EPA tried to "delist" mercury from the HAPs list. New Jersey and fourteen other states, plus various state agencies, challenged the EPA's delisting action.

IN THE LANGUAGE OF THE COURT
ROGERS, Circuit Judge.
* * * *

First, Congress required EPA to regulate more than one hundred specific HAPs, including mercury and nickel compounds. Further, EPA was required to list and to regulate, on a prioritized schedule, "all categories and subcategories of major sources and areas sources" that emit one or more HAPs. *In seeking to ensure that regulation of HAPs reflects the "maximum reduction in emissions which can be achieved by application of [the] best available control technology," Congress imposed specific, strict pollution control requirements on both new and existing sources of HAPs.* [Emphasis added.]

Second, Congress restricted the opportunities for EPA and others to intervene in the regulation of HAP sources. For HAPs that result in health effects other than cancer, as is true of mercury, Congress directed that the Administrator "may delete any source category" from the section 112(c)(1) list only after determining that "emissions from no source in the category or subcategory concerned . . . exceed a level which is adequate to protect public health with an ample margin of safety and no adverse environmental effect will result from emissions from any source."
* * * *

EPA maintains that it possesses authority to remove EGUs [electrical generating units] from * * * [the] list under the "fundamental principle of administrative law that an agency has inherent authority to reverse an earlier administrative determination or ruling where an agency has a principled basis for doing so." EPA states in its brief that it has previously removed sources listed * * * without satisfying the requirements of [the statute]. But previous statutory violations cannot excuse the one now before the court. "We do not see how merely applying an unreasonable statutory interpretation for several years can transform it into a reasonable interpretation."

DECISION AND REMEDY • *The U.S. Court of Appeals for the District of Columbia Circuit ruled in favor of New Jersey and the other plaintiffs. The EPA was required to cancel its delisting of mercury.*

WHAT IF THE FACTS WERE DIFFERENT? • *Suppose that the EPA had carried out scientific tests that showed mercury was relatively harmless as a by-product of electricity generation. How might this have affected the court's ruling?*

THE GLOBAL DIMENSION • *Because air pollution knows no borders, how did this ruling affect our neighboring countries?*

AIR-POLLUTION CONTROL STANDARDS The EPA sets primary and secondary levels of ambient standards—that is, maximum permissible levels of certain pollutants—and the states formulate plans to achieve those standards. Different standards apply depending on whether the sources of pollution are located in clean areas or polluted areas and whether they are existing sources or major new sources.

Major new sources include existing sources modified by a change in a method of operation that increases emissions. Performance standards for major sources require the use of the *maximum*

achievable control technology to reduce emissions. The EPA issues guidelines as to what equipment meets this standard.[4]

Violations of the Clean Air Act

For violations of emission limits under the Clean Air Act, the EPA can assess civil penalties of up to $25,000 per day. Additional fines of up to $5,000

---

4. The EPA has also issued rules to regulate hazardous air pollutants emitted by landfills. See 40 C.F.R. Sections 60.750–60.759.

per day can be assessed for other violations, such as failure to maintain the required records. To penalize those who find it more cost-effective to violate the act than to comply with it, the EPA is authorized to impose a penalty equal to the violator's economic benefits from noncompliance. Persons who provide information about violators may be paid up to $10,000. Private citizens can also sue violators.

Those who knowingly violate the act may be subject to criminal penalties, including fines of up to $1 million and imprisonment for up to two years (for false statements or failure to report violations). Corporate officers are among those who may be subject to these penalties.

SECTION 4
WATER POLLUTION

Water pollution stems mostly from industrial, municipal, and agricultural sources. Pollutants entering streams, lakes, and oceans include organic wastes, heated water, sediments from soil runoff, nutrients (including fertilizers and human and animal wastes), and toxic chemicals and other hazardous substances.

Federal regulations governing water pollution can be traced back to the Rivers and Harbors Appropriations Act of 1899.[5] These regulations prohibited ships and manufacturers from discharging or depositing refuse in navigable waterways without a permit.[6] In 1948, Congress passed the Federal Water Pollution Control Act (FWPCA),[7] but its regulatory system and enforcement powers proved to be inadequate.

The Clean Water Act

In 1972, amendments to the FWPCA—known as the Clean Water Act (CWA)—established the following goals: (1) make waters safe for swimming, (2) protect fish and wildlife, and (3) eliminate the discharge of pollutants into the water. The CWA also set specific schedules, which were extended by amendment in 1977 and by the Water Quality Act of 1987.[8] Under these schedules, the EPA limits the discharge of various types of pollutants based on the technology available for controlling them.

---

5. 33 U.S.C. Sections 401–418.

6. The term *navigable waters* is interpreted today as including intrastate lakes and streams used by interstate travelers and industries, as well as coastal and freshwater wetlands.

7. 33 U.S.C. Sections 1251–1387.

8. This act amended 33 U.S.C. Section 1251.

FOCUS ON POINT-SOURCE EMISSIONS The CWA established a permit system, called the National Pollutant Discharge Elimination System (NPDES), for regulating discharges from "point sources" of pollution that include industrial, municipal (such as pipes and sewage treatment plants), and agricultural facilities.[9] Under this system, any point source emitting pollutants into water must have a permit. Pollution not from point sources, such as runoff from small farms, is not subject to much regulation. NPDES permits can be issued by the EPA and authorized state agencies and Indian tribes, but only if the discharge will not violate water-quality standards. NPDES permits must be reissued every five years. Although initially the NPDES system focused mainly on industrial wastewater, it was later expanded to cover storm water discharges.

In practice, the permit system under the CWA includes the following elements:

1. National effluent (pollution) standards set by the EPA for each industry.
2. Water-quality standards set by the states under EPA supervision.
3. A *discharge permit* program that sets water-quality standards to limit pollution.
4. Special provisions for toxic chemicals and for oil spills.
5. Construction grants and loans from the federal government for *publicly owned treatment works,* primarily sewage treatment plants.

STANDARDS FOR EQUIPMENT Regulations generally specify that the *best available control technology,* or BACT, be installed. The EPA issues guidelines as to what equipment meets this standard. Essentially, the guidelines require the most effective pollution-control equipment available. New sources must install BACT equipment before beginning operations. Existing sources are subject to timetables for the installation of BACT equipment and must immediately install equipment that utilizes the *best practical control technology.* The EPA also issues guidelines as to what equipment meets this standard.

The EPA must take into account many factors when issuing and updating its rules. Some provisions of the CWA instruct the EPA to weigh the cost of the technology required relative to the benefits achieved. The provision that covers power plants, however, neither requires nor prohibits a cost-benefit analysis. The question in the following case was whether the EPA could conduct such an analysis anyway.

---

9. 33 U.S.C. Section 1342.

CASE 25.2
Entergy Corp. v. Riverkeeper, Inc.

Supreme Court of the United States, __ U.S. __, 129 S.Ct. 1498, 173 L.Ed.2d 369 (2009).
www.findlaw.com/casecode/supreme.html[a]

BACKGROUND AND FACTS • As part of its implementation of the Clean Water Act, the Environmental Protection Agency (EPA) has developed two sets of rules that apply to the cooling systems of power plants. Phase I rules require new power plants to restrict their inflow of water "to a level commensurate with that which can be attained by a closed-cycle recirculating cooling water system." Phase II rules apply "national performance standards" to more than five hundred existing plants but do not require closed-cycle cooling systems. The EPA found that converting these facilities to closed-cycle operations would cost $3.5 billion per year. The facilities would then produce less power while burning the same amount of coal. Moreover, other technologies can attain nearly the same results as closed-cycle systems. Phase II rules also allow a variance from the national performance standards if a facility's cost of compliance "would be significantly greater than the benefits." Environmental organizations, including Riverkeeper, Inc., challenged the Phase II regulations, arguing that existing plants should be required to convert to closed-cycle systems. The U.S. Court of Appeals for the Second Circuit issued a ruling in the plaintiffs' favor. Power-generating companies, including Entergy Corporation, appealed to the United States Supreme Court.

IN THE LANGUAGE OF THE COURT
Justice *SCALIA* delivered the opinion of the Court.
* * * *

In setting the Phase II national performance standards and providing for site-specific cost-benefit variances, the EPA relied on its view that [the] "best technology available" standard permits consideration of the technology's costs and of the relationship between those costs and the environmental benefits produced.

* * * The "best" technology—that which is "most advantageous"—may well be the one that produces the most of some good, here a reduction in adverse environmental impact. But "best technology" may also describe the technology that most efficiently produces some good. *In common parlance one could certainly use the phrase "best technology" to refer to that which produces a good at the lowest per-unit cost, even if it produces a lesser quantity of that good than other available technologies.* [Emphasis added.]

* * * This latter reading is [not] precluded by the statute's use of the phrase "for minimizing adverse environmental impact." *Minimizing* * * * *is a term that admits of degree and is not necessarily used to refer exclusively to the "greatest possible reduction."* [Emphasis added.]

Other provisions in the Clean Water Act also suggest the agency's interpretation. When Congress wished to mandate the greatest feasible reduction in water pollution, it did so in plain language: The provision governing the discharge of toxic pollutants into the Nation's waters requires the EPA to set "effluent limitations which shall require the elimination of discharges of all pollutants * * * ." The less ambitious goal of "minimizing adverse environmental impact" suggests, we think, that the agency retains some discretion to determine the extent of reduction that is warranted under the circumstances. That determination could plausibly involve a consideration of the benefits derived from reductions and the costs of achieving them.

* * * [Under other Clean Water Act provisions that impose standards on sources of pollution,] the EPA is instructed to consider, among other factors, "the total cost of application of technology in relation to the * * * benefits to be achieved."
* * * *

This * * * comparison of * * * statutory factors * * * leads us to the conclusion that it was well within the bounds of reasonable interpretation for the EPA to conclude that cost-benefit analysis is not categorically forbidden.

---

a. In the "Browse Supreme Court Opinions" section, click on "2009." On that page, scroll to the name of the case and click on it to access the opinion. The United States Supreme Court maintains this Web site.

CASE CONTINUES ➡

CASE 25.2 CONTINUED ➡ ★ ★ ★ ★

While not conclusive, it surely tends to show that the EPA's current practice is a reasonable and hence legitimate exercise of its discretion to weigh benefits against costs that the agency has been proceeding in essentially this fashion for over 30 years.

DECISION AND REMEDY • *The United States Supreme Court concluded that the EPA permissibly relied on a cost-benefit analysis to set national performance standards and to allow for variances from those standards as part of the Phase II regulations. The Court reversed the lower court's judgment and remanded the case.*

THE ETHICAL DIMENSION • *In this case, aquatic organisms were most directly at risk. Is it acceptable to apply cost-benefit analyses to situations in which the lives of people are directly affected? Explain.*

THE GLOBAL DIMENSION • *In analyzing the costs and benefits of an action that affects the environment, should a line be drawn at a nation's borders? Why or why not?*

WETLANDS The CWA prohibits the filling or dredging of **wetlands** unless a permit is obtained from the Army Corps of Engineers. The EPA defines *wetlands* as "those areas that are inundated or saturated by surface or ground water at a frequency and duration sufficient to support, and that under normal circumstances do support, a prevalence of vegetation typically adapted for life in saturated soil conditions." Wetlands are thought to be vital to the ecosystem because they filter streams and rivers and provide habitat for wildlife. In the past, the EPA's broad interpretation of what constituted a wetland generated substantial controversy, but the courts have considerably scaled back the CWA's protection of wetlands in recent years.[10]

In the following case, the court had to deal with the meaning of *wetlands* and whether the term included saturated land adjacent to so-called navigable-in-fact waters.

---

10. See, for example, *Rapanos v. United States,* 547 U.S. 715, 126 S.Ct. 2208, 165 L.Ed.2d 159 (2006).

✳ EXTENDED CASE 25.3 ✳
United States v. Lucas

United States Court of Appeals, Fifth District, 516 F.3d 316 (2008).

IN THE LANGUAGE OF THE COURT

Patrick E. *HIGGINBOTHAM,* Circuit Judge.
★ ★ ★ ★

Robert J. Lucas owned Big Hill Acres, Inc. (BHA, Inc.) and Consolidated Investments, Inc. Through these companies, he acquired Big Hill Acres (BHA), a large parcel of land in Jackson County, Mississippi, approximately eight miles from the Gulf of Mexico. He subdivided the property and sold mobile home lots under long-term installment plans. The property was not connected to a central municipal waste system,

and County law required Lucas to certify and install individual septic systems on each lot before they could establish electric hook-ups or sell the lots. In Jackson County, septic systems must be approved by an engineer with the Mississippi Department of Health (MDH) or by an independent licensed engineer. Lucas initially hired an MDH engineer to approve septic systems, but MDH withdrew many of its initial approvals when it found that the lots were on saturated soils. Lucas then hired a private licensed engineer, M. E. Thompson, Jr., to approve and certify the septic systems. Robbie Lucas Wrigley, Lucas's daughter, advertised the lots,

showed them to prospective buyers, and leased them.

The [U.S.] Army Corps of Engineers, the EPA [Environmental Protection Agency], the MDH, and the Mississippi Department of Environmental Quality (DEQ) became concerned that Defendants were selling house lots and installing septic systems on wetlands. These agencies issued several cease and desist orders against Lucas and Thompson, and the EPA sent letters to residents and organized a meeting of the residents to warn them of lot conditions and to tell them where wetlands were located on the property. It also met with BHA's counsel to attempt to designate

EXTENDED CASE 25.3 CONTINUED ⬇

the areas where they would allow development. These efforts were not fully successful.

The Government filed a forty-one-count indictment against Defendants * * * , charging filling of wetlands without a Section 404 permit from the [U.S. Army] Corps [of Engineers], failing to obtain Section 402 National Pollutant Discharge Elimination System (NPDES) Permits for the septic tanks, mail fraud, and conspiracy to commit mail fraud and to violate Sections 402 and 404 of the CWA [Clean Water Act]. * * * A jury convicted Defendants on all counts, and the court * * * sentenced Lucas, Wrigley, and [Thompson] to prison terms; placed BHA, Inc., and Consolidated Investments on probation; and ordered all Defendants to pay restitution, special assessments, and fines.

* * * *

The first and overarching [dominant] question is jurisdiction—whether the jury was properly required to find that the property at issue was subject to the CWA. * * * The instructions stated in relevant part,

* * * *

The term *wetlands* means those areas that are inundated or saturated by surface or groundwater at a frequency and duration sufficient to support, and that under normal circumstances do support, a prevalence of vegetation typically adapted for life in saturated soil conditions * * * . * * * Wetlands that are waters of the United States are protected by the Clean Water Act. *Wetlands are considered waters of the United States if they are adjacent to a navigable body of open water. Wetlands are adjacent to a navigable body of water if there is a significant nexus [connection] between the wetlands in question and a navigable-in-fact waterway.* Some of the factors which you may wish to consider in determining whether there is a significant nexus include, but are not limited to: * * * flow rate of surface waters from the wetlands into a navigable body of water * * * when, or to what extent, contaminants from the wetlands have or will affect a navigable body of water * * * . [Emphasis added.]

Defendants argue that the court erred in not including their requested language that:

* * * adjacency implicates a "significant nexus" between the water in question and the navigable-in-fact waterway. If the government fails to prove beyond a reasonable doubt that the wetlands at issue in this case are in fact navigable or truly adjacent to [that is,] lying near, close, contiguous, or adjoining a navigable waterway, you must find the defendants not guilty * * * .

* * * *

* * * *A district court abuses its discretion in omitting a requested* jury instruction only if the requested language *"(1) is substantively correct; (2) is not substantially covered in the charge given to the jury; and (3) concerns an important point in the trial* * * * ."* [Emphasis added.]

The court's instructions were not in error, nor was the court's omission of Defendants' requested instructions. * * * The instructions substantially covered Defendants' requested instructions by requiring adjacency as defined by a significant nexus.

* * * *

The government has shown that there is a significant nexus between the wetlands on Big Hill Acres and navigable-in-fact waters. * * * The surface from the Big Hill Acres site drains in three directions. The western portions of the site drain into Bayou Costapia. Bayou Costapia empties into the Tchoutacabouffa River, which then empties into the Gulf of Mexico. The central portions of the Big Hill Acres development drained through tributaries into Old Fort Bayou Creek. And Old Fort Bayou Creek connects to Old Fort Bayou, which is a protected coastal preserve emptying into the Gulf of Mexico. And the eastern portions drain into the headwaters of Little Bluff Creek, which then connects to Bluff Creek, which flows into the Pascagoula River and on to the Gulf of Mexico. The court did not abuse its discretion in giving the CWA instructions.

QUESTIONS

1. Assume that during most of the year, there was a solid strip of land around the property in question that was never under water or saturated. Would the outcome of this case have been the same? Why or why not?
2. According to the judge, what three characteristics of jury instructions does a federal appellate court examine to determine whether a district court has abused its discretion in omitting a requested jury instruction? Which of these three characteristics was at issue in this case?

VIOLATIONS OF THE CLEAN WATER ACT Because point-source water pollution control is based on a permit system, the permits are the key to enforcement. States have primary responsibility for enforcing the permit system, subject to EPA monitoring.

Discharging emissions into navigable waters without a permit, or in violation of pollution limits under a permit, violates the CWA. Firms that have discharge permits must monitor their own performance and file *discharge monitoring reports*. These reports are available for public inspection. Violators must report their violations and are subject to fines. Depending on the violation, civil penalties range from $10,000 to $25,000 per day, but not more than $25,000 per violation. Lying about a violation is more serious than admitting the truth about improper discharges.

Serious and intentional violations can result in criminal prosecutions, with substantial fines and imprisonment. Every year, violators—including some corporate officers—are sent to prison for dumping toxic pollutants. As with the Clean Air Act, citizens have the right to bring lawsuits for pollution that the EPA or a state environmental agency has not addressed properly. Injunctive relief and damages can also be imposed. The polluting party can be required to clean up the pollution or pay for the cost of doing so.

Drinking Water

The Safe Drinking Water Act[11] requires the EPA to set maximum levels for pollutants in public water systems. Operators of public water systems must come as close as possible to meeting the EPA's standards by using the best available technology that is economically and technologically feasible. The EPA is particularly concerned about contamination from underground sources, such as pesticides and wastes leaked from landfills or disposed of in underground injection wells. Many of these substances are associated with cancer and may cause damage to the central nervous system, liver, and kidneys.

The act was amended in 1996 to give the EPA greater flexibility in setting regulatory standards governing drinking water. These amendments also imposed certain requirements on suppliers of drinking water. Each supplier must send to every household it supplies with water an annual statement describing the source of its water, the level of any contaminants contained in the water, and any possible health concerns associated with the contaminants.

Ocean Dumping

The Marine Protection, Research, and Sanctuaries Act of 1972[12] (popularly known as the Ocean Dumping Act) regulates the transportation and dumping of material (pollutants) into ocean waters. It prohibits entirely the ocean dumping of radiological, chemical, and biological warfare agents and high-level radioactive waste.

The act also established a permit program for transporting and dumping other materials, and designated certain areas as marine sanctuaries. Each violation of any provision or permit requirement in the Ocean Dumping Act may result in a civil penalty of up to $50,000. A knowing violation is a criminal offense that may result in a $50,000 fine, imprisonment for not more than a year, or both. A court may also grant an injunction to prevent an imminent or continuing violation.

Oil Pollution

When more than 10 million gallons of oil leaked into Alaska's Prince William Sound from the *Exxon Valdez* supertanker in 1989, Congress responded and passed the Oil Pollution Act of 1990.[13] (At that time, the *Exxon Valdez* disaster was the worst oil spill in U.S. history, but the BP oil spill in the Gulf of Mexico in 2010 surpassed it.) Under this act, any onshore or offshore oil facility, oil shipper, vessel owner, or vessel operator that discharges oil into navigable waters or onto an adjoining shore may be liable for clean-up costs, as well as damages. The act created an oil clean-up and economic compensation fund, and required oil tankers using U.S. ports to be double hulled by the year 2011 (to limit the severity of accidental spills).

Under the act, damage to natural resources, private property, and the local economy, including the increased cost of providing public services, is compensable. The penalties range from $2 million to $350 million, depending on the size of the vessel and on whether the oil spill came from a vessel or an offshore facility. The party held responsible for the clean-up costs can bring a civil suit for contribution from other potentially liable parties.

<hr>

SECTION 5

TOXIC CHEMICALS

Originally, most environmental clean-up efforts were directed toward reducing smog and making water safe for fishing and swimming. Today, control of toxic chemicals used in agriculture and in industry has become increasingly important.

11. 42 U.S.C. Sections 300f to 300j-25.
12. 16 U.S.C. Sections 1401–1445.

13. 33 U.S.C. Sections 2701–2761.

Pesticides and Herbicides

The Federal Insecticide, Fungicide, and Rodenticide Act (FIFRA) of 1947[14] regulates pesticides and herbicides. Under FIFRA, pesticides and herbicides must be (1) registered before they can be sold, (2) certified and used only for approved applications, and (3) used in limited quantities when applied to food crops. The EPA can cancel or suspend registration of substances that are identified as harmful and may also inspect factories where the chemicals are made. Under 1996 amendments to FIFRA, a substance is deemed harmful if human exposure to the substance, including exposure through eating food, results in a risk of one in a million (or higher) of developing cancer.[15]

It is a violation of FIFRA to sell a pesticide or herbicide that is either unregistered or has had its registration canceled or suspended. It is also a violation to sell a pesticide or herbicide with a false or misleading label or to destroy or deface any labeling required under the act. For example, it is an offense to sell a substance that has a chemical strength different from the concentration declared on the label. Penalties for commercial dealers include imprisonment for up to one year and a fine of up to $25,000 (producers can be fined up to $50,000). Farmers and other private users of pesticides or herbicides who violate the act are subject to a $1,000 fine and incarceration for up to thirty days. Note that a state can also regulate the sale and use of federally registered pesticides.

CASE IN POINT The EPA conditionally registered Strongarm, a weed-killing pesticide. Dow Agrosciences, LLC, sold Strongarm to Texas peanut farmers. When the farmers applied it, however, Strongarm damaged their crops and failed to control the growth of weeds. The farmers sued Dow for violations of Texas law, but the lower courts ruled that FIFRA preempted their claims. The farmers appealed to the United States Supreme Court. The Court held that under a specific provision of FIFRA, a state can regulate the sale and use of federally registered pesticides so long as the regulation does not permit anything that FIFRA prohibits.[16]

Toxic Substances

The first comprehensive law covering toxic substances was the Toxic Substances Control Act of 1976.[17] The act was passed to regulate chemicals and

chemical compounds that are known to be toxic—such as asbestos and polychlorinated biphenyls, popularly known as PCBs—and to institute investigation of any possible harmful effects from new chemical compounds.

The regulations authorize the EPA to require that manufacturers, processors, and other entities planning to use chemicals first determine their effects on human health and the environment. The EPA can regulate substances that may pose an imminent hazard or an unreasonable risk of injury to health or the environment. The EPA may require special labeling, limit the use of a substance, set production quotas, or prohibit the use of a substance altogether.

SECTION 6
HAZARDOUS WASTES

Some industrial, agricultural, and household wastes pose more serious threats than others. If not properly disposed of, these toxic chemicals may present a substantial danger to human health and the environment. If released into the environment, they may contaminate public drinking water resources.

Resource Conservation and Recovery Act

In 1976, Congress passed the Resource Conservation and Recovery Act (RCRA)[18] in response to growing concern about the effects of hazardous waste materials on the environment. The RCRA required the EPA to establish regulations to determine which forms of solid waste should be considered hazardous and to establish regulations to monitor and control hazardous waste disposal. The act also requires all producers of hazardous waste materials to label and package properly any hazardous waste to be transported. The RCRA was amended in 1984 and 1986 to decrease the use of land containment in the disposal of hazardous waste and to require smaller generators of hazardous waste to comply with the act.

Under the RCRA, a company may be assessed a civil penalty of up to $25,000 for each violation.[19] The penalty is based on the seriousness of the violation, the probability of harm, and the extent to which the violation deviates from RCRA requirements. Criminal penalties include fines of up to $50,000 for each day of violation, imprisonment for up to two years (in most instances), or both.

14. 7 U.S.C. Sections 136–136y.

15. 21 U.S.C. Section 346a.

16. *Bates v. Dow Agrosciences, LLC,* 544 U.S. 431, 125 S.Ct. 1788, 161 L.Ed.2d 687 (2005).

17. 15 U.S.C. Sections 2601–2692.

18. 42 U.S.C. Sections 6901–6986.

19. 42 U.S.C. Section 6928(a).

Criminal fines and the time of imprisonment can be doubled for certain repeat offenders.

Superfund

In 1980, Congress passed the Comprehensive Environmental Response, Compensation, and Liability Act (CERCLA),[20] commonly known as Superfund. The basic purpose of Superfund is to regulate the clean-up of disposal sites in which hazardous waste is leaking into the environment.

CERCLA, as amended, has four primary elements:

1. It established an information-gathering and analysis system that enables the government to identify chemical dump sites and determine the appropriate action.
2. It authorized the EPA to respond to hazardous substance emergencies and to arrange for the clean-up of a leaking site directly if the persons responsible for the problem fail to clean up the site.
3. It created a Hazardous Substance Response Trust Fund to pay for the clean-up of hazardous sites using funds obtained through taxes on certain businesses. (The name *Superfund* is sometimes used to refer just to the trust fund, but here we use it in the broader sense to refer to CERCLA as a whole.)
4. It allows the government to recover the cost of clean-up from the persons who were (even remotely) responsible for hazardous substance releases.

POTENTIALLY RESPONSIBLE PARTIES Superfund provides that when a release or a threatened release of hazardous chemicals from a site occurs, the following persons are responsible for cleaning up the site: (1) the person who generated the wastes disposed of at the site, (2) the person who transported the wastes to the site, (3) the person who owned or operated the site at the time of the disposal, or (4) the current owner or operator. A person falling within one of these categories is referred to as a **potentially responsible party (PRP).** If the PRPs do not clean up the site, EPA can clean up the site and recover the clean-up costs from the PRPs.

Superfund imposes strict liability on PRPs and that liability cannot be avoided through transfer of ownership. Thus, selling a site at which hazardous wastes were disposed does not relieve the seller of liability, and the buyer also becomes liable for the clean-up. Liability also extends to those that merge with or buy corporations that have violated CERCLA. Although a parent corporation is not automatically liable for the violations of its subsidiary, it can be held liable if the subsidiary was merely a shell company or if it participated in or controlled the facility.[21]

JOINT AND SEVERAL LIABILITY Liability under Superfund is usually joint and several—that is, a PRP who generated *only a fraction of the hazardous waste* disposed of at the site may nevertheless be liable for *all* of the clean-up costs. CERCLA authorizes a party who has incurred clean-up costs to bring a "contribution action" against any other person who is liable or potentially liable for a percentage of the costs.

MINIMIZING LIABILITY One way for a business to minimize its potential liability under Superfund is to conduct environmental compliance audits of its own operations regularly. A business can perform internal investigations of its own operations and lands to determine whether any environmental hazards exist.

The EPA encourages companies to conduct self-audits and promptly detect, disclose, and correct wrongdoing. Companies that do so are subject to lighter penalties (fines may be reduced as much as 75 percent) for violations of environmental laws. Under EPA guidelines, the EPA will waive all fines if a small company corrects environmental violations within 180 days after being notified of the violations (or 360 days if pollution-prevention techniques are involved). The policy does not apply to criminal violations of environmental laws, though, or to actions that pose a significant threat to public health, safety, or the environment.

DEFENSES There are a few defenses to liability under CERCLA. The most important is the innocent landowner defense.[22] Under this defense, an innocent property owner may be able to avoid liability by showing that he or she had no contractual or employment relationship with the person who released the hazardous substance on the land. Thus, if the property was transferred by contract from the third

---

20. 42 U.S.C. Sections 9601–9675.

21. The landmark case establishing the liability of a parent corporation under CERCLA is *United States v. Bestfoods*, 524 U.S. 51, 118 S.Ct. 1876, 141 L.Ed.2d 43 (1998).

22. 42 U.S.C. Section 9601(35)(B).

party who disposed of the substances to the current owner, the defense normally will not be available. To assert the defense, the landowner must be able to show that at the time the property was acquired, she or he had no reason to know that hazardous substances had been disposed of on it. The landowner must also show that at the time of the purchase, she or he undertook all appropriate investigation into the previous ownership and uses of the property to determine whether there was reason to be concerned about hazardous substances. In effect, this defense protects only property owners who took precautions and investigated the possibility of environmental hazards at the time they bought the property.

REVIEWING
Environmental Law

In the early part of the first decade of the 2000s, residents of Lake Caliopa, Minnesota, began noticing an unusually high number of lung ailments among their population. A group of concerned local citizens pooled their resources and commissioned a study of the frequency of these health conditions per capita in Lake Caliopa as compared with national averages. The study concluded that residents of Lake Caliopa experienced four to seven times the rate in the frequency of asthma, bronchitis, and emphysema as the population nationwide. During the study period, citizens began expressing concerns about the large volumes of smog emitted by the Cotton Design apparel manufacturing plant on the outskirts of town. The plant had opened its production facility two miles east of town beside the Tawakoni River in 1999 and employed seventy full-time workers by 2010.

Just downstream on the Tawakoni River, the city of Lake Caliopa operated a public water works facility, which supplied all city residents with water. In August 2010, the Minnesota Pollution Control Agency required Cotton Design to install new equipment to control air and water pollution. In May 2011, citizens brought a lawsuit in a Minnesota state court against Cotton Design for various respiratory ailments allegedly caused or compounded by smog from Cotton Design's factory. Using the information presented in the chapter, answer the following questions.

1. Under the common law, what would each plaintiff be required to identify in order to be given relief by the court?
2. Are air-quality regulations typically overseen by federal, state, or local governments?
3. What standard for limiting emissions into the air does Cotton Design's pollution-control equipment have to meet?
4. What information must the city send to every household that it supplies with water?

DEBATE THIS: *The courts should reject all cases in which the wetlands in question do not consist of actual bodies of water that exist during the entire year.*

TERMS AND CONCEPTS

environmental law 555
nuisance 555

potentially responsible
  party (PRP) 566

toxic tort 556
wetlands 562

environmental impact
  statement (EIS) 556

QUESTIONS AND CASE PROBLEMS

25–1. Clean Air Act Current scientific knowledge indicates that there is no safe level of exposure to a cancer-causing agent. In theory, even one molecule of such a substance has the potential for causing cancer. Section 112 of the Clean Air Act requires that all cancer-causing substances be regulated to ensure a margin of safety. Some environmental groups have argued that all emissions of such substances must be eliminated if a margin of safety is to be reached. Such a total elimination would likely shut down many major U.S. industries. Should the Environmental Protection Agency totally eliminate all emissions of cancer-causing chemicals? Discuss.

25–2. QUESTION WITH SAMPLE ANSWER: Environmental Laws.

 Fruitade, Inc., is a processor of a soft drink called Freshen Up. Fruitade uses returnable bottles, which it cleans with a special acid to allow for further beverage processing. The acid is diluted with water and then allowed to pass into a navigable stream. Fruitade crushes its broken bottles and throws the crushed glass into the stream. Discuss fully any environmental laws that Fruitade has violated.

• **For a sample answer to Question 25–2, go to Appendix F at the end of this text.**

25–3. Environmental Laws Moonbay is a home-building corporation that primarily develops retirement communities. Farmtex owns a number of feedlots in Sunny Valley. Moonbay purchased 20,000 acres of farmland in the same area and began building and selling homes on this acreage. In the meantime, Farmtex continued to expand its feedlot business, and eventually only 500 feet separated the two operations. Because of the odor and flies from the feedlots, Moonbay found it difficult to sell the homes in its development. Moonbay wants to enjoin (prevent) Farmtex from operating its feedlot in the vicinity of the retirement home development. Under what common law theory would Moonbay file this action? Has Farmtex violated any federal environmental laws? Discuss.

25–4. Environmental Impact Statement Greers Ferry Lake is in Arkansas, and its shoreline is under the management of the U.S. Army Corps of Engineers, which is part of the U.S. Department of Defense (DOD). The Corps's 2000 Shoreline Management Plan (SMP) rezoned numerous areas along the lake, authorized the Corps to issue permits for the construction of new boat docks in the rezoned areas, increased by 300 percent the area around habitable structures that could be cleared of vegetation, and instituted a Wildlife Enhancement Permit to allow limited modifications of the shoreline. In relation to the SMP's adoption, the Corps issued a Finding of No Significant Impact, which declared that no environmental impact statement (EIS) was necessary. The Corps issued thirty-two boat dock construction permits under

the SMP before Save Greers Ferry Lake, Inc., filed a suit in a federal district court against the DOD, asking the court to, among other things, stop the Corps from acting under the SMP and order it to prepare an EIS. What are the requirements for an EIS? Is an EIS needed in this case? Explain. [*Save Greers Ferry Lake, Inc. v. Department of Defense,* 255 F.3d 498 (8th Cir. 2001)]

25–5. CERCLA Beginning in 1926, Marietta Dyestuffs Co. operated an industrial facility in Marietta, Ohio, to make dyes and other chemicals. In 1944, Dyestuffs became part of American Home Products Corp. (AHP), which sold the Marietta facility to American Cyanamid Co. in 1946. In 1950, AHP sold the rest of the Dyestuffs assets and all of its stock to Goodrich Co., which immediately liquidated the acquired corporation. Goodrich continued to operate the dissolved corporation's business, however. Cyanamid continued to make chemicals at the Marietta facility, and in 1993, it created Cytec Industries, Inc., which expressly assumed all environmental liabilities associated with Cyanamid's ownership and operation of the facility. Cytec spent nearly $25 million on clean-up costs and filed a suit in a federal district court against Goodrich to recover, under CERCLA, a portion of the costs attributable to the clean-up of hazardous wastes that may have been discarded at the site between 1926 and 1946. Cytec filed a motion for summary judgment in its favor. Should the court grant Cytec's motion? Explain. [*Cytec Industries, Inc. v. B. F. Goodrich Co.,* 196 F.Supp.2d 644 (S.D. Ohio 2002)]

25–6. CASE PROBLEM WITH SAMPLE ANSWER: Superfund.

William Gurley was the president and majority stockholder in Gurley Refining Co. (GRC). GRC bought used oil, treated it, and sold it. The refining process created a by-product residue of oily waste. GRC disposed of this waste by dumping it at, among other locations, a landfill in West Memphis, Arkansas. In February 1992, after detecting hazardous chemicals at the site, the Environmental Protection Agency (EPA) asked Gurley about his assets, the generators of the material disposed of at the landfill, site operations, and the structure of GRC. Gurley refused to respond, except to suggest that the EPA ask GRC. In October, the EPA placed the site on its clean-up list and again asked Gurley for information. When he still refused to respond, the EPA filed a suit in a federal district court against him, asking the court to impose a civil penalty. In February 1999, Gurley finally answered the EPA's questions. Under CERCLA, a court may impose a civil penalty "not to exceed $25,000 for each day of noncompliance against any person who unreasonably fails to comply" with an information request. Should the court assess a penalty in this case? Why or why not? [*United States v. Gurley,* 384 F.3d 316 (6th Cir. 2004)]

• **To view a sample answer for Problem 25–6, go to this book's Web site at www.cengage.com/blaw/cross, select "Chapter 25," and click on "Case Problem with Sample Answer."**

25–7. Clean Water Act The Anacostia River, which flows through Washington, D.C., is one of the ten most polluted rivers in the country. For bodies of water such as the Anacostia, the Clean Water Act requires states (which, under the act, include the District of Columbia) to set a "total maximum daily load" (TMDL) for pollutants. A TMDL is to be set "at a level necessary to implement the applicable water-quality standards with seasonal variations." The Anacostia contains biochemical pollutants that consume oxygen, putting the river's aquatic life at risk for suffocation. In addition, the river is murky, stunting the growth of plants that rely on sunlight and impairing recreational use. The Environmental Protection Agency (EPA) approved one TMDL limiting the *annual* discharge of oxygen-depleting pollutants and a second limiting the *seasonal* discharge of pollutants contributing to turbidity. Neither TMDL limited daily discharges. Friends of the Earth, Inc. (FoE), asked a federal district court to review the TMDLs. What is FoE's best argument in this dispute? What is the EPA's likely response? What should the court rule, and why? [*Friends of the Earth, Inc. v. Environmental Protection Agency*, 446 F.3d 140 (D.C.Cir. 2006)]

25–8. Environmental Impact Statement The fourth largest crop in the United States is alfalfa, of which 5 percent is exported to Japan. RoundUp Ready alfalfa is genetically engineered to resist glyphosate, the active ingredient in the herbicide RoundUp. The U.S. Department of Agriculture (USDA) regulates genetically engineered agricultural products through the Animal and Plant Health Inspection Service (APHIS). APHIS concluded that RoundUp Ready alfalfa does not have any harmful health effects on humans or livestock and deregulated it. Geertson Seed Farms and others filed a suit in a federal district court against Mike Johanns (then the secretary of the USDA) and others, asserting that APHIS's decision required the preparation of an environmental impact statement (EIS). The plaintiffs argued, among other things, that the introduction of RoundUp Ready alfalfa might significantly decrease the availability of or even eliminate, all nongenetically engineered varieties. The plaintiffs were concerned that the RoundUp Ready alfalfa might contaminate standard alfalfa because alfalfa is pollinated by bees, which can travel as far as two miles from a pollen source. If contamination occurred, farmers would not be able to market "contaminated" varieties as "organic," which would affect the sales of "organic" livestock and exports to Japan, which does not allow the import of glyphosate-resistant alfalfa. Should an EIS be prepared in this case? Why or why not? [*Geertson Seed Farms v. Johanns*, __ F.Supp.2d __ (N.D.Cal. 2007)]

25–9. Environmental Impact Statement The U.S. National Park Service (NPS) manages the Grand Canyon National Park in Arizona under a management plan that is subject to periodic review. In 2006, after nine years of background work and the completion of a comprehensive environmental impact statement, the NPS issued a new management plan for the park. The plan allowed for the continued use of rafts on the Colorado River, which runs through the Grand Canyon. The number of rafts was limited, however. Several environmental groups criticized the plan because they felt that it still allowed too many rafts on the river. The groups asked a federal appellate court to overturn the plan, claiming that it violated the wilderness status of the national park. When can a federal court overturn a determination by an agency such as the NPS? Explain. [*River Runners for Wilderness v. Martin*, 593 F.3d 1064 (9th Cir. 2010)]

25–10. A QUESTION OF ETHICS: Clean Air Act.

 In the Clean Air Act, Congress allowed California, which has particular problems with clean air, to adopt its own standard for emissions from cars and trucks, subject to the approval of the Environmental Protection Agency (EPA) according to certain criteria. Congress also allowed other states to adopt California's standard after the EPA's approval. In 2004, in an effort to address global warming, the California Air Resources Board amended the state's standard to attain "the maximum feasible and cost-effective reduction of GHG [greenhouse gas] emissions from motor vehicles." The regulation, which applies to new passenger vehicles and light-duty trucks for 2009 and later, imposes decreasing limits on emissions of carbon dioxide through 2016. While EPA approval was pending, Vermont and other states adopted similar standards. Green Mountain Chrysler Plymouth Dodge Jeep and other auto dealers, automakers, and associations of automakers filed a suit in a federal district court against George Crombie (then the secretary of the Vermont Agency of Natural Resources) and others, seeking relief from the state regulations. [Green Mountain Chrysler Plymouth Dodge Jeep v. Crombie, 508 F.Supp.2d 295 (D.Vt. 2007)]

(a) Under the Environmental Policy and Conservation Act (EPCA) of 1975, the National Highway Traffic Safety Administration sets fuel economy standards for new cars. The plaintiffs argued, among other things, that the EPCA, which prohibits states from adopting separate fuel economy standards, preempts Vermont's GHG regulation. Do the GHG rules equate to the fuel economy standards? Discuss.

(b) Do Vermont's rules tread on the efforts of the federal government to address global warming internationally? Who should regulate GHG emissions? The federal government? The state governments? Both? Neither? Why?

(c) The plaintiffs claimed that they would go bankrupt if they were forced to adhere to the state's GHG standards. Should they be granted relief on this basis? Does history support their claim? Explain.

LEGAL RESEARCH EXERCISES ON THE WEB

Go to this text's Web site at **www.cengage.com/blaw/cross**, select "Chapter 25," and click on "Practical Internet Exercises." There you will find the following Internet research exercises that you can perform to learn more about the topics covered in this chapter.

Practical Internet Exercise 25–1: **Legal Perspective**
Nuisance Law

Practical Internet Exercise 25–2: **Management Perspective**
Complying with Environmental Regulation

Practical Internet Exercise 25–3: **Ethical Perspective**
Environmental Justice

CHAPTER 26

Real Property and Land-Use Control

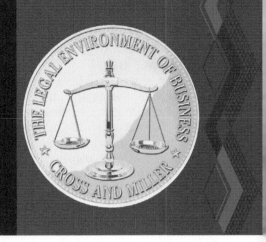

From the earliest times, property has provided a means for survival. Primitive peoples lived off the fruits of the land, eating the vegetation and wildlife. Later, as the wildlife was domesticated and the vegetation cultivated, property provided pastures and farmland. Throughout history, property has continued to be an indicator of family wealth and social position. In the Western world, the protection of an individual's right to his or her property has become one of our more important rights.

In this chapter, we first look at the nature of ownership rights in real property. We then examine the legal requirements involved in the transfer of real property, including the kinds of rights that are transferred by various types of deeds; the procedures used in the sale of real estate; and a way in which real property can, under certain conditions, be transferred merely by possession.

(For information on the financial aspects of real estate transactions, see Chapter 16.)

Realize that real property rights are never absolute. There is a higher right—that of the government to take, for compensation, private land for public use. This chapter discusses this right, as well as other restrictions on the ownership or use of property, including zoning laws. We conclude this chapter with a discussion of land-use control.

SECTION 1
THE NATURE OF REAL PROPERTY

Real property (or *realty*) consists of land and everything permanently attached to it, including structures and other fixtures. Everything else is **personal property.** Personal property is movable; real property is immovable. Real property also includes airspace and subsurface rights, as well as plant and vegetation rights.

Land and Structures

Land includes the soil on the surface of the earth and the natural products or artificial structures that are attached to it. Land further includes all the waters contained on or under its surface and much, but not necessarily all, of the airspace above it. The exterior boundaries of land extend down to the center of the earth and up to the farthest reaches of the atmosphere (subject to certain qualifications).

Airspace and Subsurface Rights

The owner of real property has relatively exclusive rights to both the airspace above the land and the soil and minerals underneath it. Any limitations on either airspace rights or subsurface rights, called *encumbrances,* normally must be indicated on the document that transfers title at the time of purchase. The ways in which ownership rights in real property can be limited will be examined later in this chapter.

AIRSPACE RIGHTS Disputes concerning airspace rights may involve the right of commercial and private planes to fly over property and the right of individuals and governments to seed clouds and produce artificial rain. Flights over private land normally do not violate property rights unless the flights are so low and so frequent that they directly interfere with the owner's enjoyment and use of the land. Leaning walls or projecting eave spouts or roofs may also violate the airspace rights of an adjoining property owner.

SUBSURFACE RIGHTS In many states, ownership of land can be separated from ownership of its subsurface. In other words, the owner of the surface may sell subsurface rights to another person. Subsurface rights can be extremely valuable, as these rights include the ownership of minerals, oil, or natural gas. But a subsurface owner's rights would be of little value if he or she could not use the surface to exercise those rights. Hence, a subsurface owner has a right, or a *profit* (see page 576), to go onto the surface of the land to, for example, find and remove minerals.

When ownership is separated into surface and subsurface rights, each owner can pass title to what she or he owns without the consent of the other owner. Of course, conflicts can arise between the surface owner's use of the property and the subsurface owner's need to extract minerals, oil, or natural gas. In that situation, one party's interest may become subservient (secondary) to the other party's interest either by statute or by case law. If the owners of the subsurface rights excavate, they are absolutely liable if their excavation causes the surface to collapse. Many states have statutes that also make the excavators liable for any damage to structures on the land. Typically, these statutes provide precise requirements for excavations of various depths.

Plant Life and Vegetation

Plant life, both natural and cultivated, is also considered to be real property. In many instances, the natural vegetation, such as trees, adds greatly to the value of realty. When a parcel of land is sold and the land has growing crops on it, the sale includes the crops, unless otherwise specified in the sales contract. When crops are sold by themselves, however, they are considered to be personal property or goods. Consequently, the sale of crops is a sale of goods and governed by the Uniform Commercial Code (discussed in Chapter 11) rather than by real property law.

SECTION 2
OWNERSHIP AND OTHER INTERESTS IN REAL PROPERTY

Ownership of property is an abstract concept that cannot exist independently of the legal system. No one can actually possess, or *hold*, a piece of land, the air above, the earth below, and all the water contained on it. One can only possess *rights* in real property. Numerous rights are involved in real property ownership, which is why property ownership is often viewed as a bundle of rights. One who possesses the entire bundle of rights is said to hold the property in *fee simple*—the most complete form of ownership. When only some of the rights in the bundle are transferred to another person, the effect is to limit the ownership rights of both the transferor of the rights and the recipient.

Traditionally, ownership interests in real property were referred to as *estates in land,* which include fee simple estates, life estates, and leasehold estates. We examine these estates in land, forms of concurrent ownership, and certain other interests in real property that is owned by others in the following subsections.

Ownership in Fee Simple

In a **fee simple absolute,** the owner has the greatest aggregation of rights, privileges, and power possible. The owner can give the property away or dispose of the property by *deed* (see page 579) or by will. When there is no will, the fee simple passes to the owner's legal heirs on her or his death. A fee simple absolute is potentially infinite in duration and is assigned forever to a person and her or his heirs without limitation or condition.[1] The owner has the rights of *exclusive* possession and use of the property.

The rights that accompany a fee simple absolute include the right to use the land for whatever purpose the owner sees fit. Of course, other laws, including applicable zoning, noise, and environmental laws, may limit the owner's ability to use the property in certain ways. A person who uses his or her property in a manner that unreasonably interferes with others' right to use or enjoy their own property can be liable for the tort of *nuisance* (discussed in Chapter 25).

In the following case, the court had to decide whether the noise—including rock and roll music, conversation, and clacking pool balls—coming from a local bar unreasonably interfered with a neighboring property owner's rights.

---

1. Another type of estate, the *fee simple defeasible*, exists in which ownership in fee simple will automatically terminate if a stated event occurs.

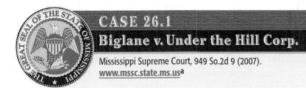

CASE 26.1
Biglane v. Under the Hill Corp.

Mississippi Supreme Court, 949 So.2d 9 (2007).
www.mssc.state.ms.us[a]

BACKGROUND AND FACTS • In 1967, Nancy and James Biglane bought and refurbished a building at 27 Silver Street in Natchez, Mississippi, and opened the lower portion as a gift shop. In 1973, Andre Farish and Paul O'Malley bought the building next door, at 25 Silver Street, and opened the Natchez Under the Hill Saloon.[b] Later, the Biglanes converted the upper floors of their building into an apartment and moved in. Although they installed insulated walls and windows, located the bedroom on the side of the building away from the Saloon, and placed the air-conditioning unit on the side nearest the Saloon, the Biglanes had a problem. The noise from the Saloon kept them wide awake at night. During the summer, the Saloon, which had no air-conditioning, opened its windows and doors, and live music echoed up and down the street. The Biglanes asked the Saloon to turn the music down, and the business complied. Additionally, thicker windows were installed, the loudest band was replaced, and the other bands were asked to keep their output below a certain level of decibels. Still dissatisfied, the Biglanes filed a suit in a Mississippi state court against the Saloon. The court enjoined the defendant from opening doors or windows when music was playing and ordered it to prevent its patrons from loitering in the street. Both parties appealed to the Mississippi Supreme Court.

IN THE LANGUAGE OF THE COURT
DIAZ, Justice, for the court.
* * * *

An entity is subject to liability * * * *when its conduct is a legal cause of an invasion of another's interest in the private use and enjoyment of land and that invasion is* * * * *intentional and unreasonable* * * * . [Emphasis added.]

* * * [The trial court] found ample evidence that the Biglanes frequently could not use or enjoy their property—significantly, that Mrs. Biglane often slept away from the apartment on weekends to avoid the noise and that she could not have her grandchildren over on the weekends because of the noise. The audiologist [one who diagnoses hearing problems] who testified for the Biglanes concluded that the noise levels were excessive and unreasonable * * * .

* * * *

* * * The trial court weighed the fact that the Biglanes knew or should have known that there was going to be some sort of noise associated with living within five feet of a * * * saloon which provides live music on the weekends.

* * * *

* * * *A reasonable use of one's property cannot be construed to include those uses which produce obnoxious noises, which in turn result in a material injury to owners of property in the vicinity, causing them to suffer substantial annoyance, inconvenience, and discomfort.* [Emphasis added.]

Accordingly, even a lawful business—which the Under the Hill Saloon certainly is—may * * * [not interfere] with its neighbors' enjoyment of their property. We recognize that each * * * case must be decided upon its own peculiar facts, taking into consideration the location and the surrounding circumstances. Ultimately, it is not necessary that other property owners should be driven from their dwellings, because it is enough that the enjoyment of life and property is rendered materially uncomfortable and annoying.

* * * *

In the case at hand, the trial court exercised its power to permit continued operation of the Saloon while setting conditions to its future operation. Namely, it found that the Saloon could not operate its business with its doors and windows opened during any time that amplified

---

a. Under "Quick Links," click on "Decisions Search" in the "Supreme Court" section. When that page opens, select "Natural Language" and enter "Biglane" and click on "Search." Select the file from the Mississippi Supreme Court (decided 2/27/07) to view the decision. The Mississippi Judiciary maintains this Web site.

b. The term *saloon* was used during the mid- to late nineteenth century in the American West to indicate an establishment that served alcohol.

CASE CONTINUES ▶

CASE 26.1 CONTINUED ➡ music is being played inside the saloon. The * * * court found that such a limitation is reasonable in that it should help contain the noise within the saloon, and should discourage the bar patrons from congregating or loitering in the streets outside of the saloon.

From a review of the record it is clear that the * * * court balanced the interests between the Biglanes and the Saloon in a quest for an equitable remedy that allowed the couple to enjoy their private apartment while protecting a popular business and tourist attraction from over-regulation.

DECISION AND REMEDY • *The Mississippi Supreme Court affirmed the lower court's injunction. The Saloon unreasonably interfered with the Biglanes' rights. "One landowner may not use his land so as to unreasonably annoy, inconvenience, or harm others."*

THE ETHICAL DIMENSION • *At one point, the Biglanes blocked off two parking lots that served the Saloon. Was this an unreasonable interference with the Saloon's rights? Explain.*

THE LEGAL ENVIRONMENT DIMENSION • *Could repulsive odors emanating from a neighbor's property constitute unreasonable interference with a property owner's rights? Discuss.*

Life Estates

A **life estate** is an estate that lasts for the life of some specified individual. A **conveyance,** or transfer of real property, "to A for his life" creates a life estate.[2] In a life estate, the life tenant's ownership rights cease to exist on the life tenant's death. The life tenant has the right to use the land, provided that he or she commits no **waste** (injury to the land). In other words, the life tenant cannot use the land in a manner that would adversely affect its value. The life tenant can use the land to harvest crops or, if mines and oil wells are already on the land, can extract minerals and oil from it, but the life tenant cannot exploit the land by creating new wells or mines.

The life tenant can create liens, *easements* (see page 576), and leases. None can extend beyond the life of the tenant, however. In addition, with few exceptions, the owner of a life estate has an exclusive right to possession during his or her lifetime.

Along with these rights, the life tenant also has some duties—to keep the property in repair and to pay property taxes. In sum, the owner of the life estate has the same rights as a fee simple owner except that she or he must maintain the value of the property during her or his tenancy.

Concurrent Ownership

Persons who share ownership rights simultaneously in particular property (including real property and personal property) are said to have **concurrent ownership.** There are two principal types of concurrent ownership: *tenancy in common* and *joint tenancy*. Concurrent ownership rights can also be held in a tenancy by the entirety or as *community property*, although these types of concurrent ownership are less common.

TENANCY IN COMMON The term **tenancy in common** refers to a form of co-ownership in which each of two or more persons owns an undivided interest in the property. The interest is undivided because each tenant has rights in the whole property. On the death of a tenant in common, that tenant's interest in the property passes to her or his heirs.

For example, four friends purchase a condominium unit in Hawaii together as tenants in common. This means that each of them has an ownership interest (one-fourth) in the whole. If one of the four owners dies a year after the purchase, his ownership interest passes to his heirs (his wife and children, for example) rather than to the other tenants in common.

Unless the co-tenants have agreed otherwise, a tenant in common can transfer her or his interest in the property to another without the consent of the remaining co-owners. Generally, it is presumed that a co-tenancy is a tenancy in common unless there is a clear intention to establish a joint tenancy (discussed next).

JOINT TENANCY In a **joint tenancy,** each of two or more persons owns an undivided interest in the property, but a deceased joint tenant's interest passes to the surviving joint tenant or tenants. The right of a surviving joint tenant to inherit a deceased joint

---

2. A less common type of life estate is created by the conveyance "to A for the life of B." This is known as an estate *pur autre vie*— that is, an estate for the duration of the life of another.

tenant's ownership interest—referred to as a *right of survivorship*—distinguishes a joint tenancy from a tenancy in common. Suppose that Jerrold and Eva are married and purchase a house as joint tenants. The title to the house clearly expresses the intent to create a joint tenancy because it says "to Jerrold and Eva as joint tenants with right of survivorship." Jerrold has three children from a prior marriage. If Jerrold dies, his interest in the house automatically passes to Eva rather than to his children from the prior marriage.

Although a joint tenant can transfer her or his rights by sale or gift to another without the consent of the other joint tenants, doing so terminates the joint tenancy. In such a situation, the person who purchases the property or receives it as a gift becomes a tenant in common, not a joint tenant. For example, three brothers, Brody, Saul, and Jacob, own a parcel as joint tenants. Brody is experiencing financial difficulties and sells his interest in the property to Beth. The sale terminates the joint tenancy, and now Beth, Saul, and Jacob hold the property as tenants in common.

A joint tenant's interest can also be levied against—that is, seized by court order—to satisfy the tenant's judgment creditors. If this occurs, the joint tenancy terminates, and the remaining owners hold the property as tenants in common. (Judgment creditors can also seize the interests of tenants in a tenancy in common.)

TENANCY BY THE ENTIRETY A **tenancy by the entirety** is a less common form of ownership that typically is created by a conveyance (transfer) of real property to a husband and wife. It differs from a joint tenancy in that neither spouse may separately transfer his or her interest during his or her lifetime unless the other spouse consents. In some states in which statutes give the wife the right to convey her property, this form of concurrent ownership has effectively been abolished. A divorce, either spouse's death, or mutual agreement will terminate a tenancy by the entirety.

COMMUNITY PROPERTY A limited number of states[3] allow property to be owned by a married couple as **community property.** If property is held as community property, each spouse technically owns an undivided one-half interest in the property. This type of ownership applies to most property acquired by the husband or the wife during the course of the marriage. It generally does not apply to property acquired prior to the marriage or to property acquired by gift or inheritance during the marriage. After a divorce, community property is divided equally in some states and according to the discretion of the court in other states.

Leasehold Estates

A **leasehold estate** is created when a real property owner or lessor (landlord) agrees to convey the right to possess and use the property to a lessee (tenant) for a certain period of time. In every leasehold estate, the tenant has a *qualified* right to exclusive, though *temporary,* possession (qualified by the landlord's right to enter onto the premises to ensure that the tenant is not causing damage to the property). The tenant can use the land—for example, by harvesting crops—but cannot injure it by such activities as cutting down timber to sell or extracting oil.

Next, we look at the types of leasehold estates, or tenancies, that can be created when real property is leased.

FIXED-TERM TENANCY OR TENANCY FOR YEARS A **fixed-term tenancy,** also called a *tenancy for years,* is created by an express contract by which property is leased for a specified period of time, such as a month, a year, or a period of years. Signing a one-year lease to occupy an apartment, for instance, creates a tenancy for years. Note that the term need not be specified by date and can be conditioned on the occurrence of an event, such as leasing a cabin for the summer or an apartment during Mardi Gras. At the end of the period specified in the lease, the lease ends (without notice), and possession of the property returns to the lessor. If the tenant dies during the period of the lease, the lease interest passes to the tenant's heirs as personal property. Often, leases include renewal or extension provisions.

PERIODIC TENANCY A **periodic tenancy** is created by a lease that does not specify how long it is to last but does specify that rent is to be paid at certain intervals. This type of tenancy is automatically renewed for another rental period unless properly terminated. For example, Jewel, LLC, enters into a lease with Capital Properties. The lease states, "Rent is due on the tenth day of every month." This provision creates a periodic tenancy from month to month. This type of tenancy can also extend from week to week or from year to year. A periodic

---

3. These states include Alaska, Arizona, California, Idaho, Louisiana, Nevada, New Mexico, Texas, Washington, and Wisconsin. Puerto Rico allows property to be owned as community property as well.

tenancy sometimes arises when a landlord allows a tenant under a tenancy for years to *hold over* (retain possession after the lease term ends) and continue paying monthly or weekly rent.

Under the common law, to terminate a periodic tenancy, the landlord or tenant must give at least one period's notice to the other party. If the tenancy is month to month, for example, one month's notice must be given. State statutes often require a different period for notice of termination in a periodic tenancy, however.

TENANCY AT WILL In a **tenancy at will,** either the landlord or the tenant can terminate the tenancy without notice. This type of tenancy can arise if a landlord rents property to a tenant "for as long as both agree" or allows a person to live on the premises without paying rent. Tenancy at will is rare today because most state statutes require a landlord to provide some period of notice to terminate a tenancy (as previously noted). States may also require a landowner to have sufficient cause (reason) to end a residential tenancy. Certain events, such as the death of either party or the voluntary commission of *waste* (harm to the premises) by the tenant, automatically terminate a tenancy at will.

TENANCY AT SUFFERANCE The mere possession of land without right is called a **tenancy at sufferance.** A tenancy at sufferance is not a true tenancy because it is created when a tenant *wrongfully* retains possession of property. Whenever a tenancy for years or a periodic tenancy ends and the tenant continues to retain possession of the premises without the owner's permission, a tenancy at sufferance is created.

Nonpossessory Interests

In contrast to the types of property interests just described, some interests in land do not include any rights to possess the property. These interests, known as **nonpossessory interests,** include *easements*, *profits*, and *licenses*. Nonpossessory interests are basically interests in real property owned by others.

An **easement** is the right of a person to make limited use of another person's real property without taking anything from the property. The right to walk across another's property, for example, is an easement. In contrast, a **profit** is the right to go onto land owned by another and take away some part of the land itself or some product of the land. For example, Akmed, the owner of Sandy View, gives Ann the right to go there and remove all of the sand and gravel that she needs for her cement business. Ann has a profit.

Easements and profits can be classified as either *appurtenant* or *in gross*. Because easements and profits are similar and the same rules apply to both, we discuss them together.

EASEMENT OR PROFIT APPURTENANT An easement or profit *appurtenant* arises when the owner of one piece of land has a right to go onto (or remove things from) an adjacent piece of land owned by another. The land that is benefited by the easement is called the *dominant estate,* and the land that is burdened is called the *servient estate*. Because easements appurtenant are intended to *benefit the land,* they run (are conveyed) with the land when it is transferred. Suppose that Owen has a right to drive his car across Green's land, which is adjacent to Owen's property. This right-of-way over Green's property is an easement appurtenant to Owen's land and can be used only by Owen. If Owen sells his land, the easement runs with the land to benefit the new owner.

EASEMENT OR PROFIT IN GROSS In an easement or profit *in gross,* the right to use or take things from another's land is given to one who does not own an adjacent tract of land. These easements are intended to *benefit a particular person or business,* not a particular piece of land, and cannot be transferred. For example, Avery owns a parcel of land with a marble quarry. Avery conveys to Classic Stone Corporation the right to come onto her land and remove up to five hundred pounds of marble per day. Classic Stone owns a profit in gross and cannot transfer this right to another. Similarly, when a utility company is granted an easement to run its power lines across another's property, it obtains an easement in gross.

CREATION OF AN EASEMENT OR PROFIT Most easements and profits are created by an express grant in a contract, deed, or will. This allows the parties to include terms defining the extent and length of time of use. In some situations, an easement or profit can also be created without an express agreement.

An easement or profit may arise by *implication* when the circumstances surrounding the division of a parcel of property imply its creation. For example, Barrow divides a parcel of land that has only one well for drinking water. If Barrow conveys the half without a well to Dean, a profit by implication arises because Dean needs drinking water.

An easement may also be created by *necessity*. An easement by necessity does not require division of property for its existence. A person who rents an apartment, for example, has an easement by necessity in the private road leading up to it.

An easement arises by *prescription* when one person exercises an easement, such as a right-of-way, on another person's land without the landowner's consent, and the use is apparent and continues for a period of time equal to the applicable statute of limitations. (In much the same way, title to property may be obtained by adverse possession, as will be discussed later in this chapter.)

TERMINATION OF AN EASEMENT OR PROFIT An easement or profit can be terminated or extinguished in several ways. The simplest way is to deed it back to the owner of the land that is burdened by it. Another way is to abandon it and create evidence of intent to relinquish the right to use it. Mere nonuse will not extinguish an easement or profit *unless the nonuse is accompanied by an overt act showing the intent to abandon.* Also, if the owner of an easement or profit becomes the owner of the property burdened by it, then it is merged into the property.

LICENSE In the context of real property, a **license** is the revocable right of a person to come onto another person's land. It is a personal privilege that arises from the consent of the owner of the land and can be revoked by the owner. A ticket to attend a movie at a theater is an example of a license. Assume that a Broadway theater owner issues a ticket to Alena to see a play. If Alena is refused entry because she is improperly dressed, she has no right to force her way into the theater. The ticket is only a revocable license, not a conveyance of an interest in property.

In essence, a license grants a person the authority to enter the land of another and perform a specified act or series of acts without obtaining any permanent interest in the land. When a person with a license exceeds the authority granted and undertakes some action on the property that is not permitted, the property owner can sue that person for trespass (discussed in Chapter 12).

CASE IN POINT A Catholic church granted Prince Realty Management, LLC, a three-month license to use a three-foot strip of its property adjacent to Prince's property. The license authorized Prince to "put up plywood panels," creating a temporary fence to protect Prince's property during the construction of a new building, and then restore the boundary line between the properties with a new brick fence.

During the license's term, Prince installed steel piles and beams on the licensed property. When Prince ignored the church's demands that these structures be removed, the church sued Prince for trespass. The court held that because the license allowed only temporary structures and Prince had exceeded its authority by installing steel piles and beams, the church was entitled to damages.[4]

SECTION 3
TRANSFER OF OWNERSHIP

Ownership interests in real property are frequently transferred by sale, and the terms of the transfer are specified in a real estate sales contract. Often, real estate brokers or agents who are licensed by the state assist the buyers and sellers during the sales transaction. (For a discussion of special duties related to brokers and agents, see Chapter 20.) Real property ownership can also be transferred by gift, by will or inheritance, by possession, or by eminent domain. In the subsections that follow, we focus primarily on voluntary sales of real property. We then consider adverse possession, which is an involuntary method of transferring title to real property. Eminent domain will be discussed later in this chapter.

Listing Agreements

In a typical real estate transaction, the seller employs a real estate agent to find a buyer for the property by entering into a listing agreement with the agent. The listing agreement specifies the duration of the listing with that agent, the terms under which the seller will sell the property, and the amount of commission the seller will pay.

There are different types of listing agreements. If the contract gives the agent an exclusive right to sell the property, then only that real estate agent is authorized to sell the property for a specified period of time. For example, a seller might give the agent thirty days of exclusive agency. If a buyer is found within the thirty-day period, the agent will be paid the full amount of the commission, even if the agent was not responsible for finding that buyer. After the thirty-day period ends, if another real estate agent procures a buyer, the listing agent may have to split the commission. In an open listing, the seller agrees

---

4. *Roman Catholic Church of Our Lady of Sorrows v. Prince Realty Management, LLC,* 47 A.D.3d 909, 850 N.Y.S.2d 569 (2008).

to pay a commission to the real estate agent who brings in a buyer. An open listing is nonexclusive, and thus agents with other real estate firms may attempt to find a buyer and share in the commission with the listing agent.

Although many sales of real estate involve listing agreements, it is not necessary for a property owner to list the property with a real estate agent. Many owners offer their properties for sale directly without an agent. The ability to advertise real properties for sale via the Internet has made it easier for an owner to find a buyer without using an agent. Because an agent is not essential, listing agreements are not shown in Exhibit 26–1 below, which summarizes the steps involved in any sale of real property.

Real Estate Sales Contracts

The sale of real estate is in some ways similar to the sale of goods because it involves a transfer of ownership, often with specific warranties. In a sale of real estate, however, certain formalities are observed that are not required in a sale of goods. The sale of real estate is a complicated transaction. Usually, after substantial negotiation between the parties (offers, counteroffers, responses), the parties enter into a detailed contract setting forth their agreement. A contract for a sale of land includes such terms as the purchase price, the type of deed the buyer will receive, the condition of the premises, and any items that will be included.

CONTINGENCIES Unless the buyer pays cash for the property, the buyer must obtain financing through a mortgage loan. Real estate sales contracts are often made contingent on the buyer obtaining financing at or below a specified rate of interest. (Chapter 16 explains the disclosures necessary for residential financing and the special disclosures required for high-interest mortgage loans.) The contract may

EXHIBIT 26–1 • Steps Involved in the Sale of Real Estate

BUYER'S PURCHASE OFFER
Buyer offers to purchase Seller's property. The offer may be conditioned on Buyer's ability to obtain financing, on satisfactory inspections of the premises, on title examination, and the like. Included with the offer is earnest money, which will be placed in an escrow account.

SELLER'S RESPONSE
If Seller accepts Buyer's offer, then a contract is formed. Seller could also reject the offer or make a counteroffer that modifies Buyer's terms. Buyer may accept or reject Seller's counteroffer or make a counteroffer that modifies Seller's terms.

PURCHASE AND SALE AGREEMENT
Once an offer or a counteroffer is accepted, a purchase and sale agreement is formed.

TITLE EXAMINATION AND INSURANCE
The examiner investigates and verifies Seller's rights in the property and discloses any claims or interests held by others. Buyer (and/or Seller) may purchase title insurance to protect against a defect in title.

FINANCING
Buyer may seek a mortgage loan to finance the purchase. Buyer agrees to grant lender an interest in the property as security for Buyer's indebtedness.

INSPECTION
Buyer has the property inspected for any physical problems, such as major structural or mechanical defects and insect infestation.

ESCROW
Buyer's purchase funds (including earnest money) are held in an escrow account by an escrow agent (such as a title company or a bank). This agent holds the deed transferring title received from Seller and any funds received from Buyer until all conditions of the sale have been met.

CLOSING
The escrow agent transfers the deed to Buyer and the proceeds of the sale to Seller. The proceeds are the purchase price less any amount already paid by Buyer and any closing costs to be paid by Seller. Included in the closing costs are fees charged for services performed by the lender, escrow agent, and title examiner. The purchase and sale of the property are complete.

also be contingent on the buyer selling other real property, the seller obtaining a survey and title insurance, and the property passing one or more inspections. Normally, the buyer is responsible for having the premises inspected for physical or mechanical defects and for insect infestation.

CLOSING DATE AND ESCROW The contract usually fixes a date for performance, or **closing,** that frequently is four to twelve weeks after the contract is signed. On this day, the seller conveys the property to the buyer by delivering the deed to the buyer in exchange for payment of the purchase price. Deposits toward the purchase price normally are held in a special account, called an **escrow account,** until all of the conditions of sale have been met. Once the closing takes place, the funds in the escrow account are transferred to the seller. The *escrow agent,* which may be a title company, bank, or special escrow company, acts as a neutral party in the sales transaction and facilitates the sale by allowing the buyer and seller to close the transaction without having to exchange documents and funds.

IMPLIED WARRANTIES IN THE SALE OF NEW HOMES The common law rule of *caveat emptor* ("let the buyer beware") held that the seller of a home made no warranty as to its soundness or fitness (unless the contract or deed stated otherwise). Today, however, most states imply a warranty—the **implied warranty of habitability**—in the sale of new homes. The seller of a new house warrants that it will be fit for human habitation even if the deed or contract of sale does not include such a warranty. Essentially, the seller is warranting that the house is in reasonable working order and is of reasonably sound construction. Under this theory, the seller of a new home can be liable if the home is defective. In some states, the warranty protects not only the first purchaser but any subsequent purchaser as well.

SELLER'S DUTY TO DISCLOSE HIDDEN DEFECTS In most jurisdictions, courts impose on sellers a duty to disclose any known defect that materially affects the value of the property and that the buyer could not reasonably discover. Failure to disclose such a material defect gives the buyer a right to rescind the contract and to sue for damages based on fraud or misrepresentation.

A dispute may arise over whether the seller knew of the defect before the sale, and there is normally a limit to the time within which the buyer can bring a suit against the seller based on the defect.

For example, in Louisiana, the prescribed limit for a suit against a seller who knew, or can be presumed to have known, of the defect is one year from the day that the buyer discovered it. If the seller did not know of the defect, the limit is one year from the date of the sale.

CASE IN POINT Matthew Humphrey paid $44,000 for a house in Louisiana and partially renovated it. He then sold the house to Terry and Tabitha Whitehead for $67,000. A few months after the Whiteheads moved in, they discovered rotten wood behind the tile in the bathroom and experienced problems with the fireplace and the plumbing. Two years later, the Whiteheads filed a suit against Humphrey seeking to rescind the sale. They argued that the plumbing problems were a latent defect that the seller had failed to disclose. Evidence revealed that prior to the sale, the parties were made aware of issues regarding the sewer system and that corrective actions were taken. At the time of the sale, the toilets flushed, and neither side realized that the latent defects had not been resolved. The court ruled that rescission was not warranted for the sewer problems because the Whiteheads had waited too long after their discovery to file a claim against Humphrey. The court did order Humphrey to pay damages for the repairs to the fireplace and for replacing some of the rotten wood, however, because Humphrey knew about these defects at the time of the sale.[5]

Deeds

Possession and title to land are passed from person to person by means of a **deed**—the instrument used to transfer real property. A deed is a writing signed by an owner of real property by which title to it is transferred to another.[6] Deeds must meet certain requirements, but unlike a contract, a deed does not have to be supported by legally sufficient consideration. Gifts of real property are common, and they require deeds even though there is no consideration for the gift. To be valid, a deed must include the following:

1. The names of the *grantor* (the donor or seller) and the *grantee* (the donee or buyer).
2. Words evidencing the intent to convey (for example, "I hereby bargain, sell, grant, or give"). No specific words are necessary, and if the deed

---

5. *Whitehead v. Humphrey,* 954 So.2d 859 (La.App. 2007).
6. Note that in some states when a person purchases real property, the bank or lender receives a *trust deed* on the property until the homeowner pays off the mortgage. A trust deed is similar to a mortgage and is not used to transfer property.

does *not* specify the type of estate being transferred, it presumptively transfers it in fee simple absolute.

3. A legally sufficient description of the land. The description must include enough detail to distinguish the property being conveyed from every other parcel of land. The property can be identified by reference to an official survey or recorded plat (a type of map), or each boundary can be described by *metes and bounds*. **Metes and bounds** is a system of measuring boundary lines by the distance between two points, often using physical features of the local geography—for example, "beginning at the southwesterly intersection of Court and Main Streets, then West 40 feet to the fence, then South 100 feet, then Northeast approximately 120 feet back to the beginning."

4. The grantor's (and usually his or her spouse's) signature.

5. Delivery of the deed.

WARRANTY DEEDS Different types of deeds provide different degrees of protection against defects of title. A **warranty deed** makes the greatest number of warranties and thus provides the most extensive protection against defects of title. In most states, special language is required to create a warranty deed.

Warranty deeds include a number of *covenants*, or promises, that the grantor makes to the grantee. These covenants include a covenant that the grantor has the title to, and the power to convey, the property; a covenant of quiet enjoyment (a warranty that the buyer will not be disturbed in her or his possession of the land); and a covenant that transfer of the property is made without knowledge of adverse claims of third parties.

Generally, the warranty deed makes the grantor liable for all defects of title by the grantor and previous titleholders. For example, Julio sells a two-acre lot and office building by warranty deed. Subsequently, a third person appears, shows that she has better title than Julio had, and forces the buyer off the property. Here, the covenant of quiet enjoyment has been breached, and the buyer can sue Julio to recover the purchase price of the land, plus any other damages incurred as a result.

SPECIAL WARRANTY DEED In contrast to a warranty deed, a **special warranty deed,** which is frequently referred to as a *limited warranty deed,* warrants only that the grantor or seller held good title during his or her ownership of the property. In other words, the grantor does not warrant that

there were no defects of title when the property was held by previous owners.

If the special warranty deed discloses all liens or other encumbrances, the seller will not be liable to the buyer if a third person subsequently interferes with the buyer's ownership. If the third person's claim arises out of, or is related to, some act of the seller, however, the seller will be liable to the buyer for damages.

QUITCLAIM DEED A **quitclaim deed** offers the least protection against defects in the title. Basically, a quitclaim deed conveys to the grantee whatever interest the grantor had. So, if the grantor had no interest, then the grantee receives no interest. Naturally, if the grantor had a defective title or no title at all, a conveyance by warranty deed or special warranty deed would not cure the defects. Such deeds, however, will give the buyer a cause of action to sue the seller.

A quitclaim deed can and often does serve as a release of the grantor's interest in a particular parcel of property. For instance, Sanchez owns a strip of waterfront property on which he wants to build condominiums. Lanz has an easement on a portion of the property that might interfere with Sanchez's plans for the development. Sanchez can negotiate with Lanz to deed the easement back to Sanchez. A quitclaim deed from Lanz would constitute such a transfer.

GRANT DEED With a **grant deed,** the grantor simply states, "I grant the property to you" or "I convey, or bargain and sell, the property to you." By state statute, grant deeds carry with them an implied warranty that the grantor owns the property and has not previously transferred it to someone else or encumbered it, except as set out in the deed.

SHERIFF'S DEED A **sheriff's deed** is a document giving ownership rights to a buyer of property at a sheriff's sale, which is a sale held by a sheriff when the owner of the property has failed to pay a court judgment against her or him. Typically, the property was subject to a mortgage or tax payments, and the owner defaulted on the payments. After a statutory period of time during which the defaulting owner can redeem the property (see Chapter 16), the deed is delivered to the purchaser.

Recording Statutes

Once the seller delivers the deed to the buyer (at closing), legal title to the property is conveyed. Nevertheless, the buyer should promptly record the deed with the state records office to establish superior ownership rights against any third parties who might make a claim to the property. Every state has a **recording statute,** which allows deeds to be recorded in the public record. Recording a deed involves a fee, which the buyer typically pays because he or she is the one who will be protected by recording the deed.

Recording a deed gives notice to the public that a certain person is now the owner of a particular parcel of real estate. By putting everyone on notice as to the true owner, recording a deed prevents the previous owners from fraudulently conveying the land to other purchasers. Deeds generally are recorded in the county in which the property is located. Many state statutes require that the grantor sign the deed in the presence of two witnesses before it can be recorded.

MARKETABLE TITLE The question of title to a particular parcel of property is especially important to the buyer. A grantor (seller) is obligated to transfer **marketable title,** or good title, to the grantee (buyer). Marketable title means that the grantor's ownership is free from encumbrances (except those disclosed by the grantor) and free of defects. If the buyer signs a real estate sales contract and then discovers that the seller does not have a marketable title, the buyer can withdraw from the contract. For example, Chan enters into an agreement to buy Fortuna Ranch from Hal. Chan then discovers that Hal has previously given Pearl an unexpired option to purchase the ranch. In this situation, the title is not marketable because Pearl could exercise the option and Hal would be compelled to sell the ranch to her. Therefore, Chan can withdraw from the contract to buy the property.

TITLE SEARCH Because each document affecting ownership of property is recorded, recording provides a chronological public record of all transactions concerning the property. A systematic examination of this record for transactions creating interests or rights in a specific parcel of real property is called a **title search.** A prospective buyer or lender generally performs a title search to determine whether the seller truly owns the interest that he or she is attempting to convey and whether anyone else has an interest in the property. A title search should—but does not always—reveal encumbrances on the property and the existence of an easement or lien.

METHODS OF ENSURING GOOD TITLE To ensure that the title is marketable, a grantee has several options depending on the state. The grantee may hire an attorney to examine an *abstract of title* (a history of what the public records show regarding the title to the property) and provide an opinion as to whether the title is marketable. If the title is defective, the attorney's opinion will specify the nature of the defects. The attorney is liable to the grantee for any loss caused by her or his negligence.

An alternative method available in a few states is the *Torrens system* of title registration. Under this system, the title is registered in a judicial proceeding. All parties claiming an interest in the property are notified of the proceeding and are given an opportunity to assert their claims. After the hearing, the court issues a certificate of title, which is similar to an automobile title, to the person found to be the owner. All encumbrances are noted on the certificate, and when the property is sold, the certificate is transferred to the grantee along with the deed.

The most common method of ensuring title is through **title insurance,** which insures the grantee against loss from defects in title to real property. When financing the purchase of real property, many lenders require title insurance to protect their interests in the collateral for the loan. Title insurance is becoming less significant because title information and records are now available electronically and thus are easy to access.

Adverse Possession

A person who wrongfully possesses (by occupying or using) the real property of another may eventually acquire title to it through adverse possession. **Adverse possession** is a means of obtaining title to land without delivery of a deed and without the consent of—or payment to—the true owner. Thus, adverse possession is a method of *involuntarily* transferring title to the property from the true owner to the adverse possessor.

Essentially, when one person possesses the real property of another for a certain statutory period of time (three to thirty years, depending on the state, with ten years being most common), that person acquires title to the land. For property to be held adversely, four elements must be satisfied:

1. *Possession must be actual and exclusive*—that is, the possessor must physically occupy the property. This requirement is clearly met if the possessor lives on the property, but it may also be met if the possessor builds fences, erects structures, plants crops, or even grazes animals on the land.

2. *The possession must be open, visible, and notorious, not secret or clandestine.* The possessor must occupy the land for all the world to see. This requirement of obviousness ensures that the true owner is on notice that someone is possessing the owner's property wrongfully.

3. *Possession must be continuous and peaceable for the required period of time.* This requirement means that the possessor must not be interrupted in the occupancy by the true owner or by the courts. *Continuous* does not mean constant—it simply means that the possessor has continuously occupied the property in some fashion for the statutory time. *Peaceable* means that no force was used to possess the land.

4. *Possession must be hostile and adverse.* In other words, the possessor cannot be living on the property with the owner's permission and must claim the property as against the whole world.

Additionally, some states have other requirements to show adverse possession. There are a number of public-policy reasons for the adverse possession doctrine. These include society's interest in resolving boundary disputes, in determining title when title to property is in question, and in assuring that real property remains in the stream of commerce. More fundamentally, the doctrine punishes owners who do not take action when they see adverse possession and rewards possessors for putting land to productive use.

In the following case, the question before the court was whether a landowner had obtained title to a portion of adjacent land by adverse possession.

CASE 26.2
Scarborough v. Rollins
Court of Appeals of Mississippi, ___ So.3d ___ (2010).
www.mssc.state.ms.us[a]

BACKGROUND AND FACTS • Charles T. Scarborough and Mildred T. Rollins were adjoining landowners, sharing one common boundary. Based on Rollins's survey of the property, Rollins believed that she owned a portion of a gravel road located to the south of the apartment buildings she owned. On the contrary, Scarborough believed that the gravel road was located totally on his property and that he owned some property north of the gravel road toward Rollins's apartment buildings. In July 2006, Scarborough filed a complaint seeking to quiet and confirm his title to the property. Rollins filed a counterclaim seeking to quiet and confirm her title. The court entered judgment for Rollins. Scarborough appealed.

IN THE LANGUAGE OF THE COURT
ISHEE, J. [Judge]
* * * *

Scarborough asserts that the trial court erred in finding that Rollins proved that she owned the property in dispute by adverse possession. Scarborough claims that Rollins failed to prove by clear and convincing evidence that her possession of the disputed grassy area down to the northern edge of the gravel road has been hostile, open, notorious, visible, continuing, exclusive, and peaceful. Scarborough also claims that Rollins's paying taxes and mowing the grass north of the gravel road by her and her predecessors in title, as well as [a prior owner's] installation of a gas line are not such adverse actions that gave him sufficient notice that he would know that Rollins was claiming the disputed area and that she was attempting to deny him ownership thereof and exclude him therefrom. Scarborough asserts that both he and Rollins used the disputed land, thus exercising joint use of the land; therefore, a claim of adverse possession is not supported. Scarborough also asserts that Rollins paid taxes only on the land situated north of her monumented south boundary line while he paid taxes on all of the land called for in his deed, including the gravel road and the land north of the gravel road up to Rollins's south boundary.

---

a. Under "Quick Links" on the right-hand side of the page, click on "Decisions Search" in the "Court of Appeals" section. On the next page, click on "Natural Language." When that page opens, type "2008-CA-01579-COA" in the box and click on "Search." In the result, click on the second item in the list. The Mississippi Judiciary maintains this Web site.

CASE 26.2 CONTINUED ➡ To succeed on a claim of adverse possession, the claimant has the burden to prove each element by clear and convincing evidence. * * * *Adverse possession requires the claimant to prove that her possession or occupancy was: (1) under claim of ownership; (2) actual or hostile; (3) open, notorious, and visible; (4) continuous and uninterrupted for a period of ten years; (5) exclusive; and (6) peaceful.*

1. Under Claim of Ownership

The deed to Rollins's property presented to the chancery court indicated that she owned the property at or near the disputed property. Evidence was provided to show that Rollins and her predecessors-in-title paid the taxes on all of the property north of the gravel road. However, Scarborough only paid taxes on the property that was south of the gravel road.

2. Actual or Hostile

Evidence was provided to the chancery court that for more than thirty-five years, no one other than Rollins and her predecessors-in-title, the Blacks, used this property.

3. Open, Notorious, and Visible

[One witness] testified at trial that his family's ownership of that land was open and obvious. He stated that everyone in Starkville, who was around the apartments, knew that the apartment complex owned the yard up to the edge of the gravel road.

4. Continuous and Uninterrupted for a Period of Ten Years

Testimony at trial from [three witnesses] all provided that Rollins and her predecessors-in-title used the property for more than thirty-five years.

5. Exclusive

Testimony at trial * * * indicated that no one, until Scarborough, claimed to have used any part of the property in dispute.

6. Peaceful

Rollins testified that until September 2007, she and her predecessors-in-title enjoyed peaceful possession of the property.

We find that Rollins satisfied the elements required for adverse possession.

* * * *

The chancery court properly held that the gravel road which is to the north of Scarborough's property and to the south of Rollins's property was the boundary between the parties and that Rollins was entitled to an award of actual and punitive damages and attorney's fees due to the conversion of her property by Scarborough.

DECISION AND REMEDY • *The Court of Appeals of Mississippi affirmed the lower court's judgment and assessed all costs of the appeal to Scarborough. Rollins had proved title to the land by adverse possession.*

WHAT IF THE FACTS WERE DIFFERENT? • *Suppose that Rollins had not paid any taxes on the disputed land and that Scarborough had done so. Would the result have been different? Explain.*

THE E-COMMERCE DIMENSION • *How might the Internet have facilitated either party's claim to the disputed property?*

SECTION 4
LIMITATIONS ON THE RIGHTS OF PROPERTY OWNERS

No ownership rights in real property can ever really be absolute—that is, an owner of real property cannot always do whatever she or he wishes on or with the property. Nuisance and environmental laws, for example, restrict certain types of activities. Holding the property is also conditional on the payment of property taxes. Zoning laws and building permits frequently restrict one's use of the realty. In addition, if a property owner fails to pay debts, the property may be seized to satisfy judgment creditors. In short, the rights of every property owner are subject to certain conditions and limitations. We look here at some of the important ways in which owners' rights in real property can be limited.

Eminent Domain

Even ownership in fee simple absolute is limited by a superior ownership. Just as the king was the ultimate landowner in medieval England, today the government has an ultimate ownership right in all land in the United States. This right, known as **eminent domain,** is sometimes referred to as the *condemnation power* of government to take land for public use. It gives the government the right to acquire possession of real property in the manner directed by the U.S. Constitution and the laws of the state whenever the public interest requires it. Property may be taken only for public use, not for private benefit.

For example, when a new public highway is to be built, the government decides where to build it and how much land to condemn. After the government determines that a particular parcel of land is necessary for public use, it will first offer to buy the property. If the owner refuses the offer, the government brings a judicial (condemnation) proceeding to obtain title to the land. Then, in another proceeding, the court determines the *fair value* of the land, which usually is approximately equal to its market value.

When the government uses its power of eminent domain to acquire land owned by a private party, a **taking** occurs. Under the *takings clause* of the Fifth Amendment to the U.S. Constitution, the government must pay "just compensation" to the owner. State constitutions contain similar provisions.

As just mentioned, the government can utilize its power of eminent domain to take property only for a public purpose. Clearly, a dam, a highway, or a national park would be considered a public purpose. But what about economic development? Is it also a public purpose that can be furthered through the use of the power of eminent domain? That was the question in the following case.

✳ EXTENDED CASE 26.3 ✳
Kelo v. City of New London, Connecticut

Supreme Court of the United States, 545 U.S. 469, 125 S.Ct. 2655, 162 L.Ed.2d 439 (2005).
www.findlaw.com/casecode/supreme.html[a]

IN THE LANGUAGE OF THE COURT

Justice *STEVENS* delivered the opinion of the Court.
* * * *
The city of New London (hereinafter City) sits at the junction of the Thames River and the Long Island Sound in southeastern Connecticut. Decades of economic decline led a state agency in 1990 to designate the City a "distressed municipality." In 1996, the Federal Government closed the Naval Undersea Warfare Center, which had been located in the Fort Trumbull area of the City and had employed over 1,500 people. In 1998, the City's unemployment rate was nearly double that of the State, and its population of just under 24,000 residents was at its lowest since 1920.

These conditions prompted state and local officials to target New London * * * for economic revitalization. * * * In February [1998] the pharmaceutical company Pfizer Inc. announced that it would build a $300 million research facility on a site immediately adjacent to Fort Trumbull; local planners hoped that Pfizer would draw new business to the area * * *.
* * * *
The city council approved [a] plan in January 2000 [to redevelop the area that once housed the federal facility]. The [City] successfully negotiated the purchase of most of the real estate in the 90-acre area, but its negotiations with [some of the property owners] failed. As a consequence, in November 2000, the [City] initiated * * * condemnation proceedings * * *.
* * * *
* * * Susette Kelo has lived in the Fort Trumbull area since 1997. * * * She prizes [her house] for its water view.

In December 2000 [Kelo and others] brought this action in [a Connecticut state court against the City and others]. They claimed, among other things, that the taking of their properties would violate the "public use" restriction in the [U.S. Constitution's] Fifth Amendment. * * * [The court issued a ruling partly in favor of both sides.]

* * * Both sides took appeals to the Supreme Court of Connecticut, [which] held * * * that all of the City's proposed takings were valid.
* * * *
We granted *certiorari* to determine whether a city's decision to take property for the purpose of economic development satisfies the "public use" requirement of the Fifth Amendment.
* * * *
* * * This Court long ago rejected any literal requirement that condemned property be put into use for the general public. * * * Not only was the "use by the public" test difficult to administer (*e.g.*, what proportion of the public

---

a. In the "Browse opinions by calendar year:" section, click on "2005." In the result, click on "Kelo v. New London" to access the opinion. The United States Supreme Court maintains this Web site.

EXTENDED CASE 26.3 CONTINUED ◆

need have access to the property? at what price?), but it proved to be impractical given the diverse and always evolving needs of society. Accordingly, * * * *this Court* * * *embraced the broader and more natural interpretation of public use as "public purpose."* [Emphasis added.]

The disposition of this case therefore turns on the question whether the City's development plan serves a "public purpose."

* * * *

Viewed as a whole, our jurisprudence has recognized that the needs of society have varied between different parts of the Nation, just as they have evolved over time in response to changed circumstances. * * * *For more than a century, our public use jurisprudence has wisely*

eschewed [avoided] rigid formulas and intrusive scrutiny in favor of affording legislatures broad latitude in determining what public needs justify the use of the takings power. [Emphasis added.]

* * * *

Those who govern the City were not confronted with the need to remove blight in the Fort Trumbull area, but their determination that the area was sufficiently distressed to justify a program of economic rejuvenation is entitled to our deference. The City has carefully formulated an economic development plan that it believes will provide appreciable benefits to the community, including—but by no means limited to—new jobs and increased tax revenue. As with other exercises in urban planning and development, the City is endeavoring to coordinate a variety of commercial, residential,

and recreational uses of land, with the hope that they will form a whole greater than the sum of its parts. To effectuate this plan, the City has invoked a state statute that specifically authorizes the use of eminent domain to promote economic development. Given the comprehensive character of the plan, the thorough deliberation that preceded its adoption, and the limited scope of our review, it is appropriate for us * * * to resolve the challenges of the individual owners, not on a piecemeal basis, but rather in light of the entire plan. *Because that plan unquestionably serves a public purpose, the takings challenged here satisfy the public use requirement of the Fifth Amendment.* [Emphasis added.]

* * * *

The judgment of the Supreme Court of Connecticut is affirmed.

 QUESTIONS

1. Why did the United States Supreme Court grant *certiorari* in this case, and what did the Court hold with respect to the principal issue?
2. Considering the impact of the majority's ruling, what are some arguments against this decision?

Legislation Prohibiting Takings for Economic Development

The increasingly widespread use of eminent domain for economic development has generated substantial controversy. Although the United States Supreme Court approved this type of taking in the *Kelo* case (just discussed), the Court also recognized that individual states have the right to pass laws that prohibit takings for economic development. Forty-three states have done exactly that, limiting the government's ability to take private property and give it to private developers. At least eight states have amended their state constitutions, and a number of other states have passed ballot measures on this issue.

Restrictive Covenants

A private restriction on the use of land is known as a **restrictive covenant.** If the restriction is binding on the party who purchases the property originally

and on subsequent purchasers as well, it is said to "run with the land." A covenant running with the land must be in writing (usually, it is in the deed), and subsequent purchasers must have reason to know about it. Suppose that in the course of developing a fifty-lot suburban subdivision, Levitt records a declaration of restrictions that effectively limits construction on each lot to one single-family house. Each lot's deed includes a reference to the declaration with a provision that the purchaser and her or his successors are bound to those restrictions. Thus, each purchaser assumes ownership with notice of the restrictions. If an owner attempts to build a duplex (or any structure that does not comply with the restrictions) on a lot, the other owners may obtain a court order enjoining the construction.

Alternatively, Levitt might simply have included the restrictions on the subdivision's map, filed the map in the appropriate public office, and included a reference to the map in each deed. In this way, each owner would also have been held to have constructive notice of the restrictions.

Inverse Condemnation

Typically, a government agency exercises the power of eminent domain in order to seize private property through litigation or negotiation. If the agency obtains the private land through agreement or judgment, it then pays compensation to the landowner. **Inverse condemnation,** in contrast, occurs when a government simply takes private property from a landowner without paying any compensation at all. In this situation, the landowner is forced to sue the government for compensation for the lost value of the land. The taking can be accomplished physically, as when a government agency simply uses or occupies the land. Regulation issued by government agency may also result in a property losing much of its value.

CASE IN POINT In Walton County, Florida, water flows through a ditch from Oyster Lake to the Gulf of Mexico. When Hurricane Opal caused the water to rise in Oyster Lake, Walton County reconfigured the drainage to divert the overflow onto the nearby property of William and Patricia Hemby. The flow was eventually restored to pre-Opal conditions, but during a later emergency, water was diverted onto the Hembys' property again. This diversion was not restored. The Hembys filed a suit against the county. After their deaths, their daughter Cozette Drake pursued the claim. The court found that by allowing the water diversion, created during emergency conditions, to remain on Drake's property long after the emergency had passed, the county had engaged in a permanent or continuous physical invasion. This invasion rendered Drake's property useless and deprived her of its beneficial enjoyment. Drake was therefore entitled to receive compensation from the county.[7]

━━━━━ **SECTION 5** ━━━━━
LAND-USE CONTROL AND ZONING

Land-use control is control over the ownership and uses of real property by authorized public agencies. Land use is subject to regulation by the state within whose political boundaries the land is located. Most states authorize control over land use through various planning boards and zoning authorities at a city or county level. The federal government does not engage in land-use control under normal circumstances, except with respect to federally owned land.[8] The federal government does influence state and local regulation, however, through the allocation of federal funds. Stipulations on land use may be a condition to the states' receiving such funds.

The rules and regulations that collectively manage the development and use of land are known as **zoning laws.** Zoning laws were first used in the United States to segregate slaughterhouses, distilleries, kilns, and other businesses that might pose a nuisance to nearby residences. The growth of modern urban areas has led to an increased need to organize uses of land. Today, zoning laws enable the government of a municipality—a town, city, or county—to control the speed and type of development within its borders by creating different zones and regulating the use of property allowed in each zone.

Police Power

The United States Supreme Court has held that zoning is a constitutional exercise of a government's police powers.[9] Therefore, as long as its zoning ordinances are rationally related to the health, safety, or welfare of the community, a municipal government has broad discretion to carry out zoning as it sees fit. A few states control land use at the state level. Hawaii, for instance, employs a statewide land-use classification scheme. Some states have a land-permit process that operates in conjunction with local control. Florida, for example, uses such a scheme in certain areas of "critical environmental concern" to permit or prohibit development on the basis of available roads and sewers. Vermont also utilizes a statewide land-permit scheme.

Usually, however, a state authorizes its city or county governments to regulate the use of land within their local jurisdictions. Local planning boards may regulate the development of subdivisions, in which private developers subdivide large tracts of land and construct commercial or residential units for resale to others. Local governments may also enact growth-management ordinances to control development in their jurisdictions.

---

7. *Drake v. Walton County,* 6 So.3d 717 (Fla.App. 2009).

8. Federal (and state) laws concerning environmental matters—such as air and water quality, the protection of endangered species, and the preservation of natural wetlands—are also a source of land-use control.

9. *Village of Euclid v. Ambler Realty Co.,* 272 U.S. 365, 47 S.Ct. 114, 71 L.Ed. 303 (1926).

SUBDIVISION REGULATIONS When subdividing a parcel of land into smaller plots, a private developer must comply not only with local zoning ordinances but also with local subdivision regulations. Subdivision regulations are different from zoning ordinances, although they may be administered by the same local agencies that oversee the zoning process. In the design of a subdivision, the local authorities may demand, for example, the allocation of space for a public park or school or may require a developer to construct streets to accommodate a specific level of traffic.

Under the equal protection clause, land-use controls cannot be discriminatory. A regulation or ordinance is discriminatory if it affects one parcel of land in a way in which it does not affect surrounding parcels and if there is no *rational basis* for the difference. For example, classifying a single parcel in a way that is not in accord with a general plan is discriminatory. Any classification that is reasonably related to the health or general welfare of the public is deemed to have a rational basis.

GROWTH-MANAGEMENT ORDINANCES To prevent population growth from racing ahead of the community's ability to provide necessary public services, local authorities may enact a growth-management ordinance to limit, for example, the number of residential building permits. A property owner may thus be precluded from constructing a residential building on his or her property even if the area is zoned for the use and the proposed structure complies with all other requirements. A growth-management ordinance may prohibit the issuance of residential building permits for a specific period of time, until the occurrence of a specific event (such as a decline in the total number of residents in the community), or on the basis of the availability of necessary public services (such as the capacity for drainage in the area or the proximity of hospitals and police stations).

Purpose and Scope of Zoning Laws

The purpose of zoning laws is to manage the land within a community in a way that encourages sustainable and organized development while controlling growth in a manner that serves the interests of the community. One of the basic elements of zoning is the classification of land by permissible use as part of a comprehensive municipal plan, but zoning extends to other aspects of land use as well.

PERMISSIBLE USES OF LAND Municipalities generally divide their available land into districts according to the land's present and potential future uses. Typically, land is classified into three types of permissible uses: residential, commercial or business, and industrial. Conservation districts are also found in some municipalities. These districts are areas dedicated to carrying out local soil and water conservation efforts—for example, *wetlands* (see page 562) might be designated as a conservation district.

In areas dedicated for **residential use,** landowners can construct buildings for human habitation. Land assigned for business activities is designated as being for **commercial use,** sometimes called business use. For example, an area with a number of retail stores, offices, supermarkets, and hotels might be designated as a commercial or business district. Land used for entertainment purposes, such as movie theaters and sports stadiums, also falls into this category, as does land used for government activities.

The third major category is **industrial use,** which typically encompasses light and heavy manufacturing, shipping, and heavy transportation. For example, undeveloped land with easy access to highways and railroads might be classified as suitable for future use by industry. Although industrial uses can be profitable for a city seeking to raise tax revenue, such uses can also result in noise, smoke, or vibrations that interfere with others' enjoyment of their property. Consequently, areas zoned for industrial use generally are kept as far as possible from residential districts and some commercial districts.

A city's residential, commercial, and industrial districts may be divided, in turn, into subdistricts. For example, zoning ordinances regulate the type, density, size, and approved uses of structures within a given district. Thus, a residential district may be divided into low-density (single-family homes with large lots), high-density (single- and multiple-family homes with small lots), and planned-unit (condominiums or apartments) subdistricts.

OTHER ZONING RESTRICTIONS Zoning rules extend to much more than the permissible use of land. In residential districts, for example, an ordinance may require a house or garage to be set back a specific number of feet from a neighbor's property line. In commercial districts, zoning rules may attempt to maintain a certain visual aesthetic. Therefore, businesses may be required to construct buildings of a certain height and width so that they conform to the style of other commercial buildings in the area. Businesses may also be required to provide parking for patrons or take other measures to manage traffic. In some instances, municipalities limit construction of new businesses to prevent traffic congestion. Zoning laws may even attempt to regulate the public morals of the community. For example, cities commonly impose severe restrictions on the location and operation of adult businesses. The ethical ramifications of zoning laws will be discussed in this unit's *Focus on Ethics* feature on pages 652–654.

Zoning Law Exceptions and Special Incentives

Zoning restrictions are not absolute. It is impossible for zoning laws to account for every contingency. The purpose of zoning is to enable the municipality to control development but not to prevent it altogether or limit the government's ability to adapt to changing circumstances or unforeseen needs. Hence, legal processes have been developed to allow for exceptions to zoning laws. Here, we look at these exceptions, known as *variances* and *special-use permits*, as well as at the *special incentives* that governments may offer to encourage certain kinds of development.

VARIANCES When a property owner wants to use his or her land in a manner not permitted by zoning rules, she or he can request a **variance,** which allows an exception to the rules. Property owners normally request variances in hardship situations. For example, a homeowner may want to replace her single-car garage with a two-car garage, but if she does so, the garage will be closer to her neighbor's property than is permitted by the zoning rules. Hence, she may ask for a variance. Similarly, a church might request a variance from height restrictions in order to erect a new steeple, or a furniture retail store might ask for a variance from footprint limitations so that it can expand its showroom (a building's *footprint* is the area of ground that it covers). Note that the hardship may not be self-created—that is, a person usually cannot buy property with zoning regulations in effect and then argue that a variance is needed for the property to be used for the owner's intended purpose.

In almost all instances, before a variance is granted, there must be a public hearing with adequate notice to neighbors who may object to the exception. The property owner requesting the variance must demonstrate that it is necessary for reasonable development, is the least intrusive solution to the problem, and will not alter the essential character of the neighborhood. After the public hearing,

a hearing examiner appointed by the municipality (or the local zoning board or commission) determines whether to grant the exception. When a variance is granted, it applies only to the specific parcel of land for which it was requested and does not create a regulation-free zone.

SPECIAL-USE PERMITS Sometimes, zoning laws permit a use, but only if the property owner complies with specific requirements to ensure that the proposed use does not harm the immediate neighborhood. In such instances, the zoning board will issue **special-use permits,** also called *conditional-use permits.*

For example, an area is designated as a residential district, but small businesses are permitted to operate there so long as they do not affect the characteristics of the neighborhood. A bank asks the zoning board for a special-use permit to open a branch in the area. At the public hearing, the bank's managers demonstrate that the branch will be housed in a building that comforms to the style of other structures in the area, that adequate parking will be available, and that landscaping will shield the parking lot from public view. Unless there are strong objections from the branch's prospective neighbors, the board will likely grant the permit.

SPECIAL INCENTIVES In addition to granting exceptions to zoning regulations, municipalities may also wish to encourage certain kinds of development. To do so, they offer incentives, often in the form of lower tax rates or tax credits. For example, to attract new businesses that will provide jobs for local citizens and increase the tax base, a city may offer incentives in the form of lower property tax rates for a period of years. Similarly, homeowners may receive tax credits for historical preservation if they renovate and maintain older homes.

Municipalities also offer incentives to further environmental goals. For example, tax incentives are used to encourage property owners to replace aging buildings with new ones that minimize energy use, reduce resource consumption, and promote green transportation choices—such as by providing outlets for plugging in electric cars. Tax credits provided by cities and towns also encourage construction firms to participate actively in "green" construction. (For further discussion of the green movement in real estate development, see this chapter's *Shifting Legal Priorities for Business* feature on the facing page.)

Like other U.S. businesses, firms in the construction industry are facing increasing pressure to "go green." Now, whenever they undertake a project, they must take into account a host of new developments, including the following:

- Innovative designs for buildings that emphasize the interconnectivity of people and structures across an entire neighborhood.
- New types of financing, including renewable energy credits, public tax credits, and other financial incentives.
- Real estate valuations based on a life-cycle analysis of a building's costs and benefits.
- Regulations that set minimum levels of performance based on changing best industry practices.

All of these are aimed at ensuring that future real estate developments will be more sustainable than those of the past. In achieving that goal, integrated design and life-cycle analysis are especially important.

Sustainability through Integrated Design and Life-Cycle Analysis

One of the hallmarks of green development is integrated design, which takes account of all of a building's stakeholders. These stakeholders include all of those who work on the design and construction of the project and those who will use the building it when it is completed. Thus, a building constructed with an integrated design will be cost-effective to build and maintain, accessible to persons with disabilities, aesthetically pleasing, safe—a matter of particular concern since 9/11—and functional.

To achieve all of these qualities requires an integrated team in which the members work together instead of focusing only on their specialties. Integrated teams include not only the architects, engineers, and contractors who do the initial design and construction but also the landscapers, maintenance personnel, and others who will maintain the building after its completion. The building's future occupants will have input as well.

Closely related to integrated design is life-cycle analysis of a building's costs and benefits. Instead of focusing only on the initial cost, life-cycle analysis takes into account all of the costs of acquiring, owning, and disposing of a building over its lifetime. Thus, an element that has a high initial cost might dramatically reduce the building's operating and maintenance costs over its lifetime. For example, a building's thermal load (the amount of heat that must be removed over a given time period) depends, in part, on its orientation to the sun. A change in the building's orientation may entail a higher cost initially but save substantially on air-conditioning expenses later.

Achieving Certified Green Building Status

Between 5 and 10 percent of the buildings started in 2010 incorporated green building techniques. A motive for building green is to obtain the LEED™ certification from the U.S. Green Building Council. (LEED stands for Leadership in Energy and Environmental Design.) To receive the certification, which was started almost two decades ago, a building or real estate development must use resources sustainably, achieve energy savings, conserve water, reduce carbon dioxide emissions, and obtain other environmentally friendly goals. A similar certification is available through the Green Globes program. To obtain either certification, the project must undergo a rigorous verification process.

The Legal Risks of Going Green

Although green building is the "right thing to do," it still may entail many risks for a construction firm or real estate developer. The builder may overpromise or fail to articulate what is meant by "green building." As a result, when the project is completed, the owner may be disappointed and threaten a lawsuit for breach of contract. If a subcontractor's work fails to conform to the requirements of the LEED rating system, certain federal, state, and local tax credits may not be available.

Some of these and other risks can be managed or limited by including express warranties and insurance provisions in contracts. Contracts should clearly identify the responsibilities of various team members to ensure that the project is truly green—or at least will meet certification requirements.

MANAGERIAL IMPLICATIONS

Wanting to help the planet is a laudable goal, but managers of real estate development projects must go further. Some will want to hire green specialists to oversee at least the preliminary stages of the project. Any manager of such a project must assess the risks. One way to do so is to hire a skilled attorney who has worked on other green projects.

REVIEWING
Real Property and Land-Use Control

Vern Shoepke purchased a two-story home from Walter and Eliza Bruster in the town of Roche, Maine. The warranty deed did not specify what covenants would be included in the conveyance. The property was adjacent to a public park that included a popular Frisbee golf course. (Frisbee golf is a sport similar to golf but using Frisbees.) Wayakichi Creek ran along the north end of the park and along Shoepke's property. The deed allowed Roche citizens the right to walk across a five-foot-wide section of the lot beside Wayakichi Creek as part of a two-mile public trail system. Teenagers regularly threw Frisbee golf discs from the walking path behind Shoepke's property over his yard to the adjacent park. Shoepke habitually shouted and cursed at the teenagers, demanding that they not throw objects over his yard. Two months after moving into his Roche home, Shoepke leased the second floor to Lauren Slater for nine months. (The lease agreement did not specify that Shoepke's consent would be required to sublease the second floor.) After three months of tenancy, Slater sublet the second floor to a local artist, Javier Indalecio. Over the remaining six months, Indalecio's use of oil paints damaged the carpeting in Shoepke's home. Using the information presented in the chapter, answer the following questions.

1. What is the term for the right of Roche citizens to walk across Shoepke's land on the trail?
2. What covenants would most courts infer were included in the warranty deed that was used in the property transfer from the Brusters to Shoepke? Explain.
3. Suppose that Shoepke wants to file a trespass lawsuit against some teenagers who continually throw Frisbees over his land. Shoepke discovers, however, that when the city put in the Frisbee golf course, the neighborhood homeowners signed an agreement that limited their right to complain about errant Frisbees. What is this type of promise or agreement called in real property law? Discuss.
4. What is the term for Roche's power to appropriate Shoepke's property for public use? Is this a restriction or a taking? Explain.

DEBATE THIS: *Under no circumstances should a local government be able to condemn a homeowner's real property in order to sell it later to real estate developers for private use.*

TERMS AND CONCEPTS

adverse possession 581
closing 579
commercial use 587
community property 575
concurrent ownership 574
conveyance 574
deed 579
easement 576
eminent domain 584
escrow account 579
fee simple absolute 572

fixed-term tenancy 575
grant deed 580
implied warranty of habitability 579
industrial use 587
inverse condemnation 586
joint tenancy 574
land-use control 586
leasehold estate 575
license 577
life estate 574
marketable title 581
metes and bounds 580

nonpossessory interests 576
periodic tenancy 575
personal property 571
profit 576
quitclaim deed 580
real property 571
recording statute 581
residential use 587
restrictive covenant 585
sheriff's deed 580
special-use permit 588
special warranty deed 580
taking 584

tenancy at sufferance 576
tenancy at will 576
tenancy by the entirety 575
tenancy in common 574
title insurance 581
title search 581
variance 588
warranty deed 580
waste 574
zoning laws 586

QUESTIONS AND CASE PROBLEMS

26–1. Property Ownership Madison owned a tract of land, but he was not sure that he had full title to the property. When Rafael expressed an interest in buying the land, Madison sold it to Rafael and executed a quitclaim deed. Rafael properly recorded the deed immediately. Several months later, Madison learned that he had had full title to the tract of land. He then sold the land to Linda by warranty deed. Linda knew of the earlier purchase by Rafael but took the deed anyway and later sued to have Rafael evicted from the land. Linda claimed that because she had a warranty deed, her title to the land was better than that conferred by Rafael's quitclaim deed. Will Linda succeed in claiming title to the land? Explain.

26–2. Zoning The county intends to rezone an area from industrial use to residential use. Land within the affected area is largely undeveloped, but nonetheless it is expected that the proposed action will reduce the market value of the affected land by as much as 50 percent. Will the landowners be successful in suing to have the action declared a taking of their property, entitling them to just compensation? Why or why not?

26–3. QUESTION WITH SAMPLE ANSWER: Deeds.

Wilfredo and Patricia are neighbors. Wilfredo's lot is extremely large, and his present and future use of it will not involve the entire area. Patricia wants to build a single-car garage and driveway along the present lot boundary. Because ordinances require buildings to be set back fifteen feet from an owner's property line, however, the placement of Patricia's existing structures prevents her from building the garage. Patricia contracts to purchase ten feet of Wilfredo's property along their boundary line for $3,000. Wilfredo is willing to sell but will give Patricia only a quitclaim deed, whereas Patricia wants a warranty deed. Discuss the differences between these deeds as they would affect the rights of the parties if the title to this ten feet of land later proves to be defective.

• **For a sample answer to Question 26–3, go to Appendix F at the end of this text.**

26–4. Subdivision Regulations Suppose that as a condition of a developer's receiving approval for constructing a new residential community, the local authorities insist that the developer dedicate, or set aside, land for a new hospital. The hospital would serve not only the proposed residential community but also the rest of the city. If the developer challenges the condition in court, under what standard might the court invalidate the condition? Explain.

26–5. Easements The Wallens family owned a cabin on Lummi Island in the state of Washington. A driveway ran from the cabin across their property to South Nugent Road. In 1952, Floyd Massey bought the adjacent lot and built a cabin. To gain access to his property, he used a bulldozer to extend the driveway without the Wallenses' permission but also without their objection. In 1975, the Wallenses sold their property to Wright Fish Co. Massey continued to use and maintain the driveway without permission or objection. In 1984, Massey sold his property to Robert Drake. Drake and his employees continued to use and maintain the driveway without permission or objection, although Drake knew it was located largely on Wright's property. In 1997, Wright sold its lot to Robert Smersh. The next year, Smersh told Drake to stop using the driveway. Drake filed a suit in a Washington state court against Smersh, claiming an easement by prescription (which is created by meeting the same requirements as adverse possession). Does Drake's use of the driveway meet all of the requirements? What should the court rule? Explain. [*Drake v. Smersh*, 122 Wash.App. 147, 89 P.3d 726 (Div. 1 2004)]

26–6. CASE PROBLEM WITH SAMPLE ANSWER: Eminent Domain.

The Hope Partnership for Education, a religious organization, proposed to build a private independent middle school in a blighted neighborhood in Philadelphia, Pennsylvania. In 2002, the Hope Partnership asked the Redevelopment Authority of the City of Philadelphia to acquire specific land for the project and sell it to the Hope Partnership for a nominal price. The land included a house at 1839 North Eighth Street owned by Mary Smith, whose daughter Veronica lived there with her family. The Authority offered Smith $12,000 for the house and initiated a taking of the property. Smith filed a suit in a Pennsylvania state court against the Authority, admitting that the house was a "substandard structure in a blighted area," but arguing that the taking was unconstitutional because its beneficiary was private. The Authority asserted that only the public purpose of the taking should be considered, not the status of the property's developer. On what basis can a government entity use the power of eminent domain to take property? What are the limits to this power? How should the court rule? Why? [Redevelopment Authority of City of Philadelphia v. New Eastwick Corp., 588 Pa. 789, 906 A.2d 1197 (2006)]

• **To view a sample answer for Problem 26–6, go to this book's Web site at www.cengage.com/blaw/cross, select "Chapter 26," and click on "Case Problem with Sample Answer."**

26–7. Ownership in Fee Simple Thomas and Teresa Cline built a house on a 76-acre parcel of real estate next to Roy Berg's home and property in Augusta County, Virginia. The homes were about 1,800 feet apart but in view of each other. After several disagreements between the parties, Berg equipped an 11-foot tripod with motion sensors and floodlights that intermittently illuminated the Clines' home. Berg also installed surveillance cameras that tracked some of the movement on the Clines' property. The cameras transmitted on an open frequency that could be received by any television within range. The Clines asked Berg to turn off, or at least redirect, the lights. When he refused, they erected a fence for 200 feet along the parties' common property line. The 32-foot-high fence consisted of 20 utility poles spaced 10 feet apart with plastic wrap stretched between the poles. This effectively blocked the lights and cameras. Berg filed a suit against the Clines in a Virginia state court, complaining that the fence interfered unreasonably with his use and enjoyment of his property. He asked the court to order the Clines to take the fence down. What are the limits on an owner's use of property? How should the court rule in this case? Why? [*Cline v. Berg,* 273 Va. 142, 639 S.E.2d 231 (2007)]

26–8. Adverse Possession In 1974, the Mansells built a shed with a dirt floor, to be used as a three-car garage, at the back of their property. This shed went beyond the Mansells' property line and encroached approximately fourteen feet on the neighboring property. The neighbor knew of the encroachment and informally approved it, but did not transfer ownership of the property. In 2001, Betty Hunter bought the neighbor's property. The survey done at that time revealed the encroachment. In 2003, Hunter's attorney notified the Mansells about the encroachment, and the parties held some informal conversations but did not reach an agreement. In 2006, the Mansells installed a concrete foundation and ran electricity to the structure. Hunter then sought a declaratory judgment that she was the fee simple owner of the property partially covered by the garage that encroached on her property, and demanded the removal of the encroaching structure. The Mansells filed a counterclaim arguing that the possession of the property from 1974 to 2001 gave them ownership by adverse possession. The trial court held that the property still belonged to Hunter, but did not order removal of the garage. Hunter and Mrs. Mansell (whose husband had died in the meantime) both appealed. Did the open occupation of the property for twenty-eight years give Mansell title by adverse possession? Why or why not? [*Hunter v. Mansell,* ___ P.3d ___ (Colo.App. 2010)]

26–9. A QUESTION OF ETHICS: Seller's Duty to Disclose.

In 1999, Stephen and Linda Kailin bought the Monona Center, a mall in Madison, Wisconsin, from Perry Armstrong for $760,000. The contract provided, "Seller represents to Buyer that as of the date of acceptance Seller had no notice or knowledge of conditions affecting the Property or transaction" other than certain items disclosed at the time of the offer. Armstrong told the Kailins of the Center's eight tenants, their lease expiration dates, and the monthly and annual rent due under each lease. One of the lessees, Ring's All-American Karate, occupied about a third of the Center's space under a five-year lease. Because of Ring's financial difficulties, Armstrong had agreed to reduce its rent for nine months in 1997. By the time of the sale to the Kailins, Ring's owed $13,910 in unpaid rent, but Armstrong did not tell the Kailins, who did not ask. Ring's continued to fail to pay rent and finally vacated the Center. The Kailins filed a suit in a Wisconsin state court against Armstrong and others, alleging, among other things, misrepresentation. [Kailin v. Armstrong, 2002 WI App 70, 252 Wis.2d 676, 643 N.W.2d 132 (2002)]

(a) Did Armstrong have a duty to disclose Ring's delinquency and default to the Kailins? Explain.

(b) What obligation, if any, did Ring's have to the Kailins or Armstrong after failing to pay the rent and eventually defaulting on the lease? Discuss.

26–10. SPECIAL CASE ANALYSIS: Eminent Domain.
Go to Extended Case 26.3, *Kelo v. City of New London, Connecticut,* 545 U.S. 469, 125 S.Ct. 2655, 162 L.Ed.2d 439 (2005), on pages 584–585. Read the excerpt and answer the following questions.

(a) **Issue:** On what issue did the Court focus?

(b) **Rule of Law:** What does the Fifth Amendment to the U.S. Constitution, which the Court applied, require with respect to the legal issue in this case?

(c) **Applying the Rule of Law:** How did the Court apply the rule of law to the facts of this case?

(d) **Conclusion:** What was the Court's conclusion?

LEGAL RESEARCH EXERCISES ON THE WEB

Go to this text's Web site at **www.cengage.com/blaw/cross**, select "Chapter 26," and click on "Practical Internet Exercises." There you will find the following Internet research exercises that you can perform to learn more about the topics covered in this chapter.

Practical Internet Exercise 26–1: **Legal Perspective**
Eminent Domain

Practical Internet Exercise 26–2: **Management Perspective**
Fair Housing

Practical Internet Exercise 26–3: **Social Perspective**
The Rights of Tenants

CHAPTER 27

Antitrust and Monopoly

The environment of business is generally one of competition among rival firms. In free and open competition, businesses attempt to develop and sell products that are more appealing to customers than are the products of rival firms. Competition among sellers therefore promotes the development of products that are attractive to consumers. When products sold by different firms are similar, firms compete by trying to sell at the lowest price possible while still earning enough after costs to make it worthwhile to continue in that particular endeavor.

For example, if Acme, Inc., develops a new Blu-ray DVD burner that has broad appeal among consumers, it will begin to earn profits greater than those of its rivals—profits commensurate with the attractiveness of its new product. All else being equal, the greater the appeal of Acme's Blu-ray burner, the greater the profits.

The legal environment of business is premised on encouraging innovative, competitive business behavior. The law attempts to prevent and correct conduct that interferes with free and open competition. The law is concerned

with two broad categories of behavior: conduct that leads to or tends to produce *monopoly power* and conduct that is an unreasonable *restraint of trade*. In this chapter, we consider the federal laws that deal with individual firms' behavior leading to or tending to create monopolies. In Chapter 28, we will discuss in detail the federal laws that regulate activities that restrain competition.

SECTION 1
MARKET POWER

To encourage innovative behavior, we might feel justified in allowing Acme to have a *monopoly* over the sale of the Blu-ray DVD burner, at least for a while—say, twenty years, which is the duration of a patent. The term **monopoly** is generally used to describe a market in which there is a single seller. In that respect, Acme would be a monopolist, albeit for a limited time, in the Blu-ray burner market. In legal terms, *monopolist* may also describe a firm that, although not the sole seller in the market, can nonetheless substantially ignore rival firms in setting a selling price for its product or can in some way limit rivals from competing in the market (possibly by preventing rivals from entering the market altogether). Acme's monopoly would give it **market power** (the power of a firm to control

the market for its product). Acme would have the power during the term of its monopoly to prevent other firms from selling the Blu-ray burner. Acme would be free to charge whatever price it chose, and it would choose a price that made its profits as large as possible.

Competitive Behavior

Another firm might seek to develop a different type of Blu-ray burner, one with appeal equal to or greater than Acme's Blu-ray burner. If it succeeded, it would draw customers away from Acme. It, too, might seek a legal monopoly over its product. There would then be two monopolies rather than one, but society would have the benefit of two unique and valued products. Moreover, Acme would be concerned that if it charged too high a price for its Blu-ray burner, it would lose customers to its rival.

Acme's rival would have the same concern about the price of its product.

Eventually, after the legal monopolies expired, numerous firms would be allowed to market identical products. Each firm would seek to attract customers by charging the lowest price. The only thing that would prevent prices from falling ever lower is that at some point the price of a Blu-ray burner would be so low that new firms would quit trying to enter the market to compete for Blu-ray burner consumers. They would instead devote their efforts and resources to alternative, more profitable ventures. Ultimately, the Blu-ray burner would sell for a competitive price—one that would, of course, cover the costs of production, as well as earn a return equal to what could be earned by employing the same resources in an alternative industry.

The Goals of Antitrust Law

The scenario described above highlights the benefits to society of having firms develop, produce, and sell goods and services, even though obtaining those benefits may involve conferring a limited monopoly. Our scenario should make clear an often overlooked point: market power is not inherently bad. Market power can correlate to high profits, which are the reward for innovation, foresight, and good management. Market power is the prize that motivates firms to benefit society with innovative products and competitive prices.

What is at issue is not market power *per se* but how firms go about acquiring market power and what firms do with that power once they acquire it. **Antitrust law** consists of the statutes and principles that regulate business conduct so as to promote the forms of competition that benefit society while simultaneously seeking to rein in the exercise of market power that often is the fruit of such competition.

SECTION 2
THE COMMON LAW AND THE RESTRAINT OF TRADE

Socially beneficial commercial activity involves cooperation, as well as competition. A business firm, for example, may compete with certain firms in some markets but cooperate with other firms in other markets. A firm that sells finished goods directly to the public may itself act as a consumer by purchasing intermediate products from a second firm. In this sense, the two firms act cooperatively rather than competitively, at least vis-à-vis one another. Similarly, two firms may cooperate to develop or market a new product.

Public Policy and Contracts

Any mutual effort that calls for more than a brief period of sustained cooperation requires commitment from all the parties. The principal means of ensuring such a sustained commitment is through a contract between the parties. Most cooperative efforts among business firms, in fact, are embodied in some form of contract. But a principle of the common law of contracts is that no contract is enforceable if it is against public policy.

ECONOMIC EFFICIENCY Many contracts between business firms promote competition. Because competition, as noted above, is beneficial to society, such contracts are not against public policy. A contract may provide assurances that one firm will be able to obtain necessary inputs from another on a long-term basis. Similarly, a contract may provide assurances to two firms entering into a joint venture that each will continue fulfilling its obligation on the project beyond the initial investment stage. In both instances, the rights and remedies afforded by contract law promote economic efficiency. Such agreements are not against public policy.

RESTRAINTS OF TRADE Some agreements between business firms, however, may reduce competition. An agreement between two bakers to coordinate their production of bread so as to limit output and charge a uniform, higher price in the market might entirely eliminate competition in the affected market. If the two bakers were the only suppliers in the market, their combining together would in effect create a joint monopoly under which they would share exclusive control over the market. Such an agreement would be condemned under the common law as an *unreasonable restraint of trade*.

Consider, though, a restaurant owner who decides to sell her restaurant to the manager. The manager might demand that, as a condition to the sale, the owner refrain from opening another restaurant across the street. Should such an agreement be condemned as being against public policy? At first glance, it is a restraint of trade: it prevents the local community from benefiting from the restauranting skills of the owner. If the agreement was not enforced, however, the manager, who was willing to pay a price commensurate with the current earnings of the restaurant, would not recover the price. Customers would probably follow the owner with the established reputation to her new restaurant across the street from the old one.

If the manager knew beforehand that the agreement would not be enforced, it would be the owner who would suffer, because the manager would not be willing to pay a price reflecting the expectation that the earnings of the restaurant would continue at the current level. Society might consider enforcing such agreements in spite of the restraint of trade so that entrepreneurs who contemplate opening new businesses will be ensured of later being able to sell those businesses at full value. If others know that sellers will be held to the promise not to compete, sellers can get a higher price for their businesses than they could if such promises were condemned as being against public policy.

Interference with Free Trade

Both agreements just discussed interfere with free trade. The first involves outright collusion between two competitors (the bakers) to completely eliminate competition between themselves. Their agreement calls for artificially driving prices higher by restricting output. The second agreement (the one between the restaurant owner and the manager) also restrains trade, but the restraint is not the primary purpose of the agreement. The restraint is really the only means of ensuring that both parties to the sale can reap the full benefit of their bargain: the sale of the restaurant for its highest value. The second agreement thus can be viewed as reasonable, given that it is the only means of achieving a legitimate end. It also has offsetting benefits in that it encourages entrepreneurship by allowing the owner to sell her business for its highest value.

SECTION 3
THE ORIGINS OF FEDERAL ANTITRUST LEGISLATION

Despite condemning anticompetitive agreements on the basis of public policy, the common law appeared to be an ineffective means of protecting free competition. Temptations exist for business firms to agree to limit competition or to harm other rivals. Such agreements, to be sure, are unenforceable, because they are held to be against public policy. But the problem under the common law is that such agreements are left unchallenged unless

one of the parties to an agreement refuses to abide by its terms. *Unenforceable* means only that a court will not sanction a party that reneges on its promise. It does not mean that a forum will be provided in which anticompetitive agreements can be challenged by others who are not parties to the agreements. These shortcomings became apparent in the United States during the latter half of the 1800s as a concentrated group of powerful individuals began to acquire market power by combining competing firms under single control.

The Trend toward Monopoly

After the Civil War ended, the nation renewed its drive westward. With the movement westward came the expansion of the railroads—which soon developed into monopolies—and the further integration of the economy. The growth of national markets also witnessed the efforts of a number of small companies to combine into large business organizations, many of which gained considerable market power.

These large organizations became known as **trusts,** the most famous—or infamous—being John D. Rockefeller's Standard Oil Trust. In general, a trust is an arrangement in which some party, referred to as a trustee, holds legal title to property for the benefit of another. As used by Standard Oil and others in the late nineteenth century, trusts were a device to amass market power. The participants transferred their stock to a trustee and in return received trust certificates. The trustee then made decisions to fix prices, control production, and determine the control of exclusive geographic markets for all of the oil companies that were members of the trust. Some argued that the trust wielded so much economic power that outside corporations could not compete effectively.

The Federal Response

Congress initially dealt with the railroad monopolies when it passed the Interstate Commerce Act of 1887.[1] It next attempted to deal with trusts in a direct, unified way by passing the Sherman Act in 1890.[2] The Sherman Act is a broadly worded pronouncement that prohibits competitors from making agreements that unreasonably restrain trade and condemns conduct leading to or tending to produce monopoly power. Violations of the Sherman Act are criminal offenses, as well as civil ones.

---

1. 49 U.S.C. Sections 1–22.
2. 15 U.S.C. Sections 1–7.

The Sherman Act, however, failed to end public concerns over monopolies. The United States Supreme Court initially construed the statute too narrowly to give it much effect and subsequently applied it so rigorously as to make the act unworkable. Lackluster enforcement also contributed to the public's dissatisfaction. Eventually, in 1914 Congress enacted the Clayton Act[3] and the Federal Trade Commission Act.[4] These laws proscribed specific acts and provided for more aggressive means of enforcement.

The Clayton Act (as amended by the Robinson-Patman Act in 1936 and the Celler-Kefauver Act of 1950) addresses specific actions that are considered to be anticompetitive. The Federal Trade Commission Act created the Federal Trade Commission and invested it with broad enforcement powers to *prevent*, as well as correct, business behavior broadly defined as *unfair trade practices*.

In the remainder of this chapter, we consider the federal legislation in more detail and examine the means of enforcement. We also examine the narrower area of antitrust law that deals with individual firms' behavior leading to or tending to create monopolies. Chapter 28 discusses the broader area of antitrust law that deals with all forms of joint activities that restrain competition.

SECTION 4
OVERVIEW OF THE MAJOR FEDERAL ANTITRUST LAWS

The major pieces of federal antitrust legislation—the Sherman Act, the Clayton Act, and the Federal Trade Commission Act—are briefly outlined next and will be discussed in more detail later in this chapter.

The Sherman Act

Sections 1 and 2 contain the main provisions of the Sherman Act:

1. Every contract, combination in the form of trust or otherwise, or conspiracy, in restraint of trade or commerce among the several States, or with foreign nations, is hereby declared to be illegal [and is a felony punishable by fine and/or imprisonment].
2. Every person who shall monopolize, or attempt to monopolize, or combine or conspire with any other person or persons, to monopolize any part of the trade or commerce among the several

States, or with foreign nations, shall be deemed guilty of a felony [and is similarly punishable].

DIFFERENCES BETWEEN SECTION 1 AND SECTION 2 These two sections of the Sherman Act are quite different. Section 1 requires two or more persons, as a person cannot contract, combine, or conspire alone. Thus, the essence of the illegal activity is *the act of joining together*. Section 2, though, can apply either to one person or to two or more persons because it refers to "every person." Thus, unilateral conduct can result in a violation of Section 2.

The cases brought to the courts under Section 1 of the Sherman Act differ from those brought under Section 2. Section 1 cases often are concerned with finding an agreement (written or oral) that leads to a restraint of trade. A **restraint of trade** is any agreement between firms that has the effect of reducing competition in the marketplace. Restraints of trade will be discussed more completely in the next chapter. Section 2 cases deal with the structure of a monopoly that exists in the marketplace. The term *monopoly* generally is used to describe a market in which there is a single seller or a very limited number of sellers. Whereas Section 1 focuses on agreements that are restrictive—that is, agreements that have a wrongful purpose—Section 2 looks at the so-called misuse of **monopoly power** in the marketplace.

Monopoly power exists when a firm has an extreme amount of market power and can affect the market price of its product. Both Section 1 and Section 2 seek to curtail market practices that result in undesired monopoly pricing and output behavior. For a case to be brought under Section 2, however, the "threshold" or "necessary" amount of monopoly power must already exist.

JURISDICTIONAL REQUIREMENTS The Sherman Act applies only to restraints that have a significant impact on interstate commerce. Courts have generally held that any activity that substantially affects interstate commerce falls within the scope of the Sherman Act. As will be discussed later in this chapter, the Sherman Act also extends to U.S. nationals abroad that are engaged in activities that affect U.S. foreign commerce. State laws regulate local restraints on competition.

The Clayton Act

In contrast to the Sherman Act's broad proscriptions, the Clayton Act's provisions deal with *specific* practices that are not expressly covered by the Sherman Act but that are considered to reduce competition or

---

3. 15 U.S.C. Sections 12–27.
4. 15 U.S.C. Sections 41–58.

lead to monopoly power. These practices are divided into four categories—price discrimination, exclusionary practices, corporate mergers, and interlocking directorates. These behaviors violate the Clayton Act only if they substantially tend to lessen competition or create monopoly power. Violations of the Clayton Act are civil, not criminal, violations.

PRICE DISCRIMINATION Section 2 of the Clayton Act prohibits **price discrimination,** which occurs when a seller charges different prices to competing buyers for identical goods or services. Congress strengthened this section by amending it with the passage of the Robinson-Patman Act in 1936. As amended, Section 2 prohibits direct and indirect price discrimination that cannot be justified by differences in production costs, transportation costs, or cost differences due to other reasons. In short, a seller is prohibited from reducing a price to one buyer below the price charged to that buyer's competitor.

Required Elements. To violate Section 2, the seller must be engaged in interstate commerce, the goods must be of like grade and quality, and goods must have been sold to two or more purchasers. In addition, the effect of the price discrimination must be to substantially lessen competition, tend to create a monopoly, or otherwise injure competition. Without proof of an actual injury resulting from the price discrimination, the plaintiff cannot recover damages.

Note that price discrimination claims can arise from discounts, offsets, rebates, or allowances given to one buyer over another. Moreover, giving favorable credit terms, delivery, or freight charges to only some buyers can also lead to allegations of price discrimination. For example, when a seller offers goods to different customers at the same price but includes free delivery for certain buyers, it may violate Section 2 in some circumstances.

Defenses. There are several statutory defenses to liability for price discrimination.

1. *Cost justification.* If the seller can justify the price reduction by demonstrating that a particular buyer's purchases saved the seller costs in producing and selling the goods, the seller will not be liable for price discrimination.
2. *Meeting the price of competition.* If the seller charged the lower price in a good faith attempt to meet an equally low price of a competitor, the seller will not be liable for price discrimination.

CASE IN POINT Water Craft was a retail dealership of Mercury Marine outboard motors. On discovering that Mercury was selling its outboard motors at a substantial discount to Water Craft's largest competitor, Water Craft filed a price discrimination lawsuit against Mercury. Mercury Marine was able show that the discounts were made in good faith to meet the low price charged by another manufacturer of marine motors. Therefore, the court found that the "meeting competition defense" applied.[5]

3. *Changing market conditions.* A seller may lower its price on an item in response to changing conditions affecting the market for or the marketability of the goods concerned. Sellers are allowed to readjust their prices to meet the realities of the market without liability for price discrimination. Thus, if an advance in technology makes a particular product less marketable than it was previously, a seller can lower the product's price.

EXCLUSIONARY PRACTICES Section 3 of the Clayton Act prohibits sellers and lessors from selling or leasing "on the condition, agreement or understanding that the . . . purchaser or lessee thereof shall not use or deal in the goods . . . of a competitor or competitors of the seller." Section 3 in effect prohibits two types of vertical arrangements involving exclusionary tactics: exclusive-dealing contracts and tie-in sales agreements.

An *exclusive-dealing contract* is one in which a seller forbids the buyer from purchasing products from the seller's competitors. For example, imagine that most soft drinks are produced by one firm, that most soft drinks are marketed by one other firm, and that the producer signs an exclusive-dealing contract with the retail seller. Because the retail seller has committed itself to the established producer, any other soft-drink producer that wants to enter the soft-drink market may find it difficult to do so. Such contracts are prohibited under Section 3 if the effect of the contract will "substantially lessen competition or tend to create a monopoly."

In a *tying arrangement,* or *tie-in sales agreement,* the seller conditions the sale of a product (the tying product) on the buyer's agreeing to purchase another product (the tied product) produced or distributed by the same seller. The legality of such agreements depends on many factors, especially on consideration of the purpose of the arrangement and its likely effect on competition in the relevant markets (consider that there are two markets, because the agreement involves both the tying and the tied product). In the next chapter,

---

5. *Water Craft Management, LLC v. Mercury Marine,* 457 F.3d 484 (5th Cir. 2006).

we will examine both exclusive-dealing contracts and tying arrangements as part of our analysis of restraints of trade.

CORPORATE MERGERS Under Section 7 of the Clayton Act, a person or business organization is forbidden to hold stock or assets in another business if "the effect . . . may be to substantially lessen competition." This section provides the statutory authorization for the government's challenging corporate mergers that could have an anticompetitive effect. We will discuss mergers in more detail in Chapter 28.

INTERLOCKING DIRECTORATES Section 8 of the Clayton Act deals with *interlocking directorates*—that is, the practice of having individuals serve as directors on the boards of two or more competing companies simultaneously. Specifically, no person may be a director for two or more competing corporations at the same time if either of the corporations has capital, surplus, or undivided profits aggregating more than $25,844,001 or competitive sales of $2,584,100 or more. The threshold amounts are adjusted each year by the Federal Trade Commission. (The amounts given here are those announced by the commission in 2010.)

The Federal Trade Commission Act

The Federal Trade Commission (FTC) Act's sole substantive provision is Section 5. It provides, in part, as follows: Unfair methods of competition in or affecting commerce, and unfair or deceptive acts or practices in or affecting commerce are hereby declared illegal. Notice that whereas the Clayton Act prohibits specific forms of anticompetitive behavior, the FTC Act is a "catchall." Section 5 condemns all forms of anticompetitive behavior that are not covered under other federal antitrust laws.

The FTC Act also created the Federal Trade Commission, an administrative agency with functions that include antitrust enforcement, as well as other duties concerning consumer protection.

_____ SECTION 5 _____
ENFORCEMENT AND EXEMPTIONS

The federal agencies that enforce the federal antitrust laws are the U.S. Department of Justice (DOJ) and the Federal Trade Commission (FTC). Section 5 of the Federal Trade Commission Act condemns all

forms of anticompetitive behavior that are not covered under other federal antitrust laws.

Agency Actions

Only the DOJ can prosecute violations of the Sherman Act, which can be either criminal or civil offenses. Either the DOJ or the FTC can enforce the Clayton Act, but violations of that statute are not crimes and can be pursued only through civil proceedings. The DOJ or the FTC may ask the courts to impose various remedies, including **divestiture** (making a company give up one or more of its operations) and dissolution. A meatpacking firm, for example, might be forced to divest itself of control or ownership of butcher shops.

The FTC has sole authority to enforce violations of Section 5 of the Federal Trade Commission Act. FTC actions are effected through administrative orders, but if a firm violates an FTC order, the FTC can seek court sanctions for the violation.

The president, of course, plays a role in establishing enforcement policies at the agencies. The Obama administration has indicated that it will take a more active antitrust stance than the Bush administration did. The current administration is vigorously enforcing antitrust regulations—similar to the approach that the European Union has taken in recent years (to be discussed shortly).

Private Actions

A private party who has been injured as a result of a violation of the Sherman Act or the Clayton Act can sue for damages and attorneys' fees. In some instances, private parties may also seek injunctive relief to prevent antitrust violations. The courts have determined that the ability to sue depends on the directness of the injury suffered by the would-be plaintiff.

Thus, a person wishing to sue under the Sherman Act must prove (1) that the antitrust violation either caused or was a substantial factor in causing the injury that was suffered and (2) that the unlawful actions of the accused party affected business activities of the plaintiff that were protected by the antitrust laws. In 2007, the United States Supreme Court limited the ability of private parties to pursue antitrust lawsuits without presenting some evidence of facts that suggest that an illegal agreement was made.

CASE IN POINT A group of subscribers to local telephone and high-speed Internet services filed a class-action lawsuit against several regional telecommunication companies (including Bell Atlantic). The plaintiffs claimed that the companies had conspired with one another and engaged in *parallel conduct*—offering similar services and pricing—over a period of years to prevent other companies from entering the market and competing. The United States Supreme Court dismissed the case, finding that "without more, parallel conduct does not suggest conspiracy." A bare assertion of conspiracy is not enough to allow an antitrust lawsuit to go forward. The Court noted that more specificity is necessary to avoid potentially "massive" discovery costs, which are especially likely to occur when the suit is brought by a large class of plaintiffs.[6]

Treble Damages

In recent years, more than 90 percent of all antitrust actions have been brought by private plaintiffs. One reason for this is that successful plaintiffs may

---

6. *Bell Atlantic Corp. v. Twombly,* 550 U.S. 544, 127 S.Ct. 1955, 167 L.Ed.2d 929 (2007).

recover **treble damages**—three times the damages that they have suffered as a result of the violation. In a situation involving a price-fixing agreement, normally each competitor is jointly and severally liable for the total amount of any damages, including treble damages if they are imposed.

Exemptions from Antitrust Laws

There are many legislative and constitutional limitations on antitrust enforcement. Most of the statutory and judicially created exemptions to the antitrust laws apply in such areas as labor, insurance, and foreign trade (see Exhibit 27–1 on page 601).

One of the most significant exemptions covers joint efforts by businesspersons to obtain legislative, judicial, or executive action. Under this exemption, for example, DVD producers can jointly lobby Congress to change the copyright laws without being held liable for attempting to restrain trade. Another exemption covers professional baseball teams.

The following case involved the exemption for professional sports teams.

✳ EXTENDED CASE 27.1 ✳
Clarett v. National Football League

United States Court of Appeals, Second Circuit, 369 F.3d 124 (2004).

IN THE LANGUAGE OF THE COURT
SOTOMAYOR, Circuit Judge.
* * * *

[Maurice] Clarett, former running back for Ohio State University ("OSU") and Big Ten Freshman of the Year, is an accomplished and talented amateur football player. After gaining national attention as a high school player, Clarett became the first college freshman since 1943 to open as a starter at the position of running back for OSU. He led that team through an undefeated season, even scoring the winning touchdown in a double-overtime victory in the 2003 Fiesta Bowl to claim the national championship. * * * Clarett is now interested in turning professional by entering the [National Football League ("NFL" or "the League")] draft. Clarett is precluded

from so doing, however, under the NFL's current rules governing draft eligibility.

* * * The eligibility rules * * * permit a player to enter the draft three full seasons after that player's high school graduation.

Clarett graduated high school on December 11, 2001, two-thirds of the way through the 2001 NFL season and is a season shy of the three necessary to qualify under the draft's eligibility rules. Unwilling to forgo the prospect of a year of lucrative professional play or run the risk of a career-compromising injury were his entry into the draft delayed until next year, Clarett filed this suit [in a federal district court] alleging that the NFL's draft eligibility rules are an unreasonable restraint of trade in violation of Section 1 of the Sherman Act and Section 4 of the Clayton Act.

* * * The major source of the parties' * * * disputes is the

relationship between the challenged eligibility rules and the current collective bargaining agreement governing the terms and conditions of employment for NFL players * * *. The current collective bargaining agreement between the NFL and its players union was negotiated between the NFL Management Council ("NFLMC"), which is the NFL member clubs' multi-employer bargaining unit, and the NFL Players Association ("NFLPA"), the NFL players' exclusive bargaining representative.

* * * *

* * * On February 5, 2004, the district court granted summary judgment in favor of Clarett and ordered him eligible to enter this year's draft. * * * [The NFL appealed to this court.]

* * * *

EXTENDED CASE CONTINUES ➡

EXTENDED CASE 27.1 CONTINUED ☞

* * * *To accommodate the collective bargaining process, certain concerted activity among and between labor and employers [is] held to be beyond the reach of the antitrust laws. [Emphasis added.]*
* * * *

Although the NFL has maintained draft eligibility rules in one form or another for much of its history, the inception of a collective bargaining relationship between the NFL and its players union some thirty years ago irrevocably altered the governing legal regime. * * *Prospective players no longer have the right to negotiate directly with the NFL teams over the terms and conditions of their employment. That responsibility is instead committed to the NFL and the players union to accomplish through the collective bargaining process, and throughout that process the NFL and the players union are to have the freedom to craft creative solutions to their differences in light of the economic imperatives of their industry. Furthermore, the NFL teams are permitted to engage in joint conduct with respect to the terms and conditions of players' employment as a multi-employer bargaining unit without risking antitrust liability.
* * * *

Clarett's argument that antitrust law should permit him to circumvent this scheme established by federal labor law starts with the contention that the eligibility rules do not constitute a mandatory subject of collective bargaining and thus cannot fall within the protection of the * * * exemption. * * * However, we find that the eligibility rules are mandatory bargaining subjects. Though tailored to the unique circumstance of a professional sports league, the eligibility rules for the draft represent a quite literal condition for initial employment and for that reason alone might constitute a mandatory bargaining subject. But moreover, the eligibility rules constitute a mandatory bargaining subject because they have tangible effects on the wages and working conditions of current NFL players. Because the unusual economic imperatives of professional sports raise numerous problems with little or no precedent in standard industrial relations, * * * many of the arrangements in professional sports that, at first glance, might not appear to deal with wages or working conditions are indeed mandatory bargaining subjects.

Furthermore, by reducing competition in the market for entering players, the eligibility rules also affect the job security of veteran players. Because the size of NFL teams is capped, the eligibility rules diminish a veteran player's risk of being replaced by either a drafted rookie or a player who enters the draft and, though not drafted, is then hired as a rookie free agent. Consequently, * * * we find that to regard the NFL's eligibility rules as merely permissive bargaining subjects would ignore the reality of collective bargaining in sports.
* * * *

For the foregoing reasons, the judgment of the district court is REVERSED and the case REMANDED with instructions to enter judgment in favor of the NFL. The order of the district court designating Clarett eligible to enter this year's NFL draft is VACATED.

QUESTIONS

1. Why are the NFL's member clubs permitted to agree that a player will not be hired until three full football seasons after the player's high school graduation?
2. Why couldn't the NFL's eligibility rules be eliminated from the list of mandatory subjects for the parties' collective bargaining agreement?

SECTION 6
U.S. ANTITRUST LAWS IN THE GLOBAL CONTEXT

U.S. antitrust laws have a broad application. Not only may persons in foreign nations be subject to their provisions, but the laws may also be applied to protect foreign consumers and competitors from violations committed by U.S. business firms. Consequently, *foreign persons,* a term that by definition includes foreign governments, may sue under U.S. antitrust laws in U.S. courts.

The Extraterritorial Application of U.S. Antitrust Laws

Section 1 of the Sherman Act provides for the extraterritorial effect of the U.S. antitrust laws. The United States is a major proponent of free competition in the global economy, and thus any conspiracy that has a *substantial effect* on U.S. commerce is within the reach of the Sherman Act. The violation may even occur outside the United States, and foreign governments as well as individuals can be sued for violation of U.S. antitrust laws. Before U.S. courts will exercise jurisdiction and apply antitrust laws, it

EXHIBIT 27-1 • Exemptions to Antitrust Enforcement

EXEMPTION	SOURCE AND SCOPE
Labor	Clayton Act—Permits unions to organize and bargain without violating antitrust laws and specifies that strikes and other labor activities normally do not violate any federal law.
Agricultural Associations	Clayton Act and Capper-Volstead Act of 1922—Allow agricultural cooperatives to set prices.
Fisheries	Fisheries Cooperative Marketing Act of 1976—Allows the fishing industry to set prices.
Insurance Companies	McCarran-Ferguson Act of 1945—Exempts the insurance business in states in which the industry is regulated.
Exporters	Webb-Pomerene Act of 1918—Allows U.S. exporters to engage in cooperative activity to compete with similar foreign associations. Export Trading Company Act of 1982—Permits the U.S. Department of Justice to exempt certain exporters.
Professional Baseball	The United States Supreme Court has held that professional baseball is exempt because it is not "interstate commerce."[a]
Oil Marketing	Interstate Oil Compact of 1935—Allows states to set quotas on oil to be marketed in interstate commerce.
Defense Activities	Defense Production Act of 1950—Allows the president to approve, and thereby exempt, certain activities to further the military defense of the United States.
Small Businesses' Cooperative Research	Small Business Administration Act of 1958—Allows small firms to undertake cooperative research.
State Actions	The United States Supreme Court has held that actions by a state are exempt if the state clearly articulates and actively supervises the policy behind its action.[b]
Regulated Industries	Industries (such as airlines) are exempt when a federal administrative agency (such as the Federal Aviation Administration) has primary regulatory authority.
Businesspersons' Joint Efforts to Seek Government Action	Cooperative efforts by businesspersons to obtain legislative, judicial, or executive action are exempt unless it is clear that an effort is "objectively baseless" and is an attempt to make anticompetitive use of government processes.[c]

a. *Federal Baseball Club of Baltimore, Inc. v. National League of Professional Baseball Clubs,* 259 U.S. 200, 42 S.Ct. 465, 66 L.Ed. 898 (1922). A federal district court has held that this exemption applies only to the game's reserve system. (Under the reserve system, teams hold players' contracts for the players' entire careers. The reserve system generally is being replaced by the free agency system.) See *Piazza v. Major League Baseball,* 831 F.Supp. 420 (E.D.Pa. 1993).

b. *Parker v. Brown,* 317 U.S. 341, 63 S.Ct. 307, 87 L.Ed. 315 (1943).

c. *Eastern Railroad Presidents Conference v. Noerr Motor Freight, Inc.,* 365 U.S. 127, 81 S.Ct. 523, 5 L.Ed.2d 464 (1961); and *United Mine Workers of America v. Pennington,* 381 U.S. 657, 89 S.Ct. 1585, 14 L.Ed.2d 626 (1965). These two cases established the exception often referred to as the *Noerr-Pennington* doctrine.

must be shown that the alleged violation had a substantial effect on U.S. commerce. U.S. jurisdiction is automatically invoked, however, when a *per se* violation (see page 611) occurs.

If a domestic firm, for example, joins a foreign cartel to control the production, price, or distribution of goods, and this cartel has a *substantial effect* on U.S. commerce, a *per se* violation may exist. Hence, both the domestic firm and the foreign cartel could be sued for violation of the U.S. antitrust laws. Likewise, if a foreign firm doing business in the United States enters into a price-fixing or other anticompetitive agreement to control a portion of U.S. markets, a *per se* violation may exist.

The Application of Foreign Antitrust Laws

Large U.S. companies increasingly need to worry about the application of foreign antitrust laws as well. The European Union (EU), in particular, has stepped up its enforcement actions against antitrust violators in recent years.

EUROPEAN UNION ENFORCEMENT The EU's laws promoting competition are stricter in many respects than those of the United States and define more conduct as anticompetitive. The EU actively pursues antitrust violators, especially individual companies and cartels that engage in monopolistic conduct. For example, in 2009, the EU fined Intel, Inc., the world's largest semiconductor chip maker, $1.44 billion in an antitrust case. According to European regulators, Intel offered computer manufacturers and retailers price discounts and marketing subsidies if they agreed to buy Intel's chips rather than the chips produced by Intel's main competitor in Europe. The EU has also fined Microsoft Corporation more than $2 billion in the last ten years for anticompetitive conduct.

ENFORCEMENT IN ASIA AND LATIN AMERICA Many other nations also have laws that promote competition and prohibit trade restraints. For example, Japanese antitrust laws forbid unfair trade practices, monopolization, and restrictions that unreasonably restrain trade. In 2008, China enacted its first antitrust rules, which restrict monopolization and price fixing (although the Chinese government may set prices on exported goods without violating these rules). Indonesia, Malaysia, South Korea, and Vietnam all have statutes protecting competition. Argentina, Brazil, Chile, Peru, and several other Latin American countries have adopted modern antitrust laws as well.

Most of the antitrust laws apply extraterritorially, as U.S. antitrust laws do. This means that a U.S. company may be subject to another nation's antitrust laws if the company's conduct has a substantial effect on that nation's commerce. For instance, in 2008, South Korea fined Intel $25 million for antitrust violations; Japan settled an antitrust case against Intel in 2005.

SECTION 7
MONOPOLIES

As noted, the impetus for the initial federal antitrust legislation was concern over monopolies—specifically, concern that in particular markets a single, dominant firm could acquire and use market power to dictate or influence prices and output. Section 2 of the Sherman Act deals broadly with such cases by condemning "every person who shall monopolize or attempt to monopolize." (Note that Section 2 applies to activities in the restraint of trade on the part of a single firm or individual. In contrast, Section 1, as will be described in the next chapter, applies to certain activities in the restraint of trade on the part of more than one individual or firm.) The essence of a single entity's violation of Section 2 is the entity's willful acquisition or maintenance of monopoly power, or its specifically

intended *attempt* to do so, provided the attempt has a reasonable chance of success.

In the remainder of this chapter, we focus on single-firm behavior that is intended either to create or to preserve a monopoly within a particular market. Notice that two distinct types of behavior are subject to sanction under Section 2. First, conduct pursued by a firm that is already a monopolist is condemned as *monopolization* if the conduct interferes with free trade and is intended to preserve the firm's monopoly. Second, conduct intended to capture monopoly power is condemned as an *attempt to monopolize*.

Another Section 2 offense is the act of *predatory pricing*. **Predatory pricing** occurs when one firm (the predator) attempts to drive its competitors from the market by selling its product at prices substantially *below* the normal costs of production. Once the competitors are eliminated, the predator presumably will raise its prices far above their competitive levels to recapture its losses and earn higher profits.

Monopolization

The United States Supreme Court has defined **monopolization** as involving the following two elements: "(1) the possession of monopoly power in the relevant market and (2) the willful acquisition or maintenance of the power as distinguished from growth or development as a consequence of a superior product, business acumen, or historic accident."[7] To establish a violation of Section 2, a plaintiff must prove both of these elements—monopoly power and an *intent* to monopolize.

MONOPOLY POWER The Sherman Act does not define *monopoly*. In economic theory, monopoly refers to control of a specific market by a single entity. It is well established in antitrust law, however, that a firm may be a monopolist even though it is not the sole seller in a market. Additionally, size alone does not determine whether a firm is a monopoly. For example, a "mom and pop" grocery located in an isolated desert town is a monopolist if it is the only grocery serving that particular market. Size in relation to the market is what matters because monopoly involves the power to affect prices and output.

Monopoly power may be proved by direct evidence that the firm used its power to control prices and restrict output.[8] Usually, however, there is not

---

7. *United States v. Grinnell Corp.,* 384 U.S. 563, 86 S.Ct. 1698, 16 L.Ed.2d 778 (1966).
8. See, for example, *Broadcom Corp. v. Qualcomm, Inc.,* 501 F.3d 297 (3d Cir. 2007).

enough evidence to show that the firm intentionally controlled prices, so the plaintiff has to offer indirect, or circumstantial, evidence of monopoly power. To prove monopoly power indirectly, the plaintiff must show that the firm has a dominant share of the relevant market and that there are significant barriers for new competitors entering that market.

RELEVANT MARKET Before a court can determine whether a firm has a dominant market share, it must define the relevant market. The relevant market consists of two elements: (1) a relevant product market and (2) a relevant geographic market.

Relevant Product Market. The relevant product market includes all products that, although produced by different firms, have identical attributes, such as sugar. It also includes products that are reasonably interchangeable for the purpose for which they are produced. Products will be considered reasonably interchangeable if consumers treat them as acceptable substitutes.[9]

What should the relevant product market include? This is often the key issue in monopolization cases because the way in which the market is defined may determine whether a firm has monopoly power. By defining the product market narrowly, the degree of a firm's market power is enhanced.

CASE IN POINT Whole Foods Market, Inc., wished to acquire Wild Oats Markets, Inc., its main competitor in nationwide high-end organic food supermarkets. The Federal Trade Commission (FTC) filed a Section 2 claim against Whole Foods to prevent the merger. The FTC argued that the relevant product market consisted of only "premium natural and organic supermarkets" rather than all supermarkets, as Whole Foods maintained. An appellate court accepted the FTC's narrow definition of the relevant market and remanded the case to the lower court to decide what remedies were appropriate, as the merger had already taken place. Whole Foods later entered into a settlement with the FTC under which it was required to divest (sell or give up control over) thirteen stores, most of which were formerly Wild Oats outlets.[10]

The main issue in the following case was whether a relevant market existed in which competitors had market power.

---

9. See, for example, *Linzer Products Corp. v. Sekar,* 499 F.Supp.2d 540 (S.D.N.Y. 2007); and *HDC Medical, Inc. v. Minntech Corp.,* 474 F.3d 543 (8th Cir. 2007).

10. *Federal Trade Commission v. Whole Foods Market, Inc.,* 548 F.3d 1028 (D.C.Cir. 2008); and 592 F.Supp.2d 107 (D.D.C. 2009).

CASE 27.2
Newcal Industries, Inc. v. IKON Office Solutions

United States Court of Appeals, Ninth Circuit, 513 F.3d 1038 (2008).
www.ca9.uscourts.gov[a]

BACKGROUND AND FACTS • Newcal Industries and IKON Office Solutions (IKON) compete in the brand-name copier equipment-leasing market for commercial customers and in the provision of service. When a lease approaches its term, these companies compete for the lease of upgraded copier equipment. When a service contract approaches its term, these companies also compete to buy out the service contract in order to provide another one. Newcal alleged that IKON "tricked" its customers by amending its lease agreements and service contracts without disclosing that such amendments would lengthen the terms of the original agreements. The purpose of these contract extensions was to shield IKON customers from competition in the aftermarkets for upgraded copier equipment and service agreements. When IKON succeeded in extending the terms of the original contract, it was able to raise that contract's value. Consequently, Newcal and other competitors had to pay higher prices to buy out such contracts in the aftermarkets for upgraded equipment and services. Newcal brought claims under the Sherman Act, alleging antitrust violations. The district court held that Newcal had failed to allege a legally recognizable "relevant market" under the Sherman Act. Newcal appealed.

---

a. Click on "Opinions" and then in "Opinions by Date" and then "2008." Go to "January" and find the decisions issued on "01/23/08." Click on the case name to access the opinion. The U.S. Court of Appeals for the Ninth Circuit maintains this Web site.

CASE CONTINUES ➡

CASE 27.2 CONTINUED ➡

IN THE LANGUAGE OF THE COURT
THOMAS, Circuit Judge.
* * * *

First and foremost, *the relevant market must be a product market. The consumers do not define the boundaries of the market; the products or producers do. Second, the market must encompass the product at issue as well as all economic substitutes for the product.* As the Supreme Court has instructed, "The outer boundaries of a product market are determined by the reasonable interchangeability of use * * * between the product itself and substitutes for it." As such, the relevant market must include "the group or groups of sellers or producers who have actual or potential ability to deprive each other of significant levels of business." [Emphasis added.]

* * * Although the general market must include all economic substitutes, it is legally permissible to premise antitrust allegations on a submarket. That is, an antitrust claim may, under certain circumstances, allege restraints of trade within or monopolization of a small part of the general market of substitutable products. *In order to establish the existence of a legally cognizable submarket, the plaintiff must be able to show (but need not necessarily establish in the complaint) that the alleged submarket is economically distinct from the general product market.* In [another case], the Supreme Court listed several "practical indicia" of an economically distinct submarket: "industry or public recognition of the submarket as a separate economic entity, the product's peculiar characteristics and uses, unique production facilities, distinct customers, distinct prices, sensitivity to price changes, and specialized vendors." [Emphasis added.]

* * * *

* * * First, the law permits an antitrust claimant to restrict the relevant market to a single brand of the product at issue. Second, the law prohibits an antitrust claimant from resting on market *power* that arises solely from contractual rights that consumers knowingly and voluntarily gave to the defendant. Third, in determining whether the defendant's market power falls in the * * * category of contractually created market power or in the * * * category of economic market power, the law permits an inquiry into whether a consumer's selection of a particular brand in the competitive market is the functional equivalent of a contractual commitment, giving that brand an agreed-upon right to monopolize its consumers in an aftermarket. The law permits an inquiry into whether consumers entered into such "contracts" knowing that they were agreeing to such a commitment.

* * * *

The relevance of this point to the legal viability of Newcal's market definition may not be intuitively obvious, but it is nevertheless significant. * * * IKON has a contractually created monopoly over services provided under *original* IKON contracts. That contractually created monopoly * * * then gives IKON a unique *relationship* with those consumers, and the contractual relationship gives IKON a unique position in the wholly derivative aftermarket for replacement equipment and lease-end services. The allegation here is that IKON is * * * exploiting its unique position—its unique contractual relationship—to gain monopoly power in a derivative aftermarket in which its power is not contractually mandated.

* * * *

* * * This case is not a case in which the alleged market power flows from contractual exclusivity. IKON is not simply enforcing a contractual provision that gives it the exclusive right to provide replacement equipment and lease-end services. Rather, it is leveraging a special relationship with its contracting partners to restrain trade in a wholly derivative aftermarket. We therefore reverse the district court's holding that * * * Newcal's complaint is legally invalid.

That holding, however, does not quite end the matter. In considering the legal validity of Newcal's alleged market, we must also determine whether IKON customers constitute a cognizable subset of the aftermarket, such that they qualify as a submarket * * *. That is, we have thus far concluded only that there is no *per se* rule against recognizing contractually created submarkets and that such submarkets are potentially viable when the market at issue is a wholly derivative aftermarket. * * * A submarket * * * must bear the "practical indicia" [indicators] of an independent economic entity in order to qualify as a cognizable submarket * * *. In this case, Newcal's complaint sufficiently alleges that IKON customers constitute a submarket according to all of those practical indicia.

CASE 27.2 CONTINUED ➡ **DECISION AND REMEDY** • *The U.S. Court of Appeals for the Ninth Circuit reversed and remanded the district court's decision. The court concluded that there existed a legally recognizable relevant market.*

THE ETHICAL DIMENSION • *Would there ever be any circumstances that could justify IKON's practice of amending customers' contracts without letting them know that the result was an extension of those original lease contracts? Explain your answer.*

WHAT IF THE FACTS WERE DIFFERENT? • *Assume that IKON's contracts allowed its customers to "opt-out" if they gave a sixty-day notice. Would the judge have ruled differently? Why or why not?*

Relevant Geographic Market. The second component of the relevant market is the geographic boundaries of the market in which the firm and its competitors sell the product or services. For products that are sold nationwide, the geographic boundaries of the market can encompass the entire United States. If transportation costs are significant or a producer and its competitors sell in only a limited area (one in which customers have no access to other sources of the product), then the geographic market is limited to that area. A national firm may thus compete in several distinct areas and have monopoly power in one geographic area but not in another.

Generally, the geographic market is that section of the country within which a firm can increase its price a bit without attracting new sellers or without losing many customers to alternative suppliers outside that area. Of course, the Internet is changing perceptions of the size and limits of a geographic market. It may become difficult to perceive any geographic market as local, except for products that are not easily transported, such as concrete.

CASE IN POINT Clear Channel Communications, Inc., owns numerous radio stations and promotes and books concert tours. Malinda Heerwagen, who had attended various rock concerts in Chicago, Illinois, filed a lawsuit against Clear Channel alleging violations of Section 2. Heerwagen claimed that the company had used anticompetitive practices to acquire and maintain monopoly power in a national ticket market for live rock concerts, causing audiences to pay inflated prices for the tickets. Heerwagen argued that because Clear Channel sold tickets nationwide, the geographic market was the entire United States. The court, however, ruled that even though Clear Channel sold tickets nationally, the relevant market for concert tickets was local. The court reasoned that "[a] purchaser of a concert ticket is hardly likely to look outside of her own area, even

if the price for tickets has increased inside her region and decreased for the same tour in other places."[11]

THE INTENT REQUIREMENT Monopoly power, in and of itself, does not constitute the offense of monopolization under Section 2 of the Sherman Act. The offense also requires an *intent* to monopolize. A dominant market share may be the result of good business judgment or the development of a superior product. It may simply be the result of historical accident. In these situations, the acquisition of monopoly power is not an antitrust violation. Indeed, it would be contrary to society's interest to condemn every firm that acquired a position of power because it was well managed and efficient and marketed a product desired by consumers.

If a firm possesses market power as a result of carrying out some purposeful act to acquire or maintain that power through anticompetitive means, then it is in violation of Section 2. In most monopolization cases, intent may be inferred from evidence that the firm had monopoly power and engaged in anticompetitive behavior.

CASE IN POINT Navigator, the first popular graphical Internet browser, used Java technology that was able to run on a variety of platforms. When Navigator was introduced, Microsoft Corporation perceived a threat to its dominance of the operating-system market. Microsoft developed a competing browser, Internet Explorer (IE), and then began to require computer makers that wanted to install the Windows operating system to install IE and exclude Navigator. Microsoft also included codes in Windows that would cripple the operating system if IE was deleted and paid Internet service providers to distribute IE and exclude Navigator. Because of this

---

11. *Heerwagen v. Clear Channel Communications*, 435 F.3d 219 (2d Cir. 2006).

pattern of exclusionary conduct, a court found that Microsoft was guilty of monopolization. The court reasoned that Microsoft's pattern of conduct could be rational only if the firm knew that it possessed monopoly power.[12]

UNILATERAL REFUSALS TO DEAL A single manufacturer acting unilaterally normally is free to deal, or not to deal, with whomever it wishes. (As will be discussed in Chapter 28, joint refusals to deal, called *group boycotts,* are subject to close scrutiny under Section 1 of the Sherman Act.)

Nevertheless, in some instances, a unilateral refusal to deal will violate antitrust laws. These instances involve offenses proscribed under Section 2 of the Sherman Act and occur only if (1) the firm refusing to deal has—or is likely to acquire—monopoly power and (2) the refusal is likely to have an anticompetitive effect on a particular market.

CASE IN POINT The owner of three of the four major downhill ski areas in Aspen, Colorado, refused to continue its participation in a jointly offered six-day "all Aspen" lift ticket. The United States Supreme Court ruled that the owner's refusal to cooperate with its smaller competitor was a violation of Section 2 of the Sherman Act. Because the company owned three-fourths of the local ski areas, it had monopoly power, and thus its unilateral refusal had an anticompetitive effect on the market.[13]

Attempts to Monopolize

Section 2 prohibits **attempted monopolization** of a market. Any action challenged as an attempt to monopolize must have been specifically intended to exclude competitors and garner monopoly power. The attempt must also have had a "dangerous" probability of success—only *serious* threats of monopolization are condemned as violations. The probability cannot be dangerous unless the alleged offender possesses some degree of market power.[14]

As mentioned earlier, predatory pricing is a form of anticompetitive conduct that, in theory, could be used by firms that are attempting to monopolize. (Predatory pricing may also lead to claims of price discrimination—see page 597.) Predatory bidding involves the acquisition and use of *monopsony power,* which is market power on the *buy* side of a market. This may occur when a buyer bids up the price of an input too high for its competitors to pay, causing them to leave the market. The predatory bidder may then attempt to drive down input prices to reap above-competitive profits and recoup any losses it suffered in bidding up the prices.

The question in the following case was whether a claim of predatory bidding is sufficiently similar to a claim of predatory pricing that the same test should apply to both.

---

12. *United States v. Microsoft Corp.,* 253 F.3d 34 (D.C.Cir. 2001). Microsoft has faced numerous antitrust claims and has settled a number of lawsuits in which it was accused of antitrust violations and anticompetitive tactics.
13. *Aspen Skiing Co. v. Aspen Highlands Skiing Corp.,* 472 U.S. 585, 105 S.Ct. 2847, 86 L.Ed.2d 467 (1985). See also *America Channel, LLC v. Time Warner Cable, Inc.,* 2007 WL 142173 (D.Minn. 2007).

14. See, for example, *Nobody in Particular Presents, Inc. v. Clear Channel Communications, Inc.,* 311 F.Supp.2d 1048 (D.Colo. 2004); and *City of Moundridge, Kansas v. Exxon Mobil Corp.,* 471 F.Supp.2d 20 (D.D.C. 2007).

CASE 27.3
Weyerhaeuser Co. v. Ross-Simmons Hardwood Lumber Co.

Supreme Court of the United States, 549 U.S. 312, 127 S.Ct. 1069, 166 L.Ed.2d 911 (2007).
www.findlaw.com/casecode/supreme.html[a]

BACKGROUND AND FACTS • Weyerhaeuser Company entered the Pacific Northwest's hardwood lumber market in 1980. By 2000, Weyerhaeuser owned six mills processing 65 percent of the red alder logs in the region. Meanwhile, Ross-Simmons Hardwood Lumber Company operated a single competing mill. When the prices of logs rose and those for lumber fell, Ross-Simmons suffered heavy losses. Several million dollars in debt, the mill closed in 2001. Ross-Simmons filed a suit in a

---

a. In the "Browse Supreme Court Opinions" section, click on "2007." On that page, scroll to the name of the case and click on it to access the opinion. The United States Supreme Court maintains this Web site.

CASE 27.3 CONTINUED ▶ federal district court against Weyerhaeuser, alleging attempted monopolization under Section 2 of the Sherman Act. Ross-Simmons claimed that Weyerhaeuser used its dominant position in the market to bid up the prices of logs and prevent its competitors from being profitable. Weyerhaeuser argued that the antitrust test for predatory pricing applies to a claim of predatory bidding and that Ross-Simmons had not met this standard. The district court ruled in favor of the plaintiff, the U.S. Court of Appeals for the Ninth Circuit affirmed, and Weyerhaeuser appealed to the United States Supreme Court.

IN THE LANGUAGE OF THE COURT
Justice *THOMAS* delivered the opinion of the Court.
* * * *

Predatory-pricing and predatory-bidding claims are analytically similar. This similarity results from the close theoretical connection between monopoly and monopsony. The kinship between monopoly and monopsony suggests that similar legal standards should apply to claims of monopolization and to claims of monopsonization.

* * * Both claims involve the deliberate use of unilateral pricing measures for anticompetitive purposes. And both claims logically require firms to incur short-term losses on the chance that they might reap supracompetitive profits [above-competitive rates] in the future.
* * * *

* * * *"Predatory pricing schemes are rarely tried, and even more rarely successful." Predatory pricing requires a firm to suffer certain losses in the short term on the chance of reaping supracompetitive profits in the future. A rational business will rarely make this sacrifice.* The same reasoning applies to predatory bidding. [Emphasis added.]
* * * *

* * * A failed predatory-pricing scheme may benefit consumers. * * * Failed predatory-bidding schemes can also * * * benefit consumers.

In addition, predatory bidding presents less of a direct threat of consumer harm than predatory pricing. A predatory-pricing scheme ultimately achieves success by charging higher prices to consumers. By contrast, a predatory-bidding scheme could succeed with little or no effect on consumer prices because a predatory bidder does not necessarily rely on raising prices in the output market to recoup its losses.
* * * *

* * * [Thus] our two-pronged [predatory pricing] test should apply to predatory-bidding claims.

* * * A plaintiff must prove that the alleged predatory bidding led to below-cost pricing of the predator's outputs. That is, the predator's bidding on the buy side must have caused the cost of the relevant output to rise above the revenues generated in the sale of those outputs. * * * Given the multitude of procompetitive ends served by higher bidding for inputs, the risk of chilling procompetitive behavior with too lax a liability standard is * * * serious * * *. Consequently, only higher bidding that leads to below-cost pricing in the relevant output market will suffice as a basis for liability for predatory bidding.

A predatory-bidding plaintiff also must prove that the defendant has a dangerous probability of recouping the losses incurred in bidding up input prices through the exercise of monopsony power. Absent proof of likely recoupment, a strategy of predatory bidding makes no economic sense because it would involve short-term losses with no likelihood of offsetting long-term gains.

Ross-Simmons has conceded that it has not satisfied [this] standard. Therefore, its predatory-bidding theory of liability cannot support the jury's verdict.

For these reasons, we vacate the judgment of the Court of Appeals and remand the case for further proceedings consistent with this opinion.

DECISION AND REMEDY • *The antitrust test that applies to claims of predatory pricing also applies to claims of predatory bidding. Because Ross-Simmons conceded that it had not met this standard, the United States Supreme Court vacated the lower court's judgment and remanded the case.*

WHAT IF THE FACTS WERE DIFFERENT? • *Logs represent up to 75 percent of a mill's total costs. Efficient equipment can increase both the speed at which lumber can be recovered from a log and the amount of lumber recovered. The Court noted that "Ross-Simmons appears to have*

CASE CONTINUES ▶

CASE 27.3 CONTINUED ▶ *engaged in little efficiency-enhancing investment." If Ross-Simmons had invested in state-of-the-art technology, how might the circumstances in this case have been different?*

THE ECONOMIC DIMENSION • *Why does a plaintiff alleging predatory bidding have to prove that the defendant's "bidding on the buy side caused the cost of the relevant output to rise above the revenues generated in the sale of those outputs"?*

REVIEWING
Antitrust and Monopoly

In 2002, Roxanna Leland, who lived in Curio Valley, an isolated town in rural Michigan, began selling fresh pies under the business name Momma Roxie's Heavenly Pies. Leland's business grew as a result of the superior quality of the pies and her willingness to carry fresh pies daily into every Curio Valley shop. Such a local desire for the pies grew that Momma Roxie's eventually garnered 80 percent of the pie sales in Curio Valley. In 2004, Leland sold the business and its name to Arnold Sachmeister under an agreement that Leland would not sell pies in Curio Valley for twenty years. Under Sachmeister, Momma Roxie's began requiring that every pie purchaser buy an "Arnie's Poem of the Day" for $1 along with each pie. In 2011, a new local pie dealer, Crusty Joe, began successfully competing with Momma Roxie's. Momma Roxie's soon began selling all pies at half the price of Crusty Joe. Using the information presented in the chapter, answer the following questions.

1. What is the term for a firm that holds such market power that it can limit rivals from competing in the market?
2. Did the agreement between Leland and Sachmeister constitute a restraint of trade? If so, would this be considered a reasonable or unreasonable restraint? Explain.
3. What is the term applicable to the requirement that each buyer purchase a poem along with a pie? Is such a requirement legal? Discuss.
4. To succeed in an action for predatory pricing against Momma Roxie's, what must Crusty Joe demonstrate?

⚙ **DEBATE THIS:** *Price discrimination should be legalized.*

TERMS AND CONCEPTS

antitrust law 594
attempted
   monopolization 606

divestiture 598
market power 593
monopolization 602
monopoly 593

monopoly power 596
predatory pricing 602
price discrimination 597
restraint of trade 596

treble damages 599
trust 595

QUESTIONS AND CASE PROBLEMS

27–1. Monopolization A car rental firm specializes in renting automobiles to insurance company customers who need temporary replacements while their cars are being repaired. Several other car rental agencies serve the same geographical area. The specialty agency substantially reduces the daily rental fee on its cars. Other firms in the area contend that the reductions amount to predatory pricing. If an antitrust action is brought against the specialty agency,

how should the case be decided? Discuss all factors that must be considered.

27–2. QUESTION WITH SAMPLE ANSWER: Market Power.

Super-Tech Industries presently controls 55 percent of the market for the manufacture and sale of computers. The balance of the market is controlled by five other manufacturers, with Alcan Corp. having 25 percent of the market. Alcan has an innovative research staff, but every time Alcan introduces a faster, more powerful, and more efficient computer into the market, Super-Tech immediately informs its customers of the upcoming development of a competing computer that it will sell at 30 percent below the Alcan price. Alcan claims that these activities on the part of Super-Tech are an antitrust violation. Discuss fully whether this unilateral action by Super-Tech violates antitrust law.

- **For a sample answer to Question 27–2, go to Appendix F at the end of this text.**

27–3. Monopolies At one time, all advertisers and advertising agencies sent their ads to newspapers by mail, courier, or some other form of physical delivery. By the mid-1980s, electronic delivery emerged as an alternative. In 1986, AD/SAT, a division of Skylight, Inc., began to deliver ads from New York and Los Angeles to newspapers through AD/SAT's high-speed facsimile system over a satellite network owned and operated by the Associated Press (AP). The AP, a cooperative association whose members include more than fifteen thousand U.S. newspapers, collects and distributes news and photographs to newspapers. AD/SAT's competitors included DigiFlex, Ad eXpress, AdStar, AdLink, and Business Link. By 1994, forty-eight of the fifty largest papers in the United States were AD/SAT customers, but 80 percent of all ads delivered to newspapers were sent by overnight couriers, such as Federal Express. That year, the AP launched AdSEND to compete in the delivery of ads to newspapers via the AP's satellite network. Unlike AD/SAT, AdSEND handled the delivery of ads using computers and charged only advertisers for the delivery. AD/SAT filed a suit in a federal district court against the AP and others. Did the AP's entry into the ad delivery business violate Section 2 of the Sherman Act? Why or why not? [*AD/SAT, a Division of Skylight, Inc. v. Associated Press,* 181 F.3d 216 (2d.Cir. 1999)]

27–4. Attempted Monopolization In 1995, to make personal computers (PCs) easier to use, Intel Corp. and other companies developed a standard, called the Universal Serial Bus (USB) specification, to enable the easy attachment of peripherals (printers and other hardware) to PCs. Intel and others formed the Universal Serial Bus Implementers Forum (USB-IF) to promote USB technology and products. Intel, however, makes relatively few USB products and does not make any USB interconnect devices. Multivideo Labs, Inc. (MVL), designed and distributed Active Extension Cables (AECs) to connect peripheral devices to each other or to a PC. The AECs were not USB compliant, a fact that Intel employees told other USB-IF members. Asserting that this caused a "general cooling of the market" for AECs, MVL filed a suit in a federal district court against Intel, claiming in part attempted monopolization in violation of the Sherman Act. Intel filed a motion for summary judgment. How should the court rule, and why? [*Multivideo Labs, Inc. v. Intel Corp.,* __ F.Supp.2d __ (S.D.N.Y. 2000)]

27–5. Monopolization Moist snuff is a smokeless tobacco product sold in small round cans from racks, which include point-of-sale (POS) ads. POS ads are critical because tobacco advertising is restricted and the number

of people who use smokeless tobacco products is relatively small. In the moist snuff market in the United States, there are only four competitors, including U.S. Tobacco Co. and its affiliates (USTC) and Conwood Co. In 1990, USTC, which held 87 percent of the market, began to convince major retailers, including Wal-Mart Stores, Inc., to use USTC's "exclusive racks" to display its products and those of all other snuff makers. USTC agents would then destroy competitors' racks. USTC also began to provide retailers with false sales data to convince them to maintain its poor-selling items and drop competitors' less expensive products. Conwood's Wal-Mart market share fell from 12 percent to 6.5 percent. In stores in which USTC did not have rack exclusivity, however, Conwood's market share increased to 25 percent. Conwood filed a suit in a federal district court against USTC, alleging in part that USTC used its monopoly power to exclude competitors from the moist snuff market. Should the court rule in Conwood's favor? What is USTC's best defense? Discuss. [*Conwood Co., LP v. U.S. Tobacco Co.,* 290 F.3d 768 (6th Cir. 2002)]

27–6. Monopolization Dentsply International, Inc., is one of a dozen manufacturers of artificial teeth for dentures and other restorative devices. Dentsply sells its teeth to twenty-three dealers of dental products. The dealers supply the teeth to dental laboratories, which fabricate dentures for sale to dentists. There are hundreds of other dealers who compete with one another on the basis of price and service. Some manufacturers sell directly to the laboratories. There are also thousands of laboratories that compete with one another on the basis of price and service. Because of advances in dental medicine, however, artificial tooth manufacturing is marked by low growth potential, and Dentsply dominates the industry. Dentsply's market share is greater than 75 percent and is about fifteen times larger than that of its next-closest competitor. Dentsply prohibits its dealers from marketing competitors' teeth unless they were selling the teeth before 1993. The federal government filed a suit in a federal district court against Dentsply, alleging in part a violation of Section 2 of the Sherman Act. What must the government show to succeed in its suit? Are those elements present in this case? What should the court rule? Explain. [*United States v. Dentsply International, Inc.,* 399 F.3d 181 (3d Cir. 2005)]

27–7. CASE PROBLEM WITH SAMPLE ANSWER: Restraint of Trade.

In 1999, residents of the city of Madison, Wisconsin, became concerned that overconsumption of liquor seemed to be increasing near the campus of the University of Wisconsin–Madison (UW), leading to more frequent use of detoxification facilities and calls for police services in the campus area. Under pressure from UW, which shared these concerns, the city initiated a new policy, imposing conditions on area taverns to discourage price reduction "specials" believed to encourage high-volume and dangerous drinking. In 2002, the city began to draft an ordinance to ban all drink specials. Tavern owners responded by announcing that they had "voluntarily" agreed

to discontinue drink specials on Friday and Saturday nights after 8 P.M. The city put its ordinance on hold. UW student Nic Eichenseer and others filed a suit in a Wisconsin state court against the Madison–Dane County Tavern League, Inc. (an association of local tavern owners), and others, alleging violations of antitrust law. On what might the plaintiffs base a claim for relief? Are the defendants in this case exempt from the antitrust laws? What should the court rule? Why? [Eichenseer v. Madison–Dane County Tavern League, Inc., 2006 WI App 226, 725 N.W.2d 274 (2006)]

- To view a sample answer for Problem 27–7, go to this book's Web site at www.cengage.com/blaw/cross, select "Chapter 27," and click on "Case Problem with Sample Answer."

27–8. Price Discrimination The customers of Sodexho, Inc., and Feesers, Inc., are institutional food service facilities, such as school, hospital, and nursing home cafeterias. Feesers is a distributor that buys unprepared food from suppliers for resale to customers who run their own cafeterias. Sodexho is a food service management company that buys unprepared food from suppliers, prepares the food, and sells the meals to the facilities, which it also operates, under contracts with its clients. Sodexho uses a distributor, such as Sysco Corp., to buy the food from a supplier, such as Michael Foods, Inc. Sysco pays Michael's list price and sells the food to Sodexho at a lower price— which Sodexho has negotiated with Michael—plus an agreed mark-up. Sysco invoices Michael for the difference. Sodexho resells the food to its facilities at its cost, plus a "procurement fee." In sum, Michael charges Sysco less for food resold to Sodexho than it charges Feesers for the same products, and thus Sodexho's customers pay less than Feesers's customers for these products. Feesers filed a suit in a federal district court against Michael and others, alleging price discrimination. To establish its claim, what does Feesers have to show? What might be the most difficult element to prove? How should the court rule? Why? [Feesers, Inc. v. Michael Foods, Inc., 498 F.3d 206 (3d Cir. 2007)]

27–9. A QUESTION OF ETHICS: Monopolization.

 Mr. Furniture Warehouse, Inc., was a company engaged in the wholesale and retail furniture business. Like many other companies in its line of business, Mr. Furniture frequently obtained its furniture products from manufacturers by making purchases on credit. Credit usually was not provided by the manufacturers them-

selves but rather by institutions engaged in "commercial factoring." Such institutions typically purchase manufacturers' accounts receivable at a discount and assume direct responsibility for collecting the outstanding debts. Moreover, factored-credit institutions often purchase debt on a nonrecourse basis, meaning that they assume the entire risk of a debtor's failure to repay. The institutions rely on credit ratings and similar criteria in deciding which purchasers should be extended credit. Barclays American/Commercial, Inc., was almost certainly the dominant factored credit institution in the market in which Mr. Furniture operated. Barclays refused to extend credit for Mr. Furniture's inventory purchases from furniture manufacturers. Mr. Furniture's president, Howard Cassett, asserted that the refusal was based on two elements: (1) Barclays's attempt to monopolize the factored-credit market and (2) the personal animosity that Barclays's manager, Jim Stenhouse, harbored toward Cassett. Mr. Furniture sued Barclays, alleging, among other things, violations of the Sherman Act. The trial court ruled that Mr. Furniture lacked standing to bring the antitrust charge; the court held that any alleged monopolization would directly injure other commercial factoring institutions that competed with Barclays, not Mr. Furniture. [Mr. Furniture Warehouse, Inc. v. Barclays American/Commercial, Inc., 919 F.2d 1517 (11th Cir. 1990)]

(a) The court's ruling, affirmed on appeal, that Mr. Furniture lacked standing was based on the contention that any antitrust violations committed by Barclays would injure its competitors—other factored-credit institutions—not Mr. Furniture. Should Mr. Furniture have been allowed to complain simply because, as a "consumer" of factored-credit services, it was harmed by the alleged monopoly over credit extension acquired by Barclays? After all, the antitrust laws are supposed to help consumers, not competitors. Does the court's ruling mean that only Barclays's rivals could bring the suit?

(b) The court explicitly held that the alleged personal animosity of the Barclays executive toward Mr. Furniture's president was irrelevant. There is something to be said for preventing the antitrust laws, which involve the mechanisms of the judicial process, from being used in a petty way to settle personal feuds. But if monopoly power—assuming Barclays had such power—is used for personal motives, would it be reasonable to allow standing on that basis? Is such abuse any less troubling just because it is done for personal rather than economic reasons?

LEGAL RESEARCH EXERCISES ON THE WEB

Go to this text's Web site at **www.cengage.com/blaw/cross**, select "Chapter 27," and click on "Practical Internet Exercises." There you will find the following Internet research exercises that you can perform to learn more about the topics covered in this chapter.

Practical Internet Exercise 27–1: **Legal Perspective**
The Standard Oil Trust

Practical Internet Exercise 27–2: **Management Perspective**
Monopolization

CHAPTER 28

Antitrust and Restraint of Trade

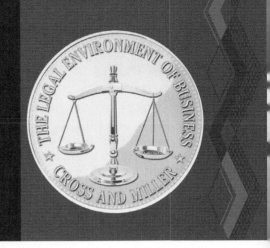

The major thrust of federal antitrust legislation has been directed at anticompetitive agreements between rival firms. Agreements to fix prices, restrict output, divide markets, exclude other competitors, and otherwise impede the dynamics of a free market have all been condemned as violations of federal antitrust laws. Such joint actions have been prosecuted as impermissible restraints of trade under Section 1 of the Sherman Act and, if the firms possess substantial market power, as conspiracies to monopolize under Section 2 of the same act.

Some agreements may be forced on an unwilling firm by another

firm possessing substantial market power. Typical of such agreements are *exclusive-dealing contracts* and *tying arrangements,* briefly described in Chapter 27. Recall that an exclusive-dealing contract conditions one firm's willingness to deal with another on the latter's continued refusal to deal with the former's rivals.

Tying arrangements normally require that the purchaser of one product also purchase a second product. Also recall that such agreements violate provisions of the Clayton Act if the contracts or arrangements harm the competitive process or interfere with free trade.

In this chapter, we continue our study of antitrust law by examining in detail the various forms of *concerted behavior* that are condemned as harmful to competition. In particular, we examine how courts attempt to distinguish between those types of trade restrictions that are necessary—perhaps even beneficial—to the competitive process and those that impede competition. We also examine the legal standards for determining whether mergers between firms should be declared illegal on the ground that the result would be to lessen competition.

SECTION 1
RESTRAINT OF TRADE: AN OVERVIEW

The underlying assumption of Section 1 of the Sherman Act is that society's welfare is harmed if rival firms are permitted to join in an agreement that consolidates their market power or otherwise restrains competition. Not all agreements between rivals, however, result in enhanced market power or *unreasonably* restrain trade. It is virtually inconceivable that an agreement to fix prices or restrict output could be designed for any purpose other than to diminish interfirm competition.

Yet there are numerous instances in which agreements among rivals might actually increase social welfare by making firms more efficient, by making

information more readily available, or by creating joint incentives to undertake risky research and development projects.

Per Se Violations

Some restraints are so substantially anticompetitive that they are deemed ***per se* violations**—illegal *per se* (inherently)—under Section 1. For example, if two competitors in a concentrated industry agree to set the prices for their products at the same level, their agreement is considered so anticompetitive that it is deemed a *per se* violation. If an agreement is found to be a *per se* violation, a court is precluded from inquiring whether the agreement should be upheld on the ground that it provides benefits that outweigh its anticompetitive effects.

611

The Rule of Reason

If an agreement is not found to be a *per se* violation of Section 1, then the court proceeds to analyze its legality by balancing the reasons for the agreement against its potentially anticompetitive effects. Using what is called the **rule of reason,** the courts analyze anticompetitive agreements that allegedly violate Section 1 of the Sherman Act to determine whether they may, in fact, constitute reasonable restraints of trade.

The need for a rule-of-reason analysis of some agreements in restraint of trade is obvious—if the rule of reason had not been developed, almost any business agreement could conceivably be held to violate the Sherman Act. Justice Louis Brandeis effectively phrased this sentiment in *Chicago Board of Trade v. United States,* a case decided in 1918:

> Every agreement concerning trade, every regulation of trade, restrains. To bind, to restrain, is of their very essence. The true test of legality is whether the restraint imposed is such as merely regulates and perhaps thereby promotes competition or whether it is such as may suppress or even destroy competition.[1]

When analyzing an alleged Section 1 violation under the rule of reason, a court will consider several factors. These factors include the purpose of the agreement, the parties' power to implement the agreement to achieve that purpose, and the effect or potential effect of the agreement on competition. A court might also consider whether the parties could have relied on less restrictive means to achieve their purpose.

In the following case, the United States Supreme Court had to decide if a Section 1 violation had occurred. In addition, the Court had to determine whether the violation should have been considered a *per se* violation or whether it should have been analyzed under the rule of reason.

---

1. 246 U.S. 231, 38 S.Ct. 242, 62 L.Ed. 683 (1918).

CASE 28.1
American Needle, Inc. v. National Football League

Supreme Court of the United States, ___ U.S. ___, 130 S.Ct. 2201, ___ L.Ed.2d ___ (2010).
www.supremecourt.gov[a]

BACKGROUND AND FACTS • The National Football League (NFL) includes thirty-two separately owned professional football teams. Each team has its own name, colors, and logo, and owns related intellectual property. In 1963, the teams formed National Football League Properties (NFLP) to develop, license, and market their trademarked items, such as caps and jerseys. Until 2000, the NFLP granted nonexclusive licenses to a number of vendors, permitting them to manufacture and sell apparel bearing team insignias. American Needle, Inc., was one of those licensees. In late 2000, the teams authorized the NFLP to grant exclusive licenses, and the NFLP granted Reebok International, Ltd., an exclusive ten-year license to manufacture and sell trademarked headwear for all thirty-two teams. It thereafter declined to renew American Needle's nonexclusive license. American Needle brought an action in a federal district court alleging that the agreements involving the NFL, its teams, the NFLP, and Reebok violated Sections 1 and 2 of the Sherman Act. In response, the defendants argued that they were incapable of conspiring within the meaning of Section 1 "because they are a single economic enterprise" as far as the marketing of trademarked goods was concerned. The district court granted summary judgment in favor of the defendants. American Needle appealed, and the U.S. Court of Appeals for the Seventh Circuit affirmed the trial court's decision. American Needle appealed to the United States Supreme Court.

IN THE LANGUAGE OF THE COURT
Justice *STEVENS* delivered the opinion of the Court.
* * * *

As the case comes to us, we have only a narrow issue to decide: whether the NFL respondents are capable of engaging in a "contract, combination * * * or conspiracy," as defined by Section 1 of the Sherman Act, or * * * whether the alleged

---

a. Click on "Opinions" in the left-hand column. When that page opens, click on "2009 Term Opinions of the Court" under the heading "2009 Term." In the results, scroll down the list of cases to "5/24/10" and click on the highlighted case title to access the opinion. The United States Supreme Court maintains this Web site.

CASE 28.1 CONTINUED ➡ activity by the NFL respondents "must be viewed as that of a single enterprise for purposes of Section 1."

* * * *

* * * The question is whether the agreement [among the teams with respect to the marketing of their intellectual property] joins together "independent centers of decision-making." If it does, the entities are capable of conspiring under Section 1, and the Court must decide whether the restraint of trade is an unreasonable and therefore illegal one.

* * * Each of the [NFL] teams is a substantial, independently owned, and independently managed business. "Their general corporate actions are guided or determined" by "separate corporate consciousnesses," and "their objectives are" not "common." The teams compete with one another, not only on the playing field, but to attract fans, for gate receipts and for contracts with managerial and playing personnel.

Directly relevant to this case, the teams compete in the market for intellectual property. To a firm making hats, the Saints and the Colts are two potentially competing suppliers of valuable trademarks. When each NFL team licenses its intellectual property, it is not pursuing the "common interests of the whole" league but is instead pursuing interests of each "corporation itself"; teams are acting as "separate economic actors pursuing separate economic interests," and each team therefore is a potential "independent center of decision-making." Decisions by NFL teams to license their separately owned trademarks collectively and to only one vendor are decisions that "depriv[e] the marketplace of independent centers of decision-making," and therefore of actual or potential competition.

* * * *

Respondents argue that * * * they constitute a single entity because without their cooperation, there would be no NFL football. * * * But the Court of Appeals' reasoning is unpersuasive.

The justification for cooperation is not relevant to whether that cooperation is [a] concerted or independent action. *A "contract, combination * * * or conspiracy" that is necessary or useful to a joint venture is still a "contract, combination * * * or conspiracy" if it "deprives the marketplace of independent centers of decision-making."* Any joint venture involves multiple sources of economic power cooperating to produce a product. And for many such ventures, the participation of others is necessary. But that does not mean that necessity of cooperation transforms concerted action into independent action; a nut and a bolt can only operate together, but an agreement between nut and bolt manufacturers is still subject to Section 1 analysis. [Emphasis added.]

* * * *

Football teams that need to cooperate are not trapped by antitrust law. * * * The fact that NFL teams share an interest in making the entire league successful and profitable, and that they must cooperate in the production and scheduling of games, provides a perfectly sensible justification for making a host of collective decisions. But the conduct at issue in this case is still concerted activity under the Sherman Act that is subject to Section 1 analysis.

When "restraints on competition are essential if the product is to be available at all," *per se* rules of illegality are inapplicable, and instead the restraint must be judged according to the flexible Rule of Reason. In such instances, the agreement is likely to survive the Rule of Reason. And depending upon the concerted activity in question, the Rule of Reason may not require a detailed analysis; it "can sometimes be applied in the twinkling of an eye."

* * * *

Accordingly, the judgment of the Court of Appeals is reversed, and the case is remanded for further proceedings consistent with this opinion.

DECISION AND REMEDY • *The United States Supreme Court reversed the judgment of the court of appeals and remanded the case for further proceedings consistent with this opinion. The agreement among the NFL teams to license their intellectual property exclusively through the NFLP to Reebok constituted concerted activity subject to Section 1 analysis.*

THE LEGAL ENVIRONMENT DIMENSION • *What did the Court mean when it stated that "the agreement is likely to survive the Rule of Reason"?*

THE ECONOMIC DIMENSION • *Does the Court's ruling mean that the NFL teams' activities with respect to the marketing of their intellectual property through the NFLP were illegal? Explain.*

SECTION 2
HORIZONTAL RESTRAINTS

The term **horizontal restraint** is encountered frequently in antitrust law. A horizontal restraint is any agreement that in some way restrains competition between rival firms competing in the same market. Whenever firms at the same level of operation and in direct competition with one another (for example, retailers of a similar product located in the same geographical market) agree to operate in a way that restricts their market activities, they are said to have imposed a horizontal restraint of trade. Some horizontal restraints are *per se* violations of Section 1, but others may be permissible; those that are not *per se* violations are tested under the rule of reason.

Price Fixing

Consider the scenario presented in Chapter 27 involving the introduction of a Blu-ray DVD burner. Suppose that our hypothetical firm, Acme, had instead sought large profits by some means other than arduous and financially risky research into innovative Blu-ray burner technology. Assume that advanced Blu-ray burner technology does not yet exist. Acme's managers decide to make life easy for themselves. They go to other Blu-ray burner producers and say, "Let's not work to one another's disadvantage. There's enough demand for Blu-ray burners for all of us to charge higher prices if we don't undercut one another's prices." Acme's plan calls for each producer to charge a price higher than an established minimum. The minimum price is set as the total cost of the least productive producer, plus a 10 percent profit margin. More efficient firms—that is, firms that can produce at lower cost—will, of course, enjoy higher profits.

Although not all such schemes are as simple or as blatant as our hypothetical example suggests, they all involve some means of eliminating competition between rivals to sell at the lowest price while still earning a normal profit—that is, one commensurate with the profit that could be earned in some alternative endeavor using the same resources. By eliminating price competition in which firms seek to sell more by charging less than their rivals, firms restrict output. This is the essence of **price fixing.**

Perhaps the definitive case regarding price-fixing agreements remains the 1940 case of *United States v. Socony-Vacuum Oil Co.,* also known as the *Madison* *Oil* case.[2] In this case, a group of independent oil producers in Texas and Louisiana were caught between falling demand due to the Great Depression and increasing supply from newly discovered oil fields in the region. In response, a group of the major refining companies agreed to buy "distress" gasoline (excess supplies) from the independents so as to dispose of it in an "orderly manner." Although there was no explicit agreement as to price, it was clear that the purpose of the agreement was to limit the supply of gasoline on the market, thereby raising prices.

There may have been good reasons for such an agreement. The refiners may simply have wanted to avoid a temporary situation that would have driven the independent suppliers out of business, thus making it difficult to secure crude oil supplies later, after the economic climate had improved. Nonetheless, the United States Supreme Court recognized the potentially adverse effects that such an agreement could have on open and free competition. The Court held that the reasonableness of a price-fixing agreement is never a defense. Any agreement that restricts output or artificially fixes price is a *per se* violation of Section 1.

CASE IN POINT The manufacturer of the prescription drug Cardizem CD, which can help prevent heart attacks, was about to lose its patent on the drug. Another company had developed a generic version in anticipation of the patent's expiration. After the two firms became involved in litigation over the patent, the first company agreed to pay the second company $40 million per year not to market the generic version until their dispute was resolved. This agreement was held to be a *per se* violation of the Sherman Act because it restrained competition between rival firms and delayed the entry of generic versions of Cardizem into the market.[3]

Group Boycotts

A **group boycott** is an agreement by two or more sellers to refuse to deal with (boycott) a particular person or firm. Traditionally, the courts have considered group boycotts to constitute *per se* violations of Section 1 of the Sherman Act because they involve concerted action. To prove a violation of Section 1, the plaintiff must demonstrate that the boycott or joint refusal to deal was undertaken with the intention of eliminating competition or preventing entry into a given market. Although most boycotts are

---

2. 310 U.S. 150, 60 S.Ct. 811, 84 L.Ed.2d 1129 (1940).
3. *In re Cardizem CD Antitrust Litigation,* 332 F.3d 896 (6th Cir. 2003).

illegal, a few, such as group boycotts against a supplier for political reasons, may be protected under the First Amendment right to freedom of expression.

Horizontal Market Divisions

Prices can be controlled indirectly through agreements to restrict output, as well as explicitly through agreements to fix prices. Because the former type of agreement operates to decrease the supplies available to consumers, it has the same effect as a direct agreement to raise prices. Efforts to control prices are often effected by **horizontal market divisions**— that is, agreements to divide up the market among rival firms.

It is a *per se* violation of Section 1 of the Sherman Act for competitors to divide up territories or customers. For example, manufacturers A, B, and C compete against one another in the states of Kansas, Nebraska, and Oklahoma. They agree that A will sell products only in Kansas, B only in Nebraska, and C only in Oklahoma. This concerted action reduces costs and allows each of the three (assuming there is no other competition) to raise the price of the goods sold in its own state. The same violation would take place if A, B, and C agreed that A would sell only to institutional purchasers (such as school districts, universities, state agencies and departments, and cities) in the three states, B only to wholesalers, and C only to retailers.

In some respects, market divisions may have an even greater impact on competition than do price-fixing agreements. Each firm has a monopoly over its allocated share of the market for that particular brand—it is the sole supplier. The sole supplier is free not only from price competition for that brand but also from competition for that brand regarding quality, customer service, and all other dimensions of competition.

Consider once again our hypothetical scenario involving Acme and its rival Blu-ray burner producers. Suppose that, flush with the initial success of their price-fixing agreement, the producers agree that each firm that begins selling Blu-ray burners to dealers in remote communities in which Blu-ray burners have not been available will thereafter have an exclusive right to sell retail or through dealers in that area. Initially, there is intense competition to find such virgin markets. After all the profitable markets have been taken, however, conditions in the exclusive markets may change. Suppliers may begin to limit the warranties they offer. Prices may begin to rise despite the lack of warranties, and service

may diminish. Because of such potential effects, agreements like that made by the Blu-ray burner producers generally are treated as *per se* violations of Section 1.

Trade Associations

Businesses in the same general industry or profession frequently organize trade associations to pursue common interests. A trade association may engage in various joint activities, such as exchanging information, representing the members' business interests before governmental bodies, conducting advertising campaigns, and setting regulatory standards to govern the industry or profession.

For example, lumber producers might be concerned about whether they are cutting more trees than expected future demand would warrant, given the cutting levels of rival firms. The market for lumber might be widely dispersed over the whole nation, making it especially difficult for small firms to gauge overall demand conditions in the lumber market. Lumber firms might thus decide to form a trade association that could amass data on the output and price levels of its members in various markets.

The association would be of economic benefit to lumber firms by reducing the costs of projecting market demand. Such knowledge could also benefit society by making the lumber market function more smoothly, dampening cycles of oversupply and undersupply of lumber output. Even if it did not make the industry function more smoothly, such knowledge would be unlikely to harm competition in the industry unless the industry was *concentrated*.

CONCENTRATED INDUSTRIES In *concentrated industries*, trade associations can be, and have been, used as a means to facilitate anticompetitive actions, such as fixing prices or allocating markets. A **concentrated industry** is one in which either a single firm or a small number of firms control a large percentage of market sales. When trade association agreements have substantially anticompetitive effects, a court will consider them to be in violation of Section 1 of the Sherman Act.

For example, consider again the lumber association. Such an association would provide information that members could use to determine whether a secret agreement to fix prices was being adhered to by the conspirators. Thus, such associations offer possibilities of both great benefit and substantial harm.

THE RULE OF REASON USUALLY APPLIED In most instances, the rule of reason is applied in evaluating such practices and agreements. If a court finds that a trade association practice or agreement that restrains trade involves no apparent intent to fix prices or limit output, and that it benefits the public as well as the association, then it may deem the restraint reasonable. If the harm to competition is substantial, however, a trade association's activities will be condemned as a violation of Section 1.

SECTION 3
VERTICAL RESTRAINTS

A **vertical restraint** of trade results from an agreement between firms at different levels in the manufacturing and distribution process. In contrast to horizontal relationships, which occur at the same level of operation, vertical relationships encompass the entire chain of production. The chain of production normally includes the purchase of inputs, basic manufacturing, distribution to wholesalers, and eventual sale of a product at the retail level. For some products, these distinct phases are carried on by different firms. In other instances, a single firm carries out two or more of the separate functional phases. Such enterprises are said to be **vertically integrated firms.**

There are two kinds of vertical integration—backward and forward. A firm that is integrated backward moves down the chain of production toward a supplier. A firm that is integrated forward moves up the chain of production toward the consumer market. For example, if the Red Ball Shoe Manufacturing Company, a shoe manufacturer, owns its source of leather, it is integrated backward. If Red Ball owns its retail outlets, it is integrated forward (see Exhibit 28–1 below).

Even though firms operating at different functional levels are not in direct competition with one another, they are in competition with other firms. Thus, agreements between firms standing in a vertical relationship may affect competition. Some vertical restraints are *per se* violations of Section 1. Others are judged under the rule of reason.

Territorial or Customer Restrictions

In arranging for the distribution of its products, a manufacturing firm often wishes to insulate dealers from direct competition with other dealers selling its products. To this end, the manufacturer may institute territorial restrictions or attempt to prohibit wholesalers or retailers from reselling the products to certain classes of buyers, such as competing retailers.

A firm may have legitimate reasons for imposing such territorial or customer restrictions. For example, a computer manufacturer may wish to prevent a dealer from reducing costs and undercutting rivals by offering computers without promotion or customer service, while relying on a nearby dealer to provide these services. In this situation, the cost-cutting dealer reaps the benefits (sales of the product) paid for by other dealers who undertake promotion and arrange for customer service. By not providing customer service, the cost-cutting dealer may also harm the manufacturer's reputation.

Territorial and customer restrictions were once considered *per se* violations of Section 1 of the Sherman Act.[4] In 1977, however, the United States Supreme Court reconsidered the treatment accorded to such vertical restrictions and held that they should be judged under the rule of reason.

CASE IN POINT GTE Sylvania, Inc., a manufacturer of television sets, limited the number of retail franchises that it granted in any given geographic area. It also required each franchisee to sell only Sylvania products from the location at which it was franchised. Sylvania retained sole discretion to increase the number of retailers in an area. When Sylvania decided to open a new franchise, it

---

4. See *United States v. Arnold, Schwinn & Co.*, 388 U.S. 365, 87 S.Ct. 1856, 18 L.Ed.2d 1249 (1967).

EXHIBIT 28–1 • Backward and Forward Vertical Integration
A firm that is integrated backward moves down the chain of production. A firm that is integrated forward moves up the chain of production.

| Circle RB Cattle Ranch (leather supplier) | ← Backward | Red Ball Shoe Manufacturing Co. (shoe manufacturer) | Forward → | Red Circle Shoes (shoe retailer) |

terminated the franchise of Continental T.V., Inc., an existing franchisee in that area that would have been in competition with the new franchise. Continental filed a lawsuit claiming that Sylvania's vertically restrictive franchise system violated Section 1 of the Sherman Act. The United States Supreme Court found that "vertical restrictions promote inter-brand competition by allowing the manufacturer to achieve certain efficiencies in the distribution of [its] products." Therefore, Sylvania's vertical system, which was not price restrictive, did not constitute a *per se* violation of Section 1 of the Sherman Act.[5]

The *Continental* case above marked a definite shift from rigid characterization of territorial and customer restrictions to a more flexible, economic analysis of these vertical restraints under the rule of reason. This rule is still applied in most vertical restraint cases.

---

5. *Continental T.V., Inc. v. GTE Sylvania, Inc.,* 433 U.S. 36, 97 S.Ct. 2549, 53 L.Ed.2d 568 (1977).

Resale Price Maintenance Agreements

An agreement between a manufacturer and a distributor or retailer in which the manufacturer specifies what the retail prices of its products must be is known as a **resale price maintenance agreement.** Such agreements were once considered to be *per se* violations of Section 1 of the Sherman Act, but in 1997 the United States Supreme Court ruled that *maximum* resale price maintenance agreements should be judged under the rule of reason.[6] The setting of a maximum price that retailers and distributors can charge for a manufacturer's products may sometimes increase competition and benefit consumers.

The question before the United States Supreme Court in the following case was whether *minimum* resale price maintenance agreements should be treated as *per se* violations.

---

6. *State Oil Co. v. Khan,* 522 U.S. 3, 118 S.Ct. 275, 139 L.Ed.2d 199 (1997).

✳ EXTENDED CASE 28.2 ✳
Leegin Creative Leather Products, Inc. v. PSKS, Inc.

Supreme Court of the United States, 551 U.S. 877, 127 S.Ct. 2705, 168 L.Ed.2d 623 (2007).
www.law.cornell.edu/supct/index.html[a]

IN THE LANGUAGE OF THE COURT
Justice *KENNEDY* delivered the opinion of the Court.
* * * *
Petitioner, Leegin Creative Leather Products, Inc. (Leegin), designs, manufactures, and distributes leather goods and accessories. In 1991, Leegin began to sell [products] under the brand name "Brighton."
Respondent, PSKS, Inc. (PSKS), operates Kay's Kloset, a women's apparel store in Lewisville, Texas. * * * It first started purchasing Brighton goods from Leegin in 1995.
* * * *

In December 2002, Leegin discovered Kay's Kloset had been marking down Brighton's entire line by 20 percent. * * * Leegin stopped selling [Brighton products] to the store.
PSKS sued Leegin in the United States District Court for the Eastern District of Texas. It alleged, among other claims, that Leegin had violated the antitrust laws by "enter[ing] into agreements with retailers to charge only those prices fixed by Leegin." * * * [The court] entered judgment against Leegin in the amount of $3,975,000.80.
The [U.S.] Court of Appeals for the Fifth Circuit affirmed. * * * We granted *certiorari* * * * .

* * * *
The rule of reason is the accepted standard for testing whether a practice restrains trade in violation of [Section] 1 [of the Sherman Act].
* * * *
Resort to per se *rules is confined to restraints * * * that would always or almost always tend to restrict competition and decrease output. To justify a* per se *prohibition a restraint must have manifestly anticompetitive effects, and lack * * * any redeeming virtue.* [Emphasis added.]
As a consequence, the *per se* rule is appropriate only after courts have had considerable experience with the type of restraint at issue, and only if courts can predict with

---

a. In the "Archive of Decisions" section, in the "By party" subsection, click on "1990–present." In the result, in the "2006–2007" row, click on "1st party." On the next page, scroll to the name of the case and click on it. On the next page, click on the appropriate link to access the opinion.

EXTENDED CASE CONTINUES ➡

EXTENDED CASE 28.2 CONTINUED ⬇

confidence that it would be invalidated in all or almost all instances under the rule of reason.

* * * *

The reasoning of the Court's more recent jurisprudence has rejected the rationales on which [the application of the *per se* rule to minimum resale price maintenance agreements] was based. * * * [These rationales were] based on formalistic legal doctrine rather than demonstrable economic effect.

* * * *

* * * Furthermore [the Court] treated vertical agreements a manufacturer makes with its distributors as analogous to a horizontal combination among competing distributors. * * * Our recent cases formulate antitrust principles in accordance with the appreciated differences in economic effect between

vertical and horizontal agreements * * *.

* * * *

The justifications for vertical price restraints are similar to those for other vertical restraints. *Minimum resale price maintenance can stimulate interbrand competition * * * by reducing intrabrand competition * * *.* The promotion of interbrand competition is important because the primary purpose of the antitrust laws is to protect this type of competition. * * * *Resale price maintenance also has the potential to give consumers more options so that they can choose among low-price, low-service brands; high-price, high-service brands; and brands that fall in between.* [Emphasis added.]

* * * *

While vertical agreements setting minimum resale prices can have procompetitive justifications, they may have anticompetitive effects in other

cases; and unlawful price fixing, designed solely to obtain monopoly profits, is an ever present temptation.

* * * *

Notwithstanding the risks of unlawful conduct, it cannot be stated with any degree of confidence that resale price maintenance always or almost always tends to restrict competition and decrease output. Vertical agreements establishing minimum resale prices can have either procompetitive or anticompetitive effects, depending upon the circumstances in which they are formed. * * * As the [*per se*] rule would proscribe a significant amount of procompetitive conduct, these agreements appear ill suited for *per se* condemnation.

* * * *

The judgment of the Court of Appeals is reversed, and the case is remanded for proceedings consistent with this opinion.

 QUESTIONS

1. Should the Court have applied the doctrine of *stare decisis* to hold that minimum resale price maintenance agreements are still subject to the *per se* rule? Why or why not?
2. What factors might the courts consider in applying the rule of reason to minimum resale price maintenance agreements? Discuss.

Refusals to Deal

Group boycotts, as mentioned, are subject to sharp scrutiny under Section 1. In contrast, basic freedom of contract has been held to support the rule that manufacturers, acting unilaterally rather than in concert (as in a group boycott), are free to deal—or not to deal—with whomever they choose. Assume that in our hypothetical example Acme acts alone to set the price for the resale of its Blu-ray burners by refusing to deal with any wholesaler that resells them at a different price. Acme has not violated the Sherman Act; it has only exercised its right to deal with whomever it chooses.

In some instances, however, a refusal to deal will violate antitrust laws. These instances involve offenses proscribed under Section 2 of the Sherman Act and occur only if (1) the firm refusing to deal has, or is likely to acquire, monopoly power and (2) the refusal is likely to have an anticompetitive effect on a particular market.

Price Discrimination

Whenever a seller charges different buyers different prices for identical goods, the seller is engaging in *price discrimination*. Recall from the preceding chapter that such behavior may violate the Robinson-Patman Act, which was enacted in 1936 and amended Section 2 of the Clayton Act. A violation of Section 2 occurs if a seller discriminates in the prices it charges different customers for commodities of like quality and grade in interstate commerce, and if the practice results in injury to competition. The act prohibits indirect discrimination, such as variations in the terms of delivery and differences in sales returns, cash discounts, and the like, as well as direct price discrimination.

CUSTOMER PREFERENCES Although the Robinson-Patman Act appears to embrace the goals of fairness and equality in the marketplace, it has often been criticized as being economically unrealistic.

For instance, a difference in packaging, labeling, or product quality normally does not exempt the pricing of the differing products from scrutiny under the act if the difference is deemed to be *negligible*. Thus, orange juice containers that differ by one-eighth inch are considered to be of like grade and quality, because they are *functionally* identical in terms of performance. Despite functional equivalence, however, customer perceptions may favor one type of container over another.

In the same vein, identical products sold under different labels are deemed to be of like quality, though some experts note that many customers exhibit strong preferences for better-known brand names even though the products are physically identical.

CASE IN POINT The United States Supreme Court addressed the issue of a milk producer's charging different prices for milk sold under different labels. Borden Company sold evaporated milk under the Borden label, a well-known brand, and at the same time, it packed and marketed evaporated milk under private labels owned by its customers. Although the milk was physically indistinguishable, Borden charged a higher price for its brand-labeled milk. In spite of obvious customer preference for the Borden brand of milk, the Court concluded that the act applied to the pricing difference because the milk was of like quality and grade in terms of physical attributes. The Court held that preferences due to brand-name recognition created through national advertising should not be considered in resolving whether goods are of like grade and quality.[7]

TIME AND COST CONSIDERATIONS Despite these examples, some economic aspects are taken into account in judging the legality of pricing practices under the Robinson-Patman Act. For example, as noted in the preceding chapter, Section 2 is not violated even though the goods sold are identical if the seller can justify the price differential on the basis of differences in cost, such as the cost of transporting the goods to buyers in disparate locations. Similarly, consideration is given to the fact that prices are not static but fluctuate as market conditions change. Thus, price discrimination occurs only if sales at different price levels are made reasonably close together in time.

Closeness in time is determined by the economic circumstances of the sales. For example, sales

of products that are not frequently sold and that involve considerable production costs may be considered close in time even if they occur years apart. Conversely, sales of low-cost products sold in high volume may be considered close in time when they occur a day or even a few hours apart. Jet aircraft typify high-cost, low-volume products. Closeness in time for sales of aircraft could be two years or more. In contrast, sales of bakery goods occur on an almost continuous basis. Closeness in time for sales of such products could be several hours or, at most, a day.

Exclusionary Practices

Recall also from the preceding chapter that Section 3 of the Clayton Act prohibits sellers and lessors from selling or leasing goods, machinery, supplies, and the like "on the condition, agreement or understanding that the . . . purchaser or lessee thereof shall not use or deal in the goods . . . of a competitor or competitors of the seller." Two types of vertical arrangements involving exclusionary tactics—*exclusive-dealing contracts* and *tying arrangements*—are within the reach of Section 3 of the Clayton Act.

EXCLUSIVE-DEALING CONTRACTS A contract under which a seller forbids a buyer to purchase products from the seller's competitors is called an **exclusive-dealing contract.** A seller is prohibited from making an exclusive-dealing contract under Section 3 if the effect of the contract is "to substantially lessen competition or tend to create a monopoly."

The United States Supreme Court's 1949 decision in the case of *Standard Oil Co. of California v. United States* provides a classic illustration of exclusive dealing.[8] In this case, the then largest gasoline seller in the nation made exclusive-dealing contracts with independent stations in seven western states. The contracts involved 16 percent of all retail outlets, whose sales were approximately 7 percent of all retail sales in that market. The Court noted that the market was substantially concentrated because the seven largest gasoline suppliers all used exclusive-dealing contracts with their independent retailers and together controlled 65 percent of the market. Looking at market conditions after the arrangements were instituted, the Court found that market shares were extremely stable, and entry into the market was apparently restricted. Thus, the Court held that the Clayton Act had been violated because competition was "foreclosed in a substantial share" of the relevant market.

---

7. *Federal Trade Commission v. Borden Co.,* 383 U.S. 637, 86 S.Ct. 1092, 16 L.Ed.2d 153 (1966).

8. 337 U.S. 293, 69 S.Ct. 1051, 93 L.Ed. 1371 (1949).

Note that since the Supreme Court's 1949 decision in the *Standard Oil* case, a number of subsequent decisions have called the holding in this case into doubt.[9] Today, it is clear that to violate antitrust law, the effect of an exclusive-dealing agreement (or a tying arrangement, discussed next) must qualitatively and substantially harm competition. To prevail, a plaintiff must present affirmative evidence that the performance of the agreement will foreclose competition and harm consumers.

TYING ARRANGEMENTS In a **tying arrangement,** or *tie-in sales agreement,* a seller conditions the sale of a product (the tying product) on the buyer's agreement to purchase another product (the tied product) produced or distributed by the same seller. The legality of a tie-in agreement depends on many factors, particularly the purpose of the agreement and the agreement's likely effect on competition in the relevant markets (the market for the tying product and the market for the tied product).

Section 3 of the Clayton Act has been held to apply only to commodities, not to services. Tying arrangements, however, can also be considered agreements that restrain trade in violation of Section 1 of the Sherman Act. Thus, cases involving tying arrangements of services have been brought under Section 1 of the Sherman Act. Although earlier cases condemned tying arrangements as illegal *per se,* courts now evaluate tying agreements under the rule of reason.

When an arrangement ties patented and unpatented products, can the relevant market and the patent holder's power in that market be presumed without proof? That was the question in the following case.

---

9. See, for example, *Illinois Tool Works, Inc. v. Independent Ink, Inc.,* which is presented as Case 28.3 below.

CASE 28.3

Illinois Tool Works, Inc. v. Independent Ink, Inc.

Supreme Court of the United States, 547 U.S. 28, 126 S.Ct. 1281, 164 L.Ed.2d 26 (2006).
www.findlaw.com/casecode/supreme.html[a]

BACKGROUND AND FACTS • Illinois Tool Works, Inc., in Glenview, Illinois, owns Trident, Inc. The firms make printing systems that include three components: a patented inkjet printhead; a patented ink container that attaches to the printhead; and specially designed, but unpatented, ink. They sell the systems to original equipment manufacturers (OEMs) that incorporate the systems into printers that are sold to other companies to use in printing bar codes on packaging materials. As part of each deal, the OEMs agree to buy ink exclusively from Illinois and Trident and not to refill the patented containers with ink of any kind. Independent Ink, Inc., in Gardena, California, sells ink with the same chemical composition as Illinois and Trident's product at lower prices. Independent filed a suit in a federal district court against Illinois and Trident, alleging, among other things, that they were engaged in illegal tying in violation of the Sherman Act. Independent filed a motion for summary judgment, arguing that because the defendants owned patents in their products, market power could be presumed. The court issued a summary judgment in the defendants' favor, holding that market power could not be presumed. The U.S. Court of Appeals for the Federal Circuit reversed this judgment. Illinois and Trident appealed to the United States Supreme Court.

IN THE LANGUAGE OF THE COURT
Justice *STEVENS* delivered the opinion of the Court.
* * * *

American courts first encountered tying arrangements in the course of patent infringement litigation [in 1912].

In the years since [1912], four different rules of law have supported challenges to tying arrangements. They have been condemned as improper extensions of the patent monopoly under the patent misuse doctrine, as unfair methods of competition under [Section] 5 of the Federal Trade Commission Act, as contracts tending to create a monopoly under [Section] 3 of the Clayton Act, and as contracts in restraint of trade under [Section] 1 of the Sherman Act. In

---

a. In the "Browsing" section, click on "2006 Decisions." When that page opens, scroll to the name of the case and click on it to read the opinion. The United States Supreme Court maintains this Web site.

CASE 28.3 CONTINUED ➡ all of those instances, the justification for the challenge rested on either an assumption or a showing that the defendant's position of power in the market for the tying product was being used to restrain competition in the market for the tied product. * * * The essential characteristic of an invalid tying arrangement lies in the seller's exploitation of its control over the tying product to force the buyer into the purchase of a tied product that the buyer either [does] not want at all, or might [prefer] to purchase elsewhere on different terms.

Over the years, however, this Court's strong disapproval of tying arrangements has substantially diminished. Rather than relying on assumptions, in its more recent opinions the Court has required a showing of market power in the tying product.

* * * *

* * * The presumption that a patent confers market power arose outside the antitrust context as part of the patent misuse doctrine.

Without any analysis of actual market conditions, [the] patent misuse [doctrine] assumed that, by tying the purchase of unpatented goods to the sale of [a] patented good, the patentee was restraining competition or securing a limited monopoly of an unpatented material. In other words, [the doctrine] presumed the requisite economic power over the tying product such that the patentee could extend its economic control to unpatented products.

* * * *

Although the patent misuse doctrine and our antitrust jurisprudence became intertwined in [a case decided in 1947], subsequent events initiated their untwining.

* * * *

Shortly thereafter, Congress * * * *excluded some conduct, such as a tying arrangement involving the sale of a patented product tied to an "essential" or "nonstaple" product that has no use except as part of the patented product or method, from the scope of the patent misuse doctrine. Thus, * * * Congress began chipping away at the assumption in the patent misuse context from whence it came.* [Emphasis added.]

It is Congress'[s] most recent narrowing of the patent misuse defense * * * that is directly relevant to this case. * * * [In 1988] Congress amended the [patent laws] to eliminate [the patent-equals-market-power] presumption in the patent misuse context.

While the 1988 amendment does not expressly refer to the antitrust laws, it certainly invites a reappraisal of the *per se* rule * * * . Given the fact that the patent misuse doctrine provided the basis for the market power presumption, it would be anomalous to preserve the presumption in antitrust after Congress has eliminated its foundation.

After considering the congressional judgment reflected in the 1988 amendment, we conclude that tying arrangements involving patented products should be evaluated under [such factors as those that apply in a rule-of-reason analysis] rather than under the *per se* rule * * *. While some such arrangements are still unlawful, such as those that are the product of a true monopoly or a marketwide conspiracy, that conclusion must be supported by proof of power in the relevant market rather than by a mere presumption thereof.

DECISION AND REMEDY • *The United States Supreme Court vacated the judgment of the lower court and remanded the case to the trial court to give Independent "a fair opportunity" to offer evidence of the relevant market and the defendants' power within it. The Supreme Court ruled that a plaintiff that alleges an illegal tying arrangement involving a patented product must prove that the defendant has market power in the tying product. A company that holds a patent in a product does not automatically possess market power in that product for antitrust purposes.*

THE LEGAL ENVIRONMENT DIMENSION • *In light of the factors that a court considers under the rule of reason, how might the court rule on remand in the Illinois case? Explain.*

THE ETHICAL DIMENSION • *What are the ethical values underpinning antitrust laws, and why are those laws applied to tying arrangements in particular?*

Mergers

As discussed in Chapter 27, Section 7 of the Clayton Act prohibits a person or business from holding stock or assets in more than one business if the effect is to substantially lessen competition. Section 7 is used to prevent mergers that could result in monopoly power or a substantial lessening of competition in the marketplace. Section 7 applies to both horizontal and vertical mergers, as discussed in the following subsections.

A crucial consideration in most merger cases is **market concentration.** Determining market concentration involves allocating percentage market shares among the various companies in the relevant market. When a small number of companies share a large part of the market, the market is concentrated. For example, if the four largest grocery stores in Chicago accounted for 80 percent of all retail food sales, that specific market clearly would be concentrated in those four firms. Competition is not necessarily diminished solely as a result of market concentration, however, and other factors must be considered to determine if a merger violates Section 7. One factor of particular importance is whether the merger will make it more difficult for *potential* competitors to enter the relevant market.

HORIZONTAL MERGERS Mergers between firms that compete with each other in the same market are called **horizontal mergers.** If a horizontal merger creates an entity with a significant market share, the merger may be considered illegal because it increases market concentration.

Factors to Determine Legality. When analyzing the legality of a horizontal merger, the courts also consider three other factors: the overall concentration of the relevant market, the relevant market's history of tending toward concentration, and whether the merger is apparently designed to establish market power or restrict competition.

The Federal Trade Commission (FTC) and the U.S. Department of Justice (DOJ) have established guidelines for determining which mergers will be challenged. Under the guidelines, the first factor to be considered is the degree of concentration in the relevant market. Other factors to be considered include the ease of entry into the relevant market, economic efficiency, the financial condition of the merging firms, and the nature and price of the product or products involved.

The Herfindahl-Hirschman Index. To determine market concentration, the FTC and the DOJ employ what is known as the **Herfindahl-Hirschman Index (HHI).** The HHI is computed by summing the squares of the percentage market shares of the firms in the relevant market. For example, if there are four firms with shares of 30 percent, 30 percent, 20 percent, and 20 percent, respectively, then the HHI equals 2,600 (900 + 900 + 400 + 400 = 2,600).

If the premerger HHI is less than 1,000, then the market is unconcentrated, and the merger is unlikely to be challenged. If the premerger HHI is between 1,000 and 1,800, the industry is moderately concentrated, and the merger will be challenged only if it increases the HHI by 100 points or more. If the HHI is greater than 1,800, the market is highly concentrated. In a highly concentrated market, a merger that produces an increase in the HHI of between 50 and 100 points raises "significant" competitive concerns. Mergers that produce an increase in the HHI of more than 100 points in a highly concentrated market are deemed likely to enhance market power. HHI figures were a factor in the following case.

CASE 28.4

Chicago Bridge & Iron Co. v. Federal Trade Commission

United States Court of Appeals, Fifth Circuit, 515 F.3d 447 (2008).
www.ca5.uscourts.gov[a]

BACKGROUND AND FACTS • Chicago Bridge & Iron Company, and its U.S. subsidiary of the same name, is a company that designs, engineers, and constructs industrial storage tanks for liquefied natural gas (LNG), liquefied petroleum gas (LPG), and liquid atmospheric gases, such as nitrogen, oxygen, and argon (LIN/LOX), as well as thermal vacuum chambers (TVCs) for testing aerospace satellites. In these four separate markets, Chicago Bridge and another company, Pitt–Des Moines, Inc., have been the dominant firms. In 2001, Chicago Bridge acquired all of Pitt–Des Moines's assets for $84 million. The Federal Trade Commission charged that Chicago Bridge's acquisition violated Section 7 of the Clayton Act and Section 5 of the Federal Trade Commission Act. An administrative law judge concurred, finding that the acquisition resulted in an undue increase in Chicago Bridge's market power that would not be constrained by the timely entry of new competitors. At issue was the use of the Herfindahl-Hirschman Index (HHI). The Federal Trade Commission calculated the HHI over a several-year period rather than on an annualized basis. Chicago Bridge appealed to the U.S. Court of Appeals for the Fifth Circuit.

---

a. On the left, click on "Opinions Page" and then in "Search for opinions where:" type "Chicago Bridge." Then click on the docket number listed. The U.S. Court of Appeals for the Fifth Circuit maintains this Web site.

CASE 28.4 CONTINUED ➡

IN THE LANGUAGE OF THE COURT
DENNIS, Circuit Judge:
* * * *

The HHIs are just one element in the Government's strong *prima facie* case. Market concentration figures should be examined in the context of the entire *prima facie* case. Here, the *prima facie* case establishes without dispute that the two dominant, and often only, players in these four domestic markets are merging. This indisputable fact "bolster[s]" the Government's market concentration figures. Where the post-merger HHI exceeds 1,800, and the merger produces an increase in the HHI of more than 100 points, the merger guidelines create a presumption of adverse competitive consequences. The increases in HHIs in this case are extremely high. HHI increases of 2,635 for the LIN/LOX tank market, 3,911 for the LPG tank market, 4,956 for the LNG tank market, and 4,999 for the TVC tank market are predicted post-merger. An HHI of 10,000 denotes a complete monopoly. Post-acquisition HHIs for the four markets are: 5,845 for LIN/LOX, 8,380 for LPG, and 10,000 for the LNG and TVC markets.

* * * The Commission agrees with the ALJ [administrative law judge] that the use of HHIs based solely on sales from the 1996–2001 period is unreliable, and therefore extended the sales-data time period to an 11-year period, 1990–2001. When sales data are sporadic, a longer historical perspective may be necessary. * * * The Commission adequately explained why it chose an extended period: (1) the extended period provided more data points, which averages out the year-to-year fluctuations and "chance outcomes" and (2) [Chicago Bridge] presents no evidence that a structural change affected the market, and thus the same market conditions persist in the 1996–2001 time-period as the 11-year period, except the 11-year period has additional data points.
* * * *

In addition to its challenge of the selection of the time period, [Chicago Bridge] also argues that the "sporadic" nature of the sales data undermines all evidence of market power. * * * We agree that reliance on very limited data, such as two data points, may undermine an entire *prima facie* case. However, we find this to be a very limited exception * * * because the academic literature has not accepted any broad conclusion that small markets are all *per se* problematic.
* * * *

We find that the record contains substantial evidence to support the Commission's finding that the HHIs are not completely irrelevant in three of the four markets. Instead of ignoring HHIs, we agree with the Commission that they should be viewed with caution and within the larger picture of long-term trends and market structure. Long-term trends in the market and the Government's other evidence favor what the HHIs also indicate: the proposed merger will substantially lessen competition.

DECISION AND REMEDY • *The U.S. Court of Appeals for the Fifth Circuit affirmed the Federal Trade Commission's decision that Chicago Bridge divest itself of its former competitor, Pitt–Des Moines.*

THE GLOBAL DIMENSION • *Assume that just prior to Chicago Bridge's acquisition of its only U.S. competitor, a multinational company based in Indonesia announced that it intended to enter all four of the markets mentioned in this case. How might this announcement affect the reasoning behind this case, if at all?*

THE LEGAL ENVIRONMENT DIMENSION • *What are some of the problems with attempting to measure industry concentration?*

VERTICAL MERGERS A **vertical merger** occurs when a company at one stage of production acquires a company at a higher or lower stage of production. Courts in the past have almost exclusively focused on "foreclosure" in assessing vertical mergers. Foreclosure occurs because competitors of the merging firms lose opportunities to either sell or to buy products from the merging firms.

Today, whether a vertical merger will be deemed illegal depends on several factors, including market concentration, barriers to entry into the market, and the apparent intent of the merging parties. Mergers that do not prevent competitors of either of the merging firms from competing in a segment of the market will not be condemned as foreclosing competition and are legal.

CONGLOMERATE MERGERS Mergers between firms that do not compete with each other because they are in different markets are called **conglomerate mergers.** There are three general types of conglomerate mergers: market-extension, product-extension, and diversification mergers. A market-extension merger occurs when a firm seeks to sell its product in a new market by merging with a firm already established

in that market. A product-extension merger occurs when a firm seeks to add a closely related product to its existing line by merging with a firm already producing that product. For example, a manufacturer might seek to extend its product line of household products to include floor wax by acquiring a leading manufacturer of floor wax. Diversification occurs when a firm merges with another firm that offers a product or service wholly unrelated to the first firm's existing activities. An example of a diversification merger would be Google's acquisition of Holiday Inns.

REVIEWING
Antitrust and Restraint of Trade

The Internet Corporation for Assigned Names and Numbers (ICANN) is a nonprofit entity organizing Internet domain names. It is governed by a board of directors elected by various groups with commercial interests in the Internet. One of ICANN's functions is to authorize an entity as a registry for certain "Top Level Domains" (TLDs). ICANN entered into an agreement with VeriSign to serve as registry for the ".com" TLD to provide registry services in accordance with ICANN's specifications. VeriSign complained that ICANN was restricting the services that it could make available as a registrar and blocking new services, imposing unnecessary conditions on those services, and setting prices at which the services were offered. VeriSign claimed that ICANN's control of the registry services for domain names violated Section 1 of the Sherman Act. Using the information presented in the chapter, answer the following questions.

1. Should ICANN's actions be judged under the rule of reason or be deemed a *per se* violation of Section 1 of the Sherman Act? Explain your answer.
2. Should ICANN's actions be viewed as a horizontal or a vertical restraint of trade? Explain.
3. Does it matter that ICANN's leadership is chosen by those with a commercial interest in the Internet? Why or why not?
4. If the dispute is judged under the rule of reason, what might be ICANN's defense for having a standardized set of registry services that must be used?

⚫ **DEBATE THIS:** *The Internet and the rise of e-commerce have rendered our current antitrust concepts and laws obsolete.*

TERMS AND CONCEPTS

concentrated industry 615
conglomerate merger 624
exclusive-dealing
   contract 619
group boycott 614

Herfindahl-Hirschman
   Index (HHI) 622
horizontal market
   division 615
horizontal merger 622
horizontal restraint 614
market concentration 622

per se violation 611
price fixing 614
resale price maintenance
   agreement 617
rule of reason 612

tying arrangement 620
vertical merger 623
vertical restraint 616
vertically integrated firm 616

QUESTIONS AND CASE PROBLEMS

28–1. Price Discrimination Most of the egg wholesalers supplying eggs to grocery stores in a particular area sell eggs to the retailers under various credit terms. The credit terms vary among the different buyers and sellers, but all of the wholesalers follow a common practice of reducing by 10 percent the price charged to a retailer if the retailer pays the wholesaler within three days of delivery. The various wholesalers agree that henceforth the 10 percent discount will be discontinued. If the agreement is indeed carried out by the wholesalers and the discount policy is discontinued, have the wholesalers violated any antitrust laws? Explain. If a suit is brought against the wholesalers, what—if any—justification could they offer for the agreement?

28–2. Market Division Suppose that the wholesale egg suppliers in the preceding problem agree that the three largest suppliers should sell exclusively to the area's large chain-store groceries, leaving the remaining suppliers to sell solely to local individual "mom and pop" stores. Does the agreement violate any antitrust laws? Is it a defense that the larger suppliers, because of their scale of operations, enjoy a cost advantage that allows them to supply the large chain buyers more efficiently? Explain.

28–3. QUESTION WITH SAMPLE ANSWER: Section 1 of the Sherman Act.

 Allitron, Inc., and Donovan, Ltd., are interstate competitors selling similar appliances, principally in the states of Illinois, Indiana, Kentucky, and Ohio. Allitron and Donovan agree that Allitron will no longer sell in Indiana and Ohio and that Donovan will no longer sell in Illinois and Kentucky. Have Allitron and Donovan violated any antitrust laws? If so, which law (or laws)? Explain.

• **For a sample answer to Question 28–3, go to Appendix F at the end of this text.**

28–4. Restraint of Trade Visa U.S.A., Inc., MasterCard International, Inc., American Express (Amex), and Discover are the four major credit- and charge-card networks in the United States. Visa and MasterCard are joint ventures, owned by the thousands of banks that are their members. The banks issue the cards, clear transactions, and collect fees from the merchants who accept the cards. By contrast, Amex and Discover themselves issue cards to customers, process transactions, and collect fees. Since 1995, Amex has asked banks to issue its cards. No bank has been willing to do so, however, because it would have to stop issuing Visa and MasterCard cards under those networks' rules barring member banks from issuing cards on rival networks. The U.S. Department of Justice filed a suit in a federal district court against Visa and MasterCard, alleging, in part, that the rules were illegal restraints of trade under the Sherman Act. Do the rules harm competition? If so, how? What relief might the court order to stop any anticompetitiveness? [*United States v. Visa U.S.A., Inc.*, 344 F.3d 229 (2d Cir. 2003)]

28–5. Price Fixing Texaco, Inc., and Shell Oil Co. are competitors in the national and international oil and gasoline markets. They refine crude oil into gasoline and sell it to service station owners and others. Between 1998 and 2002, Texaco and Shell engaged in a joint venture, Equilon Enterprises, to consolidate their operations in the western United States and a separate venture, Motiva Enterprises, for the same purpose in the eastern United States. This ended their competition in the domestic refining and marketing of gasoline. As part of the ventures, Texaco and Shell agreed to pool their resources and share the risks and profits of their joint activities. The Federal Trade Commission and several states approved the formation of these entities without restricting the pricing of their gasoline, which the ventures began to sell at a single price under the original Texaco and Shell brand names. Fouad Dagher and other station owners filed a suit in a federal district court against Texaco and Shell, alleging that the defendants were engaged in illegal price fixing. Do the circumstances in this case fit the definition of a price-fixing agreement? Explain. [*Texaco Inc. v. Dagher*, 547 U.S. 1, 126 S.Ct. 1276, 164 L.Ed.2d 1 (2006)]

28–6. CASE PROBLEM WITH SAMPLE ANSWER: Tying Arrangement.

 John Sheridan owned a Marathon gas station franchise. He sued Marathon Petroleum Co. under Section 1 of the Sherman Act and Section 3 of the Clayton Act, charging it with illegally tying the processing of credit-card sales to the gas station. As a condition of obtaining a Marathon dealership, dealers had to agree to let the franchisor process credit cards. They could not shop around to see if credit-card processing could be obtained at a lower price from another source. The district court dismissed the case for failure to state a claim. Sheridan appealed. Is there a tying arrangement? If so, does it violate the law? Explain. [Sheridan v. Marathon Petroleum Co., 530 F.3d 590 (7th Cir. 2008)]

• **To view a sample answer for Problem 28–6, go to this book's Web site at www.cengage.com/blaw/cross, select "Chapter 28," and click on "Case Problem with Sample Answer."**

28–7. Price Fixing About 80 percent of the digital music purchased in the United States was controlled by several companies that produce, license, and distribute music sold as digital files over the Internet or on compact discs. The companies formed joint ventures called MusicNet and Duet to sell music to consumers. Through these ventures, the music sellers could communicate about pricing, terms, and use restrictions. Because the prices were so high, however, most consumers avoided them. Instead, song-by-song distribution over the Internet became more common. As a result, the music companies were forced to lower prices, but most sales were still done through MusicNet as the distributor. Eventually, the music companies agreed to a price of 70 cents wholesale for songs distributed on the Internet, but they refused to sell through another distributor, eMusic, which charged 25 cents per song. A group of consumers, including Kevin Starr, brought a lawsuit alleging that the music companies engaged in a conspiracy to restrain the distribution of Internet music and to fix and maintain artificially high prices. Do the consumers have a credible antitrust case to pursue in this situation? Discuss. [*Starr v. Sony BMG Music Entertainment*, 592 F.3d 314 (2d Cir. 2010)]

28–8. A QUESTION OF ETHICS: Section 1 of the Sherman Act.

 In the 1990s, DuCoa, L.P., made choline chloride, a B-complex vitamin essential for the growth and development of animals. The U.S. market for choline chloride was divided into thirds among DuCoa, Bioproducts, Inc., and Chinook Group, Ltd. To stabilize the market and keep the price of the vitamin higher than it would otherwise have been, the companies agreed to fix the price and allocate market share by deciding which of them would offer the lowest price to each customer. At times, however, the companies disregarded the agreement. During an increase in competitive activity in August 1997, Daniel Rose became president of DuCoa. The next month, a subordinate advised him of the conspiracy. By February 1998, Rose had begun to implement a strategy to persuade DuCoa's competitors to rejoin the conspiracy. By April, the three companies had reallocated their market shares and increased their prices. In June, the U.S. Department of Justice began to investigate allegations of price fixing in the vitamin market. Ultimately, a federal district court convicted Rose of conspiracy to violate Section 1 of the Sherman Act. [United States v. Rose, 449 F.3d 627 (5th Cir. 2006)]*

(a) The court "enhanced" Rose's sentence to thirty months' imprisonment, one year of supervised release, and a $20,000 fine based, among other things, on his role as "a manager or supervisor" in the conspiracy. Rose appealed this enhancement to the U.S. Court of Appeals for the Fifth Circuit. Was it fair to increase Rose's sentence on this ground? Why or why not?

(b) Was Rose's participation in the conspiracy unethical? If so, how might Rose have behaved ethically instead? If not, could any of the participants' conduct be considered unethical? Explain.

28–9. SPECIAL CASE ANALYSIS: Resale Price Maintenance Agreements.

Go to Extended Case 28.2, *Leegin Creative Leather Products, Inc. v. PSKS, Inc.*, 551 U.S. 877, 127 S.Ct. 2705, 168 L.Ed.2d 623 (2007), on pages 617 and 618. Read the excerpt and answer the following questions.

(a) **Issue:** The dispute in this case was between which parties and turned on what legal issue?

(b) **Rule of Law:** In resolving this dispute, what common law rule did the Court overturn, and what rule did the Court create to replace this rejected precedent?

(c) **Applying the Rule of Law:** What reasons did the Court give to justify its change in the law, and how did the new rule apply in this case?

(d) **Conclusion:** In whose favor did the Court rule and why?

LEGAL RESEARCH EXERCISES ON THE WEB

Go to this text's Web site at **www.cengage.com/blaw/cross**, select "Chapter 28," and click on "Practical Internet Exercises." There you will find the following Internet research exercises that you can perform to learn more about the topics covered in this chapter.

Practical Internet Exercise 28–1: **Legal Perspective**
Mergers and Antitrust Law

Practical Internet Exercise 28–2: **Management Perspective**
Avoiding Antitrust Problems

CHAPTER 29

Investor Protection and Corporate Governance

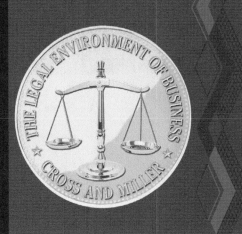

The stock market crash of October 29, 1929, and the ensuing economic depression caused the public to focus on the importance of securities markets for the economic well-being of the nation. Congress was pressured to regulate securities trading, and the result was the Securities Act of 1933[1] and the Securities Exchange Act of 1934.[2] Both acts were designed to

provide investors with more information to help them make buying and selling decisions about securities—generally defined as any instruments evidencing corporate ownership (stock) or debts (bonds)—and to prohibit deceptive, unfair, and manipulative practices in the purchase and sale of securities.

This chapter discusses the nature of federal securities regulation and its effect on the business world. We begin by looking at the federal administrative agency

that regulates securities transactions, the Securities and Exchange Commission. Next, we examine the major traditional laws governing securities offerings and trading.

We then discuss corporate governance and the Sarbanes-Oxley Act, which significantly affects certain types of securities transactions. In the concluding pages of this chapter, we look at how securities laws are being adapted to the online environment.

1. 15 U.S.C. Sections 77a–77aa.
2. 15 U.S.C. Sections 78a–78mm.

SECTION 1
THE SECURITIES AND EXCHANGE COMMISSION

The Securities Exchange Act of 1934 created the Securities and Exchange Commission (SEC) as an independent regulatory agency. The SEC administers the Securities Act of 1933 and the 1934 act. The SEC also plays a key role in interpreting the provisions of these acts (and their amendments) and in creating regulations governing the purchase and sale of securities. The basic functions of the SEC are as follows:

1. Interprets federal securities laws and investigates securities law violations.
2. Issues new rules and amends existing rules.
3. Oversees the inspection of securities firms, brokers, investment advisers, and ratings agencies.
4. Oversees private regulatory organizations in the securities, accounting, and auditing fields.
5. Coordinates U.S. securities regulation with federal, state, and foreign authorities.

Updating the Regulatory Process

The SEC is working to make the regulatory process more efficient and more relevant to today's securities trading practices. To this end, the SEC has embraced modern technology and communications methods, especially the Internet, more completely than have many other federal agencies. For example, the agency now requires companies to file certain information electronically so that it can be posted on the SEC's EDGAR (Electronic Data Gathering, Analysis, and Retrieval) database.

The SEC requires companies to make disclosures regarding climate change, as discussed in this chapter's *Shifting Legal Priorities for Business* feature on the following page.

The SEC's Expanding Regulatory Powers

Since its creation, the SEC's regulatory functions have gradually been increased by legislation granting it authority in different areas. For example, to further curb securities fraud,

The Securities and Exchange Commission (SEC) requires companies to reveal the potential financial impacts of future events such as increased competition, changes in regulatory rules, and pending lawsuits. In short, publicly traded corporations must disclose material information about future developments that might affect their earnings so that investors can make sound investment decisions. Should that information include the potential impact of climate change related to global warming?

The Risks and Opportunities of Climate Change

Since 2007, environmental groups, large institutional investors such as state pension funds, and other groups have petitioned the SEC, asking the commission to require that publicly held companies disclose climate-related information that could materially affect their operations.[a] The groups cited a number of potential costs related to climate change, such as property losses in flooded coastal areas that would affect the property owners and their insurers, increased costs for food producers due to crop losses, and increased costs for pollution-control equipment to curb greenhouse gas emissions. At the same time, climate change could also present opportunities for companies that produce goods and services that can mitigate the effects of global warming or supply energy without generating emissions.

The SEC Responds

In 2010, the SEC decided that climate change had become a sufficiently important issue that publicly held companies should disclose their exposure to it. Accordingly, the SEC issued a guidance to aid companies in deciding when and whether to disclose the potential impacts of climate change on their future profitability.[b] In announcing the decision, Mary Schapiro, the SEC chair, pointed out that "we are not opining on whether the world's climate is changing, at what pace it might be changing, or due to what causes. Nothing that the commission does today should be construed as weighing in on these topics."

The SEC's guidance suggests that companies note in their quarterly and annual reports to shareholders any significant developments in federal and state legislation and regulations regarding climate change. For example, companies should disclose estimates for any material capital expenditures for pollution-control facilities. Risk factors related to existing or pending environmental legislation or regulations should be disclosed. In particular, companies should be "sensitive to greenhouse gas legislation or regulation."

The material impact of treaties or international conventions related to climate change should also be considered and disclosed. Companies whose businesses are "reasonably likely to be affected by such agreements should monitor the progress of any potential agreements and consider the possible impact."

Finally, the SEC suggested that companies consider changes in demand for their products or services, both existing and proposed, that might occur as a consequence of climate change or environmental legislation and regulations. For example, there might be a decrease in demand for services related to carbon-based energy, such as drilling or equipment maintenance services.

MANAGERIAL IMPLICATIONS

For the moment, only managers working in publicly held companies must worry about the SEC's guidelines with respect to climate change. Nonetheless, nonpublic companies sometimes "go public." Thus, managers in those companies should also monitor pending legislation, national and international, that might affect their businesses.

a. "File No. 4-547: Request for Interpretive Guidance on Climate Risk Disclosure." *www.sec.gov.* 18 Sep. 2007: n.p. Web.

b. 17 C.F.R. Parts 211, 231, and 241 (Release Nos. 33-9106 and 34-61469; FR-82).

Congress enacted the Securities Enforcement Remedies and Penny Stock Reform Act of 1990.[3] This act expands the SEC's enforcement options and allows SEC administrative law judges to hear cases involving more types of alleged securities law violations, such as fraudulent financial reporting and financial fraud. The Securities Acts Amendments of 1990 authorized the SEC to seek sanctions against those who violate foreign securities laws.[4]

The National Securities Markets Improvement Act of 1996 expanded the power of the SEC to exempt persons, securities, and transactions from the requirements of the securities laws.[5] The Sarbanes-Oxley Act of 2002, which you will read about later

---

3. 15 U.S.C. Section 77g.

4. 15 U.S.C. Section 78a.
5. 15 U.S.C. Sections 77z-3, 78mm.

in this chapter, further expanded the authority of the SEC. The Sarbanes-Oxley Act required the SEC to adopt new rules relating to corporate disclosure requirements and created an oversight board to regulate public accounting firms.

SECTION 2
THE SECURITIES ACT OF 1933

The Securities Act of 1933 governs initial sales of stock by businesses. The act was designed to prohibit various forms of fraud and to stabilize the securities industry by requiring that investors receive financial and other significant information concerning the securities being offered for public sale. Basically, the purpose of this act is to require disclosure. The 1933 act provides that all securities transactions must be registered with the SEC unless they are specifically exempt from the registration requirements.

What Is a Security?

Section 2(1) of the Securities Act of 1933 contains a broad definition of securities, which generally include the following:[6]

1. Instruments and interests commonly known as securities, such as preferred and common stocks, treasury stocks, bonds, debentures, and stock warrants.
2. Any interests commonly known as securities, such as stock options, puts, calls, or other types of privilege on a security or on the right to purchase a security or a group of securities in a national security exchange.
3. Notes, instruments, or other evidence of indebtedness, including certificates of interest in a profit-sharing agreement and certificates of deposit.
4. Any fractional undivided interest in oil, gas, or other mineral rights.
5. Investment contracts, which include interests in limited partnerships and other investment schemes.

In interpreting the act, the United States Supreme Court has held that an **investment contract** is any transaction in which a person (1) invests (2) in a common enterprise (3) reasonably expecting profits (4) derived *primarily* or *substantially* from others' managerial or entrepreneurial efforts. Known as the *Howey* test, this definition continues to guide the

determination of what types of contracts can be considered securities.[7]

For our purposes, it is convenient to think of securities in their most common form—stocks and bonds issued by corporations. Bear in mind, though, that securities can take many forms, including interests in whiskey, cosmetics, worms, beavers, boats, vacuum cleaners, muskrats, and cemetery lots. Almost any stake in the ownership or debt of a company can be considered a security. Investment contracts in condominiums, franchises, limited partnerships in real estate, and oil or gas or other mineral rights have qualified as securities.

CASE IN POINT   Alpha Telcom sold, installed, and maintained pay-phone systems. The company guaranteed buyers of the systems a 14 percent annual return. Alpha was operating at a net loss, however, and continually borrowed funds to pay investors the fixed rate of return it had promised. Eventually, the company filed for bankruptcy, and the SEC brought an action alleging that Alpha had violated the Securities Act of 1933. A federal court concluded that the pay-phone program was a security because it involved an investment contract.[8]

Registration Statement

Section 5 of the Securities Act of 1933 broadly provides that if a security does not qualify for an exemption, that security must be *registered* before it is offered to the public. Issuing corporations must file a *registration statement* with the SEC and must provide all investors with a *prospectus*. A **prospectus** is a disclosure document that describes the security being sold, the financial operations of the issuing corporation, and the investment or risk attaching to the security. The prospectus also serves as a selling tool for the issuing corporation. Recent SEC rules allow an issuer to deliver a prospectus to investors electronically via the Internet.[9] In principle, the registration statement and the prospectus supply sufficient

---

6. 15 U.S.C. Section 77b(1). Amendments in 1982 added stock options.

7. *SEC v. W. J. Howey Co.,* 328 U.S. 293, 66 S.Ct. 1100, 90 L.Ed. 1244 (1946).

8. *SEC v. Alpha Telcom, Inc.,* 187 F.Supp.2d 1250 (2002). See also *SEC v. Edwards,* 540 U.S. 389, 124 S.Ct. 892, 157 L.Ed.2d 813 (2004), in which the United States Supreme Court held that an investment scheme offering contractual entitlement to a fixed rate of return can be an investment contract and therefore can be considered a security under federal law.

9. Basically, an electronic prospectus must meet the same requirements as a printed prospectus. The SEC rules address situations in which the graphics, images, or audio files in or accompanying a printed prospectus cannot be reproduced in an electronic form. 17 C.F.R. Section 232.304.

information to enable unsophisticated investors to evaluate the financial risk involved.

CONTENTS OF THE REGISTRATION STATEMENT The registration statement must be written in plain English and fully describe the following:

1. The securities being offered for sale, including their relationship to the registrant's other capital securities.
2. The corporation's properties and business (including a financial statement certified by an independent public accounting firm).
3. The management of the corporation, including managerial compensation, stock options, pensions, and other benefits. Any interests of directors or officers in any material transactions with the corporation must be disclosed.
4. How the corporation intends to use the proceeds of the sale.
5. Any pending lawsuits or special risk factors.

All companies, both domestic and foreign, must file their registration statements electronically so that they can be posted on the SEC's EDGAR database (mentioned previously) and investors can access the information via the Internet. The EDGAR database includes material on *initial public offerings* (IPOs), proxy statements, corporations' annual reports, registration statements, and other documents that have been filed with the SEC.

REGISTRATION PROCESS The registration statement must be reviewed and approved by the SEC before it can become effective (unless it is filed by a *well-known seasoned issuer,* as will be discussed shortly). The 1933 act restricts the types of activities that an issuer can engage in at each stage of the registration process. If an issuer violates these restrictions, investors can rescind their contracts to purchase the securities. During the *prefiling period* (before filing the registration statement), the issuer normally cannot sell or offer to sell the securities. The issuer also cannot advertise its upcoming securities offering during the prefiling period.

Waiting Period. Once the registration statement has been filed, there is a waiting period of at least twenty days during which the SEC reviews the registration statement for completeness. Frequently, the staff members at the SEC who review the registration statement ask the registrant to make numerous changes and additions, which extends the length of the waiting period.

During the waiting period, the securities can be offered for sale but cannot be sold by the issuing corporation. Only certain types of offers are allowed. All issuers can distribute a *preliminary prospectus,* called a **red herring prospectus.**[10] A red herring prospectus contains most of the information that will be included in the final prospectus but often does not include a price. General advertising is permitted, such as a **tombstone ad,** so named because historically the format resembled a tombstone. Such ads simply tell the investor where and how to obtain a prospectus.[11]

Most issuers can also use a *free-writing prospectus* during this period (although some inexperienced issuers will need to file a preliminary prospectus first).[12] A **free-writing prospectus** is any type of written, electronic, or graphic offer that describes the issuer or its securities and includes a legend indicating that the investor may obtain the prospectus at the SEC's Web site. The issuer normally must file the free-writing prospectus with the SEC no later than the first date it is used.

Posteffective Period. Once the SEC has reviewed and approved the registration statement and the waiting period is over, the registration is effective, and the *posteffective period* begins. The issuer can now offer and sell the securities without restrictions. If the company issued a preliminary or free-writing prospectus to investors, it must provide those investors with a final prospectus either before or at the time they purchase the securities. The issuer can require investors to download the final prospectus from a Web site if it notifies them of the appropriate Internet address.

Registration Process Review. To review the entire process, suppose that Delsey Corporation wants to make a public offering of its common stock. It files a registration statement and a prospectus with the SEC. On the same day, the company can make *offers* to sell the stock and start using a free-writing prospectus, but it cannot actually sell any of the stock. Delsey and its attorneys work with the SEC and provide additional information as requested for nearly six months. When the SEC finally indicates

---

10. The name *red herring* comes from the legend printed in red across the prospectus stating that the registration has been filed but has not become effective.
11. During the waiting period, the SEC also allows *road shows,* in which a corporate executive travels around speaking to institutional investors and securities analysts. In addition, electronic road shows are viewed via real-time communications methods, such as Web casting.
12. See SEC Rules 164 and 433. Note also companies that qualify as *well-known seasoned issuers* (see page 631) can even use a free-writing prospectus during the prefiling period.

that it has all the necessary information for the registration statement to be approved, Delsey can request that the twenty-day waiting period be accelerated. Only *after* the SEC declares the registration to be effective and the waiting period has elapsed or been accelerated can Delsey sell the first shares in the issue.

RESTRICTIONS RELAXED FOR WELL-KNOWN SEASONED ISSUERS In 2005, the SEC revised the registration process. The revisions created new categories of issuers based on size and presence in the market and provided a simplified registration process for large, experienced issuers.[13] The rules created new categories of issuers depending on their size and presence in the market and provided a simplified registration process for these issuers. The large, well-known securities firms that issue most securities have the greatest flexibility. A *well-known seasoned issuer* (WKSI) is a firm that has issued at least $1 billion in securities in the last three years or has at least $700 million of value of outstanding stock in the hands of the public. WKSIs can file registration statements the day they announce a new offering and are not required to wait for SEC review and approval. They can also use a free-writing prospectus at any time, even during the prefiling period.

Exempt Securities and Transactions

Certain types of securities are exempt from the registration requirements of the Securities Act of 1933. These securities—which generally can also be resold without being registered—are summarized in Exhibit 29–1 on the next page under the heading "Exempt Securities."[14] The exhibit also lists and describes certain transactions that are exempt from registration requirements under various SEC regulations.

The transaction exemptions are the most important because they are very broad and can enable an issuer to avoid the high cost and complicated procedures associated with registration. Because the coverage of the exemptions overlaps somewhat, an offering may qualify for more than one. Therefore, many sales occur without registration. Even when a transaction is exempt from the registration requirements, the offering is still subject to the antifraud provisions of the 1933 act (as well as those of the 1934 act, to be discussed later in this chapter).

REGULATION A OFFERINGS An issuer's offering of up to $5 million in securities in any twelve-month period is exempt from registration.[15] Regulation A[16] provides a simplified registration process for issues of securities by small businesses (companies with annual revenues of less than $25 million). The issuer must file with the SEC a notice of the issue and an offering circular, which must also be provided to investors before the sale. This process is much less expensive than the procedures associated with full registration.

Companies are allowed to "test the waters" for potential interest before preparing the offering circular. To *test the waters* means to determine potential interest without actually selling any securities or requiring any commitment on the part of those who express interest. Small-business issuers can also use an integrated registration and reporting system that requires simpler forms than the full registration system.

Some companies have sold their securities via the Internet using Regulation A. In 1996, the Spring Street Brewing Company became the first company to sell securities via an online IPO. Spring Street raised about $1.6 million—without having to pay any commissions to brokers or underwriters. Such online IPOs are particularly attractive to small companies and start-up ventures that may find it difficult to raise capital from institutional investors or through underwriters. By making the offering online under Regulation A, the company can avoid both commissions and the costly and time-consuming filings required for a traditional IPO under federal and state law.

REGULATION D OFFERINGS The SEC's Regulation D contains several separate exemptions from registration requirements for limited offers (offers that either involve a small dollar amount or are made in a limited manner). Regulation D provides that any of these offerings made during any twelve-month period are exempt from the registration requirements.

Rule 504. Rule 504 is the exemption used by most small businesses. It provides that noninvestment company offerings up to $1 million in any twelve-month period are exempt.[17] Noninvestment

---

13. Securities Offering Reform, codified at 17 C.F.R. Sections 200, 228, 229, 230, 239, 240, 243, 249, and 274.

14. 15 U.S.C. Section 77c.

15. 15 U.S.C. Section 77c(b).

16. 17 C.F.R. Sections 230.251–230.263.

17. 17 C.F.R. Section 230.504. Small businesses in California may also be exempt under SEC Rule 1001. California's rule permits limited offerings of up to $5 million *per transaction,* if they satisfy the conditions of Section 25102(n) of the California Corporations Code. These offerings, however, can be made only to "qualified purchasers"—that is, knowledgeable, sophisticated investors.

EXHIBIT 29-1 • Exemptions for Securities Offerings under the 1933 Securities Act

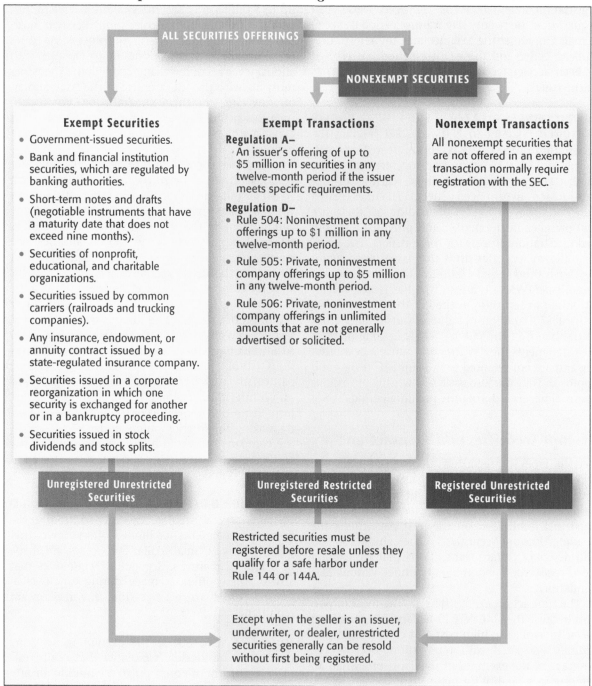

ALL SECURITIES OFFERINGS

NONEXEMPT SECURITIES

Exempt Securities
- Government-issued securities.
- Bank and financial institution securities, which are regulated by banking authorities.
- Short-term notes and drafts (negotiable instruments that have a maturity date that does not exceed nine months).
- Securities of nonprofit, educational, and charitable organizations.
- Securities issued by common carriers (railroads and trucking companies).
- Any insurance, endowment, or annuity contract issued by a state-regulated insurance company.
- Securities issued in a corporate reorganization in which one security is exchanged for another or in a bankruptcy proceeding.
- Securities issued in stock dividends and stock splits.

Exempt Transactions
Regulation A–
An issuer's offering of up to $5 million in securities in any twelve-month period if the issuer meets specific requirements.

Regulation D–
- Rule 504: Noninvestment company offerings up to $1 million in any twelve-month period.
- Rule 505: Private, noninvestment company offerings up to $5 million in any twelve-month period.
- Rule 506: Private, noninvestment company offerings in unlimited amounts that are not generally advertised or solicited.

Nonexempt Transactions
All nonexempt securities that are not offered in an exempt transaction normally require registration with the SEC.

Unregistered Unrestricted Securities

Unregistered Restricted Securities

Registered Unrestricted Securities

Restricted securities must be registered before resale unless they qualify for a safe harbor under Rule 144 or 144A.

Except when the seller is an issuer, underwriter, or dealer, unrestricted securities generally can be resold without first being registered.

companies are firms that are not engaged primarily in the business of investing or trading in securities. (In contrast, an **investment company** is a firm that buys a large portfolio of securities and professionally manages it on behalf of many smaller shareholders/owners. A **mutual fund** is a well-known type of investment company.)

For example, Zeta Enterprises is a limited partnership that develops commercial property. Zeta intends to offer $600,000 of its limited partnership interests for sale between June 1 and next May 31. The buyers will become limited partners in Zeta. Because an interest in a limited partnership meets the definition of a security (discussed earlier in this chapter), its sale is subject to the registration and prospectus requirements of the Securities Act of 1933. Under Rule 504, however, the sales of Zeta's interests are exempt from these requirements because Zeta is a noninvestment company making an offering of less than $1 million in a given twelve-month period. Therefore, Zeta can sell its interests without filing a registration statement with the SEC or issuing a prospectus to any investor.

Rule 505. Another exemption is available under Rule 505 for private, noninvestment company offerings up to $5 million in any twelve-month period. Under this exemption, the offer may be made to an unlimited number of *accredited investors* and up to thirty-five unaccredited investors. **Accredited investors** include banks, insurance companies, investment companies, employee benefit plans, the issuer's executive officers and directors, and persons whose income or net worth exceeds a certain threshold. Specific information about the offering company, its business, and the securities must be provided to all buyers before the sale if there are *any* unaccredited investors.

The SEC must be notified of the sales, and precautions must be taken because these *restricted securities* may be resold only by registration or in an exempt transaction.[18] (The securities purchased and sold by most people who handle stock transactions are called, in contrast, *unrestricted securities*.) The purchasers must buy for investment and may not sell the securities for at least a year. No general solicitation or advertising is allowed.

Rule 506. Rule 506 exempts private, noninvestment company offerings in unlimited amounts, so long as the offerings generally are not solicited or advertised. This exemption is often referred to as the *private placement exemption* because it exempts "transactions not involving any public offering."[19] There can be an unlimited number of accredited investors and up to thirty-five unaccredited investors. To qualify for the exemption, the issuer must believe that each unaccredited investor has sufficient knowledge or experience in financial matters to be capable of evaluating the investment's merits and risks.[20]

The private placement exemption is perhaps the most important exemption for firms that want to raise funds through the sale of securities without registering them. For example, Citco Corporation needs to raise capital to expand its operations. Citco decides to make a private $10 million offering of its common stock directly to two hundred accredited investors and a group of thirty highly sophisticated, but unaccredited, investors. Citco provides all of these investors with a prospectus and material information about the firm, including its most recent financial statements. As long as Citco notifies the SEC of the sale, this offering will likely qualify as an exempt transaction under Rule 506. The offering is nonpublic and not generally advertised. There are fewer than thirty-five unaccredited investors, and each of them possesses sufficient knowledge and experience to evaluate the risks involved. The issuer has provided all purchasers with the material information. Thus, Citco will *not* be required to comply with the registration requirements of the Securities Act of 1933.

RESALES AND SAFE HARBOR RULES Most securities can be resold without registration. The Securities Act of 1933 provides exemptions for resales by most persons other than issuers or underwriters. The average investor who sells shares of stock need not file a registration statement with the SEC. Resales of restricted securities acquired under Rule 505 or Rule 506, however, trigger the registration requirements *unless the party selling them complies with Rule 144 or Rule 144A*. These rules are sometimes referred to as safe harbors.

Rule 144. Rule 144 exempts restricted securities from registration on resale if all of the following conditions are met:

1. There is adequate current public information about the issuer. ("Adequate current public information" refers to the reports that certain companies are required to file under the Securities Exchange Act of 1934.)
2. The person selling the securities has owned them for at least six months if the issuer is subject to the reporting requirements of the 1934 act.[21] If

---

18. Precautions to be taken against nonexempt, unregistered resales include asking the investor whether he or she is buying the securities for others; disclosing to each purchaser in writing, before the sale, that the securities are unregistered and thus cannot be resold, except in an exempt transaction, without first being registered; and indicating on the certificates that the securities are unregistered and restricted.
19. 15 U.S.C. Section 77d(2).
20. 17 C.F.R. Section 230.506.

21. Before 2008, when amendments to Rule 144 became effective, the holding period for restricted securities was one year if the issuer was subject to the reporting requirements of the 1934 act. See the revised SEC Rules and Regulations at 72 Federal Rules 71546-01, 2007 WL 4368599, Release No. 33-8869. This reduced holding period allows nonpublic issuers to raise capital electronically from private and overseas sources more quickly.

the issuer is not subject to the 1934 act's reporting requirements, the seller must have owned the securities for at least one year.

3. The securities are sold in certain limited amounts in unsolicited brokers' transactions.
4. The SEC is notified of the resale.[22]

Rule 144A. Securities that at the time of issue were not of the same class as securities listed on a national securities exchange or quoted in a U.S. automated interdealer quotation system may be resold under Rule 144A.[23] They may be sold only to a qualified institutional buyer (an institution, such as an insurance company or a bank, that owns and invests at least $100 million in securities). The seller must take reasonable steps to ensure that the buyer knows that the seller is relying on the exemption under Rule 144A. A sample restricted stock certificate is shown in Exhibit 29–2 below.

Violations of the 1933 Act

It is a violation of the Securities Act of 1933 to intentionally defraud investors by misrepresenting or omitting facts in a registration statement or prospectus. Liability is also imposed on those who

---

22. 17 C.F.R. Section 230.144.
23. 17 C.F.R. Section 230.144A.

are negligent in not discovering the fraud. Selling securities before the effective date of the registration statement or under an exemption for which the securities do not qualify results in liability.

CRIMINAL PENALTIES Criminal violations are prosecuted by the U.S. Department of Justice. Violators may be fined up to $10,000, imprisoned for up to five years, or both.

CIVIL SANCTIONS The SEC is authorized to impose civil sanctions against those who willfully violate the 1933 act. It can request an injunction to prevent further sales of the securities involved or ask a court to grant other relief, such as ordering a violator to refund profits.

Private parties who purchase securities and suffer harm as a result of false or omitted statements or other violations may bring a suit in a federal court to recover their losses and additional damages. If a registration statement or a prospectus contains material false statements or omissions, for example, damages may be recovered from those who signed the statement or those who provided information used in preparing the statement (such as accountants and other experts).

DEFENSES There are three basic defenses to charges of violations under the 1933 act. A defendant can

EXHIBIT 29-2 • A Sample Restricted Stock Certificate

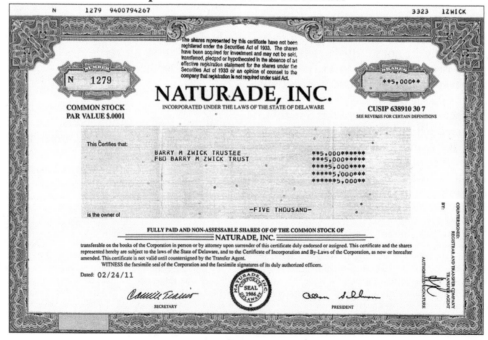

avoid liability by proving that (1) the statement or omission was not material, (2) the plaintiff knew about the misrepresentation at the time of purchasing the stock, or (3) the defendant exercised *due diligence* in preparing the registration and reasonably believed at the time that the statements were true.

The due diligence defense is the most important because it can be asserted by any defendant, except the issuer of the stock. The defendant must prove that she or he reasonably believed, at the time the registration statement became effective, that the statements in it were true and there were no omissions of material facts.

SECTION 3
THE SECURITIES EXCHANGE ACT OF 1934

The Securities Exchange Act of 1934 provides for the regulation and registration of securities exchanges, brokers, dealers, and national securities associations, such as the National Association of Securities Dealers (NASD). Unlike the 1933 act, which is a one-time disclosure law, the 1934 act provides for continuous periodic disclosures by publicly held corporations to enable the SEC to regulate subsequent trading.

The Securities Exchange Act of 1934 applies to companies that have assets in excess of $10 million and five hundred or more shareholders. These corporations are referred to as *Section 12 companies* because they are required to register their securities under Section 12 of the 1934 act. Section 12 companies are required to file reports with the SEC annually and quarterly, and sometimes even monthly if specified events occur (such as a merger).

The act also authorizes the SEC to engage in market surveillance to deter undesirable market practices such as fraud, market manipulation, and misrepresentation. In addition, the act provides for the SEC's regulation of proxy solicitations for voting (discussed in Chapter 19).

Section 10(b), SEC Rule 10b-5, and Insider Trading

Section 10(b) is one of the more important sections of the Securities Exchange Act of 1934. This section prohibits the use of any manipulative or deceptive mechanism in violation of SEC rules and regulations. Among the rules that the SEC has promulgated

pursuant to the 1934 act is **SEC Rule 10b-5,** which prohibits the commission of fraud in connection with the purchase or sale of any security.

APPLICABILITY OF SEC RULE 10b-5 SEC Rule 10b-5 applies to almost all cases concerning the trading of securities, whether on organized exchanges, in over-the-counter markets, or in private transactions. Generally, the rule covers just about any form of security, including notes, bonds, agreements to form a corporation, and joint-venture agreements. The securities need not be registered under the 1933 act for the 1934 act to apply.

SEC Rule 10b-5 applies only when the requisites of federal jurisdiction—such as the use of stock exchange facilities or any means of interstate commerce—are present. Nevertheless, this requirement is easily met because almost every commercial transaction involves interstate contacts. In addition, the states have corporate securities laws, many of which include provisions similar to SEC Rule 10b-5.

INSIDER TRADING One of the major goals of Section 10(b) and SEC Rule 10b-5 is to prevent so-called **insider trading,** which occurs when persons buy or sell securities on the basis of information that is not available to the public. Corporate directors, officers, and others, such as majority shareholders, often have advance inside information that can affect the future market value of the corporate stock. Obviously, if they act on this information, their positions give them a trading advantage over the general public and other shareholders.

The 1934 Securities Exchange Act defines inside information. It also extends liability to those who take advantage of such information in their personal transactions when they know that the information is unavailable to those with whom they are dealing. Section 10(b) of the 1934 act and SEC Rule 10b-5 apply to anyone who has access to or receives information of a nonpublic nature on which trading is based—not just to corporate "insiders."

DISCLOSURE UNDER SEC RULE 10b-5 Any material omission or misrepresentation of material facts in connection with the purchase or sale of a security may violate Section 10(b) of the 1934 act and SEC Rule 10b-5. The key to liability (which can be civil or criminal) is whether the information omitted or misrepresented is *material.*

The following are some examples of material facts calling for disclosure under SEC Rule 10b-5:

1. Fraudulent trading in the company stock by a broker-dealer.
2. A dividend change (whether up or down).
3. A contract for the sale of corporate assets.
4. A new discovery, a new process, or a new product.
5. A significant change in the firm's financial condition.
6. Potential litigation against the company.

Note that any one of these facts, by itself, is not *automatically* considered material. Rather, it will be regarded as a material fact only if it is significant enough that it would likely affect an investor's decision as to whether to purchase or sell the company's securities.

For example, Sheen, Inc., is the defendant in a class-action product liability suit that its attorney, Paula Frasier, believes that the company will lose.

Frasier has advised Sheen's directors, officers, and accountants that the company will likely have to pay a substantial damages award. Sheen plans to make a $5 million offering of newly issued stock before the date when the trial is expected to end. Sheen's potential liability and the financial consequences to the firm are material facts that must be disclosed because they are significant enough to affect an investor's decision as to whether to purchase the stock.

The case that follows is a landmark decision interpreting SEC Rule 10b-5. The SEC sued several of Texas Gulf Sulphur Company's directors, officers, and employees under SEC Rule 10b-5 after they purchased large amounts of the company's stock before the announcement of a rich ore discovery by the corporation. At issue was whether the ore discovery was a material fact that had to be disclosed under Rule 10b-5.

CASE 29.1
SEC v. Texas Gulf Sulphur Co.
United States Court of Appeals, Second Circuit, 401 F.2d 833 (1968).

BACKGROUND AND FACTS • Texas Gulf Sulphur Company (TGS) conducted aerial geophysical surveys over more than 15,000 square miles of eastern Canada. The operations indicated concentrations of commercially exploitable minerals. At one site near Timmins, Ontario, TGS drilled a hole that appeared to yield a core with an exceedingly high mineral content. TGS kept secret the results of the core sample. Officers and employees of the company made substantial purchases of TGS's stock or accepted stock options (rights to purchase stock) after learning of the ore discovery, even though further drilling was necessary to establish whether there was enough ore to be mined commercially. Several months later, TGS announced that the strike was expected to yield at least 25 million tons of ore. Subsequently, the price of TGS stock rose substantially. The Securities and Exchange Commission (SEC) brought a suit against the officers and employees of TGS for violating SEC Rule 10b-5. The officers and employees argued that the information on which they had traded had not been material at the time of their trades because the mine had not then been commercially proved. The trial court held that most of the defendants had not violated SEC Rule 10b-5, and the SEC appealed.

IN THE LANGUAGE OF THE COURT
WATERMAN, Circuit Judge.
* * * *

* * * Whether facts are material within Rule 10b-5 when the facts relate to a particular event and are undisclosed by those persons who are knowledgeable thereof *will depend at any given time upon a balancing of both the indicated probability that the event will occur and the anticipated magnitude of the event in light of the totality of the company activity.* Here, * * * knowledge of the possibility, which surely was more than marginal, of the existence of a mine of the vast magnitude indicated by the remarkably rich drill core located rather close to the surface (suggesting mineability by the less expensive openpit method) within the confines of a large anomaly (suggesting an extensive region of mineralization) might well have affected the price of TGS stock and would certainly have been an important fact to a reasonable, if speculative, investor in deciding whether he should buy, sell, or hold. [Emphasis added.]
* * * *

CASE 29.1 CONTINUED ▶   * * * A major factor in determining whether the * * * discovery was a material fact is the importance attached to the drilling results by those who knew about it. * * * The timing by those who knew of it of their stock purchases * * *—purchases in some cases by individuals who had never before purchased * * * TGS stock—virtually compels the inference that the insiders were influenced by the drilling results.

DECISION AND REMEDY • *The appellate court ruled in favor of the SEC. All of the trading by insiders who knew of the mineral find before its true extent had been publicly announced violated SEC Rule 10b-5.*

IMPACT OF THIS CASE ON TODAY'S LAW • *This landmark case affirmed the principle that the test of whether information is "material," for SEC Rule 10b-5 purposes, is whether it would affect the judgment of reasonable investors. The corporate insiders' purchases of stock and stock options indicated that they were influenced by the drilling results and that the information about the drilling results was material. The courts continue to cite this case when applying SEC Rule 10b-5 to cases of alleged insider trading.*

WHAT IF THE FACTS WERE DIFFERENT? • *Suppose that further drilling had revealed that there was not enough ore at this site for it to be mined commercially. Would the defendants still have been liable for violating SEC Rule 10b-5? Why or why not?*

The Private Securities Litigation Reform Act.

One of the unintended effects of SEC Rule 10b-5 was to deter disclosure of forward-looking information. To understand why, consider an example. A company announces that its projected earnings in a certain time period will be $15 million. It turns out that the forecast is wrong. The earnings are in fact much lower, and the price of the company's stock is affected—negatively. The shareholders then bring a class-action suit against the company, alleging that the directors violated SEC Rule 10b-5 by disclosing misleading financial information.

In an attempt to rectify this problem and promote disclosure, Congress passed the Private Securities Litigation Reform Act (PSLRA) of 1995. Among other things, the PSLRA provides a "safe harbor" for publicly held companies that make forward-looking statements, such as financial forecasts. Those who make such statements are protected against liability for securities fraud as long as the statements are accompanied by "meaningful cautionary statements identifying important factors that could cause actual results to differ materially from those in the forward-looking statement."[24]

The Securities Litigation Uniform Standards Act.

After the PSLRA was passed, a number of class-action suits involving securities were filed in state courts to skirt its requirements. In response to this problem, Congress passed the Securities Litigation Uniform Standards Act (SLUSA) of 1998.[25] This act placed stringent limits on the ability of plaintiffs to bring class-action suits in state courts against firms whose securities are traded on national stock exchanges. The SLUSA not only prevents the purchasers and sellers of securities from bringing class-action fraud claims under state securities laws, but it also applies to investors who are fraudulently induced to hold on to their securities.[26]

OUTSIDERS AND SEC RULE 10b-5 The traditional insider-trading case involves true insiders—corporate officers, directors, and majority shareholders who have access to (and trade on) inside information. Increasingly, however, liability under Section 10(b) of the 1934 act and SEC Rule 10b-5 has been extended to include certain "outsiders"—those who trade on inside information acquired indirectly. Two theories have been developed under which outsiders may be held liable for insider trading: the *tipper/ tippee theory* and the *misappropriation theory.*

The United States Supreme Court recently heard a case in which the plaintiffs attempted to assert a third theory—*scheme liability.*

CASE IN POINT In 2000, management at the cable operator Charter Communications devised an accounting scheme that would artificially inflate its reported revenues. As part of the scheme, Charter's cable converter (set top) box suppliers, Scientific-Atlanta and Motorola, agreed to overcharge Charter for the cable boxes in exchange for additional advertising on Charter's cable network. A group

---

24. 15 U.S.C. Sections 77z-2, 78u-5.
25. Pub. L. No. 105-353. This act amended many sections of Title 15 of the *United States Code.*

26. *Merrill Lynch, Pierce, Fenner & Smith, Inc. v. Dabit,* 547 U.S. 71, 126 S.Ct. 1503, 164 L.Ed.2d 179 (2006).

of investors sued Scientific-Atlanta and Motorola, alleging violation of Section 10(b) of the Securities Exchange Act of 1934 and of SEC Rule 10b-5. The United States Supreme Court affirmed the dismissal of the suit, holding that Section 10(b)'s private right of action cannot be applied to suppliers or customers who seemingly "aid and abet" a scheme to show inflated sales revenues for a publicly traded company. The Court pointed out that the suppliers had no role in preparing or disseminating Charter's financial statements. The financial statements of both Scientific-Atlanta and Motorola were correct, and their deceptive acts were not communicated to the investing public. Consequently, the plaintiffs were unable to show reliance upon any of the actions of Scientific-Atlanta and Motorola "except in an indirect chain" that the Court found too remote to justify liability.[27]

Tipper/Tippee Theory. Anyone who acquires inside information as a result of a corporate insider's breach of his or her fiduciary duty can be liable under SEC Rule 10b-5. This liability extends to **tippees** (those who receive "tips" from insiders) and even remote tippees (tippees of tippees).

The key to liability under this theory is that the inside information must be obtained as a result of someone's breach of a fiduciary duty to the corporation whose shares are traded. The tippee is liable under this theory only if (1) there is a breach of a duty not to disclose inside information, (2) the disclosure is made in exchange for personal benefit, and (3) the tippee knows (or should know) of this breach and benefits from it.[28]

Misappropriation Theory. Liability for insider trading may also be established under the misappropriation theory. Under this theory, an individual who wrongfully obtains (misappropriates) inside information and trades on it for her or his personal gain is held liable because the individual stole information rightfully belonging to another.

The misappropriation theory has been controversial because it significantly extends the reach of SEC Rule 10b-5 to outsiders who ordinarily would not be deemed fiduciaries of the corporations in whose stock they trade. It is not always wrong to disclose material, nonpublic information about a company to a person who would not otherwise be privy to it. Nevertheless, a person who obtains the information and trades securities on it can be held liable.

CASE IN POINT Patricia Rocklage was the wife of Scott Rocklage, the chief executive officer of Cubist Pharmaceuticals, Inc. Scott had sometimes disclosed material, nonpublic information about Cubist to Patricia. She had always kept the information confidential. In 2001, however, when Scott told Patricia that one of Cubist's key drugs had failed its clinical trial, Patricia refused to keep the information secret. She warned her brother, William Beaver, who owned Cubist stock. Beaver sold his Cubist shares and tipped his friend David Jones, who sold his shares. When Cubist publicly announced the trial results, the price of its stock dropped. Beaver and Jones avoided significant losses by selling when they did. The SEC filed a lawsuit against Patricia, Beaver, and Jones. The court determined that Patricia had "engaged in deceptive devices," because she had "tricked her husband into revealing confidential information to her" for trading stock. The court therefore found all three defendants guilty of insider trading under the misappropriation theory.[29]

Insider Reporting and Trading—Section 16(b)

Section 16(b) of the 1934 act provides for the recapture by the corporation of all profits realized by certain insiders on any purchase and sale or sale and purchase of the corporation's stock within any six-month period. It is irrelevant whether the insider actually uses inside information; *all such short-swing profits must be returned to the corporation.* In this context, *insiders* means officers, directors, and large stockholders of Section 12 corporations (those owning 10 percent of the class of equity securities registered under Section 12 of the 1934 act).[30] To discourage such insiders from using nonpublic information about their companies to their personal benefit in the stock market, they must file reports

---

27. *Stoneridge Investment Partners, LLC v. Scientific-Atlanta, Inc.,* 552 U.S. 148, 128 S.Ct. 761, 169 L.Ed.2d 627 (2008).

28. See, for example, *Chiarella v. United States,* 445 U.S. 222, 100 S.Ct. 1108, 63 L.Ed.2d 348 (1980); and *Dirks v. SEC,* 463 U.S. 646, 103 S.Ct. 3255, 77 L.Ed.2d 911 (1983).

29. *SEC v. Rocklage,* 470 F.3d 1 (1st Cir. 2006).

30. 15 U.S.C. Section 78*l*. Note that Section 403 of the Sarbanes-Oxley Act of 2002 shortened the reporting deadlines specified in Section 16(b).

with the SEC concerning their ownership and trading of the corporation's securities.

Section 16(b) applies not only to stock but also to warrants, options, and securities convertible into stock. In addition, the courts have fashioned complex rules for determining profits. Note that the SEC exempts a number of transactions under Rule 16b-3.[31] For all of these reasons, corporate insiders should seek the advice of competent counsel before trading in the corporation's stock. Exhibit 29–3 below compares the effects of SEC Rule 10b-5 and Section 16(b).

Regulation of Proxy Statements

Section 14(a) of the Securities Exchange Act of 1934 regulates the solicitation of proxies (see Chapter 19) from shareholders of Section 12 companies. The SEC regulates the content of proxy statements. Whoever solicits a proxy must fully and accurately disclose in the proxy statement all of the facts that are pertinent to the matter on which the shareholders are to vote. SEC Rule 14a-9 is similar to the antifraud provisions of SEC Rule 10b-5. Remedies for violations

---

31. 17 C.F.R. Section 240.16b-3.

are extensive, ranging from injunctions to prevent a vote from being taken to monetary damages.

Violations of the 1934 Act

As mentioned earlier, violations of Section 10(b) of the Securities Exchange Act of 1934 and SEC Rule 10b-5, including insider trading, may lead to both criminal and civil liability. For either criminal or civil sanctions to be imposed, however, *scienter* must exist—that is, the violator must have had an intent to defraud or knowledge of his or her misconduct (see Chapter 9). *Scienter* can be proved if it is shown that the defendant made false statements or wrongfully failed to disclose material facts.

Violations of Section 16(b) include the sale by insiders of stock acquired less than six months before the time of sale (or less than six months after the sale, if selling short—that is, selling securities that one does not yet own). These violations are subject to civil sanctions. Liability under Section 16(b) is strict liability. Neither *scienter* nor negligence is required.

In the following case (on the next page), the defendants were accused of securities fraud in violation of Section 10(b) and SEC Rule 10b-5. At issue was whether the defendants had acted with *scienter*.

EXHIBIT 29–3 • **Comparison of Coverage, Application, and Liability under SEC Rule 10b-5 and Section 16(b)**

AREA OF COMPARISON	SEC RULE 10b-5	SECTION 16(b)
What Is the Subject Matter of the Transaction?	Any security (does not have to be registered).	Any security (does not have to be registered).
What Transactions Are Covered?	Purchase or sale.	Short-swing purchase and sale or short-swing sale and purchase.
Who Is Subject to Liability?	Almost anyone with inside information under a duty to disclose—including officers, directors, controlling shareholders, and tippees.	Officers, directors, and certain shareholders who own 10 percent or more.
Is Omission or Misrepresentation Necessary for Liability?	Yes.	No.
Are There Any Exempt Transactions?	No.	Yes, there are a number of exemptions.
Who May Bring an Action?	A person transacting with an insider, the SEC, or a purchaser or seller damaged by a wrongful act.	A corporation or a shareholder by derivative action.

✳ EXTENDED CASE 29.2 ✳
Gebhart v. SEC

United States Court of Appeals, Ninth Circuit, 595 F.3d 1034 (2010).
www.ca9.uscourts.gov/opinions[a]

IN THE LANGUAGE OF THE COURT
FISHER, Circuit Judge.
* * * *

In 1994, [Alvin Gebhart] began working at Mutual of New York (MONY) in San Diego, where he sold annuities and mutual funds. While at MONY, Gebhart met Jack Archer, a fellow MONY salesperson. In 1995, Archer told Gebhart about a business venture, Community Service Group (CSG), run by James Scovie. CSG was in the business of converting mobile home parks to resident ownership. CSG purchased parks from the owners and then assisted residents in purchasing them. In late 1996, Scovie and another person, David Mounier, created MHP Conversions, LLC (MHP), to facilitate the conversion process. MHP issued promissory notes that were sold to individual investors to raise funds for CSG's purchase of the parks. The MHP notes had one-year terms with fixed interest rates of 18 percent for new investments and 14 percent for reinvested funds. Each note stated that it would "ultimately be secured by a deed of trust" on the particular park to be purchased with the funds, but that "until such time as said deed of trust is recorded, the sole asset of [the issuer] will be a deed of trust for the property known as Eastern Trailer Park."

Archer told Gebhart about the MHP program, and * * * Gebhart arranged for Archer to make a presentation of the MHP program to three of his clients, all of whom made investments in the program.

In early 1996, Gebhart moved from MONY to another financial services firm, Mutual Service Corporation (MSC), a broker-dealer and member of the NASD [National Association of Securities Dealers]. His wife, Donna Gebhart, joined him at MSC, and the two opened and operated a[n] MSC branch in Rancho Bernardo, California, where they sold insurance and annuities and provided financial planning services to clients. In October 1996, Archer approached the Gebharts about selling MHP notes to their MSC clients. * * * Archer told them that the MHP program had been approved by the compliance officer at Archer's firm, MONY. This was not true, however. Archer also told the Gebharts "that the parks were in good shape and he always assured us that they had a lot of equity in them * * * ."

The Gebharts conducted no independent investigation into the MHP program, either in 1996 or over the next four years, during which time they sold MHP [financial] notes to their clients. They failed to obtain any financial statements for CSG or MHP, ascertain who were the owners, officers, or shareholders of CSG or MHP, determine what compensation would be paid to CSG or MHP or their officers, verify that trust deeds securing the notes were being recorded, or obtain copies of recorded trust deeds. * * * Although the Gebharts believed that their clients' loans would be secured by second trust deeds, they did not inquire why they were not first trust deeds or who held the first trust deeds. In lieu of an independent investigation, the Gebharts relied on Archer's representations.
* * * *

Between the Gebharts' meeting with Archer in October 1996 and CSG's collapse in 2000, the Gebharts sold nearly $2.4 million in MHP promissory notes to 45 of their clients, earning about $105,000 in commission fees. The sales were based on several statements by the Gebharts that, it later became clear, were false. The Gebharts told their clients that the MHP notes were a proven investment that offered substantial returns and were secured by recorded deeds of trust. They said that in the worst case scenario their clients would be part owners of the mobile home parks and would be able to recover their investments. In fact, the trust deeds were not recorded and the parks were significantly over-encumbered [had excessive debt]. The Gebharts failed to disclose that their statements were based on information provided by Archer rather than their own, independent investigation.

* * * At the time of MHP's collapse [in 2000], the Gebharts' clients had over $1.5 million invested in outstanding MHP notes. MSC terminated the Gebharts' employment in August 2000.

As a result of these events, in 2002 the NASD's Department of Enforcement filed a complaint against the Gebharts for securities fraud. * * * A[n] NASD hearing panel found that the Gebharts had acted in good faith and therefore rejected the fraud charges, but the NASD National Adjudicatory Council (NAC) reversed. The NAC found that the Gebharts had committed fraud, imposed a lifetime bar on Alvin Gebhart, and imposed a one-year suspension and a $15,000 fine on Donna Gebhart. The SEC [Securities and Exchange Commission] upheld the NASD decision in 2006.

The Gebharts petitioned for review of the SEC decision.
* * * *

To establish a violation of Section 10(b) and Rule 10b-5, the SEC is required to "show that there has

---

a. Select the "Advanced Search" mode, enter "08-74943" in the "by Case No.:" box, and click on "Search." In the search results, click on the case title to access this opinion. The U.S. Court of Appeals for the Ninth Circuit maintains this Web site.

EXTENDED CASE 29.2 CONTINUED ➡

been a misstatement or omission of material fact, made with *scienter*." "The plaintiffs may establish *scienter* by proving either actual knowledge or recklessness."

* * * *

Scienter * * * *is a subjective inquiry. It turns on the defendant's actual state of mind. Thus, although we may consider the objective unreasonableness of the defendant's conduct to raise an inference of* scienter, *the ultimate question is whether the defendant knew his or her statements were false, or was consciously reckless as to their truth or falsity.* [Emphasis added.]

* * * *

The Gebharts contend that the SEC applied an erroneous *scienter* standard in this case by focusing exclusively on * * * objective inquiry and disregarding evidence of subjective good faith. We disagree. The SEC considered all of the evidence bearing on the Gebharts' actual state of mind, including the Gebharts' extreme departure from

ordinary standards of care, and found that the Gebharts were consciously aware of the risk that their statements were false. There was no error.

The SEC certainly considered the objective unreasonableness of the Gebharts' actions as *part* of its analysis. The SEC found that the Gebharts failed to perform any meaningful investigation into the MHP promissory notes—an extreme departure from ordinary standards of care that "created the substantial [and obvious] risk * * * that their representations were not true." The SEC found that the Gebharts "made no effort to investigate or understand why their clients were being sold second (and not first) deeds of trust; no effort to identify the first trust deed holders or the amounts of those outstanding trust deeds; and no effort to ensure their clients' investments were actually being secured by recorded trust deeds." The Gebharts made "no effort" to corroborate [substantiate] Archer's representations that the parks were not overly encumbered.

The SEC properly considered the objective unreasonableness of the Gebharts' actions as some evidence supporting the inference that the Gebharts acted with *scienter*, but did not treat it as dispositive [a deciding factor]. The * * * [SEC] evaluated "the evidence the Gebharts put forward to demonstrate their good faith beliefs" as "part of the complete mix of facts bearing on an evaluation of their [actual] state of mind" and concluded that the "evidence from the Gebharts about their subjective belief [was] not sufficient to overcome" the inference of *scienter* created by the evidence as a whole. The Gebharts' assertions of good faith were "not plausible" and lacked "credibility." Based on the evidence as a whole, the SEC determined that the Gebharts "knew they had no direct knowledge of the truth or falsity" of their statements, and made their statements "despite not knowing whether they were true or false." The SEC correctly applied the appropriate *scienter* standard.

* * * *

PETITION DENIED.

 QUESTIONS

1. At one point in the opinion (not included here), the court noted that "there is no evidence in the record that the Gebharts ever intended to defraud anyone." Why, then, did the court conclude that the Gebharts had acted with *scienter?*
2. According to the court, if the evidence before an agency is "susceptible to more than one rational interpretation," the court "may not substitute its judgment for that of the agency." Why do the courts show such deference to agency rulings?

CRIMINAL PENALTIES For violations of Section 10(b) and Rule 10b-5, an individual may be fined up to $5 million, imprisoned for up to twenty years, or both. A partnership or a corporation may be fined up to $25 million. Under Section 807 of the Sarbanes-Oxley Act of 2002, for a *willful* violation of the 1934 act the violator can be imprisoned for up to twenty-five years (in addition to being subject to a fine). For a defendant to be convicted in a criminal prosecution under the securities laws, there can be no reasonable doubt that the defendant knew he or she was acting wrongfully—a jury is not allowed

merely to speculate that the defendant may have acted willfully.

CASE IN POINT Martha Stewart, founder of a well-known media and homemaking empire, was once charged with intentionally deceiving investors based on statements she made at a conference. In December 2001, Stewart's stockbroker allegedly informed Stewart that the head of ImClone Systems, Inc., was selling his shares in that company. Stewart then sold her ImClone shares. The next day, ImClone announced that the Food and Drug Administration had failed to approve Erbitux, a greatly anticipated medication that the company had been developing. After the government began investigating Stewart's ImClone trades, she publicly stated at a Martha Stewart Living Omnimedia conference that she had previously instructed her stockbroker to sell her ImClone stock if the price fell to $60 per share. The government then filed a lawsuit, claiming that Stewart's statement showed she had the intent to deceive investors. The court, however, acquitted Stewart on this charge because "to find the essential element of criminal intent beyond a reasonable doubt, a rational juror would have to speculate."[32]

CIVIL SANCTIONS The SEC can also bring a civil action against anyone who violates or aids in a violation of the 1934 act or SEC rules by purchasing or selling a security while in the possession of material nonpublic information.[33] The violation must occur through the use of a national securities exchange or a broker or dealer.[34] The court

may assess as a penalty as much as triple the profits gained or the loss avoided by the guilty party.[35] The Insider Trading and Securities Fraud Enforcement Act of 1988 enlarged the class of persons who may be subject to civil liability for insider trading and gave the SEC authority to offer monetary rewards to informants.[36]

Private parties may also sue violators of Section 10(b) and Rule 10b-5. A private party may obtain rescission (cancellation) of a contract to buy securities or damages to the extent of the violator's illegal profits. Those found liable have a right to seek contribution from those who share responsibility for the violations, including accountants, attorneys, and corporations. For violations of Section 16(b), a corporation can bring an action to recover the short-swing profits.

Recall from Chapter 9 that a required element of fraud is reliance. The innocent party must justifiably have relied on the misrepresentation. If an investor is aware of misrepresentations by corporate management and purchases shares in the firm anyway, can the investor still bring a lawsuit against the corporation for a violation of Rule 10b-5? That was the question in the following case.

---

32. *United States v. Stewart,* 305 F.Supp.2d 368 (S.D.N.Y. 2004). (Stewart was later convicted on other charges relating to her ImClone trading that did not require proof of intent.)
33. 15 U.S.C. Section 78u(d)(2)(A).
34. Transactions pursuant to a public offering by an issuer of securities are excepted.
35. 15 U.S.C. Section 78u(d)(2)(C).
36. 15 U.S.C. Section 78u-1.

CASE 29.3

Stark Trading v. Falconbridge, Ltd.

United States Court of Appeals, Seventh Circuit, 552 F.3d 568 (2009).
www.ca7.uscourts.gov[a]

COMPANY PROFILE • Brian Stark's interest in investing began in high school, when he worked for his father, an independent accountant. Together, they invested in the financial markets. Stark tested his own investment theories throughout college and law school, where he met Mike Roth. In 1992, Stark and Roth formed Stark Trading. Known today as Stark Investments, the firm invests in commodities, real estate, equity, and other markets. Its principals apply hedging and portfolio management techniques on behalf of their investors, including institutions, investment funds, and wealthy individuals. The firm has offices in cities around the world, including Hong Kong, London, Singapore, and Toronto.

BACKGROUND AND FACTS • Stark Trading was a minority shareholder in Falconbridge, Inc. Noranda, Inc., owned 59 percent of Falconbridge. Both were Canadian mining companies. Noranda offered its common stockholders preferred stock for their common stock. Noranda also offered to redeem the preferred stock for $25 per share, which exceeded the market value of the common stock. On the same day, Noranda offered minority shareholders in Falconbridge 1.77 shares of Noranda common stock for each share of Falconbridge common stock. Stark knew that Noranda's value was overstated in the offer to its common stockholders. Stark thought that the Falconbridge stock was

---

a. In the left-hand column, click on "Opinions." On that page, in the "Case Number:" boxes, type in "08" and "1327," and click on "List Case(s)." In the result, click on the appropriate link to access the opinion.

CASE 29.3 CONTINUED ➡ undervalued in the market. This meant that Noranda was buying out Falconbridge's shareholders at a reduced price. Stark sent a letter explaining this to the Ontario Securities Commission. Nonetheless, Stark exchanged its Falconbridge shares for Noranda stock. Later, Noranda and Falconbridge merged to become Falconbridge, Ltd. Stark and others filed a suit in a federal district court against the new firm, alleging a violation of Rule 10b-5. The court dismissed the suit. The plaintiffs appealed.

IN THE LANGUAGE OF THE COURT
POSNER, Circuit Judge.
* * * *

In a typical Rule 10b-5 case, the plaintiff buys stock at a price that he claims was inflated by misrepresentations by the corporation's management and sells his stock at a loss when the truth comes out and the price plummets. * * * [The plaintiffs] argue that * * * the offer to swap preferred stock in Noranda for common stock inflated the apparent value of Noranda stock, and therefore made the offer of Noranda stock for Falconbridge stock look generous. But they were not fooled. They knew that the tender offer undervalued Falconbridge— that Noranda was trying to buy out the minority shareholders (thus including the plaintiffs) cheap. [Emphasis added.]

* * * *

* * * We cannot find any basis for inferring that [the plaintiffs] relied on the defendants' [offer as a representation of the value] of Falconbridge. They knew better. They knew Falconbridge was worth a lot—that's why they invested. They thought the tender offer price was too low and that Noranda had resorted to fraud to make it succeed. They had known [when they bought their Falconbridge stock] they were buying into a company that had a majority shareholder, that it was a Canadian company, and therefore that a minority shareholder would not have the same legal protections (such as appraisal rights) that minority shareholders in U.S. corporations have. They also had to know that because they thought Falconbridge undervalued, so would Noranda, which would therefore try to buy out the minority shareholders before the market revalued Falconbridge upward. * * * And a week before the deadline for tendering their shares, the plaintiffs revealed in their letter to the [Canadian] securities commission the evidence that * * * Noranda [was] trying to pull a fast one on the minority shareholders.

* * * *

* * * Sophisticated investors, they must have considered the combination of the tender-offer price and a later suit (this suit) against the defendants a better deal than holding on to their shares and by doing so, and disseminating their doubts, trying to defeat the tender offer. That is not a strategy that the courts should reward in the name of rectifying securities fraud.

DECISION AND REMEDY • *The U.S. Court of Appeals for the Seventh Circuit upheld the lower court's decision. "So implausible is an inference of reliance from the complaint in this case * * * that the dismissal of the 10b-5 claim must be affirmed."*

THE GLOBAL DIMENSION • *Noranda and Falconbridge were Canadian companies. Falconbridge, Ltd., was later bought by Xstrata, a Swiss mining company. On what basis could a U.S. court exercise jurisdiction in this case?*

THE LEGAL ENVIRONMENT DIMENSION • *Stark's assessment of the value of Falconbridge proved correct. On the day the suit in this case was filed, the Noranda shares that Stark had received in exchange for its Falconbridge shares were worth about 50 percent more than what Stark had paid in accepting the offer. In other words, the plaintiffs could not allege that they had suffered a loss as a result of the trade. What effect does this fact have on their complaint?*

SECTION 4
STATE SECURITIES LAWS

Today, every state has its own corporate securities laws, or **blue sky laws,** that regulate the offer and sale of securities within its borders. (The phrase

blue sky laws dates to a 1917 decision by the United States Supreme Court in which the Court declared that the purpose of such laws was to prevent "speculative schemes which have no more basis than so many feet of 'blue sky.'")[37] Article 8 of the Uniform

37. *Hall v. Geiger-Jones Co.,* 242 U.S. 539, 37 S.Ct. 217, 61 L.Ed. 480 (1917).

Commercial Code, which has been adopted by all of the states, also imposes various requirements relating to the purchase and sale of securities.

Requirements

Typically, state laws have disclosure requirements and antifraud provisions, many of which are patterned after Section 10(b) of the Securities Exchange Act of 1934 and SEC Rule 10b-5. State laws also provide for the registration of securities offered or issued for sale within the state and impose disclosure requirements. Methods of registration, required disclosures, and exemptions from registration vary among states. Unless an exemption from registration is applicable, issuers must register or qualify their stock with the appropriate state official, often called a *corporations commissioner.* Additionally, most state securities laws regulate securities brokers and dealers.

Concurrent Regulation

State securities laws apply mainly to intrastate transactions. Since the adoption of the 1933 and 1934 federal securities acts, the state and federal governments have regulated securities concurrently. Issuers must comply with both federal and state securities laws, and exemptions from federal law are not exemptions from state laws.

The dual federal and state system has not always worked well, particularly during the early 1990s, when the securities markets underwent considerable expansion. In response, Congress passed the National Securities Markets Improvement Act of 1996, which eliminated some of the duplicate regulations and gave the SEC exclusive power to regulate most national securities activities. The National Conference of Commissioners on Uniform State Laws then substantially revised the Uniform Securities Act to coordinate state and federal securities regulation and enforcement efforts. The new version was offered to the states for adoption in 2002. Seventeen states have adopted the Uniform Securities Act.[38]

---

38. At the time this book went to press, the Uniform Securities Act had been adopted in Georgia, Hawaii, Idaho, Indiana, Iowa, Kansas, Maine, Michigan, Minnesota, Mississippi, Missouri, New Mexico, Oklahoma, South Carolina, South Dakota, Vermont, and Wisconsin, as well as in the U.S. Virgin Islands. You can find current information on state adoptions at www. nccusl.org.

SECTION 5
CORPORATE GOVERNANCE

Corporate governance can be narrowly defined as the relationship between a corporation and its shareholders. According to a broader definition, corporate governance specifies the rights and responsibilities among different corporate participants (including stakeholders) and spells out the rules and procedures for making decisions on corporate affairs. Regardless of the way it is defined, effective corporate governance requires more than just compliance with laws and regulations.

Because corporate ownership (by shareholders) is separated from corporate control (by officers and managers), effective corporate governance is essential in large corporations. Otherwise, officers and managers may be able to advance their own interests at the expense of the shareholders. The well-publicized corporate scandals in the first decade of the 2000s clearly illustrate the reasons for concern about managerial opportunism. Indeed, corporate governance has become an issue of concern for corporate entities around the world. With the globalization of business, a corporation's bad acts (or lack of control systems) can have far-reaching consequences.

Attempts at Aligning the Interests of Officers with Those of Shareholders

Some corporations have sought to align the financial interests of their officers with those of the company's shareholders by providing the officers with **stock options,** which enable them to purchase shares of the corporation's stock at a set price. When the market price rises above that level, the officers can sell their shares for a profit. Because a stock's market price generally increases as the corporation prospers, the options give the officers a financial stake in the corporation's well-being and supposedly encourage them to work hard for the benefit of the shareholders.

Options have turned out to be an imperfect device for providing effective governance, however. Executives in some companies have "cooked" the company's books in order to keep share prices high so that they could sell their stock for a profit. Executives in other firms have had their options "repriced" so that they did not suffer any loss when the share price declined (and so that they could still profit from future increases above the lowered share price). Thus, although stock options theoretically can motivate officers to protect shareholder interests, stock option plans have sometimes become a way for officers to take advantage of shareholders.

The Goal Is to Promote Accountability

Effective corporate governance standards are designed to address problems such as those briefly discussed above and to motivate officers to make decisions that promote the financial interests of the company's shareholders. Generally, corporate governance entails corporate decision-making structures that monitor employees (particularly officers) to ensure that they are acting for the benefit of the shareholders. Thus, corporate governance involves, at a minimum:

1. The audited reporting of financial conditions at the corporation so that managers can be evaluated.
2. Legal protections for shareholders so that violators of the law who attempt to take advantage of shareholders can be punished for misbehavior and victims can recover damages for any associated losses.

Effective corporate governance can have considerable practical significance because corporate decision makers necessarily become more accountable for their actions to shareholders. Firms that are more accountable to shareholders typically report higher profits, higher sales growth, higher firm value, and other economic advantages. Thus, a corporation with better corporate governance and greater accountability to investors may also have a higher valuation than a corporation that is less concerned about governance.

Governance and Corporate Law

State corporation statutes set up the legal framework for corporate governance. Under the corporate law of Delaware, where most major companies incorporate, all corporations must have certain structures of corporate governance in place. The most important structure, of course, is the board of directors because the board makes the major decisions about the future of the corporation.

Some argue that shareholder democracy is the key to improving corporate governance. If shareholders could have more say on major corporate decisions, they presumably could have more control over the corporation. Essential to shareholder democracy is the election of the board of directors, usually at the corporation's annual meeting.

Although shareholders vote for directors, they often find it difficult to elect their nominees because organizing enough shareholders to sway an election can be very costly. In 2010, the SEC announced that it would work to modernize shareholder voting and proxy rules to reduce these costs and give shareholders direct access to other shareholders through the company's facilities for communicating with shareholders. The SEC's goal is to make the contest more even between the shareholders' candidates and the company's nominees.

THE BOARD OF DIRECTORS Under corporate law, a corporation must have a board of directors elected by the shareholders. Almost anyone can become a director, though some organizations, such as the New York Stock Exchange, require certain standards of service for directors of their listed corporations.

Directors are responsible for ensuring that the corporation's officers are operating wisely and in the exclusive interest of shareholders. Directors receive reports from the officers and give them managerial directions. In reality, though, corporate directors devote a relatively small amount of time to monitoring officers.

Ideally, shareholders would monitor the directors' supervision of the officers. In practice, however, it can be difficult for shareholders to monitor directors and hold them responsible for corporate failings. Although the directors can be sued if they fail to do their jobs effectively, directors are rarely held personally liable.

THE COMPENSATION COMMITTEE An important committee of the board of directors, mentioned in Chapter 19, is the *compensation committee,* which determines the compensation to be paid to the company's officers. As part of this process, the committee must assess the officers' performance and design a compensation system that will best align the officers' interests with those of the shareholders.

The Sarbanes-Oxley Act of 2002

As discussed in Chapter 4, in 2002 following a series of corporate scandals, Congress passed the Sarbanes-Oxley Act (see Appendix E for excerpts and explanatory comments). The act addresses certain issues relating to corporate governance. Generally, the act attempts to increase corporate accountability by imposing strict disclosure requirements and harsh penalties for violations of securities laws. Among other things, the act requires chief corporate executives to take personal responsibility for the accuracy of financial statements and reports that are filed with the SEC.

REPORTING ON EFFECTIVENESS OF INTERNAL CONTROLS The Sarbanes-Oxley Act requires all public companies to assess the effectiveness of their internal controls over financial reporting and to comply with certain procedures. Although the 2002 act initially required all public companies to have an independent auditor file a report with the SEC on management's assessment of internal controls, Congress enacted an exemption for smaller companies in 2010. In an effort to reduce compliance costs, public companies with a market capitalization, or public float, of less than $75 million no longer need to have an auditor report on management's assessment of internal controls.

OTHER PROVISIONS Additionally, the act requires that certain financial and stock-transaction reports be filed with the SEC earlier than was required under the previous rules. The act also created a new entity, called the Public Company Accounting Oversight Board, which regulates and oversees public accounting firms. Other provisions of the act established new private civil actions and expanded the SEC's remedies in administrative and civil actions. Because of the importance of this act, we present some of its key provisions relating to corporate accountability in Exhibit 29–4.

INTERNAL CONTROLS AND ACCOUNTABILITY The Sarbanes-Oxley Act includes some traditional securities law provisions but also introduces direct *federal* corporate governance requirements for public companies (companies whose shares are traded in the public securities markets). The law addresses many of the corporate governance procedures just discussed and creates new requirements in an attempt to make the system work more effectively. The requirements deal with independent monitoring of company officers by both the board of directors and the auditors.

Sections 302 and 404 of the act require high-level managers (the most senior officers) to establish and maintain an effective system of internal controls. Moreover, senior management must reassess the system's effectiveness on an annual basis. Some companies already had strong and effective internal control systems in place before the passage of the act, but others had to take expensive steps to bring their internal controls up to the new federal standards.

These include "disclosure controls and procedures" to ensure that the company's financial reports are accurate and timely. Assessment must involve documenting financial results and accounting policies before reporting the results. After the act was passed, hundreds of publicly held companies reported that they had identified and corrected shortcomings in their internal control systems.

CERTIFICATION AND MONITORING Section 906 requires that chief executive officers and chief financial officers certify the accuracy of the information in the corporate financial statements. These corporate officers are subject to both civil and criminal penalties for violations of this section. This requirement makes the officers directly accountable for the accuracy of their financial reporting and precludes any "ignorance defense" if shortcomings are later discovered.

The Sarbanes-Oxley Act also includes requirements to improve directors' monitoring of officers' activities. All members of the corporate audit committee for public companies must be outside directors. The New York Stock Exchange has a similar rule that also extends to the board's compensation committee. The audit committee must have a written charter that sets out its duties and provides for performance appraisal. At least one "financial expert" must serve on the audit committee, which must hold executive meetings without company officers being present. The audit committee must also establish procedures to encourage whistleblowers (see Chapter 21) to report violations. In addition to reviewing the internal controls, the committee also monitors the actions of the outside auditor.

SECTION 6
ONLINE SECURITIES FRAUD

A major problem facing the SEC today is how to enforce the antifraud provisions of the securities laws in the online environment. In 1999, in the first cases involving illegal online securities offerings, the SEC filed suit against three individuals for illegally offering securities on an Internet auction site.[39] In essence, all three indicated that their companies would soon go public and attempted to sell unregistered securities via the Web auction site. All of these

---

39. *In re Davis,* SEC Administrative File No. 3-10080 (October 20, 1999); *In re Haas,* SEC Administrative File No. 3-10081 (October 20, 1999); and *In re Sitaras,* SEC Administrative File No. 3-10082 (October 20, 1999).

EXHIBIT 29-4 • **Some Key Provisions of the Sarbanes-Oxley Act of 2002 Relating to Corporate Accountability**

Certification Requirements: Under Section 906 of the Sarbanes-Oxley Act, the chief executive officers (CEOs) and chief financial officers (CFOs) of most major companies listed on public stock exchanges must certify financial statements that are filed with the SEC. CEOs and CFOs have to certify that filed financial reports "fully comply" with SEC requirements and that all of the information reported "fairly represents in all material respects, the financial conditions and results of operations of the issuer."

Under Section 302 of the act, CEOs and CFOs of reporting companies are required to certify that a signing officer reviewed each quarterly and annual filing with the SEC and that it contains no untrue statements of material fact. Also, the signing officer or officers must certify that they have established an internal control system to identify all material information and that any deficiencies in the system were disclosed to the auditors.

Effectiveness of Internal Controls on Financial Reporting: Under Section 404(a), all public companies are required to assess the effectiveness of their internal controls over financial reporting. Section 404(b) requires independent auditors to report on management's assessment of internal controls, but companies with a public float of less than $75 million are exempted from this requirement.

Loans to Directors and Officers: Section 402 prohibits any reporting company, as well as any private company that is filing an initial public offering, from making personal loans to directors and executive officers (with a few limited exceptions, such as for certain consumer and housing loans).

Protection for Whistleblowers: Section 806 protects "whistleblowers"—employees who report ("blow the whistle" on) securities violations by their employers—from being fired or in any way discriminated against by their employers.

Blackout Periods: Section 306 prohibits certain types of securities transactions during "blackout periods"—periods during which the issuer's ability to purchase, sell, or otherwise transfer funds in individual account plans (such as pension funds) is suspended.

Enhanced Penalties for:

• *Violations of Section 906 Certification Requirements*—A CEO or CFO who certifies a financial report or statement filed with the SEC knowing that the report or statement does not fulfill all of the requirements of Section 906 will be subject to criminal penalties of up to $1 million in fines, ten years in prison, or both. *Willful* violators of the certification requirements may be subject to $5 million in fines, twenty years in prison, or both.

• *Violations of the Securities Exchange Act of 1934*—Penalties for securities fraud under the 1934 act were also increased (as discussed earlier in this chapter). Individual violators may be fined up to $5 million, imprisoned for up to twenty years, or both. *Willful* violators may be imprisoned for up to twenty-five years in addition to being fined.

• *Destruction or Alteration of Documents*—Anyone who alters, destroys, or conceals documents or otherwise obstructs any official proceeding will be subject to fines, imprisonment for up to twenty years, or both.

• *Other Forms of White-Collar Crime*—The act stiffened the penalties for certain criminal violations, such as federal mail and wire fraud, and ordered the U.S. Sentencing Commission to revise the sentencing guidelines for white-collar crimes (see Chapter 7).

Statute of Limitations for Securities Fraud: Section 804 provides that a private right of action for securities fraud may be brought no later than two years after the discovery of the violation or five years after the violation, whichever is earlier.

actions were in violation of Sections 5, 17(a)(1), and 17(a)(3) of the 1933 Securities Act. Since then, the SEC has brought a variety of Internet-related fraud cases and regularly issues interpretive releases to explain how securities laws apply in the online environment.

Investment Scams

As discussed in Chapter 7, the Internet has created a new vehicle for criminals to use to commit fraud and provided them with new ways of targeting innocent investors. The criminally inclined can use spam, online newsletters and bulletin boards, chat rooms, blogs, and tweets to spread false information and perpetrate fraud. For a relatively small cost, criminals can even build sophisticated Web pages to facilitate their investment scams.

Investment scams come in countless variations, but they almost always promise spectacular returns for small investments. A person might receive spam e-mail, for example, that falsely claims that a home business can "turn $5 into $60,000 in just three to six weeks." Another popular investment scam claims "a stimulus package has arrived" and promises individuals that they can make $100,000 a year using their home computer. Although most people today are dubious of the bogus claims made in spam messages, such offers can appear more attractive during times of economic recession. Often, investment scams are simply the electronic version of pyramid schemes in which the participants attempt to profit solely by recruiting new participants.

Online Investment Newsletters and Forums

Hundreds of online investment newsletters provide free information on stocks. Legitimate online newsletters can help investors gather valuable information, but some online newsletters are used for fraud. The law allows companies to pay people who write these newsletters to tout their securities, but the newsletters are required to disclose who paid for the advertising. Many fraudsters either fail to disclose or lie about who paid them. Thus, an investor reading an online newsletter may believe that the information is unbiased, when in fact the fraudsters will directly profit by convincing investors to buy or sell particular stocks.

The same deceptive tactics can be used on online bulletin boards (such as newsgroups and usenet groups), blogs, and social networking sites, including Twitter. While hiding their true identity, fraudsters may falsely pump up a company or reveal some "inside" information about a new product or lucrative contract to convince people to invest. By using multiple aliases on an online forum, a single person can easily create the illusion of widespread interest in a small stock.

Ponzi Schemes

In recent years, the SEC has filed an increasing number of enforcement actions against perpetrators of Ponzi schemes. In these scams, named after Charles Ponzi, the swindler promises high returns to investors and then uses their funds to pay previous investors. Ponzi schemes sometimes target U.S. residents and convince them to invest in offshore companies or banks. Other times, Ponzi schemes claim to offer risk-free or low-risk investments to lure investors.

CASE IN POINT Michael C. Regan told investors that he had an MBA and a proven track record of successful securities trading. As evidence, he offered fake financial statements and tax returns that showed high account balances. In reality, Regan did not have an MBA, was not a registered investment adviser, and had not traded any securities for several years. Regan promised investors returns averaging 20 percent with minimal risk and claimed to be using an investment strategy based on "short-term price trends." He used less than half of the funds entrusted to him for trading purposes and spent at least $2.4 million for his personal and family expenses. In 2009, the SEC filed a complaint alleging that Regan had engaged in a multimillion-dollar Ponzi scheme. Regan agreed to settle the case and return more than $8.7 million (plus interest) of the wrongfully acquired funds.[40]

---

40. "SEC Charges Investment Adviser in Multi-Million Dollar Ponzi Scheme." Litigation Release No. 21102. *www.sec.gov*. 24 June 2009: n.p. Web.

REVIEWING
Investor Protection and Corporate Governance

Dale Emerson served as the chief financial officer for Reliant Electric Co., a distributor of electricity serving portions of Montana and North Dakota. Reliant was in the final stages of planning a takeover of Dakota Gasworks, Inc., a natural gas distributor that operated solely within North Dakota. Emerson went on a weekend fishing trip with his uncle, Ernest Wallace. Emerson mentioned to Wallace that he had been putting in a lot of extra hours at the office planning a takeover of Dakota Gasworks. When he returned from the fishing trip, Wallace purchased $20,000 worth of Reliant stock. Three weeks later, Reliant made a tender offer to Dakota Gasworks stockholders and purchased 57 percent of Dakota Gasworks stock. Over the next two weeks, the price of Reliant stock rose 72 percent before leveling out. Wallace then sold his Reliant stock for a gross profit of $14,400. Using the information presented in the chapter, answer the following questions.

REVIEWING

Investor Protection and Corporate Governance, Continued

1. Would registration with the SEC be required for Dakota Gasworks securities? Why or why not?
2. Did Emerson violate Section 10(b) of the Securities Exchange Act of 1934 and SEC Rule 10b-5? Why or why not?
3. What theory or theories might a court use to hold Wallace liable for insider trading?
4. Under the Sarbanes-Oxley Act of 2002, who would be required to certify the accuracy of the financial statements Reliant filed with the SEC?

DEBATE THIS: *Insider trading should be legalized.*

TERMS AND CONCEPTS

accredited investor 633
blue sky laws 643

corporate governance 644
free-writing prospectus 630
insider trading 635
investment company 632

investment contract 629
mutual fund 632
prospectus 629
red herring prospectus 630

SEC Rule 10b-5 635
stock option 644
tippee 638
tombstone ad 630

QUESTIONS AND CASE PROBLEMS

29–1. Registration Requirements Estrada Hermanos, Inc., a corporation incorporated and doing business in Florida, decides to sell $1 million worth of its common stock to the public. The stock will be sold only within the state of Florida. José Estrada, the chair of the board, says the offering need not be registered with the Securities and Exchange Commission. His brother, Gustavo, disagrees. Who is right? Explain.

29–2. QUESTION WITH SAMPLE ANSWER: Registration Requirements.

Huron Corp. has 300,000 common shares outstanding. The owners of these outstanding shares live in several different states. Huron has decided to split the 300,000 shares two for one. Will Huron Corp. have to file a registration statement and prospectus on the 300,000 new shares to be issued as a result of the split? Explain.

• **For a sample answer to Question 29–2, go to Appendix F at the end of this text.**

29–3. Insider Trading David Gain was the chief executive officer (CEO) of Forest Media Corp., which became interested in acquiring RS Communications, Inc., in 2010.

To initiate negotiations, Gain met with RS's CEO, Gill Raz, on Friday, July 12. Two days later, Gain phoned his brother Mark, who bought 3,800 shares of RS stock on the following Monday. Mark discussed the deal with their father, Jordan, who bought 20,000 RS shares on Thursday. On July 25, the day before the RS bid was due, Gain phoned his parents' home, and Mark bought another 3,200 RS shares. The same routine was followed over the next few days, with Gain periodically phoning Mark or Jordan, both of whom continued to buy RS shares. Forest's bid was refused, but on August 5, RS announced its merger with another company. The price of RS stock rose 30 percent, increasing the value of Mark and Jordan's shares by $664,024 and $412,875, respectively. Did Gain engage in insider trading? What is required to impose sanctions for this offense? Could a court hold Gain liable? Why or why not?

29–4. Securities Laws In 1997, WTS Transnational, Inc., required financing to develop a prototype of an unpatented fingerprint-verification system. At the time, WTS had no revenue, $655,000 in liabilities, and only $10,000 in assets. Thomas Cavanagh and Frank Nicolois, who operated an investment banking company called U.S. Milestone (USM), arranged the financing using Curbstone Acquisition Corp. Curbstone had no assets but had registered approximately 3.5 million shares of stock with the Securities and Exchange Commission (SEC). Under the terms of the deal, Curbstone acquired WTS, and the resulting entity was named Electro-Optical Systems Corp. (EOSC). New EOSC shares were issued to all of the WTS shareholders. Only Cavanagh and others affiliated with USM could sell EOSC stock to the public, however. Over the next few months, these individuals issued false press releases, made small deceptive purchases of EOSC shares at high prices, distributed hundreds of thousands of shares to friends and relatives, and sold their own shares at inflated prices through third party companies they owned. When the SEC began to investigate, the share price fell to its actual value, and innocent investors lost more than $15 million. Were any securities laws violated in this case? If so, what might be an appropriate remedy? [*SEC v. Cavanagh*, 445 F.3d 105 (2d Cir. 2006)]

29–5. Securities Trading Between 1994 and 1998, Richard Svoboda, a credit officer for NationsBank N.A., in Dallas, Texas, evaluated and approved his employer's extensions of credit to clients. These responsibilities gave Svoboda access to nonpublic information about the clients' earnings, performance, acquisitions, and business plans in confidential memos, e-mail, credit applications, and other sources. Svoboda devised a scheme with Michael Robles, an independent accountant, to use this information to trade securities. Pursuant to their scheme, Robles traded in the securities of more than twenty different companies and profited by more than $1 million. Despite their agreement that Robles would do all of the trading, Svoboda also executed trades on his own and made profits of more than $200,000. Aware that their scheme violated NationsBank's policy, they attempted to conduct their trades so as to avoid suspicion. When NationsBank questioned Svoboda about his actions, he lied, refused to cooperate, and was fired. Did Svoboda or Robles commit any crimes? Is either of them subject to civil liability? If so, who could file a suit, and on what ground? What are the possible sanctions? What might be a defense? How should a court rule? Discuss. [*SEC v. Svoboda*, 409 F.Supp.2d 331 (S.D.N.Y. 2006)]

29–6. CASE PROBLEM WITH SAMPLE ANSWER: Duty to Disclose.

Orphan Medical, Inc., was a pharmaceutical company that focused on central nervous system disorders. Its major product was the drug Xyrem. In June 2004, Orphan merged with Jazz Pharmaceuticals, Inc., and Orphan shareholders received $10.75 per share for their stock. Before the merger was final, Orphan completed a phase of testing of Xyrem that indicated that the Food and Drug Administration (FDA) would allow the drug to proceed to the next stage of testing, which was necessary for the drug to be more widely marketed. If that happened, the value of the drug and Orphan would increase, and the stock would have been worth more than $10.75. Little Gem Life Sciences, LLC, was an Orphan shareholder that had received $10.75 per share for its stock. It sued,

claiming violations of federal securities laws because shareholders were not told, during the merger process, that the current stage of FDA tests had been successful. Little Gem claimed that if the information had been public, the stock price would have been higher. The federal district court dismissed the suit, holding that it did not meet the standards required by the Private Securities Litigation Reform Act. Little Gem appealed. Did Orphan's directors have a duty to reveal all relevant drug-testing information to shareholders? Why or why not? [Little Gem Life Sciences LLC v. Orphan Medical, Inc., 537 F.3d 913 (8th Cir. 2008)]

- **To view a sample answer for Problem 29–6, go to this book's Web site at www.cengage.com/blaw/cross, select "Chapter 29," and click on "Case Problem with Sample Answer."**

29–7. Violations of the 1934 Act To comply with accounting principles, a company that engages in software development must either "expense" the cost (record it immediately on the company's financial statement) or "capitalize" it (record it as a cost incurred in increments over time). If the project is in the pre- or post-development stage, the cost must be expensed. Otherwise it may be capitalized. Capitalizing a cost makes a company look more profitable in the short term. Digimarc Corp., which provides secure personal identification documents, announced that it had improperly capitalized software development costs over at least the previous eighteen months. The errors resulted in $2.7 million in overstated earnings, requiring a restatement of prior financial statements. Zucco Partners, LLC, which had bought Digimarc stock within the relevant period, filed a suit in a federal district court against the firm. Zucco claimed that it could show that there had been disagreements within Digimarc over its accounting. Is this sufficient to establish a violation of SEC Rule 10b-5? Why or why not? [*Zucco Partners, LLC v. Digimarc Corp.*, 552 F.3d 981 (9th Cir. 2009)]

29–8. Insider Trading Jabil Circuit, Inc., is a publicly traded electronics and technology company headquartered in St. Petersburg, Florida. In 2008, a group of shareholders who had owned Jabil stock from 2001 to 2007 sued the company and its auditors, directors, and officers for insider trading. Stock options were a part of Jabil's compensation for executives. In some situations, stock options were backdated to a point in time when the stock price was lower, making the options worth more to certain company executives. Backdating is legal as long as it is reported, but Jabil did not report the fact that backdating had occurred. Thus, expenses were understated and net income was overstated by millions of dollars. The shareholders claimed that by rigging the value of the stock options by backdating, the executives had engaged in insider trading and that there had been a general practice among the executives of selling stock before unfavorable news about the company was reported to the public. The shareholders, however, had no specific information about these stock trades or about when (or even if) a particular executive was aware of any accounting errors during the time of any backdating purchases. Were the shareholders' allegations sufficient to assert that insider trading had occurred under SEC Rule 10b-5? Why or why not? [*Edward J. Goodman Life Income Trust v. Jabil Circuit, Inc.*, 594 F.3d 783 (11th Cir. 2010)]

29–9. A QUESTION OF ETHICS: Violations of the 1934 Act.

Melvin Lyttle told John Montana and Paul Knight about a "Trading Program" that purportedly would buy and sell securities in deals that were fully insured, as well as monitored and controlled by the Federal Reserve. Without checking the details or even verifying whether the Program existed, Montana and Knight, with Lyttle's help, began to sell interests in the Program to investors. For a minimum investment of $1 million, the investors were promised extraordinary rates of return—from 10 percent to as much as 100 percent per week—without risk. They were told, among other things, that the Program would "utilize banks that can ensure full bank integrity of The Transaction whose undertaking[s] are in complete harmony with international banking rules and protocol and who guarantee maximum security of a Funder's Capital Placement Amount." Nothing was required but the investors' funds and their silence—the Program was to be kept secret. Over a four-month period in 1999, Montana raised approximately $23 million from twenty-two investors. The promised gains did not accrue, however. Instead, Montana, Lyttle, and Knight depleted investors' funds in high-risk trades or spent the funds on themselves. [SEC v. Montana, 464 F.Supp.2d 772 (S.D.Ind. 2006)]

(a) The Securities and Exchange Commission (SEC) filed a suit in a federal district court against Montana and the others, seeking an injunction, civil penalties, and refund of profits with interest. The SEC alleged, among other things, violations of Section 10(b) of the Securities Exchange Act of 1934 and SEC Rule 10b-5. What is required to establish such violations? Describe how and why the facts in this case meet, or fail to meet, these requirements.

(b) It is often remarked, "There's a sucker born every minute!" Does that phrase describe the Program's investors? Ultimately, about half of the investors recouped the amount they invested. Should the others be considered at least partly responsible for their own losses? Why or why not?

29–10. VIDEO QUESTION: Disclosure under SEC Rule 10b-5.

Go to this text's Web site at **www.cengage.com/ blaw/cross** and select "Chapter 29." Click on "Video Questions" and view the video titled *Real World Legal: Jack's Restaurant, Scene 1.* Then answer the following questions.

(a) Assuming that the companies involved in the merger are Section 12 companies, what statutory provisions prohibit Susan from trading company stock based on her inside knowledge of the merger with GTS?

(b) Did Susan breach a fiduciary duty to the corporation by telling the bartender about the proposed merger? Does the fact that she may be laid off by the company after the merger affect her duties? Explain.

(c) Under what legal theory might it be illegal for the bartender to buy shares in the company based on the information that he got from Susan? Analyze the owner's potential liability. Is there enough evidence of *scienter* in this scenario for the Securities and Exchange Commission to file criminal charges against Susan if the bartender buys the stock? Discuss.

LEGAL RESEARCH EXERCISES ON THE WEB

Go to this text's Web site at **www.cengage.com/blaw/cross**, select "Chapter 29," and click on "Practical Internet Exercises." There you will find the following Internet research exercises that you can perform to learn more about the topics covered in this chapter.

Practical Internet Exercise 29–1: **Legal Perspective**
Electronic Delivery

Practical Internet Exercise 29–2: **Management Perspective**
The SEC's Role

If this text had been written a hundred years ago, it would have had little to say about federal government regulation. Today, in contrast, just about every area of economic activity is regulated by the government. Ethical issues in government regulation arise because regulation, by its very nature, means that some traditional rights and freedoms must be given up to ensure that other rights and freedoms are protected. Essentially, government regulation brings two ethical principles into conflict. On the one hand, deeply embedded in American culture is the idea that the government should play a limited role in directing our lives. On the other hand, one of the basic functions of government is to protect the welfare of individuals and the environment in which they live.

Ultimately, almost every law or rule regulating business represents a decision to give up certain rights in order to protect other perceived rights. In this *Focus on Ethics* feature, we look at some of the ethical aspects of government regulation.

Credit Reporting Agencies and "Blacklisting"

Today, some consumer credit reporting agencies will conduct an online investigation of a person's history of credit disputes and litigation. Physicians and landlords frequently use such services to learn whether prospective patients or tenants have a history of suing their physicians or their landlords. One service, for example, allows physicians, for a fee, to perform more than two hundred online name searches to find out if a prospective patient was ever a plaintiff in a malpractice suit. Other services available to merchants (such as BadCustomer.com) keep a running tally of customers who have requested a credit-card reversal, called a *chargeback,* after paying a merchant. Even a single chargeback can cause merchants to reject a consumer's card in the future.

Users say that these services are an ideal way to screen out undesirable patients and applicants, and thereby reduce the risk of being sued. Consumer rights advocates, however, claim that the sale of such information is akin to "blacklisting"—discriminating against potential customers, patients, or tenants on the basis of previous disputes and litigation. In the last decade, these practices have led to complaints of unfairness, as well as lawsuits against reporting agencies. By and large, though, consumers have little recourse unless what is reported about them is inaccurate.

Consumer Safety

Consumers have become increasingly concerned about the safety of the products they buy, especially children's toys. Many of the toys—and other goods— sold in the United States are imported, often from China. Domestic manufacturers are unable or unwilling to compete with Chinese toy makers. After some well-publicized safety lapses with imported toys, many Americans have called for increased regulation of products from low-cost Chinese suppliers.

Certainly, there is an economic and even ethical trade-off here: accept lower-priced, less-than-perfect products from foreign low-cost producers or impose stricter regulations on imports and have the U.S. consumer pay a higher price. We might also note that not all problems are due to the foreign producers. Wal-Mart, which buys millions of Chinese toys each year, criticized its Chinese suppliers when defects were found in some toys. Later, though, Wal-Mart publicly apologized to the government of China because it turned out that the Chinese suppliers had followed Wal-Mart's specifications, which were the basis of the safety problems.

Environmental Law

Questions of fairness inevitably arise in regard to environmental law. Has the government gone too far—or not far enough—in regulating businesses in the interest of protecting the environment? At what point do the costs of environmental regulations become too burdensome for society to bear? Consider the problem of toxic waste. Although everybody is in favor of cleaning up America's toxic waste dumps, nobody knows what this task will ultimately cost. Moreover, there is no agreed-on standard as to how clean a site must be before it no longer poses any threat. Must 100 percent of the contamination be removed, or would removal of some lesser amount achieve a reasonable degree of environmental quality?

Concerns over Pharmaceuticals in Drinking Water

The amount of pharmaceuticals used by the U.S. public and in agriculture (antibiotics and hormones given to livestock) has grown substantially in recent years. Now trace amounts of many drugs have been detected in our nation's water supply. In 2008, for example, the drinking water of at least 41 million Americans in twenty-four regions across the country was found to contain small amounts of prescription drugs. Some of these trace amounts came from unmetabolized drugs that had passed through the humans and animals that ingested them, but the rest had been flushed down the toilet. For years, pharmacists, physicians, and the federal government have recommended that people dispose of unused medications by flushing them away. This prevents children from accidentally ingesting the drugs and keeps controlled substances such as the painkillers oxycodone and morphine from falling into the hands of people who might abuse them. In making these recommendations, however, no one considered the long-term effect on the environment of adding pharmaceuticals to the water supply.

The quantities present in water now are far below medicinal doses, but no one knows how long-term exposure to random combinations of drugs will affect humans or wildlife. As yet, there is little scientific evidence about the long-term effects. The federal government does not require drinking water to be tested for drugs, so Americans do not know whether their drinking water is contaminated. Requiring that water be tested and that all traces of drugs be filtered from it would be enormously expensive.

Global Environmental Issues

Pollution does not respect geographic borders. Indeed, one of the reasons that the federal government became involved in environmental protection was that state regulation alone apparently could not solve the problem of air or water pollution. Pollutants generated in one state move in the air and water to other states. Nor does pollution respect national borders. Environmental issues, perhaps more than any others, bring home to everyone the fact that the world today is truly a global community. What one country does or does not do with respect to environmental preservation may be felt by citizens in countries thousands of miles away.

Global Warming. Another challenging—and controversial—issue is potential global warming. The fear is that emissions, largely from combustion of fossil fuels, will remain in the atmosphere and create a "greenhouse effect" by preventing heat from radiating outward. Concerns over this issue have led to many attempts to force all world polluters to "clean up their acts." For example, leaders of 187 nations have already agreed to reduce emissions of greenhouse gases in their respective countries. They did this when they ratified the Kyoto Protocol, which was drawn up at a world summit meeting held in Kyoto, Japan, in 1997. The Kyoto Protocol, which is often referred to as the global warming treaty, established different rates of reduction in greenhouse emissions for different countries or regions. Most nations, however, including the United States, will not meet the treaty's objectives. Many claim the treaty is not effective because it does not address the problem of curbing greenhouse gases from most of the developing world.

Is Economic Development the Answer? Economists have shown that economic development is the quickest way to reduce pollution worldwide. After a nation reaches a certain per capita income level, the more economic growth the nation experiences, the lower the pollution output. This occurs because richer nations have the resources to pay for pollution reduction. For example, industries in the United States pollute much less per unit of output than do industries in developing nations—because we are willing to pay for pollution abatement. Even among developed nations, the United States is a leader in curbing pollution. Indeed, in the last ten years, the United States saw a much smaller increase in greenhouse gases than did the European Union (EU).

Land-Use Regulations and the "Takings Clause"

When property owners claim that a "regulatory taking" has occurred, the courts usually decide the issue on a case-by-case basis. In other words, there is no general rule that indicates whether a specific situation will be deemed a taking.

In a case decided in 2010, a group of Florida beachfront property owners challenged the constitutionality of the state's decision to add seventy-five feet of sand to the shoreline. Under Florida law, the boundary between private beachfront property and state-owned land is ordinarily the average high-water line. The state owns any land submerged beneath the ocean or other navigable waters. It is common for storms to cause some fluctuation in the shoreline, however, as sand is deposited or washed away by waves. A change that occurs gradually and imperceptibly over time is called an *accretion,* whereas a sudden change is called an *avulsion.* If an accretion deposits more sand on the shore, the owners of private beachfront property automatically acquire ownership rights to more land—to the new high-water line. If an avulsion occurs, however, the property owners' boundaries remain the same, so the state owns the land abutting the water's edge.

As a result of several hurricanes, 6.9 miles of beach were eroded (an avulsion) in the city of Destin and Walton County. The state therefore requested and received a permit from the Florida Department of Environmental Protection to add seventy-five feet of dry sand on its side (the seaward side) of the high-water line. Owners of the private beachfront property in the area formed a nonprofit corporation to fight the proposed addition of sand, but they lost at an administrative hearing. They then filed a lawsuit claiming that the state's action constituted an unlawful taking of their beachfront property.

The Courts Disagree A Florida appellate court agreed with the property owners that the state had taken their rights to receive accretions and to have their property remain in contact with the water. The Florida Supreme Court reversed, and the United States Supreme Court granted *certiorari.*

The Supreme Court held that Florida had not engaged in an unconstitutional taking. According to the high court, there was no taking because the property owners did not show that their rights to future accretions and to contact with the water were superior to Florida's right to fill in its submerged land. The state did not relocate the property line to take private property, but simply added sand to property that it already

FOCUS ON ETHICS CONTINUES ➡

owned (on the side toward the water). Therefore, the state had a right to restore the beach even though the addition of sand interfered with the property owners' rights to have their property touch the water.[1] Although a majority of the Supreme Court justices concurred in the result, there were substantial differences in their reasoning.

A Question of Fairness The question of whether private landowners should be compensated when their land is essentially "taken" for public use by environmental and land-use regulations clearly involves issues of fairness. On the one hand, states, cities, and other local governments want to preserve their natural resources and need some authority to regulate land use to achieve this goal. On the other hand, private property owners complain that they alone should not have to bear the costs of creating a benefit—such as more sandy beaches for recreation or environmental preservation[2]—that all members of the public enjoy.

Corporate Blogs and Tweets and Securities Fraud

In the fast-paced world of securities trading, there is a great demand for the latest information about companies, earnings, and market conditions. Corporations have adapted to technology by establishing Web sites and blogs, and using other interactive online media, such as Twitter and online shareholder forums. Nearly 20 percent of Fortune 500 companies sponsor blogs. Corporations that use the Internet to distribute information about the company to investors, however, need to make sure that they comply with the regulations issued by the SEC. The SEC treats statements by employees in online media, such as blogs and Twitter, the same as any other company statements for purposes of federal securities laws.

"Tweets" That Contain Financial Information Some corporate blogs include links to corporate employees' Twitter accounts so that readers can communicate directly with, and get updates from, the individual who posted the information. For example, eBay, Inc., launched its corporate blog in 2008. A few months later, Richard Brewer-Hay, a seasoned blogger that eBay hired to report online, began "tweeting" (posting updates on Twitter) about eBay's quarterly earnings and what took place at Silicon Valley technology conferences. Brewer-Hay's tweets gained him a following, but then eBay's lawyers required him to include a regulatory disclaimer with certain posts to avoid problems with the SEC. Many of his followers were disappointed by the company's oversight, which put an end to his spontaneous, personal, and informal style. Brewer-Hay is now much more reserved in his tweets on financial matters and often simply repeats eBay executives' statements verbatim.[3]

A 2008 SEC Release Provides Guidance The reaction of eBay's lawyers to Brewer-Hay's tweets was prompted in part by an interpretive release issued by the SEC in August 2008. The SEC generally embraces new technology and encourages companies to use electronic communication methods. The SEC noted that "the use of the Internet has grown such that, for some companies in certain circumstances, posting of the information on the company's Web site, in and of itself, may be a sufficient method of public disclosure."

The release also addressed company-sponsored blogs, electronic shareholders' forums, and other "interactive Web site features." The SEC acknowledged that blogs and other interactive Web features are a useful means of ongoing communications among companies, their clients, investors, shareholders, and stakeholders. The SEC cautioned, though, that all communications made by or on behalf of a company are subject to the antifraud provisions of federal securities laws. In addition, the release stated that companies cannot require investors to waive protections under federal securities laws as a condition of participating in a blog or forum.[4]

DISCUSSION QUESTIONS

1. If 90 percent of the toxic waste at a given site can be removed for $50,000, but removing the last 10 percent will cost $2 million, is it reasonable to require that the last 10 percent be removed? How would you address this question?

2. In a time of economic recession, should the government wait until there is scientific proof of the harmful effects on humans and wildlife before attempting to regulate pharmaceuticals in drinking water? Or should the government enact legislation to address the problem now—before it becomes worse? Discuss fully.

3. Can you think of a better way that the law can address the problem of global warming, which is clearly not just a national issue? Explain.

4. Is it fair for courts to decide whether a regulatory taking has occurred on a case-by-case basis and not to articulate a general rule on which landowners can rely? Why or why not?

1. *Stop the Beach Renourishment, Inc. v. Florida Department of Environmental Protection*, ___ U.S. ___, 130 S.Ct. 2592, 177 L.Ed.2d 184 (2010).
2. See, for example, *Tahoe-Sierra Preservation Council v. Tahoe Regional Planning Agency*, 535 U.S. 302, 122 S.Ct. 1465, 152 L.Ed.2d 517 (2002).
3. Cari Tuna. "Corporate Blogs and 'Tweets' Must Keep SEC in Mind. *online.wsj.com.* " 27 April 2009: n.p. Web.
4. SEC Release Nos. 34–58288, IC–28351, File No. S7–23–08. Commission Guidance on the Use of Company Web Sites.

How to Brief Cases and Analyze Case Problems

How to Brief Cases

To fully understand the law with respect to business, you need to be able to read and understand court decisions. To make this task easier, you can use a method of case analysis that is called *briefing*. There is a fairly standard procedure that you can follow when you "brief" any court case. You must first read the case opinion carefully. When you feel you understand the case, you can prepare a brief of it.

Although the format of the brief may vary, typically it will present the essentials of the case under headings such as those listed below.

1. **Citation.** Give the full citation for the case, including the name of the case, the date it was decided, and the court that decided it.
2. **Facts.** Briefly indicate (a) the reasons for the lawsuit; (b) the identity and arguments of the plaintiff(s) and defendant(s), respectively; and (c) the lower court's decision—if appropriate.
3. **Issue.** Concisely phrase, in the form of a question, the essential issue before the court. (If more than one issue is involved, you may have two—or even more—questions here.)
4. **Decision.** Indicate here—with a "yes" or "no," if possible—the court's answer to the question (or questions) in the *Issue* section above.
5. **Reason.** Summarize as briefly as possible the reasons given by the court for its decision (or decisions) and the case or statutory law relied on by the court in arriving at its decision.

An Example of a Briefed Sample Court Case

As an example of the format used in briefing cases, we present here a briefed version of the sample court case that was presented in Chapter 1 in Exhibit 1–6 on pages 23–25.

SINGER v. RAEMISCH
United States Court of Appeals, Seventh Circuit, 593 F.3d 529 (2010).

FACTS Kevin Singer, an inmate at Wisconsin's Waupun Correctional Institution, is a devoted player of Dungeons and Dragons (D&D), a fantasy role-playing game. In November 2004, the prison's gang expert received an anonymous letter stating that Singer and three other inmates were trying to recruit others to join a "gang" dedicated to playing D&D. Prison officials searched Singer's cell, confiscated all of his D&D materials, and prohibited him and other inmates from playing D&D. Singer filed a suit in a federal district court against the prison, alleging, in part, that the officials' actions violated his right to free speech under the First Amendment to the U.S. Constitution. The court concluded that the D&D ban was rationally related to a legitimate government interest and issued a judgment in the prison's favor. Singer appealed to the U.S. Court of Appeals for the Seventh Circuit.

ISSUE Can a prison, consistent with the First Amendment, restrict inmates' speech, when that restriction is reasonably viewed as promoting prison security?

DECISION Yes. The U.S. Court of Appeals for the Seventh Circuit affirmed the lower court's judgment.

REASON The court acknowledged that the prison's D&D ban was a restriction of Singer's and the other inmates' constitutional rights. But the court explained, "Prison regulations that restrict inmates' constitutional rights are nevertheless valid if they are reasonably related to legitimate penological interests,"[1] which concern prison management and the treatment of inmates. In this case, the

---

1. *Penological interests* relate to the branch of criminology dealing with prison management and the treatment of offenders.

D&D ban "bears a rational relationship" to those interests. The ban promotes prison security because games such as D&D can "mimic the organization of gangs and lead to their development." The court pointed out that this conclusion was based on the prison gang expert's testimony that D&D can "foster an inmate's obsession with escaping from the real life, correctional environment, fostering hostility, violence and escape behavior." This "can compromise not only the inmate's rehabilitation and effects of positive programming but also endanger the public and jeopardize the safety and security of the institution."

Review of Sample Court Case

Here, we provide a review of the briefed version to indicate the kind of information that is contained in each section.

CITATION The name of the case is *Singer v. Raemisch.* Singer is the plaintiff; Raemisch is the defendant. The U.S. Court of Appeals for the Seventh Circuit decided this case in 2010. The citation states that this case can be found in Volume 593 of the *Federal Reporter, Third Series,* on page 529.

FACTS The *Facts* section identifies the plaintiff and the defendant, describes the events leading up to this suit, the allegations made by the plaintiff in the initial suit, and the lower court's ruling and the party appealing (because this case is a decision of one of the federal appellate courts). The appellant's contention on appeal is also sometimes included here.

ISSUE The *Issue* section presents the central issue (or issues) decided by the court. In this case, the U.S. Court of Appeals for the Seventh Circuit considers whether a prison can restrict the speech of its inmates if that restriction is reasonably viewed as promoting prison security.

DECISION The *Decision* section includes the court's decision on the issues before it. The decision reflects the opinion of the judge or justice hearing the case. Decisions by appellate courts frequently are phrased in reference to the lower court's decision. That is, the appellate court may "affirm" the lower court's ruling or "reverse" it. Here, the court determined that the belief of the prison officials with respect to the effect of unrestricted speech was reasonable. The officials thought that unrestricted speech would compromise prison security. On that basis, the prison could legitimately ban the playing of D&D. The appellate court affirmed the ruling in the prison's favor.

REASON The *Reason* section includes references to the relevant laws and legal principles that were applied in coming to the conclusion arrived at in the case before the court. The relevant law here included the principle that prison regulations restricting inmates' constitutional rights are valid if they reasonably relate to legitimate penological interests. This section also explains the court's application of the law to the facts in this case.

Analyzing Case Problems

In addition to learning how to brief cases, students of business law and the legal environment also find it helpful to know how to analyze case problems. Part of the study of business law and the legal environment usually involves analyzing case problems, such as those included in this text at the end of each chapter.

For each case problem in this book, we provide the relevant background and facts of the lawsuit and the issue before the court. When you are assigned one of these problems, your job will be to determine how the court should decide the issue, and why. In other words, you will need to engage in legal analysis and reasoning. Here, we offer some suggestions on how to make this task less daunting. We begin by presenting a sample problem:

> While Janet Lawson, a famous pianist, was shopping in Quality Market, she slipped and fell on a wet floor in one of the aisles. The floor had recently been mopped by one of the store's employees, but there were no signs warning customers that the floor in that area was wet. As a result of the fall, Lawson injured her right arm and was unable to perform piano concerts for the next six months. Had she been able to perform the scheduled concerts, she would have earned approximately $60,000 over that period of time. Lawson sued Quality Market for this amount, plus another $10,000 in medical expenses. She claimed that the store's failure to warn customers of the wet floor constituted negligence and therefore the market was liable for her injuries. Will the court agree with Lawson? Discuss.

Understand the Facts

This may sound obvious, but before you can analyze or apply the relevant law to a specific set of facts, you must clearly understand those facts. In other words, you should read through the case problem carefully—more than once, if necessary—to make sure you understand the identity of the plaintiff(s) and defendant(s) in the case and the progression of events that led to the lawsuit.

In the sample case problem just given, the identity of the parties is fairly obvious. Janet Lawson is the one bringing the suit; therefore, she is the plaintiff. Quality Market, against whom she is bringing the suit, is the defendant. Some of the case problems you may work on have multiple plaintiffs or defendants. Often, it is helpful to use abbreviations for the parties. To indicate a reference to a plaintiff, for example, the *pi* symbol—π—is often used, and a defendant is denoted by a *delta*—Δ—a triangle.

The events leading to the lawsuit are also fairly straightforward. Lawson slipped and fell on a wet floor, and she contends that Quality Market should be liable for her injuries because it was negligent in not posting a sign warning customers of the wet floor.

When you are working on case problems, realize that the facts should be accepted as they are given. For example, in our sample problem, it should be accepted that the floor was wet and that there was no sign. In other words, avoid making conjectures, such as "Maybe the floor wasn't too wet," or "Maybe an employee was getting a sign to put up," or "Maybe someone stole the sign." Questioning the facts as they are presented only adds confusion to your analysis.

Legal Analysis and Reasoning

Once you understand the facts given in the case problem, you can begin to analyze the case. Recall from Chapter 1 that the IRAC method is a helpful tool to use in the legal analysis and reasoning process. IRAC is an acronym for Issue, Rule, Application, Conclusion. Applying this method to our sample problem would involve the following steps:

1. First, you need to decide what legal **issue** is involved in the case. In our sample case, the basic issue is whether Quality Market's failure to warn customers of the wet floor constituted negligence. As discussed in Chapter 12, negligence is a *tort*—a civil wrong. In a tort lawsuit, the plaintiff seeks to be compensated for another's wrongful act. A defendant will be deemed negligent if he or she breached a duty of care owed to the plaintiff and the breach of that duty caused the plaintiff to suffer harm.

2. Once you have identified the issue, the next step is to determine what **rule of law** applies to the issue. To make this determination, you will want to review carefully the text of the chapter in which the relevant rule of law for the problem appears. Our sample case problem involves the tort of negligence, which is covered in Chapter 12. The applicable rule of law is the tort law principle that business owners owe a duty to exercise reasonable care to protect their customers ("business invitees"). Reasonable care, in this context, includes either removing—or warning customers of—*foreseeable* risks about which the owner *knew* or *should have known*. Business owners need not warn customers of "open and obvious" risks, however. If a business owner breaches this duty of care (fails to exercise the appropriate degree of care toward customers), and the breach of duty causes a customer to be injured, the business owner will be liable to the customer for the customer's injuries.

3. The next—and usually the most difficult—step in analyzing case problems is the **application** of the relevant rule of law to the specific facts of the case you are studying. In our sample problem, applying the tort law principle just discussed presents few difficulties. An employee of the store had mopped the floor in the aisle where Lawson slipped and fell, but no sign was present indicating that the floor was wet. That a customer might fall on a wet floor is clearly a foreseeable risk. Therefore, the failure to warn customers about the wet floor was a breach of the duty of care owed by the business owner to the store's customers.

4. Once you have completed Step 3 in the IRAC method, you should be ready to draw your **conclusion.** In our sample problem, Quality Market is liable to Lawson for her injuries, because the market's breach of its duty of care caused Lawson's injuries.

The fact patterns in the case problems presented in this text are not always as simple as those presented in our sample problem. Often, for example, a case has more than one plaintiff or defendant. A case may also involve more than one issue and have more than one applicable rule of law. Furthermore, in some case problems the facts may indicate that the general rule of law should not apply. For example, suppose that a store employee advised Lawson not to walk on the floor in the aisle because it was wet, but Lawson decided to walk on it anyway. This fact could alter the outcome of the case because the store could then raise the defense of assumption of risk (see Chapter 12). Nonetheless, a careful review of the chapter should always provide you with the knowledge you need to analyze the problem thoroughly and arrive at accurate conclusions.

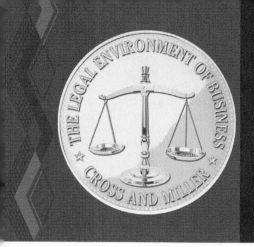

APPENDIX B

The Constitution of the United States

Preamble

We the People of the United States, in Order to form a more perfect Union, establish Justice, insure domestic Tranquility, provide for the common defence, promote the general Welfare, and secure the Blessings of Liberty to ourselves and our Posterity, do ordain and establish this Constitution for the United States of America.

Article I

Section 1. All legislative Powers herein granted shall be vested in a Congress of the United States, which shall consist of a Senate and House of Representatives.

Section 2. The House of Representatives shall be composed of Members chosen every second Year by the People of the several States, and the Electors in each State shall have the Qualifications requisite for Electors of the most numerous Branch of the State Legislature.

No Person shall be a Representative who shall not have attained to the Age of twenty five Years, and been seven Years a Citizen of the United States, and who shall not, when elected, be an Inhabitant of that State in which he shall be chosen.

Representatives and direct Taxes shall be apportioned among the several States which may be included within this Union, according to their respective Numbers, which shall be determined by adding to the whole Number of free Persons, including those bound to Service for a Term of Years, and excluding Indians not taxed, three fifths of all other Persons. The actual Enumeration shall be made within three Years after the first Meeting of the Congress of the United States, and within every subsequent Term of ten Years, in such Manner as they shall by Law direct. The Number of Representatives shall not exceed one for every thirty Thousand, but each State shall have at Least one Representative; and until such enumeration shall be made, the State of New Hampshire shall be entitled to chuse three, Massachusetts eight, Rhode Island and Providence Plantations one, Connecticut five, New York six, New Jersey four, Pennsylvania eight, Delaware one, Maryland six, Virginia ten, North Carolina five, South Carolina five, and Georgia three.

When vacancies happen in the Representation from any State, the Executive Authority thereof shall issue Writs of Election to fill such Vacancies.

The House of Representatives shall chuse their Speaker and other Officers; and shall have the sole Power of Impeachment.

Section 3. The Senate of the United States shall be composed of two Senators from each State, chosen by the Legislature thereof, for six Years; and each Senator shall have one Vote.

Immediately after they shall be assembled in Consequence of the first Election, they shall be divided as equally as may be into three Classes. The Seats of the Senators of the first Class shall be vacated at the Expiration of the second Year, of the second Class at the Expiration of the fourth Year, and of the third Class at the Expiration of the sixth Year, so that one third may be chosen every second Year; and if Vacancies happen by Resignation, or otherwise, during the Recess of the Legislature of any State, the Executive thereof may make temporary Appointments until the next Meeting of the Legislature, which shall then fill such Vacancies.

No Person shall be a Senator who shall not have attained to the Age of thirty Years, and been nine Years a Citizen of the United States, and who shall not, when elected, be an Inhabitant of that State for which he shall be chosen.

The Vice President of the United States shall be President of the Senate, but shall have no Vote, unless they be equally divided.

The Senate shall chuse their other Officers, and also a President pro tempore, in the Absence of the Vice President, or when he shall exercise the Office of President of the United States.

The Senate shall have the sole Power to try all Impeachments. When sitting for that Purpose, they shall be on Oath or Affirmation. When the President of the United States is tried, the Chief Justice shall preside: And no Person shall be convicted without the Concurrence of two thirds of the Members present.

Judgment in Cases of Impeachment shall not extend further than to removal from Office, and disqualification to hold and enjoy any Office of honor, Trust, or Profit under the United States: but the Party convicted shall nevertheless be liable and subject to Indictment, Trial, Judgment, and Punishment, according to Law.

Section 4. The Times, Places and Manner of holding Elections for Senators and Representatives, shall be prescribed in each State by the Legislature thereof; but the Congress may at any time by Law make or alter such Regulations, except as to the Places of chusing Senators.

The Congress shall assemble at least once in every Year, and such Meeting shall be on the first Monday in December, unless they shall by Law appoint a different Day.

Section 5. Each House shall be the Judge of the Elections, Returns, and Qualifications of its own Members, and a Majority of each shall constitute a Quorum to do Business; but a smaller Number may adjourn from day to day, and may be authorized to compel the Attendance of absent Members, in such Manner, and under such Penalties as each House may provide.

Each House may determine the Rules of its Proceedings, punish its Members for disorderly Behavior, and, with the Concurrence of two thirds, expel a Member.

Each House shall keep a Journal of its Proceedings, and from time to time publish the same, excepting such Parts as may in their Judgment require Secrecy; and the Yeas and Nays of the Members of either House on any question shall, at the Desire of one fifth of those Present, be entered on the Journal.

Neither House, during the Session of Congress, shall, without the Consent of the other, adjourn for more than three days, nor to any other Place than that in which the two Houses shall be sitting.

Section 6. The Senators and Representatives shall receive a Compensation for their Services, to be ascertained by Law, and paid out of the Treasury of the United States. They shall in all Cases, except Treason, Felony and Breach of the Peace, be privileged from Arrest during their Attendance at the Session of their respective Houses, and in going to and returning from the same; and for any Speech or Debate in either House, they shall not be questioned in any other Place.

No Senator or Representative shall, during the Time for which he was elected, be appointed to any civil Office under the Authority of the United States, which shall have been created, or the Emoluments whereof shall have been increased during such time; and no Person holding any Office under the United States, shall be a Member of either House during his Continuance in Office.

Section 7. All Bills for raising Revenue shall originate in the House of Representatives; but the Senate may propose or concur with Amendments as on other Bills.

Every Bill which shall have passed the House of Representatives and the Senate, shall, before it become a Law, be presented to the President of the United States; If he approve he shall sign it, but if not he shall return it, with his Objections to the House in which it shall have originated, who shall enter the Objections at large on their Journal, and proceed to reconsider it. If after such Reconsideration two thirds of that House shall agree to pass the Bill, it shall be sent together with the Objections, to the other House, by which it shall likewise be reconsidered, and if approved by two thirds of that House, it shall become a Law. But in all such Cases the Votes of both Houses shall be determined by Yeas and Nays, and the Names of the Persons voting for and against the Bill shall be entered on the Journal of each House respectively. If any Bill shall not be returned by the President within ten Days (Sundays excepted) after it shall have been presented to him, the Same shall be a Law, in like Manner as if he had signed it, unless the Congress by their Adjournment prevent its Return in which Case it shall not be a Law.

Every Order, Resolution, or Vote, to which the Concurrence of the Senate and House of Representatives may be necessary (except on a question of Adjournment) shall be presented to the President of the United States; and before the Same shall take Effect, shall be approved by him, or being disapproved by him, shall be repassed by two thirds of the Senate and House of Representatives, according to the Rules and Limitations prescribed in the Case of a Bill.

Section 8. The Congress shall have Power To lay and collect Taxes, Duties, Imposts and Excises, to pay the Debts and provide for the common Defence and general Welfare of the United States; but all Duties, Imposts and Excises shall be uniform throughout the United States;

To borrow Money on the credit of the United States;

To regulate Commerce with foreign Nations, and among the several States, and with the Indian Tribes;

To establish an uniform Rule of Naturalization, and uniform Laws on the subject of Bankruptcies throughout the United States;

To coin Money, regulate the Value thereof, and of foreign Coin, and fix the Standard of Weights and Measures;

To provide for the Punishment of counterfeiting the Securities and current Coin of the United States;

To establish Post Offices and post Roads;

To promote the Progress of Science and useful Arts, by securing for limited Times to Authors and Inventors the exclusive Right to their respective Writings and Discoveries;

To constitute Tribunals inferior to the supreme Court;

To define and punish Piracies and Felonies committed on the high Seas, and Offenses against the Law of Nations;

To declare War, grant Letters of Marque and Reprisal, and make Rules concerning Captures on Land and Water;

To raise and support Armies, but no Appropriation of Money to that Use shall be for a longer Term than two Years;

To provide and maintain a Navy;

To make Rules for the Government and Regulation of the land and naval Forces;

To provide for calling forth the Militia to execute the Laws of the Union, suppress Insurrections and repel Invasions;

To provide for organizing, arming, and disciplining, the Militia, and for governing such Part of them as may be employed in the Service of the United States, reserving to the States respectively, the Appointment of the Officers, and the Authority of training the Militia according to the discipline prescribed by Congress;

To exercise exclusive Legislation in all Cases whatsoever, over such District (not exceeding ten Miles square) as may, by Cession of particular States, and the Acceptance of Congress, become the Seat of the Government of the United States, and to exercise like Authority over all Places purchased by the Consent of the Legislature of the State in which the Same shall be, for the Erection of Forts, Magazines, Arsenals, dock-Yards, and other needful Buildings;—And

To make all Laws which shall be necessary and proper for carrying into Execution the foregoing Powers, and all other Powers vested by this Constitution in the Government of the United States, or in any Department or Officer thereof.

Section 9. The Migration or Importation of such Persons as any of the States now existing shall think proper to admit, shall not be prohibited by the Congress prior to the Year one thousand eight hundred and eight, but a Tax or duty may be imposed on such Importation, not exceeding ten dollars for each Person.

The privilege of the Writ of Habeas Corpus shall not be suspended, unless when in Cases of Rebellion or Invasion the public Safety may require it.

No Bill of Attainder or ex post facto Law shall be passed.

No Capitation, or other direct, Tax shall be laid, unless in Proportion to the Census or Enumeration herein before directed to be taken.

No Tax or Duty shall be laid on Articles exported from any State.

No Preference shall be given by any Regulation of Commerce or Revenue to the Ports of one State over those of another: nor shall Vessels bound to, or from, one State be obliged to enter, clear, or pay Duties in another.

No Money shall be drawn from the Treasury, but in Consequence of Appropriations made by Law; and a regular Statement and Account of the Receipts and Expenditures of all public Money shall be published from time to time.

No Title of Nobility shall be granted by the United States: And no Person holding any Office of Profit or Trust under them, shall, without the Consent of the Congress, accept of any present, Emolument, Office, or Title, of any kind whatever, from any King, Prince, or foreign State.

Section 10. No State shall enter into any Treaty, Alliance, or Confederation; grant Letters of Marque and Reprisal; coin Money; emit Bills of Credit; make any Thing but gold and silver Coin a Tender in Payment of Debts; pass any Bill of Attainder, ex post facto Law, or Law impairing the Obligation of Contracts, or grant any Title of Nobility.

No State shall, without the Consent of the Congress, lay any Imposts or Duties on Imports or Exports, except what may be absolutely necessary for executing its inspection Laws: and the net Produce of all Duties and Imposts, laid by any State on Imports or Exports, shall be for the Use of the Treasury of the United States; and all such Laws shall be subject to the Revision and Controul of the Congress.

No State shall, without the Consent of Congress, lay any Duty of Tonnage, keep Troops, or Ships of War in time of Peace, enter into any Agreement or Compact with another State, or with a foreign Power, or engage in War, unless actually invaded, or in such imminent Danger as will not admit of delay.

Article II

Section 1. The executive Power shall be vested in a President of the United States of America. He shall hold his Office during the Term of four Years, and, together with the Vice President, chosen for the same Term, be elected, as follows:

Each State shall appoint, in such Manner as the Legislature thereof may direct, a Number of Electors, equal to the whole Number of Senators and Representatives to which the State may be entitled in the Congress; but no Senator or Representative, or Person holding an Office of Trust or Profit under the United States, shall be appointed an Elector.

The Electors shall meet in their respective States, and vote by Ballot for two Persons, of whom one at least shall not be an Inhabitant of the same State with themselves. And they shall make a List of all the Persons voted for, and of the Number of Votes for each; which List they shall sign and certify, and transmit sealed to the Seat of the Government of the United States, directed to the President of the Senate. The President of the Senate shall, in the Presence of the Senate and House of Representatives, open all the Certificates, and the Votes shall then be counted. The Person having the greatest Number of Votes shall be the President, if such Number be a Majority of the whole Number of Electors appointed; and if there be more than one who have such Majority, and have an equal Number of Votes, then the House of Representatives shall immediately chuse by Ballot one of them for President; and if no Person have a Majority, then from the five highest on the List the said House shall in like Manner chuse the President. But in chusing the President, the Votes shall be taken by States, the Representation from each State having one Vote; A quorum for this Purpose shall consist of a Member or Members from two thirds of the States, and a Majority of all the States shall be necessary to a Choice. In every Case, after the Choice of the President, the Person having the greater Number of Votes of the Electors shall be the Vice President. But if there should remain two or more who have equal Votes, the Senate shall chuse from them by Ballot the Vice President.

The Congress may determine the Time of chusing the Electors, and the Day on which they shall give their Votes; which Day shall be the same throughout the United States.

No person except a natural born Citizen, or a Citizen of the United States, at the time of the Adoption of this Constitution, shall be eligible to the Office of President; neither shall any Person be eligible to that Office who shall not have attained to the Age of thirty five Years, and been fourteen Years a Resident within the United States.

In Case of the Removal of the President from Office, or of his Death, Resignation or Inability to discharge the Powers and Duties of the said Office, the same shall devolve on the Vice President, and the Congress may by Law provide for the Case of Removal, Death, Resignation or Inability, both of the President and Vice President, declaring what Officer shall then act as President, and such Officer shall act accordingly, until the Disability be removed, or a President shall be elected.

The President shall, at stated Times, receive for his Services, a Compensation, which shall neither be increased nor diminished during the Period for which he shall have been elected, and he shall not receive within that Period any other Emolument from the United States, or any of them.

Before he enter on the Execution of his Office, he shall take the following Oath or Affirmation: "I do solemnly swear (or affirm) that I will faithfully execute the Office of President of the United States, and will to the best of my Ability, preserve, protect and defend the Constitution of the United States."

Section 2. The President shall be Commander in Chief of the Army and Navy of the United States, and of the Militia of the several States, when called into the actual Service of the United States; he may require the Opinion, in writing, of the principal Officer in each of the executive Departments, upon any Subject relating to the Duties of their respective Offices, and he shall have Power to grant Reprieves and Pardons for Offenses against the United States, except in Cases of Impeachment.

He shall have Power, by and with the Advice and Consent of the Senate to make Treaties, provided two thirds of the Senators present concur; and he shall nominate, and by and with the Advice and Consent of the Senate, shall appoint Ambassadors, other public Ministers and Consuls, Judges of the supreme Court, and all other Officers of the United States, whose Appointments are not herein otherwise provided for, and which shall be established by Law; but the Congress may by Law vest the Appointment of such inferior Officers, as they think proper, in the President alone, in the Courts of Law, or in the Heads of Departments.

The President shall have Power to fill up all Vacancies that may happen during the Recess of the Senate, by granting Commissions which shall expire at the End of their next Session.

Section 3. He shall from time to time give to the Congress Information of the State of the Union, and recommend to their Consideration such Measures as he shall judge necessary and expedient; he may, on extraordinary Occasions, convene both Houses, or either of them, and in Case of Disagreement between them, with Respect to the Time of Adjournment, he may adjourn them to such Time as he shall think proper; he shall receive Ambassadors and other public Ministers; he shall take Care that the Laws be faithfully executed, and shall Commission all the Officers of the United States.

Section 4. The President, Vice President and all civil Officers of the United States, shall be removed from Office on Impeachment for, and Conviction of, Treason, Bribery, or other high Crimes and Misdemeanors.

Article III

Section 1. The judicial Power of the United States, shall be vested in one supreme Court, and in such inferior Courts as the Congress may from time to time ordain and establish. The Judges, both of the supreme and inferior Courts, shall hold their Offices during good Behaviour, and shall, at stated Times, receive for their Services a Compensation, which shall not be diminished during their Continuance in Office.

Section 2. The judicial Power shall extend to all Cases, in Law and Equity, arising under this Constitution, the Laws of the United States, and Treaties made, or which shall be made, under their Authority;—to all Cases affecting Ambassadors, other public Ministers and Consuls;—to all Cases of admiralty and maritime Jurisdiction;—to Controversies to which the United States shall be a Party;—to Controversies between two or more States;—between a State and Citizens of another State;—between Citizens of different States;—between Citizens of the same State claiming Lands under Grants of different States, and between a State, or the Citizens thereof, and foreign States, Citizens or Subjects.

In all Cases affecting Ambassadors, other public Ministers and Consuls, and those in which a State shall be a Party, the supreme Court shall have original Jurisdiction. In all the other Cases before mentioned, the supreme Court shall have appellate Jurisdiction, both as to Law and Fact, with such Exceptions, and under such Regulations as the Congress shall make.

The Trial of all Crimes, except in Cases of Impeachment, shall be by Jury; and such Trial shall be held in the State where the said Crimes shall have been committed; but when not committed within any State, the Trial shall be at such Place or Places as the Congress may by Law have directed.

Section 3. Treason against the United States, shall consist only in levying War against them, or, in adhering to their Enemies, giving them Aid and Comfort. No Person shall be convicted of Treason unless on the Testimony of two Witnesses to the same overt Act, or on Confession in open Court.

The Congress shall have Power to declare the Punishment of Treason, but no Attainder of Treason shall work Corruption of Blood, or Forfeiture except during the Life of the Person attainted.

Article IV

Section 1. Full Faith and Credit shall be given in each State to the public Acts, Records, and judicial Proceedings of every other State. And the Congress may by general Laws prescribe the Manner in which such Acts, Records and Proceedings shall be proved, and the Effect thereof.

Section 2. The Citizens of each State shall be entitled to all Privileges and Immunities of Citizens in the several States.

A Person charged in any State with Treason, Felony, or other Crime, who shall flee from Justice, and be found in another State, shall on Demand of the executive Authority of the State from which he fled, be delivered up, to be removed to the State having Jurisdiction of the Crime.

No Person held to Service or Labour in one State, under the Laws thereof, escaping into another, shall, in Consequence of any Law or Regulation therein, be discharged from such Service or Labour, but shall be delivered up on Claim of the Party to whom such Service or Labour may be due.

Section 3. New States may be admitted by the Congress into this Union; but no new State shall be formed or erected within the Jurisdiction of any other State; nor any State be formed by the Junction of two or more States, or Parts of States, without the Consent of the Legislatures of the States concerned as well as of the Congress.

The Congress shall have Power to dispose of and make all needful Rules and Regulations respecting the Territory or other Property belonging to the United States; and nothing in this Constitution shall be so construed as to Prejudice any Claims of the United States, or of any particular State.

Section 4. The United States shall guarantee to every State in this Union a Republican Form of Government, and shall protect each of them against Invasion; and on Application of the Legislature, or of the Executive (when the Legislature cannot be convened) against domestic Violence.

Article V

The Congress, whenever two thirds of both Houses shall deem it necessary, shall propose Amendments to this Constitution, or, on the Application of the Legislatures of two thirds of the several States, shall call a Convention for proposing Amendments, which, in either Case, shall be valid to all Intents and Purposes, as part of this Constitution, when ratified by the Legislatures of three fourths of the several States, or by Conventions in three fourths thereof, as the one or the other Mode of Ratification may be proposed by the Congress; Provided that no Amendment which may be made prior to the Year One thousand eight hundred and eight shall in any Manner affect the first and fourth Clauses in the Ninth Section of the first Article; and that no State, without its Consent, shall be deprived of its equal Suffrage in the Senate.

Article VI

All Debts contracted and Engagements entered into, before the Adoption of this Constitution shall be as valid against the United States under this Constitution, as under the Confederation.

This Constitution, and the Laws of the United States which shall be made in Pursuance thereof; and all Treaties made, or which shall be made, under the Authority of the United States, shall be the supreme Law of the Land; and the Judges in every State shall be bound thereby, any Thing in the Constitution or Laws of any State to the Contrary notwithstanding.

The Senators and Representatives before mentioned, and the Members of the several State Legislatures, and all executive and judicial Officers, both of the United States and of the several States, shall be bound by Oath or Affirmation, to support this Constitution; but no religious Test shall ever be required as a Qualification to any Office or public Trust under the United States.

Article VII

The Ratification of the Conventions of nine States shall be sufficient for the Establishment of this Constitution between the States so ratifying the Same.

Amendment I [1791]

Congress shall make no law respecting an establishment of religion, or prohibiting the free exercise thereof; or abridging the freedom of speech, or of the press; or the right of the people peaceably to assembly, and to petition the Government for a redress of grievances.

Amendment II [1791]

A well regulated Militia, being necessary to the security of a free State, the right of the people to keep and bear Arms, shall not be infringed.

Amendment III [1791]

No Soldier shall, in time of peace be quartered in any house, without the consent of the Owner, nor in time of war, but in a manner to be prescribed by law.

Amendment IV [1791]

The right of the people to be secure in their persons, houses, papers, and effects, against unreasonable searches and seizures, shall not be violated, and no Warrants shall issue, but upon probable cause, supported by Oath or affirmation, and particularly describing the place to be searched, and the persons or things to be seized.

Amendment V [1791]

No person shall be held to answer for a capital, or otherwise infamous crime, unless on a presentment or indictment of a Grand Jury, except in cases arising in the land or naval forces, or in the Militia, when in actual service in time of War or public danger; nor shall any person be subject for the same offence to be twice put in jeopardy of life or limb; nor shall be compelled in any criminal case to be a witness against himself, nor be deprived of life, liberty, or property, without due process of law; nor shall private property be taken for public use, without just compensation.

Amendment VI [1791]

In all criminal prosecutions, the accused shall enjoy the right to a speedy and public trial, by an impartial jury of the State and district wherein the crime shall have been committed, which district shall have been previously ascertained by law, and to be informed of the nature and cause of the accusation; to be confronted with the witnesses against him; to have compulsory process for obtaining witnesses in his favor, and to have the Assistance of Counsel for his defence.

Amendment VII [1791]

In Suits at common law, where the value in controversy shall exceed twenty dollars, the right of trial by jury shall be preserved, and no fact tried by jury, shall be otherwise re-examined in any Court of the United States, than according to the rules of the common law.

Amendment VIII [1791]

Excessive bail shall not be required, nor excessive fines imposed, nor cruel and unusual punishments inflicted.

Amendment IX [1791]

The enumeration in the Constitution, of certain rights, shall not be construed to deny or disparage others retained by the people.

Amendment X [1791]

The powers not delegated to the United States by the Constitution, nor prohibited by it to the States, are reserved to the States respectively, or to the people.

Amendment XI [1798]

The Judicial power of the United States shall not be construed to extend to any suit in law or equity, commenced or prosecuted against one of the United States by Citizens of another State, or by Citizens or Subjects of any Foreign State.

Amendment XII [1804]

The Electors shall meet in their respective states, and vote by ballot for President and Vice-President, one of whom, at least, shall not be an inhabitant of the same state with themselves; they shall name in their ballots the person voted for as President, and in distinct ballots the person voted for as Vice-President, and they shall make distinct lists of all persons voted for as President, and of all persons voted for as Vice-President, and of the number of votes for each, which lists they shall sign and certify, and transmit sealed to the seat of the government of the United States, directed to the President of the Senate;—The President of the Senate shall, in the presence of the Senate and House of Representatives, open all the certificates and the votes shall then be counted;—The person having the greatest number of votes for President, shall be the President, if such number be a majority of the whole number of Electors appointed; and if no person have such majority, then from the persons having the highest numbers not exceeding three on the list of those voted for as President, the House of Representatives shall choose immediately, by ballot, the President. But in choosing the President, the votes shall be taken by states, the representation from each state having one vote; a quorum for this purpose shall consist of a member or members from two-thirds of the states, and a majority of all states shall be necessary to a choice. And if the House of Representatives shall not choose a President whenever the right of choice shall devolve upon them, before the fourth day of March next following, then the Vice-President shall act as President, as in the case of the death or other constitutional disability of the President.—The person having the greatest number of votes as Vice-President, shall be the Vice-President, if such number be a majority of the whole number of Electors appointed, and if no person have a majority, then from the two highest numbers on the list, the Senate shall choose the Vice-President; a quorum for the purpose shall consist of two-thirds of the whole number of Senators, and a majority of the whole number shall be necessary to a choice. But no person constitutionally ineligible to the office of President shall be eligible to that of Vice-President of the United States.

Amendment XIII [1865]

Section 1. Neither slavery nor involuntary servitude, except as a punishment for crime whereof the party shall have been duly convicted, shall exist within the United States, or any place subject to their jurisdiction.

Section 2. Congress shall have power to enforce this article by appropriate legislation.

Amendment XIV [1868]

Section 1. All persons born or naturalized in the United States, and subject to the jurisdiction thereof, are citizens of the United States and of the State wherein they reside. No State shall make or enforce any law which shall abridge the privileges or immunities of citizens of the United States; nor shall any State deprive any person of life, liberty, or property, without due process of law; nor deny to any person within its jurisdiction the equal protection of the laws.

Section 2. Representatives shall be apportioned among the several States according to their respective numbers, counting the whole number of persons in each State, excluding Indians not taxed. But when the right to vote at any election for the choice of electors for President and Vice President of the United States, Representatives in Congress, the Executive and Judicial officers of a State, or the members of the Legislature thereof, is denied to any of the male inhabitants of such State, being twenty-one years of age, and citizens of the United States, or in any way abridged, except for participation in rebellion, or other crime, the basis of representation therein shall be reduced in the proportion which the number of such male citizens shall bear to the whole number of male citizens twenty-one years of age in such State.

Section 3. No person shall be a Senator or Representative in Congress, or elector of President and Vice President, or hold any office, civil or military, under the United States, or under any State, who having previously taken an oath, as a member of Congress, or as an officer of the United States, or as a member of any State legislature, or as an executive or judicial officer of any State, to support the Constitution of the United States, shall have engaged in insurrection or rebellion against the same, or given aid or comfort to the enemies thereof. But Congress may by a vote of two-thirds of each House, remove such disability.

Section 4. The validity of the public debt of the United States, authorized by law, including debts incurred for payment of pensions and bounties for services in suppressing insurrection or rebellion, shall not be questioned. But neither the United States nor any State shall assume or pay any debt or obligation incurred in aid of insurrection or rebellion against the United States, or any claim for the loss or emancipation of any slave; but all such debts, obligations and claims shall be held illegal and void.

Section 5. The Congress shall have power to enforce, by appropriate legislation, the provisions of this article.

Amendment XV [1870]

Section 1. The right of citizens of the United States to vote shall not be denied or abridged by the United States or by any State on account of race, color, or previous condition of servitude.

Section 2. The Congress shall have power to enforce this article by appropriate legislation.

Amendment XVI [1913]

The Congress shall have power to lay and collect taxes on incomes, from whatever source derived, without apportionment among the several States, and without regard to any census or enumeration.

Amendment XVII [1913]

Section 1. The Senate of the United States shall be composed of two Senators from each State, elected by the people thereof, for six years; and each Senator shall have one vote. The electors in each State shall have the qualifications requisite for electors of the most numerous branch of the State legislatures.

Section 2. When vacancies happen in the representation of any State in the Senate, the executive authority of such State shall issue writs of election to fill such vacancies: *Provided,* That the legislature of any State may empower the executive thereof to make temporary appointments until the people fill the vacancies by election as the legislature may direct.

Section 3. This amendment shall not be so construed as to affect the election or term of any Senator chosen before it becomes valid as part of the Constitution.

Amendment XVIII [1919]

Section 1. After one year from the ratification of this article the manufacture, sale, or transportation of intoxicating liquors within, the importation thereof into, or the exportation thereof from the United States and all territory subject to the jurisdiction thereof for beverage purposes is hereby prohibited.

Section 2. The Congress and the several States shall have concurrent power to enforce this article by appropriate legislation.

Section 3. This article shall be inoperative unless it shall have been ratified as an amendment to the Constitution by the legislatures of the several States, as provided in the Constitution, within seven years from the date of the submission hereof to the States by the Congress.

Amendment XIX [1920]

Section 1. The right of citizens of the United States to vote shall not be denied or abridged by the United States or by any State on account of sex.

Section 2. Congress shall have power to enforce this article by appropriate legislation.

Amendment XX [1933]

Section 1. The terms of the President and Vice President shall end at noon on the 20th day of January, and the terms of Senators and Representatives at noon on the 3d day of January, of the years in which such terms would have ended if this article had not been ratified; and the terms of their successors shall then begin.

Section 2. The Congress shall assemble at least once in every year, and such meeting shall begin at noon on the 3d day of January, unless they shall by law appoint a different day.

Section 3. If, at the time fixed for the beginning of the term of the President, the President elect shall have died, the Vice President elect shall become President. If the President shall not have been chosen before the time fixed for the beginning of his term, or if the President elect shall have failed to qualify, then the Vice President elect shall act as President until a President shall have qualified; and the Congress may by law provide for the case wherein neither a President elect nor a Vice President elect shall have qualified, declaring who shall then act as President, or the manner in which one who is to act shall be selected, and such person shall act accordingly until a President or Vice President shall have qualified.

Section 4. The Congress may by law provide for the case of the death of any of the persons from whom the House of Representatives may choose a President whenever the right of choice shall have devolved upon them, and for the case of the death of any of the persons from whom the Senate may choose a Vice President whenever the right of choice shall have devolved upon them.

Section 5. Sections 1 and 2 shall take effect on the 15th day of October following the ratification of this article.

Section 6. This article shall be inoperative unless it shall have been ratified as an amendment to the Constitution by the legislatures of three-fourths of the several States within seven years from the date of its submission.

Amendment XXI [1933]

Section 1. The eighteenth article of amendment to the Constitution of the United States is hereby repealed.

Section 2. The transportation or importation into any State, Territory, or possession of the United States for delivery or use therein of intoxicating liquors, in violation of the laws thereof, is hereby prohibited.

Section 3. This article shall be inoperative unless it shall have been ratified as an amendment to the Constitution by conventions in the several States, as provided in the Constitution, within seven years from the date of the submission hereof to the States by the Congress.

Amendment XXII [1951]

Section 1. No person shall be elected to the office of the President more than twice, and no person who has held the office of President, or acted as President, for more than two years of a term to which some other person was elected President shall be elected to the office of President more than once. But this Article shall not apply to any person holding the office of President when this Article was proposed by the Congress, and shall not prevent any person who may be holding the office of President, or acting as President, during the term within which this Article becomes operative from holding the office of President or acting as President during the remainder of such term.

Section 2. This article shall be inoperative unless it shall have been ratified as an amendment to the Constitution by the legislatures of three-fourths of the several States within seven years from the date of its submission to the States by the Congress.

Amendment XXIII [1961]

Section 1. The District constituting the seat of Government of the United States shall appoint in such manner as the Congress may direct:

A number of electors of President and Vice President equal to the whole number of Senators and Representatives in Congress to which the District would be entitled if it were a State, but in no event more than the least populous state; they shall be in addition to those appointed by the states, but they shall be considered, for the purposes of the election of President and Vice President, to be electors appointed by a state; and they shall meet in the District and perform such duties as provided by the twelfth article of amendment.

Section 2. The Congress shall have power to enforce this article by appropriate legislation.

Amendment XXIV [1964]

Section 1. The right of citizens of the United States to vote in any primary or other election for President or Vice President, for electors for President or Vice President, or for Senator or Representative in Congress, shall not be denied or abridged by the United States, or any State by reason of failure to pay any poll tax or other tax.

Section 2. The Congress shall have power to enforce this article by appropriate legislation.

Amendment XXV [1967]

Section 1. In case of the removal of the President from office or of his death or resignation, the Vice President shall become President.

Section 2. Whenever there is a vacancy in the office of the Vice President, the President shall nominate a Vice President who shall take office upon confirmation by a majority vote of both Houses of Congress.

Section 3. Whenever the President transmits to the President pro tempore of the Senate and the Speaker of the House of Representatives his written declaration that he is unable to discharge the powers and duties of his office, and until he transmits to them a written declaration to the contrary, such powers and duties shall be discharged by the Vice President as Acting President.

Section 4. Whenever the Vice President and a majority of either the principal officers of the executive departments or of such other body as Congress may by law provide, transmit to the President pro tempore of the Senate and the Speaker of the House of Representatives their written declaration that the President is unable to discharge the powers and duties of his office, the Vice President shall immediately assume the powers and duties of the office as Acting President.

Thereafter, when the President transmits to the President pro tempore of the Senate and the Speaker of the House of Representatives his written declaration that no inability exists, he shall resume the powers and duties of his office unless the Vice President and a majority of either the principal officers of the executive department or of such other body as Congress may by law provide, transmit within four days to the President pro tempore of the Senate and the Speaker of the House of Representatives their written declaration that the President is unable to discharge the powers and duties of his office. Thereupon Congress shall decide the issue, assembling within forty-eight hours for that purpose if not in session. If the Congress, within twenty-one days after receipt of the latter written declaration, or, if Congress is not in session, within twenty-one days after Congress is required to assemble, determines by two-thirds vote of both Houses that the President is unable to discharge the powers and duties of his office, the Vice President shall continue to discharge the same as Acting President; otherwise, the President shall resume the powers and duties of his office.

Amendment XXVI [1971]

Section 1. The right of citizens of the United States, who are eighteen years of age or older, to vote shall not be denied or abridged by the United States or by any State on account of age.

Section 2. The Congress shall have power to enforce this article by appropriate legislation.

Amendment XXVII [1992]

No law, varying the compensation for the services of the Senators and Representatives, shall take effect, until an election of Representatives shall have intervened.

APPENDIX C

The Uniform Commercial Code (Excerpts)

(Adopted in fifty-two jurisdictions—all fifty States, although Louisiana has adopted only Articles 1, 3, 4, 7, 8, and 9; the District of Columbia; and the Virgin Islands.) The Uniform Commercial Code consists of the following articles; however, this appendix only features Articles 2 & 2A.

Art.

1. General Provisions
2. Sales
2A. Leases
3. Negotiable Instruments
4. Bank Deposits and Collections
4A. Funds Transfers
5. Letters of Credit
6. Repealer of Article 6—Bulk Transfers and [Revised] Article 6—Bulk Sales
7. Warehouse Receipts, Bills of Lading and Other Documents of Title
8. Investment Securities
9. Secured Transactions
10. Effective Date and Repealer
11. Effective Date and Transition Provisions

Article 2
SALES

Part 1 Short Title, General Construction and Subject Matter

§ 2–101. Short Title.

This Article shall be known and may be cited as Uniform Commercial Code—Sales.

§ 2–102. Scope; Certain Security and Other Transactions Excluded From This Article.

Unless the context otherwise requires, this Article applies to transactions in goods; it does not apply to any transaction which although in the form of an unconditional contract to sell or present sale is intended to operate only as a security transaction nor does this Article impair or repeal any statute regulating sales to consumers, farmers or other specified classes of buyers.

§ 2–103. Definitions and Index of Definitions.

(1) In this Article unless the context otherwise requires

    (a) "Buyer" means a person who buys or contracts to buy goods.

    (b) "Good faith" in the case of a merchant means honesty in fact and the observance of reasonable commercial standards of fair dealing in the trade.

    (c) "Receipt" of goods means taking physical possession of them.

    (d) "Seller" means a person who sells or contracts to sell goods.

(2) Other definitions applying to this Article or to specified Parts thereof, and the sections in which they appear are:

"Acceptance". Section 2–606.
"Banker's credit". Section 2–325.
"Between merchants". Section 2–104.
"Cancellation". Section 2–106(4).
"Commercial unit". Section 2–105.
"Confirmed credit". Section 2–325.
"Conforming to contract". Section 2–106.
"Contract for sale". Section 2–106.
"Cover". Section 2–712.
"Entrusting". Section 2–403.
"Financing agency". Section 2–104.
"Future goods". Section 2–105.
"Goods". Section 2–105.
"Identification". Section 2–501.
"Installment contract". Section 2–612.
"Letter of Credit". Section 2–325.
"Lot". Section 2–105.
"Merchant". Section 2–104.
"Overseas". Section 2–323.
"Person in position of seller". Section 2–707.
"Present sale". Section 2–106.
"Sale". Section 2–106.
"Sale on approval". Section 2–326.

"Sale or return". Section 2–326.

"Termination". Section 2–106.

(3) The following definitions in other Articles apply to this Article:

"Check". Section 3–104.

"Consignee". Section 7–102.

"Consignor". Section 7–102.

"Consumer goods". Section 9–109.

"Dishonor". Section 3–507.

"Draft". Section 3–104.

(4) In addition Article 1 contains general definitions and principles of construction and interpretation applicable throughout this Article.

As amended in 1994 and 1999.

§ 2–104. Definitions: "Merchant"; "Between Merchants"; "Financing Agency".

(1) "Merchant" means a person who deals in goods of the kind or otherwise by his occupation holds himself out as having knowledge or skill peculiar to the practices or goods involved in the transaction or to whom such knowledge or skill may be attributed by his employment of an agent or broker or other intermediary who by his occupation holds himself out as having such knowledge or skill.

(2) "Financing agency" means a bank, finance company or other person who in the ordinary course of business makes advances against goods or documents of title or who by arrangement with either the seller or the buyer intervenes in ordinary course to make or collect payment due or claimed under the contract for sale, as by purchasing or paying the seller's draft or making advances against it or by merely taking it for collection whether or not documents of title accompany the draft. "Financing agency" includes also a bank or other person who similarly intervenes between persons who are in the position of seller and buyer in respect to the goods (Section 2–707).

(3) "Between merchants" means in any transaction with respect to which both parties are chargeable with the knowledge or skill of merchants.

§ 2–105. Definitions: Transferability; "Goods"; "Future" Goods; "Lot"; "Commercial Unit".

(1) "Goods" means all things (including specially manufactured goods) which are movable at the time of identification to the contract for sale other than the money in which the price is to be paid, investment securities (Article 8) and things in action. "Goods" also includes the unborn young of animals and growing crops and other identified things attached to realty as described in the section on goods to be severed from realty (Section 2–107).

(2) Goods must be both existing and identified before any interest in them can pass. Goods which are not both existing and identified are "future" goods. A purported present sale of future goods or of any interest therein operates as a contract to sell.

(3) There may be a sale of a part interest in existing identified goods.

(4) An undivided share in an identified bulk of fungible goods is sufficiently identified to be sold although the quantity of the bulk is not determined. Any agreed proportion of such a bulk or any quantity thereof agreed upon by number, weight or other measure may to the extent of the seller's interest in the bulk be sold to the buyer who then becomes an owner in common.

(5) "Lot" means a parcel or a single article which is the subject matter of a separate sale or delivery, whether or not it is sufficient to perform the contract.

(6) "Commercial unit" means such a unit of goods as by commercial usage is a single whole for purposes of sale and division of which materially impairs its character or value on the market or in use. A commercial unit may be a single article (as a machine) or a set of articles (as a suite of furniture or an assortment of sizes) or a quantity (as a bale, gross, or carload) or any other unit treated in use or in the relevant market as a single whole.

§ 2–106. Definitions: "Contract"; "Agreement"; "Contract for Sale"; "Sale"; "Present Sale"; "Conforming" to Contract; "Termination"; "Cancellation".

(1) In this Article unless the context otherwise requires "contract" and "agreement" are limited to those relating to the present or future sale of goods. "Contract for sale" includes both a present sale of goods and a contract to sell goods at a future time. A "sale" consists in the passing of title from the seller to the buyer for a price (Section 2–401). A "present sale" means a sale which is accomplished by the making of the contract.

(2) Goods or conduct including any part of a performance are "conforming" or conform to the contract when they are in accordance with the obligations under the contract.

(3) "Termination" occurs when either party pursuant to a power created by agreement or law puts an end to the contract otherwise than for its breach. On "termination" all obligations which are still executory on both sides are discharged but any right based on prior breach or performance survives.

(4) "Cancellation" occurs when either party puts an end to the contract for breach by the other and its effect is the same as that of "termination" except that the cancelling party also retains any remedy for breach of the whole contract or any unperformed balance.

§ 2–107. Goods to Be Severed From Realty: Recording.

(1) A contract for the sale of minerals or the like (including oil and gas) or a structure or its materials to be removed from realty is a contract for the sale of goods within this Article if they are to be severed by the seller but until severance a purported present sale thereof which is not effective as a transfer of an interest in land is effective only as a contract to sell.

(2) A contract for the sale apart from the land of growing crops or other things attached to realty and capable of severance without material harm thereto but not described in subsection (1) or of timber to be cut is a contract for the sale

of goods within this Article whether the subject matter is to be severed by the buyer or by the seller even though it forms part of the realty at the time of contracting, and the parties can by identification effect a present sale before severance.

(3) The provisions of this section are subject to any third party rights provided by the law relating to realty records, and the contract for sale may be executed and recorded as a document transferring an interest in land and shall then constitute notice to third parties of the buyer's rights under the contract for sale.

As amended in 1972.

Part 2 Form, Formation and Readjustment of Contract

§ 2–201. Formal Requirements; Statute of Frauds.

(1) Except as otherwise provided in this section a contract for the sale of goods for the price of $500 or more is not enforceable by way of action or defense unless there is some writing sufficient to indicate that a contract for sale has been made between the parties and signed by the party against whom enforcement is sought or by his authorized agent or broker. A writing is not insufficient because it omits or incorrectly states a term agreed upon but the contract is not enforceable under this paragraph beyond the quantity of goods shown in such writing.

(2) Between merchants if within a reasonable time a writing in confirmation of the contract and sufficient against the sender is received and the party receiving it has reason to know its contents, its satisfies the requirements of subsection (1) against such party unless written notice of objection to its contents is given within ten days after it is received.

(3) A contract which does not satisfy the requirements of subsection (1) but which is valid in other respects is enforceable

(a) if the goods are to be specially manufactured for the buyer and are not suitable for sale to others in the ordinary course of the seller's business and the seller, before notice of repudiation is received and under circumstances which reasonably indicate that the goods are for the buyer, has made either a substantial beginning of their manufacture or commitments for their procurement; or

(b) if the party against whom enforcement is sought admits in his pleading, testimony or otherwise in court that a contract for sale was made, but the contract is not enforceable under this provision beyond the quantity of goods admitted; or

(c) with respect to goods for which payment has been made and accepted or which have been received and accepted (Sec. 2–606).

§ 2–202. Final Written Expression: Parol or Extrinsic Evidence.

Terms with respect to which the confirmatory memoranda of the parties agree or which are otherwise set forth in a writing intended by the parties as a final expression of their agreement with respect to such terms as are included therein may not be contradicted by evidence of any prior agreement or of a contemporaneous oral agreement but may be explained or supplemented

(a) by course of dealing or usage of trade (Section 1–205) or by course of performance (Section 2–208); and

(b) by evidence of consistent additional terms unless the court finds the writing to have been intended also as a complete and exclusive statement of the terms of the agreement.

§ 2–203. Seals Inoperative.

The affixing of a seal to a writing evidencing a contract for sale or an offer to buy or sell goods does not constitute the writing a sealed instrument and the law with respect to sealed instruments does not apply to such a contract or offer.

§ 2–204. Formation in General.

(1) A contract for sale of goods may be made in any manner sufficient to show agreement, including conduct by both parties which recognizes the existence of such a contract.

(2) An agreement sufficient to constitute a contract for sale may be found even though the moment of its making is undetermined.

(3) Even though one or more terms are left open a contract for sale does not fail for indefiniteness if the parties have intended to make a contract and there is a reasonably certain basis for giving an appropriate remedy.

§ 2–205. Firm Offers.

An offer by a merchant to buy or sell goods in a signed writing which by its terms gives assurance that it will be held open is not revocable, for lack of consideration, during the time stated or if no time is stated for a reasonable time, but in no event may such period of irrevocability exceed three months; but any such term of assurance on a form supplied by the offeree must be separately signed by the offeror.

§ 2–206. Offer and Acceptance in Formation of Contract.

(1) Unless other unambiguously indicated by the language or circumstances

(a) an offer to make a contract shall be construed as inviting acceptance in any manner and by any medium reasonable in the circumstances;

(b) an order or other offer to buy goods for prompt or current shipment shall be construed as inviting acceptance either by a prompt promise to ship or by the prompt or current shipment of conforming or nonconforming goods, but such a shipment of nonconforming goods does not constitute an acceptance if the seller seasonably notifies the buyer that the shipment is offered only as an accommodation to the buyer.

(2) Where the beginning of a requested performance is a reasonable mode of acceptance an offeror who is not notified of acceptance within a reasonable time may treat the offer as having lapsed before acceptance.

§ 2–207. Additional Terms in Acceptance or Confirmation.

(1) A definite and seasonable expression of acceptance or a written confirmation which is sent within a reasonable time operates as an acceptance even though it states terms additional to or different from those offered or agreed upon, unless acceptance is expressly made conditional on assent to the additional or different terms.

(2) The additional terms are to be construed as proposals for addition to the contract. Between merchants such terms become part of the contract unless:

(a) the offer expressly limits acceptance to the terms of the offer;

(b) they materially alter it; or

(c) notification of objection to them has already been given or is given within a reasonable time after notice of them is received.

(3) Conduct by both parties which recognizes the existence of a contract is sufficient to establish a contract for sale although the writings of the parties do not otherwise establish a contract. In such case the terms of the particular contract consist of those terms on which the writings of the parties agree, together with any supplementary terms incorporated under any other provisions of this Act.

§ 2–208. Course of Performance or Practical Construction.

(1) Where the contract for sale involves repeated occasions for performance by either party with knowledge of the nature of the performance and opportunity for objection to it by the other, any course of performance accepted or acquiesced in without objection shall be relevant to determine the meaning of the agreement.

(2) The express terms of the agreement and any such course of performance, as well as any course of dealing and usage of trade, shall be construed whenever reasonable as consistent with each other; but when such construction is unreasonable, express terms shall control course of performance and course of performance shall control both course of dealing and usage of trade (Section 1–205).

(3) Subject to the provisions of the next section on modification and waiver, such course of performance shall be relevant to show a waiver or modification of any term inconsistent with such course of performance.

§ 2–209. Modification, Rescission and Waiver.

(1) An agreement modifying a contract within this Article needs no consideration to be binding.

(2) A signed agreement which excludes modification or rescission except by a signed writing cannot be otherwise modified or rescinded, but except as between merchants such a requirement on a form supplied by the merchant must be separately signed by the other party.

(3) The requirements of the statute of frauds section of this Article (Section 2–201) must be satisfied if the contract as modified is within its provisions.

(4) Although an attempt at modification or rescission does not satisfy the requirements of subsection (2) or (3) it can operate as a waiver.

(5) A party who has made a waiver affecting an executory portion of the contract may retract the waiver by reasonable notification received by the other party that strict performance will be required of any term waived, unless the retraction would be unjust in view of a material change of position in reliance on the waiver.

§ 2–210. Delegation of Performance; Assignment of Rights.

(1) A party may perform his duty through a delegate unless otherwise agreed or unless the other party has a substantial interest in having his original promisor perform or control the acts required by the contract. No delegation of performance relieves the party delegating of any duty to·perform or any liability for breach.

(2) Except as otherwise provided in Section 9–406, unless otherwise agreed, all rights of either seller or buyer can be assigned except where the assignment would materially change the duty of the other party, or increase materially the burden or risk imposed on him by his contract, or impair materially his chance of obtaining return performance. A right to damages for breach of the whole contract or a right arising out of the assignor's due performance of his entire obligation can be assigned despite agreement otherwise.

(3) The creation, attachment, perfection, or enforcement of a security interest in the seller's interest under a contract is not a transfer that materially changes the duty of or increases materially the burden or risk imposed on buyer or impairs materially the buyer's chance of obtaining return performance within the purview of subsection (2) unless, and then only to the extent that, enforcement actually results in a delegation of material performance of the seller. Even in that event, the creation, attachment, perfection, and enforcement of the security interest remain effective, but (i) the seller is liable to the buyer for damages caused by the delegation to the extent that the damages could not reasonably by prevented by the buyer, and (ii) a court having jurisdiction may grant other appropriate relief, including cancellation of the contract for sale or an injunction against enforcement of the security interest or consummation of the enforcement.

(4) Unless the circumstances indicate the contrary a prohibition of assignment of "the contract" is to be construed as barring only the delegation to the assignee of the assignor's performance.

(5) An assignment of "the contract" or of "all my rights under the contract" or an assignment in similar general terms is an assignment of rights and unless the language or the circumstances (as in an assignment for security) indicate the contrary, it is a delegation of performance of the duties of the assignor and its acceptance by the assignee constitutes a promise by him to perform those duties. This promise is enforceable by either the assignor or the other party to the original contract.

(6) The other party may treat any assignment which delegates performance as creating reasonable grounds for insecurity and may without prejudice to his rights against the assignor demand assurances from the assignee (Section 2–609).

As amended in 1999.

Part 3 General Obligation and Construction of Contract

§ 2–301. General Obligations of Parties.

The obligation of the seller is to transfer and deliver and that of the buyer is to accept and pay in accordance with the contract.

§ 2–302. Unconscionable Contract or Clause.

(1) If the court as a matter of law finds the contract or any clause of the contract to have been unconscionable at the time it was made the court may refuse to enforce the contract, or it may enforce the remainder of the contract without the unconscionable clause, or it may so limit the application of any unconscionable clause as to avoid any unconscionable result.

(2) When it is claimed or appears to the court that the contract or any clause thereof may be unconscionable the parties shall be afforded a reasonable opportunity to present evidence as to its commercial setting, purpose and effect to aid the court in making the determination.

§ 2–303. Allocations or Division of Risks.

Where this Article allocates a risk or a burden as between the parties "unless otherwise agreed", the agreement may not only shift the allocation but may also divide the risk or burden.

§ 2–304. Price Payable in Money, Goods, Realty, or Otherwise.

(1) The price can be made payable in money or otherwise. If it is payable in whole or in part in goods each party is a seller of the goods which he is to transfer.

(2) Even though all or part of the price is payable in an interest in realty the transfer of the goods and the seller's obligations with reference to them are subject to this Article, but not the transfer of the interest in realty or the transferor's obligations in connection therewith.

§ 2–305. Open Price Term.

(1) The parties if they so intend can conclude a contract for sale even though the price is not settled. In such a case the price is a reasonable price at the time for delivery if

(a) nothing is said as to price; or

(b) the price is left to be agreed by the parties and they fail to agree; or

(c) the price is to be fixed in terms of some agreed market or other standard as set or recorded by a third person or agency and it is not so set or recorded.

(2) A price to be fixed by the seller or by the buyer means a price for him to fix in good faith.

(3) When a price left to be fixed otherwise than by agreement of the parties fails to be fixed through fault of one party the other may at his option treat the contract as cancelled or himself fix a reasonable price.

(4) Where, however, the parties intend not to be bound unless the price be fixed or agreed and it is not fixed or agreed there is no contract. In such a case the buyer must return any goods already received or if unable so to do must pay their reasonable value at the time of delivery and the seller must return any portion of the price paid on account.

§ 2–306. Output, Requirements and Exclusive Dealings.

(1) A term which measures the quantity by the output of the seller or the requirements of the buyer means such actual output or requirements as may occur in good faith, except that no quantity unreasonably disproportionate to any stated estimate or in the absence of a stated estimate to any normal or otherwise comparable prior output or requirements may be tendered or demanded.

(2) A lawful agreement by either the seller or the buyer for exclusive dealing in the kind of goods concerned imposes unless otherwise agreed an obligation by the seller to use best efforts to supply the goods and by the buyer to use best efforts to promote their sale.

§ 2–307. Delivery in Single Lot or Several Lots.

Unless otherwise agreed all goods called for by a contract for sale must be tendered in a single delivery and payment is due only on such tender but where the circumstances give either party the right to make or demand delivery in lots the price if it can be apportioned may be demanded for each lot.

§ 2–308. Absence of Specified Place for Delivery.

Unless otherwise agreed

(a) the place for delivery of goods is the seller's place of business or if he has none his residence; but

(b) in a contract for sale of identified goods which to the knowledge of the parties at the time of contracting are in some other place, that place is the place for their delivery; and

(c) documents of title may be delivered through customary banking channels.

§ 2–309. Absence of Specific Time Provisions; Notice of Termination.

(1) The time for shipment or delivery or any other action under a contract if not provided in this Article or agreed upon shall be a reasonable time.

(2) Where the contract provides for successive performances but is indefinite in duration it is valid for a reasonable time but unless otherwise agreed may be terminated at any time by either party.

(3) Termination of a contract by one party except on the happening of an agreed event requires that reasonable notification be received by the other party and an

agreement dispensing with notification is invalid if its operation would be unconscionable.

§ 2–310. Open Time for Payment or Running of Credit; Authority to Ship Under Reservation.

Unless otherwise agreed

(a) payment is due at the time and place at which the buyer is to receive the goods even though the place of shipment is the place of delivery; and

(b) if the seller is authorized to send the goods he may ship them under reservation, and may tender the documents of title, but the buyer may inspect the goods after their arrival before payment is due unless such inspection is inconsistent with the terms of the contract (Section 2–513); and

(c) if delivery is authorized and made by way of documents of title otherwise than by subsection (b) then payment is due at the time and place at which the buyer is to receive the documents regardless of where the goods are to be received; and

(d) where the seller is required or authorized to ship the goods on credit the credit period runs from the time of shipment but post-dating the invoice or delaying its dispatch will correspondingly delay the starting of the credit period.

§ 2–311. Options and Cooperation Respecting Performance.

(1) An agreement for sale which is otherwise sufficiently definite (subsection (3) of Section 2–204) to be a contract is not made invalid by the fact that it leaves particulars of performance to be specified by one of the parties. Any such specification must be made in good faith and within limits set by commercial reasonableness.

(2) Unless otherwise agreed specifications relating to assortment of the goods are at the buyer's option and except as otherwise provided in subsections (1)(c) and (3) of Section 2–319 specifications or arrangements relating to shipment are at the seller's option.

(3) Where such specification would materially affect the other party's performance but is not seasonally made or where one party's cooperation is necessary to the agreed performance of the other but is not seasonally forthcoming, the other party in addition to all other remedies

(a) is excused for any resulting delay in his own performance; and

(b) may also either proceed to perform in any reasonable manner or after the time for a material part of his own performance treat the failure to specify or to cooperate as a breach by failure to deliver or accept the goods.

§ 2–312. Warranty of Title and Against Infringement; Buyer's Obligation Against Infringement.

(1) Subject to subsection (2) there is in a contract for sale a warranty by the seller that

(a) the title conveyed shall be good, and its transfer rightful; and

(b) the goods shall be delivered free from any security interest or other lien or encumbrance of which the buyer at the time of contracting has no knowledge.

(2) A warranty under subsection (1) will be excluded or modified only by specific language or by circumstances which give the buyer reason to know that the person selling does not claim title in himself or that he is purporting to sell only such right or title as he or a third person may have.

(3) Unless otherwise agreed a seller who is a merchant regularly dealing in goods of the kind warrants that the goods shall be delivered free of the rightful claim of any third person by way of infringement or the like but a buyer who furnishes specifications to the seller must hold the seller harmless against any such claim which arises out of compliance with the specifications.

§ 2–313. Express Warranties by Affirmation, Promise, Description, Sample.

(1) Express warranties by the seller are created as follows:

(a) Any affirmation of fact or promise made by the seller to the buyer which relates to the goods and becomes part of the basis of the bargain creates an express warranty that the goods shall conform to the affirmation or promise.

(b) Any description of the goods which is made part of the basis of the bargain creates an express warranty that the goods shall conform to the description.

(c) Any sample or model which is made part of the basis of the bargain creates an express warranty that the whole of the goods shall conform to the sample or model.

(2) It is not necessary to the creation of an express warranty that the seller use formal words such as "warrant" or "guarantee" or that he have a specific intention to make a warranty, but an affirmation merely of the value of the goods or a statement purporting to be merely the seller's opinion or commendation of the goods does not create a warranty.

§ 2–314. Implied Warranty: Merchantability; Usage of Trade.

(1) Unless excluded or modified (Section 2–316), a warranty that the goods shall be merchantable is implied in a contract for their sale if the seller is a merchant with respect to goods of that kind. Under this section the serving for value of food or drink to be consumed either on the premises or elsewhere is a sale.

(2) Goods to be merchantable must be at least such as

(a) pass without objection in the trade under the contract description; and

(b) in the case of fungible goods, are of fair average quality within the description; and

(c) are fit for the ordinary purposes for which such goods are used; and

(d) run, within the variations permitted by the agreement, of even kind, quality and quantity within each unit and among all units involved; and

(e) are adequately contained, packaged, and labeled as the agreement may require; and

(f) conform to the promises or affirmations of fact made on the container or label if any.

(3) Unless excluded or modified (Section 2–316) other implied warranties may arise from course of dealing or usage of trade.

§ 2–315. Implied Warranty: Fitness for Particular Purpose.

Where the seller at the time of contracting has reason to know any particular purpose for which the goods are required and that the buyer is relying on the seller's skill or judgment to select or furnish suitable goods, there is unless excluded or modified under the next section an implied warranty that the goods shall be fit for such purpose.

§ 2–316. Exclusion or Modification of Warranties.

(1) Words or conduct relevant to the creation of an express warranty and words or conduct tending to negate or limit warranty shall be construed wherever reasonable as consistent with each other; but subject to the provisions of this Article on parol or extrinsic evidence (Section 2–202) negation or limitation is inoperative to the extent that such construction is unreasonable.

(2) Subject to subsection (3), to exclude or modify the implied warranty of merchantability or any part of it the language must mention merchantability and in case of a writing must be conspicuous, and to exclude or modify any implied warranty of fitness the exclusion must be by a writing and conspicuous. Language to exclude all implied warranties of fitness is sufficient if it states, for example, that "There are no warranties which extend beyond the description on the face hereof."

(3) Notwithstanding subsection (2)

(a) unless the circumstances indicate otherwise, all implied warranties are excluded by expressions like "as is", "with all faults" or other language which in common understanding calls the buyer's attention to the exclusion of warranties and makes plain that there is no implied warranty; and

(b) when the buyer before entering into the contract has examined the goods or the sample or model as fully as he desired or has refused to examine the goods there is no implied warranty with regard to defects which an examination ought in the circumstances to have revealed to him; and

(c) an implied warranty can also be excluded or modified by course of dealing or course of performance or usage of trade.

(4) Remedies for breach of warranty can be limited in accordance with the provisions of this Article on liquidation or limitation of damages and on contractual modification of remedy (Sections 2–718 and 2–719).

§ 2–317. Cumulation and Conflict of Warranties Express or Implied.

Warranties whether express or implied shall be construed as consistent with each other and as cumulative, but if such construction is unreasonable the intention of the parties shall determine which warranty is dominant. In ascertaining that intention the following rules apply:

(a) Exact or technical specifications displace an inconsistent sample or model or general language of description.

(b) A sample from an existing bulk displaces inconsistent general language of description.

(c) Express warranties displace inconsistent implied warranties other than an implied warranty of fitness for a particular purpose.

§ 2–318. Third Party Beneficiaries of Warranties Express or Implied.

Note: If this Act is introduced in the Congress of the United States this section should be omitted. (States to select one alternative.)

Alternative A

A seller's warranty whether express or implied extends to any natural person who is in the family or household of his buyer or who is a guest in his home if it is reasonable to expect that such person may use, consume or be affected by the goods and who is injured in person by breach of the warranty. A seller may not exclude or limit the operation of this section.

Alternative B

A seller's warranty whether express or implied extends to any natural person who may reasonably be expected to use, consume or be affected by the goods and who is injured in person by breach of the warranty. A seller may not exclude or limit the operation of this section.

Alternative C

A seller's warranty whether express or implied extends to any person who may reasonably be expected to use, consume or be affected by the goods and who is injured by breach of the warranty. A seller may not exclude or limit the operation of this section with respect to injury to the person of an individual to whom the warranty extends.

As amended 1966.

§ 2–319. F.O.B. and F.A.S. Terms.

(1) Unless otherwise agreed the term F.O.B. (which means "free on board") at a named place, even though used only in connection with the stated price, is a delivery term under which

(a) when the term is F.O.B. the place of shipment, the seller must at that place ship the goods in the manner provided in this Article (Section 2–504) and bear the expense and risk of putting them into the possession of the carrier; or

(b) when the term is F.O.B. the place of destination, the seller must at his own expense and risk transport the goods to that place and there tender delivery of them in the manner provided in this Article (Section 2–503);

(c) when under either (a) or (b) the term is also F.O.B. vessel, car or other vehicle, the seller must in addition at his own expense and risk load the goods on board. If the term is F.O.B. vessel the buyer must name the vessel and in an appropriate case the seller must comply with the provisions of this Article on the form of bill of lading (Section 2–323).

(2) Unless otherwise agreed the term F.A.S. vessel (which means "free alongside") at a named port, even though used only in connection with the stated price, is a delivery term under which the seller must

(a) at his own expense and risk deliver the goods alongside the vessel in the manner usual in that port or on a dock designated and provided by the buyer; and

(b) obtain and tender a receipt for the goods in exchange for which the carrier is under a duty to issue a bill of lading.

(3) Unless otherwise agreed in any case falling within subsection (1)(a) or (c) or subsection (2) the buyer must seasonally give any needed instructions for making delivery, including when the term is F.A.S. or F.O.B. the loading berth of the vessel and in an appropriate case its name and sailing date. The seller may treat the failure of needed instructions as a failure of cooperation under this Article (Section 2–311). He may also at his option move the goods in any reasonable manner preparatory to delivery or shipment.

(4) Under the term F.O.B. vessel or F.A.S. unless otherwise agreed the buyer must make payment against tender of the required documents and the seller may not tender nor the buyer demand delivery of the goods in substitution for the documents.

§ 2–320. C.I.F. and C. & F. Terms.

(1) The term C.I.F. means that the price includes in a lump sum the cost of the goods and the insurance and freight to the named destination. The term C. & F. or C.F. means that the price so includes cost and freight to the named destination.

(2) Unless otherwise agreed and even though used only in connection with the stated price and destination, the term C.I.F. destination or its equivalent requires the seller at his own expense and risk to

(a) put the goods into the possession of a carrier at the port for shipment and obtain a negotiable bill or bills of lading covering the entire transportation to the named destination; and

(b) load the goods and obtain a receipt from the carrier (which may be contained in the bill of lading) showing that the freight has been paid or provided for; and

(c) obtain a policy or certificate of insurance, including any war risk insurance, of a kind and on terms then current at the port of shipment in the usual amount, in the currency of the contract, shown to cover

the same goods covered by the bill of lading and providing for payment of loss to the order of the buyer or for the account of whom it may concern; but the seller may add to the price the amount of the premium for any such war risk insurance; and

(d) prepare an invoice of the goods and procure any other documents required to effect shipment or to comply with the contract; and

(e) forward and tender with commercial promptness all the documents in due form and with any indorsement necessary to perfect the buyer's rights.

(3) Unless otherwise agreed the term C. & F. or its equivalent has the same effect and imposes upon the seller the same obligations and risks as a C.I.F. term except the obligation as to insurance.

(4) Under the term C.I.F. or C. & F. unless otherwise agreed the buyer must make payment against tender of the required documents and the seller may not tender nor the buyer demand delivery of the goods in substitution for the documents.

§ 2–321. C.I.F. or C. & F.: "Net Landed Weights"; "Payment on Arrival"; Warranty of Condition on Arrival.

Under a contract containing a term C.I.F. or C. & F.

(1) Where the price is based on or is to be adjusted according to "net landed weights", "delivered weights", "out turn" quantity or quality or the like, unless otherwise agreed the seller must reasonably estimate the price. The payment due on tender of the documents called for by the contract is the amount so estimated, but after final adjustment of the price a settlement must be made with commercial promptness.

(2) An agreement described in subsection (1) or any warranty of quality or condition of the goods on arrival places upon the seller the risk of ordinary deterioration, shrinkage and the like in transportation but has no effect on the place or time of identification to the contract for sale or delivery or on the passing of the risk of loss.

(3) Unless otherwise agreed where the contract provides for payment on or after arrival of the goods the seller must before payment allow such preliminary inspection as is feasible; but if the goods are lost delivery of the documents and payment are due when the goods should have arrived.

§ 2–322. Delivery "Ex-Ship".

(1) Unless otherwise agreed a term for delivery of goods "ex-ship" (which means from the carrying vessel) or in equivalent language is not restricted to a particular ship and requires delivery from a ship which has reached a place at the named port of destination where goods of the kind are usually discharged.

(2) Under such a term unless otherwise agreed

(a) the seller must discharge all liens arising out of the carriage and furnish the buyer with a direction which puts the carrier under a duty to deliver the goods; and

(b) the risk of loss does not pass to the buyer until the goods leave the ship's tackle or are otherwise properly unloaded.

§ 2–323. **Form of Bill of Lading Required in Overseas Shipment; "Overseas".**

(1) Where the contract contemplates overseas shipment and contains a term C.I.F. or C. & F. or F.O.B. vessel, the seller unless otherwise agreed must obtain a negotiable bill of lading stating that the goods have been loaded on board or, in the case of a term C.I.F. or C. & F., received for shipment.

(2) Where in a case within subsection (1) a bill of lading has been issued in a set of parts, unless otherwise agreed if the documents are not to be sent from abroad the buyer may demand tender of the full set; otherwise only one part of the bill of lading need be tendered. Even if the agreement expressly requires a full set

(a) due tender of a single part is acceptable within the provisions of this Article on cure of improper delivery (subsection (1) of Section 2–508); and

(b) even though the full set is demanded, if the documents are sent from abroad the person tendering an incomplete set may nevertheless require payment upon furnishing an indemnity which the buyer in good faith deems adequate.

(3) A shipment by water or by air or a contract contemplating such shipment is "overseas" insofar as by usage of trade or agreement it is subject to the commercial, financing or shipping practices characteristic of international deep water commerce.

§ 2–324. **"No Arrival, No Sale" Term.**

Under a term "no arrival, no sale" or terms of like meaning, unless otherwise agreed,

(a) the seller must properly ship conforming goods and if they arrive by any means he must tender them on arrival but he assumes no obligation that the goods will arrive unless he has caused the non-arrival; and

(b) where without fault of the seller the goods are in part lost or have so deteriorated as no longer to conform to the contract or arrive after the contract time, the buyer may proceed as if there had been casualty to identified goods (Section 2–613).

§ 2–325. **"Letter of Credit" Term; "Confirmed Credit".**

(1) Failure of the buyer seasonably to furnish an agreed letter of credit is a breach of the contract for sale.

(2) The delivery to seller of a proper letter of credit suspends the buyer's obligation to pay. If the letter of credit is dishonored, the seller may on seasonable notification to the buyer require payment directly from him.

(3) Unless otherwise agreed the term "letter of credit" or "banker's credit" in a contract for sale means an irrevocable credit issued by a financing agency of good repute and, where the shipment is overseas, of good international

repute. The term "confirmed credit" means that the credit must also carry the direct obligation of such an agency which does business in the seller's financial market.

§ 2–326. **Sale on Approval and Sale or Return; Rights of Creditors.**

(1) Unless otherwise agreed, if delivered goods may be returned by the buyer even though they conform to the contract, the transaction is

(a) a "sale on approval" if the goods are delivered primarily for use, and

(b) a "sale or return" if the goods are delivered primarily for resale.

(2) Goods held on approval are not subject to the claims of the buyer's creditors until acceptance; goods held on sale or return are subject to such claims while in the buyer's possession.

(3) Any "or return" term of a contract for sale is to be treated as a separate contract for sale within the statute of frauds section of this Article (Section 2–201) and as contradicting the sale aspect of the contract within the provisions of this Article or on parol or extrinsic evidence (Section 2–202).

As amended in 1999.

§ 2–327. **Special Incidents of Sale on Approval and Sale or Return.**

(1) Under a sale on approval unless otherwise agreed

(a) although the goods are identified to the contract the risk of loss and the title do not pass to the buyer until acceptance; and

(b) use of the goods consistent with the purpose of trial is not acceptance but failure seasonably to notify the seller of election to return the goods is acceptance, and if the goods conform to the contract acceptance of any part is acceptance of the whole; and

(c) after due notification of election to return, the return is at the seller's risk and expense but a merchant buyer must follow any reasonable instructions.

(2) Under a sale or return unless otherwise agreed

(a) the option to return extends to the whole or any commercial unit of the goods while in substantially their original condition, but must be exercised seasonably; and

(b) the return is at the buyer's risk and expense.

§ 2–328. **Sale by Auction.**

(1) In a sale by auction if goods are put up in lots each lot is the subject of a separate sale.

(2) A sale by auction is complete when the auctioneer so announces by the fall of the hammer or in other customary manner. Where a bid is made while the hammer is falling in acceptance of a prior bid the auctioneer may in his discretion reopen the bidding or declare the goods sold under the bid on which the hammer was falling.

(3) Such a sale is with reserve unless the goods are in explicit terms put up without reserve. In an auction with reserve the auctioneer may withdraw the goods at any time

until he announces completion of the sale. In an auction without reserve, after the auctioneer calls for bids on an article or lot, that article or lot cannot be withdrawn unless no bid is made within a reasonable time. In either case a bidder may retract his bid until the auctioneer's announcement of completion of the sale, but a bidder's retraction does not revive any previous bid.

(4) If the auctioneer knowingly receives a bid on the seller's behalf or the seller makes or procures such as bid, and notice has not been given that liberty for such bidding is reserved, the buyer may at his option avoid the sale or take the goods at the price of the last good faith bid prior to the completion of the sale. This subsection shall not apply to any bid at a forced sale.

Part 4 Title, Creditors and Good Faith Purchasers

§ 2–401. Passing of Title; Reservation for Security; Limited Application of This Section.

Each provision of this Article with regard to the rights, obligations and remedies of the seller, the buyer, purchasers or other third parties applies irrespective of title to the goods except where the provision refers to such title. Insofar as situations are not covered by the other provisions of this Article and matters concerning title became material the following rules apply:

(1) Title to goods cannot pass under a contract for sale prior to their identification to the contract (Section 2–501), and unless otherwise explicitly agreed the buyer acquires by their identification a special property as limited by this Act. Any retention or reservation by the seller of the title (property) in goods shipped or delivered to the buyer is limited in effect to a reservation of a security interest. Subject to these provisions and to the provisions of the Article on Secured Transactions (Article 9), title to goods passes from the seller to the buyer in any manner and on any conditions explicitly agreed on by the parties.

(2) Unless otherwise explicitly agreed title passes to the buyer at the time and place at which the seller completes his performance with reference to the physical delivery of the goods, despite any reservation of a security interest and even though a document of title is to be delivered at a different time or place; and in particular and despite any reservation of a security interest by the bill of lading

(a) if the contract requires or authorizes the seller to send the goods to the buyer but does not require him to deliver them at destination, title passes to the buyer at the time and place of shipment; but

(b) if the contract requires delivery at destination, title passes on tender there.

(3) Unless otherwise explicitly agreed where delivery is to be made without moving the goods,

(a) if the seller is to deliver a document of title, title passes at the time when and the place where he delivers such documents; or

(b) if the goods are at the time of contracting already identified and no documents are to be delivered, title passes at the time and place of contracting.

(4) A rejection or other refusal by the buyer to receive or retain the goods, whether or not justified, or a justified revocation of acceptance revests title to the goods in the seller. Such revesting occurs by operation of law and is not a "sale".

§ 2–402. Rights of Seller's Creditors Against Sold Goods.

(1) Except as provided in subsections (2) and (3), rights of unsecured creditors of the seller with respect to goods which have been identified to a contract for sale are subject to the buyer's rights to recover the goods under this Article (Sections 2–502 and 2–716).

(2) A creditor of the seller may treat a sale or an identification of goods to a contract for sale as void if as against him a retention of possession by the seller is fraudulent under any rule of law of the state where the goods are situated, except that retention of possession in good faith and current course of trade by a merchant-seller for a commercially reasonable time after a sale or identification is not fraudulent.

(3) Nothing in this Article shall be deemed to impair the rights of creditors of the seller

(a) under the provisions of the Article on Secured Transactions (Article 9); or

(b) where identification to the contract or delivery is made not in current course of trade but in satisfaction of or as security for a pre-existing claim for money, security or the like and is made under circumstances which under any rule of law of the state where the goods are situated would apart from this Article constitute the transaction a fraudulent transfer or voidable preference.

§ 2–403. Power to Transfer; Good Faith Purchase of Goods; "Entrusting".

(1) A purchaser of goods acquires all title which his transferor had or had power to transfer except that a purchaser of a limited interest acquires rights only to the extent of the interest purchased. A person with voidable title has power to transfer a good title to a good faith purchaser for value. When goods have been delivered under a transaction of purchase the purchaser has such power even though

(a) the transferor was deceived as to the identity of the purchaser, or

(b) the delivery was in exchange for a check which is later dishonored, or

(c) it was agreed that the transaction was to be a "cash sale", or

(d) the delivery was procured through fraud punishable as larcenous under the criminal law.

(2) Any entrusting of possession of goods to a merchant who deals in goods of that kind gives him power to transfer all rights of the entruster to a buyer in ordinary course of business.

(3) "Entrusting" includes any delivery and any acquiescence in retention of possession regardless of any condition expressed between the parties to the delivery or acquiescence and regardless of whether the procurement of the entrusting or the possessor's disposition of the goods have been such as to be larcenous under the criminal law.

(4) The rights of other purchasers of goods and of lien creditors are governed by the Articles on Secured Transactions (Article 9), Bulk Transfers (Article 6) and Documents of Title (Article 7).

As amended in 1988.

Part 5 Performance

§ 2–501. Insurable Interest in Goods; Manner of Identification of Goods.

(1) The buyer obtains a special property and an insurable interest in goods by identification of existing goods as goods to which the contract refers even though the goods so identified are non-conforming and he has an option to return or reject them. Such identification can be made at any time and in any manner explicitly agreed to by the parties. In the absence of explicit agreement identification occurs

(a) when the contract is made if it is for the sale of goods already existing and identified;

(b) if the contract is for the sale of future goods other than those described in paragraph (c), when goods are shipped, marked or otherwise designated by the seller as goods to which the contract refers;

(c) when the crops are planted or otherwise become growing crops or the young are conceived if the contract is for the sale of unborn young to be born within twelve months after contracting or for the sale of crops to be harvested within twelve months or the next normal harvest season after contracting whichever is longer.

(2) The seller retains an insurable interest in goods so long as title to or any security interest in the goods remains in him and where the identification is by the seller alone he may until default or insolvency or notification to the buyer that the identification is final substitute other goods for those identified.

(3) Nothing in this section impairs any insurable interest recognized under any other statute or rule of law.

§ 2–502. Buyer's Right to Goods on Seller's Insolvency.

(1) Subject to subsections (2) and (3) and even though the goods have not been shipped a buyer who has paid a part or all of the price of goods in which he has a special property under the provisions of the immediately preceding section may on making and keeping good a tender of any unpaid portion of their price recover them from the seller if:

(a) in the case of goods bought for personal, family, or household purposes, the seller repudiates or fails to deliver as required by the contract; or

(b) in all cases, the seller becomes insolvent within ten days after receipt of the first installment on their price.

(2) The buyer's right to recover the goods under subsection (1)(a) vests upon acquisition of a special property, even if the seller had not then repudiated or failed to deliver.

(3) If the identification creating his special property has been made by the buyer he acquires the right to recover the goods only if they conform to the contract for sale.

As amended in 1999.

§ 2–503. Manner of Seller's Tender of Delivery.

(1) Tender of delivery requires that the seller put and hold conforming goods at the buyer's disposition and give the buyer any notification reasonably necessary to enable him to take delivery. The manner, time and place for tender are determined by the agreement and this Article, and in particular

(a) tender must be at a reasonable hour, and if it is of goods they must be kept available for the period reasonably necessary to enable the buyer to take possession; but

(b) unless otherwise agreed the buyer must furnish facilities reasonably suited to the receipt of the goods.

(2) Where the case is within the next section respecting shipment tender requires that the seller comply with its provisions.

(3) Where the seller is required to deliver at a particular destination tender requires that he comply with subsection (1) and also in any appropriate case tender documents as described in subsections (4) and (5) of this section.

(4) Where goods are in the possession of a bailee and are to be delivered without being moved

(a) tender requires that the seller either tender a negotiable document of title covering such goods or procure acknowledgment by the bailee of the buyer's right to possession of the goods; but

(b) tender to the buyer of a non-negotiable document of title or of a written direction to the bailee to deliver is sufficient tender unless the buyer seasonably objects, and receipt by the bailee of notification of the buyer's rights fixes those rights as against the bailee and all third persons; but risk of loss of the goods and of any failure by the bailee to honor the non-negotiable document of title or to obey the direction remains on the seller until the buyer has had a reasonable time to present the document or direction, and a refusal by the bailee to honor the document or to obey the direction defeats the tender.

(5) Where the contract requires the seller to deliver documents

(a) he must tender all such documents in correct form, except as provided in this Article with respect to bills of lading in a set (subsection (2) of Section 2–323); and

(b) tender through customary banking channels is sufficient and dishonor of a draft accompanying the documents constitutes non-acceptance or rejection.

§ 2–504. Shipment by Seller.

Where the seller is required or authorized to send the goods to the buyer and the contract does not require him to deliver them at a particular destination, then unless otherwise agreed he must

(a) put the goods in the possession of such a carrier and make such a contract for their transportation as may be reasonable having regard to the nature of the goods and other circumstances of the case; and

(b) obtain and promptly deliver or tender in due form any document necessary to enable the buyer to obtain possession of the goods or otherwise required by the agreement or by usage of trade; and

(c) promptly notify the buyer of the shipment.

Failure to notify the buyer under paragraph (c) or to make a proper contract under paragraph (a) is a ground for rejection only if material delay or loss ensues.

§ 2–505. Seller's Shipment under Reservation.

(1) Where the seller has identified goods to the contract by or before shipment:

(a) his procurement of a negotiable bill of lading to his own order or otherwise reserves in him a security interest in the goods. His procurement of the bill to the order of a financing agency or of the buyer indicates in addition only the seller's expectation of transferring that interest to the person named.

(b) a non-negotiable bill of lading to himself or his nominee reserves possession of the goods as security but except in a case of conditional delivery (subsection (2) of Section 2–507) a non-negotiable bill of lading naming the buyer as consignee reserves no security interest even though the seller retains possession of the bill of lading.

(2) When shipment by the seller with reservation of a security interest is in violation of the contract for sale it constitutes an improper contract for transportation within the preceding section but impairs neither the rights given to the buyer by shipment and identification of the goods to the contract nor the seller's powers as a holder of a negotiable document.

§ 2–506. Rights of Financing Agency.

(1) A financing agency by paying or purchasing for value a draft which relates to a shipment of goods acquires to the extent of the payment or purchase and in addition to its own rights under the draft and any document of title securing it any rights of the shipper in the goods including the right to stop delivery and the shipper's right to have the draft honored by the buyer.

(2) The right to reimbursement of a financing agency which has in good faith honored or purchased the draft under commitment to or authority from the buyer is not impaired by subsequent discovery of defects with reference to any relevant document which was apparently regular on its face.

§ 2–507. Effect of Seller's Tender; Delivery on Condition.

(1) Tender of delivery is a condition to the buyer's duty to accept the goods and, unless otherwise agreed, to his duty to pay for them. Tender entitles the seller to acceptance of the goods and to payment according to the contract.

(2) Where payment is due and demanded on the delivery to the buyer of goods or documents of title, his right as against the seller to retain or dispose of them is conditional upon his making the payment due.

§ 2–508. Cure by Seller of Improper Tender or Delivery; Replacement.

(1) Where any tender or delivery by the seller is rejected because non-conforming and the time for performance has not yet expired, the seller may seasonably notify the buyer of his intention to cure and may then within the contract time make a conforming delivery.

(2) Where the buyer rejects a non-conforming tender which the seller had reasonable grounds to believe would be acceptable with or without money allowance the seller may if he seasonably notifies the buyer have a further reasonable time to substitute a conforming tender.

§ 2–509. Risk of Loss in the Absence of Breach.

(1) Where the contract requires or authorizes the seller to ship the goods by carrier

(a) if it does not require him to deliver them at a particular destination, the risk of loss passes to the buyer when the goods are duly delivered to the carrier even though the shipment is under reservation (Section 2–505); but

(b) if it does require him to deliver them at a particular destination and the goods are there duly tendered while in the possession of the carrier, the risk of loss passes to the buyer when the goods are there duly so tendered as to enable the buyer to take delivery.

(2) Where the goods are held by a bailee to be delivered without being moved, the risk of loss passes to the buyer

(a) on his receipt of a negotiable document of title covering the goods; or

(b) on acknowledgment by the bailee of the buyer's right to possession of the goods; or

(c) after his receipt of a non-negotiable document of title or other written direction to deliver, as provided in subsection (4)(b) of Section 2–503.

(3) In any case not within subsection (1) or (2), the risk of loss passes to the buyer on his receipt of the goods if the seller is a merchant; otherwise the risk passes to the buyer on tender of delivery.

(4) The provisions of this section are subject to contrary agreement of the parties and to the provisions of this Article on sale on approval (Section 2–327) and on effect of breach on risk of loss (Section 2–510).

§ 2–510. Effect of Breach on Risk of Loss.

(1) Where a tender or delivery of goods so fails to conform to the contract as to give a right of rejection the risk of their loss remains on the seller until cure or acceptance.

(2) Where the buyer rightfully revokes acceptance he may to the extent of any deficiency in his effective insurance coverage treat the risk of loss as having rested on the seller from the beginning.

(3) Where the buyer as to conforming goods already identified to the contract for sale repudiates or is otherwise in breach before risk of their loss has passed to him, the seller may to the extent of any deficiency in his effective insurance coverage treat the risk of loss as resting on the buyer for a commercially reasonable time.

§ 2–511. Tender of Payment by Buyer; Payment by Check.

(1) Unless otherwise agreed tender of payment is a condition to the seller's duty to tender and complete any delivery.

(2) Tender of payment is sufficient when made by any means or in any manner current in the ordinary course of business unless the seller demands payment in legal tender and gives any extension of time reasonably necessary to procure it.

(3) Subject to the provisions of this Act on the effect of an instrument on an obligation (Section 3–310), payment by check is conditional and is defeated as between the parties by dishonor of the check on due presentment.

As amended in 1994.

§ 2–512. Payment by Buyer Before Inspection.

(1) Where the contract requires payment before inspection non-conformity of the goods does not excuse the buyer from so making payment unless

(a) the non-conformity appears without inspection; or

(b) despite tender of the required documents the circumstances would justify injunction against honor under this Act (Section 5–109(b)).

(2) Payment pursuant to subsection (1) does not constitute an acceptance of goods or impair the buyer's right to inspect or any of his remedies.

As amended in 1995.

§ 2–513. Buyer's Right to Inspection of Goods.

(1) Unless otherwise agreed and subject to subsection (3), where goods are tendered or delivered or identified to the contract for sale, the buyer has a right before payment or acceptance to inspect them at any reasonable place and time and in any reasonable manner. When the seller is required or authorized to send the goods to the buyer, the inspection may be after their arrival.

(2) Expenses of inspection must be borne by the buyer but may be recovered from the seller if the goods do not conform and are rejected.

(3) Unless otherwise agreed and subject to the provisions of this Article on C.I.F. contracts (subsection (3) of Section 2–321), the buyer is not entitled to inspect the goods before payment of the price when the contract provides

(a) for delivery "C.O.D." or on other like terms; or

(b) for payment against documents of title, except where such payment is due only after the goods are to become available for inspection.

(4) A place or method of inspection fixed by the parties is presumed to be exclusive but unless otherwise expressly agreed it does not postpone identification or shift the place for delivery or for passing the risk of loss. If compliance becomes impossible, inspection shall be as provided in this section unless the place or method fixed was clearly intended as an indispensable condition failure of which avoids the contract.

§ 2–514. When Documents Deliverable on Acceptance; When on Payment.

Unless otherwise agreed documents against which a draft is drawn are to be delivered to the drawee on acceptance of the draft if it is payable more than three days after presentment; otherwise, only on payment.

§ 2–515. Preserving Evidence of Goods in Dispute.

In furtherance of the adjustment of any claim or dispute

(a) either party on reasonable notification to the other and for the purpose of ascertaining the facts and preserving evidence has the right to inspect, test and sample the goods including such of them as may be in the possession or control of the other; and

(b) the parties may agree to a third party inspection or survey to determine the conformity or condition of the goods and may agree that the findings shall be binding upon them in any subsequent litigation or adjustment.

Part 6 Breach, Repudiation and Excuse

§ 2–601. Buyer's Rights on Improper Delivery.

Subject to the provisions of this Article on breach in installment contracts (Section 2–612) and unless otherwise agreed under the sections on contractual limitations of remedy (Sections 2–718 and 2–719), if the goods or the tender of delivery fail in any respect to conform to the contract, the buyer may

(a) reject the whole; or

(b) accept the whole; or

(c) accept any commercial unit or units and reject the rest.

§ 2–602. Manner and Effect of Rightful Rejection.

(1) Rejection of goods must be within a reasonable time after their delivery or tender. It is ineffective unless the buyer seasonably notifies the seller.

(2) Subject to the provisions of the two following sections on rejected goods (Sections 2–603 and 2–604),

(a) after rejection any exercise of ownership by the buyer with respect to any commercial unit is wrongful as against the seller; and

(b) if the buyer has before rejection taken physical possession of goods in which he does not have a security interest under the provisions of this Article (subsection (3) of Section 2–711), he is under a duty after rejection to hold them with reasonable care at the seller's disposition for a time sufficient to permit the seller to remove them; but

(c) the buyer has no further obligations with regard to goods rightfully rejected.

(3) The seller's rights with respect to goods wrongfully rejected are governed by the provisions of this Article on Seller's remedies in general (Section 2–703).

§ 2–603. Merchant Buyer's Duties as to Rightfully Rejected Goods.

(1) Subject to any security interest in the buyer (subsection (3) of Section 2–711), when the seller has no agent or place of business at the market of rejection a merchant buyer is under a duty after rejection of goods in his possession or control to follow any reasonable instructions received from the seller with respect to the goods and in the absence of such instructions to make reasonable efforts to sell them for the seller's account if they are perishable or threaten to decline in value speedily. Instructions are not reasonable if on demand indemnity for expenses is not forthcoming.

(2) When the buyer sells goods under subsection (1), he is entitled to reimbursement from the seller or out of the proceeds for reasonable expenses of caring for and selling them, and if the expenses include no selling commission then to such commission as is usual in the trade or if there is none to a reasonable sum not exceeding ten per cent on the gross proceeds.

(3) In complying with this section the buyer is held only to good faith and good faith conduct hereunder is neither acceptance nor conversion nor the basis of an action for damages.

§ 2–604. Buyer's Options as to Salvage of Rightfully Rejected Goods.

Subject to the provisions of the immediately preceding section on perishables if the seller gives no instructions within a reasonable time after notification of rejection the buyer may store the rejected goods for the seller's account or reship them to him or resell them for the seller's account with reimbursement as provided in the preceding section. Such action is not acceptance or conversion.

§ 2–605. Waiver of Buyer's Objections by Failure to Particularize.

(1) The buyer's failure to state in connection with rejection a particular defect which is ascertainable by reasonable inspection precludes him from relying on the unstated defect to justify rejection or to establish breach

(a) where the seller could have cured it if stated seasonably; or

(b) between merchants when the seller has after rejection made a request in writing for a full and final written statement of all defects on which the buyer proposes to rely.

(2) Payment against documents made without reservation of rights precludes recovery of the payment for defects apparent on the face of the documents.

§ 2–606. What Constitutes Acceptance of Goods.

(1) Acceptance of goods occurs when the buyer

(a) after a reasonable opportunity to inspect the goods signifies to the seller that the goods are conforming or that he will take or retain them in spite of their nonconformity; or

(b) fails to make an effective rejection (subsection (1) of Section 2–602), but such acceptance does not occur until the buyer has had a reasonable opportunity to inspect them; or

(c) does any act inconsistent with the seller's ownership; but if such act is wrongful as against the seller it is an acceptance only if ratified by him.

(2) Acceptance of a part of any commercial unit is acceptance of that entire unit.

§ 2–607. Effect of Acceptance; Notice of Breach; Burden of Establishing Breach After Acceptance; Notice of Claim or Litigation to Person Answerable Over.

(1) The buyer must pay at the contract rate for any goods accepted.

(2) Acceptance of goods by the buyer precludes rejection of the goods accepted and if made with knowledge of a non-conformity cannot be revoked because of it unless the acceptance was on the reasonable assumption that the non-conformity would be seasonably cured but acceptance does not of itself impair any other remedy provided by this Article for non-conformity.

(3) Where a tender has been accepted

(a) the buyer must within a reasonable time after he discovers or should have discovered any breach notify the seller of breach or be barred from any remedy; and

(b) if the claim is one for infringement or the like (subsection (3) of Section 2–312) and the buyer is sued as a result of such a breach he must so notify the seller within a reasonable time after he receives notice of the litigation or be barred from any remedy over for liability established by the litigation.

(4) The burden is on the buyer to establish any breach with respect to the goods accepted.

(5) Where the buyer is sued for breach of a warranty or other obligation for which his seller is answerable over

(a) he may give his seller written notice of the litigation. If the notice states that the seller may come in and defend and that if the seller does not do so he will be bound in any action against him by his buyer by any determination of fact common to the two litigations, then unless the seller after seasonable receipt of the notice does come in and defend he is so bound.

(b) if the claim is one for infringement or the like (subsection (3) of Section 2–312) the original seller may demand in writing that his buyer turn over to him control of the litigation including settlement or else be barred from any remedy over and if he also agrees to bear all expense and to satisfy any adverse judgment, then unless the buyer after seasonable receipt of the demand does turn over control the buyer is so barred.

(6) The provisions of subsections (3), (4) and (5) apply to any obligation of a buyer to hold the seller harmless against infringement or the like (subsection (3) of Section 2–312).

§ 2–608. Revocation of Acceptance in Whole or in Part.

(1) The buyer may revoke his acceptance of a lot or commercial unit whose non-conformity substantially impairs its value to him if he has accepted it

(a) on the reasonable assumption that its nonconformity would be cured and it has not been seasonably cured; or

(b) without discovery of such non-conformity if his acceptance was reasonably induced either by the difficulty of discovery before acceptance or by the seller's assurances.

(2) Revocation of acceptance must occur within a reasonable time after the buyer discovers or should have discovered the ground for it and before any substantial change in condition of the goods which is not caused by their own defects. It is not effective until the buyer notifies the seller of it.

(3) A buyer who so revokes has the same rights and duties with regard to the goods involved as if he had rejected them.

§ 2–609. Right to Adequate Assurance of Performance.

(1) A contract for sale imposes an obligation on each party that the other's expectation of receiving due performance will not be impaired. When reasonable grounds for insecurity arise with respect to the performance of either party the other may in writing demand adequate assurance of due performance and until he receives such assurance may if commercially reasonable suspend any performance for which he has not already received the agreed return.

(2) Between merchants the reasonableness of grounds for insecurity and the adequacy of any assurance offered shall be determined according to commercial standards.

(3) Acceptance of any improper delivery or payment does not prejudice the party's right to demand adequate assurance of future performance.

(4) After receipt of a justified demand failure to provide within a reasonable time not exceeding thirty days such assurance of due performance as is adequate under the circumstances of the particular case is a repudiation of the contract.

§ 2–610. Anticipatory Repudiation.

When either party repudiates the contract with respect to a performance not yet due the loss of which will substantially impair the value of the contract to the other, the aggrieved party may

(a) for a commercially reasonable time await performance by the repudiating party; or

(b) resort to any remedy for breach (Section 2–703 or Section 2–711), even though he has notified the repudiating party that he would await the latter's performance and has urged retraction; and

(c) in either case suspend his own performance or proceed in accordance with the provisions of this Article on the seller's right to identify goods to the contract notwithstanding breach or to salvage unfinished goods (Section 2–704).

§ 2–611. Retraction of Anticipatory Repudiation.

(1) Until the repudiating party's next performance is due he can retract his repudiation unless the aggrieved party has since the repudiation cancelled or materially changed his position or otherwise indicated that he considers the repudiation final.

(2) Retraction may be by any method which clearly indicates to the aggrieved party that the repudiating party intends to perform, but must include any assurance justifiably demanded under the provisions of this Article (Section 2–609).

(3) Retraction reinstates the repudiating party's rights under the contract with due excuse and allowance to the aggrieved party for any delay occasioned by the repudiation.

§ 2–612. "Installment Contract"; Breach.

(1) An "installment contract" is one which requires or authorizes the delivery of goods in separate lots to be separately accepted, even though the contract contains a clause "each delivery is a separate contract" or its equivalent.

(2) The buyer may reject any installment which is non-conforming if the non-conformity substantially impairs the value of that installment and cannot be cured or if the non-conformity is a defect in the required documents; but if the non-conformity does not fall within subsection (3) and the seller gives adequate assurance of its cure the buyer must accept that installment.

(3) Whenever non-conformity or default with respect to one or more installments substantially impairs the value of the whole contract there is a breach of the whole. But the aggrieved party reinstates the contract if he accepts a non-conforming installment without seasonably notifying of cancellation or if he brings an action with respect only to past installments or demands performance as to future installments.

§ 2–613. Casualty to Identified Goods.

Where the contract requires for its performance goods identified when the contract is made, and the goods suffer casualty without fault of either party before the risk of loss passes to the buyer, or in a proper case under a "no arrival, no sale" term (Section 2–324) then

(a) if the loss is total the contract is avoided; and

(b) if the loss is partial or the goods have so deteriorated as no longer to conform to the contract the buyer may nevertheless demand inspection and at his option either treat the contract as voided or accept the goods with due allowance from the contract price for the deterioration or the deficiency in quantity but without further right against the seller.

§ 2–614. Substituted Performance.

(1) Where without fault of either party the agreed berthing, loading, or unloading facilities fail or an agreed type of carrier becomes unavailable or the agreed manner of delivery otherwise becomes commercially impracticable but a commercially reasonable substitute is available, such substitute performance must be tendered and accepted.

(2) If the agreed means or manner of payment fails because of domestic or foreign governmental regulation, the seller may withhold or stop delivery unless the buyer provides a means or manner of payment which is commercially a substantial equivalent. If delivery has already been taken, payment by the means or in the manner provided by the regulation discharges the buyer's obligation unless the regulation is discriminatory, oppressive or predatory.

§ 2–615. Excuse by Failure of Presupposed Conditions.

Except so far as a seller may have assumed a greater obligation and subject to the preceding section on substituted performance:

(a) Delay in delivery or non-delivery in whole or in part by a seller who complies with paragraphs (b) and (c) is not a breach of his duty under a contract for sale if performance as agreed has been made impracticable by the occurrence of a contingency the nonoccurrence of which was a basic assumption on which the contract was made or by compliance in good faith with any applicable foreign or domestic governmental regulation or order whether or not it later proves to be invalid.

(b) Where the causes mentioned in paragraph (a) affect only a part of the seller's capacity to perform, he must allocate production and deliveries among his customers but may at his option include regular customers not then under contract as well as his own requirements for further manufacture. He may so allocate in any manner which is fair and reasonable.

(c) The seller must notify the buyer seasonably that there will be delay or non-delivery and, when allocation is required under paragraph (b), of the estimated quota thus made available for the buyer.

§ 2–616. Procedure on Notice Claiming Excuse.

(1) Where the buyer receives notification of a material or indefinite delay or an allocation justified under the preceding section he may by written notification to the seller as to any delivery concerned, and where the prospective deficiency substantially impairs the value of the whole contract under the provisions of this Article relating to breach of installment contracts (Section 2–612), then also as to the whole,

(a) terminate and thereby discharge any unexecuted portion of the contract; or

(b) modify the contract by agreeing to take his available quota in substitution.

(2) If after receipt of such notification from the seller the buyer fails so to modify the contract within a reasonable time not exceeding thirty days the contract lapses with respect to any deliveries affected.

(3) The provisions of this section may not be negated by agreement except in so far as the seller has assumed a greater obligation under the preceding section.

Part 7 Remedies

§ 2–701. Remedies for Breach of Collateral Contracts Not Impaired.

Remedies for breach of any obligation or promise collateral or ancillary to a contract for sale are not impaired by the provisions of this Article.

§ 2–702. Seller's Remedies on Discovery of Buyer's Insolvency.

(1) Where the seller discovers the buyer to be insolvent he may refuse delivery except for cash including payment for all goods theretofore delivered under the contract, and stop delivery under this Article (Section 2–705).

(2) Where the seller discovers that the buyer has received goods on credit while insolvent he may reclaim the goods upon demand made within ten days after the receipt, but if misrepresentation of solvency has been made to the particular seller in writing within three months before delivery the ten day limitation does not apply. Except as provided in this subsection the seller may not base a right to reclaim goods on the buyer's fraudulent or innocent misrepresentation of solvency or of intent to pay.

(3) The seller's right to reclaim under subsection (2) is subject to the rights of a buyer in ordinary course or other good faith purchaser under this Article (Section 2–403). Successful reclamation of goods excludes all other remedies with respect to them.

§ 2–703. Seller's Remedies in General.

Where the buyer wrongfully rejects or revokes acceptance of goods or fails to make a payment due on or before delivery or repudiates with respect to a part or the whole, then with respect to any goods directly affected and, if the breach is of the whole contract (Section 2–612), then also with respect to the whole undelivered balance, the aggrieved seller may

(a) withhold delivery of such goods;

(b) stop delivery by any bailee as hereafter provided (Section 2–705);

(c) proceed under the next section respecting goods still unidentified to the contract;

(d) resell and recover damages as hereafter provided (Section 2–706);

(e) recover damages for non-acceptance (Section 2–708) or in a proper case the price (Section 2–709);

(f) cancel.

§ 2–704. Seller's Right to Identify Goods to the Contract Notwithstanding Breach or to Salvage Unfinished Goods.

(1) An aggrieved seller under the preceding section may

(a) identify to the contract conforming goods not already identified if at the time he learned of the breach they are in his possession or control;

(b) treat as the subject of resale goods which have demonstrably been intended for the particular contract even though those goods are unfinished.

(2) Where the goods are unfinished an aggrieved seller may in the exercise of reasonable commercial judgment for the purposes of avoiding loss and of effective realization either complete the manufacture and wholly identify the goods to the contract or cease manufacture and resell for scrap or salvage value or proceed in any other reasonable manner.

§ 2–705. Seller's Stoppage of Delivery in Transit or Otherwise.

(1) The seller may stop delivery of goods in the possession of a carrier or other bailee when he discovers the buyer to be insolvent (Section 2–702) and may stop delivery of carload, truckload, planeload or larger shipments of express or freight when the buyer repudiates or fails to make a payment due before delivery or if for any other reason the seller has a right to withhold or reclaim the goods.

(2) As against such buyer the seller may stop delivery until

(a) receipt of the goods by the buyer; or

(b) acknowledgment to the buyer by any bailee of the goods except a carrier that the bailee holds the goods for the buyer; or

(c) such acknowledgment to the buyer by a carrier by reshipment or as warehouseman; or

(d) negotiation to the buyer of any negotiable document of title covering the goods.

(3) (a) To stop delivery the seller must so notify as to enable the bailee by reasonable diligence to prevent delivery of the goods.

(b) After such notification the bailee must hold and deliver the goods according to the directions of the seller but the seller is liable to the bailee for any ensuing charges or damages.

(c) If a negotiable document of title has been issued for goods the bailee is not obliged to obey a notification to stop until surrender of the document.

(d) A carrier who has issued a non-negotiable bill of lading is not obliged to obey a notification to stop received from a person other than the consignor.

§ 2–706. Seller's Resale Including Contract for Resale.

(1) Under the conditions stated in Section 2–703 on seller's remedies, the seller may resell the goods concerned or the undelivered balance thereof. Where the resale is made in good faith and in a commercially reasonable manner the seller may recover the difference between the resale price and the contract price together with any incidental damages allowed under the provisions of this Article (Section 2–710), but less expenses saved in consequence of the buyer's breach.

(2) Except as otherwise provided in subsection (3) or unless otherwise agreed resale may be at public or private sale including sale by way of one or more contracts to sell or of identification to an existing contract of the seller. Sale may be as a unit or in parcels and at any time and place and on any terms but every aspect of the sale including the method, manner, time, place and terms must be commercially reasonable. The resale must be reasonably identified as referring to the broken contract, but it is not necessary that the goods be in existence or that any or all of them have been identified to the contract before the breach.

(3) Where the resale is at private sale the seller must give the buyer reasonable notification of his intention to resell.

(4) Where the resale is at public sale

(a) only identified goods can be sold except where there is a recognized market for a public sale of futures in goods of the kind; and

(b) it must be made at a usual place or market for public sale if one is reasonably available and except in the case of goods which are perishable or threaten to decline in value speedily the seller must give the buyer reasonable notice of the time and place of the resale; and

(c) if the goods are not to be within the view of those attending the sale the notification of sale must state the place where the goods are located and provide for their reasonable inspection by prospective bidders; and

(d) the seller may buy.

(5) A purchaser who buys in good faith at a resale takes the goods free of any rights of the original buyer even though the seller fails to comply with one or more of the requirements of this section.

(6) The seller is not accountable to the buyer for any profit made on any resale. A person in the position of a seller (Section 2–707) or a buyer who has rightfully rejected or justifiably revoked acceptance must account for any excess over the amount of his security interest, as hereinafter defined (subsection (3) of Section 2–711).

§ 2–707. "Person in the Position of a Seller".

(1) A "person in the position of a seller" includes as against a principal an agent who has paid or become responsible for the price of goods on behalf of his principal or anyone who otherwise holds a security interest or other right in goods similar to that of a seller.

(2) A person in the position of a seller may as provided in this Article withhold or stop delivery (Section 2–705) and resell (Section 2–706) and recover incidental damages (Section 2–710).

§ 2–708. Seller's Damages for Non-Acceptance or Repudiation.

(1) Subject to subsection (2) and to the provisions of this Article with respect to proof of market price (Section 2–723),

the measure of damages for non-acceptance or repudiation by the buyer is the difference between the market price at the time and place for tender and the unpaid contract price together with any incidental damages provided in this Article (Section 2–710), but less expenses saved in consequence of the buyer's breach.

(2) If the measure of damages provided in subsection (1) is inadequate to put the seller in as good a position as performance would have done then the measure of damages is the profit (including reasonable overhead) which the seller would have made from full performance by the buyer, together with any incidental damages provided in this Article (Section 2–710), due allowance for costs reasonably incurred and due credit for payments or proceeds of resale.

§ 2–709. Action for the Price.

(1) When the buyer fails to pay the price as it becomes due the seller may recover, together with any incidental damages under the next section, the price

(a) of goods accepted or of conforming goods lost or damaged within a commercially reasonable time after risk of their loss has passed to the buyer; and

(b) of goods identified to the contract if the seller is unable after reasonable effort to resell them at a reasonable price or the circumstances reasonably indicate that such effort will be unavailing.

(2) Where the seller sues for the price he must hold for the buyer any goods which have been identified to the contract and are still in his control except that if resale becomes possible he may resell them at any time prior to the collection of the judgment. The net proceeds of any such resale must be credited to the buyer and payment of the judgment entitles him to any goods not resold.

(3) After the buyer has wrongfully rejected or revoked acceptance of the goods or has failed to make a payment due or has repudiated (Section 2–610), a seller who is held not entitled to the price under this section shall nevertheless be awarded damages for non-acceptance under the preceding section.

§ 2–710. Seller's Incidental Damages.

Incidental damages to an aggrieved seller include any commercially reasonable charges, expenses or commissions incurred in stopping delivery, in the transportation, care and custody of goods after the buyer's breach, in connection with return or resale of the goods or otherwise resulting from the breach.

§ 2–711. Buyer's Remedies in General; Buyer's Security Interest in Rejected Goods.

(1) Where the seller fails to make delivery or repudiates or the buyer rightfully rejects or justifiably revokes acceptance then with respect to any goods involved, and with respect to the whole if the breach goes to the whole contract (Section 2–612), the buyer may cancel and whether or not he has done so may in addition to recovering so much of the price as has been paid

(a) "cover" and have damages under the next section as to all the goods affected whether or not they have been identified to the contract; or

(b) recover damages for non-delivery as pro-vided in this Article (Section 2–713).

(2) Where the seller fails to deliver or repudiates the buyer may also

(a) if the goods have been identified recover them as provided in this Article (Section 2–502); or

(b) in a proper case obtain specific performance or replevy the goods as provided in this Article (Section 2–716).

(3) On rightful rejection or justifiable revocation of acceptance a buyer has a security interest in goods in his possession or control for any payments made on their price and any expenses reasonably incurred in their inspection, receipt, transportation, care and custody and may hold such goods and resell them in like manner as an aggrieved seller (Section 2–706).

§ 2–712. "Cover"; Buyer's Procurement of Substitute Goods.

(1) After a breach within the preceding section the buyer may "cover" by making in good faith and without unreasonable delay any reasonable purchase of or contract to purchase goods in substitution for those due from the seller.

(2) The buyer may recover from the seller as damages the difference between the cost of cover and the contract price together with any incidental or consequential damages as hereinafter defined (Section 2–715), but less expenses saved in consequence of the seller's breach.

(3) Failure of the buyer to effect cover within this section does not bar him from any other remedy.

§ 2–713. Buyer's Damages for Non-Delivery or Repudiation.

(1) Subject to the provisions of this Article with respect to proof of market price (Section 2–723), the measure of damages for non-delivery or repudiation by the seller is the difference between the market price at the time when the buyer learned of the breach and the contract price together with any incidental and consequential damages provided in this Article (Section 2–715), but less expenses saved in consequence of the seller's breach.

(2) Market price is to be determined as of the place for tender or, in cases of rejection after arrival or revocation of acceptance, as of the place of arrival.

§ 2–714. Buyer's Damages for Breach in Regard to Accepted Goods.

(1) Where the buyer has accepted goods and given notification (subsection (3) of Section 2–607) he may recover as damages for any non-conformity of tender the loss resulting in the ordinary course of events from the seller's breach as determined in any manner which is reasonable.

(2) The measure of damages for breach of warranty is the difference at the time and place of acceptance between the value of the goods accepted and the value they would have had if they had been as warranted, unless special circumstances show proximate damages of a different amount.

(3) In a proper case any incidental and consequential damages under the next section may also be recovered.

§ 2–715. Buyer's Incidental and Consequential Damages.

(1) Incidental damages resulting from the seller's breach include expenses reasonably incurred in inspection, receipt, transportation and care and custody of goods rightfully rejected, any commercially reasonable charges, expenses or commissions in connection with effecting cover and any other reasonable expense incident to the delay or other breach.

(2) Consequential damages resulting from the seller's breach include

(a) any loss resulting from general or particular requirements and needs of which the seller at the time of contracting had reason to know and which could not reasonably be prevented by cover or otherwise; and

(b) injury to person or property proximately resulting from any breach of warranty.

§ 2–716. Buyer's Right to Specific Performance or Replevin.

(1) Specific performance may be decreed where the goods are unique or in other proper circumstances.

(2) The decree for specific performance may include such terms and conditions as to payment of the price, damages, or other relief as the court may deem just.

(3) The buyer has a right of replevin for goods identified to the contract if after reasonable effort he is unable to effect cover for such goods or the circumstances reasonably indicate that such effort will be unavailing or if the goods have been shipped under reservation and satisfaction of the security interest in them has been made or tendered. In the case of goods bought for personal, family, or household purposes, the buyer's right of replevin vests upon acquisition of a special property, even if the seller had not then repudiated or failed to deliver.

As amended in 1999.

§ 2–717. Deduction of Damages From the Price.

The buyer on notifying the seller of his intention to do so may deduct all or any part of the damages resulting from any breach of the contract from any part of the price still due under the same contract.

§ 2–718. Liquidation or Limitation of Damages; Deposits.

(1) Damages for breach by either party may be liquidated in the agreement but only at an amount which is reasonable in the light of the anticipated or actual harm caused by the breach, the difficulties of proof of loss, and the inconvenience or nonfeasibility of otherwise obtaining an adequate remedy. A term fixing unreasonably large liquidated damages is void as a penalty.

(2) Where the seller justifiably withholds delivery of goods because of the buyer's breach, the buyer is entitled to restitution of any amount by which the sum of his payments exceeds

(a) the amount to which the seller is entitled by virtue of terms liquidating the seller's damages in accordance with subsection (1), or

(b) in the absence of such terms, twenty per cent of the value of the total performance for which the buyer is obligated under the contract or $500, whichever is smaller.

(3) The buyer's right to restitution under subsection (2) is subject to offset to the extent that the seller establishes

(a) a right to recover damages under the provisions of this Article other than subsection (1), and

(b) the amount or value of any benefits received by the buyer directly or indirectly by reason of the contract.

(4) Where a seller has received payment in goods their reasonable value or the proceeds of their resale shall be treated as payments for the purposes of subsection (2); but if the seller has notice of the buyer's breach before reselling goods received in part performance, his resale is subject to the conditions laid down in this Article on resale by an aggrieved seller (Section 2–706).

§ 2–719. Contractual Modification or Limitation of Remedy.

(1) Subject to the provisions of subsections (2) and (3) of this section and of the preceding section on liquidation and limitation of damages,

(a) the agreement may provide for remedies in addition to or in substitution for those provided in this Article and may limit or alter the measure of damages recoverable under this Article, as by limiting the buyer's remedies to return of the goods and repayment of the price or to repair and replacement of nonconforming goods or parts; and

(b) resort to a remedy as provided is optional unless the remedy is expressly agreed to be exclusive, in which case it is the sole remedy.

(2) Where circumstances cause an exclusive or limited remedy to fail of its essential purpose, remedy may be had as provided in this Act.

(3) Consequential damages may be limited or excluded unless the limitation or exclusion is unconscionable. Limitation of consequential damages for injury to the person in the case of consumer goods is *prima facie* unconscionable but limitation of damages where the loss is commercial is not.

§ 2–720. Effect of "Cancellation" or "Rescission" on Claims for Antecedent Breach.

Unless the contrary intention clearly appears, expressions of "cancellation" or "rescission" of the contract or the like shall not be construed as a renunciation or discharge of any claim in damages for an antecedent breach.

§ 2–721. Remedies for Fraud.

Remedies for material misrepresentation or fraud include all remedies available under this Article for non-fraudulent breach. Neither rescission or a claim for rescission of the contract for sale nor rejection or return of the goods shall bar or be deemed inconsistent with a claim for damages or other remedy.

§ 2–722. Who Can Sue Third Parties for Injury to Goods.

Where a third party so deals with goods which have been identified to a contract for sale as to cause actionable injury to a party to that contract

(a) a right of action against the third party is in either party to the contract for sale who has title to or a security interest or a special property or an insurable interest in the goods; and if the goods have been destroyed or converted a right of action is also in the party who either bore the risk of loss under the contract for sale or has since the injury assumed that risk as against the other;

(b) if at the time of the injury the party plaintiff did not bear the risk of loss as against the other party to the contract for sale and there is no arrangement between them for disposition of the recovery, his suit or settlement is, subject to his own interest, as a fiduciary for the other party to the contract;

(c) either party may with the consent of the other sue for the benefit of whom it may concern.

§ 2–723. Proof of Market Price: Time and Place.

(1) If an action based on anticipatory repudiation comes to trial before the time for performance with respect to some or all of the goods, any damages based on market price (Section 2–708 or Section 2–713) shall be determined according to the price of such goods prevailing at the time when the aggrieved party learned of the repudiation.

(2) If evidence of a price prevailing at the times or places described in this Article is not readily available the price prevailing within any reasonable time before or after the time described or at any other place which in commercial judgment or under usage of trade would serve as a reasonable substitute for the one described may be used, making any proper allowance for the cost of transporting the goods to or from such other place.

(3) Evidence of a relevant price prevailing at a time or place other than the one described in this Article offered by one party is not admissible unless and until he has given the other party such notice as the court finds sufficient to prevent unfair surprise.

§ 2–724. Admissibility of Market Quotations.

Whenever the prevailing price or value of any goods regularly bought and sold in any established commodity market is in issue, reports in official publications or trade journals or in newspapers or periodicals of general circulation published as the reports of such market shall be admissible in evidence. The circumstances of the preparation of such a report may be shown to affect its weight but not its admissibility.

§ 2–725. Statute of Limitations in Contracts for Sale.

(1) An action for breach of any contract for sale must be commenced within four years after the cause of action has accrued. By the original agreement the parties may reduce the period of limitation to not less than one year but may not extend it.

(2) A cause of action accrues when the breach occurs, regardless of the aggrieved party's lack of knowledge of the breach. A breach of warranty occurs when tender of delivery is made, except that where a warranty explicitly extends to future performance of the goods and discovery of the breach must await the time of such performance the cause of action accrues when the breach is or should have been discovered.

(3) Where an action commenced within the time limited by subsection (1) is so terminated as to leave available a remedy by another action for the same breach such other action may be commenced after the expiration of the time limited and within six months after the termination of the first action unless the termination resulted from voluntary discontinuance or from dismissal for failure or neglect to prosecute.

(4) This section does not alter the law on tolling of the statute of limitations nor does it apply to causes of action which have accrued before this Act becomes effective.

Article 2A
LEASES

Part 1 General Provisions

§ 2A–101. Short Title.

This Article shall be known and may be cited as the Uniform Commercial Code—Leases.

§ 2A–102. Scope.

This Article applies to any transaction, regardless of form, that creates a lease.

§ 2A–103. Definitions and Index of Definitions.

(1) In this Article unless the context otherwise requires:

(a) "Buyer in ordinary course of business" means a person who in good faith and without knowledge that the sale to him [or her] is in violation of the ownership rights or security interest or leasehold interest of a third party in the goods buys in ordinary course from a person in the business of selling goods of that kind but does not include a pawnbroker. "Buying" may be for cash or by exchange of other property or on secured or unsecured credit and includes receiving goods or documents of title under a pre-existing contract for sale but does not include a transfer in bulk or as security for or in total or partial satisfaction of a money debt.

(b) "Cancellation" occurs when either party puts an end to the lease contract for default by the other party.

(c) "Commercial unit" means such a unit of goods as by commercial usage is a single whole for purposes of lease and division of which materially impairs its character or value on the market or in use. A commercial unit may be a single article, as a machine, or a set of articles, as a suite of furniture or a line of machinery, or a quantity, as a gross or carload, or any other unit treated in use or in the relevant market as a single whole.

(d) "Conforming" goods or performance under a lease contract means goods or performance that are in accordance with the obligations under the lease contract.

(e) "Consumer lease" means a lease that a lessor regularly engaged in the business of leasing or selling makes to a lessee who is an individual and who takes under the lease primarily for a personal, family, or household purpose [, if the total payments to be made under the lease contract, excluding payments for options to renew or buy, do not exceed $_____].

(f) "Fault" means wrongful act, omission, breach, or default.

(g) "Finance lease" means a lease with respect to which:

    (i) the lessor does not select, manufacture or supply the goods;

    (ii) the lessor acquires the goods or the right to possession and use of the goods in connection with the lease; and

    (iii) one of the following occurs:

        (A) the lessee receives a copy of the contract by which the lessor acquired the goods or the right to possession and use of the goods before signing the lease contract;

        (B) the lessee's approval of the contract by which the lessor acquired the goods or the right to possession and use of the goods is a condition to effectiveness of the lease contract;

        (C) the lessee, before signing the lease contract, receives an accurate and complete statement designating the promises and warranties, and any disclaimers of warranties, limitations or modifications of remedies, or liquidated damages, including those of a third party, such as the manufacturer of the goods, provided to the lessor by the person supplying the goods in connection with or as part of the contract by which the lessor acquired the goods or the right to possession and use of the goods; or

        (D) if the lease is not a consumer lease, the lessor, before the lessee signs the lease contract, informs the lessee in writing (a) of the identity of the person supplying the goods to the lessor, unless the lessee has selected that person and directed the lessor to acquire the goods or the right to possession and use of the goods from that person, (b) that the lessee is entitled under this Article to any promises and warranties, including those of any third party, provided to the lessor by the person supplying the goods in connection with or as part of the contract

by which the lessor acquired the goods or the right to possession and use of the goods, and (c) that the lessee may communicate with the person supplying the goods to the lessor and receive an accurate and complete statement of those promises and warranties, including any disclaimers and limitations of them or of remedies.

(h) "Goods" means all things that are movable at the time of identification to the lease contract, or are fixtures (Section 2A–309), but the term does not include money, documents, instruments, accounts, chattel paper, general intangibles, or minerals or the like, including oil and gas, before extraction. The term also includes the unborn young of animals.

(i) "Installment lease contract" means a lease contract that authorizes or requires the delivery of goods in separate lots to be separately accepted, even though the lease contract contains a clause "each delivery is a separate lease" or its equivalent.

(j) "Lease" means a transfer of the right to possession and use of goods for a term in return for consideration, but a sale, including a sale on approval or a sale or return, or retention or creation of a security interest is not a lease. Unless the context clearly indicates otherwise, the term includes a sublease.

(k) "Lease agreement" means the bargain, with respect to the lease, of the lessor and the lessee in fact as found in their language or by implication from other circumstances including course of dealing or usage of trade or course of performance as provided in this Article. Unless the context clearly indicates otherwise, the term includes a sublease agreement.

(l) "Lease contract" means the total legal obligation that results from the lease agreement as affected by this Article and any other applicable rules of law. Unless the context clearly indicates otherwise, the term includes a sublease contract.

(m) "Leasehold interest" means the interest of the lessor or the lessee under a lease contract.

(n) "Lessee" means a person who acquires the right to possession and use of goods under a lease. Unless the context clearly indicates otherwise, the term includes a sublessee.

(o) "Lessee in ordinary course of business" means a person who in good faith and without knowledge that the lease to him [or her] is in violation of the ownership rights or security interest or leasehold interest of a third party in the goods, leases in ordinary course from a person in the business of selling or leasing goods of that kind but does not include a pawnbroker. "Leasing" may be for cash or by exchange of other property or on secured or unsecured credit and includes receiving goods or documents of title under a pre-existing lease contract but does not include a transfer in bulk or as security for or in total or partial satisfaction of a money debt.

(p) "Lessor" means a person who transfers the right to possession and use of goods under a lease. Unless the context clearly indicates otherwise, the term includes a sublessor.

(q) "Lessor's residual interest" means the lessor's interest in the goods after expiration, termination, or cancellation of the lease contract.

(r) "Lien" means a charge against or interest in goods to secure payment of a debt or performance of an obligation, but the term does not include a security interest.

(s) "Lot" means a parcel or a single article that is the subject matter of a separate lease or delivery, whether or not it is sufficient to perform the lease contract.

(t) "Merchant lessee" means a lessee that is a merchant with respect to goods of the kind subject to the lease.

(u) "Present value" means the amount as of a date certain of one or more sums payable in the future, discounted to the date certain. The discount is determined by the interest rate specified by the parties if the rate was not manifestly unreasonable at the time the transaction was entered into; otherwise, the discount is determined by a commercially reasonable rate that takes into account the facts and circumstances of each case at the time the transaction was entered into.

(v) "Purchase" includes taking by sale, lease, mortgage, security interest, pledge, gift, or any other voluntary transaction creating an interest in goods.

(w) "Sublease" means a lease of goods the right to possession and use of which was acquired by the lessor as a lessee under an existing lease.

(x) "Supplier" means a person from whom a lessor buys or leases goods to be leased under a finance lease.

(y) "Supply contract" means a contract under which a lessor buys or leases goods to be leased.

(z) "Termination" occurs when either party pursuant to a power created by agreement or law puts an end to the lease contract otherwise than for default.

(2) Other definitions applying to this Article and the sections in which they appear are:

"Accessions". Section 2A–310(1).

"Construction mortgage". Section 2A–309(1)(d).

"Encumbrance". Section 2A–309(1)(e).

"Fixtures". Section 2A–309(1)(a).

"Fixture filing". Section 2A–309(1)(b).

"Purchase money lease". Section 2A–309(1)(c).

(3) The following definitions in other Articles apply to this Article:

"Accounts". Section 9–106.

"Between merchants". Section 2–104(3).

"Buyer". Section 2–103(1)(a).

"Chattel paper". Section 9–105(1)(b).

"Consumer goods". Section 9–109(1).

"Document". Section 9–105(1)(f).

"Entrusting". Section 2–403(3).

"General intangibles". Section 9–106.

"Good faith". Section 2–103(1)(b).

"Instrument". Section 9–105(1)(i).

"Merchant". Section 2–104(1).

"Mortgage". Section 9–105(1)(j).

"Pursuant to commitment". Section 9–105(1)(k).

"Receipt". Section 2–103(1)(c).

"Sale". Section 2–106(1).

"Sale on approval". Section 2–326.

"Sale or return". Section 2–326.

"Seller". Section 2–103(1)(d).

(4) In addition Article 1 contains general definitions and principles of construction and interpretation applicable throughout this Article.

As amended in 1990 and 1999.

§ 2A–104. Leases Subject to Other Law.

(1) A lease, although subject to this Article, is also subject to any applicable:

> (a) certificate of title statute of this State: (list any certificate of title statutes covering automobiles, trailers, mobile homes, boats, farm tractors, and the like);

> (b) certificate of title statute of another jurisdiction (Section 2A–105); or

> (c) consumer protection statute of this State, or final consumer protection decision of a court of this State existing on the effective date of this Article.

(2) In case of conflict between this Article, other than Sections 2A–105, 2A–304(3), and 2A–305(3), and a statute or decision referred to in subsection (1), the statute or decision controls.

(3) Failure to comply with an applicable law has only the effect specified therein.

As amended in 1990.

§ 2A–105. Territorial Application of Article to Goods Covered by Certificate of Title.

Subject to the provisions of Sections 2A–304(3) and 2A–305(3), with respect to goods covered by a certificate of title issued under a statute of this State or of another jurisdiction, compliance and the effect of compliance or noncompliance with a certificate of title statute are governed by the law (including the conflict of laws rules) of the jurisdiction issuing the certificate until the earlier of (a) surrender of the certificate, or (b) four months after the goods are removed from that jurisdiction and thereafter until a new certificate of title is issued by another jurisdiction.

§ 2A–106. Limitation on Power of Parties to Consumer Lease to Choose Applicable Law and Judicial Forum.

(1) If the law chosen by the parties to a consumer lease is that of a jurisdiction other than a jurisdiction in which the lessee resides at the time the lease agreement becomes enforceable or within 30 days thereafter or in which the goods are to be used, the choice is not enforceable.

(2) If the judicial forum chosen by the parties to a consumer lease is a forum that would not otherwise have jurisdiction over the lessee, the choice is not enforceable.

§ 2A–107. Waiver or Renunciation of Claim or Right After Default.

Any claim or right arising out of an alleged default or breach of warranty may be discharged in whole or in part without consideration by a written waiver or renunciation signed and delivered by the aggrieved party.

§ 2A–108. Unconscionability.

(1) If the court as a matter of law finds a lease contract or any clause of a lease contract to have been unconscionable at the time it was made the court may refuse to enforce the lease contract, or it may enforce the remainder of the lease contract without the unconscionable clause, or it may so limit the application of any unconscionable clause as to avoid any unconscionable result.

(2) With respect to a consumer lease, if the court as a matter of law finds that a lease contract or any clause of a lease contract has been induced by unconscionable conduct or that unconscionable conduct has occurred in the collection of a claim arising from a lease contract, the court may grant appropriate relief.

(3) Before making a finding of unconscionability under subsection (1) or (2), the court, on its own motion or that of a party, shall afford the parties a reasonable opportunity to present evidence as to the setting, purpose, and effect of the lease contract or clause thereof, or of the conduct.

(4) In an action in which the lessee claims unconscionability with respect to a consumer lease:

(a) If the court finds unconscionability under subsection (1) or (2), the court shall award reasonable attorney's fees to the lessee.

(b) If the court does not find unconscionability and the lessee claiming unconscionability has brought or maintained an action he [or she] knew to be groundless, the court shall award reasonable attorney's fees to the party against whom the claim is made.

(c) In determining attorney's fees, the amount of the recovery on behalf of the claimant under subsections (1) and (2) is not controlling.

§ 2A–109. Option to Accelerate at Will.

(1) A term providing that one party or his [or her] successor in interest may accelerate payment or performance or require collateral or additional collateral "at will" or "when he [or she] deems himself [or herself] insecure" or in words of similar import must be construed to mean that he [or she] has power to do so only if he [or she] in good faith believes that the prospect of payment or performance is impaired.

(2) With respect to a consumer lease, the burden of establishing good faith under subsection (1) is on the party who exercised the power; otherwise the burden of establishing lack of good faith is on the party against whom the power has been exercised.

Part 2 Formation and Construction of Lease Contract

§ 2A–201. Statute of Frauds.

(1) A lease contract is not enforceable by way of action or defense unless:

(a) the total payments to be made under the lease contract, excluding payments for options to renew or buy, are less than $1,000; or

(b) there is a writing, signed by the party against whom enforcement is sought or by that party's authorized agent, sufficient to indicate that a lease contract has been made between the parties and to describe the goods leased and the lease term.

(2) Any description of leased goods or of the lease term is sufficient and satisfies subsection (1)(b), whether or not it is specific, if it reasonably identifies what is described.

(3) A writing is not insufficient because it omits or incorrectly states a term agreed upon, but the lease contract is not enforceable under subsection (1)(b) beyond the lease term and the quantity of goods shown in the writing.

(4) A lease contract that does not satisfy the requirements of subsection (1), but which is valid in other respects, is enforceable:

(a) if the goods are to be specially manufactured or obtained for the lessee and are not suitable for lease or sale to others in the ordinary course of the lessor's business, and the lessor, before notice of repudiation is received and under circumstances that reasonably indicate that the goods are for the lessee, has made either a substantial beginning of their manufacture or commitments for their procurement;

(b) if the party against whom enforcement is sought admits in that party's pleading, testimony or otherwise in court that a lease contract was made, but the lease contract is not enforceable under this provision beyond the quantity of goods admitted; or

(c) with respect to goods that have been received and accepted by the lessee.

(5) The lease term under a lease contract referred to in subsection (4) is:

(a) if there is a writing signed by the party against whom enforcement is sought or by that party's authorized agent specifying the lease term, the term so specified;

(b) if the party against whom enforcement is sought admits in that party's pleading, testimony, or otherwise in court a lease term, the term so admitted; or

(c) a reasonable lease term.

§ 2A–202. Final Written Expression: Parol or Extrinsic Evidence.

Terms with respect to which the confirmatory memoranda of the parties agree or which are otherwise set forth in a writing intended by the parties as a final expression of their agreement with respect to such terms as are included therein may not be contradicted by evidence of any prior agreement or of a contemporaneous oral agreement but may be explained or supplemented:

(a) by course of dealing or usage of trade or by course of performance; and

(b) by evidence of consistent additional terms unless the court finds the writing to have been intended also as a complete and exclusive statement of the terms of the agreement.

§ 2A–203. Seals Inoperative.

The affixing of a seal to a writing evidencing a lease contract or an offer to enter into a lease contract does not render the writing a sealed instrument and the law with respect to sealed instruments does not apply to the lease contract or offer.

§ 2A–204. Formation in General.

(1) A lease contract may be made in any manner sufficient to show agreement, including conduct by both parties which recognizes the existence of a lease contract.

(2) An agreement sufficient to constitute a lease contract may be found although the moment of its making is undetermined.

(3) Although one or more terms are left open, a lease contract does not fail for indefiniteness if the parties have intended to make a lease contract and there is a reasonably certain basis for giving an appropriate remedy.

§ 2A–205. Firm Offers.

An offer by a merchant to lease goods to or from another person in a signed writing that by its terms gives assurance it will be held open is not revocable, for lack of consideration, during the time stated or, if no time is stated, for a reasonable time, but in no event may the period of irrevocability exceed 3 months. Any such term of assurance on a form supplied by the offeree must be separately signed by the offeror.

§ 2A–206. Offer and Acceptance in Formation of Lease Contract.

(1) Unless otherwise unambiguously indicated by the language or circumstances, an offer to make a lease contract must be construed as inviting acceptance in any manner and by any medium reasonable in the circumstances.

(2) If the beginning of a requested performance is a reasonable mode of acceptance, an offeror who is not notified of acceptance within a reasonable time may treat the offer as having lapsed before acceptance.

§ 2A–207. Course of Performance or Practical Construction.

(1) If a lease contract involves repeated occasions for performance by either party with knowledge of the nature of the performance and opportunity for objection to it by the other, any course of performance accepted or acquiesced in without objection is relevant to determine the meaning of the lease agreement.

(2) The express terms of a lease agreement and any course of performance, as well as any course of dealing and usage of trade, must be construed whenever reasonable as consistent with each other; but if that construction is unreasonable, express terms control course of performance, course of performance controls both course of dealing and usage of trade, and course of dealing controls usage of trade.

(3) Subject to the provisions of Section 2A–208 on modification and waiver, course of performance is relevant to show a waiver or modification of any term inconsistent with the course of performance.

§ 2A–208. Modification, Rescission and Waiver.

(1) An agreement modifying a lease contract needs no consideration to be binding.

(2) A signed lease agreement that excludes modification or rescission except by a signed writing may not be otherwise modified or rescinded, but, except as between merchants, such a requirement on a form supplied by a merchant must be separately signed by the other party.

(3) Although an attempt at modification or rescission does not satisfy the requirements of subsection (2), it may operate as a waiver.

(4) A party who has made a waiver affecting an executory portion of a lease contract may retract the waiver by reasonable notification received by the other party that strict performance will be required of any term waived, unless the retraction would be unjust in view of a material change of position in reliance on the waiver.

§ 2A–209. Lessee under Finance Lease as Beneficiary of Supply Contract.

(1) The benefit of the supplier's promises to the lessor under the supply contract and of all warranties, whether express or implied, including those of any third party provided in connection with or as part of the supply contract, extends to the lessee to the extent of the lessee's leasehold interest under a finance lease related to the supply contract, but is subject to the terms warranty and of the supply contract and all defenses or claims arising therefrom.

(2) The extension of the benefit of supplier's promises and of warranties to the lessee (Section 2A–209(1)) does not: (i) modify the rights and obligations of the parties to the supply contract, whether arising therefrom or otherwise, or (ii) impose any duty or liability under the supply contract on the lessee.

(3) Any modification or rescission of the supply contract by the supplier and the lessor is effective between the supplier and the lessee unless, before the modification or rescission, the supplier has received notice that the lessee has entered into a finance lease related to the supply contract. If the modification or rescission is effective between the supplier and the lessee, the lessor is deemed to have assumed, in addition to the obligations of the lessor to the lessee under the lease contract, promises of the supplier to the lessor and warranties that were so modified or rescinded as they existed and were available to the lessee before modification or rescission.

(4) In addition to the extension of the benefit of the supplier's promises and of warranties to the lessee under subsection (1), the lessee retains all rights that the lessee may have against the supplier which arise from an agreement between the lessee and the supplier or under other law.

As amended in 1990.

§ 2A–210. Express Warranties.

(1) Express warranties by the lessor are created as follows:

    (a) Any affirmation of fact or promise made by the lessor to the lessee which relates to the goods and becomes part of the basis of the bargain creates an express warranty that the goods will conform to the affirmation or promise.

(b) Any description of the goods which is made part of the basis of the bargain creates an express warranty that the goods will conform to the description.

(c) Any sample or model that is made part of the basis of the bargain creates an express warranty that the whole of the goods will conform to the sample or model.

(2) It is not necessary to the creation of an express warranty that the lessor use formal words, such as "warrant" or "guarantee," or that the lessor have a specific intention to make a warranty, but an affirmation merely of the value of the goods or a statement purporting to be merely the lessor's opinion or commendation of the goods does not create a warranty.

§ 2A–211. Warranties Against Interference and Against Infringement; Lessee's Obligation Against Infringement.

(1) There is in a lease contract a warranty that for the lease term no person holds a claim to or interest in the goods that arose from an act or omission of the lessor, other than a claim by way of infringement or the like, which will interfere with the lessee's enjoyment of its leasehold interest.

(2) Except in a finance lease there is in a lease contract by a lessor who is a merchant regularly dealing in goods of the kind a warranty that the goods are delivered free of the rightful claim of any person by way of infringement or the like.

(3) A lessee who furnishes specifications to a lessor or a supplier shall hold the lessor and the supplier harmless against any claim by way of infringement or the like that arises out of compliance with the specifications.

§ 2A–212. Implied Warranty of Merchantability.

(1) Except in a finance lease, a warranty that the goods will be merchantable is implied in a lease contract if the lessor is a merchant with respect to goods of that kind.

(2) Goods to be merchantable must be at least such as

(a) pass without objection in the trade under the description in the lease agreement;

(b) in the case of fungible goods, are of fair average quality within the description;

(c) are fit for the ordinary purposes for which goods of that type are used;

(d) run, within the variation permitted by the lease agreement, of even kind, quality, and quantity within each unit and among all units involved;

(e) are adequately contained, packaged, and labeled as the lease agreement may require; and

(f) conform to any promises or affirmations of fact made on the container or label.

(3) Other implied warranties may arise from course of dealing or usage of trade.

§ 2A–213. Implied Warranty of Fitness for Particular Purpose.

Except in a finance of lease, if the lessor at the time the lease contract is made has reason to know of any particular purpose for which the goods are required and that the lessee is relying on the lessor's skill or judgment to select or furnish suitable goods, there is in the lease contract an implied warranty that the goods will be fit for that purpose.

§ 2A–214. Exclusion or Modification of Warranties.

(1) Words or conduct relevant to the creation of an express warranty and words or conduct tending to negate or limit a warranty must be construed wherever reasonable as consistent with each other; but, subject to the provisions of Section 2A–202 on parol or extrinsic evidence, negation or limitation is inoperative to the extent that the construction is unreasonable.

(2) Subject to subsection (3), to exclude or modify the implied warranty of merchantability or any part of it the language must mention "merchantability", be by a writing, and be conspicuous. Subject to subsection (3), to exclude or modify any implied warranty of fitness the exclusion must be by a writing and be conspicuous. Language to exclude all implied warranties of fitness is sufficient if it is in writing, is conspicuous and states, for example, "There is no warranty that the goods will be fit for a particular purpose".

(3) Notwithstanding subsection (2), but subject to subsection (4),

(a) unless the circumstances indicate otherwise, all implied warranties are excluded by expressions like "as is" or "with all faults" or by other language that in common understanding calls the lessee's attention to the exclusion of warranties and makes plain that there is no implied warranty, if in writing and conspicuous;

(b) if the lessee before entering into the lease contract has examined the goods or the sample or model as fully as desired or has refused to examine the goods, there is no implied warranty with regard to defects that an examination ought in the circumstances to have revealed; and

(c) an implied warranty may also be excluded or modified by course of dealing, course of performance, or usage of trade.

(4) To exclude or modify a warranty against interference or against infringement (Section 2A–211) or any part of it, the language must be specific, be by a writing, and be conspicuous, unless the circumstances, including course of performance, course of dealing, or usage of trade, give the lessee reason to know that the goods are being leased subject to a claim or interest of any person.

§ 2A–215. Cumulation and Conflict of Warranties Express or Implied.

Warranties, whether express or implied, must be construed as consistent with each other and as cumulative, but if that construction is unreasonable, the intention of the parties determines which warranty is dominant. In ascertaining that intention the following rules apply:

(a) Exact or technical specifications displace an inconsistent sample or model or general language of description.

(b) A sample from an existing bulk displaces inconsistent general language of description.

(c) Express warranties displace inconsistent implied warranties other than an implied warranty of fitness for a particular purpose.

§ 2A–216. Third-Party Beneficiaries of Express and Implied Warranties.

Alternative A

A warranty to or for the benefit of a lessee under this Article, whether express or implied, extends to any natural person who is in the family or household of the lessee or who is a guest in the lessee's home if it is reasonable to expect that such person may use, consume, or be affected by the goods and who is injured in person by breach of the warranty. This section does not displace principles of law and equity that extend a warranty to or for the benefit of a lessee to other persons. The operation of this section may not be excluded, modified, or limited, but an exclusion, modification, or limitation of the warranty, including any with respect to rights and remedies, effective against the lessee is also effective against any beneficiary designated under this section.

Alternative B

A warranty to or for the benefit of a lessee under this Article, whether express or implied, extends to any natural person who may reasonably be expected to use, consume, or be affected by the goods and who is injured in person by breach of the warranty. This section does not displace principles of law and equity that extend a warranty to or for the benefit of a lessee to other persons. The operation of this section may not be excluded, modified, or limited, but an exclusion, modification, or limitation of the warranty, including any with respect to rights and remedies, effective against the lessee is also effective against the beneficiary designated under this section.

Alternative C

A warranty to or for the benefit of a lessee under this Article, whether express or implied, extends to any person who may reasonably be expected to use, consume, or be affected by the goods and who is injured by breach of the warranty. The operation of this section may not be excluded, modified, or limited with respect to injury to the person of an individual to whom the warranty extends, but an exclusion, modification, or limitation of the warranty, including any with respect to rights and remedies, effective against the lessee is also effective against the beneficiary designated under this section.

§ 2A–217. Identification.

Identification of goods as goods to which a lease contract refers may be made at any time and in any manner explicitly agreed to by the parties. In the absence of explicit agreement, identification occurs:

(a) when the lease contract is made if the lease contract is for a lease of goods that are existing and identified;

(b) when the goods are shipped, marked, or otherwise designated by the lessor as goods to which the lease contract refers, if the lease contract is for a lease of goods that are not existing and identified; or

(c) when the young are conceived, if the lease contract is for a lease of unborn young of animals.

§ 2A–218. Insurance and Proceeds.

(1) A lessee obtains an insurable interest when existing goods are identified to the lease contract even though the goods identified are nonconforming and the lessee has an option to reject them.

(2) If a lessee has an insurable interest only by reason of the lessor's identification of the goods, the lessor, until default or insolvency or notification to the lessee that identification is final, may substitute other goods for those identified.

(3) Notwithstanding a lessee's insurable interest under subsections (1) and (2), the lessor retains an insurable interest until an option to buy has been exercised by the lessee and risk of loss has passed to the lessee.

(4) Nothing in this section impairs any insurable interest recognized under any other statute or rule of law.

(5) The parties by agreement may determine that one or more parties have an obligation to obtain and pay for insurance covering the goods and by agreement may determine the beneficiary of the proceeds of the insurance.

§ 2A–219. Risk of Loss.

(1) Except in the case of a finance lease, risk of loss is retained by the lessor and does not pass to the lessee. In the case of a finance lease, risk of loss passes to the lessee.

(2) Subject to the provisions of this Article on the effect of default on risk of loss (Section 2A–220), if risk of loss is to pass to the lessee and the time of passage is not stated, the following rules apply:

(a) If the lease contract requires or authorizes the goods to be shipped by carrier

(i) and it does not require delivery at a particular destination, the risk of loss passes to the lessee when the goods are duly delivered to the carrier; but

(ii) if it does require delivery at a particular destination and the goods are there duly tendered while in the possession of the carrier, the risk of loss passes to the lessee when the goods are there duly so tendered as to enable the lessee to take delivery.

(b) If the goods are held by a bailee to be delivered without being moved, the risk of loss passes to the lessee on acknowledgment by the bailee of the lessee's right to possession of the goods.

(c) In any case not within subsection (a) or (b), the risk of loss passes to the lessee on the lessee's receipt of the goods if the lessor, or, in the case of a finance lease, the supplier, is a merchant; otherwise the risk passes to the lessee on tender of delivery.

§ 2A–220. Effect of Default on Risk of Loss.

(1) Where risk of loss is to pass to the lessee and the time of passage is not stated:

(a) If a tender or delivery of goods so fails to conform to the lease contract as to give a right of rejection, the risk of their loss remains with the lessor, or, in the case of a finance lease, the supplier, until cure or acceptance.

(b) If the lessee rightfully revokes acceptance, he [or she], to the extent of any deficiency in his [or her] effective insurance coverage, may treat the risk of loss as having remained with the lessor from the beginning.

(2) Whether or not risk of loss is to pass to the lessee, if the lessee as to conforming goods already identified to a lease contract repudiates or is otherwise in default under the lease contract, the lessor, or, in the case of a finance lease, the supplier, to the extent of any deficiency in his [or her] effective insurance coverage may treat the risk of loss as resting on the lessee for a commercially reasonable time.

§ 2A–221. Casualty to Identified Goods.

If a lease contract requires goods identified when the lease contract is made, and the goods suffer casualty without fault of the lessee, the lessor or the supplier before delivery, or the goods suffer casualty before risk of loss passes to the lessee pursuant to the lease agreement or Section 2A–219, then:

(a) if the loss is total, the lease contract is avoided; and

(b) if the loss is partial or the goods have so deteriorated as to no longer conform to the lease contract, the lessee may nevertheless demand inspection and at his [or her] option either treat the lease contract as avoided or, except in a finance lease that is not a consumer lease, accept the goods with due allowance from the rent payable for the balance of the lease term for the deterioration or the deficiency in quantity but without further right against the lessor.

Part 3 Effect of Lease Contract

§ 2A–301. Enforceability of Lease Contract.

Except as otherwise provided in this Article, a lease contract is effective and enforceable according to its terms between the parties, against purchasers of the goods and against creditors of the parties.

§ 2A–302. Title to and Possession of Goods.

Except as otherwise provided in this Article, each provision of this Article applies whether the lessor or a third party has title to the goods, and whether the lessor, the lessee, or a third party has possession of the goods, notwithstanding any statute or rule of law that possession or the absence of possession is fraudulent.

§ 2A–303. Alienability of Party's Interest Under Lease Contract or of Lessor's Residual Interest in Goods; Delegation of Performance; Transfer of Rights.

(1) As used in this section, "creation of a security interest" includes the sale of a lease contract that is subject to Article 9, Secured Transactions, by reason of Section 9–109(a)(3).

(2) Except as provided in subsections (3) and Section 9–407, a provision in a lease agreement which (i) prohibits the voluntary or involuntary transfer, including a transfer by sale, sublease, creation or enforcement of a security interest, or attachment, levy, or other judicial process, of an interest of a party under the lease contract or of the lessor's residual interest in the goods, or (ii) makes such a transfer an event of default, gives rise to the rights and remedies provided in subsection (4), but a transfer that is prohibited or is an event of default under the lease agreement is otherwise effective.

(3) A provision in a lease agreement which (i) prohibits a transfer of a right to damages for default with respect to the whole lease contract or of a right to payment arising out of the transferor's due performance of the transferor's entire obligation, or (ii) makes such a transfer an event of default, is not enforceable, and such a transfer is not a transfer that materially impairs the prospect of obtaining return performance by, materially changes the duty of, or materially increases the burden or risk imposed on, the other party to the lease contract within the purview of subsection (4).

(4) Subject to subsection (3) and Section 9–407:

(a) if a transfer is made which is made an event of default under a lease agreement, the party to the lease contract not making the transfer, unless that party waives the default or otherwise agrees, has the rights and remedies described in Section 2A–501(2);

(b) if paragraph (a) is not applicable and if a transfer is made that (i) is prohibited under a lease agreement or (ii) materially impairs the prospect of obtaining return performance by, materially changes the duty of, or materially increases the burden or risk imposed on, the other party to the lease contract, unless the party not making the transfer agrees at any time to the transfer in the lease contract or otherwise, then, except as limited by contract, (i) the transferor is liable to the party not making the transfer for damages caused by the transfer to the extent that the damages could not reasonably be prevented by the party not making the transfer and (ii) a court having jurisdiction may grant other appropriate relief, including cancellation of the lease contract or an injunction against the transfer.

(5) A transfer of "the lease" or of "all my rights under the lease", or a transfer in similar general terms, is a transfer of rights and, unless the language or the circumstances, as in a transfer for security, indicate the contrary, the transfer is a delegation of duties by the transferor to the transferee. Acceptance by the transferee constitutes a promise by the

transferee to perform those duties. The promise is enforceable by either the transferor or the other party to the lease contract.

(6) Unless otherwise agreed by the lessor and the lessee, a delegation of performance does not relieve the transferor as against the other party of any duty to perform or of any liability for default.

(7) In a consumer lease, to prohibit the transfer of an interest of a party under the lease contract or to make a transfer an event of default, the language must be specific, by a writing, and conspicuous.

As amended in 1990 and 1999.

§ 2A-304. Subsequent Lease of Goods by Lessor.

(1) Subject to Section 2A-303, a subsequent lessee from a lessor of goods under an existing lease contract obtains, to the extent of the leasehold interest transferred, the leasehold interest in the goods that the lessor had or had power to transfer, and except as provided in subsection (2) and Section 2A-527(4), takes subject to the existing lease contract. A lessor with voidable title has power to transfer a good leasehold interest to a good faith subsequent lessee for value, but only to the extent set forth in the preceding sentence. If goods have been delivered under a transaction of purchase the lessor has that power even though:

(a) the lessor's transferor was deceived as to the identity of the lessor;

(b) the delivery was in exchange for a check which is later dishonored;

(c) it was agreed that the transaction was to be a "cash sale"; or

(d) the delivery was procured through fraud punishable as larcenous under the criminal law.

(2) A subsequent lessee in the ordinary course of business from a lessor who is a merchant dealing in goods of that kind to whom the goods were entrusted by the existing lessee of that lessor before the interest of the subsequent lessee became enforceable against that lessor obtains, to the extent of the leasehold interest transferred, all of that lessor's and the existing lessee's rights to the goods, and takes free of the existing lease contract.

(3) A subsequent lessee from the lessor of goods that are subject to an existing lease contract and are covered by a certificate of title issued under a statute of this State or of another jurisdiction takes no greater rights than those provided both by this section and by the certificate of title statute.

As amended in 1990.

§ 2A-305. Sale or Sublease of Goods by Lessee.

(1) Subject to the provisions of Section 2A-303, a buyer or sublessee from the lessee of goods under an existing lease contract obtains, to the extent of the interest transferred, the leasehold interest in the goods that the lessee had or had power to transfer, and except as provided in subsection (2) and Section 2A-511(4), takes subject to the existing lease contract. A lessee with a voidable leasehold interest has

power to transfer a good leasehold interest to a good faith buyer for value or a good faith sublessee for value, but only to the extent set forth in the preceding sentence. When goods have been delivered under a transaction of lease the lessee has that power even though:

(a) the lessor was deceived as to the identity of the lessee;

(b) the delivery was in exchange for a check which is later dishonored; or

(c) the delivery was procured through fraud punishable as larcenous under the criminal law.

(2) A buyer in the ordinary course of business or a sublessee in the ordinary course of business from a lessee who is a merchant dealing in goods of that kind to whom the goods were entrusted by the lessor obtains, to the extent of the interest transferred, all of the lessor's and lessee's rights to the goods, and takes free of the existing lease contract.

(3) A buyer or sublessee from the lessee of goods that are subject to an existing lease contract and are covered by a certificate of title issued under a statute of this State or of another jurisdiction takes no greater rights than those provided both by this section and by the certificate of title statute.

§ 2A-306. Priority of Certain Liens Arising by Operation of Law.

If a person in the ordinary course of his [or her] business furnishes services or materials with respect to goods subject to a lease contract, a lien upon those goods in the possession of that person given by statute or rule of law for those materials or services takes priority over any interest of the lessor or lessee under the lease contract or this Article unless the lien is created by statute and the statute provides otherwise or unless the lien is created by rule of law and the rule of law provides otherwise.

§ 2A-307. Priority of Liens Arising by Attachment or Levy on, Security Interests in, and Other Claims to Goods.

(1) Except as otherwise provided in Section 2A-306, a creditor of a lessee takes subject to the lease contract.

(2) Except as otherwise provided in subsection (3) and in Sections 2A-306 and 2A-308, a creditor of a lessor takes subject to the lease contract unless the creditor holds a lien that attached to the goods before the lease contract became enforceable.

(3) Except as otherwise provided in Sections 9-317, 9-321, and 9-323, a lessee takes a leasehold interest subject to a security interest held by a creditor of the lessor.

As amended in 1990 and 1999.

§ 2A-308. Special Rights of Creditors.

(1) A creditor of a lessor in possession of goods subject to a lease contract may treat the lease contract as void if as against the creditor retention of possession by the lessor is fraudulent under any statute or rule of law, but retention of possession in good faith and current course of trade by the lessor for a commercially reasonable time after the lease contract becomes enforceable is not fraudulent.

(2) Nothing in this Article impairs the rights of creditors of a lessor if the lease contract (a) becomes enforceable, not in current course of trade but in satisfaction of or as security for a pre-existing claim for money, security, or the like, and (b) is made under circumstances which under any statute or rule of law apart from this Article would constitute the transaction a fraudulent transfer or voidable preference.

(3) A creditor of a seller may treat a sale or an identification of goods to a contract for sale as void if as against the creditor retention of possession by the seller is fraudulent under any statute or rule of law, but retention of possession of the goods pursuant to a lease contract entered into by the seller as lessee and the buyer as lessor in connection with the sale or identification of the goods is not fraudulent if the buyer bought for value and in good faith.

§ 2A–309. Lessor's and Lessee's Rights When Goods Become Fixtures.

(1) In this section:

(a) goods are "fixtures" when they become so related to particular real estate that an interest in them arises under real estate law;

(b) a "fixture filing" is the filing, in the office where a mortgage on the real estate would be filed or recorded, of a financing statement covering goods that are or are to become fixtures and conforming to the requirements of Section 9–502(a) and (b);

(c) a lease is a "purchase money lease" unless the lessee has possession or use of the goods or the right to possession or use of the goods before the lease agreement is enforceable;

(d) a mortgage is a "construction mortgage" to the extent it secures an obligation incurred for the construction of an improvement on land including the acquisition cost of the land, if the recorded writing so indicates; and

(e) "encumbrance" includes real estate mortgages and other liens on real estate and all other rights in real estate that are not ownership interests.

(2) Under this Article a lease may be of goods that are fixtures or may continue in goods that become fixtures, but no lease exists under this Article of ordinary building materials incorporated into an improvement on land.

(3) This Article does not prevent creation of a lease of fixtures pursuant to real estate law.

(4) The perfected interest of a lessor of fixtures has priority over a conflicting interest of an encumbrancer or owner of the real estate if:

(a) the lease is a purchase money lease, the conflicting interest of the encumbrancer or owner arises before the goods become fixtures, the interest of the lessor is perfected by a fixture filing before the goods become fixtures or within ten days thereafter, and the lessee has an interest of record in the real estate or is in possession of the real estate; or

(b) the interest of the lessor is perfected by a fixture filing before the interest of the encumbrancer or owner is of record, the lessor's interest has priority over any conflicting interest of a predecessor in title of the encumbrancer or owner, and the lessee has an interest of record in the real estate or is in possession of the real estate.

(5) The interest of a lessor of fixtures, whether or not perfected, has priority over the conflicting interest of an encumbrancer or owner of the real estate if:

(a) the fixtures are readily removable factory or office machines, readily removable equipment that is not primarily used or leased for use in the operation of the real estate, or readily removable replacements of domestic appliances that are goods subject to a consumer lease, and before the goods become fixtures the lease contract is enforceable; or

(b) the conflicting interest is a lien on the real estate obtained by legal or equitable proceedings after the lease contract is enforceable; or

(c) the encumbrancer or owner has consented in writing to the lease or has disclaimed an interest in the goods as fixtures; or

(d) the lessee has a right to remove the goods as against the encumbrancer or owner. If the lessee's right to remove terminates, the priority of the interest of the lessor continues for a reasonable time.

(6) Notwithstanding paragraph (4)(a) but otherwise subject to subsections (4) and (5), the interest of a lessor of fixtures, including the lessor's residual interest, is subordinate to the conflicting interest of an encumbrancer of the real estate under a construction mortgage recorded before the goods become fixtures if the goods become fixtures before the completion of the construction. To the extent given to refinance a construction mortgage, the conflicting interest of an encumbrancer of the real estate under a mortgage has this priority to the same extent as the encumbrancer of the real estate under the construction mortgage.

(7) In cases not within the preceding subsections, priority between the interest of a lessor of fixtures, including the lessor's residual interest, and the conflicting interest of an encumbrancer or owner of the real estate who is not the lessee is determined by the priority rules governing conflicting interests in real estate.

(8) If the interest of a lessor of fixtures, including the lessor's residual interest, has priority over all conflicting interests of all owners and encumbrancers of the real estate, the lessor or the lessee may (i) on default, expiration, termination, or cancellation of the lease agreement but subject to the agreement and this Article, or (ii) if necessary to enforce other rights and remedies of the lessor or lessee under this Article, remove the goods from the real estate, free and clear of all conflicting interests of all owners and encumbrancers of the real estate, but the lessor or lessee must reimburse any encumbrancer or owner of the real estate who is not the lessee and who has not otherwise agreed for the cost of repair of any physical injury, but not for any diminution in value of the real estate caused by the absence of the goods removed or by any necessity of replacing them. A person entitled to reimbursement

may refuse permission to remove until the party seeking removal gives adequate security for the performance of this obligation.

(9) Even though the lease agreement does not create a security interest, the interest of a lessor of fixtures, including the lessor's residual interest, is perfected by filing a financing statement as a fixture filing for leased goods that are or are to become fixtures in accordance with the relevant provisions of the Article on Secured Transactions (Article 9).

As amended in 1990 and 1999.

§ 2A–310. Lessor's and Lessee's Rights When Goods Become Accessions.

(1) Goods are "accessions" when they are installed in or affixed to other goods.

(2) The interest of a lessor or a lessee under a lease contract entered into before the goods became accessions is superior to all interests in the whole except as stated in subsection (4).

(3) The interest of a lessor or a lessee under a lease contract entered into at the time or after the goods became accessions is superior to all subsequently acquired interests in the whole except as stated in subsection (4) but is subordinate to interests in the whole existing at the time the lease contract was made unless the holders of such interests in the whole have in writing consented to the lease or disclaimed an interest in the goods as part of the whole.

(4) The interest of a lessor or a lessee under a lease contract described in subsection (2) or (3) is subordinate to the interest of

    (a) a buyer in the ordinary course of business or a lessee in the ordinary course of business of any interest in the whole acquired after the goods became accessions; or

    (b) a creditor with a security interest in the whole perfected before the lease contract was made to the extent that the creditor makes subsequent advances without knowledge of the lease contract.

(5) When under subsections (2) or (3) and (4) a lessor or a lessee of accessions holds an interest that is superior to all interests in the whole, the lessor or the lessee may (a) on default, expiration, termination, or cancellation of the lease contract by the other party but subject to the provisions of the lease contract and this Article, or (b) if necessary to enforce his [or her] other rights and remedies under this Article, remove the goods from the whole, free and clear of all interests in the whole, but he [or she] must reimburse any holder of an interest in the whole who is not the lessee and who has not otherwise agreed for the cost of repair of any physical injury but not for any diminution in value of the whole caused by the absence of the goods removed or by any necessity for replacing them. A person entitled to reimbursement may refuse permission to remove until the party seeking removal gives adequate security for the performance of this obligation.

§ 2A–311. Priority Subject to Subordination.

Nothing in this Article prevents subordination by agreement by any person entitled to priority.

As added in 1990.

Part 4 Performance of Lease Contract: Repudiated, Substituted and Excused

§ 2A–401. Insecurity: Adequate Assurance of Performance.

(1) A lease contract imposes an obligation on each party that the other's expectation of receiving due performance will not be impaired.

(2) If reasonable grounds for insecurity arise with respect to the performance of either party, the insecure party may demand in writing adequate assurance of due performance. Until the insecure party receives that assurance, if commercially reasonable the insecure party may suspend any performance for which he [or she] has not already received the agreed return.

(3) A repudiation of the lease contract occurs if assurance of due performance adequate under the circumstances of the particular case is not provided to the insecure party within a reasonable time, not to exceed 30 days after receipt of a demand by the other party.

(4) Between merchants, the reasonableness of grounds for insecurity and the adequacy of any assurance offered must be determined according to commercial standards.

(5) Acceptance of any nonconforming delivery or payment does not prejudice the aggrieved party's right to demand adequate assurance of future performance.

§ 2A–402. Anticipatory Repudiation.

If either party repudiates a lease contract with respect to a performance not yet due under the lease contract, the loss of which performance will substantially impair the value of the lease contract to the other, the aggrieved party may:

(a) for a commercially reasonable time, await retraction of repudiation and performance by the repudiating party;

(b) make demand pursuant to Section 2A–401 and await assurance of future performance adequate under the circumstances of the particular case; or

(c) resort to any right or remedy upon default under the lease contract or this Article, even though the aggrieved party has notified the repudiating party that the aggrieved party would await the repudiating party's performance and assurance and has urged retraction. In addition, whether or not the aggrieved party is pursuing one of the foregoing remedies, the aggrieved party may suspend performance or, if the aggrieved party is the lessor, proceed in accordance with the provisions of this Article on the lessor's right to identify goods to the lease contract notwithstanding default or to salvage unfinished goods (Section 2A–524).

§ 2A–403. Retraction of Anticipatory Repudiation.

(1) Until the repudiating party's next performance is due, the repudiating party can retract the repudiation unless, since the repudiation, the aggrieved party has cancelled the lease contract or materially changed the aggrieved party's position or otherwise indicated that the aggrieved party considers the repudiation final.

(2) Retraction may be by any method that clearly indicates to the aggrieved party that the repudiating party intends to

perform under the lease contract and includes any assurance demanded under Section 2A–401.

(3) Retraction reinstates a repudiating party's rights under a lease contract with due excuse and allowance to the aggrieved party for any delay occasioned by the repudiation.

§ 2A–404. Substituted Performance.

(1) If without fault of the lessee, the lessor and the supplier, the agreed berthing, loading, or unloading facilities fail or the agreed type of carrier becomes unavailable or the agreed manner of delivery otherwise becomes commercially impracticable, but a commercially reasonable substitute is available, the substitute performance must be tendered and accepted.

(2) If the agreed means or manner of payment fails because of domestic or foreign governmental regulation:

(a) the lessor may withhold or stop delivery or cause the supplier to withhold or stop delivery unless the lessee provides a means or manner of payment that is commercially a substantial equivalent; and

(b) if delivery has already been taken, payment by the means or in the manner provided by the regulation discharges the lessee's obligation unless the regulation is discriminatory, oppressive, or predatory.

§ 2A–405. Excused Performance.

Subject to Section 2A–404 on substituted performance, the following rules apply:

(a) Delay in delivery or nondelivery in whole or in part by a lessor or a supplier who complies with paragraphs (b) and (c) is not a default under the lease contract if performance as agreed has been made impracticable by the occurrence of a contingency the nonoccurrence of which was a basic assumption on which the lease contract was made or by compliance in good faith with any applicable foreign or domestic governmental regulation or order, whether or not the regulation or order later proves to be invalid.

(b) If the causes mentioned in paragraph (a) affect only part of the lessor's or the supplier's capacity to perform, he [or she] shall allocate production and deliveries among his [or her] customers but at his [or her] option may include regular customers not then under contract for sale or lease as well as his [or her] own requirements for further manufacture. He [or she] may so allocate in any manner that is fair and reasonable.

(c) The lessor seasonably shall notify the lessee and in the case of a finance lease the supplier seasonably shall notify the lessor and the lessee, if known, that there will be delay or nondelivery and, if allocation is required under paragraph (b), of the estimated quota thus made available for the lessee.

§ 2A–406. Procedure on Excused Performance.

(1) If the lessee receives notification of a material or indefinite delay or an allocation justified under Section 2A–405, the lessee may by written notification to the lessor as to any goods involved, and with respect to all of the goods if under an installment lease contract the value of the whole lease contract is substantially impaired (Section 2A–510):

(a) terminate the lease contract (Section 2A–505(2)); or

(b) except in a finance lease that is not a consumer lease, modify the lease contract by accepting the available quota in substitution, with due allowance from the rent payable for the balance of the lease term for the deficiency but without further right against the lessor.

(2) If, after receipt of a notification from the lessor under Section 2A–405, the lessee fails so to modify the lease agreement within a reasonable time not exceeding 30 days, the lease contract lapses with respect to any deliveries affected.

§ 2A–407. Irrevocable Promises: Finance Leases.

(1) In the case of a finance lease that is not a consumer lease the lessee's promises under the lease contract become irrevocable and independent upon the lessee's acceptance of the goods.

(2) A promise that has become irrevocable and independent under subsection (1):

(a) is effective and enforceable between the parties, and by or against third parties including assignees of the parties, and

(b) is not subject to cancellation, termination, modification, repudiation, excuse, or substitution without the consent of the party to whom the promise runs.

(3) This section does not affect the validity under any other law of a covenant in any lease contract making the lessee's promises irrevocable and independent upon the lessee's acceptance of the goods.

As amended in 1990.

Part 5 Default

A. In General

§ 2A–501. Default: Procedure.

(1) Whether the lessor or the lessee is in default under a lease contract is determined by the lease agreement and this Article.

(2) If the lessor or the lessee is in default under the lease contract, the party seeking enforcement has rights and remedies as provided in this Article and, except as limited by this Article, as provided in the lease agreement.

(3) If the lessor or the lessee is in default under the lease contract, the party seeking enforcement may reduce the party's claim to judgment, or otherwise enforce the lease contract by self-help or any available judicial procedure or nonjudicial procedure, including administrative proceeding, arbitration, or the like, in accordance with this Article.

(4) Except as otherwise provided in Section 1–106(1) or this Article or the lease agreement, the rights and remedies referred to in subsections (2) and (3) are cumulative.

(5) If the lease agreement covers both real property and goods, the party seeking enforcement may proceed under this Part as to the goods, or under other applicable law

as to both the real property and the goods in accordance with that party's rights and remedies in respect of the real property, in which case this Part does not apply.

As amended in 1990.

§ 2A–502. Notice After Default.

Except as otherwise provided in this Article or the lease agreement, the lessor or lessee in default under the lease contract is not entitled to notice of default or notice of enforcement from the other party to the lease agreement.

§ 2A–503. Modification or Impairment of Rights and Remedies.

(1) Except as otherwise provided in this Article, the lease agreement may include rights and remedies for default in addition to or in substitution for those provided in this Article and may limit or alter the measure of damages recoverable under this Article.

(2) Resort to a remedy provided under this Article or in the lease agreement is optional unless the remedy is expressly agreed to be exclusive. If circumstances cause an exclusive or limited remedy to fail of its essential purpose, or provision for an exclusive remedy is unconscionable, remedy may be had as provided in this Article.

(3) Consequential damages may be liquidated under Section 2A–504, or may otherwise be limited, altered, or excluded unless the limitation, alteration, or exclusion is unconscionable. Limitation, alteration, or exclusion of consequential damages for injury to the person in the case of consumer goods is *prima facie* unconscionable but limitation, alteration, or exclusion of damages where the loss is commercial is not *prima facie* unconscionable.

(4) Rights and remedies on default by the lessor or the lessee with respect to any obligation or promise collateral or ancillary to the lease contract are not impaired by this Article.

As amended in 1990.

§ 2A–504. Liquidation of Damages.

(1) Damages payable by either party for default, or any other act or omission, including indemnity for loss or diminution of anticipated tax benefits or loss or damage to lessor's residual interest, may be liquidated in the lease agreement but only at an amount or by a formula that is reasonable in light of the then anticipated harm caused by the default or other act or omission.

(2) If the lease agreement provides for liquidation of damages, and such provision does not comply with subsection (1), or such provision is an exclusive or limited remedy that circumstances cause to fail of its essential purpose, remedy may be had as provided in this Article.

(3) If the lessor justifiably withholds or stops delivery of goods because of the lessee's default or insolvency (Section 2A–525 or 2A–526), the lessee is entitled to restitution of any amount by which the sum of his [or her] payments exceeds:

(a) the amount to which the lessor is entitled by virtue of terms liquidating the lessor's damages in accordance with subsection (1); or

(b) in the absence of those terms, 20 percent of the then present value of the total rent the lessee was obligated to pay for the balance of the lease term, or, in the case of a consumer lease, the lesser of such amount or $500.

(4) A lessee's right to restitution under subsection (3) is subject to offset to the extent the lessor establishes:

(a) a right to recover damages under the provisions of this Article other than subsection (1); and

(b) the amount or value of any benefits received by the lessee directly or indirectly by reason of the lease contract.

§ 2A–505. Cancellation and Termination and Effect of Cancellation, Termination, Rescission, or Fraud on Rights and Remedies.

(1) On cancellation of the lease contract, all obligations that are still executory on both sides are discharged, but any right based on prior default or performance survives, and the cancelling party also retains any remedy for default of the whole lease contract or any unperformed balance.

(2) On termination of the lease contract, all obligations that are still executory on both sides are discharged but any right based on prior default or performance survives.

(3) Unless the contrary intention clearly appears, expressions of "cancellation," "rescission," or the like of the lease contract may not be construed as a renunciation or discharge of any claim in damages for an antecedent default.

(4) Rights and remedies for material misrepresentation or fraud include all rights and remedies available under this Article for default.

(5) Neither rescission nor a claim for rescission of the lease contract nor rejection or return of the goods may bar or be deemed inconsistent with a claim for damages or other right or remedy.

§ 2A–506. Statute of Limitations.

(1) An action for default under a lease contract, including breach of warranty or indemnity, must be commenced within 4 years after the cause of action accrued. By the original lease contract the parties may reduce the period of limitation to not less than one year.

(2) A cause of action for default accrues when the act or omission on which the default or breach of warranty is based is or should have been discovered by the aggrieved party, or when the default occurs, whichever is later. A cause of action for indemnity accrues when the act or omission on which the claim for indemnity is based is or should have been discovered by the indemnified party, whichever is later.

(3) If an action commenced within the time limited by subsection (1) is so terminated as to leave available a remedy by another action for the same default or breach of warranty or indemnity, the other action may be commenced after the expiration of the time limited and within 6 months after the termination of the first action unless the termination resulted from voluntary discontinuance or from dismissal for failure or neglect to prosecute.

(4) This section does not alter the law on tolling of the statute of limitations nor does it apply to causes of action that have accrued before this Article becomes effective.

§ 2A–507. Proof of Market Rent: Time and Place.

(1) Damages based on market rent (Section 2A–519 or 2A–528) are determined according to the rent for the use of the goods concerned for a lease term identical to the remaining lease term of the original lease agreement and prevailing at the times specified in Sections 2A–519 and 2A–528.

(2) If evidence of rent for the use of the goods concerned for a lease term identical to the remaining lease term of the original lease agreement and prevailing at the times or places described in this Article is not readily available, the rent prevailing within any reasonable time before or after the time described or at any other place or for a different lease term which in commercial judgment or under usage of trade would serve as a reasonable substitute for the one described may be used, making any proper allowance for the difference, including the cost of transporting the goods to or from the other place.

(3) Evidence of a relevant rent prevailing at a time or place or for a lease term other than the one described in this Article offered by one party is not admissible unless and until he [or she] has given the other party notice the court finds sufficient to prevent unfair surprise.

(4) If the prevailing rent or value of any goods regularly leased in any established market is in issue, reports in official publications or trade journals or in newspapers or periodicals of general circulation published as the reports of that market are admissible in evidence. The circumstances of the preparation of the report may be shown to affect its weight but not its admissibility.

As amended in 1990.

B. Default by Lessor

§ 2A–508. Lessee's Remedies.

(1) If a lessor fails to deliver the goods in conformity to the lease contract (Section 2A–509) or repudiates the lease contract (Section 2A–402), or a lessee rightfully rejects the goods (Section 2A–509) or justifiably revokes acceptance of the goods (Section 2A–517), then with respect to any goods involved, and with respect to all of the goods if under an installment lease contract the value of the whole lease contract is substantially impaired (Section 2A–510), the lessor is in default under the lease contract and the lessee may:

   (a) cancel the lease contract (Section 2A–505(1));

   (b) recover so much of the rent and security as has been paid and is just under the circumstances;

   (c) cover and recover damages as to all goods affected whether or not they have been identified to the lease contract (Sections 2A–518 and 2A–520), or recover damages for nondelivery (Sections 2A–519 and 2A–520);

   (d) exercise any other rights or pursue any other remedies provided in the lease contract.

(2) If a lessor fails to deliver the goods in conformity to the lease contract or repudiates the lease contract, the lessee may also:

   (a) if the goods have been identified, recover them (Section 2A–522); or

   (b) in a proper case, obtain specific performance or replevy the goods (Section 2A–521).

(3) If a lessor is otherwise in default under a lease contract, the lessee may exercise the rights and pursue the remedies provided in the lease contract, which may include a right to cancel the lease, and in Section 2A–519(3).

(4) If a lessor has breached a warranty, whether express or implied, the lessee may recover damages (Section 2A–519(4)).

(5) On rightful rejection or justifiable revocation of acceptance, a lessee has a security interest in goods in the lessee's possession or control for any rent and security that has been paid and any expenses reasonably incurred in their inspection, receipt, transportation, and care and custody and may hold those goods and dispose of them in good faith and in a commercially reasonable manner, subject to Section 2A–527(5).

(6) Subject to the provisions of Section 2A–407, a lessee, on notifying the lessor of the lessee's intention to do so, may deduct all or any part of the damages resulting from any default under the lease contract from any part of the rent still due under the same lease contract.

As amended in 1990.

§ 2A–509. Lessee's Rights on Improper Delivery; Rightful Rejection.

(1) Subject to the provisions of Section 2A–510 on default in installment lease contracts, if the goods or the tender or delivery fail in any respect to conform to the lease contract, the lessee may reject or accept the goods or accept any commercial unit or units and reject the rest of the goods.

(2) Rejection of goods is ineffective unless it is within a reasonable time after tender or delivery of the goods and the lessee seasonably notifies the lessor.

§ 2A–510. Installment Lease Contracts: Rejection and Default.

(1) Under an installment lease contract a lessee may reject any delivery that is nonconforming if the nonconformity substantially impairs the value of that delivery and cannot be cured or the nonconformity is a defect in the required documents; but if the nonconformity does not fall within subsection (2) and the lessor or the supplier gives adequate assurance of its cure, the lessee must accept that delivery.

(2) Whenever nonconformity or default with respect to one or more deliveries substantially impairs the value of the installment lease contract as a whole there is a default with respect to the whole. But, the aggrieved party reinstates the installment lease contract as a whole if the aggrieved party accepts a nonconforming delivery without seasonably notifying of cancellation or brings an action

with respect only to past deliveries or demands performance as to future deliveries.

§ 2A–511. Merchant Lessee's Duties as to Rightfully Rejected Goods.

(1) Subject to any security interest of a lessee (Section 2A–508(5)), if a lessor or a supplier has no agent or place of business at the market of rejection, a merchant lessee, after rejection of goods in his [or her] possession or control, shall follow any reasonable instructions received from the lessor or the supplier with respect to the goods. In the absence of those instructions, a merchant lessee shall make reasonable efforts to sell, lease, or otherwise dispose of the goods for the lessor's account if they threaten to decline in value speedily. Instructions are not reasonable if on demand indemnity for expenses is not forthcoming.

(2) If a merchant lessee (subsection (1)) or any other lessee (Section 2A–512) disposes of goods, he [or she] is entitled to reimbursement either from the lessor or the supplier or out of the proceeds for reasonable expenses of caring for and disposing of the goods and, if the expenses include no disposition commission, to such commission as is usual in the trade, or if there is none, to a reasonable sum not exceeding 10 percent of the gross proceeds.

(3) In complying with this section or Section 2A–512, the lessee is held only to good faith. Good faith conduct hereunder is neither acceptance or conversion nor the basis of an action for damages.

(4) A purchaser who purchases in good faith from a lessee pursuant to this section or Section 2A–512 takes the goods free of any rights of the lessor and the supplier even though the lessee fails to comply with one or more of the requirements of this Article.

§ 2A–512. Lessee's Duties as to Rightfully Rejected Goods.

(1) Except as otherwise provided with respect to goods that threaten to decline in value speedily (Section 2A–511) and subject to any security interest of a lessee (Section 2A–508(5)):

(a) the lessee, after rejection of goods in the lessee's possession, shall hold them with reasonable care at the lessor's or the supplier's disposition for a reasonable time after the lessee's seasonable notification of rejection;

(b) if the lessor or the supplier gives no instructions within a reasonable time after notification of rejection, the lessee may store the rejected goods for the lessor's or the supplier's account or ship them to the lessor or the supplier or dispose of them for the lessor's or the supplier's account with reimbursement in the manner provided in Section 2A–511; but

(c) the lessee has no further obligations with regard to goods rightfully rejected.

(2) Action by the lessee pursuant to subsection (1) is not acceptance or conversion.

§ 2A–513. Cure by Lessor of Improper Tender or Delivery; Replacement.

(1) If any tender or delivery by the lessor or the supplier is rejected because nonconforming and the time for performance has not yet expired, the lessor or the supplier may seasonably notify the lessee of the lessor's or the supplier's intention to cure and may then make a conforming delivery within the time provided in the lease contract.

(2) If the lessee rejects a nonconforming tender that the lessor or the supplier had reasonable grounds to believe would be acceptable with or without money allowance, the lessor or the supplier may have a further reasonable time to substitute a conforming tender if he [or she] seasonably notifies the lessee.

§ 2A–514. Waiver of Lessee's Objections.

(1) In rejecting goods, a lessee's failure to state a particular defect that is ascertainable by reasonable inspection precludes the lessee from relying on the defect to justify rejection or to establish default:

(a) if, stated seasonably, the lessor or the supplier could have cured it (Section 2A–513); or

(b) between merchants if the lessor or the supplier after rejection has made a request in writing for a full and final written statement of all defects on which the lessee proposes to rely.

(2) A lessee's failure to reserve rights when paying rent or other consideration against documents precludes recovery of the payment for defects apparent on the face of the documents.

§ 2A–515. Acceptance of Goods.

(1) Acceptance of goods occurs after the lessee has had a reasonable opportunity to inspect the goods and

(a) the lessee signifies or acts with respect to the goods in a manner that signifies to the lessor or the supplier that the goods are conforming or that the lessee will take or retain them in spite of their nonconformity; or

(b) the lessee fails to make an effective rejection of the goods (Section 2A–509(2)).

(2) Acceptance of a part of any commercial unit is acceptance of that entire unit.

§ 2A–516. Effect of Acceptance of Goods; Notice of Default; Burden of Establishing Default after Acceptance; Notice of Claim or Litigation to Person Answerable Over.

(1) A lessee must pay rent for any goods accepted in accordance with the lease contract, with due allowance for goods rightfully rejected or not delivered.

(2) A lessee's acceptance of goods precludes rejection of the goods accepted. In the case of a finance lease, if made with knowledge of a nonconformity, acceptance cannot be revoked because of it. In any other case, if made with knowledge of a nonconformity, acceptance cannot be revoked because of it unless the acceptance was on the reasonable assumption that the nonconformity would be seasonably cured. Acceptance does not of itself impair any other remedy provided by this Article or the lease agreement for nonconformity.

(3) If a tender has been accepted:

    (a) within a reasonable time after the lessee discovers or should have discovered any default, the lessee shall notify the lessor and the supplier, if any, or be barred from any remedy against the party notified;

    (b) except in the case of a consumer lease, within a reasonable time after the lessee receives notice of litigation for infringement or the like (Section 2A–211) the lessee shall notify the lessor or be barred from any remedy over for liability established by the litigation; and

    (c) the burden is on the lessee to establish any default.

(4) If a lessee is sued for breach of a warranty or other obligation for which a lessor or a supplier is answerable over the following apply:

    (a) The lessee may give the lessor or the supplier, or both, written notice of the litigation. If the notice states that the person notified may come in and defend and that if the person notified does not do so that person will be bound in any action against that person by the lessee by any determination of fact common to the two litigations, then unless the person notified after seasonable receipt of the notice does come in and defend that person is so bound.

    (b) The lessor or the supplier may demand in writing that the lessee turn over control of the litigation including settlement if the claim is one for infringement or the like (Section 2A–211) or else be barred from any remedy over. If the demand states that the lessor or the supplier agrees to bear all expense and to satisfy any adverse judgment, then unless the lessee after seasonable receipt of the demand does turn over control the lessee is so barred.

(5) Subsections (3) and (4) apply to any obligation of a lessee to hold the lessor or the supplier harmless against infringement or the like (Section 2A–211).

As amended in 1990.

§ 2A–517. Revocation of Acceptance of Goods.

(1) A lessee may revoke acceptance of a lot or commercial unit whose nonconformity substantially impairs its value to the lessee if the lessee has accepted it:

    (a) except in the case of a finance lease, on the reasonable assumption that its nonconformity would be cured and it has not been seasonably cured; or

    (b) without discovery of the nonconformity if the lessee's acceptance was reasonably induced either by the lessor's assurances or, except in the case of a finance lease, by the difficulty of discovery before acceptance.

(2) Except in the case of a finance lease that is not a consumer lease, a lessee may revoke acceptance of a lot or commercial unit if the lessor defaults under the lease contract and the default substantially impairs the value of that lot or commercial unit to the lessee.

(3) If the lease agreement so provides, the lessee may revoke acceptance of a lot or commercial unit because of other defaults by the lessor.

(4) Revocation of acceptance must occur within a reasonable time after the lessee discovers or should have discovered the ground for it and before any substantial change in condition of the goods which is not caused by the nonconformity. Revocation is not effective until the lessee notifies the lessor.

(5) A lessee who so revokes has the same rights and duties with regard to the goods involved as if the lessee had rejected them.

As amended in 1990.

§ 2A–518. Cover; Substitute Goods.

(1) After a default by a lessor under the lease contract of the type described in Section 2A–508(1), or, if agreed, after other default by the lessor, the lessee may cover by making any purchase or lease of or contract to purchase or lease goods in substitution for those due from the lessor.

(2) Except as otherwise provided with respect to damages liquidated in the lease agreement (Section 2A–504) or otherwise determined pursuant to agreement of the parties (Sections 1–102(3) and 2A–503), if a lessee's cover is by lease agreement substantially similar to the original lease agreement and the new lease agreement is made in good faith and in a commercially reasonable manner, the lessee may recover from the lessor as damages (i) the present value, as of the date of the commencement of the term of the new lease agreement, of the rent under the new lease agreement applicable to that period of the new lease term which is comparable to the then remaining term of the original lease agreement minus the present value as of the same date of the total rent for the then remaining lease term of the original lease agreement, and (ii) any incidental or consequential damages, less expenses saved in consequence of the lessor's default.

(3) If a lessee's cover is by lease agreement that for any reason does not qualify for treatment under subsection (2), or is by purchase or otherwise, the lessee may recover from the lessor as if the lessee had elected not to cover and Section 2A–519 governs.

As amended in 1990.

§ 2A–519. Lessee's Damages for Non-Delivery, Repudiation, Default, and Breach of Warranty in Regard to Accepted Goods.

(1) Except as otherwise provided with respect to damages liquidated in the lease agreement (Section 2A–504) or otherwise determined pursuant to agreement of the parties (Sections 1–102(3) and 2A–503), if a lessee elects not to cover or a lessee elects to cover and the cover is by lease agreement that for any reason does not qualify for treatment under Section 2A–518(2), or is by purchase or otherwise, the measure of damages for non-delivery or repudiation by the lessor or for rejection or revocation of acceptance by the lessee is the present value, as of the

date of the default, of the then market rent minus the present value as of the same date of the original rent, computed for the remaining lease term of the original lease agreement, together with incidental and consequential damages, less expenses saved in consequence of the lessor's default.

(2) Market rent is to be determined as of the place for tender or, in cases of rejection after arrival or revocation of acceptance, as of the place of arrival.

(3) Except as otherwise agreed, if the lessee has accepted goods and given notification (Section 2A–516(3)), the measure of damages for non-conforming tender or delivery or other default by a lessor is the loss resulting in the ordinary course of events from the lessor's default as determined in any manner that is reasonable together with incidental and consequential damages, less expenses saved in consequence of the lessor's default.

(4) Except as otherwise agreed, the measure of damages for breach of warranty is the present value at the time and place of acceptance of the difference between the value of the use of the goods accepted and the value if they had been as warranted for the lease term, unless special circumstances show proximate damages of a different amount, together with incidental and consequential damages, less expenses saved in consequence of the lessor's default or breach of warranty.

As amended in 1990.

§ 2A–520. Lessee's Incidental and Consequential Damages.

(1) Incidental damages resulting from a lessor's default include expenses reasonably incurred in inspection, receipt, transportation, and care and custody of goods rightfully rejected or goods the acceptance of which is justifiably revoked, any commercially reasonable charges, expenses or commissions in connection with effecting cover, and any other reasonable expense incident to the default.

(2) Consequential damages resulting from a lessor's default include:

(a) any loss resulting from general or particular requirements and needs of which the lessor at the time of contracting had reason to know and which could not reasonably be prevented by cover or otherwise; and

(b) injury to person or property proximately resulting from any breach of warranty.

§ 2A–521. Lessee's Right to Specific Performance or Replevin.

(1) Specific performance may be decreed if the goods are unique or in other proper circumstances.

(2) A decree for specific performance may include any terms and conditions as to payment of the rent, damages, or other relief that the court deems just.

(3) A lessee has a right of replevin, detinue, sequestration, claim and delivery, or the like for goods identified to the lease contract if after reasonable effort the lessee is unable to effect cover for those goods or the circumstances reasonably indicate that the effort will be unavailing.

§ 2A–522. Lessee's Right to Goods on Lessor's Insolvency.

(1) Subject to subsection (2) and even though the goods have not been shipped, a lessee who has paid a part or all of the rent and security for goods identified to a lease contract (Section 2A–217) on making and keeping good a tender of any unpaid portion of the rent and security due under the lease contract may recover the goods identified from the lessor if the lessor becomes insolvent within 10 days after receipt of the first installment of rent and security.

(2) A lessee acquires the right to recover goods identified to a lease contract only if they conform to the lease contract.

C. Default by Lessee

§ 2A–523. Lessor's Remedies.

(1) If a lessee wrongfully rejects or revokes acceptance of goods or fails to make a payment when due or repudiates with respect to a part or the whole, then, with respect to any goods involved, and with respect to all of the goods if under an installment lease contract the value of the whole lease contract is substantially impaired (Section 2A–510), the lessee is in default under the lease contract and the lessor may:

(a) cancel the lease contract (Section 2A–505(1));

(b) proceed respecting goods not identified to the lease contract (Section 2A–524);

(c) withhold delivery of the goods and take possession of goods previously delivered (Section 2A–525);

(d) stop delivery of the goods by any bailee (Section 2A–526);

(e) dispose of the goods and recover damages (Section 2A–527), or retain the goods and recover damages (Section 2A–528), or in a proper case recover rent (Section 2A–529)

(f) exercise any other rights or pursue any other remedies provided in the lease contract.

(2) If a lessor does not fully exercise a right or obtain a remedy to which the lessor is entitled under subsection (1), the lessor may recover the loss resulting in the ordinary course of events from the lessee's default as determined in any reasonable manner, together with incidental damages, less expenses saved in consequence of the lessee's default.

(3) If a lessee is otherwise in default under a lease contract, the lessor may exercise the rights and pursue the remedies provided in the lease contract, which may include a right to cancel the lease. In addition, unless otherwise provided in the lease contract:

(a) if the default substantially impairs the value of the lease contract to the lessor, the lessor may exercise the rights and pursue the remedies provided in subsections (1) or (2); or

(b) if the default does not substantially impair the value of the lease contract to the lessor, the lessor may recover as provided in subsection (2).

As amended in 1990.

§ 2A–524. Lessor's Right to Identify Goods to Lease Contract.

(1) After default by the lessee under the lease contract of the type described in Section 2A–523(1) or 2A–523(3)(a) or, if agreed, after other default by the lessee, the lessor may:

(a) identify to the lease contract conforming goods not already identified if at the time the lessor learned of the default they were in the lessor's or the supplier's possession or control; and

(b) dispose of goods (Section 2A–527(1)) that demonstrably have been intended for the particular lease contract even though those goods are unfinished.

(2) If the goods are unfinished, in the exercise of reasonable commercial judgment for the purposes of avoiding loss and of effective realization, an aggrieved lessor or the supplier may either complete manufacture and wholly identify the goods to the lease contract or cease manufacture and lease, sell, or otherwise dispose of the goods for scrap or salvage value or proceed in any other reasonable manner.

As amended in 1990.

§ 2A–525. Lessor's Right to Possession of Goods.

(1) If a lessor discovers the lessee to be insolvent, the lessor may refuse to deliver the goods.

(2) After a default by the lessee under the lease contract of the type described in Section 2A–523(1) or 2A–523(3)(a) or, if agreed, after other default by the lessee, the lessor has the right to take possession of the goods. If the lease contract so provides, the lessor may require the lessee to assemble the goods and make them available to the lessor at a place to be designated by the lessor which is reasonably convenient to both parties. Without removal, the lessor may render unusable any goods employed in trade or business, and may dispose of goods on the lessee's premises (Section 2A–527).

(3) The lessor may proceed under subsection (2) without judicial process if that can be done without breach of the peace or the lessor may proceed by action.

As amended in 1990.

§ 2A–526. Lessor's Stoppage of Delivery in Transit or Otherwise.

(1) A lessor may stop delivery of goods in the possession of a carrier or other bailee if the lessor discovers the lessee to be insolvent and may stop delivery of carload, truckload, planeload, or larger shipments of express or freight if the lessee repudiates or fails to make a payment due before delivery, whether for rent, security or otherwise under the lease contract, or for any other reason the lessor has a right to withhold or take possession of the goods.

(2) In pursuing its remedies under subsection (1), the lessor may stop delivery until

(a) receipt of the goods by the lessee;

(b) acknowledgment to the lessee by any bailee of the goods, except a carrier, that the bailee holds the goods for the lessee; or

(c) such an acknowledgment to the lessee by a carrier via reshipment or as warehouseman.

(3) (a) To stop delivery, a lessor shall so notify as to enable the bailee by reasonable diligence to prevent delivery of the goods.

(b) After notification, the bailee shall hold and deliver the goods according to the directions of the lessor, but the lessor is liable to the bailee for any ensuing charges or damages.

(c) A carrier who has issued a nonnegotiable bill of lading is not obliged to obey a notification to stop received from a person other than the consignor.

§ 2A–527. Lessor's Rights to Dispose of Goods.

(1) After a default by a lessee under the lease contract of the type described in Section 2A–523(1) or 2A–523(3)(a) or after the lessor refuses to deliver or takes possession of goods (Section 2A–525 or 2A–526), or, if agreed, after other default by a lessee, the lessor may dispose of the goods concerned or the undelivered balance thereof by lease, sale, or otherwise.

(2) Except as otherwise provided with respect to damages liquidated in the lease agreement (Section 2A–504) or otherwise determined pursuant to agreement of the parties (Sections 1–102(3) and 2A–503), if the disposition is by lease agreement substantially similar to the original lease agreement and the new lease agreement is made in good faith and in a commercially reasonable manner, the lessor may recover from the lessee as damages (i) accrued and unpaid rent as of the date of the commencement of the term of the new lease agreement, (ii) the present value, as of the same date, of the total rent for the then remaining lease term of the original lease agreement minus the present value, as of the same date, of the rent under the new lease agreement applicable to that period of the new lease term which is comparable to the then remaining term of the original lease agreement, and (iii) any incidental damages allowed under Section 2A–530, less expenses saved in consequence of the lessee's default.

(3) If the lessor's disposition is by lease agreement that for any reason does not qualify for treatment under subsection (2), or is by sale or otherwise, the lessor may recover from the lessee as if the lessor had elected not to dispose of the goods and Section 2A–528 governs.

(4) A subsequent buyer or lessee who buys or leases from the lessor in good faith for value as a result of a disposition under this section takes the goods free of the original lease contract and any rights of the original lessee even though the lessor fails to comply with one or more of the requirements of this Article.

(5) The lessor is not accountable to the lessee for any profit made on any disposition. A lessee who has rightfully rejected or justifiably revoked acceptance shall account to the lessor for any excess over the amount of the lessee's security interest (Section 2A–508(5)).

As amended in 1990.

§ 2A–528. Lessor's Damages for Non-acceptance, Failure to Pay, Repudiation, or Other Default.

(1) Except as otherwise provided with respect to damages liquidated in the lease agreement (Section 2A–504) or otherwise determined pursuant to agreement of the parties (Section 1–102(3) and 2A–503), if a lessor elects to retain the goods or a lessor elects to dispose of the goods and the disposition is by lease agreement that for any reason does not qualify for treatment under Section 2A–527(2), or is by sale or otherwise, the lessor may recover from the lessee as damages for a default of the type described in Section 2A–523(1) or 2A–523(3)(a), or if agreed, for other default of the lessee, (i) accrued and unpaid rent as of the date of the default if the lessee has never taken possession of the goods, or, if the lessee has taken possession of the goods, as of the date the lessor repossesses the goods or an earlier date on which the lessee makes a tender of the goods to the lessor, (ii) the present value as of the date determined under clause (i) of the total rent for the then remaining lease term of the original lease agreement minus the present value as of the same date of the market rent as the place where the goods are located computed for the same lease term, and (iii) any incidental damages allowed under Section 2A–530, less expenses saved in consequence of the lessee's default.

(2) If the measure of damages provided in subsection (1) is inadequate to put a lessor in as good a position as performance would have, the measure of damages is the present value of the profit, including reasonable overhead, the lessor would have made from full performance by the lessee, together with any incidental damages allowed under Section 2A–530, due allowance for costs reasonably incurred and due credit for payments or proceeds of disposition.

As amended in 1990.

§ 2A–529. Lessor's Action for the Rent.

(1) After default by the lessee under the lease contract of the type described in Section 2A–523(1) or 2A–523(3)(a) or, if agreed, after other default by the lessee, if the lessor complies with subsection (2), the lessor may recover from the lessee as damages:

(a) for goods accepted by the lessee and not repossessed by or tendered to the lessor, and for conforming goods lost or damaged within a commercially reasonable time after risk of loss passes to the lessee (Section 2A–219), (i) accrued and unpaid rent as of the date of entry of judgment in favor of the lessor (ii) the present value as of the same date of the rent for the then remaining lease term of the lease agreement, and

(iii) any incidental damages allowed under Section 2A–530, less expenses saved in consequence of the lessee's default; and

(b) for goods identified to the lease contract if the lessor is unable after reasonable effort to dispose of them at a reasonable price or the circumstances reasonably indicate that effort will be unavailing, (i) accrued and unpaid rent as of the date of entry of judgment in favor of the lessor, (ii) the present value as of the same date of the rent for the then remaining lease term of the lease agreement, and (iii) any incidental damages allowed under Section 2A–530, less expenses saved in consequence of the lessee's default.

(2) Except as provided in subsection (3), the lessor shall hold for the lessee for the remaining lease term of the lease agreement any goods that have been identified to the lease contract and are in the lessor's control.

(3) The lessor may dispose of the goods at any time before collection of the judgment for damages obtained pursuant to subsection (1). If the disposition is before the end of the remaining lease term of the lease agreement, the lessor's recovery against the lessee for damages is governed by Section 2A–527 or Section 2A–528, and the lessor will cause an appropriate credit to be provided against a judgment for damages to the extent that the amount of the judgment exceeds the recovery available pursuant to Section 2A–527 or 2A–528.

(4) Payment of the judgment for damages obtained pursuant to subsection (1) entitles the lessee to the use and possession of the goods not then disposed of for the remaining lease term of and in accordance with the lease agreement.

(5) After default by the lessee under the lease contract of the type described in Section 2A–523(1) or Section 2A–523(3)(a) or, if agreed, after other default by the lessee, a lessor who is held not entitled to rent under this section must nevertheless be awarded damages for non-acceptance under Sections 2A–527 and 2A–528.

As amended in 1990.

§ 2A–530. Lessor's Incidental Damages.

Incidental damages to an aggrieved lessor include any commercially reasonable charges, expenses, or commissions incurred in stopping delivery, in the transportation, care and custody of goods after the lessee's default, in connection with return or disposition of the goods, or otherwise resulting from the default.

§ 2A–531. Standing to Sue Third Parties for Injury to Goods.

(1) If a third party so deals with goods that have been identified to a lease contract as to cause actionable injury to a party to the lease contract (a) the lessor has a right of action against the third party, and (b) the lessee also has a right of action against the third party if the lessee:

(i) has a security interest in the goods;

(ii) has an insurable interest in the goods; or

(iii) bears the risk of loss under the lease contract or has since the injury assumed that risk as against the lessor and the goods have been converted or destroyed.

(2) If at the time of the injury the party plaintiff did not bear the risk of loss as against the other party to the lease contract and there is no arrangement between them for disposition of the recovery, his [or her] suit or settlement, subject to his [or her] own interest, is as a fiduciary for the other party to the lease contract.

(3) Either party with the consent of the other may sue for the benefit of whom it may concern.

§ 2A–532. Lessor's Rights to Residual Interest.

In addition to any other recovery permitted by this Article or other law, the lessor may recover from the lessee an amount that will fully compensate the lessor for any loss of or damage to the lessor's residual interest in the goods caused by the default of the lessee.

As added in 1990.

APPENDIX D

The United Nations Convention on Contracts for the International Sale of Goods (Excerpts)

Part I. SPHERE OF APPLICATION AND GENERAL PROVISIONS

* * * *

Chapter II—General Provisions

* * * *

Article 8

(1) For the purposes of this Convention statements made by and other conduct of a party are to be interpreted according to his intent where the other party knew or could not have been unaware what that intent was.

(2) If the preceding paragraph is not applicable, statements made by and other conduct of a party are to be interpreted according to the understanding that a reasonable person of the same kind as the other party would have had in the same circumstances.

(3) In determining the intent of a party or the understanding a reasonable person would have had, due consideration is to be given to all relevant circumstances of the case including the negotiations, any practices which the parties have established between themselves, usages and any subsequent conduct of the parties.

Article 9

(1) The parties are bound by any usage to which they have agreed and by any practices which they have established between themselves.

(2) The parties are considered, unless otherwise agreed, to have impliedly made applicable to their contract or its formation a usage of which the parties knew or ought to have known and which in international trade is widely known to, and regularly observed by, parties to contracts of the type involved in the particular trade concerned.

* * * *

Article 11

A contract of sale need not be concluded in or evidenced by writing and is not subject to any other requirement as to form. It may be proved by any means, including witnesses.

* * * *

Part II. FORMATION OF THE CONTRACT

Article 14

(1) A proposal for concluding a contract addressed to one or more specific persons constitutes an offer if it is sufficiently definite and indicates the intention of the offeror to be bound in case of acceptance. A proposal is sufficiently definite if it indicates the goods and expressly or implicitly fixes or makes provision for determining the quantity and the price.

(2) A proposal other than one addressed to one or more specific persons is to be considered merely as an invitation to make offers, unless the contrary is clearly indicated by the person making the proposal.

Article 15

(1) An offer becomes effective when it reaches the offeree.

(2) An offer, even if it is irrevocable, may be withdrawn if the withdrawal reaches the offeree before or at the same time as the offer.

Article 16

(1) Until a contract is concluded an offer may be revoked if the revocation reaches the offeree before he has dispatched an acceptance.

(2) However, an offer cannot be revoked:

(a) If it indicates, whether by stating a fixed time for acceptance or otherwise, that it is irrevocable; or

(b) If it was reasonable for the offeree to rely on the offer as being irrevocable and the offeree has acted in reliance on the offer.

Article 17

An offer, even if it is irrevocable, is terminated when a rejection reaches the offeror.

Article 18

(1) A statement made by or other conduct of the offeree indicating assent to an offer is an acceptance. Silence or inactivity does not in itself amount to acceptance.

(2) An acceptance of an offer becomes effective at the moment the indication of assent reaches the offeror. An acceptance is not effective if the indication of assent does not reach the offeror within the time he has fixed or, if no time is fixed, within a reasonable time, due account being taken of the circumstances of the transaction, including the rapidity of the means of communication employed by the offeror. An oral offer must be accepted immediately unless the circumstances indicate otherwise.

(3) However, if, by virtue of the offer or as a result of practices which the parties have established between themselves or of usage, the offeree may indicate assent by performing an act, such as one relating to the dispatch of the goods or payment of the price, without notice to the offeror, the acceptance is effective at the moment the act is performed, provided that the act is performed within the period of time laid down in the preceding paragraph.

Article 19

(1) A reply to an offer which purports to be an acceptance but contains additions, limitations or other modifications is a rejection of the offer and constitutes a counter-offer.

(2) However, a reply to an offer which purports to be an acceptance but contains additional or different terms which do not materially alter the terms of the offer constitutes an acceptance, unless the offeror, without undue delay, objects orally to the discrepancy or dispatches a notice to that effect. If he does not so object, the terms of the contract are the terms of the offer with the modifications contained in the acceptance.

(3) Additional or different terms relating, among other things, to the price, payment, quality and quantity of the goods, place and time of delivery, extent of one party's liability to the other or the settlement of disputes are considered to alter the terms of the offer materially.

* * * *

Article 22

An acceptance may be withdrawn if the withdrawal reaches the offeror before or at the same time as the acceptance would have become effective.

* * * *

Part III. SALE OF GOODS

Chapter I—General Provisions

Article 25

A breach of contract committed by one of the parties is fundamental if it results in such detriment to the other party as substantially to deprive him of what he is entitled to expect under the contract, unless the party in breach did not foresee and a reasonable person of the same kind in the same circumstances would not have foreseen such a result.

* * * *

Article 28

If, in accordance with the provisions of this Convention, one party is entitled to require performance of any obligation by the other party, a court is not bound to enter a judgment for specific performance unless the court would do so under its own law in respect of similar contracts of sale not governed by this Convention.

Article 29

(1) A contract may be modified or terminated by the mere agreement of the parties.

(2) A contract in writing which contains a provision requiring any modification or termination by agreement to be in writing may not be otherwise modified or terminated by agreement. However, a party may be precluded by his conduct from asserting such a provision to the extent that the other party has relied on that conduct.

* * * *

Chapter II—Obligations of the Seller

* * * *

Section II. Conformity of the Goods and Third Party Claims

Article 35

(1) The seller must deliver goods which are of the quantity, quality and description required by the contract and which are contained or packaged in the manner required by the contract.

(2) Except where the parties have agreed otherwise, the goods do not conform with the contract unless they:

  (a) Are fit for the purposes for which goods of the same description would ordinarily be used;

  (b) Are fit for any particular purpose expressly or impliedly made known to the seller at the time of the conclusion of the contract, except where the circumstances show that the buyer did not rely, or that it was unreasonable for him to rely, on the seller's skill and judgment;

  (c) Possess the qualities of goods which the seller has held out to the buyer as a sample or model;

  (d) Are contained or packaged in the manner usual for such goods or, where there is no such manner, in a manner adequate to preserve and protect the goods.

(3) The seller is not liable under subparagraphs (a) to (d) of the preceding paragraph for any lack of conformity of the goods if at the time of the conclusion of the contract the buyer knew or could not have been unaware of such lack of conformity.

* * * *

Article 64

(1) The seller may declare the contract avoided:

(a) If the failure by the buyer to perform any of his obligations under the contract or this Convention amounts to a fundamental breach of contract; or

(b) If the buyer does not, within the additional period of time fixed by the seller in accordance with paragraph (1) of article 63, perform his obligation to pay the price or take delivery of the goods, or if he declares that he will not do so within the period so fixed.

(2) However, in cases where the buyer has paid the price, the seller loses the right to declare the contract avoided unless he does so:

(a) In respect of late performance by the buyer, before the seller has become aware that performance has been rendered; or

(b) In respect of any breach other than late performance by the buyer, within a reasonable time:

(i) After the seller knew or ought to have known of the breach; or

(ii) After the expiration of any additional period of time fixed by the seller in accordance with paragraph (1) of article 63, or after the buyer has declared that he will not perform his obligations within such an additional period.

* * * *

Chapter IV—Passing of Risk

* * * *

Article 67

(1) If the contract of sale involves carriage of the goods and the seller is not bound to hand them over at a particular place, the risk passes to the buyer when the goods are handed over to the first carrier for transmission to the buyer in accordance with the contract of sale. If the seller is bound to hand the goods over to a carrier at a particular place, the risk does not pass to the buyer until the goods are handed over to the carrier at that place. The fact that the seller is authorized to retain documents controlling the disposition of the goods does not affect the passage of the risk.

(2) Nevertheless, the risk does not pass to the buyer until the goods are clearly identified to the contract, whether by markings on the goods, by shipping documents, by notice given to the buyer or otherwise.

* * * *

Chapter V—Provisions Common to the Obligations of the Seller and of the Buyer

Section I. Anticipatory Breach and Instalment Contracts

Article 71

(1) A party may suspend the performance of his obligations if, after the conclusion of the contract, it becomes apparent that the other party will not perform a substantial part of his obligations as a result of:

(a) A serious deficiency in his ability to perform or in his creditworthiness; or

(b) His conduct in preparing to perform or in performing the contract.

(2) If the seller has already dispatched the goods before the grounds described in the preceding paragraph become evident, he may prevent the handing over of the goods to the buyer even though the buyer holds a document which entitles him to obtain them. The present paragraph relates only to the rights in the goods as between the buyer and the seller.

(3) A party suspending performance, whether before or after dispatch of the goods, must immediately give notice of the suspension to the other party and must continue with performance if the other party provides adequate assurance of his performance.

Article 72

(1) If prior to the date for performance of the contract it is clear that one of the parties will commit a fundamental breach of contract, the other party may declare the contract avoided.

(2) If time allows, the party intending to declare the contract avoided must give reasonable notice to the other party in order to permit him to provide adequate assurance of his performance.

(3) The requirements of the preceding paragraph do not apply if the other party has declared that he will not perform his obligations.

Article 73

(1) In the case of a contract for delivery of goods by instalments, if the failure of one party to perform any of his obligations in respect of any instalment constitutes a fundamental breach of contract with respect to that instalment, the other party may declare the contract avoided with respect to that instalment.

(2) If one party's failure to perform any of his obligations in respect of any instalment gives the other party good grounds to conclude that a fundamental breach of contract will occur with respect to future instalments, he may declare the contract avoided for the future, provided that he does so within a reasonable time.

(3) A buyer who declares the contract avoided in respect of any delivery may, at the same time, declare it avoided in respect of deliveries already made or of future deliveries if, by reason of their interdependence, those deliveries could not be used for the purpose contemplated by the parties at the time of the conclusion of the contract.

Section II. Damages

Article 74

Damages for breach of contract by one party consist of a sum equal to the loss, including loss of profit, suffered by the other party as a consequence of the breach. Such damages may not exceed the loss which the party in breach foresaw or ought to have foreseen at the time of the conclusion of the contract, in the light of the facts and matters of which he then knew or ought to have known, as a possible consequence of the breach of contract.

Article 75

If the contract is avoided and if, in a reasonable manner and within a reasonable time after avoidance, the buyer has bought goods in replacement or the seller has resold the goods, the party claiming damages may recover the difference between the contract price and the price in the substitute transaction as well as any further damages recoverable under article 74.

Article 76

(1) If the contract is avoided and there is a current price for the goods, the party claiming damages may, if he has not made a purchase or resale under article 75, recover the difference between the price fixed by the contract and the current price at the time of avoidance as well as any further damages recoverable under article 74. If, however, the party claiming damages has avoided the contract after taking over the goods, the current price at the time of such taking over shall be applied instead of the current price at the time of avoidance.

(2) For the purposes of the preceding paragraph, the current price is the price prevailing at the place where delivery of the goods should have been made or, if there is no current price at that place, the price at such other place as serves as a reasonable substitute, making due allowance for differences in the cost of transporting the goods.

Article 77

A party who relies on a breach of contract must take such measures as are reasonable in the circumstances to mitigate the loss, including loss of profit, resulting from the breach. If he fails to take such measures, the party in breach may claim a reduction in the damages in the amount by which the loss should have been mitigated.

APPENDIX E

The Sarbanes-Oxley Act of 2002 (Excerpts and Explanatory Comments)

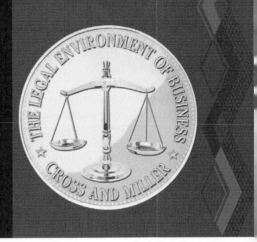

Note: The authors' explanatory comments appear in italics following the excerpt from each section.

* * * *

SECTION 302

Corporate responsibility for financial reports[1]

(a) Regulations required

The Commission shall, by rule, require, for each company filing periodic reports under section 13(a) or 15(d) of the Securities Exchange Act of 1934 (15 U.S.C. 78m, 78o(d)), that the principal executive officer or officers and the principal financial officer or officers, or persons performing similar functions, certify in each annual or quarterly report filed or submitted under either such section of such Act that—

(1) the signing officer has reviewed the report;

(2) based on the officer's knowledge, the report does not contain any untrue statement of a material fact or omit to state a material fact necessary in order to make the statements made, in light of the circumstances under which such statements were made, not misleading;

(3) based on such officer's knowledge, the financial statements, and other financial information included in the report, fairly present in all material respects the financial condition and results of operations of the issuer as of, and for, the periods presented in the report;

(4) the signing officers—

(A) are responsible for establishing and maintaining internal controls;

(B) have designed such internal controls to ensure that material information relating to the issuer and its consolidated subsidiaries is made known to such officers by others within those entities, particularly during the period in which the periodic reports are being prepared;

(C) have evaluated the effectiveness of the issuer's internal controls as of a date within 90 days prior to the report; and

(D) have presented in the report their conclusions about the effectiveness of their internal controls based on their evaluation as of that date;

(5) the signing officers have disclosed to the issuer's auditors and the audit committee of the board of directors (or persons fulfilling the equivalent function)—

(A) all significant deficiencies in the design or operation of internal controls which could adversely affect the issuer's ability to record, process, summarize, and report financial data and have identified for the issuer's auditors any material weaknesses in internal controls; and

(B) any fraud, whether or not material, that involves management or other employees who have a significant role in the issuer's internal controls; and

(6) the signing officers have indicated in the report whether or not there were significant changes in internal controls or in other factors that could significantly affect internal controls subsequent to the date of their evaluation, including any corrective actions with regard to significant deficiencies and material weaknesses.

(b) Foreign reincorporations have no effect

Nothing in this section shall be interpreted or applied in any way to allow any issuer to lessen the legal force of the statement required under this section, by an issuer having reincorporated or having engaged in any other transaction that resulted in the transfer of the corporate domicile or offices of the issuer from inside the United States to outside of the United States.

(c) Deadline

The rules required by subsection (a) of this section shall be effective not later than 30 days after July 30, 2002.

* * * *

EXPLANATORY COMMENTS: *Section 302 requires the chief executive officer (CEO) and chief financial officer (CFO) of each public company to certify that they have reviewed the company's quarterly and annual reports to be filed with the Securities and Exchange Commission (SEC). The CEO and CFO must certify that, based on their knowledge, the reports do not contain any untrue statement of a material fact or any half-truth that would make the report misleading, and that the*

---

1. This section of the Sarbanes-Oxley Act is codified at 15 U.S.C. Section 7241.

information contained in the reports fairly presents the company's financial condition.

In addition, this section also requires the CEO and CFO to certify that they have created and designed an internal control system for their company and have recently evaluated that system to ensure that it is effectively providing them with relevant and accurate financial information. If the signing officers have found any significant deficiencies or weaknesses in the company's system or have discovered any evidence of fraud, they must have reported the situation, and any corrective actions they have taken, to the auditors and the audit committee.

SECTION 306

Insider trades during pension fund blackout periods[2]

(a) Prohibition of insider trading during pension fund blackout periods

(1) In general

Except to the extent otherwise provided by rule of the Commission pursuant to paragraph (3), it shall be unlawful for any director or executive officer of an issuer of any equity security (other than an exempted security), directly or indirectly, to purchase, sell, or otherwise acquire or transfer any equity security of the issuer (other than an exempted security) during any blackout period with respect to such equity security if such director or officer acquires such equity security in connection with his or her service or employment as a director or executive officer.

(2) Remedy

(A) In general

Any profit realized by a director or executive officer referred to in paragraph (1) from any purchase, sale, or other acquisition or transfer in violation of this subsection shall inure to and be recoverable by the issuer, irrespective of any intention on the part of such director or executive officer in entering into the transaction.

(B) Actions to recover profits

An action to recover profits in accordance with this subsection may be instituted at law or in equity in any court of competent jurisdiction by the issuer, or by the owner of any security of the issuer in the name and in behalf of the issuer if the issuer fails or refuses to bring such action within 60 days after the date of request, or fails diligently to prosecute the action thereafter, except that no such suit shall be brought more than 2 years after the date on which such profit was realized.

(3) Rulemaking authorized

---

2. Codified at 15 U.S.C. Section 7244.

The Commission shall, in consultation with the Secretary of Labor, issue rules to clarify the application of this subsection and to prevent evasion thereof. Such rules shall provide for the application of the requirements of paragraph (1) with respect to entities treated as a single employer with respect to an issuer under section 414(b), (c), (m), or (o) of Title 26 to the extent necessary to clarify the application of such requirements and to prevent evasion thereof. Such rules may also provide for appropriate exceptions from the requirements of this subsection, including exceptions for purchases pursuant to an automatic dividend reinvestment program or purchases or sales made pursuant to an advance election.

(4) Blackout period

For purposes of this subsection, the term "blackout period", with respect to the equity securities of any issuer—

(A) means any period of more than 3 consecutive business days during which the ability of not fewer than 50 percent of the participants or beneficiaries under all individual account plans maintained by the issuer to purchase, sell, or otherwise acquire or transfer an interest in any equity of such issuer held in such an individual account plan is temporarily suspended by the issuer or by a fiduciary of the plan; and

(B) does not include, under regulations which shall be prescribed by the Commission—

(i) a regularly scheduled period in which the participants and beneficiaries may not purchase, sell, or otherwise acquire or transfer an interest in any equity of such issuer, if such period is—

(I) incorporated into the individual account plan; and

(II) timely disclosed to employees before becoming participants under the individual account plan or as a subsequent amendment to the plan; or

(ii) any suspension described in subparagraph (A) that is imposed solely in connection with persons becoming participants or beneficiaries, or ceasing to be participants or beneficiaries, in an individual account plan by reason of a corporate merger, acquisition, divestiture, or similar transaction involving the plan or plan sponsor.

(5) Individual account plan

For purposes of this subsection, the term "individual account plan" has the meaning provided in section 1002(34) of Title 29, except that such term shall not include a one-participant retirement plan (within the meaning of section 1021(i)(8)(B) of Title 29).

(6) Notice to directors, executive officers, and the Commission

In any case in which a director or executive officer is subject to the requirements of this subsection in connection with a blackout period (as defined in paragraph (4)) with respect to any equity securities, the issuer of such equity securities shall timely notify such director or officer and the Securities and Exchange Commission of such blackout period.

* * * *

EXPLANATORY COMMENTS: *Corporate pension funds typically prohibit employees from trading shares of the corporation during periods when the pension fund is undergoing significant change. Prior to 2002, however, these blackout periods did not affect the corporation's executives, who frequently received shares of the corporate stock as part of their compensation. During the collapse of Enron, for example, its pension plan was scheduled to change administrators at a time when Enron's stock price was falling. Enron's employees therefore could not sell their shares while the price was dropping, but its executives could and did sell their stock, consequently avoiding some of the losses. Section 306 was Congress's solution to the basic unfairness of this situation. This section of the act required the SEC to issue rules that prohibit any director or executive officer from trading during pension fund blackout periods. (The SEC later issued these rules, entitled Regulation Blackout Trading Restriction, or Reg BTR.) Section 306 also provided shareholders with a right to file a shareholder's derivative suit against officers and directors who have profited from trading during these blackout periods (provided that the corporation has failed to bring a suit). The officer or director can be forced to return to the corporation any profits received, regardless of whether the director or officer acted with bad intent.*

SECTION 402

Periodical and other reports[3]

* * * *

(i) Accuracy of financial reports

Each financial report that contains financial statements, and that is required to be prepared in accordance with (or reconciled to) generally accepted accounting principles under this chapter and filed with the Commission shall reflect all material correcting adjustments that have been identified by a registered public accounting firm in accordance with generally accepted accounting principles and the rules and regulations of the Commission.

(j) Off-balance sheet transactions

Not later than 180 days after July 30, 2002, the Commission shall issue final rules providing that each annual and quarterly financial report required to be filed with the Commission shall disclose all material off-balance sheet transactions, arrangements, obligations (including contingent obligations), and other relationships of the issuer

with unconsolidated entities or other persons, that may have a material current or future effect on financial condition, changes in financial condition, results of operations, liquidity, capital expenditures, capital resources, or significant components of revenues or expenses.

(k) Prohibition on personal loans to executives

(1) In general

It shall be unlawful for any issuer (as defined in section 7201 of this title), directly or indirectly, including through any subsidiary, to extend or maintain credit, to arrange for the extension of credit, or to renew an extension of credit, in the form of a personal loan to or for any director or executive officer (or equivalent thereof) of that issuer. An extension of credit maintained by the issuer on July 30, 2002, shall not be subject to the provisions of this subsection, provided that there is no material modification to any term of any such extension of credit or any renewal of any such extension of credit on or after July 30, 2002.

(2) Limitation

Paragraph (1) does not preclude any home improvement and manufactured home loans (as that term is defined in section 1464 of Title 12), consumer credit (as defined in section 1602 of this title), or any extension of credit under an open end credit plan (as defined in section 1602 of this title), or a charge card (as defined in section 1637(c)(4)(e) of this title), or any extension of credit by a broker or dealer registered under section 78o of this title to an employee of that broker or dealer to buy, trade, or carry securities, that is permitted under rules or regulations of the Board of Governors of the Federal Reserve System pursuant to section 78g of this title (other than an extension of credit that would be used to purchase the stock of that issuer), that is—

(A) made or provided in the ordinary course of the consumer credit business of such issuer;

(B) of a type that is generally made available by such issuer to the public; and

(C) made by such issuer on market terms, or terms that are no more favorable than those offered by the issuer to the general public for such extensions of credit.

(3) Rule of construction for certain loans

Paragraph (1) does not apply to any loan made or maintained by an insured depository institution (as defined in section 1813 of Title 12), if the loan is subject to the insider lending restrictions of section 375b of Title 12.

(l) Real time issuer disclosures

Each issuer reporting under subsection (a) of this section or section 78o(d) of this title shall disclose to the public on a rapid and current basis such additional information concerning material changes in the financial condition or operations of the issuer, in plain English, which may

---

3. This section of the Sarbanes-Oxley Act amended some of the provisions of the 1934 Securities Exchange Act and added the paragraphs reproduced here at 15 U.S.C. Section 78m.

include trend and qualitative information and graphic presentations, as the Commission determines, by rule, is necessary or useful for the protection of investors and in the public interest.

* * * *

EXPLANATORY COMMENTS: *Corporate executives during the Enron era typically received extremely large salaries, significant bonuses, and abundant stock options, even when the companies for which they worked were suffering. Executives were also routinely given personal loans from corporate funds, many of which were never paid back. The average large company during that period loaned almost $1 million a year to top executives, and some companies, including Tyco International and Adelphia Communications Corporation, loaned hundreds of millions of dollars to their executives every year. Section 402 amended the 1934 Securities Exchange Act to prohibit public companies from making personal loans to executive officers and directors. There are a few exceptions to this prohibition, such as home-improvement loans made in the ordinary course of business. Note also that while loans are forbidden, outright gifts are not. A corporation is free to give gifts to its executives, including cash, provided that these gifts are disclosed on its financial reports. The idea is that corporate directors will be deterred from making substantial gifts to their executives by the disclosure requirement—particularly if the corporation's financial condition is questionable—because making such gifts could be perceived as abusing their authority.*

SECTION 403

Directors, officers, and principal stockholders[4]

(a) Disclosures required

(1) Directors, officers, and principal stockholders required to file

Every person who is directly or indirectly the beneficial owner of more than 10 percent of any class of any equity security (other than an exempted security) which is registered pursuant to section 78l of this title, or who is a director or an officer of the issuer of such security, shall file the statements required by this subsection with the Commission (and, if such security is registered on a national securities exchange, also with the exchange).

(2) Time of filing

The statements required by this subsection shall be filed—

(A) at the time of the registration of such security on a national securities exchange or by the effective date of a registration statement filed pursuant to section 78l(g) of this title;

(B) within 10 days after he or she becomes such beneficial owner, director, or officer;

(C) if there has been a change in such ownership, or if such person shall have purchased or sold a security-based swap agreement (as defined in section 206(b) of the Gramm-Leach-Bliley Act (15 U.S.C. 78c note)) involving such equity security, before the end of the second business day following the day on which the subject transaction has been executed, or at such other time as the Commission shall establish, by rule, in any case in which the Commission determines that such 2-day period is not feasible.

(3) Contents of statements

A statement filed—

(A) under subparagraph (A) or (B) of paragraph (2) shall contain a statement of the amount of all equity securities of such issuer of which the filing person is the beneficial owner; and

(B) under subparagraph (C) of such paragraph shall indicate ownership by the filing person at the date of filing, any such changes in such ownership, and such purchases and sales of the security-based swap agreements as have occurred since the most recent such filing under such subparagraph.

(4) Electronic filing and availability

Beginning not later than 1 year after July 30, 2002—

(A) a statement filed under subparagraph (C) of paragraph (2) shall be filed electronically;

(B) the Commission shall provide each such statement on a publicly accessible Internet site not later than the end of the business day following that filing; and

(C) the issuer (if the issuer maintains a corporate website) shall provide that statement on that corporate website, not later than the end of the business day following that filing.

* * * *

EXPLANATORY COMMENTS: *This section dramatically shortens the time period provided in the Securities Exchange Act of 1934 for disclosing transactions by insiders. The prior law stated that most transactions had to be reported within ten days of the beginning of the following month, although certain transactions did not have to be reported until the following fiscal year (within the first forty-five days). Because some of the insider trading that occurred during the Enron fiasco did not have to be disclosed (and was therefore not discovered) until long after the transactions, Congress added this section to reduce the time period for making disclosures. Under Section 403, most transactions by insiders must be electronically filed with the SEC within two business days. Also, any company that maintains a Web site must post these SEC filings on its site by the end of the next business day. Congress enacted this section in the belief that if insiders are required to file reports of their transactions promptly with the SEC, companies will do more to police themselves and prevent insider trading.*

---

4. This section of the Sarbanes-Oxley Act amended the disclosure provisions of the 1934 Securities Exchange Act, at 15 U.S.C. Section 78p.

SECTION 404

Management assessment of internal controls[5]

(a) Rules required

The Commission shall prescribe rules requiring each annual report required by section 78m(a) or 78o(d) of this title to contain an internal control report, which shall—

(1) state the responsibility of management for establishing and maintaining an adequate internal control structure and procedures for financial reporting; and

(2) contain an assessment, as of the end of the most recent fiscal year of the issuer, of the effectiveness of the internal control structure and procedures of the issuer for financial reporting.

(b) Internal control evaluation and reporting

With respect to the internal control assessment required by subsection (a) of this section, each registered public accounting firm that prepares or issues the audit report for the issuer shall attest to, and report on, the assessment made by the management of the issuer. An attestation made under this subsection shall be made in accordance with standards for attestation engagements issued or adopted by the Board. Any such attestation shall not be the subject of a separate engagement.

* * * *

EXPLANATORY COMMENTS: *This section was enacted to prevent corporate executives from claiming they were ignorant of significant errors in their companies' financial reports. For instance, several CEOs testified before Congress that they simply had no idea that the corporations' financial statements were off by billions of dollars. Congress therefore passed Section 404, which requires each annual report to contain a description and assessment of the company's internal control structure and financial reporting procedures. The section also requires that an audit be conducted of the internal control assessment, as well as the financial statements contained in the report. This section goes hand in hand with Section 302 (which, as discussed previously, requires various certifications attesting to the accuracy of the information in financial reports).*

Section 404 has been one of the more controversial and expensive provisions in the Sarbanes-Oxley Act because it requires companies to assess their own internal financial controls to make sure that their financial statements are reliable and accurate. A corporation might need to set up a disclosure committee and a coordinator, establish codes of conduct for accounting and financial personnel, create documentation procedures, provide training, and outline the individuals who are responsible for performing each of the procedures. Companies that were already well managed have not experienced substantial difficulty complying with this section. Other companies, however, have spent millions of dollars setting up, documenting, and evaluating their internal financial control systems. Although initially creating the internal financial control system is a one-time-only expense, the costs of maintaining and evaluating it are ongoing. Some corporations that spent considerable sums complying with Section 404 have been able to offset these costs by discovering and correcting inefficiencies or frauds within their systems. Nevertheless, it is unlikely that any corporation will find compliance with this section to be inexpensive.

SECTION 802 (a)

Destruction, alteration, or falsification of records in Federal investigations and bankruptcy[6]

Whoever knowingly alters, destroys, mutilates, conceals, covers up, falsifies, or makes a false entry in any record, document, or tangible object with the intent to impede, obstruct, or influence the investigation or proper administration of any matter within the jurisdiction of any department or agency of the United States or any case filed under title 11, or in relation to or contemplation of any such matter or case, shall be fined under this title, imprisoned not more than 20 years, or both.

Destruction of corporate audit records[7]

(a) (1) Any accountant who conducts an audit of an issuer of securities to which section 10A(a) of the Securities Exchange Act of 1934 (15 U.S.C. 78j-1(a)) applies, shall maintain all audit or review workpapers for a period of 5 years from the end of the fiscal period in which the audit or review was concluded.

(2) The Securities and Exchange Commission shall promulgate, within 180 days, after adequate notice and an opportunity for comment, such rules and regulations, as are reasonably necessary, relating to the retention of relevant records such as workpapers, documents that form the basis of an audit or review, memoranda, correspondence, communications, other documents, and records (including electronic records) which are created, sent, or received in connection with an audit or review and contain conclusions, opinions, analyses, or financial data relating to such an audit or review, which is conducted by any accountant who conducts an audit of an issuer of securities to which section 10A(a) of the Securities Exchange Act of 1934 (15 U.S.C. 78j-1(a)) applies. The Commission may, from time to time, amend or supplement the rules and regulations that it is required to promulgate under this section, after adequate notice and an opportunity for comment, in order to ensure that such rules and regulations adequately comport with the purposes of this section.

(b) Whoever knowingly and willfully violates subsection (a)(1), or any rule or regulation promulgated by the Securities and Exchange Commission under subsection (a)(2), shall be fined under this title, imprisoned not more than 10 years, or both.

(c) Nothing in this section shall be deemed to diminish or relieve any person of any other duty or obligation imposed

---

5. Codified at 15 U.S.C. Section 7262.

6. Codified at 15 U.S.C. Section 1519.
7. Codified at 15 U.S.C. Section 1520.

by Federal or State law or regulation to maintain, or refrain from destroying, any document.

* * * *

EXPLANATORY COMMENTS: *Section 802(a) enacted two new statutes that punish those who alter or destroy documents. The first statute is not specifically limited to securities fraud cases. It provides that anyone who alters, destroys, or falsifies records in federal investigations or bankruptcy may be criminally prosecuted and sentenced to a fine or to up to twenty years in prison, or both. The second statute requires auditors of public companies to keep all audit or review working papers for five years but expressly allows the SEC to amend or supplement these requirements as it sees fit. The SEC has, in fact, amended this section by issuing a rule that requires auditors who audit reporting companies to retain working papers for seven years from the conclusion of the review. Section 802(a) further provides that anyone who knowingly and willfully violates this statute is subject to criminal prosecution and can be sentenced to a fine, imprisoned for up to ten years, or both if convicted.*

This portion of the Sarbanes-Oxley Act implicitly recognizes that persons who are under investigation often are tempted to respond by destroying or falsifying documents that might prove their complicity in wrongdoing. The severity of the punishment should provide a strong incentive for these individuals to resist the temptation.

SECTION 804

Time limitations on the commencement of civil actions arising under Acts of Congress[8]

(a) Except as otherwise provided by law, a civil action arising under an Act of Congress enacted after the date of the enactment of this section may not be commenced later than 4 years after the cause of action accrues.

(b) Notwithstanding subsection (a), a private right of action that involves a claim of fraud, deceit, manipulation, or contrivance in contravention of a regulatory requirement concerning the securities laws, as defined in section 3(a)(47) of the Securities Exchange Act of 1934 (15 U.S.C. 78c(a)(47)), may be brought not later than the earlier of—

(1) 2 years after the discovery of the facts constituting the violation; or

(2) 5 years after such violation.

* * * *

EXPLANATORY COMMENTS: *Before the enactment of this section, Section 10(b) of the Securities Exchange Act of 1934 had no express statute of limitations. The courts generally required plaintiffs to have filed suit within one year from the date that they should (using due diligence) have discovered that a fraud had been committed but no later than three years after the fraud occurred. Section 804 extends this period by specifying that plaintiffs must file a lawsuit within two years after they discover (or should have discovered) a fraud but no later than five years after the fraud's occurrence. This provision has*

prevented the courts from dismissing numerous securities fraud lawsuits.

SECTION 806

Civil action to protect against retaliation in fraud cases[9]

(a) Whistleblower protection for employees of publicly traded companies.—

No company with a class of securities registered under section 12 of the Securities Exchange Act of 1934 (15 U.S.C. 78l), or that is required to file reports under section 15(d) of the Securities Exchange Act of 1934 (15 U.S.C. 78o(d)), or any officer, employee, contractor, subcontractor, or agent of such company, may discharge, demote, suspend, threaten, harass, or in any other manner discriminate against an employee in the terms and conditions of employment because of any lawful act done by the employee—

(1) to provide information, cause information to be provided, or otherwise assist in an investigation regarding any conduct which the employee reasonably believes constitutes a violation of section 1341, 1343, 1344, or 1348, any rule or regulation of the Securities and Exchange Commission, or any provision of Federal law relating to fraud against shareholders, when the information or assistance is provided to or the investigation is conducted by—

(A) a Federal regulatory or law enforcement agency;

(B) any Member of Congress or any committee of Congress; or

(C) a person with supervisory authority over the employee (or such other person working for the employer who has the authority to investigate, discover, or terminate misconduct); or

(2) to file, cause to be filed, testify, participate in, or otherwise assist in a proceeding filed or about to be filed (with any knowledge of the employer) relating to an alleged violation of section 1341, 1343, 1344, or 1348, any rule or regulation of the Securities and Exchange Commission, or any provision of Federal law relating to fraud against shareholders.

(b) Enforcement action.—

(1) In general.—A person who alleges discharge or other discrimination by any person in violation of subsection (a) may seek relief under subsection (c), by—

(A) filing a complaint with the Secretary of Labor; or

(B) if the Secretary has not issued a final decision within 180 days of the filing of the complaint and

---

8. Codified at 28 U.S.C. Section 1658.

9. Codified at 18 U.S.C. Section 1514A.

there is no showing that such delay is due to the bad faith of the claimant, bringing an action at law or equity for de novo review in the appropriate district court of the United States, which shall have jurisdiction over such an action without regard to the amount in controversy.

(2) Procedure.—

(A) In general.—An action under paragraph (1)(A) shall be governed under the rules and procedures set forth in section 42121(b) of title 49, United States Code.

(B) Exception.—Notification made under section 42121(b)(1) of title 49, United States Code, shall be made to the person named in the complaint and to the employer.

(C) Burdens of proof.—An action brought under paragraph (1)(B) shall be governed by the legal burdens of proof set forth in section 42121(b) of title 49, United States Code.

(D) Statute of limitations.—An action under paragraph (1) shall be commenced not later than 90 days after the date on which the violation occurs.

(c) Remedies.—

(1) In general.—An employee prevailing in any action under subsection (b)(1) shall be entitled to all relief necessary to make the employee whole.

(2) Compensatory damages.—Relief for any action under paragraph (1) shall include—

(A) reinstatement with the same seniority status that the employee would have had, but for the discrimination;

(B) the amount of back pay, with interest; and

(C) compensation for any special damages sustained as a result of the discrimination, including litigation costs, expert witness fees, and reasonable attorney fees.

(d) Rights retained by employee.—Nothing in this section shall be deemed to diminish the rights, privileges, or remedies of any employee under any Federal or State law, or under any collective bargaining agreement.

EXPLANATORY COMMENTS: *Section 806 is one of several provisions that were included in the Sarbanes-Oxley Act to encourage and protect whistleblowers—that is, employees who report their employer's alleged violations of securities law to the authorities. This section applies to employees, agents, and independent contractors who work for publicly traded companies or testify about such a company during an investigation. It sets up an administrative procedure at the Department of Labor for individuals who claim that their employer retaliated against them (fired or demoted them, for example) for blowing the whistle on the employer's wrongful conduct. It also allows the award of civil damages—including back pay, reinstatement,* *special damages, attorneys' fees, and court costs—to employees who prove that they suffered retaliation. Since this provision was enacted, whistleblowers have filed numerous complaints with the Department of Labor under this section.*

SECTION 807

Securities fraud[10]

Whoever knowingly executes, or attempts to execute, a scheme or artifice—

(1) to defraud any person in connection with any security of an issuer with a class of securities registered under section 12 of the Securities Exchange Act of 1934 (15 U.S.C. 78l) or that is required to file reports under section 15(d) of the Securities Exchange Act of 1934 (15 U.S.C. 78o(d)); or

(2) to obtain, by means of false or fraudulent pretenses, representations, or promises, any money or property in connection with the purchase or sale of any security of an issuer with a class of securities registered under section 12 of the Securities Exchange Act of 1934 (15 U.S.C. 78l) or that is required to file reports under section 15(d) of the Securities Exchange Act of 1934 (15 U.S.C. 78o(d)); shall be fined under this title, or imprisoned not more than 25 years, or both.

* * * *

EXPLANATORY COMMENTS: *Section 807 adds a new provision to the federal criminal code that addresses securities fraud. Before 2002, federal securities law had already made it a crime—under Section 10(b) of the Securities Exchange Act of 1934 and SEC Rule 10b-5, both of which are discussed in Chapter 29—to intentionally defraud someone in connection with a purchase or sale of securities, but the offense was not listed in the federal criminal code. Also, paragraph 2 of Section 807 goes beyond what is prohibited under securities law by making it a crime to obtain by means of false or fraudulent pretenses any money or property from the purchase or sale of securities. This new provision allows violators to be punished by up to twenty-five years in prison, a fine, or both.*

SECTION 906

Failure of corporate officers to certify financial reports[11]

(a) Certification of periodic financial reports.—Each periodic report containing financial statements filed by an issuer with the Securities Exchange Commission pursuant to section 13(a) or 15(d) of the Securities Exchange Act of 1934 (15 U.S.C. 78m(a) or 78o(d)) shall be accompanied by a written statement by the chief executive officer and chief financial officer (or equivalent thereof) of the issuer.

---

10. Codified at 18 U.S.C. Section 1348.
11. Codified at 18 U.S.C. Section 1350.

(b) Content.—The statement required under subsection (a) shall certify that the periodic report containing the financial statements fully complies with the requirements of section 13(a) or 15(d) of the Securities Exchange Act of 1934 (15 U.S.C. 78m or 78o(d)) and that information contained in the periodic report fairly presents, in all material respects, the financial condition and results of operations of the issuer.

(c) Criminal penalties.—Whoever—

(1) certifies any statement as set forth in subsections (a) and (b) of this section knowing that the periodic report accompanying the statement does not comport with all the requirements set forth in this section shall be fined not more than $1,000,000 or imprisoned not more than 10 years, or both; or

(2) willfully certifies any statement as set forth in subsections (a) and (b) of this section knowing that the periodic report accompanying the statement does not comport with all the requirements set forth in

this section shall be fined not more than $5,000,000, or imprisoned not more than 20 years, or both.

*   *   *   *

EXPLANATORY COMMENTS: *As previously discussed, under Section 302 a corporation's CEO and CFO are required to certify that they believe the quarterly and annual reports their company files with the SEC are accurate and fairly present the company's financial condition. Section 906 adds "teeth" to these requirements by authorizing criminal penalties for those officers who intentionally certify inaccurate SEC filings. Knowing violations of the requirements are punishable by a fine of up to $1 million, ten years in prison, or both. Willful violators may be fined up to $5 million, sentenced to up to twenty years in prison, or both. Although the difference between a knowing and a willful violation is not entirely clear, the section is obviously intended to remind corporate officers of the serious consequences of certifying inaccurate reports to the SEC.*

APPENDIX F

❋

Sample Answers for End-of-Chapter *Questions* with *Sample Answer*

1–2A. Question with Sample Answer

At the time of the Nuremberg trials, "crimes against humanity" were new international crimes. The laws criminalized such acts as murder, extermination, enslavement, deportation, and other inhumane acts committed against any civilian population. These international laws derived their legitimacy from "natural law." Natural law, which is the oldest and one of the most significant schools of jurisprudence, holds that governments and legal systems should reflect the moral and ethical ideals that are inherent in human nature. Because natural law is universal and discoverable by reason, its adherents believe that all other law is derived from natural law. Natural law therefore supersedes laws created by humans (national, or "positive," law), and in a conflict between the two, national or positive law loses its legitimacy. The Nuremberg defendants asserted that they had been acting in accordance with German law. The judges dismissed these claims, reasoning that the defendants' acts were commonly regarded as crimes and that the accused must have known that the acts would be considered criminal. The judges clearly believed the tenets of natural law and expected that the defendants, too, should have been able to realize that their acts ran afoul of it. The fact that the "positivist law" of Germany at the time required them to commit these acts is irrelevant. Under natural law theory, the international court was justified in finding the defendants guilty of crimes against humanity.

2–2A. Question with Sample Answer

Trial courts, as explained in this text, are responsible for settling "questions of fact." Often, when parties bring a case to court there is a dispute as to what actually happened. Different witnesses have different versions of what they saw or heard, and there may be only indirect evidence of certain issues in dispute. During the trial, the judge and the jury (if it is a jury trial) listen to the witnesses and view the evidence firsthand. Thus, the trial court is in the best position to assess the credibility (truthfulness) of the witnesses and determine the weight that should be given to various items of evidence. At the end of the trial, the judge and the jury (if it is a jury trial) decide what will be considered facts for the purposes of the case. Trial courts are best suited to this job, as they have the opportunity to observe the witnesses and evidence, and they regularly determine the reliability of certain evidence. Appellate courts, in contrast, see only the written record of the trial court proceedings and cannot evaluate the credibility of witnesses and the persuasiveness of evidence. For these reasons, appellate courts nearly always defer to trial courts' findings of fact. An appellate court can reverse a lower court's findings of fact, however, when so little evidence was presented at trial that no reasonable person could have reached the conclusion that the judge or jury reached.

3–2A. Question with Sample Answer

Because the joint venture in Euphratia would naturally be subject to that country's laws, company lawyers would have to look to both the agreements that the joint venture had signed with the national government as well as Euphratia's laws relating to the ownership of natural resources to determine whether they would interfere with the efforts by the two companies to resolve their dispute. All countries have the right to expropriate foreign-owned property as long as they pay adequate compensation to the owners. Because the Federal Arbitration Act accords the parties significant discretion in deciding where disputes should be heard and which law should govern, virtually any dispute can be the subject of arbitration. The terms of a voluntary arbitration agreement normally will be enforced by the courts if the agreement does not compel an illegal act or contravene public policy. Assuming that Euphratia's laws did not violate U.S. public policy, the dispute itself should be arbitrable.

4–2A. Question with Sample Answer

Factors for the firm to consider in making its decision include the appropriate ethical standard. Under the utilitarian standard, an action is correct, or "right," when, among the people it affects, it produces the greatest amount of good for the greatest number. When an action affects the majority adversely, it is morally wrong. Applying the utilitarian standard requires (1) a determination of which individuals will be affected by the action in question; (2) an assessment, or cost-benefit analysis, of the negative and positive effects of alternative actions on these individuals; and (3) a choice among alternatives that will produce maximum societal utility. Ethical standards may also be based on a concept of duty—which postulates that the end can never justify the means and human beings should not be treated as mere means to an end. But ethical decision making in a business context is not always simple, particularly when it is determined that an action will affect, in different ways, different groups of people: shareholders, employees, society, and other stakeholders, such as the local community. Thus, another factor to consider is to whom the firm believes it owes a duty.

5–2A. Question with Sample Answer

As the text points out, Thomas has a constitutionally protected right to his religion and the free exercise of it. In denying his unemployment benefits, the state violated these rights. Employers are obligated to make reasonable accommodations for their employees' beliefs, right or wrong, that are openly and sincerely held. Thomas's beliefs were openly and sincerely held. By placing him in a department that made military goods, his employer effectively put him in a position of having to choose between his job and his religious principles. This unilateral decision on the part of the employer was the reason Thomas left his job and why the company was required to compensate Thomas for his resulting unemployment.

6–2A. Question with Sample Answer

The court will consider first whether the agency followed the procedures prescribed in the Administrative Procedure Act (APA). Ordinarily, courts will not require agencies to use procedures beyond those of the APA. Courts will, however, compel agencies to follow their own rules. If an agency has adopted a rule granting extra procedures, the agency must provide those extra procedures, at least until the rule is formally rescinded. Ultimately, in this case, the court will most likely rule for the food producers.

7–3A. Question with Sample Answer

This is fraud committed in e-mail sent via the Internet. The elements of the tort of fraud are (1) the misrepresentation of material facts or conditions made with knowledge that they are false or with reckless disregard for the truth, (2) the intent to induce another to rely on the misrepresentation, (3) justifiable reliance on the misrepresentation by the deceived party, (d) damages suffered as a result of the reliance, and (4) a causal connection between the misrepresentation and the injury. If any of this e-mailer's recipients reply to her false plea with money, it is likely that all of the requirements for fraud will have been met. The sort of fraud described in this problem is similar to the "Nigerian letter fraud scam" noted in the text. In this type of scam, an individual sends an e-mail promising its recipient a percentage of money held in a bank account or payable from a government agency or other source if he or she will send funds to help a fictitious official transfer the amount in the account to another bank. The details of the scam are often adjusted to current events, with perpetrators referring to news-making conflicts, tax refunds or payments, and other occurrences.

8–2A. Question with Sample Answer

Yes, it is a reasonable approach to rely on the producers' financial records, which are reasonably reflective of their costs because their normal allocation methodologies were used for a number of years. These records are historically relied upon to present important financial information to shareholders, lenders, tax authorities, auditors, and other third parties. Provided that the producers' records and books comply with generally accepted accounting principles and were verified by independent auditors, it is reasonable to use them to determine the production costs and fair market value of canned pineapple in the United States.

9–2A. Question with Sample Answer

According to the question, Janine was apparently unconscious or otherwise unable to agree to a contract for the nursing services she received while she was in the hospital. As you read in the chapter, however, sometimes the law will create a fictional contract in order to prevent one party from unjustly receiving a benefit at the expense of another. This is known as a *quasi contract* and provides a basis for Nursing Services to recover the value of the services it provided while Janine was in the hospital. As for the at-home services that were provided to Janine, because Janine was aware that those services were being provided for her, Nursing Services can recover for those services under an implied-in-fact contract. Under this type of contract, the conduct of the parties creates and defines the terms. Janine's acceptance of the services constitutes her agreement to form a contract, and she will probably be required to pay Nursing Services in full.

10–2A. Question with Sample Answer

A novation exists when a new, valid contract expressly or impliedly discharges a prior contract by the substitution of a party. Accord and satisfaction exists when the parties agree that the original obligation can be discharged by a substituted performance. In this case, Fred's agreement with Iba to pay off Junior's debt for $1,100 (as compared to the $1,000 owed) is definitely a valid contract. The terms of the contract substitute Fred as the debtor for Junior, and Junior is definitely discharged from further liability. This agreement is a *novation*.

11–2A. Question with Sample Answer

Anne has entered into an enforceable contract to subscribe to *E-Commerce Weekly*. In this scenario, the offer to deliver, via e-mail, the newsletter was presented by the offeror with a statement of how to accept—by clicking on the "SUBSCRIBE" button. Consideration was in the promise to deliver the newsletter and in the price that the subscriber agreed to pay. The offeree had an opportunity to read the terms of the subscription agreement before making the contract. Whether or not she actually read those terms does not matter.

12–2A. Question with Sample Answer

To answer this question, you must first decide if there is a legal theory under which Harley may be able to recover. You may recall from your reading the intentional tort of "wrongful interference with a contractual relationship." To recover damages under this theory, Harley would need to show that he and Martha had a valid contract, that Lothar knew of this contractual relationship between Martha and Harley, and that Lothar intentionally convinced Martha to break her contract with Harley. Even though Lothar hoped that his advertisments would persuade Martha to break her contract with Harley, the question states that Martha's decision to change bakers was based solely on the advertising and not on anything else that Lothar did. Lothar's advertisements did not constitute a tort. Note, though, that while Harley cannot collect from Lothar for Martha's actions, he does have a cause of action against Martha for her breach of their contract.

13–2A. Question with Sample Answer

The court should rule in favor of the manufacturer, finding that the gun did not malfunction but performed exactly as Clark and Wright expected. The court should also point out that Clark and Wright appreciated the danger of using the guns without protective eyewear. Clark offered no proof that the paintball gun used in the incident failed to function as expected. He was aware that there was protective eyewear available but he chose not to buy it. He was an active participant in shooting paintballs at other vehicles. The evening of the incident Clark carried his paintball gun with him for that purpose. Wright also knew it was dangerous to shoot someone in the eye with a paintball gun. But the most crucial testimony was Wright's statement that his paintball gun did not malfunction.

14–2A. Question with Sample Answer

(a) Ursula will not be held liable for copyright infringement in this case because her photocopying pages for use in scholarly research falls squarely under the "fair use" exception to the Copyright Act.

(b) While Ursula's actions are improper, they could constitute trademark infringement, not copyright infringement. Copyrights are granted for literary and artistic productions; trademarks are distinctive marks created and used by manufacturers to differentiate their goods from those of their competitors. Trademark infringement occurs when a mark is copied to a substantial degree, intentionally or unintentionally.

(c) As with the answer to (a) above, Ursula's actions fall within the "fair use" doctrine of copyright law. Her use of the taped television shows for teaching is the exact type of use the exception is designed to cover.

15–2A. Question with Sample Answer

A trustee is given avoidance powers by the Bankruptcy Code. One situation in which the trustee can avoid transfers of property or payments by a debtor to a creditor is when such transfer constitutes a *preference*. A preference is a transfer of property or payment that favors one creditor over another. For a preference to exist, the debtor must be insolvent and must have made payment for a preexisting debt within ninety days of the filing of the petition in bankruptcy. The Code provides that the debtor is *presumed* to be insolvent during this ninety-day period. If the payment is made to an insider (and in this case payment was made to a close relative), the preference period is extended to one year, but the presumption of insolvency still applies only to the ninety-day period. In this case, the trustee has an excellent chance of having both payments declared preferences. The payment to Cool Springs was within ninety days of the filing of the petition, and it is doubtful that Cool Springs could overcome the presumption that Peaslee was insolvent at the time the payment was made. The $5,000 payment was made to an insider, Peaslee's father, and any payment made to an insider within one year of the petition of bankruptcy is a preference—as long as the debtor was insolvent at the time of payment. The facts indicate that Peaslee probably was insolvent at the time he paid his father. If he was not, the payment is not a preference, and the trustee's avoidance of the transfer would be improper.

16–2A. Question with Sample Answer

The answer is likely no. A court would most likely find that this issue was novel and permitted the plaintiff to survive a motion to dismiss. However, if the loan was split without the consumer's consent, prior court cases have found that such practices violate the TILA's mandate to group all disclosures for a single transaction into one writing. Even if the plaintiff acquiesced to splitting the loan, the practice appears to circumvent the purpose of HOEPA through an artificial restructuring of the loan transaction. If loan splitting were allowed to circumvent consumer protections, lenders would have a strong incentive to divide loans as necessary to keep individual loan costs as low as possible.

17–2A. Question with Sample Answer

The court would likely conclude that National Foods was responsible for the acts of harassment by the manager at the franchised restaurant, on the ground that the employees were the agents of National Foods. An agency relationship can be implied from the circumstances and conduct of the parties. The important question is the degree of control that a franchisor has over its franchisees. Whether it exercises that control is beside the point. Here, National Foods retained considerable control over the new hires and the franchisee's policies, as well as the right to terminate the franchise for violations. That its supervisors routinely approved the policies would not undercut National Foods' liability.

18–2A. Question with Sample Answer

(a) A limited partner's interest is assignable. In fact, assignment allows the assignee to become a substituted limited partner with the consent of the remaining partners. The assignment, however, does not dissolve the limited partnership.

(b) Bankruptcy of the limited partnership itself causes dissolution, but bankruptcy of one of the limited partners does not dissolve the partnership unless it causes the bankruptcy of the firm.

(c) The retirement, death, or insanity of a general partner dissolves the partnership unless the business can be continued by the remaining general partners. Because Dorinda was the only general partner, her death dissolves the limited partnership.

19–2A. Question with Sample Answer

Directors are personally answerable to the corporation and the shareholders for breach of their duty to exercise reasonable care in conducting the affairs of the corporation. Reasonable care is defined as being the degree of care that a reasonably prudent person would use in the conduct of personal business affairs. When directors delegate the running of the corporate affairs to officers, the directors are expected to use reasonable care in the selection and supervision of such officers. Failure to do so will make the directors liable for negligence or mismanagement. A director who dissents to an action by the board is not personally liable for losses resulting from that action. Unless the dissent is entered into the board meeting minutes, however, the director is presumed to have assented. Therefore, the first issue in the case of AstroStar, Inc., is whether the board members failed to use reasonable care in the selection of the president. If so, and particularly if the board failed to provide a reasonable amount of supervision (and openly embezzled funds indicate that failure), the directors will be personally liable. This liability will include Eckhart unless she can prove that she dissented and that she tried to reasonably supervise the new president. Considering the facts in this case, it is questionable that Eckhart could prove this.

20–2A. Question with Sample Answer

Upon creation of an agency, the agent owes certain fiduciary duties to the principal. Two such duties are the duty of loyalty and the duty to inform or notify. The duty of loyalty is a fundamental concept of the fiduciary relationship. The agent must act solely for the benefit of the principal, not in the agent's own interest or in the interest of another person. One of the principles invoked by this duty is that an agent employed to sell cannot become a purchaser without the principal's consent. When the agent is a partner, contracting to sell to another partner is equivalent to selling to oneself and is therefore a breach of the agent's duty. In addition, the agent has a duty to disclose to the principal any facts pertinent to the subject matter of the agency. Failure to disclose to Peter the knowledge of the shopping mall and the increased market value of the property also was a breach of Alice's fiduciary duties. When an agent breaches fiduciary duties owed to the principal by becoming a recipient of a contract, the contract is voidable at the election of the principal. Neither Carl nor Alice can hold Peter to the contract,

and Alice's breach of fiduciary duties also allows Peter to terminate the agency relationship.

21–2A. Question with Sample Answer

The Occupational Health and Safety Act (OSHA) requires employers to provide safe working conditions for employees. The act prohibits employers from discharging or discriminating against any employee who refuses to work when the employee believes in good faith that he or she will risk death or great bodily harm by undertaking the employment activity. Denton and Carlo had sufficient reason to believe that the maintenance job required of them by their employer involved great risk, and therefore, under OSHA, their discharge was wrongful. Denton and Carlo can turn to the Occupational Safety and Health Administration, which is part of the Department of Labor, for assistance.

22–2A. Question with Sample Answer

Under Title VII of the Civil Rights Act, an employer must offer a reasonable accommodation to resolve a conflict between an employee's sincere religious belief and a condition of employment. Reasonable accommodation is required unless such an accommodation would create an undue hardship for the employer's business. In this hypothetical scenario, the only accommodation that Caldwell considered reasonable was a complete exemption from the no-facial-jewelry policy. This could be construed to impose an undue hardship on Costco. The company's dress code could be based on the belief that employees reflect on their employers, especially employees who regularly interact with customers, as Caldwell did in her cashier position. Caldwell's facial jewelry could have affected Costco's public image. Under this reasoning and in such a situation, an employer has no obligation to offer an accommodation before taking other action. Thus, Caldwell is not likely to succeed in a lawsuit against Costco for religious discrimination.

23–2A. Question with Sample Answer

The NLRB has consistently been suspicious of companies that grant added benefits during election campaigns. These benefits will be considered as an unfair labor practice that biases elections, unless the employer can demonstrate that the benefits were unrelated to the unionization and would have been granted anyway.

24–3A. Question with Sample Answer

Yes. A regulation of the Federal Trade Commission (FTC) under Section 5 of the Federal Trade Commission Act makes it a violation for door-to-door sellers to fail to give consumers three days to cancel any sale. In addition, a number of state statutes require this three-day "cooling off" period to protect consumers from unscrupulous door-to-door sellers. Because the Gonchars sought to rescind the contract within the three-day period, Renowned Books was obligated to agree to cancel the contract. Its failure to allow rescission was in violation of the FTC regulation and of most state statutes.

25–2A. Question with Sample Answer

Fruitade has violated a number of federal environmental laws if such actions are being taken without a permit. First, because the dumping is in a navigable waterway, the River and Harbor Act of 1886, as amended, has been violated. Second, the Clean Water Act of 1972, as amended, has been violated. This act is designed to make the waters safe for swimming, to protect fish and wildlife, and to eliminate discharge of pollutants into the water. Both the crushed glass and the acid violate this act. Third, the Toxic Substances Control Act of 1976 was passed to regulate chemicals that are known to be toxic and could have an effect on human health and the environment. The acid in the cleaning fluid or compound could come under this act.

26–3A. Question with Sample Answer

Wilfredo understandably wants a general warranty deed, as this type of deed will give him the most extensive protection against any defects of title claimed against the property transferred. The general warranty would have Patricia warranting the following covenants:

(a) Covenant of seisin and right to convey—a warranty that the seller has good title and power to convey.

(b) Covenant against encumbrances—a guaranty by the seller that, unless stated, there are no outstanding encumbrances or liens against the property conveyed.

(c) Covenant of quiet possession—a warranty that the grantee's possession will not be disturbed by others claiming a prior legal right. Patricia, however, is conveying only ten feet along a property line that may not even be accurately surveyed. Patricia therefore does not wish to make these warranties. Consequently, she is offering a quitclaim deed, which does not convey any warranties but conveys only whatever interest, if any, the grantor owns. Although title is passed by the quitclaim deed, the quality of the title is not warranted.

Because Wilfredo really needs the property, it appears that he has three choices: he can accept the quitclaim deed; he can increase his offer price to obtain the general warranty deed he wants; or he can offer to have a title search made, which should satisfy both parties.

27–2A. Question with Sample Answer

Super-Tech's unilateral action is a violation of the Sherman Act, Section 2. Super-Tech already controls a substantial portion of the market for computers and thus has a monopoly position in this business field. Super-Tech's action is a misuse of its monopoly power in the marketplace. Any person who shall monopolize or attempt to monopolize any part of trade or commerce may be in violation of the Sherman Act. Therefore, Alcan can file a private action seeking treble damages, costs, and reasonable attorneys' fees, and the U.S. Department of Justice can institute criminal and civil proceedings.

28–2A. Question with Sample Answer

Yes. The major antitrust law being violated is the Sherman Act, Section 1. Allitron and Donovan are engaged in interstate commerce, and the agreement to divide marketing territories between them is a contract in restraint of trade. The U.S. Department of Justice could seek fines for up to $1 million for each corporation, and the officers or directors responsible could be imprisoned for up to three years. In addition, the U.S. Department of Justice could institute civil proceedings to restrain this conduct.

29–2A. Question with Sample Answer

No. Under federal securities law, a stock split is exempt from registration requirements. This is because no sale of stock is involved. The existing shares are merely being split, and no consideration is received by the corporation for the additional shares created.

Glossary

A

Acceptance In contract law, the offeree's notification to the offeror that the offeree agrees to be bound by the terms of the offeror's proposal. Although historically the terms of acceptance had to be the mirror image of the terms of the offer, the Uniform Commercial Code provides that even modified terms of the offer in a definite expression of acceptance constitute a contract.

Accord and satisfaction An agreement for payment (or other performance) between two parties, one of whom has a right of action against the other. After the payment has been accepted or other performance has been made, the "accord and satisfaction" is complete and the obligation is discharged.

Accredited investors In the context of securities offerings, "sophisticated" investors, such as banks, insurance companies, investment companies, the issuer's executive officers and directors, and persons whose income or net worth exceeds certain limits.

Acquittal A certification or declaration following a trial that the individual accused of a crime is innocent, or free from guilt, and is thus absolved of the charges.

Act of state doctrine A doctrine that provides that the judicial branch of one country will not examine the validity of public acts committed by a recognized foreign government within its own territory.

Actionable Capable of serving as the basis of a lawsuit.

Actual authority Authority of an agent that is express or implied.

Actual malice A condition that exists when a person makes a statement with either knowledge of its falsity or a reckless disregard for the truth. In a defamation suit, a statement made about a public figure normally must be made with actual malice for liability to be incurred.

Actus reus (pronounced *ak*-tus *ray*-uhs) A guilty (prohibited) act. The commission of a prohibited act is one of the two essential elements required for criminal liability, the other element being the intent to commit a crime.

Adequate protection doctrine In bankruptcy law, a doctrine that protects secured creditors from losing their security as a result of an automatic stay on legal proceedings by creditors against the debtor once the debtor petitions for bankruptcy relief. In certain circumstances, the bankruptcy court may provide adequate protection by requiring the debtor or trustee to pay the creditor or provide additional guaranties to protect the creditor against the losses suffered by the creditor as a result of the stay.

Adhesion contract A "standard-form" contract, such as that between a large retailer and a consumer, in which the stronger party dictates the terms.

Adjudication The process of resolving a dispute by presenting evidence and arguments before a neutral third party decision maker in a court or an administrative law proceeding.

Adjustable-rate mortgage (ARM) A mortgage in which the rate of interest paid by the borrower changes periodically, often with reference to a predetermined government interest rate (the index). Usually, the interest rate for ARMs is initially low and increases over time, but there is a cap on the amount that the rate can increase during any adjustment period.

Administrative agency A federal, state, or local government agency established to perform a specific function. Administrative agencies are authorized by legislative acts to make and enforce rules to administer and enforce the acts.

Administrative law The body of law created by administrative agencies (in the form of rules, regulations, orders, and decisions) in order to carry out their duties and responsibilities.

Administrative law judge (ALJ) One who presides over an administrative agency hearing and who has the power to administer oaths, take testimony, rule on questions of evidence, and make determinations of fact.

Administrative process The procedure used by administrative agencies in the administration of law.

Administrator One who is appointed by a court to handle the probate (disposition) of a person's estate if that person dies intestate (without a valid will) or if the executor named in the will cannot serve.

Adverse possession The acquisition of title to real property by occupying it openly, without the consent of the owner, for a period of time specified by a state statute. The occupation must be actual, open, notorious, exclusive, and in opposition to all others, including the owner.

Affidavit A written or printed voluntary statement of facts, confirmed by the oath or affirmation of the party making it and made before a person having the authority to administer the oath or affirmation.

Affirm To validate; to give legal force to. *See also* Ratification

Affirmative action Job-hiring policies that give special consideration to members of protected classes in an effort to overcome present effects of past discrimination.

Affirmative defense A response to a plaintiff's claim that does not deny the plaintiff's facts but attacks the plaintiff's legal right to bring an action. An example is the running of the statute of limitations.

After-acquired evidence A type of evidence submitted in support of an affirmative defense in employment discrimination cases. Evidence that, prior to the employer's discriminatory act, the employee engaged in misconduct sufficient to warrant dismissal had the employer known of it earlier.

After-acquired property Property of the debtor that is acquired after the execution of a security agreement.

Age of majority The age at which an individual is considered legally capable of conducting himself or herself responsibly. A person of this age is entitled to the full rights of citizenship, including the right to vote. In contract law, the age at which one is no longer an infant and can no longer disaffirm a contract.

Agency A relationship between two parties in which one party (the agent) agrees to represent or act for the other (the principal).

Agency by estoppel An agency that arises when a principal negligently allows an agent to exercise powers not granted to the agent, thus justifying others in believing that the agent possesses the requisite agency authority.

Agent A person who agrees to represent or act for another, called the principal.

Agreement A meeting of two or more minds in regard to the terms of a contract; usually broken down into two events—an offer by one party to form a contract, and an acceptance of the offer by the person to whom the offer is made.

Alien corporation A designation in the United States for a corporation formed in another country but doing business in the United States.

Alienation In real property law, the voluntary transfer of property from one person to another (as opposed to a transfer by operation of law).

Allegation A statement, claim, or assertion.

Allege To state, recite, assert, or charge.

Alternative dispute resolution (ADR) The resolution of disputes in ways other than those involved in the traditional judicial process. Negotiation, mediation, and arbitration are forms of ADR.

Amend To change through a formal procedure.

American Arbitration Association (AAA) The major organization offering arbitration services in the United States.

Analogy In logical reasoning, an assumption that if two things are similar in some respects, they will be similar in other respects also. Often used in legal reasoning to infer the appropriate application of legal principles in a case being decided by referring to previous cases involving different facts but considered to come within the policy underlying the rule.

Annual percentage rate (APR) The cost of credit on a yearly basis, typically expressed as an annual percentage.

Annuity An insurance policy that pays the insured fixed, periodic payments for life or for a term of years, as stipulated in the policy, after the insured reaches a specified age.

Annul To cancel or to make void.

Answer Procedurally, a defendant's response to the plaintiff's complaint.

Anticipatory repudiation An assertion or action by a party indicating that he or she will not perform an obligation that the party is contractually obligated to perform at a future time.

Antitrust law The body of federal and state laws and statutes protecting trade and commerce from unlawful restraints, price discrimination, price fixing, and monopolies. The principal federal antitrust statues are the Sherman Act of 1890, the Clayton Act of 1914, and the Federal Trade Commission Act of 1914.

Apparent authority Authority that is only apparent, not real. In agency law, a person may be deemed to have had the power to act as an agent for another party if the other party's manifestations to a third party led the third party to believe that an agency existed when, in fact, it did not.

Appeal Resort to a superior court, such as an appellate court, to review the decision of an inferior court, such as a trial court or an administrative agency.

Appellant The party who takes an appeal from one court to another.

Appellate court A court having appellate jurisdiction.

Appellate jurisdiction Courts having appellate jurisdiction act as reviewing courts, or appellate courts. Generally, cases can be brought before appellate courts only on appeal from an order or a judgment of a trial court or other lower court.

Appellee The party against whom an appeal is taken—that is, the party who opposes setting aside or reversing the judgment.

Appraisal right The right of a dissenting shareholder, if he or she objects to an extraordinary transaction of the corporation (such as a merger or consolidation), to have his or her shares appraised and to be paid the fair value of his or her shares by the corporation.

Appraiser An individual who specializes in determining the value of certain real or personal property.

Appropriation In tort law, the use by one person of another person's name, likeness, or other identifying characteristic without permission and for the benefit of the user.

Arbitrary and capricious test A court reviewing an informal administrative agency action applies this test to determine whether or not that action was in clear error. The court gives wide discretion to the expertise of the agency and decides if the agency had sufficient factual information on which to base its action. If no clear error was made, then the agency's action stands.

Arbitration The settling of a dispute by submitting it to a disinterested third party (other than a court), who renders a decision. The decision may or may not be legally binding.

Arbitration clause A clause in a contract that provides that, in the event of a dispute, the parties will submit the dispute to arbitration rather than litigate the dispute in court.

Arraignment A procedure in which an accused person is brought before the court to answer criminal charges. The charge is read to the person, and he or she is asked to enter a plea—such as "guilty" or "not guilty."

Arson The malicious burning of another's dwelling. Some statutes have expanded this to include any real property regardless of ownership and the destruction of property by other means—for example, by explosion.

Articles of incorporation The document filed with the appropriate governmental agency, usually the secretary of state, when a business is incorporated; state statutes usually prescribe what kind of information must be contained in the articles of incorporation.

Articles of organization The document filed with a designated state official by which a limited liability company is formed.

Articles of partnership A written agreement that sets forth each partner's rights and obligations with respect to the partnership.

Artisan's lien A possessory lien given to a person who has made improvements and added value to another person's personal property as security for payment for services performed.

Assault Any word or action intended to make another person fearful of immediate physical harm; a reasonably believable threat.

Assignee The person to whom contract rights are assigned.

Assignment The act of transferring to another all or part of one's rights arising under a contract.

Assignor The person who assigns contract rights.

Assumption of risk A defense against negligence that can be used when the plaintiff was aware of a danger and voluntarily assumed the risk of injury from that danger.

Attachment (1) In the context of secured transactions, the process by which a security interest in the property of another becomes enforceable. (2) In the context of judicial liens, a court-ordered seizure and taking into custody of property prior to the securing of a judgment for a past-due debt.

Attempted monopolization Any actions by a firm to eliminate competition and gain monopoly power.

Authenticate To sign a record, or with the intent to sign a record, to execute or to adopt an electronic sound, symbol, or the like to link with the record. A

record is retrievable information inscribed on a tangible medium or stored in an electronic or other medium.

Authority In agency law, the agent's permission to act on behalf of the principal. An agent's authority may be actual (express or implied) or apparent. *See also* Actual authority; Apparent authority

Authorization card A card signed by an employee that gives a union permission to act on his or her behalf in negotiations with management. Unions typically use authorization cards as evidence of employee support during union organization.

Authorized means In contract law, the means of acceptance authorized by the offeror.

Automatic stay In bankruptcy proceedings, the suspension of virtually all litigation and other action by creditors against the debtor or the debtor's property; the stay is effective the moment the debtor files a petition in bankruptcy.

Award In the context of litigation, the amount of money awarded to a plaintiff in a civil lawsuit as damages. In the context of arbitration, the arbitrator's decision.

B

Bait-and-switch advertising Advertising a product at a very attractive price (the bait) and then informing the consumer, once he or she is in the store, that the advertised product is either not available or is of poor quality; the customer is then urged to purchase (switched to) a more expensive item.

Balloon mortgage A loan that allows the debtor to make small monthly payments for an initial period, such as eight years, but then requires a large balloon payment for the entire remaining balance of the mortgage loan at the end of that period.

Bankruptcy court A federal court of limited jurisdiction that handles only bankruptcy proceedings. Bankruptcy proceedings are governed by federal bankruptcy law.

Bankruptcy trustee A person who is either appointed by the U.S. Department of Justice or by creditors in bankruptcy cases. In all bankruptcies under Chapters 7, 12, or 13, a trustee is appointed by the U.S. Trustee, who is an officer of the Department of Justice. Chapter 11 bankruptcies allow the debtor to continue to manage the property as a "debtor in possession," but this person can be replaced for cause with a bankruptcy trustee.

Bargain A mutual undertaking, contract, or agreement between two parties; to negotiate over the terms of a purchase or contract.

Basis of the bargain In contract law, the affirmation of fact or promise on which the sale of goods is predicated, creating an express warranty.

Battery The unprivileged, intentional touching of another.

Beneficiary One to whom life insurance proceeds are payable or for whose benefit a trust has been established or property under a will has been transferred.

Beyond a reasonable doubt The standard used to determine the guilt or innocence of a person criminally charged. To be guilty of a crime, one must be proved guilty "beyond and to the exclusion of every reasonable doubt." A reasonable doubt is one that would cause a prudent person to hesitate before acting in matters important to him or her.

Bilateral contract   A type of contract that arises when a promise is given in exchange for a return promise.

Bill of lading   A document that serves both as evidence of the receipt of goods for shipment and as documentary evidence of title to the goods.

Bill of Rights   The first ten amendments to the U.S. Constitution.

Binding authority   Any source of law that a court must follow when deciding a case. Binding authorities include constitutions, statutes, and regulations that govern the issue being decided, as well as court decisions that are controlling precedents within the jurisdiction.

Blue sky laws   State laws that regulate the offer and sale of securities.

Bona fide   Good faith. A bona fide obligation is one made in good faith—that is, sincerely and honestly.

Bona fide occupational qualification (BFOQ) Identifiable characteristics reasonably necessary to the normal operation of a particular business. These characteristics can include gender, national origin, and religion, but not race.

Bond   A certificate that evidences a corporate (or government) debt. It is a security that involves no ownership interest in the issuing entity.

Botnet   Short for *robot network*—a group of computers that run an application that is controlled and manipulated only by the software source. Although sometimes a legitimate network, usually this term is reserved for a group of computers that have been infected by malicious robot software. In a botnet, each connected computer becomes a zombie, or drone.

Boycott   A concerted refusal to do business with a particular person or entity in order to obtain concessions or to express displeasure with certain acts or practices of that person or business. *See also* Secondary boycott

Breach   To violate a law, by an act or an omission, or to break a legal obligation that one owes to another person or to society.

Breach of contract   The failure, without legal excuse, of a promisor to perform the obligations of a contract.

Bribery   The offering, giving, receiving, or soliciting of anything of value with the aim of influencing an official action or an official's discharge of a legal or public duty or (with respect to commercial bribery) a business decision.

Bridge loan   A short-term loan that allows a buyer to make a down payment on a new home before selling her or his current home (the current home is used as collateral).

Brief   A formal legal document submitted by the attorney for the appellant—or the appellee (in answer to the appellant's brief)—to an appellate court when a case is appealed. The appellant's brief outlines the facts and issues of the case, the judge's rulings or jury's findings that should be reversed or modified, the applicable law, and the arguments on the client's behalf.

Browse-wrap terms   Terms and conditions of use that are presented to an Internet user at the time certain products, such as software, are being downloaded but that need not be agreed to (by clicking "I agree," for example) before being able to install or use the product.

Bureaucracy   A large organization that is structured hierarchically to carry out specific functions.

Burglary   The unlawful entry into a building with the intent to commit a felony. (Some state statutes expand this to include the intent to commit any crime.)

Business ethics   Ethics in a business context; a consensus of what constitutes right or wrong behavior in the world of business and the application of moral principles to situations that arise in a business setting.

Business invitees   Those people, such as customers or clients, who are invited onto business premises by the owner of those premises for business purposes.

Business judgment rule   A rule that immunizes corporate management from liability for actions that result in corporate losses or damages if the actions are undertaken in good faith and are within both the power of the corporation and the authority of management to make.

Business necessity   A defense to allegations of employment discrimination in which the employer demonstrates that an employment practice that discriminates against members of a protected class is related to job performance.

Business plan   A document describing a company, its products, and its anticipated future performance. Creating a business plan is normally the first step in obtaining loans or venture-capital funds for a new business enterprise.

Business tort   Wrongful interference with the business rights of another.

Business trust   A voluntary form of business organization in which investors (trust beneficiaries) transfer cash or property to trustees in exchange for trust certificates that represent their investment shares. Management of the business and trust property is handled by the trustees for the use and benefit of the investors. The certificate holders have limited liability (are not responsible for the debts and obligations incurred by the trust) and share in the trust's profits.

Buyout price   The amount payable to a partner on his or her dissociation from a partnership, based on the amount distributable to that partner if the firm were wound up on that date, and offset by any damages for wrongful dissociation.

Buy-sell agreement   In the context of partnerships, an express agreement made at the time of partnership formation for one or more of the partners to buy out the other or others should the situation warrant—and thus provide for the smooth dissolution of the partnership.

Bylaws A set of governing rules adopted by a corporation or other association.

Bystander A spectator, witness, or person who was standing nearby when an event occurred and who did not engage in the business or act leading to the event.

C

C.I.F. or C.&F. Cost, insurance, and freight—or just cost and freight. A pricing term in a contract for the sale of goods requiring, among other things, that the seller place the goods in the possession of a carrier before risk passes to the buyer.

C.O.D. Cash on delivery. In sales transactions, a term meaning that the buyer will pay for the goods on delivery and before inspecting the goods.

Cancellation The act of nullifying, or making void. *See also* Rescission

Capital Accumulated goods, possessions, and assets used for the production of profits and wealth; the equity of owners in a business.

Carrier An individual or organization engaged in transporting passengers or goods for hire. *See also* Common carrier

Case law The rules of law announced in court decisions. Case law includes the aggregate of reported cases that interpret judicial precedents, statutes, regulations, and constitutional provisions.

Case on point A previous case involving factual circumstances and issues that are similar to those in the case before the court.

Categorical imperative A concept developed by the philosopher Immanuel Kant as an ethical guideline for behavior. In deciding whether an action is right or wrong, or desirable or undesirable, a person should evaluate the action in terms of what would happen if everybody else in the same situation, or category, acted the same way.

Causation in fact An act or omission without ("but for") which an event would not have occurred.

Cause of action A situation or set of facts sufficient to justify a right to sue.

Cease-and-desist order An administrative or judicial order prohibiting a person or business firm from conducting activities that an agency or court has deemed illegal.

Certificate of deposit (CD) A note of a bank in which a bank acknowledges a receipt of money from a party and promises to repay the money, with interest, to the party on a certain date.

Certificate of limited partnership The basic document filed with a designated state official by which a limited partnership is formed.

Certification mark A mark used by one or more persons, other than the owner, to certify the region, materials, mode of manufacture, quality, or accuracy of the owner's goods or services. When used by members of a cooperative, association, or other organization, such a mark is referred to as a collective mark. Examples of certification marks include the "Good Housekeeping Seal of Approval" and "UL Tested."

Certiorari *See* Writ of *certiorari*

Chain-style business franchise A franchise that operates under a franchisor's trade name and that is identified as a member of a select group of dealers that engage in the franchisor's business. The franchisee is generally required to follow standardized or prescribed methods of operation. Examples of this type of franchise are McDonald's and most other fast-food chains.

Chancellor An adviser to the king at the time of the early king's courts of England. Individuals petitioned the king for relief when they could not obtain an adequate remedy in a court of law, and these petitions were decided by the chancellor.

Charging order In partnership law, an order granted by a court to a judgment creditor that entitles the creditor to attach profits or assets of a partner on dissolution of the partnership.

Chattel All forms of personal property.

Checks and balances The national government is composed of three separate branches: the executive, the legislative, and the judicial branches. Each branch of the government exercises a check on the actions of the others.

Choice-of-language clause A clause in a contract designating the official language by which the contract will be interpreted in the event of a future disagreement over the contract's terms.

Choice-of-law clause A clause in a contract designating the law (such as the law of a particular state or nation) that will govern the contract.

Citation A reference to a publication in which a legal authority—such as a statute or a court decision—or other source can be found.

Civil law The branch of law dealing with the definition and enforcement of all private or public rights, as opposed to criminal matters.

Civil law system A system of law derived from that of the Roman Empire and based on a code rather than case law; the predominant system of law in the nations of continental Europe and the nations that were once their colonies. In the United States, Louisiana is the only state that has a civil law system.

Claim As a verb, to assert or demand. As a noun, a right to payment.

Click-on agreement An agreement that arises when a buyer, engaging in a transaction on a computer, indicates his or her assent to be bound by the terms of an offer by clicking on a button that says, for example, "I agree"; sometimes referred to as a click-on license or a click-wrap agreement.

Closed shop A firm that requires union membership by its workers as a condition of employment. The closed shop was made illegal by the Labor-Management Relations Act of 1947.

Closely held corporation A corporation whose shareholders are limited to a small group of persons, often including only family members. The rights of shareholders of a closely held corporation usually are restricted regarding the transfer of shares to others.

Closing The final step in the sale of real estate—also called settlement or closing escrow. The escrow agent coordinates the closing with the recording of deeds, the obtaining of title insurance, and other concurrent closing activities. A number of costs must be paid, in cash, at the time of closing, and they can range from several hundred to several thousand dollars, depending on the amount of the mortgage loan and other conditions of the sale.

Closing argument An argument made after the plaintiff and defendant have rested their cases. Closing arguments are made prior to the jury charges.

Cloud computing The delivery to users of on-demand services from third-party servers over a network. Cloud computing is a delivery model. The most widely used cloud computing services are Software as a Service (SaaS), which offers companies a cheaper way to buy and use packaged applications that are no longer run on servers in house.

Codicil A written supplement or modification to a will. A codicil must be executed with the same formalities as a will.

Collateral Under Article 9 of the Uniform Commercial Code, the property subject to a security interest.

Collateral promise A secondary promise that is ancillary (subsidiary) to a principal transaction or primary contractual relationship, such as a promise made by one person to pay the debts of another if the latter fails to perform. A collateral promise normally must be in writing to be enforceable.

Collective bargaining The process by which labor and management negotiate the terms and conditions of employment, including working hours and workplace conditions.

Collective mark A mark used by members of a cooperative, association, or other organization to certify the region, materials, mode of manufacture, quality, or accuracy of the specific goods or services. Examples of collective marks include the labor union marks found on tags of certain products and the credits of movies, which indicate the various associations and organizations that participated in the making of the movies.

Comity A deference by which one nation gives effect to the laws and judicial decrees of another nation. This recognition is based primarily on respect.

Comment period A period of time following an administrative agency's publication or a notice of a proposed rule during which private parties may comment in writing on the agency proposal in an effort to influence agency policy. The agency takes any comments received into consideration when drafting the final version of the regulation.

Commerce clause The provision in Article I, Section 8, of the U.S. Constitution that gives Congress the power to regulate interstate commerce.

Commercial impracticability A doctrine under which a seller may be excused from performing a contract when (1) a contingency occurs, (2) the contingen-cy's occurrence makes performance impracticable, and (3) the nonoccurrence of the contingency was a basic assumption on which the contract was made. Despite the fact that UCC 2–615 expressly frees only sellers under this doctrine, courts have not distinguished between buyers and sellers in applying it.

Commercial use Use of land for business activities only; sometimes called business use.

Commingle To put funds or goods together into one mass so that the funds or goods are so mixed that they no longer have separate identities. In corporate law, if personal and corporate interests are commingled to the extent that the corporation has no separate identity, a court may "pierce the corporate veil" and expose the shareholders to personal liability.

Common carrier A carrier that transfers people or goods for hire to the general public.

Common law That body of law developed from custom or judicial decisions in English and U.S. courts, not attributable to a legislature.

Community property A form of concurrent ownership of property in which each spouse technically owns an undivided one-half interest in property acquired during the marriage. This form of joint ownership occurs in only a minority of states and Puerto Rico.

Comparative negligence A theory in tort law under which the liability for injuries resulting from negligent acts is shared by all parties who were negligent (including the injured party), on the basis of each person's proportionate negligence.

Compensatory damages A money award equivalent to the actual value of injuries or damages sustained by the aggrieved party.

Complaint The pleading made by a plaintiff alleging wrongdoing on the part of the defendant; the document that, when filed with a court, initiates a lawsuit.

Complete performance Performance of a contract strictly in accordance with the contract's terms.

Composition agreement *See* Creditors' composition agreement

Computer crime Any wrongful act that is directed against computers and computer parties, or wrongful use or abuse of computers or software.

Concentrated industry An industry in which a large percentage of market sales is controlled by either a single firm or a small number of firms.

Concurrent conditions Conditions in a contract that must occur or be performed at the same time; they are mutually dependent. No obligations arise until these conditions are simultaneously performed.

Concurrent jurisdiction Jurisdiction that exists when two different courts have the power to hear a case. For example, some cases can be heard in either a federal or a state court.

Concurrent ownership Joint ownership.

Concurring opinion A written opinion outlining the views of a judge or justice to make or emphasize a point that was not made or emphasized in the majority opinion.

Condemnation The process of taking private property for public use through the government's power of eminent domain.

Condition A possible future event, the occurrence or nonoccurrence of which will trigger the performance of a legal obligation or terminate an existing obligation under a contract.

Condition precedent A condition in a contract that must be met before a party's promise becomes absolute.

Confession of judgment The act of a debtor in permitting a judgment to be entered against him or her by a creditor, for an agreed sum, without the institution of legal proceedings.

Confiscation A government's taking of privately owned business or personal property without a proper public purpose or an award of just compensation.

Conforming goods Goods that conform to contract specifications.

Confusion The mixing together of goods belonging to two or more owners so that the separately owned goods cannot be identified.

Conglomerate merger A merger between firms that do not compete with each other because they are in different markets (as opposed to horizontal and vertical mergers).

Consent Voluntary agreement to a proposition or an act of another. A concurrence of wills.

Consequential damages Special damages that compensate for a loss that is not direct or immediate (for example, lost profits). The special damages must have been reasonably foreseeable at the time the breach or injury occurred in order for the plaintiff to collect them.

Consideration Generally, the value given in return for a promise or a performance. The consideration, which must be present to make the contract legally binding, must be something of legally sufficient value and bargained for.

Consignment A transaction in which an owner of goods (the consignor) delivers the goods to another (the consignee) for the consignee to sell. The consignee pays the consignor for the goods when they are sold by the consignee.

Consolidation A contractual and statutory process in which two or more corporations join to become a completely new corporation. The original corporations cease to exist, and the new corporation acquires all their assets and liabilities.

Constitutional law Law that is based on the U.S. Constitution and the constitutions of the various states.

Construction loan A loan obtained by the borrower to finance the building of a new home. Construction loans are often set up to release funds at particular stages of the project.

Constructive condition A condition in a contract that is neither expressed nor implied by the contract but rather is imposed by law for reasons of justice.

Constructive delivery An act equivalent to the actual, physical delivery of property that cannot be physically delivered because of difficulty or impossibility; for example, the transfer of a key to a safe constructively delivers the contents of the safe.

Constructive discharge A termination of employment brought about by making an employee's working conditions so intolerable that the employee reasonably feels compelled to leave.

Consumer credit Credit extended primarily for personal or household use.

Consumer-debtor An individual whose debts are primarily consumer debts (debts for purchases made primarily for personal or household use).

Consumer goods Goods that are primarily for personal or household use.

Consumer law The body of statutes, agency rules, and judicial decisions protecting consumers of goods and services from dangerous manufacturing techniques, mislabeling, unfair credit practices, deceptive advertising, and so on. Consumer laws provide remedies and protections that are not ordinarily available to merchants or to businesses.

Contract An agreement that can be enforced in court; formed by two or more parties, each of whom agrees to perform or to refrain from performing some act now or in the future.

Contract implied in law *See* Quasi contract

Contractual capacity The threshold mental capacity required by the law for a party who enters into a contract to be bound by that contract.

Contribution *See* Right of contribution

Contributory negligence A theory in tort law under which a complaining party's own negligence contributed to or caused his or her injuries. Contributory negligence is an absolute bar to recovery in a minority of jurisdictions.

Conversion The wrongful taking, using, or retaining possession of personal property that belongs to another.

Conveyance The transfer of a title to land from one person to another by deed; a document (such as a deed) by which an interest in land is transferred from one person to another.

Conviction The outcome of a criminal trial in which the defendant has been found guilty of the crime.

"Cooling-off" laws A set of federal and state laws designed to protect purchasers and leasees of goods or property. For example, the Federal Trade Commission's cooling-off period is three business days for purchases of goods or services from door-to-door salespersons. Cooling off periods vary for loans, mortgages, leases, etc.

Co-ownership Joint ownership.

Copyright The exclusive right of authors to publish, print, or sell an intellectual production for a statutory period of time. A copyright has the same monopolistic nature as a patent or trademark, but it differs in that it applies exclusively to works of art, literature, and other works of authorship, including computer programs.

Corporate governance The relationship between a corporation and its shareholders—specifically, a system that details the distribution of rights and responsibilities of those within the corporation and spells out the rules and procedures for making corporate decisions.

Corporate social responsibility The concept that corporations can and should act ethically and be accountable to society for their actions.

Corporation A legal entity formed in compliance with statutory requirements. The entity is distinct from its shareholders-owners.

Cosign The act of signing a document (such as a note promising to pay another in return for a loan or other benefit) jointly with another person and thereby assuming liability for performing what was promised in the document.

Cost-benefit analysis A decision-making technique that involves weighing the costs of a given action against the benefits of the action.

Co-surety A joint surety. One who assumes liability jointly with another surety for the payment of an obligation.

Counteradvertising New advertising that is undertaken pursuant to a Federal Trade Commission order for the purpose of correcting earlier false claims that were made about a product.

Counterclaim A claim made by a defendant in a civil lawsuit that in effect sues the plaintiff.

Counteroffer An offeree's response to an offer in which the offeree rejects the original offer and at the same time makes a new offer.

Course of dealing Prior conduct between parties to a contract that establishes a common basis for their understanding.

Course of performance The conduct that occurs under the terms of a particular agreement; such conduct indicates what the parties to an agreement intended it to mean.

Court of equity A court that decides controversies and administers justice according to the rules, principles, and precedents of equity.

Court of law A court in which the only remedies that could be granted were things of value, such as money damages. In the early English king's courts, courts of law were distinct from courts of equity.

Covenant not to compete A contractual promise to refrain from competing with another party for a certain period of time and within a certain geographic area. Although covenants not to compete restrain trade, they are commonly found in partnership agreements, business sale agreements, and employment contracts. If they are ancillary to such agreements, covenants not to compete will normally be enforced by the courts unless the time period or geographic area is deemed unreasonable.

Covenant of quiet enjoyment A promise by a grantor (or landlord) that the grantee (or tenant) will not be evicted or disturbed by the grantor or a person having a lien or superior title.

Covenant running with the land An executory promise made between a grantor and a grantee to which they and subsequent owners of the land are bound.

Cover A buyer or lessee's purchase on the open market of goods to substitute for those promised but never delivered by the seller. Under the Uniform Commercial Code, if the cost of cover exceeds the cost of the contract goods, the buyer or lessee can recover the difference, plus incidental and consequential damages.

Cram-down provision A provision of the Bankruptcy Code that allows a court to confirm a debtor's Chapter 11 reorganization plan even though only one class of creditors has accepted it. To exercise the court's right under this provision, the court must demonstrate that the plan does not discriminate unfairly against any creditors and is fair and equitable.

Creditor A person to whom a debt is owed by another person (the debtor).

Creditors' composition agreement An agreement formed between a debtor and his or her creditors in which the creditors agree to accept a lesser sum than that owed by the debtor in full satisfaction of the debt.

Crime A wrong against society proclaimed in a statute and punishable by society through fines and/or imprisonment—or, in some cases, death.

Criminal act *See Actus reus*

Criminal intent *See Mens rea*

Criminal law Law that defines and governs actions that constitute crimes. Generally, criminal law has to do with wrongful actions committed against society for which society demands redress.

Cross-border pollution Pollution across national boundaries; air and water degradation in one nation resulting from pollution-causing activities in a neighboring country.

Cross-examination The questioning of an opposing witness during a trial.

Cumulative voting A method of shareholder voting designed to allow minority shareholders to be represented on the board of directors. With cumulative voting, the number of members of the board to be elected is multiplied by the total number of voting shares held. The result equals the number of votes a shareholder has, and this total can be cast for one or more nominees for director.

Cure Under the Uniform Commercial Code, the right of a party who tenders nonconforming performance to correct his or her performance within the contract period.

Cyber crime A crime that occurs online, in the virtual community of the Internet, as opposed to the physical world.

Cyber fraud Fraud that involves the online theft of credit card information, banking details, and other information for criminal use.

Cyber mark A trademark in cyberspace.

Cyber tort A tort committed via the Internet.

Cyberlaw An informal term used to refer to all laws governing electronic communications and transactions, particularly those conducted via the Internet.

Cybernotary A legally recognized authority that can certify the validity of digital signatures.

Cybersquatting The act of registering a domain name that is the same as, or confusingly similar to, the trademark of another and then offering to sell that domain name back to the trademark owner.

D

Cyberterrorist A hacker whose purpose is to exploit a target computer for a serious impact, such as the corruption of a program to sabotage a business.

Damages Money sought as a remedy for a breach of contract or for a tortious act.

Debtor Under Article 9 of the Uniform Commercial Code, any party who owes payment or performance of a secured obligation.

Debtor in possession (DIP) In Chapter 11 bankruptcy proceedings, a debtor who is allowed to continue in possession of the estate in property (the business) and to continue business operations.

Deceptive advertising Advertising that misleads consumers, either by making unjustified claims concerning a product's performance or by omitting a material fact concerning the product's composition or performance.

Declaratory judgment A court's judgment on a justiciable controversy when the plaintiff is in doubt as to his or her legal rights; a binding adjudication of the rights and status of litigants even though no consequential relief is awarded.

Decree The judgment of a court of equity.

Deed A document by which title to property (usually real property) is passed.

Deed in lieu of foreclosure An alternative to foreclosure in which the mortgagor, rather than fighting to retain possession, voluntarily conveys the property to the lender in satisfaction of the mortgage.

Defalcation The misuse of funds.

Defamation Any published or publicly spoken false statement that causes injury to another's good name, reputation, or character.

Default judgment A judgment entered by a court against a defendant who has failed to appear in court to answer or defend against the plaintiff's claim.

Defendant One against whom a lawsuit is brought; the accused person in a criminal proceeding.

Defense Reasons that a defendant offers in an action or suit as to why the plaintiff should not obtain what he or she is seeking.

Deficiency judgment A judgment against a debtor for the amount of a debt remaining unpaid after collateral has been repossessed and sold.

Delegatee One to whom contract duties are delegated by another, called the delegator.

Delegation The transfer of a contractual duty to a third party. The party delegating the duty (the delegator) to the third party (the delegatee) is still obliged to perform on the contract should the delegatee fail to perform.

Delegation doctrine A doctrine based on Article I, Section 8, of the U.S. Constitution, which has been construed to allow Congress to delegate some of its power to make and implement laws to administrative agencies. The delegation is considered to be proper as long as Congress sets standards outlining the scope of the agency's authority.

Delegator One who delegates his or her duties under a contract to another, called the delegatee.

Delivery In contract law, one party's act of placing the subject matter of the contract within the other party's possession or control.

De novo Anew; afresh; a second time. In a hearing *de novo*, an appellate court hears the case as a court of original jurisdiction—that is, as if the case had not previously been tried and a decision rendered.

Deposition The testimony of a party to a lawsuit or a witness taken under oath before a trial.

Destination contract A contract in which the seller is required to ship the goods by carrier and deliver them at a particular destination. The seller assumes liability for any losses or damage to the goods until they are tendered at the destination specified in the contract.

Dilution With respect to trademarks, a doctrine under which distinctive or famous trademarks are protected from certain unauthorized uses of the marks regardless of a showing of competition or a likelihood of confusion. Congress created a federal cause of action for dilution in 1995 with the passage of the Federal Trademark Dilution Act.

Direct examination The examination of a witness by the attorney who calls the witness to the stand to testify on behalf of the attorney's client.

Directed verdict *See* Motion for a directed verdict

Disaffirmance The legal avoidance, or setting aside, of a contractual obligation.

Discharge The termination of an obligation. (1) In contract law, discharge occurs when the parties have fully performed their contractual obligations or when events, conduct of the parties, or operation of the law releases the parties from performance. (2) In bankruptcy proceedings, the extinction of the debtor's dischargeable debts.

Discharge in bankruptcy The release of a debtor from all debts that are provable, except those specifically excepted from discharge by statute.

Disclosed principal A principal whose identity is known to a third party at the time the agent makes a contract with the third party.

Discovery A phase in the litigation process during which the opposing parties may obtain information from each other and from third parties prior to trial.

Dishonor To refuse to accept or pay a draft or a promissory note when it is properly presented. An instrument is dishonored when presentment is properly made and acceptance or payment is refused or cannot be obtained within the prescribed time.

Disparagement of property An economically injurious false statement made about another's product or property. A general term for torts that are more specifically referred to as slander of quality or slander of title.

Disparate-impact discrimination A form of employment discrimination that results from certain employer practices or procedures that, although not discriminatory on their face, have a discriminatory effect.

Disparate-treatment discrimination A form of employment discrimination that results when an employer intentionally discriminates against employees who are members of protected classes.

Dissenting opinion   A written opinion by a judge or justice who disagrees with the majority opinion.

Dissociation   The severance of the relationship between a partner and a partnership when the partner ceases to be associated with the carrying on of the partnership business.

Dissolution   The formal disbanding of a partnership or a corporation. It can take place by (1) acts of the partners or, in a corporation, of the shareholders and board of directors; (2) the death of a partner; (3) the expiration of a time period stated in a partnership agreement or a certificate of incorporation; or (4) judicial decree.

Distributed network   A network that can be used by persons located (distributed) around the country or the globe to share computer files.

Distribution agreement   A contract between a seller and a distributor of the seller's products setting out the terms and conditions of the distributorship.

Distributorship   A business arrangement that is established when a manufacturer licenses a dealer to sell its product. An example of a distributorship is an automobile dealership.

Diversity of citizenship   Under Article III, Section 2, of the Constitution, a basis for federal court jurisdiction over a lawsuit between (1) citizens of different states, (2) a foreign country and citizens of a state or of different states, or (3) citizens of a state and citizens or subjects of a foreign country. The amount in controversy must be more than $75,000 before a federal court can take jurisdiction in such cases.

Divestiture   The act of selling one or more of a company's parts, such as a subsidiary or plant; often mandated by the courts in merger or monopolization cases.

Dividend   A distribution to corporate shareholders of corporate profits or income, disbursed in proportion to the number of shares held.

Docket   The list of cases entered on a court's calendar and thus scheduled to be heard by the court.

Document of title   Paper exchanged in the regular course of business that evidences the right to possession of goods (for example, a bill of lading or a warehouse receipt).

Domain name   The series of letters and symbols used to identify site operators on the Internet; Internet "addresses."

Domestic corporation   In a given state, a corporation that does business in, and is organized under the laws of, that state.

Domestic relations court   A court that deals with domestic (household) relationships, such as adoption, divorce, support payments, child custody, and the like.

Double jeopardy   A situation occurring when a person is tried twice for the same criminal offense; prohibited by the Fifth Amendment to the Constitution.

Double taxation   A feature (and disadvantage) of the corporate form of business. Because a corporation is a separate legal entity, corporate profits are taxed by state and federal governments. Dividends are again taxable as ordinary income to the shareholders receiving them.

Down payment   The part of the purchase price of real property that is paid in cash up front, reducing the amount of the loan or mortgage.

Draft   Any instrument (such as a check) drawn on a drawee (such as a bank) that orders the drawee to pay a certain sum of money, usually to a third party (the payee), on demand or at a definite future time.

Dram shop act   A state statute that imposes liability on the owners of bars and taverns, as well as those who serve alcoholic drinks to the public, for injuries resulting from accidents caused by intoxicated persons when the sellers or servers of alcoholic drinks contributed to the intoxication.

Due diligence   A required standard of care that certain professionals, such as accountants, must meet to avoid liability for securities violations. Under securities law, an accountant will be deemed to have exercised due diligence if he or she followed generally accepted accounting principles and generally accepted auditing standards and had, "after reasonable investigation, reasonable grounds to believe and did believe, at the time such part of the registration statement became effective, that the statements therein were true and that there was no omission of a material fact required to be stated therein or necessary to make the statements therein not misleading."

Due process clause   The provisions of the Fifth and Fourteenth Amendments to the Constitution that guarantee that no person shall be deprived of life, liberty, or property without due process of law. Similar clauses are found in most state constitutions.

Dumping   The selling of goods in a foreign country at a price below the price charged for the same goods in the domestic market.

Duress   Unlawful pressure brought to bear on a person, causing the person to perform an act that he or she would not otherwise perform.

Duty of care   The duty of all persons, as established by tort law, to exercise a reasonable amount of care in their dealings with others. Failure to exercise due care, which is normally determined by the "reasonable person standard," constitutes the tort of negligence.

E

E-agent   A computer program, electronic, or other automated means used to perform specific tasks without review by an individual.

E-commerce   Business transacted in cyberspace.

E-contract   A contract that is entered into in cyberspace and is evidenced only by electronic impulses (such as those that make up a computer's memory), rather than, for example, a typewritten form.

E-evidence   A type of evidence that consists of computer-generated or electronically recorded information, including e-mail, voice mail, spreadsheets, word-processing documents, and other data.

E-signature As defined by the Uniform Electronic Transactions Act, "an electronic sound, symbol, or process attached to or logically associated with a record and executed or adopted by a person with the intent to sign the record."

Early neutral case evaluation A form of alternative dispute resolution in which a neutral third party evaluates the strengths and weakness of the disputing parties' positions; the evaluator's opinion forms the basis for negotiating a settlement.

Easement A nonpossessory right to use another's property in a manner established by either express or implied agreement.

Emancipation In regard to minors, the act of being freed from parental control; occurs when a child's parent or legal guardian relinquishes the legal right to exercise control over the child. Normally, a minor who leaves home to support himself or herself is considered emancipated.

Embezzlement The fraudulent appropriation of money or other property by a person to whom the money or property has been entrusted.

Eminent domain The power of a government to take land for public use from private citizens for just compensation.

Employee A person who works for an employer for a salary or for wages.

Employer An individual or business entity that hires employees, pays them salaries or wages, and exercises control over their work.

Employment at will A common law doctrine under which either party may terminate an employment relationship at any time for any reason, unless a contract specifies otherwise.

Employment discrimination Treating employees or job applicants unequally on the basis of race, color, national origin, religion, gender, age, or disability; prohibited by federal statutes.

Enabling legislation A statute enacted by Congress that authorizes the creation of an administrative agency and specifies the name, composition, purpose, and powers of the agency being created.

Encryption The process by which a message (plaintext) is transformed into something (ciphertext) that the sender and receiver intend third parties not to understand.

Entrapment In criminal law, a defense in which the defendant claims that he or she was induced by a public official—usually an undercover agent or police officer—to commit a crime that he or she would otherwise not have committed.

Entrepreneur One who initiates and assumes the financial risks of a new enterprise and who undertakes to provide or control its management.

Entrustment The transfer of goods to a merchant who deals in goods of that kind and who may transfer those goods and all rights to them to a buyer in the ordinary course of business [UCC 2–403(2)].

Environmental impact statement (EIS) A statement required by the National Environmental Policy Act for any major federal action that will significantly affect the quality of the environment. The statement must analyze the action's impact on the environment and explore alternative actions that might be taken.

Environmental law The body of statutory, regulatory, and common law relating to the protection of the environment.

Equal dignity rule In most states, a rule stating that express authority given to an agent must be in writing if the contract to be made on behalf of the principal is required to be in writing.

Equal protection clause The provision in the Fourteenth Amendment to the Constitution that guarantees that no state will "deny to any person within its jurisdiction the equal protection of the laws." This clause mandates that state governments treat similarly situated individuals in a similar manner.

Equitable maxims General propositions or principles of law that have to do with fairness (equity).

Equitable right of redemption The right of a mortgagor who has breached the mortgage agreement to redeem or purchase the property prior to foreclosure proceedings.

Equity of redemption The right of a mortgagor who has breached the mortgage agreement to redeem or purchase the property prior to foreclosure proceedings.

Equity participation loan A loan that allows the lender to participate in some percentage of the increase in the equity value of a business or property; any loan that gives the lender the right to obtain an ownership interest in the project being financed.

Escrow account An account that is generally held in the name of the depositor and escrow agent; the funds in the account are paid to a third person only on fulfillment of the escrow condition.

Establishment clause The provision in the First Amendment to the U.S. Constitution that prohibits Congress from creating any law "respecting an establishment of religion."

Estop To bar, impede, or preclude.

Estoppel The principle that a party's own acts prevent him or her from claiming a right to the detriment of another who was entitled to and did rely on those acts. *See also* Agency by estoppel; Promissory estoppel

Ethical reasoning A reasoning process in which an individual links his or her moral convictions or ethical standards to the particular situation at hand.

Ethics Moral principles and values applied to social behavior.

Eviction A landlord's act of depriving a tenant of possession of the leased premises.

Evidence Proof offered at trial—in the form of testimony, documents, records, exhibits, objects, and so on—for the purpose of convincing the court or jury of the truth of a contention.

Exclusionary rule In criminal procedure, a rule under which any evidence that is obtained in violation of the accused's constitutional rights guaranteed by the Fourth, Fifth, and Sixth Amendments, as well as any evidence derived from illegally obtained evidence, will not be admissible in court.

Exclusive distributorship A distributorship in which the seller and the distributor of the seller's products agree that the distributor has the exclusive right to distribute the seller's products in a certain geographic area.

Exclusive jurisdiction Jurisdiction that exists when a case can be heard only in a particular court or type of court, such as a federal court or a state court.

Exclusive-dealing contract An agreement under which a seller forbids a buyer to purchase products from the seller's competitors.

Exculpatory clause A clause that releases a contractual party from liability in the event of monetary or physical injury, no matter who is at fault.

Executed contract A contract that has been completely performed by both parties.

Execution An action to carry into effect the directions in a court decree or judgment.

Executive agency An administrative agency within the executive branch of government. At the federal level, executive agencies are those within the cabinet departments.

Executory contract A contract that has not as yet been fully performed.

Export To sell products to buyers located in other countries.

Express authority Authority expressly given by one party to another. In agency law, an agent has express authority to act for a principal if both parties agree, orally or in writing, that an agency relationship exists in which the agent had the power (authority) to act in the place of, and on behalf of, the principal.

Express contract A contract in which the terms of the agreement are fully and explicitly stated in words, oral or written.

Express warranty A seller's or lessor's oral or written promise, ancillary to an underlying sales or lease agreement, as to the quality, description, or performance of the goods being sold or leased.

Expropriation The seizure by a government of privately owned business or personal property for a proper public purpose and with just compensation.

Extension clause A clause in a time instrument that allows the instrument's date of maturity to be extended into the future.

F

F.A.S. Free alongside. A contract term that requires the seller, at his or her own expense and risk, to deliver the goods alongside the ship before risk passes to the buyer.

F.O.B. Free on board. A contract term that indicates that the selling price of the goods includes transportation costs (and that the seller carries the risk of loss) to the specific F.O.B. place named in the contract. The place can be either the place of initial shipment (for example, the seller's city or place of business) or the

place of destination (for example, the buyer's city or place of business).

Family limited liability partnership (FLLP) A limited liability partnership (LLP) in which the majority of the partners are persons related to each other, essentially as spouses, parents, grandparents, siblings, cousins, nephews, or nieces. A person acting in a fiduciary capacity for persons so related could also be a partner. All of the partners must be natural persons or persons acting in a fiduciary capacity for the benefit of natural persons.

Federal form of government A system of government in which the states form a union and the sovereign power is divided between a central government and the member states.

Federal question A question that pertains to the U.S. Constitution, acts of Congress, or treaties. A federal question provides a basis for federal jurisdiction.

Federal Rules of Civil Procedure (FRCP) The rules controlling procedural matters in civil trials brought before the federal district courts.

Fee simple An absolute form of property ownership entitling the property owner to use, possess, or dispose of the property as he or she chooses during his or her lifetime. On death, the interest in the property passes to the owner's heirs; a fee simple absolute.

Fee simple absolute An ownership interest in land in which the owner has the greatest possible aggregation of rights, privileges, and power. Ownership in fee simple absolute is limited absolutely to a person and his or her heirs.

Felony A crime—such as arson, murder, rape, or robbery—that carries the most severe sanctions, usually ranging from one year in a state or federal prison to the forfeiture of one's life.

Fiduciary As a noun, a person having a duty created by his or her undertaking to act primarily for another's benefit in matters connected with the undertaking. As an adjective, a relationship founded on trust and confidence.

Fiduciary duty The duty, imposed on a fiduciary by virtue of his or her position, to act primarily for another's benefit.

Filtering software A computer program that includes a pattern through which data are passed. When designed to block access to certain Web sites, the pattern blocks the retrieval of a site whose URL or key words are on a list within the program.

Final order The final decision of an administrative agency on an issue. If no appeal is taken, or if the case is not reviewed or considered anew by the agency commission, the administrative law judge's initial order becomes the final order of the agency.

Firm offer An offer (by a merchant) that is irrevocable without consideration for a period of time (not longer than three months). A firm offer by a merchant must be in writing and must be signed by the offeror.

Fitness for a particular purpose *See* Implied warranty of fitness for a particular purpose

Fixed-rate mortgage A standard mortgage with a fixed, or unchanging, rate of interest. The loan payments on these mortgages remain the same for the duration of the loan, which ranges between fifteen and forty years.

Fixed-term tenancy A type of tenancy under which property is leased for a specified period of time, such as a month, a year, or a period of years; also called a *tenancy for years*.

Fixture A thing that was once personal property but that has become attached to real property in such a way that it takes on the characteristics of real property and becomes part of that real property.

Forbearance An agreement between the lender and the borrower in which the lender agrees to temporarily cease requiring mortgage payments, to delay foreclosure, or to accept smaller payments than previously scheduled.

Force majeure clause A provision in a contract stipulating that certain unforeseen events—such as war, political upheavals, acts of God, or other events—will excuse a party from liability for nonperformance of contractual obligations.

Foreclosure A proceeding in which a mortgagee either takes title to or forces the sale of the mortgagor's property in satisfaction of a debt.

Foreign corporation In a given state, a corporation that does business in the state without being incorporated therein.

Foreseeable risk In negligence law, the risk of harm or injury to another that a person of ordinary intelligence and prudence should have reasonably anticipated or foreseen when undertaking an action or refraining from undertaking an action.

Forgery The fraudulent making or altering of any writing in a way that changes the legal rights and liabilities of another.

Formal contract A contract that by law requires a specific form, such as being executed under seal, to be valid.

Forum A jurisdiction, court, or place in which disputes are litigated and legal remedies are sought.

Forum-selection clause A provision in a contract designating the court, jurisdiction, or tribunal that will decide any disputes arising under the contract.

Franchise Any arrangement in which the owner of a trademark, trade name, or copyright licenses another to use that trademark, trade name, or copyright, under specified conditions or limitations, in the selling of goods and services.

Franchise tax A state or local government tax on the right and privilege of carrying on a business in the form of a corporation.

Franchisee One receiving a license to use another's (the franchisor's) trademark, trade name, or copyright in the sale of goods and services.

Franchisor One licensing another (the franchisee) to use his or her trademark, trade name, or copyright in the sale of goods or services.

Fraud Any misrepresentation, either by misstatement or omission of a material fact, knowingly made with the intention of deceiving another and on which a reasonable person would and does rely to his or her detriment.

Fraudulent misrepresentation (fraud) Any misrepresentation, either by misstatement or omission of a material fact, knowingly made with the intention of deceiving another and on which a reasonable person would and does rely to his or her detriment.

Free exercise clause The provision in the First Amendment to the U.S. Constitution that prohibits Congress from making any law "prohibiting the free exercise" of religion.

Free writing prospectus A free writing prospectus is any type of written, electronic, or graphic offer that describes the issuing corporation or its securities and includes a legend indicating that the investor may obtain the prospectus at the SEC's Web site.

Frustration of purpose A court-created doctrine under which a party to a contract will be relieved of his or her duty to perform when the objective purpose for performance no longer exists (due to reasons beyond that party's control).

Full faith and credit clause A clause in Article IV, Section 1, of the U.S. Constitution that provides that "Full Faith and Credit shall be given in each State to the public Acts, Records, and Judicial Proceedings of every other State." The clause ensures that rights established under deeds, wills, contracts, and the like in one state will be honored by the other states and that any judicial decision with respect to such property rights will be honored and enforced in all states.

Full warranty A warranty as to full performance covering generally both labor and materials.

Fungible goods Goods that are alike by physical nature, by agreement, or by trade usage. Examples of fungible goods are wheat, oil, and wine that are identical in type and quality.

G

Garnishment A legal process used by a creditor to collect a debt by seizing property of the debtor (such as wages) that is being held by a third party (such as the debtor's employer).

General jurisdiction Exists when a court's subject-matter jurisdiction is not restricted. A court of general jurisdiction normally can hear any type of case.

General partner In a limited partnership, a partner who assumes responsibility for the management of the partnership and liability for all partnership debts.

General partnership *See* Partnership

Generally accepted accounting principles (GAAP) The conventions, rules, and procedures that define accepted accounting practices at a particular time. The source of the principles is the Financial Accounting Standards Board.

Generally accepted auditing standards (GAAS) Standards concerning an auditor's professional qualities and the judgment exercised by him or her in the performance of an examination and report. The source of the standards is the American Institute of Certified Public Accountants.

Genuineness of assent Knowing and voluntary assent to the terms of a contract. If a contract is formed as a result of a mistake, misrepresentation, undue influence, or duress, genuineness of assent is lacking, and the contract will be voidable.

Good faith Under the Uniform Commercial Code, good faith means honesty in fact; with regard to merchants, good faith means honesty in fact *and* the observance of reasonable commercial standards of fair dealing in the trade.

Good faith purchaser A purchaser who buys without notice of any circumstance that would put a person of ordinary prudence on inquiry as to whether the seller has valid title to the goods being sold.

Good Samaritan statute A state statute that provides that persons who rescue or provide emergency services to others in peril—unless they do so recklessly, thus causing further harm—cannot be sued for negligence.

Goodwill In the business context, the valuable reputation of a business viewed as an intangible asset.

Grand jury A group of citizens called to decide, after hearing the state's evidence, whether a reasonable basis (probable cause) exists for believing that a crime has been committed and whether a trial ought to be held.

Grant deed A deed that simply recites words of consideration and conveyance. Under statute, a grant deed may impliedly warrant that at least the grantor has not conveyed the property's title to someone else.

Grantee One to whom a grant (of land or property, for example) is made.

Grantor A person who makes a grant, such as a transferor of property or the creator of a trust.

Group boycott The refusal to deal with a particular person or firm by a group of competitors; prohibited by the Sherman Act.

Guarantor A person who agrees to satisfy the debt of another (the debtor) only after the principal debtor defaults; a guarantor's liability is thus secondary.

H

Habitability *See* Implied warranty of habitability

Hacker A person who uses one computer to break into another. Professional computer programmers refer to such persons as "crackers."

Hearsay An oral or written statement made out of court that is later offered in court by a witness (not the person who made the statement) to prove the truth of the matter asserted in the statement. Hearsay is generally inadmissible as evidence.

Herfindahl-Hirschman Index (HHI) An index measuring market concentration for purposes of antitrust enforcement; calculated by summing the squares of the percentage market shares held by the respective firms.

Historical school A school of legal thought that emphasizes the evolutionary process of law and that looks to the past to discover what the principles of contemporary law should be.

Holding company A company whose business activity is holding shares in another company.

Home equity loan A loan in which the lender accepts a person's home equity (the portion of the home's value that is paid off) as collateral, which can be seized if the loan is not repaid on time. Borrowers often take out home equity loans to finance the renovation of the property or to pay off debt that carries a higher interest rate, such as credit-card debt.

Homeowners' insurance Insurance that protects a homeowner's property against damage from storms, fire, and other hazards. Lenders may require that a borrower carry homeowners' insurance on mortgaged property.

Homestead exemption A law permitting a debtor to retain the family home, either in its entirety or up to a specified dollar amount, free from the claims of unsecured creditors or trustees in bankruptcy.

Horizontal merger A merger between two firms that are competing in the same market.

Horizontal restraint Any agreement that in some way restrains competition between rival firms competing in the same market.

Hot-cargo agreement An agreement in which employers voluntarily agree with unions not to handle, use, or deal in nonunion-produced goods of other employers; a type of secondary boycott explicitly prohibited by the Labor-Management Reporting and Disclosure Act of 1959.

Hybrid (two-step) mortgage A mortgage that starts as a fixed-rate mortgage and then converts to an adjustable-rate mortgage.

I

I-551 Alien Registration Receipt Proof that a noncitizen has obtained permanent residency in the United States; the so-called green card.

I-9 verification A form from the Department of Homeland Security, U.S. Citizenship and Immigration Services, used for employment eligibility verification; a form that documents that each new employee is authorized to work in the United States

Identification In a sale of goods, the express designation of the specific goods provided for in the contract.

Identity theft The act of stealing another's identifying information—such as a name, date of birth, or Social Security number—and using that information to access the victim's financial resources.

Immunity A status of being exempt, or free, from certain duties or requirements. In criminal law, the state may grant an accused person immunity from prosecution—or agree to prosecute for a lesser offense—if the accused person agrees to give the state information that would assist the state in prosecuting other individuals for crimes. In tort law, freedom from liability for defamatory speech. *See also* Privilege

Implied authority Authority that is created not by an explicit oral or written agreement but by implication. In agency law, implied authority (of the agent) can be conferred by custom, inferred from the position the agent occupies, or implied by virtue of being reasonably necessary to carry out express authority.

Implied contract A contract formed in whole or in part from the conduct of the parties (as opposed to an express contract). Also known as implied-in-fact contract.

Implied warranty A warranty that the law derives by implication or inference from the nature of the transaction or the relative situation or circumstances of the parties.

Implied warranty of fitness for a particular purpose A warranty that goods sold or leased are fit for a particular purpose. The warranty arises when any seller or lessor knows the particular purpose for which a buyer or lessee will use the goods and knows that the buyer or lessee is relying on the skill and judgment of the seller or lessor to select suitable goods.

Implied warranty of habitability An implied promise by a landlord that rented residential premises are fit for human habitation—that is, in a condition that is safe and suitable for people to live in.

Implied warranty of merchantability A warranty that goods being sold or leased are reasonably fit for the ordinary purpose for which they are sold or leased, are properly packaged and labeled, and are of fair quality. The warranty automatically arises in every sale or lease of goods made by a merchant who deals in goods of the kind sold or leased.

Impossibility of performance A doctrine under which a party to a contract is relieved of his or her duty to perform when performance becomes impossible or totally impracticable (through no fault of either party).

Imposter One who, by use of the mail, telephone, or personal appearance, induces a maker or drawer to issue an instrument in the name of an impersonated payee. Indorsements by imposters are not treated as unauthorized under Article 3 of the Uniform Commercial Code.

In personam jurisdiction Court jurisdiction over the "person" involved in a legal action; personal jurisdiction.

In rem jurisdiction Court jurisdiction over a defendant's property.

Incidental beneficiary A third party who incidentally benefits from a contract but whose benefit was not the reason the contract was formed; an incidental beneficiary has no rights in a contract and cannot sue to have the contract enforced.

Indemnify To compensate or reimburse another for losses or expenses incurred.

Independent contractor One who works for, and receives payment from, an employer but whose working conditions and methods are not controlled by the employer. An independent contractor is not an employee but may be an agent.

Independent regulatory agency An administrative agency that is not considered part of the government's executive branch and is not subject to the authority of the president. Independent agency officials cannot be removed without cause.

Indictment (pronounced in-*dyte*-ment) A charge by a grand jury that a reasonable basis (probable cause) exists

for believing that a crime has been committed and that a trial should be held.

Industrial use Land use for light or heavy manufacturing, shipping, or heavy transportation.

Informal contract A contract that does not require a specified form or formality in order to be valid.

Information A formal accusation or complaint (without an indictment) issued in certain types of actions (usually criminal actions involving lesser crimes) by a law officer, such as a magistrate.

Information return A tax return submitted by a partnership that only reports the income earned by the business. The partnership as an entity does not pay taxes on the income received by the partnership. A partner's profit from the partnership (whether distributed or not) is taxed as individual income to the individual partner.

Infringement A violation of another's legally recognized right. The term is commonly used with reference to the invasion by one party of another party's rights in a patent, trademark, or copyright.

Initial order In the context of administrative law, an agency's disposition in a matter other than a rulemaking. An administrative law judge's initial order becomes final unless it is appealed.

Injunction A court decree ordering a person to do or refrain from doing a certain act or activity.

Innkeeper An owner of an inn, hotel, motel, or other lodging.

Innocent misrepresentation A false statement of fact or an act made in good faith that deceives and causes harm or injury to another.

Inside director A person on the board of directors who is also an officer of the corporation.

Insider A corporate director or officer, or other employee or agent, with access to confidential information and a duty not to disclose that information in violation of insider-trading laws.

Insider trading The purchase or sale of securities on the basis of "inside information" (information that has not been made available to the public) in violation of a duty owed to the company whose stock is being traded.

Insolvent Under the Uniform Commercial Code, a term describing a person who ceases to pay "his debts in the ordinary course of business or cannot pay his debts as they become due or is insolvent within the meaning of federal bankruptcy law" [UCC 1–201(23)].

Installment contract Under the Uniform Commercial Code, a contract that requires or authorizes delivery in two or more separate lots to be accepted and paid for separately.

Insurable interest An interest either in a person's life or well-being or in property that is sufficiently substantial that insuring against injury to (or the death of) the person or against damage to the property does not amount to a mere wagering (betting) contract.

Insurance A contract in which, for a stipulated consideration, one party agrees to compensate the other for loss on a specific subject by a specified peril.

Intangible property Property that is incapable of being apprehended by the senses (such as by sight or touch); intellectual property is an example of intangible property.

Integrated contract A written contract that constitutes the final expression of the parties' agreement. If a contract is integrated, evidence extraneous to the contract that contradicts or alters the meaning of the contract in any way is inadmissible.

Intellectual property Property resulting from intellectual, creative processes. Patents, trademarks, and copyrights are examples of intellectual property.

Intended beneficiary A third party for whose benefit a contract is formed; an intended beneficiary can sue the promisor if such a contract is breached.

Intentional tort A wrongful act knowingly committed.

Interest-only (IO) mortgage A mortgage that gives the borrower the option of paying only the interest portion of the monthly payment and forgoing the payment of principal for a specified period of time, such as five years. After the interest-only payment option is exhausted, the borrower's payment will increase to include payments on the principal.

Intermediary bank Any bank to which an item is transferred in the course of collection, except the depositary or payor bank.

International Financial Reporting Standards (IFRS) A set of accounting standards created by the International Accounting Standards Board (IASB). Today, more than 120 nations and reporting jurisdictions either permit or require IFRS for domestically listed companies. The Securities and Exchange Commission is working towards a convergence between the IASB and U.S. accounting standards.

International law The law that governs relations among nations. International customs and treaties are generally considered to be two of the more important sources of international law.

International organization In international law, a term that generally refers to an organization composed mainly of nations and usually established by treaty. The United States is a member of more than one hundred multilateral and bilateral organizations, including at least twenty through the United Nations.

Interpretive rule An administrative agency rule that simply declares a policy or explains the agency's position and does not establish any legal rights or obligations.

Interrogatories A series of written questions for which written answers are prepared and then signed under oath by a party to a lawsuit, usually with the assistance of the party's attorney.

Inverse condemnation The taking of private property by the government without payment of just compensation as required by the U.S. Constitution. The owner must sue the government to recover just compensation.

Investment company A company that acts on behalf of many smaller shareholder-owners by buying a large portfolio of securities and professionally managing that portfolio.

Investment contract In securities law, a transaction in which a person invests in a common enterprise reasonably expecting profits that are derived primarily from the efforts of others.

Invitee A person who, either expressly or impliedly, is privileged to enter onto another's land. The inviter owes the invitee (for example, a customer in a store) the duty to exercise reasonable care to protect the invitee from harm.

Irrevocable offer An offer that cannot be revoked or recalled by the offeror without liability. A merchant's firm offer is an example of an irrevocable offer.

J

Joint and several liability In partnership law, a doctrine under which a plaintiff may sue, and collect a judgment from, one or more of the partners separately (severally, or individually) or all of the partners together (jointly). This is true even if one of the partners sued did not participate in, ratify, or know about whatever gave rise to the cause of action.

Joint liability Shared liability. In partnership law, partners incur joint liability for partnership obligations and debts. For example, if a third party sues a partner on a partnership debt, the partner has the right to insist that the other partners be sued with him or her.

Joint tenancy The joint ownership of property by two or more co-owners in which each co-owner owns an undivided portion of the property. On the death of one of the joint tenants, his or her interest automatically passes to the surviving joint tenants.

Joint venture A joint undertaking of a specific commercial enterprise by an association of persons. A joint venture is normally not a legal entity and is treated like a partnership for federal income tax purposes.

Judgment The final order or decision resulting from a legal action.

Judgment *n.o.v.* *See* Motion for judgment *n.o.v.*

Judgment rate of interest A rate of interest fixed by statute that is applied to a monetary judgment from the moment the judgment is awarded by a court until the judgment is paid or terminated.

Judicial foreclosure A court-supervised foreclosure proceeding in which the court determines the validity of the debt and, if the borrower is in default, issues a judgment for the lender.

Judicial lien A lien on property created by a court order.

Judicial process The procedures relating to, or connected with, the administration of justice through the judicial system.

Judicial review The process by which courts decide on the constitutionality of legislative enactments and actions of the executive branch.

Jurisdiction The authority of a court to hear and decide a specific action.

Jurisprudence The science or philosophy of law.

Justiciable controversy A controversy that is not hypothetical or academic but real and substantial. A requirement that must be satisfied before a court will hear a case.

K

King's court A medieval English court. The king's courts, or *curiae regis,* were established by the Norman conquerors of England. The body of law that developed in these courts was common to the entire English realm and thus became known as the common law.

L

Laches The equitable doctrine that bars a party's right to legal action if the party has neglected for an unreasonable length of time to act on his or her rights.

Landlord An owner of land or rental property who leases it to another person, called the tenant.

Larceny The wrongful taking and carrying away of another person's personal property with the intent to permanently deprive the owner of the property. Some states classify larceny as either grand or petit, depending on the property's value.

Law A body of enforceable rules governing relationships among individuals and between individuals and their society.

Lawsuit The litigation process. *See* Litigation

Lease In real property law, a contract by which the owner of real property (the landlord, or lessor) grants to a person (the tenant, or lessee) an exclusive right to use and possess the property, usually for a specified period of time, in return for rent or some other form of payment.

Lease agreement In regard to the lease of goods, an agreement in which one person (the lessor) agrees to transfer the right to the possession and use of property to another person (the lessee) in exchange for rental payments.

Leasehold estate An estate in realty held by a tenant under a lease. In every leasehold estate, the tenant has a qualified right to possess and/or use the land.

Legal positivists Adherents to the positivist school of legal thought. This school holds that there can be no higher law than a nation's positive law—law created by a particular society at a particular point in time. In contrast to the natural law school, the positivist school maintains that there are no "natural" rights; rights come into existence only when there is a sovereign power (government) to confer and enforce those rights.

Legal rate of interest A rate of interest fixed by statute as either the maximum rate of interest allowed by law or a rate of interest applied when the parties to a contract intend, but do not fix, an interest rate in the contract. In the latter case, the rate is frequently the same as the statutory maximum rate permitted.

Legal realism A school of legal thought that was popular in the 1920s and 1930s and that challenged many existing jurisprudential assumptions, particularly the assumption that subjective elements play no part in judicial reasoning. Legal realists generally advocated a less abstract and more pragmatic approach to the law, an approach that would take into account customary practices and the circumstances in which transactions take place. The school left a lasting imprint on American jurisprudence.

Legal reasoning The process of reasoning by which a judge harmonizes his or her decision with the judicial decisions of previous cases.

Legislative rule An administrative agency rule that affects substantive legal rights and carries the same weight as a congressionally enacted statute.

Letter of credit A written instrument, usually issued by a bank on behalf of a customer or other person, in which the issuer promises to honor drafts or other demands for payment by third persons in accordance with the terms of the instrument.

Levy The obtaining of money by legal process through the seizure and sale of property, usually done after a writ of execution has been issued.

Liability Any actual or potential legal obligation, duty, debt, or responsibility.

Libel Defamation in writing or other form (such as in a videotape) having the quality of permanence.

License A revocable right or privilege of a person to come on another person's land.

Licensee One who receives a license to use, or enter onto, another's property.

Lien (pronounced *leen*) A claim against specific property to satisfy a debt.

Lien creditor One whose claim is secured by a lien on particular property, as distinguished from a general creditor, who has no such security.

Life estate An interest in land that exists only for the duration of the life of some person, usually the holder of the estate.

Limited jurisdiction Exists when a court's subject-matter jurisdiction is limited. Bankruptcy courts and probate courts are examples of courts with limited jurisdiction.

Limited liability Exists when the liability of the owners of a business is limited to the amount of their investments in the firm.

Limited liability company (LLC) A hybrid form of business enterprise that offers the limited liability of the corporation but the tax advantages of a partnership.

Limited liability limited partnership (LLLP) A type of limited partnership. The difference between a limited partnership and an LLLP is that the liability of the general partner in an LLLP is the same as the liability of the limited partner. That is, the liability of all partners is limited to the amount of their investments in the firm.

Limited liability partnership (LLP) A form of partnership that allows professionals to enjoy the tax benefits of a partnership while limiting their personal liability for the malpractice of other partners.

Limited partner In a limited partnership, a partner who contributes capital to the partnership but has no right to participate in the management and operation of the business. The limited partner assumes no liability for partnership debts beyond the capital contributed.

Limited partnership (LP) A partnership consisting of one or more general partners (who manage the business and are liable to the full extent of their personal assets for debts of the partnership) and one or more limited partners (who contribute only assets and are liable only to the extent of their contributions).

Limited warranty A written warranty that fails to meet one or more of the minimum standards for a full warranty.

Liquidated damages An amount, stipulated in the contract, that the parties to a contract believe to be a reasonable estimation of the damages that will occur in the event of a breach.

Liquidated debt A debt that is due and certain in amount.

Liquidation (1) In regard to bankruptcy, the sale of all of the nonexempt assets of a debtor and the distribution of the proceeds to the debtor's creditors. Chapter 7 of the Bankruptcy Code provides for liquidation bankruptcy proceedings. (2) In regard to corporations, the process by which corporate assets are converted into cash and distributed among creditors and shareholders according to specific rules of preference.

Litigant A party to a lawsuit.

Litigation The process of resolving a dispute through the court system.

Long arm statute A state statute that permits a state to obtain personal jurisdiction over nonresident defendants. A defendant must have "minimum contacts" with that state for the statute to apply.

M

Magistrate's court A court of limited jurisdiction that is presided over by a public official (magistrate) with certain judicial authority, such as the power to set bail.

Mailbox rule A rule providing that an acceptance of an offer becomes effective on dispatch (on being placed in a mailbox), if mail is, expressly or impliedly, an authorized means of communication of acceptance to the offeror.

Main purpose rule A rule of contract law under which an exception to the Statute of Frauds is made if the main purpose in accepting secondary liability under a contract is to secure a personal benefit. If this situation exists, the contract need not be in writing to be enforceable.

Majority *See* Age of majority

Majority opinion A court's written opinion, outlining the views of the majority of the judges or justices deciding the case.

Malpractice Professional misconduct or the failure to exercise the requisite degree of skill as a professional. Negligence—the failure to exercise due care—on the part of a professional, such as a physician or an attorney, is commonly referred to as malpractice.

Manufacturing or processing-plant franchise A franchise that is created when the franchisor transmits to the franchisee the essential ingredients or formula to make a particular product. The franchisee then markets the product either at wholesale or at retail in accordance with the franchisor's standards. Examples of this type of franchise are Coca-Cola and other soft-drink bottling companies.

Mark *See* Trademark

Market concentration A situation that exists when a small number of firms share the market for a particular good or service. For example, if the four largest grocery stores in Chicago accounted for 80 percent of all retail food sales, the market clearly would be concentrated in those four firms.

Market power The power of a firm to control the market price of its product. A monopoly has the greatest degree of market power.

Marketable title Title to real estate that is reasonably free from encumbrances, defects in the chain of title, and other matters that affect title, such as adverse possession.

Market-share liability A method of sharing liability among several firms that manufactured or marketed a particular product that may have caused a plaintiff's injury. Each firm's liability is proportionate to its respective share of the relevant market for the product. Market-share liability applies only if the injuring product is fungible, the true manufacturer is unidentifiable, and the unknown character of the manufacturer is not the plaintiff's fault.

Market-share test The primary measure of monopoly power. A firm's market share is the percentage of a market that the firm controls.

Material alteration *See* Alteration

Material fact A fact to which a reasonable person would attach importance in determining his or her course of action.

Mechanic's lien A statutory lien on the real property of another, created to ensure payment for work performed and materials furnished in the repair or improvement of real property, such as a building.

Mediation A method of settling disputes outside of court by using the services of a neutral third party, called a mediator. The mediator acts as a communicating agent between the parties and suggests ways in which the parties can resolve their dispute.

Member The term used to designate a person who has an ownership interest in a limited liability company.

Mens rea (pronounced *mehns ray*-uh) Mental state, or intent. A wrongful mental state is as necessary as a wrongful act to establish criminal liability. What constitutes a mental state varies according to the wrongful action. Thus, for murder, the *mens rea* is the intent to take a life. For theft, the *mens rea* must involve both the knowledge that the property belongs to another and the intent to deprive the owner of it.

Merchant A person who is engaged in the purchase and sale of goods. Under the Uniform Commercial Code, a person who deals in goods of the kind involved in the sales contract; for further definitions, see UCC 2–104.

Merger A contractual and statutory process in which one corporation (the surviving corporation) acquires all of the assets and liabilities of another corporation (the merged corporation). The shareholders of the merged corporation receive either payment for their shares or shares in the surviving corporation.

Meta tags Words inserted into a Web site's keywords field to increase the site's appearance in search engine results.

Minimum-contacts requirement The requirement that before a state court can exercise jurisdiction over a foreign corporation, the foreign corporation must have sufficient contacts with the state. A foreign corporation that has its home office in the state or that has manufacturing plants in the state meets this requirement.

Minimum wage The lowest wage, either by government regulation or union contract, that an employer may pay an hourly worker.

Mini-trial A private proceeding in which each party to a dispute argues its position before the other side and vice versa. A neutral third party may be present and act as an adviser if the parties fail to reach an agreement.

Mirror image rule A common law rule that requires, for a valid contractual agreement, that the terms of the offeree's acceptance adhere exactly to the terms of the offeror's offer.

Misdemeanor A lesser crime than a felony, punishable by a fine or imprisonment for up to one year in other than a state or federal penitentiary.

Misrepresentation A false statement of fact or an action that deceives and causes harm or injury to another. *See also* Fraudulent misrepresentation (fraud); Innocent misrepresentation

Mitigation of damages A rule requiring a plaintiff to have done whatever was reasonable to minimize the damages caused by the defendant.

Money laundering Falsely reporting income that has been obtained through criminal activity as income obtained through a legitimate business enterprise—in effect, "laundering" the "dirty money."

Monopolization The possession of monopoly power in the relevant market and the willful acquisition or maintenance of that power, as distinguished from growth or development as a consequence of a superior product, business acumen, or historic accident.

Monopoly A term generally used to describe a market in which there is a single seller or a limited number of sellers.

Monopoly power The ability of a monopoly to dictate what takes place in a given market.

Moral minimum The minimum degree of ethical behavior expected of a business firm, which is usually defined as compliance with the law.

Mortgage A written instrument that gives a creditor (the mortgagee) an interest in, or lien on, the debtor's (mortgagor's) real property as security for a debt. If the debt is not paid, the property can be sold by the creditor and the proceeds used to pay the debt.

Mortgage assignee An entity that purchases a mortgage from the current mortgage holder and assumes all rights and liabilities of that mortgage, including the right to collect and foreclose.

Mortgage bond A bond that pledges specific property. If the corporation defaults on the bond, the bondholder can take the property.

Motion A procedural request or application presented by an attorney to the court on behalf of a client.

Motion for a directed verdict In a state court, a party's request that the judge enter a judgment in her or his favor before the case is submitted to a jury because the other party has not presented sufficient evidence to support the claim. The federal courts refer to this request as a *motion for judgment as a matter of law.*

Motion for a new trial A motion asserting that the trial was so fundamentally flawed (because of error, newly discovered evidence, prejudice, or other reason) that a new trial is necessary to prevent a miscarriage of justice.

Motion for judgment as a matter of law In a federal court, a party's request that the judge enter a judgment in her or his favor before the case is submitted to a jury because the other party has not presented sufficient evidence to support the claim. The state courts refer to this request as a *motion for a directed verdict.*

Motion for judgment *n.o.v.* A motion requesting the court to grant judgment in favor of the party making the motion on the ground that the jury verdict against him or her was unreasonable and erroneous.

Motion for judgment on the pleadings A motion by either party to a lawsuit at the close of the pleadings requesting the court to decide the issue solely on the pleadings without proceeding to trial. The motion will be granted only if no facts are in dispute.

Motion for summary judgment A motion requesting the court to enter a judgment without proceeding to trial. The motion can be based on evidence outside the pleadings and will be granted only if no facts are in dispute.

Motion to dismiss A pleading in which a defendant asserts that the plaintiff's claim fails to state a cause of action (that is, has no basis in law) or that there are other grounds on which a suit should be dismissed.

Multiple product order An order issued by the Federal Trade Commission to a firm that has engaged in deceptive advertising by which the firm is required to cease and desist from false advertising not only in regard to the product that was the subject of the action but also in regard to all the firm's other products.

Municipal court A city or community court with criminal jurisdiction over traffic violations and, less frequently, with civil jurisdiction over other minor matters.

Mutual assent The element of voluntary consent in the formation of a contract. The manifestation of contract parties' mutual assent to the same bargain is required to establish a contract.

Mutual fund A specific type of investment company that continually buys or sells to investors shares of ownership in a portfolio.

Mutual rescission An agreement between the parties to cancel their contract, releasing the parties from further obligations under the contract. The object of the agreement is to restore the parties to the positions they would have occupied had no contract ever been formed. *See also* Rescission

N

National law Law that pertains to a particular nation (as opposed to international law).

Natural law The belief that government and the legal system should reflect universal moral and ethical principles that are inherent in human nature. The natural law school is the oldest and one of the most significant schools of legal thought.

Necessity In criminal law, a defense against liability; under Section 3.02 of the Model Penal Code, this defense is justifiable if "the harm or evil sought to be avoided" by a given action "is greater than that sought to be prevented by the law defining the offense charged."

Negative amortization Occurs when the payment made by the borrower is less than the interest due on the loan and the difference is added to the principal. The result of negative amortization is that the balance owed on the loan increases rather than decreases over time.

Negligence The failure to exercise the standard of care that a reasonable person would exercise in similar circumstances.

Negligence *per se* An act (or failure to act) in violation of a statutory requirement.

Negligent misrepresentation Any manifestation through words or conduct that amounts to an untrue statement of fact made in circumstances in which a reasonable and prudent person would not have done (or failed to do) that which led to the misrepresentation. A representation made with an honest belief in its truth may still be negligent due to (1) a lack of reasonable care in ascertaining the facts, (2) the manner of expression, or (3) the absence of the skill or competence required by a particular business or profession.

Nominal damages A small monetary award (often one dollar) granted to a plaintiff when no actual damage was suffered or when the plaintiff is unable to show such loss with sufficient certainty.

Nonconforming goods Goods that do not conform to contract specifications.

Normal trade relations (NTR) status A status granted through an international treaty by which each member nation must treat other members at least as well as it treats the country that receives its most favorable treatment. This status was formerly known as most-favored-nation status.

Notary public A public official authorized to attest to the authenticity of signatures.

Notice-and-comment rulemaking An administrative rulemaking procedure that involves the publication of a notice of a proposed rulemaking in the *Federal Register,* a comment period for interested parties to express their views on the proposed rule, and the publication of the agency's final rule in the *Federal Register.*

Notice of default A formal notice to a borrower who is behind in making mortgage payments that the

borrower is in default and may face foreclosure if the payments are not brought up to date. The notice is filed by the lender in the county where the property is located.

Notice of Proposed Rulemaking A notice published (in the *Federal Register*) by an administrative agency describing a proposed rule. The notice must include information on when and where agency proceedings on the proposed rule will be held, a description of the nature of the proceedings, the legal authority for the proceedings (which usually is the agency's enabling legislation), and the terms or the subject matter of the proposed rule.

Notice of sale A formal notice to a borrower who is in default on a mortgage that the mortgaged property will be sold in a foreclosure proceeding. The notice is sent to the borrower by the lender and is also typically recorded with the county, posted on the property, and published in a newspaper.

Novation The substitution, by agreement, of a new contract for an old one, with the rights under the old one being terminated. Typically, there is a substitution of a new person who is responsible for the contract and the removal of an original party's rights and duties under the contract.

Nuisance A common law doctrine under which persons may be held liable for using their property in a manner that unreasonably interferes with others' rights to use or enjoy their own property.

O

Objective theory of contracts A theory under which the intent to form a contract will be judged by outward, objective facts (what the party said when entering into the contract, how the party acted or appeared, and the circumstances surrounding the transaction) as interpreted by a reasonable person, rather than by the party's own secret, subjective intentions.

Offer A promise or commitment to perform or refrain from performing some specified act in the future.

Offeree A person to whom an offer is made.

Offeror A person who makes an offer.

Online Dispute Resolution (ODR) The resolution of disputes with the assistance of organizations that offer dispute-resolution services via the Internet.

Opening statement A statement made to the jury at the beginning of a trial by a party's attorney, prior to the presentation of evidence. The attorney briefly outlines the evidence that will be offered and the legal theory that will be pursued.

Operating agreement In a limited liability company, an agreement in which the members set forth the details of how the business will be managed and operated.

Opinion A statement by the court expressing the reasons for its decision in a case.

Option contract A contract under which the offeror cannot revoke his or her offer for a stipulated time period and the offeree can accept or reject the offer during this period without fear that the offer will be made to another person. The offeree must give consideration for the option (the irrevocable offer) to be enforceable.

Order for relief A court's grant of assistance to a complainant. In bankruptcy proceedings, the order relieves the debtor of the immediate obligation to pay the debts listed in the bankruptcy petition.

Ordinance A law passed by a local governing unit, such as a municipality or a county.

Original jurisdiction Courts having original jurisdiction are courts of the first instance, or trial courts—that is, courts in which lawsuits begin, trials take place, and evidence is presented.

Output contract An agreement in which a seller agrees to sell and a buyer agrees to buy all or up to a stated amount of what the seller produces.

Outside director A person on the board of directors who does not hold a management position at the corporation.

P

Parol evidence A term that originally meant "oral evidence," but that has come to refer to any negotiations or agreements made prior to a contract or any contemporaneous oral agreements made by the parties.

Parol evidence rule A substantive rule of contracts under which a court will not receive into evidence the parties' prior negotiations, prior agreements, or contemporaneous oral agreements if that evidence contradicts the terms of the parties' written contract.

Participation loan A loan that gives the lender some equity rights in the property, such as the right to receive a percentage of revenue, rental income, or resale income. Also called an equity participation loan.

Partner A co-owner of a partnership.

Partnering agreement An agreement between a seller and a buyer who frequently do business with each other on the terms and conditions that will apply to all subsequently formed electronic contracts.

Partnership An agreement by two or more persons to carry on, as co-owners, a business for profit.

Partnership by estoppel A judicially created partnership that may, at the court's discretion, be imposed for purposes of fairness. The court can prevent those who present themselves as partners (but who are not) from escaping liability if a third person relies on an alleged partnership in good faith and is harmed as a result.

Pass-through entity Any entity that does not have its income taxed at the level of that entity; examples are partnerships, S corporations, and limited liability companies.

Past consideration Something given or some act done in the past, which cannot ordinarily be consideration for a later bargain.

Patent A government grant that gives an inventor the exclusive right or privilege to make, use, or sell his or her invention for a limited time period. The word *patent* usually refers to some invention and designates either the instrument by which patent rights are evidenced or the patent itself.

Peer-to-peer (P2P) networking The sharing of resources (such as files, hard drives, and processing styles) among multiple computers without necessarily requiring a central network server.

Penalty A sum inserted into a contract, not as a measure of compensation for its breach but rather as punishment for a default. The agreement as to the amount will not be enforced, and recovery will be limited to actual damages.

Per curiam By the whole court; a court opinion written by the court as a whole instead of being authored by a judge or justice.

Per se A Latin term meaning "in itself" or "by itself."

Per se violation A type of anticompetitive agreement—such as a horizontal price-fixing agreement—that is considered to be so injurious to the public that there is no need to determine whether it actually injures market competition; rather, it is in itself (*per se*) a violation of the Sherman Act.

Perfect tender rule A common law rule under which a seller was required to deliver to the buyer goods that conformed perfectly to the requirements stipulated in the sales contract. A tender of nonconforming goods would automatically constitute a breach of contract. Under the Uniform Commercial Code, the rule has been greatly modified.

Perfection The legal process by which secured parties protect themselves against the claims of third parties who may wish to have their debts satisfied out of the same collateral; usually accomplished by the filing of a financing statement with the appropriate government official.

Performance In contract law, the fulfillment of one's duties arising under a contract with another; the normal way of discharging one's contractual obligations.

Periodic tenancy A lease interest in land for an indefinite period involving payment of rent at fixed intervals, such as week to week, month to month, or year to year.

Personal jurisdiction See In personam jurisdiction

Personal property Property that is movable; any property that is not real property.

Petition in bankruptcy The document that is filed with a bankruptcy court to initiate bankruptcy proceedings. The official forms required for a petition in bankruptcy must be completed accurately, sworn to under oath, and signed by the debtor.

Petitioner In equity practice, a party that initiates a lawsuit.

Petty offense In criminal law, the least serious kind of criminal offense, such as a traffic or building-code violation.

Phishing An online fraud action that allows criminals to pretend to be legitimate companies either by using e-mails or malicious Web sites that trick individuals and companies into providing useful information, such as bank account numbers, Social Security numbers, or credit card numbers.

Pierce the corporate veil To disregard the corporate entity, which limits the liability of shareholders, and hold the shareholders personally liable for a corporate obligation.

Plaintiff One who initiates a lawsuit.

Plea In criminal law, a defendant's allegation, in response to the charges brought against him or her, of guilt or innocence.

Plea bargaining The process by which a criminal defendant and the prosecutor in a criminal case work out a mutually satisfactory disposition of the case, subject to court approval; usually involves the defendant's pleading guilty to a lesser offense in return for a lighter sentence.

Pleadings Statements made by the plaintiff and the defendant in a lawsuit that detail the facts, charges, and defenses involved in the litigation; the complaint and answer are part of the pleadings.

Police powers Powers possessed by states as part of their inherent sovereignty. These powers may be exercised to protect or promote the public order, health, safety, morals, and general welfare.

Policy In insurance law, a contract between the insurer and the insured in which, for a stipulated consideration, the insurer agrees to compensate the insured for loss on a specific subject by a specified peril.

Positive law The body of conventional, or written, law of a particular society at a particular point in time.

Positivist school A school of legal thought whose adherents believe that there can be no higher law than a nation's positive law—the body of conventional, or written, law of a particular society at a particular time.

Possessory lien A lien that allows one person to retain possession of another's property as security for a debt or obligation owed by the owner of the property to the lienholder. An example of a possessory lien is an artisan's lien.

Potentially responsible party (PRP) A potentially liable party under the Comprehensive Environmental Response, Compensation and Liability Act (CERCLA). Any person who generated the hazardous waste, transported the hazardous waste, owned or operated a waste site at the time of disposal, or currently owns or operates a site may be responsible for some or all of the cleanup costs involved in removing the hazardous chemicals.

Power of attorney A written document, which is usually notarized, authorizing another to act as one's agent; can be special (permitting the agent to do specified acts only) or general (permitting the agent to transact all business for the principal).

Power of sale foreclosure A foreclosure procedure that is not court supervised; available only in some states.

Preauthorized transfer A transaction authorized in advance to recur at substantially regular intervals. The terms and procedures for preauthorized electronic fund transfers through certain financial institutions are subject to the Electronic Fund Transfer Act.

Precedent A court decision that furnishes an example or authority for deciding subsequent cases involving identical or similar facts.

Predatory pricing The pricing of a product below cost with the intent to drive competitors out of the market.

Predominant-factor test A test courts use to determine whether a contract is primarily for the sale of goods or for the sale of services.

Preemption A doctrine under which certain federal laws preempt, or take precedence over, conflicting state or local laws.

Preemptive rights Rights held by shareholders that entitle them to purchase newly issued shares of a corporation's stock, equal in percentage to shares presently held, before the stock is offered to any outside buyers. Preemptive rights enable shareholders to maintain their proportionate ownership and voice in the corporation.

Preference In bankruptcy proceedings, property transfers or payments made by the debtor that favor (give preference to) one creditor over others. The bankruptcy trustee is allowed to recover payments made both voluntarily and involuntarily to one creditor in preference over another.

Preferred creditor One who has received a preferential transfer from a debtor.

Prejudgment interest Interest that accrues on the amount of a court judgment from the time of the filing of a lawsuit to the court's issuance of a judgment.

Preliminary hearing An initial hearing used in many felony cases to establish whether it is proper to detain the defendant. A magistrate reviews the evidence and decides if there is probable cause to believe that the defendant committed the crime with which he or she has been charged.

Preponderance of the evidence A standard in civil law cases under which the plaintiff must convince the court that, based on the evidence presented by both parties, it is more likely than not that the plaintiff's allegation is true.

Pretrial conference A conference, scheduled before the trial begins, between the judge and the attorneys litigating the suit. The parties may settle the dispute, clarify the issues, schedule discovery, and so on during the conference.

Pretrial motion A written or oral application to a court for a ruling or order, made before trial.

Price discrimination Setting prices in such a way that two competing buyers pay two different prices for an identical product or service.

Price-fixing agreement An agreement between competitors in which the competitors agree to fix the prices of products or services at a certain level; prohibited by the Sherman Act.

Prima facie case A case in which the plaintiff has produced sufficient evidence of his or her conclusion that the case can go to a jury; a case in which the evidence compels the plaintiff's conclusion if the defendant produces no evidence to disprove it.

Prime offer rate An interest rate that banks historically charged their most reliable customers. Today, it serves as a basis for pricing other commercial and residential loans.

Principal In agency law, a person who agrees to have another, called the agent, act on his or her behalf.

Principle of rights The principle that human beings have certain fundamental rights (to life, freedom, and the pursuit of happiness, for example). Those who adhere to this "rights theory" believe that a key factor in determining whether a business decision is ethical is how that decision affects the rights of others. These others include the firm's owners, its employees, the consumers of its products or services, its suppliers, the community in which it does business, and society as a whole.

Privatization The replacement of government-provided products and services by private firms.

Privilege In tort law, the ability to act contrary to another person's right without that person's having legal redress for such acts. Privilege may be raised as a defense to defamation.

Privileges and immunities clause Special rights and exceptions provided by law. Article IV, Section 2, of the Constitution requires states not to discriminate against one another's citizens. A resident of one state cannot be treated as an alien when in another state; he or she may not be denied such privileges and immunities as legal protection, access to courts, travel rights, and property rights.

Privity of contract The relationship that exists between the promisor and the promisee of a contract.

Pro rata Proportionately; in proportion.

Probable cause Reasonable grounds to believe the existence of facts warranting certain actions, such as the search or arrest of a person.

Probate The process of proving and validating a will and the settling of all matters pertaining to administration, guardianship, and the like.

Probate court A state court of limited jurisdiction that conducts proceedings relating to the settlement of a deceased person's estate.

Procedural due process The requirement that any government decision to take life, liberty, or property must be made fairly. For example, fair procedures must be used in determining whether a person will be subjected to punishment or have some burden imposed on him or her.

Procedural law Rules that define the manner in which the rights and duties of individuals may be enforced.

Procedural unconscionability Occurs when, due to one contractual party's vastly superior bargaining power, the other party lacks knowledge or understanding of the contract terms due to inconspicuous print or the lack of an opportunity to read the contract or to ask questions about its meaning. Procedural unconscionability often involves an *adhesion contract,* which is a contract drafted by the dominant party and then presented to the other—the adhering party—on a take-it-or-leave-it basis.

Product liability The legal liability of manufacturers, sellers, and lessors of goods to consumers, users, and bystanders for injuries or damages that are caused by the goods.

Product misuse A defense against product liability that may be raised when the plaintiff used a product in a manner not intended by the manufacturer. If the misuse is reasonably foreseeable, the seller will not escape liability unless measures were taken to guard against the harm that could result from the misuse.

Professional corporation A corporation formed by professional persons, such as physicians, lawyers, dentists, or accountants, to gain tax benefits. Subject to certain exceptions (when a court may treat a professional corporation as a partnership for liability purposes), the shareholders of a professional corporation have the limited liability characteristic of the corporate form of business.

Profit In real property law, the right to enter onto and remove things from the property of another (for example, the right to enter onto a person's land and remove sand and gravel therefrom).

Promise A person's assurance that he or she will or will not do something.

Promisee A person to whom a promise is made.

Promisor A person who makes a promise.

Promissory estoppel A doctrine that applies when a promisor makes a clear and definite promise on which the promisee justifiably relies; such a promise is binding if justice will be better served by the enforcement of the promise. *See also* Estoppel

Promissory note A written promise made by one person (the maker) to pay a fixed sum of money to another person (the payee or a subsequent holder) on demand or on a specified date.

Promoter A person who takes the preliminary steps in organizing a corporation, including (usually) issuing a prospectus, procuring stock subscriptions, making contract purchases, securing a corporate charter, and the like.

Property Legally protected rights and interests in anything with an ascertainable value that is subject to ownership.

Prospectus A document required by federal or state securities laws that describes the financial operations of the corporation, thus allowing investors to make informed decisions.

Protected class A class of persons with identifiable characteristics who historically have been victimized by discriminatory treatment for certain purposes. Depending on the context, these characteristics include age, color, gender, national origin, race, and religion.

Proximate cause Legal cause; exists when the connection between an act and an injury is strong enough to justify imposing liability.

Proxy In corporation law, a written agreement between a stockholder and another under which the stockholder authorizes the other to vote the stockholder's shares in a certain manner.

Proxy fight A conflict between an individual, group, or firm attempting to take control of a corporation and the corporation's management for the votes of the shareholders.

Public corporation A corporation owned by a federal, state, or municipal government—not to be confused with a publicly held corporation.

Public figures Individuals who are thrust into the public limelight. Public figures include government officials and politicians, movie stars, well-known businesspersons, and generally anybody who becomes known to the public because of his or her position or activities.

Public policy A government policy based on widely held societal values and (usually) expressed or implied in laws or regulations.

Publicly held corporation A corporation for which shares of stock have been sold to the public.

Puffery A salesperson's exaggerated claims concerning the quality of goods offered for sale. Such claims involve opinions rather than facts and are not considered to be legally binding promises or warranties.

Punitive damages Money damages that may be awarded to a plaintiff to punish the defendant and deter future similar conduct.

Purchase-money security interest (PMSI) A security interest that arises when a seller or lender extends credit for part or all of the purchase price of goods purchased by a buyer.

Q

Quantum meruit (pronounced *kwahn*-tuhm *mehr*-oo-wuht) Literally, "as much as he deserves"—an expression describing the extent of liability on a contract implied in law (quasi contract). An equitable doctrine based on the concept that one who benefits from another's labor and materials should not be unjustly enriched thereby but should be required to pay a reasonable amount for the benefits received, even absent a contract.

Quasi contract A fictional contract imposed on parties by a court in the interests of fairness and justice; usually, quasi contracts are imposed to avoid the unjust enrichment of one party at the expense of another.

Question of fact In a lawsuit, an issue involving a factual dispute that can only be decided by a judge (or, in a jury trial, a jury).

Question of law In a lawsuit, an issue involving the application or interpretation of a law; therefore, the judge, and not the jury, decides the issue.

Quiet enjoyment *See* Covenant of quiet enjoyment

Quitclaim deed A deed intended to pass any title, interest, or claim that the grantor may have in the property but not warranting that such title is valid. A quitclaim deed offers the least amount of protection against defects in the title.

Quorum The number of members of a decision-making body that must be present before business may be transacted.

Quota An assigned import limit on goods.

R

Ratification The act of accepting and giving legal force to an obligation that previously was not enforceable.

Reaffirmation agreement An agreement between a debtor and a creditor in which the debtor reaffirms, or promises to pay, a debt dischargeable in bankruptcy. To be enforceable, the agreement must be made prior to the discharge of the debt by the bankruptcy court.

Real property Land and everything attached to it, such as foliage and buildings.

Reamortize Restart the amortization schedule (a table of the periodic payments the borrower makes to pay off a debt), changing the way the payments are configured.

Reasonable care The degree of care that a person of ordinary prudence would exercise in the same or similar circumstances.

Reasonable doubt *See* Beyond a reasonable doubt

Reasonable person standard The standard of behavior expected of a hypothetical "reasonable person." The standard against which negligence is measured and that must be observed to avoid liability for negligence.

Rebuttal The refutation of evidence introduced by an adverse party's attorney.

Receiver In a corporate dissolution, a court-appointed person who winds up corporate affairs and liquidates corporate assets.

Record According to the Uniform Electronic Transactions Act, information that is either inscribed on a tangible medium or stored in an electronic or other medium and that is retrievable. The Uniform Computer Information Transactions Act uses the term *record* instead of *writing*.

Recording statutes Statutes that allow deeds, mortgages, and other real property transactions to be recorded so as to provide notice to future purchasers or creditors of an existing claim on the property.

Red herring prospectus A preliminary prospectus that can be distributed to potential investors after the registration statement (for a securities offering) has been filed with the Securities and Exchange Commission. The name derives from the red legend printed across the prospectus stating that the registration has been filed but has not become effective.

Redemption A repurchase, or buying back. In secured transactions law, a debtor's repurchase of collateral securing a debt after a creditor has taken title to the collateral due to the debtor's default but before the secured party disposes of the collateral.

Reformation A court-ordered correction of a written contract so that it reflects the true intentions of the parties.

Regulation Z A set of rules promulgated by the Federal Reserve Board to implement the provisions of the Truth-in-Lending Act.

Rejection In contract law, an offeree's express or implied manifestation not to accept an offer. In the law governing contracts for the sale of goods, a buyer's manifest refusal to accept goods on the ground that they do not conform to contract specifications.

Rejoinder The defendant's answer to the plaintiff's rebuttal.

Release A contract in which one party forfeits the right to pursue a legal claim against the other party.

Relevant evidence Evidence tending to make a fact at issue in the case more or less probable than it would be without the evidence. Only relevant evidence is admissible in court.

Remainder A future interest in property held by a person other than the original owner.

Remanded Sent back. If an appellate court disagrees with a lower court's judgment, the case may be remanded to the lower court for further proceedings in which the lower court's decision should be consistent with the appellate court's opinion on the matter.

Remedy The relief given to an innocent party to enforce a right or compensate for the violation of a right.

Remedy at law A remedy available in a court of law. Money damages are awarded as a remedy at law.

Remedy in equity A remedy allowed by courts in situations where remedies at law are not appropriate. Remedies in equity are based on settled rules of fairness, justice, and honesty, and include injunction, specific performance, rescission and restitution, and reformation.

Replevin (pronounced rih-*pleh*-vin) An action to recover specific goods in the hands of a party who is wrongfully withholding them from the other party.

Reply Procedurally, a plaintiff's response to a defendant's answer.

Reporter A publication in which court cases are published, or reported.

Repudiation The renunciation of a right or duty; the act of a buyer or seller in rejecting a contract either partially or totally. *See also* Anticipatory repudiation

Requirements contract An agreement in which a buyer agrees to purchase and the seller agrees to sell all or up to a stated amount of what the buyer needs or requires.

Res ipsa loquitur (pronounced *rehs ehp*-suh *low*-quuh-tuhr) A doctrine under which negligence may be inferred simply because an event occurred, if it is the type of event that would not occur in the absence of negligence. Literally, the term means "the facts speak for themselves."

Resale price maintenance agreement An agreement between a manufacturer and a retailer in which the manufacturer specifies the minimum retail price of its products. Resale price maintenance agreements are illegal *per se* under the Sherman Act.

Rescind (pronounced rih-*sihnd*) To cancel. *See also* Rescission

Rescission (pronounced rih-*sih*-zhen) A remedy whereby a contract is canceled and the parties are returned to the positions they occupied before the contract was made; may be effected through the mutual consent of the parties, by their conduct, or by court decree.

Residential use Use of land for construction of buildings for human habitation only.

Respondeat superior (pronounced ree-*spahn*-dee-uht soo-*peer*-ee-your) In Latin, "Let the master respond." A doctrine under which a principal or an employer is held liable for the wrongful acts committed by agents or employees while acting within the course and scope of their agency or employment.

Respondent In equity practice, the party who answers a bill or other proceeding.

Restitution An equitable remedy under which a person is restored to his or her original position prior to loss or injury, or placed in the position he or she would have been in had the breach not occurred.

Restraint of trade Any contract or combination that tends to eliminate or reduce competition, effect a monopoly, artificially maintain prices, or otherwise hamper the course of trade and commerce as it would be carried on if left to the control of natural economic forces.

Restrictive covenant A private restriction on the use of land that is binding on the party that purchases the property originally as well as on subsequent purchasers. If its benefit or obligation passes with the land's ownership, it is said to "run with the land."

Retained earnings The portion of a corporation's profits that has not been paid out as dividends to shareholders.

Retainer An advance payment made by a client to a law firm to cover part of the legal fees and/or costs that will be incurred on that client's behalf.

Reverse To reject or overrule a court's judgment. An appellate court, for example, might reverse a lower court's judgment on an issue if it feels that the lower court committed an error during the trial or that the jury was improperly instructed.

Reverse discrimination Discrimination against majority groups, such as white males, that results from affirmative action programs, in which preferences are given to minority members and women.

Reverse mortgage A loan product typically provided to older homeowners that allows them to extract cash (in either a lump sum or multiple payments) for the equity in their home. The mortgage does not need to be repaid until the home is sold or the owner leaves or dies.

Reversible error An error by a lower court that is sufficiently substantial to justify an appellate court's reversal of the lower court's decision.

Revocation In contract law, the withdrawal of an offer by an offeror. Unless an offer is irrevocable, it can be revoked at any time prior to acceptance without liability.

Right of contribution The right of a co-surety who pays more than his or her proportionate share on a debtor's default to recover the excess paid from other co-sureties.

Right of first refusal The right to purchase personal or real property—such as corporate shares or real estate—before the property is offered for sale to others.

Right of reimbursement The legal right of a person to be restored, repaid, or indemnified for costs, expenses, or losses incurred or expended on behalf of another.

Right of subrogation The right of a person to stand in the place of (be substituted for) another, giving the substituted party the same legal rights that the original party had.

Right-to-work law A state law providing that employees are not to be required to join a union as a condition of obtaining or retaining employment.

Robbery The act of forcefully and unlawfully taking personal property of any value from another; force or intimidation is usually necessary for an act of theft to be considered a robbery.

Rule of four A rule of the United States Supreme Court under which the Court will not issue a writ of *certiorari* unless at least four justices approve of the decision to issue the writ.

Rule of reason A test by which a court balances the positive effects (such as economic efficiency) of an agreement against its potentially anticompetitive effects. In antitrust litigation, many practices are analyzed under the rule of reason.

Rule 10b-5 *See* SEC Rule 10b-5

Rulemaking The process undertaken by an administrative agency when formally adopting a new regulation or amending an old one. Rulemaking involves notifying the public of a proposed rule or change and receiving and considering the public's comments.

Rules of evidence Rules governing the admissibility of evidence in trial courts.

S

S corporation A close business corporation that has met certain requirements as set out by the Internal Revenue Code and thus qualifies for special income tax treatment. Essentially, an S corporation is taxed the same as a partnership, but its owners enjoy the privilege of limited liability.

Sale The passing of title (evidence of ownership rights) from the seller to the buyer for a price.

Sales contract A contract for the sale of goods under which the ownership of goods is transferred from a seller to a buyer for a price.

Satisfaction *See* Accord and satisfaction

Scienter (pronounced *sy-en-ter*) Knowledge by the misrepresenting party that material facts have been falsely represented or omitted with an intent to deceive.

Search warrant An order granted by a public authority, such as a judge, that authorizes law enforcement personnel to search particular premises or property.

Seasonably Within a specified time period, or, if no period is specified, within a reasonable time.

SEC Rule 10b-5 A rule of the Securities and Exchange Commission that makes it unlawful, in connection with the purchase or sale of any security, to make any untrue statement of a material fact or to omit a material fact if such omission causes the statement to be misleading.

Secondary boycott A union's refusal to work for, purchase from, or handle the products of a secondary employer, with whom the union has no dispute, for the purpose of forcing that employer to stop doing business with the primary employer, with whom the union has a labor dispute.

Secured party A lender, seller, or any other person in whose favor there is a security interest, including a person to whom accounts or chattel paper has been sold.

Secured transaction Any transaction in which the payment of a debt is guaranteed, or secured, by personal property owned by the debtor or in which the debtor has a legal interest.

Securities Generally, corporate stocks and bonds. A security may also be a note, debenture, stock warrant, or any document given as evidence of an ownership interest in a corporation or as a promise of repayment by a corporation.

Security agreement An agreement that creates or provides for a security interest between the debtor and a secured party.

Security interest Any interest "in personal property or fixtures which secures payment or performance of an obligation" [UCC 1–201(37)].

Self-defense The legally recognized privilege to protect one's self or property against injury by another. The privilege of self-defense protects only acts that are reasonably necessary to protect one's self or property.

Seniority system In regard to employment relationships, a system in which those who have worked longest for the company are first in line for promotions, salary increases, and other benefits; they are also the last to be laid off if the workforce must be reduced.

Service mark A mark used in the sale or the advertising of services, such as to distinguish the services of one person from the services of others. Titles, character names, and other distinctive features of radio and television programs may be registered as service marks.

Service of process The delivery of the complaint and summons to a defendant.

Severance pay A payment by an employer to an employee that exceeds the employee's wages due on termination.

Sexual harassment In the employment context, the granting of job promotions or other benefits in return for sexual favors or language or conduct that is so sexually offensive that it creates a hostile working environment.

Share A unit of stock. *See also* Stock

Share exchange In a share exchange, some or all of the shares of one corporation are exchanged for some or all of the shares of another corporation, but both corporations continue to exist. Share exchanges are often used to create *holding companies* (companies that own part or all of other companies' stock).

Shareholder One who purchases shares of a corporation's stock, thus acquiring an equity interest in the corporation.

Shareholder's derivative suit A suit brought by a shareholder to enforce a corporate cause of action against a third person.

Sharia Civil law principles of some Middle Eastern countries that are based on the Islamic directives that follow the teachings of the prophet Muhammad.

Sheriff's deed The deed given to the purchaser of property at a sheriff's sale as part of the foreclosure process against the owner of the property.

Shipment contract A contract in which the seller is required to ship the goods by carrier. The buyer assumes liability for any losses or damage to the goods after they are delivered to the carrier. Generally, all contracts are assumed to be shipment contracts if nothing to the contrary is stated in the contract.

Short sale A sale of real property for an amount that is less than the balance owed on the mortgage loan, usually due to financial hardship. Both the lender and the borrower must consent to a short sale. Following a short sale, the borrower still owes the balance of the mortgage debt (after the sale proceeds are applied) to the lender unless the lender agrees to forgive the remaining debt.

Short-swing profits Profits made by officers, directors, and certain large stockholders resulting from the use of nonpublic (inside) information about their companies; prohibited by Section 12 of the 1934 Securities Exchange Act.

Shrink-wrap agreement An agreement whose terms are expressed in a document located inside a box in which goods (usually software) are packaged; sometimes called a *shrink-wrap license.*

Signature Under the Uniform Commercial Code, "any symbol executed or adopted by a party with a present intention to authenticate a writing."

Slander Defamation in oral form.

Slander of quality The publication of false information about another's product, alleging that it is not what its seller claims.

Slander of title The publication of a statement that denies or casts doubt on another's legal ownership of any property, causing financial loss to that property's owner. Also called trade libel.

Small claims courts Special courts in which parties may litigate small claims (usually, claims involving $2,500 or less). Attorneys are not required in small claims courts, and in many states attorneys are not allowed to represent the parties.

Sociological school A school of legal thought that views the law as a tool for promoting justice in society.

Sole proprietorship The simplest form of business, in which the owner is the business; the owner reports business income on his or her personal income tax return and is legally responsible for all debts and obligations incurred by the business.

Sovereign immunity A doctrine that immunizes foreign nations from the jurisdiction of U.S. courts when certain conditions are satisfied.

Spam Bulk, unsolicited (junk) e-mail.

Special-use permit A permit that allows for a specific exemption to zoning regulations for a particular piece of land in a location that has a particular zoning characteristic. Local zoning authorities grant special-use permits.

Special warranty deed A deed in which the grantor only covenants to warrant and defend the title against claims and demands of the grantor and all persons claiming by, through, and under the grantor.

Specific performance An equitable remedy requiring the breaching party to perform as promised under the contract; usually granted only when money damages would be an inadequate remedy and the subject matter of the contract is unique (for example, real property).

Spot zoning A zoning classification granted to a parcel of land that is different than the classification given to other land in the immediate area.

Standing to sue The requirement that an individual must have a sufficient stake in a controversy before he or she can bring a lawsuit. The plaintiff must demonstrate that he or she either has been injured or threatened with injury.

Stare decisis (pronounced *ster*-ay dih-*si*-ses) A common law doctrine under which judges are obligated to follow the precedents established in prior decisions.

Statute of Frauds A state statute under which certain types of contracts must be in writing to be enforceable.

Statute of limitations A federal or state statute setting the maximum time period during which a certain action can be brought or certain rights enforced.

Statute of repose Basically, a statute of limitations that is not dependent on the happening of a cause of action. Statutes of repose generally begin to run at an earlier date and run for a longer period of time than statutes of limitations.

Statutory law The body of law enacted by legislative bodies (as opposed to constitutional law, administrative law, or case law).

Statutory lien A lien created by statute.

Statutory period of redemption A time period (usually set by state statute) during which the property subject to a defaulted mortgage, land contract, or other contract can be redeemed by the debtor after foreclosure or judicial sale.

Statutory right of redemption A right provided by statute in some states under which mortgagors can redeem or purchase their property back after a judicial foreclosure for a limited period of time, such as one year.

Stock An equity (ownership) interest in a corporation, measured in units of shares.

Stock buyback Sometimes, publicly held companies use funds from their own treasuries to repurchase their own stock, with the result being that the price of the stock usually goes up.

Stock certificate A certificate issued by a corporation evidencing the ownership of a specified number of shares in the corporation.

Stock option *See* Stock warrant

Stock warrant A certificate that grants the owner the option to buy a given number of shares of stock, usually within a set time period.

Stockholder *See* Shareholder

Strict liability Liability regardless of fault. In tort law, strict liability may be imposed on defendants in cases involving abnormally dangerous activities, dangerous animals, or defective products.

Strike An extreme action undertaken by unionized workers when collective bargaining fails; the workers leave their jobs, refuse to work, and (typically) picket the employer's workplace.

Subject-matter jurisdiction Jurisdiction over the subject matter of a lawsuit.

Sublease A lease executed by the lessee of real estate to a third person, conveying the same interest that the lessee enjoys but for a shorter term than that held by the lessee.

Subpoena A document commanding a person to appear at a certain time and place or give testimony concerning a certain matter.

Subprime mortgage A high-risk loan made to a borrower who does not qualify for a standard mortgage because of his or her poor credit rating or high debt-to-income ratio. Lenders typically charge a higher interest rate on subprime mortgages.

Substantial performance Performance that does not vary greatly from the performance promised in a contract; the performance must create substantially the same benefits as those promised in the contract.

Substantive due process A requirement that focuses on the content, or substance, of legislation. If a law or other governmental action limits a fundamental right, such as the right to travel or to vote, it will be held to violate substantive due process unless it promotes a compelling or overriding state interest.

Substantive law Law that defines the rights and duties of individuals with respect to each other, as opposed to procedural law, which defines the manner in which these rights and duties may be enforced.

Substantive unconscionability Results from contracts, or portions of contracts, that are oppressive or overly harsh. Courts generally focus on provisions that deprive one party of the benefits of the agreement or leave that party without remedy for nonperformance by the other. An example of substantive unconscionability is the agreement by a welfare recipient with a fourth-grade education to purchase a refrigerator for $2,000 under an installment contract.

Suit *See* Lawsuit; Litigation

Summary judgment *See* Motion for summary judgment

Summary jury trial (SJT) A method of settling disputes in which a trial is held, but the jury's verdict is not binding. The verdict acts only as a guide to both sides in reaching an agreement during the mandatory negotiations that immediately follow the summary jury trial.

Summons A document informing a defendant that a legal action has been commenced against him or her and that the defendant must appear in court on a certain date to answer the plaintiff's complaint. The document is delivered by a sheriff or any other person so authorized.

Superseding cause An intervening force or event that breaks the connection between a wrongful act and an injury to another; in negligence law, a defense to liability.

Supremacy clause The provision in Article VI of the Constitution that provides that the Constitution, laws, and treaties of the United States are "the supreme Law of the Land." Under this clause, state and local laws that directly conflict with federal law will be rendered invalid.

Surety A person, such as a cosigner on a note, who agrees to be primarily responsible for the debt of another.

Suretyship An express contract in which a third party to a debtor-creditor relationship (the surety) promises to be primarily responsible for the debtor's obligation.

Syllogism A form of deductive reasoning consisting of a major premise, a minor premise, and a conclusion.

Symbolic speech Nonverbal conduct that expresses opinions or thoughts about a subject. Symbolic speech is protected under the First Amendment's guarantee of freedom of speech.

T

Tag In the context of the World Wide Web, a code in an HTML document. *See* Meta tags.

Takeover The acquisition of control over a corporation through the purchase of a substantial number of the voting shares of the corporation.

Taking The taking of private property by the government for public use. Under the Fifth Amendment to the Constitution, the government may not take private property for public use without "just compensation."

Tangible employment action A significant change in employment status, such as firing or failing to promote an employee, reassigning the employee to a position with significantly different responsibilities, or effecting a significant change in employment benefits.

Tangible property Property that has physical existence and can be distinguished by the senses of touch, sight, and so on. A car is tangible property; a patent right is intangible property.

Tariff A tax on imported goods.

Technology licensing Allowing another to use and profit from intellectual property (patents, copyrights, trademarks, innovative products or processes, and so on) for consideration. In the context of international business transactions, technology licensing is sometimes an attractive alternative to the establishment of foreign production facilities.

Tenancy at sufferance A type of tenancy under which one who, after rightfully being in possession of leased premises, continues (wrongfully) to occupy the property after the lease has been terminated. The tenant has no rights to possess the property and occupies it only because the person entitled to evict the tenant has not done so.

Tenancy at will A type of tenancy under which either party can terminate the tenancy without notice; usually arises when a tenant who has been under a tenancy for years retains possession, with the landlord's consent, after the tenancy for years has terminated.

Tenancy by the entirety The joint ownership of property by a husband and wife. Neither party can transfer his or her interest in the property without the consent of the other.

Tenancy in common Co-ownership of property in which each party owns an undivided interest that passes to his or her heirs at death.

Tenant One who has the temporary use and occupation of real property owned by another person, called the landlord; the duration and terms of the tenancy are usually established by a lease.

Tender An unconditional offer to perform an obligation by a person who is ready, willing, and able to do so.

Tender of delivery Under the Uniform Commercial Code, a seller's or lessor's act of placing conforming goods at the disposal of the buyer or lessee and giving the buyer or lessee whatever notification is reasonably necessary to enable the buyer or lessee to take delivery.

Tender offer An offer to purchase made by one company directly to the shareholders of another (target) company; often referred to as a "takeover bid."

Third party beneficiary One for whose benefit a promise is made in a contract but who is not a party to the contract.

Time draft A draft that is payable at a definite future time.

Tippee A person who receives inside information.

Title insurance Insurance commonly purchased by a purchaser of real property to protect against loss in the event that the title to the property is not free from liens or superior ownership claims.

Tombstone ad An advertisement, historically in a format resembling a tombstone, of a securities offering. The ad informs potential investors of where and how they may obtain a prospectus.

Tort A civil wrong not arising from a breach of contract. A breach of a legal duty that proximately causes harm or injury to another.

Tortfeasor One who commits a tort.

Toxic tort A personal injury caused by exposure to a toxic substance, such as asbestos or hazardous waste. Victims can sue for medical expenses, lost wages, and pain and suffering.

Trade dress The image and overall appearance of a product—for example, the distinctive decor, menu, layout, and style of service of a particular restaurant. Basically, trade dress is subject to the same protection as trademarks.

Trade libel The publication of false information about another's product, alleging it is not what its seller claims; also referred to as slander of quality.

Trade name A term that is used to indicate part or all of a business's name and that is directly related to the business's reputation and goodwill. Trade names are protected under the common law (and under trademark law, if the name is the same as the firm's trademark).

Trade secret Information or a process that gives a business an advantage over competitors who do not know the information or process.

Trademark A distinctive mark, motto, device, or implement that a manufacturer stamps, prints, or otherwise affixes to the goods it produces so that they may be identified on the market and their origins made known. Once a trademark is established (under the common law or through registration), the owner is entitled to its exclusive use.

Treasury securities Government debt issued by the U.S. Department of the Treasury. The interest rate on Treasury securities is often used as a baseline for measuring the rate on loan products with higher interest rates.

Treasury shares Corporate shares that are authorized by the corporation but that have not been issued.

Treaty An agreement formed between two or more independent nations.

Treble damages Damages consisting of three times the amount of damages determined by a jury in certain cases as required by statute.

Trespass to land The entry onto, above, or below the surface of land owned by another without the owner's permission or legal authorization.

Trespass to personal property The unlawful taking or harming of another's personal property; interference with another's right to the exclusive possession of his or her personal property.

Trespasser One who commits the tort of trespass in one of its forms.

Trial court A court in which trials are held and testimony taken.

Trust An arrangement in which title to property is held by one person (a trustee) for the benefit of another (a beneficiary).

Trust indorsement An indorsement for the benefit of the indorser or a third person; also known as an agency indorsement. The indorsement results in legal title vesting in the original indorsee.

Two-step mortgage A mortgage that starts as a fixed-rate mortgage and then converts to an adjustable-rate mortgage (ARM).

Tying arrangement An agreement between a buyer and a seller in which the buyer of a specific product or service becomes obligated to purchase additional products or services from the seller.

U

U.S. trustee A government official who performs certain administrative tasks that a bankruptcy judge would otherwise have to perform.

Ultra vires (pronounced *uhl*-trah *vye*-reez) A Latin term meaning "beyond the powers"; in corporate law, acts of a corporation that are beyond its express and implied powers to undertake.

Unanimous opinion A court opinion in which all of the judges or justices of the court agree to the court's decision.

Unconscionable (pronounced un-*kon*-shun-uh-bul) **contract or clause** A contract or clause that is void on the basis of public policy because one party, as a result of his or her disproportionate bargaining power, is forced to accept terms that are unfairly burdensome and that unfairly benefit the dominating party. *See also* Procedural unconscionability; Substantive unconscionability

Undisclosed principal A principal whose identity is unknown by a third person, and the third person has no knowledge that the agent is acting for a principal at the time the agent and the third person form a contract.

Unenforceable contract A valid contract rendered unenforceable by some statute or law.

Unidentified principal A principal whose identity is unknown by a third person, but the third person knows that the agent is or may be acting for a principal at the time the agent and the third person form a contract.

Uniform law A model law created by the National Conference of Commissioners on Uniform State Laws and/or the American Law Institute for the states to consider adopting. If the state adopts the law, it becomes statutory law in that state. Each state has the option of adopting or rejecting all or part of a uniform law.

Unilateral contract A contract that results when an offer can only be accepted by the offeree's performance.

Union shop A place of employment in which all workers, once employed, must become union members within a specified period of time as a condition of their continued employment.

Unliquidated debt A debt that is uncertain in amount.

Unreasonably dangerous product In product liability, a product that is defective to the point of threatening a consumer's health and safety. A product will be considered unreasonably dangerous if it is dangerous beyond the expectation of the ordinary consumer or if a less dangerous alternative was economically feasible for the manufacturer, but the manufacturer failed to produce it.

Usage of trade Any practice or method of dealing having such regularity of observance in a place, vocation, or trade as to justify an expectation that it will be observed with respect to the transaction in question.

Usury Charging an illegal rate of interest.

Utilitarianism An approach to ethical reasoning in which ethically correct behavior is not related to any absolute ethical or moral values but to an evaluation of the consequences of a given action on those who will be affected by it. In utilitarian reasoning, a "good" decision is one that results in the greatest good for the greatest number of people affected by the decision.

V

Valid contract A contract that results when elements necessary for contract formation (agreement, consideration, legal purpose, and contractual capacity) are present.

Validation notice An initial notice to a debtor from a collection agency informing the debtor that he or she has thirty days to challenge the debt and request verification.

Variance A form of a relief from zoning and other laws that is granted to a property owner; used to make up for any deficiency in real property so that it could prevent the property from complying with zoning regulations.

Venue (pronounced *ven*-yoo) The geographical district in which an action is tried and from which the jury is selected.

Verdict A formal decision made by a jury.

Vertical merger The acquisition by a company at one stage of production of a company at a higher or lower stage of production (such as its supplier or retailer).

Vertical restraint Any restraint on trade created by agreements between firms at different levels in the manufacturing and distribution process.

Vertically integrated firm A firm that carries out two or more functional phases—such as manufacture, distribution, retailing—of a product.

Vesting Under the Employee Retirement Income Security Act of 1974, a pension plan becomes vested when an employee has a legal right to the benefits purchased with the employer's contributions, even if the employee is no longer working for this employer.

Vicarious liability Legal responsibility placed on one person for the acts of another.

Virtual courtroom A courtroom that is conceptual and not physical. In the context of cyberspace, a virtual courtroom could be a location on the Internet at which judicial proceedings take place.

Virtual property Property that, in the context of cyberspace, is conceptual, as opposed to physical. Intellectual property that exists on the Internet is virtual property.

Virus Any program transmitted between computers via the Internet generally without the knowledge or consent of the recipient. Viruses attempt to do deliberate damage to systems and data.

Vishing The voice counterpart of phishing; vishers use an e-mail or a notice on a Web site that encourage persons to make a phone call which then triggers a voice response system that asks for valuable personal information such as credit card numbers.

Void contract A contract having no legal force or binding effect.

Voidable contract A contract that may be legally avoided (canceled, or annulled) at the option of one of the parties.

Voidable preference In bankruptcy law, a preference that may be avoided, or set aside, by the trustee.

Voir dire (pronounced *vwahr deehr*) A French phrase meaning, literally, "to see, to speak." In jury trials, the phrase refers to the process in which the attorneys question prospective jurors to determine whether they are biased or have any connection with a party to the action or with a prospective witness.

Voting trust An agreement (trust contract) under which legal title to shares of corporate stock is transferred to a trustee who is authorized by the shareholders to vote the shares on their behalf.

W

Waiver An intentional, knowing relinquishment of a legal right.

Warranty A promise that certain facts are truly as they are represented to be.

Warranty deed A deed in which the grantor guarantees to the grantee that the grantor has title to the property conveyed in the deed, that there are no encumbrances on the property other than what the grantor has represented, and that the grantee will enjoy quiet possession of the property; a deed that provides the greatest amount of protection for the grantee.

Warranty disclaimer A seller's or lessor's negation or qualification of a warranty.

Warranty of fitness *See* Implied warranty of fitness for a particular purpose.

Warranty of merchantability *See* Implied warranty of merchantability.

Warranty of title An implied warranty made by a seller that the seller has good and valid title to the goods sold and that the transfer of the title is rightful.

Waste The abuse or destructive use of real property by one who is in rightful possession of the property but who does not have title to it. Waste does not include ordinary depreciation due to age and normal use.

Watered stock Shares of stock issued by a corporation for which the corporation receives, as payment, less than the fair market value of the shares.

Whistleblowing An employee's disclosure to government, the press, or upper-management authorities that the employer is engaged in unsafe or illegal activities.

White-collar crime Nonviolent crime committed by individuals or corporations to obtain a personal or business advantage.

Willful Intentional.

Winding up The second of two stages involved in the termination of a partnership or corporation. Once the firm is dissolved, it continues to exist legally until the process of winding up all business affairs (collecting and distributing the firm's assets) is complete.

Workers' compensation laws State statutes establishing an administrative procedure for compensating workers' injuries that arise out of—or in the course of—their employment, regardless of fault.

Workout agreement A formal contract between a debtor and his or her creditors in which the parties agree to negotiate a payment plan for the amount due on the loan instead of proceeding to foreclosure.

Worm A type of virus that is designed to copy itself from one computer to another without human interaction. Unlike the typical virus, a computer worm can copy itself automatically and can replicate in great volume and with great speed. Worms, for example, can send out copies of themselves to every contact in your e-mail address book.

Writ of attachment A court's order, prior to a trial to collect a debt, directing the sheriff or other officer to seize nonexempt property of the debtor; if the creditor prevails at trial, the seized property can be sold to satisfy the judgment.

Writ of *certiorari* (pronounced sur-shee-uh-*rah*-ree) A writ from a higher court asking the lower court for the record of a case.

Writ of execution A court's order, after a judgment has been entered against the debtor, directing the sheriff to seize (levy) and sell any of the debtor's nonexempt real or personal property. The proceeds of the sale are used to pay off the judgment, accrued interest, and costs of the sale; any surplus is paid to the debtor.

Wrongful discharge An employer's termination of an employee's employment in violation of an employment contract or laws that protect employees.

Z

Zoning The division of a city by legislative regulation into districts and the application in each district of regulations having to do with structural and architectural designs of buildings and prescribing the use to which buildings within designated districts may be put.

Zoning laws The rules and regulations that collectively manage the development and use of land.

Table of Cases

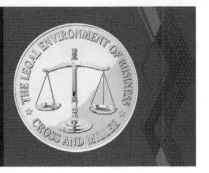

For your convenience and reference, here is a list of all the cases mentioned in this text, including those within the footnotes, features, and case problems. Any case that was an excerpted case for a chapter is given special emphasis by having its title **boldfaced.**

D

E

F

G

Index